Automobile History
Day By Day

FIRST EDITION

Douglas A. Wick

One of the joys of researching automobile history is the everpresent chance of discovering something that was previously unknown. This photograph, taken in 1910, came to light just before the publication of this book, and while nothing is known about the subject that can be included in the main text, it does make a good title page illustration! Rev. Charles S. Sayre, an avid tinkerer, built this vehicle in 1907 while serving the Seventh Day Baptist Church in Dodge Center, MN. His car, tentatively called a 1907 Sayre, featured a 10-hp engine, friction transmission, and a clever if primitive front wheel drive.

HEDEMARKEN COLLECTIBLES
Publisher & Wholesaler

First Printing 1997

Copyright 1997 by Hedemarken Collectibles

Wick, Douglas A. (1947-   )

Automobile History Day By Day: a chronological listing of automotive events and vital statistics for people involved with the industry.
Includes five indexes.

ISBN 0-9620968-1-4 (Hardbound)
ISBN 0-9620968-2-2 (Softbound)

Printed and bound in the United States of America

Published and distributed by:

HEDEMARKEN COLLECTIBLES
P. O. Box 7399 - Northbrook Station
Bismarck, ND 58507-7399
(701) 258-5794

About the cover...

The only difference between men and boys,
Is the size of their toys.

Four rather grown-up boys gathered with their toys on the grounds of the North Dakota State Capitol in Bismarck on September 22, 1996, their cars representing four distinct automotive categories. From left to right:

Cover photo by Bob Link

ANTIQUE - 1910 Pratt-Elkhart Model 1, Hon. Edward T. Schafer

The current Governor of North Dakota, Ed Schafer has compiled a successful business career including serving as President of the Gold Seal Company, the household products firm founded by his father. Closely associated with the promotion of historic Medora, ND and nearby Theodore Roosevelt National Park, both the elder and younger Schafers appropriately own Marmon-built Roosevelts. Gov. Schafer likes cars, pure and simple, although a survey of his present collection indicates a soft spot for 1960's Pontiacs.

CLASSIC - 1939 Rolls-Royce Wraith, Douglas A. Wick

After a sixteen-year career as an accountant in the electric utility industry Doug Wick founded Hedemarken Collectibles, which among other things has become a leading international dealer of postal history. His automotive preferences center on the Rolls-Royce in particular and cars built between the two world wars in general. His first new car was also his boyhood dream car - a 1969 Buick Riviera. Doug's everyday transportation for the past 18 years has been a 1979 Volkswagen Beetle convertible with a license plate frame proclaiming "My Other Car Is A Rolls-Royce".

MILESTONE - 1957 Ford Thunderbird, Russel Kruger

Rusty Kruger is a Registered Pharmacist and proprietor of Mandan Drug Inc. Although a very successful pharmacy his store is probably best known for its old-fashioned soda fountain and Lindy Sue's Candies, a line of specialty chocolates developed and marketed by his wife. Rusty's first car was a well used 1946 Ford Business Coupe and his loyalty to this marque continues. A fan of 50's-era cars in general, his collection is bracketed by a 1930 Model A and a 1966 Shelby Mustang.

CONTEMPORARY - 1996 Dodge Viper, LeeRoy Mitzel

Lee Mitzel is the founder of Mitzel Builders Inc., a successful builder of custom homes, apartment complexes, and commercial properties. His first car was a 1963 Chevrolet Impala coupe. The Impala remains a personal favorite, especially those variants that are now classified as "muscle cars". Lee has also developed a fondness for modern exotics, including such diverse cars as a Mercedes-Benz 600SL V-12 and a neo-classic Zimmer Golden Spirit.

Dedication

Glen Wick and his first car, a 1937 Ford Deluxe Coupe.

The Dalles, OR January 1942 - Glen Wick and "his" Jeep, a very early version of the universal military vehicle. Guard duty against a potential Pacific Coast invasion preceded hard combat on Guadalcanal and Bougainville.

To my father, Glen Wick (1915-1995),
who taught me many things,
including how to drive.

Among his earliest memories were times spent in his Dad's office at the Wick Brothers Ford and Dodge dealership in Robinson, ND (see July 15 in the main body of this book).

Although he loved cars and loved to drive as much as I do, my Dad's experiences with the Great Depression and World War II no doubt instilled in him a conservative approach to things automotive. In almost seven decades of driving he owned only seven cars, all of which would be considered as rather conventional forms of transportation. Not included in this count is a brief possession of an Austin-Healey (see back cover) that forty years later has become a surrealistic memory.

During the early 1970's my Dad was at an age when many men realize their automotive fantasies. He lusted for a Continental Mark IV (which he easily could have afforded) but opted instead for a Mercury Montego. Twelve years later when it was time to trade he drooled over a Buick Riviera but purchased a 1984 LeSabre sedan that would prove to be his last car. Shortly before he lost 95% of his eyesight in 1991 he had an attack of "new car fever". Always one to go for

the gusto I actually got him to test drive of all things, a Sterling, but the trusty LeSabre remained in his garage.

On the night before he died one of the things that my Dad and I talked about was this book which at the time would have been only about half its present size. I was preparing it for publication knowing that my Dad's life was nearing its end. The book's format, while quite logical, was chosen with him in mind - my hope was that my Mom could read it to him quite literally one day at a time. After his fatal heart attack I decided to pursue some rather obvious "uncovered stones" that had been left for a possible second edition.

There remain many uncovered stones but after two years of addititional work I felt that it was time to put it in gear. *Automobile History Day by Day* is a reference book that hopefully will become a useful tome for professionals, historians, and hobbyists. Most of all I hope that users of this book will find simple pleasures in some of its entries. My Dad was anxiously looking forward to this book - please use it in his memory.

Glen Wick's first post-World War II car, a 1949 Ford Tudor with the author "at the wheel"

Somewhere west of Laramie (it actually is in Wyoming) in 1959 - Glen Wick making a roadside repair to his 1956 Buick Special 4-door sedan.

June 5, 1963 - Cadet Harry J. Pearce, U.S. Air Force Academy, accepts delivery of his 1963 Chevrolet Corvette Sting Ray convertible.

FORWARD

This chronology of automotive events outlines an important part of industrial history. No other industry has played such an important role in world development and along the way so captured the hearts of the people. This love affair with the automobile continues. Mine began in 1963 when I was a cadet at the U. S. Air Force Academy. In exchange for the cost of my government paid education, my father agreed to provide a car of my choice. The choice seemed preordained. The new Corvette Sting Ray convertible had been introduced and surely seemed the embodiment of every young man's dream. To assess the progression of that dream, one only has to examine the new 1997 Corvette that has just been introduced. A third of a century later the extraordinary advances in performance, ride, and handling will attest to the vitality of the automobile industry. I salute Mr. Wick's meticulous chronicling of that industry. In Detroit at General Motors, we would consider it a labor of love.

Harry J. Pearce
Vice Chairman
General Motors Corporation

ACKNOWLEDGMENTS

In his forward Harry J. Pearce states that the production of this book was a labor of love. Indeed it was! A compilation of this type could best be done by an large number of contributors. Much of the research, however, was done as a solo effort. My personal library of over 700 automobile books, countless magazines, and file drawers full of sales brochures and magazine advertisements were utilized to assemble the initial draft of *Automobile History Day By Day*.

I next sought additional material at libraries, both public and academic. The bulk of this effort was conducted in Bismarck, ND and Albuquerque, NM. While neither of these cities would qualify as an "automotive hotbed", my findings were quite substantial. I did contact a limited number of sources worldwide to hopefully fill in some holes, but this effort was modest and so were the results.

Two people in particular contributed well beyond the call of duty. Carl F. W. Larson, the dean of North Dakota automobile historians whose "day job" finds him teaching English at Dickinson State University, became involved in my project late in 1996 and offered many new entries as well as sage advice on the overall concept of the book.

Stuart R. Blond of Fords, NJ has for some years been compiling a similar chronology for The Packard Club with listings limited to that marque. He generously shared these efforts with the result that Packard is extremely well represented in this book.

Others who contributed one or more entries are in alphabetical order: Peter Baines of the Rolls-Royce Enthusiasts' Club, Shamrock Shelley Cleaver of the Edsel Owners Club, Inc., Mark Coir of Cranbrook Archives, Scripps Downing of the Scripps-Booth Register, Bob Nelson, Ed Parsil of the Subaru 360 Drivers' Club, Jerry Peoples, Jeff Shapiro and John H. Willard.

Photographs, advertisements, and other illustrations used in this book are primarily from my personal collection. The few that were supplied by others are credited as they appear.

INTRODUCTION

"The history of the American automobile is a can of worms that would make any self-respecting bilateral invertebrate blanche."

- Beverly Rae Kimes

This statement from the Introduction to the *Standard Catalog of American Cars 1805-1942* (First Edition 1985) cannot be argued. When one expands the parameters from the United States to the world, the task becomes even more daunting.

The inspiration for this book dates from the mid-1970's. I was an infrequent contributor to *Old Cars Weekly* who quite by chance found himself in the vicinity of that journal's Iola, WI offices. On a whim I stopped at the new Krause Publications building and was treated to the fine hospitality of then Editor Robert Lemke.

One of the many items that we discussed was the annual *Old Cars* calendar. I noted that it might be improved by including an automotive event in each daily block of the monthly grid. Bob acknowledged that this idea had been studied, but a suitable list of events did not exist and the cost of compiling such a list was prohibitive on company time.

I have a habit of getting involved in "labors of love", so needless to say within a few weeks *Old Cars* was in possession of such a list. Only high points were covered in my original effort, and only 363 out of a possible 366 dates had an entry, but it was a good beginning.

The following year the *Old Cars* calendar did indeed have automotive history included in the monthly grids. Alas, while the general reception of this addition was positive a few people complained that the trivia inclusion made the calendar's usefulness as an appointment book somewhat restricted. After two years, the *Old Cars* calendar returned to its original format.

Life goes on. I married, had a son, changed careers, and got older. At some forgotten date in 1993 while searching in our basement for something else I stumbled across my old 15-page typewritten manuscript. This document took up residence on a corner of the desk in my home-based office where it languished for several weeks.

At some point the seed that became this book was planted. My freelance writing career had continued on a sporadic basis in several fields including the 1988 publication of my first book, *North Dakota Place Names*. During this 15-year period my personal automotive library had grown by at least 1,000%, and I had graduated from typewriter to word processor. Late in 1993 I entered the original 15-page document into my personal computer and began the task of going through my personal automotive library. Information from material acquired since 1978 was added, plus a revisiting of my older material yielded countless items of a more minor nature that had been intentionally skipped during my first effort.

I wasn't exactly sure what I had started or where it would end, but the computer file soon became quite a monster. By the summer of 1994 I had become a regular visitor at the Bismarck Public Library and the North Dakota State Library, both of which yielded surprising amounts of new data. My parents lived in Albuquerque, NM, so I seized the opportunity of our annual visits to the Duke City to utilize the resources of the Albuquerque Public Library and the libraries of the University of New Mexico. Contacts were limited to a few automotive historians, personalities, and their relatives. By late 1996 my manuscript had reached the point where *Automobile History Day By Day* was ready to become a reality.

"Strive for perfection in everything you do."

- Sir F. H. Royce

Soon after I began compiling this book I became aware of some of the pitfalls that can bedevil such an effort - read again the Kimes quotation on the previous page.

Ideally I would like to have started my research with a blank sheet of paper and original source documents. Because such material is literally scattered throughout the world this was out of the question. Most of my research had to be done by combing thousands of previously published works. The well known, not so well known, and anonymous men and women who authored these works have given the automotive world a mother lode of material that surely has no equal.

Automobile History Day By Day, when each individual entry is broken down into segments, contains literally thousands of elements that are presented as both chronologically precise and factually true. Unfortunately such a goal is a pipe dream.

A major problem I had to deal with was duplicate entries. I first became aware of this pitfall when I entered the death of famed stylist Raymond H. Dietrich. Having met and visited with Mr. Dietrich in the mid-1970's, this item had more personal significance than most and I had the uneasy feeling that I had already recorded this event. Indeed I had!

When I prepared the indexes for this book I encountered over six hundred events that were recorded on two or more dates. Former Indianapolis Speedway owner Tony Hulman set a record of sorts by, according to various sources, dying on five different dates. Many of these were solved by consulting original records or contemporary accounts (most often newspapers), but some simply required me to make a call. This was not easy - even my favorite automotive historian, Griffith Borgeson, recorded the birth date of Nicola Romeo on two different dates in his book *The Alfa Romeo Tradition*. No event has intentionally been included in the book on two or more dates, but despite my efforts it is quite likely that this has occurred.

Relying on another's research efforts is always risky and carries with it the reality that if an erroneous fact, to use an oxymoron, is repeated enough times it will become virtually impossible to set the record straight. A common error that I had to deal with was a death being recorded by the date of the newspaper obituary which usually is one or two days after the actual event.

Even original source records can be suspect. Enzo Ferrari related the story, often repeated in print, that his birth certificate is dated as of the time its filing two days after the actual event had taken place. United States Social Security records are supposed to list birth and death dates for all deceased beneficiaries, yet in a test of this data base I discovered that my father's birth date is erroneously recorded ten days earlier than the true date.

Purely factual errors may forever be subject to debate. When absolute precision is sought for such things as full names, exact locations in a changing world, first, last, etc., the goal of perfection becomes unattainable. But we should continue to strive for that elusive quality.

> "The word complete has been used and misused to the breaking point and
> is not a good choice of wording as nothing is ever complete."
>
> *- Keith Marvin*

I think that I've captured most of the high points and a lot of the more obscure points of automotive history that can be precisely dated. Yet *Automobile History Day By Day* is NOT a complete history of the automobile nor can it ever be. Some would argue that its not even a "history". It is at the very least an accumulation of automotive facts, many of which are very difficult to find or had never appeared in print at any time. I hope that you share my belief that this book will become a valuable and useful reference.

The cover of this book optimistically states "First Edition". Its chronological scope is open-ended, not just limited to "old" cars. As long as automobiles are manufactured, driven, raced, collected, etc., automobile history will continue to be made. No doubt many of the automotive leaders of the 21st century have been born during the time that this book was being written.

I expect to renew my own efforts at adding new material literally before the actual production of this book is complete. While the list of contributors noted in the Acknowledgents is very brief it is my belief that hundreds, if not thousands, of you could supply me with additions, corrections, and enhancements.

In short, a second edition and beyond is a distinct possibility as we work together to make this book as complete and completely accurate as is humanly possible. If updated material continues to become available and the reality of business make such an effort financially feasible, new editions will occur from time to time.

Persons interested in contributing to a possible second edition can contact me in care of the publisher:

HEDEMARKEN COLLECTIBLES
P. O. Box 7399 - Northbrook Station
Bismarck, ND 58507-7399

Douglas A. Wick
June 1997

Postscript -

While the predetermined mission of this book was to collect and organize events of automotive history that could be assigned to an exact date, the mischievous side of my personality plus my enthusiasm for the Rolls-Royce marque led me to commit one violation of the self-imposed rules.

According to this book the famous meeting of Hon. C. S. Rolls and F. H. Royce occurred on May 4, 1904. Detailed notes from this encounter have survived but, unfortunately, they are not dated. Numerous attempts to pinpoint the exact date have been conducted, and circumstantial evidence points strongly to May 4, but unless new discoveries are made it is quite improper to offer this date as fact.

Rolls-Royce has probably had more words written about it on a per capita basis than any other marque with the possible execption of Duesenberg. To any future Rolls-Royce historians I only ask that you approach the inclusion of this entry as a personal indulgence. Please do not use this book to perpetuate as fact a date that as of today is unproven.

JANUARY 1

1870 Francis E. Stanley marries Augusta May Walker

1873 Wilhelm Maybach is named Chief Design Engineer for Gasmotorenfabrik Deutz AG in Cologne, Germany

1879 Carl Benz successfully operates his two-stroke gasoline engine for the first time

1884 Arthur Boquer Domonoske, Chief Engineer of Doble Steam Motors 1922-1923, is born in Germantown (now Artois), CA

1892 Samuel Broers of the Firestone Tire & Rubber Company is born in Amsterdam, Holland

1894 Charles Trepardoux leaves his partnership with Count Albert de Dion and Georges Bouton because of a dispute over the relative merits of steam power versus internal-combustion gasoline engines

1900 Construction of the new Autocar Company factory in Ardmore, PA begins

1902 Paul Daimler assumes the top management role for Osterreichisches Daimler Motoren AG, manufacturers of the Austro-Daimler

1904 The Motor Car Act becomes law in Great Britain, requiring the licensing of all drivers and the registration of all vehicles

1906 Pennsylvania's state-issued license plates debut

1906 The Walter Car Company of New York City is reorganized as the Walter Automobile Company i nTrenton, NJ with Frederick Kuser as President, William Walter as Vice President, Washington A. Roebling II as Secretary, and John L. Kuser as Treasurer - this firm would evolve into the Mercer Automobile Company in 1909

1908 Coachbuilder Hermann C. Brunn is born in New York state

1908 Factory Superintendent Terry Stafford and Sales Manager J. F. Billings resign from the Smith Automobile Company, builders of the Great Smith

1909 Racer Marcel Balsa is born in Saint-Frion, France

1910 The (Societa) Anonima Lombarda Fabbrica Automobili is founded in Milan, Italy by Ugo Stella to manufacture the A.L.F.A., with Giuseppe Merosi officially named as Technical Director

1910 The Ford Motor Company occupies its new Highland Park, MI factory that was designed by architect Albert Kahn

1910 Ettore Bugatti Automobilfabrik is established in Molsheim, France with the financial backing of Augustin de Vizcaya, a Spanish baron living in the area

1911 The Studebaker Brothers Manufacturing Company and the Everitt-Metzger-Flanders Company, builders of the E-M-F, merge as the Studebaker Corporation

1912 Victor George Reuther of the United Auto Workers is born in Wheeling, WV

1913 George W. Killebrew is elected President of the Marathon Motor Works, the struggling Nashville, TN automobile manufacturer

1914 Nicholas Dykstra of Mack Trucks, Inc. is born

1914 W. O. Bentley weds Leonie Withers in his first of three marriages (she would die during the great 1918 influenza epidemic)

1915 The Patent Cross-License Agreement is finalized among the members of the National Automobile Chamber of Congress

1915 The Dort Motor Car Company is incorporated with J. Dallas Dort as President, David M. Averill as Vice President, Fred A. Aldrich as Secretary-Treasurer, John D. Mansfield as General Manager, and Etienne Planche as Chief Engineer

1916 B. W. Burtsell resigns as Production Manager of the Packard Motor Car Company to become an independent consulting engineer - E. S. Hare joins the company as a special sales representative for Packard trucks in New York City

1919 Edsel B. Ford is named President of the reorganized Ford Motor Company succeeding his father, Henry Ford

1919 The Ford Motor Company announces a minimum daily wage of $6.00

1919 Col Jesse G. Vincent rejoins the Packard Motor Car Company as Vice President of Engineering following his World War I military service

1922 Massachusetts becomes the first state to require automobile insurance

1924 Duesenberg Automobile & Motors Company is declared bankrupt

1926 Rolls-Royce of America, Inc. purchases the Long Island City, NY coachbuilding firm of Brewster & Company

1926 Ernest Wooler is named Chief Engineer of the Timken Roller Bearing Company

1927 Assar Gabrielsson is named Managing Director of AB Volvo

1927 Racer James R. "Hap" Sharp is born in Tulsa, OK - his nickname noted his HAPpy New Years birthday

1928 Capt. Edward V. Rickenbacker joins General Motors as a "trouble-shooter" for Cadillac and LaSalle

1928 The 1928 Hudson and Essex Super-Sixes are introduced - this was the first time since 1916 that the Hudson Motor Car Company had officially used a model year designation

1928 The Dixi-built Austin Seven is introduced, an event often cited as the automotive beginning of BMW

1929 The 1929 Lincolns are introduced

1930 The First Dodge straight-8, the Series DC, is introduced along with the Series DB and DD - the Series DA was continued as the "second series"

1930 The Road Traffic Act of 1930 takes effect in Great Britain requiring compulsory automobile insurance

1930 Charles A. Chayne joins Buick as a design engineer

1931 The 1931 DeSoto Six Series SA is introduced

1931 General Motors closes the original Fleetwood Metal Body Company works in Fleetwood, PA, transferring its functions to a former World War I airplane factory in Detroit, MI

1932 The 1932 Dodge Series DK "New Eight" is introduced

1932 The Packard Series 900 Light Eight is introduced

1932 Auto Union AG acquires Wanderer-Werke AG of Siegmar-Schonau, Germany

1932 Herbert Venediger joins DKW as Chief Development Engineer

1932 Production of GAZ Model A cars and GAZ Model AA trucks (based on the Ford Model A and Model AA) begins at the Gor'kiy (USSR) Automotive Plant

1932 Frederick Seale Addy of the Amoco Corporation is born in Boston, MA

1932 Tadashi Kume of Honda is born in Shizuoka Prefecture, Japan

1932 Classic car collector Dr. Peter C. Kesling is born in LaPorte, IN

1932 A merger of Praga, Skoda, and Tatra becomes effective for a projected twenty years, but the Czech combine would last only two months

1933 The Dodge Series DO is introduced, a car that was destined to be the marque's last straight-8

1933 The Pierce Silver Arrow is introduced at the New York Automobile Show

1934 Frederic G. Donner is named Assitant Treasurer of General Motors

1934 Automotive journalist LeRoi Tex Smith (nee Charles Scott Welch Smith, aka LeRoi Ugama) is born in Cleveland, OK

1935 The 1936 Nashes are introduced - senior series cars featured the marque's first hydraulic brakes and all-steel bodies

1937 Great Britain requires safety-glass windshields on all cars

1937 Pat Fairfield wins the South African Grand Prix in East London driving an E.R.A. R.4A, the first victory for the marque in the hands of a private owner

1938 Racer Picko Troberg is born in Sundsvall, Sweden

1938 Herr Stadtbaurat Dr. Hans Kolzow succeeds Conrad Matschoss as Director of the Verein Deutscher Ingenieure (Society of German Engineers)

1942 The United States government bans the sale of "nonessential" new cars and trucks, and prohibits the use of chrome trim

1942 The Olds Motor Works officially becomes the Oldsmobile Division of General Motors

A 1942 Oldsmobile Town Sedan is parked at left on Superior Avenue in Tomah, WI.

1943 Emil C. Fink, President and Chairman of Mack Trucks, Inc., dies in New York City at age 61

1944 The Motor Truck Division of the International Harvester Company is created

1945 Racer Jacques-Bernard "Jacky" Ickx is born in Brussels, Belgium, the son of racing journalist Jacques Ickx

1945 Journalist Carlton C. Magee is named President of the Magee-Hale Parking Meter Company of Oklahoma City, OK

1947 Benjamin Anibal retires as Chief Engineer of Pontiac, with George A. Delaney named as his successor

1947 The virtually unchanged Plymouth P15 officially becomes a 1947 model

1948 The 1948 Chryslers and Plymouths are introduced

1948 Wilhelm Haspel returns as Managing Director of Daimler-Benz AG after being cleared of suspected Nazi associations during World War II

1948 Colonel C. R. Radclyffe, the military governor of the British Zone of occupied Germany, hires Dr. Heinz Nordhoff, formerly director of Opel's truck plant in Brandenburg, to be Volkswagen's chief executive

1950 Hugh J. Ferry officially becomes the sixth President of the Packard Motor Car Company

1951 Jack F. Wolfram is elected General Manager of Oldsmobile

1951 Arnold W. Lenz is elected General Manager of Pontiac

1951 Racer Hans-Joachim Stuck is born in Gronau, West Germany, the son of racer Hans Stuck

1952 The 1952 Fords are introduced - engine options included the marque's first overhead valve six

1952 The Lotus Engineering Company is founded by Colin Chapman, Hazel Williams Chapman, and Michael Allen

1952 Retired General Motors executive George C. Carhart dies in Pasadena, CA at age 81 while watching the annual Tournament of Roses parade

1953 Harold Crist, the creator of the original Jeep, is hired as Project Manager for the Mid-America Research Corporation of Wheatland, PA to develop the Mighty Mite, a smaller, more powerful version of the Jeep

1955 Studebaker modifies its 1955 lineup by changing the windshield to a wraparound design on all sedans and station wagons - the Speedster Hardtop Coupe is introduced during the Rose Bowl football game in Pasadena, CA

1957 Cadillac names James M. Roche as General Manager and Fred H. Murray as General Sales Manager

1957 Regie Nationale des Usines Renault contracts with Amedee Gordini to design sporting versions of its popular Dauphine model

1959 The 1959 Opels are introduced to the United States market

1959 The California Texas Corporation changes its name to the California Texas Oil Corporation

1962 Trevor Taylor records his first major racing victory, winning the Cape Grand Prix of the South African Springbok Series in his Lotus

1963 Racer Jean-Marc Gounon is born in Aubenas, Ardeche, France

1964 The United States government requires front seat belts as standard equipment in all newly-manufactured domestic cars

1966 The Dodge Charger is introduced as a mid-year model

1967 F. T. Hopkins is named General Sales Manager of Cadillac

1967 Virgil E. Boyd is elected President of the Chrysler Corporation

1967 Great Britain imposes a 70 mph speed limit

1968 Shoulder harnesses are required in all new cars manufactured in the United States

1968 Jim Clark, driving a Lotus-Ford, wins the South African Grand Prix for his record 25th Grand Prix victory

1968 The California Texas Oil Corporation changes its name to the Caltex Petroleum Corporation

1969 The 1969 British Fords are introduced to the United States market

1972 Richard C. Gerstenberg is elected Chairman and Chief Executive Officer of General Motors

1972 The Pontiac Owners Club International is organized, later changing its name to the Pontiac-Oakland Club International

1973 Robert D. Lund is named General Manager of Cadillac, succeeding George R. Elges

1974 Mack Trucks, Inc., a Delaware corporation, reorganizes in Pennsylvania

1974 Publisher Chester L. Krause sells Car Classics magazine to Frank Taylor of Compton, CA

1975 The Honda Civic CVCC is introduced to the United States market

1980 SA des Automobiles Peugeot and Automobiles Talbot SA of Spain merge

1981 Roger B. Smith is elected Chairman and Chief Executive Officer of General Motors

1981 Mauri Rose, a three-time winner of the Indianapolis 500, dies in Michigan at age 74

1982 Daimler-Benz of North America is created

1982 Treser Automobiltechnik und Design is founded in Ingolstadt, West Germany by Walter Treser to manufacture special high-quality components for Audi cars

1982 Volvo assumes responsibility to market the Renault 5 through its dealer network

1984 Edsel B. Ford II is named Advertising Manager of the Ford Division, Ford Motor Company

1984 Haakan Frisinger is elected President of AB Volvo, with Roger Holtback succeeding him as President of the automobile division

1985 Switzerland begins charging its citizens for use of public highways

1988 Dr. Ferdinand Piech, grandson of Ferdinand Porsche, is named Chairman of Audi NSU Auto Union AG

1990 Saab Automobile AB is established as a subsidiary of Saab-Scania AB

1996 John F. Smith Jr. succeeds John G. Smale as Chairman of General Motors - John D. Rock retires as General Manager of Oldsmobile

JANUARY 2

1447 The Memmiger Chronicle mentions the trial of a carriage "without horse, oxen or people, yet the man who built it sat in it", an event often cited as the first reference to a self-propelled road vehicle

1860 John M. Studebaker marries Mary Jane Stull

1861 Nikolaus A. Otto and Wilhelm Otto apply for a German patent on their internal combustion engine

1864 Albert Fisher, a builder of bodies for motor trucks and an uncle of the Fisher brothers of General Motors, is born in Peru, OH

1878 Frederic John Fisher is born in Sandusky, OH

1881 J. Lester Dryden, the developer of the automobile grill and the Long single-plate clutch, is born in Carrolton, OH

1884 Frank Charles Campsall of the Ford Motor Company is born in Essex, ON, Canada

1885 Race car designer Ernest Henry is born in Geneva, Switzerland

1897 A steam-powered London-built Thornycroft truck is sold to the South Wales Motor Car & Cycle Company of Cardiff, the first sale of a motor truck in Great Britain

1901 The Cleveland Cap and Screw Company is founded - in 1903 the firm was purchased by Alexander Winton to manufacture automobile parts, and today has evolved into TRW Inc.

1902 James Melton, opera singer & antique automobile collector, is born in Moultrie, GA

1904 Charles Schmidt, driving the Packard Gray Wolf race car at Daytona Beach, FL, breaks the United States 1-mile and 5-mile sprint records

1915 Cadillac's "Penalty of Leadership" magazine advertisement appears

1923 Duesenberg Automobile & Motors Company is forced into receivership

1923 Ernest R. Breech joins the Yellow Cab Manufacturing Company as Controller

1934 The Chevrolet 1934 "Eagle" mascot is patented by designers William Schnell and Eric S. Carlson

1934 The 1934 Dodge Series DR and DS are introduced

1935 Auburn introduces their Series 851 "Super-Charged" line of six models, including the Speedster, at the New York Auto Show

1935 The 1935 Chryslers are introduced

1935 The 1935 DeSotos are introduced

A brand new 1935 DeSoto Airstream Model SF Sedan, one of 6,027 built, is
photographed in the North Dakota Badlands

1935 The 1935 Dodges are introduced

1935 The 1935 Pierce-Arrows are introduced

1946 Stylist Paul W. Gillan joins General Motors

1947 Production of 1947 Cadillacs officially begins, although the cars are essentially identical to the 1946 models

1951 Carl E. Heussner of the Chrysler Corporation and an authority on electroplating dies in Detroit, MI at age 51

1953 The Hudson Jet is introduced

1954 Samuel A. Fulton, automotive accessories manufacturer and longtime President of the Gideon Society, dies in Milwaukee, WI at age 76

1957 The Chrysler Crown Imperial Ghia-bodied limousine is introduced

1957 Racer Giuseppe "Beppe" Gabbiani is born in Piacenza, Italy

1962 Sir William Lawrie Welsh, North American Representative for the Society of (British) Motor Manufacturers 1948-1955, dies in Farmington, CT at age 70

1964 Studebaker transfers all automobile production to its Canadian factory in Hamilton, ON

1969 Terry Ehrich purchases *Hemmings Motor News* from magazine founder E. R. "Ernie" Hemmings of Quincy, IL

1969 Racer Robby Gordon is born in Cerritos, CA

1974 E. L. Cord dies in Reno, NV at age 79

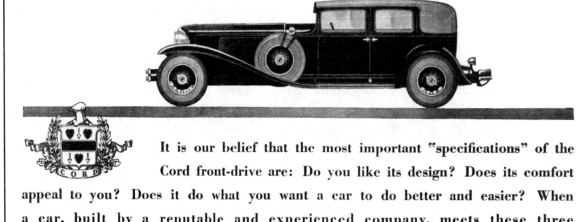

It is our belief that the most important "specifications" of the Cord front-drive are: Do you like its design? Does its comfort appeal to you? Does it do what you want a car to do better and easier? When a car, built by a reputable and experienced company, meets these three requirements, you can safely depend upon that company to adequately provide for all mechanical details.—E. L. CORD

CORD FRONT DRIVE

SEDAN $3095 .. BROUGHAM $3095 .. CABRIOLET $3295 .. PHAETON $3295   Prices F.O.B. Auburn, Indiana. *Equipment other than standard, extra*
AUBURN AUTOMOBILE COMPANY . AUBURN, INDIANA

The original Cord and later "coffin-nose" model of 1936-1937 were America's most successful pre-World War II front wheel drive cars.

1974 The United States Congress enacts legislation to impose a national 55 mph speed limit

1994 Chrysler Corporation's Neon compact goes on sale as a 1995 model

1995 Rudolf Hruska, longtime Alfa Romeo engineer and the designer of the Alfasud, dies at age 79

1997 William T. Cameron, historian of the Cameron marque although unrelated to that Cameron family, dies at age 92

JANUARY 3

1900 George Kirkham of Warren, OH purchases a Packard Model A, most likely the first sale of that marque

1901 Leo George Jacques of the Motor Products Corporation is born in Pontiac, MI

1902 Custom coach builder Enos J. Derham is born

1905 Dante Giacosa, a Fiat stylist 1928-1975, is born in Rome, Italy

1911 Racer Fritz Huschke von Hansten is born in Halle, Germany

1918 William A. McConnell of the Ford Motor Company is born

1919 Peter E. Martin is appointed as General Superintendent of Production for the Ford Motor Company

1920 The Martin Wasp is introduced at the Hotel Commodore in New York City

1921 The Studebaker Corporation announces that they have ended farm wagon production

1925 The Hupmobile Model E-1 is introduced, the marque's first 8-cylinder car

1926 General Motors introduces their new marque and Oakland companion, the Pontiac, to the public

1928 The LaSalle 1927-1930 "Sieur de LaSalle" mascot is patented by designer E. E. Burr

1928 The Oakland 1927-1928 "Eagle" mascot is patented by designer William Schnell

1928 The Packard Custom 443 is introduced along with a rumble seat coupe and a convertible coupe as additional body styles in all series

1929 Sir Herbert Austin arrives in New York City to arrange for the production of the Austin Seven in the United States

1931 The Marmon Sixteen is introduced at 31st Annual New York Auto Show

From the frontispiece of The Designer's Story, *a small hardcover booklet written by Walter Dorwin Teague, designer of the Marmon Sixteen.*

1931 The 1931 Mercer debuts at the Hotel Montclair in New York City - the convertible coupe shown plus a show chassis would be the total output of a thinly-disguised attempt by the moribund Elcar Motor Company to survive by reviving the marque that had died in 1925

1931 E. L. Cord, a widower for less than four months, marries Virginia Kirk "Gigi" Tharpe

1939 The experimental Rolls-Royce "Big Bertha", a Wraith chassis with a straight-8 engine, is completed

1939 Oscar Bruno Marx III of the Ford Motor Company is born in Detroit, MI

1939 Guiseppe Busso joins Alfa Romeo as an assistant to Orazio Satta

1940 Garnet McKee, inventor of the automobile windshield wiper, dies in Madison, WI at age 62

1941 William J. Lane, one of three brothers that designed and built the Lane Steam car 1900-1911, dies in Poughkeepsie, NY at age 100

1943 Racer Alfredo Costanzo is born in Australia

1944 Robert Lacey, biographer of the Ford family, is born in Guildford, Surrey, England

1946 C. A. Musselman, Chairman of the Chilton Company, publishers of automtive manuals, dies at age 73

CHILTON AUTOMOBILE DIRECTORY

1948 Frank Alborn, a designer of the Locomobile Vanderbilt Cup race cars who later was Chief Engineer of the White Motor Company, dies

1949 Henry G. Weaver, Director of Customer Research for General Motors, dies at age 59

1954 Racer Christian Lautenschlager dies in Unterturkheim, West Germany at age 77

1955 Reo Motors, Inc. President John C. Tooker announces that the firm will resume the manufacture of motor trucks

1957 Stewart McDonald of the Moon Motor Car Company dies in New York City at age 77

1960 Racer Russell Spence is born in Great Britain

1963 The first Ford Thunderbird Limited Edition Landau is produced

1969 Racer Michael Schumacher is born in Hurth-Hermuhlheim, West Germany

1975 Volkswagenwerk AG announces plans to build a new factory in Brazil

1982 Howard A. "Dutch" Darrin, a partner in the custom coachbuiling firms of Hibbard & Darrin 1922-1932 and Fernandez & Darrin 1932-1937, a consultant with many automobile companies in the United States and Europe, and a stylist with Nash, Packard, Kaiser, and others, dies in Santa Monica, CA at age 84

1989 Robert L. Banks, a research chemist with the Phillips Petroleum Company 1946-1989, dies in Bartlesville, OK at age 67

1996 Automotive artist Terence Cuneo dies at age 89

JANUARY 4

1868 Matthew Frederick Bramley, President of the Templar Motors Corporation, is born in Independence, OH

1872 Aerodynamics pioneer Edmund Rumpler is born in Vienna, Austria

1890 George Hathaway Taber Jr. of the Sinclair Refining Company is born in Franklin, PA

1893 Mason M. Roberts of General Motors is born in Anderson, IN

1897 Jack J. Timpy of American Motors is born in Ludington, MI

1898 Societe A. Darracq is founded in Suresnes, France by Alexandre Darracq

1917 Frank J. Enger of the Enger Motor Car Company commits suicide in Cincinnati, OH at age 58

Manufactured 1909-1917, the Enger was always a good car and their offerings included a V-12 in 1916.

Mr. Enger's suicide note discussed his failing health and included detailed plans to continue operations, but the firm was bankrupt within two months.

1918 Construction begins onthe Rouge plant of the Ford Motor Company

1930 The 1930 Auburns are introduced at the New York Automobile Show

1930 The Cadillac V-16 is introduced at the New York Automobile Show

1936 Harry L. Horning, founder of the Waukesha Motor Company and an advocate of the Ricardo L-head engine, dies in Battle Creek, MI at age 55

1937 The Nash Motors Company and the Kelvinator Corporation, manufacturers of household appliances, merge as the Nash-Kelvinator Corporation with Charles W. Nash as Chairman and George W. Mason as President

1942 Racer Jim Downing is born in Atlanta, GA

1944 David W. Rodger, Vice President and Secretary of the Federal-Mogul Corporation and an employee of the firm since 1915, dies at age 50

1947 Elisha H. Cooper, Chairman of the Fafnir Bearing Company 1926-1947, dies at age 77

1950 The 1950 Dodges are introduced

1952 The 1952 Plymouths are introduced

1954 The first 1954 Cadillac is produced

1955 The 1955 Packards are introduced, featuring the marque's first V-8 engines and the "cathredral" taillights designed by Richard A. Teague

1962 Chung Mong Kyu, Vice President of the Hyundai Motor Company and only son of cofounder Chung Se Yung, is born

1967 Ormond E. Hunt, a former Chief Engineer of Packard and longtime executive with General Motors, dies in Detroit, MI at age 83

1967 Donald Campbell is killed at age 45 attempting a water speed record at Coniston Water, Lancashire, England

1971 Racer Richie Hearn is born in Glendale, CA

1974 Yves Boisset, an Argentine Peugeot official, is kidnapped by guerillas

1975 Fire destroys the T.V.R. Engineering Ltd. factory in Blackpool, Lancashire, England **TVR**

1979 Harry H. Bennett of the Ford Motor Company dies in Los Gatos, CA at age 86

1980 Dodge Main, the huge Hamtramck, MI factory designed by Albert Kahn in 1910, closes after nearly 70 years of use

1990 The Lincoln Town Car is named Car of the Year by *Motor Trend* magazine, the first time in 38 years that the honor had been given to a luxury sedan

1995 Brooks Stevens, automobile stylist, classic car collector, and creator of the neo-classic Excalibur, dies in Milwaukee, WI at age 83

1996 General Motors Chairman John F. Smith Jr. announces that the General Motors EV-1 electric-powered coupe will be marketed through Saturn dealers beginning in the fall, with an electric-powered version of the Chevrolet S-10 pickup truck to be available soon afterwards

JANUARY 5

1872 Gasmotorenfabrik Deutz AG is incorporated in Cologne, Germany

1873 Carlton Cole Magee, the inventor of the parking meter, is born in Fayette, IA

1883 Clyde Tingley, an official of the Gramm Motor Company who later served as Mayor of Albuquerque, NM and Governor of New Mexico, is born in London, OH

1891 Glenn Dale Angle, Chief Draftsman of the Welch Motor Car Company 1909-1911 and for the Dort Motor Car Company 1916, is born in Imlay City, MI

1904 Ransom E. Olds retires from the Olds Motor Works, primarily due to his disagreement with the desire of Samuel L. and Frederick L. Smith to manufacture larger, more expensive cars

1912 John Samuel French of the Ford Motor Company is born in Toronto, ON, Canada

1914 James Couzens of the Ford Motor Company announces a $5.00 wage per 8-hour day, replacing the old scale of $2.34 per 9-hour day

1914 The first Lincoln Highway prototype automobile, designed by H. D. W. Mackaye, is tested in Detroit, MI

1914 The first Rayfield Cyclecar is completed amid great optimism, but only one more car would be built

1919 Ernest Ballot announces plans to manufacture a 2-litre automobile

1920 Racer Andre Simon is born in Paris, France

1924 Walter P. Chrysler officially introduces the first Chrysler, an event would lead to the formation of the Chrysler Corporation

1925 The Seagrave Corporation is incorporated in Michigan to succeed the Seagrave Company incorporated in Ohio in 1904

1925 Ralph DePalma drives a stripped down Chrysler Model B-70 touring car 1,000 miles in 786 minutes at the Culver City, CA track to set numerous stock car records

1928 Six months after construction had begun, the first truck rolls off the assembly line at the new GMC factory in Pontiac, MI

1928 The Graham-Paige Motors Corporation is organized in Dearborn, MI by brothers Joseph B., Robert C., and Ray A. Graham

THE SATURDAY EVENING POST

An

INVITATION

from the

three Graham brothers

The public and the automobile trade are cordially invited to the first showing of passenger cars bearing our name.

SPACE A-5
GRAND CENTRAL PALACE
NEW YORK
JANUARY 7-14, 1928
Also in the main lobbies of the
Roosevelt and Pennsylvania hotels

Joseph B. Graham
Robert C. Graham
Ray A. Graham

GRAHAM-PAIGE

THE SATURDAY EVENING POST

1929 The Auburn 120 is introduced at the National Automobile Show in New York City

1931 Arthur W. Herrington and Fred E. Moskovics enter into a partnership to develop and market Herrington's invention of an all-wheel drive vehicle

1932 The Hupmobile 1931-1934 "Stylized H" mascot is patented by designer Raymond Loewy

1933 The Packard Tenth Series Eight, Super Eight and Twelve are introduced

1938 Racer Keith Greene is born in London, England

1940 Sherrod E. Skinner, General Manager of Oldsmobile, is elected as a Vice President of General Motors

1942 Harry J. Klingler, General Manager of Pontiac, is elected as a Vice President of General Motors - Vice President of Finance Frederic G. Donner is elected to the Board of Directors

1950 The 1950 Chryslers are introduced

1955 The Chrysler Town & Country station wagons are introduced as mid-year models

1955 The 1955 Packards are previewed by the automotive press

1955 The first A.C. Ace is imported into the United States by Joe Bojalad of Pittsburgh, PA

1958 The 1958 DeSoto Adventurers are introduced

1962 Buick announces that it will resume importing the German-built Opel

Read all about it.

Opel's return to the United States market consisted primarily of uninspiring economy sedans and coupes - an exception was the GT Coupe of 1969-1973 often described as a low budget alternative for a Corvette, Porsche, etc., but in truth a unique little car in its own right and a hot collectible of today.

1965 Racer Billy Wade is killed at age 34 at the Daytona International Speedway in Daytona Beach, FL during a testing session for Goodyear tires

1975 Arthur B. Domonoske of Doble dies at age 91

1981 Majority interest in Aston Martin Lagonda Ltd. is acquired by Pace Petroleum and CH Industrials, with Victor Gauntlett and Tim Hearley named as Joint Chairmen

1988 Gunnar Engellau, President of AB Volvo 1956-1971 and Chairman 1971-1978, dies in Goteborg, Sweden at age 80

1995 The Ford Mustang Cobra R is introduced

JANUARY 6

1887 James Harmon Marks of Packard is born in Grand Rapids, MI

1896 Edward P. Cowles is hired by James W. Packard to assist in the design of a "motor wagon"

1899 Heinrich "Heinz" Nordhoff of Volkswagen is born in Hildesheim, Germany

1911 Earl Howard of the Cadillac Motor Car Company delivers a new Cadillac to Delco to facilitate development of the self-starter by Charles F. Kettering and associates

1915 Joseph Edward Lundy of the Ford Motor Company born in Clarion, IA

1917 Studebaker's famous "gold car", a standard touring car with most of the chassis and body plated in gold, is unveiled at the New York Automobile Show

1920 Walter P. Chrysler joins the Willys-Overland Company as Executive Vice President and General Manager

1924 Racer Pablo Birger is born in Buenos Aires, Argentina

1925 John Zachary DeLorean is born in Detroit, MI

1925 Eleven prominent pioneers of the United States automobile industry are given silver medals during the Silver Anniversary Dinner of the National Automobile Chamber of Commerce's "The Decoration of the Pioneers"

1926 Racer George Francis Patrick "Pat" Flaherty is born in Glendale, CA

1926 Stanley Carleton Gault of the Goodyear Tire & Rubber Company is born in Wooster, OH

1929 E. L. Cord test drives the prototype Cord L 29

*The parking lot at Prospect Point in Vancouver, BC, Canada provides
a study of 1930's rear views. The white car is a Cord L 29 convertible coupe.*

1930 The Graham-Paige Motors Corporation of Dearborn, MI registers its logo as a trademark

1931 John A. Betti of the Ford Motor Company is born in Ottawa, IL

1934 The Graham Custom Eight Model 69 is introduced as a Second Series 1934 offering, featuring a supercharger designed by F. F. Kishline

1935 The Packard 120 is introduced on the Lawrence Tibbett radio show

1941 Charles E. Wilson is elected President of General Motors, replacing William S. Knudsen who had resigned the previous year to enter government service

1942 The first Mercury 305 cid Series H V-8 engine is produced

1943 Eugene Holman is elected to the Board of Directors of the Standard Oil Company of New Jersey

1944 C. H. Warner, a cofounder of the Stewart-Warner Speedometer Corporation, dies in San Marino, CA at age 71

1953 Earle S. MacPherson is issued a United States patent for his vehicle wheel suspension system

1954 The North American debut of the Swallow Doretti is held at the Ambassador Hotel in Los Angeles, CA

1954 The 1954 Fords are introduced featuring three new models, the Crestline Skyliner, Cresline Sunliner, and the Ranch Wagon, plus the marque's first OHV V-8 engine

1954 The Kaiser-Darrin sports car is released for public sale after several delays during the previous two months

1955 The 1955 Kaisers are introduced

1955 The 1955 Willys Bermuda hardtop coupe and Custom 4-door sedan are introduced

1956 "Packard" script is added to all Clipper trunks, ending the attempt to establish Clipper as a separate marque

Clipper for 1956
—America's Finest Medium Price Car—
Built by Packard Craftsmen

1957 Louis S. Clarke, the cofounder of the Autocar Company in 1899 who is credited with inventing the sparkplug in the United States and building the first automobile with shaft drive, dies in Palm Beach, FL at age 90

1960 The General Motors Acceptance Corporation elects Charles G. Stradella as Chairman and Thomas W. Towell as President

1960 Racer Fernando Croceri is born in Argentina

1972 Robert S. McLaughlin, founder of the McLaughlin Motor Car Company and longtime President of General Motors of Canada Ltd., dies in Oshawa, ON at age 100

1973 Fowler McCormick, President of the International Harvester Company 1941-1946 and its Chairman 1946-1951, dies at age 74

1973 A Mercedes-Benz 770K, the so-called "Adolf Hitler parade car", is sold to Earl Clark of Lancaster, PA for an auction record of $153,000

1978 John F. Gordon, President of General Motors 1958-1965, dies in Royal Oak, MI at age 77

1989 Racer Jim Hurtubise dies from a heart attack in Port Arthur, TX at age 56

JANUARY 7

1866 William Benson Mayo of the Ford Motor Company is born in Chatham, MA

1868 Gustav Otto Ludolf Heine of Heine-Velox is born in Vierkrug, Germany

1887 Canadian automobile pioneer Henry Seth Taylor dies at age 55

1894 Clyde R. Paton, Chief Engineer of Packard and Willys, is born in Almont, MI

1900 The Plass Motor-Wagon Company is founded in Pierre, SD by Reuben H. Plass and J. S. Reynolds of Brooklyn, NY and Charles S. DeLand of Pierre

1912 Jack Forker Chrysler, son of Walter P. Chrysler and an official with the W. P. Chrysler Building Corporation, is born in Bellevue, PA

1914 Christian Hamilton Gray and Thomas Sloper are issued a British patent for their radial tire, although actual production was minimal at the time

1916 Elliott Marantette "Pete" Estes of General Motors is born in Mendon, MI

1917 Tom Killefer of the Chrysler Corporation is born in Los Angeles, CA

1918 Victor Lasky, biographer of Henry Ford II, is born in Liberty, NY

1921 The Rolls-Royce Ltd. Board of Directors approve production plans for the "Goshawk", which would be marketed as the 20 HP

1924 The custom coachbuilding firm of LeBaron Inc. is formed by the merger of LeBaron Carrossiers and the Bridgeport Body Company with Clarence W. Seward as President, Raymond H. Dietrich as Vice President, Ralph S. Roberts as Secretary, and James H. Hinman as Treasurer

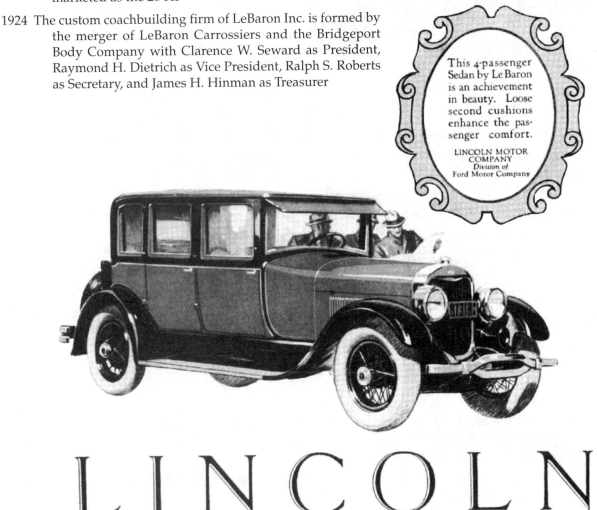

This 4-passenger Sedan by LeBaron is an achievement in beauty. Loose second cushions enhance the passenger comfort.

LINCOLN MOTOR COMPANY
Division of
Ford Motor Company

LINCOLN

1928 The Dodge Brothers Victory Six is introduced to the public at the New York Auto Show

1929 W. Dale Compton of the Ford Motor Company is born is Chrisman, IL

1929 The first Plymouth Model U is produced

1932 Bernard Hanon of Renault is born in Bois-Colombes, France

1936 The Pontiac "Indian Head in oval" mascot is patented by designer Franklin Q. Hershey

1936 James E. DeLong is appointed General Manager of the Waukesha Motor Company

1939 Racer Brausch Niemann is born in Durban, South Africa

1946 Racer Mike Wilds is born in Great Britain

1950 The 1950 Chevrolets are introduced

The Coffee County Court House in Manchester, TN is the site of a chance gathering of from left, 1949, 1951, and 1950 Chevrolets.

1954 Harold F. Howard, former General Manager of Chevrolet, dies at age 57

1956 The Plymouth Fury sport coupe is introduced as a mid-year model

1957 The Mercury Turnpike Cruiser convertible Indianapolis 500 Pace Car replica is introduced

1958 Goffredo Zehender, winner of the 1931 24 Hours of Spa (Belgium), dies at age 56

1962 Edward Riley of General Motors dies at age 67

1963 The 60,000,000th Ford Motor Company-built vehicle, a Mercury S-55, is produced

1964 Racer Paulo Carcasci is born in Brazil

1964 Racer Reg Parnell dies at age 52 of peritonitis in Derby, England

1969 Fiat acquires a 50% ownership of Ferrari

1974 Edsel B. Ford II joins the Ford Motor Company as a product analyst

1976 The historic Ormond Garage in Ormond Beach, FL, known as the "Birthplace of Speed", is destroyed by fire

1980 President Jimmy Carter signs legislation granting $1.5 billion in federal loan guarantees to the ailing Chrysler Corporation

1985 General Motors launches their semi-autonomous Saturn Corporation with Joseph J. Sanchez named as its first President

1985 Arthur W. Soutter of Rolls-Royce of America, Inc. dies

1986 International Trucks, the non-agricultural side of the defunct International Harvester Company, is reorganized as the Navistar International Corporation

1987 General Motors reorganizes the Cadillac Group

1989 The Dodge Viper is introduced at the North American International Automobile Show

1991 Racer Henri Louveau dies in France at age 80

1994 Race car sponsor J. W. Hunt dies at age 74

JANUARY 8

1888 Walter Samuel Carpenter Jr., a Director of General Motors, is born in Wilkes-Barre, PA

1897 Robert Lowry Biggers of the Chrysler Corporation is born in Webster Groves, MO

1904 Cartoonist Peter Arno, founder in 1939 of the Albatross Motor Car Company and designer of its single prototype, is born in New York City

1907 Thomas E. Rush succeeds Jacob Sulzbach as President of the Mack Brothers Motor Car Company

1915 The Cadillac Motor Car Company's two-speed rear axle is ruled to be an infringement of patent rights held by Walter S. Austin of the Austin Automobile Company in Grand Rapids, MI, with damages and costs awarded

1916 Rembrandt Bugatti commits suicide in Paris, France at age 30

1920 Automobile spring manufacturer James Martin McInerney is born in Chicago, IL

1927 The Little Marmon is introduced in New York City - by July the car would be marketed as the "Marmon Eight"

1944 William K. Vanderbilt Jr., patron of automobile racing and the Long Island Motor Parkway, dies in New York City at age 65

1947 Racer Greg Pickett is born in Alamo, CA

1948 Racer Jas Patterson is born on Long Island, NY

1951 Jack F. Wolfram, General Manager of Oldsmobile, is elected as a Vice President of General Motors

*This 1953 Oldsmobile 98 hardtop coupe parked at left in Glenwood, MN was
manufactured early in Jack F. Wolfram's 13 year term as
General Manager of the division.*

1957 William A. Siler of the Delco-Remy Division of General Motors dies at age 63

1960 B. Frank Jones, retired Chief Engineer of the White Motor Company, dies at age 68

1970 John J. Riccardo is elected President of the Chrysler Corporation

1972 Racer Bryon Faloon is killed during the New Zealand Grand Prix in Auckland

1975 Automotive historian Louis P. Lochner dies in Wiesbaden, West Germany at age 87

1980 Thomas Raymond Mays, longtime racer and developer of the BRM race cars, dies in Bourne, England

JANUARY 9

1835 Yataro Iwasaki, founder of Mitsubishi, is born in Tosa, Japan

1844 George Pope is born in Boston, MA

1846 George Norman Pierce, founder of Pierce-Arrow, is born in Friendsville, PA

*A Pierce-Arrow from the early 1920's earning its keep not
as luxury automobile but as a tour bus, a task for which
the great car was eminently qualified.*

1870 HSH Prince Francis Joseph Leopold Frederick of Teck, Chairman of the Royal Automobile Club, is born at Kensington Palace in London

1877 James Carroll Blair of the Libbey-Owens-Ford Glass Company is born in Toledo, OH

1887 Racer and automotive historian Sidney Charles Houghton "Sammy" Davis is born in London, England

1889 Charles Leaming Tutt, President of the Pikes Peak Auto Highway Company, is born in Colorado Springs, CO

1894 Canadian axle manufacturer William H. Watkins is born near Britton, MI

1901 Gioachino Colombo of Alfa Romeo is born in Legnano, Italy

1903 Henry B. Joy contracts with architect Albert Kahn to construct a new factory in Detroit, MI for the Packard Motor Car Company

1906 Jacob Sulzback succeeds Otto E. Mears as President of the Mack Brothers Motor Car Company

1907 The Luverne Automobile Company is incorporated in Minnesota with A. D. LaDue as President, E. A. Brown as Vice President, S. C. Rea as Secretary, Jay A. Kennicott as Treasurer, F. A. "Al" Leicher as Manager, his brother Edward L. Leicher as Mechanical Engineer, and S. B. Nelson, William Jacobsen Jr., Dr. C. O. Wright, and J. W. Gerber as minority stockholders

1908 John N. Willys is named President of the Overland Automobile Company

1909 The Badger Four Wheel Drive Auto Company organized in Clintonville, WI

1911 Judge W. C. Noyes of the United States Circuit Court of Appeals rules in favor of the Ford Motor Company, effectively making the Selden patent invalid and spelling the end of the ALAM

1912 The first Ahrens-Fox piston pumper fire truck is delivered to the Rockford (IL) Fire Department

1915 Earl Cooper scores his first victory, winning the 305-mile Point Loma Road Race in San Diego, CA driving his famous Stutz No. 8

1924 The Ford Motor Company announced a standard cab for their trucks

1926 The Pontiac is introduced at New York Automobile Show as a companion marque for the Oakland

1930 Paul A. Heinen of the Chrysler Corporation is born in Teaneck, NJ

1930 Raymond Horrocks of British Leyland is born

1932 The Packard 900 Light Eight and Twin-Six are introduced, expanding its market coverage in both directions (the Twin-Six was actually a quickly assembled show car, with the specification much-modified by the time actual production began in April)

1948 The last 1947 Pontiac is produced, twelve days after production of the 1948 Pontiacs had begun, one of the few times that two model years had been produced concurrently

1948 Neste OY is incorporated in Finland

1950 Production of the 1950 Kaisers officially begins, although unsold and virtually identical 1949 models had been recoded as 1950's since the previous November

1953 Henry T. Ewald, cofounder of the Campbell-Ewald Company that pioneered national automobile advertising campaigns, dies in Detroit, MI at age 67

1953 Edward Beach Gallaher, the designer of the 1900 Keystone who was later involved with the Searchmont and Motorette, dies in Norwalk, CT at age 79

1953 Fabbrica Automobili Isotta-Fraschini is declared bankrupt

1956 Lewis N. Rosenbaum of the Continental Motors Corporation dies at age 74

1958 The Toyota and Datsun marques debut in the United States at the Imported Motor Car Show in Los Angeles, CA

1959 Racer Mark Martin is born in Batesville, AR

1960 Racer Pascal Fabre is born in Lyon, France

1962 Walter C. Teagle, President of the Standard Oil Company of New Jersey 1917-1937 and its Chairman 1937-1942, dies at age 83

1963 The first of fourteen "Swiss Cheese" Pontiac Catalinas is built featuring various weightsaving techniques to make the car competitive on the race circuits

1967 Roy D. Chapin Jr. is named Chairman of American Motors to succeed the retiring Robert B. Evans - AMC President Roy Abernethy also retires and is succeeded by William V. Luneburg

1967 Construction begins on the Volga Automobile Works in Tol'iatti, USSR

1977 The Wolf, sponsored by Walter Wolf and driven by Jody Scheckter, wins its Formula 1 debut in the Argentinian Grand Prix

1981 Racer and automobile historian S. C. H. "Sammy" Davis dies in Guildford, Surrey, England on his 94th birthday

1981 Antique automobile collector Bernard J. "Barney" Pollard Sr. dies in Detroit, MI at age 84

JANUARY 10

1870 Frederick Kearney Parke of Studebaker is born in St. Louis, MO

1870 The Standard Oil Company of Ohio is organized

1888 James Gillespie Blaine, a Director of the Studebaker-Packard Corporation, is born in New York City

1889 Automotive artist John Held Jr. is born in Salt Lake City, UT

1896 Edgar Charles Row of the Chrysler Corporation is born in St. Marys, OH

1901 Oil is discovered at Spindletop Field near Beaumont, TX, an event that in many ways made the United States automobile industry feasible

1905 Automobiles Delage is established in Courbevoie, France by Louis Delage

1912 The 1912 Velies are introduced at the Grand Central Palace Show in New York City

1913 Robert S. Olson of the Ford Motor Credit Company is born in Columbus Junction, IA

1913 Ten White automobiles and trucks arrive in Libau, Russia (now Liepaja, Latvia), the first of about 4,000 to be purchased by the Czarist government

Colorado high school student Ernie Peyton drove this 20-year-old White truck between Fort Collins and Estes Park while working for the Rocky Mountain Transportation Company in the late 1940's. In the 1960's Peyton purchased the truck from a junkyard and restored it.

1914 Robert Blythin of Packard is born in Cleveland, OH

1914 Airplane pilot Lincoln Beachey and automobile racer Barney Oldfield stage their first match race in Emeryville, CA

1917 Chocolate manufacturer William Klein Jr., a noted collector of classic Rolls-Royce and Bentleys, is born in Elizabethtown, PA

1918 The Hebb Motors Company, Inc. is organized to manufacture Patriot motor trucks in Havelock, NE (now a part of Lincoln, NE) with A. G. Hebb as President, Elmer C. Hammond as Vice President, Loyd A. Winship as Secretary-Treasurer, and Laurence F. Seaton as Chief engineer

1918 Charles F. Kettering is elected President of the Society of Automotive Engineers

1921 Racer Rodger Morris Ward is born in Beloit, KS

1923 Production of the Star shifts from Long Island City, NY to the former Willys-Overland Company plant in Elizabeth, NJ

1930 Henry A. Nadig, whose gasoline-powered car was completed as early as 1891, dies in Allentown, PA

1934 The Nash LaFayette is introduced as a low-priced sub-marque

1934 Racer Neil "Soapy" Castles is born

1935 Ferry Porsche marries Dorothea Reitz

1940 Racer Harry Gant is born in Taylorsville, NC

1941 Harry G. Carmichael, Vice President and General Manager of General Motors of Canada Ltd., resigns to direct World War II mobilization on behalf of the Canadian government

1942 The Ford Motor Company signs a government contract to produce 15,000 Willys-designed GPW's, the utility car that would become the "Jeep"

1946 Lloyd P. Lochridge of the Sinclair Refining Company dies at age 56

1949 The 1949 Willys Model VJ3-4 Jeepster is introduced

1950 The Hyundai Engineering & Construction Company, Ltd. is incorporated in Seoul, Korea

1952 Racer Jochen Dauer is born in Nuremberg, West Germany

1953 Racer Robert W. "Bobby" Rahal is born in Medina, OH

1955 Donald R. Stuart joins the Studebaker-Packard Corporation as Packard Divisional Sales Manager under the supervision of LeRoy Spencer

1956 John M. Wood, owner of the Albany Hardware Specialty Manufacturing Company whose previous automotive career included positions with Packard, Lincoln, White, and the Stout Engineering Laboratories, dies

1958 The Ford Motor Company announces plans to enter the heavy and extra-heavy truck field

1958 Racer Eddie Cheever is born in Phoenix, AZ

1967 The Pontiac Saint Moritz convertible show car is unveiled at the Toledo (OH) Auto Show

1968 Roy L. Reuther of the United Auto Workers dies in Detroit, MI at age 58

1971 Racer Ignazio Giunti is killed at age 29 when his Ferrari crashes into the stalled Matra of Jean-Pierre Beltoise at the Buenos Aires 1000 km race at the now renamed Autodromo Municipal in Buenos Aires, Argentina

1972 Nubar Gulbenkian, oil magnate and exotic Rolls-Royce fancier, dies in Cannes, France at age 75

1975 Toni Schmuecker is named Managing Director of Volkswagenwerk AG

1979 The last Volkswagen Beetle convertible is produced

1981 The first Annual Southwest Unique Little Car Meet is staged in Phoenix, AZ by the Subaru 360 Drivers' Club

1990 James R. Shipley, a General Motors stylist 1936-1938 and a longtime professor of art and design at the University of Illinois, dies at age 79

JANUARY 11

1889 Calvin Blackman Bridges, a pioneer designer of streamlined cars, is born in Schuyler Falls, NY

1897 Frank Arthur Patty of General Motors is born in Lawrence, KS

1902 Rome, Italy issues its first drivers license to Giulio de Leonardis

1913 The Hudson Motor Car Company introduces the Model 54 sedan, claimed to be the world's first production closed car, at the 13th National Automobile Show in New York City

1913 The Maxwell Motor Corporation is formed in Detroit, MI to salvage the marque from the defunct United States Motor Company

1917 The Ford Model T truck is introduced

1919 Hudson's new companion marque, the Essex, is publicly unveiled at the Los Angeles (CA) Auto Show

1921 Frederick Haynes is elected President and General Manager of Dodge Brothers, Inc.

1923 Carroll Shelby is born in Leesburg, TX

1925 Rene Dreyfus makes his major racing debut, winning the Falicon Hillclimb in a Bugatti Brescia

1925 George L. Lavery, a proponent of metal automobile wheels, dies in Elkins Park, PA at age 68

1926 Burton J. Westcott, founder of the Westcott Motor Car Company, dies in Springfield, OH at age 57

1940 The 25,000,000th General Motors car is produced, a silver Chevrolet Master DeLuxe four-door town sedan - that evening a celebratory banquet is hosted by Alfred P. Sloan Jr. and William S. Knudsen, with a nostalgic appearance by corporation founder William C. Durant

1944 J. Walter Christie, a pioneer designer of front-wheel-drive cars, dies in Falls Church, VA at age 77

1946 Edgar F. Kaiser is named General Manager of the Kaiser-Frazer Corporation

1950 Harry M. Bramberry Sr., the inventor of nitrided steel piston rings and a consultant to the White Motor Company, dies in New York City at age 56

1952 Nathaniel M. Aycock, an employee and official of The Texas Company since 1923, dies in Bronxville, NY at age 64

1954 Alfred E. Grater, German-born former Assistant Chief Engineer of the Reo Motor Car Company, dies at age 65

1956 The 1956 Chevrolet Corvette is introduced

1956 The DeSoto Pacesetter convertible is introduced as a limited-production replica of the unique car that would be produced to serve as pace car for the upcoming Indianapolis 500 race

1957 Pontiac introduces its top of the line Series 28 Star Chief Custom Bonneville convertible coupe, and the equally exclusive Series 27 Star Chief Custom Safari 4-door station wagon, later dubbed the "Transcontinental"

1958 The Studebaker-based 1958 Packard sedan, hardtop, and station wagon are introduced, which along with the Hawk sport coupe introduced nearly three months earlier would be the last of the marque

1959 Racer Brett Bodine is born in Elmira, NY

1959 Racer Thierry Tassin is born in Belgium

1968 Matra unveils its new V-12 racing engine

1975 Stylist Raymond H. Dietrich is named the first honorary member of the Classic Car Club of America

1977 Henry Ford II resigns from the Ford Foundation

1982 Jiro Horikoshi of Mitsubishi dies

JANUARY 12

1822 Jean Joseph Etienne Lenoir, internal combustion engine pioneer, is born in Mussy-la-Ville, Belgium

1874 Carl Graham Fisher is born in Greensburg, IN

1877 Louis Renault is born in Paris, France

1879 Ray Harroun, winner of the first Indianapolis 500 in 1911, is born in Spartansburg, PA

1899 Ralph Edward Oakland, Vice President and Treasurer of the Checker Cab Manufacturing Corporation, is born in Chicago, IL

1900 The Detroit Automobile Company completes its first vehicle, a delivery wagon largely designed by Henry Ford which is sold to Newcomb, Endicott and Company

1904 Henry Ford drives the Ford Arrow to a new land speed record of 91.370 mph on frozen Lake St. Clair, MI, breaking the record set ten days earlier by the Packard Gray Wolf

1912 The Mason Automobile Company is reorganized with Edward R. Mason returning as President

1921 Durant Motors, Inc. is organized in New York by William C. Durant

1922 The Jewett is introduced by Jewett Motors Inc. of Detroit, MI, a subsidiary of the Paige-Detroit Motor Car Company, and named for Harry M. Jewett, President of the parent company

1922 The last Scripps-Booth is produced

1923 The 7,000,000th Ford Model T is produced

1924 Racer Olivier Gendebien is born in Brussels, Belgium

1928 Racer Lloyd Ruby is born in Wichita Falls, TX

1934 The Auto Union "p-wagen" laps the Avus track at better than 200 kph to validate the contract between the company and Ferdinand Porsche

1936 Erik Ekstrom, Swedish-born Vice President of the Borg-Warner Corporation, dies in Rockford, IL at age 47

1938 Racer Alan Binely Rees is born in Newport, Monmouthshire, Wales

1949 The 1949 Pontiacs are introduced, featuring the marque's first post-World War II styling by Herman Kaiser, Bob Lauer, and Joe Schemansky

1950 The 1950 Plymouths are introduced

1951 The 1951 Plymouths are introduced

1954 August Frykman, the Souris, ND blacksmith whose automotive efforts consisted of two 1907 Frykmans featuring his patented Frykman Friction Drive transmission, dies in Minneapolis, MN at age 76

1957 Racer Ken Wharton is killed at age 40 when his Ferrari Monza crashes during a sports car race in Ardmore, New Zealand

1962 Racer Emanuele Pirro is born in Rome, Italy

1963 Racer Kerry Teague is born in Concord, NC

1970 George Brough, manufacturer of the 1935-1939 Hudson-powered Brough Superior, dies

1973 Clifton R. Wharton Jr. becomes the first black to be elected to the Ford Motor Company Board of Directors

1975 The Fittipaldi makes its Formula 1 debut in the Argentinian Grand Prix in Buenos Aires, but the car driven by Wilson Fittipaldi is involved in a minor crash and is forced to retire

1988 Racer Piero Taruffi dies in Rome, Italy at age 81

JANUARY 13

1862 William Edmund Warwick of the Standard Oil Company of Indiana is born in Oshkosh, WI

1906 The first American Motor Car Manufacturers Association (AMCMA) auto show opens at the 69th Regiment Armory in New York City

1907 The Isotta-Fraschini is introduced in the United States

1920 Harry H. Bassett is elected President of the Buick Motor Company

1920 Charles F. Kettering is named as a Vice President of General Motors

1928 William A. Simonds joins the Ford Motor Company as a member of the Advertising and Publicity department

1937 Anthony Paul Saint John of the Chrysler Corporation is born in Washington, DC

1941 Carleton Ellis, the inventor in 1925 of the first durable lacquer for automobile painting, dies in Miami Beach, FL at age 64

1941 Paul M. Marko, holder of many patents relating to automotive storage batteries, dies at age 63

1942 Henry Ford is issued a United States patent for a plastic automobile body

1948 The last 1947 Cadillac is produced

A 1947 Cadillac convertible, one of the era's most nostalgic cars, is parked at far left in the parking lot of the Frontier Motel in McAllen, TX

1950 Racer Bob Earl is born in Great Bend, KS

1953 Alfa Romeo purchases the aerodynamic B.A.T. 7 from Carrozzeria Bertone to display at the New York Auto Show

1954 Frederic S. Glover of Reo dies in Detroit, MI at age 74

1957 Alejandro de Tomaso makes his Formula 1 racing debut, finishing ninth in the Argentine Grand Prix in Buenos Aires driving a Ferrari 500/625

1959 Racer Ernie Irvan is born in Salinas, CA

1968 Racer Gianni Morbidelli is born in Pesaro, Italy

1984 Racer and automotive historian John Bolster dies at age 73

1988 Donald Mitchell Healey dies in Cornwallshire, England at age 89

JANUARY 14

1883 Roy Edward Cole of Dodge and Studebaker is born in Columbia Station, OH

1896 The Daimler Motor Syndicate, Ltd. is founded in Coventry, Warwickshire, England by Harry J. Lawson

1897 Clarance Stanley of General Motors is born in Pittsfield, MA

1902 Andrew L. Riker begins developing the first gasoline-powered Locomobile as authorized by company President Samuel T. Davis

1914 The moving assembly line is implemented at the Ford Motor Company

1920 John F. Dodge dies in New York City at age 55

1929 Arthur F. Sidgreaves is designated by Rolls-Royce, Ltd. to succeed Basil Johnson as Managing Director at month's end

Mr. Peter Helck, internationally-known artist and automobile connoisseur, is the owner of "Old 16." This car was designed by A. L. Riker and driven to its greatest triumphs by "Dare-devil" Joe Tracy and George Robertson.

1933 Racer Stuart Turner is born in England

1934 Racer Alberto Rodriguez Larreta is born in Buenos Aires, Argentina

1946 Edward J. Cutler, the principal developer of the Henry Ford Museum and Greenfield Village, transfers to the Ford Motor Company as "architectural engineer" primarily to allow him to qualify for retirement benefits

Demand
CHAMPIONS

1949 The first long wheelbase 1949 Plymouth Deluxe is produced

1950 Robert T. Hazell, Vice President and General Manager of the Fruehauf Trailer Company of Canada Ltd., dies

From a 1953 Champion Spark Plug Company magazine advertisment.

1954 The boards of directors of the Nash-Kelvinator Corporation and the Hudson Motor Car Company agree to merge as the American Motors Corporation

1955 Col. Horatio Nelson Jackson, a banker who made the first trans-United States automobile trip in 1903, dies in Burlington, VT at age 82

1966 Automobile historian Arthur Pound dies at age 81

1975 The Deutsche Bank acquires a controlling interest in Daimler-Benz AG

1985 James L. Conlon, General Manager of the Buick-Oldsmobile-Pontiac Assembly Division 1952-1960, dies in Columbus, OH at age 89

1986 Jaguar announces the creation of the Silk Cut Jaguar Team, a three year commitment to campaign the Jaguar XJR in international motor racing

1986 Thierry Sabine, founder of the Paris-Dakar Rally, dies at age 36 in a helicopter crash in Timbuktu, Mali

1987 The Collins & Aikman Corporation reorganizes as the Wickes Companies, Inc. - the principal products of the company are fabrics and other materials used for automobile interiors

1988 Bill Casstevens elected Secretary-Treasurer of the United Auto Workers

1996 Formula 1 race car designer Mo Gomm dies at age 74

JANUARY 15

1870 Pierre Samuel DuPont of General Motors is born in Wilmington, DE

1877 Alden L. McMurtry, a founder of the Society of Automotive Engineers, is born in Pittsburgh, PA

1887 David Herrick Goodwillie of the Libbey-Owens-Ford Glass Company is born in Oak Park, IL

1894 Rodger Joseph Emmert of General Motors is born in Piqua, OH

1902 The first automobile race in Japan is staged at Uyeno Park in Yokohama and won by T. Sudo driving an Auto-Bi motorcycle, a predecessor of the Thomas Flyer

1907 Brothers Everett S. and Forrest F. Cameron are awarded a United States patent for their automobile transmission design

1909 H. D. Ludlow of Chicago, IL becomes the first funeral director to use a motorized hearse

1909 Gianoberto Carlo Rembrandt "Jean" Bugatti is born in Mulheim-am-Rhein, Germany

1911 W. O. Bentley enters the automobile industry as a partner in Lecoq and Fernie, London agents for La Licorne, Buchet, and D.F.P. cars

1918 Frank Winchell of General Motors is born in Evansville, IN

1919 Racer Bill Stroppe is born in Long Beach, CA

1924 William S. Knudsen is named President and General Manager of Chevrolet, Vice President of General Motors and is elected to the Board of Directors

1941 and 1939 Chevrolets, both somewhat battered, are processed through Canadian customs south of Boissevain, Manitoba. The cars represented the final years of William S. Knudsen's career with Chevy.

1925 The Ford Airport opens in Dearborn, MI

1926 Automobile parts manufacturer James Sims Reid Jr. is born in Cleveland, OH

1929 A Series 6-80 sedan is the first Auburn produced at the Central Manufacturing Company facility in Connersville, IN

1934 Racer Mario Araujo de Cabral is born in Portugal

1936 The Ford Foundation is established primarily to circumvent new tax laws and ensure that control of the Ford Motor Company would remain with the Ford family after Henry Ford's death

1936 Ralph Garfield Lewis, Technical Advisor of the General Motors Export Corporation and a former official with Buick, Hudson, Carhart, and Kingston, dies at age 59

1941 Charles Cheers Wakefield, 1st Viscount Wakefield, founder and Governing Director of C. C. Wakefield & Company Ltd., manufacturers of lubricating oils, dies at age 81

1942 The first "blackout" Cadillac is produced with painted rather than chrome plated trim due to World War II rationing

1942 Racer Jacque Coulon is born in France

1943 Chevrolet Corvette engineer David C. Hill is born in Rochester, NY

1948 The 20,000th Volkswagen is produced

1950 General Motors opens its "Mid-Century Motorama" at the Waldorf-Astoria Hotel in New York City, featuring the Cadillac Debutante convertible with leopard skin upholstery and gold plated interior hardware

1953 The 100,000th 1953 Dodge is produced

1953 The 1953 Willys Aero-Falcon is introduced as a mid-year model

1953 Racer David Kennedy is born in Sligo, Ireland

1954 The 1954 Packards are introduced

1957 Frank T. Armstrong of the Wagner Electric Corporation dies

1958 The Ford Motor Company creates the Lincoln-Edsel-Mercury Division, hiring former Packard President James J. Nance as a Vice President in charge of the division

1964 Volkswagen de Mexico is established

1978 The ATS makes its Formula 1 debut at the Argentinian Grand Prix in Buenos Aires, with the cars driven by Jochen Mass and Jean-Pierre Jarier finishing 11th and 12th - the Merzario makes its Formula 1 debut, but the car designed and driven by Arturo Merzario retires with a faulty differential

1981 Racer Graham Whitehead dies in Basildon, Berkshire, England at age 58

1982 Gerald C. Meyers resigns as Chairman and Chief Executive Officer of the American Motors Corporation - W. Paul Tippett Jr. succeeds him as Chairman and Jose J. Dedeurwaerder is named President

1984 The Hyundai Pony is introduced in Canada as the first Korean car to be marketed in North America

1988 Edsel B. Ford II and William Clay Ford Jr., great-grandsons of Henry Ford, are elected to the Board of Directors of the Ford Motor Company

1995 William Digneit of the Ford Motor Company dies at age 73

JANUARY 16

1853 Tire manufacturer Andre Michelin is born

1867 Thomas E. Rush of Mack and International is born in New York City

1899 Fritz Konecke of Daimler-Benz AG is born in Hannover, Germany

1900 James W. Packard applies for a patent on an "Automatic Spark Control", his first relating to automobiles

1905 The Sunbeam Motor Car Company Ltd. is registered in Wolverhampton, England with John Marston as Chairman and Thomas Cureton as Managing Director

1905 The Autocar Type XI, featuring the marque's first 4-cylinder engine, is introduced

1913 The world's first 4-passenger closed car, a Duryea built in Coventry, England, is introduced at the Stanley Motor Show

1916 The Hudson Super Six is officially introduced to the public

1917 Fred Lloyd Hartley of the Union Oil Company of California is born in Vancouver, BC, Canada

1919 The Essex is announced as a lower-priced companion for the Hudson

1925 David Samuel Potter of General Motors is born in Seattle, WA

1927 L. L. Woodward, President since 1916 of Fitz Gibbon & Crisp, Inc., manufacturers of bodies for commercial vehicles, and President of the Autocar Company since April 1926, dies in Trenton Junction, NJ at age 47

1930 Racer Luki Botha is born in South Africa

1934 Joseph B. Graham announces that all Graham six-cylinders cars will be outfitted with superchargers, although actual implementation of this plan would require 21 months

Partially cut off, the car parked at far left in Petoskey, MI is a rare 1937 Graham.

1935 Racer Anthony Joseph "A. J." Foyt is born in Houston, TX

1936 The Packard Motor Car Company and the Henney Motor Company sign a contract whereby Henney will have exclusive rights to Packard's commercial chassis

1937 Walter S. Rogers of White and Chrysler dies

1941 Col. W. G. Wall, cofounder, Vice President, and Chief Engineer of the National Motor Vehicle Company and President of the Society of Automotive Engineers in 1928, dies in Indianapolis, IN at age 64

1944 The Divco-Twin Truck Company changes its name to the Divco Corporation

1944 Racer Bill Tempero is born in Milwaukee, WI

1947 Claire L. Barnes, an official of the Willys-Overland Company who in 1929 was a cofounder and later President of the Houdaille-Hershey Corporation, dies in New York City at age 66

1952 Alvan Macauley, President 1916-1939 and Chairman 1939-1948 of the Packard Motor Car Company, dies in Clearwater, FL one day short of his 80th birthday

The unmistakable radiator shell of a classic Packard and the Orpheum Theatre with "talkies" give period charm to this circa-1930 view of Ortonville, MN.

1952 Racer Piercarlo Ghinzani is born in Riviera d'Adda, Bergamo, Lombardy, Italy

1953 The Chevrolet Corvette and Pontiac Parisienne show cars are introduced to the press at the Waldorf-Astoria Hotel in New York City

1954 General Motors unveils the Pontiac Strato Streak Sedan, Pontiac Bonneville Special GT Coupe, and the Firebird XP-21 jet-powered car at the General Motors Motorama at the Waldorf-Astoria Hotel in New York City

1955 Juan Manuel Fangio in a Mercedes-Benz W196 wins the 1955 Argentine Grand Prix in Buenos Aires - Eugenio Castellotti makes his Formula 1 Grand Prix debut driving a new Lancia D50, but crashes after suffering heat stroke

1957 Paul E. Gery of the Engineering and Foundry Division of the Ford Motor Company and a former Buick test engineer dies

1958 The first Scarab sports car is tested

1965 United States President Lyndon B. Johnson and Canadian Prime Minister Lester Pearson sign the United States & Canada Automotive Trade Agreement

1966 Racers Jose-Luis Pampyn and Rafael Taravilla are killed during the Monte Carlo Rally when their Fiat crashes between Ales and Uzes, France

1968 Alfa Romeo approves Rudolf Hruska's masterplan to develop and manufacture the Alfasud

1978 The Ford Econoline Super Wagon and Super Van are introduced

1984 The Ford Motor Company purchases the Dearborn Inn in Dearborn, MI

1992 William Rootes, 2nd Baron Rootes of Ramsbury, Chairman of Chrysler United Kingdom 1967-1973, dies in Hungerford, England at age 74

JANUARY 17

1872 James Alvan Macauley of the Packard Motor Car Company is born in Wheeling, WV

1879 John Thomas Smith of General Motors is born in New Haven, CT

1882 Roy Donaldson McClure, the first Chief Surgeon of the Henry Ford Hospital and Henry Ford's longtime personal physician, is born in Bellebrook, OH

1892 Harry Herbert Bennett of the Ford Motor Company is born in Ann Arbor, MI

1895 Sir William Sinclair of Dunlop Rubber Company (Scotland) Ltd. is born in Wick, Scotland

1896 Alva W. Phelps of General Motors is born in Buena Vista, GA

1899 Camille Jenatzy, driving an electric Jenatzy of his own design at Acheres Park, France, raises the land speed record to 41.42 mph - former land speed record holder Count Gaston de Chasseloup-Laubat then regained the record reaching 43.69 mph in his Jeantaud electric

1903 The third annual National Automobile Show (the first since 1900) opens at Madison Square Garden in New York City

1908 The Harrison Wagon Works of Grand Rapids, MI, manufacturers of the Harrison that was equipped with an unsuccessful attempt at the first self-starter, is declared to be bankrupt

1917 John Vallery Banks of Kaiser is born in Boise, ID

1920 The Motor Wheel Corporation is incorporated in Michigan

1921 The first United States-built Rolls-Royce is completed

Fifth Avenue, New York City circa 1936. Partly obscured by a light pole,
a United States-built Rolls-Royce is parked at lower left.
The recently completed Empire State Building looms in the background.

1922 George B. Selden dies in Rochester, NY at age 75

1924 Racer John Riseley-Pritchard is born in Hereford, Hereford, England

1933 The Kelsey-Hayes Wheel Company is incorporated in Delaware to succeed the Kelsey-Hayes Wheel Corporation

1936 The first long-chassis Squire, with a custom Ranalah body, is delivered to Val E. Zethrin of Chislehurst, Kent, England

1938 Racer Rauno Aaltonen is born in Turku, Finland

1940 The Shell Marketing Company Ltd. changes its name to the Shell Refining and Marketing Company Ltd.

1945 Renault is nationalized by the French government as a result of the alleged Nazi-collaboration of Louis Renault - the Regie Nationale des Usines Renault formed in Billancourt would be run as a private business by the government appointed President, Pierre Lefaucheux

1948 Racer Lake Speed is born in Jackson, MS

1948 Maurice Goudard, past President of the Societe des Ingenieurs de l'Automobile and a leading automotive engineer in his native France, dies in Paris at age 66

1949 The first Volkswagen Beetle is imported into the United States

1952 Coachbuilder Walter O. Briggs, Chairman of the Briggs Manufacturing Company and owner of the Detroit Tigers baseball team, dies in Miami Beach, FL at age 74

1954 The Maserati 250F records its first racing victory as Juan Manuel Fangio wins the Argentine Grand Prix in Buenos Aires - Giuseppe Farina, who finished second in a Ferrari 625, qualified for the pole position, at age 47 years, 80 days the oldest driver to accomplish this feat in a Formula 1 championship race

1955 The 1955 Packards are introduced to the public, featuring the marque's first V-8 engines and new Torsion-Level suspension

1956 Ford Motor Company common stock is offered to the public for the first time

The student parking lot at Bismarck (ND) High School in 1963. The 1956 Ford Fairlane Sunliner convertible was manufactured during the year that Ford Motor Company stock was first offered to the public.

Hon. Edward T. Schafer

1958 Wilfred Leland dies in Detroit, MI at age 88

1964 The 1964 Opels are introduced to the United States market

1964 The first Porsche Carrera GTS is delivered to Otto Zipper in Los Angeles, CA

1966 Leonard P. Steuart, longtime Washington, DC automobile dealer, dies in Washington at age 86

1968 The British Leyland Motor Corporation is formed by the merger of the Leyland Group and British Motor Holdings Ltd.

1972 Edward F. Fisher of General Motors dies in Detroit, MI at age 80

1996 The British automobile industry celebrates its centennial with a program in Coventry Cathedral

JANUARY 18

1883 Warren Courtland MacFarlane, Acting General Manager and Treasurer of the Auburn Automobile
        Company 1922-1923, is born in Miles City, MT

1886 Robert Wentworth Lea, Vice President and General Manager of the Stephens Motor Car Company
        1919-1924, is born in Woodville, WI

1896 The Duryea Motor Wagon Company contracts with Charles B. King to have the latter manufacture
        Duryea-designed engines in Detroit, MI

1902 Byron J. Carter applies for a United States patent on his three-cylinder steam engine

1904 The Society of Automobile Engineers is organized in New York City

1907 The Hispano-Suiza is introduced in England at the Midland Motor Show in Bingley Hall, Birmingham

1919 Bentley Motors, Ltd. is established in London, England by W. O. Bentley, H. M. Bentley, A. H. M. J.
        Ward, F. T. Burgess, and Harold F. Varley

1919 Keith Wilson of the Champion Spark Plug Company is born in Indianapolis, IN

1931 Carl H. L. Flintermann, an advocate and manufacturer of steel automobile wheels, dies in Jackson, MI at
        age 54

1936 John Vernon Pugh, an official with many British automobile firms, dies at age 64

1937 The 25,000,000th Ford is produced

1939 Nicola Materazzi, Chief Engineer of Bugatti Automobili and designer of the Bugatti 110, is born in
        Salerno, Italy

1940 The Packard Eighteenth Series 120 is introduced

A 1940 Packard 120 convertible coupe passes a 1920's sedan in Elizabeth, MN.
The effect of the low-priced 120 on the Packard Motor Car Company will be
debated as long as people are interested in automobile history.

1940 Racer Pedro Rodriguez is born in Mexico City, DF, Mexico

Mexico City about the time of the birth of Pedro Rodriguez.
At this time nearly 100% of the automobiles in Mexico originated in the United States.

1941 Jose Ignacio Lopez de Arriotua of Opel and Volkswagen is born in Amorebieta, Spain

1942 Racer Georges-Francis "Johnny" Servoz-Gavin is born in Grenoble, France

1945 Automotive historian Jonathan Wood is born in Reading, Berkshire, England

1948 The Tri-Wheel Motor Company, manufacturers of the Thrif-T subcompact commercial vehicle, reorganizes as the Tri-Wheel Motor Corporation

1950 Racer Gianfranco Brancatelli is born in Turin, Italy

1950 Racer Gilles Villeneuve is born in Berthierville, PQ, Canada, the elder brother of race Jacques Villeneuve Sr. and father of racer Jacques Villeneuve Jr.

1952 The 1952 Hudsons are introduced

1952 The Willys-Overland Company reenters the automobile business with the Willys Aero, a compact two-door sedan designed by Phil Wright and engineered by Clyde R. Paton

1953 The first Argentian Grand Prix is held at the 17 de Octubre Circuit in Buenos Aires and won by Alberto Ascari in a Ferrari 500

1955 August S. Duesenberg dies in Camby, IN at age 75

1955 Charles Russell Feldmann, Chairman of the Henney Motor Company, announces that the firm will cease production of professional cars "temporarily"

1955 The Tri-Wheel Motor Corporation, now located in Springfield, MA, files for bankruptcy

1956 Claud L. Stevens of the Ford Motor Company dies

1961 The International Scout is introduced to the public

1963 The Chrysler Corporation acquires a majority interest in the Societe Industrielle de Mecanique et Carrosserie Automobile (Simca)

1966 Racer Andre Ribeiro is born in Sao Paulo, Brazil

1971 Racer Christian Fittipaldi is born in Sao Paulo, Brazil, the son of racer Wilson Fittipaldi and nephew of racer Emerson Fittipaldi

1971 Walter A. Olen of FWD dies in Clintonville, WI at age 95

1978 The last Volkswagen "Beetle" is produced at the Emden, Germany factory

1984 Frank O. Prior of the Standard Oil Company of Indiana dies at age 88

1996 Andrew L. Freeman, the inventor of the headbolt heater, dies in Grand Forks, ND at age 86

JANUARY 19

1736 James Watt, a principal figure in the development of the steam engine, is born in Greenock, Renfrewshire, Scotland

1808 Rubber pioneer Nathaniel Manley Hayward is born in Easton, MA

1875 Harry Austin Knox is born in Westfield, MA

1880 Walter Turner Fishleigh of Packard and Ford is born in Chicago, IL

1894 Henry G. Morris & Pedro G. Salom apply for a patent on their electric car

1904 The reorganized Buick Motor Company in corporates in Flint, MI

1909 The H. S. Houpt Manufacturing Company of New York City registers its "H" within three concentric circles logo as a trademark - their car was conceived as the Houpt, but first appeared as the Houpt-Rockwell to recognize partners Harry S. Houpt and Albert F. Rockwell

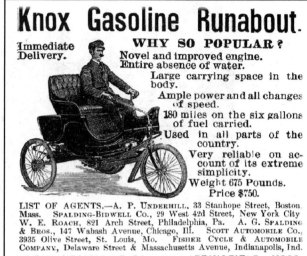

1914 Racer Bob Gerard is born in Leicester, Leicestershire, England

1925 The Aerolite Piston Company, Ltd. is liquidated by E. G. Davies

1927 John Kelsey, President of the Kelsey Wheel Company, dies in Detroit, MI at age 60

1928 The Pep Auto Supply Company is organized in Pennsylvania

1929 William Joseph "Billy" Hayden of Ford and Jaguar is born in London, England

1932 Alfredo "Dino" Ferrari is born

1946 James D. Mooney is named President of the Willys-Overland Company

1950 General Motors opens the Midcentury Motorama at the Waldorf Astoria in New York City for a nine-day run - this was the first use of the name "Motorama"

1952 The 1952 Chevrolets are introduced

1954 Ward M. Canaday is elected President and Chairman of the Willys-Overland Company

1955 The Cadillac Park Avenue show car is unveiled at the New York Motorama in the Waldorf-Astoria Hotel - the car became a prototype for the ultra-luxury Eldorado Brougham

1956 Racer Garrett Evans is born

1956 Frederick V. Bott of General Motors dies in New York City while attending the opening of the General Motors Motorama

1957 Pontiac drops plans to build an assembly plant in Sunnyvale, CA

1958 Stirling Moss, driving a Cooper-Climax 1.96-litre, wins the Argentine Grand Prix in Buenos Aires, the first Formula 1 victory for the marque and the first in the post-World War II era by a rear-engined car - Juan Manuel Fangio driving a Maserati 250F records the fastest lap, at age 46 years, 210 days the oldest driver to accomplish this feat in a Formula 1 championship race

1960 Mrs. James W. (Elizabeth A. Gillmer) Packard dies in New York City

1968 Ray Harroun, winner of the first Indianapolis 500, dies in Anderson, IN at age 89

1969 Carlo Salamano, winner of the 1923 Italian Grand Prix, dies in Italy

1981 Landscape architect and amateur automobile racer Sidney Shurcliff dies at age 74

1984 Frank T. Malumphy, a prominent restorer of vintage Packards, dies in Kent, CT at age 64

JANUARY 20

1849 Steam engine pioneer Nathan Read dies in Belfast, ME at age 89

1876 Josef Casimir Hofmann, a concert pianist who designed the Hofmann car in 1909, is born in Krakow, Poland

1910 The Detroit-Dearborn "pentagon" logo is registered as a trademark, but the company would be bankrupt before the end of the year

1912 Automobile body manufacturer Walter Owen Briggs Jr. is born in Detroit, MI

1914 The assets of the bankrupt Amplex Motor Car Company of Mishawaka, IN are sold at auction by receiver M. W. Mix

1914 Automobile historian Richard Crabb is born in Wabash, IN

1916 The Denby Truck Company acquires the Detroit, MI factory of the Briggs-Detroiter Company

Adapted from a 1915 magazine advertisement - Denby trucks were manufactured 1914-1930.

1920 Darwin S. Hatch, Managing Editor of *Motor Age* magazine, dies in Chicago, IL at age 36

1926 Ernest C. Kanzler sends a memorandum to Henry Ford recommending the end of Ford Model T production

1927 Racer and automotive writer Denise McCluggage is born in El Dorado, KS

1928 The Ford Motor Company administrative offices are relocated to their new building

1929 Racer Edward Glenn "Fireball" Roberts is born in Apopka, FL

1930 The M.G. Car Company Ltd. stages a grand inaugural luncheon at its new factory in Abingdon-on-Thames, Berkshire, England

1934 Racer Giorgio Bassi is born in Milan, Italy

1935 Fred O. Paige, founder and first President of the Paige-Detroit Motor Car Company, dies in Hollywood, CA

1937 Henry W. Spaulding, founder of the Spaulding Manufacturing Company, dies in Grinnell, IA at age 90

1945 Sidney Waldon, a Director of the Packard Motor Car Company 1903-1915, dies in Hamilton, ON, Canada at age 71

1946 The first Kaiser and Frazer automobiles are unveiled in the Grand Ballroom of the Waldorf-Astoria Hotel in New York City

Kaiser and Frazer mounted the most serious post-World War II challenge to the United States automobile establishment, but production after 1955 was limited to a few cars built in Argentina. This 1947 Frazer is parked near the Public School in Crosby, ND.

1947 The Cities Service Oil Company Ltd. changes its name to Fina Petroleum Products Ltd.

1949 The Buick Riviera hardtop coupe is introduced at the Waldorf Astoria Hotel in New York City

1949 The 1949 Chevrolets and Pontiacs are introduced at the Waldorf Astoria Hotel in New York City

1951 The 1951 Dodges are introduced

1953 The Kaiser-Frazer Corporation announces plans to build the Kaiser-Darrin sports car

1954 The 1954 Oldsmobiles are introduced - the unusual late date has perpetuated a theory that the new cars had actually been planned for the 1955 model year but were moved up because General Motors President Harlow H. Curtice was unhappy with the planned 1954 models

1954 Ralph Lex Adams, a truck body designer with the Edward G. Budd Manufacturing Company since 1917, dies at age 65

1955 Industrias Kaiser Argentina SA (IKA) is organized to manufacture Jeeps in Buenos Aires, Argentina

1955 Nathan Lazarnick, a pioneer in photographing automobiles and automotive equipment for catalogue illustration, dies

1957 Racer Jeff Wood is born in Wichita, KS

1959 Automotive writer C. Edward Packer dies at age 61

1967 Racer Billy Foster is killed

1968 Racer Luciano Lombardini is killed when his Lancia Fulvia crashes near Skopje, Macedonia, Yugoslavia during the Monte Carlo Rally

1971 The Jaguar XJ13 is unveiled at Lindley, England - test driver Norman Dewis crashes during its first test run, ending the development program, but the unique, badly damaged car is retained and later restored by the company

1977 Nils Wahlberg, Vice President of Engineering for the Nash Motors Company 1916-1952 who previously had worked for Maxwell-Briscoe, Thomas, Packard, and Oakland, dies in Washington, DC at age 91

JANUARY 21

1843 Emile Levassor is born in Marolles-en-Hurepoix, France

1844 William Livingstone Jr., a prominent Detroit businessman who was involved in the formation of the Ford Motor Company, is born in Dundas, ON, Canada

1864 James Jackson Storrow of Nash is born in Boston, MA

1886 George Freers of Marmon is born in Terre Haute, IN

1888 Otto M. Burkhardt of Pierce-Arrow is born in Meissen, Germany

1888 Alfred E. Grater of Reo is born in Germany

1899 The five Opel brothers acquire the rights to the Lutzmann, and begin the manufacture of automobiles in Russelsheim, Germany

1903 The German-American Automobile Company of New York City is forced into bankruptcy after one year of limited production

1912 A. B. C. Hardy succeeds William H. Little as President of the Little Motor Car Company

1918 Emil Jellinek-Mercedes, the Austro-Hungarian consul in Nice, France and former patron of the Mercedes marque, dies in Geneva, Switzerland at age 64

1920 Theodore Douglas, President of the Duplex Engine Governor Company, dies in Scarborough, NY at age 51

1921 Ralph Mulford, driving a Paige roadster at Daytona Beach, FL, sets a new Class B stock car record by covering a mile at 102.83 mph

1923 Racer Jud Larson is born in Grand Prairie, TX

1925 Automotive parts manufacturer Ralph James Weiger is born in Hammond, IN

1930 Racer John Campbell-Jones is born in Epsom, England

1935 Dr. Masakazu Negishi of the Miyata Works, Ltd. of Toyko, Japan dies

1947 Ford truck production at the Highland Park Plant resumes after an absence of nearly twenty years

1954 General Motors introduces the XP-21 Firebird show car, powered by the world's first gas-turbine engine

1964 Racer Joe Weatherly is killed at age 41 when his Mercury crashes during a race at the Riverside (CA) International Speedway

1966 K. T. Keller, Chrysler Corporation President 1935-1950 and Chairman of the Board 1950-1956, dies in London, England at age 80

1971 The Antique Truck Club of America is founded in College Point, NY with Raymond L. Richenbaugh as President

1972 Henry J. Nave is named President of Mack Trucks, Inc., with Zenon C. R. Hansen continuing as Chairman and Chief Executive Officer

1975 Coachbuilder William E. Biddle of the Biddle & Smart Company dies in Concord, MA at age 92

1982 William V. Luneburg, President of American Motors 1967-1977, dies in Detroit, MI at age 69

1985 Bernard Hanon resigns as Chairman of Regie Naitonale des Usines Renault, with Georges Besse named as his successor

JANUARY 22

1847 Industrialist Alexander Siemens, a patron of pioneer British motoring, is born in Hannover, Germany

1870 Matteo Ceirano of Fiat is born in Cuneo, Italy

1894 Roscoe Martin Smith of the Ford Motor Company is born in Johnson County, IN

1901 The Irish Automobile Club (later the Royal Irish Automobile Club) is founded in Dublin

1902 The German-American Automobile Company is organized in New York City with William N. Beach as President, John L. Schultz as Superintendent, and James MacNaughton as General Manager

1908 Harry Fergusson-Wood of Rolls-Royce is born in Chester, England

1922 Alfred William Pelletier of Mack Trucks, Inc. is born in Toronto, ON, Canada

1923 The Kenworth Motor Truck Corporation is founded in Seattle, WA with Edgar K. Worthington as President and H. W. Kent as First Vice President

1931 Montague Stanley Napier dies

1942 Packard President Max M. Gilman is involved in a serious automobile accident in Royal Oak, MI

1944 Arthur Giles Bishop, a Director of General Motors, dies in Flint, MI at age 92

1944 Ernest E. Wilson, Director of the General Motors Proving Ground, dies at age 45

1950 Preston Tucker is found innocent of fraud

1954 General Motors demonstrates the XP21 Firebird, the world's first gas-turbine automobile, in New York City

1954 Pontiac announces plans to add 1,300,000 square feet to its main factory

1956 Luigi Musso, driving a Lancia-Ferrari D50, records his only Formula 1 victory at the Argentine Grand Prix in Buenos Aires

1957 The 1957 Packard Clippers are introduced - the 57th Series cars were basically badge-engineered Studebakers available only as a 4-door sedan or a station wagon

1959 Racer Mike Hawthorn is killed at age 29 when his Jaguar crashes on a public road near Guildford, Surrey, England

1962 Edward W. Isom of the Sinclair Refining Company dies at age 76

1968 Rev. Homer Martin, first President of the United Auto Workers, dies in Los Angeles, CA at age 66

1970 Automotive historian Floyd Clymer dies in Los Angeles, CA at age 75

1981 Racer Cuth Harrison dies in Sheffield, Yorkshire, England at age 74

1986 The General Motors Europe-Passenger Car Unit is established in Zurich, Switzerland with Ferdinand P. J. Beickler as President

1986 General Motors acquires a 59.7% ownership of Group Lotus PLC

1990 Stylist Gordon M. Buehrig dies at age 85

1995 James Holden is named Executive Vice President of Chrysler Corporation

JANUARY 23

1884 Racer Ralph DePalma is born in Troia, Foggia, Apulia, Italy

1890 Arthur T. Murray, a pioneer employee of Locomobile and Lozier who later was an executive in the automobile parts industry, is born in Norwalk, CT

1902 Henry B. Joy increases his investment in the Ohio Automobile Company, manufacturers of the Packard, to $25,000

1907 Glenn H. Curtiss, driving a V-8 motorcycle of his own design at Ormond Beach, FL, reaches an unofficial 136.3 mph, a record speed for a motor vehicle

1912 A United States patent is issued for the Aermore Exhaust Horn manufactured by the Aermore Manufacturing Company of Chicago, IL

1919 Harry S. Harkness, owner of the Sheepshead Bay Speedway Corporation, dies in New York City from influenza at age 38

1919 Walter H. Strom, President of the U. S. Ball Bearing Manufacturing Company, dies in Chicago, IL from influenza at age 28

1926 Automotive parts manufacturer Joseph Vernon Scott is born in Scranton, PA

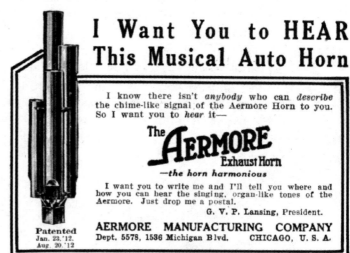

1933 Arthur L. Garford, a chassis manufacturer associated with the early Studebaker and manufacturer of the 1908/1913 Garford, dies in Elyria, OH at age 74

1935 Racer Jerry Grant is born

1945 William F. Krenzke, a design engineer with Mitchell who later made his name in the power lawn mower industry, dies at age 59

1946 Racer Don Whittington is born in the United States, the elder brother of racers Bill and Dale Whittington

1951 A German patent is issued to Bela Barenyi for his chassis design that was quickly adopted by Mercedes-Benz and is considered to be the first conceived primarily with safety in mind

1954 The World Motor Sports Show opens in Madison Square Garden in New York City

1955 Fred Bodley, Technical Editor of *Motor Trend* magazine, dies at age 51 in Santa Monica, CA

1958 Merrill C. Horine, a consulting engineer with Mack since 1918, dies at age 64

1961 William Clay Ford is elected President of the Detroit Lions football team

1967 Sam Adelman, the legendary Ukrainian-born dealer of junked car parts in Mount Vernon, NY, dies at age 72

1972 Racer Orlando Dall'Ave is killed during near Millau, France during the Monte Carlo Rally

1976 Carole Vico of Buffalo, NY wins the grand prize, a new Rolls-Royce Silver Shadow sedan, on the television game show *High Rollers*

JANUARY 24

1860 Jean Lenoir is issued French patent #43,624 for his internal combustion engine

1871 Albert Russel Erskine of Studebaker is born in Huntsville, AL

1887 Louis R. Mack of Packard is born

1900 The Societa Milanese d'Automobili Isotta-Fraschini & C. is organized

1902 Henry B. Joy attends his first Packard board meeting

1907 Senator Russell Alger (R-MI), a former Vice President of the Packard Motor Car Company, dies in Washington, DC at age 70

1912 A Hupmobile Model D touring car returns to Detroit, MI, completing a promotional 48,600-mile, 26-country around-the-world trip

1914 Dr. Joachim Zahn, Chairman of the Management Board for Daimler-Benz AG 1965-1979, is born in Wuppertal (now Wuppertal-Elberfeld), Germany

1924 Ford Motor Company's planned community of Kingsford, MI is incorporated as a village - the company owned vast forest reserves in the area to supply its needs for station wagon bodies, etc., and the new village was named for the manager of the works, Edward G. Kingsford

1929 Benjamin Anibal applies for a patent on his V-8 engine design, destined to be used in the 1930-1931 Oaklands

1929 General Manager Perley H. Ford of Casco Motors Inc., a Sanford, ME truck manufacturer, dies

1942 The last 1942 Willys is produced

1943 Racer Tony Trimmer is born in West Kingsdown, Kent, England

1954 Racer Jo Gartner is born in Vienna, Austria

1956 Dr. Heinz Hordhoff of Volkswagen announces that his company has dropped its plans to assemble cars at the former Studebaker factory in New Brunswick, NJ

1956 The 100,000th Volvo PV444 is produced

1957 The 10,000,000th Plymouth is produced

1957 The Studebaker-based 1957 Packard Clippers are introduced

1958 Racer Altfrid Heger is born in Essen, West Germany

1960 Racer Gary Collins is born

1966 Charles Balough, President of the Hercules Motors Corporation 1915-1955, dies in Youngstown, OH at age 82

JANUARY 25

1830 Thomas Witherell Palmer of the Detroit Automobile Company is born in Detroit, MI

1883 David Abbot "Ab" Jenkins Jr. is born in Spanish Fork, UT

1905 Arthur E. MacDonald of Scotland, driving a 90 hp Napier at Daytona Beach, FL, raises the land speed record to 104.65 mph - later in the day Herbert L. Bowden of Boston, MA, driving his own Mercedes twin-engined "Flying Dutchman", makes a run at 109.75 mph, although his time is not recognized because his car exceeds the weight limitation in effect at the time

1906 Racer Toni Ulmen is born in Dusseldorf, Germany

1907 Captain Lord Herbert Scott joins Rolls-Royce Ltd. as a Director

1908 Frank Peter Kurtis, designer of race cars and the 1949/1955 Kurtis sports car, is born in Crested Butte, CO

1909 The Rainier Motor Company of Saginaw, MI is sold at auction to George C. Comstock, an attorney representing company founder John T. Ranier in an attempt to save the company - General Motors took over the company four months later, and produced the Rainier until 1911

1910 Racer Henri Louveau is born in France

1914 Hugh Graham Conway, Rolls-Royce executive and automotive historian, is born

1921 Rev. Samuel S. Marquis resigns from the Sociological Department of the Ford Motor Company

1925 Automobile parts manufacturer Adolph E. Brion dies in New York City at age 61

1926 The factory of the bankrupt Earl Motors, Inc. in Jackson, MI is sold at auction

1926 John B. Beltz of Oldsmobile is born in Lansing, MI

1930 Racer Major Melton is born in Laurinburg, NC

1930 Racer Heinz Schiller is born in Frauenfeld, Switzerland

1932 Alexis de Sakhnoffsky joins Packard as Consulting Art Director

1941 Racer Elzie Wylie "Buddy" Baker Jr. is born in Florence, SC

1943 Walter C. Keys, a mechanical product engineer with the United States Rubber Company whose previous experience included stints with Buick, Cadillac, and Chalmers, dies

1950 William R. Angell, President of the Continental Motors Corporation 1930-1939, dies in Detroit, MI at age 72

1952 The last DeSoto Carry-All Sedan is produced

1952 General Motors introduces its "Autronic Eye", the industry's first automatic headlight control

1955 Ernest R. Breech is elected Chairman of the Board of the Ford Motor Company, the first person to officially hold that title

1956 Racer Johnny Cecotto is born in Caracas, Venezuela of Italian ancestry

1958 Robert R. Young, a General Motors executive 1922-1929, dies at age 60

1958 L. T. Hill of the Shell Oil Company of Canada Ltd. dies at age 48

1959 Henry R. Lansdale, a Packard and Hare's Motors, Inc. official who served as Vice President and General Manager of the National Automotive Parts Association 1930-1955 and its Chairman 1955-1957, dies in Detroit, MI at age 76

1962 Racer Jorge de Abreu Novais dies in Oporto, Portugal at age 62

1965 Racer Larry Thomas is killed at age 28 in a highway accident near Tifton, GA

1971 Racer Luca Badder is born in Montebelluna, Treviso, Venetia, Italy

1976 The Ligier makes its Formula 1 debut in the Brazilian Grand Prix, but the Type JS5 car financed by Guy Ligier, designed by Gerard Ducarouge, Michel Beaujon, and Paul Carillo, and driven by Jacques Laffite is forced to retire with gear linkage problems

1989 Donald J. Atwood, General Motors Vice Chairman, resigns to become Deputy Secretary of Defense in the administration of President George Bush

1991 The United States Postal Service issues a 4-cent coil stamp in Tucson, AZ designed by Richard Schlecht and picturing the 1866 Dudgeon Steam Wagon

JANUARY 26

1851 Charles Valton, a sculptor and designer of automobile mascots, is born in Pau, France

1861 Tire manufacturer Charles Willard Seiberling is born in Des Moines, IA

1862 Steam automobile pioneer Edwin Franklin Brown is born in Auburn, ME

1871 Sir Arthur Philip Du Cros of the Dunlop Rubber Company Ltd. is born in Dublin, Ireland

1885 Automobile engine designer Harry Ralph Ricardo is born in London, England

1888 Maurizio Temperino is born in Limone, Piemonte, Italy

1891 Fred Lee Black of the Ford Motor Company is born in Battle Creek, MI

1902 Elliott Gordon Ewell of Mack Trucks, Inc. is born in Washington, NC

1906 Fred H. Marriott, driving the Stanley steam-powered "Wogglebug" at Ormond Beach, FL, raises the land speed record to 127.659 MPH - this would be the last time that a steam-powered vehicle would hold this record

1911 Thomas Neal succeeds James J. Storrow as President of General Motors

1917 Jorma O. Sarto of the Chrysler Corporation is born

1917 The Goodyear Tire & Rubber Company, Ltd. (Java) is established in Buitzenzorg, West Java, Dutch East Indies (now Bogor, Indonesia)

1920 The Lincoln Motor Company is founded

1922 Sidney Kelly of the Ford Motor Company is born in New York City

1923 Thomas Oliver Mathues of General Motors is born in Dayton, OH

1925 Actor and racer Paul Leonard Newman is born in Cleveland, OH

1926 Automotive journalist Warren Weith is born in New York City

1930 Ramsey Manners, a Director of Bentley Motors, Ltd., dies at age 37 from the effects of combat injuries received in France in 1915

1932 Automotive parts manufacturer James D. Sutherland dies in New Haven, CT at age 59

1934 The Rolls-Royce 1936-1955 "Kneeling Spirit of Ecstasy" mascot is designed by Charles Sykes as an option to traditional standing mascot

1943 Christopher Sinsabaugh, Editor of *Automotive News*, dies in Detroit, MI at age 71

1945 Racer David Purley is born in Bognor Regis, Sussex, England

1950 Charles H. Fox, founder in 1902 of the Ahrens-Fox Company and a pioneer designer of motorized fire engines, dies in Cincinnati, OH at age 89

1953 Charles E. Wilson resigns as President of General Motors to become Secretary of Defense in the cabinet of President Dwight D. Eisenhower

1955 The Chevrolet Nomad station wagon is introduced as a mid-year model

1956 Marvin N. Schneider of the Willard Storage Battery Company dies at age 38

1966 Glenn D. Angle, an aeronautics executive whose early career had been as Chief Draftsman for Welch and Dort, dies at age 75

1970 Herman L. Weckler of Buick, DeSoto, and Dodge, dies at age 81

1979 The first episode of *The Dukes of Hazard* television show airs, "starring" an orange 1969 Dodge Charger

1985 Joseph J. Sanchez, first President of the Saturn Corporation, dies in Lansing, MI just 18 days after accepting that position - William E. Hoglund is named as his successor

1990 Racer Bob Gerard dies in South Croxton, Leicestershire, England at age 76

JANUARY 27

1881　Tire manufacturer Piero Pirelli is born in Milan, Italy

1884　Leigh R. Evans of Thomas, Franklin, and Russell is born in Easton, PA

1889　Gordon Lefebvre of Chevrolet and Pontiac is born in Richmond, VA

1892　Oil company executive Robert Giffen Stewart is born in Marion, IA

1899　Camille Jenatzy, driving his electric Jenatzy at Acheres Park, France, raises the land speed record to 49.92 mph

1903　William A. Hatcher resigns from the Packard Motor Car Company

1904　William K. Vanderbilt, Jr. raises land speed record to 92.307 mph at Daytona Beach, FL driving his 11.9-litre Mercedes 90

1914　The American Cyclecar Manufacturers' Association meets for the first time in Chicago, IL

1920　Philip A. Caldwell of the Ford Motor Company is born in Bourneville, OH

1925　Tony Jefferson Hogg of *Road & Track* magazine is born in London, England

1926　The Standard Oil Company of California and the Pacific Coast Oil Company merge as a Delaware corporation, the Standard Oil Company of California (Socal)

1931　The Hudson/Essex 1931 "Stylized Bird" mascot is patented by designer F. C. Ruppel

1931　The Hudson 1932 "Eagle" mascot is patented by designer F. C. Ruppel

1934　Racer George Follmer is born in Phoenix, AZ

1934　C. T. Klug, Sales Manager of the Willard Storage Battery Company, dies

1936　Production of the Cord 810 begins

1951　The 1951 DeSotos are introduced

Wall Drug, a popular stopping point in Wall, SD. The second car from left is a 1951 DeSoto convertible with its Plymouth cousin parked to its right.

1960　Samuel Conner Pandolfo, founder of the Pan Motor Company, dies in Fairbanks, AK at age 84

1965　The Shelby GT350, based on the Ford Mustang, is introduced by designer Carroll Shelby in Riverside, CA

1966　Groudbreaking ceremonies are held in Indianapolis, IN for the factory of the new Duesenberg Corporation

JANUARY 28

1688 Ferdinand Verbiest, an early proponent of self-propelled road vehicles, dies

1864 Charles Williams Nash is born near DeKalb, IL

1871 Charles Belden Van Dusen, an S. S. Kresge Company official who was the son-in-law of David D. Buick and a cofounder of the Automobile Club of Michigan, is born in Detroit, MI

1896 Walter Arnold of East Peckham, Kent, England is cited for exceeding the speed limit by 2 mph eight days prior in the first such arrest in Great Britain - the following year, with other family members, he began manufacturing Arnold cars

1918 Automotive engineer Aldebert De Queiroz is born in Brazil

1920 The Delaware charter of the defunct Kent Motors Corporation is repealed for nonpayment of taxes

1921 Erwin Herman Graham of the Chrysler Corporation is born in Detroit, MI

1927 Racer James Ernest "Jimmy" Bryan is born in Phoenix, AZ

1935 Charles S. Crawford, Chief Engineer of Opel, dies in Indianapolis, IN at age 51

1937 The prototype Rolls-Royce Wraith is given its first road test

1938 Rudolf Caracciola raises the land speed record to 268.496 mph driving a Mercedes-Benz on the Frankfurt-Darmstadt Autobahn, his time remaining unbroken as the highest speed ever attained on a public highway - later that day Bernd Rosemeyer is killed at age 28 at the same venue when he crashes near Morfelden while attempting to raise the record in his Auto Union

1942 The Ford Rotunda in Dearborn, MI closes for the duration of World War II

1944 Racer Harald Grohs is born in Essen, Germany

1947 Racer Ian Taylor is born in Great Britain

1949 The last Plymouth P15 is produced ending a 39-month run of essentially identical cars

1949 Racer Jean-Pierre Wimille is killed at age 39 when his Simca-Gordini 10GC crashes during a practice run for the General Peron Grand Prix at Palermo Park in Buenos Aires, Argentina

1951 The Ford Victoria, a two-door hardtop coupe designed by Gordon M. Buehrig, is introduced as a midyear model

1953 The Jeep CJ-3B is introduced

1957 Forrest H. Kane, a design engineer with Oakland and Pontiac, dies at age 58

1958 Racer David Green is born in Owensboro, KY

1958 Clinton R. Boothby, Chief Electrical Engineer of the Electric Autolite Company, dies at age 57

1959 Automobile insurance pioneer Vern Moulton dies at age 78

1960 Automotive engineer Earle S. MacPherson, whose career included stints with Chalmers, Liberty, Hupmobile, and Chevrolet before executive roles with General Motors and the Ford Motor Company, dies at age 68

1964 Mead L. Bricker of the Ford Motor Company dies at age 78

1966 The 27-month public testing program of the semi-production Chrysler Turbine Cars concludes

1970 Maurice Sizaire dies at age 92

1970 The Japan Automatic Transmission Company is formed as a joint venture of the Ford Motor Company, Nissan Motor Company, Ltd., and Toyo Kogyo Company, Ltd.

1980 Pat Griffith, winner of the 1953 Tourist Trophy race, dies at age 55

1985 Racer Sidonio Cabenelas is murdered

JANUARY 29

1864 Milton Barlow Ochs, Publisher of the *Chattanooga* (TN) *Times* and a staunch promoter of the Dixie Highway, Taft Memorial Highway, and Lookout Mountain Scenic Highway, is born in Cincinnati, OH

1871 Ira Adalbert Weaver, a developer of automobile maintenance equipment, is born in Polk County, IA

1873 Sidney Dunn Waldon, a director of the Packard Motor Car Company 1903-1915, is born in London, England

1880 Automobile design engineer Joseph A. Anglada is born in New York City

1886 Carl Benz is issued German patent #37435 for his "Motorwagen", in many ways the world's first complete automobile

1891 Ignaz Schustala, founder of the business that would evolve into the Tatra automobile works, dies in Vienna, Austria at age 68

1898 Charles Gillet Stradella of the General Motors Acceptance Corporation is born in North Tonawanda, NY

1906 Victor Demogeot, driving a V-8 Darracq at Ormond Beach, FL, reaches 122.449 mph to set a record for internal-combustion engined cars

1907 Artist John Ford Clymer, best remembered for his Chrysler advertisements in the late 1940's, is born in Ellensburg, WA

1912 Prominent classic car collector Mills Bee Lane Jr. is born in Savannah, GA

1914 The Association of Spark Plug Manufacturers is organized in Chicago, IL

1915 Racer Brian Shawe-Taylor is born in Dublin, Ireland

1919 Elbert L. Smith of McIntyre and Barley dies in France at age 24

1939 Howard W. Simpson resigns from the Ford Motor Company to pursue a career as an independent design engineer

1940 Racer Kunimitsu Takahashi is born in Tokyo, Japan

1941 John J. Burke of the General Tire & Rubber Company dies at age 51

1942 The last pre-World War II Chrysler is produced

1942 The last pre-World War II Dodge produced

1945 Racer Tommy Houston is born

1945 Albert G. Lindenthal of Buick dies at age 50

1949 Automobile parts manufacturer J. A. Grass dies in York, PA at age 56

1950 Racer Jody Scheckter is born in East London, South Africa

1950 D. McCall White, designer of the first Cadillac V-8 whose long career also included stints with Daimler, Napier, and Crossley in his native Great Britain, and Nash, Lafayette, and Tucker in the United States, dies in Hartford, CT at age 69

1954 The 1954 Kaisers are introduced

1957 Ray L. Howard, pioneer aviator, automobile racer, and designer of improved automobile clutches, dies

1969 Racer Paul Warwick is born in Great Britain, the younger brother of racer Derek Warwick

1978 The Arrows makes its Formula 1 debut in the Brazilian Grand Prix in Rio de Janeiro, with the car driven by Riccardo Patrese finishing ninth behind the winning Ferrari of Carlo Reutemann

1981 Nissan announces plans to build a factory in Great Britain

1989 Global Motors, Inc., the United States importer of the Yugo, files for bankruptcy

JANUARY 30

1807 Isaac de Rivaz is issued a French patent for his explosion motor, an important ancestor of the modern internal combustion engine

1856 William Harold Mullins, who built the first all-steel automobile body for the 1905 Pope-Toledo and is credited with manufacturing the first one-piece stamped fenders, is born in East Palestine, OH

1879 Robert Powell Page Jr. of Autocar is born in Boyce, VA

1901 Racer Rudolph Caracciola is born in Remagen, Germany

1905 The Detroit-Oxford Motor Company is organized in Oxford, MI by William H. Radford, Clyde J. Smith, and Clarence H. Crawford to manufacture the Oxford touring car and S and R Automatic Carburetors

1906 Howard C. Marmon is issued a United States patent for his hollow crankshaft lubrication system, considered by many to be his most significant invention

1917 Racer and journalist Paul Frere is born in Le Havre, France

1917 William Warwick and family complete their over 9,000-mile round trip to New York City as their GMC truck reaches Seattle, WA

1920 Toyo Kogyo Company Ltd. is founded in Hiroshima, Japan - in 1960 the firm would begin manufacturing the Mazda automobile

1921 Donald Edward Kidder of Ford, Kaiser, Chrysler, and Studebaker is born in Detroit, MI

1923 Racer Norm Nelson is born

1925 Race car designer Harry A. Miller files for a United States patent on his front-wheel-drive "Drive Mechanism for Vehicles"

1929 The Houdaille-Hershey Corporation is formed as a consolidation of the Houdaille Corporation, Hershey Corporation, and the Oakes Products Corporation

1930 Alfred Herrhausen of Daimler-Benz AG is born in Diplom-Kaufmann, Germany

1930 Osamu Suzuki of the Suzuki Motor Company, Ltd. is born in Cero, Gifu, Japan

1937 Racer Bruce Johnstone is born in Durban, South Africa

1939 The first Studebaker Champion is produced, a Morocco Gray 4-door sedan

1942 The last pre-World War II Chevrolet, a black coupe, is produced

1942 The last pre-World War II DeSoto is produced

1948 Benson Ford is elected Vice President of the Ford Motor Company and General Manager of the Lincoln-Mercury Division

1951 Ferdinand Porsche dies in Stuttgart, Germany at age 75

1954 Automotive designer Charles F. Herreshoff dies in San Diego, CA at age 77

1959 Henry D. "Harry" Collier, President of the Standard Oil Company of California 1940-1945, dies in San Francisco, CA at age 83

1966 Harold H. Seaman, cofounder of the Seaman Body Corporation that produced automobile bodies primarily for Nash and Pierce-Racine, dies in Chandler, AZ at age 86

A 1942 Chevrolet Aero Sedan, a new body style for the marque, is parked in front of the Public School in Hot Springs (now Truth or Consequences), NM. Behind it is a 1939 Plymouth Roadking Business Coupe.

1968 International introduces its Fleetstar-A trucks to replace the R and V series

1995 David Boole, Jaguar's Director of Communications, dies at age 48

JANUARY 31

1862 Curtis Hussey Veeder, inventor of the odometer and tachometer and the founder of the Veeder Manufacturing Company, is born in Allegheny (now part of Pittsburgh), PA

1874 Auguste Jean Paris Jr., an independent inventor of improvements to the internal combustion engine, is born in New York City

1875 Walter Alfred Olen of the Four Wheel Drive Auto Company is born in Winneconne, WI

1888 Karl Hamlen Martin, builder of the Martin Wasp, is born in Buffalo, NY

1892 Leon E. Briggs of the Ford Motor Company is born in Syracuse, NY

1897 The world's first speed hillclimb, held in Nice, France as the concluding stage of the Marseille-Nice race, is won by M. Pary in a DeDion-Bouton steam car with Michelin pneumatic tires

1901 David Fergusson joins the George N. Pierce Company ten days after first viewing the company's prototype steam carriage

1902 Alfred Marcel Ney of the Bendix Corporation is born in St. Petersburg, Russia of French parents

1905 Clement Smith is issued a United States patent for his steering gear and linkage design

1921 The assets of the Yellow Cab Manufacturing Company and the Walden W. Shaw Corporation are split into separate entities

A circa-1925 Yellow taxicab awaits its next call in Jamestown, ND.

1929 Basil Johnson retires as Managing Director of Rolls-Royce, Ltd., although it is now known that his departure was requested by F. H. Royce

1930 Racer Joakim "Jo" Bonnier is born in Stockholm, Sweden

1930 The Fordson, MI post office at the Fordson factory closes

1931 Sir Walrond Sinclair, Managing Director of the British Goodrich Rubber Company Ltd., and Richard S. Witchell, Works Manager since 1921, are elected as Directors of Bentley Motors, Ltd.

1934 Racer Ernesto "Tino" Brambilla is born in Monza, Italy

1935 Automotive parts manufacturer Raymond Frank Vodovnik is born in Chisholm, MN

1942 The last pre-World War II Chrysler is produced

1942 The last pre-World War II Plymouth is produced

1942 The last pre-World War II Studebaker produced, a President Skyway Sedan

1942 Daniel Goeudevert of Ford-Werke AG is born in Reims, France

1942 William A. Simonds is named Director of Public Relations at the Willow Run (MI) bomber plant of the Ford Motor Company

1945 William M. Packer resigns as Vice President-Distribution for the Packard Motor Car Company

1946 Carlton C. Magee, the inventor of the parking meter, dies at age 73

The legacy of Carlton C. Magee is prominently displayed in this circa-1950 view of Weslaco, TX.

1954 The 1954 Willys Aeros are introduced

1955 The Pontiac Star Chief Custom Safari two-door Station Wagon is introduced

1957 Racer Mauro Baldi is born in Milan, Italy

1957 Lawson H. Frew, Senior Staff Engineer of the Shell Oil Company and a former project engineer with DeSoto, dies at age 47

1960 Racer Harry Blanchard is killed when his Porsche crashes during a 1000 km race in Buenos Aires, Argentina

1960 The Daytona International Speedway in Daytona Beach, FL stages special races for United States compact cars - Valiant sweeps the top seven positions in the 10-lap event, and takes the top three spots in the nationally televised 20-lap event with drivers Marvin Panch, Roy Schecter and Larry Frank

1966 Racer Jyrki Jarvilehto "J. J." Lehto is born in Finland

1967 Racer Carlos J. Martin dies from injuries suffered two days earlier in a crash during the Gran Premio International in Mar del Plata, Argentina - three spectators also died as a result of the accident

1968 Semon E. Knudsen resigns as Executive Vice President of General Motors

1975 AB Volvo acquires a majority interest in Van Doorne's Automobielfabrik NV of Eindhoven, the Netherlands, manufacturers of the Daf

1975 Marizio Temperino dies at age 87

1979 White Consolidated Industries, Inc. purchases Frigidaire from General Motors

1981 Elliott M. Estes retires as President of General Motors

FEBRUARY 1

1880 Frederick Kenton Thayer of Rayfield is born in Chrisman, IL

1885 Donaldson Brown of General Motors is born in Baltimore, MD

1898 The Travelers Insurance Company issues the first automobile insurance policy to Dr. Truman J. Martin of Buffalo, NY

1901 The Edison Storage Battery Company is organized primarily to develop a nickel-iron alkaline battery to improve the feasibility of electric automobiles

1902 Ralph Gwin Follis of the Standard Oil Company of California is born in San Francisco, CA

1905 The Mack Brothers Motor Car Company is incorporated in Pennsylvania

1907 Leon Serpollet dies in Paris, France at age 48

1913 Pierce-Arrow applies for a patent on its fender-mounted headlights

1919 David J. Abodaher, a biographer of Lee Iacocca, is born in Streator, IL

1921 Racer Jose Maria Ibanez is born in Argentina

1921 17-year-old Carmen Fasanella obtains his taxicab driver's license in Princeton, NJ, beginning a record-setting 68-year career

1922 The Locomobile Company of America is placed into receivership

1923 James W. Ford of the Ford Motor Company is born in Alameda, CA

1923 "Ethyl" gasoline, a name coined by Charles F. Kettering, is introduced in Dayton, OH at a service station owned by Willard Talbott

1924 Pierce-Arrow offers its first four-wheel brakes

1924 Herschel B. Knap, Service Engineer for the Packard Motor Car Company, dies in Detroit, MI at age 35

1925 Alfred R. Glancy is named General Manager of the Oakland Division of General Motors

1930 Earl D. Sirrine is named Sales Engineer for the Autocar Company

An influential pioneer automobile marque, Autocar later devoted itself entirely to the manufacturing of heavy duty trucks such as this circa-1940 unit hauling logs in Washington state.

1930 The first Soviet-built Ford is produced at AMO factory in Moscow

1931 W. E. Hosac, Vice President in charge of sales for Rolls-Royce of America, Inc., resigns and is succeeded by John S. Inskip

1932 Racer Xavier Perrot is born in Zurich, Switzerland

1942 The last pre-World War II Nash is produced

Nash-Kelvinator Corporation advertising during World War II noted their pre-war civilian products as well their military products.

1944 William B. Mayo of the Ford Motor Company dies in Detroit, MI at age 78

1945 Francis Seiberling, a director of the Goodyear Tire & Rubber Company and former United States Congressman, dies in Akron, OH at age 74

1947 Ferrari announces its first production automobiles

1953 James C. Blair, President of the Libbey-Owens-Ford Glass Company 1923-1930, dies at age 76

1955 The design for the 1956 Chevrolet Corvette is approved

1961 Sherwood H. Egbert is elected President of the Studebaker-Packard Corporation, replacing the retiring Harold E. Churchill

1962 The 2,000,000th "new" Rambler is produced (pre-World War I Ramblers were excluded in tabulating this milestone)

1963 Mobil Oil Australia PTY Ltd. changes its name to Mobil Oil Australia Ltd.

1965 The Firestone Tire & Rubber Company acquires the Seiberling Tire & Rubber Company

1969 John Z. DeLorean is named General Manager of Chevrolet

1971 Rolls-Royce Ltd. voluntarily enters into receivership

1971 Ernest S. Starkman is appointed to the top environmentalist position at General Motors

1972 Paccar, Inc., manufacturers of Kenworth trucks, and the Pacific Car & Foundry Company merge

1981 F. James McDonald is elected President of General Motors

1982 Robert C. Stempel is named General Manager of Chevrolet

1984 Ford of Spain produces its 3,000,000th Ford Fiesta

1985 Philip Caldwell retires as Chairman of the Ford Motor Company and is succeeded by Donald E. Petersen, who is succeeded as President by Harold A. "Red" Poling

1989 Chrysler Corporation and the Hyundai Motor Company sign a marketing agreement whereby Chrysler dealers will offer Hyundai motor cars in the United States

1997 Edward H. Mertz, General Manager of Buick, retires and is succeeded by Robert Coletta - John Grettenberger, General Manager of Cadillac, also retires and is succeeded by John F. Smith, unrelated namesake of General Motors Chairman John F. Smith Jr.

FEBRUARY 2

1861   Josiah Dallas Dort is born in Inkster, MI

1869   Charles Brady King is born in Angel Island, CA

1876   Benjamin Basil Lovett, Henry Ford's longtime personal dancing instructor, is born in West Swanzey, NH

1885   Axel Julius Jansson, a design engineer with many automobile firms, is born in Sweden

1897   A prototype Daimler parcel van, the first gasoline-powered truck to be manufacutured in Great Britain, completes a successful 70-mile round trip between Coventry and Birmingham with a full payload

1902   David Michael Klausmeyer of Barley, Chevrolet, and Marmon-Herrington is born in Norwood, OH

1906   Edward S. "Ned" Jordan marries Charlotte Hannahs

1915   Owen M. Nacker and Alanson P. Brush are issued United States patent for their rear suspension design used on the Marmon Model 34

1916   The A. G. Hebb Auto Company incorporates in Nebraska to manufacture truck bodies with A. G. Hebb as President, Elmer C. Hammond as Vice President, F. R. Hussong as Secretary-Treasurer, and King W. Gillespie as Manager

1919   Charles Calvert Ellis of the Ford Motor Company is born in Baltimore, MD

1920   Nelson S. Pringle, Engineer of Tests for the Autocar Company, dies in Ardmore, PA from pneumonia at age 34

1923   Howard Harmon Kehrl of General Motors is born in Detroit, MI

1925   The Packard Second Series Eight and Third Series Six are introduced

1926   E. L. Cord is elected President of the Auburn Automobile Company

1926   The Marmon Motor Car Company is established as a separate corporation from the parent Nordyke & Marmon Company

1926   The Stutz 1926-1935 "Goddess Ra" mascot is patented by designers Aurelius M. Renzetti and D. Carlton Brown

1937   Racer Tony Shelly is born in Wellington, New Zealand

1942   The last 1942 Pontiac Eight and Torpedo Six are produced

1942   The United States government orders rationing of all new cars held by dealers

1948   Racer Roger Williamson is born in Leicester, Leicestershire, England

1949   The Lloyd Motoren-Werke GmbH is founded in Bremen, Germany by Carl F. W. Borgward

1953   Harlow H. Curtice is elected President of General Motors succeeding Charles E. Wilson who had resigned to become Secretary of Defense

1953   Racer Kazuo Mogi is born in Japan

1955   The Chrysler Corporation legally makes Imperial a separate marque

1960   The compact Mercury Comet is introduced, the first of the marque to have a 6-cylinder engine

1967   William I. Stieglitz resigns as head of the United States Traffic Safety Agency to protest "inadequate" rules

1974   The Bricklin is introduced at the National Association of Automobile Dealers convention in Las Vegas, NV

1979   Otto Zipper, a racing enthusiast and collector of antique automobiles, dies in Daytona Beach, FL at age 64

1984   Harold K. Sperlich is elected President of the Chrysler Corporation

1992   A prototype Nissan R91 driven by Masahiro Hasemi, Toshio Suzuki, and Kazuyoshi Hoshino wins the 24 Hours of Daytona in Daytona Beach, FL, the first Japanese car to win an international 24-hour race

FEBRUARY 3

1870 William J. Walsh of the Buda Company is born in Chicago, IL

1872 Alburn Edward Skinner, the Nash distributor for New York and New Jersey 1920-1936, is born in Westfield, NY

1881 Joseph A. Galamb of the Ford Motor Company is born in Mako, Hungary

Joseph A. Galamb was one of several "invisible" designers of Henry Ford's Model T. On May 22, 1914 Rev. J. Bruce Wylie's touring car collided with a train in Hecla, SD. Despite its appearance the Model T Ford became legendary for its ruggedness, but was no match for a locomotive.

1882 Wallace Ronald Campbell of the Ford Motor Company of Canada, Ltd. is born in Windsor, ON

1891 Col. Edgar Staley Gorrell of the Stutz Motor Car Company of America is born in Baltimore, MD

1899 George Harley Bates of the Ford Motor Company of Canada Ltd. is born in Aylmer, ON

1903 The Reading Automobile Company of Reading, PA is reorganized as the Relay Motor Car Company

1904 The first 10-hp Royce engine is tested by designer F. H. Royce

1910 The Lozier Motor Company reorganizes with plans to relocate from Plattsburg, NY to Detroit, MI and challenge Packard for leadership in the United States luxury car market

1916 J. Gordon Dawson, a test engineer with Rolls-Royce Ltd. 1938-1946, is born

1917 The Cartercar Company is officially dissolved

1919 The Cummins Engine Company is incorporated in Columbus, IN to build diesel engines under license from the Hvid Company in the Netherlands

1920 Racer Tony Gaze is born in Melbourne, Victoria, Australia

1926 Racer and land speed record holder Arthur E. Arfons is born in Akron, OH

1926 Automobile parts distributor Edward Marshall Jones is born in Decatur, GA

1930 Carl W. Burst forms the Moon-Ruxton Company, a merger of the old Moon Motor Car Company and New Era Motors, Inc.

1931 E. L. Cord is elected Chairman of the Cord Corporation, with Roy H. Faulkner succeeding him as President

1938 Ross Hooven Roberts of Lincoln-Mercury is born in Gainesville, TX

1941 The Buick Special Series 40-A, a smaller Special utilizing Chevrolet bodies, is introduced

1942 Buick's Plant #11 produces its last pre-World War II automobile engine

1943 Theodore A. Willard, the inventor of the storage battery and founder of the Willard Storage Battery Company, dies in Beverly Hills, CA at age 80

WILLARD SERVICE STATIONS

1243 Blue Hill Avenue
MATTAPAN, MASS.
Tel. Milton 1031

Willard STORAGE BATTERY

635 Columbia Road
DORCHESTER, MASS.
Tel. Columbia 9733

SALES AND SERVICE

1946 Joseph Cermak of the Gramm Motor Company and the Cleveland Graphite Bronze Company dies at age 69

1947 The first regular production Volvo PV444 is completed

1947 Charles G. Morgan Jr., an official of the American Trucking Associations who was an advocate of highway safety and a cofounder of the National Truck Driving Rodeo, dies at age 53

1948 The first 1948 Cadillac is produced, beginning the age of tailfins

1948 The Packard Motor Car Company Board of Directors rejects a proposed merger with Nash Motors Company

1950 Racer Rocky Moran is born in Pasadena, CA

1951 Dr. August Horch dies in Munchberg, Bavaria, Germany at age 82

1954 The 1954 Kaiser Manhattan is introduced along with the first series Kaiser Special - these cars were actually slightly modified and recoded 1953 models

1954 T. C. Huxley Jr., Vice President of the Diamond T Motor Car Company and an employee of the company since 1919, dies at age 63

1954 D. Myrle Smith of the McQuay-Norris Manfacturing Company dies in St. Louis, MO at age 58

1956 Racer Johnny Claes dies in Brussels, Belgium of tuberculosis at age 39

1957 Racer Francisco "Chico" Serra is born in Sao Paulo, Brazil

1969 The Edsel Owners Club, Inc. is founded as a non-profit organization by Perry Piper and Edsel Henry Ford

1972 Racer Jamie Galles is born in Albuquerque, NM

1981 On the centenary of his birth the citizens of Mako, Hungary dedicate a memorial plaque to Joseph A. Galamb noting his major contributions to the design of the Ford Model T and the Fordson farm tractor

1990 General Motors unveils their first prototype "Impact" electric car

1993 Racer Paul Emery dies in Epsom, England at age 76

FEBRUARY 4

1873 Racer George Schuster is born

1876 William H. Little, a founder of the Little Motor Car Company and the first President of the Chevrolet Motor Company, is born in Westboro, MA

1901 David Fergusson, newly hired Chief Engineer of the George N. Pierce Company, begins his design career with Pierce-Arrow

1907 Rolls-Royce records its first sale of a Silver Ghost in Canada, a Roi-des-Belges tourer with Barker body ordered by George Gillies of Toronto, ON

1909 Automobile parts manufacturer John Jacob Bohmrich is born in Milwaukee, WI

1913 Louis Henry Perlman of New York City is issued a United States patent for his demountable tire-carrying rim

1913 Racer Richard John Beattie-Seaman, known professionally as Dick Seaman, is born in Chichester, Sussex, England

1922 The Ford Motor Company purchases the Lincoln Motor Company for $8 million

1924 Doble Steam Motors of Emeryville, CA registers their logo as a trademark

1927 Malcolm Campbell, driving the "Bluebird" at Pendine Sands, Wales, raises the land speed record to 174.88 mph

1929 The 1,000,000th Ford Model A is produced

1929 The last Plymouth Model Q is produced

1932 Production of the 1932 Plymouth Model PB begins, the first of the marque officially identified by model year and the last 4-cylinder until the 1978 Horizon compact

1939 Rolls-Royce historian John Webb de Campi is born in Chicago, IL

1941 76-year-old Ransom E. Olds is issued his last automotive patent for an internal combustion engine design

1942 The last pre-World War II Buick is produced at its Flint, MI factory

1942 The last pre-World War II Cadillac is produced

1942 Frank R. Schubert, an industrial engineer who managed the first bearing factory in Moscow, USSR 1930-1931 and later served as Assistant General Manager of the Houde Engineering Corporation, dies at age 47

1945 Pioneer black racer Benny Scott is born in Los Angeles, CA

1945 Cecil Kimber of M.G. is killed in a railway accident at age 56

1950 Theodore Schneider of Rochet-Schneider dies in Paris, France

1953 Paul G. Hoffman is elected Chairman of the Studebaker Corporation

1960 Corlis G. Keyes, founder and Chairman of the Board of the Keyes Supply Company Ltd., dies at age 79

1968 Rolf Stommelen and Jochen Neerpasch, driving a Porsche 907, win the 24 Hours of Daytona in Daytona Beach, FL, the first time that a German car had won a race of that type

1970 American Motors shareholders approve the acquisition of the Kaiser-Jeep Corporation

1970 Hugh J. Ferry, former Treasurer, President, and Chairman of the Packard Motor Car Company, dies in Detroit, MI at age 85

1970 Racer Sigmund Haugdahl, often cited as the first to use weights on the wheel rims as a means to balance tires, dies in Jacksonville, FL

1971 Rolls-Royce Ltd. declares bankruptcy with E. Rupert Nicholson named as receiver

1982 Race car designer Riley Brett dies at age 87

1988 Harold K. Sperlich retires as President of Chrysler Corporation, and is succeeded by Bennett E. Bidwell

FEBRUARY 5

1840 John Boyd Dunlop, a veterinary surgeon credited with inventing the pneumatic tire, is born in Dreghorn, Ayrshire, Scotland

1845 Thomas Buckland Jeffery, founder of the company bearing his name that manufactured the Rambler, is born in Stoke Damerel, Devonshire, England

1852 Frederick Samuel Fish of Studebaker is born in Newark, NJ

1853 James Thompson McCleary, a United States Congressman 1893-1907 (R-MN) who later was an official with the Lincoln Highway association, is born in Ingersoll, ON, Canada

1878 Andre Gustave Citroen is born in France of Dutch/Jewish ancestry

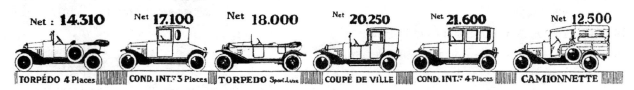

1880 Gabriel Voisin is born in Belleville-sur-Saone, France

1884 Aaron L. Sapiro of the Ford Motor Company is born in San Francisco, CA

1888 John Moyes Lessells, a Rolls-Royce design engineer who later was a professor of mechanical engineering at the Massachusetts Institute of Technology in Cambridge, MA, is born in Dunfermline, Scotland

1903 The Packard board approves the design and manufacture of the Model M, a low-priced 1-cylinder car to compete with the Oldsmobile "Curved Dash" - this was the company's first board meeting in Detroit, MI

1914 F. C. Ball, glass jar manufacturer, purchases the Inter-State Motor Company of Muncie, IN

1919 The first Voisin is completed and test driven by Gabriel Voisin

1931 Malcolm Campbell, driving the Napier-Campbell "Blue Bird III" at Daytona Beach, FL, raises the land speed record to 246.086 mph

1936 The 1936 Chrysler Series C-11 is introduced as a mid-year model

1942 The last pre-World War II Hudson is produced

1945 Marcel Doret, a holder of various automobile and airplane speed records, dies in Abbeville, France at age 48

1947 The stockholders of the Graham-Paige Motors Corporation approve the sale of the firm's automotive assets to the Kaiser-Frazer Corporation

1947 Racer Darrell Lee Waltrip is born in Owensboro, KY

1951 Automobile parts manufacturer Joseph N. Smith dies at age 63

1952 The first "Don't Walk" sign is erected in New York City

1953 Indianapolis 500 promoter Steven Hannagan dies in Nairobi, Kenya at age 53

1953 Racer Dorsey Schroeder is born in Kirkwood, MO

1954 Carl Eric Wickman, a Hupmobile dealer who founded the Greyhound Corporation, dies

1956 Racer Hector Rebaque is born in Mexico City, DF, Mexico

1970 American Motors purchases the Kaiser-Jeep Corporation

1986 Stylist John Reinhart dies at age 70

FEBRUARY 6

1895 Arthur Nutt, the manager of the Toledo, OH plant of the Packard Motor Car Company, is born in New Rochelle, NY

1898 Charles Augustine Chayne of General Motors is born in Harrisburg, PA

1911 Thomas Henry Oster of the Ford Motor Company is born in Braddock, PA

1911 The "Spirit of Ecstasy" mascot designed by Charles Sykes is adopted as standard equipment by the Rolls-Royce Ltd. Board of Directors

1928 Gerry Bouwer leaves Capetown, South Africa in his Chrysler in what would be the first overland car trip to London, England

The heart and soul of a masterpiece

1937 Captain Matt Payne, a design engineer with Clement-Talbot, Ltd., dies at age 46

1950 Racer Paul Gentilozzi is born in Detroit, MI

1951 The second-series Kaiser Dragon is introduced

1952 The 1952 Lincolns are introduced featuring a new overhead-valve V-8 engine and styling by William F. Schmidt and assistants Don DeLaRossa, Don Beyreis, and L. David Ash

1952 Harlan J. Oakes of Pontiac and GMC dies at age 41

1954 The Mercedes-Benz 300SL "gullwing coupe" and 190SL roadster are introduced at the International Motor Sports Show in New York City, the first production cars of the marque to have their world premiere in the United States

1955 Herb Thomas, driving a 1954 Hudson Hornet, wins a 100-mile race at West Palm Beach, FL, the last of 79 NASCAR victories for the marque

1955 E. O. Holmgrain, Chief Draftsman of the Velie Motor Corporation who later was a design truck engineer with Ford and Federal, dies

1961 Ousted executive Robert Markewich sues the Chrysler Corporation

1964 Richard A. Teague is elected Vice President of Automotive Styling for American Motors

1966 The Daytona Continental, the first 24-hour automobile race staged in the United States, is won by Ken Miles and Lloyd Ruby driving a Ford Mark II

1968 General Motors Executive Vice President Semon E. "Bunkie" Knudsen is hired by Henry Ford II to be President of the Ford Motor Company, succeeding Arjay R. Miller who is named Vice Chairman of the Board

1971 Racer Jean-Christophe "Jules" Boullion is born in France

1976 Sir William Sinclair, Director and Chief Executive of Dunlop Rubber Company (Scotland) Ltd., and a Director of Bentley Motors, Ltd., dies at age 81

1979 James H. Marks, Executive Vice President of the Packard Motor Car Company 1944-1946, dies at age 92

1985 Walter L. Jacobs, President of the Hertz Corporation 1926-1960, dies in Miami, FL at age 88 - he founded the first car rental company in 1918, sold it to John D. Hertz in 1923, but remained an employee of the firm

1995 The Ferrari 412 T2 is introduced by Chairman Luca di Montezemolo

FEBRUARY 7

1885 Yataro Iwasaki, the founder of Mitsubishi, dies in Tokyo, Japan at age 50

1901 The Detroit Automobile Company, Henry Ford's first official venture in this industry, dissolves

1908 William Daniel Singleton of the Ford Motor Company is born in Dallas, TX

1909 Thomas Archibald Bedford of the Kaiser-Frazer Corporation is born in San Diego, CA

1919 Henry Ford is ordered by the courts to distribute profits to stockholders back to August 1916 with interest

1920 The Amerada Corporation is incorporated in Delaware

1921 The ReVere Motor Car Company is forced into receivership

1921 The Societe Generale des Huiles de Petrole is incorporated in Paris, France - the firm adopted the name BP France in 1987

1931 Dave Evans, driving the Cummins Diesel Special at Daytona Beach, FL, raises the land speed record for this type of vehicle to 100.755 mph - the car was a racing chassis built by Fred Duesenberg with a diesel engine designed by Clessie L. Cummins

1938 Harvey S. Firestone dies in Miami Beach, FL at age 69

The simple yet effective Firestone logo -
a close friend of Henry Ford, neither mogul would live to
witness the marriage of their
grandchildren and the legal union of the two families.

1938 The first bench tests of the new Mercedes-Benz 3-litre V-12 engine are conducted prior to its installation in the W154 chassis

1939 M. D. Reardon of the Standard Oil Company of New Jersey dies in Richmond, VA

1942 The last pre-World War II Buick produced within the entire division is completed at the Southgate, CA factory

1952 Racer Will Hobgood is born in Cedar Creek, SC

1954 Dodge begins its lavish 40th anniversary celebration

1956 Racer John Nielsen is born in Varde, Denmark

1958 The 2,000,000th Cadillac is produced, a Sedan DeVille that is met at the end of the assembly line by division General Manager James M. Roche and Joe Malachinski, a Cadillac employee since 1903

1960 Karl Maybach, son of Wilhelm Maybach and designer of the Maybach Zeppelin of the 1930's, dies in Friedrichshafen, West Germany at age 80

1973 American Motors announces plans to market automobiles powered by Wankel rotary engines

1975 Canada imposes a 55 mph speed limit

1980 The Ford Motor Company dedicates its Engineering Computer Center in Dearborn, MI

1985 The first Ford Tempo with an air bag is delivered to the United States Department of Transportation for testing

FEBRUARY 8

1861 Harry Ward Leonard, a pioneer developer of automobile lighting systems, is born in Cincinnati, OH

1884 Lieutenant-Colonel the Right Honorable John Theodore Cuthbert Moore-Brabazon, PC, GBE, MC, 1st Lord Brabazon of Tara of Sandwich in the County of Kent (better known as the racer Lord Brabazon) is born in Kent county, England

1898 Charles Russell Feldman of the Henney Motor Company, a manufacturer of hearses long affiliated with the Packard Motor Car Company, is born in Philadelphia, PA

1911 Charles F. Kettering installs his reduced size starter-generator in a Cadillac and conducts the first successful tests on the system

1911 The American Motor Car Manufacturers Association (AMCMA) disbands in Chicago, IL as pending legal actions against the Selden patent appear to be heading toward an unsuccessful conclusion

1912 The Army Road Test to prove the reliability of motor trucks begins in Washington, DC

1914 Automotive historian Frank Xavier Ross Jr. is born in Manhattan, NY

1916 Charles F. Kettering receives the second of two patents for his Engine Starting, Lighting, and Ignition System

1916 The assets of the bankrupt Rayfield Motor Car Company are sold at auction

1917 Glenn H. Curtiss unveils his Autolandplane, probably the world's first roadable airplane, at the Pan-American Aeronautic Exposition in New York City

1922 The Shell Union Oil Company is incorporated in Delaware to consolidate the parent company's North American operations

1925 Automotive artist Edward Penfield dies in Beacon, NY at age 58

1932 Racer Henry Clifford "Cliff" Allison is born in Cumberlandshire, England

1936 General Motors founder William C. Durant files a personal bankruptcy petition in Federal District Court in New York City

1937 Harry C. Wiess is elected President of the Humble Oil Company

1939 Bill Cummings, winner of the 1934 Indianapolis 500 and holder of the land speed record for diesel-powered cars, dies at age 24

1939 The Hupp Motor Car Corporation acquires the Cord 810/812 dies and enough spare parts to enable production of about 600 Hupmobile Skylarks

1942 Maj. Gen. Fritz Todt, builder of the German Autobahns, is killed in an airplane crash at age 50

1946 The 1946 Lincolns and Mercurys are introduced to the public after several months of retooling difficulties and supply shortages

1947 The 1947 Chevrolets are introduced

1948 Automobile bearing designer Carlos H. Allen dies at age 56

1951 J. R. Heller, a cofounder and executive of the Elco Lubricant Corporation and an authority on hypoid bear lubrication, dies in Tucson, AZ at age 50

1960 The AVCO Corporation, founded as the Cord Corporation, sells its last remaining Connersville, IN properties to end the firm's historic link with the time of E. L. Cord

1960 Racer Steve Kempton is born in Nottingham, Nottinghamshire, England

1964 Finlay Robertson Porter of Mercer and F.R.P. dies in Southampton, NY at age 92

1964 Racer Frank Biela is born in Neuss, West Germany

1964 The Iraq National Oil Company is incorporated in Baghdad, Iraq

1966 The Briggs Cunningham Automotive Museum opens in Costa Mesa, CA

1968 British Motor Holdings Ltd. and Leyland Motor Corporation Ltd. merge to form the British Leyland Motor Corporation Ltd., which evolved into BL Public Limited Company

1974 William J. Muller, the front-wheel-drive pioneer associated with the Ruxton, dies in Metairie, LA at age 79

1974 Automobile parts manufacturer Nicholas P. Thul dies in Plainfield, NJ at age 83

1985 Sir William Lyons of Jaguar dies in Warrenbury Hall, Warwick, Warwickshire, England at age 83

FEBRUARY 9

1820 Moses Gerrish Farmer, an electrician whose inventions made pioneer electric automobiles feasible, is born in Boscawen, NH

1846 August Wilhelm Maybach is born in Heilbronn am Neckar, Germany

1883 Earle Wayne Webb, President of the Ethyl Gasoline Corporation 1925-1947, is born in Morehead City, NC

1886 Owen R. Skelton of the Chrysler Corporation is born in Edgerton, OH

1899 Lyndon Walkup Burch, a test engineer for the Packard Motor Car Company 1925-1930, is born in Grand Rapids, MI

1900 Abraham Burlingame, builder of the 1896 Burlingame steam car, dies in Worcester, MA at age 58

1901 Louis Clifford Goad of General Motors is born in Petersburg, IN

1909 The Indianapolis Motor Speedway Company is incorporated with Carl G. Fisher as President, Arthur C. Newby as First Vice Presidnet, Frank H. Wheeler as Second Vice President, and James A. Allison as Secretary-Treasurer

1911 Mercer records its first major racing victory as Charles Bigelow in a Type 35R raceabout wins the Panama Pacific Light Car Race in San Francisco, CA

1927 Automotive parts manufacturer Donald Waddington Manning is born in Philadelphia, PA

1927 Automotive writer Frederick Wilson Henry McComb is born in Northern Ireland

1933 The 1933 Fords are introduced

1933 The Packard Formal Sedan is introduced

1937 Racer Anthony Francis O'Connell "Tony" Maggs is born in Pretoria, South Africa

1939 Racer Jan Opperman is born

1942 The last pre-World War II DeSoto is produced

1942 The last pre-World War II Packard is produced, a Clipper sedan

1950 Edwin Foster Blair is elected to the Board of Directors of the Packard Motor Car Company

1951 The 1951 Chryslers are introduced

1953 Life membership in the Society of Automotive Engineers is awarded to Peter M. Heldt, 51 years after his editorial in Horseless Age had led to the organization of the society

1955 Racer Eddie Hearne dies in Los Angeles, CA at age 67

1959 The former Packard factory on East Grand Boulevard in Detroit, MI is heavily damaged by fire

1962 Robert A. Stranahan, President and Chairman of the Champion Spark Plug Company 1908-1962, dies in Toledo, OH at age 75

1978 William D. Thompson, a design engineer with Elcar, Stutz, Duesenberg, and Pierce-Arrow, dies in San Diego, CA at age 79

1978 Racer Hans Stuck dies in Gronau, West Germany at age 77

1993 Sydney Enever, longtime M.G. designer, dies at age 86

FEBRUARY 10

1877 William Robert Angell of the Continental Motors Corporation is born in Jesup, IA

1878 Alanson Partridge Brush is born in Detroit, MI

1880 Jesse Gurney Vincent of Packard is born in Charleston, AR

1893 Automobile insurance pioneer Hathaway Gasper Kemper is born in Van Wert, OH

1895 Sir John Paul Black, Managing Director of Standard Motor Company Ltd. and onetime owner of Triumph, is born

1895 Automobile parts manufacturer Fred J. Campbell is born in Freeport, IL

1895 The first Panhard et Levassor gasoline-powered truck is given its initial test run in Paris, France by M. Mayade, Chief Engineer of the company

1901 Henri Farman records his first racing victory, winning the Pau-Peyrehorade-Pau road race for touring cars in an 8-hp Darracq

1903 Racer Franco Cortese is born in Oggebbio, Novara, Piedmont, Italy

1910 Siro Vazquez of the Exxon Corporation is born in Caracas, Venezuela

1917 Automobile stylist Elwood Paul Engel is born in Newark, NJ

1919 Racer Eddie Johnson is born in Richmond, VA

1920 Eugene Bordinat Jr., a longtime stylist with General Motors and the Ford Motor Company, is born in Toledo, OH

1922 John Hugh Liedtke of the Pennzoil Company is born in Tulsa, OK

1926 General Motors directors approve the purchase of a site for a new truck production facility - the 160-acre Alfred Howland farm just south of Pontiac, MI was purchased in March, but announcement of the transaction would be withheld until June 1927

1927 Franklin's 1925-1928 "Lion" mascot is changed from polished nickel silver to nickel-plated bronze

Air-Cooled

The 25th Anniversary Franklin

The Literary Digest for May 14, 1927

Now on the Crest of a New Wave of Success - THE FRANKLIN COUPÉ

1928 Jean-Luc Lagardere of Matra is born in Aublet, Gers, France

1940 S. F. Edge of Napier dies in Gallops, England at age 71

1941 The first experimental Highway Post Office begins service between Washington, DC and Harrisonburg, VA using a specially-built White Model 788 transit bus

1942 The last pre-World War II Ford and Mercury are produced

1942 The last pre-World War II Pontiac is produced, a Streamline Six sedan

1947 The Kaiser-Frazer Corporation acquires the automotive assets of the Graham-Paige Motors Corporation

1950 The 1950 Hudson Super-Sixes are introduced nearly three months after the introduction of the Pacemakers, completing the marque's lineup

1951 Charles W. Churchill, President of Chrysler Corporation Ltd. of Canada, dies in Detroit, MI at age 70

1952 The DeSoto V-8 is introduced

1953 Alan P. Good of Lagonda dies at age 46

1955 The Chrysler C-300 hardtop coupe is introduced as a mid-year model

1955 The first 1955 Canadian Ford is produced following a 100-day strike

1958 The Arabian Oil Company Ltd. is incorporated in Tokyo, Japan

1960 The American Bugatti Club is organized

1963 Racer Didier Artzet is born in Nice, France

1988 Matra SA completes a 7-month process of privatization

1989 The Ford Motor Company announces a 1988 net income of $5.3 billion, a world's record for an automotive manufacturer

1996 Early Ford V8 Club of America official Earl Martin dies at age 68

FEBRUARY 11

1847 Thomas Alva Edison is born in Milan, OH

1868 John W. Wilkinson of Franklin is born in Syracuse, NY

1875 Ross Shaw Sterling, Chairman of the Humble Oil & Refining Company 1917-1925 and Governor of Texas 1931-1932, is born in Anahuac, TX

1886 Roy H. Faulkner, an executive with Oakland, Nash, Auburn, Studebaker, and Pierce-Arrow, is born in Allegheny (now part of Pittsburgh), PA

1888 Race car engine designer Fred Offenhauser is born

1895 George A. Delaney of Paige, Graham-Paige, Graham, and Pontiac is born in Centerview, MO

1907 The Brush Runabout prototype is introduced at the Detroit Automobile Show

1910 Automobile historian Lionel Thomas Caswell Rolt is born in Chester, England

1912 E. T. Reynolds of the Studebaker-Packard Corporation is born in Auburn, NY

1919 Joseph William Moon of the Moon Motor Car Company dies at age 68

1924 The Winton Motor Car Company announces that it is leaving the automobile business

1932 George R. Rowland, Chief Engineer of The Texas Company and an authority on lubrication and lubricants, dies in Elizabeth, NJ at age 64

1933 The first German built and designed Ford is introduced

1934 Racer John Surtees is born at Tatsfield, Surrey, England

1935 John W. Brussel is named Manager of the Federal-Mogul Corporation

1936 Encouraged by its success at the 1933-1934 Chicago Century of Progress, General Motors opens its "Parade of Progress" in Lakeland, FL as eight streamlined vans plus support vehicles embark on a four-year odyssey throughout North America

1937 The Fisher Body Division of General Motors and the United Auto Workers (UAW) reach a tentative agreement to end a 44-day strike, opening the way the industry-wide unionization of factory workers

1938 The Cord Corporation reorganizes as the Aviation and Transportation Corporation (ATCO)

1948 Hugh J. Ferry is elected to the Packard Motor Car Company Board of Directors

1949 The Ford Division of the Ford Motor Company is established

1951 Marshall Teague wins the Daytona Beach (FL) 160-mile race, the first of 79 NASCAR victories for the Hudson Hornet

1955 Pierre-Andre Lefaucheux, President of Renault, is killed at age 56 in a car accident in Saint-Dizier, France at age 56

1959 Racer Roberto Moreno is born in Rio de Janeiro, Brazil

1959 Racer Marshall Teague is killed at age 37 during an attempt to raise the closed-course speed record at Daytona Beach, FL

1962 Automobili Serenissima SpA is founded in Bologna, Italy by Giorgio Billi and Count Giovanni Volpi Di Misurata - the firm would evolve into Automobile Turismo e Sport, manufacturers of the 1962-1964 ATS sports car

1967 Frank F. Matheson, designer of the 1903-1912 Matheson who later was a distributor for Dodge, Oakland, Pontiac, and GMC, dies in Grand Rapids, MI at age 95

1994 Racer Neil Bonnett is killed at age 47 during a practice run at Daytona Beach, FL

FEBRUARY 12

1809 Abraham Lincoln, 16th President of the United States and namesake of the United States luxury marque, is born in Hodgenville, KY

1866 Charles Beebe Raymond of the the B. F. Goodrich Company is born in Akron, OH

1887 Labor mediator James F. Dewey is born in Locustdale, PA

1891 Henry Hoyt Gilbert of Cadillac, Lincoln, and Mercury is born in Bridgeport, IN

1901 James W. Packard is awarded his first automobile patent

1902 The first Studebaker automobile is sold, an electric-powered runabout purchased by R. W. Blees of Macon, MO

1903 The first Overland is test driven in Terre Haute, IN

The Overland was one of America's most popular pioneer marques. This 1914 Model 79-R roadster was typical of its era - and very sporty.

1907 The Bailey Automobile Company is organized in Springfield, MA by Bertram Bailey, Henry G. Whitman, and Willis L. Van Sicklin to produce the Bailey, designed by brothers James A. & Julian L. Perkins

1908 The New York to Paris Race begins as six cars leave Times Square in New York City with an estimated 50,000 spectators looking on

1914 The Mississippi Supreme Court rules that a 1912 law requiring automobile registration is unconstitutional, and orders refunds of $28,040

1919 Ralph DePalma, driving a special 905-cid V-12 Packard, raises the land speed record to 149.875 mph at Daytona Beach, FL

1920 Herman J. Hass, Vice President and General Manager of the Peru Auto Parts Manufacturing Company, dies in Peru, IN at age 57

1925 Dietrich, Inc. is founded by Raymond H. Dietrich in Detroit, MI to design and build custom automobile bodies

1929 The Pontiac 1928 "Indian Head" mascot is patented by designer William Schnell

1932 Robert Anthony Lutz of the Ford Motor Company and Chrysler Corporation is born in Zurich, Switzerland (his father, a United States citizen, was serving as a director of a Swiss bank)

1935 Sidney Joseph Reso of the Exxon Corporation is born in New Orleans, LA

1938 The Aviation & Transportation Corporation, formerly the Cord Corporation, announces that they have withdrawn completely from the manufacturing of automobiles, officially ending the Auburn, Cord, and Duesenberg marques

1942 Robert Archibald Speir Gray, author of *Rolls On The Rocks* chronicling the 1971 Rolls-Royce, Ltd. receivership, is born in Kibworth Beauchamp, Leicestershire, England

1948 Patrick J. Flaherty, Chairman of the Board of the Johnson Bronze Company and a pioneer in the manufacture of bronze automobile bearings, dies in Miami Beach, FL

1951 Automobile parts distributor Lester Hutchings dies at age 54

1952 Racer Patrick Gaillard is born in Paris, France

1953 The Willys-Overland Company celebrates its Golden Anniversary

1953 The Rev. Canon Frederick W. Hassard-Short, Chairman of the British Automobile Association 1942-1953, dies in London at age 79

1957 Jaguar's Browns Lane factory and several hundred cars are destroyed by fire

1958 Modernistic Industries, Inc., a manufacturer of recreational vehicles, is incorporated in Iowa

1962 American Motors elects Richard E. Cross as Chairman and Roy Abernethy as President, replacing George W. Romney, who had held both positions - Romney was named Vice Chairman, in effect granting him a leave of absence to explore a political career

1962 The Ford Motor Company announces that their "FoMoCo" glass trademark will be renamed "Car-Lite"

1964 Henry Ford II and Anne McDonnell Ford divorce

1971 Robert M. Rodger of the Chrysler Corporation dies of cancer at age 53

1976 Nissan purchases Volkswagen's factory in Australia

1987 Racer Dennis Poore dies in London, England at age 70

1992 General Motors of Canada Ltd. announces a new marque, the Asuna

1993 Racer Joe Booher is killed at the Daytona International Speedway

FEBRUARY 13

1871 Designer Joseph Vollmer is born in Baden-Baden, Germany

1883 Automobile and truck designer Charles Balough is born in Nagylak, Hungary (now Nadlac, Romania)

1898 Henry Lindfield of Brighton, England dies in the hospital one day after being involved in an automobile accident to become the first driver fatality in Great Britain

1901 George Jeffries Harrington, Plant Engineer of the Somerville (NJ) Ford Motor Company factory 1925-1928, is born in Boston, MA

1922 Racer Willi Heeks is born in Moorlage, Germany

1925 Stuart Macklin Frey of the Ford Motor Company is born in Peoria, IL

1927 John Joseph Nevin, an executive with the Ford Motor Company and the Firestone Tire & Rubber Company, is born in Jersey City, NJ

1929 Heinz W. Hahn of Iveco is born in Russelsheim, Germany

1934 The 1934 Pontiac "Indian Maiden" mascot is patented by designer B. E. Lemm

A 1934 Pontiac is the lone car visible in this view of the busy harbor in Port-au-Prince, Haiti.

1940 Robert James Eaton of the Chrysler Corporation is born in Buena Vista, CO

1946 B. E. Sibley of the Continental Oil Company dies in Needles, CA at age 59

1948 Racer Jim Crawford is born in Dunfermline, Great Britain

1948 Andrew McNally 3rd is elected President of Rand McNally & Company, road map publishers

1953 William C. Mack of Mack Trucks, Inc. dies in New York City at age 94

1953 Chrysler Corporation Ltd. of Canada President E. C. Row announces major expansions of the company's factories in Windsor, ON to accomodate increased demand

1958 The 1958 Ford Thunderbird, the first of the submarque with four seats, is introduced as a hardtop coupe (a convertible would be added later)

1960 Delmar G. "Barney" Roos dies in Philadelphia, PA at age 72

1961 Enzo Ferrari introduces the mid-engined Ferrari Dino 156 Forumla 1 car and the mid-engined Ferrari Dino 246SO sports car

1962 Roy F. McConnell of the Standard Oil Company dies at age 77

1968 The Lincoln Continental Mark III is introduced in Chicago, IL

1969 The Iso Fidia, a four-door sedan and successor to the F4, is introduced in Athens, Greece

1971 Roger M. Kyes, Executive Vice President of General Motors, dies in Columbus, OH at age 64

FEBRUARY 14

1793 Goldsworthy Gurney is born in Treator, Cornwall, England

1877 William Oliver Cooper of the Templar Motors Corporation is born in Wellsville, OH

1878 Hans Ledwinka of Tatra is born in Klosterneuburg, Austria

1880 Vern Moulton, a cofounder in 1916 of the Auto-Owners Insurance Company, is born in LeRoy, MI

1885 Benjamin B. Hotchkiss, firearms manufacturer and namesake of the 1903-1955 French automobile, dies in Paris, France at age 58

1896 The Prince of Wales, later King Edward VII, is given a ride in a Canstatt Daimler by owner Frederick R. Simms during the Imperial Institute of London show, the first time that a member of the British royal family had ridden in a motor car

1897 Robert Ralph Young of General Motors is born in Canadian, TX

1911 The Studebaker Corporation is reorganized in South Bend, IN combining the assets of the Studebaker Brothers Manufacturing Company and the Everitt-Metzger-Flanders Company

1912 The Lozier Motor Company officially withdraws from racing

1912 The Rayfield Motor Car Company elects Frederick K. Thayer as President, Charles Hoult as Vice President, A. E. Schnitker as Secretary-Treasurer, and E. E. Staley as Sales Manager - the brothers John, William, George, and Frederick Rayfield worked for their namesake firm, but were not corporate officers

1912 H. M. Bentley joins his younger brother W. O. as a partner in the London automobile dealership of Lecoq and Fernie

1913 The Morris is introduced at the North of England Motor Show in Manchester

1913 The last Thomas is produced

1913 James R. Hoffa of the United Auto Workers is born

1921 Nash increases the size of the Series 40 4-cylinder engine from 165.9 cid to 178.9 cid

1927 Ford standardizes 21-inch wire wheels on all Model T cars

1929 The St. Valentine's Day Massacre in Chicago, IL centers around a Packard disguised as a police car

1932 Racer Edwin K. "Banjo" Matthews is born in Akron, OH

1932 Frederic W. Warner, President and General Manager of the Oakland Motor Car Company 1917-1925 and a Director of General Motors, dies in Clearwater, FL at age 65

1942 Racer Ricardo Valentine Rodriguez de la Vega is born in Mexico City, DF, Mexico

1944 Racer Bengt Ronald "Ronnie" Peterson is born in Orebro, Sweden

1949 NV Koninklijke Nederlandsche Mij tot Exploitatie van Petroleumbronnen in Nederlandsch-Indie changes its name to Royal Dutch/Shell Group

1957 American Motors registers a stylized "Metropolitan" as a trademark for its British-built subcompact car

1962 The Jaguar Mark X is introduced to the United States market

1965 Racer James Marcenac dies in Van Nuys, CA at age 69

1965 Racer Lex Davison is killed in Sandown Park, Victoria, Australia when he crashes while practicing for the Australian Grand Prix

1968 Racer Scott Sharp is born in Norwalk, CT

1974 Automotive journalist Julian Chase dies in New York City at age 95

1976 Racer Piero Scotti dies at age 66

1992 Automobile historian J. Ditlev Scheel dies at age 73

1994 Racer Rodney Orr is killed at age 31 during a practice run at the Daytona International Speedway in Daytona Beach, FL

1996 Michael Schumacher takes the Ferrari F310 for its initial test drive at the Fiorano track in Italy

FEBRUARY 15

1882 Automobile engineer Clarence Willard Avery is born in Dansville, MI

1886 Antone Lyman Lott of the Motor Products Corporation is born in Chicago, IL

1894 Stylist and coachbuilder Raymond Henri Dietrich is born in Brooklyn, NY

1896 Donald Kirk David, a Director of the Ford Motor Company, is born in Moscow, ID

1900 Charles Allen Thomas, a General Motors research chemist who was involved in the development of Ethyl gasoline, is born in Scott County, KY

1902 Oldsmobile places its first national auto advertisement in the *Saturday Evening Post*

1911 Leonard Freel Woodcock, President 1970-1977 of the United Auto Workers, is born in Providence, RI

1913 The Knox Automobile Company is declared bankrupt

1920 Packard announces the Fuelizer, a fuel preheating device developed by Lionel M. Woolson

1920 David Allan Wickins of Lotus is born

1926 The Ford Motor Company is awarded the first United States Post Office Department contract for the commercial carrying of air mail

1927 The Fordson, MI post office is established at the Fordson factory

1929 Racer Norman Graham Hill is born in Hampstead, London, England

1931 Harold Lee Elfes, Sales Engineer for the Motor Products Corporation, dies in Detroit, MI at age 41 from pneumonia

1932 William Doyle of Texaco, Inc. is born in Seattle, WA

1933 The Willys-Overland Company is forced into receivership

1934 James W. Cottrell, Technical Editor of the *Commercial Car Journal*, dies

1936 The Mercedes-Benz 170H, an ancestor of the Volkswagen Beetle, the 260D, the world's first production diesel-powered passenger car, and the top-of-the-line supercharged 500K all debut at the Berlin Automobile Show

1936 Albert L. Douglas of the Mack-International Motor Truck Corporation dies

1937 Vincenzo Lancia dies in Turin, Italy at age 55

1937 Stylist Amos E. Northup dies at age 47 at Harper Hospital in Detroit, MI two day after slipping on the ice and breaking his skull

1939 The 27,000,000th Ford is produced

1947 The Packard Motor Car Company Zone Office assumes the wholesale end of the company's Boston, MA business

1948 Bernd Pischetsrieder of BMW is born in Munich, West Germany

1948 The first NASCAR-sanctioned race, staged on the sands at Daytona Beach, FL, is won by Red Byron of Atlanta, GA driving a Ford

1949 The Ford Division of the Ford Motor Company is established

1950 Henry D. Eisengrein, Vice President and General Manager of the Ward LaFrance Tuck Corporation and a former official with Maccar, White, and Diamond T, dies at age 57

1951 Racer Richard Dallest is born in France

1952 Packard contracts with the Henney Motor Company to produce the Pan American showcar

A 1939 Ford Deluxe convertible coupe and the "Oldest House in the U.S.A." in St. Augustine, FL.

1952 Studebaker Corporation President Harold S. Vance drives the 7,130,874th and "Last Vehicle of Studebaker's First Century", a 1952 Commander State Starliner Hardtop Coupe, off the assembly line with Walter C. Zientowski, the factory's senior employee, as his passenger

1953 The 1953 Willys Aero-Ace is introduced as a mid-year model

1954 The Thunderbird name is chosen for the new Ford sports car

1955 James J. Nance of the Studebaker-Packard Corporation is elected President of the Automobile Manufacturers Association

1956 Racer Hitoshi Ogawa is born in Tokyo, Japan

1957 Racer Jimmy Spencer is born in Berwick, PA

1963 Studebaker announces that all of their new cars will be fitted with front seat belts

1965 The Chevrolet Caprice is introduced as an upscale Impala Sport Sedan

1967 J. Frank Duryea dies in Old Saybrook, CT at age 97

1968 Subaru of America, Inc. is organized in Pennsylvania and begins importing the Subaru 360, a 2-cylinder mini sedan

1973 Racer Giancarlo Fisichella is born in Rome, Italy

1976 Racer Paul Russo dies in Daytona Beach, FL at age 61

1977 The 500,000th Chevrolet Corvette is produced, a white coupe with red interior to match the first 1953 Corvette - it was purchased by 22-year-old Francis Patric Meraw of Detroit, MI

1982 Cruise control inventor Ralph R. Teetor dies in Hagerstown, IN at age 91

1984 Groundbreaking ceremonies are held for the new 2.38-mile Grand Prix circuit in Dallas, TX

FEBRUARY 16

1843 Henry Martyn Leland is born in Danville, VT

1852 H. & C. Studebaker, a blacksmith and wagon building partnership, is founded by Henry and Clement Studebaker in South Bend, IN

1856 Carlo Bugatti, the father of Ettore Bugatti, is born in Milan, Italy

1878 Thomas S. Merrill of General Motors is born in Washington, DC

1880 Charles Thomas Fisher is born in Sandusky, OH

1894 Harold Taylor Ames, an executive with Auburn, Cord, and Duesenberg, is born in Antioch, IL

1907 The Angus Automobile Company of Angus, NE begins producing the Fuller - the firm would produce about 500 cars before closing in 1910

1911 Thomas Neal, a Detroit paint manufacturer, is elected President of General Motors

1920 The Astra is introduced at the St. Louis (MO) Automobile Show

1920 Racer Anthony "Tony" Crook is born in Manchester, England

1920 Racer Walt Faulkner is born in the United States

1921 John Friece Adamson of American Motors is born in Chicago, IL

1921 Racer Jean Behra is born in Nice, France

1928 Edzard Reuter, Chairman of Daimler-Benz AG 1987-1995, is born in Berlin, Germany

1928 Pioneer British motoring enthusiast Alexander Siemens dies at age 81

1930 Frank Victor John Darin of the Ford Motor Company is born in Detroit, MI

1930 Racer Jack George Stanley Sears is born in Northampton, England, the son of well known motor car enthusiast Stanley E. Sears and the father of racer David Sears

1931 David Robert Markin, President of Checker Motors Corporation 1970-1984, is born in New York City

1936 Roy D. Chapin of Hudson dies from pneumonia in Detroit, MI at age 55

1950 The new Kaisers designed by Howard A. "Dutch" Darrin are introduced as 1951 models

1955 The Willys Six 2-door sedan is introduced as a mid-year model

1957 Concert pianist Josef Hofmann, designer of the 1909 Hofmann automobile, dies at age 81

1962 The first A.C. Ace, as modified to Carroll Shelby's specifications, is shipped to Dean Moon's shop in Santa Fe Springs, CA, where a Ford 260-cid V-8 is installed to create the prototype Cobra

1964 The Porsche Carrera GTS makes its racing debut at Daytona Beach, FL

1965 S. C. van Pantheleon Baron Van Eck, founder of the Shell Oil Company, dies in Santa Barbara, CA at age 84

1967 Perry H. Gentzel, Vice President for Engineering of the Stanley Motor Carriage Company, dies in State College, PA

1994 Lynn H. Steele, a manufacturer of reproduction rubber parts for antique cars, dies

FEBRUARY 17

1872 Fred Rollin White, an executive with the Baker Motor Vehicle Company, the Baker Rauch & Lang Company, and the Baker-Raulang Company, is born in Cleveland, OH

1877 Sir Kenneth Irwin Crossley is born

1884 Paul Silvestre, a sculptor and designer of automobile mascots, is born

1890 The first Panhard et Levassor is test driven in Paris, France

1901 Maurice Farman records his first racing victory, winning the Grand Prix de Pau in a 24-hp Panhard - his brother, Henri Farman, finished second in a 12-hp Darracq

1911 The first self-starter, based on patents of Clyde J. Coleman and Charles F. Kettering, is installed on a Cadillac and successfully tested

1912 Frank Kulick, driving a modified Ford Model T on frozen Lake St. Clair, MI, covers a flying mile at 103.45 mph

1927 Melbert W. Taber, an electrical engineer with the Packard Motor Car Company 1911-1917 who later was associated with the Motor Wheel Corporation, dies in Detroit, MI at age 45

1934 The first high school drivers' education class begins at State College High School in State College, PA with Amos Earl Neyhart as the teacher

1936 Hiram P. Maxim, Chief Engineer of the Electric Vehicle Company 1895-1907, dies in LaJunta, CO at age 66

1941 Automotive historian and journalist David Wheaton Brownell is born in Fall River, MA

1942 Racer John Morton is born in the United States

1951 The United States government bans the production of white sidewall tires because of the Korean War effort

1953 Racer Steve Millen is born in New Zealand

1965 George Willis Dunham, designer of the first Hudson, dies in Norwalk, CT

1966 John G. Perrin, designer of the Lozier, dies in Springfield, MA at age 88

LOZIER

"The Choice of Men Who Know"

1966 Alfred P. Sloan Jr., President 1923-1937 and Chairman 1937-1956 of General Motors, dies in New York City at age 90

Hon. Edward T. Schafer

This 1951 Cadillac 75 limousine was one of the largest cars built during the legendary General Motors career of Alfred P. Sloan Jr.

The 5 year old "hanging" out of the rear door is Eddie Schafer who would grow up to become a car enthusiast and Governor of North Dakota.

1972 Volkswagen Beetle #15,007,034 is produced at the Wolfsburg, Germany factory to surpass the Ford Model T record, although controversy would linger about amended production quantities bor both cars

1972 Racer Friday Hassler is killed during practice at Daytona Beach, FL

1982 The 1983 aerodynamically designed Ford Thunderbird and Mercury Cougar are introduced

1983 The Toyota Motor Company, Ltd. and General Motors announce a joint venture, the New United Motor Manufacturing, Inc. (NUMMI), to convert an old plant in Fremont, CA to manufacture small cars

FEBRUARY 18

1856 George Louis Lavery, a proponent of metal automobile wheels, is born in Boston, MA

1884 James David Mooney, President of the Willys-Overland Company 1946-1949, is born in Cleveland, OH

1898 Enzo Anselmo Ferrari is born near Modena, Italy

1902 Eugene C. Richard files a patent application for his "valve-in-head" engine on behalf of the Buick Manufacturing Company

1915 Harry Ward Leonard, an associate of Thomas A. Edison who built the Century, Knickerbocker, and Ward Leonard automobiles 1901-1903, and later was a developer of improved automobile lighting systems who held over 100 patents in the field, dies in Bronxville, NY at age 54

1917 Automobile designer Philippe Charbonneaux is born in France

1918 The Edward G. Budd Manufacturing Company of Philadelphia, PA produces its 200,000th all-steel body for the Dodge Brothers touring car

1919 Ralph DePalma, driving the Packard 905 at Daytona Beach, FL, records a one-way flying mile at 149.887 mph, a world's record although not officially recognized as a new land speed record

1925 The Stutz Motor Car Company of America authorizes development of the Vertical Eight chassis designed by new President Frederic E. Moskovics

1926 William C. Durant announces that he will leave an active role in the daily management of Durant Motors, Inc.

1928 Racer Jimmy McElreath is born in Arlington, TX

1930 Automobile parts manufacturer Stanley Wendell Gustafson is born in Lansing, MI

1930 Edsel B. Ford purchases a M.G. M-Type, possibly the first United States sale for this marque, which he used frequently for three years before adding it to the collection of the Henry Ford Museum

1932 Sir Harry Brittain replaces H. T. Vane as Chairman and Managing Director of D. Napier & Son, Ltd., with the express goal of reentering the motor car business after an absence of eight years

1940 The Buick Town Master, a custom-bodied Brunn town car, is introduced

1952 The Studebaker Corporation begins its official centenary celebration

1953 Racer Ingo Hoffmann is born in Sao Paulo, Brazil

1955 Frederick C. Chandler, founder of the Chandler Motor Car Company, dies in Cleveland, OH at age 71

1956 The DeSoto Adventurer, a high-powered 2-door hardtop similar to the Chrysler 300, is introduced as a mid-year model - model year production would total just 996 units

1963 John B. Long is elected President of Harmon-Herrington Company, Inc.

1965 The Mercury Cougar design is approved for production

1967 Frederic E. Moskovics dies in Greenwich, CT at age 86

1973 Richard Petty wins the Daytona 500 at Daytona Beach, FL in a Dodge before a crowd of more than 103,000, the first time that a stock car race had drawn in excess of 100,000 fans

1979 Richard Petty, driving an Oldsmobile, becomes the first six-time winner of the Daytona (Beach, FL) 500

1988 The Ford Motor Company announces a 1987 net income of $4.6 billion, a world's record for an automotive manufacturer

1994 Donovan "Don" Cummins, a charter member of the United States Auto Club and longtime Vice President of Engineering for the Cummins Engine Company, dies at age 91

FEBRUARY 19

1862 George L. Weiss, a Cleveland, OH automobile enthusiast who was prominent in the early histories of Winton and Packard, is born in Allentown, PA

1878 Edward Peter "Garet" Garrett, a biographer of Henry Ford, is born in Pana, IL

1883 Darwin S. Hatch of *Motor Age* magazine is born in Kentland, IN

1886 Francis Edgar Rice of the Phillips Petroleum Company is born in Council Bluffs, IA

1886 William Starling Sullivan Rodgers of The Texas Company is born in Columbus, OH

1901 James John Nance of the Studebaker-Packard Corporation is born in Ironton, OH

1901 Roy D. Chapin quits college to join the Olds Motor Works, beginning an illustrious automotive career

1903 Carmen Fasanella, whose 68-year career as a taxicab owner/driver is often cited as a world's record, is born in Princeton, NJ

1906 The prototype Mason automobile is given its first test drive in Des Moines, IA by designer Frederick S. Duesenberg

1906 Longtime NASCAR official Johnny Bruner is born in Birmingham, AL

1913 William Mitchell Lewis retires as President and General Manager of the Mitchell-Lewis Motor Company

Manufactured 1903-1923 in Racine, WI, the Mitchell was a very popular marque, especially in the plains states. This 1917 Model C-42 touring is ready for a patriotic event somewhere in Minnesota.

1923 The Checker Cab Manufacturing Corporation is reorganized in New Jersey to acquire the stock of the Delaware corporation of the same name

1923 Racer Giulio Cabianca is born in Verona, Italy

1924 George S. Cawthorne, a onetime Rambler official and later a designer with several different motor truck companies, dies in Chicago, IL at age 49

1928 Sir Malcolm Campbell, driving the Napier-Campbell V-12 "Blue Bird II", raises the land speed record to 206.96 mph at Daytona Beach, FL

1932 The British Ford Model Y is introduced at Dagenham as the first "British" Ford rather than an assembled car with United States specifications

1934 David Colville takes delivery of the first Rolls-Royce produced Bentley, a 3 1/2 Litre Hooper Saloon, to reach private hands

1937 Donald E. Hackworth of General Motors is born in Circleville, OH

1941 As part of the reorganization of the Auburn Automobile Company, the assets of the Lycoming Motors Corporation are transferred to the Aviation Corporation, which basically were the remains of the former parent Cord Corporation

1941 Automotive valve manufacturer William W. Crawford dies in Miami Beach, FL at age 58

1947 Although essentially unchanged, the Ford Motor Company begins titling new Mercurys as 1947 models

A 1947 Mercury convertible is parked at far left on Bank Street (US 10) in Wallace, ID.

1950 Racer Jean-Pierre Malcher is born in France

1952 Racer Stephen South is born in Harrow, Middlesex, England

1955 Herman Stoll of General Motors, an authority on forging and casting problems, dies

1957 Edward Ringwood Hewitt, namesake of the Hewitt made 1906-1907 in New York City, and the Adams-Hewitt made 1905-1914 in Bedford, England, dies in New York City at age 90

1957 J. Allan Mahoney, Sales Engineer of the Hercules Motors Corporation, dies at age 65

1960 The International Harvester Corporation acquires the former plant of the United States Rubber Company in Fort Wayne, IN

1960 Racer John Paul Jr. is born in Muncie, IN, the son of racer John Paul Sr.

1961 Racer Andy Wallace is born in Oxford, Oxfordshire, England

1965 Henry Ford II marries Maria Christina Vettore Austin

1970 Racer Talmadge Prince is killed during practice at Daytona Beach, FL

1982 The DeLorean Manufacturing Company Ltd. is declared insolvent by the British government, with Sir Kenneth Cork appointed as receiver

1986 An Austin Seven produced at the Longbridge, England factory is the 5,000,000th car produced using the "Mini" design of Alec Issigonis

1990 Siro Vazquez, Senior Vice President of the Exxon Corporation 1970-1975, dies at age 80

1991 Autombilie historian Don Butler dies at age 79

FEBRUARY 20

1880 Emil A. Nelson, a design engineer with Packard, Oldsmobile, and Hupmobile and namesake of the 1917-1921 Nelson, is born in Cleveland, OH

1890 Russell Hudson McCarroll of the Ford Motor Company is born in Detroit, MI

1895 Racer Louis Vorow Zborowski is born at Melton Mowbray, England

1895 Clarence Oramel Skinner, a onetime Oldsmobile employee who later was an executive with the Automotive & Aviation Parts Mfrs., Inc., is born in Lansing, MI

1907 The Biddle-Murray Manufacturing Company of Oak Park, IL closes its doors after three years of limited automobile production

1918 Automotive historian Vernon Pizer is born in Boston, MA

1920 The Jones Motor Car Company of Wichita, KS is destroyed by fire

1929 The first Roosevelt, a companion of the Marmon and the first 8-cylinder car to sell for less than $1000, is produced

1930 Kenneth Coleman Merrill of the Ford Motor Credit Company is born in South Bend, IN

1934 Racer Robert William "Bobby" Unser is born in Albuquerque, NM

1935 The 1935 Auburn Custom Eight and Salon Six are introduced

1937 The first Arrowbile is completed by Waldo D. Waterman of Santa Monica, CA - this vehicle is often credited as being the world's first practical combination airplane/automobile

1937 Racer Roger Penske is born in Shaker Heights, OH

1941 John Eddy Utley of the Kelsey-Hayes Company is born in Evanston, IL

1953 Dean Alvin Walters, Technical Service Manager for Willys Motors Inc. and an employee of the company since 1909, dies at age 63

1954 The Dodge Firearrow show car is introduced

1954 The prototype Ford Thunderbird is unveiled

1955 Cedric P. Lockton, Chief Engineer of Chloride Batteries Ltd. and an employee of that firm since 1924, dies in England

1958 Herdis G. English, Chief Engineer of the Transmission and Axle Group, Ford Motor Company, dies at age 43

1959 Racer Scott Everts Brayton is born in Coldwater, MI

1968 The 266-cid V-8 engine is introduced as an option for the International Scout

1969 Walter Pyke Johnson, President of the Automotive Safety Foundation 1942-1953, dies in Skokie, IL at age 80

1971 Chrysler Corporation establishes an Office of Public Responsibility headed by Virgil E. Boyd, with Byron J. Nichols and Philip Buckminster as his assistants

1973 Charles S. Mott, a director of General Motors 1913-1973, dies in Flint, MI at age 97

1993 Ferruccio Lamborghini dies in Perugia, Italy at age 76

1996 Clare M. MacKichan, a General Motors stylist 1939-1978 best remembered for the 1955-1957 Chevrolets, Chevrolet Nomad, and Opel GT, dies in Nokomis, FL at age 77

Many people feel that the 1957 Chevrolet best captures the essence of late-1950's styling.

FEBRUARY 21

1831 Sir Charles Dance begins steam carriage service between Cheltenham and Gloucester, England using vehicles designed by Sir Goldsworthy Gurney

1888 Steam engine pioneer George H. Corliss dies in Providence, RI at age 70

1895 Automobile parts manufacturer H. Gray Muzzy is born in Detroit, MI

1905 The Christie Direct Action Motor Car Company is organized to manufacture the front wheel drive cars developed by J. Walter Christie

1907 Hendrik Spijker of Spyker drowns when his North Sea steamer breaks up in a storm off the coast of the Hook of Holland, the Netherlands

1909 Bob Burman in a Buick Model 17 wins the Mardi Gras Speed Contest in New Orleans, LA

1912 Isotta-Fraschini is issued an Italian patent for their 4-wheel brakes

1912 Automobile historian George Walter Risley is born in Chicago, IL

1913 Racer Roger Laurent is born in Liege, Belgium

1916 The Dixie Flyer is introduced in Louisville, KY

1922 Alfred P. Sloan Jr. of General Motors gives the Oakland Motor Division a four-point directive specifying that no drastic changes should be made until June 30, 1923

1934 Spark plug manufacturer Jack Gray dies

1940 Racer Peter Kenneth Gethin is born in Ewell, Surrey, England

1943 Automotive patent expert Elmer H. Schwarz dies in New Jersey

1944 Coachbuilder Giacinto Ghia dies in Turin, Italy at age 56

1948 Six days after its first race, the National Association for Stock Car Auto Racing (NASCAR) is formally incorporated in Daytona Beach, FL with Bill France Sr. as President

Descended from bootleggers and disliked by some purists, NASCAR racing nevertheless developed into one of the world's most popular spectator sports.

1949 Col. George A. Green, Australian-born Vice President of General Motors and General Manager of the GMC Truck & Coach Division who previously had worked for Thornycroft and Vanguard in England, dies in Miami Beach, FL at age 66

1958 Comfort A. Adams, a consulting engineer with the Edward G. Budd Manufacturing Company 1934-1947, dies at age 89

1960 George W. Borg, inventor of automobile clutch improvements and Chairman of the Borg-Warner Corporation, dies in Janesville, WI at age 71

1968 Iso is granted an international copyright for the Grifo name

1979 The 100,000,000th Chevrolet, a 1979 Monza coupe, is produced

FEBRUARY 22

1895 John Quayle McClure, President of the National Automobile & Casualty Company 1927-1956, is born in Los Angeles, CA

1904 Earle C. Anthony opens the Western Motor Car Company in Los Angeles, CA as a dealer for the National, Northern, and Thomas marques - the following year he acquired the distributorship for Packard, with whom he would play a major role for over 50 years

1910 Isotta-Fraschini applies for a patent on 4-wheel brakes

1914 Clinton Firestone of Firestone-Columbus dies

1918 Racer George Constantine is born in the United States

1921 The Washington is introduced in Eaton, OH by the local Methodist minister and his wife dressed as George and Martha Washington - the marque would become defunct in 1924 after production of no more than 40 cars

1922 Charles S. Mott of General Motors hires William S. Knudsen, formerly Production Manager for the Ford Motor Company, as his assistant

1922 Racer Jesus Iglesias is born in Pergamino, Argentina

1923 The 1,000,000th Chevrolet is produced

1926 The Fulford Speedway in Miami Beach, FL stages its first and only major event, the 300-mile Carl G. Fisher Cup Race won by Peter DePaolo in a Duesenberg

1933 Sir Malcolm Campbell, driving the Campbell Special "Blue Bird IV" at Daytona Beach, FL, raises the land speed record to 272.46 mph

1938 Racer Tim Mayer is born in Dalton, PA

1941 R. J. O'Toole of the A. O. Smith Corporation is born in Chicago, IL

1947 Dr. J. Harry Clo, Director of Research for A. Schrader's Son and an authority on air controlled automotive devices, dies in Waynesville, NC at age 65

1947 Henry E. Romberg, Assistant Chief Engineer for the Hayes Manufacturing Company whose earlier career included stints with Diamond T and Nash, dies

1949 Racer Andreas-Nikolaus "Niki" von Lauda is born in Vienna, Austria

1950 Automotive historian Sir Max Pemberton dies at age 86

1952 Neal G. Adair, Editor of *Motor* magazine, dies in New York City at age 65

1953 Severt Sundberg is killed when his Ferrari 166 crashes during an ice race in Burtrask, Sweden

1953 The prototype of the Kaiser-Darrin sports car is introduced

1959 The first Daytona 500 is staged at the new Daytona International Speedway in Daytona Beach, FL and won by Lee Petty in an Oldsmobile

1969 Racer Don MacTavish is killed at age 36 when his Mercury Comet crashes during a race in Daytona Beach, FL

1973 Winthrop Rockefeller, the Governor of Arkansas and a famous collector of antique automobiles, dies in Palm Springs, CA at age 60

1990 Victor Lasky, the critical biographer of Henry Ford II, dies in Washington, DC at age 72

1995 Stylist Richard Arbib dies in New York City at age 77

FEBRUARY 23

1852 Harry John Lawson, founder of the Daimler Motor Syndicate, Ltd. in Coventry, Warwickshire, England, is born in London

1880 Roy Dikeman Chapin of the Hudson Motor Company is born in Lansing, MI

1881 William Stamps Farish of the Standard Oil Company of New Jersey is born in Mayersville, MS

1891 Edward Francis Fisher, a cofounder of the Fisher Body Company, is born in Norwalk, OH

1893 Rudolf Diesel receives a German patent for the diesel engine

1906 The Aerocar Motor Company of Detroit, MI registers its "Aerocar" logo, but the firm failed in 1908 and its factory was taken over by Hudson

1909 General Motors declares the first dividend on its preferred stock

1912 The Carroll Motor Car Company of Strasburg, PA completes its one and only car, a 40-hp touring designed by Carroll Aument

1914 The first Saxon is sold and shipped to its new owner

1924 Patrick L. Hussey, a cofounder of the Cadillac Motor Car Company and founder of the Husey Drop Forging & Manufacturing Company, dies in Cleveland, OH

1925 Willard L. Velie Jr. of the Velie Motor Corporation marries Martha Kelly, heiress of the Kelly-Springfield Tire & Rubber Company

1928 Racer Hans Herrmann is born in Stuttgart, Germany

1929 Baroness Mercedes Adrienne Manuela Ramona von Schlosser Weigl (nee Jellinek), namesake of the Mercedes and Mercedes-Benz, dies in Vienna, Austria at age 40

1939 Edward F. Hallock of the Socony-Vacuum Oil Company dies at age 50

1946 Racer Alberto Colombo is born in Varedo, Liano, Italy

1947 Walter T. Fishleigh of Packard and Ford dies in Detroit, MI at age 67

1953 Ernesto Ceirano of Fiat, winner of the 1911 and 1914 Targo Florio, dies in Turin, Italy at age 79

1953 Racer Satoru Nakajima is born in Okazaki, Japan

1954 The 500,000th post-World War II Jeep is produced

1954 A. Ludlow Clayden, a Sun Oil Company official 1922-1953 who previously had worked for Daimler in his native England, dies in Daytona Beach, FL at age 71

1955 The Nash-based Hudson Hornet and Wasp are introduced at the Chicago Auto Show, completing Hudson's model lineup

1958 Racing champion Juan Manuel Fangio is kidnapped in Havana, Cuba by Communist guerrillas

1959 Jean-Louis-Eugen Groff, Scientific Advisor to the Institut Francasis du Petrole, dies in France at age 65

1960 Racer Arthur Legat dies in Haine St. Pierre, Belgium at age 61

1964 Richard Petty wins the Daytona (Beach, FL) 500 in a Plymouth, the first racing victory for Chrysler Corporation's new "Hemispherical Combustion Chamber Maximum Performance Engine", or simply the Hemi

1964 Racer Peter Kox is born in the Netherlands

1966 The 1,000,000th Ford Mustang is produced

1967 The Pontiac Firebird is introduced

1968 Artist Peter Arno, the creator of the unique 1939 Albatross, dies at age 64

1971 23 days after Rolls-Royce Ltd. had entered receivership, a new company, Rolls-Royce (1971) Ltd., is registered

1976 The Bahrain National Oil Company is organized in Awali, Bahrain

FEBRUARY 24

1871 James Indus Farley of Auburn is born near Hamilton, IN

1878 Joseph Winterbotham Jr., President of the Mitchell-Lewis Motor Company 1914-1916 and later a Director of the Nash Motors Company, is born in Joliet, IL

1897 Ernest Robert Breech of the Ford Motor Company is born in Lebanon, MO

1905 The organizational meeting of the American Motor Car Manufacturers Association is held at the Ford Motor Company with Ford executive James Couzens presiding - the 23 charter member companies were opponents of the Association of Licensed Automobile Manufacturers and the Selden patent

1909 The Hudson Motor Car Company is incorporated in Detroit, MI with its cars to be named for cofounder Joseph L. Hudson

1912 Charles Lewis, President of the Jackson Automobile Company and President of the Lewis Spring and Axle Company which later built the Hollier, dies in Jackson, MI at age 61

1914 Herbert M. Dawley of Pierce-Arrow is issued a United States patent for his fender-mounted headlights that would become the marque's signature styling feature

1921 Automobile parts manufacturer Charles Edwin Drury is born in Albany, IL

1931 Lucius Morton Wainwright, President of the Diamond Chain & Manufacturing Company since 1905 and longtime Treasurer of the Motor & Accessory Manufacturers Association, dies in Miami Beach, FL at age 71

1932 Malcolm Campbell, driving the Napier-Campbell "Blue Bird III" at Daytona Beach, FL, raises the land speed record to 253.97 mph

1936 Lance Reventlow, builder of the Scarab sports car, is born in London, England, the son of Danish Count Kurt von Haugwitz-Reventlow and F. W. Woolworth heiress Barbara Hutton

1942 General Motors Vice President Ernest R. Breech resigns to become President of the Bendix Aviation Corporation

1947 Robert W. Stewart of the Standard Oil Company of Indiana dies at age 80

1950 The Walter M. Murphy Company, Coachbuilders former premises in Pasadena, CA is destroyed by fire

1951 Fred M. Zeder of the Chrysler Corporation dies in Miami Beach, FL at age 64

1955 Racer Alain Marie Pascal Prost, the Formula 1 alltime leader with 51 victories and 798.5 points, is born in Saint-Chamond, France

1955 Racer Clemente Biondetti dies of cancer in Florence, Italy at age 56

1958 The Studebaker-Packard Corporation Board of Directors, without an official vote, accepts Chairman Harold E. Churchill's proposal to terminate the Packard marque and direct the anticipated savings toward the production and promotion of the Studebaker Lark

1962 Harrah's Automobile Collection in Sparks, NV opens to the public

1963 Eugene J. Farkas, a longtime design engineer with the Ford Motor Company, dies in South Laguna Beach, CA at age 81

1964 Tiny Lund, driving a Ford, records his first major racing victory at the Daytona (Beach, FL) 500

1968 American Motors introduces the AMX as a mid-year model

1968 Racer Emanuele Naspetti is born in Ancona, Italy

1978 United States-born automobile photojournalist Caroline Nostrand and Scotch-Irish automobile journalist F. Wilson McComb are married in Chichester, Sussex, England

1992 Robert S. Miller resigns as Vice Chairman of the Chrysler Corporation

FEBRUARY 25

1837 Thomas Davenport of Brandon, VT is issued a United States patent for his electric motor first successfully demonstrated in 1834

1895 Lewis D. Crusoe of the Ford Motor Company is born in Mora, MN

1899 Harold Raymond Boyer of Maxwell, Oakland, and Cadillac is born in Springfield, OH

1899 The first motor vehicle accidental death in Great Britain occurs in London

1905 The first crossing of the Andes Mountains between Argentina and Chile is completed by Jose M. Piquero and Pedro Rusinol

1906 The first automobile show in Canada opens in Toronto, ON

1907 Ettore Bugatti marries Barbara Mascherpa in Milan, Italy

1919 Oregon imposes the first state gasoline tax (1%)

1920 Henry Russel of Oldsmobile dies at age 67

1920 Cie Financiere Belge des Pertoles Petrofina SA is incorporated in Brussels, Belgium - the firm would evolve into Petrofina SA in June 1957

1926 Frederick E. Muller, a French-born tool designer for Panhard et Levassor who later was a ball bearing designer with the Norma-Hoffmann Bearings Corporation, dies in Mount Vernon, NY at age 52

1932 Racer Tony Brooks is born in Dukinfield, Cheshire, England

1936 A. E. Barit is elected President of the Hudson Motor Car Company, succeeding the late Roy D. Chapin

1943 Racer Jurgen Lassig is born in Tuttlingen, Germany

1944 Racer Albert Francois Cevert is born in Paris, France

1945 The Scarab "Project Y" prototype is completed by designer William B. Stout and Owens-Corning Fiberglass officials R. Games Slayter and Walter F. Krause - the car is often cited as the world's firt fiberglass-bodied automobile

1948 Fabbrica Automobili Isotta-Fraschini is placed into receivership

1955 Robert B. Haynes, Vice President of the Dana Corporation and a former design engineer with Packard, Studebaker, and Cadillac, dies

1957 Sir William M. Letts, pioneer Britsh automobile designer and founder of the Automobile Association, dies in Llandudno, Wales one day short of his 84th birthday

1960 Robert W. Renwick of the Ford Motor Company dies at age 38

1961 Racer Davey Allison is born in Hollywood, FL, the son of racer Bobby Allison

1961 The Yanama Diesel Company of Japan acquires a license to build Wankel rotary engines to be used in stationary applications only

1962 Racer T. J. Clark is born

1864 Maurice Farman, pioneer racer, luxury automobile manufacturer, and airplane designer, dies in Paris France at age 86

1970 The 70,000,000th Chevrolet is produced

1979 Christie's, the London, England auction firm, stages its first collector car auction in Los Angeles, CA - a 1936 Mercedes-Benz 500K roadster from the collection of the late M. L. "Bud" Cohn sells for a record $400,000

1983 Thomas H. Keating, General Manager of Chevrolet 1949-1956, dies in Bal Harbour, FL at age 88

1997 Guiseppe "Nuccio" Bertone, Chairman of Carrozzeria Bertone, dies in Turin, Italy at age 82

FEBRUARY 26

1853 Charles Trepardoux, an early partner of de Dion et Bouton, is born in Paris, France

1873 Pioneer British automobilist Sir William Malesbury Letts is born

1873 Frederick Sayward Fales of the Standard Oil Company is born in Rockland, ME

1875 Lee Sherman Chadwick, designer of the 1904-1916 Chadwick, is born in East Braintree, VT

1885 Irving Jacob Reuter of General Motors is born in Indianapolis, IN

1886 Howard Earl Blood, a General Motors of Canada Ltd. executive who in 1927 founded the Norge Corporation, makers of household appliances, is born in Petoskey, MI

1888 Mario Castoldi of Fiat is born in Zibido San Giacomo, Milan, Lombardy, Italy

1888 Ernest Wooler of Royce, Rolls-Royce, Crossley, Chandler, Cleveland, and the Timken Roller Bearing Company is born in Farnsworth, Lancashire, England

1900 Joseph Athanasius Anderson of General Motors is born in Ishpeming, MI

1900 The National Cycle & Automobile Company, Ltd. opens a showroom in Toronto, ON, the first automobile dealership in Canada, to sell bicycles and Locomobile steamers

1903 Alexander Winton in his Winton "Bullet" sets a 1 kilometer speed record at Daytona Beach, FL, the first record to be set at this venue

1908 Racer Jean-Pierre Wimille is born in Paris, France

1912 Gordon Edward Grundy of the Studebaker Corporation of Canada Ltd. is born in Toronto, ON

1913 Joseph Elkan Adams of the White Motor Company is born in Cleveland, OH

1913 Harry Deets Weller Jr. of the Firestone Tire & Rubber Company, General Motors, and the White Motor Company is born in Lancaster, PA

1916 The Scripps-Booth Company files papers to dissolve the corporation

1917 Racer Robert la Caze is born in Paris, France

1922 Vincenzo Lancia and Felice Nazzaro are the guests of honor at groundbreaking ceremonies for the Monza track in Italy

1923 Forrest Kenneth Poling of the Ford Motor Company is born in Dixon, OH

1924 Kissel engineers Herman D. Palmer and Joseph A. Tarkington are issued a United States patent for their "Automatic Oil Control", a throttle-controlled device to regulate the amount of oil supplied to the engine

1935 The 1935 Pontiac "Indian Maiden" mascot is patented by designers Chris Klein and C. Karnstadt

1935 Howard C. Marmon and George H. Freers receive a United States patent for their "Motor Vehicle", a front-wheel-drive V-12 two-door sedan - a single prototype known officially as the HCM Special was built, but this car is usually considered to be the last Marmon automobile produced

1941 The post office at the Ford Motor Company Navy Service School opens in Dearborn, MI

1943 Racer Francois Mazet is born in Paris, France

1944 The Sports Car Club of America (SCCA) is formed in Boston, MA by seven vintage sports car enthusiasts initially with preservation, not racing, as their prime motivation

1952 The 1952 Henry J Corsair is introduced as a mid-year replacement for the Vagabond line

1954 Joseph W. Frazer resigns from the Willys Motors Inc.

1954 Edwin Fox of Vanden Plas, British coachbuilders, dies at age 69

1954 P. A. Watson, a production engineer with Packard, Rutenber, and Auburn, dies at age 73

1955 Racer Rupert Keegan is born in London, England

1965 Lee Roy Yarbrough sets a new world closed course speed record in his hemi-powered Dodge, reaching 181.818 mph at Daytona Beach, FL

1970 The second-generation 1970 1/2 Chevrolet Camaro is introduced

1970 The second-generation 1970 1/2 Pontiac Firebird is introduced

1973 The Ford International Finance Corporation is incorporated in Delaware as a subsidiary of the Ford Motor Company

1996 Nancy E. Polis is named Secretary of General Motors, succeeding Sharlene A. Vickery who is named General Director for Marketing, Sales, and Service for the corporation's Pontiac-GMC Division

FEBRUARY 27

1836 Russell Alexander Alger, a Packard official and United States Senator (R-MI 1902-1907), is born in LaFayette Township, Medina County, OH

1877 Walter Owen Briggs, a manufacturer of mass-produced automobile bodies, is born in Ypsilanti, MI

1878 Alvan Tufts Fuller, the Boston Packard dealer 1903-1947 and Governor of Massachusetts 1925-1929, is born in Malden, MA

1879 E. R. Thomas marries Flora Lozier, sister of Henry A. Lozier, a Toledo, OH bicycle manufacturer who would later produce the Lozier car

1905 Elmer Elijah Richards of Studebaker is born in Dallas, PA

1910 Racer Eylard Theodore von Horn "Ted Horn" is born in Cincinnati, OH

1914 Ralph DePalma edges Barney Oldfield in the ninth Vanderbilt Cup race in Santa Monica, CA in what DePalma always called his greatest race

1917 The Hanson Six debuts at the Southeastern Automobile Show in Atlanta, GA, albeit a prototype built at the Puritan Machine Company in Detroit, MI

1918 The Fruehauf Trailer Company is incorporated in Michigan

1919 S. L. Blackburn, Vice President and Director of Sales and Advertising for the Anderson Motor Company, dies in Rock Hill, SC at age 36

1920 E. S. Hare forms Hare's Motors, Inc., a holding company controlling the affairs of Locomobile, Mercer, and Crane-Simplex

1924 The Nash Motors Company purchases the plant of the bankrupt Mitchell Motor Company in Racine, WI

1925 Shoichiro Toyoda of Toyota is born in Nagoya, Japan

Championed by Toyota Vice President Shoichiro Toyoda, the Corolla, such as this 1974 S-5 coupe, played a major role in establishing the firm as the largest Japanese automobile manufacturer.

1933 Electric automobile advocate Joseph John DiCerto is born in New York City

1934 Ralph Nader, critic of the Chevrolet Corvair, is born Winsted, CT

1934 William Kirn Tell Jr. of Texaco, Inc. is born in Evanston, IL

1939 Racer Peter Jeffrey Revson is born in New York City

1939 The Bentley "Scalded Cat", with experimental straight-8 engine mounted in a standard Mark V chassis, is completed

1946 George W. Mason, President of the Nash-Kelvinator Corporation, is elected President of the Automobile Manufacturers Association to succeed Alvan Macauley, Chairman of the Packard Motor Car Company, who resigned after a 18-year tenure

1948 The Federal Trade Commission issues a restraining order prohibiting the Willys-Overland Company from representing that it had developed the Jeep

1950 The 500th Austin Princess is completed

1954 Racer Bobby Ball dies in Phoenix, AZ at age 28 from injuries suffered during a race April 1, 1953

1960 Racer Ettore Chimeri is killed at age 35 during a practice run for the Cuban Sports Car Grand Prix

1960 Racer Dennis Setzer is born in Newton, NC

1960 Robert J. Peters, Chief Metallurgist of the Warner Gear Division of the Borg-Warner Corporation, dies at age 63

1961 The Toyo Kogyo Company, Ltd. of Hiroshima, Japan acquires a license to manufacture Wankel rotary engines

1964 Racer Todd Bodine is born in Chemung, NY

1965 Racer Pedro Chaves is born in Oporto, Portugal

1965 Racer Dennis Wing is killed at age 25 during a practice run for the Australian Grand Prix in Hobart, Tasmania

1967 The United States Rubber Company changes its name to Uniroyal, Inc.

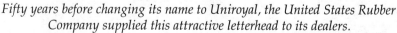

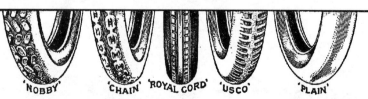

JOHN ZACHER
Ford Cars and Supplies, Auto and Team Livery
Heil, North Dakota

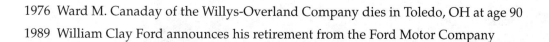

Fifty years before changing its name to Uniroyal, the United States Rubber Company supplied this attractive letterhead to its dealers.

1976 Ward M. Canaday of the Willys-Overland Company dies in Toledo, OH at age 90

1989 William Clay Ford announces his retirement from the Ford Motor Company

FEBRUARY 28

1835 Steam car pioneer Enos Merrill Clough is born in Springfield, NH

1875 Sir Goldsworthy Gurney, designer of pioneer steam-powered road vehicles, dies in Reeds, Cornwall, England at age 81

1880 Charles S. Howard, pioneer racer, traveler, racehorse owner, and Buick dealer, is born in Marietta, GA

1892 George H. Ellis, a 26-year-old employee of the Deering Harvester Company, successfully tests his automobile in Ravenswood, IL, how a part of Chicago - although additional production was ruled out, this vehicle is considered to be the ancestor of the International truck

1892 Rudolf Diesel is issued a German patent for his "rational heat engine"

1903 Henry Ford and Alexander Y. Malcomsom enter into an agreement with John F. and Horace E. Dodge to have the brothers supply chassis and running gear for 650 Ford automobiles

1905 Howard C. Marmon and Jesse Warrington are issued a United States patent for their "Running Gear for Motor Vehicles", the basis of all 1904-1908 Marmons

1906 Roy D. Chapin, Howard E. Coffin, James J. Brady, and Frederick O. Bezner sign a written agreement and contribute $1,500 each to establish a firm to produce their own automobile, realized in September as the Thomas-Detroit, produced in Detroit, MI as a companion car to the Thomas Flyers produced by the E. R. Thomas Motor Company in Buffalo, NY

1908 Racer Albert Scherrer is born in Switzerland

1911 The factory of the Haynes Automobile Company in Kokomo, IN is heavily damaged by fire

1914 Brothers Charles L., Frank L., and George Parker announce that the Parker Motor Company of Seattle, WA would soon begin production of the Ajax - the firm, soon renamed Ajax Motors Company, would fail in 1915

1914 Eddie Pullen, driving a Mercer Type 45, wins the Grand Prize Race in Santa Monica, CA - this is often cited as the first Grand Prix victory by a United States driver and car

1914 Racer Elie Bayol is born in Marseille, France

1920 The Beverly Hills (CA) Board Speedway stages its first event, a 250-mile race won by Jimmy Murphy in a Duesenberg

1921 The first United States-built Rolls-Royce is completed and delivered in chassis form to Wallace Potter of Pawtucket, RI

1925 The last Aston (England) Hill Climb is staged

1929 The American Austin Car Company is incorporated in Delaware

1932 The last Ford Model A is produced

An aging Ford Model A Tudor Sedan awaits its owner in Yankton, SD.

1933 Gordon M. Buehrig joins General Motors Styling

1933 James R. Hughes is issued a United States patent for the basic body shell of the Pierce Silver Arrow show car

1934 General Motors registers "GM" as a trademark

1936 Ford introduces its steel-spoked "banjo" steering wheel as an option

1940 Racers Aldo and Mario Gabriel Andretti are born in Montona, Italy (now Motovun, Croatia)

1940 DeWitt Page, a Vice President of General Motors and former President of the New Departure Manufacturing Company, dies in Hialeah Park, FL at age 70

1941 Alfonso XIII, the deposed King of Spain who was closely associated with the Hispano-Suiza, dies in Rome, Italy at age 54

1941 Edsel B. Ford drives the first Ford Model GP Command Reconnaissance Truck off the assembly line - this was Ford's version of what would evolve into the Jeep

1946 The Commission Sportive Internationale (CSI) holds its first post-World War II meeting and elects Augustin Perouse as President

1948 French automobile designer and racer Jean-Pierre Wimille signs a contract with Ford SA Francaise (FSAF) to develop a series of Ford-based prototypes

1951 William S. Ballenger, Treasurer of the Chevrolet Motor Company 1911-1925, dies in Flint, MI at age 84

1956 Howard A. Coffin, an official with Warren, Cadillac, the Firestone Tire & Rubber Company, and the Socony-Vacuum Oil Company who later served as a Congressman from Michigan, dies in Washington, DC at age 78

1960 John Grabner of the Continental Motors Corporation dies at age 60

1961 Modernistic Industries, Inc., a manufacturer of recreational vehicles, changes its name to Winnebago Industries, Inc.

1961 Racer Eric Bachelart is born in Brussels, Belgium

1965 Max M. Gilman, the disgraced General Manager and President of the Packard Motor Car Company who later was an official of the General Tire & Rubber Company, dies in South Laguna, CA at age 76

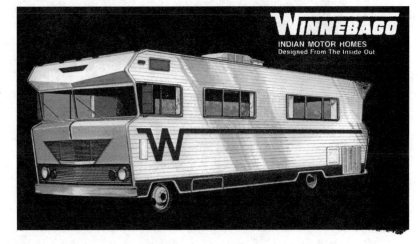

1969 Racer Butch Leitzinger is born in State College, PA

1969 Edward P. "Doc" White, the official chauffeur for United States Presidents Woodrow Wilson, Warren G. Harding, Calvin Coolidge, and Herbert Hoover, dies in Palm Beach, FL

1975 The AMC Pacer is introduced as a mid-year model

1977 Roy Abernethy, President of American Motors 1962-1976, dies in Tequesta, FL at age 70

1981 Clifford Sklarek, the inventor of the Lorraine spotlight and a longtime automotive historian, dies in California at age 92

1984 Ferrari's new GTO is introduced at the Salon de l'Auto Geneve

1986 Weldon C. Kocich, a test driver for the Goodyear Tire & Rubber Company, retires after having driven 3,141,946 miles over a 33-year career - he is often cited as the world's most durable driver

1987 Frederic G. Donner, Chairman and Chief Executive Officer of General Motors 1958-1967, dies in Greenwich, CT at age 84

FEBRUARY 29

1908   The Standardization Test of three random Cadillacs begins at the new Brooklands track in England under the supervision of the Royal Automobile Club

A Cadillac, Rambler, and Dolson lead a 1908 parade in Mandan, ND. The Cadillac, a one-cylinder 1905 Model M Touring Car, was essentially the same car as those in the RAC Standardization Test that would elevate the status of American motor cars in general and validate the concept of interchangeable parts.

1928   The first Dodge Standard Six is produced

1932   Racer Masten Gregory is born in Kansas City, MO

1940   Automotive parts manufacturer Gordon J. Monahan dies in Peterborough, Ontario, Canada at age 44

1944   William L. "Will" Kissel, the lone survivor of the four Kissel brothers, sells the remaining assets of the Kissel Motor Car Company to the West Bend Aluminum Company

1952   The Henry J Corsair is introduced as the first true 1952 model

1964   William S. James, a design engineer with Hupmobile, Studebaker, and Ford who served as Vice President for Research and Engineering with the Fram Corporation 1948-1955, dies at age 71

1964   Racer Tim Mayer is killed at age 26 when his Cooper-Climax crashes during a practice run at the Longford Course in Tasmania, Australia

1968   Jean-Pierre Beltoise takes the Matra MS11 race car for its first test run at the Aerodrome de Villacoublay-Velizy in Velizy-Villacoublay, France

1980   The White Motor Company closes its Exton, PA plant acquired in 1953 with the purchase of the Autocar Company

1980   The Craven Foundation automobile museum in Toronto, ON, Canada closes its doors

MARCH 1

1875 Edward A. Johnston, designer of the first International trucks, is born in Brockport, NY

1885 Thomas P. Archer of General Motors is born in Centerburg, OH

1897 The Winton Motor Carriage Company is organized in Cleveland, OH with Alexander Winton as President, Thomas W. Henderson as Vice President, George H. Brown as Secretary-Treasurer, and Leo Melanowski as Chief Engineer

1900 Monroe Jackson Rathbone of the Exxon Corporation is born in Parkersburg, WV

1902 The first Rambler is sold by the Thomas B. Jeffery Company during the Chicago (IL) Auto Show

1905 Katsui Kawamata of Nissan is born in Ibaraki Prefecture, Japan

1906 Roy D. Chapin resigns from the Olds Motor Works

1907 The Daihatsu Motor Company Ltd. is founded in Osaka, Japan

1907 Officials Nathan M. Kaufman, Daniel W. Kaufman, and C. H. Blomstrom of the DeLuxe Motor Car Company of Detroit, MI register its trademark for its marque, called The Car DeLuxe - the company legally dissolved in 1912, although production had ended in 1909 when its factory was taken over by Flanders

1909 George W. Dunham, Chief Engineer of the Olds Motor Works, resigns to accept a similar position with the Hudson Motor Car Company

1911 Joseph I. Andreini of Mack and White is born in New York City

1911 A Saurer 4 1/2-ton truck, built by Adolphe Saurer in Arbon, Switzerland, arrives in San Francisco, CA, completing a demonstration drive from Denver, CO - this truck was later shipped to Pueblo, CO and driven to New York City in what the company claimed to be the first trans-United States trip by a motor truck

1920 Kanichiro Ishibashi, Chairman of the Bridgestone Tire Company Ltd. 1973-1985, is born in Kurume, Fukuoka, Japan

1923 Hudson discontinues its 4-passenger Coupe

1923 The Kenworth Motor Truck Corporation moves into its new Seattle, WA plant

1924 William A. Simonds is appointed Advertising Manager of the Seattle, WA branch of the Ford Motor Company

1928 The Packard Standard Model 443 is introduced

1932 BMW cancels its licensing agreement with Austin, opening the way for Max Friz to develop the first BMW of in-house design

1932 The Dodge 1932-1934 "Ram" mascot is patented by designer Herbert V. Henderson

1932 The 1932 Nash Series 1000 is introduced, the first time that the marque had introduced two different series in one model year

1934 Earl H. Smith, formerly Assistant Chief Engineer of Pontiac, joins the Packard Motor Car Company to oversee the implementation of mass production techniques required for the upcoming Packard One Twenty

1936 Harry J. Carmichael succeeds H. A. Brown as Vice President and General Manager of General Motors of Canada Ltd.

1937 Claude S. Briggs, founder of the Briggs-Detroiter Company, dies in Detroit, MI at age 64

1937 Connecticut issues the first "permanent" automobile license plates updated annually with colored inserts

1941 Racer Dave Marcis is born in Wausau, WI

1949 Automotive engineer Mihai P. Ciobanu is born in Romania

1951 The Kaiser-Frazer Corporation purchases the Detroit Engine Division of Continental Motors Corporation, having leased the facilities since 1947

1955 Donald R. Stuart is named National Sales Manager, Packard Division of the Studebaker-Packard Corporation

1955 Napco Industries, Inc. is formed through the merger of the Berghoff Brewing Corporation of Fort Wayne, IN, Northwestern Auto Parts Company of Minneapolis, MN, the Federal Motor Truck Company of Detroit, MI, Napco Detroit, Inc. and the R. W. M. Investment Company - the primary business of the new firm is the manufacture of heavy duty equipment for commercial vehicles

1957 Kenneth W. Hildenbrand, Chief Inspector of the Monroe Auto Equipment Company, dies at age 58

1965 Carl A. Rasmussen is named Chief Engineer of Cadillac

1965 Ferrari contracts with Fiat to produce its V-6 Dino engine

1965 Racer Rocky Trosize is killed at age 25 when he crashes during the Australian Grand Prix in Hobart, Tasmania - photographer Robin Dabrera is also killed in the accident

1965 Racer Giuseppe Bugatti is born in Brescia, Italy

1969 Pontiac General Manager John Z. DeLorean transfers to the same position at Chevrolet, with F. James McDonald becoming the new General Manager of Pontiac

1971 Automatic transmission is standardized for all full-sized Pontiacs

1975 The Honda Civic is introduced to the United States market

1977 George Walter Risley retires as Assistant Curator of the National Automotive History Collection at the Detroit Public Library

1978 The Boston, MA Cadillac dealership, the marque's first, is closed by owner Peter Fuller, son of founder Alvan T. Fuller

1979 Eugene A. Cafiero resigns as Vice President of the Chrysler Corporation

The Honda Civic. More miles per gallon than anybody.

1980 The Osella makes its Formula 1 debut in the South African Grand Prix in Kyalami, but the designed by Enzo Osella and Giorgio Stirano and driven by Eddie Cheever is involved in an accident and is forced to retire

1984 British racer Peter Walker dies in Worcester, Worcestershire, England at age 70

1985 Richard A. Teague retires as Vice President-Styling of American Motors

1985 The 40,000,000th Toyota vehicle, a Tercel, is produced on the same day that the 10,000,000th Toyota Corolla is produced

1986 The first Shelby GLH-S, a Dodge-based performance car designed by Carroll Shelby, is produced at the Shelby Automobiles, Inc. plant in Whittier, CA

1987 Wolfgang Seidel, winner of the 1959 Targa Florio, dies at age 60

1990 Harold A. Poling succeeds Donald E. Petersen as Chairman of the Board and Chief Executive Officer for the Ford Motor Company - Philip E. Benton Jr. is named President and Chief Operating Officer, and Allan D. Gilmour is named President of the Ford Automotive Group

1992 The Larrousse makes its Formula 1 debut at the South African Grand Prix at Kyalami, with the Type LC92 driven by Ukyo Katayama taking 12th place

MARCH 2

1863 Custom coachbuilder Justus Vinton Locke is born in Watertown, MA

1866 Firetruck manufacturer Peter Pirsch is born in Kenosha, WI

1868 Theodore Douglas, the inventor of the duplex engine governor, is born in Washington, DC

1897 Renowned sculptor Avard Tennyson Fairbanks, a favorite of Chrysler Corporation engineer Fred M. Zeder and the creator of the Clifton Award given at the 1946 Automotive Golden Jubilee banquet, is born in Provo, UT

1904 Thornton Edward Waterfall of the Chrysler Corporation is born in Detroit, MI

1919 The first regular production ReVere is completed

1925 Benjamin Anibal joins the Oakland Division of General Motors as Chief Engineer

1926 Bentley Motors, Ltd. is reorganized with Woolf Barnato as Chairman, W. O. Bentley as Managing Director, and Hubert Pike, Ramsey Manners, and John Kennedy Carruth as Directors

1927 Col. Charles Clifton of Pierce-Arrow retires as President of the National Automobile Chamber of Commerce

1935 Bill Cummings, driving the Cummins Diesel Special that had finished 12th in the 1934 Indianapolis 500, raises the land speed record for diesel powered cars to 137.195 mph in Daytona Beach, FL

1939 John Phillip Frazier of the Cummins Engine Company is born in Indianapolis, IN

1942 The United States government implements automobile rationing due to World War II

1943 Frank C. Campsall fires Charles E. Sorensen from the Ford Motor Company

1945 Racer Raymond Mays contacts key British motor industry figures with plans that would lead to the 1947 formation of British Racing Motors, Ltd., builders of BRM racing cars

1958 John Held Jr., an artist who worked for Packard 1925-1931, dies at age 69

1962 The Ford Motor Company announces that the Cardinal, a sub-compact with front wheel drive and a German-built V-4 engine, would go into production at its Louisville, KY plant in July

1962 Racer Gabriele Tarquini is born in Guilianova Lido, Italy

1966 At a ceremony in Dearborn, MI the 1,000,000th Ford Mustang, a white convertible, is traded to Captain Stanley Tucker of Saint John's, Newfoundland, Canada who had purchased the first Mustang three days before the car was officially introduced in 1964

1967 Hans Ledwinka of Tatra dies in Munich, Germany at age 89

1970 Sir Reay Geddes, Chairman of the Dunlop Rubber Company Ltd., and Leopoldo Pirelli, Chairman of Pirelli SpA, announce a merger of their firms

1972 John Dykstra of the Ford Motor Company dies in Southfield, MI at age 73

1980 Bruce K. Brown of the Standard Oil Company of Indiana dies at age 80

1985 Jack N. Humbert, a General Motors stylist 1948-1984 who designed the Pontiac GTO, Firebird, and Grand Prix, dies

1988 J. Michael Losh, General Manager of Pontiac, announces that the Fiero will be discontinued at the end of the current model year

1990 A Chevrolet Corvette ZR-1 driven at Fort Stockton, TX by the team of Tommy Morrison, John Henricy, Scott Lagasse, Stuart Hayner, Jim Minneker, Scott Allman, Don Knowles, and Kim Baker sets numerous speed records, including the 24-hour record average of 175.885 mph, breaking the 50-year-old record established by Ab Jenkins in the Mormon Meteor III at the Bonneville Salt Flats, UT

MARCH 3

1908 Sir George William Harriman of the Austin Motor Company Ltd. is born

1909 The Manufacturers Contest Association (MCA) and the American Automobile Association (AAA) agree to form the AAA Contest Board, whereby the latter group would sanction and manage various car racing events

1912 Takashi Ishihara of Nissan is born in Tokyo, Japan

1914 Automobile parts manufacturer Willard Frederick Rockwell Jr. is born in Boston, MA

1915 Automobile parts manufacturer Frank Joseph Ehringer is born in Newark, NJ

1917 George Marion Lhamon of Paccar, Inc. is born in Los Angeles, CA

1919 Automobile parts manufacturer Chester Devenow is born in Detroit, MI

1924 Henry R. Nolte Jr. of the Ford Motor Company is born in New York City

1927 J. G. Parry Thomas is killed at the Pendine Sands, Wales during an attempt to raise the land speed record - his car, nicknamed "Babs" was buried at the site but exhumed in April 1969, restored and put into a museum

1932 Alfieri Maserati dies at age 44 from complications resulting from a 1927 racing accident

1936 D. J. Wilber of the Scintilla Magneto Company dies at age 39

1939 The Bugatti Royale Binder Coupe de Ville is completed

1940 Paul C. Sauerbrey, Vice President and General Manager of the Plymouth Division of Chrysler Corporation, dies in Fort Lauderdale, FL at age 53

1942 The Auburn Central Manufacturing Company, formerly the Auburn Automobile Company, changes its name to the American Central Manufacturing Company

1942 Production of civilian trucks is halted by the United States government for the duration of World War II

1947 The Kaiser-Frazer Corporation begins production of its own engines in the leased Continental Motors, Inc. plant in Detroit, MI

1949 The Tucker Corporation is forced into receivership

1956 Ernst Loof of Veritas dies of cancer at age 48 in Bonn, West Germany

1962 Racer Perry McCarthy is born in London, England

1963 Henry R. Bodman, longtime General Counsel of the Packard Motor Car Company, dies at age 88

1964 Carrozzeria Touring of Milan, Italy enters voluntary receivership

1972 Sir William Lyons retires as Chairman of Jaguar Cars Ltd.

1973 The Shadow makes its Formula 1 debut in the South African Grand Prix at Kyalami, with the Type DN1A driven by George Follmer finishing sixth

1976 Walter Hubert Beal, President of the Auburn Automobile Company 1932-1934, dies

Fiat 124 Cabriolet with custom coachwork by Carrozzeria Touring.

1977 The former factory of the Chandler Motor Car Company in Cleveland, OH is destroyed by fire

1984 Racer Mike Mosley dies at age 39

1992 Racer Lella Lombardi dies in Milan, Italy from cancer at age 48

MARCH 4

1880 J. G. Utz, Chief Engineer of the Chalmers-Detroit Motor Company 1907-1912 and later a manufacturer of automotive parts, is born in Marshalltown, IA

1887 The Daimler "benzin motor carriage" makes its first test run in Esslingen and Cannstatt, Germany - this was Gottlieb Daimler's first four-wheeled motor vehicle, and the event was celebrated by the Daimler Motoren- Gesellschaft for many years as the birth of the gasoline automobile

1888 Knute Kenneth Rockne, Notre Dame University football coach and namesake of the Rockne, a 1932-1933 low-priced companion marque of the Studebaker, is born in Voss, Norway

THE ROCKNE "75" CONVERTIBLE ROADSTER

South Bend, IN was the home of Studebaker and Notre Dame, so naming the new marque for the late coach was an easy decision. Unfortunately the grips of the great depression were too strong and Rockne production ended after just fourteen months.

1889 Luis de Florez, a mechanical and chemical engineer who is credited with many inventions in the oil refining industry, is born in New York City

1891 Joseph Washington Frazer is born in Nashville, TN

1894 Ray R. Rausch of the Ford Motor Company is born in Cleveland, OH

1896 Graeme Keith Howard of General Motors is born in Los Angeles, CA

1899 Count Gaston de Chasseloup-Laubat, driving his streamlined Jeantaud electric car at Acheres Park, France, raises the land speed record to 57.60 mph

1900 The Automobile Club of America (ACA) stages its first race, a round trip between Springfield, Long Island, NY and Babylon, NY - the winner is Andrew L. Riker driving a Riker of his own design, the only electric car in the field

1902 The American Automobile Association is organized

1910 The Firestone Tire & Rubber Company, originally incorporated in West Virginia in 1900, is reorganized as an Ohio corporation

1916 Arjay Ray Miller of the Ford Motor Company is born in Shelby, NE

1919 Racer Elzie Wylie "Buck" Baker Sr. is born in Hartville, SC

1921 Warren Gamaliel Harding becomes the first President of the United States to ride to his inauguration in an automobile (a Packard Twin Six)

1927 Col. James W. Furlow, Deputy Chief of the U. S. Army Motor Transport Corps during World War I, dies in Pittsburgh, PA at age 54

1932 Sir Henry Birkin, driving a 4 1/2 litre "Blower" Bentley, sets the alltime Brooklands record for Class C (under 5000 cc) of 137.96 mph

1933 Racer Nino Vaccarella is born in Palermo, Sicily, Italy

1933 Roy D. Chapin returns to his position as Chairman of the Board of the Hudson Motor Car Company after serving for seven months as Secretary of Commerce in the administration of United States President Herbert Hoover

1936 Racer James "Jim" Clark Jr. is born in Kilmany, Fifeshire, Scotland

1941 The Packard Clipper is introduced

1950 The 100,000th Volkswagen is produced

1956 Ernest G. Liebold of the Ford Motor Company dies in Grosse Pointe Woods, MI at age 71

1957 Racer Rick Mast is born in Lexington, VA

1966 L. Irving Woolson of DeSoto dies at age 61

1966 The Studebaker Corporation announces that it is abandoning automobile production as the last Canadian-built car is completed

1972 Racer Jos Verstappen is born in Montfort, Ille-et-Vilaine, France of Dutch ancestry

1972 The Eifelland makes its Formula 1 debut in the South African Grand Prix at Kyalami, with the Type 21 driven by Rolf Stommelen finishing 13th

1974 Racer Bill Aston dies in Lingfield, Great Britain at age 73

1978 The Theodore makes its Formula 1 debut in the South African Grand Prix, but the Type TR1 driven by Keke Rosberg retires with clutch problems

1985 Automobile safety advocate Dr. J. William Haddon dies in Washington, DC at age 58

1986 The Chrysler Corporation is reorganized in Delaware

1992 Paul Schweizer, driving a Horlacher Na-S Sport battery-powered car designed and built by Horlacher AG of Mohlin, Switzerland, sets a world's record by driving 339.898 miles on a single charge - the run was done on public roadways between Zurich, Berne, Lausanne, and Geneva, Switzerland

1994 Mercedes-Benz introduces its subcompact prototypes, Eco-Sprinter and Eco-Speedster in Stuttgart, Germany prior to the Geneva Motor Show - the two cars were developed in cooperation with Nicolas Hayek, President of the Swiss watch conglomerate SMH

MARCH 5

1658 Antoine de la Mothe, Le Sieur de Cadillac, namesake of the United States luxury marque, is born in the province of Gascony, France

1875 The Wisconsin state legislature offers a bounty of $10,000 to any state resident who could produce "a cheap and practical substitute for use of horses and other animals on the highway and farm"

1897 Rhys Manley Sale, President of the Ford Motor Company of Canada, Ltd. 1950-1961, is born in Windsor, ON

1903 The Association of Licensed Automobile Manufacturers (ALAM) is organized with 18 manufacturers as charter members following a successful patent infringement lawsuit against the Winton Motor Carriage Company on behalf of George B. Selden

1907 The North Carolina General Assembly requires automobile owners in Guilford, Wake and Wayne Counties to register their vehicles - this bizarre situation lasted until 1909 when registration was required in all counties

1911 Automobile designer Edward Joel Pennington dies in Springfield, MA at age 52

1924 Race sponsor R. Kenneth "Ken" Tyrrell is born

1925 William Merrill Chester Jr. of the Heil Company is born in Milwaukee, WI

1926 John David Caplan of General Motors is born in Weiser, ID

1926 Quentin Eugene Wood of the Quaker State Corporation is born in Mechanicsburg, PA

1927 The LaSalle is formally introduced as a companion marque to Cadillac

1929 The Los Angeles (CA) Automobile Show is destroyed by fire with over 320 new cars, including the one-off Auburn Cabin Speedster, lost

1929 Rally driver Erik Carlsson is born in Trollhattan, Sweden

1929 Allen Edward Murray of the Mobil Corporation is born in New York City

1932 William Robert Wilson resigns as General Manager of the Reo Motor Car Company

A 1931 Reo Flying Cloud at the Doust Tree near Garberville, CA.

1934 Woolf Barnato becomes a Director of Bentley Motors (1931) Ltd.

1934 The Tatra 77 is introduced in Prague, Czechoslovakia

1934 Racer Ernie Triplett dies at age 27 from injuries suffered the previous day during a race at the Imperial Valley Fair in El Centro, CA

1936 A. O. Dunk, prolific buyer of defunct automobile manufacturer inventories, dies in Los Angeles, CA at age 62

1940 Racer Graham Peter McRae is born in Wellington, New Zealand

1942 Automotive parts manufacturer Robert Gregory Paul is born in Rockford, IL

1948 Kenneth N. Cook, Assistant Sales Manager of the Rollway Bearing Company, dies

1952 The Willys Aero Ace is introduced as a mid-year model

1952 Robert H. Duff, a Scottish-born truck engineer with the Chrysler Corporation since 1926, dies in Detroit, MI at age 54

1956 The Hudson Hornet Special V-8, a cheaper version of the Hornet Custom, is introduced as a mid-year model

THE BIG CAR WITH BIG CHANGES IS THE STYLE SENSATION OF '56

**Hudson Hornet V-8
Hollywood Hardtop**

1956 The Packard Executive is announced as a replacement for the Clipper Custom

1959 Charles Henry Lewis of the Standard Oil Company of California dies at age 52

1961 Sennet W. Gilfillan, credited with many improvements in automobile ignition systems, dies in Los Angeles, CA at age 71

1962 The Studebaker-Packard Corporation acquires Schaefer, Inc.

1971 Automobile historian Allan Nevins dies in Menlo Park, CA at age 80

1977 Racer Tom Pryce is killed at age 27 when his Shadow-Cosworth DN8 crashes during the South African Grand Prix at Kyalami

1986 Sir Austin Bide retires as Chairman of Rover Group PLC (formerly the British Leyland Motor Corporation Ltd.), with Canadian-born Graham Day named as his successor

1991 The Bentley Continental R is introduced

1995 Racer Gregg Hansford dies in Phillip Island, Australia

MARCH 6

1856 Elihu Herbert Cutler, a cofounder of the Knox Automobile Company, is born in Ashland, MA

1896 Charles B. King tests his car in Detroit, MI, the first time that a motor car had been driven on the streets of that city

1896 John Brown of Longhurst, Ireland accepts delivery of a Serpollet steamer, the first automobile to be imported into Ireland

1900 Gottlieb Daimler dies in Canstatt, Germany at age 65

1906 Roger M. Kyes of General Motors is born in East Palestine, OH

1909 The Hudson Motor Car Company holds its first Board of Directors meeting

1909 Racer William Lawrence "Bill" Schindler is born in Summitville, NY

1909 North Carolina requires all automobiles to registered with the Secretary of State, except New Hanover County where motorists are required to register with the Superior Court

1915 The tenth Vanderbilt Cup is held at the Pan-Pacific International Exposition in San Francisco, CA and won by Dario Resta in a Peugeot

1917 Racer Oswald Karch is born in Ludwigshafen, Germany

1921 Racer Piero Carini is born in Sondrio, Italy

1923 Theodore Hart Mecke Jr. of the Ford Motor Company is born in Philadelphia, PA

1927 Herbert C. Harrison, founder of the Harrison Radiator Company which in 1918 became part of General Motors, dies in London, England at age 50

1928 William Francis Nolan, biographer of Barney Oldfield, is born in Kansas City, MO

1929 David D. Buick dies in Detroit, MI at age 74

*This Buick 5-passenger coupe photographed in Black River Falls, WI
dates from 1929, the year of David D. Buick's death. Mr. Buick had left his
namesake company 25 years earlier and died in relative poverty.*

1930 The Italian government extends the 25-year charter given to Fiat in 1906 until 1980

1931 Racer James "Jimmy" Stewart is born in Bowling, Dunbartonshire, Scotland, the elder brother of racer Jackie Stewart

1932 William H. Mullins, credited with manufacturing the first one-piece stamped automobile fenders, dies in Salem, OH at age 76

1934 The Auto Union Type C Grand Prix car makes its public debut at the Avus track in Berlin, Germany with Hans Stuck setting a world record by covering 134.90 miles in one hour

1934 Basil H. Joy, Secretary of the Institution of Automobile Engineers (London) since 1910, retires and is succeeded by Brian G. Robbins

1935 Fred Crawford Thompson of the Borg-Warner Corporation dies at age 51

1936 Racer Bob Akin is born

1940 Edwin W. M. Bailey, the builder of the Bailey Electric 1908-1916 and Superintendent of the coachbuilding firm Biddle & Smart Company 1915-1920 (both firms were located in Amesbury, MA), dies in Barbados, West Indies at age 76

1941 Pontiac's World War II effort begins with a government order for Oerlikon anti-aircraft cannons

1942 John M. O'Malley, an employee of the Pope Manufacturing Company who drove the company's Portola race cars in the first Vanderbilt Cup Races and later was an official of the California Department of Public Works, Division of Highways, dies at age 67

1950 R. S. Burgin, a design engineer and member of the first motorized unit to survey the original Lincoln Highway, dies in Wichita, KS at age 55

1952 Alanson P. Brush, designer of the first 4-cylinder Cadillac, namesake of the Brush, and a longtime designer for Oakland and Buick, dies in Detroit, MI at age 74

1954 The 10,000th Saab is produced

1955 Racer Jesus Pareja is born in Madrid, Spain

1956 Buick President Ivan L. Wiles is elected to the new position of Executive Vice President of General Motors in charge of dealer relations

A longtime leader in straight-8 engines, Buick switched to a V-8 in 1953 with great success. Well over 1,000,000 Buick V-8's were on the road when this 1956 Super 4-door sedan, photographed in Canby, MN, was manufactured.

1956 The Hudson Hornet Special V-8 is introduced to fill the price bracket between the Hornet and Wasp

1956 The Renault Dauphine, designed mostly by Fernand Picard, is introduced at Le Palais de Chaillot in Paris, France

1956 William G. Sternberg Jr., President of the Sterling Motor Truck Company 1924-1955, dies at age 70

1967 Glenn Pray sells the Cord Automobile Company to a group of Tulsa, OK businessmen who announce plans to continue manufacturing the Cord 8/10 replicar

1995 The Ferrari F50 is introduced at the Geneva Motor Show

1996 Huschke von Hansten, winner of the 1940 Mille Miglia and 1956 Targa Florio and Porsche racing director 1952-1968, dies in Stuttgart, Germany at age 85

MARCH 7

1818 Pioneer British motoring patron Sir Frederick Joseph Bramwell is born

1886 Racer Rene Thomas is born in Perigueux, France

1903 Hon. C. S. Rolls, driving a Mors on a private estate in Clipston, Nottinghamshire, England, records a flying kilometer at 82.84 mph, but Rolls himself disallows the record because of favorable wind and slope

1907 The Chadwick Engineering Works is incorporated in Pottstown, PA

1908 Hugo Pfau, a coachbuilder with LeBaron Inc. and later an automotive historian, is born in Kreutzlingen, Switzerland

1916 The Bayerische Flugzeugwerke AG (Bavarian Aircraft Works) is founded by Gustav Otto and Karl Rapp by a merger of their firms - this company would evolve into the Bayerische Motoren-Werke GmbH (BMW)

1934 Herman J. Jaeger, an inventor and manufacturer of automobile lights, dies in Weehawken, NJ at age 68

1935 Sir Malcolm Campbell, driving the Campbell Special "Blue Bird V" at Daytona Beach, FL, raises the land speed record to 276.82 mph

1938 Racer Janet Guthrie is born in Iowa City, IA

1939 Consulting lubrication engineer William Francis Parish dies at age 65

1947 Walter Rohrl, a four-time winner of the Monte Carlo Rally, is born in Regensburg, Germany

1963 Willys Motors Inc. and the Kaiser-Jeep Corporation are reorganized as the Kaiser Industries Corporation

1968 The Ford International Capital Corporation is incorporated in Delaware as a subsidiary of the Ford Motor Company

1969 Racer Hideki Noda is born in Osaka, Japan

1970 The March makes its Formula 1 debut with four cars entered in the South African Grand Prix at Kyalami - Jackie Stewart finished third and Jo Siffert tenth in the Robin Herd-designed cars

1970 The Corvair Society (CORSA) holds its organizational meeting

1978 Racer Rudolf Schoeller dies at age 75

1985 Robert W. Woodruff, Chairman of the Board of the Coca-Cola Company and a director of the White Motor Company, dies at age 95

1990 William Clay Ford Jr., a great grandson of Henry Ford, is promoted by the Ford Motor Company to oversee strategic planning for worldwide operations

1995 The Bentley Azure convertible is introduced at the Geneva (Switzerland) Auto Show

MARCH 8

1876 Automotive journalist William Fletcher Bradley is born in Scarborough, Yorkshire, England

1878 Marc Birkigt of Hispano-Suiza is born in Geneva, Switzerland

1881 Hiram James Leonard of Stearns-Knight and Willys is born in Rock Island, IL

1889 Automotive battery manufacturer Samuel Wyman Rolph is born in Ottawa, ON, Canada

1903 C. J. Moore of Westfield, MA is hired as factory manager of the Ohio Automobile Company, manufacturers of the Packard

1906 Fiat SpA is incorporated to succeed the Fabbrica Italiana Automobili Torino, at which time its cars change from F.I.A.T. to simply Fiat

1907 Peugeot records its first official racing victory, with Giosue Guippone winning the Corsa Vetturette at Turin, Italy

1911 The Ford Motor Company Ltd. is established in Manchester, England

1917 Paul Henry Wendler of General Motors is born in Grand Rapids, MI

1920 The Duesenberg Automobile & Motors Company is organized as a Delaware corporation with Newton E. van Zandt as President, Luther M. Rankin as Vice President, Frederick S. Duesenberg as Chief Engineer, and August S. Duesenberg as Assistant Chief Engineer

1920 Reggio Zunino of Chevron Oil Italiana SpA is born in Venice, Italy

1927 The Studebaker 1927-1929 "Atalanta" mascot is patented by designer Carl C. Mose

1928 Jonathan D. Maxwell dies in Worton, MD at age 64

1928 The Pontiac 5-passenger Sport Phaeton is introduced

1929 The 1,000,000th Oakland is produced

1931 Journalist and engineer Charles R. Thomas Jr., an advocate of better roads, dies at age 42

1933 The Studebaker Corporation is placed into receivership

1936 Daytona Beach, FL, on a beach/public roadway course measured off by Sig Haugdahl, stages its first road race for stock cars - this race is cited as the impetus that led to the creation of NASCAR

1937 Thomas M. Bradley is named President of the Hupp Motor Car Corporation

1941 John M. Schaefer, a pioneer employee with Pope-Hartford, Corbin, and Knox who later was affiliated with the Cities Service Oil Company, dies at age 52

1946 Frederick W. Lanchester dies at age 77

1949 The first short wheelbase 1949 Plymouth Deluxe is produced

1954 Racer James Lewis Brundage is killed

1957 The Renault Dauphine is introduced at the Geneva Auto Show

1961 Edward J. Cutler of the Ford Motor Company dies in Plymouth, MI at age 78

1967 The Ford Motor Company dedicates its Automotive Safety Research Center and its Service Research Center

1968 Racer Michael Bartels is born in Plettenberg, Germany

1969 The high-performance Pontiac Firebird Trans Am is introduced

1980 Congressman J. Irving Whalley (R-PA 1960-1973), a strong supporter of automobile industry issues, dies in Pompano Beach, FL at age 77

MARCH 9

1856 Count Jules-Felix-Philippe-Albert de Dion de Malfiance is born in Carquefou, France

1887 Joseph Newton Smith of the Boston Woven Hose & Rubber Company is born in born in Lynn, MA

1899 Arthur W. Soutter of Rolls-Royce of America, Inc. is born

1901 Fire destroys the Olds Motor Works factory in Detroit, MI, an event that led to Oldsmobile's return to Lansing - an enduring legend states that employee James J. Brady pushed a Regular Runabout, unofficially called the "Curved Dash", out of the building, and with the car's drawings protected in the office safe the company had no choice but to pursue a one-model policy

1902 Coachbuilder James B. Brewster dies in New York City at age 84

1903 The Eckhardt & Souter 25-hp touring car designed by John Eckhardt is introduced at the Buffalo (NY) Automobile Show

1910 The Studebaker Corporation acquires 100% ownership of the Everitt-Metzger-Flanders Company

1911 The Ford Motor Company opens its first overseas factory at Trafford Park, Manchester, England

1918 Earl A. Thompson applies for a United States patent on his synchro-mesh transmission

1921 John Sagan of the Ford Motor Company is born in Youngstown, OH

1932 The first Ford V-8 is produced

1935 A reorganized Studebaker Corporation is formed two years and a day after going into receivership with Harold S. Vance as Chairman and Paul G. Hoffman as President

1937 Racer Brian Herman Thomas Redman is born in Burnley, Lancashire, England

1939 Robert Schwartz, President of Rolls-Royce Motors, Inc. (USA) 1986-1989 and a former American Motors Corporation executive, is born in Atlantic City, NJ

1942 Robert Bosch dies in Stuttgart, Germany at age 80

1942 The United States government authorizes the production of a limited number of light trucks and buses to be released to users on a priority basis

1942 Ray C. Sackett, an advertising executive and former official of the Studebaker Corporation and Chrysler Corporation, joins the Society of Automotive Engineers to assist in their World War II programs

1947 Joseph A. Donnelly of Mack and Autocar dies in Chicago, IL

1947 Franco Cortese wins the first and only "world tour" all-Cisitalia race at Gezira Island in Cairo, Egypt

1950 Racer Danny Sullivan is born in Louisville, KY

1952 The last DeSoto Suburban 9-passenger sedan is produced

1952 The El Autodrom 17 de Octobre racetrack in Buenos Aires, Argentina opens

1955 Racer Teo Fabi is born in Milan, Italy

1958 Eugen Benz, elder son of Carl Benz and a partner in C. Benz Sohne, makers of the Benz Sohne 1906-1926, dies at age 84

1964 The first Ford Mustang is produced, a white convertible with a 260-cid V-8

1966 Racer Pablo Birger dies in Buenos Aires, Argentina at age 42

1987 Lee Iacocca announces that the Chrysler Corporation and Renault have signed an agreement whereby Chrysler will purchase and absorb American Motors

1996 Rally driver Adolphe Conrath dies at age 68

MARCH 10

1884 Wallace Trevor Holliday of the Standard Oil Company is born in Cleveland, OH

1895 Russell A. Crist of GMC is born in Wells County, IN

1902 Edward Randolph Dye, the inventor of the "cloverleaf" highway interchange and an advocate of automobile seat belts, is born in Linton, IN

1903 Byron J. Carter is issued a United States patent for his three-cylinder steam engine

1903 Racer Joe Tracy is issued a United States patent for his combined exhaust valve and igniter

1904 Frederic Andrew Bush of the Sinclair Petroleum Company is born in Silver City, NM

1905 John Lothrop Brown Jr. of American Motors is born in Winchester, MA

1909 Karl H. Effmann of the Perfect Circle Company is born in Akron, OH

1909 Andrew L. Freeman, the inventor of the headbolt heater, is born in Upham, ND

1910 The American LaFrance Fire Engine Company of Elmira, NY announces their first motorized truck

1913 The North Carolina General Assembly passes legislation requiring the Secretary of State to register all automobile and issues license plates to their owners

1922 The Star marque is introduced in Washington, DC by Durant Motors, Inc.

1934 Benjamin F. Wright, Assistant Chief Engineer of the Dodge Brothers Corporation, dies following a brief illness

1939 Racer Charles Crichton-Stuart is born in London, England

1939 James H. Walker, founder and President of the Walker Body Company in Merrimac, MA, dies in Pinehurst, NC at age 66

1939 Tranquillo Zerbi of Fiat dies in Turin, Italy at age 48

1940 Lee Hammond Runk of the Chrysler Corporation is born in Buffalo, NY

1941 The Auburn Central Manufacturing Company, formerly the Auburn Automobile Company, receives a contract to produce Jeep bodies for the Willys-Overland Company

1942 Walter M. Nones, founder in 1914 of the Norma-Hoffmann Bearings Corporation and its Chairman until 1941, dies in New York City at age 67

1947 Detroit department store official W. Tom ZurSchmiede, Henry C. Bogle, a law partner of former Packard General Counsel Henry E. Bodman, and longtime dealer Earle C. Anthony are elected to the Board of Directors of the Packard Motor Car Company

1953 Volkswagen adopts an oval rear window for its standard sedan, replacing the original split rear window - The Volkswagen Transporter adds a rear bumper as standard equipment

1955 Racer Toshio Suzuki is born in Saitama Prefecture, Japan

1959 Racer Mike Wallace is born in Saint Louis, MO

1960 The Gordon (later Gordon-Keeble) GT is introduced as a new marque at the Geneva (Switzerland) Autoshow

1962 E. S. Hare, a Packard executive who formed Hare's Motors, Inc. in 1920 as a corporate umbrella for Mercer, Locomobile, and Simplex, dies in New York City at age 79

1964 The first Ford Mustang is produced

1965 Archibald Goodman Frazer-Nash dies in Kingston-upon-Thames, England

1966 The Alfa Romeo Spider, the last car designed by Battista "Pinin" Farina, is introduced at the Geneva (Switzerland) Motor Show

1969 Stylist Harley J. Earl of General Motors dies at age 75

1983 The Ford Bronco II utility vehicle is introduced

1991 The Jordan makes its Formula 1 debut in the United States Grand Prix in Phoenix, AZ, with the Type 191 financed by Eddie Jordan, designed by Gary Anderson, and driven by Bertand Gachot finishing in 10th place - Lamborghini makes its Formula 1 debut, with the Type 291 driven by Nicola Larini finishing in 7th place

MARCH 11

1866 Robert Wright Stewart, Chairman of the Standard Oil Company of Indiana 1918-1929, is born in Cedar Rapids, IA

1885 Land speed record holder Sir Malcolm Campbell is born in Chislehurst, Kent, England

1889 Automotive streamling pioneer Paul Jaray is born in Vienna, Austria of Hungarian parents

1890 Eugene F. McDonald Jr., a onetime Franklin official who later became President of the Zenith Radio Corporation, is born in Syracuse, NY

1895 Pneumatic tires are installed on a Duryea, often cited as the first such application in the industry

1899 John Nevin Bauman of the White Motor Company is born in Jeanette, PA

1908 The Standardization Test is completed on three Cadillacs as the cars are reassembled and driven 500 miles at Brooklands in England

1911 F. Donald Butler, an automobile historian who earlier had been a stylist with Hudson, Nash, AMC, and Chrysler, is born in Paulding County, OH

1914 Andrew L. Pomeroy of Thompson Products Inc. is born in Philadelphia, PA

1929 Sir Henry Segrave, driving the 925-hp Napier "Golden Arrow" designed by Capt. J. S. Irving, raises the land speed record to 231.446 mph at Daytona Beach, FL,

1930 Racer Troy Ruttman is born in Mooreland, OK

1930 John D. Cutter of the Fafnir Bearing Company dies at age 44

1940 Automobile bearing manufacturer R. E. Clingan dies in Saint Petersburg, FL at age 60

1943 Racer Arturo Francesco Merzario is born in Civenna, Italy

1944 Richard H. Scott, former President of the Reo Motor Car Company, dies in Lansing, MI at age 75

1949 David R. Wilson, a manufacturer of cylinder blocks and President of Willys-Overland Company 1934-1939, dies in Pontiac, MI at age 74

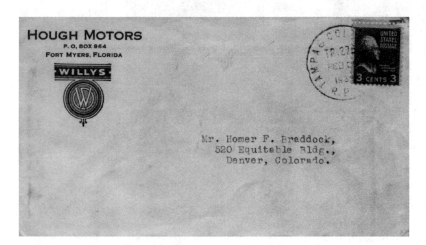

A dealer's envelope from Fort Myers, FL displays the art deco logo that Willys adopted in November 1936.

1953 Racer Derek Daly is born in Dublin, Ireland

1953 Packard announces a custom limousine, executive sedan, and formal sedan as mid-year additions in an effort to recapture their former segment of the luxury market

1956 Peter M. Heldt, German-born automotive journalist whose 1902 *Horseless Age* editorial led to the formation of the Society of Automotive Engineers, dies in Miami, FL

1958 Racer Eddie Lawson is born in Upland, CA

1971 The mid-sized Pontiac Ventura is introduced

1974 Coachbuilder Enos J. Derham dies in Bryn Mawr, PA at age 72

1977 Racer Alberto Rodriguez dies at age 43

1985 Racer Lee Shepherd dies at age 40 when he crashes during a race in Ardmore, OK

MARCH 12

1790 John Frederic Daniell, credited with many improvements in electric battery technology, is born in London, England

1831 Clement Studebaker is born in Gettysburg, PA

1874 Edward Andrew Deeds, a cofounder of the Delco Corporation, is born in Granville, OH

1882 Erwin George "Cannon Ball" Baker is born in Lawrenceburg, IN

1891 George Walter Mason, first Chairman of American Motors, is born in Valley City, ND

1902 Henry Ford resigns from the Henry Ford Company, receiving $900 for his interest in the firm plus the right to use his name in any future business ventures

1904 Colonel Harley Tarrant wins the first automobile race staged in Australia

1921 Giovanni "Gianni" Agnelli II, grandson and namesake of the founder of Fiat SpA and Chairman of the company 1966-1994, is born in Turin, Italy

1928 Kurt Volkhart takes the Opel RAK-1 rocket-powered car for its first test run in Russelsheim, Germany

1938 Racer John Sherman "Johnny" Rutherford III is born in Coffeyville, KS

1940 The Alfa Romeo Tipo 162 engine undergoes its first dynamometer tests, recording a world's record 164 bhp per litre

1951 Joseph E. Fields, President of DeSoto 1931-1937, dies in Palm Springs, CA at age 72

A 1937 DeSoto convertible enters the traffic flow on Colby Avenue in Everett, WA. Production of this rare car totalled just 992 units.

1952 The Mercedes-Benz 300 SL is introduced to the press

1952 Albert G. Partridge of the Goodyear Tire & Rubber Company dies at age 71

1953 Joseph Fewsmith, a cofounder of the Meldrum & Fewsmith, Inc. agency and the developer of the Jordan advertising campaigns of the 1920's, dies at age 63

1953 Augustin Legros of Delage dies at age 72

1954 Tire manufacturer Arthur B. Newhall dies at age 69

1958 Willard L. Huppert, Technical Service Manager of the Motor Coach Division, General Motors and an employee of the firm since 1928, dies at age 61

1963 Racer John Andretti is born in Bethlehem, PA

1964 Mercedes-Benz acquires a license to manufacture diesel Wankel rotary engines

1965 Vittorio Jano of Alfa-Romeo commits suicide at age 73

1967 Dan Gurney's Eagle records its first major victory, winning the Race of Champions at Brands Hatch, England

1969 Automotive artist Frank Quail Jr. dies in West Palm Beach, FL

1969 Racer Gareth Rees is born in Great Britain

1982 The Ford Ranger pickup truck is introduced

1990 Roy S. Roberts is named General Manufacturing Manager of Cadillac, making him the highest ranking black in the United States auto industry

MARCH 13

1845 J. F. Daniell, inventor of the constant electric battery, dies at age 55

1864 N. A. Otto & Cie is organized to manufacture gasoline engines

1872 Charles Henry Warner, a cofounder of the Warner Instrument Company and the Stewart-Warner Speedometer Corporation, is born in Clinton, WI

1882 Torkild Rieber, Chairman of The Texas Company (Texaco) 1935-1940, is born in Voss, Norway

A Texaco station, post office, and general store shared the same building in the late 1930's, and pretty much comprised the entire town of Virginia Dale, CO.

1898 The South African Motor Car Company begins offering round trip bus excursions from Cape Town to Somerset West-Strand

1905 Carl E. Allen of General Motors is born in Carbondale, IL

1908 Rolls-Royce Ltd. announces that it will henceforth produce only the 40/50 hp chassis, later called the Silver Ghost

1913 The Vanden Plas (England) Ltd. (with which is incorporated Theo Masui Ltd.) coachbuilding firm is founded, although the cumbersome legal name would be shortened within a few weeks

1913 Racer Joe Kelly is born in Ireland

1914 Leon Hess of the Amerada Hess Corporation is born in Asbury Park, NJ

1917 Carl Kelsey is issued a United States patent for his friction drive transmission

1920 Hebb Motors Company, Inc. is reorganized as the Hebb Motor Company

1920 Marmon successfully meets a challenge to lap the Indianapolis Motor Speedway in a stock, fully equipped sedan at a mile-a-minute, as a Model 34 sedan records a lap at 63.2 mph

1923 Donald Nelson Frey of the Ford Motor Company is born in St. Louis, MO

1924 President Robert Gray and Vice President William M. Gray resign from Gray-Dort Motors Ltd. as the company is forced into bankruptcy following the demise of the Dort Motor Car Company, its United States counterpart

1926 James J. Storrow, Chairman of the Nash Motors Company 1916-1926, dies in Lincoln, MA at age 62

1928 The Luxford, a taxicab built on the Ford Model A chassis, is introduced

1929 Lee Bible is killed attempting a land speed record at Daytona Beach, FL in the White Triplex powered by three V-12 Liberty engines

1931 The Marmon-Herrington Company, Inc. is incorporated in Indiana

MARMON-HERRINGTON *All-Wheel-Drive* **TRUCKS**

1932 Mitsubishi executive Tsuneo Ohinouye, Chief Executive Officer of its Normal, IL subsidiary Diamond-Star Motors, is born in Tokyo, Japan

1935 Hilmar Kopper of Daimler-Benz AG is born

1944 Charles E. Sorensen resigns as Vice President of the Ford Motor Company

1947 Racer Lyn St. James (nee Evelyn Cornwall) is born in Willoughby, OH

1948 The Playboy is introduced at the Waldorf-Astoria Hotel in New York City

1949 Racer Hiroshi Kazato is born in Japan

1951 John J. Wallbillich, Manager of Planning and Development for Adam Opel AG, dies in Russelsheim, Germany at age 64

1953 Hudson introduces its new small cars, the Jet and upscale Super Jet, as designed by Frank S. Spring with considerable input from corporation President A. E. Barit

1954 Indianapolis Motor Speedway executive Theodore E. "Pop" Myers dies

1964 Derek Bell makes his racing debut, winning a race at Goodwood in his Lotus Seven

1966 Automobile historian Roderic M. Blood, a charter member of the Veteran Motor Car Club of America (VMCCA), dies in West Newton, MA

1973 The Mercedes-Benz ESF 22, the fourth of five experimental safety vehicles, is unveiled to the public

1980 Robert T. Griffin is named Staff Executive to the President, Chrysler Corporation

1980 Henry Ford II resigns as Chairman of the Ford Motor Company and names Philip Caldwell as his successor

1980 The Ford Motor Company is found not guilty by a jury in Winimac, IN in the first criminal trial of a United States corporation in a product liability suit - the case involved the 1978 deaths of three women killed when their Ford Pinto was involved in an automobile accident

1983 The RAM makes its Formula 1 debut in the Brazilian Grand Prix, with the RAM-March Type 1 driven by Eliseo Salazar finishing in 15th place

MARCH 14

1875 William M. Colby, founder of the Colby Motor Company in Mason City, IA, is born in rural Dane County, WI

1899 The Verona-Brescia-Brescia race is staged in Italy - Ettore Bugatti wins the single-seater class in a Prinetti & Stucchi

1902 Henry B. Joy takes delivery of his first Packard, a Model F

1903 The first Boston Auto Show is held in Symphony Hall

1903 The Packard Motor Car Company board authorizes the development of a racing car from one of the first group of Model K's

1903 Harry Shulman of the United Auto Workers is born in Krugloye, Russia (now Belarus)

1904 Hermann Ahrens, Daimler-Benz AG stylist, is born in Uslar, Germany

1909 Prosper L'Orange (1876-1939), Benz engineer, is issued a patent for a pre-combustion chamber type diesel engine that would lead to the manufacturing of diesel-powered automobiles

1910 Antonio Santoni is issued an Italian patent for his centrifugal supercharger

1914 Racer Lee Arnold Petty is born near Randleman, NC, the father of racer Richard Petty and grandfather of racer Kyle Petty

1921 Fred Morrell Zeder II of Chrysler-Zeder, Inc. is born in Orange, NJ

1923 The Brooks (Steam) Motors Ltd. is incorporated in Stratford, Ontario, Canada

1924 John M. Mack, the founder of Mack Trucks, Inc., is killed at age 58 when his Chandler coupe is hit by a trolley car near Weatherly, PA

1925 William Clay Ford is born in Detroit, MI

1927 Racer William J. "Bill" Rexford is born in Conewango Valley, NY

1931 Durant Motors of Canada reorganizes as Dominion Motors Ltd. and would build the Frontenac, based on the old Durant 619, until 1933

1933 The 1933 Chevrolet "Eagle" mascot is patented by designers William Schnell and J. R. Morgan

1933 The 1933 Pontiac "Indian Head in circle" mascot is patented by designer William Schnell

1934 Walter D'Arcy Ryan, a consulting engineer with the General Electric Company and an authority on motor vehicle illumination problems, dies in Schenectady, NY

1940 Robert Cornelius Lannert of the International Harvester Company is born in Chicago, IL

1951 Bess Hannah (Mrs. Henry J.) Kaiser dies

1951 J. Russell Winch of the Lubrizol Corporation and a former employee of the Firestone Tire & Rubber Company dies in Cleveland, OH at age 59

1952 The 1952 Kaiser DeLuxe and Manhattan are introduced as mid-year models - these were the first true 1952 Kaisers, as earlier cars were unsold 1951's that had been slightly modified and recoded as 1952's

1952 The 1952 Nash Ambassador and Statesman are introduced

1953 Packard introduces a limousine on an extended wheelbase Patrician chassis

1953 Plymouth introduces its XX500 prototype showcar

1956 The Kaiser Motors Corporation changes its name to the Kaiser Industries Corporation

1957 Racer Eugenio Castellotti is killed at age 26 when his Ferrari crashes during a practice run in Modena, Italy

1958 The Checker Cab Manufacturing Corporation changes its name to Checker Motors Corporation

A name change after 35 years signalled the company's 1959 entry into the passenger car business. The already outdated styling remained unchanged right to company's demise in 1982.

1961 Racer Hiro Matsushita is born in Kobe, Japan

1962 General Motors produces its 75,000,000th car, a 1962 Pontiac Bonneville convertible

1966 Edwin C. Klotzburger of General Motors dies at age 59

1975 Howard A. "Dutch" Darrin is presented with honorary membership in the Classic Car Club of America (CCCA) during the club's regional meeting in Minneapolis, MN

1993 The Sauber makes its Formula 1 debut in the South African Grand Prix at Kyalami with the Type C12 driven by J. J. Lehto finishing in fifth place

MARCH 15

1864 Precision machinist Carl Edvard Johansson, a longtime associate of Henry Ford, is born in Frotuna, Gotlunda, Vastmanland, Sweden

1878 Anton Johan Lovstad issued Norwegian patent for "torsion springs for carriages", closely resembling modern torsion bar suspension

1886 William Felton Barrett of the Prest-O-Lite Company is born in Dayton, OH

1905 George Russell of General Motors is born in Glasgow, Scotland

1906 Rolls-Royce Ltd. is registered with Ernest Alexander Claremont as Chairman, John de Looze as Secretary, and Hon. C. S. Rolls, F. H. Royce, Claude Johnson, and A. H. Briggs as Directors

1909 Herbert H. Hills begins his employment with the Packard Motor Car Company

1911 Draftsman Etienne Planche begins design work for the first Chevrolet

1911 Gustav Otto, son of internal combustion engine pioneer Nikolaus A. Otto, organizes Gustav Otto Flugmaschinenfabrik Munchen, a company that would into Bayerische Motoren-Werke GmbH (BMW) in 1917

1913 Racer Jack Fairman is born in Smallfield, Surrey, England

1919 C. Harold Wills resigns as Chief Engineer of the Ford Motor Company

1925 Wilfred "Roy" Milner joins the Oakland Divison of General Motors as an assistant to Chief Engineer Benjamin Anibal

1927 Rome, Italy issues its first automobile registration

1932 The Plymouth 1931-1932 "Goddess" mascot is patented by designer Herbert V. Henderson

1937 Automotive historian William G. Holder is born in Richmond, IN

1942 Albert Fisher, an uncle of the seven Fisher brothers and a cofounder of the Fisher Body Company, dies in Detroit, MI at age 78

1949 Stockholders of the Tri-Wheel Motor Corporation vote to put the company into receivership

1951 Harold G. Carron, an official with the Electric Storage Battery Corporation since 1910, dies at age 60

1953 Marc Birkigt of Hispano-Suiza dies in Versoix, Switzerland at age 75

1954 Plymouth offers power brakes as a $36.55 option

1954 The 5,000th Porsche is produced

1956 Willys Motors Inc. acquires the Kaiser Industries Corporation

1956 Erik Carlsson joins Saab as a professional test driver

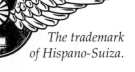

The trademark of Hispano-Suiza.

1960 Noel H. Miller of the Modine Manufacturing Company dies at age 55

1961 Soviet automotive engineer N. R. Briling dies in Moscow at age 84

1964 The first Marmon highway truck is completed by the recently formed Marmon Motor Company of Denton, TX

1977 The 500,000th Corvette is produced and driven off the St. Louis, MO assembly line by Chevrolet General Manager Robert D. Lund

1977 General Motors announces that production of the Chevrolet Vega and Pontiac Astre will cease at the end of the current model year

1982 Martin P. Winther, manufacturer of Winther truck 1917-1927 and Winther automobile 1921-1923, dies in Clermont, FL

1988 Automobile historian Henry N. Manney III of *Road and Track* magazine dies at age 65

1990 The Ford Explorer is introduced as a 1991 model

MARCH 16

1866 Russell Eugene Gardner, founder of the Gardner Motor Company in 1919, is born in Hickman, KY

1869 Charles B. Whittelsey of the Hartford Rubber Works Company is born in New Haven, CT

1884 Ernest Gustav Liebold of the Ford Motor Company is born in Detroit, MI

1880 William Bushnell Stout, builder of the revolutionary Stout Scarab, is born in Quincy, IL

1888 The Rheinische Gasmotorenfabrik Benz & Cie of Mannheim, Germany records its first sale as Emile Roger of Paris, France purchases a Benz 2-hp, 1-cylinder three-wheeler

1893 F. H. Royce marries Minnie Grace Punt

1901 The California Legislature authorizes counties, cities, and incorporated towns to tax and license motor vehicles

1906 Rolls-Royce Distributing Ltd. is incorporated

1909 Bearing manufacturer Henry Timken dies in San Diego, CA at age 77

1910 Barney Oldfield, driving his Blitzen Benz, raises the land speed record to 131.724 mph in Daytona Beach, FL, reclaiming the record for gasoline-powered vehicles

1911 Rolls-Royce Ltd. purchases exclusive rights to the "Spirit of Ecstasy" mascot from sculptor Charles Sykes

1911 The Oklahoma State Legislature requires automobile owners to register their vehicles with the State Highway Commissioner

1912 Edward Dumas Rollert of Buick is born in Crete, IL

1916 Packard closes its factory to visitors because of military secrecy

1917 John M. Studebaker dies at age 83

1918 William C. Wenk of Franklin and Pierce-Arrow dies at age 49

1926 Sir Henry Segrave, driving a Sunbeam at Southport, Lancashire, England, raises the land speed record to 152.33 mph

1926 Edward James Blanch of the Ford Motor Company is born in Utica, NY

1927 The first Falcon-Knight is produced

1928 Goetz Grimm of Volkswagen is born in Gotha, Germany

1936 Racer Piet "Peter" de Klerk is born in Pilgrims Rest, South Africa

1942 Racer Jonkheer Gijs Van Lennep is born in Bloemendaal, the Netherlands

1942 Bearing manufacturer Herrman A. Schatz dies at age 65

1943 Racer Hans Heyer is born in Munchengladbach, Germany

1946 Frank C. Campsall of the Ford Motor Company dies in Savannah, GA at age 62

1950 Motor coach executive John A. Ritchie, a former executive with General Motors and that company's taxicab business, dies

1951 The Packard 250 series is introduced as a mid-year addition, featuring the Mayfair hardtop coupe and a new convertible

1955 The 1,000,000th Buick V-8 is produced

1957 Max L. Howard, an experimental engineer with the Studebaker-Packard Corporation, dies at age 28

1958 The 50,000,000th Ford, a Thunderbird, is produced

1958 Racer Kees Nierop is born in Canada

1961 The Jaguar E-Type is introduced at the Geneva (Switzerland) Auto Show

1962 Racer Franck Freon is born in Paris, France

1966 General Motors produces its 100,000,000th worldwide automobile, an Oldsmobile Toronado

1984 The last rear-wheel-drive Oldsmobile is produced, a Ninety-Eight sedan

1988 Racer Mickey Thompson and his wife are murdered in Bradbury, CA

1992 Robert J. Eaton is named Vice Chairman and Chief Operating Officer of the Chrysler Corporation

MARCH 17

1834 Gottlieb Wilhelm Daimler is born in Schorndorf, Wurttemberg, Germany

1876 Bennett Major Leece, a pioneer manufacturer of automotive lighting equipment, is born in Cleveland, OH

1889 George L. Brown of the Reo Motor Car Company is born in Tillsonburg, ON, Canada

1894 Gen. William Frederick Marquat, a career United States Army officer who was the automobile editor for the *Seattle* (WA) *Times* 1919-1920, is born in St. Louis, MO

1911 The North Dakota State Legislature requires the Secretary of State to register all vehicles with state-issued license plates - plate number one is issued to Senator Charles Ellingson of Sharon, the original sponsor of the bill, for his 1910 Parry touring car

1914 A United States patent is issued for the Boyce Moto Meter

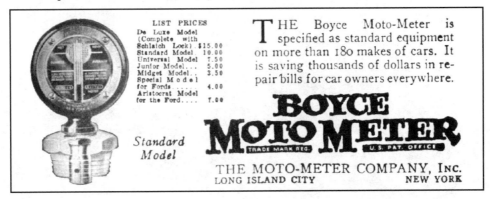

1930 John N. Willys is sworn in as the first United States ambassador to Poland

1930 James Benson Irwin, a United States astronaut who was first to drive the Lunar Roving Vehicle on the surface of the Moon, is born in Pittsburgh, PA

1932 Robert J. Sinclair, President of Saab-Scania of America, is born in Philadelphia, PA

1932 Racer Fred Gamble is born in Pittsburgh, PA

1942 Buick breaks ground for a new factory in Melrose Park, IL to build Pratt & Whitney aircraft engines

1947 Packard directors Henry E. Bodman and Robert Parker resign, in part due to their disappointment over the failed merger with Nash

1948 Alvan Macauley retires as Chairman of the Packard Motor Car Company

1949 The Porsche is introduced at the 19th International Automobile Show in Geneva, Switzerland

1954 The Willys Aero Ace DeLuxe, Eagle Custom, and DeLuxe Six station wagon are introduced to complete the marque's 1954 lineup

1957 The Cadillac Eldorado Brougham, a four-door hardtop sedan designed by Ed Glowacke and based on the Orleans and Park Avenue showcars, is introduced

1960 The compact Mercury Comet, the first of the marque to have a 6-cylinder engine, is introduced as a new series

1966 The International Harvester Company of Delaware merges with the International Harvester Corporation

1972 The Ford Courier mini-pickup truck, manufactured in Japan by the Toyo Kogyo Company, Ltd., is introduced for sale in the western United States market

1978 Theodore P. Hall, developer of the Hall flying automobile, dies in San Diego, CA at age 79

1989 Racing official Mary Momo, the wife of race car designer Alfred Momo, dies in New York City at age 85

1995 The United States Postal Service issues a non-denominated 15-cent coil stamp in New York City to cover the presorted first-class post card rate - the unidentified design by Bill Nelson pictures the tailfin of a 1959 Cadillac

MARCH 18

1853 Rudolf Christian Karl Diesel is born in Paris, France of Bavarian parents

1878 Sir Percival Lea Dewhurst Perry, longtime chairman of the Ford Motor Company Ltd., is born in Bristol, England

1879 Frederic Samuel Glover, President of the Timken-Detroit Axle Company 1919-1933 and of the Reo Motor Car Company 1938-1940, is born in Delaware, OH

1881 Rudolph Carl Norberg of the Willard Storage Battery Company is born in Stockholm, Sweden

1886 George Ebling of the Ford Motor Company is born in Detroit, MI

1895 The world's first gasoline-powered bus service begins between Seigen, Netphen, and Deuz, Germany - the first bus is a 5-hp Benz driven by Hermann Golze

1896 Henry Michael Hogan of General Motors is born in Torrington, CT

1908 The Ford Model T is announced to dealers

The Model T Ford would quite literally change the world, but at the time it was announced to dealers Ford's "bread and butter" was the Model S, such as this roadster photographed in Rapid City, SD.

1917 The steamer "Vigilancia" with 84 FWD trucks on board is torpedoed by a German U-boat leading to United States entry into World War I

1919 Prosper L'Orange, on behalf of Benz & Cie, is issued a German patent for his diesel engine design

1923 Anthony "Andy" Granatelli is born in Dallas, TX

1927 Wade Morton sets a United States stock car record, driving an Auburn 8-88 1,000 miles at an average speed of 68.37 mph at the Atlantic City (NJ) Speedway

1928 Roy Frederick Bennett, President and Chief Executive Office of the Ford Motor Company of Canada, Ltd. 1970-1981, is born in Winnipeg, MB

1929 General Motors announces plans to acquire Adam Opel AG of Germany

1932 Automobile parts manufacturer David Keith Leak is born in Flint, MI

1933 The Studebaker Corporation is forced into receivership

1934 King George V, riding in a 1931 Daimler Double-Six limousine, officially dedicates the Mersey Tunnel between Liverpool and Birkenhead in England

1936 The new research laboratories of the Institution of Automobile Engineers opens in Bretford, Warwickshire, England

1937 Racer Mark N. Donohue Jr. is born in Summit, NJ

1938 Racer Timo Makinen is born near Helsinki, Finland

1947 William C. Durant dies in New York City at age 85

One of William C. Durant's bad ideas was the Samson truck, manufactured only 1920-1922. This Colorado couple converted a used Samson into a motor home, a rarity in that era.

1947 Racer Michel Leclere is born in Paris, France

1950 Racer Larry Perkins is born in Cowangie, Victoria, Australia

1953 The Chrysler Imperial Newport hardtop coupe is introduced as a mid-year model

1953 The Dodge Coronet Sixes are introduced as mid-year models, replacing the Meadowbrook Special series

1959 Paul W. Litchfield, President of the Goodyear Tire & Rubber Company 1926-1940 and its Chairman 1930-1958, dies in Phoenix, AZ at age 83

1962 The Studebaker-Packard Corporation acquires Paxton Products Company

1962 Racer Volker Weidler is born in Heidelberg, West Germany

1964 Racer Alex Caffi is born in Rovato, Italy

1974 Yves Boisset, kidnapped Argentine Peugeot executive, is released by his guerilla captors following the payment of a ransom

1977 Racer Carlos Pace is killed at age 32 in a private airplane crash in Mairipora, Brazil

1981 The 23,000,000th Buick, a 1981 Regal coupe, is produced at the Flint, MI factory and driven off the assembly line by owner Mrs. Edna Cunningham of Frankenmuth, MI

1982 Racer Theo Fitzau dies

1983 The Unocal Corporation is incorporated to succeed the Union Oil Company of California

1994 Automotive historian Carey S. Bliss dies at age 79

MARCH 19

1861 Jean-Joseph Etienne Lenoir is issued a patent for his "Air Engine", an important ancestor of the modern internal-combustion engine

1861 Henry May of Pierce-Arrow is born in Tetrow, Germany

1863 Automobile parts manufacturer Adolph E. Brion is born in Brooklyn, NY

1879 John J. Raskob, financier and political activist who was heavily involved with General Motors during the 1920's, is born in Lockport, NY

1886 Fred Morrell Zeder of the Chrysler Corporation is born in Bay City, MI

This 1946 Chrysler photographed in West Union, IA was a typical design of Zeder, Breer, and Skelton - "The Three Musketeers" - who dominated engineering at the Chrysler Corporation until the 1950's.

1891 Frederick Coolidge Crawford, automobile parts manufacturer and founder of the Frederick C. Crawford Auto-Aviation Museum in Cleveland, OH, is born in Watertown, MA

1892 Delmar S. Harder, an executive with Durant Motors, Inc., the Ford Motor Company, and General Motors, is born in Delhi, NY

1892 The Standard Oil Company of New Jersey changes its name to simply the Standard Oil Company as part of their anti-trust reorganization

1900 The new Fiat plant in Turin, Italy is officially opened by the Duke of Genoa

1908 The first race in Savannah, GA, the 342-mile Challenge Trophy for stock cars, is won by Lewis Strang in an Isotta-Fraschini

1910 Automobile historian Reynold M. Wik is born in Norbeck, SD

1911 Teddy Tetzlaff, driving a 46-hp Lozier, defeats the 90-hp Fiat of Ralph DePalma in a match race staged at the Playa del Rey Motordrome in Los Angeles, CA

1932 The Sydney Harbour Bridge in Sydney, NSW, Australia officially opens to the public - the bridge remains at 160 feet the world's widest bridge

1941 Matteo Ceirano of Fiat dies in Turin, Italy at age 71

1943 Racer Vern Schuppan is born in Booleroo, South Australia, Australia

1949 France ends World War II sales restrictions on automobiles

1949 Sir Harold Snagge, Chairman of D. Napier & Son, Ltd. 1932-1943, dies at age 76

1952 The 1,000,000th Jeep is produced

1956 Joe Oros is appointed Chief Stylist for all Ford cars and trucks, a position he would hold until 1968

1956 The Wayne Corporation of Piqua, OH, manufacturers of Meteor hearses, purchases the A. J. Miller Company of Bellefontaine, OH

1964 Racer Nicola Larini is born in Lido di Camaiore, Italy

1970 Racer Michael Krumm is born in West Germany

1980 Automobile stylist Raymond H. Dietrich dies in Albuquerque, NM at age 86

MARCH 20

1687 Rene Robert Cavalier, Sieur de La Salle, North American explorer and namesake of the 1927-1940 General Motors automobile, is murdered at age 43 in present-day Texas

1853 Henry Edmunds Jr., entrepeneur and inventor famous for arranging the first meeting of F. H. Royce and Hon. C. S. Rolls, is born in Halifax, Yorkshire, England

1856 Frederick Winslow Taylor, the "father of scientific management" and a developer of assembly line techniques, is born in Philadelphia, PA

1871 Charles Paillet, a sculptor and designer of automobile mascots with an animal theme, is born in Moulins, France

1873 Fenton Alfred "Al" Leicher of Luverne is born in Loganville, WI

1882 James T-B Bowles of the Crown Central Petroleum Corporation is born in Paris, IL

1888 Louis Ruthenburg of GMC is born in Louisville, KY

1894 Walter C. Jerome, creator of the 1959 Sir Vival, a twin-sectioned safety inspired car based on a 1948 Hudson, is born in Ohio

1894 George Everett Whitlock, a Dodge Brothers, Inc. official 1914-1929 before entering the steel business, is born in Georgetown, IL

1904 Dean Anderson McGee of the Kerr-McGee Corporation is born in Humboldt, KS

1908 Australian autombile manufacturer Edward W. Holden marries Hilda May Lavis

1910 John Gustav Staiger of American Motors is born in Chase, WI

1920 The first 16-valve Bugatti is delivered to a customer in Basel, Switzerland

1926 Roland Peugeot is born in Valentigney, France

1926 Automotive historian Michael Sedgwick is born

1928 James W. Packard dies in Cleveland, OH at age 64

1929 Willard Lamb Velie Jr. dies

1930 Clessie L. Cummins set the first official land speed record for Diesel-powered cars, reaching 80.389 mph at Daytona Beach, FL in the Cummins Diesel Special

1935 Rudolph M. Hunter, a pioneer designer of electric automobiles, dies at age 78

1939 Racer John Martin is born

1947 Tom O. Duggan, a pioneer racer who became Vice President of Thompson Products Inc. and an authority on automotive replacement parts marketing, dies in Orange, CA at age 52

1950 Arthur H. Timmerman retires as Vice President of the Wagner Electric Corporation after fifty years with the company

1951 The last of 46 Porsches manufactured in Gmund, West Germany is completed as production is shifted to Stuttgart

1952 The Fiat "Otto Vu" with a 2-litre V-8 is introduced at the Geneva Show

1952 Racer Geoff Brabham is born in Sydney, NSW, Australia, the eldest of the three racing sons of three-time World Champion Driver Sir Jack Brabham

1953 The 1953 Kaiser Carolina, a stripped version of the Kaiser Deluxe, is introduced as a mid-year model

1955 Harry Shulman, a United Auto Workers attorney and mediator, dies in Hamden, CT at age 52

1956 William B. Stout, a designer of all forms of transportation including the futuristic Stout Scarab of 1932-1936, dies in Phoenix, AZ at age 76

1957 Mercury discontinues the Turnpike Cruiser convertible Indianapolis 500 Pace Car replica after producing 1,265 units

1959 Racer Joe Tracy dies in Long Island City, NY at age 75

1967 Dr. J. William Haddon calls for an 80 mph maximum for all cars

1972 Racer Pedro Lamy is born in Aldeia Galega, Portugal

1985 The Ford Scorpio is introduced as the European successor to the Ford Granada

1988 The last Pontiac Fiero is produced

1996 John R. Horne succeeds James C. Cotting as President and Chief Executive Office of the Navistar International Corporation, and assumes the additional title of Chairman

MARCH 21

1869 Industrial architect Albert Kahn, designer of many United States automobile factories, is born in Rhaunen, Westphalia, Germany

1876 Charles Walter Matheson is born in Grand Rapids, MI

1877 Maurice Farman is born in Paris, France of British parents

1877 Martin L. Pulcher of the Federal Motor Truck Company is born in Mount Clemens, MI

1895 Racer Robert Benoist is born in Auffargis, France

1898 Robert Allison of Port Carbon, PA places the first order for a Winton

1911 Automobile historian John Bell Rae is born in Glasgow, Scotland

1913 Racer George Abecassis is born in Chertsey, England

1915 Factory management consultant Frederick W. Taylor dies at age 59

1916 Racer Ken Wharton is born in Smethwick, Staffordshire, England

1921 Racer Truman Fontell "Fonty" Flock is born in Fort Payne, AL

1921 Racer Francesco "Chico" Godia-Sales is born in Barcelona, Spain

1923 The 1,000,000th Buick is produced

1923 was a milestone year for Buick, and the most popular 1923 Buick was the Model 45 touring - this is one of 45,227 manufactured.

1928 James Wesley Kinnear III of Texaco, Inc. is born in Pittsburgh, PA

1936 Automotive electrical equipment manufacturer George Faulkner dies

1940 Racer Felice Nazzaro dies in Turin, Italy at age 59

1947 Earle S. MacPherson applies for a United States patent for his vehicle wheel suspension system

1948 The Tucker Corporation acquires the Air Cooled Motors Company of Syracuse, NY, a successor to the defunct Franklin Automobile Company

1948 The Gordini 8 GC race car is completed and road tested by designer Amedee Gordini

1949 Racer Keiichi Suzuki is born in Japan

1950 Preston Tucker files a lawsuit against his former prosecutors

1951 The 500th Porsche is completed and driven from the leased Reutter coachworks in Zuffenhausen, Germany by Hans Klauser, research and personnel manager

you can forget the weather

PORSCHE AIR COOLED ENGINE

Forget anti-freeze. Forget engine overheating. Forget costly radiator and water pump troubles. The fast, never-failing flow of air over the PORSCHE engine assures maximum cooling efficiency in any climate. PORSCHE air-cooling actually keeps the engine *cooler* at lowest speeds!

Continental

A luxuriously hand - finished coupe of limousine comfort, incor- porating every famous feature of PORSCHE race- tested engineering.

PORSCHE

Various Porsche models now available from $2995, delivered N. Y. C.

Dealers from Coast to Coast

U. S. A. Distributor: HOFFMAN-PORSCHE CAR CORPORATION, 443 Park Ave., New York 22

1951 Pirelli SpA applies for a patent for its Cinturato radial tire

1952 The Willys Aero Lark is introduced as a base-trim mid-year model

1957 Arthur J. Wieland of General Motors, the Willys-Overland Company, and the Ford Motor Company dies at age 61

1960 Racer Ayrton Senna da Silva is born in Sao Paulo, Brazil

1964 The Iso Rivolta Grifo prototype makes its racing debut in the Sebring (FL) 12-Hour Grand Prix of Endurance for sports cars

1966 Racer Kenny Brack is born in Sweden

1966 Robert Blythin, General Counsel of the Packard Motor Car Company 1952-1956, dies at age 52

1970 American Motors creates AM General to assume the functions of the former Defense & Government Products Division of Kaiser Industries Corporation

1971 The Ferrari 312B2 makes its racing debut with Clay Regazzoni driving at the Brands Hatch Grand Prix in England

1972 Oberdan Sallustro, an Argentine Fiat executive, is kidnapped by guerillas

1977 Subaru of America, Inc. is reorganized as a New Jersey corporation

MARCH 22

1831 Steam engine pioneer William Symington dies in London, England at age 67

1853 Herman Henry Kohlsaat, patron of the first automobile race in the United States in 1895, is born in Albion, IL

1873 Racer Joseph "Joe" Tracy is born in County Waterford, Ireland

1874 Louis Delage is born in Cognac, France

1892 Eugene C. Hoelzle of Packard is born in Lansing, MI

1895 Automotive artist Walter Wallace Seaton is born in San Francisco, CA

1905 The California Legislature approves an act requiring registration of all motor vehicles with the Secretary of State

1909 The Royal Automobile Club begins a test of two Daimler engines featuring the sleeve valve design of Charles Y. Knight - favorable results would garner the coveted Dewar Award plus a 100% commitment by the Daimler Motor Company, Ltd. to use Knight engines until 1933

1914 Sir Donald Gresham Stokes, Chairman and Managing Director of the British Leyland Corporation Ltd. 1968-1973, is born in London, England

1920 Automotive journalist Douglas Albert Armstrong is born in Windsor, Berkshire, England

1922 Hot rod pioneer Alex Xydias, founder of the So-Cal Speed Shop in 1946, is born in Los Angeles, CA

1926 The Ford Motor Company's River Rouge factory is renamed the Fordson Plant

1927 Production of the Dodge Brothers Series 124 begins

1930 Racer Gastone Brilli-Peri is killed at age 36 when he crashes during a practice run for the Tripoli Grand Prix

1932 The last Oakland-derived Pontiac V-8 is produced

1932 The Rockne 1931-1933 "Winged R" mascot is patented by designer G. R. Johnson

1934 The Brewster-Ford is introduced by John S. Inskip as an attempt to salvage the depression-wracked remains of Rolls-Royce of America, Inc.

1938 Peter John Pestillo of the Ford Motor Company is born in Bristol, CT

1948 Racer Per Stureson is born in Sweden

1952 Wingate M. Anderson of the Standard Oil Company of Brazil dies in Sharon, CT at age 57

1953 Racer Rick Miaskiewicz is born in the United States

1957 A. P. Warner, founder of the Warner Instrument Company, cofounder of the Stewart-Warner Speedometer Company, and the inventor of the automobile speedometer, dies in Beloit, WI at age 87

1961 Maurice Schwartz, a employee of the Walter M. Murphy Company, Coachbuilders, and a partner with Bohman & Schwartz 1931-1939, dies

1974 Racer Peter Revson is killed at age 35 when his Shadow-Cosworth crashes during a practice run at the Kyalami track in South Africa

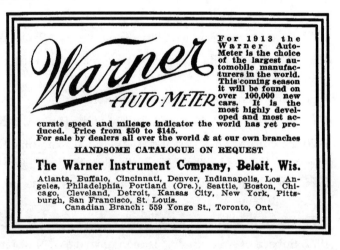

MARCH 23

1899 The first Nice (France) Speed Trials are held on the Promenade des Anglais with Georges Lemaitre winning in a 20-hp Peugeot, the first sprint race victory by a gasoline-powered vehicle

1901 The first Chicago (IL) Auto Show opens under the sponsorship of Samuel Miles, Editor of *Motor Age* magazine

1902 Automobile body manufacturer Edward Gowan Budd Jr. is born in Philadelphia, PA

1903 Joaquin F. dos Reis of the Kaiser-Frazer Corporation is born in Wailuku, Maui, HI

1903 The Missouri General Assembly requires all automobiles to be registered with the city license commissioner or county clerk

1908 David Bruce-Brown makes his racing debut at age 18, hitting 109 mph at Daytona Beach, FL in a 90-hp Fiat

1909 Wilhelm and Karl Maybach form the Luftfahrzeug-Motoren GmbH in Bissingen, Germany to manufacture engines for Zeppelin airships - the Maybach Motoren-Werke GmbH, a subsidiary facility in Friedrichshafen, Germany, would manufacture luxury Maybach automobiles 1921-1941

1915 The British Army orders 50 FWD trucks to be delivered in 40 days

War Proved the Four-Wheel-Drive Principle as Developed in the F-W-D

Four-Wheel-Drive Auto Company
Clintonville :: Wisconsin

1915 Racer Arthur Owen is born in London, England

1921 Donald Malcolm Campbell, land speed record setter and the only son of land speed record setter Malcolm Campbell, is born in Kingston Hill, Surrey, England

1922 Henry Hess, German-born manufacturer of automobile bearings who was a founder of the Society of Automotive Engineers and its President in 1909, dies in Atlantic City, NJ at age 57

1928 Volkswagen historian Walter Henry Nelson is born in Munich, Germany

1929 Attorney Raymond S. Pruitt files a patent application on behalf of the Auburn Automobile Company for the Cord crest trademark

1931 Automotive machine-tool manufacturer Stanley H. Bullard dies in Fairfield, CT at age 53

1932 Louis Robert Ross of the Ford Motor Company born in Detroit, MI

1933 Automotive artist Ken Dallison is born in Hounslow, England

1933 Racer John Taylor is born in Leicester, England

1937 Land speed record setter Craig Norman Breedlove is born in Costa Mesa, CA

1945 Automotive historian Charles Keith Hyde is born in Pittsfield, MA

1946 The Ford Motor Company of Canada, Ltd. introduces the Monarch, a new marque combining Ford and Mercury styling and engineering features

1947 The Frazer Manhattan is introduced as a mid-year model reaturing an upgraded interior designed by Carleton B. Spencer

1952 Roger L. Morrison, a developer of improved highway construction techniques, dies at age 68

1953 The Kaiser-Frazer Corporation announces plans to purchase the Willys-Overland Company

1954 The second series Kaiser Special is introduced as true 1954 models, replacing the slightly modified and recoded 1953's that had been marketed as 1954's

1956 The Studebaker-Packard Corporation puts merger talks with the Ford Motor Company and Textron Corporation on hold pending talks with the Curtiss-Wright Corporation

1958 Earle W. Pughe, retired President of the Ludlow Valve Manufacturing Company, dies at age 60

1959 The first Daf 600 is produced

1969 The first Formula Ford race is staged at Willow Springs International Raceway in Rosamond, CA and won by Jules Williams in a Lotus 51

1972 Fred L. Black, a public relations executive for the Ford Motor Company 1918-1942 and later for the Nash-Kelvinator Corporation and American Motors, dies in Sedona, AZ at age 81

1970 American Motors introduces the AMX/3, an upscale sports car, in Rome, Italy, but production would end after six pre-production prototypes

1976 Fred Hofmann, Service Manager of Bentley Motors, Ltd., dies

1981 Racer Mike Hailwood dies at age 40 from injuries suffered two days earlier when his Rover was involved in a traffic accident near Tamworth-in-Arden, England

MARCH 24

1881 George Cooper Lees, producer of the first front wheel brakes in 1921, is born in Hyde, England

1882 J. H. Hunt of Packard, the Delco Corporation, and General Motors is born in Saranac, MI

1890 Automobile parts manufacturer Brainerd F. Phillipson is born in Chicago, IL

1893 Racer Gastone Brilli-Peri is born in Montevarchi, Florence, Tuscany, Italy

1899 Georges Lemaitre wins the La Turbie Hillclimb in a Peugeot, the first time that a hillclimb had been won by a gasoline powered vehicle

1903 Harry Parsons is issued a patent for his "Armor for Pneumatic Tires", a non-skid device resembling modern tire chains

1906 Landscape architect and amateur automobile racer Sidney Nichols Shurcliff is born in Boston, MA

1908 Otto Zachow is issued a United States patent for his 4-wheel drive system

1913 Adolf Daimler, the middle son of Gottlieb Daimler who was active in his father's company, dies at age 41

1914 Wright Tisdale of the Ford Motor Company is born in Taunton, MA

1915 Racer Eugene Martin is born in Suresnes, Hauts-de-Seine, France

1917 Nobuhiko Kawamoto of Honda is born in Hyogo, Japan

1923 Racer Brian Naylor is born in Salford, Oxfordshire, England

1925 Fred H. Berger of Oakland and Yellow Cab dies in Detroit, MI at age 45

1925 Automobile upholstery manufacturer Jared Warner Stark dies in Florida at age 49

1932 Chief Engineer Carl Doman takes the Series 17 Franklin V-12 for its first test drive in Syracuse, NY

1933 William M. Colby, founder of the Colby Motor Company in Mason City, IA, dies in Mount Pleasant, IA at age 58

1935 Horst Klingmann of the Michelin Tire Corporation is born in Loerrach, Germany

1935 William J. McAneeny of Hudson dies at age 62

1945 The 20,000th tank is produced by the Chrysler Corporation

1947 Racer Pierre Dieudonne is born in Brussels, Belgium

1948 The last Lincoln Continental Mark I is produced

1954 Stockholders of the Hudson Motor Car Company and the Nash-Kelvinator Corporation approve a proposed merger of the two firms

1954 George E. Daniels, the first President of General Motors and a founder of the Daniels Motor Car Company, dies in Danbury, CT

1964 Edward V. Rippingille Sr., the British-born General Motors scientist who helped develop the first mechanical human heart, dies in Toronto, ON, Canada at age 77

1965 Racer Rob MacCachren is born

1970 Racer Buddy Baker sets a world closed course speed record at the Alabama International Speedway in Talladega, reaching 200.447 mph in his Hemi-powered Dodge Charger Daytona

1971 A VAZ 2102 based on the Fiat 124 is the first car produced at the Volga Automobile Works in Tol'iatti, USSR

1974 The National Corvette Restorers Society is organized in Angola, IN

1985 The Marlboro/Daily Express International Trophy at Silverstone, the first Formula 3000 race, is won by Mike Thackwell in a Ralt-Cosworth

1988 Elliott M. "Pete" Estes of General Motors dies in Chicago, IL at age 72

1988 Racer Roger Loyer dies in France at age 80

MARCH 25

1872 Oscar Bernhardt Mueller, pioneer racer and automobile parts manufacturer, is born in Decatur, IL

1879 Signius Wilhelm Poul Knudsen (later "Americanized" to William S. Knudsen) of the Ford Motor Company and General Motors is born in Copenhagen, Denmark

1883 Robert E. Healy of Martin Wasp is born in Bennington, VT

1890 Clarence Earl Bleicher of DeSoto is born in Dayton, OH

1901 The Mercedes is introduced at the 5-day "Week of Nice" in France, with the car driven by Wilhelm Werner dominating the events

1906 Albert Sydney Enever of M.G. is born in Colden Common, England

1920 Walter P. Chrysler resigns from General Motors

1924 Wolfgang R. Habbel of Audi is born in Dillenburg, Germany

1930 Lawrence Kiyoshi "Larry" Shinoda, Chevrolet Corvette Stingray designer, is born in Los Angeles, CA

1931 Lord Howe (born Edward Richard Assheton), driving a Delage, sets the alltime Brooklands record for Class F (under 1500 cc) of 127.05 mph

1935 Frank L. Morse, cofounder of the Morse Chain Company and a Director of the Borg-Warner Corporation, dies in Orlando, FL at age 70

1937 Thomas S. Monaghan, pizza executive and prolific collector of classic automobiles, is born

1938 Racer Fritz d'Orey is born in Brazil

1945 Clyde W. Stringer of Cadillac dies at age 62

1947 The remaining divisions of the former Cord Corporation evolve into the AVCO Manufacturing Corporation

1949 Ross Sterling, President and Chairman of the Board of the Humble Oil & Refining Company 1917-1925 and a former Governor of Texas, dies at age 74

1951 Dr. Charles E. Lucke, head of the mechanical engineering department at Columbia University for 33 years, an authority on thermodynamics, and holder of 130 patent relating to internal combustion engines, dies at age 74

1953 Chrysler Corporation Ltd. of Canada introduces the Dodge Mayfair and the Plymouth Belvedere as a full series seven months before similar action in the United States

1954 The experimental turbine-engined Plymouth is announced to the public some six months after George J. Huebner Jr. had taken it for its first test drive

1956 Racer Lou Moore dies at age 51

1956 Carlton F. Stanley, a nephew of F. E. and F. O. Stanley who was himself active in the affairs of the Stanley steamer, dies

1966 The first Trans-Am Championship race staged by the Sports Car Club of America (SCCA) is won by Jochen Rindt driving an Alfa Romeo GTA over the Sebring, FL track

1968 Leon C. Greenebaum, Chairman of the Hertz Corporation 1956-1968, dies in New York City at age 60

1968 The 1,000,000th Lincoln, a metallic blue Continental 4-door sedan, is produced

1973 Frederick Matthaei Sr., founder of the American Metal Products Company, a producer of automobile parts, dies in Ann Arbor, MI at age 80

1973 Photographer Edward Steichen, affiliated with Packard 1932-1933, dies at age 93

1981 The Jeep Scrambler CJ-8 is introduced as a midyear model

MARCH 26

1852 David MacLean Parry, founder of the Parry Automobile Company, is born on a farm near Pittsburgh, PA

1863 George A. Brockway, founder of the Brockway Motor Truck Corporation, is born in Homer, NY

1877 Automobile battery manufacturer Taliaferro Milton is born in Berryville, VA

1879 Thomas Hancock, the father of the British rubber industry whose efforts paralleled those of Charles Goodyear in the United States, dies in Stoke Newington, England at age 78

1879 Othmar Hermann Ammann, the designer of the George Washington Bridge in New York City, is born in Schaffhausen, Switzerland

1885 Ernest Ingold, a longtime San Francisco, CA automobile dealer, is born in Chicago, IL

1896 James Hamilton Smith of General Motors is born in Jackson, MI

1914 Steam car pioneer James H. Bullard dies at age 71

1919 Samuel B. Dusinberre of the New Departure Manufacturing Company dies in Detroit, MI at age 54

1923 Construction begins on the Milan-Varese (Italy) Autostrada, the world's first inter-urban limited access highway

1927 Frederick L. Maytag, appliance manufacturer and Iowa state senator, dies at age 69 - with his son, Elmer H. Maytag, he purchased a controlling interest in the ailing Mason Motor Car Company in 1910 and manufactured the car as the Maytag through 1911 before switching to washing machines

1927 The first Mille Miglia race begins as Count Aymo Maggi and Bindo Maserati leave Brescia, Italy in their Isotta-Fraschini - the race was won by Ferdinando Minoia and Guiseppe Morandi in an O.M.

1930 The Master Tire & Rubber Corporation is organized in Delaware

1930 Russell Huff, Chief Engineer of the Packard Motor Car Company who later served as a consulting engineer for Dodge Brothers, Inc. and was President of the Society of Automotive Engineers in 1916, dies in Saint Petersburg, FL at age 52

1932 Henry M. Leland dies in Detroit, MI at age 89

America's two dominant luxury marques, Cadillac and Lincoln, both claim Henry M. Leland as a founder. This 1921 Lincoln coupe is parked beside the Lutheran Hospital in Hampton, IA.

1933 Racer Renato Pirocchi is born in Notaresco, Teramo, Abruzzi, Italy

1935 Automotive historian Albert Dee Drake is born in Portland, OR

1940 Construction and development of the Mercedes-Benz W165 racing car ends due to World War II, with the completed cars hidden in Dresden until the end of the war

1943 Lella Lombardi, the first woman to earn points in Formula 1 Grand Prix competition, is born in Frugarolo, Alessandria, Piedmont, Italy

1952 Racer Didier Pironi is born in Villecresnes, France

1952 James J. Nance is elected to the Packard Motor Car Company Board of Directors as a prelude to his election as President of the company

1955 Fonty Flock, driving a Chevrolet V-8, wins a 100-mile race in Columbia, SC, the first NASCAR victory for the marque

1958 Racer Elio de Angelis is born in Rome, Italy

1959 Louis W. Shank of the Ethyl Gasoline Corporation dies at age 58

1960 Racer Brian Till is born in Houston, TX

1960 Racer Jim Hughes is killed at age 29 during a race in Sebring, FL

1962 The Studebaker-Packard Corporation directors ask company stockholders to approve dropping the Packard name from the corporate title

1964 Racer Martin Donnelly is born in Belfast, Northern Ireland

1966 Racer Bob McLean is killed at age 30 and four others also die when his Ford GT40 crashes during a 12-hour race in Sebring, FL

1979 Dr. Fritz Konecke, Chairman of the Daimler-Benz AG Supervisory Board 1953-1960, dies in Stuttgart, Germany at age 80

1984 The Ford Escort is named the world's best selling car for the third year in a row

1985 The first United States-built Nissan is produced at the new Nissan Motor Manufacturing Company factory in Smyrna, TN, the largest automobile plant in the country

1985 Privatization of Volkswagenwerk AG is approved by the West German government

1989 Boris Yeltsin is elected to the Soviet parliament, defeating Communist Party candidate Yevgeny A. Brakov, manager of the Zavod Imieni Likhacheva, manufacturers of the ZIL

1997 The 1998 Lincoln Town Car is introduced at the New York Autoshow

Under the leadership of Dr. Fritz Konecke, negotiations began in 1956 with the Studebaker-Packard Corporation that resulted in Mercedes-Benz cars being sold through S-P dealers 1958-1963, firmly reestablishing the German marque in the United States.

MARCH 27

1863 Frederick Henry Royce is born in Alwalton, Lincolnshire, England

1879 Automobile photographer Edward Jean Steichen is born in Luxembourg

1900 The Magyar Autoklub (Hungarian Automobile Club) is founded

1901 Albert R. Shattuck is awarded the Packard agency for the northeastern United States

1907 Vauxhall Motors Ltd. is registered in Great Britain

1907 The Prague Automobile Factory, Ltd. is organized to produce the PAT-PAF

1908 James Samuel Owens of the Champion Spark Plug Company is born in McKinney, KY

1910 Father Joseph Staggi, a Roman Catholic priest and pioneer automobile designer in his native Italy, dies in Los Gatos, CA at age 85

1920 Jervis Bell McMechan of the Ford Motor Company is born in Detroit, MI

1922 William S. Livezey, promoter of the Texmobile, is convicted of mail fraud and sentenced to five years in a federal prison

1922 Automotive journalist Henry N. Manney III is born

1922 Robert Dale Rowan of the Fruehauf Corporation is born in Holland, MI

1925 Cecil Kimber registers his modified Morris as the first M.G., now known as "Old Number One" although not universally accepted as the true first M.G.

1929 Lammot DuPont is elected Chairman of General Motors succeeding his brother, Pierre S. DuPont

1932 Lee R. Miskowski of Lincoln-Mercury is born in Stevens Point, WI

1936 The first production four-wheeled Morgan is completed after assembling four rather different prototypes

1939 Racer William Caleb "Cale" Yarborough is born in Timmonsville, NC

1940 Sandro Munari, a four-time winner of the Monte Carlo Rally, is born in Cavarzere, Venetia, Italy

1944 James G. Bruce, Editor of *Canadian Automotive Trade*, dies at age 55

1945 Vincent H. Bendix, the inventor of four-wheel brakes and President of the Society of Automotive Engineers in 1931, dies in New York City at age 62

1949 James W. Bryce, an associate of J. Walter Christie and heavily involved in the development of front wheel drive, dies in Montclair, NJ at age 68

1951 Racer Rodney Combs is born in Lost Creek, WV

1952 Kiichiro Toyoda, the founder of the Toyota Motor Company, Ltd., dies at age 57

1955 Lancia scores its first Grand Prix victory as Alberto Ascari wins at Valentino

1956 The Ford Motor Company releases their first public annual report

1956 The 2,000,000th American Motors automobile is produced

1961 Racer Parker Johnstone is born in Atlanta, GA

1965 Racer Gregor Foitek is born in Zurich, Switzerland

1971 Racer David Coulthard is born is Twynholm, England

1990 Billy Hayden is named Chairman of Jaguar, now a subsidiary of the Ford Motor Company, succeeding the retiring Sir John Egan

1994 The Pacific makes its Formula 1 debut in the Brazilian Grand Prix, but the car driven by Bertrand Gachot is forced to retire - the Simtek makes its debut, with the Type S941 driven by David Brabham finishing twelfth

MARCH 28

1851 Murray Edward Gordon Finch-Hatton, the 12th Earl of Winchilsea, a patron of pioneer motoring in Great Britain, is born

1875 Viggo Falbe-Hansen of the Ford Motor Company A-S (Denmark) is born in Copenhagen, Denmark

1880 Harry LeVan Horning, founder of the Waukesha Motor Company, is born in Wauwatosa, WI

1892 Charles E. Duryea and Erwin F. Markham sign a contract to design and finance the construction of a gasoline-powered motor vehicle

1899 Camille Jenatzy completes the *La Jamais Contente* (The Never Satisfied), his radically streamlined Jenatzy electric built specifically to regain the land speed record

1900 The British royal family receives its first motor car, a Daimler 6-hp Mail Phaeton

1903 The first Daytona Beach, FL speed trials are staged with Alexander Winton in his Winton Bullet defeating Horace T. Thomas in the Oldsmobile Pirate

1904 The last Nice (France) Speed Trials on a straight course are won by Louis Rigolly in a Gobron-Brillie

1912 Consalvo Sanesi of Alfa Romeo is born in Terranova Bracciolini, Italy

1912 The (US) Army Road Test to prove the reliability of motor trucks ends at Fort Benjamin Harrison near Indianapolis, IN after a 1,509-mile trip from Washington, DC via Atlanta, GA

1913 The first Morris is produced by W. R. M. Motors, Ltd. of Cowley, Oxford, England

1920 Elmer Apperson, President of the Apperson Brothers Automobile Company 1901-1920, dies in Los Angeles, CA at age 58 while attending an automobile race

1925 The Alvis Tadpole, a front-wheel-drive sports car, is introduced

1925 The last speed hillclimb held on a public road in Great Britain is staged at Kop Hill, Buckinghamshire

1927 The 100,000th Pontiac is produced and presented to Pontiac, MI mayor C. L. Rockwell

A tourist camp in Spicer, MN about 1930. The three most visible cars are 1928 coupe versions of low-priced rivals Chevrolet and Ford, and at the right a 1929 Pontiac Model 6-29 Sedan. Though still offically the companion marque of Oakland, Pontiac was already established as one of the industry's great success stories.

1928 Filippo Surace of Alfa Romeo is born in Reggio, Calabria, Italy

1929 Racer Paul England is born in Australia

1932 Lewis Harris Kittredge, President of the Peerless Motor Car Company 1905-1921, commits suicide in Cleveland, OH

1935 Racer Hubert Hahne is born in Moers, Germany

1935 Louis Mendelssohn, Treasurer and Chairman of the Board of the Fisher Body Company 1909-1926, dies at age 80

1938 Federal Judge John Knight rules that the Pierce-Arrow Motor Company is insolvent and orders its assets to be liquidated

1941 Construction of Ford Motor Company's Willow Run (MI) factory begins

1947 The Kaiser-Frazer Corporation names John Hallett as Works Manager and Dean B. Hammond as Vice President-Engineering

1949 Edgar F. Kaiser is elected President of the Kaiser-Frazer Corporation

1951 Franklin R. Hight of the Edward G. Budd Manufacturing Company dies in Miami, FL at age 57

1952 Racer Tony Brise is born in Dartford, Kent, England

1952 James W. Flynn of the Edward G. Budd Manufacturing Company dies at age 56

1953 The defunct Crosley Motors Inc. merges with the Aerojet Engineering Company of Azusa, CA, with majority ownership in both firms being held by the General Tire and Rubber Company

1956 MGA #13355, a black roadster, is pulled off the assembly line and shipped to the Bodies Branch at Coventry for conversion into the prototype MGA coupe

1960 Racer Steve Kosiski is born in Omaha, NE

1960 Frank Lanchester dies at age 89

1961 Powel Crosley Jr., founder and namesake of the Crosley automobile, Crosley radios, and longtime owner of the Cincinnati Reds baseball team, dies in Cincinnati, OH at age 74

1966 The 1966 Duesenberg Model D is unveiled at the Indianapolis Motor Speedway - promoted by Fred A. "Fritz" Duesenberg, son of August S. Duesenberg, and designed by Virgil M. Exner, only a single prototype was produced

1970 Racer D. Ndahura is killed in Uganda during the East Africa Safari when his car is struck by a flash flood

1976 The first United States Grand Prix West is staged in Long Beach, CA and won by Clay Regazzoni driving a Ferrari 312T

1979 The Jaguar XJ6 Series III and Daimler Double-Six Series III are introduced

1979 Rose Ann Hollertz, the manager of Chevyland USA, an old car museum near Elm Creek, NE, is murdered at age 37

1991 Volkswagenwerk AG agrees to purchase a 70% controlling interest in Skoda from the Czech government

1992 Volkswagenwerk AG announces that Ferdinand Piech will succeed Carl Hahn as Chairman in 1993

MARCH 29

1868 Selwyn Francis Edge is born in Sydney, NSW, Australia

1876 Henry DeWard Collier of the Standard Oil Company is born in San Francisco, CA

1876 Mary Litogot Ford, mother of Henry Ford, dies in Dearborn, MI at age 36

1881 Lewis Newman Rosenbaum of the Continental Motors Corporation is born in Homak, Hungary

1888 Charles Randolph Thomas, a longtime proponent of better highways, is born in Beaufort, NC

1891 Alfred Neubauer of Daimler-Benz AG is born in Bohemia

1900 Racer Bill Aston is born in Stafford, Great Britain

1901 Frank Reynolds Pierce of General Motors, the Nash-Kelvinator Corporation, and the Dearborn Motors Corporation is born in Monticello, AR

1901 Wilhelm Werner wins the LaTurbie (France) hillclimb driving a new 35-hp Mercedes, the first racing victory for the new Daimler marque

1902 Alanson P. Brush marries Jane Deming Marsh

1909 Automotive historian William Robert Nitske is born in Germany

1910 C. N. Teetor is granted a patent for his "Oil-Regulating Piston Rings", leading to his founding of the Perfect Circle Company

1919 The first Tatra vehicle, a TL4 truck, is completed

1922 The Ford-owned Lincoln Motor Company is reorganized as a Michigan corporation

1927 Henry Segrave, driving the Sunbeam Mystery S designed by Louis Coatalen at Daytona Beach, FL, breaks the 200 mph barrier in raising the land speed record to 203.7928 mph

1933 Harry E. Pence, a Minneapolis, MN automobile dealer who was influential in Buick affairs, dies in Dayton, OH

1939 Mercury offers special "spring colors" as an option

1940 Automotive artist Earl Horter dies at age 54

1940 John T. Rainier, manufacturer of the 1905-1911 Rainier, dies in Hewlett Harbor, NY at age 79

1944 Racer William John "Billy" Vukovich is born in Fresno, CA, the son of two-time Indianapolis 500 winner Bill Vukovich and father of racer Bill Vukovich III

1948 The modern era of Formula 1 racing begins with the Grand Prix de Pau (France), which is won by Nello Pagani in a Maserati 4CL

1949 Bion Cole Place, an attorney, inventor, and sales executive associated with the automotive industry since 1913, dies at age 73

1952 The Packard Pan American show car designed by Richard Arbib is introduced at the New York International Motor Sports Show

1954 Packard introduces the Clipper Special Sedan and Club Sedan as mid-year, lower-priced additions to its Clipper line

1954 Racer Chip Robinson is born in the United States

1961 Racer Gary Thomas Brabham is born in Wimbledon, England, the second son of racer racer Sir Jack Brabham

1961 Racer Doug Heveron is born in Liverpool, NY

1971 The Jaguar V-12 engine is announced

1977 Roland Bugatti dies in Aix-en-Provence, France at age 54

1977 The Cortland, NY factory of Brockway Motor Trucks Division of Mack Trucks, Inc. is shut down by the parent organization

1981 Racer David Prophet is killed at age 43 in a helicopter crash near the Silverstone circuit in England

1986 Katsuji Kawamata, Nissan Motor Company, Ltd. President 1957-1973 and Chairman 1973-1985, dies in Tokyo, Japan at age 81

MARCH 30

1890 Tire manufacturer Arthur Whiting Carpenter is born in Wellsville, NY

1891 Arthur William Sydney Herrington of Marmon-Herrington is born in Coddenham, England

1892 The United States Rubber Company is organized in New Jersey

1897 Edison Lothair Teetor, President of the Perfect Circle Compay 1938-1946, is born in Hagerstown, IN

1899 The Societe Renault Freres is founded in Billancourt, France by brothers Louis, Marcel, and Fernand Renault

1900 Wilhelm Bauer becomes the first driver to be killed in a speed hill climb when his Daimler, owned by Emil Jellinek, crashes into a cliff at La Turbie, France, and Bauer dies the next day

1907 Racer Rudolf Krause is born in Germany

1910 Racer Peter Hirt is born in Switzerland

1917 The Monroe Auto Equipment Company is incorporated in Michigan

1919 John E. Johnson, Secretary and Treasurer of the Warner Gear Company of Muncie, IN, dies at age 45

1927 Tom S. Sligh Jr., a research engineer with Studebaker, dies in South Bend, IN at age 36 from an accidental gunshot wound

1929 Pioneer British motoring enthusiast Douglas-Scott-Montagu, 2nd Baron Montagu, dies in London at age 62

1932 Joseph Patrick Flannery of Uniroyal, Inc. is born in Lowell, MA

1935 Electric automobile advocate Elliott John DeWaard is born in Sault Sainte Marie, MI

1947 The Tucker automobile is announced

1947 Jean-Pierre Wimille introduces the JPW prototype at Nimes, France

1948 Giovanni Battista Ceirano of Fiat dies in LaCassa, Turin, Piedmont, Italy at age 82

1948 Tire manufacturer Frank G. Schenuit dies in Baltimore, MD at age 53

1956 Chrysler Corporation's third Plymouth-based gas-turbine car completes a four-day promotional trip from New York City to Los Angeles, CA

1958 Len Sutton wins his Championship Trail debut at Trenton, NJ

1961 Racer Michael Christopher Thackwell is born in Auckland, New Zealand

1964 The Bugatti collection of John W. Shakespeare is loaded onto a train in Hoffman, IL for shipment to new owner Fritz Schlumpf in Malmerspach, France

1969 Racer Lucien Bianchi is killed at age 34 when his Alfa Romeo T33 crashes during a practice run at Le Mans, France

1971 Racer Fabrizio de Simone is born in Italy

1974 The Hesketh makes its Formula 1 debut in the South African Grand Prix at Kyalami, but the Type 308 designed by Harvey Postlethwaite and driven by James Hunt is forced to retire

1975 Kenneth S. Adams, Chairman of the Phillips Petroleum Company 1951-1968, dies at age 75

1979 British Leyland Motors, Inc., the United States subsidiary of BL PLC, changes its name to Jaguar Rover Triumph Inc.

MARCH 31

1878 Benjamin Samuels of the Yellow Cab Manufacturing Company and the Benzoline Motor Fuel Company is born in Chicago, IL

1888 Willard Frederick Rockwell of the Timken-Detroit Axle Company is born in Boston, MA

1900 The W. A. Roach Company of Philadelphia, PA, a distributor for the Waverley Electric, places the first national automobile advertisement in the United States in the *Saturday Evening Post*

1904 Louis Rigolly, driving a Gobron-Brillie at Nice, France, raises the land speed record to 94.78 mph

1904 The Vacuum Oil Company Ltd. is incorporated in Victoria, Australia

1906 The Overland Automobile Company is organized in Terre Haute, IN by David M. Parry and Claude E. Cox

1910 Alvan Macauley is named General Manager of the Packard Motor Car Company

1912 Antique automobile collector D. Cameron Peck is born in Illinois

1914 Walter S. Austin of the Austin Automobile Company in Grand Rapids, MI is issued a United States patent for his two-speed rear axle

1915 The Flugwerke Deutschland (German Aircraft Works) is reorganized by financier Julius Auspitzer - this firm would evolve into the Bayerische Motoren-Werke GmbH (BMW)

1919 Packard completes their government order for 15,000 war trucks

1921 Automobile parts manufacturer Edward Mandell DeWindt is born in Great Barrington, MA

1925 The Ford Motor Company of Australia, Proprietary, Ltd. and the Ford Manufacturing Company of Australia are incorporated

1931 Knute Rockne, Notre Dame University football coach and namesake of the Rockne automobile manufactured by Studebaker, is killed at age 43 in a plane crash near Bazaar, KS

1932 The Ford V-8 is introduced

1942 Howard A. Fisher, youngest of the seven brothers who founded the Fisher Body Company, dies in Detroit, MI at age 40

1944 Albert C. Corr of the Gates Rubber Company dies at age 46

1945 Wifredo P. Ricart completes his contract as a technical advisor to Alfa Romeo and returns to his native Spain

1945 Pierre Lefaucheux is appointed Director-General of the nationalized Regie Nationale des Usines Renault

1948 Hudson McCarroll of the Ford Motor Company dies in Bay City, MI at age 58

1951 The Plymouth Belvedere hardtop coupe is introduced as a mid-year model

1951 Dr. Roy D. McClure, Henry Ford's longtime personal physician, dies in Detroit, MI at age 69

1952 Racer Anders Olofsson is born in Sweden

1956 Racer Kevin Cogan is born in Culver City, CA

1956 Racer Ralph DePalma dies in South Pasadena, CA at age 72

1958 Racer David Coyne is born in Great Britain

1960 Racer Jon Beekhuis is born Zurich, Switzerland

1966 Racer Jose Luis di Palma is born in Argentina

1973 Racer Yves Giraud-Cabantous dies at age 69

1996 Dante Giacosa, stylist for Fiat 1928-1975, dies in Turin, Italy at age 91

Fiat 124 Spider.

For nearly half a century every Fiat displayed the artistic talents of Dante Giacosa.

APRIL 1

1826 Samuel Morey of Oxford, NH is issued a patent for a his "gas and vapor engine"

1836 Peter E. Studebaker is born in Ashland, OH

1894 Edgar Wadsworth Smith of General Motors is born in Bethel, CT

1894 Raymond Walker Stanley, son of Francis E. Stanley and a longtime promoter of the legacy of the Stanley steamer, is born in Newton, MA

1898 The Winton Motor Carriage Company completes its first sale as Robert Allison of Port Carbon, PA receives a one cylinder Winton phaeton

1901 The first White is sold, a steam-powered Model A stanhope

1903 Count Eliot Zborowski is killed when his Mercedes crashes during a speed hillclimb in La Turbie, France - the winner of the race was Otto Hieronimus in another Mercedes

1904 Emil Mathis and Ettore Bugatti agree to a joint venture where the latter would design a Mathis model known as the Hermes which would be built at the Societe Alsacienne de Construction Mecanique (SACM) in Illkirch- Grafenstaden, France and marketed by Mathis

1904 The first Royce is completed and test driven 13 miles from the Cooke Street works in Manchester, England to F. H. Royce's home in Knutsford

1905 Jean-Marie Letourneur and Jean-Arthur Marchand form a partnership in Paris, France to design and construct custom automobile bodies

1906 Edwin Carl Klotzburger of General Motors is born in St. Louis, MO

1907 The Brush Runabout Company begins taking orders for the Brush, an early attempt at producing a small, economical automobile

1907 Wilhelm Maybach resigns as Chief Engineer of the Daimler Motoren-Gesellschaft, having held that position since 1895, and is succeeded by Paul Daimler, eldest son of company founder Gottlieb Daimler

1908 De Industrieele Maatschappij Trompenburg of Amsterdam, the Netherlands, producers of the Spyker, declares bankruptcy and begins reorganizing under the leadership of Johan Bienfait

1909 The Welch Motor Car Company of Pontiac, MI registers "Welch" as a trademark

1909 The Fleetwood Metal Body Company is founded in Fleetwood, PA

1909 Racer Bill Whitehouse is born in London, England

1913 The moving assembly line is introduced by the Ford Motor Company

1913 A. G. Hebb forms the A. G. Hebb Auto Company in Lincoln, NE, taking over the premises of the E. L. Pratt Automobile Company, a Ford dealership

1919 The first Cleveland is produced by the Cleveland Automobile Company, a subsidiary of the Chandler Motor Car Company

1921 General Motors stylist Edward E. Glowacke is born in Detroit, MI

1922 The Lincoln Motor Company is incorporated as a subsidiary of the Ford Motor Company

1926 K. T. Keller joins the Chrysler Corporation as Vice-President of Manufacturing

1927 Durant Motors, Inc. sells their Long Island City, NY factory to the Ford Motor Company

1927 Race car mechanic Herb Nab is born in Fruita, CO

1928 Richard Joseph Stegemeier of the Unocal Corporation is born in Alton, IL

1930 Anthony Keith Gill of Lucas Industries PLC is born in Colchester, England

1930 Meldrum & Fewsmith, Inc., an advertising agency specializing in automotive accounts, is founded by Barclay Meldrum and Joseph Fewsmith

1931 The first DeVaux is produced at the
      Grand Rapids, MI factory

1932 The Franklin V-12 is introduced

1932 The Martin-Wasp Corporation is declared
      null and void by the State of Vermont

1941 The first Packard Clipper is produced

1944 Forrest M. Keeton, a design engineer with
      Pope-Toledo and Car DeLuxe and
      namesake of the 1909-1910 Croxton-Keeton
      and 1912-1914 Keeton, dies

1944 Samuel O. White, Director of Engineering for the Borg-Warner Corporation, dies at age 61 having started
      with the predecessor Warner Gear Company in 1904

1945 P. H. "Mr. Mac" MacGregor of Pontiac retires

1946 Production of 1946 Oldsmobiles resumes after the UAW strike ends

A 1946 Oldsmobile convertible has arrived at the Sherwood Inn in
Skaneateles, NY, a popular resort in the Finger Lakes region.

1947 Col. Victor Wilfred Page, a prolific author of books on automobile and airplane maintenance, dies in
      New Bedford, MA at age 61

1948 The 1949 Mercurys are introduced

1948 George W. Romney joins the Nash-Kelvinator Corporation

1950 Racer Loris Kessel is born in Lugano, Switzerland

1952 Norman K. VanDerzee of Hudson announces "Twin-H Power", the first United States manufacturer to
      offer twin carburetion and dual manifolding on a 6-cylinder car

1952 The 1952 Nash Ramblers are introduced

1955 John T. Gallatin, an official of the Edward G. Budd Manufacturing Company who later was an
      advertising consultant in the farm implement business, dies at age 50

1958 The White Motor Company acquires the Diamond T Motor Car Company for $10,400,000

1960 The Shell Refining Company Ltd. changes its name to the Shell Company of the United Kingdom Ltd.

1961 The German-built Amphicar is introduced in the United States

1964 The first Ford GT-40 race car is completed

1964 The Plymouth Barracuda is introduced

1966 Kenneth N. Scott is named General Manager of Cadillac, succeeding Harold G. Warner

1967 The Ford Mark IV race car makes a successful debut, with Mario Andretti and Bruce McLaren winning the annual 12-hour race at Sebring, FL

1967 Great Britain requires seat belts for both front seats in all new cars

1968 Pennzoil United Inc. is incorporated in Delaware

1969 The Mercedes-Benz C111 makes its first test run at the Daimler-Benz AG test track in Unterturkheim, Germany

1969 The British-American Oil Company Ltd. changes its name to Gulf Oil Canada Ltd.

1969 Petrofina (Great Britain) Ltd. changes its name to Petrofina (UK) Ltd.

1970 The AMC Gremlin is introduced as the first subcompact car manufactured in the United States

If you had to compete with GM, Ford and Chrysler what would you do? American Motors

We started a small car revolution by coming out with America's first subcompact: the Gremlin.

1971 The Nigerian National Oil Corporation is incorporated

1972 Neil "Soapy" Castles wins the 200-mile Grand National NASCAR Eastern Division race at Greenville, SC, his first victory in over 400 starts dating back to 1950

1976 The Automotive Affair, Canada's first collector car dealership, is opened in London, ON by Denny Plowright and Terry Cannon

1977 The Nigerian National Oil Corporation changes its name to the Nigerian National Petroleum Corporation

1980 John Egan is appointed as Chairman of Jaguar Cars, Ltd.

1981 Racer Harlan Fengler dies

1988 The Chevrolet Corvette 35th Anniversary Edition is introduced at the New York Auto Show

1989 William Clay Ford retires from the Ford Motor Company

1989 George F. Kachlein Jr., President of the American Automobile Association 1962-1964, dies at age 81

1989 Porsche Leasing GmbH is established

1993 Alan Kulwicki, the 1992 NASCAR champion, is killed at age 38 in an airplane crash in Bristol, TN

1996 Charles Szews is named Vice President & Chief Financial Officer of the Oshkosh Truck Corporation

APRIL 2

1841 Clement-Agnes Ader, a pioneer automobile/airplane designer, is born in Muret, France

1872 George Brayton is issued a United States patent for his internal combustion engine

1873 George Preston Dorris is born in Nashville, TN

1875 Walter Percy Chrysler is born in Wamego, KS

1878 Albert Champion, pioneer automobile racer and sparkplug manufacturer, is born in Paris, France

1900 Emil Jellinek contracts with the Daimler Motoren-Gesellschaft to be the sole agent for Daimler cars in France and is elected to the board of the company

1902 Rodolphe Peugeot is born

1905 Rodney Lewis de Burgh Walkerley, Editor of *MoToR* magazine 1928-1958, is born in Oundle, Northamptonshire, England

1909 Race promoter James Hensley "Jim" Lamb is born in Elkton, VA

1910 Thomas B. Jeffery of Rambler dies in Pompeii, Italy at age 65

1914 Otto von Bachelle resigns as Chief Engineer of Hupmobile

1919 The 3,000,000th Ford Model T is produced

Model T Ford production was nearing 3,000,000 when these Nevada tourists visited the Wawona tree in Yosemite National Park, CA.

1922 The Mercedes 28/95 equipped with a Roots supercharger makes its racing debut at the Targa Florio

1923 Steam car historian John Heafield Bacon is born in Wellesley Hills, MA

1924 The Nash Motors Company purchases the Mitchell Motor Company of Racine, WI primarily to acquire additional production capacity

1926 Racer John Arthur "Jack" Brabham is born in Hurstville, NSW, Australia

1928 Racer Gino Munaron is born in Turin, Italy

1929 The Chrysler 1930 "Winged Cap" mascot is patented by designer by Oliver H. Clark

1929 The Stewart-Warner Speedometer Corporation changes its name to the Stewart-Warner Corporation

1932 The Plymouth PB is introduced, the first of the marque to officially have an assigned model year

1935 Lincoln announces a 160-inch wheelbase professional car chassis

1940 Racer Stanley Michael Bailey "Mike" Hailwood is born in Great Milton, Oxfordshire, England

1943 The first issue of the revived *Ford Times*, edited by B. Mark Mulcahy, appears

1947 Harry C. Beaver of Stevens-Duryea and Rolls-Royce dies at age 70

1953 Col. Will H. Brown, chief of the Army Motor Transport Corps in World War I, dies in Indianapolis, IN at age 81

1953 Racer Will Hoy is born in Royston, England

1956 Alfred P. Sloan Jr. retires after nineteen years as Chairman of General Motors, with Albert Bradley elected as his successor

1957 Carl J. Bock, Chief Engineer of GMC 1948-1956, dies at age 61

1958 Herbert Allen "Bert" Pierce, Automobile Editor for the *New York Herald-Tribune* 1921-1944 and the *New York Times* 1944-1947, dies in New York City at age 76

1959 Rally driver Juha Kankkunen is born in Finland

1961 Allen B. Laing, a longtime Plainfield, NJ dealer of Stevens-Duryea, Little, Chalmers, Brush, Oakland, Hupmobile, Cadillac, and Oakland, and the developer of the first successful antifreeze, dies in Plainfield at age 86

1962 The Vacuum Oil Company Ltd. changes its name to Mobil Oil Australia PTY Ltd.

1963 Civil engineer Martin W. Torkelson, a developer of improved highway bridge designs, dies at age 84

1963 Racer Fabrizio Barbazza is born in Monza, Italy

1964 The Chrysler Corporation announces that the Plymouth Barracuda will be available in May

1964 Saab directors approve the development of the Gudmund prototype that would evolve into the Model 99

1972 Racer Speedy Thompson dies one day before his 46th birthday, suffering a heart attack while driving in a NASCAR event in Charlotte, NC

1973 John Z. DeLorean resigns from General Motors

1979 The Budd Automotive Company of Canada changes its name to Budd Canada Inc.

1984 Automotive engineer George J. Liddell, an authority on lubricants and fuels, dies in Lima, PA at age 82

1985 The United States Postal Service issues a 12-cent coil stamp in Kingfield, ME designed by Ken Dallison and depicting a 1909 Stanley Steamer

1987 The United States government allows individual states to raise the speed limit on rural Interstate highways to 65 mph

APRIL 3

1851 George Herbert Day of Columbia is born in Brooklyn, CT

1883 Charles Sharp Crawford of Lozier, Empire, Westcott, Cole, Premier, and Opel is born in Indianapolis, IN

1885 Gottlieb Daimler is issued a German patent for his 1-cylinder engine

1906 Maryland requires all automobile owners to make white-on-black license plates for their vehicles

1924 William T. Burns of the Timken Roller Bearing Company dies at age 36

1926 Racer Alfred "Speedy" Thompson is born in Monroe, NC

1937 The Stutz Motor Car Company of America files for bankruptcy

1937 Racer Peter Bryant is born in London, England

1941 Electric vehicle historian Sheldon Rubin Shacket is born in Chicago, IL

1947 President Louis Horowitz and Vice President Charles D. Thomas of the Playboy Motor Car Corporation of Buffalo, NY announce plans to produce a subcompact car, the Playboy

1948 The Jeepster is introduced as a mid-year model

1948 Daniel J. Moran, President of the Continental Oil Company, dies at age 59

1951 Racer Oscar Pedersoli is born in Italy

1955 Egon G. Berg, German-born transmission designer with the Barber-Greene Company, dies at age 53

1959 Racer Fermin Velez is born in Barcelona, Spain

1959 Racer Mike Hurlburt is born

1960 Racer Pedro van Dory is killed at age 41 during the Riverside (CA) Grand Prix

1961 Peter Arundell driving a Lotus 20 achieves his first win, a rare shared victory as he finishes in a dead heat with Tony Maggs driving a Cooper at a race in Goodwood, England

1966 Battista "Pinin" Farina, the founder of Carrozzeria Pininfarina, dies in Lausanne, Switzerland at age 70

1971 Racer Emmanuel Collard is born in Paris, France

1981 Chrysler Corporation closes their Lynch Road plant in Detroit, MI

1985 Racer Helmut Niedermayr dies at age 69

1987 Daf B.V. is organized to succeed Van Doorne's Bedrifswagenfabrick Daf B.V.

1988 The EuroBrun makes its Formula 1 debut in the Brazilian Grand Prix in Rio de Janeiro, but the Type ER188 designed by Mario Tolentino and Bruno Zava and driven by Stefano Modena retires with a faulty fuel pump - the Rial makes its debut, but the ARC1 driven by Andrea de Cesaris retires with engine problems

1989 Duesenberg enthusiast Jerry Gebby dies in Tucson, AZ at age 91

1990 General Motors Chairman Roger B. Smith retires - Robert C. Stempel is elected Chairman and Chief Executive Officer and Lloyd E. Reuss is elected President

1996 A Jaguar E-type roadster goes on permanent exhibit at the Museum of Modern Art in New York City, just the third car to receive this honor

APRIL 4

1878 Channing Rice Dooley, longtime executive with the Standard Oil companies, is born in Rockville, IN

1878 Harry Ezekiel Harris Sr., an inventor of precision machine tools that made mass production of automobiles and airplanes possible, is born in Glenham, NY

1894 Orville Harden of the Standard Oil Company of New Jersey is born in Chicago, IL

1905 The first New Hampshire license plate is issued to Gov. John McLane for his Franklin 20-hp

1924 The Voisin "Stylized Eagle" mascot is patented

1924 Racer Bob Christie is born near Grants Pass, OR

1925 The last sprint races on public roads in Great Britain are staged at Whitecross Road near Hereford and Brentner Straight in Tavistock

1928 Racer Bud Tingelstad is born in Frazee, MN

1929 Carl Benz dies in Ladenburg, Germany at age 84

1930 John Marley Fleming of Vauxhall is born in Boston, MA

1931 Andre Michelin, cofounder of the Compagne Generale des Etablissements Michelin in 1888, dies atage 78

1932 The second Bugatti Royale Type 41 is delivered to Armand Esders with a 2-seat roadster body designed by Jean Bugatti - the car was rebodied as a Coupe de Ville by Binder of Paris in the late 1930's

1936 William Hoeler, Body Engineer for the International Motor Company, dies

1940 Racer Richard James David Attwood is born in Wolverhampton, Staffordshire, England

1943 Howard C. Marmon dies in Fort Lauderdale, FL at age 66

1944 Racer Craig T. Nelson is born in Spokane, WA

1948 Clemente Biondetti driving a Ferrari wins the first post-World War II Targa Florio

1948 Harlow Hyde, an advertising executive connected with the Indianapolis Motor Speedway who did publicity work for Stevens-Duryea, Empire, Marmon, and Stutz, dies in Indianapolis, IN at age 74

1950 Automotive historian Ray Thursby is born in Altadena, CA

1955 Racer James Weaver is born in London, England

1958 Racer Christian Danner is born in Munich, Germany

1962 Arthur E. Twohey, a cofounder of the Horseless Carriage Club of America, dies in Los Angeles, CA

1966 Racer Mark Skaife is born in Australia

1964 The Plymouth Barracuda is introduced at the New York Automobile Show

1966 NASCAR official James A. "Pat" Purcell dies at age 59

1967 The Shell Company of the United Kingdom Ltd. changes its name to Shell UK Ltd.

1979 Dr. Hans Niebold, driving the Mercedes-Benz C111/IV gasoline-engined test car at the Nardo track in Italy, sets several records including the closed track record of 250.918 mph

1981 The "last full-size Chrysler" is produced as the Chrysler Corporation discontinues the Chrysler New Yorker, Chrysler Newport, Dodge St. Regis, and Plymouth Grand Fury, and permanently closes the Lynch Road plant in Detroit, MI where these cars had been assembled

1996 The Jaguar SK8 convertible is introduced at the New York International Auto Show as a 1997 model

APRIL 5

1869 Racer Frank Alderman Garbutt is born in Mason City, IL

1870 Alfred Harris Swayne of General Motors is born in Washington, DC

1887 Lucius D. Copeland of Phoenix, AZ is issued a United States patent for his steam-powered bicycle

1888 Arthur George Drefs, longtime executive with the McQuay-Norris Manufacturing Company of St. Louis, MO, manufacturers of pistons, piston rings, pins, and bearings, is born in Buffalo, NY

1916 Groundbreaking ceremonies are held for the new Jordan Motor Car Company factory in Cleveland, OH

1920 Sydney L. Terry of the Chrysler Corporation is born

1921 The Chevrolet Brothers Manufacturing Company is formed by Louis and Arthur Chevrolet to market their Frontenac high-performance overhead-valve cylinder head conversion kits

1921 Veteran racer Dominique Lamberjack drives a Voisin from Paris to Nice, France, beating the fastest train by about six hours

1923 The Firestone Tire & Rubber Company of Akron, OH begins production of the world's first balloon tires

1927 Ford historian David Lanier Lewis is born in Bethalto, IL

1927 The Twin Coach Company is incorporated in Delaware to manufacture buses and other commercial vehicles, and acquires the plant of the Fageol Motors Company in Kent, OH

1928 The Howard Motor International Corporation of New York City begins production of the Howard Silver Morn, but production is very limited during its two-year existance

1929 Dr. Gerhard Prinz, Chairman of the Management Board for Damiler-Benz AG 1980-1983, is born in Solingen, Germany

1930 The 1930 Plymouth Model U is replaced by the slightly modified Model 30U

1933 The second series 1933 Dodge Series DP is introduced with longer 115-inch wheelbase

1936 Racer Ronnie Bucknum is born in Alhambra, CA

1940 The Buick "Y-Job" dream car is unveiled to the press

1946 A. W. McCalmont of the Jackson Automobile Company and the Sinclair Refining Company dies at age 64

1954 Pierre S. DuPont, President of General Motors 1920-1923 and its Chairman 1923-1929, dies in Wilmington, DE at age 84

1955 The 8,000,000th Buick is produced

1957 Racer David Ashley is born

1958 Clyde H. Britten, Vice President of Manufacturing for the Lubrizol Corporation, dies at age 52

1961 Hubert Charles French, Managing Director of the Ford Motor Company of Australia, PL 1925-1950, dies at age 78

1962 Autocostruzioni Societa per Azioni is organized in Milan, Italy by Gerino Gerini, Lorenzo Bandini, Giancarlo Baghetti, and Giotto Bizzarini to produce a small Ferrari-based sports car, the A.S.A.

1964 Fred Lorenzen wins the Atlanta 500, the first time that a driver had won the same NASCAR race three years in a row

1965 Racer Mike Bliss is born

1966 Journalist H. Massac Buist, a pioneer promoter of British automotive and aeronautical development, dies at age 87

1968 The Lincoln Continental Mark III is introduced

1973 Racer David Murray dies in Las Palmas, Canary Islands, Spain at age 63

1984 Elaine Bond of *Road & Track* magazine dies at age 59

1990 The last Oldsmobile Rocket V-8 engine is produced

APRIL 6

1835 Benton Hanchett, a lawyer and banker who was a cofounder of the Argo Electric Vehicle Company, is born in Oneida County, NY

1853 Emil Jellinek is born in Leipzig, Germany of Moravian ancestry

1860 Artist Rene Lalique, noted for his custom glass automobile radiator mascots, is born in Ay, France

1865 Automobile parts manufacturer John B. Foote is born in Chicago, IL

1885 John Godfrey Parry Thomas, designer of the Leyland Eight and a challenger for the land speed record, is born in Wrexham, Denbigh, Wales

1892 George Montague Williams, President of the Marmon Motor Car Company 1924-1933, born in Nanaimo, Vancouver Island, BC, Canada

1898 Winton becomes an "international" marque thirteen days after selling its first car, as a sale is made to John Moodie of Hamilton, ON, Canada

FROM CLEVELAND TO NEW YORK.
A Winton
Motor Phaeton

Made the run from Cleveland to New York City May 22d to 26th. Distance traveled, 707.4 miles. Actual running time, 47 hrs. and 34 min. Average speed per hour 15 miles. A convincing demonstration and a record that will stand. Hydro-Carbon System. ☞ *Write us for particulars.*
THE WINTON MOTOR CARRIAGE CO.,
472-478 Belden St., Cleveland, O.

Alexander Winton was a pioneeer believer in advertising his products — these appeared in the Scientific American *in 1899.*

SELF=MOVING

That's the English of the French word Automobile, as the new conveyance is called.
Of all those made, the
Winton Motor Carriage
is acknowledged by experts to be the best. To ride in one is a delightful experience, to own one, •write for catalogue and get date of delivery. Hydrocarbon system at a cost of about one-half cent per mile.

Price $1,000. *No Agents.*

THE WINTON MOTOR CARRIAGE CO., Cleveland, Ohio.

1900 The Duryea Power Company is incorporated in Reading, PA with Herbert M. Sternbergh as President to build automobiles designed by Charles E. Duryea

1908 Byron J. Carter of Cartercar dies in Pontiac, MI at age 44

1909 Racer Hermann Lang is born in Bad Canstatt, Germany

1910 Charles L. McIntosh, President of the Pierce Motor Company of Racine, WI, dies - McIntosh was also Treasurer of the J. I. Case Threshing Machine Company, and shortly after his death the Case firm assumed control of Pierce with its Pierce-Racine automobiles now marketed as the Case

1912 Racer Tommy Hinnershitz is born in Alsace Township, PA near Reading

1915 Charles W. Gadd, a research engineer with General Motors 1937-1976, is born

1922 The Sterling-Knight Motors Company purchases the Accurate Machine Company in Cleveland, OH as a facility for manufacturing the cars designed by former Stearns Chief Engineer James Gilman "Pete" Sterling

1923 Racer Herbert Watson "Herb" Thomas is born in Barbecue Township, Hartnett County, NC

1923 H. S. McDewell, Research Engineer for the Maxwell Motor Corporation, dies in Washington, DC at age 37

1926 Automobile parts manufacturer Robert Worst Hague is born in Findlay, OH

1932 John Edwin Foxworth Jr. of General Motors is born in Bishopville, SC

1934 The Ford Motor Company announces white sidewall tires as an option on new vehicles at $11.25 per set over standard blackwalls

A 1934 Ford coupe in picturesque Kanab, UT - its owner seems to have liked the above offer. American collectors almost universally mount whitewalls on cars of this era, but when these cars were new blackwalls were the dominant choice by a wide margin.

1934 Franklin F. "Fay" Chandler, Vice President of the Ross Gear & Tool Company, dies in Lafayette, IN at age 57

1938 John Francis Smith Jr. of General Motors is born in Worcester, MA

1939 F. F. Beall, Vice President and General Manager of the Packard Motor Car Company 1907-1920 and Vice President of the Gray Motor Company 1921-1926, dies in Detroit, MI at age 61

1944 William M. More, head of the automobile department at the New York Trade School since 1919, dies at age 73

1945 Raymond Haskell of The Texas Company dies in New York City at age 66

1947 R. A. Watson of the Federal-Mogul Corporation dies in San Francisco, CA

1949 The first Plymouth Series P-17 3-passenger coupe is produced

1952 Edward E. Berg, an official of GMC since 1924, dies in Buffalo, NY at age 54

1953 Dodge introduces air conditioning as an option

1954 The Lehman Brothers report *Benefits of a Merger* is given to Packard and Studebaker executives and directors

1957 Leo Donovan, Automotive Editor of the *Detroit Free Press*, dies

1968 The Ford Motor Company "Wide World of Ford" exhibit opens for six months at HemisFair in San Antonio, TX

1983 Automobile engineer and designer W. Everett Miller dies in Los Angeles, CA at age 78

1987 Roy S. Roberts is named Personnel Director for General Motors

1992 General Motors names Louis R. Hughes as President of European Operations

APRIL 7

1889 Arthur Middleton Hughes of the Phillips Petroleum Company is born in Holland, TX

1896 Lester Hutchings of the Western Auto Supply Company is born in Excelsior Springs, MO

1902 E. T. Stead in a Mercedes wins the La Turbie, France, speed hillclimb to become the first Englishman to win such an event on the European continent

1907 Vernon Wesley Sherman, a project engineer with Chrysler Corporation 1933-1942, is born in Oscoda, MI

1907 Raymond C. Dahlinger is hired by the Ford Motor Company to drive finished cars off the assembly line

1922 Sig Haugdahl, driving the Wisconsin Special at Daytona Beach, FL, records a one-way run of 180.27 mph, increasing the world record by over 24 mph, although not officially recognized as a new land speed record

1924 Automotive parts manufacturer Thomas Frank Russell is born in Detroit, MI

1926 Cruse Watson Moss of American Motors and the Kaiser-Jeep Corporation is born in Kent, OH

1927 The Consolidated Motors Corporation is formed by William C. Durant

1930 President Carl W. Burst and Vice President Stanley Moon are removed from their positions in the Moon Motor Car Company as part of a takeover by New Era Motors, Inc. - new officers are Archie M. Andrews as Chairman, William J. Muller as President, Helm Walker as Vice President, and Frederic E. Welsh as Treasurer

1930 Brainerd F. Phillipson, founder in 1919 and President of the Climax Molybdenum Company, dies at age 40

1931 The first production Marmon Sixteen is completed

1936 The Fiat Topolino is introduced

1937 Vernon I. Shobe of the Zenith Carburetor Company dies in Ann Arbor, MI at age 52

1939 The Mercedes-Benz W165 Grand Prix racing car is given its first test runs by Rudolf Caracciola and Hermann Lang at Hockenheim, Germany

1939 Movie director and producer Francis Ford Coppola, a devotee of the Tucker marque, is born in Detroit, MI

1941 Automotive machine tool manufacturer J. W. Wilford dies at age 63

1947 Henry Ford dies in Dearborn, MI at age 83

*A Model A pickup, a 1941 V-8, a late Model T, and a Van Ette delivery congregate
at the Ford dealership in Elburn, IL - a fitting tribute to Henry.*

1947 The Ford Motor Company hires baseball great Babe Ruth as a consultant

1955 The Plymouth Belvedere Turbine car is first shown to the public at the Waldorf-Astoria Hotel in New York City

1957 Ricardo Rodriguez makes his racing debut at age 15 driving a 1500-cc OSCA to a third-place finish at Avandaro

1958 The Ferrari Dino 206S V-6 front-engined sports car is introduced in Goodwood, England

1959 Edward S. Janicke of the Ford Motor company dies at age 58

1962 Automotive battery manufacturer Samuel W. Rolph dies at age 73

1963 Racer Bob Marvin dies at age 24 from injuries incurred during a race in Langhorne, PA

1966 Racer Loy Allen is born in Raleigh, NC

1966 Racer Walt Hansgen dies in Orleans, Loiret, France at age 46 from injuries suffered five days earlier during a practice run at Le Mans in his Ford MkII

1966 Pioneer racer and Marmon-Herrington executive Bert Dingley dies

1966 The 11,000,000th Volkswagen is produced

1968 Jim Clark, the 1963 and 1965 World Champion Driver, is killed at age 32 when his Lotus-Ford crashes during a Formula 2 race in Hockenheim, West Germany

1969 Robert L. Kessler is named General Manager of the Fisher Body Division of General Motors

1982 Racer Harald Ertl is killed at age 33 in a private airplane crash near Giessen, West Germany

1985 The Minardi makes its Formula 1 debut in the Brazilian Grand Prix, but the Type M185 designed by Giacomo Caliri and driven by Pierluigi Martini retires with engine problems

APRIL 8

1805 Isaac de Rivaz applies for a French patent on his explosion motor, an important ancestor of the modern internal combustion engine

1867 Eugene C. Richard, the inventor of the "valve-in-head" engine, is born in Savoie province, France

1882 Elbert John Hall, a pioneer designer of V-8 aviation engines who was also associated with the Fageol and DeVaux marques, is born in San Jose, CA

1900 Theodore Otte Yntema of the Ford Motor Company is born in Holland, MI

1901 The first formal automobile race in Great Britain is staged at the Crystal Palace in London and won by Charles Jarrott driving an 8-hp Panhard et Levassor

1902 Frank Jaskowiak of Bismarck, ND completes the first Jaskowiak, a two-seat roadster powered by a Palmer 3-hp engine

1907 Henry J. Kaiser marries Bessie Hannah Fosburgh

1908 A White steam racer driven by Walter C. White wins the Fort George Hill Climb in New York City, defeating 70 other cars

1908 Sir Alfred George Beech Owen, financial patron of BRM, is born

1910 The first race is held at the Playa del Rey Motordrome in Los Angeles, CA, the first of twenty-four board tracks that would be built between 1910 and 1924 in the United States - the winner of the 1-mile speed trial was Barney Oldfield in his "Blitzen" Benz at 128.88 mph

1910 Automotive parts manufacturer Samuel E. MacArthur is born in Philadelphia, PA

1914 Yoshiki Yamasaki of Toyo Kogyo Company, Ltd., manufacturers of the Mazda, is born in Hiroshima, Japan

1916 Racer Bob Burman is killed at age 31 when his Peugeot crashes during the last boulevard race in Corona, CA - also killed in the accident were his riding mechanic Eric Schroeder, track policeman William H. Speers, and five spectators

1918 Harrison Clark of the Ford Motor Company is born in Renssalaer, NY

1928 The first Dodge Standard Six export model (with RHD) is produced

1930 Robert Marland Bailey of the Midas International Corporation is born in Chicago, IL

1930 The 1,000th Cadillac V-16 is produced

1940 The 28,000,000th Ford is produced, a Deluxe Fordor Sedan with body by Ford built at the Edgewater, NJ plant

1941 Automotive historian Paul Van Valkenburgh is born in Marysville, KS

1948 The first 1949 Ford is produced

1953 James B. Fisher, Vice President of the Waukesha Motor Company 1935-1949, dies at age 69

1954 Harry L. Keller, a design engineer with Overland, Oakland, and Buick, dies at age 67

1955 Rene M. Petard, Chief Engineer of the Mitchell-Lewis Motor Company and later the French representative for Studebaker, dies in Neville en Caux, Seine, Inferieure, France at age 69

1958 Oldsmobile produces its 4,000,000th car with Hydra-Matic transmission

1959 Watt L. Moreland, founder of the Moreland Motor Truck Company, dies at age 79

1959 Racer Robert Pressley is born in Asheville, NC

1966 Racer Mark Blundell is born in Barnet, England

1971 Fritz von Opel of Adam Opel AG dies in Saint Moritz, Switzerland at age 71

APRIL 9

1831 Steam car pioneer Henry Seth Taylor is born in Stanstead Plain, PQ, Canada

1878 James Frederic Bourquin of the Continental Motors Corporation is born in Detroit, MI

1885 Civil engineer Roy Winchester Crum, a longtime advocate of concrete and concrete aggregate road construction, is born in Galesburg, IL

1890 Andrew L. Riker marries Edith Whiting

1901 Frederick W. Ball is issued a United States patent for his planetary transmission

1902 Hon. C. S. Rolls, driving a 60 hp Mors at Acheres Park, France, makes four attempts at a new land speed record, but his fastest run of 63.10 mph is slower than the 1899 record by Camille Jenatzy

1904 Automotive historian William T. Cameron is born in New Rochelle, NY

1904 William R. Morris (later Lord Nuffield) marries Elizabeth Maud Anstey

1905 Ralph H. Isbrandt of Buick, Nash, Kaiser-Frazer, and American Motors is born in Milwaukee, WI

1906 Alan Paul Good of Lagonda is born

1909 General Motors completes acquisition of the Oakland Motor Car Company

1909 The first enclosed double-deck bus, a Commer, is introduced

1912 The Marquette Motor Car Company, a General Motors subsidiary, registers its logo as a trademark, but the marque was discontinued later in the year

1912 Fiat executives Ludovico Scarfiotti and Giovanni Agnelli are acquitted of stock fraud charges following a 450-day trial

1917 The "Wingfoot Express", a Packard Model E 5-ton truck sponsored by the Goodyear Tire & Rubber Company, begins a promotional tour from Akron, OH to Boston, MA and back

Packard was almost as well known for its trucks as for its luxury cars.
This pre-World War I chassis was used as a tour bus in San Francisco, CA.

1920 Marie Luhring of the International Harvester Company is admitted as the first female member of the Society of Automotive Engineers (SAE)

1922 Racer Johnny Thomson is born in the United States

1923 John Cote Dahlinger, the alleged illegitimate son of Henry Ford, is born in Detroit, MI

1927 The Wire Wheel Corporation is organized

1935 The Alfa Romeo Bimotore 16-cylinder race car is unveiled to the press

1937 Tokyo Ishikawajima Shipbuilding & Engineering Company, Ltd. is founded in Toyko, Japan - the firm would evolve into Isuzu Motors Ltd.

1940 James W. Hume, a manufacturer of automobile wheels and an authority on wheel balance weights, dies in Ypsilanti, MI at age 61

1941 Racer Amos Johnson is born in the United States

1943 Rita Miller Grisham of T & N Industries Inc. is born in Woodbury, TN

1944 Lucius B. Manning, an associate of E. L. Cord, dies at age 49

1956 The 1956 Metropolitans are introduced to the United States market at Nash and Hudson dealerships

1956 The Packard Executive sedan and coupe are introduced as mid-year additions to fill the price gap between the senior Packard and the Clipper

1956 Ernst & Ernst, a national accounting and consulting firm, issues a report to the Studebaker-Packard Corporation with three options: (1) move all production to Studebaker's South Bend, IN facilities, (2) drop production of the Packard marque, or (3) liquidate the entire corporation

1957 The first three Edsel dealerships are selected

1958 Windsor T. White, President 1915-1921 and Chairman 1921-1927 of the White Motor Company, dies at age 91

1959 Racer George Amick is killed at Daytona Beach, FL at age 34

1959 The AVCO Manufacturing Corporation, evolved from the former Cord Corporation, changes its name to the AVCO Corporation

1961 Porsche makes its Formula 1 debut at the Brussels Grand Prix, but the two cars driven by Jo Bonnier and Dan Gurney are unsuccessful

1964 Racer Dale Shaw is born in Center Conway, NH

1969 The last Jaguar 2.4-litre saloon is produced before being replaced in the marque's lineup by the new XJ6 saloon

1971 Racer Jacques Villeneuve (Jr.) is born in Canada, the son of racer Gilles Villeneuve and nephew of racer Jacques Villeneuve (Sr.)

1976 Louis Giron, a onetime employee of Bugatti and longtime chief of restoration for the National Motor Museum in Beaulieu, England, retires

1981 Pontiac introduces the T1000, a sub-compact based on the Chevrolet Chevette

1981 The Ford Motor Company dedicates its Diversified Products Technical Center in Dearborn, MI

1986 The French government rules against the privatization of Renault

1991 The Ford Motor Company announces that Edsel B. Ford II will succeed Kenneth C. Merrill as President of the Ford Motor Credit Company when the latter retires on May 1

APRIL 10

1804 Isaac de Rivaz test drives his road carriage with an internal combustion engine

1853 Charles Lewis, a cofounder of the Jackson Automobile Company, is born in Winscombe, England

1879 John Daniel Hertz, founder of the Hertz Rent-A-Car System, Inc. and the Yellow Cab Company, is born in Ruttka, Bohemia, Austria (now the Czech Republic)

1881 Frank W. Edwards of the Delco Corporation is born in Georgetown, OH

1891 George Gunn Jr., Vice President and Sales Manager of the White Motor Company 1925-1930, is born in Tacoma, WA

1902 Guy Claude Gerard Maria de las Mercedes Jellinek, biographer of his father Emil Jellinek-Mercedes, is born in Nice, France - his godfather was the expatriate English racer Claude Loraine-Barrow

1909 The Rolls-Royce Silver Rogue, driven by Percy Northey to a first place finish in the 1908 Scottish Reliability Trial, is sold as a used car in London, England

1910 Alvan Macauley is named General Manager of the Packard Motor Car Company

*Packard was America's leading luxury car during most of
Alvan Macauley's long tenure with the company.*

1913 Racer J. Carlyle "Duke" Dinsmore is born in Williamstown, WV

1914 Racer Paul Russo is born in Kenosha, WI

1916 Ralph Mulford breaks the stock car speed record at Daytona Beach, FL, covering a flying mile at 102.53 mph in a Hudson Super Six

1920 Gray-Dort Motors Ltd. produces its last horse-drawn vehicle under the sentimental watch of company President Robert Gray

1920 The Snap-On Wrench Company is founded in Milwaukee, WI by Joseph Johnson and William A. Seidemann

1922 Horsedrawn fire fighting apparatus is used in Detroit, MI for the last time

1929 Racer John Michael "Mike" Hawthorn is born in Mexborough, Yorkshire, England

1933 Germany drops driver's license fees, part of Adolf Hitler's plan to enable all Germans to acquire and operate an automobile

1934 Racer Count Jonkheer Carel Pieter Anthonie Jan Hubertus Godin de Beaufort is born at Maarsbergen Castle, the Netherlands

1936 The Continental-Divco Company changes its name to the Divco-Twin Truck Company

1938 The Mercedes-Benz W154 makes its racing debut in the Pau (France) Grand Prix, with Hermann Lang finishing second to the Delahaye 145 of Rene Dreyfus

1944 Henry Ford II is elected Executive Vice President of the Ford Motor Company

1944 Joseph A. Galamb retires from the Ford Motor Company to end a 39-year career with the firm

1946 Norman F. Wanger of the Gulf Oil Company dies in Conyngham, PA at age 47

1947 Ford Motor Company's factories and offices are closed for the day and all other automobile plants shut down their assembly lines for one minute as a tribute to Henry Ford during his funeral in Detroit, MI - Mr. Ford's last automobile ride, ironically, is in a 1942 Packard hearse

1950 The Pau (France) Grand Prix, the first official International Formula 1 race, is won by Juan Manuel Fangio in a Maserati

1950 Tazio Nuvolari competes in his last automobile race, winning the 1.5 litre class at the Circuit of Monte Pellegrino in a Cisitalia

1951 Henry J. Kaiser marries Alyce Chester less than one month after the death of his first wife

1953 Otto R. Lehmann, an early associate of Henry Ford who claimed to have suggested the Model T, dies in Hartford, CT at age 77

1954 Fiat's experimental gas-turbine car is completed

1954 George E. Martin, a retired brake engineer with General Motors and former Chief Engineer with the Diamond T Motor Car Company, dies at age 75

1963 The Ford Motor Company announces that Arjay R. Miller will assume the presidency of the firm after the retirement of John Dykstra

1965 Racer Lloyd "Lucky" Casner is killed at age 39 during a practice run at Le Mans, France

1967 Racer Mark Smith is born in the United States

1967 Horace Milner Bentley, business partner and older brother of W. O. Bentley, dies

1969 Alvin M. Bentley, a Michigan Congressman who inherited a large block of General Motors stock, dies in Tucson, AZ at age 50

1972 Argentine Fiat executive Oberdan Sallustro is murdered by guerillas twenty days after he had been kidnapped

1980 William Clay Ford is named Vice Chairman of the Ford Motor Company

1981 Henry Ford II rejects Chrysler Corporation's offer to merge

APRIL 11

1866 Clara Jane Bryant, wife of Henry Ford, is born in Greenfield, MI

1888 Henry Ford marries Clara Bryant in Greenfield, MI on her 22nd birthday

1899 James W. Packard writes a letter to George L. Weiss of Winton, suggesting that they establish their own automobile company, an act often cited as the conception of the Packard

1908 The Rockford Automobile & Engine Company of Rockford, IL registers "The Federal" as a trademark - the Federal marque, occasionally known as the Rockford, was produced 1907-1909 in three different cities, but the firm ultimately failed

1913 Ettore Bugatti first proposes designing a super car that would result in the Type 41 Royale

1920 The first post-World War I race at Brooklands, the Short Essex Easter Handicap, is won by Malcolm Campbell driving a Lorraine-Dietrich

1926 Claude Johnson, Managing Director of Rolls-Royce, Ltd., dies in London, England of pneumonia at age 63

1926 Racer Pete Lovely is born in the United States

1928 The Opel RAK 1 rocket car driven by Kurt Volkhart is publicly demonstrated for the first time in Russelsheim, Germany

1933 William E. Metzger dies in Detroit, MI at age 64

1954 George C. Lees, President and General Manager of the United States Axle Company, its founder in 1920, and the producer of the first front wheel brakes in 1921, dies in Pottstown, PA at age 73

1957 William G. Skelly, founder of the Skelly Oil Company, dies in Tulsa, OK at age 78

"The Little Place on the Hill", a Skelly Oil Company service station overlooking Turner Falls, OK. The building still exists.

1958 Friedrich Flick announces a merger of Daimler-Benz AG and Auto Union AG

1965 Albert M. Wibel of the Ford Motor Company dies in Detroit, MI at age 79

1971 Noted car collector John Algie, a founder of Packard Automobile Classics in 1953, dies

1979 Racer John "Johnny" Gerber dies in Davenport, IA at age 82

1983 Racer Rudolf Krause dies in East Germany

1991 Robert E. Dauch resigns as Chrysler Corporation Executive Vice President in charge of manufacturing operations, with Dennis K. Pawley designated to assume most of his former duties

1991 Duesenberg historian J. L. Elbert dies in Clinton, MO at age 72

APRIL 12

1856 Electric car pioneer Pedro G. Salom is born in Philadelphia, PA

1875 Hubert Wingfield Egerton, a cofounder in 1901 of the custom coachbuilding firm of Mann Egerton, Ltd., is born in Norfolkshire, England

1888 Cecil Kimber, the founder of M.G., is born in Dulwich, England

1899 William Holmes Doerfner of General Motors is born in Saginaw, MI

1902 Charles Schmidt, a Frenchman formerly associated with the Mors, joins the Ohio Automobile Company, manufacturers of the Packard

1905 Walter "Wally" Hassan of Bentley and Jaguar is born

1907 Racer Eugene Chaboud is born in Lyon, France

1917 Racer Robert Manzon is born in Marseilles, France

1922 The International Motor Truck Corporation changes its name to Mack Trucks, Inc.

1924 Leopold Arthur "Walter" Hayes of Ford of Europe, Inc. is born in England

1924 Racer Curtis Turner is born in Floyd, VA

1930 Fred V. McGraw, Sales Manager of the Ray Day Piston Company, dies in Columbus, OH at age 41 from injuries suffered in an automobile accident

1932 The 1931-1934 Studebaker "Goose" mascot is patented by designer G. R. Johnson

1942 Racer Carlos Alberto Reutemann is born in Santa Fe, Argentina

1951 Racer Ray Mallock is born in Great Britain

1953 Harold A. Hicks of the Ford Motor Company dies at age 58

1954 The Hudson Jet Family Club Sedan, Hudson's lowest priced 1954 car, is introduced as a mid-year model

1955 Racer Eduardo Dibos is born in Lima, Peru

1961 John Dykstra is elected President of the Ford Motor Company

1961 Racer Corrado Fabi is born in Milan, Italy, the younger brother of racer Teo Fabi

1962 Studebaker's prototype notchback sedan, based on the Avanti, is completed by Pichon-Parat of France

1962 Racer Ron Flockhart is killed at age 38 when his former RAAF Mustang crashes into the Dandenong Range near Melbourne, Australia while practicing for a Melbourne-London air speed record attempt

1964 Racer Ross Cheever, the younger brother of racer Eddie Cheever, is born in Rome, Italy of United States ancestry

1966 Sydney Herbert Allard dies in Surrey county, England at age 55

1968 Dr. Heinz Nordhoff of Volkswagen dies in Wolfsburg, West Germany at age 69 - Kurt Lotz is appointed as the new President

1971 Graham Hill wins the Yellow Pages Jochen Rindt Trophy at the Thruxton circuit in a Brabham-Ford, at age 42 years, 56 days the oldest drive to win a Formula 2 race

1971 The Customer Service Division of the Ford Motor Company is formed

1973 Meade F. Moore, a 46-year veteran of the Nash Motors Company and American Motors who is credited with developing unit-body construction and Nash's noted "Weather Eye", dies in Phoenix, AZ at age 78

1975 G. Elizabeth Carmichael, President of Twentieth Century Motor Car Company and developer of the 3-wheel Dale, is arrested in Miami, FL

1977 General Motors announces that they are dropping plans to produce a Wankel rotary engine

APRIL 13

1771 Steam road vehicle pioneer Richard Trevithick is born in Illogan, Cornwall, England

1877 Racer Christian Lautenschlager is born in Magstadt, Germany

1879 Oswald Bruce "Oz" Cooper of Packard is born in Mount Gilead, OH

1883 Lucas Petrou Kyrides (originally Kyriakides), a pioneer researcher of synthetic rubber while with the Hood Rubber Company, Watertown, MA 1911-1914, is born in Bursa, Asia Minor (now Turkey)

1887 Daniel Stonewall Eddins of Plymouth is born in Waco, TX

1891 Philo Woodworth Parker of the Standard Oil Company is born in Georgetown, NY

1900 The first production Packard, a Model B, is shipped to company official George L. Weiss

1902 Leon Serpollet, driving his steam-powered Serpollet *La Baleine* (The Whale), raises the land speed record to 75.06 mph at Nice, France, the first time that this record had been held by a non-electric vehicle

1904 The Cadillac Motor Car Company's factory in Detroit, MI is heavily damaged by fire

1907 The Rolls-Royce Silver Ghost is introduced to the press

1913 The Chandler Motor Car Company occupies its factory in Cleveland, OH

1913 Automotive cartoonist Russell Brockbank is born in Niagara Falls, ON, Canada

1925 Elwood Haynes dies in Kokomo, IN at age 67

Blue Ribbon Speedster

For sheer beauty, for the suggestion of eager liveliness in every line, for calm expression of confident excellence, we doubt if the Haynes 77 Blue Ribbon Speedster will ever be equalled. With its out-reaching hood, its sweeping fenders and graceful perfection of contour, it completely conveys the sense of quickly responding to the whim or will of its owners.

The great Haynes-built 77 motor is almost human in its supply of power that provides a gentle pace or a vibrant, racing, determined rush which annihilates distance. You should give yourself a real pleasure by inspecting it at your Haynes dealer.

THE HAYNES AUTOMOBILE COMPANY, *Kokomo, Indiana*
EXPORT OFFICE: 342 Madison Avenue, New York City, U.S.A.

One of America's more successful pre-1900 automotive pioneers, these advertisements from 1899 and 1923 virtually bracket the career of Elwood Haynes.

The New Improved Haynes 77 Blue Ribbon Speedster, Two-Passenger

1925 Automobile parts manufacturer Walter W. Carpenter dies in Detroit, MI at age 39

1926 The first Salmson GSS is sold

1928 Racer Giannino Marzotto is born in Italy

1929 The Bendix Corporation reorganizes as the Bendix Aviation Corporation with General Motors owning 24% of the new company - the company would revert to its original name in 1960

1931 Racer Daniel Sexton "Dan" Gurney is born in Port Jefferson, NY

1937 Racer Larry Cannon is born

1942 George L. Norris, a pioneer in developing automotive usages for vanadium, dies in New York City at age 76

1942 Racer Xavier Lapeyre is born in France

1943 Racer Michael "Mike" Beuttler is born in Cairo, Egypt (his mother and Army father were stationed there at the time)

1945 Anton F. Brotz Sr., builder in 1902 of the Brotz Special and later a steam engineer with the Kohler Company, dies at age 69

1948 Paul G. Hoffman resigns as President of the Studebaker Corporation

A 1948 Studebaker sedan in Wiarton, Ontario, Canada.

1949 Racer Ricardo Zunino is born in Buenos Aires, Argentina

1951 Zbigniew Joseph Karczewski, a Polish-born research engineer with the Ford Motor Company who had worked for Renault and Citroen prior to World War II, dies at age 57

1959 Milton H. Van Alstyne of the Harrison Radiator Division of General Motors dies at age 48

1965 The 10,000,000th Pontiac is produced, a 1965 gold Catalina

1974 The lowest numbered Duesenberg Model J, a LeBaron dual-cowl phaeton with serial J-101, sets an auction record of $205,000 in Atlanta, GA

APRIL 14

1629 Internal combustion engine pioneer Christian Huygens is born in the Hague, the Netherlands

1878 Carburetor manufacturer George Malvin Holley Sr. is born in Port Jervis, NY

HOLLEY CARBURETOR
Best I Can Buy

1891 Joseph Day applies for a British patent for his two-stroke engine

1897 Emile Levassor dies at age 54 from complications arising from injuries suffered near Lapalud, France during the Paris-Marseille road race - four days later a daughter is born to Anna and Gottlieb Daimler in Stuttgart, Germany who is christened Emillie in his honor

1899 Herr Beissbarth of Munich, Germany is issued a license plate for his Wartburg - this plate survives today and is believed to be the oldest such artifact in existance

1907 James H. Woodhead of the Kaiser-Frazer Corporation is born in Lafayette, CO

1909 The Anglo-Persian Oil Company, Ltd. is registered in Great Britain - the firm would evolve into British Petroleum Company PLC

1914 Stacy G. Carkhuff of the Firestone Tire & Rubber Company is issued a United States patent for "Nonskid" tires

1915 The Meccas Manufacturing & Specialty Company of New York City registers "Mecca 400" as a trademark, but the firm would dissolve in 1916

1919 Frank Timothy Malumphy, a New Milford, CT Volkswagen dealer and restorer of classic Packards, is born

1923 F. T. Burgess, Chief Designer for Bentley Motors, Ltd., is issued a British patent for his front brakes design

1927 The first regular production Volvo is introduced in Goteborg, Sweden

1929 The first Monaco Grand Prix, conceived by cigarette manufacturer Antony Nogues, is held in Monte Carlo and won by "Williams" in a Bugatti T35B

1929 Warren M. Wiese of the Harrison Radiator Division of General Motors is born in Rochester, MN

1931 The 20,000,000th Ford is produced, a Model A Fordor Town Sedan

1931 Racer Vic Wilson is born in Kingston-upon-Hull, Yorkshire, England

1933 Racer Paddy Hopkirk is born in Belfast, Northern Ireland

1943 Stephen B. Tompkins of Mack and Autocar dies at age 52

1943 Racer Toine Hezemans is born in Eindhoven, the Netherlands

1946 The first post-World War II automobile race in the United States is a stock car event held in Daytona Beach, FL and won by Red Byron in a Ford

1949 The Playboy Motor Car Corporation of Buffalo, NY files for bankruptcy

1950 The Nash Rambler Airflyte Convertible Landau, usually identified as simply the Rambler, is introduced as the first compact convertible

1952 The 1952 Willys station wagons are introduced

1954 Willys workers agree to take a pay cut in a desperate attempt to keep the company solvent

1954 The Fiat experimental gas-turbine car is given its first road test

1957 The Ford Skyliner with retractable hardtop is introduced, with the first car presented to United States President Dwight D. Eisenhower

1962 The Ford Motor Company drops plans to produce the sub-compact Cardinal in the United States - the car would debut in Germany as the 1963 Taunus 12M

1962 Harold Linder Pope of the Pope Manufacturing Company dies in Chula Vista, CA

1964 The first Ford Mustang is inadvertently sold to Stanley Tucker of Saint John's, Newfoundland, Canada three days before the car's official introduction - Tucker refused the company's request for its return, but did sell it to the company two years later with considerable publicity

1965 The 1,500,000th Volkswagen Transporter is produced

Three Volkswagen Transporters dominate this view of Paramaribo, Surinam.

1967 Racer "Gimax" (nee Carlo Franchi) is born in Italy

1977 The Ford Motor Company announces a three-member "Office of the Chief Executive" comprised of Henry Ford II, Lee A. Iacocca, and Philip Caldwell

1979 The former administration building of the Willys-Overland Company in Toledo, OH is demolished to make room for a parking lot

1988 Cedar Rapids, IA collector car dealer Duffy Schamberger holds a grand opening at his new facility

APRIL 15

1819 Oliver Evans, pioneer steam carriage designer, dies in New York City at age 63

1865 Abraham Lincoln, 16th President of the United States and namesake of the United States luxury marque, dies in Washington, DC at age 56

1880 Eleanor Thornton, believed to be Charles Sykes' model for his Rolls-Royce "Spirit of Ecstasy" mascot, is born in Stockwell, England

1891 Georges Henry Roesch of Talbot is born in Geneva, Switzerland

1898 Racer Peter DePaolo is born in Roseland, NJ

1901 The first motorized hearse in Great Britain, a Coventry-built Daimler, is used for the first time in the funeral of William Drakeford, an official of the Daimler Motor Company, Ltd.

1902 The Holsman Automobile Company of Chicago, IL receives a patent for its "high wheel" automobile

1905 The first completed Mathis, as designed by Ettore Bugatti, is sold

1908 Walter E. Flanders resigns from the Ford Motor Company, partly in protest to Henry Ford's pending one-model policy and partly to help organize the Everitt-Metzger-Flanders Company

1908 The first issue of *Ford Times* is published

1909 The first DeWitt auto-buggy is completed by designer Virgil L. DeWitt at his North Manchester, IN factory

1912 Washington August Roebling II of the Mercer Automobile Company is one of 1,517 people killed in the sinking of the RMS Titanic in the North Atlantic Ocean

1916 *Flivver Ten Million*, composed by Frederick Converse to honor the Ford Model T, is debuted by the Boston (MA) Symphony Orchestra under the direction of Serge Koussevitsky

1921 General Motors transfers all management functions of the Chevrolet Motor Company from Flint, MI to its corporate headquarters in Detroit

1922 Racer Graham Whitehead is born in Harrogate, Yorkshire, England

1925 The first factory-assembled Ford Model T pickup truck is introduced

Main Street in Oakfield, WI about 1930. The Model T Ford pickup at right (with modified box) and sedan driving toward the camera illustrate the rather spindly appearance of these vehicles.

1927 The first Salmson GP is sold

1928 Racer Pietro Bordino is killed at age 40 when his Bugatti Type 35B crashes during a practice run at the Circuit of Alessandria in Italy

1929 The last Chandler is produced as DuBois Young, President of the parent Hupp Motor Car Corporation, decides to discontinue the 17-year old marque

An unkown Chandler-Cleveland dealership during the mid-1920's.

1931 Klaus Liesen of Volkswagen is born

1932 Cecil Jesse Silas of the Phillips Petroleum Company is born in Miami, FL

1933 Racer Mel Kenyon is born in DeKalb, IL

1936 J. C. R. Armstrong, an official of the General Vehicle Company and later a consulting engineer, dies

1937 S. C. H. "Sammy" Davis covers 102.22 miles in an hour at Brooklands in a BMW 328 to begin a short-lived tradition of attempting 1-hour records with stock sports cars

1945 Drag racer Sam Miller is born in Wayne, NJ

1951 Edwin B. Jackson, a Canadian-born executive Packard, Willys-Overland, Locomobile, and Stutz, dies in St. Simons Island, GA at age 74

1954 Harry L. Bill, Vice President and General Manager of the Greenfield Tap & Die Corporation whose previous automotive experience included positions with Metzger, Chalmers, and Corbin, dies in Amersfoort, the Netherlands at age 72

1956 General Motors announces the XP-500 show car featuring the world's first free-piston engine

1961 The Jaguar E-Type makes its racing debut with Graham Hill winning a race at Oulton Park, England

1964 The Chesapeake Bay Bridge-Tunnel between Kiptopeke and Chesapeake Beach, VA, the world's longest such structure at 17.65 miles, opens to traffic

1973 Racer Ernst Klodwig dies in East Germany

1977 The Lincoln Versailles, a luxury-compact based on the Ford Granada chassis, is introduced as a competitor of the Cadillac Seville during the grand opening ceremonies for the Renaissance Center in Detroit, MI

1988 Global Motors, Inc. founder Malcolm Bricklin sells his majority interest in the firm for $20,000,000

1996 Dodge truck executive W. G. "Bill" Kincaid dies in St. Louis, MO at age 74

APRIL 16

1875 The Marcus automobile designed by Siegfried Marcus makes its maiden run in Vienna, Austria

1878 Automotive journalist Hugo Massac Buist is born in Hampstead, England

1883 H. D. Church of Mercer, Packard, Locomobile, Kelly-Springfield, and Chevrolet is born in Waltham, MA

1886 Albert W. Scarratt of the International Harvester Company is born in St. Paul, MN

1898 John Dykstra of the Ford Motor Company is born in Stiens, the Netherlands

1903 James Allen Barke, Vice Chairman of the Ford Motor Company Ltd. 1965-1990, is born in Rhodes Green, England

1908 The first Oakland is sold to a private owner

Frank E. Fithen of Steubenville, OH lost both of his arms as a child in a railroad accident, yet was able to perform many tasks including driving his modified 1913 Oakland Model 6-60 speedster.

1913 Automotive historian Charles Lam Markmann is born in Philadelphia, PA

1918 Racer Dick Gibson is born in Bourne, England

1923 Ernest W. Seaholm is named Chief Engineer of Cadillac

1923 The duPont Model C is introduced, featuring the marque's first 6-cylinder engine

1925 Justus V. Locke, founder of the custom coachbuilding firm of Locke & Company, dies in New York City at age 62

1925 Automobile parts manufacturer John McGrath, Vice President of the Eberhard Manufacturing Company of Cleveland, OH, dies at age 63

1929 New Era Motors, Inc. is awarded a corporate charter in Delaware with Archie M. Andrews as President

1930 Professor E. H. Lockwood of Yale University, an authority fuel usage in internal combustion engines, dies at age 63

1933 Racer Bob Carey is killed at age 27 when his Miller 255 crashes during a track record attempt at the Ascot Speedway in Los Angeles, CA

1935 Racer Leon Duray "Jigger" Sirois is born in Hammond, IN, the son of race car mechanic Frenchy Sirois and namesake of the pioneer United States racer Leon Duray (real name George Stewart)

1937 Alfred H. Swayne of General Motors dies at age 67

1946 Arthur Chevrolet commits suicide at age 60 in Slidell, LA

1946 Joseph C. Coulombe, Canadian-born holder of 200 patents relating to fuel feeding equipment for automobiles, dies in Del Mar, CA at age 63

1950 Sterling Edwards introduces his new Edwards R-26 sports car at the first Palm Springs (CA) road race, winning the 40-lap race

1950 The first races held at the new Brands Hatch circuit near Farningham, Kent, England are won by Ken Carter, Don Parker, and Bill Whitehouse

1950 To commemorate its 75th anniversary, the original Marcus automobile is driven in Vienna, Austria, reaching a speed of 3 mph

1951 Homer A. Vilas is elected to the Packard Motor Car Company Board of Directors

1953 Ford Motor Company officials select the basic design for the Continental Mark II

1954 Racer John Bowe is born in Australia

1956 Herbert Henry Franklin dies in Syracuse, NY at age 89

The Syracuse, NY factory of the H.H. Franklin Manufacturing Company as it appeared in 1907. The Franklin was America's most successful air-cooled car.

1957 Richard H. Long, builder of the 1922-1926 Bay State, dies at age 91

1957 The Studebaker-Packard Corporation announces a sales agreement with Daimler-Benz AG to market Mercedes-Benz automobiles in the United States

1958 Walter Ferris, Vice President of the Oilgear Company and a cofounder of the firm in 1921, dies at age 89

1961 The Ford Parts Division of the Ford Motor Company is formed

1967 William L. Hughson of the National Automobile Dealers Association, dies in Sonoma, CA - in 1903 he became the first Ford dealer, later relocating his agency from Buffalo, NY to San Francisco, CA

1978 Francis W. Davis, a Pierce-Arrow engineer who later invented power steering, dies in Cambridge, MA at age 90

1988 Racer Jose Dolhem is killed at age 43 in a private airplane crash near Saint-Etienne, France

1991 Roscoe M. Smith of the Ford Motor Company dies in San Diego, CA at age 97

1997 Vasek Polak, a racing enthusiast closely associated with Porsche, dies in Great Falls, MT at age 82

APRIL 17

1843 Steam engine pioneer Samuel Morey dies in Fairlee, VT at age 80

1867 Vickers Son & Company Ltd. is founded - since 1980 the firm has been the owner and manufacturer of the Rolls-Royce and Bentley marques

1877 Thomas Alexander Russell, manufacturer of the 1905-1916 Toronto-built Russell, is born in Exeter, Ontario, Canada

1882 Peter Edmund Martin of the Ford Motor Company is born in Wallaceburg, ON, Canada

1888 Robert C. Enos of the Eaton Axle & Spring Company is born in Ashtabula, OH

1900 James C. Zeder, youngest brother of Chrysler Corporation engineer Fred M. Zeder and himself an engineering executive with the company, is born in Bay City, MI

1901 J. S. Critchley, General Manager of the Daimler Motor Company, Ltd., is elected as a Director of the firm

1907 Custom coachbuilder Rudolph Robert "Rudy" Stoessel, an associate of Howard A. "Dutch" Darrin and a cofounder of Coachcraft, Ltd., is born in Herzogenaurach, Bavaria, Germany

1911 Charles F. Kettering applies for his first United States patent for the self-starter

1919 The first Ballot race car is completed

1924 James Kendall Bakken of the Ford Motor Company is born in Mount Horeb, WI

1928 Kurt Volkhart takes the Opel RAK 1 for its third test run, reaching a top speed of 62 mph

1933 Virgil Max Exner Jr., son of the automobile stylist of the same name and a successful stylist in his own right, is born in South Bend, IN

1934 Richard H. Scott retains his title of President of the Reo Motor Car Company, but real power is transferred to new General Manager Clarence W. Avery and an executive committee of Ransom E. Olds, Donald E. Bates and George H. Smith

1934 Racer Brian Gubby is born in Epsom, England

1936 Elwood Thomas Ickes, a prominent automotive metallurgist, dies in Philadelphia, PA at age 58

1939 The Packard Motor Car Company elects Alvan Macauley as Chairman of the Board and Max M. Gilman as President

1945 Raymond F. Cook, a tool and die maker for the Studebaker Corporation since 1931, dies

1952 Racer Mike Chase is born

1954 Racer Riccardo Patrese, holder of the record for most Formula 1 starts, is born in Padua, Italy

1956 K. T. Keller retires as Chairman of the Chrysler Corporation

1957 The assets of the Powell Manufacturing Company, manufacturers since 1955 of the Powell Sport Wagon, are sold at auction - although marketed as a new car, the Powell was manufactured almost totally from refurbished Plymouth parts dating back to 1941

1964 The Ford Mustang is introduced in conjunction with opening day of the New York World's Fair

1965 The GT Equipment Group is offered as an option on the Ford Mustang

1967 M. S. "Matt" McLaughlin is named General Manager of the Ford Division of the Ford Motor Company, succeeding Donald N. Frey

1969 The Ford Maverick is introduced

1970 The British-built Ford Capri is introduced to the United States market

1972 Alvin J. Arnheim, historian of the McFarlan marque, dies in New York City

1978 Earle S. Eckel, a cofounder of the Antique Automobile Club of America in 1935, dies in Easton, PA at age 87

APRIL 18

1863 Edwin Warren Marble Bailey, builder of the Bailey Electric, is born in East Pittston, ME

1870 Arthur Pratt Warner, the inventor of the automobile speedometer, is born in Jacksonville, FL

1882 Wilhelm Maybach and Gottlieb Daimler reach a partnership agreement to develop a high speed internal combustion engine for the express purpose of powering vehicles

1898 Sir Patrick Hennessey, Chairman of the Ford Motor Company Ltd., is born

1906 The factory of the Sunset Automobile Company is destroyed by fire as a result of the San Francisco, CA earthquake - production of the Sunset never resumed, although the firm was not legally dissolved until 1909

1911 Ray A. Graham marries Eugenia Winston

1915 Thomas Francis O'Neil, Chairman 1960-1981 of the General Tire & Rubber Company, is born in Kansas City, MO

1920 Robert John Brotje Jr. of the Champion Spark Plug Company is born in Toledo, OH

1925 The first Grand Premio di Tripoli (Libya) is won by Renato Balestrero in a 1990cc O.M.

1928 The Hispano-Suiza driven by Charles Weymann and Robert Bloch defeats the Stutz Black Hawk driven by Tom Rooney and Gil Anderson in a match race staged at the Indianapolis Motor Speedway

1928 William Paul Panny, a design engineer with the Chrysler Corporation 1951-1960 who later was an executive in the aerospace industry, is born in New York City

1929 The 500,000th Pontiac is produced

1939 The Packard 1939-1942 "Goddess of Speed" mascot is patented by designer John D. Wilson

1940 The Alfa Romeo Type 162 prototype race car is completed

1940 Racer Gordon Spice is born in London, England

1942 Racer Karl Jochen Rindt is born in Mainz, Germany

1946 The Packard Clipper Six, Super Clipper, and Custom Super Clipper are introduced as mid-year models

1949 The Hudson Motor Car Company launches its 40th anniversary celebration with a nationwide radio broadcast opened by Michigan Governor G. Mennen Williams

1949 Racer Geoff Bodine is born in Elmira, NY

1949 Archibald M. Maxwell of the Standard Oil Company of Ohio dies at age 53

1950 The 2,000,000th Nash is produced

1952 Racer Enzo Calderari is born in Bienne, Switzerland

1954 Richard A. Teague completes the design of his "cathedral" taillights as used on 1955 and 1956 Packards

1955 Ford Motor Company establishes the Special Products Division to develop the Edsel under the leadership of Benson Ford and Richard E. Krafve

1955 The Ford Motor Company splits its Lincoln-Mercury Division into two separate divisions and establishes the Special Products Division

1957 The Ford Skyliner, the first production retractable hardtop, is introduced

1958 Automobile parts manufacturer William F. Wise dies at age 62

1967 Rolland Jay Thomas, President of the United Auto Workers 1939-1946, dies in Muskegon, MI at age 66

1971 Jackie Stewart wins the Spanish Grand Prix driving a Tyrrell-Cosworth Type 003, the first Formula 1 victory for the marque

1989 The Toyota Motor Company, Ltd. announces plans to build a factory in Burnaston, Derbyshire, England

1990 Roger B. Smith, Chairman of General Motors, announces the corporation's intention to produce the Impact electric car

1990 Racer Bob Drake dies at age 65

1996 The new General Motors Truck Product Center is dedicated in Pontiac, MI

APRIL 19

1870 Frederick J. Forsyth is issued a United States patent for his spring-powered velocipede

1875 Morgan J. Hammers, an associate of Abner Doble, is born in Secor, IL

1876 Halstead Harley Seeley, a manufacturer of automobile windshields, is born in Livingston County, MI

1878 Joseph E. Fields of the Chrysler Corporation is born in Fargo, Dakota Territory (now ND)

1892 L. Ray Buckendale of the Timken-Detroit Axle Company is born in Detroit, MI

1892 Charles E. Duryea, according to his later claims, drives the first successful gasoline-powered United States-built automobile in Springfield, MA - brother and frequent rival J. Frank Duryea later sets the date of this event as September 21, 1893, which is supported by local newspaper accounts

1893 Walter L. Goodman of the General Petroleum Corporation is born in Parsons, KS

1902 The Baldwin Automobile Company of Connellsville, PA, former manufacturers of the Baldwin Steam car, is purchased by J. C. Kurtz

1912 Racer Rudolf "Rudi" Fischer is born in Zurich, Switzerland

1918 George Pope of Pope-Hartford dies at age 75

1922 A. B. C. Hardy is elected as a Director of General Motors

1924 The first Hispano-Suiza 8-Litre Type H6C is delivered to Andre Dubonnet

1925 Pioneer British motoring patron Sir David Salomans dies at age 73

1932 W. O. Bentley officially becomes an employee of Rolls-Royce Ltd. and agrees to allow the company to register his family name as a trademark

1937 The unique Airmobile conceived by Paul M. Lewis and designed with the assistance of former Franklin engineers Carl Doman and Ed Marks, is given its first road test in Syracuse, NY

1938 Racer Basil van Rooyen is born in Johannesburg, South Africa

1940 The Alfa Romeo Tipo 162 is given its first road test

1940 Racer Kurt Ahrens Jr. is born in Brunswick (Braunschweig), Germany

1945 Saturn historian Joe Sherman is born in Lebanon, NH

1946 Barbara Jean Mahone of General Motors, the highest ranking black woman in the automobile industry, is born in Notasulga, AL

1946 Racer Alain Cudini is born in France

1948 Alvan Macauley retires as Chairman of the Packard Motor Car Company, having been with the firm since 1910

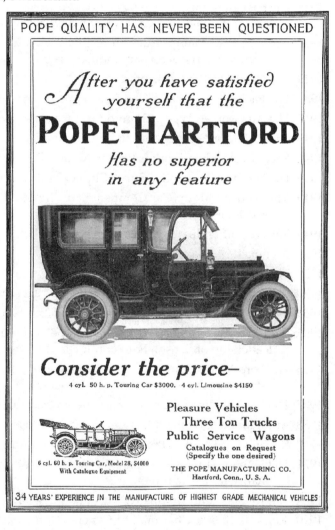

POPE QUALITY HAS NEVER BEEN QUESTIONED

After you have satisfied yourself that the

POPE-HARTFORD

Has no superior in any feature

Consider the price—

4 cyl. 50 h. p. Touring Car $3000. 4 cyl. Limousine $4150

Pleasure Vehicles
Three Ton Trucks
Public Service Wagons
Catalogues on Request
(Specify the one desired)

6 cyl. 60 h. p. Touring Car, Model 28, $4000
With Catalogue Equipment

THE POPE MANUFACTURING CO.
Hartford, Conn., U. S. A.

34 YEARS' EXPERIENCE IN THE MANUFACTURE OF HIGHEST GRADE MECHANICAL VEHICLES

1950 Roy E. Cole, Chief Engineer for Dodge 1928-1930 and for Studebaker 1930-1948 where he designed the low priced Champion series of 1939, dies in South Bend, IN at age 67

1952 Automobile windshield manufacturer Halstead H. Seeley dies in Ann Arbor, MI on his 76th birthday

1954 Joseph Winterbotham (Jr.) of Mitchell and Nash dies at age 76

1955 The Plymouth-based gas-turbine car developed by George John Huebner Jr. makes its public debut on the streets of Detroit, MI

1955 Volkswagen of America is established

The high school in Aurora, NE circa 1960 and an ominous sign - a Volkswagen "Beetle" in front of a 1958 Chevrolet. Detroit would react, but its virtual monopoly of the domestic market was over.

1959 Racer Dick Linder is killed when his Varga Special crashes during a race in Trenton, NJ

1959 The Kaiser-Frazer Owners Club International is founded in Chicago, IL

1962 Racer Alfred "Little Al" Unser Jr. is born in Albuquerque, NM

1966 Lynn A. Townsend is elected President of the Chrysler Corporation

1968 The 14,000,000th Buick is produced

1970 Jackie Stewart wins the Spanish Grand Prix driving a March, the first victory for the marque in just its second Formula 1 appearance

1971 Racer Luigi Piotti dies at age 57

1979 Production of the Chevrolet Citation, the marque's first front-wheel-drive car, begins

1979 The mid-sized Pontiac Phoenix is discontinued with the series name being assigned to the compact-sized front-wheel-drive chassis shared with the Chevrolet Citation

1989 Automobile historian F. Wilson McComb dies at age 62 in East Marden, Sussex, England

1990 Antique automobile collector D. Cameron Peck dies in Tucson, AZ at age 78

APRIL 20

1769 Chief Pontiac, legendary Indian leader and namesake of the General Motors marque, is murdered at Cahokia, IL

1865 James Thayer McMillan, a director of the Packard Motor Car Company 1914-1946, is born in Detroit, MI

1885 Pioneer automobile advertising executive Henry Theodore Ewald is born in Detroit, MI

1889 Arthur Warren Ambrose of the Cities Service Oil Company is born in Lockeford, CA

1898 Tire manufacturer Harvey Samuel Firestone Jr. is born in Chicago, IL

1906 Wilson Decatur Patterson of the White Motor Company is born in Jacksonville, FL

1908 William L. Grout, financial backer of the Grout Brothers Automobile Company and father of Carl, Fred and C. B. (the brothers), dies

1914 Thomas Roy Reid of the Ford Motor Company is born in Monticello, AR

1921 The first and only Corsican Grand Prix is staged to commemorate thecentenary of the death of Napoleon Bonaparte - the winner is Albert Guyot driving a Bignan-Sport, and the event is often cited as the birth of sports car racing

1922 The Packard Single Six Series 126 and 133 are introduced

1924 Peter Joseph Sherry of the Ford Motor Company is born in Mahanoy City, PA

1924 Racer Peter DePaolo, driving a Duesenberg at the Culver City (CA) board track, records his first racomg victory

1927 Philip Toll "Phil" Hill Jr., the first United States-born Formula 1 World's Champion Driver and a prominent classic car collector, is born in Miami, FL

1930 Clessie L. Cummins, driving a diesel-powered Packard roadster at Daytona Beach, FL, reaches 80.398 mph to establish a land speed record for this type of vehicle

1930 Racer Stuart Lewis-Evans is born in Beckenham, Great Britain

1931 Matilda Dodge Wilson, widow of John F. Dodge, is elected to the Board of Directors of the Graham-Paige Motors Corporation, becoming the first woman to serve on the board of a major automobile manufacturer

1935 Delage & Cie. is forced into receivership

1935 Brewster & Company, in the first of two such sales, liquidates its inventory of used Rolls-Royce cars and other luxury marques in an attempt to remain solvent

1940 A reorganization plan for the Auburn Automobile Company is approved by a federal court

1940 James William Stryker of General Motors is born in Grand Rapids, MI

1949 James D. Mooney resigns as President of the Willys-Overland Company

1949 Racer Chuck Gurney is born

1952 The Edwards R-62 makes its racing debut, competing without success in the Pebble Beach (CA) road races - also making its debut at this venue was the modified Porsche driven by Johnny von Neumann that inspired the production Porsche Speedster of 1954

1952 Racer Gordon Reid and four spectators are killed during a race in Dayton, OH

1957 Racer Mario Hytten is born in Switzerland

1961 Racer Paolo Barilla is born in Milan, Italy

1962 Jesse G. Vincent, Packard Vice President of Engineering 1912-1950, dies in Detroit, MI at age 82

1963 Racer Mauricio Gugelmin is born in Joinville, Brazil

1965 Racer Adrian Fernandez is born in Mexico City, DF, Mexico

1984 San Diego, CA hotel owner William D. Evans, a longtime antique automobile collector, dies while preparing his 1902 Mercedes for the Great American Race

APRIL 21

1867 F. W. Gurney, founder in 1903 and Chief Engineer of the Gurney Ball Bearing Company, is born in New Braintree, MA

1879 Commercial vehicle body manufacturer Lion L. Woodward is born in Lancaster, PA

1886 Ernest Walter Hives, 1st Baron Hives of Duffield, Chairman of Rolls-Royce Ltd. 1950-1957, is born in Reading, Berkshire, England

1899 Automotive historian James Wentworth Day is born in Exning, Suffolk, England

1902 William K. Vanderbilt Jr., driving a Mercedes-Simplex at Ablis, France, makes land speed record runs of 67.78 mph and 69.04 mph - although setting a new standard for gasoline-powered cars the runs were not offically recognized and failed to exceed Leon Serpollet's 8-day-old record of 75.06 mph in a steam-powered Serpollet

1903 Carl Benz resigns from the Board of Directors of Benz & Cie

1906 The first Montreal (PQ, Canada) Automobile Show opens

1911 Roland Fox of Alvis and the coachbuilding firm of Vanden Plas (England) Ltd., is born

1927 Lionel Mason Chicoine of the Ford Motor Company is born in Detroit, MI

1929 Charles McGee Pigott of Paccar, Inc. is born in Seattle, WA

1934 Lawrason Dale Thomas of the Amoco Corporation is born in Saginaw, MI

Alvis and Vanden Plas logos

1939 The 2,000,000th Studebaker is produced

1944 Automobile historian Paul Carroll Wilson is born in Washington, DC

1955 Paul E. Lewis, Assistant Chief Engineer of the Leece-Neville Company, dies

1956 Henry J. Fuller of Rolls-Royce of America, Inc. dies at age 82

1961 James Melton, an opera singer who collected antique automobiles and operated an old car museum, dies in New York City at age 59

1962 Ford Motor Company's "An Adventure in Outer Space" exhibit opens at the Seattle World's Fair

1965 Renault and Peugeot agree to form an "association for immediate close cooperation" in research, design, investment, and purchasing

1967 The 100,000,000th General Motors car is produced, a 1967 Chevrolet Caprice Custom coupe assembed at the Janesville, WI plant

1970 The Timken Roller Bearing Company changes its name to The Timken Company

1971 Eaton Yale & Towne Inc. changes its name to the Eaton Corporation

1972 Irving J. Reuter of General Motors dies in Asheville, NC at age 87

1976 The last 1976 Cadillac Eldorado convertible is produced, promoted at the time as the last United States convertible

1979 Racer Ira Vail dies at age 84

1980 Joe Thompson, Ford stylist involved with the Ford Model A and the Lincoln-Zephyr, dies in Glendale, CA at age 92 - he is credited with developing the clay modeling technique for automobile styling

1983 The 1984 Chevrolet Corvette is introduced as the first completely restyled Corvette since 1968

1985 Ayrton Senna, driving a Lotus-Renault, wins the Portuguese Grand Prix in Estoril, the first of his 41 Formula 1 Championship victories - the Zakspeed makes its Formula 1 debut, but the Type 841 driven by Jonathan Palmer retires with suspension problems

1996 Zora Arkus-Duntov, the first Chevrolet Corvette Chief Engineer and a pioneer of fuel injection, dies in Grosse Pointe, MI at age 86

APRIL 22

1803 George Antoine Belcourt, a Roman Catholic priest, Indian missionary, and one of Canada's earliest motorists, is born in Bay du Febvre, Lower Canada (now Quebec)

1833 Steam road vehicle pioneer Richard Trevithick dies in Dartford, Kent, England at age 62

1844 (Sir) William John Crossley, cofounder of Crossley Brothers, Ltd. is born

1881 Arthur Josiah Mountford Baker, Chief Engineer in charge of car design for the Willys-Overland Company 1920-1932, is born in Birmingham, England

1891 Vittorio Jano of Alfa Romeo is born in San Giorgio Canavese, Italy

1895 Archibald McIntyre Maxwell of the Standard Oil Company of Ohio is born in Knoxville, TN

1898 Leo Dewey Welch of the Standard Oil Company of New Jersey is born in Rochester, NY

1911 The Packard Six, later called the Model 1-48, is introduced

1913 James T. McCleary, President of the Lincoln Memorial Road Association, grants Carl G. Fisher permission to use the Lincoln Highway name for the cross-country road that he is promoting

1919 John Norman Romney Barber of British Leyland Motors, Inc. is born

1921 Leland F. Goodspeed, Chief Engineer of the Roamer Motor Car Company, sets an unofficial stock car speed record of 105.08 mph at Daytona Beach, FL driving a Roamer D-4-75 with 4-cylinder Rochester-Duesenberg engine

1922 General Motors ships the last Scripps-Booth, a Model F, as the plant is converted to producing bodies for Buick

1925 Racer Fred Wells is killed at age 26 when the Wells Hornet, a car he had designed, crashed during a test run on the Long Island Motor Parkway between Central islip and Brentwood, NY

1928 Ray Keech raises the land speed record to 207.5526 mph at Daytona Beach, FL driving the White Triplex powered by three V-12 Liberty engines

1933 Sir Frederick Henry Royce dies in West Wittering, West Sussex, England at age 70

1935 Raymond Eugene Goodson of the Oshkosh Truck Corporation is born in Canton, NC

1936 Racer James R. "Bunkie" Blackburn is born

1937 Frank E. Watts is named Vice President of Engineering for Hupmobile

1942 George T. Christopher is named President and General Manager of the Packard Motor Car Company succeeding Max M. Gilman, who resigned after he and Ruth Adams, wife of another Packard executive, were injured in an automobile accident on January 22, 1942 - officially due to health reasons, Gilman's resignation resulted from his adulterous affair and was demanded by Chairman Alvan Macauley who effectively blackballed him from future positions in the automobile industry

1944 Frederick R. Simms, founder of the Daimler Motor Syndicate, Ltd. in 1893, the Royal Automobile Club, and the first person to drive a motor car in Great Britain, dies in London at age 81

1948 The 1949 Lincoln Cosmopolitan and Mercury lines are introduced as the first post-World War II designs of the Ford Motor Company

1954 F. Alexander Riegel of General Motors dies at age 50

1956 Ernie McAfee is killed when his Ferrari crashes during a 100-mile sports car race in Pebble Beach, CA

1956 Walt Faulkner is killed at age 35 when he crashes during a race in Vallejo, CA

1964 Ford Motor Company's Wonder Rotunda opens at New York World's Fair

1966 Sir Alfred Owen unveils the BRM Type 83 race car at Bourne, England

1970 The Mitsubishi Motors Corporation is established as a wholly owned subsidiary of Mitsubishi Heavy Industries Ltd.

1975 Racer Greg Moore is born in Maple Ridge, BC, Canada

1988 Peter Helck, automotive artist and longtime owner of the Locomobile Vanderbilt Cup racer "Old 16", dies in Boston Corners, NY at age 94

1992 Racer Ronnie Bucknum dies in California at age 56 from diabetes

APRIL 23

1840 Steam car pioneer Henry Alonzo House is born in Brooklyn, NY

1869 Hector Jay Hayes, the developer of the first all-metal automobile body, is born in Muir, MI

1884 Charles W. Nash marries Jessie Halleck

1884 Racer Robert "Bob" Burman is born in Imlay City, MI

1898 Nelson Corkish Dezendorf of General Motors is born in Portland, OR

1900 The Thousand Miles Trial begins - 65 entries leave Bristol, England and 23 cars manage to complete the course, with Hon. Charles S. Rolls winning in his 12-hp Panhard

1903 The Pennsylvania General Assembly requires all motor vehicles not registered with a city or municipality to register with a county official

1911 Bob Burman, driving the "Blitzen" Benz at Daytona Beach, FL on his 27th birthday, reaches 141.732 mph in a one-way run that is unofficial but 10 mph faster than Barney Oldfield's land speed record set in 1910

1919 W. O. and H. M. Bentley join brother-in-law A. H. M. J. Ward as Directors of the Aerolite Piston Company, Ltd.

1921 Toni Schmuecker of Volkswagenwerk AG is born in Frechen, Germany

1926 Rolls-Royce Ltd. appoints Basil Johnson as Managing Director to succeed his late brother Claude Johnson, along with William M. Cowen as General London Manager, Arthur F. Sidgreaves as General Sales Manager, and Major Len W. Cox as Sales Manager

1927 C. M. Hough, a federal judge involved in the Selden Patent suit with the Ford Motor ompany, dies at age 68

1928 Dow Jones Services announces the pending introduction of a new car by the Chrysler Corporation, the DeSoto

1929 Heinz Branitzki of BMW is born in Zulz, Germany (now Biala, Poland)

1929 The Volvo PV651 is introduced, the marque's first 6-cylinder car

1930 Packard engineer Lionel M. Woolson dies in Attica, NY at age 42

1940 Automotive brake manufacturer Hugh A. Gillies dies in New York City at age 58

1944 Clement O. Miniger, a developer of automobile batteries who served on the board of the Willys-Overland Company, dies in Toledo, OH at age 69

1947 The 1,000,000th Packard is produced

Packard

"Ask the man who owns one"

1953 The last Allstate is produced

1961 Racer Pierluigi Martini is born in Lugo, Bologna, Emila-Romagna, Italy, the nephew of racer Giancarlo Martini

1962 Jo Siffert driving a Lotus finishes 6th in a race at Pau, France in his Formula 1 debut

1962 Stirling Moss crashes during a practice run at Goodwood, England and his injuries effectively end his racing career

1963 Racer Paul Belmondo is born in Paris, France

1969 Racer P. J. Jones is born in Torrance, CA, the son of racer Parnelli Jones

1970 Racer Jason Keller is born

1970 Herb Shriner, age 51, a humorist and longtime owner of the one-off Phantom Corsair, and his wife Eileen Joy are killed in an automobile accident near Delray Beach, FL

1976 Toni Schmuecker, Chairman of Volkswagenwerk AG, announces plans to build an assembly plant in the United States

1978 Eight USAC officials are killed in an airplane crash near Rushville, IN

1985 The Standard Oil Company of Indiana is reorganized as the Amoco Corporation

1986 Alec Ulmann, organizer of the first Sebring (FL) races in 1950 and the first United States Grand Prix in 1959, dies in Southampton, NY at age 82

1987 The Chrysler Corporation announces their pending purchase of Lamborghini

1992 The Smithsonian Institution acquires a Miller 1500-cc race car

1993 The Chrysler Corporation introduces its Neon line of compact cars

APRIL 24

1885 Mead L. Bricker, Vice President and Director of Manufacturing for the Ford Motor Company, is born in Youngstown, OH

1893 Ray Putnam Dinsmore of the Goodyear Tire & Rubber Company is born in Tewksbury, MA

1904 John Perrin receives authorization to develop the first Lozier automobile

1908 Ralph DePalma makes his racing debut, driving an Allen-Kingston at the Briarcliff Trophy Race in Westchester, NY

1913 Prince Edward Island, Canada lifts its ban on automobiles

1915 Ben Davis Mills of the Ford Motor Company is born in Vian, OK

1917 The Monroe Motor Company reorganizes, and President R. F. Monroe moves his company from Flint, MI to the former Welch plant in Pontiac, MI

1931 Yves Georges Rapilly of Peugeot is born in Saint-Brieuc, France

1934 Automotive historian Karl Erik Ludvigsen (aka Elliott Miles & Eric Nielssen) is born in Kalamazoo, MI

1934 Racer Mike Taylor is born in London, England

1937 Racer Reinhold Jost is born in Abtsteinach, Germany

1941 Racer Silvio Moser is born in Bellinzona, Switzerland

1941 Oscar Mueller, winner of the first automobile race in the United States (the *Chicago Times-Herald* Contest on November 2, 1895), a partner with five brothers and his father, Hieronymus Mueller, in the Mueller Manufacturing Company, builders of the Mueller 1896-1899, and later an automobile parts executive, dies in Bradenton, FL at age 70

1946 H. J. Stambaugh Jr., a Canadian manufacturer of automotive steel, dies at age 58

1949 Automobile parts manufacturer Arthur T. Murray dies at age 59

1953 Racer Naoki Nagasaka is born in Japan

1954 Racer Guy Mairesse is killed at age 43 when he crashes during a practice run for the Coupe de Paris at the Montlhery circuit in France

1960 Mike Spence records his first racing victory, winning a Formula Junior race at Snetterton, England in his 998-cc Cooper-Austin

1962 American Motors announces that it will stop importing the English-built Metropolitan sub compact

1964 King Gustav Adolf VI of Sweden dedicates Volvo's new Torslanda plant at Sorredsdalen

1965 Ernest Walter, Lord Hives, Chairman of Rolls-Royce Ltd. 1950-1957, dies in London at age 79

1967 Fred Lorenzen announces his retirement from NASCAR stock car racing, although he would return to the tracks in 1970

1969 Racer Hermie Sadler is born

1970 Racer Jean-Philippe Belloc is born in France

1975 The last Citroen DS produced, ending a run of nearly 20 years

1980 The General Motors Advance Studio releases the Pontiac Fiero for planned production

1987 Gioachino Colombo, an Alfa Romeo design engineer who also worked briefly for Ferrari, Maserati, and Bugatti, dies at age 84

1992 In a massive reorganization, General Motors establishes the North American Car Platforms Division headed by E. Michael Mutchler, the North American Truck Platforms Division headed by Clifford J. Vaughan, and the Vehicle Sales and Marketing Division headed by J. Michael Losh - in separate actions J. T. Battenberg III is named as head of component operations, and Jose Ignacio Lopez is named as head of worldwide parts purchasing

1995 The last Chevrolet Corvette ZR-1 is produced, although the "offical" ceremony would be staged four days later

1996 The Ellingson Car Museum opens in Rogers, MN

APRIL 25

1861 William Ford and Mary O'Hern Litogot, the parents of Henry Ford, are married in Detroit, MI

1874 Allen Blackwell Laing, a longtime automobile dealer who is credited with the development of antifreeze, is born in Plainfield, NJ

1881 Automobile parts manufacturer Charles Anderson Dana is born

1894 Donald P. Hess, an official of the Timken Roller Bearing Company and later President of the American Bosch Corporation, is born in Cleveland, OH

1901 New York state passes the first automobile licensing laws, requiring owners to pay a $1.00 registration fee and make their own plates

1913 Masaji Iwasawa of the Toyo Kogyo Company, Ltd., manufacturers of the Mazda, is born in Odate, Japan

1913 Automobile historian Allen Andrews is born in London, England

1917 Racer Jean Lucas is born in Le Mans, France

1922 A. B. C. Hardy is elected as a Vice President of General Motors

1925 Maserati's first car, the Tipo 26, makes its racing debut by winning its class in the Targa Florio with co-designer Alfieri Maserati at the wheel

1926 Racer Giulio Masetti is killed at age 30 when his Delage crashes in Madonie, Italy during the Targa Florio

1927 The first Dodge Convertible Cabriolet is produced

1928 Frank Lockhart, winner of the 1926 Indianapolis 500, is killed at age 25 in Daytona Beach, FL while attempting to raise the land speed record driving the Miller-powered 16-cylinder Black Hawk

1929 The Kelsey-Hayes Wheel Corporation is incorporated in New York

1938 Automotive ball bearing manufacturer Judd W. Spray dies at age 51

1940 The last Duesenberg J is completed and delivered to artist Rudolf Bauer

1941 Robert Henley Combs, President of the Prest-O-Lite Storage Battery Company of Canada Ltd., dies in Toronto, Ontario at age 65

1944 Owens-Corning Fiberglas of Toledo, OH begins construction of an experimental plastic-bodied automobile under the direction of Dr. R. Games Slayter, Walter F. Krause, and William B. Stout

1945 William H. Clark, an authority on automotive oil additives, dies at age 59

1957 Racer Cor Euser is born in Haarlem, the Netherlands

1959 Mario Andretti makes his racing debut, winning a race at the Nazareth (PA) Speedway driving his own 1948 Hudson

1962 Fred Frame, winner of the 1932 Indianapolis 500, dies at age 66

1965 Swiss racer Tommy Spychiger is killed at age 30 when his Ferrari crashes during a race at Monza, Italy

1967 John Wyer's Mirage, based on the Ford GT40, makes its racing debut in a 1000 km race at Monza, Italy, but the car is plagued with minor breakdowns as Ferrari captures the top two places

1967 The Kuhlman Electric Company is reorganized as the Kuhlman Corporation, manufacturers of automobile parts

1977 The International S-series trucks are introduced at the Superdome in New Orleans, LA

1984 The Austin Montego and badge-engineered M.G. Montego are introduced

1988 The Ford Motor Company completes the sale of its business interests in South Africa

1989 The Ford Motor Company stages a gala celebration to note the 25th anniversary of the Ford Mustang

1996 General Motors founder William C. Durant is posthumously inducted into the Business Hall of Fame

APRIL 26

1859 Samuel Holland, pioneer automobile manufacturer in Park River, ND, is born in Norway

1875 Thomas Lynch Raymond, a cofounder of the Kent Motors Corporation, is born in East Orange, NJ

1887 Danish automobile pioneer Albert Hammel receives patent for his internal combustion engine

1891 Paul Gray Hoffman of Studebaker is born in Chicago, IL

1893 Automobile aerodynamics pioneer Wunibald Kamm is born in Basel, Switzerland

1906 The George N. Pierce Company purchases a 16-acre plot that had been the site of the 1901 Pan-American Exposition for their new factory

1908 John Stephen Bugas of the Ford Motor Company is born in Rock Springs, WY

1917 Automotive historian Anthony Cobb Bird is born in London, England

1921 Racer Francois Picard is born in Villefranche-sur-Saone, France

1922 Automotive historian Robert F. Karolevitz is born in Yankton, SD

1937 Racer Jean-Pierre Maurice Georges Beltoise is born in Paris, France

1937 Racer Gus Hutchison is born in Atlanta, GA

1938 The Studebaker Corporation Board of Directors approves the development of a "new model passenger car in the low-price field" that would emerge as the 1939 Studebaker Champion

A 1939 Studebaker Champion sedan at the post office in Carpinteria, CA.

1944 Racer Jose Dolhem is born in Paris, France

1945 Racer Dick Johnson is born in Australia

1948 Frederick Cameron, the youngest of four Cameron brothers involved with the 1903-1920 Cameron as well as many others marques, dies at age 63

1953 Racer Pierre Gilbert Ugnon is killed during the annual Mille Miglia, won by Giannino Marzotto in a Ferrari

1954 Leroy V. Cram, a General Motors design engineer 1908-1949, dies at age 70

1955 Walter C. Baker, manufacturer of Baker Electric automobiles 1899-1916, dies in Cleveland, OH at age 86

Baker Electrics

1958 Racer Johnny Dumfries is born in Rothesay, Great Britain

1962 Studebaker-Packard Corporation's stockholders vote to drop "Packard" from the corporate title effective July 2

1965 The White Motor Company changes its name to the White Motor Corporation

1970 Chris Amon records his first Formula 1 victory at Silverstone, England

1973 The Ford Motor Company announces plans to build a factory in Spain

1983 The Honda Motor Company Ltd. dedicates their new Ohio assembly plant

APRIL 27

1888 Anglo American Oil Ltd. is registered in Great Britain - the firm would evolve into Esso UK PLC

1893 Norman Melancthon Bel Geddes, designer of the General Motors Futurama exhibit at the 1939-1940 New York World's Fair, is born in Adrian, MI

1899 Edwin Joel Thomas of the Goodyear Tire & Rubber Company is born in Akron, OH

1902 Racer Rudolf Schoeller is born in Switzerland

1907 The first production Chadwick is given its initial road test with company Sales Manager Harold B. Larzelere driving in the company of journalist "Hugh Dolnar"

1913 Frederick S. Duesenberg marries Isle Denny

1913 Automotive equipment manufacturer Lee Hunter is born in St. Louis, MO

1913 Ryoichi Nakagawa of the Nissan Motor Company, Ltd. is born

1915 William Frederick Burrows of the White Motor Company is born in Gates Mills, OH

1920 Tommy Milton, driving a 16-cylinder Duesenberg Special at Daytona Beach, FL, records a one-way run of 156.046 mph, a world record although not officially recognized as a new land speed record

1921 T. G. John Ltd. moves to larger premises in Coventry, England and changes its name to the Alvis Car and Engineering Company Ltd.

1924 The Targa Florio is won by Christian Werner in a Mercedes Type PP designed by Dr. Ferdinand Porsche, the first major racing victory for the marque with a supercharged car

1924 Richard R. Zimmer of Crane-Simplex dies at age 40

1926 J. G. Parry Thomas raises the land speed record to 169.238 mph at the Pendine Sands, Wales driving the V-12 400-hp Liberty-engined Thomas Special nicknamed "Babs"

1926 The Packard Motor Car Company is given trademark protection for its "Ask The Man Who Owns One" advertising slogan

1928 Designer Fritz von Opel takes his rocket-powered RAK 1 for its fourth test drive at Russelsheim, Germany, reaching 59 mph

1933 Racer Robert "Bob" Bondurant is born in Evanston, IL

1934 The 1,000,000th Nash is produced, a Series 1227 Town Sedan that was later presented to Dr. E. O. Nash (no relation) of Pueblo, CO, whose 1918 car was the oldest Nash still being used by its original owner

1934 Erwin Komenda completes drawings for the "Volkswagen Project, Porsche Type 60"

1939 Automotive steel manufacturer J. Albert Roesch Jr. dies in Pittsburgh, PA at age 57

1943 Racer Helmut Marko is born in Graz, Austria

1946 Racer Marc Sourd is born in France

1948 William S. Knudsen of the Ford Motor Company and General Motors dies in Detroit, MI at age 69

1951 The third-series Kaiser Dragon is introduced

1951 David Fergusson of Pierce-Arrow dies in Rochester, NY at age 81

1959 The Ford Motor Company announces that they will no longer abide by the Automobile Manufacturers Association (AMA) safety agreement and will market high-performance options

1964 Automobile stylist Alexis de Sakhnoffsky dies in Atlanta, GA at age 62

1966 Racer Marco Werner is born in West Germany

1973 Racer Carlos Menditeguy dies in Buenos Aires, Argentina at age 57

1974 Frost & French Inc. of Los Angeles, CA, the world's last Studebaker dealer, quits business eight years after last new Studebaker had been produced

1975 Lella Lombardi driving a March places 6th in the Spanish Grand Prix at Montjuich Park, becoming the first woman to earn world championship points in a Formula 1 race - the Hill GH1, based on the Lola T371 by designer Andy Smallman, makes its debut, but cars driven by Rolf Stommelen and Francois Migault fail to finish

1997 Heinz-Harald Frentzen records his first Formula 1 victory at the San Marino Grand Prix in Imola, Italy driving a Williams-Renault

APRIL 28

1876 Nicola Romeo is born in Sant'Antimo, Italy

1882 Tire manufacturer Alberto Pirelli is born in Milan, Italy

1887 Paul Faussier, President of the Sport Velocipedique Metropolitaine, stages the first automobile race in France, but the only entrant is Georges Bouton in a steam-powered DeDion, Bouton et Trepardoux quadricycle who averages 14 mph for the nearly 20-mile race in and around Paris

1900 Hendry Stuart Mackenzie Burns of the Shell Oil Company is born in Aberdeen, Scotland

1903 Ten automobile manufacturers, including Cadillac, Northern, Thomas, and Pope, join the Association of Licensed Automobile Manufacturers (ALAM) to comply with Selden Patent rights

1907 Stanley Harold "Wacky" Arnolt II is born in Indiana

1908 Ludwig "Louis" Kissel, father of the Kissel brothers and a manager at the Kissel Motor Car Company, dies in Milwaukee, WI at age 69 from a gunshot wound inflicted nine days earlier by an angry employee

1912 Pioneer automobile manufacturer Charles Abresch dies

1913 Automotive historian Ken William Purdy is born in Chicago, IL

1916 Ferruccio Lamborghini is born in Renazzo di Cento, Ferrara, Italy

1922 The Ford Motor Company begins manufacturing its own storage batteries

1926 J. G. Parry Thomas, driving the Thomas Special "Babs" at the Pendine Sands in Wales, raises the land speed record to 170.624 mph to break his own one-day-old record

1935 Pehr-Gustaf Gyllenhammar, Chairman of AB Volvo 1983-1990, is born in Goteborg, Sweden

1940 Alberto Ascari makes his automobile racing debut driving the new Ferrari 815 in the closed-circuit Mille Miglia

1940 Morgan J. Hammers, an associate of steam car designer Abner Doble, dies in Stamford, CT at age 65

1943 Norman Bell of the Norma-Hoffmann Bearings Corporation dies

1945 Ugo Gobbato of Alfa Romeo is killed at age 56 by the Italian Partigiani during a period of post-World War II anti-Fascist violence

1945 Thomas A. Weir, Vice Consul of the United States Consulate in the Canary Islands and a former executive with the Socony-Vacuum Oil Company, dies at age 45

1949 Dodge announces the pending introduction of the Wayfarer Roadster, the first post-World War II car to be built with that bodystyle

1950 James Douglas Muir "Jay" Leno, television personality and prominent car collector, is born in New Rochelle, NY

1953 The Kaiser Manufacturing Corporation, a subsidiary of the Kaiser-Frazer Corporation, purchases the Willys-Overland Company for $62,381,175 and centralizes all Kaiser and Willys production at the Willys factory in Toledo, OH

1958 The Ferrari Dino 156 makes its racing debut with Luigi Musso finishing third at the Naples (Italy) Grand Prix

1959 Piano manufacturer Gustav Heine, patron of the luxury Heine-Velox, dies in Sunol, CA at age 91

1960 William C. Newberg is elected President of the Chrysler Corporation

1973 Racer Piero Drogo dies in Bologna, Italy at age 46

1974 The Amon makes its only Formula 1 appearance in the Spanish Grand Prix at the Jarama circuit north of Madrid, but the car driven by Chris Amon retires with brake failure - the Trojan makes its debut with the Type T103 driven by Tim Schenken finishing in 14th place

1975 The last International light truck is built, a model 500 4x4 cab and chassis, ending 68 years of production of such vehicles

1995 Bowling Green (KY) Plant Manager Will Cooksey drives the last Chevrolet Corvette ZR-1 off the assembly line after a six-year run of 6,938 cars

APRIL 29

1865 Herman Joseph Jaeger, an inventor and manufacturer of automobile lights, is born in New York City

1870 The Atlantic Refining Company is incorporated in Pennsylvania

1894 Automobile radiator manufacturer Fred Matthew Young is born in Muskegon, MI

1898 The Goodyear Tire & Rubber Company is established in Akron, OH

1899 Camille Jenatzy, driving his Jenatzy electric *La Jamais Contente* at Acheres Park, France, becomes the first driver to break the 60 mph barrier in raising the land speed record to 65.79 mph - the metric equivalent for this run, 105.904 km/h, also marked the first time the 100 km/h barrier had been broken

1905 Otto E. Mears is elected President of the Mack Brothers Motor Car Company

1915 The Chevrolet Model 490 is introduced

1916 The Emerson Motors Company is incorporated in Delaware with Theodore A. Campbell as President, Robert C. Hupp as Vice President and Chief Engineer, and George N. Campbell as Treasurer to manufacturer automobiles designed by Col. Willis George Emerson

1922 Frank W. Edwards, Sales Engineer for the Delco Corporation, dies in Dayton, OH at age 41

1923 The first Salmson Grand Sport is completed and sold to dealers Ring & Hoffman of Strasbourg, Alsace, France

1925 The Standardised Closed Cab is introduced for the Ford Model TT truck chassis

Ford Motor Company

Detroit, Michigan

See the Nearest Authorized Ford Dealer

Ford

CARS · TRUCKS · TRACTORS

1931 Racer Larry J. Frank is born in Mountain City, TN

1933 August Horch is reinstated as Chief Executive Officer of A. Horch & Cie, Motorwagenwerke AG

1933 Frank Alfred McPherson of the Kerr-McGee Corporation is born in Stilwell, OK

1934 George Eyston, driving the Flying Spray at the Bonneville Salt Flats, UT, sets a land speed record for diesel-powered vehicles, covering the flying kilometer at 159.0004 mph

1937 Racer Hugh Palliser Kinglsey Dibley is born in Hong Kong where his father was serving in the Royal Navy

1939 The compact Crosley is introduced to the press and dealers by Powel Crosley Jr. at the Indianapolis (IN) Motor Speedway

1941 The 29,000,000th Ford is produced, a 1941 Super Deluxe Station Wagon that is presented to the American National Red Cross by Edsel B. Ford

1941 Racer Jerry Karl is born

1941 John G. Rumney, a designer and manufacturer of automobile springs, dies in Grosse Pointe, MI at age 90

1943 Raymond M. Owen, designer of the Owen 1899-1901 and the Owen Magnetic 1915-1921, and a pioneer Oldsmobile and Reo dealer during the interim, dies in Westport, CT at age 70

1951 Racer Ralph Dale Earnhardt is born in Kannapolis, NC

1955 The Socony-Vacuum Oil Company changes its name to the Socony Mobil Oil Company

1958 Chester G. Luby, a Chevrolet dealer in Forest Hills, NY, contracts to be sole distributor for 22 eastern states to become the first Datsun dealer in the United States

1959 The 50,000,000th Ford Motor Company vehicle, a 1959 Ford Galaxie Town Sedan, is produced at the Dearborn, MI plant

1959 William R. "Bill" Perkins of Sunbeam dies

1962 Racer Herman "The Turtle" Beam, known for driving in the slow lane but always finishing, records his best-ever finish - 6th, but 31 laps behind the winner - in the Volunteer 500

1962 Harry R. Fruehauf of the Fruehauf Trailer Company dies at age 65

1963 Racer Chad Little is born in Spokane, WA

1967 Earl A. Thompson, head of the General Motors design team that developed the Hydramatic transmission, dies in Bloomfield Hills, MI at age 75

CADILLAC-ENGINEERED
HYDRA-MATIC DRIVE
*OPTIONAL ON ALL MODELS AT EXTRA COST

AUTOMATIC GEARSHIFTING

NO CLUTCH PEDAL

1976 The Opel Isuzu manufactured in Tokyo, Japan by Isuzu Motors Ltd. for General Motors Europe, is introduced to the United States market by Buick dealers

1978 Racer Theo Helfrich dies at age 64

1982 Henry Ford II sells the Renaissance Center in Detroit, MI

1983 Lee Iacocca's attempt to revive the Imperial fails as the last of 12,285 "modern" Imperials rolls off the Windsor, ON, Canada assembly line

1994 Geoffrey Healey, son of Donald Healey and himself a respected automobile designer, dies at age 72

1996 Arthur Ross, retired Director of Dealer Relations for Volkswagen of America, dies in Middletown, NJ at age 75

APRIL 30

1894 Racer Leon Duray (nee George Gardener Stewart) is born in Cleveland, OH

1896 Diesel engine designer Hans List is born in Austria

1898 William H. Graves of Packard is born in Leslie, MI

1908 Automobile historian Sidney Olson is born in Salt Lake City, UT

1910 H. Kerr Thomas begins designing the Pierce-Arrow 5-ton truck

1911 Henry Kearns, a longtime Chevrolet dealer in Pasadena, CA, is born in Salt Lake City, UT

1915 The Shell Marketing Company Ltd. is registered in Great Britain

1920 The first Studebaker Light Six is produced

1920 Racer J. Duncan Hamilton is born in Cork, Ireland

1921 The Miller 183 8-cylinder engine makes its racing debut in a 150-mile race in Fresno, CA

1923 Ferdinand Porsche returns to the Osterreichisches Daimler Motoren AG in Wiener-Neustadt, Austria, manufacturers of the Austro-Daimler

1924 Racer Peter DePaolo records his first major victory, winning a 150-mile race at the Fresno (CA) board track

1925 Dodge Brothers, Inc. is sold to the New York City banking firm of Dillon, Read & Company for $146 million, the largest cash sale in United States history to date - E. J. Wilmer is appointed as President by the new owners

1937 Peter Walker sets the alltime lap record for the Campbell circuit at Brooklands, reaching 72.74 mph in his E.R.A.

1948 The Land Rover is introduced at the Amsterdam Auto Show

1949 Carl M. Breer retires from the Chrysler Corporation ending a 33-year career in automotive engineering

1958 Alvan T. Fuller, longtime Boston Packard dealer and Governor of Massachusetts 1925-1929, dies in Boston at age 80

1959 The Texas Company changes its name to Texaco, Inc.

1960 James C. Zeder retires as Vice President-Engineering for the Chrysler Corporation after 35 years with the company

1962 The 47,000,000th Chevrolet is produced

1963 John Dykstra retires as President of the Ford Motor Company

1963 Racer Michael Waltrip is born in Owensboro, KY

1973 Automobile stylists Raymond Loewy and Howard A. "Dutch" Darrin accept the first two honorary memberships in the Milestone Car Society

1975 The Ford Motor Company introduces the extra-heavy Transcontinental truck line

1978 The Mercedes-Benz C-111/3 research car sets nine world records for Diesel-engined cars, including 2,345 miles in 12 hours (an average of 195.39 mph)

1980 Mitsubishi purchases Chrysler Corporation's Australian facilities

1991 Charles F. Jones, President of the Humble Oil & Refining Company 1964-1970, dies at age 79

1994 Racer Roland Ratzenberger is killed at age 31 when his Simtek Ford crashes during practice at the Dino and Enzo Ferrari Autodrome in Imola, Italy, site of the next day's San Marino Grand Prix

1996 Ford historian and restoration authority Bob Zewalk dies

1996 Racer Scott Brayton donates a 1952 Cisitalia 202 Gran Sport convertible to the Auburn-Cord-Duesenberg Museum in Auburn, IN

MAY 1

1873 Eugen Benz, elder son of Carl Benz, is born

1878 Walter Clark Teagle of the Standard Oil Company of New Jersey is born in Cleveland, OH

1879 Everit Jay Sadler of the Standard Oil Company of New Jersey is born in Brockport, NY

1880 The B. F. Goodrich Company is organized in Ohio

1883 Count Albert de Dion receives a patent for a steam generator, the first of 394 patents issued to him or to his company

1890 Max Kaspar Rose and Friedrich Wilhelm Esslinger withdraw from Benz & Cie because of disagreements with Carl Benz regarding his efforts toward automobile manufacturing - Friedrich von Fischer and Julius Ganss soon join the Benz firm in their place

1892 Harold T. Youngren, a design engineer with Oakland, Studebaker, Buick, Pierce-Arrow, and Oldsmobile who ended his long career as Vice President of Engineering for the Ford Motor Company 1946-1952, is born in Oakland, CA

1893 The Daimler exhibit opens at the Columbian Exposition in Chicago, IL

1898 Automobile racing's first fatalities are recorded during a 90-mile race in Perigueux, France when the Benz Parisienne of M. de Montariol and the Landrey-et-Beyroux of the Marquis de Montaignac are involved in a crash - the Marquis and both riding mechanics are killed

1901 The first Pierce Motorette is completed

1901 The world's first postage stamp picturing an automobile is issued in Buffalo, NY by the United States Post Office Department as part of the Pan-American commemorative series - the vignette of the 4c stamp is unidentified, but is now generally identified as an 1899 Columbia electric

1902 The first prototype gasoline-powered Locomobile is completed

1905 Vermont issues the state's first automobile license to Charles C. Warren of Waterbury for his Packard

1912 Winthrop Rockefeller, Governor of Arkansas 1967-1970 and an antique car collector who founded the Museum of Automobiles in Morrilton, AR, is born in New York City

1914 A. H. M. J. Ward, an electrical engineer and brother-in-law of W. O. and H. M. Bentley, joins the board of Bentley and Bentley Ltd.

1914 The Knox Automobile Company is sold in a bankruptcy auction to Edward O. Sutton, who reorganizes the firm as the Knox Motors Company

1915 Ford begins the practice of using identical car numbers and engine numbers on its Model T assembly line

1915 The Packard Twin Six is introduced

1916 The Sterling-New York, a low-priced roadster designed by Joseph A. Anglada, is introduced

1917 The first Nelson is completed

1917 The Wisconsin Duplex Auto Company is formed in Clintonville, WI by William A. Besserdich and Bernhard A. Mosling - the firm would evolve into the Oshkosh Truck Corporation, builders of specialty trucks with all-wheel drive

1918 Automotive parts manufacturer Walter James Turner is born in Vanderbilt, MI

1919 Harry H. Bassett is named General Manager of Buick

1923 Newton E. Van Zandt of ReVere dies in New York City

1924 The Federal-Mogul Corporation is incorporated in Michigan as a merger of the Muzzy-Lyon Company and the Federal Bearing & Bushing Corporation

1925 Lawrence P. Fisher is named President of Cadillac

1925 Ettore Bugatti registers the slogan "Le pur sang des Automobiles" and the thoroughbred horse profile as French trademarks

1925 The Nash Motors Company introduces the Ajax as a new marque, and the first United States car priced under $1,000 with four-wheel brakes

1926 The Ajax marque is dropped by the Nash Motors Company, with the car continuing as the Nash Light Six (Series 220)

1926 The Atlantic City Board Speedway in Amatol, NJ stages its first event, a 300-mile race won by Harry Hartz in a Miller

1927 Charles L. Sheppy, Chief Engineer of the Pierce-Arrow Motor Car Company, dies in Summerville, SC at age 55

1928 Racer Desmond Titterington is born in Cultra, Down, Northern Ireland

1931 The Ford Model A Deluxe Pickup is introduced - production would end in September after just 293 units had been manufactured

1932 Automobile historian James John Flink is born in Joliet, IL

1933 The Marmon Motor Car Company is declared bankrupt

1935 The 1935 Chrysler DeLuxe Airstream is introduced as a mid-year model

1935 J. E. Crane joins the Standard Oil Company of New Jersey as Assistant Treasurer

1936 The first Cord 810 Phaetons are shipped to dealers

1938 The Hudson 112 DeLuxe is introduced as an extra trim version of the now "standard" Hudson 112 introduced at the beginning of the model year

1939 The 6,000,000th Ford V-8 is produced

1946 The first post-World War II Chevrolet truck with chrome trim is produced, reflecting the easing of wartime restrictions

1947 The Advance Design Chevrolet trucks are introduced, the first built with post-World War II styling features

1950 The Chrysler Imperial is announced as a mid-year model to supplement the long-wheelbase Crown Imperial line

1951 Cadillac discontinues its low-priced Series 61, which had replaced the LaSalle in 1941

1951 Racer Geoff Lees is born in Atherstone, Great Britain

1952 James J. Nance becomes President and General Manager of the Packard Motor Car Company and is elected to the Board of Directors replacing Henry C. Bogle - Hugh J. Ferry is elected Chairman of the Board

1952 Earle S. MacPherson is named Vice President in charge of engineering for the Ford Motor Company, succeeding the retiring Harold T. Youngren

1952 Hugh Dean, Vice President of General Motors and a former executive with the Chevrolet division, retires after 37 years with the company

1953 Zora Arkus-Duntov is hired by Chevrolet Chief Engineer Edward N. Cole to be the first Chief Engineer for the new Corvette sports car

1954 The Nash-Kelvinator Corporation and the Hudson Motor Car Company officially merge to form the American Motors Corporation with George W. Mason as Chairman and President - Hudson President A. E. Barit retires

1954 Royce G. Martin, President and Chairman of the Board of the Electric Autolite Company, dies in Lexington, KY at age 69

1955 Stirling Moss, driving a Mercedes-Benz 300SLR with navigator Denis Jenkinson, wins the Mille Miglia and sets the alltime speed record for the event

1955 Arthur G. Phelps, Executive Assistant to the General Manager of the Delco-Remy Division of General Motors and an employee of the division for 43 years, dies at age 63

1955 Arthur B. Schultz, Senior Mechanical Engineer since 1951 with the Argonne National Laboratory who previously had held engineering positions with Ford, Pontiac, and Packard, dies

1955 Leigh R. Evans, design engineer with Thomas and Franklin, Chief Engineer for the Canadian-built Russell, and later an official in the automobile parts industry, dies at age 71

1955 Racer Mike Nazaruk is killed at age 33 when he crashes during a race in Langhorne, PA

1957 Automatic transmission becomes available in Ford trucks

1958 The Chrysler Corporation choses an in-line six cylinder design for the engine of its new compact car currently under development

1963 Arjay R. Miller is named President of the Ford Motor Company

1964 Race Paolo delle Piane is born in Bologna, Italy

1967 John Wyer's Mirage wins its first race, with Jacky Ickx and Dick Thompson outrunning the Ferrari P4 of Ludovico Scarfiotti and Mike Parkes to win the 1000 km Grand Prix de Francorchamps in Spa, Belgium

1968 The International R series truck line is discontinued after 18 years of production - also deleted from the lineup was the V series that had been introduced in 1956 with the marque's first gasoline V-8 engines

1969 John B. Beltz is elected General Manager of Oldsmobile and Howard H. Kehrl is named Chief Engineer, replacing Beltz in that position

1975 Cadillac introduces the 1975 1/2 Seville, a "small" four-door sedan based on the Chevrolet Nova platform

1976 The Phantom III Technical Society, an affiliate of the Rolls-Royce Owners' Club, holds first meeting

1978 Claudio Ferrari, President and Chief Executive Officer of Fiat Motors of North America, Inc., announces the appointment of automobile journalist Karl E. Ludvigsen as Vice President for Corporate Relations

1980 Stephen P. Malone retires as Chief Engineer of Pontiac, with former Cadillac chief body engineer Robert L. Dorn named to replace him

1984 The Toyo Kogyo Company, Ltd. changes its name to the Mazda Motor Corporation

1985 The Musee de l'Anthologie Automobile relocates to Reims, France

1987 Mitsubishi Motors Corporation acquires Todd Motors Corporation Ltd. of New Zealand, later renamed Mitsubishi Motors New Zealand Ltd.

1988 The Dallara makes its Formula 1 debut at the San Marino Grand Prix in Imola, Italy, but the Type F188 financed by Gianpaolo Dallara, designed by Sergio Rinland, and driven by Alex Caffi retires with gearbox problems

1989 Bob Burger retires as General Manager of Chevrolet - Jim Perkins of Lexus is hired as his replacement

1991 Kenneth C. Merrill retires as President of the Ford Motor Credit Company

1994 Racer Ayrton Senna is killed at age 32 when his Williams crashes during the San Marino Grand Prix at the Dino and Enzo Ferrari Autodrome in Imola, Italy

1994 The Ford Motor Company names William Clay Ford Jr. as Vice President - Commercial Truck Vehicle Center

MAY 2

1882 James Dinsmore Tew of the B. F. Goodrich Tire & Rubber Company is born in Jamestown, NY

1883 Racer Alessandro Cagno is born in Turin, Italy

1883 Harold F. Sheets of the Socony-Vacuum Oil Company in born in Rochelle, IL

1894 R. S. Burgin, a design engineer and member of the surveying crew for the original Lincoln Highway, is born in Old Fort, NC

*Cars from Ohio, New York, Pennsylvania, and Indiana gather on July 16, 1916
"in the sagebrush 100 miles east of Rock Springs, WY" with no road in sight.*

*The scene below showing the Lincoln Highway entering Fort Lupton, CO dates
from only about five years later than the above, and clearly shows the importance
of good roads to the automobile movement.*

1895 Eugene Holman of the Standard Oil Company of New Jersey is born in San Angelo, TX

1904 Norval Hawkins conducts his first audit of the Ford Motor Company, an event that would lead to a position as General Sales Manager of the firm during a period when it rose to dominance in the automobile industry

1912 The B. F. Goodrich Tire & Rubber Company is reorganized in New York, succeeding the original company organized in Ohio in 1880

1918 The General Motors Corporation acquires the Chevrolet Motor Company of Delaware in what was in effect a merger paving the way for William C. Durant to regain control of General Motors

1923 The first Triumph is completed

1925 The Rolls-Royce New Phantom, later called the Phantom I, is introduced

1930 Construction begins on the Gor'kiy Automobile Plant in Nizhni Novgorod (now Gor'kiy), Russia, USSR

1932 Elmer William Johnson of General Motors is born in Denver, CO

1932 The Continental-Divco Company is incorporated in Michigan to manufacture commercial motor vehicles

1936 Brewster & Company conducts the second of two clearance sales to dispose of excess inventory in an attempt to remain solvent

1937 C. N. Teetor, founder of the Teetor-Hartley Motor Company who designed the first enbloc 4-cylinder engine in 1909 and later founded the Perfect Circle Company, manufacturers of piston rings, dies in Hagerstown, IN at age 66

1938 Neil Allen Springer of the International Harvester Company is born in Fort Wayne, IN

1939 Automobile parts engineer Clifford L. Snyder dies at age 47

1941 Racer Tony Adamowicz is born in Torrance, CA

1946 Racer Dany Snobeck is born in France

1948 Wilhelm von Opel dies in Wiesbaden, Germany at age 76

1949 The 1949 Packard Twenty-Third Series is introduced

1952 Herb Thomas, Al Keller, Dick Rathman, Joe Eubanks, and Paul Pettit, all driving Hudson Hornets, sweep the first five places in a 150-mile NASCAR race in Langhorne, PA

1952 The Mercedes-Benz 300SL make its racing debut at the Mille Miglia

1955 George W. Walker is appointed Vice President in charge of styling for the Ford Motor Company

1956 Racer Robb Gravett is born in London, England

1959 The Aston Martin DBR4/250 makes its debut at the BRDC International Trophy race in Silverstone, England, with the car driven by Roy Salvadori finishing second behind the Cooper-Climax of Jack Brabham

1961 Henry John Kaiser Jr., Vice President of the Kaiser Industries Corporation, dies in Oakland, CA at age 44

1963 The Fruehauf Trailer Company changes its name to the Fruehauf Corporation

1971 Racer Buzz Calkins is born in Denver, CO

1972 Buddy Baker becomes the first driver to finish a 500-mile race in less than three hours, winning the NASCAR-sponsored Winston Select 500 at the Alabama International Motor Speedway in Talladega

1977 Edward N. Cole, Chairman of the Checker Motors Corporation and President and Chief Operating Officer of General Motors 1967-1974, is killed in an airplane crash near Mendon, MI at age 67

1986 Finnish racer Henri Toivonen, age 29, and his United States-born navigator Sergio Cresto, age 30, are killed when their Lancia Delta 54 crashes near Corte, Corsica, France during a rally

MAY 3

1884 Dean Milton Gillespie of the White Motor Company is born in Salina, KS

1889 Alvin G. Tanner of the Socony-Vacuum Oil Company is born in Pittsfield, MA

1890 Alonzo William Peake of the Standard Oil Company is born in Kansas City, MO

1904 New York requires the state's abbreviation to be included on automobile license plates

1909 The Ayres Gasoline Engine & Automobile Works of Rochester, MI files for dissolution, having ceased production of the Ayres in 1905

1912 Albert M. Wibel joins the Ford Motor Compay

1933 Sir Judson Graham Day of British Leyland Motor Corporation Ltd. and the Rover Group PLC is born in Canada

1936 Ludvik Frank Koci of General Motors is born in Chicago, IL

1937 Lammot DuPont retires as Chairman of General Motors and is succeeded by Alfred P. Sloan Jr. - Sloan is succeeded as President by William S. Knudsen

1940 Ford offers two-tone paint schemes as an option

1940 Racer Jean-Pierre Paoli is born in France

1941 The second experimental Highway Post Office begins service between South Bend, Peru, and Indianapolis, IN using an International Model KD-8-F-COE tractor-trailer rig - this vehicle was soon rejected primarily due to the inability of the postal clerks in the trailer to communicate with the driver

1942 The speed limit in United States is reduced to 40 mph to conserve fuel

1943 Race car designer Harry A. Miller dies in Detroit, MI at age 67

1945 The 31,000,000th Ford is produced, a Model 59C half-ton pickup truck

1948 George W. Davis, President of the George W. Davis Motor Car Company 1908-1928, dies in Richmond, IN at age 80

1949 Racer Boy Hayje is born in Amsterdam, the Netherlands

1951 The first sketch of 1953 Buick Skylark is developed

1953 Bill Stroppe wins the first Phoenix (AZ) National Road Race driving a Mercury-powered Kurtis 500-S

1954 Buick produces it 2,000,000th Dynaflow transmission

1956 Victor A. Wegner, an automotive sales engineer with the Gulf Oil Company 1933-1956, dies

1956 Racer Ed Pimm is born in the United States

1966 The Atlantic Refining Company and Richfield Oil Corporation merge as the Atlantic Richfield Company

1967 The 70,000,000th United States-built Ford Motor Company vehicle is produced

1967 Racer Heinz-Harald Frentzen is born in Munich, West Germany

1968 Van Doorne Automobielfabrik NV, manufacturers of the Daf, dedicate their new factory in Born, Limburg, the Netherlands

1969 Harold L. Hamilton of General Motors dies at age 78

1987 Davey Allison records his first NASCAR victory, winning the Winston 500 in Talladega, AL driving a Ford Thunderbird

1988 Automotive historian Andrew Whyte dies

1992 Sidney J. Reso of the Exxon Corporation dies at age 57

1993 Jerome B. York, Chrysler Corporation Executive Vice President, resigns to join International Business Machines (IBM)

MAY 4

1880 Harry W. Ford, first President of Saxon, is born in Knob Knoster, MO

1897 Alexander Winton is issued a United States patent for his "Explosive Engine"

1898 Bruce K. Brown of the Standard Oil Company of Indiana is born in Columbus, OH

1899 Fritz von Opel, grandson of company founder Adam von Opel, is born in Russelsheim, Germany

1904 The Prvni Ceskomoravska Tovarna na Stroje v Praze (First Czecho-Moravian Machinery Factory) Board of Directors approve a feasibility study to consider the production of automobiles, resulting in the birth of the Praga marque

1904 F. H. Royce and Hon. C. S. Rolls meet for the first time at the Midland Hotel in Manchester, England - the encounter had been arranged after some difficulty by Henry Edmunds and would lead to the formation of Rolls-Royce, Ltd. (See Postscript to the Introduction)

1905 Tennessee requires registration of all automobiles with the Secretary of State

1905 The Paris, France coachbuilding firm of Letourneur & Marchand receives its first order

1912 Race car mechanic Takeo "Chick" Hirashima is born in Glendale, CA

1920 Harry A. Miller is issued a United States patent for a race car incorporating many features later copied by other manufacturers

1928 Formula 1 racer Count Wolfgang Graf Berghe von Trips is born in a 50-room castle in Horrem, near Cologne, Germany

1928 The last Salmson GSC is sold

1930 Theodore N. Louckes of Oldsmobile is born in Lansing, MI

1931 Ford-Werke AG transfers its operations from Berlin to its new plant in in Cologne, Germany with a Model AA truck as the first vehicle produced

1940 Racer Peter Holden Gregg is born in New York City

1940 Charles Yale Knight, inventor of the sleeve-valve engine, dies in Mendocino, CA

1946 Racer John Watson is born in Belfast, Northern Ireland

1948 Racer Hurley Haywood is born in Chicago, IL

1953 Edgar F. Kaiser is elected President of Willys Motors Inc.

1954 The General Motors Board of Directors authorizes the development of an ultra-luxury car, the Cadillac Eldorado Brougham, under the direction of stylist Ed Glowacke and engineer Fred Arnold

1954 Lehman Brothers issues a report *Suggested Basis of Consolidation*, detailing Packard's possible purchase of Studebaker

1956 B. W. Cooke, founder in 1921 and President of the Cooke Auto School and President 1931-1940 of the Motor Institute of America, dies

1959 The first Austin Mini is produced

1963 Herbert R. Straight of the Cities Service Oil Company dies at age 88

1966 Vittorio Valletta of Fiat signs a contract with Soviet Minister of Automobile Production Aleksandr N. Tarasov to construct a factory in the USSR

1974 The Ford Motor Company exhibit opens at Expo '74 in Spokane, WA

1979 A prototype 1979 Packard is introduced at the All Packard Invitational Meet in Perrysburg, OH - the car, a heavily reworked 1979 Cadillac Coupe deVille, was designed by Bud Bayliff and Dale Shellenbarger

1980 Didier Pironi records his first Grand Prix victory, winning the Belgian Grand Prix at Zolder

MAY 5

1874 Oil producer Earle Westwood Sinclair is born in Wheeling, WV

1884 Christian Fred Sauereisen, inventor of spark plug improvements, is born in Pittsburgh, PA

1892 Spencer Drummond Hopkins of General Motors is born in Onancock, VA

1902 Charles Schmidt is given full charge of the Packard shops

1909 Richard Lester Johnson of the Ford Motor Company is born in Walshville, IL

1910 The DeWitt Motor Car Company factory in North Manchester, IN is destroyed by fire

1912 John Emmett Judge of the Ford Motor Company is born in Grafton, ND

1913 Racer Duane Carter Sr. is born in Fresno, CA

1915 Cannon Ball Baker begins his record-setting trans-United States trip in San Diego, CA driving a Stutz

1927 The Graham Brothers Company, manufacturers of motor trucks, purchases the Paige-Detroit Motor Car Company from Harry M. Jewett, reorganizing as the Graham-Paige Motors Corporation

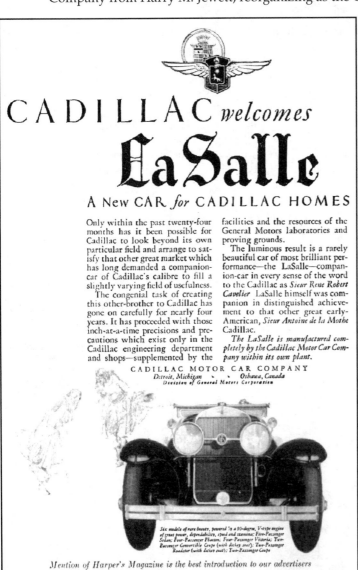

1927 The LaSalle is introduced as a companion marque of the Cadillac

1927 Racer Art Pollard is born

1932 Racer Boris "Bob" Said is born in New York City of Syrian-Russian parents

1932 Automotive historian Bareld Harmannus "Bart H." Vanderveen is born in Assen, the Netherlands

1938 The 5,000,000th Ford V-8 is produced

1940 The last Gran Premio di Tripoli (Libya) is won by Giuseppe "Nino" Farina driving an Alfa Romeo

1944 Racer Dave McMillen is born in New Zealand

1944 Berta Benz, wife of Carl Benz and an important associate in his early work, dies

1945 Rene Lalique, an artist noted for his custom glass automobile radiator mascots, dies in Paris, France at age 85

1948 Albert S. Matthews, President of the Packard Federal Corporation, the distributors of the marque's taxicabs, dies in New York City at age 67

24-hour Service   Anywhere

Any Place   Any Time
NEXT TIME CALL CITY CAB
Phone 1316
CITY CAB and BUS CO.
Busses For Charter   Custom Built Cabs
214 Sixth   Bismarck

*One of the clients of Packard's short-lived taxicab business was the
City Cab and Bus Company of Bismarck, ND.*

1957 Nino Vaccarella makes his racing debut, placing eighth in an Italian hillclimb in a Lancia 2500

1958 The first 1958 Ford Thunderbird convertible is produced

1958 Arman J. Kearfott, a research engineer with General Motors since 1920, dies at age 62

1959 Arthur S. Randak of the Sinclair Refining Company dies at age 46

1960 Harvey S. Firestone III, heir to the Firestone tire fortune, dies in Havana, Cuba at age 30

1965 Racer Glenn Seton is born in Australia, the son of racer Barry Seton

1978 The first national meeting of the Marmon Club opens in Thomasville, GA

1982 BL Cars, Ltd. reintroduces the M.G. marque as a non-sporting variant of its Metro

1984 Race car sponsor "J.C." Agajanian dies in Los Angeles, CA at age 70

1991 Richard A. Teague, automobile stylist and collector of antique cars, dies in Fallbrook, CA at age 67

MAY 6

1865 John Walter Christie, designer of front-wheel-drive race cars, is born in Old Bridge (now River Edge), NJ

1882 Publisher William Edmund Scripps, a cofounder and first President of the Scripps-Booth Company, is born in Detroit, MI

1885 Fred Rockelman of Ford, Plymouth, and Tucker, is born in Detroit, MI

1885 Reinier Gerrit Anton van der Woude of the Shell Union Oil Company is born in Amsterdam, the Netherlands

1886 Power brakes pioneer Robert Potter Breeze is born in New York City

1889 The Benz automobile is exhibited at Paris (France) World's Fair

1891 William Vernon Chickering Ruxton, the New York City stockbroker who was the namesake of the front-wheel-drive 1929 Ruxton, is born in Milton, MA

1905 Racer Rene Dreyfus is in Nice, France

1909 The Belmont Automobile Manufacturing Company is organized in New Rochelle, NY

1910 Elmer W. Bernitt of American Motors is born in Detroit, MI

1910 Groundbreaking ceremonies are held for the new Lozier Motor Company factory in Detroit, MI

1913 Vanden Plas (England) Ltd. is formed by a merger of the firm founded two months earlier and the parent Theo Masui Ltd. organization

1919 Racer Andre Guelfi is born in France

1923 The first Circuit of Mantua (Italy) race is won by Antonio Ascari in an Alfa Romeo RLTF

1925 Donald Frederick McCullough, a manufacturer of textiles for automobile interiors, is born in Montclair, NJ

1928 The DeSoto is introduced as a new marque from the Chrysler Corporation

1930 The last of 32,642 Dodge Senior Sixes is produced

1933 Richard L. Strombotne of the National Highway Traffic Safety Administration is born in Watertown, SD

1935 Achille Varzi wins the Tunis Grand Prix in Carthage, Tunisia, his first race with the Auto Union team

1939 The Maserati 4CL race car debuts in the Brooklands International Trophy dash as the entry of private owner Reggie Tongue, finishing third

1941 Victor Lee Emerson, the inventor of bevel-gear drive and the universal joint, dies in Philadelphia, PA at age 78

1941 Diesel engine authority Charles B. Jahnke dies in Mount Vernon, OH at age 54

1941 Racer Peter Gaydon is born in Great Britain

1958 Racer Tommy Byrne is born in Drogheda, Ireland

1961 Vanwall makes its final racing appearance, as John Surtees finishes fifth at the Intercontinental Formula International Trophy race in Silverstone, England in the unique rear-engined VW14, known as "The Whale"

1962 Racer Mike Cope is born

1964 Racer Andrea Chiesa is born in Milan, Italy of Swiss ancestry

1972 Henri Pescarolo, driving a Matra-Simca MS670 Group 5 at the 8.76-mile Spa-Francorchamps circuit in Belgium, sets a road circuit lap record by averaging 163.086 mph

1977 Volvo and Saab announce plans to merge

1984 Lloyd Van Horn opens Van Horn's Truck Museum near Mason City, IA

1991 Harry Gant, age 51, wins the Winston 500 in Talladega, AL to extend his own record as the oldest winner of a NASCAR race

1993 Gary C. Valade is named Executive Vice President of the Chrysler Corporation, replacing Jerome B. York

MAY 7

1868 British statesman and jurist Henry Peter Brougham, Baron Brougham and Vaux, dies in Cannes, France at age 89 - his name became synonymous with the closed carriages that he preferred and is perpetuated as a type of formal automobile body style

1877 Truck manufacturer Harry Holman Linn (nee Flannery), founder of the Linn Manufacturing Company, is born in Washburn, ME

1912 Sir Anthony Reay Mackay Geddes of the Dunlop Rubber Company Ltd. is born

1915 Isaac B. Trumbull, President of Trumbull Motor Car Company, is among the victims of the sinking of the SS Lusitania

1917 Samuel L. Smith, principal financial backer of the Olds Motor Works, dies at age 86

The OLDSMOBILE
"The Best Thing on Wheels"
The OLDSMOBILE is the cheapest reliable automobile in the world as well as the most economical in operation. Its premier position has been won by inventive genius and is maintained by progressive methods of manufacture.
Price $650.
Write for Illustrated Book to Dept. 21.
OLDS MOTOR WORKS. - DETROIT, MICH.
Factories: DETROIT and LANSING.

1927 The first DKW production automobile is completed

1932 Bo Rydin of Volvo is born

1937 Professor Wunibald Kamm introduces his first "K-Car" in Munich, Germany, incorporating many of his theories on automobile streamlining

1938 Tom Murray Jamieson, designer of the E.R.A. racing car, is killed at Brooklands when A. C. Lace's Darracq crashes through the railing

1939 The Mercedes-Benz W165 makes its racing debut, with Hermann Lang and Rudolf Caracciola taking the top two places in the Tripoli Grand Prix

1946 Automobile safety expert David Charles Viano is born in San Mateo, CA

1947 Prominent highway engineer Thomas R. Agg dies at age 68

1950 The first Heart Trophy Race is held at the Suffolk County (NY) Airport and won by Brett Hannaway in an M.G. TC

1952 James J. Nance resigns his position at Hotpoint to become President and General Manager of the Packard Motor Car Company

1952 Racer Stanley Dickens is born in Farila, Sweden

1953 The Ford Archives is dedicated at Fair Lane, the Dearborn, MI home of the late Henry Ford

1958 Sam Hanks is named Racing Director for the Indianapolis Motor Speedway Company

1959 Walter E. Titchener, Vice President and Factory Manager of the Hackney Brothers Body Company, dies at age 65

1967 Don Prudhomme, driving a modified Ford, becomes the first dragster to break the seven-second barrier for the quarter-mile, reaching 226 mph during the National Hot Rod Association (NHRA) World Series in Carlsbad, CA

1968 Racer Mike Spence is killed at age 31 when his Lotus crashes during a practice run at the Indianapolis Motor Speedway

1979 Stylists complete the full-sized clay model of the Pontiac Fiero

1989 Prominent classic car collector Mills B. Lane Jr. dies in Savannah, GA at age 76

MAY 8

1786 Thomas Hancock, the father of the indiarubber industry in Great Britain and a contemporary rival of Charles Goodyear in the United States, is born in Marlborough, Wiltshire, England

1879 George B. Selden applies for a patent for his automobile - unproven, unbuilt, and generally known to be unworkable, this patent nevertheless dominated the United States automobile industry until Henry Ford's legal challenge ended successfully in 1911

1880 Georges Charles Sizaire is born in Paris, France

1892 Howard Woodworth Simpson, a designer of automobile transmissions, is born in Kalmazoo, MI

1899 The Olds Motor Works is incorporated for $500,000, acquiring the assets of the Olds Motor Vehicle Company and the Olds Gasoline Engine Works with Samuel L. Smith as President, Ransom E. Olds as Vice President and General Manager, and Frederick L. Smith as Secretary and Treasurer

1903 Clement Ader applies for a patent for his V-6 and V-8 automobile engines

1907 J. Dallas Dort marries Marcia Webb

1916 The first Stephens is completed by the Stephens Motor Car Company, a subsidiary of the Moline Plow Company, Freeport, IL that manufactured cars until 1924

1921 David H. Spiller of Echlin Inc. is born in Chicago, IL

1924 Racer Abram Joseph "A. J." Watson is born in Mansfield, OH

1931 The Ford Model AA Type 239-A Packers' Express is introduced

1931 Frederick Van Z. Lane, Chief Transport Engineer with the Packard Motor Car Company who later worked as an independent consultant, dies in New York City at age 50

1932 Donald Lewis Stivender of General Motors is born in Chicago, IL

1939 Packard completes its famous production line bridge over Grand Avenue at its factory in Detroit, MI

1940 William R. Mitchell, Executive Vice President of the National Acme Company and an employee of that firm for 42 years, dies in Cleveland Heights, OH at age 62

1948 Dr. Frank O. Clements, former Director of the General Motors Research Corporation, dies in Columbus, OH at age 73

1955 Dr. Gustav Egloff, Director of Reearch for the Universal Oil Products Company, dies

1955 Dr. Charles R. Short, General Motors research engineer for 35 years, bank president, and inventor holding 388 patents, dies

1956 Henry Ford II retires as Chairman of the Ford Foundation

1956 The Curtiss-Wright Corporation offers a "Joint Program" to the directors of the Studebaker-Packard Corporation

1957 The last of 2,996 Lincoln Continental Mark II's is produced

1957 The Shell Refining and Marketing Company Ltd. changes its name to the Shell Refining Company Ltd.

1958 Norman Bel Geddes, designer of the General Motors Futurama at the 1939-1940 New York World's Fair, dies in New York City at age 65

1958 John Robert Fish, research engineer and President of the Fish Carburetor Corporation since 1946, dies at age 63

1959 Charles E. Hering of the White Motor Company dies at age 47

1964 Racer Bobby Labonte is born in Corpus Christi, TX

1966 Harry J. Seaman, developer of improved roadbuilding techniques, dies in Milwaukee, WI at age 67

1966 Carl Duerr of Jensen resigns due to policy differences with new owner Kjell Qvale

1982 Racer Gilles Villeneuve dies in Leuven, Belgium at age 32 from injuries caused when his Ferrari 126C2 crashed during a practice run for the Belgian Grand Prix at Zolder

1984 Nudie Cohn, an automobile customizer known for restyling with a western motif, dies in North Hollywood, CA at age 81

1996 Race car designer Brian Lovell dies at age 68

MAY 9

1850 Clark Sintz, manufacturer of the Sintz 2-cylinder high-wheeler 1902-1904, is born in Clark County, OH - although just six Sintz cars were built, the engine design was utilized by the first Pungs-Finch in 1904

1876 Nikolaus A. Otto tests his four-stroke internal combustion engine for the first time

1879 Felix Benneteau-Desgrois, a sculptor and designer of automobile mascots, is born in Paris, France

1882 Henry John Kaiser is born in Sprout Brook, NY

LaSalle Avenue in Barron, WI circa 1949. The slab-sided sedan parked at far left is a 1947 Kaiser.

1892 Warren Lowe Baker of the Socony-Vacuum Oil Company is born in Washington, DC

1896 Manuel Gregorio Escobedo, a Director of the General Motors Acceptance Corporation de Mexico, is born in Zacatecas, Zacatecas, Mexico

1896 The International Horseless Carriage Exhibition, the first motor show to be staged by the manufacturers themselves, opens in London, England with ten exhibitors

1906 The first Targo Florio, a 276.8-mile race staged in Sicily, is won by Alessandro Cagno in an Itala

1907 George Frederick Kachlein Jr. of the American Automobile Association is born in Tacoma, WA

1907 Nova Scotia issues the province's first automobile license plate to W. M. Black of Wolfville

1909 The Fleetwood Metal Body Company is incorporated with Harold C. Urich as President, Nicholas J. Kutz as Secretary, and Alfred Schlegel as Treasurer

1909 Daniel Marmon dies in Indianapolis, IN at age 65

1922 Wallace Winfield Edwards of GMC is born in Pontiac, MI

1928 Packard begins the development of a speedster - the building of two prototypes are authorized using Series 526 roadster bodies on a modified chassis

1928 The Borg-Warner Corporation is organized in Illinois through the merger of the Borg & Beck Company, the Marvel Carburetor Company, and the Warner Gear Company

1932 David Arnold Stuart Plastow of Rolls-Royce is born in Grimsby, Lindsey, Lincolnshire, England

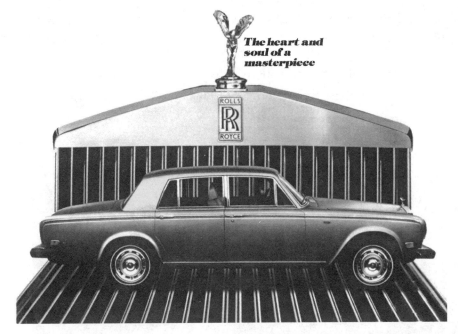

The heart and soul of a masterpiece

Sir David Plastow led Rolls-Royce from its financial debacle of 1971 through its separation from the aero division, and continued on after merging with Vickers in 1980.

This 1977 Silver Shadow II bridged the transition from Silver Shadow to Silver Spirit.

1933 The 1933 LaSalle "Stylized Bird" mascot is patented by designer Thomas L. Hibbard

1934 Frederick A. Leisen of LeBaron Inc. is issued a United States patent for his "Ring of Fire" mascot

1935 The Duesenberg Motor Company announces that production of the Model J is over after having " delivered 428 new cars with a remaining 22 cars as cars unsold or chassis"

1941 Walter S. Cochrane, a design engineer with Buick 1913-1926 and a diesel engine designer with the Chrysler Corporation since 1926, dies in Detroit, MI at age 55

1947 Racer Andy Sutcliffe is born in Mildenhall, Suffolk, England

1948 Stirling Moss makes his racing debut driving his 500-cc Cooper in a hillclimb at Prescott, England sponsored by the Bugatti Owners' Club

1949 Racer Carlo Felice Trossi dies in Milan, Italy from cancer at age 40

1960 The sale of Volkswagenwerk AG stock to the public is authorized, ending eleven years of ownership by the West German government

1960 The last Volvo PV445 chassis is produced

1962 The Ford Motor Company initiates a formal program to develop a small, sporty type car - the final result would be the 1964 1/2 Mustang

1965 Walter S. Austin Sr., manufacturer of the 1903-1920 Austin and inventor of the two-speed rear axle, dies in Grand Rapids, MI at age 99

1967 Racer Tim Fedewa is born

1970 Walter Reuther, President of the United Auto Workers since 1946, is killed in an airplane crash near Pellston, MI at age 62

1973 The first Bricklin prototype begins a series of road tests

1974 Automotive historian and vintage car enthusiast L. T. C. Rolt dies at age 64

1983 The Nissan Motor Manufacturing Company opens their Smyrna, TN factory

1992 Roberto Guerrero driving a Lola-Buick sets an Indianapolis 500 qualifying record of 232.482 mph, including a one-lap record of 232.618 mph

MAY 10

1841 James Gordon Bennett Jr., publisher of the *New York Herald* and sponsor of the Gordon Bennett Cup automobile races 1900-1905, is born in New York City

1885 Edward Lewis Estabrook of the Standard Oil Company is born in Brandon, Dakota Territory (now SD)

1888 The Nippon Oil Company Ltd. is incorporated in Japan

1904 Sir David Brown, owner of Aston-Martin 1947-1972, is born in Huddersfield, Yorkshire, England

1906 Charles Baillairge dies in Quebec, PQ, Canada at age 79 - among his many varied accomplishments was the construction of a steam-powered automobile in 1844 at age 19

1914 Racer John James is born in Packwood, Warwickshire, England

1920 John W. Hyatt, an inventor who founded the Hyatt Roller Bearing Company in 1891 and was it President 1891-1917, dies in Newark, NJ at age 82

1922 The 1,000th Rickenbacker is produced

Announcing

A new refined Rickenbacker 4 door Coach-Brougham. The world's most beautiful car—at the world's most attractive price.

$1595
f. o. b. factory
plus war tax

Rickenbacker Motor Company   Detroit, Michigan

Rickenbacker
A · CAR · WORTHY · OF · ITS · NAME

1923 General Motors Chairman and President Pierre S. DuPont retires from an active management role in the company, naming Alfred P. Sloan Jr. to succeed him as President

1927 E. L. Cord purchases the Lexington Motor Company and Arnsted Engineering Company, both located in Connersville, IN

1927 The first Dodge Senior Six is produced

1928 E. L. Cord purchases the Central Manufacturing Company of Connersville, IN

1928 Coachbuilder James Frank de Causse dies in Paris, France at age 48

1930 The Plymouth Model 30-U is introduced as the "New Finer Plymouth"

1931 Automotive parts manufacturer and electomotive automobile advocate Lowell Sherman Bain is born in Chicago, IL

1932 Sir Harold Snagge, new Chairman of D. Napier & Son, Ltd., annouces that efforts to employ W. O. Bentley and return to automobile production have been terminated

1939 The Maserati 4CL race car makes its official factory-sponsored debut in the Grand Prix of Tripoli

1941 Col. Oliver Brunner Zimmerman of the International Harvester Company dies at age 67

1945 O. O. Rieser, an authority on automotive battery cases, dies at age 51

1949 Sam Breadon, a St. Louis, MO car dealer 1903-1949 and the owner of the St. Louis Cardinals baseball team, dies at age 72

1956 Andrew L. Pomeroy of Thompson Products Inc. dies in Cleveland, OH at age 42

1960 Erwin G. "Cannon Ball" Baker dies in Indianapolis, IN at age 78

1960 E. P. DeBerry of the Studebaker-Packard Corporation dies at age 46

1963 Racer Gianfranco Comotti dies in Bergamo, Italy at age 56

1967 Racer Lorenzo Bandini dies at age 31 three days after his Ferrari 312/67 had crashed during the Monaco Grand Prix in Monte Carlo

1975 Automotive journalist Tom McCahill dies

1975 The first Formula 3 race is staged in Monte Carlo, Monaco, and won by Renzo Zorzi in a GRD-Lancia

1979 Henry Ford II announces his plans to retire as Chairman of the Ford Motor Company

1980 The Excalibur Series IV is introduced at the Los Angeles (CA) Auto Expo

1982 General Motors' new J-car plant in Janesville, WI opens with production of its first Cadillac Cimarron and Chevrolet Cavalier

1982 P. H. Zimmer, Chairman and President of Princess Homes, Inc., announces that the company name has been changed to the Zimmer Corporation, partly to recognize the introduction of the Zimmer Quick Silver, a neo-classic luxury sports coupe that the firm is producing in its Pompano Beach, FL plant

1985 Racer Toni Branca dies in Sierre, Switzerland at age 68

1990 The Honda Motor Company Ltd. names Nobuhiko Kawamoto as President, and Shoichiro Irimajiri and Yoshihide Munekuni as Executive Vice Presidents

MAY 11

1883 Sir Algernon Arthur St. Lawrence Lee Guinness, Steward of the Royal Automobile Club and brother of land speed record holder K. Lee Guinness, is born

1895 Arthur J. Wieland of General Motors, the Willys-Overland Company, and the Ford Motor Company is born in Sandusky, OH

1900 George Andrew Brooks of General Motors is born in New York City

1900 The first competitive English sprint race held at Welbeck Park as part of the Thousand Miles Trial is won by Hon. C. S. Rolls driving a Panhard

1902 John Mervin Cochrane of the Ford Motor Company of Canada, Ltd. is born in Ailsa Craig, ON

1904 The first speed hillclimb on the Isle of Man is staged in Port Vuillen and won by S. F. Edge in a Napier

1908 Henry Ford informs William C. Durant of his terms to add the Ford Motor Company to Durant's new General Motors, but lack of cash causes that deal and a similar one with Ransom E. Olds of Reo to fall through - Durant would later successfully negotiate with Samuel L. Smith for the takeover of the Olds Motor Works

1908 The Ohio Secretary of State requires all automobiles to be registered and display state-issued license plates - plate #1 is issued to Thomas B. Paxton, a prominent Cincinnati attorney, for his Franklin

1916 Charles F. Kettering and Edward A. Deeds agree to sell the Delco Corporation to United Motors Corporation, a William C. Durant entity created as part of his plan to regain control of General Motors

1920 The 4,000,000th Ford Model T is produced

1920 The Grant Motor Car Corporation of Cleveland, OH registers its "Grant Six" oval logo as a trademark

1920 Automotive journalist C. H. Gurnett dies in Chicago, IL at age 53

1921 Racer Geoffrey Crossley is born in Baslow, Derbyshire, England

1924 Racer Julius Timothy "Tim" Flock is born in Fort Payne, AL

1926 Racer Rob Schroeder is born in the United States

1927 Packard officially enters the custom-bodied market with a New York City exhibit of nine cars by six coachbuilders

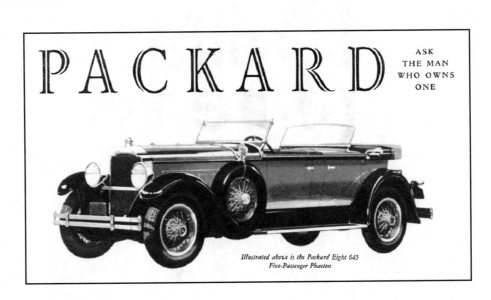

PACKARD
ASK
THE MAN
WHO OWNS
ONE

Illustrated above is the Packard Eight 645
Five-Passenger Phaeton

1931 Iain Mair Anderson, an executive with Ford, AMC, and Volkswagen, is born in Calcutta, India

1936 Earle V. Hennecke, founder in 1933 and President of the Automotive Equipment Company and a former official of the Motometer Company, dies at age 52

1940 Racer Herbert Muller is born in Reinach, Switzerland

1945 The United States government authorizes the production of 40,000 passenger cars for priority users beginning July 1

1945 Henry Ford II is named to the Board of Directors of the Automotive Council for War Production, replacing Charles E. Sorensen

1947 Franco Cortese drives the Ferrari 125 Sport in a race in Piacenza, Italy, the first racing appearance for the marque

1947 The B. F. Goodrich Tire & Rubber Company of Akron, OH begins test marketing of the world's first tubeless tires

1948 The Packard 1946-1950 "Goddess of Speed" mascot is patented by designer Howard F. Yeager

1948 Ferrari makes its major racing debut at the Italian Grand Prix in Turin

1953 Production begins at the new Ford Motor Company of Canada, Ltd. plant in Oakville, ON

1953 F. Malcolm Reid, Vice President and Director of Engineering for the Fruehauf Trailer Company who previously had worked for Packard and Cadillac, dies at age 53

1954 The Hindustan Ambassador, a badge-engineered variant of the Morris Oxford Series 11, is introduced by Hindustan Motors Ltd. of Calcutta, India

1970 Racer Marcos Gueiros is born in Brazil

1978 The 2,000,000th Chevrolet Camaro is produced, a gold coupe driven off the Van Nuys, CA assembly line by General Manager Robert D. Lund

1988 Christie's sells an Alfa Romeo 8C-35 for $2,850,000 at an auction in Monte Carlo, Monaco, a record for a Grand Prix car

MAY 12

1842 James H. Whiting, founder of the Flint (MI) Wagon Works which would evolve into the Buick Motor Company, is born in Torrington, CT

1881 Joseph Ebstein, a sculptor and designer of automobile mascots, is born in Batna, Algeria

1890 Paul G. Zimmerman, a design engineer with the Knox Automobile Company who later was a successful aeronautical and marine engineer, is born in Iroquois, SD

1891 Earl J. Bush of Diamond T is born in Topeka, KS

1904 The first and only speed trials staged at Douglas Promenade, Isle of Man are won by S. F Edge in a Napier at 57.3 mph

1906 E. R. Hollander, G. P. Tangeman, and C. H. Tangeman register the coined "Hol-Tan" name as a trademark for their New York City car dealership - the firm sold a badge-engineered Moon as a "Hol-Tan" in 1908, but thereafter returned to being a dealership exclusively as agents for the Delaunay-Belleville and Lancia

1914 Vauxhall Motors (1914) Ltd. is registered in Great Britain to succeed the company of the same name founded in 1907

1914 A United States patent is issued for the Pierce-Arrow fender-mounted headlights

1914 Racer Willy Poege dies in Bad Nauheim, Germany

1915 Automotive historian Lyle Kenyon Engel is born in New York City

1915 Prominent antique automobile collector William Brewster is born in Hamden, CT

1915 David M. Parry of the Parry Automobile Company dies at age 63

1919 Lynn Alfred Townsend of the Chrysler Corporation is born in Flint, MI

1921 Herbert H. Rice is named President of Cadillac

1922 Racer Roy Francesco Salvadori is born in Dovercourt, Essex, England of Italian ancestry

1925 Burt J. Craig is appointed Controller of the Ford Motor Company

1933 David A. Shaw, Treasurer of the Simplex Automobile Company and the Amplex Motor Car Company, and a cofounder and Secretary-Treasurer of the Grant Motor Car Corporation, dies in Cleveland, OH at age 62

1934 The smaller, low-priced Buick Series 40 is introduced, evolving two years later into the Special

A 1934 Buick Series 40 approaches the camera in this mid-1930's scene in Iron Mountain, MI.

1934 Georges Sizaire dies in Courbevoie, France at age 54

1935 The Alfa Romeo 16-cylinder Bimotore race cars debut at the 9th Tripoli Grand Prix in Libya, with two cars driven by Tazio Nuvolari and Louis Chiron finishing 4th and 5th

1935 The Cape Cod Challenge Cup Race, the first race held at the Marston's Mills track in Massachusetts, is won by Sidney Shurcliff in a Ford

1936 The 3,000,000th Ford truck is produced

1942 Claudio Lombardi of Abarth is born in Alessandria, Piedmont, Italy

1943 J. H. McDuffee, a pioneer racer of Stanley steamers, receiver of the first shipment of Ford automobiles, and the first licensed driver in New York City who later was an executive with Willys-Overland and in the automotive electrical equipment industry, dies at age 64

1946 William F. Marande, Chief Metallurgist of the Eaton Manufacturing Company and a former employee of Buick, dies in Saginaw, MI at age 46

1948 The Packard Motor Car Company Board of Directors authorizes the development of an automatic transmission

1951 The Rolls-Royce Owners' Club is founded in Wilkes-Barre, PA

1952 James J. Nance is elected President and General Manager of the Packard Motor Car Company

1953 William Clay Ford is elected Vice President of the Ford Motor Company and General Manager of Special Product Operations

1953 The third and last General Motors Parade of Progress featuring 44 Futurliners begins its three-year journey in Dayton, OH

1954 The Ford Motor Company of Canada,Ltd. consolidates production of its Mercury and Monarch marques

1956 Racer Leon Duray dies at age 62

1957 The last Mille Miglia is completed as Piero Taruffi takes the checkered flag in his Ferrari 315S V-12 - Joseph Gottingus is killed at age 44 when his Triumph crashes near Florence - at Guidizzolo, Italy, just 30 miles from the finish, the 3.8-litre Ferrari of Alfonso de Portago and Edmund "Gunner" Nelson crashes killing both men plus ten spectators, causing the Italian government to ban the road race

1957 A. J. Foyt records his first major victory, winning a midget car race in Kansas City, MO

1959 Edgar Apperson dies in Phoenix, AZ at age 89

1959 Jack Brabham records his first major victory at the Monaco Grand Prix

1961 Racer Tony Bettenhausen (Sr.) is killed at age 44 when he crashes during a practice run at the Indianapolis (IN) Motor Speedway

1963 Racer Stefano Modena is born in San Prospero, Italy

1969 General Motors announces that is is discontinuing production of the Chevrolet Corvair

1973 Racer Art Pollard is killed at age 46 during a practice run for the Indianapolis 500

1974 The Token makes its Formula 1 debut in the Belgian Grand Prix, but the Type RJ02 driven by Tom Pryce retires after colliding with the Tyrrell of Jody Scheckter

1975 The Hispano-Suiza Society is organized in Glen Cove, Long Island, NY with Alec Ulmann of New York City as President, Jules Heumann of San Francisco, CA as Secretary and Registrar, and John Sebert of Toronto, ON, Canada as Treasurer

1984 The Nurburgring race track near Koblenz, Germany reopens after a major remodeling

1985 Hoover Universal, Inc., founded in 1913 as a manufacturer of automotive parts, is acquired by Johnson Controls, Inc.

1988 The Ford Probe, a new front-wheel drive sporty car, is introduced

1992 Automobile historian John W. Burgess dies at age 80

MAY 13

1873 Leonard Huntress Dyer, inventor of many improvements in automobile technology including the "H-pattern" gearshift gate, is born in Washington, DC

1897 The Pope Manufacturing Company unveils its first automobile in what is often cited as the world's first automotive press preview

1899 The five-day old Olds Motors Works purchases a factory site in Detroit as part of a planned relocation from Lansing, MI

1902 The Vacuum Oil Company Ltd. is registered in London, England

1904 George Alonzo Jacoby of General Motors is born in Pleasureville, KY

1908 Sir Lovedin George Thomas Farmer of Rover is born

1913 Ford Motor Company of Canada, Ltd. produces its first engines

1913 Racer Theo Helfrich is born in Frankfurt am Main, Germany

1915 H. F. S. Morgan is issued a British patent for a four-wheeled version of the three-wheeler Morgan, but actual production is shelved due to World War I

1923 The racing debut of Tatra is successful as Josef Vermirovsky wins the Ledec Alej flying kilometer in Brno, Czechoslovakia driving a T11

1926 Renwick & Bertelli, Ltd. of Birmingham, England introduces its first car, affectionately known as the "Buzzbox", although plans for mass production are scrapped when they acquire Aston Martin

1927 Racer William Archibald "Archie" Scott-Brown is born in Paisley, Renfrew, Scotland

1928 Racer Dave Lewis dies in Los Angeles, CA

1936 Fred R. White, an executive with the Baker Motor Vehicle Company 1897-1915, the Baker Rauch & Lang Company 1915-1925, and the Baker-Raulang Company 1925-1936, dies in Cleveland, OH at age 64

1938 The Pierce-Arrow Motor Car Company is liquidated

1940 The Auburn Automobile Company is reorganized as the Auburn Central Manufacturing Company

1942 The last pre-World War II Buick Estate Wagon conversion is completed

1944 John M. Devine of the Ford Motor Company is born in Pittsburgh, PA

1949 Clarence W. Avery, Chairman of the Murray Body Company 1928-1949 and a former Ford Motor Company executive, dies in Plainwell, MI at age 67

1950 Raymond Mays competes in his last automobile race, driving a BRM at the British Grand Prix in Silverstone - this was the first race under the new FIA Formula 1 world championship rules, with Giuseppe "Nino" Farina winning in an Alfa Romeo Tipo 158 - the Alta designed by Geoffrey Taylor and driven by Geoffrey Crossley made its debut but failed to finish

1960 Racer Harry Schell is killed at age 38 when his Cooper-Climax crashes during a practice run at Silverstone, England

1962 Racer Mikael "Micke" Johansson is born in Sweden

1966 Racer Peter Zakowski is born in West Germany

1980 Douglas A. Fraser, President of the United Auto Workers, is elected to the Board of Directors of Chrysler Corporation, the first union official to sit on the board of a major United States corporation

1986 The Jeep Wrangler is introduced as a 1987 model, replacing the Jeep CJ

1987 The Standard Oil Company of Ohio and BP North America Inc. merge as BP America Inc.

1991 Drag racing engine designer Keith Black dies at age 64

1994 Duncan Hamilton, winner of the 1953 24 Hours of Le Mans race, dies in Sherborne, Dorset, England at age 74

MAY 14

1842 James Henry Bullard, whose steam car ran in Springfield, MA in 1886, is born in Poultney, VT

1872 Marcel Renault is born

1912 Leon A. Fults, longtime executive with the Western Auto Supply Company of Kansas City, MO, is born in Center, TX

1913 Norman Howard of Kaiser and Willys is born in New York City

1914 George A. Matthews, a cofounder of the Jackson Automobile Company, dies in Jackson, MI at age 61

1918 James Gordon Bennett, Publisher of the *New York Herald* and a patron of pioneer automobile racing, dies at age 77

1925 Racer Ninian Sanderson is born in Great Britain

1931 The first Bentley 4 Litre is completed

1949 Porsche Salzburg is established in Salzburg, Austria to import, distribute, and service Volkswagens in that country

1960 Mickey Thompson, driving the "Assault" at March Air Force Base, CA, breaks Bernd Rosemeyer's 22-year-old records reaching 132.94 mph in the standing kilometer and 149.93 mph in the standing mile

1962 Racer Dave Scott is born in Petersfield, Hampshire, England

1965 Christian F. Sauereisen, the inventor of an improved spark plug, dies in Aspinwall, PA at age 81

1966 Racer Chuck Rodee is killed at age 38 when he crashes during a practice run at the Indianpolis Motor Speedway

1969 The last Chevrolet Corvair is produced

1969 Racer Stephan Gregoire is born in Neufchateau, France

Jackson

No hill too steep
No sand too deep

Experts in Comfort—

The Jackson heads the list of comfortable cars because it has always been comfortable; and because its builders' long experience makes them comfort experts.

"Olympic" Four $1500
"Majestic" Four 1975
"Sultanic" Six 2650

Jackson Automobile Company
1316 E. Main St.,
Jackson, Mich.

1972 John B. Beltz, Oldsmobile General Manager 1969-1972 and "father of the Toronado", dies in Lansing, MI at age 46

1974 The Ford Motor Company adopts a worldwide metrification plan

1976 Automobile stylist Vincent Edward Gardner dies near Auburn, IN at age 63

1978 Inventor William P. Lear, developer of the first practical automobile radio and an advocate of modern steam-powered cars, dies in Reno, NV at age 75

1991 The last Buick Reatta is produced

1994 Helmuth Bott of Porsche dies in Munsingen-Buttenhausen, Germany at age 68

MAY 15

1897 Edward Tillottson Ragsdale of Buick is born in Hopkinsville, KY

1897 Wifredo Pelayo Ricart y Medina, an Alfa Romeo design engineer and later the designer of the Pegaso sports car, is born in Barcelona, Spain

1898 Journalist Henry Sturmey resigns as a Director of the Daimler Motor Company, Ltd.

1900 John Franklin Gordon of Cadillac is born in Akron, OH

1900 New York City issues its first driver's license

1902 The Burmah Oil Company (now Burmah Oil PLC) is organized in Edinburgh, Scotland

1903 New York state's homemade license plates with owner's initials are replaced by number plates, with #1 assigned to G. P. Chamberlain of Harrison

1903 Racer Paul Albert is killed near Nieder-Ingelheim, Germany (now Ingelheim) when his 60-hp Mercedes crashes while enroute from Weisbaden, Germany to Paris, France to compete in the upcoming Paris-Madrid race

1903 Charles Emory Nelson, cofounder in 1939 with E. E. Bryant and O. F. Gusloff of the Nelson Muffler Corporation, is born in LaPorte, IN

1908 The Fryckman automobile is unveiled in Souris, ND

1909 Minnesota state-issued license plates debut

1911 Robert C. Graham marries Bertha E. Hack

1918 Nantucket Island, MA votes to lift the ban on motorized vehicles ending the controversial twelve year old policy

1920 Richard Burkett Stoner of the Cummins Engine Company is born in Ladoga, IN

1922 Automotive historian Richard Alexander Hough is born in Brighton, Sussex, England

1923 The Clymer Manufacturing Company of Rockford, IL is issued a United States patent for its "through-the-windshield" spotlight

1929 The 10,000th Roosevelt is produced

THE NEW IMPROVED
MARMON
Roosevelt
STRAIGHT-EIGHT

1929 Racer Peter Broeker is born in Canada

1932 Wendell M. Williams Jr., a Test & Developmental Engineer with the Chrysler Corporation 1955-1958 and a longtime Professor of Mechanical Engineering at the Georgia Institute of Technology, is born

1938 The Mercedes-Benz W154 race car records its first victory as Hermann Lang, Manfred von Brauchitsch, and Rudolf Caracciola take the first three places in the Tripoli (Libya) Grand Prix - Eugenio Siena, winner of the 1932 Spa (Belgium) 24-hour race, is killed during the race

1943 Racer Alan Rollinson is born in Walsall, Staffordshire, England

1947 Chevrolet announces that plans to build a compact car, the Cadet, have been indefinitely deferred because of material shortages and the strong sales of existing models

1947 Piero Dusio drives his Cisitalia SMM spyder to a third-place finish at the Sassi-Superga hillclimb in Turin, Italy, the first competitive event for the new model

1953 The first power steering-equipped Kaiser is produced

1953 Racer Chet Miller is killed at age 50 when his Novi crashes during a practice session for the Indianapolis 500

1957 Racer Keith Andrews is killed at age 36 when he crashes during a practice session for the Indianapolis 500

1958 Eugene F. McDonald Jr., a former Franklin Automobile Company official who became President of the Zenith Radio Corporation, dies at age 68

1959 Racer Luis Perez Sala is born in Barcelona, Spain

1961 Henry K. Holsman, designer of the 1902-1910 Holsman highwheeler, dies in Genoa City, WI at age 94

1962 The semi-production Chrysler Turbine Car, designed by Elwood P. Engle and built by Carrozzeria Ghia, is introduced to Chrysler dealers at the Waldorf-Astoria Hotel in New York City

1966 Myron Edson Forbes of Studebaker and Pierce-Arrow dies at age 86

1975 Automotive historian Jonathan Norton Leonard dies at age 71

1977 The Ragtime Car and Boat Museum opens in Emeryville, CA featuring the collection of Owen Owens

1981 The 20,000,000th Volkswagen Beetle is produced at the Puebla, Mexico plant

1982 Racer Gordon Smiley is killed at age 33 when he crashes during a practice run for the Indianapolis 500

1986 Racer Elio De Angelis dies in Marseille, France at age 28 from injuries suffered when his Brabham BT55-BMW 4 crashed during a practice run at the Paul Ricard circuit in Le Castellet, France

1990 Michael N. Hammes, International Vice President of the Chrysler Corporation, resigns to become Executive Vice President of Black & Decker with Joseph E. Cappy named as his successor

1991 The Buick Reatta is officially discontinued

1991 The main facility of H. J. Mulliner, Park Ward Ltd. is closed due to a severe decline in custom coachbuilding activities

Bentley T Series 2-Door Saloon
with Coachwork by H. J. Mulliner, Park Ward

1992 Racer Jovy Marcelo is killed at age 26 when he crashes during a practice run for the Indianapolis 500

MAY 16

1852 Henry Russel, a pioneer Oldsmobile executive, is born in Detroit, MI

1876 Maurice Wolfe is born in Rosewood, IN

1891 The first Daimler engine is imported into England by Frederick R. Simms

1897 Howard Addison "Dutch" Darrin, custom body designer and automobile stylist, is born in Cranford, NJ

1907 The Ardsley Motor Car Company of Yonkers, NY is officially dissolved

1909 Racer Luigi "Gigi" Villoresi is born in Milan, Italy

1918 The first automobile legally enters Nantucket, MA

1921 Frank C. Clement, driving the second experimental Bentley 3-litre, wins the Brooklands Whitsun race, the first victory for the marque

1928 The Nash Motors Company of Kenosha, WI registers its modernized logo as a trademark

1932 Nash Ambassador Eight 4-Door Convertible Sedan

1928 Edward Macauley, son of corporation President Alvan Macauley, joins the Packard Motor Car Company

1929 Edsel B. Ford breaks ground for the new Ford Motor Company Ltd. factory in Dagenham, England

1930 August C. Fruehauf, founder and Chairman of the Fruehauf Trailer Company, dies in Grosse Pointe, MI at age 61

1936 The Ford Rotunda opens in Dearborn, MI

1938 Alan Giles Altenau of Bridgestone/Firestone Inc. is born in Cincinnati, OH

1946 Charles F. Carroll, the inventor of many improvements in automobile design, dies in Cleveland, OH at age 69

1948 Racer Ralph Hepburn is killed at age 51 when his Novi crashes during a practice run at the Indianapolis Motor Speedway

1948 Dwight Heinmuller, post-World War II Packard collector and historian, is born in Baltimore, MD

1949 Racer Steve Shelton is born in the United States

1952 Porsche and Studebaker sign an agreement calling for the German firm to design a small car for the South Bend, IN company - three prototypes were all that resulted from this effort

1956 John J. Caton, founder of the Chrysler Institute of Engineering, dies in Phillipsburg, NJ at age 76

1956 The General Motors Technical Center in Warren, MI is dedicated - among the highlights is the public unveiling of the XP-500 show car featuring the world's first free-piston engine

1967 Racer Stevie Reeves is born

1970 Stylist Alex Tremulis drives an aerodynamic Ramona Travoy motor home at El Mirage Dry Lake, CA to a speed of 97.613 mph, a record for this type of vehicle

1995 Saab-Scania AB splits into two separate companies, Saab AB and Scania AV

MAY 17

1868 Horace Elgin Dodge is born in Niles, MI

1878 Augustine Joseph Cunningham of Cunningham is born in Rochester, NY

1878 Thomas Radford Agg, a pioneer builder and promoter of good roads, is born in Fairfield, IA

1882 Tire and automobile parts manufacturer Clarence Clay Carlton is born in Akron, OH

1883 Louis G. Bissell, Chairman of Mack Trucks, Inc., is born in Brooklyn, NY

1886 Alfonso XIII, King of Spain and prominent automobile enthusiast, is born in Madrid, Spain

1890 Tom S. Sligh Jr. of Studebaker is born in Ruston, LA

1890 Emile Levassor marries Louise Sarazin, widow of Edouard Sarazin and the French distributor of Daimler engines, setting the stage for the Panhard et Levassor motor car as a successful business venture

1899 The Austrian Automobile Association (ARBO) is organized

1904 Clement Smith and Terry Stafford are issued a United States patent for their clutch and planetary transmission design

1909 Concert pianist Josef Hofmann completes the first and only Hofmann, a large six-cylinder car built at his home in Aiken, SC

1917 The Macon Motor Car Company in Macon, MO is destroyed by fire just as production is about to begin

1917 Harry S. Harkness becomes the sole owner of the Sheepshead Bay Speedway in New York City

1918 Paul Franklin Chenea of General Motors is born in Milton, OR

1921 The Earl of Shrewsbury, the financial backer of Clement-Talbot, Ltd., London manufacturers of the Talbot, dies at age 60

The British-built Talbot evolved from the French-built Clement in 1903. The proud owner of this circa-1905 one-eyed 12/16 hp tourer replaced his chauffeur for the photograph. Talbot became the Sunbeam-Talbot in 1938.

1922 Kenelm Ernest Lee "K. Lee" Guinness, driving a Sunbeam at Brooklands, England, raises the land speed record to 133.75 mph, the first official increase in twelve years

1924 Walter C. Marmon resigns as President of the Nordyke & Marmon Company, and is succeeded by George M. Williams

1925 J. Dallas Dort dies in Flint, MI at age 64

1930 Construction begins on the new Ford-Werke AG factory in Niehl, Germany, near Cologne

1930 Rocket-powered automobile pioneer Max Valier is killed in Berlin, Germany when an engine explodes during testing

1934 Gordon M. Buehrig files a patent application for his automobile design that would evolve into the 1936 Cord 810

1948 H. J. Leonard, President of the F. B. Stearns Company 1925-1930 and President of the Willys-Overland Company 1936-1948, dies in Toledo, OH at age 67

1948 Racer Mikko Kozarowitsky is born in Helsinki, Finland

1950 David M. Goodrich, Chairman of the B. F. Goodrich Company, dies in Mount Kisco, NY at age 73

1953 Thomas O. Richards of General Motors dies at age 53

1954 S. Frank Baker, President and General Manager of the Detroit Automotive Products Corporation and an authority on the Thornton four-rear-wheel drive system for motor trucks, dies at age 58

The finest car that money can buy
The finest transportation of today

STEARNS·KNIGHT SALES CORPORATION . . CLEVELAND

STEARNS·KNIGHT

The claims stated in this 1928 advertisement would certainly be disputed by Packard, Cadillac, Pierce-Arrow, and others. Stearns-Knight, the once proud luxury marque was now a subsidiary of Willys-Overland and less than two years from oblivion.

Carl F. W. Larson

1955 Racer Manuel Ayulo is killed at age 33 during a practice run at the Indianapolis Motor Speedway

1958 Jackie Lewis makes his racing debut, finishing second in his Cooper-Norton in a race at Brands Hatch

1959 Racer Jerry Unser is killed at age 26 during a practice run at the Indianapolis Motor Speedway

1961 Mechanical engineering professor John M. Lessells, a design engineer with Rolls-Royce, Ltd. 1917-1919, dies at age 73

1962 The last Volvo P2101 chassis is produced

1964 Lord Brabazon, automobile racer, pioneer airplane pilot, sportsman, and political associate of Winston Churchill, dies in Chertsey, England at age 80

1964 Racer Mauro Martini is born in Italy

1970 Cadwallader Washburn "Carl" Kelsey, a Maxwell-Briscoe Motor Company executive who later built the 1911-1914 three-wheeled Motorette and the 1920-1921 Kelsey, dies at age 89

1993 Robert Doehler, a stylist for Ford and Studebaker, dies in Milwaukee, WI at age 70

1994 Racer Al Unser Sr. announces his retirement

1996 Racer Scott Brayton is killed at age 37 when his Lola crashes during a practice run at the Indianapolis Motor Speedway

1997 Troy Ruttman, winner of the 1952 Indianapolis 500, dies in Lake Havasu City, AZ at age 67

MAY 18

1858 Charles Merrill Hough, a federal judge involved in the Selden Patent lawsuit with the Ford Motor Company, is born in Philadelphia, PA

1887 Sidney Albert Cook of Diamond T is born near Ipswich, East Suffolk, England

1889 Thomas Midgley Jr. of General Motors is born in Beaver Falls, PA

1889 Joseph Fewsmith, a public relations official with the Peerless Motor Car Company who later formed his own advertising agency, is born in Cleveland, OH

1891 Carl Barker, longtime executive with the Shell Oil Company, is born in Selma, AL

1901 The Overman Wheel Company of Chicopee Falls, MA registers the name "Victor" as a trademark for its steam cars - the firm merged with the Locomobile Company of America in 1903 and the Victor was discontinued

The Victor Automobile

Marks a new era in the use of steam, and steam is pre-eminently the power to use on Automobiles.

We have solved the problems which have heretofore prevented the use of steam in the hands of the general public.

With a Victor Automobile it is possible to go for 25 miles and do absolutely nothing, except put the power on by opening the throttle, and steering it.

The water is maintained automatically in the boiler, and is guaranteed not to vary one inch.

The pressure on the fuel tank is maintained automatically, and is guaranteed not to vary one pound.

Other details have been put to rights, and we are prepared to guarantee satisfaction in road work.

Orders will be received for the wagon illustrated herewith at $1,000, to be delivered in July, and guaranteed to be satisfactory in road work before payment.

These wagons will have four horse power, and will be geared according to the hill climbing or speeding necessities of the purchaser.

Victor bicycle riders will know that our twenty years' experience as bicycle builders has enabled us to produce an Automobile fit to take its place in the family of Victors.

OVERMAN WHEEL CO.,
Chicopee Falls, Mass.

1906 H. Moreland of Gloucester, England orders a 6-cylinder 30-hp Rolls-Royce, but this order was later amended to a new 40/50-hp car, the first sale of the chassis that would later be known as the Silver Ghost

1907 Automotive artist Steven Dohanos is born in Lorain, OH

1914 Baron Emmanuel de Graffenried, winner of the 1949 British Grand Prix, is born in Paris, France of Swiss ancestry

1915 Cannon Ball Baker, driving a Stutz Bearcat, arrives in New York City 11 days, 7 hours and 15 minutes after leaving San Diego, CA, breaking all existing cross-country records

1916 The Libbey-Owens Glass Company is organized in Ohio

1921 A. B. C. Hardy is appointed President and General Manager of the Olds Motor Works

1922 The 6,000,000th Ford Model T is produced

1928 Racer Jo Schlesser is born in Liouville, Meuse, France

1931 Racer Bruce Halford is born in Hampton-in-Arden, Warwickshire, England

1936 The Board of Directors of the Reo Motor Car Company votes to shift truck production to the main factory in Lansing, MI

1941 Racer Maurizio de Narvaez is born in Colombia

1946 Hall of Fame baseball player Reginald Martinez "Reggie" Jackson, a collector of antique and classic cars, is born in Wyncote, PA

1946 Racer Kenji Takahashi is born in Japan

1951 Pierce A. Weyl, a design engineer with the Ford Motor Company since 1927, dies

1952 Piero Taruffi records his only Grand Prix victory at the Bremgarten Circuit near Berne, Switzerland driving a Ferrari 500 - the AFM designed by Alex von Falkenhausen makes its debut, but the car driven by Hans Stuck retires with engine problems

1958 The Lotus makes its Formula 1 debut in the Monaco Grand Prix, with the car driven by Cliff Allison finishing in 6th place

1966 The Socony Mobil Oil Company Inc. changes its name to the Mobil Oil Corporation

1971 Dr. G. von Opel sets electric car standing-start 1/4-mile (16.87 seconds) and flying-start kilometre (117.35 mph) records at Hockenheim, West Germany

1972 Racer Jim Malloy dies at age 36 from injuries suffered four days earlier during a practice run at the Indianapolis Motor Speedway

1973 Dr. Ing. Rudolf Uhlenhaut, former Chief Engineer of Daimler-Benz AG, is chosen as the third honorary member of the Milestone Car Society

1973 Giulio de Leonardis, Rome, Italy's first licensed driver, dies at age 93

1974 Automobile engine designer Sir Harry Ricardo dies at age 89

1980 Hunt House in Paulerspury, England, home of the Rolls-Royce Enthusiasts Club and the Sir Henry Royce Foundation, opens

1983 Owen Bieber is elected as President of the United Auto Workers

MAY 19

1787 The Maryland House of Delegates issues a patent to Oliver Evans for his "Steam Carriage"

1824 Henry Brewster, whose carriage building company would evolve into a custom coachbuilding firm in the twentieth century, is born in New Haven, CT

1874 Gustav E. Franquist of Simplex is born in Ishpeming, MI

1888 Clifford Sklarek, builder of the 1905 Sklarek, inventor and manufacturer of the Lorraine spotlight, and a historian of the automobile industry, is born in Canton, IL

1892 Racer Christian Werner is born in Stuttgart, Germany

1896 The first Benz in the Netherlands is sold to Adolphe Zimmermans

1901 The first automobile appears in Moline, IL leading to the production of the Velie by Willard Lamb Velie, grandson of farm implement manufacturer John Deere

1902 The first seaside speed trials are staged in Great Britain at Bexhill-on-Sea, Sussex, England and won by Leon Serpollet in the Gardner-Serpollet "Easter Egg" steam car

1903 The Buick Motor Company is organized in Detroit, MI

1903 The Packard Motor Car Company Board of Directors approves the purchase of a factory site in Detroit, MI

1905 Howard O. Carter establishes the Carter Motor Car Corporation in Washington, DC to produce his unusual Carter Two-Engine Car

1905 Lammot du Pont Copeland of General Motors is born in Wilmington, DE

1908 The first automobile race in Russia, a 438-mile run from St. Petersburg to Moscow, is won by Victor Hemery in Benz

1917 D. McCall White resigns as Chief Engineer of Cadillac

1927 The Dodge Senior Six is introduced

1928 Anthony Colin Bruce Chapman of Lotus is born in Richmond, Surrey, England

1931 Racer Robert Hugh Fearson "Bob" Anderson is born in Hendon, England

1933 Otto Merz, winner of the 1927 German Grand Prix, is killed at age 43 when he crashes at the Avus circuit in Germany

1934 Racer Paddy Driver is born in Johannesburg, South Africa

1935 The Frankfurt-Darmstadt (Germany) Autobahn opens to the public

1939 Percival S. Tice, a carburetor authority and patent consultant with the Stewart-Warner Corporation, dies at age 58

1949 Ward M. Canaday is elected Chairman of the Willys-Overland Company

1953 Packard completes two White House fleet cars with air conditioning, a first for the marque - the option would become available to the general public six weeks later

1954 John Joseph Wydler, a Cities Service Oil Company engineer who was an authority on supercharging, dies at age 67

1957 Masten Gregory makes his Formula 1 debut finishing third at the Monaco Grand Prix in his Maserati 250F - Stuart Lewis-Evans makes his Formula 1 debut in the same race finishing fourth in his Connaught-Alta, although the remainder of his career would with the Vanwall team

1958 Racer Archie Scott-Brown dies at age 31 from injuries suffered the previous day when his Lister crashed during a sports car race at the Spa circuit in Belgium

1959 Carl F. Norberg, President of the Electric Storage Battery Company, dies at age 60

1966 Fiat announces plans to build a factory in Poland

1990 The International Trophy race at Silverstone is won by Allan McNish in a Lola-Mugen, at age 20 years, 141 days the youngest driver to win a Formula 3000 event

1991 Racer Willy T. Ribbs becomes the first black driver to qualify for the Indianapolis 500

MAY 20

1843 Albert Augustus Pope of Pope-Hartford is born in Boston, MA

1875 Karl Mobius, a sculptor and designer of automobile mascots, is
      born in Borna, Germany

1877 James A. Kline, manufacturer of the 1910-1923 Kline Kar who
      previously had designed the Pullman, is born near Hummelstown, PA

1890 Automobile historian Joseph Allan Nevins is born in Camp Point, IL

1899 New York City makes the world's first speeding arrest, as Jacob German is stopped for driving 12 mph

1903 The first commercial vehicle race begins in New York City, with two races on two days sponsored by the
      Automobile Club of America (ACA) - the light truck winner for both races was a Waterless Knox
      driven by Harry A. Knox, while the heavy truck winner for both races was a Herschmann steamer

1904 The first Buick engine is successfully tested

*A Barnesville, MN couple with their 1908 Buick Model F Touring. Buick was the
ninth largest United States automobile manufacturer in their first full year
(1905) and held the number two ranking 1907-1910 trailing only Ford.*

1905 The first races are staged at the Hippodrome in Morris Park, Bronx, NY - Louis Chevrolet makes his
      racing debut, and wins two of the three races in his 90-hp Fiat - the White steam-powered race car
      "Whistling Billy", driven by Webb Jay, makes its debut and covers a mile in 53 seconds during an
      exhibition run

1907 The Hatfield Motor Vehicle Company of Miamisburg, OH registers the "Buggyabout" name as a
      trademark - founded by Charles B. Hatfield Sr. and Jr., the firm would fail in 1908

1911 Automobile textiles manufacturer Jerome Morton Comar is born in Chicago, IL

1913 Marshall Merkes, post-World War II owner of the rights to the Duesenberg name, is born

1917 Charles Donald Graef of the Ford Motor Company is born in New York City

1920 Sir Henry Segrave, driving his 1914 Opel 4.5-litre Grand Prix car, wins his debut race at Brooklands

1921 Yutaka Kume of Nissan is born in Tokyo, Japan

1921 Racer Aldo Gordini is born in Bologna, Italy

1926 Racer Bob Sweikert is born in Los Angeles, CA

1927 The first Austin Swallow is completed, becoming the direct lineal ancestor of what would become the Jaguar marque

1935 The 1936 Nash Series 3640 is introduced

1937 Franz Steinkuhler of Volkswagen is born in Wurzburg, Germany

1948 The Playboy Motor Car Corporation goes public, offering twenty million shares of common stock at $1 per share

1954 Road map publisher Andrew McNally Jr. dies in Chicago, IL at age 67

RAND McNALLY
ROAD ATLAS
OF THE
UNITED STATES

1955 George A. Sloan, a Director of the Goodyear Tire & Rubber Company, dies in New York City at age 61

1957 The Jeep FC-170 pickup truck is introduced as a midyear model

1957 The Studebaker-Packard Corporation and Daimler-Benz AG sign an agreement whereby Studebaker dealers would begin selling Mercedes-Benz automobiles in the United States following the expiration of the contract with Max Hoffman

1961 The Ford Motor Company completes a highly modified Lincoln Continental convertible sedan for the United States Secret Service to be used as a presidential limousine - it was in this car that John F. Kennedy was riding when he was assassinated in Dallas, TX in 1963

1962 The Lola designed by Eric Broadley makes its Formula 1 debut in the Dutch Grand Prix in Zandvoort, but the car driven by John Surtees is involved in an accident after which the car driven by Roy Salvadori is withdrawn

1964 Enzo Ferrari abruptly pulls out of a near-agreement with the Ford Motor Company for the takeover of his firm, an event often cited as the catalyst through which an angry Henry Ford II authorized Ford's return to racing

1965 Racer Edgar Barth dies of cancer at age 48 in Ludwigsburg, West Germany

1971 Edward G. Budd Jr., President of the Edward G. Budd Manufacturing Company 1946-1967, dies at age 69

1971 Racer Tony Stewart is born in Rushville, IN

1972 After four years of development, Alfa Romeo begins production of the Alfasud

1984 Bill Holland, winner of the 1949 Indianapolis 500, dies in Tucson, AZ at age 76

1987 The American Motors Corporation approves Chrysler Corporation's purchase offer

1994 The Rolls-Royce Flying Spur is introduced featuring the marque's first turbocharging

MAY 21

1542 Don Hernando de Soto, Spanish explorer and namesake of Chrysler Corporation's 1928-1961 DeSoto marque, dies near present-day Arkansas City, AR

1847 Carburetor manufacturer Frank H. Ball is born in Oberlin, OH

1878 Glenn Hammond Curtiss, a V-type engine pioneer who made his greatest contributions in aviation, is born in Hammondsport, NY

1892 Charles Parker Fiske of the General Motors Acceptance Corporation is born in Lynn, MA

1898 The Nesseldorf Prasident makes a test run from Nesseldorf, Moravia to Vienna, Austria - this was the first car built in what is now the Czech Republic, and is also often cited as the first car to be equipped with a front bumper

1901 Connecticut passes the first automobile speed limit legislation, imposing a maximum speed of 12 mph in rural areas and 8 mph within city limits

1912 Rinehart Sensing Bright of the Chrysler Corporation is born in Plaindealing, LA

1916 Flying ace Georges Boillot, a pre-World War I member of the Peugeot racing team, is killed at age 30 when his plane is shot down over Verdun, France

1918 Duesenberg historian J. L. Elbert is born

1918 Charles Valton, a designer of automobile mascots, dies in Chinon, France at age 67

1924 The last French GN manufactured under license by Salmson, chassis #1563, is sold to racer Andre Lombard

1924 Automobile parts manufacturer Albert Frank Humlhanz is born in Chalfont, PA

1924 Racer Cotton Owens is born

1927 Barney Oldfield, driving a Hudson Super Six 2-door coach at the Culver City (CA) track, establishes a non-stop 1,000-mile record for stock cars of 13 hours, 8 minutes (average speed 76.4 mph)

1929 The Ford Model A Fordor sedan is introduced

THE NEW THREE WINDOW FORDOR SEDAN

1930 The first American Austin is produced at the Butler, PA factory

1935 Racer Hartwell "Stubby" Stubblefield is killed when he crashes during a practice session at the Indianapolis Motor Speedway

1939 Werner Bigalke makes his debut with the Auto Union team finishing sixth in the Eifelrennen at the Nurburgring in Germany

1942 Racer Danny Ongais is born in Honolulu, HI

1945 Hudson Motor Car Company President A. E. Barit announces that the Fisher brothers, having resigned from General Motors in August 1944, are attempting to gain control of Hudson

1950 Juan Manuel Fangio wins the Monaco Grand Prix in an Alfa Romeo 158, the first of 24 Formula 1 Grand Prix victories in his career

1956 William E. Ireland, Vice President-Sales for the B. F. Goodrich Tire & Rubber Company of Canada Ltd., dies

1957 The last of 67 Volvo Sport 2-seat sports cars is produced

1959 After denying rumors for several years, the Chrysler Corporation confirms that the development of a compact car is in progress

1962 Racer Enrique Contreras is borrn in Mexico

1965 The Matra MS1 race car makes its initial test run at Montlhery, France

1969 Crankshaft manufacturer Harry G. Stoddard, a longtime executive of the Wyman-Gordon Company, dies in Worcester, MA at age 95

1976 The "last" Jensen is built, although production of the Interceptor would soon resume on a limited basis

1976 Edwin H. Metz, President of the Metz Company 1916-1921, dies

1978 The Martini makes its Formula 1 debut in the Belgian Grand Prix at Zolder, with the car designed by Tico Martini and driven by Rene Arnoux finishing in ninth place

1981 The "Cimarron by Cadillac" is introduced

1981 Pontiac introduces its 1982 J2000 "world car"

1983 The first Great American Race, a rally for 1941 and earlier cars sponsored by the Dallas, TX-based Interstate Battery System of America, begins in Anaheim, CA

1986 The Ford Motor Company announces plans to acquire an interest in Alfa Romeo

MAY 22

1872 Raymond Moses Owen, manufacturer and designer of the 1915-1921 Owen Magnetic, is born in Bedford, OH

1879 Frank E. Watts of Hupmobile is born in West Falmouth, ME

1882 S. L. Blackburn, Vice President of the Anderson Motor Company 1917-1919, is born in Vaughndale, NC

1892 Orville Swan Caesar of the Greyhound Corporation is born in Rice Lake, WI

Orville S. Caesar became President of the Greyhound Corporation in 1946,
the year this coach was photographed at the Greyhound Inn in Somerest, KY.
The car is a rare 1942 Studebaker.

1892 Charles LeRoy McCuen of Oldsmobile is born in Stockton, CA

1895 Racer Gus Schrader is born in Iowa

1900 The Nesseldorf Rennzweier, the marque's first true race car, is completed

1905 Cecil Hopkins of the Ford Motor Company is born in Hartford, CT

1909 The first Palace House Speed Hillclimb is held in Beaulieu, England, now the site of the National Motor Museum

1915 General Motors management closes the Cartercar factory in Jackson, MI

1921 Tazio Nuvolari makes his racing debut, finishing second in an Ansaldo at the Circuit of Garda in Italy

1921 Racer Marshall Teague is born in Daytona Beach, FL

1928 The 1928 Chevrolet "Griffin" mascot is patented by designer F. C. Ruppel

1929 The Packard Motor Car Company creates the Custom Body Division

1929 Racer Sergio Mantovani is born in Milan, Italy

1931 William J. Gaffke, German-born engineer with Franklin and Pierce-Arrow who later worked in the automobile parts industry, dies in Buffalo, NY at age 44

1934 Racer Robert "Bobby" Johns is born

1937 The Fram Corporation is incorporated in Rhode Island as a consolidation of the Fleming Manufacturing Company and the Fram Oil Filter Company

1944 L. J. Cronkhite of the Fruehauf Trailer Company dies at age 46

1946 John F. Maxwell, founder of the Plymouth Factory Service School, dies in Lansing, MI at age 54

1949 W. D. Allen of Ford is killed

1950 The Nash-Kelvinator Corporation registers the "Rambler" and "Statesman" names as trademarks - the Statesman was the 1950 version of the economy Nash 600, while the Rambler name, used by its ancestral company 1900-1913, was reintroduced for the firm's new compact car

1953 Volvo introduces the Philip prototype, a large sedan looking very much like the United States-built Kaiser

1955 Louis Chiron, at age 55 years, 292 days the oldest driver ever to compete in a Grand Prix, places sixth at Monaco driving a Lancia D50

1959 Lee Petty wins the 100-mile race at Charlotte, NC in an Oldsmobile, the last victory for the marque until 1978

1966 McLaren makes its Formula 1 debut in the Monaco Grand Prix, but the Type M2B driven by Bruce McLaren retires with an oil leak

1970 Racer Pedro Diniz is born in Sao Paulo, Brazil

1970 Racer Steve Portenga is born

1972 Henry Ford II and architect John Portman announce plans to rebuild the Detroit, MI riverfront area

1973 Antique car collector Mort Kresteller, known as "Mr. Auburn", dies in San Francisco, CA at age 47

1975 Maserati stockholders vote in Milan, Italy to file for bankruptcy

MASERATI REDEFINES THE SEDAN...AT 145 MPH

1977 Janet Guthrie becomes the first woman to qualify for the Indianapolis 500

1977 Jody Scheckter wins the Monaco Grand Prix, the 100th Formula 1 win for a car powered by the Ford-Cosworth DFV engine

1977 Automotive supply company executive James M. Hannan dies at age 68

1978 Sir Bernard Docker of Daimler dies at age 81

1985 The merger of the Ford Motor Company and Amcar of South Africa is completed with the new subsidiary being named the South African Motor Corporation (SAMCOR)

MAY 23

1875 Alfred Pritchard Sloan Jr. of General Motors is born in New Haven, CT

1879 Frederic Ewen Moskovics is born in Budapest, Hungary

1903 Col. H. Nelson Jackson and Sewall K. Crocker begin the first trans-United States trip by automobile leaving San Francisco, CA in a 2-cylinder Winton

1903 Racer Ernst Klodwig is born in Germany

1905 The first Rolls-Royce 30-hp 6-cylinder is completed

1910 George N. Pierce dies in Buffalo, NY at age 64

1912 Richard Webber Jackson of Hudson is born in Detroit, MI

1925 Henry Segrave makes only appearance at the Shelsley Walsh, England hillclimb and wins in a Sunbeam

1925 Automobile parts manufacturer Fred J. Campbell dies at age 30

1928 The rocket-powered Opel RAK 2 makes its debut at the Avus track near Berlin, Germany with designer Fritz von Opel exceeding 125 mph before 2,000 invited spectators

1933 John Froelich, inventor of the gasoline-powered farm tractor, dies

1934 Clyde Barrow and Bonnie Parker are killed by law enforcement officials in rural Bienville Parish, LA - their stolen, bullet-riddled 1934 Ford V-8 would become a valuable collectible

1935 Ernest W. Hives offically announces the termination of Rolls-Royce Phantom II production

1937 John D. Rockefeller of the Standard Oil Company dies in Ormond Beach, FL at age 97

1940 Racer Gerard Larrousse is born in Lyon, France

1941 Sir Herbert Austin dies in Bromsgrove, England at age 74

1944 Enoch J. Egginton of the Pure Oil Company dies at age 49

1949 Racer Jerry Sneva is born

1950 The Chrysler Town & Country Newport hardtop coupe is introduced as a mid-year model

1955 Walter L. Goodman of the General Petroleum Corporation dies at age 62

1956 Charles E. Nelson, President and General Manager of the Nelson Muffler Corporation, is killed at age 53 in an automobile accident in Madison, WI

1958 Racer Frank Jelinski is born in Hannover, West Germany

1962 Louis Coatalen dies in Paris, France at age 82

1963 Racer Wally Dallenbach Jr. is born in New Brunswick, the son of racer Wally Dallenbach (Sr.)

1965 Racer Honore Wagner dies at age 44 when he crashes during a race at the Nurburgring in Germany

1967 Racer Didier Cottaz is born in Bourgoin, France

1969 Racer Laurent Aiello is born in Montrouge, France

1970 Racer Bryan Herta is born in Warren, MI

1972 Racer Rubens Barrichello is born in Sao Paulo, Brazil

1979 Hub van Doorne of Daf dies at age 79

1985 Antique automobile collector William Dube dies in Zephyrhills, FL

1988 The 3,000,000th United States-built Ford Escort is produced at the Wayne, MI plant

MAY 24

1867 Benjamin Briscoe is born in Detroit, MI

1876 Howard Carpenter Marmon is born in Richmond, IN

1899 The Paris-Bordeaux race is won by Fernand Charron driving a Panhard et Levassor

1899 The Back Bay Cycle & Motor Company opens the world's first public garage in Boston, MA

1903 Marcel Renault, age 31, and his riding mechanic, Vauthier, are killed during the Paris-Madrid race race in a crash near Couhe-Verac, France, with later crashes killing racer E. T. Stead and the riding mechanic Pierre Rodez - after completion of the first leg of the race to Bordeaux, France, officials cancelled the remainder of the event, declared leader Fernand Gabriel driving a Mors to be the winner, and the era of city-to-city races essentially ended

1913 The first hillclimb staged at Craigantlet, near Belfast, (Northern) Ireland is won by Harry G. Ferguson, later a tractor manufacturer and proponent of four-wheel-drive automobiles

1914 A modified Singer driven by Lionel Martin wins its class at the Aston Clinton (England) Hillclimb, an event that led to the creation of the Aston Martin sports car

1917 The Enger Motor Car Company facilities in Cincinnati, OH are sold at auction

1924 W. DeGroff Wilcox of the Edward G. Budd Manufacturing Company dies at age 44

1926 Automobile safety advocate Dr. J. William Haddon is born in Orange, NJ

1932 Craig Snover Thompson of the White Motor Company is born in Brooklyn, NY

1936 Horace L. Hirschler, a mechanical and automotive consulting engineer, dies in San Francisco, CA at age 44

1939 Rolf L. Olsen, Norwegian-born engine designer and consultant, dies in New Rochelle, NY

1942 Rally driver Hannu Mikkola is born in Finland

1953 Racer Lamberto Leoni is born in Argenta, Italy

1956 The Ford Motor Company convenes its first public shareholders' meeting

1960 Racer Scott Pruett is born in Sacramento, CA

1963 Racer Ivan Capelli is born in Milan, Italy

1964 Racer Fireball Roberts is critically injured during a 600-mile NASCAR race in Charlotte, NC, dying 37 days later from his injuries

1966 Racer Ricky Craven is born in Newburgh, ME

1981 Herbert Muller, 1966 and 1973 winner of the Targa Florio, is killed at age 41 when he crashes during a race at the Nurburgring in Germany

1983 Racer Rolf Stommelen is killed at age 39 when his Porsche crashes during a race in Riverside, CA

1986 The Belgian Grand Prix Formula 3000 race at Spa-Francorchamps is won by Phillippe Alliot is a March-Cosworth, at age 31 years, 302 days the oldest driver to win such an event

1987 Al Unser (Sr.) wins his fourth Indianapolis 500 driving a March-Cosworth, at age 47 years, 360 days the oldest winner of the race

1989 Driving a Mitsubishi Colt GTi-16V at Rattvik, Sweden, stunt driver Bengt Norberg sets world's records for driving a car on two side wheels for 192.873 miles and 27.842 miles in one hour

1990 Racer Dries van der Lof dies in Enschede, the Netherlands at age 70

1992 Racer Hitoshi Ogawa is killed at age 36 during a F3000 race at the Suzuka circuit in Japan

MAY 25

1874 Simon Mery, builder with his brother-in-law Leon Turcat of the 1898-1928 Turcat-Mery, is born in Marseille, France

1890 Edward R. Godfrey of General Motors is born in Maynard, MA

1893 Moses G. Farmer, an electrician whose inventions made pioneer electric automobiles feasible, dies in Chicago, IL at age 73

1898 The Haynes-Apperson Company is organized in Kokomo, IN with Elwood Haynes, Elmer Apperson, G. W. Charles, J. W. Polley, and W. H. Reed as Directors

1903 Jonathan Norton Leonard, a biographer of Henry Ford, is born in Somerville, MA

1904 Baron Pierre deCaters, driving a Mercedes at Ostend, Belgium, raises the land speed record to 97.25 mph

1914 Ettore Bugatti is issued a French patent for his "pursang" trademark

1915 The Lozier Motor Company factory in Plattsburgh, NY is sold at auction

1923 John Weitz, women's fashion designer and sports car enthusiast, is born in Berlin, Germany

1924 Donald Jesse Atwood Jr. of General Motors is born in Haverhill, MA

1927 Horace W. Potter joins the Packard Motor Car Company as Custom Body Specifications Manager

1935 The Aston Martin Owners Club is organized in London, England by Mort Morris-Goodall, Charles Jarrott, and S. C. H. "Sammy" Davis

1939 Racer Mike Harris is born in Mufulira, Northern Rhodesia (now Zambia)

1940 Racer Kevin Bartlett is born in Australia

1940 Racer and BRM designer Tony Southgate is born in Coventry, England

1940 Robert E. Fries, an employee of the Lozier Motor Company who later was a manufacturer of automobile axles and clutches, dies in Cleveland, OH at age 53

1945 KdF-Staadt, Germany, site of the Volkswagen factory, is renamed Wolfsburg

1947 Franco Cortese driving a Ferrari 125 Sport wins a race at the Carcalla circuit in Rome, the marque's first racing victory

1947 Roy Salvadori makes his bigtime racing debut, finishing fifth in his 2.9-litre Alfa Romeo in the Grand Prix des Frontieres at Chimay, Belgium

1947 Hyundai Construction, the first of the Hyundai companies, is founded by Chung Ju Yung

1950 Abraham M. Babitch, a design engineer with the AC Spark Plug Division of General Motors since 1924, dies in Flint, MI

1955 The 1955 Willys four-wheel-drive wagons are introduced

1956 Cesare Barbieri, the Italian-born inventor of automotive antifreeze, dies in New York City at age 78

1956 John Holman joins the Ford Motor Company to manage its national racing program

1962 General Motors stylist Ed Glowacke dies from leukemia at age 41

1970 Racer Ido Marang is killed in Panama City during an auto rally

1972 The International Automotive Hall of Fame opens in Wisconsin Dells, WI

1975 James C. Zeder of the Chrysler Corporation dies in Bloomfield Hills, MI at age 75

1985 Darrell Waltrip wins the first race staged at the Charlotte (NC) Motor Speedway

1987 Robert C. Stempel is elected as President of General Motors

MAY 26

1844 Jacob F. Studebaker is born in Ashland, OH

1862 Isaac Babbitt, the inventor in 1839 of the anti-friction metal that bears his name and is essential in modern bearing technology, dies at age 62

1868 The Studebaker Brothers Manufacturing Company is organized

1873 Automobile manufacturer Ernest Willoughby Petter is born in Great Britain

1880 Ernest John Sweetland, inventor of the Purolator oil filter, is born in Carson City, NV

1906 Racer Mauri Rose is born in Columbus, OH

1907 The world's first 24-hour race, the Endurance Derby staged at the Point Breeze dirt track in Philadelphia, PA, concludes with winners, J. L. Brown and Robert Maynes covering 791 miles in their Autocar for an average speed of just under 33 mph

1909 Joseph Irwin Miller of the Cummins Engine Company is born in Columbus, IN

1910 The Rayfield Motor Car Company is incorporated in Springfield, IL with Bruce Vancil as President, J. F. Miller as Vice President, E. E. Staley as Secretary, and William Rayfield as Treasurer - the later two men were also officers of the defunct Springfield Motor Car Company, whose factory was taken over by the new firm

1912 Cyril Snipe of England driving a S.C.A.T. becomes the first non-Italian winner of the Targa Florio

1923 The first Le Mans (France) 24-hour Grand Prix d'Endurance begins

1926 Race car mechanic Walter "Bud" Moore is born in Spartanburg, SC

1927 The 15,000,000th Ford Model T is produced

1932 The third Bugatti Royale Type 41 is delivered to Dr. A. J. Fuchs in Germany with a drop head coupe body by Weinberger of Munich

1934 The Ford Rotunda designed by Albert Kahn opens at the Chicago (IL) Century of Progress exposition

1936 The 3,000,000th Ford V-8 is produced

Madelia, MN circa 1937 - the car nearest the camera at left is a 1936 Ford Tudor powered by the famous flat-head V-8.

1937 Ford Motor Company personnel and United Auto Workers leaders clash in the "Battle of the Overpass"

1937 Automotive historian Lawrence Robert Gustin is born in Flint, MI

1938 Adolf Hitler lays the cornerstone for the "people's car" factory in the new city of KdF-Stadt, Germany (later renamed Wolfsburg for the nearby castle of Count von der Schulenberg) - the car was initially called the KdF-Wagen (*Kraft durch Freude* - strength through joy), but was later renamed Volkswagen

1938 Racer Peter Westbury is born in London, England

1943 Edsel B. Ford dies in Grosse Pointe Shores, MI at age 49

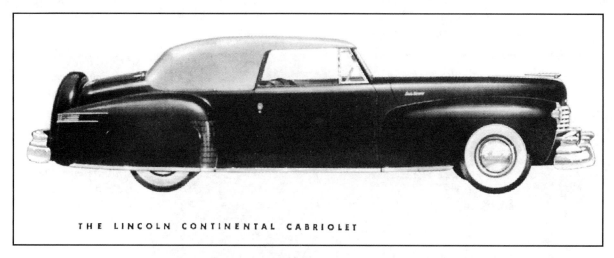

THE LINCOLN CONTINENTAL CABRIOLET

Edsel B. Ford's most enduring legacy is probably the Lincoln Continental.

1943 A. E. Bronson, Vice President and Secretary of the Dill Manufacturing Company and an employee of the firm since 1911, dies

1944 Racer Sam Posey is born in New York City

1949 The 20/Ghost Club is organized by Dr. Adrian Belsey and Stanley E. Sears to promote the preservation of Rolls-Royce Silver Ghost and 20 hp cars

1950 Great Britain ends World War II gasoline rationing

1953 The Kaiser-Frazer Corporation changes its name to the Kaiser Motors Corporation

1955 Racer Alberto Ascari, the 1952 and 1953 World Champion Driver, is killed at age 36 when his Ferrari 750 crashes during a practice run at Monza, Italy

1955 Donald H. Merry, a manufacturing official with the Packard Motor Car Company, Ford Motor Company, Kaiser-Frazer Corporation, and Avco Manufacturing Corporation, dies at age 35

1957 Racer Roberto Ravaglia is born in Mestre, Italy

1959 Automotive publisher Andrew Lee Dyke dies in St. Louis, MO

1960 Jaguar Cars Ltd. acquires the Daimler Motor Company, Ltd. of Coventry, England

1969 Racer Paul Hawkins is killed at age 31 when his Lola T70 crashes during the Tourist Trophy race at Oulton Park, England

1971 The Mercedes-Benz ESF 03, the first of five special cars produced to accent safety features, is unveiled to the public

1974 Racer Silvio Moser dies at age 33 from injuries received when his Lola crashed during the previous month's Monza (Italy) 1000 km race

1981 Chrysler and Peugeot announce plans to jointly produce automobiles and engines

1983 The Ford Tempo and Mercury Topaz are introduced

1996 The first U. S. 500 is staged at the Michigan International Speedway in Brooklyn, MI and won by Jimmy Vasser driving a Reynard-Honda 250

MAY 27

1826 Samuel Brown successfully drives his 40-litre internal combustion engined car in London, England

1841 Rene Panhard is born in Paris, France

1881 Ralph W. Gallagher of the Standard Oil Company is born in Salamanca, NY

1903 The Pope Motor Car Company announces that they have acquired the factory of the International Motor Car Company in Toledo, OH, manufacturers of the 1901-1903 Toledo steam and gasoline cars, and that their new cars will be marketed as the Pope-Toledo

Pope-Toledo automobiles would be manufactured here until 1909 when the marque was discontinued. The building itself began its third life as the home of the new Overland built by Willys.

1904 The first Buick "Valve-in-Head" engine is completed

1905 White's "Whistling Billy" steam race car makes its racing debut, with Webb Jay winning the open ten-mile race at Chicago's Harlem Racetrack

1914 The first issue of *GMC Truck Talk* is published

1923 The first Le Mans 24-hour race concludes, with winners Andre Lagache and Rene Leonard covering 1,372.928 miles in their Chenard-Walcker

1927 Production of the Ford Model T officially ends after 15,007,033 units had been built, although truck production continued on a limited basis

1929 Sir Henry Segrave, holder of the land speed record, is knighted by King George V

1934 The Auto-Union makes its debut in a race at the Avus circuit near Berlin, Germany, with August Momberger taking third place

1939 T. Morey Rude, Vice President and General Manager of the Bundy Tubing Company and a former employee of Fiat and Scripps-Booth, dies at age 54

1939 Charles Bryant Drake Wood, President of the Pressed Steel Company and an authority on pressed steel stampings for automobiles, dies at age 54

1942 Racer Piers Raymond Courage is born in Colchester, England

1942 Racer Robin Michael Widdows is born in Witney, Oxfordshire, England

1951 Stirling Moss makes his Formula 1 debut, finishing eighth at the Swiss Grand Prix in Bremgarten in an HWM-Alta - the Veritas makes it Formula 1 debut, but the car driven by Peter Hirt retires with a faulty fuel pump

1954 American Motors officials announce that Hudson production will end in Detroit, MI and shift to the Nash factory in Kenosha, WI

1961 Racer Pierre-Henri Raphanel is born in Algiers, Algeria of French ancestry

1962 Automotive consultant Charles B. Rose dies at age 82

1969 Racer Jeremy Mayfield is born in Owensboro, KY

1975 T. J. Ross, a longtime public relations consultant for the Chrysler Corporation, dies in Rye, NY at age 81

MAY 28

1870 Shock absorber manufacturer Edward Vassallo Hartford is born in Orange, NJ

1876 Charles Frederick Herreshoff, a prominent boatbuilder and inventor of automobile improvements who built the Herreshoff motor car 1909-1914, is born in Nice, France

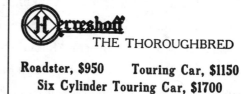

1882 J. V. Whitbeck of Chandler, Franklin, Oldsmobile, Thomas, and Lozier is born in Sodus, NY

1887 Ray Austin Graham of Graham-Paige is born in Washington, IN

1900 Frederick A. LaRoche registers "Multimobile" as a trademark - he was the head of the American Darracq Automobile Company of New York City, importers of this French marque

1902 The magazine *Car Illustrated* debuts

1903 Henry Abram Lozier Sr. of the Lozier Motor Company dies

1914 The last pre-World War I Irish hillclimb is staged at Ballinascorney near Dublin and won by J. T. Wood in a G.W.K.

1916 Barney Oldfield driving his old front-wheel-drive Christie laps the Indianapolis (IN) Motor Speedway at 102.6 mph, the first time that the 100 mph barrier had been broken at that track

1917 NASCAR mechanic Ray Fox is born in Pelham, NH

1919 Andre Citroen introduces his first car, the Model A

1920 Racer Jim Russell, better known as an instructor and developer of young drivers, is born in Downham Market, Norfolk, England

1921 The 5,000,000th Ford Model T is produced

1922 The Dodge Brothers Series Two commercial vehicles are introduced

1926 Racer Marvin Panch is born in Menominee, WI

1927 The last Rolls-Royce Silver Ghost is completed at the Springfield, MA factory

1927 Racer Edward Julius "Eddie" Sachs Jr. is born in Bethlehem, PA

1930 The 7,000,000th Chevrolet is produced, a 1930 2-door Coach

1930 The Libbey-Owens Glass Company changes its name to the Libbey-Owens-Ford Glass Company

1932 Heinrich-Joachim von Morgen, winner of the 1930 Masaryk Grand Prix, is killed in a crash during a practice run at the Nurburgring in Germany

1936 The 3,000,000th Buick is produced, a Series 40 Special 4-door sedan

1937 The Golden Gate Bridge in San Francisco, CA is opened to vehicular traffic

1938 Racer Eppie Wietzes is born in Canada

1939 Grover Ira Mitchell, a design engineer with the Streator Motor Car Company, manufacturers of the Halliday automobile, and later a professor of mechanical engineering, dies at age 50 from injuries suffered in an automobile accident

1940 The 250,117th 1940 Buick is produced, breaking the company's model year record set in 1928

1952 The first Dodge V-8 engine is produced

1953 The last Kaiser Dragon is produced

1970 The last International Loadstar truck is built at the Fort Wayne, IN plant as production of this model shifts to the new plant in Springfield, OH

1975 G. Elizabeth Carmichael, transexual promoter of the 3-wheel Dale, is convicted of fraud in Los Angeles, CA

1976 Volkswagenwerk AG announces the purchase of the unfinished Chrysler Corporation factory in New Sharon, PA for the purpose of manufacturing Volkswagens in the United States

1989 The Onyx makes its Formula 1 debut in the Mexican Grand Prix in Mexico City, but the Type ORE1 driven by Stefan Johansson retires with transmission problems

1990 Taiichi Ohno of Toyota dies in Toyota City, Japan at age 78

MAY 29

1767 Internal combustion engine pioneer Philippe Lebon is born in Brachay, France

1868 William Carleton Wenk of Franklin and Pierce-Arrow is born in Hartford, CT

1883 Stuart Andros de la Rue of Bentley is born

1891 Albert Bradley of General Motors is born in Blackburn, England

1892 Ernest Carlton Kanzler of the Ford Motor Company is born in Saginaw, MI

1895 The first automobile race in Italy, a 62-mile round trip between Turin and Asti, is won by Simone Federmann in a Daimler omnibus

1901 The Paris-Bordeaux race is won by Henri Fournier driving a Mors - the second Gordon Bennett Trophy race, run concurrently over the same course, is won by the only finisher, Leonce Girardot in a Panhard et Levassor

1903 Racer Mark Everard Pepys, the 6th Earl of Cottenham, is born

1912 The Smith Automobile Company factory in Topeka, KS is sold to the Perfection Metal Silo Company of Kansas City, MO

1917 Frederick H. Clarke and Dr. Henry F. Clarke of the Kent Motors Corporation are arrested in Newark, NJ for stock fraud

1918 Humorist Herb Shriner, the longtime owner of the one-off Phantom Corsair, is born in Toledo, OH

1922 Racer Joseph Herbert "Joe" Weatherly is born in Oak Grove, VA

1934 John Baptist Curcio of Mack Trucks, Inc. is born in Hazleton, PA

1934 The Cadillac 1933-1936 "Goddess" mascot is patented by designers Chris J. Klein and J. R. Morgan

1935 The Ford Motor Company pavilion designed by Walter Dorwin Teague opens at the California-Pacific Exposition in San Diego, CA

1939 Racer Alfred "Al" Unser Sr. is born in Albuquerque, NM

1944 Hiram J. Halle, a principal in the development of high octane gasoline and President of the Universal Oil Products Company, dies at age 77

1946 The first production Kaisers and Frazers are built at the Willow Run factory near Ann Arbor, MI

1950 Preston Tucker's lawsuit against his former prosecutors is dismissed

1955 Racer Ken Schrader is born in Fenton, MO

1957 Racer Bobby Hamilton is born in Nashville, TN

1957 Ivan W. Hansen, Sales Engineer of the Hyatt Bearings Division of General Motors, dies at age 33

1960 Richie Ginther makes his Formula 1 debut, driving an experimental rear-engined Ferrari-Dino 246P to a sixth place finish in the Monaco Grand Prix in Monte Carlo - the front-engined Scarab of Lance Reventlow debuts, but is outclassed by the new rear-engined cars and fails to qualify - the race is won by Stirling Moss in a Lotus, the first Formula 1 victory for the marque

1960 Maj. Gen. William F. Marquat, a United States Army officer who served as Automobile Editor for the *Seattle* (WA) *Times* 1919-1920, dies at age 66

1961 Benjamin Samuels of the Yellow Cab Company dies at age 83

1963 Racer Ukyo Katayama is born in Tokyo, Japan

1964 Racer Osvaldo Negri Jr. is born in Brazil

1963 Grover E. Reuckstell, founder of Ruckstell Sales & Manufacturing Company and inventor of the two-speed axle often fitted to the Ford Model T, dies in Palm Springs, CA

1965 Matra makes its racing debut, but the two MS1 cars perform poorly in the Monaco Grand Prix

1969 Harold F. Sheets, former Chairman of the Board of the Socony-Vacuum Oil Company, Inc., dies at age 86

1971 Al Unser (Sr.) becomes the first Indianapolis 500 winner to receive a purse of more than $200,000

1973 Sir George Harriman of Austin dies at age 65

1863 Automobile parts manufacturer Walter F. Rockwell dies at age 73

1977 A. J. Foyt, driving a Coyote-Foyt of his own design, becomes the first four-time winner of the Indianapolis 500 - Janet Guthrie becomes the first woman driver in the event but retires with mechanical problems

1978 Alfa Romeo President Gaetano Cortesi and three other executives are sentenced to prison terms for fraud

MAY 30

1886 C. F. Scott, the inventor of the first electric dynamometer for testing a complete automobile, is born in New York City

1893 George A. Sloan, a Director of the Goodyear Tire & Rubber Company, is born in Nashville, TN

1896 The first automobile accident recorded in the United States occurs in New York City when a Duryea driven by Henry Wells of Springfield, MA collides with Evelyn Thomas' bicycle

1896 *Cosmopolitan* magazine publisher John Brisben Walker stages the second automobile race in the United States, a 15-mile run from New York City to Irvington-on-Hudson, NY - the only finisher was J. Frank Duryea, who won the entire purse of $3,000

1897 The Erie & Sturgis gasoline carriage designed and built by James Philip Erie & Samuel D. Sturgis is given its first test drive in Los Angeles, CA

1897 The first Winton is publicly demonstrated with a one mile trial run in Cleveland, OH, and achieves a top speed of 33.8 mph

1903 The first of the streamlined Stanley steam "Wogglebug" racers makes its debut at the Readville Track near Boston, MA - F. E. Stanley would defeat all comers and set a United States one-mile speed record

1903 Barney Oldfield, driving the Ford 999 at the Empire City Track in New York City, defeats Charles Wridgway in a 40-hp Peerless, in the process becoming the first United States citizen to hit 60 mph and breaking the record set just hours earlier by F. E. Stanley

1905 The Packard Gray Wolf, now owned by Col. E. R. Green, makes its last racing appearance, with Jesse Ellingsworth driving in a 10-mile race in Chicago, IL

1905 Reo makes its racing debut as Daniel Wurges wins two of three races driving the Reo Bird at the Empire City track in Yonkers, NY

1906 Rudolf Hasse, winner of the 1937 Belgian Grand Prix, is born in Saxony province, Germany

1908 A Chadwick Six driven by Willie Haupt sets a track record at the Giant's Despair hillclimb in Wilkes-Barre, PA, becoming the first supercharged automobile to compete in (and win) a race

1909 Julien Potterat, the Swiss-born designer of the Riga, Latvia-built Russo-Baltique, drives one of his cars to victory in the Riga-St. Petersburg race

1911 Ray Harroun wins the first Indianapolis 500 averaging 74.602 mph in the Marmon Wasp, often cited as the first car with a rearview mirror

1911 William C. Durant and Louis Chevrolet announce plans to build a new automobile, the Chevrolet

1913 Jules Goux wins the Indianapolis 500 in his Peugeot Type L76 to become the first foreign winner, both driver and car, of this race

1914 William "Coal-Oil Billy" Carlson finishes ninth in the Indianapolis 500 in the Maxwell 140-hp special, the first kerosene-powered car to compete in the race - the winner was Rene Thomas driving a Delage

1916 Eddie Rickenbacker and Peter Henderson are the first drivers to wear protective headgear during the Indianapolis 500

1919 Col. Jesse G. Vincent drives a Packard Twin Six as the pace car for the Indianapolis 500 - a special Packard with a 299-cid V-12 driven by Ralph DePalma finishes sixth, the only time a V-12 engined car finished this race - racers Louis LeCocq of France and Arthur Thurman of Washington state are killed during the event, which was won by Howdy Wilcox in a Peugeot

1921 Tommy Milton wins the Indianapolis 500 in the Frontenac Special

1921 Johnny Gerber of Meriden, KS, driving a homemade speedster powered by a Chevrolet 490 engine, finishes second in a 25-mile race in St. Joseph, MO in his personal racing debut as well as for the Chevrolet marque

1922 Bentley enters its first international race and makes its only appearance in the Indianapolis 500 with the 3-litre driven by W. D. Hawkes finishing 13th behind winner Jimmy Murphy in a Duesenberg-Miller - the Frontenac Four designed by Louis Chevrolet is introduced to the public during the pre-race festivities

1923 During the Indianapolis 500 Tom Alley crashes through a fence killing spectator Bert Schoup, the first time that such an event had occurred at this site

1924 Barney Oldfield introduces the prototype Oldfield coupe prior to the running of the 14th Indianapolis 500

1924 Co-drivers Lora "L. L." Corum and Joe Boyer win the Indianapolis 500 in a Duesenberg, the marque's first victory of this race

1925 Co-drivers Peter DePaolo and Norman Batten win the Indianapolis 500 in a Duesenberg, becoming at 101.13 mph the first to break the 100 mph barrier in the race

1929 Racer Bill Spence is killed during the Indianapolis 500 race, which was won by Ray Keech in a Miller

1930 The first two 16-cylinder cars appear in the Indianpolis 500 - a Cord L29 driven by E. L. Cord is the first pace car to have front-wheel-drive

1931 The Cummins Diesel Special driven by Dave Evans finishes 13th in the Indianapolis 500, becoming the first car to complete the race non-stop

1932 John N. Willys resigns as United States ambassador to Poland at the request of President Herbert Hoover who wants him to return to Toledo, OH and resume management of the troubled Willys-Overland Company

John N. Willy's entry into the low-priced field was the Whippet. This 1928 Model 98 sedan was owned by the author's maternal grandfather, Fred Allan - his mother and uncle are pictured with the car at their home in Tuttle, ND.

1933 Racers Lester Spangler and Mark Billman along with riding mechanic G. L. "Monk" Gordon are killed during the Indianapolis 500, which was won by Louis Meyer in a Miller

1935 Racer Clay Weatherly is killed during the Indianapolis 500, which was won by Kelly Petillo is a Wetteroth-Offenhauser

1936 Louis Meyer becomes the first three-time winner of the Indianapolis 500

1939 Victor W. Kliesrath is issued a United States patent for an automobile transmission

1939 Defending champion Floyd Roberts is killed at age 37 during the Indianapolis 500, which was won by Wilbur Shaw in a Maserati 8CTF

1939 Racer Dieter Quester is born in Vienna, Austria

1941 Matthew F. Bramley of Templar dies in Lakewood, OH at age 73

1947 George W. Mason is named President of the Nash-Kelvinator Corporation and drives a Nash Ambassador sedan as the pace car for the 31st Indianapolis 500 - William "Shorty" Cantlon is killed during the race which was won by Mauri Rose in a Deidt-Offenhauser

1949 A Jaguar XK120, driven by R. M. V. Sutton in Jabbeke, Belgium, sets a stock car speed record of 132.596 mph

1950 Martin J. Brennan, an official of the Willard Storage Battery Company since 1913, dies in Detroit, MI at age 56

1952 Troy Ruttman, driving the Seal Fast Kuzma-Offenhauser, wins the Indianapolis 500 at age 22 years, 81 days to become the youngest winner of the race

1953 The Dearborn Motors Corporation, distributors of Ford tractors, is reorganized as a division of the Ford Motor Company

1953 Racer Carl Scarborough is killed during the Indianapolis 500, which is won by Bill Vukovich in a Kurtis KK500A-Offenhauser

1955 Walter C. Reid, Chairman of the Mack Trucks, Inc. dies in Portland, OR at age 86

IT'S PART OF THE LANGUAGE...BUILT LIKE A

TRUCKS • BUSES • FIRE APPARATUS
AND ELECTRONIC EQUIPMENT

1955 Racer Bill Vukovich is killed at age 36 while leading the Indianapolis 500 in his quest to become the first to win the race three years in a row

1956 Pat Flaherty wins the Indianapolis 500 in the John Zink Special - this was the first race sanctioned by the United States Auto Club (USAC)

1957 Racer Piero Carini is killed at age 35 when his Ferrari Testa Rossa crashes during a 1500-cc sports car race near Saint-Etienne, France

1958 Racer Pat O'Connor is killed at age 29 during the Indianapolis 500, which was won by Jimmy Bryan in an Epperly-Offenhauser

1959 Rodger Ward becomes the first Indianapolis 500 winner to receive more than $100,000

1964 Eddie Sachs, age 37, and Dave MacDonald, age 26, are killed during the Indianapolis 500, which was won by A. J. Foyt in a Watson-Offenhauser

1964 Racer Andrea Montermini is born in Sassuolo, Italy

1965 Jim Clark, driving a Lotus 38-Ford, wins the Indianapolis 500

1967 The Mazda Cosmo is introduced, featuring the world's first production twin-rotor Wankel engine

1975 Diamond Reo Trucks, Inc. is declared bankrupt

1976 Racer Elmer George dies in Terre Haute, IN at age 47

1978 The 20,000,000th Oldsmobile is produced

1989 James V. Rose of the Chrysler Corporation dies at age 63

1990 Gerald Greenwald, Vice Chairman of the Chrysler Corporation, resigns

1995 F. R. W. "Lofty" England, longtime Jaguar executive, dies in Gmunden, Austria at age 83

MAY 31

1841 William Rockefeller, younger brother of John D. Rockefeller and an official with the Standard Oil Company, is born in Richford, NY

1863 Automobile parts manufacturer John H. Dohner is born in Champaign, OH

1874 Father George A. Belcourt, a Roman Catholic Indian missionary and pioneer Canadian automobile enthusiast, dies in Shediac, New Brunswick

1888 Automobile designer James Scripps Booth is born in Detroit, MI

1888 Daniel James Moran of the Continental Oil Company is born in Cygnet, OH

1889 James Edwin Delong, Assistant Engineer of the Rutenber Motor Company 1912-1914, Factory Manager of the Indiana Truck Corporation 1919-1923, and a longtime official of the Waukesha Motor Company of Waukesha, WI, is born in Zionsville, IN

1895 Oscar H. Banker, an inventor of automotive components and crusader for automobile safety, is born in Moonjoosoon, Turkey

1903 Joseph William Eskridge of Hudson and American Motors is born in Winona, MS

1904 Byron J. Carter is issued a United States patent for his friction drive transmission

1907 The first motorized taxicab service in the United States is started in New York City

1908 Bert Jones Mitchell, the designer of the first automobile air conditioner (installed in a 1939 Packard), is born in Thayer, MO

1909 The Walter Automobile Company is reorganized as the Mercer Automobile Company with Ferdinand W. Roebling as President, Charles Roebling as Vice President, John L. Kuser as Secretary-Treasurer, R. I. Kingston as General Manager, and Etienne Planche as Chief Designer

1912 Edmund Dangerfield opens the world's first automobile museum in London, England

1914 John Henry Brinker of the A. O. Smith Corporation is born in Cleveland, OH

1923 The Sterling-Knight Motors Company announces the purchase of the Supreme Motor Company of Warren, OH and its intent to begin production of a 6-cylinder car designed by Pete Sterling

1927 The Falcon Motor Corporation of Elyria, OH produces its 3,000th Falcon-Knight

1927 The Willys-Knight 1927-1928 "Knight with Lance" mascot is patented by designer F. C. Ruppel

Lahr Motor Sales Company was the Willys-Overland dealer in Bismarck, ND.
The building later served as a Montgomery-Ward retail store and is today largely
occupied by professional offices.

1929 The Ford Motor Company signs a "Technical Assistance" contract to produce cars in the Soviet Union

1934 Lawrence P. Fisher retires as President and General Manager of the Cadillac Motor Car Company

1934 The Socony-Vacuum Corporation changes its name to the Socony-Vacuum Oil Company

1934 Louis H. Palmer, an authority on motor coach operation and urban transportation problems, dies at age 53

1939 Goldie Gardner, driving the MG EX135 on the Dessau (Germany) Autobahn, raises his own Class G speed record to 203.2 mph

1939 Racer Rod Banting is born in Great Britain

1942 Racer Joseph "Jo" Vonlanthen is born in Saint-Ursanne, Switzerland

1948 Thomas S. Derr, a Stanley steam car mechanic who sporadically built the American Steam Car 1926-1942 using rebuilt Stanley engines and Hudson chassis, dies in Waban, MA at age 51

1948 Racer Jack Baldwin is born

1955 Gustav A. Lillieqvist, Swiss-born Research Director for American Steel Foundries and an internationally known automotive metallugist, dies

1955 B. H. McMillan of Chevrolet dies at age 49

1959 Racer Andrea de Cesaris is born in Rome, Italy

1959 Jo Bonnier wins the Dutch Grand Prix at Zandvoort in his BRM P25, the first Grand Prix victory for the British marque after ten years of effort - Innes Ireland makes his Grand Prix debut in this race, finishing fourth in his Lotus-Climax 16 - Aston Martin makes its Formula 1 debut, but cars driven by Carroll Shelby and Roy Salvadori are forced to retire

1962 Racer Philippe Gache is born in Avignon, France

1965 John F. Gordon retires as President of General Motors

1966 Renault announces plans to become involved with the enlargement of the Moskovskii Zavod Malolitrajnikh Automobilei factory in Moscow, USSR, manufacturers of the Moskvitch

1968 Mario Castoldi of Fiat dies at age 80

1972 The Mercedes-Benz ESF 05, the third of five experimental safety vehicles, is unveiled to the public

1973 The Audi Fox is introduced

1974 The Antique Automobile Club of America (AACA) votes to include all cars 25 years old or more plus selected orphan marques as eligible for club activities

1977 Floyd Davis, winner of the 1941 Indianapolis 500, dies

1985 The Ford Aerostar minivan introduced as a 1986 model

1992 A monument noting the accomplishments of automobile pioneer Sephaniah Reese is dedicated in Plymouth, PA

1992 The Andrea Moda makes its only Formula 1 appearance, but the car designed by Nick Wirth and driven by Roberto Moreno retires from the Monaco Grand Prix with mechanical problems

JUNE 1

1796 Internal combustion engine pioneer Nicolas Leonard Sadi Carnot is born in Paris, France

1828 Warren Packard, the father of William D. Packard and James W. Packard, is born in Lordstown, OH

1849 Twins Francis Edgar and Freelan Oscar Stanley are born in Kingfield, ME

1878 Childe Harold Wills of the Ford Motor Company, and later builder of the Wills Sainte Claire, is born in Fort Wayne, IN

1882 Automotive engineer William T. Murphy is born in Providence, RI

1884 Automobile historian Arthur Pound is born in Pontiac, MI

1885 Armstrong Alexander Stambaugh of the Standard Oil Company of Ohio is born in New Germantown, PA

1899 Automobile pioneer Sylvester Hayward Roper dies from heart failure in Boston, MA at age 72 while riding a steam bicycle of his own invention

1902 The Velie Carriage Company begins construction of its factory in Moline, IL

1903 Sizaire Freres et Naudin is organized in Puteaux, France by brothers Maurice and George Sizaire along with Louis Naudin

1905 Germany begins motorized postal service

1906 Ohio requires all automobile owners to prepare homemade license plates including the letters "OH" and register their cars with the Secretary of State

1909 Six cars leave New York City at the exact moment that the Alaska-Yukon-Pacific Exposition opens in Seattle, WA in "The Great Race" to that city

1912 Mississippi issues its first license plates for automobiles, but in a unique development the State Supreme Court in 1914 rules that the law requiring registration is unconstitutional

1913 Thomas W. Palmer, a United States Senator 1883-1889 (R-MI) who was an original partner in the Detroit Automobile Company, dies in Detroit, MI at age 83

1915 The Chevrolet 490 is placed on sale

1915 The Packard Twin Six Series 1-25 is introduced

1915 The Kuhlman Electric Company, manufacturers of automobile parts, is incorporated in Michigan

1916 William C. Durant is elected President of General Motors to succeed Charles W. Nash whose resignation would become effective in two months

1916 Edward T. Strong is named General Sales Manager of the Buick Motor Company

1916 E. S. Hare is promoted to Supervisor of the Truck Division, Packard Motor Car Company just five months after joining the firm as a salesman

1917 Henry M. Leland resigns as President of the Cadillac Motor Car Company

1917 Paul Francis Lorenz of the Ford Motor Company is born in St. Joseph, MO

1918 Artaud and Louis Dufresne, formerly with Panhard et Levassor, join with Gabriel Voisin to begin creating the first Voisin based on a large car design purchased from Andre Citroen

1921 Duesenberg, Inc. officially opens its new factory in Indianapolis, IN

1923 The Tarkington Motor Company of Rockford, IL dissolves after producing just six cars

1925 The 1926 Nash Series 260 is introduced

1926 The 1927 Nash Series 260 is introduced

1926 Racer Darel Eugene "Yancy" Dieringer is born in Indianapolis, IN

1928 The 1929 Nashes are introduced with top-of-the-line models featuring twin ignition

1929 Tatsuro Toyoda of Toyota is born in Nagoya, Japan

1929 The first Marquette, a companion marque of the Buick, is produced

1930 Andrew L. Riker dies in Fairfield, CT at age 61

Among Andrew L. Riker's many credits is the design of the first gasoline-powered Locomobile.

1931 The 1932 Nash Series 900 is introduced

1931 Automotive historian Mira Wilkins is born in New York City

1934 The 1934 Dodge Series DRXX is introduced as a mid-year economy line

1934 Nicholas Dreystadt is named General Manager of Cadillac

1937 The Packard 1936-1937 "Goddess of Speed" mascot is patented by designer Werner H. A. Gubitz

1940 GMC acquires the facilities of the Wilson Foundry & Machine Company to increase their Pontiac, MI production capabilities

1943 John F. Gordon is named Chief Engineer of Cadillac

1943 Henry Ford returns to the office of President of the Ford Motor Company, Charles E. Sorensen is named Vice President, Burt J. Craig is named Vice President and Treasurer plus given a seat on the Board of Directors, and Frank C. Campsall is named to the new position of Assistant General Manager

1943 Automobile historian Lawrence J. White is born in New York City

1944 The first issue of *Packard News* is published

1946 Boris Peter Sergay, an authority on automobile traction and a former design engineer with the Reo Motor Car Company, dies at age 46

1948 Racer Thomas Edsol "Tom" Sneva is born in Spokane, WA

1949 Raymond H. Laird retires from the Ford Motor Company

1950 Vernon C. Hoover of Revere Copper & Brass, Inc. dies at age 45

1951 The White Motor Company acquires the Sterling Motor Truck Company

1951 James M. Crawford retires from General Motors

1952 Walter R. Grant replaces Hugh J. Ferry as Treasurer of the Packard Motor Car Company, and Milton E. Tibbetts retires as Vice President and Patent Counsel after 45 with the company

1952 Pat Purcell joins NASCAR as Executive Director

1956 The Brunswick Ordnance Corporation, Mack Manufacturing Corporation, Mack Motor Truck Corporation, Mack Motor Truck Company, Mack Motor Car Company, and International Plainfield Motor Company, all subsidiaries of Mack Trucks, Inc., are merged into the parent firm

1959 Bobby Allison records his first major victory in an automobile race at Montgomery, AL

1959 Racer Martin Brundle is born in King's Lynn, England

1960 Harold G. Warner is named General Manager of Cadillac replacing James M. Roche

1961 The Fiat 600D and 1100 Special are introduced to the United States market

1963 The Greenfield, MI Post Office at Henry Ford Museum changes its name to Greenfield Village

1964 Racer Davy Jones is born in Chicago, IL

1965 The Fiat 1500 Spider is introduced to the United States market

1965 James M. Roche is elected President of General Motors

1970 Bill Smyth is named Director of Competition for USAC

1972 Pennzoil United Inc. changes its name to the Pennzoil Company

1973 Tire manufacturer Harvey S. Firestone Jr. dies in Akron, OH at age 75

1977 American Motors Chairman Roy D. Chapin Jr. hosts a gala premier for AMC's "Concept Cars for the 80's" at the Hilton Hotel in New York City

1986 Racer Jo Gartner is killed at age 32 when his Porsche crashes during the Le Mans (France) 24-Hour race

1994 Ray Carr driving his 1902 Northern arrives in Jekyll Island, GA 24 days and 2,489 miles after leaving San Diego, CA - this car has the distinction of being the oldest car to cross the United States under its own power

JUNE 2

1817 Steam engine pioneer George Henry Corliss is born in Easton, NY

1866 Automotive artist Edward Penfield is born in Brooklyn, NY

1866 William Brewster of Brewster & Company, a manufacturer of custom automobile bodies and complete luxury cars, is born in New York City

COACH work designed and built by Brewster & Co. was awarded a gold medal at the World's Exposition in Paris in 1878, and the *Légion d'Honneur* was conferred on the senior member of the firm. . . . American carriage makers celebrated the occasion with a banquet. . . . "In beauty, style and workmanship, I believe their carriages are unsurpassed," said the speaker of the evening, "but in one respect I take exception to them and I will state it confidentially to you gentlemen here, their carriages never wear out! I am like a boy with a toy; I like a new one now and then." . . . This statement, made about the famous Brewster carriages of fifty years ago, is even more impressively true of Brewster automobile coach work today. Indeed, it has been no uncommon thing for Brewster-built coach work to outlast two chassis; and cases are on record where it has been used on as many as five chassis. . . . The recent purchase of Brewster by Rolls-Royce places at the disposal of the American motorist a car unrivaled in beauty, staunchness, and riding comfort—a car with coach work as well as chassis to keep alive the tradition of "never wearing out." The illustration shows a Nottingham by Rolls-Royce and Brewster. Rolls-Royce/Brewster, Fifth Avenue at 56th Street, New York. Also at all Rolls-Royce Branches.

ROLLS-ROYCE
BREWSTER

1874 George Brayton is issued a United States patent for his "Gas-Engines"

1875 Charles Stewart Mott of General Motors is born in Newark, NJ

1877 Robert Craig Hupp is born in Grand Rapids, MI

1884 Ferdinando Minoia, a factory racer for Isotta-Fraschini and Alfa Romeo, is born in Milan, Italy

1897 Oil magnate and Rolls-Royce fancier Nubar Sarkis Gulbenkian is born

1900 The Salzburg-Linz-Vienna trial is won by Richard Ritter von Stern driving a 4-cylinder, 24-hp Daimler

1908 The Everitt-Metzger-Flanders Company, makers of the E-M-F, is founded by Barney Everitt, William E. Metzger, and Walter E. Flanders with William E. Kelly as Chief Engineer

1911 The first Pierce-Arrow truck is sold to the International Brewing Corporation

1913 Stylist and coachbuilder Pietro Frua is born in Piedmont, Italy

1914 Robert William Mullin Jr. of Mack Trucks, Inc. is born in Brooklyn, NY

1919 The Martin-Wasp Corporation is formed in Bennington, VT by Karl H. Martin, Robert E. Healy and E. H. Holden

1920 Racer Don Branson is born in Rantoul, IL

1930 Wallace Boyd Askins of the White Motor Corporation is born in Chicago, IL

1931 Harry W. Bundy, a manufacturer of automobile tubing and hoses, dies in Beaver Island, MI at age 55

1932 Hugh Chalmers, President of the Chalmers Motor Company 1910-1916 and Chairman of the reorganized Chalmers Motor Corporation 1916-1922, dies in Beacon, NY at age 58

1934 Reginald G. Burr, an authority on urban motor bus operations, dies at age 35 from acute appendicitis

1935 The 2,000,000th Ford V-8 is produced

1936 The American Bantam Car Company is incorporated with Roy S. Evans as President

1937 Otto C. Rohde, Vice President and Chief Engineer of the Champion Spark Plug Company, dies five days after being injured while watching practice runs for the Indianapolis 500 race

1939 Goldie Gardner driving the MG EX135 on the Dessau (Germany) Autobahn raises his own Class G record for the mile to 203.85 mph

1939 Automotive historian Peter Collier is born in Hollywood, CA

1944 GMC receives the Army-Navy "E" award for production efficiency and achievement in supplying war equipment

1947 Charles L. McCuen is named General Manager of Research for General Motors, succeeding the retiring Charles F. Kettering

1952 The plaster model of the original Chevrolet Corvette is completed

1954 The Volvo Sport, a 2-seat sports car with fibreglass body by Glasspar of USA, is introduced at the Torslanda Airport near Goteborg, Sweden

1956 Racer Jan Lammers is born in Zandvoort, the Netherlands

1957 Harry A. Knox dies in Miami, FL at age 82

1958 Racer Erwin Bauer is killed at age 45 during a 1000 km race at the Nurburgring circuit in Germany

1960 Racer Kyle Petty is born in Randleman, NC, the son of racer Richard Petty

1962 Racer Dennis Taylor is killed at age 41 when he crashes during a Formula Junior race in Monte Carlo, Monaco

1968 Henry M. Hogan of General Motors dies at age 72

1970 Mrs. Anna Thompson Dodge, widow of Horace E. Dodge, dies in Grosse Pointe, MI at age 98 (contemporary accounts erroneously listed her age as 103)

1970 Racer Bruce McLaren is killed at age 32 when his McLaren M8D crashes during a practice run at the Goodwood track in England

1972 Chrysler Corporation drops plans to purchase a controlling interest in Mitsubishi

1983 Harold T. Ames, a longtime associate of E. L. Cord, dies in Rancho Mirage, CA at age 89

JUNE 3

1837 Rollin Charles White, the first President of the Baker Motor Vehicle Company, is born in Putney, VT

1864 Ransom Eli Olds is born in Geneva, OH

1867 Automotive steel manufacturer A. D. Dorman is born in Wheatland, PA

1873 Automobile battery designer Bruce Ford is born in Brooklyn, NY

1878 Racer Bernd Eli "Barney" Oldfield is born in Wauseon, OH

1896 Roy T. Hurley, the Chairman of the Curtiss-Wright Corporation 1952-1961 who was prominent in the affairs of the Studebaker-Packard Corporation during the late 1950's, is born in New York City

1917 Hugo Fischer von Roslerstamm, longtime Technical Director of the Nesselsdorfer Wagenbau-Fabriks-Gesellschaft, dies in Vienna, Austria

1924 The Chrysler 1924-1927 "Winged Cap" mascot is patented by designer Oliver H. Clark

1925 The 100,000th Chevrolet built at the former Samson factory in Janesville, WI, a Series M 1-ton Utility Express truck chassis, is produced

1925 The last British-built Rolls-Royce Silver Ghost actually sold, a Barker touring car ordered by J. Henry Thomas, is completed by the coachbuilder and delivered to its owner

1927 Thomas E. Rush of Mack and International dies at age 60

1930 The first American Austins are delivered to dealers

1930 The Cadillac 1930-1932 "Goddess" mascot is patented by designer William Schnell

1934 The Mercedes-Benz W25 makes a successful debut at the Nurburgring with Manfred von Brauchitsch winning the 12th International Eifel race

1937 Racer Jean-Pierre Jaussaud is born in France

1939 Raymond Mays, 21-time winner of the Shelsley Walsh (England) hillclimb, sets his personal record of 37.36 seconds driving an E.R.A.

1941 Harold Kenneth Skramstad Jr. of the Henry Ford Museum and Greenfield Village is born in Washington, DC

1946 Charles E. Wilson is named Chief Executive Officer of General Motors succeeding Alfred P. Sloan Jr., who would retain the office of Chairman of the Board

1948 The Playboy subcompact is introduced by the Playboy Motor Car Corporation of Buffalo, NY

1952 Risaburo Toyoda, the first President of the Toyota Motor Company, Ltd., dies at age 68

1954 The new Buick-Oldsmobile-Pontiac assembly plant opens in Arlington, TX

1956 Racer Jim Clark driving a Sunbeam scores his first major victory

1956 Peter Collins driving a Lancia-Ferrari D50 records his first of three Formula 1 Grand Prix victories in winning the Belgian Grand Prix at Spa-Francorchamps

1959 Ford Motor Company acquires a majority ownership of the semi-independent Ford Motor Company of Canada, Ltd.

1974 The Mercedes-Benz ESF 24, the last of five experimental cars built to test safety features, is introduced to the public

1974 Argentine Peugeot executive Jose Choheco is kidnapped by guerillas

1983 The Ford Motor Company announces that they have dropped plans to build a factory in Portugal

1983 Antique car collector Charles N. Harris dies in Cape Girardeau, MO

1987 Jack C. Fox, historian of the Indianapolis 500 motor car race, dies in Palo Alto, CA at age 61

1995 Automobile photographer Milton Gene Kieft is killed in an automobile accident near Portage, MI

JUNE 4

1867 Tyrrell Hubert Augustus Duncombe, a medical doctor and motoring enthusiast who invented free wheeling, is born in Waterford, Ontario, Canada

1871 Rene Gregoire, a sculptor and designer of automobile mascots, is born in Samer, France

1883 Horace Elmer Rice of the American Bosch Magneto Corporation is born in Philadelphia, PA

1896 The Ford Quadricycle, the first car built by Henry Ford, is taken for its first test drive by its designer on the streets of Detroit, MI

1899 Franklin Hall Marmon, son of Walter C. Marmon, is born in Indianapolis, IN

1902 Auburn stylist Alan Huet Leamy Jr. is born in Arlington, MD

1905 The American Locomotive Company enters the automobile business with President Albert J. Pitkin announcing the construction of a new factory in Providence, RI to build the Alco

1917 The Emerson Motors Company is charged with stock fraud by a federal grand jury

1919 The first Citroen sold to M. Testemolle

1923 The design for the new Chrysler by Oliver H. Clark is approved by the Maxwell-Chalmers Board of Directors

1924 The 10,000,000th Ford Model T is produced

1928 Gerry Bouwer arrives in London, England in his Chrysler to completing the first overland trip by automobile from Capetown, South Africa

1930 Automotive historian Richard Lewis Knudson is born in Newton, MA

1930 Coker Fifield Clarkson, Secretary and General Manager of the Society of Automotive Engineers since 1910, dies in Scarborough, NY

1940 The 7,000,000th Ford V-8 is produced

1940 Racer Robs Lamplough is born in Gloucester, England

1946 Nicholas Dreystadt is named General Manager of Chevrolet

1946 Michelin & Cie. applies for a French patent for its new radial tires

1947 Oldsmobile unveils its high compression, overhead valve V-8 engine at the summer meeting of the Society of Automotive Engineers

1948 The Ford Motor Company sells the Johansson Gage Division to the Brown & Sharpe Manufacturing Company of Providence, RI - William Clay Ford is elected to the Board of Directors

1949 Walter Bergius, manufacturer of the Bergius automobile in Glasgow, Scotland in 1904 and later an associate of engine designer Harry Ricardo, dies at age 67

1950 Nello Pagani makes his only Formula 1 racing appearance finishing seventh in the Swiss Grand Prix at the Bremgarten circuit near Berne in a supercharged Maserati 4CLT/48

1957 United States automakers agree to delete speed and performance references from its advertising and stress safety features

1958 William A. Chryst, a cofounder of Delco and associate of Charles F. Kettering, dies at age 80

1959 The American Honda Motor Company is established in Los Angeles, CA, initially to develop a market for Honda motorcycles

1959 Leonidas Doty Jr., Vice President-Engineering and Research for the Wausau Motor Parts Company, dies at age 47

1960 Racer Sammy Weiss is killed during a race at Laguna Seca near Salinas, CA

1984 The Honda Motor Company Ltd. announces plans to build a plant in Alliston, ON, Canada

1990 Petrofina (UK) Ltd. changes it name to Fina PLC

1993 Helmut Panke is named Chairman and Chief Executive Officer of the BMW (US) Holding Corporation

JUNE 5

1888 Ransom E. Olds marries Metta Ursula Woodward in Lansing, MI

1890 Hanson Ames Brown, Vice President and General Manager of General Motors of Canada Ltd. 1927-1936 is born in Pierceton, IN

1890 The Packard Electric Company is incorporated in Warren, OH with James W. Packard as President and William D. Packard as Secretary-Treasurer

1908 Racer Franco Rol is born in Italy

1909 The Timken Roller Bearing Axle Company reorganizes as two distinct businesses, the Timken Roller Bearing Company and the Timken-Detroit Axle Company

1917 Fire destroys the original factory of the Fleetwood Metal Body Company in Fleetwood, PA

1923 Racer Jorge Daponte is born in Buenos Aires, Argentina

1927 Isotta-Fraschini makes its last official racing appearance with Aymo Maggi in a Tipo 8A recording the fastest lap at Modena

1928 Racer Umberto Maglioli is born in Biella, Italy

1940 The B. F. Goodrich Tire & Rubber Company of Akron, OH introduces "Ameripol" tires, the world's first to be made from synthetic rubber

1941 Racer Bubby Jones is born

1946 Cadillac names John F. Gordon as General Manager and Edward N. Cole as Chief Engineer

1948 Stirling Moss driving a 500-cc Cooper wins his class at Stanmer Park, near Brighton, England, for his first racing victory

1950 Pakistan Petroleum Ltd. is incorporated in Karachi, Pakistan

1951 Gordon M. Buehrig is issued a United States patent for his "vehicle top with removable panels", an idea that appeared on 1968 Chevrolet Corvette

1952 A test run from Canada to Mexico is completed by a Kenworth conventional truck powered by an experimental gas turbine Model 502 engine developed by the Boeing Aircraft Company

1955 Racer Bob Slater is killed at age 32 when he crashes during the Hawkeye Futurity in Des Moines, IA

1956 Carl W. Johnson, a cofounder of the Cleveland Graphite Bronze Company in 1919, dies in Detroit, MI at age 70

1956 Harvey D. Carbiener, a design engineer for the Automotive Division, Excel Corporation and an employee of the firm since 1939, dies

1960 Racer Jim Clark makes his Formula 1 debut driving a Lotus in the Dutch Grand Prix

1961 The first Chaparral is tested in Riverside, CA by designer Jim Hall

1963 Racer Mel Hansen dies

1964 Racer Bobby Hillin is born in Midland, TX

1971 Racer Nicolas Leboissetier is born in France

1977 The Lec makes its Formula 1 debut at the Belgian Grand Prix in Zolder, with the Type CRP1 driven by David Purley finishing in 13th place

1985 Henry Kearns, a longtime Pasadena, CA Chevrolet dealer who later was an international business consultant, dies at age 74

JUNE 6

1864 Metta Ursula Woodward, wife of Ransom E. Olds, is born in Pinckney, MI

1889 Rubber chemist and compounder A. L. Freedlander of the B. F. Goodrich Company is born in Wooster, OH

1897 Sutton & Company of Manchester, England purchases a Daimler parcel van, the first sale of a gasoline-powered motor truck in Great Britain

1901 Walter P. Chrysler marries Della Viola Forker in Ellis, KS

1906 Automotive historian Frank Robert Donovan is born in New York City

1907 Construction begins on the Long Island Motor Parkway as General Manager A. R. Pardington performs the groundbreaking ritual

1908 Charles Yale Knight is issued a British patent for his sleeve valve engine design

1908 Racer Giovanni Bracco is born in Biella, Italy

1923 Racer Ivor Bueb is born in London, England

1925 The Maxwell Motor Corporation is reorganized in Delaware as the Chrysler Corporation

1926 Giotto Bizzarrini is born in Quercianella, Italy

1928 The first Dodge Victory Six Sport Roadster is produced

1932 Lydia B. Lazurenko of General Motors is born

1933 The first drive-in motion picture theatre, the Automobile Movie Theatre, is opened in Camden, NJ by Richard M. Hollingshead Jr.

1936 Racer Bill Puterbaugh is born

1938 Construction begins on the new Rolls-Royce factory in Crewe, England

1940 Charles E. Wilson is named acting President of General Motors

1941 Louis Chevrolet dies in Detroit, MI at age 62

1947 Karl M. Wise, the last Vice President of Engineering for the Pierce-Arrow Motor Car Company who previously was an official with Studebaker and Chalmers, dies near South Bend, IN at age 61

1948 Charles W. Nash dies in Beverly Hills, CA at age 84

1950 Charles S. Howard Sr., a highly successful Buick dealer and owner of prized racehorses, dies in Hillsborough, CA at age 69

1951 Racer Noritake Takahara is born in Tokyo, Japan

1964 The first McLaren race car, a modified Cooper with an Oldsmobile engine, makes its debut at Mosport Park, ON and takes the victory in the hands of designer Bruce McLaren

1964 The Daimler and Lanchester Owners' Club is founded

1966 Richard E. Cross retires as Chairman of American Motors and is succeeded by Robert Beverley Evans

1982 The first Detroit (MI) Grand Prix is won by John Watson driving a McLaren MP4/1B-Ford

1995 Female racer Doris "Geordie" Anderson dies in Australia at age 87

JUNE 7

1864 Waldo H. Marshall of Alco is born

1865 Alexander Young Malcomson of the Ford Motor Company is born in Dalry, Ayrshire, Scotland

1884 Automobile parts manufacturer Royce George Martin is born in Clint, TX

1895 Frederick R. Simms is authorized by a syndicate of investors to begin forming the Daimler Motor Company, Ltd. to manufacture Daimler cars under license in England

1904 Clement Smith is issued a United States patent for his "leader iron front-axle"

1910 Ernest Lawrence Barcella of General Motors is born in Hamden, CT

1921 Benjamin F. Gregory and William H. Craun are issued a United States patent for their "front drive and steering wheel for automobiles"

1925 Robert C. Graham of the Ford Motor Company is born in Minneapolis, MN

1926 The first 1927 Oakland Model 6-54D is produced

1926 John Phillip Cartwright, Executive Vice President of the Studebaker Corporation 1964-1965, is born in Ellwood City, PA

1927 Racer Charles de Tornaco is born in Brussels, Belgium

1928 Production of the Plymouth, Chrysler Corporation's new low priced marque, begins in Detroit, MI

1928 The last Salmson GP is sold

1929 Derek Donald Barron of the Ford Motor Company Ltd. is born

1934 Peter Monteverdi is born in Binningen, Switzerland

1934 Ferdinand A. Bower, Chief Engineer of the Buick Motor Company since 1928, is awared an honorary Doctor of Science degree from Villanova University

1938 Frank H. McKinney, Advertising Manager for the Packard Motor Car Company, dies in Birmingham, MI at age 54

1944 Racer Robert Benoist, an active member of the French underground, is arrested by the Gestapo in Paris

1947 Allied headquarters in Tokyo authorizes the production of 300 Japanese automobiles per year

1948 Sir Arthur F. Sidgreaves, Managing Director of Rolls-Royce Ltd. 1929-1946, commits suicide in a London subway station at age 65

1948 E. D. Johnson, an official of the Wagner Electric Corporation and an authority on automotive braking equipment, is killed in a train accident in Columbus, OH at age 45

1951 Harry A. Marchant, a charter official with the Chrysler Corporation in 1924 who previously had held positions with the Paige-Detroit Motor Car Company, Cadillac Motor Car Company, and Lincoln Motor Company, dies in Detroit, MI at age 66

1954 George T. Christopher, President of the Packard Motor Car Company 1942-1949, dies in Tipp City, OH at age 66

1954 The Ford Motor Company forms a styling team to undertake the conception of an entirely new car, the as yet unnamed Edsel

1963 Randolph H. Guthrie is elected Chairman of the Studebaker Corporation

1964 Racer Earl "Bomber" Balmer makes his Grand National racing debut, driving a Dodge in the Dixie 400

1966 G. James Allday, a cofounder of the Veteran Car Club of Great Britain, dies in Fowey, Cornwall, England

1970 Automotive historian St. John C. Nixon dies in Germany at age 84

1972 Automotive writer Ken Purdy commits suicide in New York City at age 59

1980 The Keystone Region Chapter of the Studebaker Drivers Club places a bronze plaque near New Chester, PA to note the location of the original 1820's wagon making shop of John Clement Studebaker

1989 Racer Chico Landi dies in Sao Paulo, Brazil at age 81

1992 Racer Ian Taylor is killed at age 45 when he crashes during a practice run in Spa-Francorchamps, Belgium

JUNE 8

1817 James Benjamin Brewster, founder of J. B. Brewster and Company, a predecessor of the Brewster custom coachbuiling firm, is born in New Haven, CT

1866 Samuel Simpson Marquis, an Episcopalian minister closely associated with Henry Ford, is born in Sharon, OH

1892 Racer Giuseppe Campari is born in Fanfullo, Lodi, Lombardy, Italy

1896 Harry Richard Fruehauf of the Fruehauf Trailer Company is born in Detroit, MI

1908 A match race at Brooklands is won by Felice Nazzaro in the Fiat "Mephistopheles" over Frank Newton in the Napier "Samson"

1912 The New Mexico State Legislature passes an act requiring registration of automobiles with the Secretary of State

1912 W. O. Bentley competes in his first automobile race, the Aston Clinton Hillclimb, and wins the 2-litre class in a D.F.P.

1919 Racer Frank Mundy (nee Francis Eduardo Menendez) is born in Atlanta, GA

1920 Francis Albert "Frank" Costin, developer of the Marcos sports car, is born

1923 The Hercules Motors Corporation incorporates in Ohio to succeed the Hercules Motor Manufacturing Company

1930 George Edmund Merryweather, a pioner in the automobile machine-tool industry, dies in Cleveland, OH at age 57

1931 The last of 75,510 Plymouth Model 30-U's is produced

1948 The 1949 Fords are introduced in a press preview at the Waldorf Astoria Hotel in New York City

1948 Construction of the first Porsche begins in Gmund, Austria

1951 Racer Franz Konrad is born in Graz, Austria

1955 The Mercedes-Benz 220 6-cylinder sedan is introduced to the United States market

1958 The 1,000,000th Plymouth V-8 engine is produced

When this rather spartan 1959 Savoy 4-door sedan parked in Long Prairie, MN was built, Plymouth had just began manufacturing its second million V-8's.

1959 Racer Leslie Johnson dies in Withington, Gloucestershire, England at age 47

1968 Racer Ludovico Scarfiotti is killed at age 34 when his Porsche crashes during a practice run for the Rossfeld hillclimb in Germany

1974 The 54-car collection of Judge Roy M. Hofheinz, owner of the Houston Astros National League baseball team, is sold at auction in the Astrodome in Houston, TX

1978 Philip Caldwell is named Deputy Chief Executive Officer of the Ford Motor Company

JUNE 9

1861 Automobile parts manufacturer John McGrath is born in Philadelphia, PA

1889 Gottlieb Daimler is issued a German patent for his twin-cylinder V-type engine

1898 Racer Luigi Fagioli is born in Osimo, Ancona, Marche, Italy

1898 B. Brewster Jennings, longtime executive with the Standard Oil Company of New York and the Socony-Vacuum Oil Company, is born in New York City

1899 The first English speed hillclimb is staged at Petersham Hill near London

1900 Rolland Jay Thomas of the United Auto Workers is born in East Palestine, OH

1900 The Baden-Graz-Baden trial for touring cars is won by Rudolf Struhatschek and Karl Ritter von Skoda driving a 9-hp Nesseldorf

1903 The Acme Motor Car Company is incorporated in Reading, PA with James C. Reber as President and Victor Jakob as Chief Engineer

1903 Racer Felice Bonetto is born in Manerbio, Brescia, Lombardy, Italy

1909 Alice Huyler Ramsey with four female passengers leaves New York City in a Maxwell Model 30, beginning the first trans-United States automobile trip by a woman driver

1912 Alan G. Loofbourrow of the Chrysler Corporation is born in Columbus, OH

1916 Robert Strange McNamara of the Ford Motor Company is born in San Francisco, CA

1920 Martin Valentine Roberts, an original director of the second Bentley Motors, Ltd., resigns

1921 General Motors establishes a "pricing ladder" for their car lines to ensure complete coverage of the market

1922 William C. Durant purchases the Duesenberg factory in Elizabeth, NJ to produce the Flint automobile, outbidding Walter P. Chrysler who was seeking a location to develop and manufacture the first Chrysler

1924 The 1925 Franklins are introduced

1924 The Alfa Romeo P2 designed by Vittorio Jano makes its racing debut as Antonio Ascari drives it to victory in the Circuito de Cremona (Italy)

1925 The Powell Muffler Company of Utica, NY is issued a United States patent for its blow-out proof muffler

1930 The second-generation Ford Model A commercial vehicles are introduced

1930 S. C. H. "Sammy" Davis sets a lap record for the Mountain Course at Brooklands (England) reaching 66.86 mph in his supercharged Riley Nine

1939 Racer David Wishart Hobbs is born in Leamington Spa, Warwickshire, England

1941 Packard historian James Arthur Ward is born in Buffalo, NY

1943 Racer John Fitzpatrick is born in Birmingham, England

1944 The first Volvo B4B engine is completed

1948 The 1949 Fords, featuring the marque's first post-World War II design, are previewed by the press at the Waldorf-Astoria Hotel in New York City

A 1949 Ford 2-door sedan in Tularosa, NM.

1951 Clarence C. Carlton, Vice President and Secretary of the Motor Wheel Corporation, dies at age 69

1953 Stuart Nixon, a research engineer for the Sealed Power Corporation who held many patents involving piston ring improvements, dies at age 53

1954 Raymond E. Plimpton, a journalist and design engineer involved in the motor bus industry, dies at age 67

1956 Racer Jeff MacPherson is born in Santa Ana, CA

1963 Chris Amon driving a Lola-BRM competes in the Belgian Grand Prix, at age 19 the youngest driver ever to compete in a Grand Prix race - the ATS makes its debut, but cars driven by Phil Hill and Giancarlo Baghetti are forced to retire - the BRP makes its debut, but the car driven by Innes Ireland is forced to retire - the Scirocco makes its debut, with driver Tony Settember finishing in eighth place

1968 Bruce McLaren, driving a McLaren Type M7A designed by Robin Herd and Gordon Coppuck, wins the Belgian Grand Prix in Spa-Francorchamps, the first Formula 1 victory for the marque

1968 Racer Ronnie Duman is killed at age 36 when he crashes during a race in West Allis, WI

1979 The last 1979 Lincoln Continental is produced at the Wixom, MI plant - this car is often cited as the last "big" car produced and the culmination of the United States automobile industry's "downsizing" efforts following the Arab oil embargo of 1973

JUNE 10

1862 Steam car pioneer George Eli Whitney is born in Boston, MA

1866 John Walter Edward Douglas-Scott-Montagu, 2nd Baron Montagu of Beaulieu, a prominent figure in early British motoring circles, is born in London

1878 Oil and gasoline producer William Grove Skelly is born in Erie, PA

1896 Thomas Sieger Derr, a prolific inventor and rebuilder of Stanley steam cars who built the American Steam Car 1926-1942, is born in Brookline, MA

1899 Alexander Winton offers a challenge to unsatisfied customer James W. Packard to build a better automobile, leading to the birth of the Packard Motor Car Company

1903 The Daimler factory in Canstatt, Germany is destroyed by fire, including three Mercedes 90-hp race cars being prepared for the upcoming Gordon Bennett race is Ireland

1907 The Peking-Paris Rally begins in Peking, China with five entrants

1910 Thomas B. Jeffery & Company, builders of the Rambler, incorporates as the Thomas B. Jeffery Company with the late founder's son, Charles T. Jeffery, as President

1911 The first American LaFrance rotary gear pumping engine fire truck is sold to the San Antonio (TX) Fire Department

1912 Giampaolo Garcea of Alfa Romeo is born in Padua, Italy

1917 Automobile parts manufacturer David Bernstein is born in Omaha, NE

1927 The Graham brothers purchase the Paige-Detroit Motor Car Company from Harry M. Jewett, reorganizing the firm as Graham-Paige Motors Corporation with Joseph B. Graham as President, Robert C. Graham as Vice President-Sales, and Ray A. Graham as Secretary-Treasurer

Ethel M. Myers of Coleta, IL and her 1915 Paige roadster. Descended from the Paige-Detroit and evolving into the Graham-Paige, the self-described "Most Beautiful Car in America" was built 1911-1927.

1932 Racer Andre Boillot dies in Chateauroux, France from injuries suffered five days earlier when his Peugeot-Bugatti hybrid crashed during the La Chatre Hill Climb

1934 Hans Stuck wins the Felsberg Hill Climb in Germany, the first victory for the new Auto Union race cars

1934 Henry Ford is awarded an honorary Doctor of Laws degree by Colgate University in Hamilton, NY

1935 Racer Vic Elford is born in Peckham, Great Britain

1938 John Anthony Donaldson of Mack Trucks, Inc. is born in Miami, FL

1940 John Swinscoe, an English-born designer of automotive jigs and tools who was associated with Buick and Oldsmobile, dies at age 59

1941 Racer Dave Walker is born in Sydney, NSW, Australia

1942 Racer Peter Ryan is born in Canada

1946 The Pontiac Torpedo is introduced, completing the marque's 1946 lineup

1946 Christian Girl, an automobile spring manufacturer whose various business ventures evolves into the Houdaille-Hershey Corporation, dies at age 71

1947 Saab introduces its first car, the model 92 prototype

1948 The 1949 Fords are introduced to the public

A 1949 Ford sedan leads oncoming traffic in this scene of a busy day in Huntsville, Ontario, Canada.

1949 Preston Tucker is indicted for fraud

1950 H. O. K. Meister, General Manager of the Hyatt Bearings Division of General Motors, dies in Shelter Island, NY at age 62

1963 Anita King, a silent screen actress who in 1915 driving a KisselKar was the first woman to make a solo trans-United States automobile trip, dies in Hollywood, CA at age 74

1966 The last 1966 Ford Thunderbird is produced

1968 The 3,000,000th post-World War II Cadillac is produced, a gold DeVille convertible

1981 The last "der Grosser" Mercedes-Benz 600 is produced ending a production run of 2,677 units over 18 years

1981 Racer Bud Clusserath is killed in a helicopter crash

1985 Classic car collector and former automobile museum co-owner Edgar Clarke dies in Manchester, CT

1989 Alain Ferte establishes a new race lap record at Le Mans, reaching 150.429 mph in his Jaguar SRJ-9

1995 Masaya Hanai, Chairman of the Toyota Motor Company, Ltd. 1978-1982, dies in Toyota City, Japan at age 82

JUNE 11

1871 Leonidas Carstarphen Dyer, a ten term Missouri Congressman who authored the Auto Theft Act of 1919, is born in Warren County, MO

1877 Howard Aldridge Coffin, Controller for the Warren Motor Car Company 1911-1913, Cadillac executive 1921-1925, holder of other positions in the automobile industry, and Michigan Congressman, is born in Middleborough, MA

1886 Bridge designer David Barnard Steinman is born in New York City

1891 William D. Packard marries Annie Storer

1895 Charles E. Duryea is issued a patent for his "Road Vehicle"

1895 The Paris-Bordeaux-Paris race begins - a 4-hp Daimler driven by Edouard Michelin is often cited as the world's first automobile to have pneumatic tires

1927 John Richard Hall, an Irish-born production manager with Lozier, Chandler, and Cleveland, dies in Cleveland, OH at age 60

1928 The first production Plymouth is built in the Highland Park, MI factory

1928 Domenico Chirico of Alfa Romeo is born in Reggio, Calabria, Italy

1931 Alfred Charles DeCrane Jr. of Texaco, Inc. is born in Cleveland, OH

1932 Pierre Peugeot is born in Valentigney, France

1939 Racer John Young "Jackie" Stewart is born in Milton, Dunbartonshire, Scotland

1940 George M. Kryder of the Firestone Tire & Rubber Company dies at age 46

1947 Racer Bob Evans is born in Newent, Gloucestershire, England

1947 Racer Tom Gloy is born in the United States

1949 The first post-World War II Bridgehampton (NY) 100-mile SCCA Sports Car Race is won by George Huntoon in a 1934 Alfa Romeo 8C 2300

1949 Racer Tom Pryce is born in Ruthin, Denbighshire, Wales

1949 William Robert Timken, cofounder of the Timken Roller Bearing Company, dies in Croton on the Hudson, NY at age 83

1950 The Dodge Diplomat two-door hardtop is introduced as a mid-year model

1950 Racer Duane "Pancho" Carter Jr. is born in Racine, WI, the son of racer Duane Carter Sr.

1955 Racer Pierre Levegh is killed at age 49 during the 24 Hours of Le Mans when his Mercedes-Benz 300SLR collided with the Austin-Healey driven by Lance Macklin, hurtled into the crowd and killed 83 spectators

1956 Cecil B. Thomas, President of the Chrysler Export Corporation 1942-1956, dies in Grosse Pointe, MI at age 61

1957 Fred L. Sage, retired Director of Engineering for the Truck Division, Chrysler Corporation, dies at age 69

1958 Racer Andrew Gilbert-Scott is born in Cookham Dean, Berkshire, England

1964 Racer Jean Alesi is born in Avignon, France of Sicilian descent

1966 Racer Jimmy Davies is killed at age 36 during a race in Chicago, IL

1966 Racer Jud Larson dies in Reading, PA at age 43

1972 Racer Jo Bonnier is killed at age 42 when his Lola T280 crashes at Le Mans, France

1974 Jose Choheco, the Argentine Peugeot executive kidnapped eight days earlier, is freed by his guerilla captors after payment of a ransom

1974 The Musee de l'Anthologie Automobile opens in Villiers-en-Lieu, France

1985 The United States Postal Service issues an 11-cent coil stamp in Baton Rouge, LA designed by Ken Dallison and picturing a 1933 Stutz (Super) Bearcat

1989 Mercedes-Benz returns to Le Mans 34 years after the 1955 tragedy and wins the race

1994 The Petersen Automotive Museum opens in Los Angeles, CA

JUNE 12

1874 Frederick Alvin Van Fleet, Advertising Manager for the Peerless Motor Car Company 1925-1928, is born in Cambria Mills, MI

1882 Sir Arthur Frederick Sidgreaves of Rolls-Royce is born in the Straits Settlements where his father was a British colonial official

1889 Maurice Olley of Rolls-Royce and General Motors is born in Scarborough, England

1889 Packard Motor Car Company Director William Tom ZurSchmiede is born

1892 The steam-powered Harris omnibus is demonstrated in Baltimore, MD with limited success by designer George T. Harris

1899 The Automatic Air Carriage Company is incorporated in Albany, NY by Edward A. Willard, Robert R. Blood, Charles J. Hensley and Seymour L. Husted Jr., all of New York City - production was limited to a single prototype

1901 The first Peerless is introduced

1903 Racer Claude Loraine-Barrow dies in Libourne, France from injuries suffered when his De Dietrich crashed during the recent Paris-Madrid race - his riding mechanic, Pierre Rodez, had been killed instantly

1909 The first races sanctioned by the American Automobile Association (AAA) are also the first races staged at the Portland (OR) Road Course - the main event, a 7-lap affair for the Wemme Cup, is won by Bert Dingley in a Chalmers-Detroit

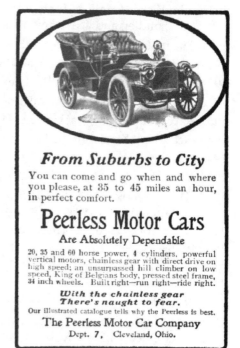

From Suburbs to City

You can come and go when and where you please, at 35 to 45 miles an hour, in perfect comfort.

Peerless Motor Cars

Are Absolutely Dependable

20, 35 and 60 horse power, 4 cylinders, powerful vertical motors, chainless gear with direct drive on high speed; an unsurpassed hill climber on low speed, King of Belgians body, pressed steel frame, 34 inch wheels. Built right—run right—ride right.

With the chainless gear There's naught to fear.

Our illustrated catalogue tells why the Peerless is best.

The Peerless Motor Car Company

Dept. 7, Cleveland, Ohio.

1911 Robert E. Hunter of Graham-Paige, Pontiac, and the Ford Motor Company is born in Nunda, NY

1911 The Pueblo (CO) Fire Department orders its first motorized fire truck, an American LaFrance pumper

1912 Elmer Apperson marries Catherine Elizabeth Clancy

1912 Alfred N. Mayo, President of the Knox Automobile Company, dies

1914 The Kentucky General Assembly requires automobile license plates to be issued annually

1916 Paul Wilson Wyckoff of the Chrysler Corporation is born in Detroit, MI

1920 The General Motors Research Corporation is created with Charles F. Kettering as its first General Manager

1921 Racer Dennis Taylor is born in Great Britain

1926 George H. Kleinert of the Kelsey Wheel Company dies in Mount Clemens, MI at age 62

1927 Racer Bill Cheesbourg is born in Tucson, AZ

1930 Racer Robert McGregor Innes Ireland is born in Kirkcudbright, Kirkcudbrightshire, Scotland

1932 Giustino Cattaneo is elected to the Isotta-Fraschini Board of Directors

1933 Greenfield Village opens adjacent to the Henry Ford Museum in Dearborn, MI

1936 Robert Jardine, an authority on internal combustion engine valves whose career included stints with Panhard et Levassor, DeDion-Bouton, Berg, Royal Tourist, Jeffery, and Mitchell, dies at age 60

1937 Etorre Bugatti registers "Pursang" as an international trademark

1943 Earle D. Parker, Vice President of the Barber-Colman Company, dies at age 63

1948 Racer Hans Binder is born in Zell-am-Ziller, Austria

1949 Racer Len Koenig of Palmyra, NJ is killed when he crashes during a race in Langhorne, PA

1950 Racer Chris Hodgetts is born in Tamworth-in-Arden, Worcestershire, England

1952 Publisher William E. Scripps, a cofounder of the Scripps Motor Company, dies at age 70

1952 Maurice Olley completes his chassis with code-name "Opel" which with minor modifications would be the platform for the new Chevrolet Corvette

LET IT TALK! The Chevrolet Corvette speaks your language; why not hear what it has to say? . . . Hear it whisper on the straightaway . . . sigh gently as it smooths a turn . . . laugh a little as it levels out a hill . . . speak of planes and wild blue yonders as it ghosts into a valley. . . . Yes, *why not* listen! Your Chevrolet dealer can probably give you the keys to a Corvette today. Try out the first all-American sports car to go into production. . . .

Chevrolet Division of General Motors, Detroit 2, Michigan

1964 Ronald K. Evans of General Motors dies in Cadillac, MI at age 74

1971 The last Lincoln Continental Mark III is produced

1975 The "last" Chrysler Imperial is produced, although the marque would be reintroduced in 1981

1976 The 5-cylinder diesel-powered Mercedes-Benz C111 establishes three absolute speed records at the Nardo circuit in southern Italy

1995 Duane O. Mackie, Editor-in-Chief of *Collectible Automobile* magazine, dies in Chicago, IL at age 53

JUNE 13

1876 Benjamin Franklin Hopkins, founder in 1919 and President of the Cleveland Graphite Bronze Company, is born in Cleveland, OH

1898 Ivan Lester Wiles of Marmon, Oakland, and Buick is born in Goodland, IN

1899 Eugene Anthony Casaroll of Dual-Ghia is born

1902 Charles Minshall, President of the Standard Wheel Company of Terre Haute, IN, hires Claude E. Cox to be Superintendent of the newly formed automobile department - Cox would design and build the first Overland

1905 Lester Lum "Tex" Colbert of the Chrysler Corporation is born in Oakwood, TX

1911 Cadillac commits to develop and utilize the self-starter designed by Charles F. Kettering

1914 The Cyclecar Club of New Jersey stages the first United States races for cyclecars at a farm near Teaneck, NJ - all events were won by Scripps-Booth Rockets

1915 The first race staged at the Milwaukee Dirt Track in West Allis, WI is won by Louis Disbrow in a Case

1917 The Phillips Petroleum Company in incorporated in Delaware

1920 The first Circuit of Mugello (Italy) race is won by Giuseppe Campari in an Alfa Romeo, the first racing victory for that marque

1922 Henry M. Leland and Wilfred Leland resign from the Lincoln Motor Company four months after the firm had been purchased by the Ford Motor Company - their positions of President and Vice President were filled by Edsel B. Ford and Ernest C. Kanzler

1924 Rene Dreyfus makes his racing debut driving the family's Mathis

1926 Eugene Anthony Cafiero of the Chrysler Corporation is born in New York City

1928 Paul Ritchie Wheaton of American Motors is born in Kenosha, WI

1930 Sir Henry Segrave is killed at age 33 when his boat Miss England II crashes shortly after officially raising the water speed record to 98.76 mph on Lake Windermere, England

1933 Horace H. Rackham, an original shareholder in the Ford Motor Company and a director of the firm 1903-1919, dies

1936 SA des An. Ets. Chenard et Walcker declares bankruptcy - the firm would reorganize offering Chenard-Walcker automobiles until 1946, after which they would limit their product range to light commercial vehicles

1937 The Mercedes-Benz W125 race car designed by Fritz Nallinger, Rudolf Uhlenhaut, and Albert Ress makes its debut at the Nurburgring

1938 Robert E. Haylett of the Union Oil Company of California dies in Los Angeles, CA at age 46

1940 Racer Bob Swanson dies at age 27 from injuries suffered the previous day during a race in Toledo, OH

1940 Harry E. Figgie, Vice President of the Standard Steel Spring Company, dies in White Sulphur Springs, WV at age 53

1946 The first post-World War II Lincoln Continental, a 1946 convertible, is produced and presented to Ford Motor Company President Henry Ford II for use as his personal car

1962 Racer Davey Hamilton is born in Nampa, ID

1966 Racer and motor sport journalist Naoki Hattori is born in Yokkaichi, Japan

1970 Racer Dick Brown is killed at age 40 during the Can-Am trials in Mosport Park, ON

1971 Dr. Helmut Marko and Gijs van Lennep, driving a Porsche 917K, set a new record for the 24-hour Grand Prix d'Endurance at Le Mans, France, covering 3,315.203 miles

1978 Lee Iacocca is fired as President of Ford Motor Company by Chairman Henry Ford II

1981 Racer Jean-Louis Lafosse is killed when his Rondeau crashes during the 24 Hours of Le Mans - also killed in the incident was race marshall Jean Pierre Mobila

1982 Racer Riccardo Paletti is killed at age 23 when his Osella-Cosworth crashes during the Canadian Grand Prix in Montreal, PQ

1996 The United States-built Toyota Avalon is introduced to the South Korean market with a gala showing in Seoul

JUNE 14

1832 Internal combustion engine pioneer Nikolaus August Otto is born in Cologne, Germany

1865 Giovanni Battista Ceirano of Fiat is born in Cuneo, Italy

1890 Harold Lee Hamilton of General Motors is born in Little Shasta, CA

1891 John Stanley Dempsey, a longtime official with the Buda Company, a manufacturer of automobile engines in Harvey, IL, is born in Buda, IL

"The Part That Sells the Car"

1892 Erwin A. Weiss of Packard is born

1899 The first sprint races in England are staged on public roads near Colchester, Essex, but only one car, a French Delahaye, is entered

1900 The first Gordon Bennett Cup, a run from Paris to Lyon in France, is staged with only five cars entered - the winner is Fernand Charron driving a 40-hp Panhard et Levassor

1904 The Sociedad Hispano-Suiza Fabrica de Automoviles SA is organized in Spain with a capitalization of 250,000 Pesetas

1910 The seventh Glidden Tour begins in Cincinnati, OH, with a planned route to Fort Worth, TX and back to Chicago, IL

1913 Henry Banks, racer and USAC official, is born in London, England, although he moved to Royal Oak, MI as an infant

1916 An International Model F truck becomes first commercial vehicle to reach the summit of Pikes Peak, CO

1917 The 2,000,000th Ford Model T is produced

1917 William Geoffrey Rootes is born in Loose, Kent, England

1923 The Packard Single Eight is introduced including a new body style, the Touring Sedan

1928 The first Plymouth is produced

1928 Leon Duray in his Miller Special sets a new world's closed-course record of 148.173 mph at the unfinished Packard Proving Grounds in Utica, MI which would hold the "World's Fastest Speedway" title until 1952 when the title would go to the new Monza track in Italy

1931 Enzo Ferrari wins the Bobbio-Passo del Penice reliability trial in an Alfa Romeo 8C2300 for his last victory as a driver

1934 George Zoltan Libertiny, a Ford Motor Company research engineer, is born in Szolnok, Hungary

1936 The BMW 328 makes its racing debut, as Ernst Henne wins the class race for unsupercharged cars at the Nurburgring in Germany

1942 Racer Jim Busby is born in the United States

1943 Racer John Miles is born in Islington, England

1946 Edwin H. Ehrman, Chief Engineer of the Standard Screw Company and an authority on national screw threads standards, dies in Chicago, IL at age 80

1949 Lee Petty makes his racing debut, driving the family Buick in a stock car event at the Charlotte (NC) Fairgrounds dirt track

1953 Racer Tom Cole of Sayville, NY is killed in Le Mans, France at age 31 - winners Tony Rolt and Duncan Hamilton, driving a Jaguar C-type, become the first to average over 100 mph in the event

1956 The Zavod Imieni Molotova (Molotov Automobile Plant) in Gor'kiy, USSR, manufacturers of the luxury ZIM, changes its name to the Gor'kiy Automobile Plant, with its product now called the Volga

1958 W. W. Brown, designer, builder, and driver of race cars and President of the W. W. Brown Machine Works in Kansas City, MO, dies at age 71

1961 Racer Jack Miller is born in Indianapolis, IN

1969 Racer John Woolfe is killed at age 34 when his Porsche crashes in Le Mans, France

1985 Hans-Joachim Stuck sets a lap record of 156.377 during a practice run at Le Mans, France

1988 The frontal appearance of the Bentley is altered to further separate the marque from its Rolls-Royce cousin

1995 Stephen P. Yokich is elected President of the United Auto Workers

JUNE 15

1886 Robert H. Colley of the Atlantic Refining Company is born in Bridgeport, CT

1896 Walter L. Jacobs of the Hertz Corporation is born in Chicago, IL

1896 Ivan Alexeevich Likhachev, Director of Zavod Imieni Stalina 1936-1950, is born in Ozertsy (now Venev Raion), Russia

1901 Cleveland, OH issues the first automobile license in Ohio to C. E. Burke

1902 The first Italian speed hillclimb, the Consuma Cup staged near Florence is won by Nourry in a DeDion-Bouton

1909 Crane & Breed of Cincinnati, OH introduces the first commercially-built motorized hearse

1911 Charles F. Kettering applies for the second United States patent on his self-starter

Charles F. Kettering used a 1911 Cadillac Model 30 similar to this touring as a test bench for developing the first successful self-starter.

1913 Coachbuilder Alfredo Vignale is born in Turin, Italy

1915 Nicola Romeo assumes general management duties for Alfa Romeo

1918 The first production Hanson Six is completed at the Atlanta, GA factory of the Hanson Motor Company

1919 Charles C. Hanch is named General Manager of the Maxwell Motor Corporation

1920 Rudolf Schiske and Dore Pordes apply for an Austrian patent for their "vehicle springing by rods under torsion", an ancestor of modern torsion bar suspension

1920 Racer Keith Andrews is born in Denver, CO

1924 Horace M. Swetland, an automobile journalist who founded the Society of Automotive Engineers in 1904, dies at age 70

1929 Ray Keech, winner of the 1929 Indianapolis 500 and former land speed record holder, is killed at age 30 when his Miller "Simplex Piston Ring Special" crashes while leading a 200-mile race in Altoona, PA - the event was terminated and Keech was posthumously declared to be the winner

1930 Frederick Robertson Smith, Chief Engineer of Armstrong-Siddeley Motors Ltd. since 1910, dies at age 48

1933 Plymouth opens its new assembly plant in Los Angeles, CA

1935 The 1936 Nash LaFayettes are introduced

1937 Harold T. Ames is issued a United States patent for retractable headlights as used on the Cord 810 and 812

1938 Dallas E. Winslow, Inc. purchases the Auburn and Cord parts stock plus related equipment for $85,000

1943 Thos Lee Bryant of *Road & Track* magazine is born in Daytona Beach, FL

1950 Automotive historian Roger William Hicks is born in Cornwall, England

1951 Daimler-Benz AG authorizes the construction of five new Mercedes-Benz W165 race cars, signaling the marque's return to Formula 1 competition

1952 Steel company executive John Francis Havemeyer, a longtime proponent of marketing United States automobiles in Europe, dies in New York City at age 76

1953 Racer Eje Elgh is born in Karlskoga, Sweden

1955 Harry J. Erickson, Vice President and General Manager of Gray Line Tours 1919-1941, dies in Seattle, WA at age 60

1958 Maria-Teresa de Filippis driving a Maserati 250F finishes 10th at the Belgian Grand Prix in Spa, the first start in a World Championship Formula 1 race by a woman driver

1958 Racer Riccardo Paletti is born in Milan, Italy

1959 Henry Frederick Stanley Morgan, founder in 1910 of the Morgan Motor Company Ltd., dies at age 78

1961 Racer Giulio Cabianca is killed at age 38 when his Cooper-Climax crashes during a test run in Modena, Italy

1963 Brazilian racer Christian "Bino" Heins is killed when his Alpine crashes during the 24-Hours of Le Mans in France

1965 Bert J. Mitchell, an associate of stylist Howard A. Darrin who designed the first automobile air conditioner, dies in Dallas, TX at age 57

1982 Jaguar/Group 44 unveils the Jaguar XJR-5 race car

1986 Richard Petty starts his 1,000th race, the Miller American 400 in Brooklyn, MI

1993 James Hunt, the 1976 World Champion Driver, dies from a heart attack in London, England at age 45

JUNE 16

1863 Edmund Prior Horton, a pioneer salesman for the Maxwell-Briscoe Motor Company and later a manufacturer of automobile parts, is born in New Castle, NY

1874 Henry Middlebrook Crane of Crane-Simplex and General Motors is born in New York City

1888 Jean Baptiste August Kessler of the Shell Oil Company is born in the Hague, the Netherlands

1890 NV Koninklijke Nederlandsche Mij tot Exploitatie van Petroleumbronnen in Nederlandsch-Indie is incorporated in the Hague, Netherlands - the firm would evolve into Royal Dutch/Shell Group

1895 Leonidas Theodore Barrow of the Humble Oil and Refining Company is born in Manor, TX

1898 Sir Henry Spurrier of the Leyland Motors Corporation Ltd. is born

1903 The Ford Motor Company is incorporated, combining the short-lived firms of the Ford & Malcomson Company and the Fordmobile Company, Ltd.

1903 Alexander Edward "Alec" Ulmann, United States race promoter and classic car collector, is born in St. Petersburg, Russia

1910 The first issue of *The Packard* is published with E. Ralph Estep as Editor

1913 Race promoter Joshua James "J. C." Agajanian is born

1915 The Packard Twin Six is awarded the grand prize at the Panama-Pacific International Exposition in San Francisco, CA

1917 Harry A. Miller completes the Golden Submarine race car

1923 Templar Motors Corporation reorganizes with its former receiver T. L. Hausmann as President

1923 Racer William Ronald "Ron" Flockhart is born in Edinburgh, Scotland

1923 Walter E. Flanders dies at age 52 from injuries suffered in an automobile accident three weeks earlier

1924 The second series 1924 Hudson Super Sixes are introduced

1928 A monument honoring racer Louis Zborowski is dedicated at Le Mans, France

1930 Elmer A. Sperry, inventor of the Sperry Gyroscope and cofounder of the Sperry Rand Corporation, but remembered in automotive circles as the designer of the Sperry Electric of 1899-1901 and pioneering the usage of disc brakes, dies in Brooklyn, NY at age 69

1930 Racer Mike Sparken (nee Michel Poberejsky) is born in Neuilly-sur-Seine, France

1937 The Long Island Motor Parkway Company dissolves after 31-years and deeds its pioneering toll highway to the public

1941 Joseph Patrick Wright Jr., co-author with John Z. DeLorean about the latter's account of his career with General Motors, is born in Detroit, MI

1941 Automotive parts manufacturer Witt H. Braley dies

1941 Edward M. Schick, Pitesti, Romania-born design engineer with General Motors in Germany and later an Oldsmobile dealer in the United States, dies

1945 The Willys Universal, in effect the first civilian Jeep, is introduced

1947 Henry Ford II announces that the 1948 Ford will be as different from the 1947 as the Model A was from the Model T

1948 James I. Farley, an executive with the Auburn Automobile Company 1906-1926 who served as a United States Representative (D-IN) 1933-1939, dies in Bryn Mawr, PA at age 77

1949 Albert Marestaing unveils the new JPW prototype at the Bois de Boulogne concours in Paris, France, based on the designs of the late racer/engineer Jean-Pierre Wimille

1950 Ernest W. Hives, Executive Chairman of Rolls-Royce Ltd., is elevated to the peerage by King George VI, becoming Lord Hives of Duffield

1953 Ford introduces Master Guide power steering as an option

One of the first Fords with Master Guide power steering was this 1953 Customline Country Sedan purchased new by the author's uncle, Marvin Wick, of St. Louis Park, MN.

1953 The Ford Rotunda reopens in Dearborn, MI on the company's 50th anniversary and the Ford Research and Engineering Center is dedicated

1953 A. E. Barit of Hudson and George W. Mason of Nash meet over lunch at the Book-Cadillac Hotel in Detroit, MI and work out the basics for a merger of their companies

1954 The Chrysler Corporation opens its new Chelsea (MI) Proving Grounds - Jack McGrath sets a world's closed-track record of 179.386 mph and Betty Skelton establishes a womens land speed record of 143.44 mph, both of whom were driving the Dodge Firearrow show car

1957 George Ronald Donaldson of the B. F. Goodrich Tire & Rubber Company of Canada Ltd. dies at age 62

1958 Stanley H. Franklin, Director of Research for the Fram Corporation, dies at age 60

1964 The 8,000,000th Volkswagen is produced

1968 Racer Jean Lagrace is killed at age 33 during a race in Mont-Tremblant, PQ, Canada

1973 The automotive holdings of the Magee Museum in Bloomsburg, PA are sold at auction by Omar Landis

1973 *Old Cars* newspaper becomes a twice-monthly publication

1984 Automotive historian Bill Libby dies in Westminster, CA at age 56

1989 Holmes P. Tuttle, a Ford dealer for 67 years, dies at age 83

1991 The Fondmetal makes its Formula 1 debut in the Mexican Grand Prix in Mexico City, but the car driven by Olivier Grouillard retires

JUNE 17

1867 George M. Tinker of the Waltham Manufacturing Company, a design engineer involved with the 1899 Orient Electric and 1898-1902 Waltham Steam, is born in Nashua, NH

1876 William Chauncey Geer, a research chemist with the B. F. Goodrich Tire & Rubber Company, is born in Ogdensburg, NY

1879 Fred H. Berger of Oakland and Yellow Cab is born in Bingen, Germany

1879 Charles Henry Widman of the Murray Body Company is born in Rochester, NY

1885 William C. Durant marries Clara Pitt in Flint, MI

1889 Henry E. Koopman of the Phillips Petroleum Company is born in Pittsburg, KS

1893 Automotive artist Clarence Peter Helck is born in New York City

1898 The first regular motorized mail service in Great Britain begins between Inveraray and Ardrishaig, Argyllshire, Scotland using Coventry-built Daimlers

1899 George L. Weiss sells his interest in Winton for $12,000 and invests $3,000 into the new Packard concern

1899 The Automobile Company of America is formed in Bridgeport, CT by John Brisben Walker, Editor of *Cosmopolitan* magazine, and asphalt paving magnate Amzi Lorenzo Barber to produce the Locomobile steam car based on designs purchased from F. E. and F. O. Stanley

1900 Charles R. Beacham of the Ford Motor Company is born in McRae, GA

1904 The fifth Gordon Bennett Trophy race staged at the Homburg circuit in Germany is won by Leon Thery driving a Richard-Brasier

1905 Holmes Paul Tuttle, a Ford dealer for 67 years, is born in Tuttle, OK

1907 The Hillman-Coatalen Motor Car Company Ltd. registered by William Hillman and Louis Coatalen to produce the Hillman automobile

1907 The Brooklands motor course opens in Weybridge, England

1912 Theo Masui Ltd., an English coachbuilding firm, is founded by Warwick Wright, Theo Masui, and Edmond de Prelle de la Nieppe of Belgium - the firm would evolve the following year into Vanden Plas (England) Ltd.

1914 The first all-steel automobile body is patented by Joseph Ledwinka, the Vienna, Austria-born associate of Edward G. Budd

1920 Walter Sharrat Keigwin, a London merchant, and A. H. M. J. Ward become Directors of Bentley Motors, Ltd.

1922 Malcolm Campbell, driving the 18.3-litre Sunbeam, sets a venue record for the Saltburn Sands, Redcar, Yorkshire of 133.75 mph

1923 Enzo Ferrari records his first racing victory, winning a 166-mile event at the Circuito del Savio near Ravenna, Italy in an Alfa Romeo RL TF - it was at this race that Ferrari met the Count and Countess Baracca who suggested that he use the prancing horse emblem of their son, a World War I pilot, a logo that would grace all Ferrari cars in later years

1925 Chrysler Corporation Ltd. of Canada is organized with John D. Mansfield as President and Walter P. Chrysler as Chairman of the Board

1926 The Langhorne (PA) Dirt Track stages it first event, a 50-mile race won by Fred Winnai in a Duesenberg

1926 Charles G. Young of Willys dies in San Juan, PR at age 59

1928 Lodwrick Monroe Cook of the Atlantic Richfield Company is born in Castor, LA

1929 The Cord Corporation is organized in Chicago, IL with E. L. Cord as President, Lucius B. Manning as Vice President, Raymond S. Pruitt as Secretary, and Hayden Hodges as Treasurer

1931 The first Packard Light Eight (Model 900) is produced

The Packard Light Eight Coupe Sedan for five, with graceful new lines, priced at the factory at
$1795

1931 Packard introduces the Ninth Series Standard Eight

1931 The second-generation Packard Twin Six is introduced

1932 Christian Werner, winner of the 1924 Targa Florio and the 1928 German Grand Prix, dies of throat cancer in Bad Cannstatt, Germany at age 40

1934 Allan Dana Gilmour of the Ford Motor Company is born in Burke, VT

1935 Alan P. Good purchases the bankrupt Lagonda Ltd., immediately hiring W. O. Bentley as his Technical Director

1937 Automotive diesel engine designer Ion Alexandru Voiculescu is born in Romania

1944 Lord Herbert Scott, Chairman of Rolls-Royce Ltd. since 1936, dies in Winchester, England at age 71

1944 Racer Lucien Guitteny is born in France

1956 The last Detroit-built Packard is produced

1956 Sir Percival Perry of the Ford Motor Company Ltd. dies in Nassau, New Providence Island, Bahamas at age 78

1956 Bob Sweikert, winner of the 1955 Indianapolis 500, is killed at age 30 when he crashes during the Midwest Spring Feature race in Milwaukee, WI

1960 Racer Adrian Campos is born in Valencia, Spain

1960 Clarence H. Parrish Jr. of the Ford Motor Company dies at age 47

1962 Racer Jim Clark records his first Formula 1 victory, winning the Belgian Grand Prix at Spa-Francorchamps in his Lotus - Ricardo Rodriguez places fourth in a Ferrari 156 to become at age 20 years, 123 days the youngest driver to earn points in a Formula 1 championship race

1964 Sir Henry Spurrier, President of the Leyland Motors Corporation Ltd., dies in Preston, England at age 66

1971 Edward T. Ragsdale, a Buick employee 1923-1959 who rose to be the division's General Manager 1956-1959 and is credited with developing the hardtop body style, dies in Sarasota, FL at age 74

1990 Harry Gant wins the Miller 500 in Long Pond, PA at age 50, becoming the oldest racer to win a NASCAR event

1992 Bill France Sr., the founder and first President of NASCAR, dies at age 82

JUNE 18

1889 The Standard Oil Company of Indiana is incorporated as a subsidiary of the Standard Oil Company of New Jersey

1893 Edwin Dagobert Bransome, Chairman of the Vanadium Corporation of America who was with General Motors 1919-1921 and was President of Mack Trucks, Inc. 1949-1955, is born in Philadelphia, PA

1902 Locke & Company, a New York City custom coachbuilder, is incorporated

1904 Automobile stylist Gordon Miller Buehrig is born in Mason City, IL

1904 Lawrence Randolph Hafstad of General Motors is born in Minneapolis, MN

1916 A Haynes Light Six Model 34, driven by Samuel Grier and R. M. McKenna, completes a Pacific Ocean to Atlantic Ocean trip in twelve hours (actual running time was less than six hours) - something of a promotional stunt, the run was made on roadways and railroad tracks from Panama City, Panama to Colon, Canal Zone along the newly constructed Panama Canal

1920 Edmund Rumpler makes the first test drive of his Tropfen-Auto to coincide with the 35th birthday of his wife

1923 The first Checker taxicab is produced

1927 The first race held at the Nurburgring in Germany is won by Rudolf Caracciola in a Mercedes-Benz S type

1936 Racer Denis Clive Hulme is born in Nelson, New Zealand

1937 New York City banker Jefferson Seligman, the purchaser in 1906 of the first Rolls-Royce Silver Ghost to be exported, dies at age 78

1939 Dr. Harold Firth Haworth, Technical Representative and former Chief Engineer of Leyland Motors Ltd., dies in Manchester, England at age 56

1940 Alfa Romeo test driver Attilio Marinoni is killed on the Milan-Varese Autostrada when his modified Tipo 158 collides with a truck

1940 James D. Mooney, President of the General Motors Export Corporation since 1922, is relieved of his responsibilities to allow his return to Detroit to take charge of all corporate negotiations involving national defense work

1943 Chrysler Corporation stylist Thomas Charles Gale is born in Flint, MI

1946 Race car designer Ian Gordon Murray is born in Durban, South Africa

1946 Joe Dawson, winner of the 1912 Indianapolis 500, dies at age 57

1947 The Nash-Kelvinator Corporation opens their new automobile assembly plant in Mexico City

1947 Hon. Sir Edward W. Holden dies at age 61

1949 Robert P. Page Jr., Chairman of the Autocar Company, dies in Bryn Mawr, PA at age 70

1954 The 5,000,000th Pontiac, a 1954 Star Chief Custom Catalina hardtop coupe, is produced in the Pontiac, MI assembly plant

1955 Fuller F. Barnes, President and Chairman of the Board of the Associated Spring Corporation until 1954, dies

1958 Cliff Allison makes his Formula 1 debut, finishing sixth in the Monaco Grand Prix at Monte Carlo in a Lotus-Climax - Graham Hill also debuts in this race, but his Lotus-Climax retires with a lost wheel

1958 Andrew D. Grey, Editor of the Chilton automobile manuals and an employee of the Chilton Company since 1934, dies at age 47

1966 Bruce McLaren and Chris Amon, driving a Ford GT40 Mk2, win the Le Mans 24-hour race, becoming the first to exceed 3000 total miles during the event

1967 Dan Gurney, driving an Eagle Type T1G, wins the Belgian Grand Prix at Spa-Francorchamps, the marque's first and only victory and the first for a United States car since Jimmy Murphy's Duesenberg won the French Grand Prix in 1921

1967 A Formula 3 race at Caserta, Italy results in two deaths - Swiss racer Fehr Beat, attempting to warn oncoming cars of a multiple car pileup, is struck and killed by Geki (nee Giacomo Russo), who then is killed at age 29 when his Matra crashes into the wall

1968 Adolph G. Miller, General Manager of Rolls-Royce of America, Inc., dies in Springfield, MA

1972 The first race is staged at the new circuit near Estoril, Portugal

1976 The Mobil Oil Corporation changes its name to the Mobil Corporation

1977 Racer Franco Rol dies at age 69

JUNE 19

1863 Sir Max Pemberton, biographer of Sir F. H. Royce, is born in Birmingham, Warwickshire, England

1902 The first Franklin is produced

The FRANKLIN

Four=cylinder　　　　　　**Air=cooled**

France has honored the makers of the *Franklin* by adopting some of the features used in the *Franklin* cars.

Some of these are

Dynamo Ignition　　　　**Self-Adjusting Transmission**
Compensation Carbureter　**Direct Drive on High Gear**
Flexible Frame

The most important and valuable feature of the *Franklin*, however, is air-cooling. While the construction of every part of the *Franklin* proves our engineer to be a genius of high order, his magnificent success in building a powerful and effective air-cooled, four-cylinder motor, has freed all motorists from the repairs, the delay, the loss of power and other unnecessary troubles that result from water-cooling.

Send for literature on the

Light Car　　　　**Light Tonneau**
24 H. P. Touring Car

Made with aluminum bodies, dash and bonnet, luxuriously upholstered, and finished in every particular.

H. H. FRANKLIN MFG. CO., 314 Geddes St., Syracuse, N. Y.

Member of the Association of Licensed Automobile Manufacturers.

1902 The Locomotive & Machine Company of Montreal Ltd. is founded - the firm would evolve into Bombardier, Inc., a manufacturer of off-road vehicles designed for winter conditions

1903 Barney Oldfield sets a 1-mile speed record of 60.4 mph in the Ford "999" at the Indianapolis (IN) Fairgrounds, the first time the 60 mph barrier had been broken on a closed track

1913 Racer Paolo "Paul" Zuccarelli is killed at age 28 along with his riding mechanic, Fanelli, when their Peugeot crashes between Thomery and Tivoli, France during a practice run for the upcoming French Grand Prix at Amiens

1917 Ernest C. Kanzler of the Ford Motor Company marries Josephine Hudson Clay to become the brother-in-law of Edsel B. Ford

1927 The Mercedes-Benz Type S makes its racing debut with Rudolf Caracciola, Christian Werner, and Adolf Rosenberger taking the top three places in the sports car class in the inaugural races at the Nurburgring in Germany

1928 The Falcon-Knight "Falcon on Dog Bone" mascot is patented by designer F. C. Ruppel

1934 The 1,000,000th Ford V-8 is produced

1938 Racer Charlie Glotzbach is born

1939 The R. H. Macy Company begins selling subcompact Crosleys in its New York City department store

1940 United States government representatives visit the American Bantam Car Company in Butler, PA for a meeting that would lead to the development of the Jeep

1945 Graham-Paige President Joseph W. Frazer hires William B. Stout to design a "Scarab-type" car for possible production, but only a single prototype of the fibreglass-bodied car would be built

1946 The Packard Twenty-First Series Clipper Six Taxi is introduced

1947 The Tucker '48 is introduced before over 5,000 people at the Tucker plant in Chicago, IL

1949 NASCAR stages its first Winston Cup event, a Grand National race at the Charlotte (NC) Fairgrounds won by Jim Roper in a Lincoln

1950 James J. Nance meets with Hugh J. Ferry and the Packard board at the Detroit (MI) Athletic Club to discuss Nance's terms required to leave Hotpoint and become the automaker's President

1952 Ford Motor Company's management receives a special committee report detailing the pros and cons of developing a new Continental

1953 Racer Jean-Michel Martin is born in Belgium

1954 Lester C. Hunt, designer of Wyoming's famous "bucking bronco" license plate in 1936 before serving as that state's Governor 1943-1949 and as a United States Senator 1949-1954, dies at age 61

1956 The first 1957 Hudson Hornet is produced

1956 Ford sets a 500-mile stock car record at the Indianapolis Motor Speedway

1960 Racer Chris Bristow is killed at age 22 when his Cooper-Climax crashes during the Belgian Grand Prix at Spa - later in the same race Alan Stacey is killed at age 26 when he is struck in the face by a bird and loses consciousness, causing his Lotus 18-Climax to crash - the Scarab makes its Formula 1 debut, but cars driven by Chuck Daigh and sponsor Lance Reventlow retire with engine problems

1960 Racer Jimmy Bryan is killed at age 33 when he crashes during a 100-mile USAC race in Langhorne, PA

1964 Racer Enrico Bertaggia is born in Noale, Italy

1966 Ford GT Mark II's finish 1-2-3 at the annual Le Mans, France 24-hour race

1969 The 4,000,000th Cadillac is produced, a light blue Coupe de Ville that is driven off the assembly line by owner Lee Mannes of Saint Clair Shores, MI

1969 The 2,000,000th Morris Mini is produced

1973 Henry Ford II opens the new Ford Motor Company plant in Bordeaux, France

1974 The last Vanden Plas 1300 Princess is produced

1977 Jacques Laffite wins the Swedish Grand Prix in Anderstorp, the first Formula 1 victory for the Ligier marque

1988 Bobby Allison competes in his last race, the Miller High Life 500 in Pocono, PA, and is involved in a near-fatal accident during the first lap

1993 Alfa Romeo stylist Franco Scaglione dies in Suvereto, Tuscany, Italy at age 76

JUNE 20

1856 Rudolph Melville Hunter, a leading pioneer in electric car technology, is born in New York City

1860 Alexander Winton is born in Grangemouth, Stirling, Scotland

The Packard brothers may not have been happy with their 1898 Winton, but the pioneer marque was generally held in high regard until its demise in 1924. This 1905 Model K is very typical.

1866 Edward Ringwood Hewitt, grandson of locomotive pioneer Peter Cooper, is born in Ringwood Manor, NJ - Hewitt designed the 1905-1906 Hewitt, often cited as the first United States production car with a V-8 engine and the British Adams-Hewitt motor car, was involved with the Metzger Motor Car Company, and founded the Hewitt Motor Company that later was absorbed by the International Motor Company, builders of Mack trucks

1866 Automobile wheel manufacturer John Kelsey is born in Detroit, MI

1876 Edward George Seubert of the Standard Oil Company of Indiana is born in Syracuse, NY

1884 Harold Brown Harvey, founder of The Harvey Metal Corporation and a pioneer in manufacturing aluminum and brass automobile parts, is born in Parkman, ME

1893 Byron Cecil Foy of DeSoto is born in Dallas, TX

1897 Captain George Edward Thomas Eyston, racer and land speed record setter, is born in Oxfordshire, England

1903 Tom Fetch & Marius C. Krarup leave San Francisco, CA in the Packard Model F "Old Pacific" to begin the second trans-United States automobile trip

1911 Racer Paul Pietsch is born in Neustadt, Germany

1913 Sizaire-Berwick (France) Ltd. is formed by Scottish businessman Alexander Keiller, London used-car dealer F. W. Berwick, Maurice and Georges Sizaire, and Louis Naudin with home offices in London, England and its factory in Courbevoie, France

1914 Assistant Research Engineer William R. McCulla drives a Packard Model 5-48 70.447 miles in one hour at the Indianapolis Speedway

1914 Victor Gino Raviolo, a design engineer with the Chrysler Corporation, Packard Motor Car Company, Ford Motor Company, and American Motors, is born in New York City

1917 Harold C. MacDonald of the Ford Motor Company is born in Virginia, MN

1918 Charles C. Hanch is named Chief of Automotive Products for the United States War Industries Board

1922 The 175,000th Hudson is produced, a 7-passenger phaeton that was shipped to the Hudson dealer in the Hague, Netherlands

1925 The 12,000,000th Ford is produced

1926 Automotive historian Leon A. Harris Jr. is born in New York City

1927 Pierre Semerena of American Motors is born

1937 Jean-Pierre Wimille and Robert Benoist win the Le Mans 24-hour race in a Bugatti Type 57G, becoming the first to exceed 2000 total miles during the event

1941 The Ford Motor Company signs its first domestic union contract with the United Auto Workers (UAW)

1945 Shekhar Mehta, the only five-time winner of the Safari Rally, is born in Kenya

1951 Charles E. Fogg of Autocar dies in Havertown, PA at age 65

1952 Racer Luigi Fagioli dies at age 54 three weeks after his Lancia Aurelia had crashed during a practice run in Monte Carlo, Monaco

1953 The Gordon Bennett Golden Jubilee Rally is held in Ireland to commemorate the original 1903 event that introduced automobile racing to that country

1957 Pontiac announces plans to sell British-made Vauxhalls through its dealer network

1958 Racer Ron Hornaday Jr. is born

1964 Three spectators are killed when the A.C. driven by Peter Bolton crashes during the Le Mans (France) 24-hour race - the winners are Umberto Maglioli and Giancarlo Baghetti in a Ferrari

1969 The Amerada Petroleum Corporation changes its name to the Amerada Hess Corporation

1970 Racer Andre Willem is killed at age 26 when he crashes during a race in Carpentras, France

1970 Francois Cevert makes Formula 1 racing debut driving a March-Ford in the Dutch Grand Prix

1971 Gar Wood, designer of racing boats who was closely associated with the Packard Motor Car Company, dies in Miami, FL at age 90

1980 The Ford Motor Company closes their Mahwah, NJ plant

1987 Earl "Madman" Muntz dies in Rancho Mirage, CA at age 73

British craftsmanship and distinction . . .

Vauxhall

. . . with more of the features Americans want

You might know such a *practical* car would be British! Nimble as a hedgerow hare, the Vauxhall is at the same time austerely English in fuel economy. It parks you deftly where others give up—yet gives you four-door convenience with room for five and all their vacation luggage. What's more, there's nothing new to learn for it has an American type gearshift. In short—it's the ideal family import. Drive it and see—soon!

SOLD AND SERVICED BY **PONTIAC DEALERS** COAST TO COAST

For colour catalogue, write Pontiac Motor Division, Dept. 22, Pontiac, Mich.

The 1959 Vauxhall was marketed in the United States by Pontiac dealers and looked more than a little like a scaled-down Pontiac.

JUNE 21

1891 Donald Alexander of the Edward G. Budd Manufacturing Company is born in Canton, OH

1891 Anthony J. Langhammer, a Mechanical Engineer for Packard 1916-1920 who spent most of his career as a metallurgist with the Chrysler Corporation, is born in Covington, KY

1904 The Maxwell-Briscoe Motor Company is incorporated by Jonathan D. Maxwell and Benjamin Briscoe with financial help from banker John Pierpont Morgan

An anonymous Wisconsin farmer poses proudly with his 1906 Maxwell, one of America's most popular cars in that era.

1907 The Rolls-Royce Silver Ghost begins its 15,000 Miles Official Trial

1911 A stock Metz roadster leaves Iron Hill, MD at 12:01 AM, and arrives in Winchester, NH before days end, having crossed Delaware, Pennsylvania, New Jersey, New York, Connecticut, Massachusetts, and Vermont - the well planned exhibition resulted in the car being marketed as "The Car that Covered Nine States in a Single Day"

1920 John Ambrose Ford of the Chrysler Corporation is born in New Haven, CT

1922 The Hudson Motor Car Company announces that 1922 Hudson and Essex production has surpassed the total for 1921

1924 Automotive equipment manufacturer Walter Bernhard Kissinger is born in Fuerth, Germany

1928 Col. Charles Clifton, Chairman of the Pierce-Arrow Motor Car Company 1919-1928, dies in Buffalo, NY at age 74

1929 Bentleys sweep the first four places at the 24 Hours of Le Mans (France)

1929 The last M.G. 14/40 Mk IV is completed

1930 William Lyman Stewart of the Union Oil Company dies at age 62

1936 E. H. Cutler, Vice President of the Knox Automobile Company, dies in New York City at age 80

1936 The first Hungarian Grand Prix is staged in Budapest and won by Tazio Nuvolari in an Alfa Romeo Tipo-C 8C-35

1937 Racer John Cannon is born in London, England

1941 Max Hoffman, a 36-year-old Austrian already established as a dealer and promoter of automobiles, arrives in New York City to begin his United States career as an importer of European automobiles

1943 Racer Al Loquasto is born

1946 Former General Motors executive William S. Knudsen joins the Hupp Corporation, former makers of the Hupmobile and now a division of White Consolidated Industries, Inc.

1947 William Clay Ford marries Martha Firestone - their grandfathers, Henry Ford and Harvey S. Firestone were close friends and giants of the automobile and tire industries

1947 The first post-World War II Mille Miglia begins

1948 Rev. Samuel S. Marquis, a longtime associate of Henry Ford, dies in Cranbrook, MI at age 82

1952 Louis Thoms, Chief Engineer of the Graham Brothers Company and the Graham-Paige Motors Corporation before joining General Motors, dies at age 57

1956 Henry M. Crane, designer of the Crane and Crane-Simplex and a longtime technical advisor to General Motors, dies in New York City at age 82

1957 Racer Phil Parsons is born

1958 Racers Guido Zerneri and Luigi Mora are killed during the Mille Miglia

1959 Racer Anthony Reid is born in Great Britain

1965 Claud H. Foster, inventor of the automobile horn and the founder of the Gabriel Manufacturing Company, dies in Bellevue, OH at age 92

1966 Ferdinando Innocenti, Chairman of the Societa Generale per l'Industria Metallurgica e Meccanica, dies in Milan, Italy at age 74 - the motor scooter firm introduced a range of Innocenti cars in 1961, all based loosely on various British vehicles

1969 Fiat SpA acquires a fifty percent ownership of Ferrari SEFAC

1970 Racer Piers Courage is killed at age 28 when his DeTomaso-Cosworth crashes during the Dutch Grand Prix at Zandvoort

1972 The Craven Foundation automobile collection opens to the public in Niagara Falls, ON, Canada

1975 The first national meeting of the International Truck Restorers Club is held in Fort Wayne, IN

1978 The Aston Martin Volante convertible is announced

Aston Martin

Every great automobile reflects a dream. From a beginning in 1914, Lionel Martin's goal was to build a fast touring car for which the primary consideration was Quality.

From the hand formed all aluminum body to the 4-cam, aluminum V8 engine built by one man proud enough to put his name on it; from the interior trimmed with the finest Connolly hides, Wilton wool carpets and burled walnut to the awesome strength of the steel platform chassis and the masterful feel of the rack and pinion steering and four wheel disc brakes, today's Aston Martin brilliantly reflects the original goal.

If you have driven a succession of expensive automobiles but have yet to find one that conforms to your unyielding demand for excellence, the time has come to experience an Aston Martin.

1990 Automotive parts manufacturer John M. Burke dies at age 51

1992 A Jaguar XJ220 driven by Martin Brundle on the Nardo track in Italy reaches 217.1 mph, the highest speed ever attained by a stock production car

JUNE 22

1843 Amzi Lorenzo Barber, a leader in the asphalt paving industry and a cofounder of Locomobile, is born in Saxtons River, VT

1876 David Marvin Goodrich of the B. F. Goodrich Tire & Rubber Company is born in Akron, OH

1899 Automotive artist Haddon Hubbard Sundblom is born in Muskegon, MI

1900 James William Watson of the Chrysler Corporation, General Motors, and American Motors is born in Marietta, OH

1902 The first Sassi-Superga Hillclimb staged near Turin, Italy is won by Vincenzo Lancia in a F.I.A.T. 24-hp, the marque's racing debut

1909 The Cole Motor Car Company is founded in Indianapolis, IN by Joseph Jaret Cole

This is the
Cole "50" Electric Starting
Touring Car
$1985

1910 Charles E. Test, President of the National Motor Vehicle Company 1900-1910, dies in Waukesha, WI at age 53

1910 Dr. Herbert Quandt of BMW is born in Pritzwalk, Germany

1912 The 1913 Packard Model 2-48 is introduced

1915 Volvo, a Latin word meaning "I roll", is registered as a trademark by Svenska Kullargerfabriken (SKF), manufacturers of ball bearings

1915 Racer Robin Montgomerie-Charrington is born in London, England

1922 The 75,000th Essex is produced, a 5-passenger, 2-door Coach

1927 The first Oakland All-American Six is produced

1927 Bennett E. Bidwell of the Chrysler Corporation is born in Plymouth, IN

1930 Woolf Barnato and Glen Kidston win the Le Mans 24-hour race in their Bentley Speed Six, the fourth consecutive win for the marque in this event - Barnato, in his third and last appearance, recorded his third victory to complete a perfect record

1932 Alexander Winton dies at age 72

1933 Sir Henry "Tim" Birkin, a member of the Bentley racing team, dies in London at age 36 from complications arising from burning his arm during the Tripoli Grand Prix

1934 Ferdinand Porsche contracts with the Automobile Manufacturers' Association (RDA) of Germany to build three prototype "people's cars" within ten months

1936 Sir Herbert Austin, Chairman of the Austin Motor Company Ltd., receives the title of Baron from King Edward VIII

1937 Powel Crosley Jr. presides over groundbreaking ceremonies for the new Crosley Motors Inc. factory in Richmond, IN

1940 The American Bantam Car Company of Butler, PA agrees to supply seventy prototype Jeeps to the United States government for testing

1944 Automotive parts manufacturer Philip Alphonse Dur is born in Bethesda, MD

1946 The first shipment of Kaiser and Frazer cars leaves the Willow Run, MI factory

1948 American Locomotive Company executive Allen C. Connor is appointed as Controller for the Tri-Wheel Motor Corporation

1952 Mike Hawthorn makes his major racing debut, finishing fourth at the Belgian Grand Prix in Spa-Francorchamps in his Cooper-Bristol - the Aston-Butterworth makes its debut, but the car driven by Robin Montgomerie-Charrington retires with mechanical problems

1954 The Packard Motor Car Company announces that an agreement has been signed whereby Packard will purchase the Studebaker Corporation

1956 The last Packard and Clipper V-8 engines are produced at the Utica, MI factory

1962 Reese H. Taylor, President of the Union Oil Company of California 1938-1956 and its Chairman since 1956, dies at age 61

1972 The 1,000,000th Ford Thunderbird is produced, a gold coupe from the Pico Rivera, CA plant that was sold to George Watts, owner of the oldest known Thunderbird, a black 1955 convertible

1972 The last Volvo 1800E sports coupe is produced

1975 James Hunt wins the Dutch Grand Prix in Zandvoort driving a Hesketh 308, the only Formula 1 victory for the marque financed by Lord Alexander Fermor-Hesketh

1975 Alumni Day at the General Motors Institute in Flint, MI is celebrated with a mock race featuring General Motors President Elliott M. "Pete" Estes in a 1910 Buick Model 10, Buick General Manager George R. Elges in a 1910 Buick Bug race car, and GMI President Harold P. Rodes in a 1975 Buick Indianapolis 500 Pace Car

1977 Benjamin Anibal, longtime General Motors engineer and the designer of the original 1926 Pontiac, dies in suburban Detroit, MI at age 90

1979 Racer Louis Chiron dies in Monte Carlo, Monaco at age 79

1988 Dr. Pier Giorgio Cappelli of Fiat assumes management of the Ferrari racing program

1989 Prominent automobile collector Rick Carroll is killed at age 51 in a car accident in South Carolina

1996 Walter Stillman, a Buick dealer since 1929 and a Director of the National Automobile Dealers Association, dies in Hanover, NH at age 90

JUNE 23

1859 Tire manufacturer and racer Edouard Michelin is born

1899 Amedee Gordini, racer, rallyist, race car designer and builder, team manager, and development engineer, is born in Bazzano, Italy

1902 S. G. Averell of New York City purchases the second Franklin built, but the first of the marque to be sold

1902 The "Mercedes" name (with accents) is registered as a trademark by the Daimler Motoren-Gesellschaft

1909 Ford No. 2, a Model T driven by Bert Scott and Jimmy Smith, arrives at the Alaska-Yukon-Pacific Exposition in Seattle, WA, winning the "race" that had started in New York City 23 days earlier

1911 Automobile parts manufacturer Thomas Jefferson Ault is born in Portland, IN

1916 Automotive historian Menno Duerksen is born in Weatherford, OK

1916 Racer Leslie Thorne is born in Greenock, Renfrewshire, Scotland

1916 The Modine Manufacturing Company, a leading manufacturer of automobile radiators, is founded in Racine, WI

1917 The 4-passenger Disbrow Quad Express is announced

1921 The assets of the Hebb Motor Company are sold at auction

1923 Jordan's "Somewhere West of Laramie" magazine advertisement debuts

1924 Second series 1924 Essex Sixes are introduced

1927 The General Motors Arts & Colour Section is formed under the direction of Harley M. Earl

1930 Racer Bob Harkey is born

1931 Packard Ninth Series Eights are introduced

1935 The second and last of the modern Briarcliff Trophy Races is staged in Briarcliff, NY, after which town leaders decide to discontinue the series

1936 Hugh Edward Norton of the British Petroleum Company PLC is born in London

1937 Racer Herbert Mackay-Fraser is born in Connecticut

1945 The Ford Motor Company ends operations at its Willow Run factory

1950 The Mercury Monterey and Lincoln Lido hardtop coupes are introduced as mid-year models

1950 The 1950 Nash Rambler station wagon is introduced as a mid-year model

1957 Charles B. King dies in Larchmont, NY at age 88

1959 Racer Michel Trolle is born in France

1963 Worth McMillion makes his Grand National racing debut driving a Pontiac at South Boston, VA

1968 Jackie Stewart, driving a Matra MS10, wins the Dutch Grand Prix in Zandvoort, the first Formula 1 victory for the marque

1973 Racer Gerry Birrell dies in Rouen, France at age 28

1978 Bombardier, Inc. is organized in Canada succeeding the original company founded in 1902 by Joseph-Armand Bombardier

1991 Bertrand Gachot, Johnny Herbert, and Volker Weidler, driving a Mazda, win the 24 Hours of Le Mans, the first victory in this race by a Japanese car

1996 Alex Zanardi records his first IndyCar victory, winning a race in Portland, OR in his Target Reynard Honda

JUNE 24

1888 Lewis Powell Kalb, an employee of the Pierce-Arrow Motor Car Company 1911-1915 and the Kelly-Springfield Truck & Bus Corporation 1915-1921, and an executive with the Continental Motors Corporation 1921-1950, is born in Bellefontaine, OH

1889 Frank Whittemore Abrams of the Standard Oil Company of New Jersey is born in Rockville Center, Long Island, NY

1895 Reid Anthony Railton is born in Alderley Edge, Cheshire, England

1900 Oliver Lippincott, driving a Locomobile steamer, becomes the first motorist to enter Yosemite National Park, CA

RAILTON

1902 The Paris-Vienna race begins with 137 entries and 10,000 spectators

1911 Racer Juan Manuel Fangio y Cia is born in Balcarce, Argentina

1914 L. G. "Cupid" Hornsted, driving a 200 hp Benz at Brooklands, England makes several land speed record runs, recording a best two-way average of 124.10 mph - although slower than several earlier unrecognized runs, this was the first effort using the now standard two-way average requirement

1922 William Rockefeller of the Standard Oil Company dies in Tarrytown, NY at age 81

1923 Cesare Romiti of Fiat SpA is born in Rome, Italy

1923 Opel records it finest racing moment when the 12-litre car built in 1913 wins a beach race on Fano Island, Denmark at a speed of 128 mph

1924 The Alvis Car and Engineering Company Ltd. formally closes down, but later reopens under the management of liquidator Sir Gilbert Gansey

1927 Archie Merrill Long of Cadillac is born in Altoona, PA

1928 The rocket-powered Opel RAK 3 makes its debut on a section of railroad track near Hannover, Germany with about 20,000 spectators in attendance, and sets a Rail Speed Record of 157.8 mph on its first run - "manned" only by a caged cat, the car crashes during its second run when too many rockets fire at once

1931 Benton Hanchett, a cofounder of the Argo Electric Vehicle Company, dies at age 96

1931 Frank N. Nutt, a spark plug manufacturer and Chief Engineer of the Haynes Automobile Company 1899-1914, dies in Rochester, MN at age 51

1934 Racer Tommy Bridger is born in Welwyn, England

1936 The Springfield Manufacturing Company, the successor of Rolls-Royce of America, Inc. and Brewster & Company coachbuilders, is liquidated

1941 Herman H. A. Schmidt Jr., a design engineer with the Ward Motor Vehicle Company and an authority on electric automobiles, dies

1949 G. A. Kraus of the Champion Spark Plug Company is killed in an automobile accident at age 60

1953 Racer Takao Wada is born in Japan

1954 The New York Thruway opens

1956 Automobile executive Ivan A. Likhachev dies in Moscow, USSR at age 60

1959 Aeronutronic Systems, Inc. becomes the Aeronutronic Division of the Ford Motor Company

1960 Racer Jim Bown is born

1961 Racer Hut Stricklin is born in Calera, AL

1965 Buick President Edward D. Rollert is promoted to Vice President of General Motors in charge of the car and truck group

1968 Racer Vittorio Zoboli is born in Bologna, Italy

1969 Ernest Wooler, a Rolls-Royce design engineer in his native England and later Chief Engineer of the Cleveland Automobile Company, dies in Fort Lauderdale, FL at age 81

1971 The International Scout II is introduced

1977 The United States government drops plans to convert all highway signs to the metric system

JUNE 25

1891 Irving Brown Babcock of General Motors is born in Milwaukee, WI

1895 William Francis Hufstader of Dort, Mason, Graham, Dodge, and Buick is born in Jersey City, NJ

1900 The Automobile Club of Western New York is founded in Buffalo, NY

1906 The Kissel Motor Car Company is organized in Hartford, WI with H. K. Butterfield as President, Otto P. Kissel as Vice President, and George A. Kissel as Secretary-Treasurer

1914 The Salem, MA bicycle shop of Lucius B. Packard is destroyed by fire - in the late 1890's three prototype Packard automobiles had been built here, but actual production did not occur

1915 The Daniels Motor Car Company is incorporated in Reading, PA by George E. Daniels and Neff E. Parish

1919 The Auburn Automobile Company is reorganized with Morris Eckhart as President, A. P. Kemp as First Vice President and Treasurer, and James I. Farley as Second Vice President and General Sales Manager

1925 The first Diana is produced by the Diana Motors Company of St. Louis, MO, a wholly owned subsidiary of the Moon Motor Car Company

1927 The second series Essex Super-Sixes are introduced

1929 The 6,000,000th Chevrolet is produced

1930 The Packard board of directors approves development of a front-drive V-12 prototype under the direction of consultant C. W. Van Ranst

1932 Racer Tim Parnell is born in Derby, England, the son of racer Reg Parnell

1935 The first Lincoln-Zephyr, based largely on the designs of John Tjaarda, is produced

A 1939 Lincoln-Zephyr prepares to drive through the Chandelier Tree
in northern California.

1938 The first Southern Irish Rally is staged for "veteran" motor cars

1939 Racer Dick Seaman is killed at age 26 when his Mercedes-Benz W154 crashes in heavy rain during the Belgian Grand Prix in Spa-Francorchamps - the redesigned Alfa Romeo Type 316 race car makes its debut with driver Nino Farina - Georg Meier makes his Auto Union debut, but retires with mechanical problems

1940 Henry Ford is awarded the James Watt International Medal by the British Institution of Mechanical Engineers at a dinner in Detroit, MI

1946 Packard Motor Car Company Chairman Alvan Macauley is inducted into the Automotive Hall of Fame

1946 Calvin C. Williams is issued a United States patent for his high compression steam engine

1949 The first post-World War II 24 Hours of Le Mans (France) begins

1949 Racer Patrick Tambay is born in Paris, France

1950 The first automobile races are held at the former United States Navy blimp base in Santa Ana, CA

1951 John Wilkinson of Franklin dies in Syracuse, NY at age 83

*A view of I. & L. Grant's Store in Pennelville, NY
taken in 1924 - the touring car at left in a John Wilkinson-designed
Franklin displaying the "Renault" style hood used 1911-1920.*

1952 Peter Wilks takes the Rover Jet I, featuring a rear-mounted gas turbine engine, on its debut test drive at Jabbeke, Belgium

1952 Frederick A. Van Fleet, Advertising Manager for the Peerless Motor Car Company 1925-1928, dies at age 78

1953 A full-sized clay model of the proposed Lincoln Continental Mark II is completed

1956 The last 1956 Packard is produced, marking the end of production at the Conner Avenue plant in Detroit, MI and the last "real" Packard

1956 Channing Rice Dooley of the Standard Oil Company dies at age 78

1957 The last Hudson is produced at the American Motors plant in Kenosha, WI - during the marque's 48-year history, nearly 4,000,000 vehicles (including companion marques and commerical units) had been manufactured

1964 Racer Johnny Herbert is born in Brentwood, Essex, England

1974 The Bricklin SV-1 is introduced to the public in Livonia, MI

1979 J. C. Whitney & Company, the Chicago, IL auto parts mail order firm, is forced into Chapter XI bankruptcy

1980 Rolls-Royce Motors Ltd. and Vickers Son & Company Ltd. announce plans to merge

1981 The United States Postal Service issues a 17-cent regular coil stamp picturing an "Electric Auto" at the Greenfield Village, MI post office - the design by Chuck Jaquays was based on a photograph of a 1917 Detroit Electric coupe

1990 The new Peugeot 905 race car makes its first test run at the Montlhery track in the hands of Jean-Pierre Jabouille

JUNE 26

1885 Automobile parts manufacturer Walter W. Carpenter is born in Chicago, IL

1889 Race promoter and official George Morton Levy is born in Seaford, LI, NY

1898 The Prince of Wales (later King Edward VII) takes the first actual royal journey in a motor car, traveling with J. S. Critchley in his Coventry Daimler from Warwick Castle to Compton Verney

1898 Willy Emil Messerschmitt, the German aviation industrialist whose name graced the Messerschmitt bubble car of 1953-1962, is born in Frankfurt am Main, Germany

1898 Automobile headlamp manufacturer Elmer Ellsworth Wood Jr. is born in Newark, NJ

1902 Inventor William Powell Lear, a proponent of modern steam-powered automobiles, is born in Hannibal, MO

1902 The Paris-Vienna automobile race begins - the first leg, a 351.46-mile run to Innsbruck doubles as the third Gordon Bennett Trophy race, and is won by S. F. Edge driving a Napier 50-hp

1902 Ettore Bugatti and Baron Eugene de Dietrich reach an agreement whereby Bugatti will manufacture cars of his design as the De Dietrich-Bugatti at the de Dietrich factory in Niederbronn, Alsace, Germany (now France)

1904 Ettore Bugatti files for his first patent (German) relating to the yoke end for a steering gear

1905 The Automobile Association (AA) is organized in Great Britain

1906 The French Grand Prix, the world's first such race, is staged in Le Mans by the Automobile Club de France (ACF) and won by the Hungarian driver Ferenc Szisz in a 13-liter, 90-hp Renault

1915 The first race is held at the Maywood Speedway in Chicago, IL and 85,000 people see Dario Resta win the 500-mile race in a Peugeot at 97.58 mph

1917 Richard H. Collins is named President of Cadillac

1925 The Chrysler Corporation is incorporated in Delaware as a reorganized Maxwell Motor Corporation with Nicholas Kelley as interim President

1929 Racer Rodney Nuckey is born in London, England

1930 Harry C. Stutz dies from appendicitis in Indianapolis, IN at age 53

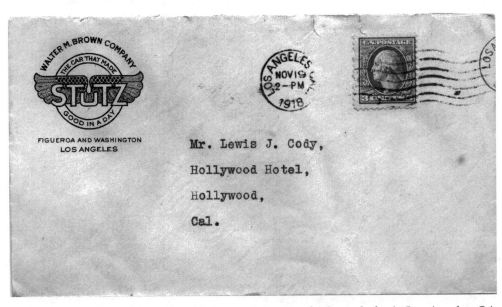

A business envelope of the Walter M. Brown Company, the Stutz dealer in Los Angeles, CA.

1930 F. H. Royce is knighted by King George V, becoming Sir Frederick Henry Royce, Bart., O.B.E., M.I.M.E

1933 Giustino Cattaneo resigns from Isotta-Fraschini

1935 Racer Carlo Facetti is born in Cormano, Milan, Lombardy, Italy

1937 Racer Erwin Kremer is born in Germany

1944 Ivan Gregory Fallon, biographer of John Z. DeLorean, is born in Wexford, Ireland

1951 Leon A. Chaminade, a design engineer with Studebaker and Chevrolet, dies in Detroit, MI at age 61

1951 James J. Shanley, an advocate for standardized sealed beam headlights and flashing turn signals, dies in Elizabeth, NJ at age 64

1952 Packard President James J. Nance gives his first "Key Man" speech

1953 The last Henry J is produced

1955 Racer Phillippe Streiff is born in Grenoble, France

1955 Ira Garfunkel, a General Motors development test engineer who designed an improved compressor for automobile air conditioners, is killed in an automobile accident

1956 The Zavod Imieni Stalina (Stalin Automobile Plant) in Moscow, USSR changes its name to the Zavod Imieni Likhacheva, with the former ZIS marque renmaed as the ZIL - the new name honored Ivan A. Likhachev, the Road Transport Minister and former director of the factory who had died two days ago, instead of Joseph Stalin who had fallen out of favor with the current Communist regime

1956 Paul J. Rhoads, Assistant Chief Engineer of the Detroit Transmission Division of General Motors, dies in La Paz, Mexico

1962 Racer Kevin Lepage is born

1963 Racer Steve Grissom is born in Gadsden, AL

1977 The Grand Prix de Rouen-les-Essarts is won by Eddie Cheever in a BMW, at age 19 years, 168 days, the youngest winner of a Formula 2 race

1983 The Horseless Carriage Club of America dedicates a monument in Des Moines, IA to mark the 1906 assembly site of the first Mason car by Frederick S. Duesenberg

Designer Frederick S. Duesenberg drives the prototype Mason up the steps of the Iowa State Capitol. He then drove down the same steps and ascended a second time in reverse gear. The publicity stunt was sanctioned by the state legislature as a means of promoting the new business venture.

JUNE 27

1868 Walter Charles Baker, founder of the Baker Motor Vehicle Company, is born in Hinsdale, NH

1871 Frank F. Matheson is born in Kalamazoo, MI

*Brothers Frank F. and Charles W. Matheson manufactured cars under
their own name 1903-1912 before becoming succcessful distributors of
Oaklands and Pontiacs, among others.*

1873 Joseph Arthur Jeffery, credited with many improvements in spark plug technology, is born in
San Francisco, CA

1876 Following its relocation from Richmond, IN to Indianapolis, Nordyke, Marmon & Company
reorganizes as the Nordyke & Marmon Company

1881 Gustave Baumann, an artist affiliated with Packard 1914-1920, is born in Magdeburg, Germany

1897 William Lyman Stewart Jr. of the Union Oil Company of California is born in Santa Paula, CA

1901 Camille du Gast makes her racing debut in the Paris-Berlin race driving a 20-hp Panhard et Levassor

1902 The first Susa-Mont Cenis (Italy) speed hillclimb is won by Vincenzo Lancia in a Fiat

1904 L. Irving Woolson of DeSoto is born in New York City

1905 Howard C. Marmon is issued a United States patent for his friction braking system with internal brake
shoes

1907 The Seagrave prototype Model AC-30 combination chemical and hose car, their first motorized fire truck, makes a 55-mile test run from Chillicothe and Columbus, OH

1908 The American Locomotive Automobile Company of Providence, RI, manufacturers of the Alco, merges with its parent company, the American Locomotive Company

1910 Luxury automobile manufacturer SA Minerva Motors of Antwerp, Belgium registers its logo as a trademark in the United States

1922 Julian S. Friede is issued a United States patent for an air-tight seat cushion with adjustable vent on behalf of the Moon Motor Car Company, thought to be the only patent ever issued to this firm

1923 A statue of F. H. Royce sculpted by F. Derwent Wood is unveiled in Derby, England, partly to honor the man and partly to bring publicity and potential sales to Rolls-Royce Ltd.

1925 Automotive steel manufacturer A. D. Dorman dies at age 58

1938 Archie Moulton Andrews, an executive with Moon, Ruxton, Hupmobile, and other independents, dies at age 59

1940 Ferdinando Minoia of Isotta-Fraschini dies at age 56

1942 Racer Christopher Frank Stuart "Chris" Irwin is born in London, England

1945 Benjamin Briscoe dies in Dunnellon, FL at age 78

1948 The Maserati 4CLT/48 race car makes its debut at the San Remo Grand Prix in Ospedaletti, Italy with Alberto Ascari and Luigi Villoresi finishing first and second - the car would thereafter be known as the Tipo San Remo

1952 Howard Cooper of the Sinclair Refining Company dies at age 61

1955 Henry Ford II is elected to the Board of Directors of the General Electric Company

1955 Illinois passes the first seat belt legislation in the United States

1955 Holden W. Rightmyer of the Standard Products Company since 1951, and the designer of all door locks used by the Chrysler Corporation 1933-1936 while with the American Swiss Company, dies

1957 Gordon Lefebvre of Chevrolet and Pontiac dies at age 68

1957 The Chevrolet Division of General Motors registers the "Impala" name as a trademark

1958 The Mackinac Bridge connecting the two Michigan peninsulae is dedicated - the first cars to officially cross the bridge are 83 white 1958 Oldsmobile 98 convertibles carrying beauty queens representing each of Michigan's counties

1962 The Alfa Romeo Giulia is introduced in Monza, Italy

1962 Renzo Rivolta introduces his new marque, the Iso Rivolta, in Bresso, Italy

1963 George M. Holley, founder of the Holley Carburetor Company in 1918 and its Chairman 1930-1963, dies in Warren, MI at age 85

1963 Racer Johnny Benson Jr. is born in Grand Rapids, MI

1964 Production of the Sunbeam Tiger begins

1967 The last Sunbeam Tiger II is produced

1973 The 5,000,000th Cadillac is produced, a blue Sedan DeVille

1973 The last of 8,078 Volvo 1800ES sport wagons is produced

1974 The 2,000,000th visitor is received at Harrah's Automobile Collection in Sparks, NV

1978 The Japan Petroleum Development Corporation changes its name to the Japan National Oil Corporation

1986 Jerry J. Moore of Houston, TX purchases the ex-Harrah 1931 Bugatti Royale double berline de voyage for an auction record $6.5 million

1988 Elmer W. Johnson, General Motors Executive Vice President, resigns

1994 Sam Hanks, winner of the 1957 Indianapolis 500, dies at age 79

1996 Yoshikazu Hanawa becomes President of the Nissan Motor Company, Ltd.

JUNE 28

1830 Samuel Latta Smith of Oldsmobile is born in Algonac, MI

1851 Pioneer British motoring enthusiast Sir David Lionel Goldsmid-Stern Salomans is born in Brighton, Sussex, England

1877 Charles Arthur Tilt, founder in 1905 of the Diamond T Motor Car Company, is born in Chicago, IL

Towering above the field in speed, power, economy
...that's DIAMOND T *reliability*

IT'S Redding to Yreka and Alturas, then all the way down to Richmond—the roads of northern California are hilly and winding, as this view of Mt. Shasta suggests. Over these roads this extra-heavy-duty Diamond T has rolled up 280,000 miles in the last two years, hauling 5,000-gallon loads of gasoline. Owner E. B. Hinkle is very happy about the whole thing.

He stresses the economy and complete satisfaction of his Diamond T experience, and adds, "Your parts service has been exceptional. Never, even during the most critical times, have our Diamond T's been laid up for want of parts."

Today's Diamond T trucks are the finest we have ever built. The complete line includes 19 models from one ton upwards, and every model has the built-in reliability for which Diamond T has been famous since 1905. We sincerely believe that the new Diamond T Super-Service engines set an entirely new standard for performance and long life in hard service.

See your Diamond T dealer—he is an expert on motor transport. Let him recommend the Diamond T that will do *your* job best for you. See him for truck service, too.

DIAMOND T MOTOR CAR COMPANY CHICAGO
Established 1905

DIAMOND T TRUCKS

1888 Ray Adrian Long of Chalmers, Columbia, and Divco is born in Detroit, MI

1897 A German-built Benz Velo, appearing in a Grand Forks parade to promote cigars, is the first automobile to be driven in North Dakota

1898 Henry Timken and Reginald Heinzelman are issued a United States patent for their "Roller Bearing for Vehicles"

1902 The first Packard Model G is completed - this was the marque's first and only 2-cylinder car, but just four would be produced

1907 Rolls-Royce historian Harold Nockolds is born

1908 Adam Kramer Stricker Jr. of General Motors is born in New York City

1914 Archduke Franz Ferdinand is assassinated in Sarajevo, Bosnia, an action that resulted in the outbreak of World War I, while riding in an Austro-Daimler that was being chauffered by racer Otto Merz, a Mercedes team driver

1914 The grandstands at the Baden-Baden (Germany) racetrack are destroyed by fire

1918 The AMO automotive plant in Moscow is nationalized by the new Communist govenment

1923 Racer Adolfo J. Cruz Schwelm is born in Buenos Aires, Argentina

1924 The last speed hillclimb at Spread Eagle, England is staged

1925 The first Belgian Grand Prix is staged in Spa-Francorchamps, and won by Antonio Ascari in an Alfa Romeo P2

1926 The Daimler Motoren-Gesellschaft and Benz & Cie formally merge as Daimler-Benz Aktiengesellschaft, manufacturers of the Mercedes-Benz, with Wilhelm Kissel of Benz as Managing Director of the new firm

1926 Racer Betty Skelton is born in Pensacola, FL

1927 Raymond Haim Levy of Renault is born in Paris, France

1931 Racer Junior Johnson is born in Ronda, NC

1936 Alberto Ascari makes his motorcycle racing debut as a prelude to his automobile racing career

1939 Automobile parts manufacturer Morton F. Judd dies at age 54

1940 Racer Dieter Schornstein is born in Aachen, Germany

1945 The last B-24 bomber is produced by the Ford Motor Company at its Willow Run, MI plant that would become the home of the Kaiser-Frazer Corporation

1947 Thomas Clive DeLaval-Crow, Chief Engineer of the New Departure Manufacturing Company who previously had been a draftsman with Alldays & Onions in his native England, dies at age 61

1951 The Nash Rambler Country Club hardtop coupe is introduced as a mid-year model

1955 The Dodge Firebomb convertible, in effect the prototype Dual-Ghia, is introduced in Grosse Pointe, MI by Gene Casaroll

1957 Racer Mike Skinner is born in Ontario, CA

1963 The FWD Corporation of Clintonville, WI acquires the Columbus (OH) Division of the Seagrave Corporation, manufacturers of firetrucks, for $4,000,000

1964 Racer Tim Hubman is born in El Dorado, CA

1964 Dan Gurney wins the French Grand Prix in his Brabham Type BT7, the first of 35 Formula 1 victories for the marque

1970 Byron C. Foy of DeSoto dies at age 77

1983 Stylist and coachbuilder Pietro Frua dies in Turin, Italy at age 70

1987 David Scott-Moncreiff, automotive historian and longtime dealer/restorer of pre-World War II Rolls-Royce, dies at age 79

1988 William E. Hoglund, Robert T. O'Connell, and John F. Smith Jr. are named Vice Chairmen of General Motors

1996 Automotive journalist Len Frank dies in Long Beach, CA at age 60

JUNE 29

1895 Motorola executive Paul Vincent Galvin, a leading pioneer in promoting car radios, is born in Harvard, IL

1901 The 3-day Paris-Berlin race is won by Henri Fournier driving a Mors

1902 The 4-day Paris-Vienna race is won by Marcel Renault driving a Renault

1907 S. F. Edge drives a Napier for 24 hours at average speed of 60 mph

1911 Ettore Bugatti is issued a German patent for the "pursang" trademark

1916 The Aerolite Piston Company, Ltd. is incorporated by A. H. M. J. Ward, James Tolley, and Alfred Bentley to take over the piston business of Bentley and Bentley Ltd.

1920 The Walden W. Shaw Livery Corporation changes its name to the Yellow Cab Manufacturing Company

1921 Racer Henry O'Reilly "Harry" Schell is born in Paris, France, the son of United States citizens

1923 Alessandro Cagno driving a Fiat 803 with a Wittig vane-type supercharger wins the 340-mile Gran Premio Vetturette at Brescia, Italy for the first racing victory in Europe by a supercharged car

1927 The 1928 Nashes are introduced

1929 The "Blower" Bentley, a 4.5-litre chassis with Villiers supercharger, makes its racing debut with Tim Birkin's car retiring in the Brooklands (England) 6 Hour Race due to bearing failure

1932 Auto Union AG is formed by Danish-born Jorgen Skafte Rasmussen and Dr. Richard Bruhn, with the company's legal status dated retroactively to November 1, 1931

1935 The first Cape Cod Grand Prix is staged at the Marston's Mills track and won by a Bentley 3-litre

1937 Charles H. Metz dies in Glendale, CA at age 73

1938 G. D. Boerlage of the Royal Dutch/Shell Group dies at age 52

1939 The Ford-Ferguson tractor is introduced

1939 Racer Jimmy Snyder dies in Cahokia, IL

1944 Racer Frank Sytner is born in Liverpool, Lancashire, England

1946 The first Kaiser and Frazer cars are introduced by Los Angeles, CA dealer Earl Muntz

1948 A. K. Brumbaugh, a design engineer with Autocar and White, dies in Palo Alto, CA at age 64

1953 The last Kaiser Deluxe is produced

1957 Giuseppe Bacciagaluppi, Managing Director of the Autodromo Nazionale di Monza in Italy, stages the first race at the newly remodeled track, a match race between ten top European Formula 1 drivers and ten top Indianapolis car drivers - Jimmy Bryan of the United States in the Salih roadster wins the Two Worlds Trophy at 160.060 mph

1957 Elmer F. Heimbach, Vice President of Engineering for the Brummer Seal Company, dies at age 58

1967 Racer Jeff Burton is born in South Boston, VA

1979 Chevrolet collector Bob Van Etten dies

1985 The plant of the former Gotfredson Truck Corporation Ltd. in Windsor, ON, Canada is destroyed by fire along with more than 70 collector vehicles stored in the building

1985 A Rolls-Royce Phantom V limousine once owned by Beatle John Lennon and sporting psychedelic paintwork is sold in New York City to Jim Pattison for $2,225,000, a record price for a "used" Rolls-Royce

JUNE 30

1882 Gottlieb Daimler resigns as Technical Director of Langen, Otto, & Rosen

1894 Edward Riley of General Motors is born in Lawrence, MA

1901 Lon A. Fleener of General Motors and the White Motor Company is born in Morgantown, IN

1908 The H. H. Franklin Manufacturing Company of Syracuse, NY registers the "Franklin" name as a trademark

1910 The seventh Glidden tour ends in Chicago, IL and is won by Ray McNamara in a Premier

1922 Edward V. Hartford, the inventor of the Hartford Shock Absorber, dies in New York City at age 52

1923 The Ford Model T officially becomes a 1924 model

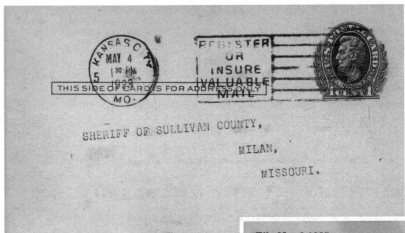

During the 1920's government postal cards were sent to area law enforcement personnel to alert them of stolen vehicles.

File No. 6-1287
May 4th, 1923.

Motor No. **6631910**

Ford Coupe Stolen

1923 Model—Black body and wheels. 1923 Kansas State License No. 30-433. Firestone tires all around, including spare. Extra large chain locks spare tire on. Chip out of upper windshield on right side. Pads around foot pedals. Stolen from Arkansas City, Kansas, about 10:30 P. M., May 3rd, 1923. Owner, Boyd Mohler.

$25.00 reward for recovery of car not burned or destroyed.
$25.00 reward for arrest and conviction of the thief.

NOTIFY
AUTOMOBILE UNDERWRITERS CLUB OF KANSAS AND MISSOURI
416 American Bank Bldg., Kansas City, Mo.
At Our Expense.
Telephone MAin 4635

1926 General Motors purchases the Fisher Body Corporation, retaining William A. Fisher as General Manager of the new Fisher Body Division

1930 General Motors acquires the Winton Engine Company of Cleveland, OH, gaining the services of Alexander Winton, his firm's expertise with marine engines, and his designs for improvements in fuel injection systems

1931 George Freers is issued a United States patent for his "double-dome" combustion chamber as introduced in the 1930 Marmon

1931 The last regular production Peerless is built

1933 The third (and last to be sold) Bugatti Royale Type 41 is delivered to Capt. Cuthbert Foster in London, England with limousine coachwork by Park Ward & Company Ltd.

1934 The Peerless Motor Car Company reorganizes as the Peerless Corporation, brewers of Carlings beer

1937 Groundbreaking ceremonies are held for the new Chrysler Corporation Ltd. of Canada factory in Windsor, ON

1937 The 25,000th Volvo is produced, a dark blue PV52 sedan

1939 The Bentley Corniche prototype is completed

1944 Henry Ford II is elected Vice President of the Ford Motor Company of Canada, Ltd.

1946 Bert Dingley retires as President of the Marmon-Herrington Company, Inc. and is succeeded by former Chevrolet executive David M. Klausmeyer

1948 Racer Achille Varzi is killed at age 43 when his experimental supercharged Alfa Romeo crashes during a practice run for the Swiss Grand Prix at the rain-soaked Bremgarten circuit in Berne, Switzerland

1953 The first Chevrolet Corvette is produced, a white roadster with red interior built at the temporary facilities in Flint, MI

1954 Kaiser Motors Corporation terminates production of its 1954 models

1956 Carl J. Snyder of the Chrysler Corporation is killed in an airplane crash

1956 Alfredo "Dino" Ferrari dies in Modena, Italy at age 34 from muscular dystrophy

1957 Racer Sterling Marlin is born in Columbia, TN

1960 William C. Newberg is fired as President of the Chrysler Corporation because of alleged conflicts-of-interest caused by owning stock in various corporate suppliers

1960 Diadema Argentina SA de Petroleo changes its name to Shell Cia Argentina de Petroleo SA

1966 Giuseppe "Nino" Farina, the 1950 World Champion Driver, is killed at age 59 when he loses control of his Lotus Cortina on an icy road near Chambery, France,

1969 The last of 4,204,925 Ramblers is produced in Kenosha, WI as the marque officially becomes the AMC

1970 Kelly Petillo, winner of the 1935 Indianapolis 500, dies at age 68

1972 The last 1972 Pontiac is produced

1978 William Fisk Harrah, casino/hotel owner and builder of the world's largest automobile collection, dies in Rochester, MN at age 67

Only those lucky enough to have visited Harrah's can understand it.
The collection was probably the greatest - of anything - ever privately assembled.

1980 Members of the Subaru 360 Drivers' Club complete a 2,600-mile trip with their arrival in Tucson, AZ

JULY 1

1829 Willem van Bakel establishes a carriage shop in Amsterdam, Holland that would evolve into Carrosserie Schutter & van Bakel

1860 Charles Goodyear, inventor of vulcanization, dies in New York City at age 59

1873 Alfred Owen Dunk, a prolific buyer of defunct automobile company inventories, is born in Saginaw, MI

1888 Herschel Blake Knap of Packard is born in Bloomington, IL

1892 Automobile parts manufacturer John Aaron Grass is born in York, PA

1893 Brothers John F. "Jack" Mack and Augustus F. "Gus" Mack acquire the wagonmaking business of Christian Fallesen in Brooklyn, NY

Following their successes during World War I, the "Bulldog" Mack became a leader in the heavy truck field for many years.

1899 Fabbrica Italiana Automobili Torino (F.I.A.T.) is founded by Giovanni Agnelli, Ludovico Scarfiotti, Count E. C. di Bricherasio, Count Biscaretti di Ruffia, Cesare Gatti, Enrico Marchesi, and Gustav Deslex in Turin, Italy

1899 Mme. Labrousse, believed to be the first woman to compete in an automotive speed event, finishes fifth in the Paris-Spa race

1900 Vincenzo Lancia makes his racing debut, winning a speed-trial at Padua, Italy in a 6-hp Fiat - the winner of the quadricycle class in the Padua-Vicenza-Padua road race is Ettore Bugatti in what would be his last known racing competition as a driver

1901 William King White, son of Rollin H. White and himself an official in the White Motor Company, is born in Cleveland, OH

1901 John Wilkinson joins the H. H. Franklin Manufacturing Company as Chief Engineer

1904 The first Buick is test driven in Flint, MI

1907 David William Hardy Scott-Moncreiff, automotive historian and dealer in pre-World War II Rolls-Royce, is born

1907 The Illinois General Assembly requires license plates for all cars

1908 Pliny Fisk Olds, father and first business partner of Ransom E. Olds, dies in Lansing, MI at age 80

1908 The Brush Model B is introduced

1909 A contract is signed by William C. Durant and Henry M. Leland leading to the acquisition of the Cadillac Motor Car Company by General Motors

1910 Maryland state-issued license plates are introduced

1913 The Lincoln Highway Association is incorporated "to produce the establishment of a continuous improved highway from the Atlantic to the Pacific, open to lawful traffic of all description without toll charges"

1914 Dodge Brothers, Inc. is incorporated to manufacture Dodge Brothers automobiles

1915 Tennessee state-issued license plates are introduced

1916 The Packard Second Series 2-25 Twin Six is introduced

1917 Automobile historian William Greenleaf is born in Brooklyn, NY

1917 Texas state-issued license plates are introduced

1917 The 1918 Dodges are introduced

1918 The 1919 Dodges are introduced, including a 4-door sedan, 5-window coupe, town car taxicab, and limousine as new models

1919 The 1920 Dodges are introduced

1920 The 500,000th Dodge is produced

1920 The prototype Handley-Knight, designed by J. I. Handley, is completed by Handley Motors, Inc. of Kalamazoo, MI

1922 Morris Eckhart retires as President of the Auburn Automobile Company - Treasurer A. P. Kemp assumes the additional roles of President and General Manager with James I. Farley as First Vice President and General Sales Manager, E. A. Johnson as Secretary, Z. B. Walling as Assistant Treasurer, and John Zimmerman as Assistant Treasurer

1923 James F. Bourquin, Vice President and General Manager of the Continental Motors Corporation, dies in Detroit, MI at age 45 following an operation for appendicitis

1925 The Chrysler Four, essentially a badge-engineered continuation of the Maxwell, is introduced

1925 The 1926 Nash Series 230 Special Six is introduced

1925 Groundbreaking ceremonies are held for the Ford Motor Company of Australia, PL factory in Geelong, Victoria

1926 Carl Horst Hahn, Chairman of Volkswagenwerk AG 1982-1993, is born in Chemnitz, Germany

1927 The second series 1927 Hudson Super-Sixes are introduced

1927 The Packard Fourth Series Custom Eight 443 is introduced along with the Fifth Series Six 526 and 533

1927 Production of the Protos ends after 27 years

1928 The second series 1928 Hudson and Essex Super-Sixes are introduced

1928 Wade Morton and Eddie Miller set a world's record driving a stock Auburn 115 speedster (sans fenders) 2,017 miles in 24 hours at Atlantic City, NJ

1929 The Dodge Series DA is introduced as the "first series 1930 Dodge"

1929 The second series Hudson and Essex Super-Sixes are introduced - they were originally marketed as "1930" cars, but the company redesignated them as "1929" cars in the early 1930's

1929 The Hudson Motor Car Company introduces the Dover light commercial vehicles, based on the Essex chassis

1930 The Plymouth Model 30U officially becomes a 1931 model

1931 The 1932 Dodge Series DC and Series DG are introduced

1931 The Quaker State Oil Refining Corporation is incorporated in Delaware to acquire, merge, and operate 19 smaller businesses

1932 Robert Allen Link of the Chrysler Corporation is born in Detroit, MI

1933 Albert R. Erskine, President of the Studebaker Corporation, commits suicide at his home in South Bend, IN at age 62

1935 Lord Nuffield (Sir William R. Morris) sells the M.G. Car Company, Ltd. and Wolseley Motors Ltd. to the public corporation Morris Motors Ltd.

1937 Maurice Olley of General Motors is named Passenger Vehicle Engineer for Vauxhall Motors Ltd.

1946 Ernest R. Breech is named Executive Vice President of the Ford Motor Company

1946 The Hupp Motor Car Corporation is reorganized as the Hupp Corporation with former General Motors President William S. Knudsen as Chairman, but its products do not include automobiles

1946 Dr. Frederick E. Searle retires after 30 years with the Henry Ford Trade School

1946 The Master Tire & Rubber Corporation changes its name to the Cooper Tire & Rubber Company

1947 Racer Kazuyoshi Hoshino is born in Tokyo, Japan

1948 Gregory Houston Bowden, historian of the Morgan marque, is born in London, England

1949 Volkswagen announces the four-seater convertible with coachwork by Karmann

1951 Luigi Fagioli and Juan Manuel Fangio, driving an Alfa Romeo Type 159, win the French Grand Prix - at age 53 years, 21 days Fagioli is the oldest driver to win a Formula 1 championship race

1951 Robert B. Schenck, Chief Metallurgical Engineer for Buick, retires after 36 years of service with General Motors

1951 George B. Allen retires as a design engineer with the Chrysler Corporation 42 years after beginning his automotive career with the Hudson Motor Car Company

1952 The Ford Motor Company establishes the Special Products Group under the direction of William Clay Ford to develop the Lincoln Continental Mark II

1953 The Ford Motor Company signs a licensing agreement with former employee Howard W. Simpson for use of his "Simpson gear train" transmission design

1953 Packard introduces air conditioning as a $625 option, and hires Ray Powers of Lincoln-Mercury as Vice President for Manufacturing

1954 American Motors signs a contract with the Packard Motor Car Company to purchase V-8 engines and Ultramatic transmissions from Packard

1956 Bugatti makes its last Formula 1 appearance at the French Grand Prix, but the Type 251 driven by Maurice Trintignant retires with a faulty throttle

1956 Semon E. "Bunkie" Knudsen is named General Manager of Pontiac

1956 The Highway Act of 1956 is implemented, authorizing construction of the 41,000-mile Interstate Highway System

1959 The Chrysler Corporation reorganizes into three automotive divisions - Chrysler-Imperial, Dodge, and Plymouth-DeSoto

1960 Edward A. Deeds, cofounder of the Dayton Engineering Laboratories Company (Delco) with Charles F. Kettering, dies in Dayton, OH at age 86

1960 John A. C. Warner retires as Secretary and General Manager of the Society of Automotive Engineers after 33 years with the organization, and is succeeded by Joseph Gilbert

1962 Racer Hugh Randall dies at age 29 when his Vargo Special crashes during a 100-mile USAC Championship Race in Langhorne, PA

1963 The Shell Oil Company of Canada Ltd. changes its name to Shell Canada Ltd.

1965 Pontiac General Manager Elliott M. "Pete" Estes transfers to the same position at Chevrolet, with Pontiac Chief Engineer John Z. DeLorean being promoted to the top position with Pontiac

John Z DeLerean's "roller coaster" career in the automobile industry was highlighted by the stainless steel sports car bearing his name and the legendary Pontiac GTO.

1965 Racer Tony Hegbourne dies at age 33, more than a month after crashing in his Alfa Romeo during the Belgian Grand Prix at Spa

1965 Matra records its first racing victory, with Jean-Pierre Beltoise winning the Formula 3 International Trophy race at Reims, France

1969 George R. Elges is named General Manager of Cadillac, succeeding Calvin J. Werner

1973 The Ensign makes its Formula 1 debut at the French Grand Prix, with the car driven by Rikki von Opel finishing 15th

1979 Jean-Pierre Jabouille wins the French Grand Prix driving a Renault RS11, the first Formula 1 victory for the marque in the modern era

1982 The Toyota Motor Corporation is established by merging the Toyota Motor Company, Ltd. and the Toyota Motor Sales Company

1983 Inventor R. Buckminster Fuller, designer of the Dymaxion automobile and the Ford Rotunda, dies in Los Angeles, CA at age 87

1984 The Standard Oil Company of California changes its name to the Chevron Corporation

1985 W. Paul Tippett Jr. resigns as Chairman of American Motors to join Spring Industries

1987 The Quaker State Oil Refining Corporation changes its name to the Quaker State Corporation

1996 Robert Oswald is named Chairman of Robert Bosch North America and becomes the first non-German to be a Director of the parent Robert Bosch GmbH

JULY 2

1759 Steam engine pioneer Nathan Read is born in Warren, MA

1899 The first motorized mail service begins in Buffalo, NY, with Dr. Truman J. Martin supplying his own 1898 Columbia Electric - Dr. Martin was the father of Karl H. Martin, builder of the 1919-1924 Martin Wasp

1900 Cesare Isotta makes his racing debut driving a Renault in time trials in Padua, Italy

1903 Camille Jenatzy, driving a 60-hp Mercedes, wins the 4th Gordon Bennett Cup, a 327.5-mile road race staged in Athy, Ireland and often called the first Irish Grand Prix

1904 Buick, Studebaker, and Worthington join the ALAM to comply with Selden patent rights

1905 The world's first 24-hour race begins at the Driving Park track in Columbus, OH - the Soules brothers win in their Pope-Toledo, covering 828.50 miles

1908 The Velie Motor Vehicle Company is incorporated by Willard Lamb Velie, grandson of farm implement manufacturer John Deere

Velie manufactured automobiles 1909-1929 and trucks 1911-1923.

1909 Robert Galbraith Dunlop of the Sun Oil Company is born in Boston, MA

1911 Racer Reginald "Reg" Parnell is born in Derby, England

1912 William LeRoy Mitchell of General Motors is born in Cleveland, OH

1915 Rudolf Hruska of Alfa Romeo is born in Vienna, Austria

1921 William B. and George B. Pratt retire after a 12-year period of building the Pratt-Elkhart, Pratt, and Elcar

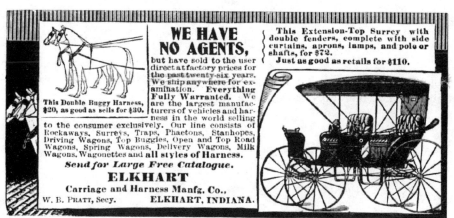

Like many pioneer automobile manufacturers, the Pratt brothers were established carriage builders before entering the motorized era. (1899 advertisement)

1921 Peugeot ends its 15-year factory-sponsored racing program as a Type L25 driven by Reville wins the 235-mile Meeting de Boulogne-sur-Mer

1924 John Joseph Riccardo of the Chrysler Corporation is born in Little Falls, NY

1928 Chrysler Corporation acquires Dodge Brothers, Inc. and establishes the Dodge Brothers Corporation as a subsidiary

1928 Chrysler Corporation dedicates its new Engineering Building

1932 Driving an early Model SJ convertible, Frederick S. Duesenberg is involved in an automobile accident on Ligonier Mountain, PA, and dies 24 days later from the effects of his injuries

1932 Racer Jacques Pollet is born in France

1933 Racer Tazio Nuvolari signs a contract to drive for the Maserati racing team

1935 Ab Jenkins, driving the Duesenberg Special at the Bonneville Salt Flats, UT, sets a Class B super-stock record for the flying mile of 145.44 mph

1937 Racer Richard Lee Petty is born in Level Cross, NC, the father of racer Kyle Petty

1938 Geoffrey Taylor, driving a 2-litre Alfa Romeo, sets a 1/2-mile record of 80.18 mph at the Brighton Speed Trials

1939 Automotive historian Carl Frederick William Larson is born near Parkers Prairie, MN

1948 Brig. Gen. Albert J. Browning, a Vice President of the Ford Motor Company, dies in Detroit, MI at age 48

1954 Charles S. Davis, Chairman of the Board of the Borg-Warner Corporation and its former President, dies in Paris, France at age 77

1954 Racer Mike White is born in South Africa

1961 The DeTomaso makes its Formula 1 debut in the French Grand Prix, but the Type F1/001 driven by Giorgio Scarlatti retires with engine failure

1962 The 30,000,000th Ford V-8 engine is produced

1962 The Studebaker-Packard Corporation officially becomes the Studebaker Corporation, legally terminating the Packard marque

1962 Racer Peter Ryan is killed at age 20 when his Lotus-Climax crashes during the Coupe de Vitesse des Juniors at Reims, France

1964 Racer Glenn "Fireball" Roberts dies at age 35 from injuries suffered during a NASCAR race on May 24 in Charlotte, NC

1967 The first Formula Ford race is staged at Brands Hatch, England

1967 Vanden Plas (England) 1923 Ltd. becomes a division of the British Motor Corporation

1973 Racer Swede Savage dies at age 26 from injuries suffered five weeks earlier during the Indianapolis 500

1974 The reference library of the late automotive journalist Ken Purdy is sold at auction in New York City

1985 Racer David Purley is killed at age 40 when his Pitts Special biplane crashes into the sea off Bognor Regis, England

1992 The 1,000,000th Chevrolet Corvette is produced and is driven off the Bowling Green, KY assembly line by Zora Arkus-Duntov, the sub-marque's first Chief Engineer

JULY 3

1885 Raymond Charles Dahlinger of the Ford Motor Company is born in Detroit, MI

1886 The "Motorwagen" of Carl Benz makes its public debut in Mannheim, Germany

1893 Automobile body manufacturer William John Meinel is born in Philadelphia, PA

1898 James Penfield Seiberling of the Seiberling Rubber Company is born in Akron, OH

1898 The Nederlandsche Automobiel Club is founded in Utrecht

1899 William A. Hatcher of Winton joins Packard to help design the new firm's first automobile

1899 Hon. John Scott-Montagu in his Coventry Daimler is first to enter the grounds of the Houses of Parliament in London in an automobile

1909 The first Hudson is produced, a 20-hp 4-cylinder roadster

1912 The 1913 American Scout, Tourist, and Traveler are introduced, featuring a chassis with underslung springs designed by Fred I. Tone - officially the marque name was simply American, but through common usage these cars are today almost universally referred to as "American Underslung"

1914 Ernest R. Sternberg, a truck design consultant with Sterling, White, and Autocar, is born

AMERICAN UNDERSLUNG

WE have published a very interesting book on the advantages of Underslung construction. It is of value to dealer or individual. It tells of our full line which ranges in price from $1475 to $4500. Write for a copy today.

American Motors Company
Dept. H   Indianapolis, Indiana

1916 The first Jordan is produced

1916 John McDougall of the Ford Motor Company is born in Belfast, (Northern) Ireland

1917 Robert Thomas Griffin of the Chrysler Corporation is born in Somerville, MA

1920 The first post-World War I Shelsley Walsh Hillclimb is won by C. A. Bird in a Sunbeam followed by Guy Anthony "Tony" Vandervell, later the creator of the Vanwall Grand Prix race car, in a Clement-Talbot

1921 Oreste Fraschini dies in Turin, Italy at age 54

1922 The Allen Motor Car Company is liquidated - production had ceased in 1921

1922 Stuart A. de la Rue becomes a Director of Bentley Motors, Ltd. - he would serve as Chairman for a brief time in 1923

JORDAN

I want to be happy—

THERE is still a country where a cowboy can spread his loop without getting it caught in a fence post—where the mountains tickle the sky and ten million stars just almost scare you.

Give me a horse or a car that has a little of

the lighted match and stick of dynamite about it. Give me a little more health than there is in the daily dozen—a little more air than you will find in Atlantic City—and a lot more poetry than I ever found in Browning.

I want to go in a Playboy. Then I'll be happy.

JORDAN MOTOR CAR COMPANY, Inc., CLEVELAND, OHIO

There's a place out west that stretches hundreds of miles north and south of wherever you are—where even the water holes are forty miles apart—and you can just keep on going any direction you choose.

The Jordan was a good, if not great, car but the marque is best remembered for its advertising - Jordan quite simply reinvented the art form.

1924 Frank Winston Wylie of the Chrysler Corporation is born in New York City

1926 Tire manufacturer Francois Michelin is born in Clermont-Ferrand, France

1935 Andre Citroen dies in Paris, France at age 57

1945 The first post-World War II United States automobile is produced, a 1946 Ford Super Deluxe Tudor that was later presented to President Harry S. Truman

1950 Automobile chain manufacturer Frank A. Bond dies in Erie, PA at age 67

1952 The last Crosley is produced at their Marion, IN factory

1953 The 500,000th Volkswagen is produced

1954 William B. Livingston of GMC dies in Chicago, IL at age 56

1955 George Hepburn Robertson, the winner of the 1908 Vanderbilt Cup, dies in New York City at age 71

1959 Dan Gurney makes his Formula 1 debut, driving a Ferrari in the French Grand Prix

1960 Francis C. "Jack" Reith, General Manager of Mercury 1955-1957, dies in Cincinnati, OH at age 45

1963 Racer Markus Ostreich is born in Fulda, West Germany

1970 Walter O. Briggs Jr., an heir of the Briggs Manufacturing Company automobile body firm and the owner of the Detroit Tigers baseball team, dies in Detroit, MI at age 58

1970 The last Volvo Amazon is produced - the car is now in the Volvo museum

1971 The Pocono Raceway in Long Pond, PA stages its first event, a 500-mile USAC Championship Race that is won by Mark Donohue driving the Sunoco McLaren-Offy Special

1975 Lynn A. Townsend resigns as Chairman of the Chrysler Corporation

1978 Ernest R. Breech, Chairman 1955-1960 of the Ford Motor Company, dies in Royal Oak, MI at age 81

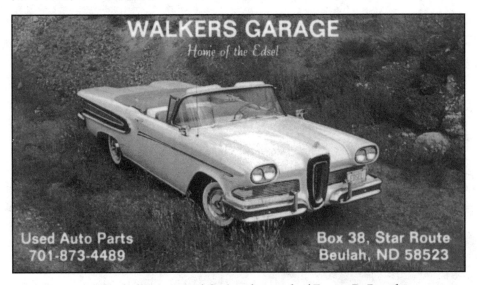

The Edsel affair occurred during the watch of Ernest R. Breech.
The colorful business card of Beulah, ND automobile parts dealer Leroy Walker
pictures his 1958 Citation convertible - as this book goes to press
Walker owns 201 examples of the marque.

1984 Jaguar Cars Holdings Ltd. changes its name to Jaguar PLC

1987 Herbert Edward Hill, the developer of the constant velocity joint that made front-wheel-drive practicable, dies at age 86

1996 Richard Gary Stauffer, cofounder in 1959 with Arthur Turner of the Northwood Institute in Midland, MI, the only university in the United States to offer a four-year degree in automotive marketing, dies in Midland, MI at age 68

JULY 4

1877 Automotive machine-tool manufacturer Stanley Hale Bullard is born in Hoboken, NJ

1894 Elwood Haynes test drives the first Haynes in Kokomo, IN with associates Elmer Apperson and Warren Wrightsman as passengers

1903 Benjamin Briscoe, Jonathan D. Maxwell, and C. W. Althouse organize the Maxwell-Briscoe Motor Company, with manufacturing facilities initially in Tarrytown, NY, to manufacture Maxwell automobiles

1903 The first Irish Speed Trials held in Phoenix Park, Dublin are won by Baron deForest in a Mors

1905 The White "Whistling Billy" racer, driven by Webb Jay, defeats Fiat and Thomas in a match race at the Morris Park Dirt Track in the Bronx, NY, lowering the world's mile record to 48.6 seconds

1907 Ernst Loof, designer of the Veritas and an occasional racer, is born in Neindorf, Germany

1909 The first rural paved road in the United States is completed

1911 Etablissements Ballot is founded in Paris, France by Ernest Ballot

1914 A Saxon roadster arrives in San Francisco, CA, 30 days after leaving New York City, completing the first transcontinental automobile trip using the newly completed Lincoln Highway

1914 The inaugural race at the Sioux City (IA) Speedway is won by Eddie Rickenbacker in a Duesenberg with Eddie O'Donnell as his riding mechanic

1914 Mercedes takes the first three places at the French Grand Prix in Lyon - the Delage Type S makes its racing debut, but only the Arthur Duray car completes the race, finishing in eighth place

1915 Racer Willie Carlson dies in Tacoma, WA

1918 Racer Johnnie Parsons is born in Los Angeles, CA

1920 DuPont's Duco Satin Finish proxylin enamel paint is announced - this quick-drying paint was introduced by Oakland in late 1923 and would soon revolutionize automobile production techniques

1920 Harry W. DuPuy, President of the Pennsylvania Rubber Company of Jeannette, PA, dies at age 39

1924 George Fredericks of the Walter M. Murphy Company, Coachbuilders drowns while attempting to rescue a company secretary during a beach holiday

1926 Racer Wolfgang Seidel is born in Germany

1936 Automotive historian Michael Frederick Lister "Mike" Allison is born in London, England

1938 Racer Ernest Pieterse is born in Parow-Bellville, South Africa

1939 Creston, WY dedicates a monument to honor Henry B. Joy for his efforts in building the Lincoln Highway

1946 Racer Dave Champeau is killed during a race in Lincoln, NE

1948 Racer Rene Arnoux is born in Pontcharra, France

1948 Racer Christian Kautz is killed when his Maserati crashes during the Swiss Grand Prix at the Bremgarten circuit near Berne - later in the race Omobono Tenni is killed in a separate accident

1952 Troy Ruttmann, driving the Offenhauser-powered Agajanian Special, wins the inaugural 200-mile race at the Southland Speedway, later known as the Raleigh (NC) Speedway

1953 The first Volvo Duett 445DH light truck is produced

1953 Earl Wallace Winans, an engineering executive with Regal and Federal, dies in Wheatley, Ontario, Canada at age 72

1954 Mercedes-Benz makes its first post-World War II racing appearance at the French Grand Prix in Reims-Gueux, with Juan Manuel Fangio and Karl Kling taking the top two places in identical W196's

1961 The Japanese government ratifies a contract between the Toyo Kogyo Company, Ltd., and Wankel GmbH of Germany, giving the manufacturer of the Mazda rights to the Wankel rotary engine

1962 Racer Roland Ratzenberger is born in Salzburg, Austria

1965 Jean-Pierre Beltoise wins the Reims Grand Prix in a Matra, the first major Grand Prix victory by a French car since 1952

1965 Racer Steve Robertson is born in London, England

1969 The International Motor Sports Association (IMSA) is founded by John Bishop

1969 Racer Cesar Tiberio Jimenez is born in Mexico

1972 George Schuster, the final driver of the winning Thomas Flyer in the New York to Paris race in 1908, dies in Springville, NY at age 99

1972 The National Motor Museum in Beaulieu, Hampshire, England opens

1973 Racer Jan Magnusson is born in Denmark

1984 Richard Petty records his 200th NASCAR victory, winning the Firecracker 400 at the Daytona International Speedway in Daytona Beach, FL with Ronald Reagan, the first sitting President of the United States to attend a NASCAR event, looking on - Petty's Pontiac would later be exhibited at the Smithsonian Institution in Washington, DC

1984 Autoworld entertainment park opens in Flint, MI

JULY 5

1866 Father George A. Belcourt of Rusticoville, Prince Edward Island, Canada displays the Ware Steam Car built by Elijah Ware of Bayonne, NJ that he had recently purchased - this was the first automobile on the island and is often cited as the first United States-built automobile to be exported

1889 Harry J. Klingler of Pontiac is born in Saint Clair, MI

1905 The sixth and final Gordon Bennett Trophy race is staged at the Auvergne Circuit near Clermont-Ferrand, France, and is won by Leon Thery driving a Brasier

1912 The main event of the first Montamara Fiesta Road Races in Tacoma, WA, a 250-mile "Free-for-all Race", is won by Teddy Tetzlaff in a Fiat

1915 The Omaha, NE 1 1/4-mile board track opens with a 302-mile race won by Eddie Rickenbacker in a Maxwell

1915 Racer Billy "Coal-Oil" Carlson and his riding mechanic, Paul Franzen, are killed when their Maxwell crashes during the 200-mile Golden Potlach Trophy Race in Tacoma, WA

1917 The Moon Motor Car Company reincorporates in Delaware

1920 Rollin C. White, founder and President of the White Sewing Machine Company in 1876 that later manufactured White cars and trucks, and the first President of the Baker Motor Vehicle Company 1899-1915, dies in Cleveland, OH at age 83

1927 Construction begins on the new GMC truck factory and headquarters building in Pontiac, MI

1933 Robert C. Stempel of General Motors is born in Trenton, NJ

1933 Fritz Todt is appointed General Inspector for German Highways with his primary assignment the design of the Autobahn system

This late 1930's view of the Mannheim-Heidelberg Autobahn clearly shows the revolutionary divided four-lane design that would become universal.

1937 Jean-Paul-Christophe Parayre of Renault is born in Lorient, France

1937 The second and last Vanderbilt Trophy race is staged at the Roosevelt Raceway in Westbury, Long Island, NY and won by Bernd Rosemeyer in a Type C Auto Union

1942 Commander Walter George Windham, credited with many firsts in British automobile and aviation history, dies in Builth Wells, Radnorshire, Wales at age 74

1945 Julius Dorpmuller, the head of the Autobahn project, dies in Malente, Germany at age 75

1946 Preston Tucker obtains a letter of intent to sell, clearing the way to legally prepare for manufacture of the Tucker Torpedo

1953 Mike Hawthorn records his first major victory, winning the French Grand Prix at Reims-Gueux in a Ferrari 500

1954 Racer Bob Scott is killed at age 25 when he crashes during a 200-mile AAA Championship race in Darlington, SC

1955 Frank B. Stearns dies in Cleveland, OH at age 76

1956 Oscar C. Kreis, a design draftsman with the Packard Motor Car Company 1902-1908, Chief Engineer with the Gray Motor Company 1908-1916, Chief Research Engineer with Continental Motors Corporation 1916-1932, and later a consulting engineer to the Studebaker Corporation and General Motors, dies at age 78

1959 Dan Gurney makes his Formula 1 debut at the French Grand Prix in Reims-Gueux, but his Ferrari-Dino 246 retires with radiator failure

1968 Herbert Willetts, President of the Mobil Oil Corporation 1961-1968, dies in New York City at age 68

1970 Joseph B. Graham dies at age 87

1973 The Ford Motor Company produces its "last" convertible, a 1973 Mercury Cougar XR7

1974 Ralph Hamlin, driver of the first car to reach the summit of Mount Washington, NH and later a Franklin dealer, dies in Los Angeles, CA at age 93

1981 Alain Prost wins his first Formula 1 championship race, the 67th French Grand Prix at Dijon-Prenois, in his Renault RE30

1986 Racer Albert Scherrer dies at age 78

JULY 6

1851 Electric motor pioneer Thomas Davenport dies in Salisbury, VT at age 48

1876 Petroleum producer Harry Ford Sinclair is born in Wheeling, WV

1879 Karl Maybach is born in Cologne-Deutz, Germany

1888 Racer Charles Cleveland Merz is born in Indianapolis, IN

1891 Automotive engineer Earle Steele MacPherson is born in Highland Park, IL

1900 Reese Hale Taylor of the Union Oil Company of California is born in Los Angeles, CA

1903 Lester L. Whitman and Eugene I. Hammond leave San Francisco, CA in a curved dash Oldsmobile nicknamed "Old Scout", beginning the third trans-United States automobile trip

1906 John S. Gray, President of the Ford Motor Company 1903-1906, dies in Detroit, MI at age 64

1906 Racer T. C. "Cuth" Harrison is born in Sheffield, Yorkshire, England

1907 The first 1908 Packard Thirty Model UA is produced

1907 The first race held at Brooklands is won by H. C. Tryon in a Napier

1910 The Argo Electric Vehicle Company is organized in Saginaw, MI by Fred Buck, Theodore Huss, Benton Hanchett, Otto Schupp, and Albert M. Marshall

1910 Franz Heinrich Ulrich, Chairman of the Daimler-Benz AG Supervisory Board 1970-1976, is born in Germany

1912 The Hudson Series 37 is introduced

1914 Dodge Brothers, Inc. grants its first retail franchise to J. D. Picksley Cheek Sr. of Nashville, TN

1923 The 10,000th Rickenbacker is produced

1923 General Motors ends active production of its copper-cooled engines, but approves continued research efforts on the concept

1924 Rene Thomas, driving the Delage Type DH "La Torpille" at Arpajon, France, raises the land speed record to 143.31 mph

1926 The 1927 Nash Series 220 is introduced

1930 Racer Ian Burgess is born in London, England

1935 The Squire makes its racing debut at Brooklands, but does not finish

1936 The Squire Car Manufacturing Company Ltd. is declared bankrupt

1936 Theodule Guilbaud, French-born General Manager of the Societa Anonima Carburatore Zenith in Turin, Italy, dies at age 48

1941 Milton J. Budlong, the Packard distributor in Philadelphia, PA and New York City and a pioneer proponent of 6-cylinder engines, dies at age 72

1942 Robert F. Runge, Vice President of SKF Industries, Inc. since 1920, dies at age 56

1954 Karl H. Martin of Martin-Wasp dies in Bennington, VT at age 66

1958 Racer Luigi Musso is killed at age 33 when his Ferrari Dino 246 crashes during the French Grand Prix at Reims-Gueux - Phil Hill makes his Formula 1 debut in the race, finishing seventh in a Maserati 250F - five-time World Champion Driver Juan Manuel Fangio announces his retirement from racing after finishing fourth in his Maserati 250F

1958 Racer Art Bisch dies in Atlanta, GA at age 31

1969 The Dover (DE) Downs Speedway stages its first race, the Mason-Dixon 300 sponsored by NASCAR and won by Richard Petty in a Ford

1971 The 15,000,000th Pontiac is produced, a black Grand Ville 4-door hardtop

1974 The Auburn-Cord-Duesenberg Museum opens in the restored 1930 headquarters building of the Auburn Automobile Company in Auburn, IN

JULY 7

1870 George R. Beamer of the United States Gauge Company is born in Ontario, Canada

1876 The White Sewing Machine Company is organized - the firm as it evolved would later make White cars and trucks

1886 Robert Allen Stranahan, the founder of the Champion Spark Plug Company in 1908, is born in Buffalo, NY

1897 The Roots Oil Motor & Motor Car Company, Ltd. is registered in London, England by J. D. Roots to manufacture Roots & Venables motorcars

1899 William A. Hatcher completes the drawings for the first Packard

1903 In action taken in Vienna, Austria, Emil Jellinek legally changes his family name to Jellinek-Mercedes

1907 Albert Francis Davis of Graham-Paige Motors Corporation and General Motors is born in Evansville, IN

1908 Christian Lautenschlager driving a 12.8-litre Mercedes in the car's racing debut records his first major victory winning the French Grand Prix at Dieppe

1915 The Simplex Automobile Company of New Brunswick, NJ purchases the Crane Motor Car Company of Bayonne, NJ

1919 Roger J. Helder of the Chrysler Corporation is born in Grand Rapids, MI

1928 The Chrysler Corporation holds a private showing for the new DeSoto marque, at the time existing only as a single prototype

1928 The Plymouth is formally introduced as the Chrysler Plymouth, with famed aviatrix Amelia Earhart driving the car onto a stage at Madison Square Garden in New York City

1931 John Brisben Walker of Locomobile dies at age 83

1936 Wallace Swiener, President of Hupp Motor Car Corporation, dies

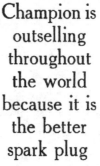

Hupmobile produced just 1,556 cars in 1936. This 4-door sedan features "Aerodynamic" styling and unusual center-hinged doors.

Todd Hanson

1936 Racer Eldon Rasmussen is born

1936 Racer Josef "Jo" Siffert is born in Fribourg, Switzerland

1938 Robert Thomas O'Connell of General Motors is born in New Haven, CT

1941 Racer Mike Hiss is born in Norwalk, CT

1941 Automotive historian Richard Michael Langworth is born in Rye, NY

1944 Racer Steve Krisiloff is born

1947 The 4,000,000th United States post-World War II automobile is produced

1947 The Tucker '48 is shown in an exclusive preview at the Hotel Statler in Washington, DC

1951 Arthur J. Moulton, codesigner with Charles Lanier Lawrence and Sidney S. Breese of the B.L.M. automobile and a charter member of the Society of Automotive Engineers, dies in Newport, RI at age 68

1953 The Ford Motor Company Board of Directors approve final development and production of the Continental Mark II

1958 Joeph F. Merkel, designer/manufacturer of the 1905-1907 Merkel, dies in Rochester, NY

1958 William B. Wachtler, a General Motors executive developing plans for the company to begin manufacturing in Brazil, dies at age 66

1959 Racer Alessandro Nannini is born in Siena, Italy

1965 Ethyl Gasoline Corporation executive Earle W. Webb dies in Baden-Baden, West Germany at age 82

1967 Racer Tom Kristensen is born in Denmark

1968 Racer Jo Schlesser is killed at age 40 when his Honda RA302 crashes during the French Grand Prix at Rouen which was staged in a heavy rain - the race is won by Jackie Ickx driving a Ferrari 312/68, his first of eight Formula 1 victories

1969 Karl A. Roesch of White and Autocar dies at age 65

1970 Morris Markin, President of the Checker Motors Corporation, dies at age 76

1972 The last 1972 Cadillac is produced

1982 The Musee National de l'Automobile in Mulhouse, France, featuring the collection of Fritz Schlumpf, opens to the public

1984 Carl Solheim is elected President of the Crosley Automobile Club succeeding Jim Bollman

JULY 8

1695 Internal combustion engine pioneer Christian Huygens dies in the Hague, the Netherlands at age 66

1839 John Davison Rockefeller, the founder of the Standard Oil Company in 1870, is born in Richford, NY

1882 Robert B. Elliott of the Nash Motors Company is born in Toledo, OH

1883 James Ernest Auten, a longtime corporate executive whose automotive career included stints with White, Cadillac, Lafayette, and Nash, is born in Berlin Township, Knox County, OH

1892 Lester Callaway Hunt, who as Wyoming Secretary of State in 1936 designed that state's "bucking bronco" license plate, is born in Isabel, IL - the model for his design was A. G. "Stub" Farlow riding the horse known as Deadman

A 1939 view of the Washakie County Court House in Worland, WY - the cars display Wyoming's famous "bucking bronco" license plate.

1893 Gottlieb Daimler marries Lina Hartmann as his second wife

1906 The first Klink is produced by Harvey Toms for Dansville, NY photographer John F. Klink - the car's success would lead to the formation of the Klink Motor Car Manufacturing Company in March 1907

1909 George Wilcken Romney of American Motors is born in Colona Dublan, Chihuahua, Mexico

1912 A Packard 3-ton truck driven by Walter T. Fishleigh, E. L. Burnett, and Arnold Haener leaves New York City beginning the first continuous trans-United States trip by a motor truck

1912 Automotive parts manufacturer John Fredrich Schweikert is born in Philadelphia, PA

Wall Drug in Wall, SD has long been a favorite stopping point. The small station wagon in the center of this mid-1950's view is a 1951 Nash Rambler, a car championed by George W. Romney.

1919 Wilfried Guth, Chairman of the Daimler-Benz AG Supervisory Board 1976-1985, is born in Germany

1919 Automobile restoration authority Brian Morgan is born in Birmingham, England

1919 Bentley Motors, Ltd. is reorganized with W. O. Bentley as Chairman and Joint Managing Director with his brother H. M. Bentley

1922 Wayne Horace Smithey of the Ford Motor Company is born in Ogallala, NE

1927 The Cities Service Oil Company Ltd. is registered in Great Britain

1930 Electric automobile advocate Aaron E. Klein is born in Atlanta, GA

1931 Automobile body manufacturer Leo I. Heintz dies in Philadelphia, PA at age 52

1933 The Harry A. Miller Manufacturing Company of Los Angeles, CA, builders of high performance racing engines, is forced into bankruptcy

1936 Ford offers an optional "Deluxe Package" for all of its pickups and light trucks

1942 Louis Schweitzer of Renault is born in Geneva, Switzerland

1944 Automotive parts manufacturer Clarence B. Swift dies at age 54

1944 The first vehicle, a ZIS 5-V truck, is produced at the Urals Automotive Plant in Miass, USSR

1948 Frederick W. Barker, Henry Ford's defense attorney in the Selden patent lawsuit, dies at age 83

1950 Maurice L. Kerr, a chassis engineer with the White Motor Company, dies at age 62

1951 Eccentric racer Joel Thorne rents a Cadillac from the local agency, then proceeds to drive it in a 150-mile stock car race in Milwaukee, WI

1952 Charles Merz, a pioneer racer with the National and Stutz factory teams, dies in New Augusta, IN at age 64

1959 Edmund Hans, credited with many improvements in automobile heating systems, dies in Mount Vernon, IL at age 72

1961 The front-engined, four-wheel drive Ferguson-Climax Project 99 makes its racing debut in the Intercontinental British Empire Trophy race at Silverstone with Jack Fairman driving

1962 Dan Gurney wins the French Grand Prix driving a Porsche 804, the only Formula 1 victory for the marque

1964 The last 1964 Cadillac is produced

1970 Harrah's Automobile Collection in Sparks, NV receives its 1,000,000th visitor

1975 John J. Riccardo is elected Chairman of the Chrysler Corporation, with Eugene A. Cafiero succeeding him as President

1980 The Bentley Mulsanne is introduced in Paris, France

1983 Erwin A. Weiss, Packard's Chief Chassis Engineer 1936-1954, dies at age 91

1985 The first Dallas (TX) Grand Prix is staged

1991 John H. Gerstenmaier, President of the Goodyear Tire & Rubber Company 1974-1978, dies at age 74

JULY 9

1802 Electric motor pioneer Thomas Davenport is born in Williamstown, VT

1885 H. S. McDewell of Maxwell is born in Winthrop, MA

1887 Automobile bearing manufacturer William T. Burns is born in Philadelphia, PA

1889 Gottlieb Daimler is issued a German patent for his V-2 gasoline engine

1904 The first Buick Model B is driven from Flint to Detroit by Walter L. Marr and Thomas Buick (son of the car's namesake David D. Buick) to convince Buick Motor Company principal owner James H. Whiting to approve the manufacturing of complete automobiles

1904 Automotive parts manufacturer Ballard Alton Yates is born in Williamsport, OH

1908 The fifth Glidden Tour begins in Buffalo, NY with a planned route into Pennsylvania, the New England states, and finishing in Saratoga Springs, NY

1908 Lord Montagu of Beaulieu officially opens the new Rolls-Royce Ltd. factory in Derby, England, ending the company's stay in Manchester

1909 C. K. Batchelder and his riding mechanic, John Twohey, are killed when their Stearns 60-hp crashes during a race at the Blue Bonnets track in Montreal, PQ, Canada

1919 The Ford Motor Company is reorganized as a Delaware corporation with Edsel B. Ford as President - the Henry Ford family now owned 100% of the company's stock

1922 Automotive engineer William T. Murphy, President and General Manager of the Standard Machinery Company of Auburn, RI, dies at age 40

1931 Edward A. Ross, President of the Ross Gear & Tool Company, dies at age 47 in London, England after becoming ill on a business trip to Europe

1933 The groundbreaking ceremony is held for San Francisco-Oakland Bay Bridge

1939 The first Montauk (NY) Grand Prix is won by Foote in an Alfa Romeo

1951 Ronald J. Waterbury, Assistant Chief Engineer of Chevrolet who previously had worked for Oakland, Packard, and Studebaker, dies in Detroit, MI at age 52

1952 Louis Charles Huck, an official of Diamond T and General Motors who organized the Huck Axle Corporation in 1923 to develop and manufacture the Huck double reduction axle, dies at age 56

1955 Don Beauman is killed at age 26 when his Connaught crashes during the Leinster Trophy race in Wicklow, Ireland

1960 Otis Presbrey, President of Otis Auto Dynatester, Inc., dies at age 70

1963 Swedish-born rally champion Erik Carlsson marries Pat Moss, sister of British racer Stirling Moss and herself a world-class rally driver

1965 The last 1965 Ford Thunderbird is produced

1974 Sir Harry Brittain, Chairman of D. Napier & Son, Ltd. who attempted to put Napier back into the automobile business through acquisition of Bentley Motors, Ltd., dies at age 101

1976 A recreated 1904 Buick built to celebrate the United States bicentennial successfully retraces the original 1904 trip made by the first Buick

1981 Patrick Jacquemart is killed at age 35 when his Renault R5 Turbo crashes during a practice run at the Mid-Ohio race course

1982 Checker Motors Corporation of Kalamazoo, MI announces that they are withdrawing from automobile production after 60 years

1989 Racer Craig Arfons, son of Walt Arfons, dies in Sebring, FL during a WSR attempt

JULY 10

1867 Norval Abiel Hawkins of the Ford Motor Company and General Motors is born in Ypsilanti, MI

1874 Henry Cave, pioneer automotive designer and the founder of the SKF
    Ball Bearing Company, is born in Nottingham, England

1883 George Alexander Long of Northfield, MA is issued a United States
    patent for his "Steam Road Vehicle"

1883 Emile Adolphe Monier, a sculptor and designer of automobile
    mascots, is born in Paris, France

1904 Automotive engineer Ralph H. Kress is born

1907 The fourth Glidden Tour begins in Cleveland, OH, with an
    indirect route to Chicago, IL, then back to New York City

1907 The Oldsmar, FL post office is established - this model townsite
    on the north end of Tampa Bay was a pet project of automobile
    manufacturer Ransom E. Olds, with its name coined from "Olds"
    plus "mar", the Spanish word for "sea"

1912 The White "Whistling Billy" steamer race car is totaled when Chris Dundee crashes during a race in
    Portland, OR

1914 Neville Reiners of the Cummins Engine Company is born in Fort Dodge, IA

1916 Woodrow Wilson tours the Highland Park, MI plant of the Ford Motor Company, marking the first time
    that a sitting President had visited an automobile factory

1918 Racer Fred Wacker Jr. is born in Chicago, IL

1919 The reorganized Bentley Motors, Ltd. is registered

1920 The Available Truck Company of Chicago, IL registers "Available" as a trademark

1923 Robert B. McCurry Jr. of Dodge is born in Reynoldsburg, OH

1926 Sol Witner Sanders, biographer of Soichiro Honda, is born in Atlanta, GA

1928 Alejandro De Tomaso is born in Buenos Aires, Argentina

SKF Puts the Right Bearing in the Right Place

The de Tomaso Pantera. Around $10,000.*

Pantéra by de Tomaso
Imported for
Lincoln-Mercury

LINCOLN · MERCURY

1928 John Newcombe Maltby of Burmah Oil PLC is born in Esher, England

1931 Automobile parts manufacturer Richard Alan Hansen is born in Berwyn, IL

1932 Racer Carlo Abate is born in Turin, Italy

1940 The Graham-Paige Motors Corporation reopens its factory to build a final run of Series 133 Graham Hollywood Custom sedans using on the old Cord 810 body dies

1941 Ford Motor Company Vice President Peter E. Martin resigns because of health reasons

1946 Racer Jean-Pierre Jarier is born in Charenton-le-Pont, France

1947 John Tjaarda, the designer of the Lincoln-Zephyr, announces that North American Motors Inc. of Grand Prairie, TX would begin manufacturing the economy North American in 1948

1950 Cadillac names Don E. Ahrens as General Manager and James M. Roche as General Sales Manager

1950 New York City imported car dealer Max Hoffman receives a shipment of twenty Volkswagens, the first to be imported into the United States

1956 Burton A. Becker, manufacturer of the 1899-1912 Elmore, dies in Sandusky, OH

1957 The 250,000th Meteor is produced by the Ford Motor Company of Canada, Ltd.

A United States-built 1955 Ford Fairlane 2-door Club Sedan and a Canadian
1955 Meteor 4-door Sedan provide an interesting contrast, differing
primarily in side trim, while parked in Abbotsford, BC.

1958 The first parking meters in Great Britain are installed outside the United States embassy in London

1958 The East German Trabant goes into regular production

1960 Joseph F. Gettrust, Sales Manager for the Nelson Muffler Corporation, dies at age 47

1962 Racer Thomas W. "Tommy" Milton is found dead near Mount Clemens, MI from a gunshot wound at age 69

1967 Abram vanderZee, whose 50-year automotive career included positions with Chevrolet, Durant, Plymouth, and Dodge, dies at age 73

1968 The first Alfa Romeo Alfasud engine is tested

1972 Race car designer Dale Drake dies at age 69

1989 William Heynes of Jaguar dies at age 85

1996 Richard H. Stout, an automotive historian and a stylist with General Motors, the Studebaker-Packard Corporation, and the Ford Motor Company, dies at age 76

1996 The Toyota Motor Corporation opens its new Tokyo Design Research Laboratory in Hachioji City, Tokyo, Japan

JULY 11

1872 Rollin Henry White is born in Cleveland, OH

1898 Thomas Cook & Son and the Compagnie Nationale d'Automobiles begin the first six-day bus excursion, leaving Paris in a DeDion et Bouton steam-powered omnibus and reaching Aix-le-Bains on schedule - although successful, the firms decided against additional trips

1899 Giovanni Agnelli purchases the Welleyes prototype, the patents held by Giovanni Battista Ceirano, and the services of Aristide Faccioli, leading to the founding of the Fabbrica Italiana Automobili Torino (Fiat)

1902 Aloysius Francis Power of General Motors is born in Worcester, MA

1905 The second Glidden Tour begins in New York City with a planned route through the New England states and returning to New York

1907 Texas requires the registration of all automobiles with county clerk

1910 Hon. Charles S. Rolls is killed at Bournemouth, England when his French-built Wright biplane crashes during a demonstration flight

1913 The tenth Glidden Tour begins in Minneapolis, MN, with a planned route to Glacier National Park, MT

1916 President Woodrow Wilson signs the Federal Road Aid Act to establish a national highway system

1922 Racer Fritz Riess is born in Nuremburg, Germany

1922 Jerald F. terHorst of the Ford Motor Company is born in Grand Rapids, MI

1923 The 8,000,000th Ford Model T is produced

1925 The Laurel (MD) Board Speedway stages its first event, a 250-mile race that is won by Peter DePaolo in a Miller

1926 The first German Grand Prix is staged at Avus and won by Rudolf Caracciola in a Mercedes

1931 Bentley Motors, Ltd. is forced into receivership with Patrick Roper Frere named to oversee the affairs of the company

1931 The 1932 Plymouth Model PA is introduced

1931 Dick Seaman and Whitney Straight make their racing debuts in the Shelsley Walsh Hillclimb in England

1933 Automotive historian Wallace Binny "Tad" Burness is born in Berkeley, CA

1937 Barron Collier Jr. competes in his last race, winning the Climb to the Clouds at Mt. Washington, NH in his 2300-cc Alfa Romeo

1938 Thomas M. Bradley resigns as President of The Hupp Motor Car Corporation, manufacturers of the Hupmobile

1943 Racer Rolf-Johann Stommelen is born in Siegen, Germany

1954 Frank B. Chadwick, Secretary of the Air Cooled Motors Company and a former official of the H. H. Franklin Manufacturing company, dies in Syracuse, NY at age 60

1955 Charles W. Kynoch of the Chrysler Corporation, largely responsible for Dodge entering the motor truck business, dies

1959 Charles A. Chayne presents Bugatti Royale #41121, the Weinberger cabriolet, to the Henry Ford Museum

1960 A unique stainless steel 1960 Ford Thunderbird is completed at the Ford Motor Company factory in Wixom, MI in collaboration with the Allegheny Ludlum Steel Corporation and The Budd Company

1960 Racer Bobby Dotter is born

1961 A. A. Stambaugh, Chairman of the Board of the Standard Oil Company of Ohio 1950-1955, dies at age 76

1971 Racer Pedro Rodriguez is killed at age 31 when his Ferrari 512M crashes during a sports car race at the Norisring in Germany

1975 Oldsmobile produces its "last" convertible, a red Delta 88 Royale

JULY 12

1857 Lemuel Warner Bowen, a pioneer associate of Henry Ford and the first President of the Cadillac Motor Car Company, is born in Green Bay, WI

1862 Automobile parts manufacturer Chester E. Clemens is born in Troy, NY

1885 Nicholas Kelley, the interim President of the Chrysler Corporation at its formation in 1925 and later its Vice President and General Counsel, is born in Zurich, Switzerland

1893 John A. Carpenter Warner, Assistant Research Manager for the Studebaker Corporation 1926-1930 and longtime official with the Society of Automotive Engineers, is born in Putnam, CT

1895 Inventor Richard Buckminster Fuller is born in Milton, MA

1895 Hon. Evelyn Ellis and Frederick R. Simms driving a Panhard et Levassor cover 56 miles during a round trip between Micheldever, Hampshire and Datchet, Buckinghamshire in the first cross country automobile trip to occur in Great Britain

1904 The first Mount Washington, NH "Climb to the Clouds" is won by Harry Harkness in a Mercedes

1906 The third Glidden Tour begins in Buffalo, New York with a side trip into Quebec, Canada enroute to Bretton Woods, NH

1906 Alexander Y. Malcomson sells his 255 shares of the Ford Motor Company to Henry Ford for $175,000

1909 The sixth Glidden Tour begins in Detroit, MI with a planned route to Kansas City, MO

1915 The Empire Motor Car Company acquires the former Federal Motor Company factory in Indianapolis, IN

EMPIRE
"The Little Aristocrat"

1916 Mr. & Mrs. William Warwick and 4-year-old daughter Daisy leave Seattle, WA in a GMC truck loaded with Carnation Milk products on a trip sponsored by the Seattle Chamber of Commerce to promote the National Parks Highway - they would arrive in New York City 70 days later

1916 Racer Phil Cade is born in Charles City, IA

1921 Gordon Blair MacKenzie of the Ford Motor Company is born in Kalamazoo, MI

1923 Jacques Lombard of Citroen is born in Auxerre, France

1923 Racer Bill Lloyd is born in New York City

1924 Ernest A. D. Eldridge driving the Fiat "Mephistopheles" at Arpajon, France raises the land speed record to 146.01 mph

1925 Roger Bonham Smith, Chairman of General Motors 1981-1990, is born in Columbus, OH

1927 The 1926 Packard "Goddess of Speed" mascot is patented by in-house designer Joseph E. Corker

1930 Racer Guy Ligier is born in Vichy, France

1937 Siegfried Buschmann of the Edward G. Budd Manufacturing Company is born in Essen, Germany

1939 Racer Warwick Banks is born in Great Britain

1941 Racer Benny Parsons is born in Detroit, MI

1944 George E. Vogelsong, a sales executive with Studebaker, Twyman, and Wills Sainte Claire, dies at age 58

1951 Hon. Nicholas Geoffrey Rootes, heir to the Rootes automotive empire, is born

1958 The Studebaker-Packard Corporation announces that 1959 production will consist only of Studebakers

1958 Richard Petty makes his racing debut

1958 Edward R. Mason, former Chief Engineer of Mechanical Research for the Chrysler Corporation and an employee of the company since 1932, dies at age 47

1966 Jaguar Cars Ltd. and the British Motor Corporation merge to form the British Motor Holdings Ltd.

1970 Racer Herbert Schultze is killed when his Alfa Romeo crashes during a race at the Nurburgring in Germany

1970 The Chaparral 2J "sucker car" with vacuum-assisted road holding features makes its racing debut in the Can-Am Challenge race in Watkins Glen, NY, but driver Jackie Stewart retires with minor mechanical problems

1982 The last Checker is produced

JULY 13

1805 Oliver Evans tests his Evans Steam "Orukter Amphibolos" in Philadelphia, PA

1897 Harry A. Knox files a United States patent application for his 2-cylinder gasoline engine

1898 The Paris-Amsterdam-Paris race concludes on its seventh day when winner Fernand Charron returns to Paris in his Panhard et Levassor

1899 The Pontiac Spring & Wagon Works are organized in Pontiac, MI with Albert G. North as President and Harry G. Hamilton as Secretary-Treasurer

1899 John D. Davis and his wife, Louise Hitchcock Davis, leave New York City in an attempt to make the first transcontinental automobile trip - after numerous mechanical and other problems they abandoned the attempt near Toledo, OH

1909 Harry E. Chesebrough, General Manager of the Plymouth-DeSoto-Valiant Division of the Chrysler Corporation and former Chief Engineer of DeSoto and Dodge, is born in Ludington, MI

1914 Racer Samuel Dwight "Sam" Hanks is born in Columbus, OH

1916 Walker Ryan Allen Graham of the Chrysler Corporation is born in Muncie, IN

1916 Gerard Wellington Brooks of Mack Trucks, Inc. is born in Evanston, IL

1916 Charles W. Nash purchases the Thomas B. Jeffery Company following a meeting with company officials in Chicago, IL

1918 Racer Alberto Ascari, the son of racer Antonio Ascari, is born in Milan, Italy

1922 Production of the Rolls-Royce 20-hp begins

1924 The first Coppa Acerbo race is staged in Pescara, Italy and won by Enzo Ferrari driving an Alfa Romeo RL

1927 The Hudson Motor Car Company announces a new one-day production record of 1,831 cars

1940 Henry Ford II marries Anne McDonnell

1940 The last Hupmobile is produced

1941 The Willys-Overland Company is awarded a United States government contract for 16,000 Jeeps at $749 per unit

1947 Raymond Sommer makes his debut as a member of the Gordini racing team at the Albi Grand Prix

1952 Pontiac General Manager Arnold W. Lenz is killed at age 64 in an automobile accident near Lapeer, MI

1957 Racer Thierry Boutsen is born in Brussels, Belgium

1958 The last Packard is produced in South Bend, IN

1960 Ernest R. Breech resigns as Chairman of the Board of the Ford Motor Company and is succeeded by Henry Ford II who also continues as President

1968 The Mazda R-100 is introduced, the world's first volume-production car powered by a Wankel rotary engine

1969 The Trenton (NJ) Speedway stages its first event, the Northern 300 NASCAR race, which is won by David Pearson in a Ford

1971 A. P. Buquor, the Martin-Parry Corporation executive who designed the first 6-wheeled truck, dies in Washington, DC at age 77

1978 Henry Ford II fires Lee Iacocca as President of Ford Motor Company

1983 The Chrysler Corporation repays its federal loan guarantees totalling $813,487,500

1987 Werner Breitschwerdt resigns as Chairman of Daimler-Benz AG

1989 The Honda Motor Company Ltd. announces plans to build a factory in Swindon, Wiltshire, England

1993 Racer Davey Allison is killed at age 32 in a helicopter crash near Talladega, AL

1993 Racer Leslie Thorne dies in Troon, Ayrshire, Scotland at age 77

1995 The Chrysler Corporation opens a new car dealership in Hanoi, Vietnam, the first United States-built automobile agency ever in this country

JULY 14

1835 Pioneer automobile designer Albertus Friedericus Leopoldus Hammel is born in Copenhagen, Denmark

1857 Frederick Louis Maytag is born in Elgin, IL

1873 Augustus F. Mack, the youngest of the five Mack brothers, is born in Mount Cobb, PA

1889 Oil company executive Frederick Bowers Koontz is born in New Martinsville, WV

1900 Miss Wemblyn, driving a 6-hp Panhard et Levassor, wins the special Ladies Race at Ranelagh - although for women only, this race is often cited as the first female racing victory in Great Britain

1907 Racer Francisco "Chico" Landi is born in Sao Paulo, Brazil

1908 The Rolls-Royce "Silver Ghost" is sold as a used car to a London, England taxicab company

1914 Howard C. Marmon is issued a United States patent for his "Power Train Mounting for Automobiles", a system incorporating a universal joint between the engine and the frame

1915 Charles Joseph Scanlon of General Motors is born in Chicago, IL

1915 The Chevrolet Motor Company purchases the Mason Motor Company

1919 William G. Belfry of Texaco Canada Inc. is born

1920 Engineers Fred M. Zeder, Carl M. Breer, and Owen R. Skelton resign from the Studebaker Corporation to join Walter P. Chrysler in his efforts to revive the ailing Willys-Overland Company

1921 Sturgis Muirhead Fay of the Ford Motor Company is born in Waltham, MA

1925 The world's largest electric sign, "CITROEN", debuts on the sides of the Eiffel Tower in Paris, France, a reward to Andre Citroen for designing a system of traffic lights for the French capital - it would be dismantled in 1936

1931 The Cord Corporation is issued a United States patent for its 1931 Auburn radiator shell design

1931 The Chevrolet 1931-1932 "Eagle" mascot is patented by designers William Schnell and Frederick Giuntini

1935 Edoardo Agnelli, son and heir-apparent of Fiat founder Giovanni Agnelli, is killed in a seaplane crash off the coast of Genoa, Italy

There was a time when the advantages of a Straight Eight motor versus other types, needed selling to the public. Auburn, with one or two others, was a successful pioneer in this field about five years ago. Today, the demand for the superior performance, smoother and more flexible flow of power, possible only with a Straight Eight, has swept the entire country, forcing other manufacturers to follow Auburn's leadership. There is assurance to buyers in the fact that Auburn has had so many years of experience ahead of others, in which to improve and perfect not only its Straight Eight motor itself, but also priority in designing and strengthening the entire car to meet the requirements peculiar to this type of motor. It is only natural, therefore, that a rapidly increasing number of people look to Auburn for bigger value, better performance, longer endurance and a better investment. To meet this demand, and more important, to deserve it, Auburn is offering two New Series of Straight Eights; 100 h. p., 125 inch wheelbase, Sport Sedan—$1195; and 125 h.p., 130 inch wheelbase, Sport Sedan — $1495. The more competent you are to judge motor cars the more you will realize the desirability and economy of owning an Auburn.

AUBURN
POWERED BY LYCOMING

—294—

1936 Robert Gray Weeks of the Mobil Corporation is born in Camden, NJ

1941 Frederic J. Fisher, the eldest of the seven brothers who founded the Fisher Body Company, dies in Detroit, MI at age 63

1943 General Motors announces plans to acquire the assets of the Yellow Truck & Coach Manufacturing Company

1945 Automobiles Deutsch-Bonnet of Champigny-sur-Marne, France unveils its D.B.4, the first post-World War II racing car

1946 Tazio Nuvolari wins the Albi (France) Grand Prix driving a Maserati 4CL, his first post-World War II victory - at age 53 his victory set a record for the oldest winner of a Grand Prix race

1951 Froilan Gonzalez, driving a Ferrari 375, records his first Formula 1 victory in the British Grand Prix at Silverstone and the first victory for the marque under the new World Championship Driver system

1953 The Chevrolet Corvette is introduced

1954 Peter Pirsch, founder in 1919 of Peter Pirsch & Company, manufacturers of firetrucks, dies in Kenosha, WI at age 88

1955 The Volkswagen Karmann-Ghia coupe is introduced at the Kasino Hotel in North Rhine-Westphalia, West Germany

1955 Claude Sintz, a designer and manufacturer of automotive parts since 1895, dies - he assisted his father, Clark Sintz, in building the 1902-1904 Sintz high-wheeler

1956 The Emeryson makes its Formula 1 debut in the British Grand Prix at Silverstone, but the Mark 1 designed and driven by Paul Emery retires with ignition problems

1957 Racer Herbert Mackay-Fraser is killed at age 20 when his Lotus crashes during the Coupe de Vitesse at Reims, France - later in the same race Bill Whitehouse is killed at age 48 when his Cooper-Climax crashes

1969 Development of the Holden GTR-X sports car begins, but production would end with the prototype completed in 1973

1972 The 1973 International Scout II is introduced

1974 A. E. Barit, President of the Hudson Motor Car Company 1936-1954, dies in Grosse Pointe Park, MI at age 83

1979 Clay Regazzoni wins the British Grand Prix driving a Williams-Cosworth Type FW07, the first Formula 1 victory for the marque

1986 Industrial designer Raymond Loewy, closely associated with Studebaker for many years, dies in Monte Carlo, Monaco at age 90

1994 Henry B. Schacht retires as Chairman of the Cummins Engine Company

1996 Racer Jeff Krosnoff is killed at age 31 when he crashes during an Indy-Car race in Toronto, Ontario, Canada - also killed in the accident was course worker Gary Avrin

JULY 15

1865 Alfred Charles William Harmsworth, Lord Northcliffe, a prominent British journalist who was a great promoter of the Rolls-Royce, is born in Chapelizod, Ireland

1867 Oreste Fraschini is born in Milan, Italy

1883 Carl C. Hinkley, founder in 1914 of the Hinkley Motors Corporation and later an official of the Buda Company, is born in Lima, OH

1893 Morris Markin of Checker is born in Russia

1903 Dr. Ernst Pfennig of Chicago, IL purchases a Ford Model A, the first sale for the Ford Motor Company

1908 The first Ford Model T is sold

The most important car ever produced - the Model T Ford. The man seated nearest the camera in the rear seat of this 1911 touring is the author's grandfather, Carl J. Wick, who was a Ford dealer 1916-1922.

1908 Clarence E. Bonner of Chrisman, IL introduces the Bonner six-cylinder touring car by making a promotional drive to Paris, IL, but production was limited to this prototype and possibly one additional unit

1912 Joseph L. Hudson, Detroit retail store owner and first President of the Hudson Motor Car Company, dies at age 65

1913 Byron John Nichols of the Chrysler Corporation is born in Beloit, WI

1914 Racer Birabongse Bhanudej Bhanubandh, Prince of Siam, known as B. Bira, is born in Bangkok, Thailand

1915 The Briggs-Detroiter Company is reorganized as the Detroiter Motor Car Company with A. O. Dunk as President

1916 The United States Army orders 150 Dodge cars for use in the Mexican campaign

1917 Production begins at the ReVere Motor Car Company in Logansport, IN

1922 The first all-steel Dodge Brothers 4-door sedan body is completed by the Edward G. Budd Manufacturing Company of Philadelphia, PA

1922 The Bugatti Type 30 makes its racing debut, with Pierre de Vizcaya and Pierre Marco taking second and third places at the French Grand Prix in Strasbourg

1924 E. L. Cord resigns his sales position with Quinlan Motors in Chicago, IL, the Moon distributorship owned by John Quinlan

1924 George R. Beamer, Sales Manager of the United States Gauge Company, dies at age 54

1928 The Mercedes-Benz SS makes its racing debut at the German Grand Prix at the Nurburgring and sweeps the top three places - Halle in an Amilcar and Vinzenz Junek in a Bugatti are killed in accidents during the race

1928 Francis Birtles arrives in Sydney, Australia in his 14-hp Bean, having completed the first overland automobile trip from England

1928 Racer Elmer George is born in Hockerville, OK

1929 Racer Ian Stewart is born in Edinburgh, Scotland

1934 Ernst Gunther Burgaller makes his debut with the Auto Union team at the Germany Grand Prix staged at the Nurburgring, but retires with mechanical problems

1935 General Sales Manager Abram vanderZee addresses all Dodge dealers and salesmen over the CBS national radio network

1935 Robert C. Graham of the Graham-Paige Motors Corporation attends the Reo Motor Car Company board meeting in Lansing, MI to propose a merger of the two firms, but Reo rejects his offer

1938 The last 1938 Pontiac Six and Eight are produced

1939 Carl G. Fisher, a cofounder of the Prest-O-Lite Company and the Indianapolis Motor Speedway Company and the developer of Miami Beach, dies in Miami, FL at age 65

1952 Racer John Cleland is born in Wishaw, Scotland

1953 Willys offers the General Motors Hydra-Matic transmission as an option due to a shortage of the Borg-Warner Corporation units caused by a strike at the latter firm

1953 Fuji Heavy Industries, Ltd. is organized in Japan, manufacturers since 1958 of the Subaru

1954 Clifford B. Longley of the Ford Motor Company dies in Detroit, MI at age 65

1959 The first Jaguar Mark 2 saloon is produced

1960 Racer Wayne Taylor is born in Port Elizabeth, South Africa

1961 Tony Maggs, driving a Lotus in his Formula 1 debut, finishes 13th in the British Grand Prix at Aintree - the Ferguson, financed by Harry Ferguson, designed by Claude Hill, and driven by Jack Fairman and Stirling Moss, makes its only Formula 1 appearance but is disqualified for receiving an illegal push start - the Gilby also makes its debut with the car driven by Keith Greene finishing 15th, the marque's best result in its three Formula 1 appearances

1965 The International Scout 80 is discontinued

1969 The Mercedes-Benz C111 is completed in its initial configuration

1972 The Williams makes its Formula 1 debut in the British Grand Prix, but the car driven by Henri Pescarolo retires after being involved in an accident

1972 Racer Fonty Flock dies in Atlanta, GA at age 51

1974 George A. Delaney, Chief Engineer of Pontiac 1947-1956 who had previously been associated with Paige, Graham-Paige, and Graham, dies at age 79

1983 The last International truck, a Transtar conventional semi-tractor, is completed at the Fort Wayne, IN plant as all production is shifted to the Springfield, OH plant

1984 Michael Humenik, a Ford Motor Company research engineer 1952-1984 who developed many new automotive usages for plastics and ceramics, dies at age 59

1987 Matra SA begins the process of privatization

1993 The last Cadillac Allante is produced

1994 John Thornley of M.G. dies at age 85

JULY 16

1870 Automobile parts manufacturer Charles Edwin Thompson is born in McIndoe Falls, VT

1878 The Green Bay-Madison (WI) automobile race begins with two competitors, the Oshkosh steamer built by Frank A. Shomer, A. M. Farrand, A. Gallinger, and O. F. Morse in that city and the Green Bay steamer built by Edward P. Cowles of Wequiock, WI

1888 Ugo Gobbato of Alfa Romeo is born in Volpago del Montello, Italy

1895 Fortunato Felice Barberis of General Motors is born in Milan, Italy

1900 F. P. Nehrbas, a Buffalo, NY bicycle mechanic, joins the E. R. Thomas Motor Company to build the prototype automobile designed by Erwin Ross Thomas

1905 Societa Petrolifera Italiana SpA is incorporated in Piacenza, Italy

1908 Rene Panhard dies at age 67 and is succeeded as Managing Director of the Societe des Anciens Etablissements Panhard et Levassor by Hippolyte Panhard, his 37-year-old son

1923 John Robert Nyland of the Holley Carburetor Company is born in Saginaw, MI

1924 Chrysler makes its racing debut with Ralph DePalma winning the Mount Wilson Hillclimb near Los Angeles, CA - his 22.1 mph speed for the 9.5-mile course established an event record for stock cars, but was the slowest speed for all of DePalma's many victories

1928 Racer Jim Rathmann is born in Valparaiso, IN

1951 James E. Ellor, Assistant Chief Engineer of Rolls-Royce Ltd., dies in London, England at age 59

1951 Frank G. Oberle of the American Bosch Corporation dies in Chicago, IL at age 44

1951 Everett H. Shepard, carburetor engineer for Chevrolet 1932-1947, dies in Banning, CA at age 69

1955 Jack Brabham makes his Formula 1 debut at the British Grand Prix in Aintree, but his Cooper retires with valve problems - Stirling Moss wins the race in his Mercedes-Benz W196, the first of sixteen Grand Prix victories in his career

1956 Stylists complete work on the "real" 1957 Packards, which were destined to be scrapped in favor of Studebaker-based cars built in South Bend, IN

1956 Ron W. Todghma becomes the first native-born President of the Chrysler Corporation Ltd. of Canada

1958 Robert P. Breeze, designer of the Breeze-Paris race car while on military duty in France and of the 1919 Breeze Midget upon his return to the United States, a developer of power braking systems, and an official of the Sebring (FL) International Raceway, dies at age 72 while swimming of the coast of Lido Beach, NY

1960 Diesel engine designer Emil R. Marten of the White Motor Company dies at age 31

1961 Abner Doble dies in Santa Rosa, CA at age 66

1966 Racer Chris Irwin makes his Formula 1 debut, driving a Brabham-Climax to a 7th place finish in the British Grand Prix - the Shannon makes its only Formula 1 appearance, but the Type SH1 driven by Trevor Taylor retires with a split fuel tank

DOBLE-DETROIT STEAM CAR

1969 The last 1969 Pontiac is produced

1971 The 15,000,000th Pontiac is produced

1977 Renault makes its modern Formula 1 debut in the British Grand Prix, but the Type RS01 driven by Jean-Pierre Jabouille retires with turbocharger problems

1983 The Spirit makes its Formula 1 debut in the British Grand Prix, but the Type 201 driven by Stefan Johansson retires because of a fuel pump belt failure

JULY 17

1879 N. B. Pope, Managing Editor of *Automobile Topics* magazine, is born in Thomaston, ME

1881 Alfred Robinson Glancy of Oakland is born in Miamiville, OH

1898 The 119-mile Turin-Asti-Alessandria-Turin cross country event is staged

1901 Luigi Chinetti, a racer, exotic car dealer, and motor sports promoter, is born in Milan, Italy

1903 Arthur Duray, driving a Gobron-Brillie at Ostend, Belgium, raises the land speed record to 83.47 mph

1912 Racer Erwin Bauer is born in Germany

1913 A 1910 Buick Model 10 "Bear Cat" driven by W. W. Brown becomes the first car to reach summit of Pikes Peak, CO without the aid of horses

1914 Dodge Brothers Inc. is organized with John F. Dodge as President and Horace E. Dodge as Vice President

1927 The second German Grand Prix is staged at the Nurburgring, the first race held at the new German speedway

1928 The Plymouth Division of Chrysler Corporation is created

1934 The Plymouth 1934-1935 "Mayflower" mascot is patented by designer Herbert V. Henderson

A 1934 Plymouth 2-door sedan is parked near the non-commissioned officers
quarters on Governors Island in Upper New York Bay.

1938 David M. Averill of Dort, Chevrolet, Ajax, and Nash dies at age 59

1940 Harry M. Rugg, credited with the design of the engine for the first Stanley steamer and later a design engineer with Dodge Brothers and several oil companies, is killed at age 61 in an automobile accident near Penfield, PA

1941 Albert M. Wibel is named Vice President in Charge of Purchasing for the Ford Motor Company

1943 M. W. McConkey, a former patent attorney for General Motors and President of the Hydraulic Brake Company, dies

1945 The first Jeep CJ-2A is produced

1945 Henry J. Kaiser and Joseph W. Frazer meet in San Francisco, CA to lay plans for the formation of the Kaiser-Frazer Corporation

1947 Hudson McCarroll of the Ford Motor Company is appointed as Director of Chemical and Metallurgical Engineering and Research

1950 The Volkswagen is officially introduced in the United States as New York City imported car dealer Max Hoffman unveils his first shipment of twenty cars in his showroom at 487 Park Avenue

1951 General Motors previews its Sabre showcar, a two-seat roadster capable of 180 mph, at the Milford, MI proving grounds

1952 Ford Motor Company establishes the Special Product Operations headed by William Clay Ford to develop the Continental Mark II

1953 George A. Spoon of the Muskegon Motor Specialties Company, an authority in the design and manufacture of camshafts, dies in Milwaukee, WI at age 58

1954 The Vanwall makes its Formula 1 debut in the British Grand Prix, but the car driven by Peter Collins retires with a blown cylinder head gasket

1956 A 1956 Plymouth Savoy is the 100,000th model year automobile produced by the Chrysler Corporation Ltd. of Canada

1956 Dewey H. Campbell, Chief Engineer of the P & G Manufacturing Company and the inventor of the valve gapper, a tool which checks valve gaps on overhead valves, dies

1959 Racer William P. Buckert is killed at age 52 during a midget race in Waterloo, NY

1959 Simon J. Vos of the Trinidad Oil Company dies in London, England at age 62

1963 The last 1963 Ford Thunderbird is produced

1964 Donald Campbell, driving the Proteus Bluebird at the Bonneville Salt Flats, UT, sets a land speed record for wheel-driven cars and gasoline-powered cars with two identical runs of 403.10 mph

1974 Dean B. Hammond of the Kaiser-Frazer Corporation dies at age 65

1976 Frank W. Abrams, Chairman of the Standard Oil Company of New Jersey 1946-1954, dies in Greenport, NY at age 87

1981 Automotive historian Tom Mahoney dies in Poughkeepsie, NY at age 75

1984 Antique automobile collector Granville S. Watson dies

1985 The first Ford Aerostar minivan is produced at the St. Louis (MO) Assembly Plant

1995 Racer Juan Manuel Fangio dies at age 84

JULY 18

1833 John Squire and Francis Macerone of Paddington Wharf, England are issued a patent for their Steam Carriage for Common Roads

1865 Rubber pioneer Nathaniel Hayward, whose work with vulcanization was taken over and continued by Charles Goodyear, dies in Colchester, CT at age 57

1868 Burton J. Westcott, founder of the Westcott Motor Car Company, is born in Richmond, IN

1890 Charles Erwin Wilson of General Motors is born in Minerva, OH

1893 Benjamin Richard Donaldson of the Ford Motor Company is born in Grand Rapids, MI

1911 The 1909 Thomas Flyer "Eagle on a Globe" mascot to commemorate the marque's win in the 1908 New York-Paris race is patented by designer George T. Verreault

1916 Martin Joseph Caserio of Pontiac is born in Laurium, MI

1920 Racer Eric Brandon is born in London, England

1926 Otto Merz, Rudolf Caracciola, and Willy Walb, all driving Mercedes-Benz K tourers, sweep the first three places in the touring car race preceding the Grand Prix of Europe in San Sebastian, Spain in the first racing event for the new Daimler-Benz AG firm

1927 The Hudson Motor Car Company announces plans to constuct an assembly plant in Berlin, Germany

1929 The Plymouth Model U is officially declared to be a "1930" model

1939 George Eyston covers 114.638 miles in an hour at Brooklands in a Bentley 4 1/4 Liter streamlined coupe, setting the track record for a stock sports car

1941 John Martin Schreiber, inventor of a passenger bus that could operate on either overhead electric wires of on motor fuel, dies in Orange, NJ at age 65

1942 Dr. Wilhelm Kissel, Chairman of the Daimler-Benz AG Supervisory Board 1926-1942, dies in Überlingen, Germany at age 56

1946 Fred L. Eberhardt, President of Gould & Eberhardt, Inc. for 45 years, dies at age 78

1948 Juan Manuel Fangio makes his Grand Prix debut, finishing twelfth at the Grand Prix de l'ACF at Reims-Gueux in a Simca-Gordini T15

1950 Arthur H. Timmerman, recently retired Vice President of the Wagner Electric Corporation and a pioneer in the automotive electronics field, dies in Dallas, TX at age 79

1952 Joseph Albert Chamasrour of Renault, AMC, and Chrysler is born in Beirut, Lebanon

1954 Sir Ernest W. Petter, who with his brother Percival W. Petter in 1895 built the first internal combustion engined automobile in Great Britain, dies in New Milton, England at age 81 - their Yeovil, Somerset venture ended in 1898 after about a dozen varied vehicles had been produced

1958 Henri Farman, pioneer racer, luxury automobile manufacturer, and airplane designer, dies in Paris, France at age 84

1959 The David Fry-designed Fry Formula 2 car makes its only Grand Prix appearance at Aintree, but the car driven by Michael Parkes fails to qualify - the JBW makes its Formula 1 debut, but the car designed by Fred Wilkinson and driven by Brian Naylor retires with transmission problems - Bruce McLaren, driving a Cooper, records the fastest lap, at age 21 years, 322 days the youngest driver to accomplish this feat in a Formula 1 championship race

1970 The Surtees makes its Formula 1 debut in the British Grand Prix, but the Type TS7 driven by sponsor and designer John Surtees is forced to retire with oil pressure problems

1975 The "last" Buick convertible, a LeSabre, is built at the Fairfax, KS plant - the marque would reenter the open car market with its 1982 Riviera convertible

1980 Chrysler Corporation Chairman Lee Iacocca announces the pending return of the Imperial marque

JULY 19

1888 Max M. Gilman of Packard is born in Plymouth, WI

1897 Daniel Rugg Dodge, father of John F. and Horace E. Dodge, dies at age 78

1899 A. C. Nelson of Berea, OH is hired to help build the first Packard

1902 The Jackson Automobile Company is organized in Jackson, MI by Byron J. Carter, George A. Matthews, and Charles Lewis - the firm built the Jackson 1903-1923, the Jaxon steam car in 1903, and the Orlo in 1904

1904 Automotive parts manufacturer Vernon C. Hoover is born in Sunbury, PA

1905 The first Brighton (England) Speed Trials, a 4-day event, begin

1913 The tenth Glidden Tour ends in Glacier National Park, MT - the only cars to record perfect scores are the three 1914 Metz Model 22's driven by Charles H. Metz, Walter Metz, and George Vatter

1925 Edward Eugene Brewer of the Cooper Tire & Rubber Company is born in Findlay, OH

1927 The Mercedes-Benz Type S makes its racing debut at the Eifel race at the Nurburgring, with Rudolf Caracciola winning the sports-car class

1930 Automobile historian Charles Edward Edwards is born in Charleston, SC

1934 Harold T. Ames files a patent application for his retractable headlights, the design becoming one of the hallmarks of the Cord 810/812

1935 The first parking meter, invented by Carlton C. Magee, is installed in Oklahoma City, OK

1943 Racer Mark Everard Pepys, the 6th Earl of Cottenham, dies in London at age 40

1947 John A. Lux of the Stewart Motor Company dies in East Aurora, NY

1952 The Connaught makes its Formula 1 debut at the British Grand Prix in Silverstone, with cars driven by Dennis Poore, Eric Thompson, Ken Downing, and Ken McAlpine finishing 4th, 5th, 9th, and 16th

1954 Kaiser lays off about 400 workers as its Toledo, OH assembly lines that are utilized for building Willys commercial vehicles and Jeeps

1955 The first Volvo 445PH estate car is produced

1955 Ernest E. Minard, retired President of the National Sales Engineering Corporation whose previous automotive career included stints with Oldsmobile and Studebaker, dies at age 83

1959 Racer Van Johnson is killed when his rebuilt Varga Special crashes during a race in Harrisburg, PA, three months to the day after Dick Linder had been killed in the same car

1969 S. H. Grylls retires from Rolls-Royce Ltd. after 39 years with firm

1974 The first national meeting of the Tucker Automobile Club is held at the home of Stan Gilliland in Wellington, KS

1975 The Lyncar makes its only Formula 1 appearance in the British Grand Prix in Silverstone, with the car designed by Martin Slater and driven by John Nicholson finishing in 17th place

1977 George M. Levy, a longtime official of the Roosevelt Raceway in Westbury, NY, dies at age 88

JULY 20

1872 Carl Benz marries Berta Ringer in Pforzheim, Germany

1878 Ernest Solon Cowie, an inventor of automotive electrical equipment, is born in Kansas City, MO

1880 Cadwallader Washburn "Carl" Kelsey is born in Clarens, Switzerland, the son of United States citizens

1894 Errett Lobban Cord is born in Warrensburg, MO

1904 Racer Harry Harkness wins the Climb to the Clouds in Mount Washington, NH in a Mercedes, beating the Stanley of F. E. Stanley and setting a record for the event

1909 The Ford Motor Company registers its "Ford" script logo as a trademark

1911 Racer Lewis Strang dies

1919 Benson Ford, originally named Edsel Bryant Ford Jr., is born in Detroit, MI

1923 The 1924 Nashes are introduced, featuring the industry's first electric dashboard clock as an option

1926 The Apperson Brothers Automobile Company of Kokomo, IN is liquidated at auction after 25 years of production

1931 Racer Tony Marsh is born in Stourbridge, Gloucestershire, England

1942 Racer Peter Goodwill "Pete" Hamilton is born in Maine

1943 Charles H. Tremear, operator of the photographic studio at the Henry Ford Museum and Greenfield Village, dies in Detroit, MI at age 77

1943 Racer Christopher Arthur "Chris" Amon is born in Bulls, New Zealand

1945 B. W. Burtsell, Production Manager for the Packard Motor Car Company 1910-1916 and later an independent consulting engineer, dies in North Tonawanda, NY at age 63

1955 Calouste Sarkis Gulbenkian, Turkish born Shell Oil Company executive, dies in Lisbon, Portugal at age 86

1957 William Dean Robinson, President of the Briggs Manufacturing Company, dies in Detroit, MI at age 59

1957 Tony Brooks and Stirling Moss, driving a Vanwall, win the British Grand Prix at Aintree to record the marque's first major racing victory

1959 Donald Alexander of the Edward G. Budd Manufacturing Company dies at age 68

1960 Racer Claudio Langes is born in Brescia, Italy

1960 Racer Kris Nissen is born in Arnum, Denmark

1962 Racer Giovanna Amati is born in Rome, Italy

1964 Racer Bernd Schneider is born in Saarbrucken, West Germany

1967 The last Panhard, a blue Model 24b coupe, is completed to end 78 years of automobile production

1968 Jo Siffert, driving a Lotus 49B, wins the British Grand Prix at Brands Hatch to record his first Grand Prix victory and the first by a Swiss driver since 1949

1971 The last 1971 Pontiac is produced

1990 John R. Bond of *Road & Track* magazine dies in Escondido, CA at age 77

JULY 21

1888 Robert Snyder King, President of the Pennzoil Company 1936-1940, is born in Dayton, OH

1904 Louis Rigolly, driving a 15-litre Gobron-Brillie on the Ostend-Nieuwpoort road in Belgium, raises the land speed record to 103.55 mph, becoming the first to break the 100 mph barrier in an automobile

1917 The Bayerische Flugzeugwerke AG (BFW) is reorganized as the Bayerische Motoren-Werke GmbH (Bavarian Motor Works) in Munich, Germany by Karl Friedrich Rapp, a former designer with Daimler

1925 Malcolm Campbell, driving a Sunbeam at the Pendine Sands in Wales, raises the land speed record to 150.87 mph

1926 Frederick John Mancheski of Echlin Inc. is born in Stevens Point, WI

1930 The M.G. Car Company reorganizes as the M.G. Car Company Ltd. with Sir William R. Morris as Governing Director and Cecil Kimber as Managing Director, severing the last legal link with Morris Garages

1932 The Essex Terraplane is introduced, with car #1 christened by aviatrix Amelia Earhart and given to Orville Wright

1932 Georg Heuer of Karosserie Glaser dies in Dresden, Germany

1934 William Hastings Bassett, Chairman of the SAE Non-Ferrous Metals Division and a manufacturer of brass automobile parts, dies

1936 The 1934 DeSoto "Winged Goddess" mascot is patented by designer Herbert V. Henderson

1943 Racer Pierre Chauvet, who also raced under the names Fritz Glatz and Umberto Calvo, is born in Austria

1944 Barbara Mascherpa (Mrs. Ettore) Bugatti dies in Paris, France at age 62

1946 The first post-World War II speed event in Germany is staged in Ruthestein and won by Hermann Lang in a BMW

1948 United States automobile production for the calendar year reaches 2,000,000

1949 The first Jaguar XK120 released for public sale (serial #66002) is shipped to Sydney, NSW, Australia

1953 Herman Mathis of the Gulf Oil Company dies at age 65

1956 The Lincoln and Continental divisions of the Ford Motor Company are consolidated

1960 The first automobile race is held at the Atlanta (GA) International Raceway

1961 Nicholas Dykstra is elected President of Mack Trucks, Inc.

1965 Racer Jovy Marcelo is born in the Philippines

1974 The last Volkswagen Karmann-Ghia is produced at the Wilhelm Karmann GmbH plant in Osnabruck, West Germany - total production for the 19-year run amounted to 363,401 coupes and 80,899 convertibles

1984 Henry Ford is enshrined in the National Aviation Hall of Fame, Dayton, OH

1985 Alan B. Couture, an experimental engineer and test driver with the Chrysler Corporation 1923-1956, dies in Southfield, MI at age 95

1987 The Ferrari F40 is introduced in Maranello, Italy

1991 Racer Paul Warwick is killed at age 22 when he crashes during the Gold Cup race at the Oulton Park circuit in England

JULY 22

1862 The Reed Steam wagon built by John A. Reed of New York City begins a planned journey from Nebraska City, NE to Denver, CO, but the vehicle is disabled and abandoned after completing just seven miles

1870 Frank Lanchester is born in Hove, Sussex, England

1874 E. A. DeWaters of Thomas, Cadillac, and Buick is born in Kalamazoo, MI

1894 The Paris-Rouen automobile race, the first such event held in Europe, begins at the Porte Maillot in Paris under the sponsorship of journalist Pierre Giffard - 19 of 21 cars completed the course, with the huge 20-hp de Dion-Bouton steam tractor driven by Count Albert de Dion the first to finish, but this machine was disqualified as an "industrial vehicle" with the official winner declared to be the Peugeot driven by Georges Lemaitre

1898 James W. Packard is taken for a test ride in a Winton motor car by Alexander Winton

1898 Automobile advertising executive Ross Roy is born in Kingston, ON, Canada

1904 The first gasoline-powered Studebaker-Garford is produced, driven into the street and sold on the spot to H. D. Johnson, who just happened to be passing by - Johnson was the son-in-law of John M. Studebaker and the whole transaction was a carefully staged "event"

1905 The second Glidden Tour concludes with a return to New York City after a route through the New England states - the winner is Percy Pierce in a Pierce-Arrow

1908 The Fisher Body Company is organized in Detroit, MI by brothers Frederic J. and Charles T. Fisher, along with their uncle, Albert Fisher

1909 The Dayton Engineering Laboratories Company is incorporated by Charles F. Kettering and Edward A. Deeds after receiving an order from Cadillac for 8,000 automobile ignition units - the name of the company, intentionally coined to allow the "Delco" acronym, was suggested by associate William A. Chryst

1909 Racer Dorino Serafini is born in Pesaro, Italy

1911 Racer and USAC official Emil Andres is born in Chicago, IL

1916 Tire manufacturer Edwin Herbert Sonnecken is born in New Haven, CT

1933 Alexander J. Trotman of the Ford Motor Company is born in Middlesex, England

1935 K. T. Keller is elected President of the Chrysler Corporation succeeding founder Walter P. Chrysler who remained as Chairman of the Board

1936 Francois Lecot, driving a Citroen 11CV, ends his one-year marathon after completing approximately 250,000 miles

1940 Ab Jenkins, driving the Duesenberg "Mormon Meteor" at the Bonneville Salt Flats, UT, sets new speed records for 500 and 1000 miles

1945 Harlow H. Curtice announces Buick's post-World War II expansion plans

1947 Gary Davis, President of the Davis Motor Car Company of Van Nuys, CA introduces the prototype Davis D-2 3-wheeled automobile

1948 The Willys-Overland Company introduces the Jeepster, a sporty variant of the standard Jeep designed by Brooks Stevens

1949 Automotive engineer Ion P. Tabacu is born in Romania

1953 Joseph Russell Corace, President and Chief Executive Office of Inalfa Hollandia Inc. and a former design engineer with General Motors and Volvo, is born in Mount Clemens, MI

1953 Automotive journalist Harold W. Slauson is killed in an automobile accident at age 70

1961 Racer Calvin Fish is born in Norwich, England

1969 Owen R. Skelton of the Chrysler Corporation dies in Palm Beach, FL at age 83

1970 Racer Craig Baird is born in New Zealand

1984 James J. Nance, President and General Manager of the Packard Motor Car Company 1952-1954, and the successor Studebaker-Packard Corporation 1954-1956, dies in Bellaire, MI at age 84

1987 Edzard Reuter is named Chairman of Daimler-Benz AG

JULY 23

1869 Richard Hugh Scott of Reo is born in Renfrew County, Ontario, Canada

1881 Herbert H. Hills of Packard is born in Davidson, MI

1901 Ransom E. Olds is issued a United States design patent for his "Vehicle Body", now commonly called the Curved Dash Oldsmobile

1903 The first 2-cylinder Ford Model A to be sold is delivered to its new owner, Dr. Ernst Pfennig of Chicago, IL

1908 Automobile stylist Franklin Quick Hershey is born in Detroit, MI

1909 Zenon Clayton Raymond Hansen, Chairman of Mack Trucks, Inc. 1967-1972, is born in Hibbing, MN

1919 The Luverne Motor Truck Company is incorporated in Minnesota by F. A. "Al" Leicher, his brother Edward L. Leicher, and their sons Robert and Larry Leicher

1919 The first post-World War I speed trials in England are staged at Westcliff, Essex

1921 The bankrupt Hebb Motor Company is reorganized as the Patriot Manufacturing Company with William E. Hardy as President, William H. Ferguson as Vice President, and Charles C. Quiggle as Secretary-Treasurer

1926 The Studebaker Model ES Big Six Custom Sedan is introduced - the car was marketed as the "President", the marque's first usage of this name

1926 H. C. Moser, General Manager of the Chicago Motor Coach Company and Transportation Engineer for the Yellow Truck & Coach Manufacturing Company, dies in Baltimore, MD at age 43

1930 Glenn H. Curtiss, a V-type engine pioneer who was best known for his career in aviation, dies in Buffalo, NY at age 52

1935 Francois Lecot in his Citroen 11CV begins his one-year marathon drive of approximately 250,000 miles

1935 Racer John Cordts is born in Canada

1935 Racer James Ellis "Jim" Hall is born in Abilene, TX

1941 Racer Richard Ernest "Richie" Evans is born in Westernville, NY

1947 The Davis Motor Car Company of Van Nuys, CA announces plans to begin production of the 3-wheeled Davis in 1948

1947 Racer Torsten Palm is born in Kristinehamn, Sweden

1950 The first Dutch Grand Prix is staged in Zandvoort and won by Louis Rosier in a Talbot-Lago Type 26C

1950 The first races are held at Elkhart Lake, WI, and the main event is won by Jim Kimberly in a Ferrari

1973 Edward V. Rickenbacker dies in Zurich, Switzerland at age 82

Best know in the automotive world as a pre-World War I racing champion and later as the owner of Indianapolis Motor Speedway, Eddie Rickenbacker did little more than lend his name to the car manufactured 1922-1927 in Detroit, MI.

JULY 24

1866 Automotive journalist C. H. Gurnett is born in Ingersoll, ON, Canada

1869 Harvey G. Shafer of Marmon is born in Indianapolis, IN

1869 Julius Heinrich Dorpmuller, the head of the Autobahn project, is born in Elberfeld (now Wuppertal-Elberfeld), Germany

1876 Julius Peter Heil of the Heil Company is born in Dusemond-on-the-Mosel, Germany

1878 The Green Bay-Madison (WI) automobile race concludes after six days elapsed time but just 33 hours, 27 minutes of actual running time for an average of 6 mph - the winners are Frank A. Shomer and A. M. Farrand in the Oshkosh steamer

1899 The 9-day Tour de France Automobile is won by Rene de Knyff driving a Panhard et Levassor

1902 Robert Schwenke is issued a German patent for his front-wheel-drive system for cars

1906 Racer Gianfranco Comotti is born in Brescia, Italy

1907 The fourth Glidden Tour ends in New York City - the four cars of the Buffalo (NY) Automobile Club are declared joint winners

1913 Soldier and diplomat Henry Albert Byroade, a longtime classic car enthusiast, is born in Allen County, IN

1915 The Velie, LA post office is established and named by local postmaster Charles M. Hutchinson for his Velie automobile

1916 Samuel B. Stevens and four relief drivers leave New York City in a newly-introduced Marmon 34 attempting to break the trans-United States record using the just completed Lincoln Highway

1917 The Pullman Motor Company is liquidated

1920 Sherwood Harry Egbert, President of the Studebaker-Packard Corporation 1961-1963, is born in Seattle, WA

1923 The 100,000th Star is produced

1924 The second series 1924 Essex Sixes are introduced

1929 The 2,000,000th Ford Model A is produced

1931 Racer Anthony V. "Tony" Hegbourne is born in Great Britain

1938 Dick Seaman records his first Grand Prix victory finishing ahead of teammates Rudolf Caracciola and Hermann Lang in a sweep for the Mercedes-Benz W154 trio in the German Grand Prix at the Nurburgring

1939 David Alec Gwyn Simon of the British Petroleum Company PLC is born in London, England

1942 Helmut Becker, West German importer of the Iso, is born in Berlin

1950 Clyde R. Paton is named Director of Engineering for the Willys-Overland Company

1950 Goldie Gardner becomes the first driver to exceed 120 mph in Class J (below 350 cc) when he reaches 121.048 mph on the Jabbeke road in Belgium - later that day he reaches 104.725 mph in a M.G. YA sedan to claim the "World's Fastest Saloon" title for the marque

1952 Lammot DuPont of General Motors dies in New London, CT at age 71

1952 Frederick Wilhelm Hohensee, the German-born associate of William C. Durant who helped design and build the first Chevrolet, dies in Yonkers, NY at age 83

1952 The Special Products Division of the Ford Motor Company is established under the direction of William Clay Ford

1953 Joseph S. Mack of Mack trucks dies in San Diego, CA at age 82

1958 Earle F. Johnson of General Motors dies at age 71

1960 Racer Jean Blanc (nee Jean Saveniers) is killed at age 37 when he crashes during a race in Salerno, Italy

1962 Racer Johnny O'Connell is born in Poughkeepsie, NY

1964 The last 1964 Ford Thunderbird is produced

1969 Racer Stan Wattles is born in Glen Cove, NY

1972 Lance Reventlow, creator of the Scarab sports car, is killed at age 36 in a plane crash in the Colorado Rockies

JULY 25

1885 Stewart Southworth Hathaway of the Buda Company, manufacturers of automobile engines, is born in East Orange, NJ

1895 G. F. Shaver of New York City wins a $500 prize to coin a new name for the horseless carriage - "motor-cycle"

1903 Barney Oldfield, making his final appearance with the Ford "999", raises the closed-course speed record to 65.0 mph at the Empire City track in Yonkers, NY

1904 The first Glidden Tour begins in New York City enroute to St. Louis, MO

1905 Racer Georges Grignard is born in Paris, France

1909 Frederick Llewellyn Smith, Chairman of Rolls-Royce Motors Ltd. 1971-1972 and an employee of Rolls-Royce since 1933, is born

1912 John R. Bond of *Road & Track* magazine is born in Muncie, IN

1913 The Hupp Corporation, manufacturers of the R.C.H., is placed into receivership

R-C-H "Twenty-Five" 5-Passenger Touring Car

110-inch Wheel Base

1921 The Rickenbacker Motor Company is incorporated in Lansing, MI by Barney Everitt, William E. Metzger, and Walter E. Flanders, with its cars named for racer and World War I flying ace Eddie Rickenbacker, who had little actual input into the affairs of the business

1925 Automotive historian Jack Curtis Fox is born in Los Angeles, CA

1935 Racer Tony Lanfranchi is born in Great Britain

1936 Racer Gerry Ashmore is born in Great Britain

1945 Henry J. Kaiser and Joseph W. Frazer announce plans to form a corporation to manufacture automobiles following the conclusion of World War II

1947 The 1948 Packard Twenty-Second Series Super Eight and Custom Eight convertibles are introduced, the marque's first open-bodied cars of the post-World War II era

1948 Earl D. "Ed" Sirrine, former Sales Engineer for the Autocar Company, dies in Marianna, FL at age 61

1949 Edward Coverly Newcomb, a consultant to the Studebaker Corporation and a onetime associate of Henry M. Crane with the Simplex Automobile Company, dies in Boston, MA at age 77

1953 George L. Kelley, Massachusetts-born Deputy Chairman of the Pressed Steel Company, manufacturers of automobile bodies in Cowley, Oxfordshire, England, dies at age 74

1963 Karl K. Probst, designer of the original Jeep, dies in Dayton, OH at age 79

1969 Racer Guillaume Gomez is born in Orleans, Loiret, France

1983 William Balderston, a longtime executive of the Philco Corporation who was a leader in the automobile radio movement, dies at age 86

1991 George Hutchinson Love, Chairman of the Chrysler Corporation 1961-1966, dies in Pittsburgh, PA at age 90

JULY 26

1799 Isaac Babbitt, the inventor of Babbitt Metal, is born in Taunton, MA

1847 Moses G. Farmer of Dover, NH demonstrates his "electromagnetic locomotive", the ancestor of the electric automobile

1858 Peugeot Freres registers its "a lion with or without arrows" trademark, a logo widely used in later years on its automobiles

A young French girl poses proudly with her family's new Peugeot Model 401 in a snapshot dated July 14, 1934. An automobile manufacturer since 1889, the company remains in the control of the Peugeot family.

1875 Paul Weeks Litchfield, Chairman of Goodyear Tire & Rubber Company 1930-1958, is born in Boston, MA

1876 Sam Breadon, longtime Saint Louis, MO car dealer and owner of the St. Louis Cardinals major league baseball team, is born in New York City

1880 Arthur Grainger Hebb, manufacturer of the Patriot truck, is born in Vermont

1894 Rudolf Diesel announces the successful completion and testing of his kerosene engine

1894 William J. Muller, the principal designer of the front-wheel-drive Ruxton, is born in Port Morris, NY

1896 Sir Henry Ralph Stanley "Tim" Birkin, one of the "Bentley Boys" racing team, is born

1901 The Mack Brothers Company is incorporated in New York State

1903 Col. H. Nelson Jackson and his chauffeur Sewall K. Crocker arrive in New York City in their 2-cylinder Winton 63 days after leaving San Francisco, CA to complete the first trans-United States automobile trip - in 1944 Jackson would donate the car to the Smithsonian Institution in Washington, DC

1908 The German 40-hp Protos, driven by Lt. Hans Koeppen, Hans Knape and Ernest Maas, arrives in Paris, France as the first car to complete the New York to Paris race, but is penalized thirty days for being transported from Kelton, UT to Seattle, WA by train and refusing to go through Alaska

1913 Bob Burman, driving his Blitzen Benz in Vancouver, BC, establishes a Canadian record for the flying mile of 50.8 seconds in an exhibition sponsored by E. B. Conner of the Imperial Oil Company, Ltd.

1916 The Studebaker Series 18 is announced

1921 Jimmy Murphy in a Duesenberg wins the French Grand Prix in Le Mans to become the first United States citizen driving a United States-built car to win a major foreign race

1924 Alden L. McMurtry, a pioneer builder of steam and gasoline automobiles who was a founder of the Society of Automotive Engineers, dies in Greenwich, CT at age 47

1924 The last speed hillclimb at South Harting, England is staged

1925 Racer Antonio Ascari is killed at age 36 when his Alfa Romeo P2 crashes while leading the French Grand Prix at Montlhery

1926 Ernest C. Kanzler resigns from the Ford Motor Company six months to the day after his memo to Henry Ford recommended replacing the Ford Model T

1928 Racer Don Beauman is born in Great Britain

1928 Max Valier, formerly associated with Opel, tests his experimental rocket- powered car on railroad tracks near Steige, Germany - he had moderate success, but the car crashed on its third run

1930 The 1931 Buicks are introduced

1930 Victor Herbert Sussman of the Ford Motor Company is born in New York City

1932 Frederick S. Duesenberg dies in Johnstown, PA from injuries suffered in a July 2, 1932 automobile accident

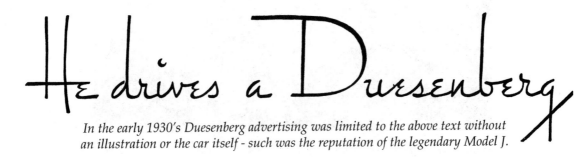

In the early 1930's Duesenberg advertising was limited to the above text without an illustration or the car itself - such was the reputation of the legendary Model J.

1937 Racer Ernst von Delius dies at age 27 from injuries suffered the previous day when his Auto Union crashed during the German Grand Prix at the Nurburgring

1942 Racer Teddy Pilette is born in Brussels, Belgium, the son of racer Andre Pilette

1945 The Kaiser-Frazer Corporation is organized with Henry J. Kaiser as Chairman of the Board and Joseph W. Frazer as President and General Manager

1946 Racer Emilio de Villota is born in Madrid, Spain

1952 Hubert K. Dalton, one of the designers of the original Chevrolet car in 1911 and later a manufacturer of automotive tools, dies in Honolulu, HI at age 86

1956 The Studebaker-Packard Corporation board approves the "Joint Program" with the Curtiss-Wright Corporation - James J. Nance and Paul G. Hoffman resign, and Harold E. Churchill is named as the corporation's new President

1958 J. Lansford McCloud, a retired Ford Motor Company executive and employee of the firm for 41 years, dies at age 66

1964 Francis Richard Henry Penn Curzon, a racer for Sunbeam and Talbot in the 1920's and later a member of Parliament, dies in Buckinghamshire at age 80

1969 Racer Leon Dernier is killed at age 57 when his Mazda R100 crashes during a race in Spa-Francorchamps, Belgium

1973 The 1,000,000th Chrysler is produced, a 1973 Newport 4-door sedan

1976 George Souders, winner of the 1927 Indianapolis 500, dies at age 73

1995 George W. Romney, Chairman of American Motors 1954-1962 and a former Governor of Michigan, dies in Bloomfield Hills, MI at age 88

JULY 27

1879 Milton E. Tibbetts, Patent Counsel and Vice President for the Packard Motor Car Company, is born in Washington, DC

1888 The Kimball electric tricycle, often cited as the first electric automobile built in the United States, is given its inaugural road test in Boston, MA - the car was built by Fred W. Kimball, but primarily designed by its owner, Philip W. Pratt

1893 Thomas Joseph Ross, a public relations consultant for the Chrysler Corporation, is born in Brooklyn, NY

1900 Dale Roeder of the Ford Motor Company is born in Lima, OH

1904 The first Buick is sold to Dr. Herbert H. Hills of Flint, MI according to contemporary journalist Hugh Dolnar, although most later references cite August 13, 1904 as the actual date of sale

1917 The first Ford Model T 1-ton truck is produced

1917 Henry Ford and Son Inc. is organized to produce the Fordson tractor

1919 William Herbert Davis of the British Motor Corporation is born in Birmingham, England

1925 The Ford Model T officially becomes a 1926 model

1928 The "last" 4-cylinder Dodge is produced, until the introduction of the sub-compact Omni in 1978

1932 Automobile historian Stephen W. Sears is born in Lakewood, OH

1933 Racer Chris Lawrence is born in Great Britain

1938 James K. Wagner, Ford Motor Company engineer and automotive historian, is born in Dover, OH

1938 Hupmobile and Graham acquire the dies, jigs, fixtures, and other assets of the bankrupt Auburn Automobile Company including spare body, fender, and frame stampings for the Cord 810/812 that would be used to produce the Hupmobile Skylark and Graham Hollywood

1947 Racer Jean Max is born in Marseille, France

1948 Woolf Barnato, winner of the 24 Hours of Le Mans in 1928, 1929, and 1930 in his only three entries in the race, and a Director of both Bentley Motors, Ltd. and Bentley Motors (1931) Ltd., dies at age 53 following a medical operation

1950 SAEIC is incorporated in France to produce the Ford-based JPW

1951 Clifton Hugh Carlisle, founder of the Goodyear Tire & Rubber Company of Canada Ltd., dies in Toronto, ON at age 81

1952 Les Leston driving a Cooper-Norton at Prescott (England) in his first hillclimb breaks the 500-cc record in three successive runs

1954 Racer Philippe Alliot is born in Voves, France

1954 Automotive parts manufacturer Walter S. Howard dies at age 67

1955 The 5,000,000th Oldsmobile is produced, a Holiday 4-door hardtop

1956 The Studebaker-Packard Corporation enters into a joint management agreement with the Curtiss-Wright Corporation

1961 L. L. Colbert resigns as President and Chairman of the Chrysler Corporation and is succeeded by Lynn A. Townsend

1969 Racer Moises Solana is killed at age 36 when his McLaren M6B crashes during the Valle de Bravo hillclimb in Mexico

1978 Benson Ford dies at age 59, suffering a heart attack while aboard his cruiser Onika on Lake Huron off the coast of Cheboygan, MI

1981 A 1917 Liberty Class B military truck is donated to the Smithsonian Institution by Paul W. Mowrey of Edina, MN

1987 The Ferrari F40 is introduced

1990 The last of over 7,000,000 Citroen 2CV "Deux Chevaux" is produced at the Mangualde, Portugal factory

1990 The Musee National de l'Automobile in Mulhouse, France unveils the "seventh" Bugatti Royale, a recreation of the Armand Esders roadster mounted on a chassis made largely from spare parts

1995 Gerhard Liener, Finance Director for Daimler-Benz AG, resigns

JULY 28

1873 Joseph Oriel Eaton, founder of the Torbensen Gear & Axle Company in 1911 and of the Eaton Axle & Spring Company in 1919, is born in Yonkers, NY

1883 Vittorio Valletta of Fiat is born in Sampierdarena, Genoa, Liguria, Italy

1891 Ransom E. Olds is issued a patent for a governor for steam engines, the first of his approximate 33 patents

1897 Warren Packard, father of William D. Packard and James W. Packard, dies at age 69

1897 Duesenberg enthusiast Jerry E. Gebby is born

1900 The 4-day Paris-Toulouse-Paris race is won by Pierre Levegh driving a Mors

1905 Clifford Earp driving a 90-hp Napier equals the land speed record of 104.53 mph at Blackpool Promenade, England

1906 The third Glidden Tour ends in Bretton Woods, NH and is won by Percy Pierce in a Pierce-Arrow

1908 The fifth Glidden Tour ends in Saratoga Springs, NY and is won by E. A. Renting in a Pierce-Arrow

1909 The Parry Automobile Company is organized in Indianapolis, IN by David M. Parry

1916 The Scripps-Booth Company is reorganized as the Scripps-Booth Corporation, partly to facilitate the acquisition of the Sterling Motor Car Company later in the year

1922 William C. Durant acquires a controlling interest in Locomobile

1927 The 1928 Buicks are introduced

1927 Racer Heini Walter is born in Ruti, Switzerland

1928 The Plymouth, named by Chrysler Sales Division Vice President Joseph W. Frazer, is introduced at Madison Square Garden in New York City

1929 The 1930 Buicks are introduced

1935 Racer Massimo Natili is born in Ronciglione, Viterbo, Latium, Italy

1938 Thomas John Wagner of the Ford Motor Company is born in Peoria, IL

1939 The last 1939 Studebaker Champion is produced

1941 The Richardson Pan-American Highway Expedition is completed when a modified 1941 Plymouth driven by Sullivan Richardson, Arnold Whitaker, and Kenneth C. Van Hee reaches Punta Arenas, Magallanes, Chile after an 8-month journey from Detroit, MI

1946 Racer Robert Mazaud is killed when his Maserati 4CL crashes during the 24 Hours of Le Mans (France) held this year only at Nantes, France - this was the first racing fatality in major post-World War II competition

1952 Racer Leon Malon dies in Le Havre, France at age 71

1955 The Chrysler Corporation Ltd. of Canada begins production of V-8 engines

1956 Racer Louis Hery is killed when his Panhard overturns during a race in Le Mans, France

1957 Jean Behra driving a BRM P25 wins the Grand Prix de Caen (France), the marque's first major racing victory

1961 Racer Yannick Dalmas is born in Le Beausset, Toulon, France

1963 Carl F. W. Borgward dies in Bremen, Germany at age 72

1968 Racer Chris Lambert is killed

1973 The "Bonnie & Clyde Death Car", a bullet-riddled 1934 Ford V-8 Sedan, is sold at auction for a record $175,000 to Peter Simon of Jean, NV

JULY 29

1891 John Lansford McCloud of the Ford Motor Company is born in Detroit, MI

1896 Horace E. Dodge marries Christina Anna Thompson in Windsor, ON, Canada

1898 Ellis S. Hoglund of General Motors is born in Chicago, IL

1899 Werner H. A. Gubitz of Packard is born in Hamburg, Germany

1899 The Automobile Company of America officially adopts "Locomobile" as its tradename

1902 Pierre de Caters breaks the 75 mph barrier

1908 Edgar Fosburgh Kaiser is born in Spokane, WA

1909 The Buick Motor Company acquires the Cadillac Motor Car Company for $4.5 million, the purchase actually being made on behalf of newly-formed General Motors

1912 Jesse G. Vincent joins the Packard Motor Car Company

1912 Harry M. Jewett succeeds Henry A. "Harry" Lozier Jr. as President of the Lozier Motor Company

1916 The Nash Motors Company is incorporated in Maryland as the successor to the Thomas B. Jeffery Company with James J. Storrow as Chairman and Charles W. Nash as President

1916 Samuel B. Stevens and four relief drivers arrive in San Francisco, CA in their Marmon 34, breaking the trans-United States record recently set by "Cannon Ball" Baker by forty-one hours

1919 Emlen S. Hare resigns as Vice President of the Packard Motor Car Company

1924 Racer Luigi Musso is born in Rome, Italy

1928 The 1929 Buicks are introduced

1928 The Mercedes-Benz SSK makes its racing debut as Rudolf Caracciola wins a hillclimb event at Gabelbach, Germany

1932 Racer Colin Davis is born in London, England, the son of racer and automotive journalist S. C. H. "Sammy" Davis

1945 Charles B. Raymond of the B. F. Goodrich Company dies at age 79

1946 Racer Stig Blomqvist is born in Lindesberg, Sweden

1950 Racer Joe Fry dies

1951 Racer Walt Brown dies in Williams Grove, NY at age 49

1952 LeRoy Spencer resigns as Executive Vice President of the Packard Motor Car Company and is appointed West Coast Manager for the firm

1953 The last 1953 Hudson is produced

1953 The Kaiser-Willys Sales Division of Kaiser Motors Corporation is established

1958 Herbert G. Freeston, Chief Engineer of Shell Research Ltd. England, dies at age 46

1969 William D. Singleton of the Ford Motor Company dies at age 61

1973 Racer Roger Williamson is killed at age 25 when his March-Cosworth crashes during the Dutch Grand Prix at Zandvoort

JULY 30

1828 Internal combustion engine pioneer Isaac de Rivaz dies at age 76

1863 Henry Ford is born in Springwells Township, MI

1876 A. J. Rowledge of Rolls-Royce is born in Peterborough, England

1887 Harry Carothers Wiess, a cofounder of the Humble Oil Company in 1917, is born in Beaumont, TX

1903 The Packard K Special race car is given its first road test in Warren, OH

1908 George Schuster arrives in Paris in the Thomas Flyer to win the New York to Paris Race having covered 13,341 miles - the German Protos had arrived four days earlier, but was penalized thirty days for rules violations

1909 The sixth Glidden Tour ends in Kansas City, MO and is won by W. S. Winchester in a Pierce-Arrow

1912 Jesse G. Vincent is named Chief Engineer of the Packard Motor Car Company

1923 Henry M. Crane is appointed Technical Assistant to the President of General Motors

1927 The 1928 Chandlers, featuring 25 different models, are introduced by Frederick C. Chandler

1928 The Chrysler Corporation purchases Dodge Brothers, Inc. from the New York City banking firm of Dillon, Read & Company for $170 million

1930 The Cadillac V-12 is introduced by division President Lawrence P. Fisher

1934 John N. Willys weds Mrs. Florence Dingler Dolan in his second marriage

1941 The last 1941 Pontiac is produced

This Streamliner Torpedo 4-door sedan clearing United States customs at Porthill, ID was one of 330,061 1941 Pontiacs produced.

1944 Racer Gerry Birrell is born in Glasgow, Scotland

1945 Pioneer automobile designer Frank Jaszkowiak dies at age 78

1946 Racer Neil Bonnett is born

1953 Racer Brett Riley is born in New Zealand

1967 Racer Ian Raby is injured when his Lotus crashes during a Formula 2 race in Zandvoort, the Netherlands - he would die November 7, 1967

1981 Racer Bud Tingelstad dies in Indianapolis, IN at age 53

1985 The Saturn Corporation announces that their factory will be built in Spring Hill, TN

1991 Racer Tommy Bridger dies in Aboyne, Aberdeenshire, Scotland at age 57

JULY 31

1886 Road map publisher Andrew McNally (Jr.) of Rand McNally & Company is born in Chicago, IL

1887 Raymond S. Pruitt, General Counsel of the Auburn Automobile Company, is born in Gettysburgh, Dakota Territory (now Gettysburg, SD)

1890 P. F. Olds & Son, Inc., manufacturers of gasoline engines, is established in Lansing, MI with Pliny F. Olds as President and Ransom E. Olds as Secretary, Treasurer, and General Manager

1894 Otto August Kuhler, pioneer motoring journalist and a designer of streamlined automobiles before World War I, is born in Reimscheid, Germany

1902 The Circuit des Ardennes staged near Bastogne, Belgium and often cited as the first true circuit race is won by Charles Jarrott in a Panhard et Levassor

1911 The Mason Motor Company is incorporated in Flint, MI by Arthur C. Mason, Charles Byrne, and Charles E. Wetherald to produce engines for the new Chevrolet Classic Six

1914 The Ford Motor Company announces a plan to return between $40 and $60 to each purchaser of a new Ford Model T should sales exceed 300,000 units during the following twelve months - this action is often cited as the industry's first rebate program

Model T Ford sales would indeed exceed 300,000 and Henry Ford's rebates would enhance his folkhero status. One of these cars was this touring used by two young couples in Lineville, IA.

1916 Pioneer female NASCAR racer Louise Smith is born

1918 Francis E. "Frank" Stanley is killed at age 69 in a car accident in Wenham, MA

1922 Wolfgang Klemperer publishes test results showing the advantages of Paul Jaray's aerodynamic automobile bodies

1923 The first prototype Chrysler, with styling by Oliver H. Clark, is completed

1923 Edson Poe Williams of the Ford Motor Company is born in Minneapolis, MN

1923 The Hercules Motors Company changes its name to the Hercules Motors Corporation

1928 Automotive journalist Leon Mandel is born in Chicago, IL

1936 The last 1936 Pontiac Deluxe Eight is produced

1938 The Alfa Romeo Tipo 158 makes its racing debut winning the first two places in the Coppa Ciano at Livorno, Italy

1948 Everett E. Richmond, an electrical engineer and tool designer for Locomobile who later was a designer of speed boats and submarines, dies in Wanamassa, NJ at age 64

1952 Gustaf Larson retires as Vice President and Director of Engineering for AB Volvo

1952 Ralph W. Gallagher, President of the Standard Oil Company of New Jersey, dies in New York City at age 71

1954 Onofre Marimon is killed at age 30 when his Maserati 250F crashes during a practice run for the German Grand Prix at the Nurburgring

1955 Edgar M. Clark of the Standard Oil Company of New Jersey dies in Phoenix, AZ at age 85

1957 A. J. Cunningham, President of James Cunningham & Son Company, Inc., manufacturers of the luxury Cunningham marque 1907-1936, dies in Rochester, NY at age 79

1969 Sherwood H. Egbert, President of the Studebaker-Packard Corporation 1961-1963 (Studebaker Corporation after 1962), dies in Los Angeles, CA at age 49

1971 David R. Scott and James B. Irwin drive the Lunar Roving Vehicle (LRV) 17.20 miles to the edge of Hadley Rille on the surface of the Moon, the first time that an "automobile" had been driven in an alien world

1972 Ferrari announces its withdrawal from racing

1972 The 1973 International trucks are introduced seventeen days after the introduction of the 1973 Scout II

1977 Stylist William L. Mitchell retires after 42 years with General Motors

1978 Volkswagen of America and the Volkswagen Manufacturing Corporation of America merge

1980 L'Ebe Bugatti dies in Milan, Italy at age 76, having spent the last years of her life working to ensure the legacy of her father Ettore Bugatti

1981 The last of 695,124 Chevrolet Corvettes is produced at the St. Louis, MO factory as production is transferred to the new plant in Bowling Green, KY

1984 Automotive historian Philip Van Doren Stern dies in Sarasota, FL at age age 83

1990 The first Saturn is produced and driven off the Spring Hill, TN assembly line by General Motors Chairman Roger B. Smith

1996 William Boddie succeeds Albert Caspers as Chairman of Ford-Werke AG

AUGUST 1

1871 Frederick Edwards Searle of the Henry Ford Trade School is born in Westfield, MA

1872 Gottlieb Daimler joins Deutz AG to work with Nikolaus A. Otto and Eugen Langen in the design and construction of gasoline engines

1878 Dugald Clark receives a British patent for his two-stroke engine

1879 Ralph A. Hankinson, a longtime race promoter and official with the American Automobile Association (AAA) and the International Motor Contest Association (IMCA), is born in Russell, KS

1894 Piston ring manufacturer Allen Waller Morton is born in Richmond, VA

1896 Edward Buddrus of the Phillips Petroleum Company is born in Kansas City, MO

1898 The National Motor Carriage Company is incorporated in New Jersey with Ernest E. Lorrilard as President, General O. O. Howard as Vice President, Arthur S. Winslow as Secretary, David Allen Reed as Treasurer, and J. W. Howard as Consulting Engineer

1900 Sidney A. Swensrud of the Standard Oil Company of Ohio is born in Northwood, IA

1902 Henry Clay Alexander, a Director of General Motors, is born in Murfreesboro, TN

1910 New York state-issued license plates are introduced

1911 William C. Durant registers a stylized "GMC" logo as the trademark of the General Motors Truck Company, organized to handle marketing for the Rapid and Reliance truck lines

1912 Masaya Hanai of Toyota is born

1913 Nesseldorf Technical Director Hugo von Roslerstamm resigns after a series of strikes had damaged the company's production capabilities

1914 The Monroe Motor Company is organized in Flint, MI by William C. Durant and R. F. Monroe of the Monroe Body Company in Pontiac, MI

1915 The Ford Motor Company announces that Model T sales for the previous twelve months were 308,213 units, and that they will honor their rebate offer by mailing $50 "Profit Sharing" checks to each buyer for a total payout of $15,410,650

1916 William C. Durant officially becomes President of General Motors, succeeding Charles W. Nash who had left two months earlier to form the Nash Motors Company

1917 The General Motors Corporation acquires the stock of the General Motors Company, dissolving the latter to become an "operating" company

1917 The Oakland Motor Car Company reorganizes as the Oakland Motor Division of the General Motors Corporation

1917 The Olds Motor Works becomes a division of General Motors rather than a separate company owned by General Motors

1919 The 1920 Winton Model 24 and Model 25 are introduced, the marque's first totally redesigned cars since 1916

1920 Duesenberg Brothers is organized to manage the racing activities of Frederick S. and August S. Duesenberg

1921 Durant Motors, Inc. purchases the Sheridan factory in Muncie, IN from General Motors

1923 The 1924 Buicks are introduced on "Buick Day", staged to commemorate the 25th anniversary of David D. Buick's Buick Auto-Vim and Power Company which would evolve into the Buick Motor Company in 1904

1923 The 1924 Chevrolets are introduced

1923 Alexander Y. Malcomson, Treasurer 1903-1906 and a cofounder of the Ford Motor Company, dies in Ann Arbor, MI at age 58

1924 The 1925 Nashes are introduced, featuring the marque's first four-wheel brakes

1925 The 1926 Buicks are introduced

This mid-1920's Buick dealership in Ovid, CO featured curbside
gasoline pumps - and a Model T Ford center door sedan!

1925 The 1926 Chevrolets are introduced

1925 The General Motors Research Corporation is relocated from Dayton, OH to Detroit, MI and reorganized as the Research Section, General Motors Corporation

1925 The Ford Motor Company acquires the Stout Metal Airplane Company

1926 The 1927 Nash Series 230 is introduced

1926 The 1927 Stars are introduced

1927 John Gray Smale of General Motors is born in Listowel, Ontario, Canada

1928 Packard introduces the Sixth Series Eight - production of the Fifth Series Six ends after a thirteen-month run, with 6-cylinder engines not reappearing in a Packard until the depression-inspired 110 of 1937

1929 The 1930 Chryslers are introduced

1929 The first prototype Ruxton front-wheel-drive car is completed

1930 Philip Patrick Crimmins, a metallurgical engineer with the Ford Motor Company 1954-1958, is born in Poughkeepsie, NY

1931 Stylist James S. McDaniel joins the General Motors Art and Colour Section

1933 The Terraplane DeLuxe Eights are introduced with extra features compared to the original 1933 Terraplanes, now marketed as Standard Eights

1934 Racer Robert Vance "Bobby" Isaac is born in Catawba, NC

1934 Automotive historian Lewis Herbert Carlson is born in Muskegon, MI

1935 The last Rolls-Royce Phantom II Continental is completed

1939 Clarence Reese is elected President of the Continental Motors Corporation

1944 Automotive journalist John George Dinkel is born in Brooklyn, NY

1947 Harold T. Youngren joins the Ford Motor Company

1948 Henry Austin Clark opens the Long Island Automotive Museum in Southampton, NY

1950 James F. Dewey, a labor mediator noted for his work in the 1946 General Motors strike, dies in Frackville, PA at age 63

1953 Ernst Loof, the pre-World War II German motorcycle racing champion who is best remembered as a designer for BMW and Veritas, makes his only Formula 1 appearance as a driver in the German Grand Prix at the Nurburgring, but his Veritas Meteor retires with a faulty fuel pump

1954 Hermann Lang makes his final racing appeareance, but his effort in the German Grand Prix at the Nurburgring ends in disappointment when his Mercedes-Benz W196 crashes while challenging for second place - in its only Formula 1 appearance, the Klenk Meteor, built by Hans Klenk based on the design of the pre-World War II BMW 328 and driven by Theo Helfrich, retires with engine troubles

1957 The first Volkswagen Karmann-Ghia convertible is produced

1959 Racer Jean Behra is killed at age 38 when his Porsche crashes during the Grand Prix of Berlin at Avus

1959 Racer Ivor Bueb is killed at age 36 when his Cooper-Borgward crashes during the Auvergne Trophy race at the Clermont Ferrand circuit

1961 Racer Allen Berg is born in Calgary, Alberta, Canada

1963 William L. Stewart Jr. of the Union Oil Company dies at age 66

1964 The first Ford Mustang 2+2 GT fastback coupe is produced

1966 The last Ferrari Superfast Type 500 is completed

1966 Prominent antique automobile collector William Brewster, best remembered for importing the Duesenberg SJ Gurney Nutting roadster from India, dies in Stonington, CT at age 51

J·GURNEY NUTTING&C0L͆

1968 The 1969 Jaguars are introduced to the United States market

1969 Gerhard Mitter, winner of the 1969 Targa Florio, is killed at age 33 when his BMW 269-4 crashes during a practice run at the Nurburgring circuit in Germany

1970 The International Scout 800B is introduced as a transitional model between the Scout 800A and the Scout II that would be introduced in March 1971

1971 Richard Petty becomes the first stock car racer to reach $1 million in career winnings

1974 Buick General Manager George R. Elges announces that the marque will reintroduce its V-6 engine for the 1975 model year

1974 The last 1974 International Scout II is produced

1977 Patricia Montgomery is named Cadillac's Director of Public Relations, the first woman to hold such a position in any General Motors division

1978 The financially stressed Automobili Ferruccio Lamborghini is placed under the "controlled administration" of Italian government official Alessandro Artese

1980 Racer Patrick Depailler is killed at age 35 when his Alfa Romeo 179 crashes during a practice run for the German Grand Prix at Hockenheim

1981 Fred A. MacArthur of Packard dies is Mount Clemens, MI at age 78

1990 Robert C. Stempel is elected Chairman of General Motors, replacing the retiring Roger B. Smith

AUGUST 2

1800 English inventor George Medhurst is issued a British patent for his "vehicle powered by compressed air"

1871 Automotive artist Frederick R. Gruger is born in Philadelphia, PA

1881 Giustino Cattaneo of Isotta-Fraschini is born in Caldogno, Italy

1898 The Llandudno Motor Touring Company begins bus excursions between Llandudno, Penmaenmawr, Bethesda, Penryhn, and Llanrwst, Wales

1900 Horace Elgin Dodge Jr. is born in Detroit, MI

1906 Andree Yvonne Odette Maya Jellinek-Mercedes, youngest child of Emil Jellinek-Mercedes, is born in Vienna, Austria - like her older sister, Mercedes, she became the namesake of an automobile, the Maja, designed by Ferdinand Porsche and manufactured by the Osterreichische Automobil- Gessellschaft in 1907-1908

1909 A Rapid truck reaches the summit of Pikes Peak, the first time that a commercial vehicle had successfully completed the trip

1911 A Saurer 4 1/2-ton truck arrives in New York City, completing a five- month odyssey throughout the United States - the company claimed this as the first trans-United States truck trip, although it was not a continuous run or done completely under its own power

1916 Enos Clough, builder of the 1869 Clough "Faerie Queen", is killed in an automobile accident in Laconia, NH at age 81

1917 A special Chalmers Speedster driven by Joe Dawson and Joe Gardham at the Sheepshead Bay Speedway in New York City completes a 24-hour run that set 15 speed and endurance records for stock cars

1922 Ganga Prasad Birla of Hindustan Motors Ltd. is born in Calcutta, India

1926 Packard discontinues the Second Series Eight and Third Series Six after an eighteen-month production run, replacing them with the Third Series Eight and Fourth Series Six

1931 The DeSoto 1932 "Goddess" mascot is patented by designer Herbert V. Henderson

1933 Constantine Stavros Nicandros of Conoco Inc. is born in Port Said, Egypt

1943 William Grover-Williams, a British secret agent who raced as "Williams", is arrested in France by the Gestapo - the two-time winner of the French Grand Prix would be executed in Paris later in the year

1944 General Motors Chairman Alfred P. Sloan Jr. announces that brothers Alfred J., Edward F., Lawrence P., and William A. Fisher have retired from the corporation

1944 Pierre Schon, an design engineer with GMC 1914-1940, dies at age 64

1945 Yoshito Hirahara of Toyota is killed in Tokyo, Japan during a bombing raid

1949 Racer John Winter (nee Louis Krages) is born in Bremen, Germany

1950 The Ford Motor Company creates the Defense Products Division to handle government contracts related to Korean War materiel

1950 George W. Rumford of the Chrysler Corporation dies in Detroit, MI at age 68

1953 Hans Herrmann makes his major racing debut, finishing ninth in the German Grand Prix at the Nurburgring in his privately owned Veritas Meteor - the EMW, manufactured in Eisenach, DDR and based largely on the pre-World War II BMW Type 328, makes its only Formula 1 appearance, but Edgar Barth retires with exhaust problems

1964 Honda makes its Formula 1 debut in the German Grand Prix at the Nurburgring, with Ronnie Bucknum driving the Model RA270 V-12 to a 13th-place finish

1965 The first 1966 Ford Thunderbird is produced

1971 The 1972 Mercedes-Benz models are introduced to the United States market

1976 Monroe J. Rathbone, Chairman of the Exxon Corporation, dies in Baton Rouge, LA at age 76

1985 The 100,000th Rolls-Royce is produced, a royal blue Silver Spur sedan

1990 Stunt driver Sven-Erik Soderman, driving an Opel Kadett at Mora, Sweden, sets a world's record by reaching 102.14 mph while driving the car on two side wheels

1996 The 100,000th Toyota Corolla is produced by the Toyota Motor Philippines Corporation

AUGUST 3

1888 Dr. Benjamin F. Goodrich dies in Manitou Springs, CO at age 46

1899 Racer Louis Alexandre Chiron is born in Monte Carlo, Monaco

1900 The Firestone Tire & Rubber Company is organized in Akron, OH with James Christy Jr. as President, James A. Swinehart as Vice President, Louis E. Sisler as Secretary, and Harvey S. Firestone as Treasurer and General Manager

1909 The Waltham Manufacturing Company reorganizes as the Metz Company with John Robbins as President and Charles J. Spiegelberg as Treasurer - company namesake Charles H. Metz was a major shareholder and would succeed Robbins as President within a few months

1917 The original General Motors Company founded as a New Jersey firm in 1908 is legally dissolved after all of its stock had been acquired by the newly formed General Motors Corporation

1922 Francis James McDonald of General Motors is born in Saginaw, MI

1924 Alfa Romeo, appearing in its first major race outside Italy, becomes the first marque to win in its initial grand prix event as Giuseppe Campari wins the French Grand Prix in Lyon - the Bugatti Type 35 also makes its racing debut in this event

1928 The rocket-powered Opel RAK 4 explodes during a test on railroad tracks near Hannover, Germany and local authorities forbid any more testing with the already-completed RAK 5

1937 Michael A. Leonard of the Chrysler Corporation is born in Cadillac, MI

1938 Samuel L. Davis is elected President of Hupmobile

1938 The last race is held at Brooklands ending the 32-year history of the famous English circuit

1941 Gasoline rationing begins in parts of the eastern United States

1947 John Randolph Rines of General Motors is born in Baltimore, MD

1952 The Mercedes-Benz 300SL sweeps the first four places in the German Grand Prix at the Nurburgring - BMW makes its Formula 1 debut, but cars driven by Marcel Balsa and Bernd Nacke are forced to retire - the Greifzu, based on the pre-World War II BMW 328 by designer Paul Greifzu, makes its only Formula 1 appearance, but the car driven by Rudolf Krause is forced to retire - the Heck, also based on the BMW 328 by designer and driver Ernst Klodwig, makes its debut but is forced to retire

1955 The American Automobile Association abolishes its Contest Board, leaving United States car racing without a governing body

1958 Racer Kurt Thiim is born in Vojens, Denmark

1958 Racer Peter Collins is killed at age 26 when his Ferrari Dino crashes during the German Grand Prix at the Nurburgring

1963 Henry Ford II and Anne McDonnell Ford separate

1964 The first 1965 Ford Thunderbird is produced

1964 Racer Carel de Beaufort dies at age 30 three days after his Porsche had crashed at the Nurburgring circuit during a practice run for the German Grand Prix

1990 The Nissan Motor Company, Ltd. and Siam Motors Company, Ltd. sign a joint venture agreement designed to double Nissan production in Thailand over the next two years

AUGUST 4

1858 Arthur Lovett Garford of Garford and Studebaker is born in Elyria, OH

1872 Col. James Wadsworth Furlow, Deputy Chief of the Motor Transport for the United States Army during World War I, is born in Americus, GA

1877 Nikolaus A. Otto is issued German patent #532 for his four-stroke engine

1884 James W. Packard graduates from Lehigh University in Bethlehem, PA with a Bachelor of Science degree in Mechanical Engineering

1894 Thomas Holden White of the White Motor Company is born in Cleveland, OH

1897 L. Z. Morris Strauss, a director of the Studebaker Corporation, is born in Charleston, WV

1898 William D. Packard is taken for a demonstration ride in a Winton automobile by company representative George L. Weiss

1900 Internal-combustion pioneer Jean Lenoir dies in Varenne-St. Hilaire, France at age 78

1917 John Cooper Fitch, race car driver and designer, is born in Indianapolis, IN

1922 Horace E. Rice, Assistant to the President of the American Bosch Magneto Corporation, is killed at age 39 when his automobile is struck by a train in Oxford, PA

1923 The American LaFrance Fire Engine Company of Elmira, NY registers it stylized name with Maltese Cross logo as a trademark

1925 Noel Westwood and G. L. Davies, driving a Citroen 5CV, begin the first circumnavigation of Australia by automobile

1928 The DeSoto is formally introduced by the Chrysler Corporation as a new marque

1928 Racer Christian Goethals is born in Belgium

1934 Racer Joseph Paul "Joe" Leonard is born in San Diego, CA

1935 Dietrich, Inc. suspends production of custom bodies

1936 The last 1936 Pontiac Deluxe Six is produced

1936 Racer Claude Ballot-Lena is born in Paris, France

1937 E. L. Cord sells his holdings in the Cord Corporation

1940 Alex McLean Warren Jr. of Toyota Motor Mfg. USA is born in Augusta, GA

1941 The last Ford Model T engine is produced

1941 The third experimental Highway Post Office begins service between San Francisco and Pacific Grove, CA using a specially-built Mack bus

1952 Harry H. Hooker, Assistant Chief Engineer of the Eaton Manufacturing Company and an authority on the manufacture and design of axles, dies at age 58

1955 William J. Cameron of the Ford Motor Company of Canada, Ltd. dies in Oakland, CA at age 76

1957 Juan Manuel Fangio wins the German Grand Prix at the Nurburgring in a Maserati 250F for the last of his twenty-four Formula 1 Grand Prix victories and the last Formula 1 win for the marque - this win clinched his fifth and last World Champion Driver title, at age 46 the oldest person to accomplish this feat

1959 Alfred R. Glancy of Oakland and General Motors dies at age 78

1967 Racer Niclas Jonsson is born in Sweden

1971 Racer Jeff Gordon is born in Vallejo, CA

1976 Eugene M. "Gino" Caraffa, an Abingdon, MD classic car dealer, is found murdered in Staten Island, NY

1983 Tony Hogg, car enthusiast and Editor-in-Chief of *Road & Track* magazine 1979-1983, dies from a heart attack at age 58

AUGUST 5

1873 Frederick Winning Hassard-Short of the British Automobile Association is born

1882 The Standard Oil Company of New Jersey is organized

1885 Albert Sobey of the General Motors Institute is born in Hancock, MI

1899 The Detroit Automobile Company is organized with Clarence A. Black as President, Albert E. F. White as Vice President, William H. Murphy as Secretary, and Frank R. Alderman as Treasurer - the Mechanical Superintendent (and also a Director) was Henry Ford

1902 William K. Vanderbilt Jr., driving a 60-hp Mors at Ablis, France, raises the land speed record to 76.08 mph, the first time that the record had been set by a gasoline-powered vehicle and the first time that it was held by a United States citizen

1907 Racer Roger Loyer is born in France

1910 Robert Douglas Reinhardt of General Motors is born in Boston, MA

1914 The first electric traffic signal is installed in Cleveland, OH at the corner of Euclid Avenue and 105th Street

1920 The assets of the Little Motor Kar Company, Fort Worth, TX, manufacturers of the Texmobile, are ordered to be sold at auction

1924 The Ford Motor Company begins public tours of its Rouge plant

1930 Racer Paul Richard "Richie" Ginther is born in Hollywood, CA

1935 Oliver Bertram, driving the Barnato-Hassan Special, sets the alltime Brooklands record for Class B (under 8000 cc) of 142.60 mph

1940 Sherrod E. Skinner is elected General Manager of Oldsmobile

1942 The Marmon-Herrington Company, Inc. names Arthur W. Herrington as Chairman, Bert Dingley as President, and William B. Nottingham as Secretary

1943 Racer Leo Juhani Kinnunen is born in Tampere, Finland

1947 Ferdinand Porsche is released from prison, having been held as a suspected Nazi collaborater by United States and French occupation authorities in the aftermath of World War II

1951 Amedee Gordini's supercharged Simca-Gordini makes its racing debut with Maurice Trintignant winning the Albi Grand Prix

1953 The first 1954 Hudson is produced

1953 The Classic Car Club of America holds their first CARavan at the Packard Proving Grounds in Utica, MI

1955 The 1,000,000th Volkswagen, a standard sedan painted gold to commemorate the occasion, is produced

1956 Cadillac announces the purchase of Hudson's Detroit facilities

1962 The Brabham Formula 1 race car makes its debut in the German Grand Prix at the Nurburgring, but the Type BT3 driven by namesake Jack Brabham is forced to retire - the ENB, built in Brussels, Belgium by Paul Emery and driven by Lucien Bianchi makes its only Formula 1 appearance and finishes 16th

1963 Craig Breedlove, driving the 3-wheel turbojet-powered Spirit of America, raises the land speed record to 407.45 mph at the Bonneville Salt Flats, UT

1968 The last 1968 Pontiac is produced

1970 Racer Jerry Titus dies at age 41 from injuries suffered a month earlier at Road America in Elkhart Lake, WI

1971 Racer Patrick Crinelli is born in Italy

1973 Jackie Stewart wins the Dutch Grand Prix at Zandvoort in a Tyrrell- Cosworth, his 27th and last Grand Prix victory

1974 The Ford Guest Center opens to the public

1987 Chrysler Corporation purchases the American Motors Corporation from Renault, recreating it as the Jeep-Eagle Division of Chrysler

1991 Soichiro Honda, founder in 1948 and President until 1973 of the Honda Motor Company Ltd. and the firm's Supreme Advisor 1973-1991, dies in Tokyo, Japan at age 84

AUGUST 6

1788 James Brewster, founder of the carriage building firm that would evolve into the 20th-century manufacturer of automobiles and custom coachwork, is born in Preston, CT

1861 John Kenrick Fisher is issued a patent for a steam-powered fire engine

1875 Jujiro Matsuda, founder of the Toyo Kogyo Company, Ltd. that has manufactured the Mazda automobile since 1960, is born near Hiroshima, Japan

1887 Racer John Dudley Benjafield is born in London, England

1891 George C. Reifel of Packard is born in West Unity, OH

1897 Chad F. Calhoun of Kaiser and Willys is born in Springfield, NE

1903 United Automobile Workers official Douglas Alan Strachan is born in London, England

1904 Barney Oldfield joins the Peerless Motor Car Company and makes his first appearance in the Peerless Green Dragon race car in a series of match races at the Canadian National Exhibition track in Toronto, ON, the first major racing event staged in Canada

1906 The Mechanical Branch of the Association of Licensed Automobile Manufacturers adopts their first standard specifications covering screws, nuts, and bolts

1907 The Imperial Motor Car Company is founded in Jackson, MI by brothers Theodore A. and George N. Campbell, producing cars until 1916

Sporting a 1913 Wisconsin license plate, this 1911 Imperial was a good value during its eight year lifespan. It was unrelated to the later luxury marque manufactured by the Chrysler Corporation.

1913 The Michigan Buggy Company of Kalamazoo, MI, manufacturers since 1911 of the Michigan, is forced into bankruptcy

1928 Hyundai Motor Company cofounder Chung Se Yung is born in Asan, Tongcho, Kangwon Province, Korea

1929 Glenn Andrew Cox Jr. of the Phillips Petroleum Company is born in Sedalia, MO

1935 Ab Jenkins, driving the Duesenberg Special at the Bonneville Salt Flats, UT, sets a Class B super-stock record by covering 153.96 miles in one hour

1935 Mrs. Gwenda Stewart, driving a Derby-Miller, sets the alltime Brooklands record for Class E (under 2000 cc) of 135.95 mph

1947 Paul W. Gaebelein of the Chrysler Corporation dies in Pasadena, CA at age 59

1953 Peter Lambertus, President of the American Bearing Company, dies at age 66

1956 The Curtiss-Wright Corporation signs an agreement to provide management advisory services to the Studebaker-Packard Corporation for three years

1956 Alvin Carr McCord, an inventor of devices for both automobiles and railways, dies in Detroit, MI at age 88

1959 The Chevrolet Division of General Motors registers the "Corvair" name as a trademark - the name had first been used for a Corvette-based one-off show car, but was now earmarked for the division's new and soon to be controversial rear-engined compact car

the happiest driving compact car
corvair
by Chevrolet

Corvair 700 5-Passenger Club Coupe

1959 Daryl F. Lemaux, Assistant Experimental Engineer with the Truck & Coach Division of General Motors, dies at age 57

1961 Earle C. Anthony, the longtime Packard dealer in California and a director of the Packard Motor Car Company, dies in San Francisco at age 80

1967 Traffic safety specialist Norman C. Damon dies at age 69

1968 Giovanni Bracco, winner of the 1952 Mille Miglia, dies at age 60

1973 The first 1974 International Scout II is produced

1976 The first national meet of the Cadillac-LaSalle Club begins on the grounds of the Indianapolis (IN) Motor Speedway

1980 The first Chrysler Corporation "K" car, a Plymouth Reliant, is produced at the Jefferson Assembly Plant in Detroit, MI

1983 The 153 vintage cars and trucks from the estate of Charles N. Harris are sold at auction in Cape Girardeau, MO

1984 Fernand Vadier of Ballot dies

1991 Peugeot SA announces their withdrawal from the United States market

1994 NASCAR debuts at the Indianapolis Motor Speedway as Jeff Gordon wins the inaugural Brickyard 400 in a Chevrolet

1996 The Toyota Motor Corporation announces that it will construct a Toyota Corolla manufacturing plant in Indaiatuba, Sao Paulo, Brazil

AUGUST 7

1876 William Guy Wall of National is born in Baltimore, MD

1885 Burt John Craig of the Ford Motor Company is born in Detroit, MI

1897 Frank William Jenks of the International Harvester Company is born in Richmond, VA

1906 The Cadillac crest is granted registered trademark status

1909 Alice Huyler Ramsey arrives in San Francisco, CA in her Maxwell Model 30, completing the first trans-United States automobile trip by a woman driver

1912 Jakob Knudsen Jakobsen, a staff engineer involved in the design of the Chrysler turbine engine 1955-1960, is born in Bording Sogn, Denmark

1915 Dario Resta, driving a Peugeot, wins the 100-mile Chicago Cup Challenge Race at the Maywood Board Speedway in Chicago, IL averaging 101.86 mph, the first time that 100 mph barrier had been attained in the United States for a race of this length

1915 The Des Moines (IA) Board Speedway opens with a 300-mile race won by Ralph Mulford in a Duesenberg at 87.00 mph

1919 The Continental Motors Corporation produces its first type 7-R 6-cylinder engine

THE COAT OF ARMS OF ANTOINE DE LA MOTHE CADILLAC WHO FOUNDED IN 1701, UNDER COMMISSION FROM LOUIS XIV, THE COLONY ON THE SITE WHERE NOW STANDS THE CITY OF DETROIT.

THE TYPE 53 CADILLAC CAR IS DISTINGUISHED BY THIS COAT OF ARMS MOUNTED UPON ITS RADIATOR.

A view of the Continental Motors Corporation factory in Detroit, MI - Continental produced its own car, actually a disguised DeVaux, only in 1933-1934, but manufactured engines for other marques for many years. The type 7-R engine was used by Auburn, Case, Jordan, Moon, and Velie plus several minor marques.

1922 The Barley, named for Albert C. Barley of the Roamer Motor Car Company, is introduced in Kalamazoo, MI

1925 The Shell Company of Canada Ltd. is incorporated

1926 The second series Hudson Super Sixes are introduced

1926 The first British Grand Prix is staged at Brooklands - the winners are Robert Senechal and Louis Wagner driving an 8-cylinder Delage 15S8

1927 The last Dodge Convertible Cabriolet is produced as the sporty car is discontinued less than four months after its introduction

1927 Giulio Ramponi competes in his first major racing event, finishing third in the Cuneo-Colle della Maddelena Hillclimb in an Alfa Romeo

1927 Arden Ramon Haynes of the Imperial Oil Company, Ltd. is born in Saskatchewan, Canada

1928 The Pierce-Arrow Motor Car Company is reorganized as a subsidiary of the Studebaker Corporation, with A. Russell Erksine of Studebaker named as Chairman of the Board and Myron E. Forbes continuing as President

1930 The 2,000,000th 6-cylinder Chevrolet is produced

1934 The Klausen Hillclimb in Switzerland is won by Louis Chiron in a 4.9-litre Bugatt Bugatti, the first four-wheel-drive car to compete in a hillclimb

1935 The 1,000,000th 1935 General Motors vehicle, a Chevrolet, is produced

1935 John Cobb's Napier-Railton, holder of the alltime lap record at Brooklands, makes its initial appearance in the Byfleet Lightning Short Handicap

1937 The Auburn Automobile Company produces its last car, a 1937 Cord

1938 Stylist Giorgetto Giugiaro is born in Cuneo, Italy

1938 The Alfa Romeo Type 158 race car makes its racing debut at Livorno

1939 The last races are held at Brooklands - the Third August Outer-Circuit Handicap is won by G. L. Baker in a Graham-Paige, the Mountain Handicap is won by band leader Billy Cotton in an E.R.A., and the Campbell Circuit Race is won by Raymond Mays in an E.R.A.

1940 Charles D. Hastings, an executive with the Olds Motor Works 1902-1908 and the Hupp Motor Car Corporation 1908/1935, dies in Detroit, MI at age 81

1944 Racer Dave Morgan is born in Shepton Mallet, Somerset, England

1945 Longtime General Motors executives Alfred P. Sloan Jr. and Charles F. Kettering establish the Sloan-Kettering Institute in New York City to conduct medical research

1947 Ferdinand Porsche approves the final design for the Cisitalia Grand Prix race car just two days after being released from prison

1951 Ernest S. Cowie, and inventor of automotive electrical equipment, dies in Kansas City, MO at age 73

1956 Mack Trucks, Inc. purchases the Brockway Motor Truck Corporation of Cortland, NY

1956 Tire manufacturer Piero Pirelli dies in Milan, Italy at age 75

1957 Neil H. McElroy, President of the Proctor & Gamble Company and a Director of the Chrysler Corporation, is nominated as Secretary of Defense by President Dwight D. Eisenhower

1960 Milivoj Bozic, personal chauffeur for Marshal Josip Broz Tito of Yugoslavia, competes in the Freiburg (Germany) Hillclimb and places ninth in a Porsche

1971 Joseph W. Frazer dies in Newport, RI at age 79

AUGUST 8

1874 Henry Edward Bodman, General Counsel for the Packard Motor Car Company 1924-1952 and a Director of same 1917-1948, is born in Toledo, OH

1877 August Frykman is born in Torsby, Sweden

1903 The Packard Model L completes a 1,000 mile trial at Grosse Pointe, MI

1904 Racer Achille Varzi is born in Galliate, Italy

1904 The Peerless Green Dragon becomes the first car to exceed 60 mph in Canada

1907 The Rolls-Royce Silver Ghost completes a 15,000 Miles Official Trial

1912 Leonard Dyer establishes the Enterprise Automobile Company in Hoboken, NJ to manage his various automotive patents

1913 Henry John Nave of the White Motor Company is born in Attica, IN

1919 Gray-Dort Motors Ltd. of Chatham, ON, Canada absorbs the Gray-Campbell Company to obtain additional production capacity

1919 The Hispano-Suiza "Stork" mascot is patented by designer F. Bazin

1926 Racer Gaston Andrey is born in Switzerland

1926 Racer Piero Drogo is born in Vignale Monferrato, Venezuela

1932 Roy D. Chapin, Chairman of the Hudson Motor Car Company, is sworn in as Secretary of Commerce in the administration of United States President Herbert Hoover

1934 The 1,000,000th Plymouth, a DeLuxe 4-Door Sedan, is produced - Mrs. Ethel Miller of Turlock, CA, who had purchased the first Plymouth in 1928 and still owned it, drove her car to the Century of Progress Exposition in Chicago, IL where she exchanged it for the newer milestone car

1935 Doc MacKenzie clinches the Eastern AAA racing title by winning the 50-mile feature in Langhorne, PA

1938 Mrs. Walter P. (Della V. Forker) Chrysler dies

1938 The Ford Motor Company registers "Ford-Mercury" and "Mercury" as trademarks - at the time it was unclear if their new car would be a distinct marque or simply an upscale Ford

A circa-1940 business card notes that Midtown Motors in San Francisco, CA handled Ford, Lincoln-Zephyr, and the new Mercury. Van Ness Avenue is still the center of automobile sales in the city by the bay.

1939 Darrell L. Davis, Chrysler Corporation executive and United States distributor of the Alfa Romeo 1988-1991, is born in Sharon, PA

1939 The Packard Eighteenth Series 110, Super Eight 160, and Custon Super Eight 180 are introduced

1939 The last Packard V-12 is produced

1939 The first 1940 Plymouth is produced

This 1940 Plymouth 4-door sedan served the authorities at the
White Sands National Monument in southern New Mexico.

1939 Raymond Mays breaks the lap record for the Campbell circuit at Brooklands in England, reaching 77.79 mph in his E.R.A.

1943 A. C. Hoof, founder in 1932 and President of Hoof Products Company, a manufacturer of automotive engine governors, dies in Hinsdale, IL at age 55

1944 Racer Robert Benoist, an active member of the French underground, is deported to Germany by his Gestapo captors

1946 Edward Thomas Schafer, Governor of North Dakota 1992-date whose various business ventures include a collectible car dealership, is born in Bismarck, ND

1947 Ewald K. Schadt of Cadillac dies

1949 The 1949 Buick Special, exhibiting most of the 1950 styling features, is introduced to challenge lower-priced competitors

1954 Racer Nigel Mansell is born in Upton-on-Severn, Worcestershire, England

1955 Racer Michael Roe is born in Ireland

1957 Ernest L. Maxim, founder and Chairman of the Board of the Maxim Motor Company, dies at age 71

1957 Frank Gregory Stewart, President of the Standard Automobile Supply Company and a cofounder and first President of Automobile Old Timers, dies at age 71

1959 Racer Charles Prince is killed at age 35 during a race in Xenia, OH

1959 The 39-day-old Plymouth-DeSoto Division of the Chrysler Corporation is renamed the Plymouth-DeSoto-Valiant Division to herald the impending arrival of the new compact Valiant, at first marketed as a new marque

1962 The last 1962 Ford Thunderbird is produced

1963 Charles T. Fisher of the Fisher Body Division of General Motors dies in Detroit, MI at age 83

1963 Racer Masahiko Kageyama is born in Japan

1975 SA Andre Citroen sells the Officine Alfieri Maserati SpA to the Italian government

1975 The last Fiat 500 is produced

1980 The first Chrysler Corporation "K-car", a 1981 Plymouth Reliant, is driven off the assembly line by Chairman Lee Iacocca

1982 Racer Eric Brandon, the 1952 British Formula 3 champion, dies at age 62

1986 The last episode of the televsion show *Knight Rider* airs featuring a Pontiac Firebird with fictional capabilities

1989 Racer Brian Naylor dies in Marbella, Spain at age 66

1991 James B. Irwin, a United States astronaut who drove the Lunar Roving Vehicle on the surface of the Moon in 1971, dies at age 61

1995 Oldsmobile historian Dennis Casteele dies at age 49

AUGUST 9

1871 Carl Benz & August Ritter Mechanische Werkstatte is founded in Mannheim, Germany, the first business venture of Carl Benz

1874 Horace Tucker Thomas of Oldsmobile and Reo is born in Newbury, VT

1888 David Bullock Harris of the Humble Oil and Refining Company is born in Dallas, TX

1894 Robert Elliott of the Ford Motor Company is born in Troy, TX

1896 Sir Bernard Dudley Frank Docker, a British businessman known for his numerous one-off custom Daimlers, is born

1900 The Paige automobile built by Edison W. Paige is driven from Batavia to Rochester, NY

1901 The Irish Automobile Club sponsors the first rally in Ireland as twelve automobiles attempt an organized journey from Dublin to Waterford

1906 Nello Ugolini of Maserati and Ferrari is born in Vignola, Italy

1910 Automotive design engineer Frank J. Olender is born in Buffalo, NY

1912 The Sterling Motor Company is incorporated by William C. Durant, J. Dallas Dort, Curtis R. Hatheway, Edwin R. Campbell, and Fred A. Aldrich as part of the corporate web created with the Chevrolet Motor Car Company

1916 Barney Oldfield sets ten non-competitive speed records from 1-mile to 50-miles at the St. Louis (MO) Dirt Track driving the Miller "Golden Submarine" special

1918 United States automobile production is ordered to halt by January 1, 1919 and convert to military production - the World War I armistice signed on November 11, 1918 would allow the order to be lifted

1925 Racer Len Sutton is born in Aims, OR

1926 Joseph McElroy Dunn of Paccar, Inc. is born in Toledo, OH

1926 Joseph W. Eskridge joins the Hudson Motor Car Company

1931 Enzo Ferrari competes in his last automobile race driving an Alfa Romeo 8C2300 to a second-place finish behind Tazio Nuvolari in the Circuito delle Tre Province

1944 The Soviet State Defense Committee approves construction of the Minsk (Byellorussian SSR) Automotive Plant - production of MAZ trucks would begin in 1946

1944 Racer Patrick Depailler is born in Clermont-Ferrand, France

1945 The Kaiser-Frazer Corporation is incorporated in Nevada with Henry J. Kaiser as Chairman of the Board and Joseph W. Frazer as President

1948 Norman John Stewart of General Motors of Canada Ltd. is born in Toronto, ON

1954 The 1,000,000th Buick hardtop, a 1955 Century 4-door Riviera, is produced

1956 David Abbot "Ab" Jenkins Jr., Mayor of Salt Lake City, UT 1939-1943 and a holder of many marathon driving records, dies in Milwaukee, WI at age 73

1959 Racer Werner Kuehn is killed during a race at the Hanseatenring near Rostock, DDR

1962 The Chrysler Corporation announces that its 1963 cars and trucks will carry a 5-year, 50,000-mile warranty

1963 Racer Alain Menu is born in Geneva, Switzerland

1967 Vittorio Valletta of Fiat dies at age 84

1968 William P. Lear announces that he will invest $10,000,000 to develop a steam automobile that he will have on the market within 15 months

1968 Charles P. Fiske of the General Motors Acceptance Corporation dies at age 76

1982 Robert S. Olson of the Ford Motor Credit Company dies at age 69

1984 Jaguar Cars Ltd. of Coventry, England is separated from government-owned British Leyland Ltd. and privatized with John Egan remaining as Chairman

1990 Al Unser Jr. sets a world's record for a 500-mile race in winning the Michigan 500 at an average speed of 189.727 mph

1991 The Rover Group PLC, manufacturers of the Sterling, withdraws from the United States market

1992 Edward E. Brewer, President and Chairman of the Board of the Cooper Tire & Rubber Company 1977-1982 and an employee of the firm since 1949, dies at age 67

When Edward E. Brewer began his 33-year career with the Cooper Tire & Rubber Company, dealers' envelopes displayed the firm's orange oval logo.

AUGUST 10

1882 The Standard Oil Company of New York is incorporated under the laws of New York state

1897 The Automobile Club of Great Britain and Ireland (ACGBI) is founded by C. Harrington Moore and Frederick R. Simms, and holds its first meeting at Whitehall Court in London - the club evolved into the Royal Automobile Club (RAC), and is the oldest existing automobile club in the world

1898 Racer Frederick Hollis Wells is born in Newark, NJ

1904 The first Glidden Tour ends in St Louis, MO and is won by tour sponsor Charles J. Glidden in his Napier

1905 Automobile parts manufacturer William Joseph Joyce Jr. is born in Columbus, OH

1907 Prince Scipione Borghese wins the Peking-Paris Rally, arriving in Paris in his 40-hp Itala exactly two months after the race began and 21 days ahead of his nearest competitors

1909 Col. Albert A. Pope, President of the Pope Manufacturing Company 1877/1907, dies in Cohasset, MA at age 66

1910 Racer Guy Mairesse is born in La Capelle, Aisne, France

1911 Stanley James Gillen of the Ford Motor Company is born in Toledo, OH

1913 President Woodrow Wilson, a strong supporter of improved roads, purchases Membership Certificate No. 1 in the Lincoln Highway Association

1913 Paul Arthur Miller of General Motors is born in Buffalo, NY

1915 Racer Carlos Alberto Menditeguy is born in Buenos Aires, Argentina

1927 Edsel B. Ford officially announces that "a new Ford automobile is an accomplished fact", referring to the pending replacement of the Model T with the Model A

1928 Gerino Gerini, winner of the 1958 Mille Miglia and designer of the A.S.A., is born in Rome, Italy

1931 Bruce Ford, holder of more than 50 patents relating to automotive batteries, dies in Philadelphia, PA at age 58

1932 The first British Ford Model Y is produced by the Ford Motor Company, Ltd.

1935 The Packard Fourteenth Series Eight, Super Eight, and Twelve are introduced (per common superstition, there was no Thirteenth Series)

1937 C. C. McConville, Superintendent of the Four Wheel Drive Auto Company, dies in Clintonville, WI at age 63

1938 J. E. Crane is elected Treasurer of the Standard Oil Company of New Jersey

1940 The last Alexandria Bay (NY) Round the Houses race is won by Alfa Romeo

1944 Frederick C. Kroeger, a Vice President of General Motors, dies at age 56

1946 The first major post-World War II race is held in the British Isles - the Ulster Trophy race at Ballyclare, Northern Ireland, is won by B. Bira in the E.R.A. R3B known as "Romulus"

1947 Ford Motor Company of Canada, Ltd. Chairman Wallace R. Campbell dies in Windsor, ON at age 65

1948 Goliath-Werke GmbH is founded in Bremen, Germany by Carl F. W. Borgward

1949 Thomas P. Archer of General Motors dies in Detroit, MI at age 64

1953 Racer Tazio Nuvolari dies in Mantua, Italy at age 60

1953 Louis M. Klinedinst, retired Vice President of the Timken Roller Bearing Company, dies at age 70

1961 The last 1961 Ford Thunderbird is produced

1966 Racer Eric Helary is born in Paris, France

1968 Torkild Rieber, Chairman of The Texas Company (Texaco) 1935-1940, dies at age 86

1969 Lamonte J. Belnap, President of Rolls-Royce of America, Inc. 1920-1923, dies at age 92

1970 The first 1971 Pontiac is produced

1978 Chrysler Corporation announces plans to sell its entire European operations to PSA Peugeot-Citroen for $426 million

1985 The FWD Corporation stages a 75th anniversary celebration in Clintonville, WI

1986 Automotive historian Lyle K. Engel dies in Miami, FL of leukemia at age 71

1986 The Hungarian Grand Prix, the first such race held behind the Iron Curtain, is won by Nelson Piquet in a Williams-Honda

AUGUST 11

1871 Clement Studebaker Jr. is born in South Bend, IN

1891 Automobile pioneer John S. Connelly is granted a United States patent for his "Gas Motor"

1896 H. Ivan F. Evernden of Rolls-Royce is born

1896 Ransom E. Olds tests his first gasoline-powered automobile in Lansing, MI - the body for the vehicle was designed and built by Olds' friend Frank G. Clark

1916 Racer Johnny Claes is born in Fulham, England of Belgian ancestry

1923 The Ford Motor Company plant for glass manufacturing goes into operation

1927 J. Sheppard Smalley, owner 1909-1915 of the Smalley Auto Company in Muscatine, IA, is killed at age 42 in a train accident near Buffalo, NY

1931 Leonard Allen Haba of Paccar, Inc. is born in Carrington, ND

1931 Ferdinand Porsche applies for German patent for his torsion-bar suspension

1932 Ray A. Graham of Graham-Paige drowns in Chatham, ON, Canada at age 45

1938 The 1939 Studebaker Commanders and State Presidents are introduced

1939 Jean Bugatti is killed at age 30 during a road test of the Type 57C Bugatti "Tank" race car used by Jean-Pierre Wimille earlier that year in winning the 24-Hours of Le Mans (France)

1940 Stanley P. Rockwell, an authority on automotive metallurgy, is killed at age 54 when his yacht explodes while cruising in Long Island Sound

1945 Henry C. McCaslin joins the Kaiser-Frazer Corporation as Chief Engineer

1946 The Buick Super convertible is introduced

1951 The 4,000,000th Pontiac is produced, a Catalina hardtop coupe

1955 The 500,000th 1955 Pontiac, a Star Chief Custom Safari two-door Station Wagon, is produced and presented to Professor Amos E. Neyhart, a pioneer in developing high school driver education programs

1955 Frank A. Seiberling, President of the Goodyear Tire & Rubber Company 1898-1921, President and founder of the Seiberling Tire & Rubber Company 1921-1938 and its Chairman 1938-1950, dies in Akron, OH at age 95

1955 John Clifford Pope of the Ethyl Gasoline Corporation dies at age 55

1959 E. R. Carolin, Sales Manager of the Kelsey-Hayes Company, dies at age 50

1964 John J. Schumann Jr., President of the General Motors Acceptance Corporation 1929-1954, dies in Madison, WI at age 74

1965 The Ford Bronco, a 4-wheel-drive sports utility truck, is introduced

1966 The first Chevrolet Camaro, a 1967 coupe, is produced at the Norwood, OH plant

1967 Dr. J. William Haddon is confirmed as Director of the National Highway Safety Bureau

1968 Charles E. Sorensen of the Ford Motor Company dies in Bethesda, MD at age 86

1972 The Chicago Historical Antique Automobile Museum opens to the public

1975 British Leyland Motors, Inc. is nationalized and renamed British Leyland Ltd.

1980 The Ford Motor Company produces the first "World Car", a 1981 Ford Escort, at its Fort Wayne, IN factory - local UAW leader John Barson drives the car off the assembly line

1980 The Chrysler Corporation revives the Imperial marque after a five-year lapse as Frank Sinatra drives a 1981 metallic silver coupe off the assembly line in Windsor, ON, Canada

1984 Racer Marcel Balsa dies at age 75

1987 Ford stylist Eugene "Gene" Bordinat (Jr.) dies at age 67

1991 Racer John Delphus "J. D." McDuffie is killed at age 52 when he crashes during a NASCAR race in Watkins Glen, NY

AUGUST 12

1854 Louis Mendelssohn of the Fisher Body Company is born in Germany

1878 The George N. Pierce Company is founded in Buffalo, NY

1882 Vincent Hugo Bendix is born in Moline, IL

Vincent H. Bendix, the inventor of four-wheel brakes, organized the Bendix Corporation in 1924 and was its first President. This advertisement dates from 1926.

1882 Edward James Cutler of the Ford Motor Company is born in London, ON, Canada

1901 An 1899 Locomobile steamer driven by Charles A. Yont and W. B. Felker completes the first automobile trip to the summit of Pikes Peak, CO

1902 The International Harvester Company is organized

1905 The first Shelsley Walsh speed hillclimb is staged in Worcestershire, England under the sponsorship of the Midlands Automobile Club and is won by E. M. C. Instone in a 35-hp Daimler

1914 Teddy Tetzlaff driving the "Blitzen" Benz covers a flying mile at 142.85 mph at the Bonneville Salt Flats, UT

1916 The first Pikes Peak, CO hillclimb, staged to celebrate the completion of the new road to the summit built by Spencer Penrose, is won by Rea Lentz in a Romano Eagle

1933 Racer Rufus Parnell "Parnelli" Jones is born in Texarkana, AR

1940 Charles W. Matheson of Matheson, Dodge, Oakland, and Pontiac is killed at age 64 in an automobile accident in Brodhead, WI

1947 The first Renault 4CV is produced - all first-year cars were painted desert-sand yellow, using a paint supply captured with the fall of Gen. Erwin Rommel's Afrika Korps

1952 George W. Stephens, Chairman of the Mansfield Tire & Rubber Company, dies age 72

1952 James E. Hurn, holder of many patents concerning automotive oil filters, dies at age 49

1953 Fire badly damages the General Motors Hydra-Matic transmission plant in Livonia, MI

1954 The Hudson Motors Division of American Motors announces that the Hudson Itala is in limited production

1962 Eugene Holman of the Standard Oil Company of New Jersey dies in New York City at age 67

1963 The first 1964 Ford Thunderbird is produced

1971 The first 1972 Pontiac is produced

1981 Isuzu, Suzuki, and General Motors sign an agreement in Tokyo, Japan to share information on the development of small four-wheeled vehicles

1985 Racer Manfred Winkelhock is critically injured when his Porsche crashes during a 1000 km race at Mosport Park, ON, Canada, and dies at age 32 later that day in a Toronto hospital

AUGUST 13

1861 Elmer Apperson is born near Kokomo, IN

1866 Giovanni Agnelli, the founder of Fiat, is born in Villar Perosa, Italy

1872 Claude Strait Briggs, founder of the Briggs-Detroiter Company, is born in Battle Creek, MI

1873 Arthur Henry Hoffman, a college professor and authority on automotive air cleaners, carburetors, and oil filters, is born in Washington, IA

1876 Harry C. Beaver of Stevens-Duryea and Rolls-Royce of America, Inc. is born in McAllisterville, PA

1884 Charles E. Duryea marries Rachel Steer

1898 James W. Packard purchases Winton automobile #12 - dissatifaction with the car would lead to the building of his own car and the founding of the Packard Motor Car Company

1902 Felix Wankel, rotary engine developer, is born in Lahr, Germany

1904 The first production Buick is sold to Dr. Herbert H. Hills of Flint, MI

1912 Tom Lilley of the Ford Motor Company is born in Bluefield, WV

1918 The Bayerische Motoren-Werke GmbH is restructured as the Bayerische Motoren-Werke AG, with Camillo Castiglioni as principal investor

1920 The Hilton Four, named for founder Hilton W. Sofield, is introduced by the Motor Sales & Service Corporation of Riverton, NJ - production ended in 1921 after the factory had been destroyed by fire

1925 A. B. C. Hardy of General Motors retires due to ill health

1926 Howard P. Freers of the Ford Motor Company is born

1928 Fernand Charron, winner of the first Gordon Bennett, dies at age 62

1930 Tom Hans Barrett of the Goodyear Tire & Rubber Company is born in Topeka, KS

1935 The Moon Motor Car Company plant in St. Louis, MO is sold to the Cupples Company for use as a wooden match factory

1936 Automobile parts manufacturer Richard Allen Heise is born in Chicago, IL

1936 Frederick S. Fish of Studebaker dies in South Bend, IN at age 84

1936 The Ford Motor Company's soy bean plastics factory begins operations

1938 Lee R. Raymond of the Exxon Corporation is born in Watertown, SD

1940 Racer Jean-Claude Andruet is born in France

1946 Racer Divina Galica is born in Malmesbury, Wiltshire, England

1951 William F. Kenny of the Chrysler Corporation dies in Stroudsburg, PA at age 83

1952 Racer Dan Marvin is born in the United States

1954 The last 1954 Plymouth is produced

1955 Racer Hideo Fukuyama is born in Owase, Japan

1971 Racer Patrick Carpentier is born in Ville Lasalle, PQ, Canada

1971 W. O. Bentley dies in Woking, Surrey, England at age 82

1989 Racer Tim Richmond dies in Miami, FL at age 34 from AIDS

AUGUST 14

1865 Walter Lorenzo Marr of Buick is born in Lexington, MI

1877 Nikolaus A. Otto is issued a United States patent for his "Gas-Motor Engine" ten days after receiving a German patent for the same - his design defined the modern four-stroke internal-combustion engine

1885 Hon. Sir Edward Wheewall Holden is born in Adelaide, South Australia

1893 The world's first automobile license plates are issued in Paris, France

1901 The Ellis & Turner Company of Peoria, IL completes a 600-mile test run in their Duryea-inspired prototype

1902 Max von Duttenhofer, a cofounder of the Daimler Motoren Gesellschaft, dies and is succeeded in his top management position by Wilhelm Korenz

1909 Lew Schwitzer, driving a Stoddard-Dayton Model 9H, wins the first speed event at the Indianapolis Motor Speedway

1911 Hickman Price Jr. of Graham-Paige, Kaiser, Frazer, and Willys is born in Nashville, TN

1918 Ford historian James Brough is born in London, England

1921 The first race held at the Cotati Speedway in Santa Rosa, CA, a 150-mile event, is won by Eddie Hearne in a Duesenberg-Distil

1922 Racer Leslie Marr is born in Durham, Durhamshire, England

1922 Journalist Lord Northcliffe (nee A. C. W. Harmsworth), famous for coining the Rolls-Royce slogan "The Best Car In The World", dies in London at age 57

ROLLS-ROYCE
THE BEST CAR IN THE WORLD

1922 John Lloyd Chadwick of the Champion Home Builders Company, manufacturers of recreational vehicles and motor homes, is born in Windsor, Ontario, Canada

1930 The Packard Eighth Series Eight is introduced

1935 The last new United States-built Rolls-Royce Phantom I is delivered to Mrs. M. S. Morrow of Whitestone, NY

1937 Ball bearing manufacturer George Robert Bott dies near New Canaan, CT at age 58

1942 Racer Jack Keith Oliver is born in Chaswell Heath, Romford, Essex, England

1946 Racer Tom Walkinshaw is born in Mauldslie, Scotland

1948 George C. "Chet" Collins, Fleet Sales Manager for Thompson Products Inc. and an authority on the maintenance of heavy-duty trucks and buses, dies in Columbus, OH at age 51

1952 Stanwood W. Sparrow, Vice President of Engineering for the Studebaker Corporation, dies

1953 Magnus M. Burgess, an official of the C. R. Wilson Body Company and the Murray Corporation, dies at age 56

1956 Racer Rusty Wallace is born in Fenton, MO

1956 Racer Jacques Isler is born in Zurich, Switzerland

1957 H. Jay Hayes, often credited with building the first all-metal automobile body in 1898, dies in Forest Hills, NY at age 88

1958 Steam car historian John H. Bacon is killed at age 35 in an airplane crash over the North Atlantic Ocean

1962 A 1963 Studebaker Avanti driven by Andy Granatelli at the Bonneville Salt Flats, UT sets 29 national stock car records

1967 Racer Bob Anderson is killed at age 36 in Silverstone, England while testing his Brabham-Climax for the upcoming first Canadian Grand Prix

1974 The Twentieth Century Motor Car Company is incorporated in Nevada to manufacture the 3-wheeled Dale - the company, along with its transexual Chief Executive Officer G. Elizabeth Carmichael (nee Jerry Dean Michael), would collapse within months under allegations of fraud

1977 Racer Bobby Isaac dies in Hickory, NC at age 43

1977 Michael F. Widman Jr., leader of the campaign to unionize the Ford Motor Company, dies in Silver Spring, MD at age 77

1977 Alan Jones wins the Austrian Grand Prix driving a Shadow-Cosworth DN8A, the only Formula 1 victory for the marque

1977 The Singapore Airlines London-Sydney Rally, the longest such event ever held, begins in London, England

1980 The Buick foundry in Flint, MI is phased out

1988 Enzo Ferrari dies in Modena, Italy at age 90

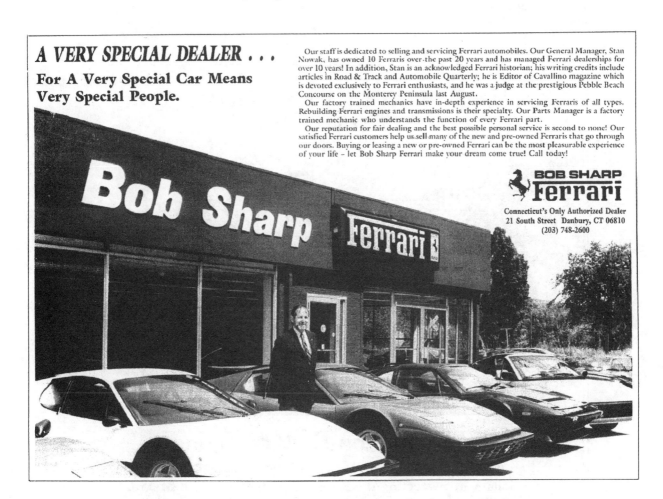

AUGUST 15

1883 Wilhelm Kurtz of Stuttgart, Germany completes the world's first light, high-speed gasoline engine for designer Gottlieb Daimler

1884 Pioneer racer Guy W. Vaughan, an official of the Desberon Motor Company of New Rochelle, NY, the designer of the 1909 Vaughan car in Kingston, NY, and a longtime associate of Frank B. Stearns and the Stearns-Knight, is born in Bayshore, Long Island, NY

1888 Paul Waldo Seiler of GMC is born in Hudson, IN

1892 Charles Robert Musgrave of the Phillips Petroleum Company is born in Sedan, KS

1893 Harlow Herbert Curtice of Buick and General Motors is born in Petrieville, MI

1899 Henry Ford resigns as Chief Engineer of the Edison Illuminating Company in Detroit, MI to concentrate on automobile production

1901 Warren Homer Martin of the United Auto Workers is born in Goreville, IL

1905 Racer Manfred von Brauchitsch is born in Hamburg, Germany

1912 The F. B. Stearns Company announces the discontinuance of its poppet-valve Model 30-60, with all future production to be called Stearns-Knight featuring the Charles Y. Knight-designed sleeve-valve engine

1917 Charles L. Nedoma of the Chalmers Motor Corporation joins the Cadillac Motor Car Company as Secretary to the Chief Engineer

1922 Bernard Allen Weisberger, a biographer of William C. Durant, is born in Hudson, NY

1927 Edward V. Rickenbacker purchases the Indianapolis (IN) Motor Speedway from Carl G. Fisher and James A. Allison for about $700,000

1928 The Studebaker Corporation and the Pierce-Arrow Motor Car Company agree to a merger

1929 The DeSoto Model K is officially designated a 1930 model

1934 Guy Moll, winner of the 1934 Monaco Grand Prix, is killed at age 24 when his Alfa Romeo P3 crashes during the Coppa Acerbo voiturette race in Pescara, Italy

1936 The first Alexandria Bay (NY) Round the Houses race is staged

1938 Nicola Romeo dies in Magreglio, Italy at age 62

1939 Rene Dreyfus in a Delahaye wins the "Million Franc" challenge run at the Montlhery (France) circuit beating a Bugatti and a Sefac

1941 Robert Stevens "Steve" Miller, Jr. of the Chrysler Corporation is born in Portland, OR

1941 Racer Colin Bond is born in Australia

1945 World War II gasoline rationing ends in the United States

1947 Ferrari makes its racing debut finishing second in a race at Pescara, Italy

1949 E. P. Horton, founder of the Automotive Gear Works of Richmond, IN, manufacturers of the Double Diamond transmission, diffentials, and axles, dies in Greenwich, CT at age 86

1949 Stylist Gordon M. Buehrig joins the Ford Motor Company

1956 Roy H. Faulkner of Oakland, Nash, Auburn, Studebaker, and Pierce-Arrow dies at age 70

1956 51 days after producing its last car, Packard's Conner Avenue plant in Detroit, MI closes with all activity shifting to the Studebaker factory in South Bend, IN

1957 The 1958 Willys CJ, Jeeps, and pickup trucks are introduced

1957 Racer Per-Gunnar "Peggan" Andersson is born in Falkenberg, Sweden

1961 The first 1962 Pontiac is produced

1962 The Michigan Rivet Corporation relocates from Detroit, MI to Warren, MI

1962 The 1963 Hillmans are introduced to the United States market

1964 The Fiat 1100D sedan is introduced to the United States market

1970 Herbert M. Dawley of Pierce-Arrow dies at age 90

1973 Gary Davis, creator of the 1948 Davis three-wheel car, dies in Palm Springs, CA at age 68

1976 John Watson wins the Austrian Grand Prix driving a Penske PC4, the first and only Formula 1 victory for the marque

AUGUST 16

1831 Bearing manufacturer Henry H. Timken is born in Bremen, Germany

TIMKEN
Tapered
ROLLER BEARINGS

1873 John Edgar Johnson of the Warner Gear Company is born in Ashtabula, OH

1889 Herbert Edward Smith of the United States Rubber Company is born in San Jose, CA

1904 The R. E. Olds Company, builders of Reo cars and trucks, incorporates in Lansing, MI with Ransom E. Olds as President and General Manager, Reuben Shettler as Vice President, and Edward F. Peer as Secretary and Treasurer

1906 The first production Mason, financed by Edward R. Mason and designed by Frederick S. Duesenberg, is completed at the Mason Motor Car Company factory in Des Moines, IA

1908 Racer George Connor is born in San Bernardino, CA

1908 George Schuster, winner of the New York to Paris Race, is honored in a parade in New York City

1921 Henry Innes, a Canadian who manufactured the Innes 1920-1921 in Jacksonville, FL, dies at age 46

1923 The Alfa Romeo P1 race car is given its first speed test with Antonio Ascari reaching 112 mph

1925 Edward Y. Davidson Jr., Illuminating Engineer for the Macbeth-Evans Glass Company of Charleroi, PA, dies in Chicago, IL at age 27

1934 Master modeler Gerald Wingrove is born in Loudwater, Buckingham, England

1937 G. A. Schreiber, a consulting engineer whose automotive career included stints with Adler, Daimler, Spyker, E-M-F, Paige, Willys-Overland, GMC, and White, dies at age 56 from injuries suffered when struck by an automobile on July 21

1937 Joseph C. Halbleib, inventor with his brother Edward C. Halbleib of an improved electric starter-generator, dies at age 58

1938 Roque Edward Lipford of the Monroe Auto Equipment Company is born in Monroe, MI

1947 Racer Giancarlo Martini is born in Lavezzola, Italy

1948 Samuel W. Rushmore, holder of more than 80 patents related to automotive cooling systems, dies in Plainfield, NJ at age 77

1958 Charles B. Van Dusen, son-in-law of David D. Buick and a cofounder of the Automobile Club of Michigan, dies at age 87

1968 Racer Yvan Muller is born in France

1970 The Bellasi makes it Formula 1 debut in the Austrian Grand Prix, but the car designed by Vittorio Bellasi and driven by Silvio Moser is forced to retire with radiator problems

1983 Automobile advertising pioneer Ross Roy dies in Grosse Pointe Shores, MI at age 85

1984 John Z. DeLorean's drug trafficking trial ends with a not guilty verdict

1985 The last episode of the television show *The Dukes of Hazzard* airs

1993 Racer Rene Dreyfus dies in New York City at age 88

AUGUST 17

1863 Byron J. Carter of Cartercar is born near Jackson, MI

1867 Everett Welles Frazar, an import-export consultant who represented Henry Ford in Japan, is born in Shanghai, China

1884 Arthur Brock Newhall of the Hood Rubber Company is born in Lynn, MA

1885 Automobile historian St. John Cousins Nixon is born in Beckenham, Kent, England

1889 Ronald Krake Evans of General Motors is born in Big Rapids, MI

1890 Ralph R. Teetor, President of the Perfect Circle Company and the inventor of cruise control, is born in Hagerstown, IN

1894 Sir William Edward Rootes is born in Kent county, England

1896 Arthur James Edsell, demonstrating a Roger-Benz at the Crystal Palace in London, runs over and kills Mrs. Bridget Driscoll resulting in the first motoring fatality in Great Britain

1903 C. Kenneth Baxter, Chairman and President of the Deep Rock Oil Company of Tulsa, OK, is born in Lafayette, IN

1904 The Ford Motor Company of Canada Ltd. is established near Windsor, ON

1904 Ralph Murray Buzard of the International Harvester Corporation is born in Greenwich, OH

1909 Road map publisher Andrew McNally 3rd of Rand McNally & Company is born in Chicago, IL

1913 Racer Oscar Galvez is born in Buenos Aires, Argentina

1915 Charles F. Kettering receives the first of two United States patents for an "Engine Starting Device", the first successful automobile self-starter

1925 The stockholders of the Yellow Cab Manufacturing Company approve a merger of their firm with General Motors

1937 The last 1937 Pontiac Deluxe Six is produced

1938 Racer Francis McNamara is born in Galesburg, IL

1939 Automotive historian Beverly Rae Kimes is born in Aurora, IL

1945 Racer Peter Brock is born in Australia

1950 John S. Dempsey, President of the Buda Company, dies at age 59

Chief Pontiac in silhouette as used in the late 1930's.

1952 Racer Nelson Piquet is born in Rio de Janeiro, Brazil

1952 The E.R.A. makes its final Formula 1 appearance in the Dutch Grand Prix at Zandvoort, but the G Type designed by David Hodkin and driven by Stirling Moss is forced to retire - the Frazer-Nash also makes its final appearance, but the Model 421, patterned on the pre-World War II BMW 328 by designer H. J. Aldington and driven by Ken Wharton, retires with transmission problems

1954 Stockholders of both corporations approve the plan for the Packard Motor Car Company to purchase the Studebaker Corporation

1955 The 1956 Jeep pickup trucks are introduced

1956 The 6,000,000th Pontiac is produced, a 1956 Star Chief Custom Catalina

1957 Orville Harden, Vice President of the Standard Oil Company of New Jersey, dies at age 63

1962 John H. Watson Jr., a longtime director of the White Motor Company and the Studebaker Corporation, dies at age 78

1966 Racer Ken Miles is killed at age 47 when his Ford J-car racing prototype crashes during a test run at the Riverside (CA) International Raceway

1969 The Porsche 917 makes its racing debut, with Jo Siffert competing in the Can-Am Mid-Ohio race in Lexington, OH without success

1975 Racer DeWayne "Tiny" Lund is killed at age 45 during the Talladega 500 in Talladega, AL

1976 Jensen closes its doors after 42 years although production of the Interceptor would soon resume on a limited basis

1985 Racer Niki Lauda announces his retirement

1994 Luigi Chinetti, racer, exotic car dealer, and promoter closely associated with the Ferrari marque, dies at age 93

AUGUST 18

1883 Abram vanderZee of the Chrysler Corporation is born in Jersey City, NJ

1884 Henri Toutee of Chenard-Walcker is born in Bleneau, Burgundy, France

1894 Lucius Bass Manning, a securities trader closely linked with the career of E. L. Cord, is born in Tacoma, WA

1905 Attorney Newell S. Wright files an application to register the Cadillac crest as a trademark

1927 Racer John Rhodes is born in Wolverhampton, Staffordshire, England

1929 Racer Jimmy Davies is born in Glendale, CA

1934 Racer Michael May is born in Stuttgart, Germany of Swiss ancestry - following a 1961 accident during a practice run at the Nurburgring circuit in Germany he was affiliated with both Porsche and Ferrari in the development of improved fuel injection systems

1936 Norval Hawkins, General Sales Manager of the Ford Motor Company 1907-1919 and later a General Motors consultant, dies in Detroit, MI at age 69

Ten cars line up in Lusk, MY in 1914 - eight are Model T Fords,
a tribute to General Sales Manager Norval Hawkins.

1937 Brewster & Company, formerly Rolls-Royce of America, Inc., is liquidated by owner Dallas E. Winslow

1937 The Toyota Motor Company, Ltd. is established by separating the automotive department from the parent Toyoda Automatic Loom Works

1938 Arnold N. Taylor, Chief Engineer of the C. M. Hall Lamp Company and an authority on automotive lighting equipment, dies in Detroit, MI at age 45

1939 Robert Baynes Horton of the British Petroleum Company PLC is born in Bushey, England

1940 Walter P. Chrysler dies of cancer at age 65 in Great Neck, Long Island, NY

1944 Racer Larry McCoy is born

1945 The first post-World War II speed event in England is staged on a 1/2-mile grass and earth course at Naish House, near Portishead

1957 The first and only Pescara (Italy) Grand Prix is won by Stirling Moss in a Vanwall - 46-year old Juan Manuel Fangio, driving for Maserati finishes second and clinches his fifth and final World Champion Driver title in Formula 1 to become the oldest racer to accomplish this feat

1959 The last 1959 Pontiac is produced

1963 Jim Clark driving a Lotus-Ford wins the 200-mile USAC race at the Milwaukee Speedway in West Allis, WI - this was the first major United States race won by a rear-engined car

1966 Frank Jay, former President of the Stanley Motor Carriage Company, dies in Newton, MA at age 91

1967 Racer Uwe Alzen is born in Germany

1968 Clessie L. Cummins, founder of the Cummins Engine Company and an early proponent of diesel engines, dies in Sausalito, CA at age 79

1973 Race car engine designer Fred Offenhauser dies at age 85

AUGUST 19

1887 Francis Wright Davis, a Pierce-Arrow design engineer and the inventor of power steering, is born in Germantown, PA

1887 Lloyd L. Smith of the B. F. Goodrich Company is born in Copley, OH

1897 The London Electric Cab Company begins the first motorized taxicab service in Great Britain utilizing a fleet of Bersey electrics

1909 The first automobile races are held at Indianapolis (IN) Motor Speedway - William A. Bourque and his riding mechanic Harry Holcomb, both from Springfield, MA, are killed during the 250-mile stripped-chassis contest, the fifth event of the day

1912 The E. R. Thomas Motor Car Company is placed into receivership

1912 Smith Hempstone Oliver, Curator of Land Transportation for the Smithsonian Institution 1946-1956, a cofounder of the Veteran Motor Car Club, and a prolific automotive journalist, is born in Newport, RI

1916 Racer Dennis Poore is born in London, England

1922 Andre Pierre Jacques Benard of Royal Dutch/Shell Group is born in Draveil, Essone, France

1926 Racer Johnny Boyd is born

1933 The first All-American Soap Box Derby is held in Akron, OH

1935 The 1936 Buicks are unveiled to national field service personnel, with a few cars released for promotional drives throughout the country

1939 Sam W. Hardee, Vice President of the Universal Motor Oils Company, dies at age 30 from injuries suffered in an automobile accident

1942 Racer Raymond Marvin "Ray" Elder is born in Caruthers, CA

1946 Count Albert de Dion dies in Paris, France at age 90

1954 Racer Oscar "Poppy" Larrauri is born in Rosario, Argentina

1958 The Studebaker-Packard Corporation announces that they are dropping the Packard marque, and introducing the compact Studebaker Lark

1959 Great Britain makes its first conviction for speeding as a result of police use of radar

1972 Frederick E. Searle of the Henry Ford Trade School dies in Farmington, MI at age 101

1974 Wifredo P. Ricart of Alfa Romeo and Pegaso dies at age 77

1975 Racer Mark Donohue dies at age 38 in Graz, Austria from injuries sustained two days earlier when his March-Cosworth crashed during a practice run for the Austrian Grand Prix at the Osterreichring in Zeltweg

1985 Robert E. "Bob" Barber, driving the "Steamin' Demon" built by James D. Crank of Redwood City, CA, raises the steam car land speed record to 145.607 mph at the Bonneville Salt Flats, UT, breaking the record held by Fred Marriott's Stanley since 1906

AUGUST 20

1885 Nils Erik Wahlberg of Nash is born in Finland of Swedish parents

1890 Soviet automobile engineer Evgenii Alekseevich Chudakov is born in Sergievskoe, Russia

1902 Alexander Y. Malcomson, a Detroit, MI coal dealer and friend of Henry Ford, agrees to a partnership with Ford for the purpose of building a prototype automobile that would attract other investors

1904 Charles Ellsworth Nelson of the Waukesha Motor Company is born in Waukesha, WI

1910 The Great Chadwick Six sets a world's record for ten miles covering the distance in 8 minutes, 23 seconds

1912 Racer Bob Swanson is born in Minneapolis, MN

1921 Paul Ferdinand Hartz of the Fram Corporation is born in Denmark

1924 Automobile parts manufacturers Oscar A. Smith and Edwin C. Henn are killed when their car is struck by a train near Painesville, OH

1928 Alan H. Leamy's basic design for Duesenberg Model J sheetmetal is approved by management

1929 Bradfield Motors, Inc. of Chicago, IL registers its trademark - the Kissel-based luxury taxicab manufacturer founded by H. C. Bradfield would cease production in 1931 with the demise of its chassis supplier

1929 The Packard Seventh Series 740 and 745 are introduced

1930 Rene Cozette, a design engineer with Sizaire-Berwick who later invented the Cozette carburetor and supercharger, is killed at age 34 when he crashed during a test run at the Montlhery circuit in France

1937 The last 1937 Pontiac Deluxe Eight is produced

1938 James L. Dunlap of Texaco Canada Inc. is born in Bakersfield, CA

1938 Racer Bill Winn is killed when he crashes during a race in Springfield, IL

1941 Stefano Iacoponi of Alfa Romeo is born in Cascina, Italy

1941 Automotive journalist Patrick Joseph Bedard is born in Waterloo, IA

1942 Harry Jonathan Pearce of General Motors is born in Bismarck, ND

1945 The first post-World War II Chevrolet truck for civilian use is produced

1945 George H. Coulson, an employee of Mercer before beginning a successful career in the automotive parts business, dies

1946 World War II civilian truck restrictions are lifted in the United States

1954 Plymouth officially drops its Hy-Drive semi-automatic transmission

1954 George H. Taber Jr. of the Sinclair Refining Company dies at age 64

1954 Racer Osami Nakako is born in Japan

1956 Plans are announced to continue the Packard marque as a badge-engineered Studebaker for the 1957 model year

1957 Thelma Chrysler Foy, daughter of Walter P. Chrysler and wife of former DeSoto executive Byron C. Foy, dies in New York City

1962 The first 1963 Ford Thunderbird is produced

1991 Mazda Motor Corporation announces that they will enter the luxury car market in 1994 with the Amati

1992 Doug McCombs of Spokane, WA driving the Endeavor III, a modified International truck powered by a Detroit Diesel V-12 engine, at the Bonneville Salt Flats, UT sets a land speed record of 223.084 mph for diesel-powered trucks

AUGUST 21

1754 Steam-powered vehicle pioneer William Murdock is born at Bellow Mill, near Old Cumnock, Scotland

1881 Edouard Marcel Sandoz, a sculptor and designer of automobile mascots, is born in Basel, Switzerland

1883 Automobile frame manufacturer Lloyd Raymond Smith is born in Chicago, IL

1885 Robert Cabel Graham is born in Washington, IN

1885 William Francis O'Neil of the General Tire & Rubber Company is born in Akron, OH

1887 Paul Whitefield Gaebelein of the Chrysler Corporation is born in Hoboken, NJ

1897 The Olds Motor Vehicle Company, the first automobile manufacturer in Michigan, is organized with principal investor Edward W. Sparrow elected as President, Eugene F. Cooley as Vice President, Arthur C. Stebbins as Secretary, and Ranson E. Olds as Treasurer and General Manager

1900 The first Pierce steam vehicle is tested without success - subsequent problems led the company to abandon steam power in favor of gasoline

1903 Tom Fetch & Marius C. Krarup arrive in New York City in the Packard Model F "Old Pacific", completing the second trans-United States automobile trip

1904 Automotive restoration authority Richard Charles Wheatley is born in Handsworth, Birmingham, England

1913 Racer Fred Agabashian is born in Modesto, CA

1914 Automobile parts manufacturer Robert Earl Valk is born in Muskegon, MI

1916 The Fisher Body Corporation is established by merging the assets of the Fisher Body Company, Fisher Closed Body Company, and Fisher Body Company of Canada Ltd.

1926 Donald Ferris Kopka of the Ford Motor Company is born in Lansing, MI

1932 John Charles Curran Jr., Financing Manager for the Ford Motor Credit Company 1962-1969 and later an executive with the White Motor Company, is born in New York City

1933 The Packard Eleventh Series is introduced

1937 The last 1937 Cord 812 is produced

1943 Automotive artist F. Gordon Crosby dies at age 58

1947 Ettore Bugatti dies in Neuilly, France at age 65

1948 Racer Cliff Hucul is born

1950 The 1951 Packard Twenty-Fourth Series 200, 300 and Patrician 400 are introduced

1951 Warren J. Iliff of Oldsmobile and Pontiac dies at age 49

1952 Sherman L. Kelly, founder of the Electric Autolite Company, dies in Toledo, OH at age 89

1959 Racer Stuart Crow is born in the United States

1961 The first 1962 Ford Thunderbird is produced

1964 The 1965 Hillman Husky is introduced to the United States market

1966 Renzo Rivolta of Iso Rivolta dies in Pavia, Italy at age 58

1967 The first 1968 Pontiac is produced

1968 The Mazda Cosmo 110S, featuring a Wankel rotary engine, makes its racing debut at the Nurburgring in Germany

1980 The 1981 AMC Eagles are introduced

1991 Al Teague, driving the Speed-O-Motive/Spirit of 76 at the Bonneville Salt Flats, UT, raises the flying mile record for wheel-driven cars to 425.230 mph

AUGUST 22

1647 Denis Papin, a physicist who in 1690 constructed the first steam engine with a piston, is born in Blois, France

1869 William L. Walton, builder of the 1902 Walton in Neche, ND, is born in Peterborough, ON, Canada

1890 Harold Sines Vance of Studebaker is born in Port Huron, MI

1892 John Cuthbert Long, the biographer of Roy D. Chapin, is born in Babylon, Long Island, NY

1901 Hugh Chalmers marries Frances Lucretia Houser

1902 Henry M. Leland meets with officers of the struggling Henry Ford Company, after which the firm was reestablished as the Cadillac Motor Car Company with Lem W. Bowen as President, William E. Metzger as Sales Manager, and Henry M. Leland on the Board of Directors

1902 President Theodore Roosevelt tours Hartford, CT in a Columbia Electric Victoria, becoming the first president to ride in an automobile - some sources indicate that his predecessor, William McKinley, drove his own Stanley Steamer in his hometown of Canton, OH during the summer of 1899

1913 American Locomotive Company President W. H. Marshall announces that the firm is ending production of the Alco automobile

1914 Spencer Wishart is killed when his Mercer Type 45 crashes while leading the Elgin National Trophy Race in Elgin, IL

1922 Diadema Argentina SA de Petroleo is incorporated

1923 W. H. Marshall, President of the American Locomotive Company 1906-1917 who was instrumental in producing the Alco automobile, dies at age 59

1927 Brothers Alfred J., Lawrence P., Charles T., Frederick J., William A., Howard A., and Edward F. Fisher perform the groundbreaking ritual for the new Fisher Building in Detroit, MI

1934 William Elis Hoglund of Pontiac and Saturn is born in Stockholm, Sweden

1935 Walter Watney, the new owner of Delage & Cie., contracts with Delahaye to produce a badge-engineered Delage from mostly Delahaye parts

1938 Perry L. Tenney of General Motors, a principal developer of the automatic transmission, dies in East Lansing, MI at age 54

1947 Racer Ian Scheckter is born in East London, South Africa, the elder brother of racer Jody Scheckter

1948 Steam automobile advocate Andrew Jamison is born in Santa Monica, CA

1954 American Motors and the Packard Motor Car Company sign a reciprocity accord whereby Packard would supply AMC with V-8 engines, and AMC would supply automobile bodies to Packard - the deal quickly was found to be one-sided in Packard's favor, and AMC Chairman George W. Romney ordered Meade F. Moore to initiate a crash program to develop their own V-8

1957 Oscar L. Maag, a consulting engineer with the Timken Roller Bearing Company, dies

1959 The last 1959 Ford Thunderbird is produced

1960 David B. Steinman, designer of the Mackinac Bridge in Michigan, dies at age 74

1963 William R. Morris, Baron Nuffield of Nuffield, dies in Huntercombe, Henley-on-Thames, England at age 85

1964 Racer Bill Horstemeyer is killed at age 36 when he crashes during the Tony Bettenhausen Memorial Race in Springfield, IL

AUGUST 23

1866 Louis Semple Clarke, cofounder of the Autocar Company, is born in Pittsburgh, PA

1904 Harry D. Weed of Canastota, NY is issued a patent for his tire chains

1913 Automobiles legally enter Yosemite National Park, CA for the first time

1916 The Kelsey Wheel Company is organized in New York state

1917 Harry Larrowe Swan of the Ford Motor Company is born in Detroit, MI

1917 Tore Browaldh of Volvo is born in Vasteras, Sweden

1919 Racer Andre "Dries" van der Lof is born in Emmen, the Netherlands

1922 The first Southsea (England) Speed Carnival is won by Count Louis Zborowski in the 23-litre " Chitty-Chitty-Bang-Bang" at 73.1 mph

1923 Don Heinisch of the FWD Corporation is born in Chicago, IL

1923 Coachbuilder Vanden Plas (England) 1923 Ltd. reorganizes and takes over the former premises of The Kingsbury Aviation Company in northwest London

1925 Helmuth Bott of Porsche is born in Kirchheim, Germany

1932 The last Pontiac Series 402 Six is produced

1935 The first 1936 Auburns are shipped to dealers

1936 Carl C. Hinkley, Executive Engineer of the Buda Company and an authority on diesel engines, dies in Detroit, MI at age 53

1939 John R. Cobb, driving a Railton Special at the Bonneville Salt Flats, UT, raises the land speed record to 369.70 mph

1950 Frank Phillips, founder of the Phillips Petroleum Company, dies in Atlantic City, NJ at age 76

1951 William H. Wallace, an authority on the production of automotive springs, dies at age 64

1954 Karl H. Effmann of the Perfect Circle Company dies in Colorado Springs, CO at age 45 from accidental carbon monoxide poisoning

1956 Col. Charles Buhl, Assistant Body Engineer with the Edward G. Budd Manufacturing Company and a former employee of the Ford Motor Company and Studebaker Corporation, dies

1959 Stirling Moss wins the Portuguese Grand Prix at the Monsanto circuit near Lisbon driving a Cooper-Climax, the only Formula 1 race ever staged at this venue

1963 Racer Kenny Wallace is born in Saint Louis, MO

1966 Wyndham Mortimer, founder of the United Auto Workers trade union, dies in Hawthorne, CA at age 82

1966 The Packard Club's first national meet, a three-day affair, begins in Colorado Springs, CO

1967 Racer Georges Berger is killed at age 48 when he crashes during a race at the Nurburgring in Germany

1974 Roger Hedlund, driving the Battery Box, sets a land speed record for electric automobiles of 175 mph at the Bonneville Salt Flats, UT

1974 General Motors closes its assembly plant in Copenhagen, Denmark

1987 Racer Didier Pironi is killed at age 35 in a speedboat crash off the Isle of Wight in the English Channel - a severe accident during the German Grand Prix at Hockenheim in 1982 had ended his automobile racing career

1987 Racer Sheila Van Damm dies

AUGUST 24

1832 Internal combustion engine pioneer Nicolas Carnot dies in Paris, France at age 36

1870 David Alexander Shaw of Amplex and Grant is born in Hamden, NY

1872 James Hume Walker, founder of the Walker Body Company, is born in Amesbury, MA

1878 Frederick Michael Small, founder of the Martin-Parry Corporation, is born in York, PA

1881 Vincenzo Lancia is born in Fobello di Valsesia, Italy

1883 Clark Harry Kountz of the Sinclair Refining Company is born near Bradford, PA

1891 Emile Levassor is issued his first automobile patent, protecting his improvements to the ignition system

1911 A Packard 3-ton truck driven by Walter T. Fishleigh, E. L. Burnett, and and Arnold Haener reaches San Francisco, CA 46 days after leaving New York City, finishing the first trans-United States trip by a motor truck made completely under its own power

1911 Frank Raymond Wilton "Lofty" England of Jaguar is born

1916 John Herbert Gerstenmaier of the Goodyear Tire & Rubber Company is born in Saint Paul, MN

1920 Automobile parts manufacturer Lewis Edward Fleuelling is born in Saint Thomas, Ontario, Canada, the son of United States citizens

1921 Racer Sam Tingle is born in Manchester, England of Rhodesian parents

1925 Automotive journalist Bob Fendell is born in Bayonne, NJ

1930 Racer Roger McCluskey is born in Texas

1931 Eugene John McMullen of Oldsmobile dies at age 44 from injuries resulting from an automobile accident

1934 Roy H. Faulkner is appointed President of the Auburn Automobile Company, having resigned from that position in 1931 to join Studebaker

1934 The 1935 Auburns are previewed by dealers in Auburn, IN

1935 Terry Lamar Emrick of the Champion Spark Plug Company is born in Bowling Green, OH

1945 The last Cadillac-built M-24 tank is produced, ending the marque's World War II effort

1946 Charles H. McCrea, President of the National Malleable & Steel Castings Company since September 1942, dies in Cleveland, OH at age 56

1949 Alex Xydias sets a stock-powered automobile speed record, reaching 156.390 mph at the Bonneville Salt Flats, UT in his So-Cal streamliner powered by a 1939 Ford V-8

1950 Packard introduces its all-new 1951 models (24th Series) as styled by John Reinhart

1954 The 1,000,000th 1954 Ford is produced

1956 The last 1956 Ford Thunderbird is produced

1957 Daniel S. Eddins, President of Oldsmobile 1925-1933 and President of Plymouth 1934-1952, dies at age 70

1959 The Ford Motor Credit Company is organized in Delaware as the corporate financial subsidiary with Theodore O. Yntema as Chairman and Robert S. Olson as President

1964 The first 1965 Cadillac is produced

1964 The first 1965 Pontiac is produced

1964 Racer Eric Bernard is born in Istres, France

1967 Henry J. Kaiser dies in Honolulu, HI at age 85

1972 J. Byron Hull of Hingham, MA, Secretary of the Veteran Motor Car Club of America 1952-1972, dies

1983 Yukiyasu Togo is named President of Toyota USA, succeeding Isao Makino

1987 The 1988 Chevrolet S-10 pickup is introduced

1988 The 1989 Ford Tempo is introduced

AUGUST 25

1819 James Watt, the principal inventor of the modern steam engine, dies at Heathfield Hall near Birmingham, Staffordshire, England at age 83

1858 Charles Douglas Hastings, a longtime executive with Oldsmobile and Hupmobile, is born in Hillsdale, MI

1864 Milton Othello Reeves, creator of the Reeves Octoauto and Sextoauto, is born in Rush County, IN

1869 Emanuele Cacherano, Count di Bricherasio of Fiat is born in Turin, Italy

1880 Albert Gerry Partridge of the Goodyear Tire & Rubber Company is born in Jamestown, NY

1900 Clarence Reese, whose automotive career included positions with Chevrolet and DeVaux before joining the Continental Motors Corporation, is born in Muncie, IN

1901 Clare E. Briggs of Plymouth is born in Port Huron, MI

1903 Robert Wendell Conder of the Chrysler Corporation is born in Indianapolis, IN

1903 A Phelps touring car driven by designer L. J. Phelps sets the first official record (1 hour, 46 minutes) for the Mount Washington, NH hillclimb

1910 Walden W. Shaw and John D. Hertz form the Walden W. Shaw Livery Company, ancestor of the Yellow Cab Company

1911 Racer David Buck and his riding mechanic, Steve Jacobs, are killed when a tire blowout causes their Pope-Hartford to overturn during the 2nd Elgin (IL) Road Races

1917 The first ReVere, in bare chassis form, is tested in Logansport, IN

1918 Donald Herbert Edward Carlson of the Ford Motor Company of Canada, Ltd. is born in Edmonton, Alberta, Canada

1921 Six-Cylinder Love, the first full-length play based on the motor car, opens at the Sam H. Harris Theatre in New York City

1922 Fred Gilbert Secrest of the Ford Motor Company is born in Lakewood, OH

1928 Heber W. Peters is appointed Vice President of Distribution for the Packard Motor Car Company, replacing the retired Herbert H. "Doc" Hills

1931 The 8,000,000th Chevrolet is produced

1936 Racer Gordon Walter Johncock is born in Hastings, MI

1940 Edouard Michelin, cofounder of the Compagnie Generale des Etablissements Michelin in 1888, dies at age 81

1941 The Packard Twentieth Series is introduced

1942 Ernest F. Davis, Chief Metallurgist of the Borg-Warner Corporation, dies in Chicago, IL

1953 The White Motor Company acquires the Autocar Company

1953 The Hudson Itala is previewed to the press

1954 The first Highway Post Office bus, a 1941 White Model 788, is retired after more than 13 years of service - the vehicle was later restored and is now displayed in the National Postal Museum in Washington, DC

1958 The Volvo PV544 is introduced

1958 Racer Lt. Col. Alfred Thomas "Goldie" Gardner dies in Eastbourne, East Sussex, England at age 69

1959 The 3,000,000th Volkswagen is produced

1965 Iso Grifo production begins

1983 The Ford Escort cabriolet, the first Ford convertible manufactured in Europe in 25 years, is introduced

1985 All six Bugatti Royales are exhibited at the Pebble Beach (CA) Concours, the first and only time that the celebrated cars have appeared together

1987 Wilton John Oldham, Rolls-Royce historian and collector, dies

1988 The United States Postal Service issues a Classic Cars booklet of twenty 25c stamps in five different designs - 1928 Locomobile, 1929 Pierce-Arrow, 1931 Cord, 1932 Packard, and 1935 Duesenberg - in Detroit, MI as designed by artist Ken Dallison

1990 Racer David Hampshire dies in Newton Solney, Derbyshire, England at age 72

AUGUST 26

1791 Nathan Read of Warren, MA is issued a United States patent for his steam- powered land carriage

1872 James Joseph Couzens Jr. of the Ford Motor Company is born in Chatham, ON, Canada

1872 Walter Carpenter Marmon is born in Richmond, IN

1891 William Guy "Bill" Hardy of Rolls-Royce is born

1905 The Smith Automobile Company, a Kansas corporation, reorganizes as a Missouri corporation

1913 Henry B. Joy presents the chosen route for the Lincoln Highway to the Conference of West and Middle West Governors at their meeting in Colorado Springs, CO

1914 Anthony George DeLorenzo of General Motors is born in Edgerton, WI

1914 Riding mechanic John C. Jenter dies four days after the Mercer Type 45 driven by Spencer Wishart crashed during the 5th Elgin (IL) Road Races

1921 The Locomobile Company of America regains its independent status

1925 Racer Bobby Ball is born in Phoenix, AZ

1926 The Cord Corporation purchases the Ansted Motor Company of Connersville, IN

1926 As part of the process of merging with General Motors, the Yellow Cab Manufacturing Company changes its name to the Yellow Truck & Coach Manufacturing Company with John D. Hertz as Chairman and John A. Ritchie as President

1926 The Texas Corporation is organized in Delaware as the successor of The Texas Company

1929 Warren Packard II dies in Detroit, MI at age 36

1929 The first Rolls-Royce Phantom II Continental is completed

1931 The Shell Company of Canada Ltd. changes its name to the Shell Oil Company of Canada Ltd.

1933 The Studebaker Corporation sells the Pierce-Arrow Motor Car Company to a group of Buffalo businessmen for $1 million, reestablishing Pierce-Arrow as an independent firm

1934 The first Swiss Grand Prix is staged at the Bremgarten circuit in Berne and won by Hans Stuck in an Auto Union Type A - racer Hugh Hamilton is killed during the race

1935 Racer James Harvey Hylton is born

1935 John North Willys dies in Riverdale, NY at age 61

1937 Charles S. McIntyre, President of the Monroe Auto Equipment Company since 1923, dies at age 59

1938 The Mercury is introduced as a new marque by the Ford Motor Company

1940 The last LaSalle is produced after 14 years as the companion of Cadillac

1940 Percy Pierce of Pierce-Arrow dies

1943 George W. Christ, developer of steel-backed bearings and a design engineer with E-M-F and Studebaker, dies at age 59

1944 Racer Johnny Parsons (Jr.) is born in Newhall, CA, the son of racer Johnnie Parsons

1946 Racer David Earle "Swede" Savage Jr. is born

1948 Harry C. Wiess, President of the Humble Oil Company, dies at age 61

1950 Ransom E. Olds dies in Lansing, MI at age 86

1955 The last 1955 Ford Thunderbird is produced

1958 Racer Craig Huartson is born

1959 The Austin Seven and Morris Minor are introduced as badge-engineered versions of the famous "Mini" design of Alec Issigonis

1968 The first 1969 Pontiac is produced

1972 Clyde R. Paton, Chief Engineer of Packard 1932-1942, dies in Birmingham, MI at age 78

1982 Automotive historian Harry Barnard dies in Wilmette, IL at age 75

1986 Walter Treser Automobilbau GmbH is founded by Walter Treser in Berlin, Germany to develop and manufacture Treser cars, basically upscale versions of stock Audis

1985 The Yugo is introduced to the United States market

1992 The first Moscow (Russia) International Motor Show opens

AUGUST 27

1859 Edwin Drake strikes oil at 69 feet near Titusville, PA with the world's first successful oil well

1872 Pliny Eastman Holt, credited with building the first automobile in California in 1896, is born in London, NH

1877 Hon. Charles Stewart Rolls is born in London, England

1891 William J. Haley of the Standard Oil Company of New Jersey is born in Philadelphia, PA

1897 Cyrus Richard Osborn of General Motors is born in Dayton, OH

1900 The first long distance bus service in Great Britain is founded by A. E. Wynn of Knaresborough, West Riding, Yorkshire to serve the route from London to Leeds

1902 After producing twenty cars, the Henry Ford Company is reorganized as the Cadillac Motor Car Company

1904 Newport, RI imposes the first jail sentence for a speeding violation

1907 Calvin J. Werner of Cadillac is born in Dayton, OH

1909 The Houpt-Rockwell makes its debut in a 24-hour race at Brighton Beach, NY, but the car driven by George Robertson fails to finish

1909 Racer Charles Pozzi is born in Paris, France

1910 The first Elgin (IL) Road Races are staged - the 305-mile National Stock Chassis Championship is won by Ralph Mulford in a Lozier

1910 The first American LaFrance motorized fire truck is sold to the Lenox (MA) Fire Department and is still owned by the department

1911 Mercer records its first racing victory as Hughie Hughes wins a race in Elgin, IL

1912 Thomas Wilby begins the first trans-Canada automobile trip

1917 Antique automobile collector and historian Henry Austin Clark is born

1915 Harry S. Harkness succeeds Carl G. Fisher as President of the Sheepshead Bay Speedway Corporation

1925 Tire manufacturer Leopoldo Pirelli is born

1927 Joan Potter Elwart, biographer of John and Horace Dodge, is born in Detroit, MI

1930 The Kinetic Chemical Company is formed as a joint venture of the DuPont Company and General Motors to manufacture and market freon

1935 Automotive historian Norman S. Barrett is born in London, England

1936 Goldie Gardner driving an M.G. sets the alltime Brooklands record for Class G (under 1100 cc) of 124.40 mph

1938 Captain George Eyston driving the Rolls-Royce powered Thunderbolt at the Bonneville Salt Flats, UT raises his own land speed record to 345.49 mph

1942 Racer Tom Belso is born in Copenhagen, Denmark

1948 Henry Austin Clark opens the Long Island Automotive Museum in Southampton, NY on his 31st birthday

1954 Racer Derek Warwick is born in Alresford, Essex, England

1954 C. Stanley Sundling, President of the Laboratory Equipment Company and a member of the AAA Contest Board Technical Committee for the Indianapolis 500 Mile Race, is killed at age 45 in an automobile accident near Crystal Lake, IL - also killed at age 40 in the accident is William S. Powell, Vice President of the firm and a member of the AAA Contest Board

1959 Milton E. Tibbetts, longtime patent attorney and Packard executive, dies in Whittier, CA at age 80

1959 Racer Gerhard Berger is born in Worgl, Austria

1963 Ford introduces the fiberglass Allego sport coupe, a one-off styling exercise that would greatly influence the Mustang

1964 Andrew C. Maier, manufacturer of automobile paints and varnishes, dies in Pontiac, MI at age 81

1967 The first Canadian Grand Prix is staged at Mosport Park, ON and won by Jack Brabham

1968 Ford-Werke AG introduces the new Ford Escort

1968 The Libbey-Owens-Ford Glass Company changes its name to the Libbey-Owens- Ford Company

1988 General Motors introduces the Opel Vectra and Vauxhall Cavalier for the western European market

1993 General Motors sells its Group Lotus subsidiary to Bugatti International S.A.H., the new Bugatti group's financial holding company headquartered in Luxembourg

AUGUST 28

1866 Windsor Thomas White of White is born in Orange, MA

1883 Roger Leroy Morrison, a longtime highway engineering educator and developer of improved roadbuilding methods, is born in Winnetka, IL

1891 Stuart Gordon Baits of Hudson and American Motors is born in Dowagiac, MI

1895 Frank O. Prior of the Standard Oil Company of Indiana is born in Escondido, CA

1897 Major-General Montgomery of Winchester purchases a Coventry-built Daimler in the first British sale of a vehicle to a person outside of the automobile industry

1899 The Pittsburgh Motor Vehicle Company reorganizes as the Autocar Company

1902 Andrew L. Riker is elected Vice President of Locomobile

1904 The Louisiana Purchase Trophy Race at the Saint Louis (MO) World's Fair is won by Barney Oldfield driving the Peerless Green Dragon

1905 John H. Middlekamp of Mack and Reo is born in Brooklyn, NY

1907 The Oakland Motor Car Company is organized in Pontiac, MI by Edward M. Murphy, Frank E. Kirby, Alanson P. Brush, R. F. Monroe, M. J. Hallinan, C. J. Cram, and James Dempsey

1921 Construction of the Paragon Motor Company factory begins in Cumberland, MD - the building was never completed and Paragon production would consist of just four prototypes

1922 The Monza circuit in Italy opens

1922 Roland Cesare Maria Carlo Bugatti, youngest son of Ettore Bugatti, is born in Dorlisheim, France

1929 The last Bentley 3 Litre produced, a tourer with body by Wylder, is registered by its first owner

1936 Lord Herbert Scott is elected Chairman of Rolls-Royce Ltd.

1936 Gordon M. Buehrig resigns as Chief Stylist for the Cord Corporation and is succeeded by Alex Tremulis

1937 The Toyota Motor Company, Ltd. is organized in Japan

1942 William Samuels, a German-born design engineer with Chevrolet, dies at age 56

1946 The Packard Twenty-First Series Custom Super Eight is introduced, featuring a 148" wheelbase

1948 Allen Rae of A. Schrader's Son and a former executive of the Dunlop Tire & Rubber Goods Company Ltd. dies

Toyota's trademark contains Japanese characters representing the founding family's name - Toyoda.

1951 The 1,000th Porsche is produced

1957 Automobile windshield manufacturer Dana Elisha Seeley dies on Mackinac Island, MI at age 88

1957 Pontiac stages its 50th Anniversary celebration, based on the founding of the division's original car, the Oakland

1958 Alonzo William Peake, President of the Standard Oil Company of Indiana 1945-1955, dies in Dundee, Scotland at age 68

1959 Halsey R. Jones of the Timken Roller Bearing Company dies at age 55

1961 Bob Osiecki sets a closed course record of 181.565 mph at the Daytona Speedway in Daytona Beach, FL in the Chrysler-powered "Mad Dog IV"

1968 The first Iso Grifo 7-litre is produced

1969 Oliver E. Barthel, a pioneer designer with King, Ford, Oldsmobile, and Cadillac, the designer of the Ford 999 race car, the holder of 35 patents relating to the automobile, and the inventor of the taper frame allowing more streamlined bodies, dies in Detroit, MI at age 91

1972 General Motors announces that it will market a Wankel rotary engine as an optional power unit for the Chevrolet Vega within two years

1977 The merger of Volvo and Saab is called off

1977 Racer Mike Parkes is killed at age 35 in a traffic accident near Turin, Italy

1994 Rubens Barrichello qualifies for the pole position in the Belgian Grand Prix, at age 22 years, 97 days the youngest driver to accomplish this feat in a Formula 1 championship race

AUGUST 29

1857 Charles Jasper Glidden, telephone magnate, automobile enthusaist, and creator of the Glidden Tour reliability runs, is born in Manchester, NH

1876 Charles Franklin Kettering of General Motors is born on the family farm north of Loudonville, OH

1885 Gottlieb Daimler is issued a German patent for his first vehicle, often cited as the world's first motorcycle

1886 James Mark Crawford of Allen, Auburn, and Chevrolet is born in Indianapolis, IN

1888 Automobile historian Frank Ernest Hill is born in San Jose, CA

1898 The Goodyear Tire & Rubber Company is incorporated in Ohio

1901 J. Frank Duryea contracts with the J. Stevens Arms and Tool Company to design a line of automobiles to be called Stevens-Duryea

"STEVENS-DURYEA"

"Individual Distinction" is written all over our gasoline machine.
The fame of this automobile is rapidly growing, as the
"STEVENS-DURYEA" embodies all desirable features that contribute toward the making of a superior vehicle.

PRICE AT FACTORY
$1,300

This includes complete equipment.
Our illustrated catalog should be in the hands of every automobilist.
Mailed FREE upon request.

J. STEVENS ARMS & TOOL COMPANY
925 Main Street
Member Association Licensed Automobile Manufacturers.   CHICOPEE FALLS, MASS.

1902 John Harold Shields of the Superior Coach Corporation is born in Shawnee Township, OH

1914 The last pre-World War I English hillclimb is staged at Style Kop, Staffordshire and won by William R. Morris (later Lord Nuffield) in a Morris-Oxford

1917 The Lincoln Motor Company is founded by Henry M. Leland to manufacture Liberty airplane engines

1919 Automotive parts manufacturer Steven Stanley Gordon is born in Detroit, MI

1921 Pioneer black racer Wendell Scott is born in Virginia

1929 The first Rolls-Royce Phantom II is completed

1933 Racer Alan Stacey is born in Broomfield, Essex, England

1934 Rolls-Royce of America, Inc. reoganizes as the Springfield Manufacturing Company to avoid involving the Rolls-Royce name in bankruptcy proceedings

1940 Land speed record setter Gary Gabelich is born in San Pedro, CA

1940 Walter C. Marmon dies in Indianapolis, IN at age 68

1945 Racer Jean Ragnotti is born in Carpentras, France

1947 Racer James Simon Wallis Hunt is born in Sutton, Surrey, England

1948 The first 1949 Kaiser is produced

1957 Edgar L. Longaker, inventor of the automobile ignition battery, dies in Norristown, PA at age 75

1959 Rudolf Caracciola, the 1935, 1937, and 1938 European Grand Prix champion, dies in Lugano, Switzerland at age 58

1968 Raymond H. Laird of the Ford Motor Company dies in Punta Gorda, FL at age 69

1977 Racer Brian McGuire is killed at age 31 when the McGuire-Cosworth of his own design crashes during a practice run in Brands Hatch, England

1993 Racer Roger McCluskey dies in Indianapolis, IN at age 63

AUGUST 30

1879 John Evon Nelson of the Gulf Oil Company is born in Helensburgh, Scotland

1888 Automotive parts manufacturer Frederick V. McGraw is born in San Francisco, CA

1890 Abraham Edward Barit of Hudson is born

1892 John Allan Rolls, father of Hon. C. S. Rolls of Rolls-Royce, is raised to the peerage as Lord Llangattock

1905 Louis Bancel Warren of the Chrysler Corporation is born in Monmouth Beach, NJ

1916 Studebaker announces the Heaslet Special, a semi-custom touring car named in honor of James G. Heaslet, Vice President of Engineering

1918 Alvin Morell Bentley, a United States Congressman from Michigan and an heir to a General Motors fortune, is born in Portland, ME

The famous "Step Down" Hudsons of 1948-1954 were produced under the leadership of A.E. Barit. This 2-door Brougham, rarely photographed from the rear, looks positively modern between a pickup and a Plymouth in front of Mercy Hospital in Valley City, ND.

1920 The Coupe Internationale des Voiturettes, the first post-World War I race in France, is staged in Le Mans and won by Ernest Friderich in a Bugatti Type 13

1932 The Ford Sedan Delivery Car Type 130-B is introduced

1934 Automotive products manufacturer Daniel Boyd Griffith is born in Albuquerque, NM

1934 The Packard Twelfth Series Eight is introduced with a factory bulletin to dealers that they would be called 1935 Packards, the first time that the company had officially used year dates to identify cars

1935 Racer Gerhard Mitter is born in Schonlinde, Sudetenland, Czechoslovakia

1935 Erick Arthur Reickert, President and Chief Executive Officer of New Venture Gear Inc. and a former Ford Motor Company and Chrysler Corporation executive, is born in Newport, TN

1936 Automobile parts manufacturer G. Ronald Morris is born in East Saint Louis, IL

1937 Racer Bruce Leslie McLaren is born in Auckland, New Zealand

1941 Racer Ignazio Giunti is born in Rome, Italy

1945 The first post-World War II Hudson is produced, a pale green Super Six coupe

1946 D. Sulprizio, President and General Manager of the United Engine & Machine Company and a former engineer with Fiat and Tosi in his native Italy, dies in San Leandro, CA

1952 Sir Walrond Sinclair, Chairman of the British Tire & Rubber Company Ltd., dies in London, England at age 72

1952 Edmund B. Neil, a truck engineer with the Pierce-Arrow Motor Car Company and later an independent consulting engineer, dies at age 62

1955 The last 1955 Ford is produced

1958 Raymond A. Schakel of the Diamond Chain & Manufacturing Company dies at age 58

1959 Racer Ed Elisian is killed at age 32 when he crashes during a race in West Allis, WI

1970 Byers A. Burlingame of Studebaker dies in South Bend, IN at age 70

AUGUST 31

1888 Herman L. Weckler of Buick and the Chrysler Corporation is born in Pittsburgh, PA

1899 F. O. Stanley, driving a Stanley Steamer, becomes the first to reach the summit of Mount Washington, NH by automobile

1899 Kenneth Stanley Adams of the Phillips Petroleum Company is born in Horton, KS

1901 John Roby Benson, 2nd Lord Charnwood, the onetime owner of Aston-Martin Ltd., is born

1904 James W. Packard marries Elizabeth Achsah Gillmer

1906 Racer Raymond Sommer is born in Paris, France

1912 The first Rayfield, a Light Six touring car, is completed at the firm's new Chrisman, IL factory

1915 Samuel Todd Davis, President of the Locomobile Company of America, dies at age 42 following a stroke

1921 William J. Walsh, Assistant Sales Manager for the Buda Company, dies at age 51

1922 The Marmon Model 34C is introduced

1935 Ab Jenkins, with Tony Gulotta as relief driver, covers 3,253 miles in 24 hours (average 135.47 mph) at the Bonneville Salt Flats, UT in the Duesenberg Special

1939 Walter M. Jones of the Waukesha Motor Company dies in Pittsburgh, PA at age 52

1942 Racer Alessandro Pesenti-Rossi is born in Bergamo, Italy

1946 Colin Strang, driving his own Strang special, wins the Prescott (England) Hillclimb, the first time that a car with a 500-cc or smaller engine had won a hillclimb outright against larger competitors

1948 Racer Harald Ertl is born in Mannheim, Germany

1952 Racer Jim Rigsby of Lennox, CA is killed during a sprint race in Dayton, OH

1953 General Motors sells its Hertz Drivurself subsidiary to the Omnibus Corporation

1953 The Packard Balboa show car is unveiled

1953 Racer Miguel Angel Guerra is born in Buenos Aires, Argentina

1955 The world's first solar-powered automobile, designed by William G. Cobb, is demonstrated at the General Motors Powerama in Chicago, IL

1956 The Oldsmobile Golden Rocket show car is introduced

1956 Automotive journalist J. Howard Pile dies

1957 The Lincoln and Mercury divisions of the Ford Motor Company are combined

1957 James E. Lynch, organizer of the "Jimmie Lynch Daredevils" stunt drivers show, dies in Texarkana, AR at age 50

1958 Chairman Albert Bradley and President Harlow H. Curtice retire from General Motors

1958 J. Rush Snyder of Thompson Products Inc. dies at age 72

1959 The first 1960 Pontiac is produced

1959 Harold S. Vance of the Studebaker-Packard Corporation dies in Washington, DC at age 69

1975 The last 1975 Dodge is produced

1977 Leslie R. Henry retires as Curator of Transportation at the Henry Ford Museum and is succeeded by John A. Conde, formerly of American Motors

1987 F. James McDonald retires as President of General Motors

SEPTEMBER 1

1880 James Frank Drake, longtime President of the Gulf Oil Company, is born in Pittsfield, NH

1882 H. C. Moser of the Yellow Truck & Coach Manufacturing Company is born in New york City

1883 John H. Watson Jr., a Cleveland, OH attorney who was a longtime director of the Studebaker Corporation and the White Motor Company, is born in Bradford, VT

1888 George Harold Brodie of the Studebaker-Packard Corporation is born in Pittsfield, MA

1888 William Brewster marries Marie Munger in New York City

1893 Don Emery of the Phillips Petroleum Company is born in Delmont, PA

1897 Hans Ledwinka joins the Nesselsdorfer Wagenbau-Fabriks-Gessellschaft

1902 The city of Chicago, IL issues its first automobile license plate to Arthur L. Eddy

1903 Massachusetts issues the first state-issued automobile license plate in the United States to Frederic Tudor of Brookline

License plates were "old hat" in Massachusetts by 1908 when plate 064B was mounted on this 1907 Maxwell Model R Tourabout. The number is repeated on the lens of the right cowl lamp.

1907 Ettore Bugatti signs a formal license agreement with Gasmotorenfabrik Deutz AG of Cologne, Germany to design and produce Deutz cars for a term of five years

1907 Walter Philip Reuther of the United Auto Workers is born in Wheeling, WV

1907 The George N. Pierce Company moves into its new Elmwood Plant in Buffalo, NY

1908 Emil A. Nelson begins designing the first Hupmobile

1909 The Packard Motor Car Company reincorporates in Michigan, succeeding the West Virginia corporation formed in 1903

1912 The Brockway Motor Truck Corporation is organized in Cortland, NY with George A. Brockway as President and General Manager and Dr. Frederick R. Thompson as Secretary-Treasurer

1912 William L. Day is named General Manager of the General Motors Truck Company

1917 The first Nash is produced

1918 The 1919 Nashes are introduced

1919 The 1920 Nashes are introduced

1920 The 1921 Nashes are introduced

1920 The Packard Single Six First Series is introduced

1920 Dirk de Bruyne of Royal Dutch/Shell Group is born in Rotterdam, Holland

NASH
Leads the World in Motor Car Value

1921 The Lancia Lambda is introduced

1921 Sir Austin William Pearce, Chairman of Esso Petroleum Company 1972-1980 and a Director of Jaguar PLC, is born in Plymouth, Devonshire, England

1923 H. D. Church joins the Chevrolet Motor Company

1924 Racer Joe Boyer dies in Altoona, PA after being injured during a 250-mile race at the Altoona Board Speedway in Tipton, PA earlier in the day

1927 Automotive historian Paul Richard Woudenberg is born in Highland Park, IL

1928 Boy Scouts across the United States install about 3,000 concrete markers along the route of the Lincoln Highway

1929 The SA Scuderia Ferrari is incorporated primarily to manage the racing activities of Alfa Romeo

1929 Raymond B. Birge joins Packard as head of the Custom Body Division

1929 B. E. Sibley is named Chief Technologist for the Continental Oil Company, a position he would hold until his death in 1946

1935 Irving B. Babcock is named General Manager of the Yellow Truck & Coach Manufacturing Company, replacing Paul W. Seiler

1937 The 1938 DeSotos are introduced

1940 Paul W. Litchfield retires as President of the Goodyear Tire & Rubber Company, but continues to serve as that company's Chairman of the Board

1941 The 1942 DeSotos are introduced, featuring hidden "Airfoil" headlights

1941 The 1942 Hudsons are introduced

1943 Harry C. Tillotson, founder and President of the Tillotson Manufacturing Company and inventor of the Tillotson carburetor, dies

1944 James M. Novak of the Ford Motor Company is born

1946 Racer George Barringer is killed when he crashes during a 200-mile race at Lakewood Park in Atlanta, GA that was halted at 98 miles because of the accident - George Robson, also involved in the crash, would die the next day

1950 The first Porsche is completed

1950 Ward M. Canaday is elected President of the Willys-Overland Company

1950 Charles F. Arnold is named Chief Engineer of Cadillac

1950 Mrs. Ransom E. Olds, the former Metta Woodward who was three days younger than her husband, dies six days after her husband's death

1950 Arthur H. Kannady of the Standard Oil Company of California dies at age 50

1950 Alvin F. Knoblock, a retired Vice President of General Motors and a veteran of 65 years in the automotive business, dies in Detroit, MI

1955 The Cadillac Division of General Motors registers the "Seville" name as a trademark - the name originally was used for the coupe version of its top- of-the-line Eldorado, but since the 1975 model year Seville has been a separate series of the marque

1955 The 1956 Jaguars are introduced to the United States market

1956 The Studebaker-Packard Corporation initiates the "Joint Program" with the Curtiss-Wright Corporation

1956 The 1957 Jaguars are introduced to the United States market

1956 The Volvo Amazon/120 is introduced

1956 Charles O. Guernsey retires as Vice President and Manager of the Transit Equipment Division, Marmon-Herrington Company, Inc.

1956 William H. Graves, Vice President and Director of Engineering for the Studebaker-Packard Corporation, is appointed a professor of automotive engineering at the University of Michigan and head of its new Automotive Engineering Laboratory

1957 The 1958 Jaguars are introduced to the United States market

1957 Raymond S. Pruitt of the Auburn Automobile Company dies at age 70

1958 Frederic G. Donner is elected Chairman and Chief Executive Officer of General Motors, the first person to hold both titles - John F. Gordon is elected President and Chief Operating Officer

1958 The first 1959 Pontiac is produced, featuring "Wide-Track" stance
1958 The 1959 Jaguars are introduced to the United States market
1958 The 1959 Lloyds are introduced to the United States market
1959 The 1960 Jaguars are introduced to the United States market
1959 The 1960 Opels are introduced to the United States market
1960 The 1961 Jaguars are introduced to the United States market
1960 The first 1961 Pontiac is produced
1961 The 1962 Jaguars are introduced to the United States market
1961 The first Volkswagen 1500 Type-3 is produced
1962 The 1963 British Fords are introduced to the United States market
1962 The 1963 Jaguars are introduced to the United States market
1962 L. N. Mays is named General Sales Manager of Cadillac
1963 The 1964 Fiats are introduced to the United States market
1963 The 1964 British Fords are introduced to the United States market
1963 The 1964 Jaguars are introduced to the United States market
1964 The 1965 Fiats are introduced to the United States market
1964 The 1965 British Fords are introduced to the United States market
1964 The 1965 Jaguars are introduced to the United States market, including the new 3.8S sedan
1965 The 1966 Fiats are introduced to the United States market
1965 The 1966 British Fords are introduced to the United States market
1965 The 1966 Jaguars are introduced to the United States market
1966 The 1967 Fiats are introduced to the United States market
1966 The 1967 British Fords are introduced to the United States market
1966 Calvin J. Werner is named General Manager of Cadillac, succeeding Kenneth N. Scott
1968 Racer Franck Lagorce is born in L'Hay-les-Roses, France
1969 The 1970 Checkers are introduced
1970 The 1971 Checkers are introduced
1971 The 1972 Checkers are introduced
1972 The 1973 Checkers are introduced
1973 The 1974 Checkers are introduced
1974 The 1975 Checkers are introduced
1974 The 1975 Chevrolet Blazer is introduced
1980 Henry Austin Clark closes his Long Island Automotive Museum in Southampton, NY, ending the 32-year life of the first major antique automobile musuem in the United States
1980 24-year-old Patrick Mimran is named President of Nuova Automobili Ferruccio Lamborghini SpA
1983 The Lorain-Carnegie Bridge in Cleveland, OH is rededicated as the Hope Memorial Bridge in honor of Harry Hope, one of the stonecutters who made the four art-deco pylons used on the bridge and the father of comedian Bob Hope
1985 Racer Stefan Bellof is killed at age 27 when his Porsche crashes during a 1000 km race at the Spa circuit in Belgium
1987 Robert Stempel is elected President of General Motors
1989 The 1990 Chevrolet Blazer and Astro are introduced - the Astro is the first minivan to offer all-wheel-drive as an option
1990 The 1991 Chevrolet Blazer and S-10 Pickup are introduced
1991 The 1992 Chevrolet S-10 Pickup is introduced
1991 Harry Gant, age 51, wins the Heinz Southern 500 in Darlington, SC, to extend his record as the oldest winner of a NASCAR race
1992 The 1993 GMC Jimmy is introduced
1996 The Toyota RAV4 L Electric Vehicle is offered to the Japanese public on a limited basis

SEPTEMBER 2

1869 Hiram Percy Maxim of Columbia is born in Brooklyn, NY

1896 Rollin H. White marries Katharine King in Brooklyn, NY

1898 The National Motor Carriage Company acquires the Duryea Motor Wagon Company

1899 Automotive artist James W. Williamson is born in Omaha, NE

1911 William Fisk Harrah, casino/hotel operator and builder of the world's largest automobile collection, is born in South Pasadena, CA

1913 Emil Jellinek-Mercedes, writing from his villa in Nice, France, announces that he now considers the Rolls-Royce to be the "best car at present", a statement that caused a sensation in automotive circles

1919 Racer Lance Macklin is born in London, England

1919 Karl Schopper begins building the first Roots supercharger, later to be installed in a Mercedes 10/30 chassis

1921 The retail price of new Ford Model T drops to $355, its alltime low point

1924 The Haynes Automobile Company suspends production

1924 Dario Resta, winner of the 1916 Indianapolis 500, is killed at age 40 when his Sunbeam crashes during a speed record attempt at Brooklands

1936 Helmut Werner of Mercedes-Benz is born in Cologne, Germany

1937 The 1938 Hupmobiles are introduced after a one-year hiatus in the production of the marque

1940 William Joseph Lovejoy of the General Motors Acceptance Corporation is born in Brooklyn, NY

1944 Leo New, a mechanic with the Packard Motor Car Company before beginning a successful career in the gas pipe line business, dies at age 54

1946 Racer George Robson, winner of the 1946 Indianapolis 500, dies from injuries suffered the previous day when he crashed during a race at Lakewood Park in Atlanta, GA

1947 Racer Jim Richards is born in New Zealand

1948 The 1949 Kaisers are announced to dealers

1949 The Michigan Rivet Corporation is founded by K. M. Knuppenburg and Gene P. Giulioli to manufacture automotive parts

1950 Mike Hawthorn, driving a Riley Nine, wins the 1,100-cc class at the Brighton Speed Trials for his first racing victory

1950 Raymond Mays, driving a 2-litre E.R.A., wins the standing-start kilometre event at the Brighton Speed Trials in the last sprint event of his career

1952 James Gilman "Pete" Sterling, former Chief Engineer of Stearns-Knight and the designer of the 1920-1926 Sterling-Knight, dies in Cleveland Heights, OH at age 72

1952 Benjamin B. Lovett, Henry Ford's longtime personal dancing instructor, dies in Weymouth, MA at age 76

1954 Burt J. Craig of the Ford Motor Company dies in Detroit, MI at age 69

1955 The Studebaker-Packard Corporation holds the first meeting of its Dealer-Factory Planning Committee at the Packard Proving Grounds in Utica, MI

1958 Racer Olivier Grouillard is born in Toulouse, Haute-Garonne, France

1959 The Ford Falcon is introduced in the first nationwide closed-circuit television news conference

1959 Stylist Richard A. Teague joins American Motors

1960 Harold E. Churchill resigns as President of the Studebaker-Packard Corporation

1963 Donna Mae Mims, driving an Austin-Healey, wins the Class H Production Race in Thompson, CT to become the first woman to win a SCCA Class Championship

1963 Racer Robbie Buhl is born in Detroit, MI

1966 Racer Olivier Panis is born in Lyon, France

1969 Semon "Bunkie" Knudsen is fired as President of the Ford Motor Company although the action would not be officially announced for nine days

1969 Racer Willy Mairesse dies in Ostend, Belgium at age 40 from an overdose of sleeping pills

1973 The 1974 Chevrolet Blazer is introduced

1976 Leyland Historic Vehicles Ltd. stages a grand opening for its new museum in Donington, Derbyshire, England, established to preserve and display cars manufactured by various units of British Leyland, Ltd.

1976 Racer Michel Jourdian Jr. is born in Mexico City

1994 The National Corvette Museum opens in Bowling Green, KY under the management of Dan Gale

SEPTEMBER 3

1835 Sibrandus Stratingh takes his steam-powered vehicle for its first test drive in Groningen, the Netherlands

1864 Jonathan Dixon Maxwell is born near Russiaville, IN

1875 Ferdinand Porsche is born in Maffersdorf, Austria (now Liberec, Czech Republic)

1892 William Stubbs James, a design engineer with Hupmobile and Studebaker before becoming Director of Research for the Ford Motor Company in 1945, is born in Asbury Park, NJ

1892 Theodore V. Houser, a Sears, Roebuck & Company executive 1928-1958 who was responsible for the Allstate marque, a badge-engineered Henry J, is born in Kansas City, MO

1896 Roy Jackson, a Ford Motor Company executive in Trieste, Italy and Paris, France during the 1920's, is born in Kingston, ON, Canada

1898 Clement Ader files for his first automobile patent

1900 The first automobile built in Flint, MI, the Wisner designed by Charles H. Wisner, is introduced in that city's Labor Day parade

1903 The Buick Motor Company is organized

1903 Danish automobile pioneer Albert Hammel dies at age 68

1903 Charles Schmidt demonstrates the new Packard K Special race car at the Trumbull County (OH) Fair, after which the Cleveland Plain Dealer dubs the car the "Gray Wolf"

1909 The Krit Motor Car Company is organized in Detroit, MI by Claude S. Briggs and W. S. Piggins to manufacture cars per the designs of Kenneth Crittenden

This 1911 Krit is typical of the marque built 1910-1915. Its swastika logo was a symbol of good luck in those days.

1922 The first major race at Monza, the Italian Grand Prix, is won by Pietro Bordino in a Fiat 804

1923 Richard Arthur Yealin of Checker is born in Pittsburgh, PA

1925 Chrysler Corporation purchases the American Motor Body Company of Detroit, MI to eliminate body shortages on the assembly line

1931 Racer William George "Bill" Sadler is born in St. Catherines, Ontario

1934 Louis Unser wins his first Pikes Peak Hill Climb near Colorado Springs, CO driving a Stutz Special

1935 Sir Malcolm Campbell, driving the Campbell Special "Bluebird V" at the Bonneville Salt Flats, UT, raises the land speed record to 301.129 mph - this was the ninth and last time he would raise the record over a span of eleven years

1936 Packard introduces the Fifteenth Series Super Eight and Twelve, the 1937 medium-range 120, and the new low-priced, 6-cylinder 115C

1936 Reo officially leaves the automobile business and turns exclusively to the manufacture of motor trucks

1939 The first and only Yugoslavian Grand Prix and the last major race before World War II is held at Kalemagdan Park in Belgrade and won by Tazio Nuvolari in an Auto Union Type D - Manfred von Brauchitsch finishes third in a Mercedes-Benz W163 in what would be his last race

1940 The Dearborn, MI plant of the Graham-Paige Motors Corporation is closed "temporarily" to prepare for the manufacture of the Cord 810/812-based Graham Clipper - later commitments to national defense contracts would in effect result in the end of the Graham marque

1940 Williams S. Knudsen resigns as President of General Motors to enter government service

1940 Harley J. Earl is appointed as a Vice President of General Motors

1946 Cisitalia makes its racing debut at the Coppa Brezzi, the first post- World II closed circuit race in Italy - Piero Dusio wins driving the D.46 1100-cc monoposto of his own design

1948 Nicholas Dreystadt of General Motors dies of cancer at age 59 in Detroit, MI

1950 The Ferrari 375F1 4.5-litre race car makes its debut at the Italian Grand Prix in Monza with Alberto Ascari at the wheel, but the car retires with engine trouble - Philippe Etancelin, driving a Talbot-Lago T26C, places fifth, at age 53 years, 248 days the oldest driver to earn points in a Formula 1 championship race

1954 The last 1954 Pontiac is produced, ending the division's straight-8 era

A group of 1950's cars parked in front of the Municipal Auditorium in Minot, ND includes a 1954 Pontiac Chieftain Custom Catalina hardtop coupe at far right.

1960 Clarence Francis is elected Chairman of the Studebaker-Packard Corporation

1961 Lawrence P. Fisher, one of the seven brothers who founded the Fisher Body Company and a former President of Cadillac, dies in Detroit, MI at age 72

1963 The first 1964 Pontiac is produced

1969 The 1970 Fords are introduced

1969 Racer Jorg Muller is born in West Germany

1981 The 1982 full-sized Pontiacs are introduced

1989 Teo Fabi, driving a Porsche-March 89P, wins the CART Red Roof Inns 200 at the Mid-Ohio Speedway for the marque's first Indy-Car victory

SEPTEMBER 4

1865 Richard Henry Long, builder of the 1922-1926 Bay State automobile, is born in South Weymouth, MA

1887 Mechanical engineer Earle Buckingham, whose career included a stint with the Veeder Manufacturing Company of Hartford, CT, makers of automobile odometers, is born in Bridgeport, CT

1890 Clarence Edward Olmsted of Texaco, Inc. is born in Santa Paula, CA

1891 Fritz Todt, the principal designer of the autobahn system, is born in Pforzheim, Germany

1901 Sir William Lyons, founder of Jaguar, is born in Blackpool, England

1904 William C. Durant test drives a Buick while considering the purchase of the ailing Buick Motor Company

1904 Groundbreaking ceremonies are held for the first Reo Motor Car Company buildings in Lansing, MI

Charley Schwiddle of Essex, IA appears quite pleased with his 1906 Reo, one of the first cars manufactured by Ransom E. Olds' second automotive empire.

1906 Terry Stafford is issued a United States patent for his 3-speed progressive transmission

1908 The Imperial Motor Car Company of Williamsport, PA files for bankruptcy

1912 James Otis Wright of the Ford Motor Company is born in Norfolk, VA

1914 Francis C. "Jack" Reith, General Manager of the Mercury Division of the Ford Motor Company 1955-1957, is born in Des Moines, IA

1915 The Twin City Concrete Speedway in Fort Snelling, MN stages its first event, a 500-mile race won by Earl Cooper in a Stutz

1916 The Cincinnati (OH) Board Speedway opens with a 300-mile race won by John Aitken in a Peugeot - Wilbur D'Alene finishes second in his Duesenberg which is numbered "13" over the objections of many superstitious drivers who subsequently persuade the AAA to permanantly ban number "13"

1917 Henry Ford II is born in Detroit, MI

1920 Racer Clemar Bucci is born in Santa Fe, Argentina

1921 The first Italian Grand Prix is staged in Brescia and won by Jules Goux in a Ballot 3L

1922 The Swallow Sidecar Company is founded by William Lyons (on his 21st birthday) and William Walmsley - the company would evolve into Jaguar Cars, Ltd.

1923 The Altoona (PA) Board Speedway stages its first event, a 200-mile race won by Eddie Hearne in the Durant Special

1924 Racer Robert "Bobby" Grim is born in Coal City, IN

1924 Willard C. Lipe, Vice President of the Brown-Lipe Gear Company of Syracuse, NY, dies at age 62

1926 Donald Eugene Petersen, President 1980-1985 and Chairman 1985-1991 of the Ford Motor Company, is born in Pipestone, MN

1927 The Fiat 806 makes its racing debut, with Pietro Bordino driving the car to victory in the Grand Prix of Milan at Monza, Italy - this would be the marque's last official appearance in international racing

1934 George T. Christopher is named Vice-President of Manufacturing for the Packard Motor Car Company, replacing the retiring E. F. Roberts

1935 The White Motor Company of Cleveland, OH introduces the world's first streamlined motor truck

1936 The 1937 Studebakers are introduced

1940 Ab Jenkins, driving the Duesenberg "Mormon Meteor" at the Bonneville Salt Flats, UT, sets a world's 1-hour record of 190.68 miles (306.87 km)

1945 Boyce Nelson of the Sinclair Refining Company is killed in an automobile accident at age 44

1946 James T. McMillan, a Director of the Packard Motor Car Company 1914-1946, dies in Detroit, MI at age 61

1947 Steven James Germann of the Alfred P. Sloan Museum is born in Dayton, OH

1950 NASCAR's first superspeedway race, the Southern 500 at the Darlington (SC) International Raceway, is won by Johnny Mantz in a Plymouth P19 two-door sedan

1950 Ab Jenkins records a one-hour run of 195.95 miles at the Bonneville Salt Flats, UT in the Mormon Meteor III, a Curtiss-engined car built by August S. Duesenberg in 1938 and now enshrined in the Utah State Capitol in Salt Lake City

1950 William Joseph Davidson of General Motors, the President of the Society of Automotive Engineers in 1939, dies in Goderich, Ontario, Canada at age 69

1957 "E-Day" marks the introduction of the Edsel, Ford Motor Company's much heralded new marque named for Edsel B. Ford and introduced on the 40th birthday of his son Henry Ford II - the first sale is to Dr. Frank Zeller Jr. of Winter Haven, FL who purchases a turquoise and white Pacer convertible

1958 James J. Nance resigns as General Manager of the Lincoln-Edsel-Mercury Division of the Ford Motor Company

1960 Phil Hill records his first Formula 1 World Championship title winning the Italian Grand Prix at Monza in his Ferrari Dino 246 - his efforts marked the final World Championship-qualifying Grand Prix victory, pole position, and fastest lap to be achieved by a front-engined Formula 1 car

1960 William F. O'Neil, founder of the General Tire & Rubber Company, dies in Akron, OH at age 75

1962 The first 1963 Pontiac is produced

1962 Frederick J. Hooven of the Ford Motor Company is issued a United States patent for his front-wheel-drive design

1966 Ludovico Scarfiotti wins the Italian Grand Prix at Monza, his first and only Grand Prix victory, and the first Grand Prix won using tires made by the Firestone Tire & Rubber Company

1966 Racer Chris Smith is born in the United States

1972 A 1933 Duesenberg Model J Convertible Victoria by Fernandez & Darrin and originally owned by Greta Garbo is purchased for $90,000 by Charles Wood of Lake George, NY to establish a new auction record

1980 The White Motor Company files for Chapter XI bankruptcy protection

1984 Peugeot SA Chairman Jean-Paul Parayre resigns, with Jacques Calvet named as his successor

1988 The 1989 Chevrolet S-10 pickup is introduced

1990 The Czechosloviakian government authorizes the privatization of Skoda

SEPTEMBER 5

1880 James Wares Bryce, an associate of J. Walter Christie and the development of front wheel drive, is born in New York City

1901 Willis Grant Murray and Walter Clement sign a contract agreeing to build a "gasoline motor-car to be known as the Murray Motor-Car"

1903 The Packard Motor Car Company Board of Directors approve a plan to relocate from Warren, OH to Detroit, MI

1906 Harry Barnard, the biographer of James Couzens, is born in Pueblo, CO

1914 Ira Vail makes his major racing debut driving an Otto at Brighton Beach, NY

1916 Barney Oldfield sets a closed-circuit speed record of 112.9 mph at the Chicago, IL board track driving a Christie front-wheel-drive race car

1926 Automotive parts manufacturer Lauritz F. Nielsen dies in Minneapolis, MN at age 51

1930 Charles Creighton and James Hargis of Maplewood, MO arrive back in New York City having completed a 42-day round trip to Los Angeles, CA driving their 1929 Ford Model A roadster the entire 7,180 mile distance in reverse gear

1938 LeRoy E. Pelletier of E-M-F dies in Detroit, MI at age 70

1938 Fay Leone Faurote, an official with Oldsmobile and Thomas before starting his own automobile advertising business in 1921, dies at age 57

1939 Racer Gianclaudio Guiseppe "Clay" Regazzoni is born in Lugano, Switzerland

1942 Royal Air Force Captain F. W. Hartman, a partner of Lendrum & Hartman, sole concessionaires for Buicks in Great Britain, is killed in combat

1948 Ferrari makes its Grand Prix debut finishing third at the Italian Grand Prix in Turin behind an Alfa Romeo and a Maserati

1953 F. W. Wilcock competes without success in the Brighton (England) Speed Trials in the Swandean Spitfire Special powered by a 27-litre Rolls-Royce Merlin engine, the largest car ever to appear at the venue

1956 Jean Herbert driving the Renault Etoile Filante (Shooting Star) at the Bonneville Salt Flats, UT sets a land speed record for turbine-powered cars of 195 mph

1960 Mechanics Paul McDuffe and Charles Sweatlund along with race official Joe Taylor are killed when two cars crash into the pit area during a NASCAR race in Darlington, SC

1963 Racer Taki Inoue is born in Kobe, Japan

1965 Racer David Brabham is born in Wimbledon, England, the third son of racer Sir Jack Brabham

1970 Racer Jochen Rindt is killed at age 28 when his Lotus-Cosworth crashes during a practice run for the Italian Grand Prix at Monza - he had already amassed enough points to win the World Championship Driver title to become Formula 1's first posthumous champion

1973 The 1974 AMC models are introduced

1977 Daimler-Benz AG executive Hans-Martin Schleyer is kidnapped by the so-called Baader-Meinhof terrorists

1980 The St. Gothard Tunnel, the world's longest highway tunnel at 10.14 miles, opens between Goschenen and Airolo, Switzerland

1991 Lee Iacocca announces that he will retire as Chairman of the Chrysler Corporation at the end of the year

SEPTEMBER 6

1873 Howard Earle Coffin, a cofounder of the Hudson Motor Car Company, is born in West Milton, OH

1891 The Peugeot Type 3 quadricycle is introduced, the company's first product that is marketed to the public

1896 Alvan Macauley Jr., son of the longtime Packard executive and himself an automobile industry official, is born in Dayton, OH

1900 Andrew L. Riker sets a 5-mile speed record for electric cars of 10 minutes, 20 seconds at Newport, RI

1907 A Stearns 30-60 with seven passengers on board becomes the first motor vehicle to reach the summit of Pikes Peak, CO under its own power for the entire distance

1908 Raymond Christy Firestone of the Firestone Tire & Rubber Company is born in Akron, OH

1911 Charles Deutsch of D.B. is born in Champigny-sur-Marne, France

1912 Clayton Blaine Leach of Pontiac is born in Birch Run, MI

1915 The first prototype army tank is completed by William Foster & Company Ltd. of Lincoln, Lindsey, Lincolnshire, England and is given its intitial test drive

1916 Stewart James Wolfe of General Motors and American Motors is born in Kings, NY

1928 Barton Lee Peck, builder of the 1897-1899 Peck, drowns in Daytona Beach, FL

1928 Sidney Watkins, longtime Grand Prix on-site medical doctor, is born in Liverpool, England

1935 James Leonard Pate of the B. F. Goodrich Company and the Pennzoil Company is born in Mount Sterling, IL

1938 Racer Larry Dickson is born in Marietta, OH

1938 V. G. Barford, Chief Designer for J. I. Thornycroft & Company, Ltd., dies at age 66

1938 Dr. Ing. Ferdinand Porsche is awarded the National Culture Prize for his design of a German "people's car"

1940 Everett W. Turley, an employee of the Haynes Automobile Company who later was an executive in fleet management, dies at age 49

1941 Jonkheer Hugo Loudon of the Royal Dutch Oil Company dies in the Netherlands at age 81

1941 J. Ross St. Germain of the Ethyl Gasoline Corporation dies at age 41

1945 Richard Vryling Le Sueur, President of the Imperial Oil Company, Ltd., dies in Toronto, ON, Canada at age 64

1949 British occupation forces transfer ownership of Volkswagenwerk AG to the government of Lower Saxony

1954 The Hudson Itala, featuring a custom-built body by Carrozzeria Touring of Milan, Italy mounted on a Jet chassis, is introduced

1954 Race mechanic Clay Smith is killed at age 39 in a pit accident during a 100-mile race in DuQuoin, IL

1955 Jean-Marc Borel of Bugatti Automobili, manufacturers of the Bugatti 110, is born in Gap, Hautes Alpes, France

1958 Rudolph C. Norberg, President of the Willard Storage Battery Company 1928-1941, dies at age 77

1964 Joe Leonard, driving a Dodge at DuQuoin, IL, records his first major racing victory

1970 Arthur W. Herrington of Marmon-Herrington dies at age 79

1970 The Ontario (CA) Motor Speedway stages its first event, the California 500, an Indycar event won by Jimmy McElreath in a Coyote-Ford

1971 The 10,000,000th Opel is produced, a Rekord L6 sedan

1972 William L. Kissel, a cofounder of the Kissel Motor Car Company of Hartford, WI, dies at age 93

1981 Teruo Tojo is named President of Mitsubishi

1990 Renault SA acquires Mack Trucks, Inc.

SEPTEMBER 7

1859 Francois Pilain, founder of the Societe des Automobiles Pilain, is born in Saint-Berain, Saone-et-Loire, France

1871 Automobile parts manufacturer Oscar A. Smith is born in Meriden, CT

1877 Garnet Wolseley McKee, the inventor of the automobile windshield wiper, is born in Sandwich, Ontario, Canada

1881 Charles Emil Sorensen of the Ford Motor Company is born in Copenhagen, Denmark

1896 A Riker Electric Trap driven by Andrew L. Riker and C. H. Whiting wins the first closed-course automobile race in United States at the Rhode Island State Fair in Narragansett Park

One of the greatest automotive engineers of the pioneer era, Andrew L. Riker is best remembered for his work with Locomobile and the cars and trucks that bear his name

1898 The 12th Earl of Winchilsea, a pioneer British motoring enthusiast, dies at age 47

1899 Newport, RI stages the first automobile parade with nineteen flower-bedecked cars participating

1908 The first Lowell (MA) Road Race, a 254.4-mile event, is won by Lewis Strang in an Isotta-Fraschini

1908 Automotive historian Victor Boesen is born in Plainfield, IN

1910 Racer Lee Wallard is born in Schenectady, NY

1910 Automotive artist Ben Stahl is born in Chicago, IL

1912 The Continental Motors Corporation is formed in Buffalo, NY by Gordon L. Matthews, Frank V. Whyland, Allen E. Choate, Walter F. Schmiding, and Reverdy L. Hurd to produce the Comet automobile - the venture failed in 1914

1912 The Blitzen Benz makes its racing debut, as Bob Burman sets a track record at the Brighton Beach (NY) Speedway time trials

1914 The Mercer Automobile Company officially withdraws from racing

1915 William A. Besserdich is awarded a patent for his Steering Mechanism, a design used on most 4-wheel-drive vehicles

1924 Elisabeth Junek makes her racing debut, winning the Plzen-Tremosna hillclimb in a Bugatti

1930 The Maserati 8C 3000 makes its racing debut, with Achille Varzi taking it to victory in the Italian Grand Prix at Monza

1936 Racer Brian Hart is born in Enfield, England

1936 Raymond Mays breaks the lap record for the Mountain Course at Brooklands, reaching 84.31 mph in his E.R.A.

1939 Racer Donnie Joseph Allison is born in Miami, FL

1940 Edmund Rumpler dies in Berlin, Germany at age 68

1945 Thomas P. Henry, President of the American Automobile Association 1923-1945, dies in Detroit, MI at age 67

1946 John Cooper, driving a 500-cc prototype Cooper, wins the 850-cc class at the first post-World War II Brighton Speed Trials, the first victory for the marque

1951 The first Allard J2X is sold

1951 Racer Rad Dougall is born in South Africa

1956 Charles W. Good, a professor of mechanical engineering at the University of Michigan since 1918, dies

1957 Phil Hill makes his Ferrari racing debut, finishing third at Monza in a Dino 246 Formula 1 car

1961 John S. Inskip, who was involved with Rolls-Royce in the United States for 30 years as an executive, coachbuilder, importer, dealer, and service representative, dies in Westport, CT

1967 Racer Kelvin Burt is born in Birmingham, England

1984 Governor George Deukmejian signs legislation making California the first state to allow collector cars to be registered with license plates from the car's year of manufacture

1986 The 1987 Chevrolet Blazer and S-10 pickup are introduced

1986 The AGS makes its debut in the Italian Grand Prix at Monza, but the car designed by Christian Vanderpleyn and driven by Ivan Capelli retires

1988 Fiat SpA increases its ownership of Ferrari SpA to 90%

1991 Harry Gant, age 51, wins the Miller Genuine Draft 400 in Richmond, VA to extend his own record as the oldest winner of a NASCAR race

1992 Automobile stylist Clare E. Hodgman dies in Daytona Beach, FL at age 81

1993 Chrysler Corporation's new Neon compact cars are officially introduced at the Frankfurt Auto Show in Germany

The Neon introduced itself to the world with clever advertisements such as this.
For different markets they would be badge engineered as a
Plymouth, Dodge, or Chrysler.

1996 William Brownlie, Chrysler Corporation stylist 1953-1980, dies at age 70

SEPTEMBER 8

1871 Adolf Daimler, middle son of Gottlieb Daimler, is born

1871 Robert Samuel McLaughlin, founder of the McLaughlin Motor Car Company and the long-time President of General Motors of Canada Ltd., is born in Enniskillen, ON, Canada

1876 Walter Charles White, President of the White Motor Company 1921-1929, is born in Cleveland, OH

1879 Harold Hibbard Seaman, cofounder of the Seaman Body Corporation, is born in Milwaukee, WI

1880 The Imperial Oil Company, Ltd. is incorporated in Canada

1884 Edwin Fox of Vanden Plas (England) 1923 Ltd. is born in Edgware, Middlesex, England

1895 Adam Opel dies of typhus at age 58

1899 Mervin Franklin Cotes of the Motor Wheel Corporation is born in Peoria, IL

1903 The Packard Motor Car Company re-elects James W. Packard as President, and elects Russell Alger as Vice President and Philip H. McMillan as Secretary-Treasurer

1923 The Daniels Motor Car Company is declared bankrupt

1923 Ugo Sivocci, winner of the 1923 Targa Florio, is killed during practice for the Italian Grand Prix at Monza when his Alfa Romeo P1 leaves the track and crashes into a tree

1925 The 2,000,000th Chevrolet is produced, a Superior Series K 2-door Coach

1927 Herbert A. Temple, an experimental engineer with the Hupp Motor Car Corporation who previously had worked for Sheffield, Studebaker, and Packard, dies in Detroit, MI at age 44

1937 The first 1938 Pontiac Six is produced

1041 The first 1942 Chevrolet is produced

1947 The 1948 Packard Twenty-Second Series closed cars are introduced, completing the marque's model year lineup

1953 The first Pontiac is produced with a Chevrolet Powerglide transmission, a move necessitated by the Hydra-Matic plant fire of August 12th

1954 The 3,000,000th vehicle is produced by Ford Motor Company of Canada, Ltd.

1954 Frank J. Olender, President of the Olender Sales & Engineer Company and a former design engineer with Hudson and Plymouth, dies at age 44

1954 Richard Simonsen, a longtime Australian importer of General Motors cars and parts, dies in Perth, Western Australia at age 49

1954 William W. Sloane, Vice President of the Goodman Manufacturing Company, dies at age 68

1955 Gosta Vennerholm, Swedish-born Manager of the Manufacturing Research Department of the Ford Motor Company and an employee of the firm since 1924, dies

1956 Racer Stefan Johansson is born in Vaxjo, Sweden

1959 The first 1960 Ford Thunderbird is produced

1960 Racer Aguri Suzuki is born in Tokyo, Japan

1966 Racer John Taylor dies in Koblenz, West Germany at age 33 from injuries suffered earlier in the year when his Brabham-BRM crashed during the German Grand Prix at the Nurburgring

1976 Millard H. Toncray, Chief Engineer of the Hudson Motor Car Company 1942-1954, dies in Onaway, MI at age 83

1984 Johnnie Parsons, winner of the 1950 Indianapolis 500, dies in Van Nuys, CA at age 66

1986 The Nissan Motor Company Ltd. opens its Sunderland, England factory, the first Japanese automobile plant in Europe

1994 Ford Motor Company announces that William Clay Ford Jr. will succeed his namesake father as Chairman of the Board's Finance Committee

SEPTEMBER 9

1873 Ernesto Ceirano of Fiat is born in Cuneo, Italy

1897 Ralph Kenneth Davies, longtime executive with the various Standard Oil companies, is born in Cherrydale, VA

1900 Cesare Isotta, driving a 5CV Renault, wins the 400 kg class in the 5 km time trials in Brescia, Italy

1901 The American Car Association (ACA) sponsors its first hill climb, a contest at Nelson Hill near Peekskill, NY that is won by a steam-powered Grout Stanhope

1904 William Thomas Gossett of the Ford Motor Company is born in Gainesville, TX

1906 A Buick Model F arrives in San Francisco, CA, completing the first trans-United States trip by a touring car

1909 The Selden patent is upheld as legal and valid, causing a stampede of manufacturers seeking to acquire ALAM licenses

1910 Charles W. Nash is named President of the Buick Motor Company

1913 The first Corona (CA) Road Races are staged on the city's unique circular track - winner of the main event, a 301.81-mile "Free-for-all Race", is Earl Cooper in a Stutz

Corona's famous circular race track, Grand Boulevard, appears very prominently in this aerial photograph of the city taken nearly three decades after its closure.

1915 Theodore Johnathan Emmert of the Ford Motor Company of Canada, Ltd. is born in Smithboro, IL

1917 John Richard Parker of the A. O. Smith Corporation is born in Three Rivers, MI

1918 Lt. George R. Mason of the Mason Motor Company dies in France at age 29

1923 Carlo Salamano, driving a Fiat 805 fitted with a Roots-type supercharger, wins the European Grand Prix at Monza, Italy, the first grand prix victory for a supercharged car

1928 Racer Emilio Materassi is killed at age 39 along with 20 spectators when his Talbot crashes during the Italian Grand Prix in Monza

1932 James Gordon Buick, Controller of the Lincoln-Mercury Division of the Ford Motor Company 1959-1975, is born in Beecher City, IL

1945 The first post-World War II motor race in Europe is held at the Bois de Boulogne in Paris, France and won by Jean-Pierre Wimille in the unique Bugatti Type 50B 4.7-litre

1949 The Volvo PV445, basically a PV444 chassis on which a specialty body could be mounted, is introduced

1950 Racer Victor Hemery dies

1953 The Ford Motor Company produces its 40,000,000th vehicle, a 1954 Mercury convertible

A 1954 Mercury leads traffic in Manchester, GA.

1954 The first regular production Ford Thunderbird is built

1955 Dr. Graham Edgar, first Director of Research for the Ethyl Gasoline Corporation and developer of the octane scale for motor fuels, dies at age 67

1956 Racer Oscar Manautou is born in Mexico

1960 Mickey Thompson, driving the Challenger I at the Bonneville Salt Flats, UT, records a one-way run of 406.60 mph, becoming the first driver to break the 400 mph barrier although the run is unrecognized as a land speed record

1963 George W. Risley joins the Detroit Public Library as Assistant Curator of the National Automotive History Collection

1966 The National Traffic and Motor Vehicle Safety Act becomes law in the United States

1968 Malcolm Sayer's memorandum to Sir William Lyons results in the development of what would be the Jaguar XJ-S coupe

1970 The first Zhiguli, a Fiat-based compact car, is produced at the new plant in Tol'iatti, USSR

1978 Ronald Haynes of Rolls-Royce, Ltd. dies

1982 Henry Ford II retires from all involvement with the Ford Motor Company

SEPTEMBER 10

1847 John Brisben Walker, founder of *Cosmopolitan* magazine, patron of pioneer automobile racing, and a cofounder of the Automobile Company of America, manufacturers of the Locomobile, is born in Whitpain, PA

1897 George Smith, a London taxicab driver, is the first person arrested for drunken driving in Great Britain

1898 J. Frank Duryea joins the American Automobile Company to design a three-cylinder surrey-type automobile

1898 Waldo Lonsbury Semon, a B. F. Goodrich Company research chemist who was a leader in the development of synthetic rubber, is born in Demopolis, AL

1898 Gervais William Trichel of the Chrysler Corporation is born in Trichel, LA

1900 The Warren, OH partnership of Packard & Weiss incorporates as the Ohio Automobile Company, manufacturers of the Packard motor car

1900 Automotive historian Philip Van Doren Stern is born in Wyalusing, PA

1905 The first Coppo Florio race is staged on the island of Sicily with twenty-one competitors including the patron, Vincenzo Florio, in a Mercedes - the winner is Carlo Raggio driving an Itala

1908 Curtis R. Hatheway, an attorney with Ward, Hayden & Satterlee advises William C. Durant not to incorporate as "International Motor Company", offer reserved approval of "United Motors Company", and suggest "General Motors Company" as a name that would not receive legal challenges

1910 William C. Durant loses control of General Motors for the first time

1912 General Motors receives a patent for its "GMC" trademark

1913 J. Dallas Dort recommends the formation of a company independent of the control of William C. Durant to produce the Dort automobile

1921 The Avus Autobahn, the world's first controlled-access highway, opens near Berlin, Germany - promoted by Karl Friedrich Fritsch, the highway has frequently been used as a race track

1926 Robert E. Petersen of *Motor Trend* magazine is born in Los Angeles, CA

1926 The last Salmson GSS is sold

1933 Giuseppe Campari, age 41, and Baconin Borzacchini, age 35, are killed when their Alfa Romeos are involved in a four-car accident during the second qualifying heat of the Italian Grand Prix at Monza - later in the day Count Stanislaus Czaykowski is killed when his Bugatti Type 54 crashes near the end of the main event

1934 The 1935 Auburn 653 Six and 851 Eight are introduced to the public

1937 The Packard Sixteenth Series Twelves are introduced

1940 The Alfa Romeo Tipo 512 is bench tested for the first time, exactly three months after Italy officially entered World War II

1942 Racer Guido Dacco is born in Limiate, Italy

1942 President Franklin D. Roosevelt orders gas rationing in the United States

1950 The first Sandberg Speed Hill Climb staged at the Sandberg Ranch north of Los Angeles, CA

1950 Racer Raymond Sommer is killed at age 44 when his 1100-cc Cooper crashes during the Grand Prix du Haute Garonne at the Cadours, France circuit

1950 The Cummins Diesel Special No. 61 driven by Jimmy Jackson sets a land speed record for diesel-powered cars of 165.23 mph at the Bonneville Salt Flats, UT

1952 Two Packard Mayfairs arrive at the Henney Motor Company factory in Freeport, IL for conversion into Monte Carlo showcars

1952 Racer Bruno Giacomelli is born in Borgo Pancarale, Brescia, Lombardy, Italy

1955 Racer Armin Hahne is born in Moers, West Germany

1959 Dr. Raymond Henry Hobrock, retired Vice President of the Bundy Tubing Company, dies at age 59

1961 Count Wolfgang von Trips is killed at age 33 when his Ferrari crashes during the Italian Grand Prix at Monza - Nino Vaccarella makes his Grand Prix debut, driving a Scuderia Serenissima de Tomaso-OSCA

1962 Rollin H. White dies in Hobe Sound, FL at age 90

1962 Racer Glenn Leasher is killed at age 25 during a land speed record attempt at the Bonneville Salt Flats, UT

1962 The Ford Motor Company authorizes production of the Ford Mustang as designed by Joe Oros, Gail Halderman, and L. David Ash

1967 John Surtees wins the Italian Grand Prix at Monza in a Honda, a race often referred to as "The Race of the Century"

1970 The 1971 Chevrolet Vega, a new sub-compact, is introduced

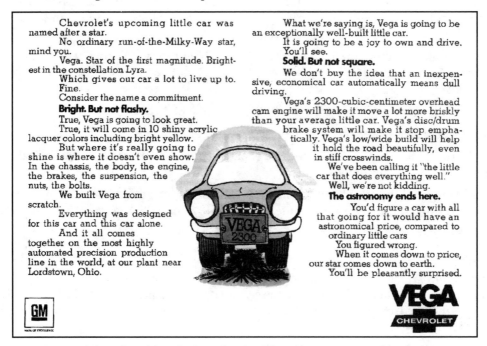

For several weeks prior to its introduction Chevrolet ran teaser advertisements to generate interest in its new sub-compact.

1970 The 1971 Oldsmobiles, including the second-generation Toronado, are introduced

1972 Marsden Ware of Packard dies in Bloomfield Hills, MI at age 75

1972 25-year old Emerson Fittipaldi, driving for Lotus-Cosworth, clinches the World Champion Driver title in Formula 1 to become the youngest person to accomplish this feat

1983 Alice Huyler Ramsey, the first woman to drive an automobile across the United States, dies in Covina, CA at age 96

SEPTEMBER 11

1875 Harry Hoxie Bassett of Buick is born in Utica, NY

1875 George Washington Hanson is born in Monroe County, GA

1879 Louis Herve Coatalen of Sunbeam is born in Concarneau, France

1884 Phillip Halsey Patchin of the Standard Oil Company is born in Des Moines, IA

1889 John Joseph Schumann Jr. of the General Motors Acceptance Corporation is born in New York City

1903 The Buick Motor Company of Detroit, MI announces plans to relocate to Flint, MI

1903 The Wisconsin State Fair Park in Milwaukee, the oldest permanent racing circuit in the world, opens

1903 Henry B. Joy is named General Manager of the Packard Motor Car Company, assuming principal management of the firm from President James W. Packard

1909 Soviet automobile executive Vasilii Nikolaevich Doenin is born in Yalta, Crimea, Ukraine

1915 Sir Austin Ernest Bide of the British Leyland Motor Corporation Ltd. is born in London, England

1916 Roscoe M. Smith joins the Ford Motor Company as an electrician in the flywheel department

1918 Packard suspends automobile production for the duration of World War I

1927 Charles J. Glidden, creator of the Glidden Tours, dies in Boston, MA at age 70

1935 The first 1936 Pontiac Deluxe Eight is produced

1935 Gerald Greenwald of the Chrysler Corporation is born in St. Louis, MO

1938 The V-16 Alfa Romeo Type 316 makes its racing debut in the Italian Grand Prix at Monza as Guiseppe Farina finishes second to the Auto Union Type D driven by Tazio Nuvolari

1949 Racer Bill Whittington is born in the United States

1951 The Shell-D'Arcy Petroleum Company of Nigerian Ltd. is incorporated

1966 The 1967 Chevrolet trucks are introduced

1967 Peter Monteverdi introduces his first automobile, the Monteverdi 375 S High Speed, at the Frankfurt (West Germany) Automobile Show

1967 The 1968 Oldsmobiles are introduced

1969 Henry Ford II fires Ford Motor Company President Semon E. "Bunky" Knudsen just 19 months after hiring him away from General Motors - Lee Iacocca is named President of Ford North American Automotive Operations and Robert J. Hampson is named President of Ford Non-Automotive Operations

1970 The sub-compact Ford Pinto is introduced

1972 The Mercedes-Benz 280C introduced to the United States market

1978 Racer Ronnie Peterson dies at age 34 in Milan, Itlay from injuries suffered when his Lotus-Cosworth crashed during the Italian Grand Prix at Monza

1983 Albert Bradley, Chairman of General Motors 1956-1958, dies in Greenwich, CT at age 92

1983 Racer Brian Muir dies

1995 British racer Keith Odor is killed during the Super Touring Car race at the Avus track in Germany when his disabled Nissan is broadsided by an Audi driven by Frank Biela

SEPTEMBER 12

1874 William V. Hartmann of the Gulf Oil Company is born in Cincinnati, OH

1876 Harry Clayton Stutz is born in Ansonia, OH

1882 Joseph Bolden Graham, President of the Graham Brothers Company truck manufacturers 1917-1926, President of Graham-Paige Motors Corporation 1927-1941, and the holder of patents related to the making of hollow glassware and bottles, is born in Washington, IN

1896 Alfred Momo is born in Turin, Italy

1897 The Arona-Stresa-Arona race is staged, the second ever held in Italy

1904 Racer Lou Moore is born in Hinton, OK

1912 The United States Motor Company is forced into receivership

1912 Carl G. Fisher and James A. Allison announce in Indianapolis, IN that they plan to promote the building of a transcontinental highway to be completed before the 1915 Panama-Pacific Exposition in San Francisco, CA

1913 Eiji Toyoda of Toyota is born in Kinjo, Nishi Kasugai, Aichi, Japan

1914 Charles Colmery Gibson, Vice President of the Goodyear Tire & Rubber Company and a 36-year employee of the firm, is born in Edwards, MS

1916 Racer Melvin E. "Tony" Bettenhausen (Sr.) is born in Tinley Park, IL

1918 E. G. "Cannonball" Baker completes a 17,000-mile, 77-day promotional trip to all 48 state capitals in a ReVere touring car powered by a Duesenberg engine

1924 The assets of the bankrupt Mitchell Motor Company are sold at auction, with the main factory going to the Nash Motors Company for production of its new Ajax marque

1924 The world's first inter-urban highway, the Milan-Varese Autostrada, is officially opened by King Victor Emmanuel III of Italy

1926 Alfred Neubauer introduces a code system for communicating with drivers during his first appearance as manager of the Mercedes-Benz racing team in a race at the Solitude circuit near Stuttgart, Germany - Otto Merz led the team to a one-two-three finish

1931 Racer Jimmy Gleason dies one day after crashing during a race in Syracuse, NY

1932 Hermann Ahrens joins the Daimler-Benz AG special car department

1940 The Alfa Romeo Tipo 512 monoposto race car is given its first road test with Consalvo Sanesi at the controls

1941 The 1942 Fords are introduced

1944 Philip G. Johnson, President of the Kenworth Motor Truck Corporation since 1937, dies in Wichita, KS

1944 Racer Eddie Keizan is born in Johannesburg, South Africa

1952 Racer Jean-Louis Schlesser is born in Nancy, France, a nephew of racer Jo Schlesser

1955 Automotive maintenance journalist G. van Twist dies in Dordrecht, Holland

1956 Racer Ricky Rudd is born in Chesapeake, VA

1958 Harold P. Henning, Manager of Engineering Operations and Inspection for General Motors, dies at age 57

1959 Racer Glen Rocky is killed at age 32 during a race in Marne, MI

1959 Racer Frederick Bliven is killed at age 19 during a race in Middletown, NY

1959 Walter H. Roesing of the Champion Spark Plug Company dies at age 59

1960 Great Britain initiates the Roadworthiness Test for all vehicles ten or more years old

1961 Carlyle Fraser, President of the Genuine Parts Company 1925-1947 and its Chairman 1947-1961, dies in Atlanta, GA at age 66

1962 The 1963 Buick Riviera is introduced as a new series, available only as a sport coupe

1965 Jackie Stewart records his first Grand Prix victory, winning the Italian Grand Prix at Monza in a BRM

1968 The 1969 Oldsmobiles are introduced

1969 Racer Giampiero Simoni is born in Italy

1988 The Ford Motor Company and the Nissan Motor Company, Ltd. announce plans to design a minivan and build a jointly-owned factory in Avon Lake, OH

1988 William L. Mitchell, former General Motors Vice President-Design, dies at age 76

1994 The first Toyota Avalon is produced at the Georgetown, KY plant

1995 The 250,000th Australian-built Toyota Camry is produced at the Toyota Motor Corporation Australia Ltd. plant in Altona, Victoria

SEPTEMBER 13

1755 Steam power pioneer Oliver Evans is born in Newport, DE

1869 Paul Daimler, eldest son of Gottlieb Daimler and the successor of Wilhelm Maybach as Chief Engineer of Mercedes, is born in Karlsruhe, Germany

1873 Crankshaft manufacturer Harry Galpin Stoddard is born in Athol, MA

1891 Jay Everett Crane of the Standard Oil Company of New Jersey is born in Newark, NJ

1892 Achille Philion is issued a United States patent for his "Steam Carriage"

1898 W. L. Elliott of Oakland, CA completes a 56-mile trip to the summit of Mt. Hamilton in his Elliott Gasoline Carriage, one of the first cars built in California

1899 Arthur Smith strikes and kills New York City pedestrian Henry B. Bliss in the first recorded fatality from an automobile accident in the United States

1916 A Hudson Super-Six Series H phaeton begins a promotional "Twice Across America" run from San Francisco, CA to New York City and back to San Francisco

1932 Racer Mike MacDowel is born in Great Yarmouth, Norfolkshire, England

1936 E. R. Thomas of Thomas and Thomas-Detroit dies in Buffalo, NY at age 85

1938 James H. Ross of BP America Inc. is born in London, England

1945 Packard begins construction of its new final car assembly factory

1945 The first post-World War II Pontiac is produced, a Streamliner Sedan Coupe

1945 The first post-World War II Lincoln is introduced to the press

1953 OSCA makes its final Formula 1 appearance in the Italian Grand Prix in Monza, with Louis Chiron finishing tenth

1954 James Scripps Booth, designer of the Biautogo, Scripps-Booth, and daVinci, dies at age 66

1957 The last 1957 Pontiac is produced

1958 Benjamin H. Blair, retired Chief Engineer-Leaf Springs of the Easton Manufacturing Company, dies at age 70

1960 The last 1960 Ford Thunderbird is produced

1961 The first Ford Thunderbird Sports Roadster, a 1962 model, is produced

1961 Henry Ford II signs a pact whereby the Ford Motor Company will purchase the Philco Corporation

1961 Racer Jim Guthrie is born in Gadsden, AL

1965 The first 1966 Pontiac is produced

1967 Lord Lambury of Northfield (nee Leonard P. Lord), Chairman of the British Motor Corporation, dies in London, England at age 71

1969 The Alabama Speedway in Talladega, AL stages its first event, a 401.66 mile NASCAR race won by Ken Rush in a Chevrolet Camaro

1971 Kurt Lotz resigns as Chairman of Volkswagenwerk AG

1973 AB Volvo announces plans to build a plant in Chesapeake, VA

1977 Oldsmobile introduces the first United States-built diesel-powered automobiles

1981 The Toleman makes its Formula 1 debut in the Italian Grand Prix with the Type TG181 driven by Brian Henton finishing tenth

1982 Marcus Wallenberg of Saab-Scania AB dies at age 82

1990 The 1991 Ford Ranger pickup is introduced

SEPTEMBER 14

1846 George Baldwin Selden, whose controversial automobile patent dominated the United States automobile industry until 1911, is born in Clarkson, NY

George B. Selden's claim of inventing the automobile was, at best, exaggerated. The cars bearing his name that were built 1907-1914 were quite ordinary and met with limited commercial success. Selden trucks, however, enjoyed a brief period of fame beginning with their introduction in 1913, but the marque faded away about 1932.

The Beginning of the World's Second Largest Industry

GEORGE B. SELDEN invented, in 1877, the first internal combustion gasoline engine for road locomotion. This was the beginning of the world's second largest industry.

History affords no more startling record of achievement than the development of the automotive industry, which resulted from this remarkable invention by Selden.

SELDEN TRUCKS have shared in the development of this second largest industry. Wherever in the world there has existed a need for dependable, economical, profitable haulage of commodities, SELDEN TRUCKS have served and proved their ability.

SELDEN TRUCKS possess tremendous strength of construction and enormous pulling power. Actual records of users prove their cost of operation and maintenance to be low. There are no better trucks than SELDEN TRUCKS.

Ask us to give you facts that will show how SELDEN TRUCKS are effecting economies in your line of business.

1½, 2½, 3½, 5 Ton Models—All Worm Drive

WRITE for Booklet, "Yesterday, Today, Tomorrow," a brief history of the early days of the automobile

SELDEN TRUCK CORPORATION, Rochester, N.Y., U. S. A.

1882 Frank Raymond Fageol, the founder of Fageol Motors Company of Oakland, CA in 1917 and the Twin Coach Company of Kent, OH in 1927, is born in Polk County, IA

1902 John Irving Whalley, a United States Congressman noted for supporting automobile industry causes, is born in Barnesboro, PA

1902 Orville Wick of General Motors is born in Malcolm, ND

1903 The Packard Motor Company begins removing the machinery at its Warren, OH facility for transfer to the new factory in Detroit, MI

1905 The first Tourist Trophy race is staged by the Royal Automobile Club on the Isle of Man and won by an Arrol-Johnston driven by designer John S. Napier

1914 The first FWD firetruck is sold to Minneapolis (MN) Fire Department

1918 Racer Georges Berger is born in Brussels, Belgium

1920 The first Lincoln is completed, a 7-Passenger Touring

1923 General Motors holds the first meeting of its General Technical Committee, formed to prevent problems within the corporation similar to those encountered during the development of the copper-cooled engine

1924 The Studebaker Standard Six and Big Six Model EP are introduced

1927 Dancer Dora Angela "Isadora" Duncan is accidently strangled in Nice, France at age 49 when her long scarf gets caught in the rear wheel of a Bugatti driven by factory mechanic Benoit Falchetto

1935 Dick Shuttleworth, driving a 2.9-litre Alfa Romeo, sets a 1/2-mile record of 79.36 mph at the Brighton (England) Speed Trials

1938 C. L. Jacobsen, Sales Manager for the Chrysler Division of the Chrysler Corporation, announces the availability of a sun roof

1939 The Graham-Paige Motors Corporation contracts with Hupmobile to build its Cord-based Skylark, also acquiring the right to manufacture its own Cord-based car, the Hollywood

1940 Carl W. Weiss, the German-born design engineer whose universal joint was the basis of the front-wheel-drive Ruxton, dies

1944 Racer Robert Benoist, a key member of the French underground during World War II, is executed at Buchenwald, Germany by his Gestapo captors

1949 Racer John Bauer is born in the United States

1950 Racer Masami Kuwashima is born in Japan

1953 Bayard D. Kunkle of General Motors dies at age 70

1955 William Fisher Jennings, President and Treasurer of the Bound Brook Oil-Less Bearing Company and an employee of the firm for 41 years, dies

1956 Donald L. McClure of the Libbey-Owens-Ford Glass Company dies in Houston, TX

1958 Albert Beauchamp, Senior Product Design Checker for the Fisher Body Division of General Motors, dies at age 59

1958 Ben J. Smith of the International Harvester Company dies at age 52

1960 The Organization of the Petroleum Exporting Countries (OPEC) is founded in Baghdad, Iraq

1967 The 1968 Plymouths are introduced, including the new Road Runner coupe

1968 Patsy Burt, driving a McLaren-Oldsmobile, wins the standing start kilometre at the Brighton (England) Speed Trials, the first and only victory by a woman at that venue

1978 Philip Caldwell is elected President of the Ford Motor Company

1979 The new Lundhurst, NJ headquarters of Rolls-Royce Motors, Inc. is officially opened by HRH The Duke of Kent

1982 Rev. Gregory A. Bezy, founder of the Sacred Heart Auto League in 1954, dies in Victorville, CA at age 68

1982 The Chevrolet S-10 Blazer is introduced as a 1983 model

1982 The 1983 GMC Jimmy is introduced

1991 Bugatti SpA of Campogalliano, Italy, a company founded by Romano Artioli, introduces the Bugatti EB110 in Paris, France - the model noted its debut 110 years after the birth of Ettore Bugatti

1992 The 1993 Ford Ranger pickup and Aerostar minivan are introduced

SEPTEMBER 15

1877 Frank Forrest Beall of Packard and Gray is born in Derwood, MD

1881 Ettore Arco Isidoro Bugatti is born in Milan, Italy

1882 Andrew Cornelius Maier, a manufacturer of automobile paints and varnishes, is born in Saginaw, MI

1888 Racer Antonio Ascari is born in Moratica di Bonferraro, Lombardy, Italy

1908 The Republic Rubber Company of Youngstown, OH is issued a United States patent for its tire tread pattern marketed as "Staggard"

1909 Judge C. M. Hough of New York rules that George B. Selden is the inventor of the automobile, his patent if valid, and the Ford Motor Company has infringed that patent

1909 Charles F. Ketterling applies for a patent on his automobile ignition improvements

1909 Yutaka Katayama of Nissan is born in Tokyo, Japan

1916 Racer Antonio "Toni" Branca is born

1918 Automobile historian Alfred DuPont Chandler Jr. is born in Guyencourt, DE

1923 The last race at the Janesville (WI) Fair Grounds, a 100 mile event, is won by Red Parkhurst

1924 Racer James Anthony "Jimmy" Murphy is killed at age 30 when his Miller front-wheel-drive prototype race car crashes during a test run in Syracuse, NY

1924 Gustav E. Franquist, a founder of the Society of Automotive Engineers who designed the first Simplex, dies in Philadelphia, PA at age 50

1927 E. L. Cord and the Auburn Automobile Company purchase the Lycoming Motors Corporation of Williamsport, PA and the Limousine Body Company of Kalamazoo, MI

1930 The new administration building of the Auburn Automobile Company opens in Auburn, IN - the Auburn-Cord-Duesenberg Museum now occupies the restored building

A bulk mail card from 1938 pictures the former Auburn Automobile Company administration building, still virtually new but her days of glory long gone.

1936 Ernest E. Sweet, former Chief Engineer of the Cadillac Motor Car Company, dies at age 63

1937 The first 1938 Pontiac Eight is produced

1938 The 1939 Hupmobile Senior Six and Eight are shown to automotive editors at the Grosse Pointe Yacht Club near Detroit, MI

1938 John R. Cobb, driving a Railton Special at the Bonneville Salt Flats, UT, raises the land speed record to 350.20 mph

1939 The 1940 Nashes are introduced

1944 Jurgen E. Schrempp of Daimler-Benz AG is born in Freiburg, Wurttemberg, Germany

1946 Racer Adelbert William "Al" Putnam is killed at age 37 when his Palmer Special crashed during a qualifying run in Indianapolis, IN

1946 Victor R. Heftler, French-born President of the Zenith Carburetor Company, dies in Grosse Pointe Park, MI

1950 The first race staged at the Opa Locka (FL) Speedway is won by Bob Gegen in a supercharged M.G. TC

1951 The Aston Martin DB3/1 makes its racing with debut at the RAC Tourist Trophy race at Dunrod, Ireland, but the car driven by Lance Macklin had to retire due to bearing failure

1952 George H. Eaton, Automotive Field Supervisor for the Atlantic Refining Company, dies at age 63

1955 The 1956 Hillman Minx is introduced to the United States market

1956 The 1957 British Fords are introduced to the United States market

1957 The 1958 British Fords are introduced to the United States market

1959 The 1960 Lloyds are introduced to the United States market

1964 The 1965 Cadillacs are introduced by division General Manager Harold G. Warner at the Cadillac National Press Preview in Detroit

1965 The 10,000,000th Volkswagen is produced

1966 Racer Antonio Tamburini is born in Arezzo, Italy

1970 The 1971 Plymouth Valiant compacts are introduced three weeks before the appearance of the full-sized models

1972 The 1973 Opels are introduced to the United States market

1976 Volkswagenwerk AG purchases Chrysler Corporation's assembly plant in Westmoreland, PA

1978 Production of the International Loadstar truck ends after 16 years and 940,660 units

1978 The 1979 Pontiac Sunbird is introduced, thirteen days before the other models

1978 Willy Messerschmitt, airplane designer/manufacturer and namesake of the 1953-1962 Messerschmitt bubblecar, dies in Munich, Germany at age 80

1989 The 1990 Ford Tempo is introduced

1989 Dean A. McGee, Chairman of the Kerr-McGee Corporation 1963-1983, dies at age 85

1991 Harry Gant, age 51, wins the Peak Antifreeze 500 in Dover, DE to extend his own record as the oldest winner of a NASCAR race

SEPTEMBER 16

1883 Tire manufacturer Francis Breese Davis Jr. is born in Fort Edward, NY

1888 Walter Owen Bentley is born in London, England

1888 Better roads advocate Herbert Sinclair Fairbank is born in Baltimore, MD

1895 James Edward Trainer of the Firestone Tire & Rubber Company is born in New York City

1896 Peter Olai Peterson of Studebaker, Rockne, and Mack is born in Kristiansund, Norway

1901 Testing is completed for the Packard Model F

1903 The first gasoline engine designed by F. H. Royce, a 2-cylinder, 10-hp unit, is successfully tested

1908 The General Motors Company is incorporated in New Jersey by William C. Durant

The administrative office building of the Buick Motor Company in Flint, MI as it looked in 1908 - Buick was the original building block of General Motors, and much of the giant corporation's organization no doubt was planned in this building.

1910 Racer Karl Kling is born in Giessen, Germany

1910 Racer Giosue Guippone (aka Cesare Giuppone) is killed when his Peugeot crashes during a practice run near Desvres, France

1914 Racer Josef Peters is born in Dusseldorf, Germany

1915 William C. Durant regains control of General Motors

1916 The Kent Motors Corporation is organized in Newark, NJ by Frederick H. Clarke, Dr. Henry F. Clarke, R. J. Cosgrove, Lloyd H. Foster, Wallace A. Hood, F. J. Nagel, Thomas L. Raymond, L. A. D. Percival, J. H. Simpson, and A. U. Conquest

1922 Kenichi Yamamoto of Mazda, the designer of the world's most successful Wankel rotary-engined cars, is born in Kumamoto, Japan

1922 Automotive engineer Arthur B. Browne dies in Cambridge, MA at age 55

1931 A GMC T-95-C tractor/trailer unit operated by the Southern California Freight Lines Ltd. arrives in New York City eight days after leaving Los Angeles, CA with a load of perishable fruit and vegetables, completing the first trans-United States trip by a refrigerated truck

1935 The first 1936 Pontiac Deluxe Six is produced

One of a series of post cards produced in 1936 by the Pontiac Motor Company.

1938 George Eyston driving the Thunderbolt at the Bonneville Salt Flats, UT raises the land speed record to 357.50 mph, breaking the record set the previous day by John R. Cobb at the same site

1939 Great Britain imposes gasoline rationing because of World War II

1940 The Packard Nineteenth Series 110, 120, and Super Eight 160 are introduced

1942 The post office at the Ford Motor Company Navy Service School closes

1947 John R. Cobb driving the Railton Mobil Special at the Bonneville Salt Flats, UT raises land speed record to 394.196 mph - his fastest run was 403.135, the first time that the 400 mph barrier had been broken

1947 The Cisitalia 202 Gran Sport coupe with the trend-setting body designed by Carrozzeria Pininfarina is introduced at the Fiera de Milano (Italy)

1947 Racer Gary Balough is born

1954 The last 1954 Packard body is produced at the Conner Avenue plant in Detroit, MI

1955 The United States Auto Club (USAC) is organized with Duane Carter as Director of Competition

1955 The last 1955 Pontiac is produced

1958 The last 1958 Ford Thunderbird is produced

1958 The 1959 Buicks are unveiled in the earliest post-World War II introduction of a complete line of cars

1960 Racer Steve McEachern is bom

1963 The 7,000,000th Volkswagen is produced

1963 Racer Darin Brassfield is born in Porterville, CA

1965 The 1966 Ford Mustangs are introduced

1967 The 1968 Fiats are introduced to the United States market

1968 Henry A. Barnes, a designer of traffic control equipment, dies in New York City at age 61

1973 The 1974 Cadillacs are introduced

1991 John H. Brinker of the A. O. Smith Corporation dies at age 77

SEPTEMBER 17

1854 David Dunbar Buick is born in Arbroath, Scotland

1859 Joseph Saunders Coates, founder of the Coates-Goshen Automobile Company, is born in Goshen, NY

1880 Harriet Frismuth, a sculptor and designer of automobile mascots, is born in Philadelphia, PA

1892 Automobile parts manufacturer Frederick Carl Matthaei Sr. is born in Detroit, MI

1903 Lester L. Whitman and Eugene I. Hammond arrive in New York City to complete the third trans-United States automobile trip which included a route from Windsor to Niagara Falls in Ontario, Canada to give the journey an international flavor

1904 The first British speed trials held on sand are staged at Portmarnock, near Dublin, Ireland

1908 The Italian Zust arrives in Paris, France 49 days after the victorious Thomas Flyer as the third and last of the six starters to complete the New York to Paris Race

1909 Edward Nicholas Cole of General Motors is born in Berlin (now Marne), MI

1918 The factory of the A. G. Hebb Auto Company is destroyed by fire

1919 Henry, Clara, and Edsel B. Ford become sole owners of the Ford Motor Company

1921 John W. Swan, founder of the Swan Carburetor Company of Cleveland, OH, applies for a United States patent for an improved automobile intake manifold

1922 The Kansas City (MO) Board Track stages its first event, a 300-mile race won by Tommy Milton driving a Leach - Roscoe Sarles is killed during the event

1924 Ralph DePalma driving a stock Chrysler covers 1,000 miles in 1,007 minutes at the board track in Fresno, CA

1926 The Fulford Speedway in Miami Beach, FL is destroyed by a hurricane

1929 Racer Stirling Craufurd Moss is born in London, England

1932 Malcolm Campbell sets a standing 1/2-mile record of 76.27 mph driving his land speed record Sunbeam at the Brighton (England) Speed Trials

1934 The first prototype Squire chassis is unveiled to the public

1938 Russell E. Gardner, President of the Gardner Motor Company 1919-1926 and its Chairman 1926-1930, dies in Memphis, TN at age 72

1938 Racer Lee Roy Yarbrough is born in Jacksonville, FL

1940 The Packard Custom Super Eight 180 is introduced

1942 The new Buick factory built for manufacturing Pratt & Whitney aircraft engines opens in Melrose Park, IL

1948 Dr. Heinz Nordhoff of Volkswagen and Dr. Ferry Porsche sign a contract in Bad Reichenhall, West Germany providing for material supply and marketing cooperation between the two firms

1951 Eugene E. Etzler, an official of the White Motor Company and an authority on truck transportation for the petroleum industry, dies in Los Angeles, CA at age 67

1956 The first 1957 Ford Thunderbird is produced

1960 Edgar W. Smith, an executive with General Motors 1919-1954, dies in Morristown, NJ at age 66

1960 Racer Fabien Giroix is born in Saint-Maur-des-Fosses, Val-de-Marne, France

1960 Racer Damon Hill is born in Hamstead, England, the son of racer Graham Hill

1963 Carlton R. Mabley, the "M" of the 1904-1907 S & M Simplex, dies at age 84

1971 The Lincoln Continental Mark IV is introduced

1974 The British Motor Corporation introduces the Vanden Plas 1500, a luxury version of the Austin Allegro

1980 Racer Egbert "Babe" Stapp dies at age 76

1986 The Bentley Turbo R sets 16 records for speed and endurance by a stock car at the Millbrook, Bedfordshire, England high-speed banked circuit

1988 The Ford Motor Company announces plans to build a plant in Cadiz, Spain

1988 Stanley Edward Sears, English motor car enthusiast and historian most closely associated with the Bentley, dies in Algarve, Portugal

1991 The 1992 Ford Ranger pickup and Aerostar minivan are introduced

SEPTEMBER 18

1831 Siegfried Marcus is born in Malchin, Mecklenburg-Schwerin, Germany

1886 Powel Crosley Jr. is born in Cincinnati, OH

1887 Coachbuilder Giacinto Ghia is born in Turin, Italy

1887 Jonathan D. Maxwell marries Nora Cockley

1893 John Lyon Collyer of the B. F. Goodrich Company is born in Chelsea-on- Hudson, NY

1900 Andrew L. Riker, driving a Riker electric, covers one mile in 1 minute, 46 seconds at Guttenberg, NJ to set a United States speed record of 33.962 mph

1904 Mr. and Mrs. Charles J. Glidden arrive in Vancouver, BC, Canada in their 24-hp Napier, completing a 3,536-mile trip from Boston, MA - the venture included what is often cited as the first crossing of the Canadian Rockies by an automobile

1907 Automotive artist Walter Richards is born in Penfield, OH

1912 Kurt Lotz of Volkswagen is born in Lenderscheid, Germany

1915 The Narragnasett Park Asphalt Speedway in Providence, RI stages its first races - the 100-mile main event is won by Eddie Rickenbacker in a Maxwell

1918 Racer Johnny Mantz is born in Hebron, IN

1920 Automobile parts manufacturer John Corwin Fergus is born in Columbus, OH

1932 Ab Jenkins begins a solo 24-hour drive in a new Pierce-Arrow V-12 at the Bonneville Salt Flats, UT

1935 Societe Nouvelle des Automobiles Delage is founded to assure service for the Delage marque by the Delahaye organization

1939 Diesel engine authority Dr. Ing. Adolph Nagel dies at age 63

1940 Ralph Erich Reins of ITT Automotive Inc. is born in Detroit, MI

1951 Racer Marc Surer is born in Aresdorf, Switzerland

1953 The last 1953 Plymouth is produced

1953 The Veteran Car Club of Great Britain stages a reenactment of the 1903 Thousand Miles Trial - Frederick Stanley Bennett and his Cadillac are the only original contestant and car to participate

1953 Racer Charles de Tornaco is killed at age 26 when his Ferrari crashes during a practice run in Modena, Italy

1955 The Ford Motor Company of Canada, Ltd. produces its 2,000,000th V-8 engine

1955 Winslow Byron Pope, a 25-year product engineer with the Edward G. Budd Manufacturing Company who previously had held engineering positions with Stutz, Jordan, and White, dies at age 49

1956 The North Indiana Toll Road opens to the public

1962 Racer Boris Said is born in Stamford, CT

1964 The last episode of the television program *Route 66* airs

1967 Matilda Rausch Dodge Wilson, widow of John F. Dodge, dies in Brussels, Belgium at age 83

1969 The 1970 Cadillacs are introduced

1969 The 1970 Chevrolets are introduced, including the new Monte Carlo coupe

1969 The 1970 Pontiacs are introduced

1970 The 1971 Fords are introduced one week after the debut of the new Pinto subcompact

1979 John J. Riccardo resigns as Chairman of Chrysler Corporation

1985 Theodore O. Yntema of the Ford Motor Company dies at age 85

1991 Paul R. Verkuil is named head of the American Automobile Association

1996 The Ford Motor Company announces that Murray L. Reichenstein will retire as a Vice President at the end of the year

SEPTEMBER 19

1778 Henry Peter Brougham, whose name is perpetuated in the Brougham body style, is born in Edinburgh, Scotland

1887 Dr. Graham Edgar of the Ethyl Gasoline Corporation, the developer of the octane rating system for motor fuels, is born in Fayetteville, AR

1887 Carriage manufacturer Henry Brewster, whose company would evolve into a custom automobile body firm, dies in New York City at age 63

1887 William Adams Simonds, a biographer of Henry Ford and longtime Editor of *Ford News*, is born in Central City, NE

1888 Albert Vidal Alexandre Boudarel, a sculptor and designer of animal mascots for automobiles, is born in Paris, France

1888 Hugh Dean of General Motors is born in Chicago, IL

1890 Leland, Faulconer, and Norton is organized in Detroit, MI to do precision machine work with Robert C. Faulconer as President, Henry M. Leland as Vice President and General Manager, and Charles A. Strelinger as Treasurer, with Charles H. Norton as a stockholder - this was the first business in which Henry M. Leland had equity

1891 B. Frank Jones, a truck engineer with Pierce-Arrow, White, and Autocar, is born in Philadelphia, PA

1897 Richard Ashton Hutchinson of Studebaker is born in Spokane, WA

1898 Harry Joseph Seaman, founder of Seaman Motors and developer of improved roadbuilding techniques, is born in Berlin, WI

1904 Earle C. Anthony acquires the Packard agency for Los Angeles, CA, which would be one of the nation's most successful through 1955

1909 Ferdinand Anton "Ferry" Porsche (Jr.), son of Ferdinand Porsche, is born in Wiener-Neustadt, Austria

1913 Frank Goodell Armstrong of American Motors is born in Waukesha, WI

1914 E. L. Cord marries Helen Marie Frische in Santa Ana, CA

1916 Mr. and Mrs. William Warwick and daughter Daisy arrive in New York City in a GMC truck loaded with Carnation Milk products after a 70-day trip from Seattle, WA to promote the National Parks Highway

1918 The International Harvester Company of New Jersey and the International Harvester Corporation merge

A circa-1920 International 5-ton truck in Mandan, ND.

1919 The Buick, CO post office opens in the home of rancher August Beuck, who used the name of the General Motors automobile because of the unpopularity of "German-sounding" names in the post-World War I era

1930 George A. Kissel announces that a friendly receivership of the Kissel Motor Car Company is underway

1931 Jacques Calvet of Peugeot is born in Boulogne-sur-Seine, France

1932 Ab Jenkins completes a 24-hour solo run at the Bonneville Salt Flats, UT in a stock Pierce-Arrow V-12 roadster, covering 2,710 miles for an average speed of 112.94 mph - this was the first 24-hour run done at Bonneville

1941 Anthony Loring Hines, Vice President-Honda of America Manufacturing Company 1993-date at their factory in Marysville, OH, is born in Altus, OK

1941 J. Ernest Andrew, inventor of many devices used in the manufacture of automobile springs, dies

1944 Automotive historian Wallace Alfred Wyss is born in Detroit, MI

1946 Racer Brian Henton is born in Derby, England

1948 The 1949 Kaisers are introduced

1951 Joseph S. Coates, builder of the 1909-1910 Coates-Goshen, dies in Goshen, NY at age 92

1952 Racer Bernard de Dryver is born in Brussels, Belgium

1953 Soviet automotive engineer E. A. Chudakov dies in Moscow, USSR at age 63

1953 Walt Hansgen wins the Watkins Glen Grand Prix in a Jaguar XK120 Special

1955 Richard Benz, younger son of Carl Benz who joined his father as a partner in C. Benz Sohne, makers of the Benz Sohne 1906-1926, dies at age 80

1955 The last 1955 Ford Thunderbird is produced

1956 Racer Juan Manuel Fangio II, nephew and namesake of five-time World Champion Driver Juan Manuel Fangio, is born in Balcarce, Argentina

1956 Charles A. Tilt, President 1905-1945 and Chairman 1945-1956 of the Diamond T Motor Car Company, dies in Trout Lake, WI at age 79 - the company built automobiles 1907-1910 and heavy trucks until 1966

1957 The 1958 Studebakers and Packards are introduced

1959 Dr. Max R. Burnell, Medical Director for General Motors 1949-1958, dies in Flint, MI at age 65

1968 The 1969 Plymouths are introduced, including the full-sized Fury III series with new "fuselage" styling

1969 Professor Ferry Porsche, in celebration of his 60th birthday, is presented with the unique Porsche 914/8

1969 The 1970 Ford Bronco is introduced

1970 The 1971 Ford Mustangs are introduced

1974 The 1975 Cadillacs are introduced

1975 Ford Motor Company announces plans to purchase Jaguar

1983 Carl L. Hoban of Mountain Home, AR, founder and past President of the Midstates Jeepster Association, dies at age 75

1988 Walter Percy Chrysler Jr., who had a brief career in his father's company but is best remembered as the manager of the Chrysler Building in New York City and as an art collector, dies

SEPTEMBER 20

1853 Col. Charles Clifton of Pierce-Arrow is born in Buffalo, NY

*This 1914 Vestibule Brougham Landaulet displays the artwork of the Clifton era
that made Pierce-Arrow advertising as respected as the cars themselves.*

1870 Francis Seiberling, a United States Congressman 1929-1933 (R-OH) and a Director of the Goodyear Tire
      & Rubber Company, is born in Des Moines, IA

1876 Harry Thurber Woolson, longtime Chrysler Corporation engineer whose early career included stints
      with Packard, Studebaker, and Willys-Overland, is born in Passaic, NJ

1876 Carleton Ellis, the inventor of the first durable lacquer for automobile painting, is born in Keene, NY

1889 Taine Gilbert McDougal of the AC Spark Plug Company is born in New Lexington, OH

1893 Adolph Paschal Buquor of the Martin-Parry Corporation, the designer of the first 6-wheel truck, is born
      in Silver City, NM

1908 Gerald Francis Jones of Mack Trucks, Inc. is born in the Bronx, NY

1909 The Metzger Motor Car Company is organized in Detroit, MI by William E. Metzger and Barney Everitt to manufacture Everitt cars

1910 Richard Eugene Cross of American Motors is born in Madison, WI

1921 Racer Horace Gould is born in Southmead, England

1930 Grace Emery of Bradford, PA accepts delivery of the first United States-built Rolls-Royce Phantom I (Serial S101FR) with the new aluminum cylinder head

1937 The Packard Sixteenth Series Sixes, Eights, and Super Eights are introduced

1938 The Packard Seventeenth Series is introduced

1940 Continental is designated as a marque separate from Lincoln by the Ford Motor Company

1940 Adrian Squire, designer of the 1934-1936 Squire sports car, is killed in Bristol, England during a German air raid

1940 Harley C. Loney, an official of the Allen Motor Car Company who later founded the Harley C. Loney Company, manufacturers of automotive parts, dies at age 48

1945 Packard ends its World War II military production program with the completion of its 55,523rd and last Rolls-Royce Merlin engine

1946 Charles W. Seiberling, Vice President of the Goodyear Tire & Rubber Company 1898-1921, dies at age 85

1947 Buick registers its stylized stencil "BUICK" logo as a trademark

1947 Heatley Green, an automobile parts manufacturer since 1901, dies in Detroit, MI

1952 Racer Bill Schindler is killed at age 43 during a race in Allentown, PA

1957 Racer Montague H. Roberts, driver from New York City to Cheyenne, WY of the winning Thomas Flyer in the 1908 New York to Paris race, dies in Newark, NJ at age 74

1958 S. Clifford Merrill of the Timken Roller Bearing Company dies at age 61

1963 The 1964 Chryslers are introduced

1963 The 1964 Plymouths are introduced

1970 The Tyrrell makes its Formula 1 debut in the Canadian Grand Prix, but the Type 001 driven by Jackie Stewart retires with a broken axle after taking the pole position in qualifying

1973 The 1974 Buicks are introduced

1973 The 1974 Chevrolets are introduced

1973 The 1974 Oldsmobiles are introduced, including the Cutlass Salon series, Ninety-Eight Regency coupe, and the Toronado Brougham as new models

1974 Buick Electra Custom Hardtop Coupe

1973 The 1974 Pontiacs are introduced

1979 Lee Iacocca is elected Chairman of the Chrysler Corporation

1985 Raymond W. Stanley, son of steam car pioneer Francis E. Stanley, dies in York Harbor, ME at age 91, having spent his later years preserving and promoting the legacy of the Stanley Steamer

SEPTEMBER 21

1756 John Loudon Macadam, a developer of road paving materials, is born in Ayr, Scotland

1871 Charles L. Sheppy of Pierce-Arrow is born in Gratwick, NY

1886 William Andrew Fisher is born in Norwalk, OH

1893 The first Duryea automobile is tested in Springfield, MA by J. Frank Duryea

1895 Stanley W. Ostrander of General Motors and the Ford Motor Company is born in Whittemore, MI

1895 The Duryea Motor Wagon Company of Springfield, MA is incorporated in Maine with Charles E. Duryea as President

1903 Byron J. Carter applies for a patent on his friction drive transmission

1903 Preston Thomas Tucker is born in Capac, MI

1915 Roy Dikeman Chapin Jr. of American Motors is born in Detroit, MI

1915 The (Societa) Anonima Lombarda Fabbrica Automobile (A.L.F.A.) is forced into receivership, leading to the creation of the Societa Anonima Italiana Nicola Romeo e C., manufacturers of the Alfa Romeo

1920 Kenneth "Ken" McAlpine, a businessman and occasional racer who was the principal benifactor of the Connaught racing team, is born in Chobham, Surrey, England

1924 Barton Brown of General Motors is born in Glen Cove, NY

1926 The Marmon 1927-1928 "Eagle" mascot is patented by designer William Schnell

1930 Attorney Arthur J. Sabin, an occasional automobile historian, is born in Chicago, IL

1930 Jean-Pierre Wimille makes his major racing debut in the French Grand Prix at Pau, but his Bugatti Type 37A retires after just two laps with supercharger problems

1930 The first Czech Grand Prix is staged in Brno and won by co-drivers Hermann Prinz zu Leiningen and Heinrich-Joachim von Morgen driving a Bugatti Type 35B

1933 Racer Dick Simon is born in Seattle, WA

1934 The first Ford-Gregorie speedster is delivered to Edsel B. Ford

1935 The Cord 810 is previewed to dealers

1935 The SS 4-door saloon is introduced

1938 The first hand assembled Mercury is completed in Richmond, CA

1940 Albert L. Clough, an automotive journalist, consulting engineer, and founding member of the Society of Automobile Engineers, dies at age 71

1941 Custom coachbuilder Hermann A. Brunn dies at age 67

1944 Earle W. Sinclair, President of the Sinclair Refining Company and founder of the Sinclair Oil Corporation, dies in New York City at age 70

1945 Henry Ford II is elected President of the Ford Motor Company

1945 The Kaiser-Frazer Corporation signs a 5-year lease on Willow Run factory

1947 France stages its first major post-World War II race, as Louis Chiron in a Talbot-Lago wins the French Grand Prix at Lyon-Parilly - the Albert Lory-designed CTA-Arsenal made an unsuccessful debut in this event and was never raced again

1949 The 1,000,000th post-World War II Buick is produced, a Model 43-D Special Deluxe Sedan featuring new 1950 styling

1952 Racer Frank Luptow dies from injuries suffered the previous day during a race in Atlanta, GA

1953 Racer Arie Luyendyk is born in Sommelsdyk, the Netherlands

1957 James D. Mooney, President of the General Motors Overseas Corporation 1923-1941 and President of the Willys-Overland Company 1946-1949, dies in Tucson, AZ at age 73

The parking lot at Eaton's Inn in Big Timber, MT includes two Willys vehicles.
The Jeep-based cars were very popular in the post-World War II era.

1958 Odbert P. Wilson, retired President of the Norma-Hoffmann Bearings Corporation, dies at age 75

1958 Racer Peter Whitehead is killed at age 43 when his half-brother Graham Whitehead crashes their Jaguar during the Tour de France

1959 The first Valiant is produced at the Dodge plant in Hamtramck, MI - the new compact car was introduced as a separate marque and would not become a "Plymouth" until the 1961 model year

1961 George H. Love is elected Chairman of the Chrysler Corporation

1961 The 1962 Pontiacs are introduced

1963 The Plymouth Barracuda is introduced

1967 The 1968 Cadillacs are introduced

1967 The 1968 Chevrolets are introduced

1967 The 1968 Pontiacs are introduced

1971 The 1972 Chevrolet trucks, including the Blazer, are introduced

1971 The 1972 Opels are introduced to the United States market

1972 The 1973 Cadillacs are introduced

1972 The 1973 Chevrolet cars and trucks are introduced

1972 The 1973 Pontiacs are introduced

1973 The 1974 Ford Mustang II and Bronco are introduced

1984 The 1985 Chevrolet Blazer and S-10 pickup are introduced

SEPTEMBER 22

1892 John F. Dodge marries Ivy S. Hawkins

1893 Hines Holt Baker of the Humble Oil and Refining Company is born in Goldthwaite, TX

1896 Racer and land speed record holder Sir Henry O'Neal de Hane Segrave is born in Baltimore, MD of English parents

1900 George Blackmore of Painesville, OH becomes the first Packard dealer

1903 The new Packard Motor Car Company factory in Detroit, MI opens

1907 Richard Ernest Krafve, General Manager of Edsel, is born in Minneapolis, MN

1907 Racer Philip Fotheringham-Parker is born in Great Britain

1908 George E. Daniels becomes the first President of General Motors

1919 Claude Johnson of Rolls-Royce announces plans to manufacture cars in the United States

1919 The Sinclair Oil & Refining Company and the Sinclair Gulf Corporation consolidate as the Sinclair Consolidated Oil Company with Harry F. Sinclair as President

1921 Racer Ian Raby is born in London, England

1922 The Ford Model T officially becomes a 1923 model

1936 Lloyd Edwin Armin Reuss of Buick is born in Belleville, IL

1939 The 1940 Buicks are introduced

1941 Racer Roger Manderville is born in the United States

1944 Racer Richard Robarts is born in Steeple, Essex, England

1949 Dodge announces that its Wayfarer Roadster will be available with optional regulator-type side windows

White's City, NM is the gateway to Carlsbad Caverns National Park.
Over twenty late-1940's cars occupy the parking lot including, at far left,
a 1949 Dodge Wayfarer Roadster.

1949 Peter Whitehead, driving a Ferrari 125, wins the Czechoslovakian Grand Prix in Brno to gain the first Grand Prix victory by a British driver in the post-World War II era

1949 The Shell Union Oil Company changes its name to the Shell Oil Company

The world's largest banyan tree shadows this Shell service station in West Palm Beach, FL.

1950 The 1951 Nashes and Nash Ramblers are introduced

1954 Racer Randy Lanier is born in the United States

1955 Henry Plonski, Chief Inspector for the Peninsular Metal Products Corporation and an employee of the firm for 19 years, dies

1955 Fred G. Folberth, Transylvania-born engineer with the Automotive Development Company and internationally known as a carburetor designer, dies

1958 Racer Franco Forini is born in Switzerland

1961 The 1962 Cadillacs are introduced

1961 The 1962 Oldsmobiles are introduced

1962 Racer A. W. Faust is killed at age 48 when his Lotus-Buick crashes during a 101-mile sports car race in Watkins Glen, NY

1965 Bridge designer Othmar H. Ammann dies at age 86

1967 The 1968 Fords are introduced

1967 The 1968 Mercury Montego is introduced as a new model

1967 Racer Rickard Rydell is born in Sweden

1971 The 1972 AMC lines are introduced

1971 The first regular issue of *Old Cars* newspaper is published

1972 The 1973 Fords are introduced

1973 The 1974 Chevrolets are introduced

1974 The Parnelli makes its Formula 1 debut in the Canadian Grand Prix in Mosport Park, with the Type VPJ4 driven by Mario Andretti finishing in seventh place - the Penske also makes its debut with the Type PC1 driven by Mark Donohue finishing in twelfth place

Ford promoted their 1968 cars with a deck of playing cards, each of which was face different.

1980 Bjoern Lundvall of Saab dies

1989 Chrysler Corporation sells 50% of its interest in the Mitsubishi Motors Corporation

1991 Harry Gant, age 51, wins the Goody's 500 in Martinsville, VA, his fourth consecutive victory and an extension of his own record as the oldest winner of a NASCAR race

1991 Riccardo Patrese wins the Portuguese Grand Prix in his Williams-Renault, the 50th Formula 1 victory for the marque

1995 L. L. "Tex" Colbert, longtime Chrysler Corporation executive, dies in Naples, FL at age 90

SEPTEMBER 23

1861 Robert August Bosch, developer of improved automotive electrical systems, is born in Albeck, Wurttemburg, Germany

1885 Clarence E. Rogers of Amplex, Sun, and Crow-Elkhart is born in St. Joseph County, IN

1897 Great Britain records its first traffic fatality on a public highway when nine-year-old Stephen Kempton is killed on Stockmar Road near Hackney - he had stolen a ride by hanging from a spring on a taxicab operated by the Electric Cab Company, fell off and was crushed by a wheel of the vehicle

1908 Alan Lewis Gornick of the Ford Motor Company is born in Leadville, CO

1915 William C. Durant incorporates the Chevrolet Motor Company of Delaware as a holding company with the eventual goal of allowing the new firm to purchase a controlling interest in General Motors

1915 The first Patterson-Greenfield is produced by C. R. Patterson & Sons of Greenfield, OH to the design of the founder's son, Fred Patterson, who is often cited as the first black to play football at Ohio State University

1923 Howard "Howdy" Wilcox, winner of the 1919 and 1923 Indianapolis 500's, is killed at age 34 when he crashes during a race in Altoona, PA

1924 Major C. Court Treatt and party leave Capetown, South Africa in two military-type Crossleys, beginning the first overland trip across Africa to Cairo, Egypt

1927 Werner Breitschwerdt of Daimler-Benz AG is born in Stuttgart, Germany

1931 Willis Joseph Price of the Chevron Corporation is born in Louisville, KY

1931 Hamilton Morton Stephens, Western Sales Manager of the Oakland Motor Car Company, dies in Detroit, MI at age 48

1935 General Motors de Mexico, SA is founded with Ivan C. Dresser as General Manager

1935 The Packard Fourteenth Series 120 is introduced, replacing the Twelfth Series (per commonsu perstition, there was no Thirteenth Series)

1939 The last pre-World War II Irish hillclimb staged at Ballinascorney, near Dublin, is won by A. P. MacArthur in an M.G.

1940 The American Bantam Car Company completes the first Jeep prototype and delivers it to United States government testers at Camp Holabird, MD

1950 Racer Samuel Carnes "Sam" Collier is killed at age 38 when he loses control of his Ferrari 166 during the Watkins Glen (NY) Grand Prix

1952 Clarence E. Bleicher, President of DeSoto 1944-1952, dies in Detroit, MI at age 62

1953 Norman K. VanDerzee announces that dealers can place orders for the Italia, a custom-bodied luxury sports car to be produced by the Hudson Motor Car Company

1955 Irven E. Coffey of the Carter Carburetor Corporation and the inventor of the automatic choke, dies at age 67

1956 Frank W. Szanto of the Continental Motors Corporation dies at age 29

1960 James M. Crawford of Auburn and Chalmers dies in LaJolla, CA at age 74

1961 Stirling Moss wins the Gold Cup race at Oulton Park, England in a Ferguson-Climax P99, the final victory in a major race by a front-engined car

1967 Fiat SpA acquires the Officine Meccaniche SA in Brescia, Italy, builders of O.M. trucks and onetime manufacturers of cars of the same name, and Autobianchi SA of Milan, Italy, manufacturers since 1957 of the Bianchi

1969 The 1970 Chryslers and Imperials are introduced

1969 The 1970 Dodges are introduced

1969 The 1970 Plymouths are introduced

1971 The 1972 Chevrolets are introduced

1971 The 1972 Pontiacs are introduced

1972 The Crystal Palace circuit in south London, England is closed by the Greater London Council because of noise objections and safety concerns

1975 Racer Rene Thomas, winner of the 1914 Indianapolis 500 and former holder of the land speed record, dies in Paris, France at age 89

1979 A commemorative plaque honoring F. H. Royce is unveiled in West Wittering, England by Donald Pepper, Vice Chairman of Rolls-Royce Ltd.

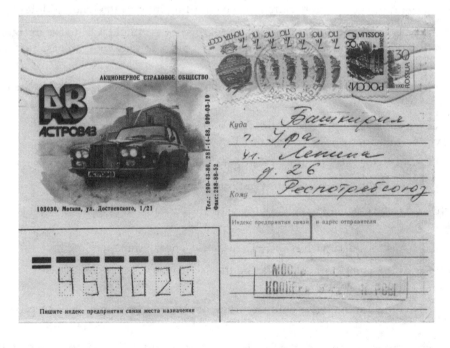

A 1992 envelope from independent Russia with inflationary additional postage paid with mixed Russian and old USSR stamps. The cachet promotes Astrovas, an acronym of the Automobile Insurance Company of Moscow. The car is a Rolls-Royce Silver Shadow, perhaps an unrealistic choice to imply a touch of class, but certainly more appropriate then a Communist-associated ZIL limousine.

1982 The Citroen BX is introduced

1990 Peugeot's unblown V-10 905 race car makes its racing debut in the World Sports-Prototype Championships in Montreal, PQ, Canada, but the car driven by Keke Rosberg retires due to fuel pump failure

SEPTEMBER 24

1864 Publisher George Gough Booth, a cofounder of the Scripps-Booth Company and father of its chief designer, James Scripps Booth, is born in Toronto, ON, Canada

1894 Charles Fayette Taylor, a professor of automotive engineering at the Massachusetts Institute of Technology, is born in New York City

1896 The Paris-Marseille-Paris race begins with 31 entrants

1898 John Hatton Berry of the General Motors Export Corporation is born in Wallasey, Cheshire, England

1902 The Daimler Motoren-Gesellschaft takes delivery of its first magneto ignition system as designed by Gottlob Honold and Robert Bosch

1905 Racer Bob Carey is born in Anderson, IN

1908 The first factory-built Ford Model T is completed

1909 Automobile stylist Virgil Max Exner Sr. is born in Ann Arbor, MI

1910 Automotive parts manufacturer John Donald Reindel is born in Detroit, MI

1912 The Goodyear Tyre & Rubber Company (Great Britain) Ltd. is registered in Wolverhampton, England

1916 The Hudson Super-Six completes a promotional "Twice Across America" run from San Francisco, CA to New York City and back to San Francisco

1921 The first race at the Avus circuit in Germany is won by Fritz Von Opel driving an Opel

1936 Wills Sainte Claire, Inc., the last legal entity related to the automotive career of C. Harold Wills, is liquidated

1938 K. J. Howell, a design engineer with the Mercer Motors Company, Rolls-Royce of America, Inc., the Studebaker Corporation, and the General Motors Export Corporation, dies at age 38

1948 The Honda Motor Company Ltd. is founded

1949 The assets of Fabbrica Automobili Isotta-Fraschini are liquidated

1951 Anna S. Kretz of Buick is born in Poland

1954 Fred W. Cederleaf, Swedish-born official with the Borg-Warner Corporation and a former design engineer with Studebaker, Buick, and Dodge, dies at age 66

1955 Frederick S. Fales, President of the Standard Oil Company of New York 1932-1940, dies in New Rochelle, NY at age 82

1957 Richard H. Grant, Vice President of Chevrolet 1924-1929 and Vice President of General Motors 1929-1944, dies at age 78

1958 Edward F. Roberts, retired General Superintendent of the Packard Motor Car Company, dies at age 83

1960 The 1961 Chryslers and Imperials are introduced

1960 Racer Akio Morimoto is born in Hyogo, Japan

1960 Racer Johnny Thomson is killed at age 38 when he crashes during a race in Allentown, PA

1963 The 1964 Oldsmobiles are introduced

1964 The 1965 Chevrolets cars and trucks are introduced including the second-generation Corvair

1964 The 1965 Oldsmobiles are introduced

1964 The 1965 Pontiacs are introduced

1964 Racer Jeff Krosnoff is born in Tulsa, OK

1966 Racer Christophe Bouchut is born in Voiron, France

1971 The 1972 Ford cars and trucks are introduced

1971 Kurt Lotz resigns as Chairman of Volkswagenwerk AG

1974 General Motors announces that production of its rotary-engined sports compact, the "Monza", will be postponed because of problems complying with emissions standards

1981 The 1982 Cadillacs are introduced

1982 The Bendix Corporation is acquired by the Allied Corporation

1992 The 1993 Chevrolet Astro and S-10 pickup are introduced

SEPTEMBER 25

1725 Steam vehicle pioneer Nicolas Joseph Cugnot is born in Void, Austrian Lorraine (now France)

1860 Brothers Philander H. and Francis M. Roots of Connersville, IN are issued a United States patent for their supercharger, a design that would be extensively adopted by the automobile industry many years later

1867 Henry M. Leland and Ellen Hull are married

1868 Dana Elisha Seeley, a manufacturer of automobile windshields, is born in Livingston County, MI

1891 Max G. Paulus of the Standard Oil Company of Indiana is born in Baltimore, MD

1891 Henry and Clara Ford move to Detroit, MI

1897 The first gas-powered bus service in Great Britain is started in Bradford by J. E. Tuke of the Yorkshire Motor Car Company, Ltd.

1899 Automobile historian Ralph Cecil Epstein is born in Chicago, IL

1919 General Motors acquires the Dayton Metal Products Company, one of the many businesses started by Charles F. Kettering

1924 Malcolm Campbell, driving a Sunbeam at Pendine Sands, Wales, raises the land speed record to 146.157 mph - this was the first of nine times that he would raise the record

1927 Joe H. King of the Chrysler Corporation is born

1931 The 25,000th BMW, a Dixi 3/15, is produced at the Eisenach, Germany plant

1936 Racer Bill Schindler crashes during a sprint race in Mineola, NY, an accident that three days later would result in the loss of his left leg but would not end his career

1937 Charles W. Svenson, a Swedish-born mechanical superintendent who spent 54 years with the Corbin Screw Corporation and was involved in the design of the first Corbin automobile in 1905, dies at age 73

1939 Racer Neville Lederle is born in Theunissen, South Africa

1942 Racer Henri Pescarolo is born in Paris, France

1945 George L. Weiss, a cofounder of the Packard Motor Car Company, dies in Garden Grove, CA at age 83

1947 The Kaiser Custom, an upscale version of the basic Kaiser Special, is introduced as a mid-year model - the first Custom was also the 100,000th Kaiser automobile produced

1957 William J. Haley of the Standard Oil Company of New Jersey and the Esso Export Corporation dies in Rye, NY at age 66

1962 General Motors announces a two-year, 24,000-mile blanket warranty on all of its 1963 cars and trucks

1963 The 1964 Imperials are introduced

1964 The 1965 Dodges are introduced

1964 The Ford Mustang 2+2 GT fastback coupe is introduced as a 1965 model

1964 The 1965 Plymouths are introduced

1965 The 1966 Ford Thunderbirds are introduced

1967 Racer Mika Salo is born in Helsinki, Finland

1969 The 1970 AMC models are introduced

1973 The 1974 Dodges are introduced

1973 The 1974 Plymouths are introduced

1975 Bricklin Canada Ltd. declares bankruptcy and ends production after a two-year run of 2,872 cars

1978 Robert F. Lemke is named Editor of *Old Cars* newspaper

1980 The 1981 Pontiacs are introduced

1983 The first Grand Prix of Europe is staged at Brands Hatch, England with Nelson Piquet winning in his Brabham BT52B-BMW

1987 The United States Postal Service issues a 17.5-cent coil stamp at Indianapolis, IN depicting a "Racing Car 1911" - designed by Tom Broad, the car pictured is the Marmon Wasp with which Ray Harroun won the first Indianapolis 500 race

SEPTEMBER 26

1854 George W. Atterbury, manufacturer and namesake of the 1910-1935 Atterbury truck, is born in Litchfield, IL

1905 The Motorcar Company, manufacturers of the Cartercar, is incorporated in Detroit, MI by Byron J. Carter, Frank T. Caughey, Fred Postal, Randall A. Palmer, Harry R. Radford, and George A. Young

1908 The first automobile races in Montreal, PQ, Canada are held at Delormier Park

1909 William Henry Getty France Sr., the founder and first President of NASCAR, is born in Horsepen, VA

1910 William C. Durant loses control of General Motors

1916 Franco Vittorio Scaglione, automobile streamlining proponent and longtime Alfa Romeo stylist, is born in Florence, Italy

1920 The Ranger automobile is announced in Houston, TX

1921 The Eagle Motor Truck Corporation of St. Louis, MO registers its "eagle" logo as a trademark

1921 Automobile spring manufacturer William Keller McInerney is born in Chicago, IL

1930 Philippe Etancelin, driving a Bugatti Type 35C, wins the French Grand Prix at Pau

1933 The 1933 Buick "Winged 8" mascot is patented by designer C. L. Sislo

1933 The 1933 Oldsmobile "Goddess" mascot is patented by designer B. E. Lemm

1943 Racer Tim Schenken is born in Sydney, NSW, Australia

1946 Max Grabowsky, founder in 1902 and President 1902-1908 of the Rapid Motor Vehicle Company, a truck manufacturing firm that would evolve into the GMC marque of General Motors, dies in Detroit, MI at age 72

1949 Robert A. Weinhardt, a design engineer with Ford, Packard, Kaiser-Frazer, and Willys who had helped design the first demountable disc wheels and shock absorbers, dies at age 66

1950 E. Paul duPont, founder of the DuPont Motor Manufacturing Company and later President of the Indian Motorcycle Company, dies at age 63

1952 The Kaiser-Frazer Corporation announces plans to produce a plastic-bodied sports car designed by Howard A. "Dutch" Darrin

1954 Matthew C. Kuepfer, Vice President of the Hercules Motor Corporation and an employee of the firm for 35 years, dies

1954 Elmer Siegling of Thompson Products Inc. dies at age 62

1955 Yrjo "George" Leiviska, an employee of Buick, Cadillac, and GMC in the 1930's prior to a government service career in his native Finland, dies

1956 The new 12-story central office building of the Ford Motor Company is dedicated in Dearborn, MI

1960 Stunt driver Sven-Erik Soderman is born in Sweden

1961 Charles E. Wilson, President of General Motors 1941-1953, dies in Norwood, LA at age 71

1961 The 1962 Chryslers are introduced

1962 The 1963 Chryslers are introduced

1962 The Ford Motor Company announces a two-year, 24,000-mile warranty on all of its 1963 cars and trucks

1963 Racer Joe Nemechek is born in Naples, FL

1963 The 1964 Chevrolets are introduced

1964 The 1965 Ford Thunderbirds are introduced

1966 The Sportop option for the International Scout is introduced

1967 The 1968 AMC models are introduced, including the new Javelin sport coupe

1968 The 1969 Cadillacs are introduced

1968 The 1969 Chevrolets are introduced

1972 The 1973 Plymouths are introduced

1974 Racer Harry Hartz dies at age 78

1975 Automotive historian Frank Donovan dies at age 69

1982 The first episode of the television show *Knight Rider* airs "starring" a modified Pontiac Firebird

1990 Charles C. Ellis, a Ford Motor Company official 1952-1959, dies at age 71

SEPTEMBER 27

1858   Thomas Neal, President of General Motors 1910-1912 and Chairman of same 1913-1915, is born in Corunna, ON, Canada

1875   John Walter Drake, first President of the Hupp Motor Car Corporation, is born in Sturgis, MI

1880   Tire manufacturer Harry Wilfred DuPuy is born in Allegheny (now part of Pittsburgh), PA

1887   Stylist Joe Thompson is born

1899   Albert Jesse Browning of Ford is born in Ogden, UT

1900   Packard's first magazine advertisement appears in *The Motor Vehicle Review*

1904   The R. E. Olds Company changes its name to the Reo Car Company (later amended to the Reo Motor Car Company) to avoid a legal confrontation with the Olds Motor Works

1906   William D. Packard marries Kathryn Bruder in his second marriage

1906   Hon. C. S. Rolls, driving a 20-hp Rolls-Royce, wins the Tourist Trophy race on the Isle of Man

1913   The Wagenhals Motor Car Company reorganizes with William Pflum as President, W. G. Wagenhals as Vice President and Treasurer, and Hughes C. Turner as Secretary

1925   Construction begins at the Nurburgring circuit in Germany

1928   The cornerstone of what would become the Henry Ford Museum is laid

1932   The last Plymouth Model PB is produced

1940   The 1941 Fords are introduced in three series, Special, Deluxe, and Super Deluxe

1942   Louis Schneider, winner of the 1931 Indianapolis 500, dies at age 43

1945   Henry Ford II fires Harry H. Bennett, the longtime associate of his grandfather, Henry Ford

1945   Racer Bruce Leven is born in the United States

1951   Racer Steve Soper is born in Harrow, Middlesex, England

1955   Paul W. Gillan is issued a United States patent for his "Combined Bumper & Grille" design as used on the 1955 Pontiacs

1957   Racer Pierre Petit is born in France

1960   The Ford Econoline trucks are introduced

1961   Marvin E. Coyle of Chevrolet dies at age 73

1963   The 1964 Fords are introduced

1968   The 1969 Fords are introduced

1972   Mack Trucks, Inc. contributes $1 million to establish the American Truck Museum and Library in Allentown, PA

1974   The 1975 Buicks are introduced

1974   The 1975 Chevrolets are introduced

1974   The 1975 Fords are introduced

1974   The 1975 Oldsmobiles are introduced

1974   The 1975 Pontiacs are introduced

1975   The 1976 Pontiacs are introduced, including the new Sunbird compact

1979   The 1980 AMC Eagles are introduced

1982   James W. McLernon resigns as President and Chief Executive Officer of Volkswagen USA, with Noel Phillips named as his successor

1987   Coloni makes its Formula 1 debut at the Spanish Grand Prix, but the Type FC187 driven by Nicola Larini retires with suspension problems

1989   Coachbuilder Hermann C. Brunn dies in San Mateo, CA at age 81

1990   Renault and Volvo sign an agreement of industrial cooperation, with the eventual goal of a merger of the two firms - the merger plans were abandoned in 1993

SEPTEMBER 28

1799 Philippe Lebon d'Humbersin is issued a French patent for his two-stroke internal combustion coal-gas motor featuring many principals of the modern two-stroke engine

1873 Gustave Gurschner, a sculptor and designer of automobile mascots, is born in Muhldorf, Bavaria, Germany

1888 William C. Durant and J. Dallas Dort organize the Flint Road Cart Company

1894 Fernand Marie-Charles Vadier, an associate of engine designer Ernest Henry, is born in Poitiers, France

1898 Racer Baconin Borzacchini is born in Terni, Italy

1901 Thomas William Towell of the General Motors Acceptance Corporation is born in Caneadea, NY

1917 John Richard Eastman of the Sheller-Globe Corporation is born in Ottawa, OH

1929 Maserati's new V4, a 16-cylinder race car driven by Baconin Borzacchini, sets a world's record for ten kilometres of 152.6 mph during a race in Cremona, Italy

1930 The Auburn Automobile Company of Auburn, IN hosts a community open house at its new headquarters building designed by A. M. Strauss of Fort Wayne

1935 The 1936 Buicks are officially introduced featuring "Turret-Top" styling and for the first time, series names - Special, Century, Roadmaster, and Limited

1936 The first 1937 Pontiac Deluxe Six is produced

1938 Charles E. Duryea dies in Philadelphia, PA at age 76

1943 Racer Win Percy is born in Tolpuddle, Dorset, England

1944 Charles G. Black of the Standard Oil Company dies in New York City at age 76

1947 John T. Smith, General Counsel and Vice President of General Motors, dies at age 68

1947 Alberto "Ciccio" Ascari records his first automobile racing victory at Modena, Italy driving a Maserati

1950 The Kaiser-Frazer Corporation introduces the compact Henry J as a new marque

A 1951 Henry J joins a Plymouth and Ford in front of the Washington Country Court House in Hillsboro, OR. The compact car's major fault was that it was ahead of its time.

1952 German coachbuilder Wilhelm Karmann Sr. dies

1957 American Motors officially announces the termination of the Hudson and Nash marques

1958 Racer Jimmy Reece is killed during a 100-mile USAC race in Trenton, NJ

1958 Lorenzo Bandini makes his Formula Junior racing debut driving his own Volpini in the 7th Annual Sicilian Gold Cup race

1959 Racer Ron Fellows is born in Windsor, ON, Canada

1960 The Nissan Motor Corporation in USA is founded with Takashi Ishihara as President, and Soichi Kawazoe and Yutaka Katayama as Vice Presidents

1961 The 1962 Dodges are introduced

1961 The 1962 Plymouths are introduced

1962 The 1963 Chevrolet cars and trucks are introduced on the same day the 48,000,000th Chevrolet is produced

1962 The 1963 Ford Thunderbirds are introduced

1963 Racer Erik Comas is born in Romans-sur-Isere, France

1967 John W. Anderson, an inventor and manufacturer of automobile parts, dies at age 83

1968 Racer Mika Hakkinen is born in Helsinki, Finland

1969 Racer Sasha Maassen is born in Aachen, West Germany

1970 Racer Gaulter Salles is born in Rio de Janeiro, Brazil

1971 The 1972 Plymouths are introduced

1975 The Long Beach Grand Prix for Formula 5000 cars is staged as a trial for the Long Beach Grand Prix for Formula One to be held in six months- the winner is Brian Redman in a Lola-Chevrolet

1977 The Singpore Airlines London-Sydney Rally, the longest such event ever held, concludes in Sydney, NSW, Australia after 45 days - the winner is a Mercedes-Benz 280SE driven by Michael Broad, Andrew Cowan, and Colin Malkin

1978 The 1979 Pontiacs are introduced except for the Sunbird which had debuted thirteen days earlier

1978 A Mazda RX7 driven by *Road & Track* Editor Don Sherman sets a Class E record at the Bonneville Salt Flats, UT, reaching 183.904 mph

1980 Mike Thackwell qualifies for the Canadian Grand Prix, at age 19 years, 182 days the youngest driver to start a Formula 1 championship race

1982 The UAW-Ford National Development and Training Center opens in Dearborn, MI

1984 Jose J. Dedeurwaerder succeeds W. Paul Tippett Jr. as Chief Executive Officer of American Motors

1988 The United States Postal Service issues a 20.5-cent stamp in San Angelo, TX for the Zip+4 Presort rate - the stamp, designed by Chris Calle, pictures a 1913 Ahrens-Fox Model AC fire engine purchased new by the San Angelo Fire Department

1989 Racer Richie Ginther dies at age 59 while vacationing in Touzac, France

1995 Brian Jackson, a co-owner of the Barrett-Jackson Collector Car Auction, dies from cancer at age 49

SEPTEMBER 29

1826 Steam-powered automobile pioneer Charles Baillairge is born in Quebec, PQ, Canada

1860 Monsieur Barvajel purchases a Lenoir gasoline engine, thought to be the first sale of an internal combustion engine

1888 The Daimler Motor Company of New York is established in Long Island City, NY by piano manufacturer William Steinway with United States rights to all of Gottlieb Daimler's German patents

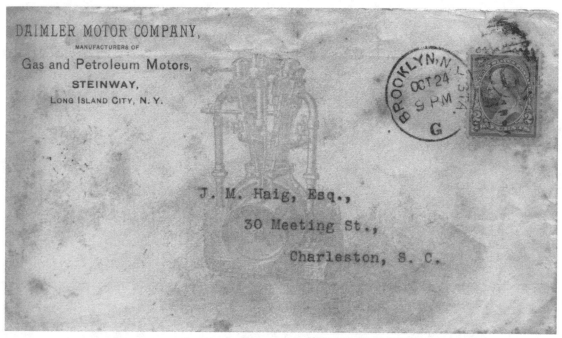

An 1895 envelope from the Diamler/Steinway concern displays the famous Daimler V-twin motor. Steinway was importing Daimler cars in 1891, fully two years before the Duryea brothers "invented" the automobile.

1903 Henry B. Wick of Youngstown, OH offers to purchase a 50% equity in the Ohio Automobile Company, but the offer is rejected by the board

1906 Roy Abernethy of American Motors is born in West Monterey, PA

1908 General Motors purchases the Buick Motor Company for about $3,750,000, in effect a sale from and to William C. Durant to become the cornerstone of the new corporation

1913 Rudolf Diesel commits suicide at age 55, jumping from the cruiser Dresden while crossing the English Channel

1914 William A. Besserdich and Bernhard A. Mosling are issued a United States patent for their Locking Device for Differential Gears, an invention that was the basis of modern four-wheel drive

1919 The Pan Motor Company of Saint Cloud, MN registers the "Pan" name as a trademark

1924 General Motors President Alfred P. Sloan Jr. singles out Oakland and Chevrolet for failure to keep up with consumer demands

1929 The Packard 734 Speedster Eight is introduced

1929 Walter C. White, President of the White Motor Company, is killed at age 53 in an automobile accident near Cleveland, OH

1931 Automobile battery manufacturer Chester M. Angell dies at age 46

1933 John Doyle Ong of the B. F. Goodrich Company is born in Uhrichsville, OH

1950 Mrs. Henry (Clara Bryant) Ford dies at age 83

1952 Land speed record holder John R. Cobb is killed at age 52 while trying to raise the water speed record at Loch Ness, Scotland

1960 The 1961 Fords are introduced

1960 The 1961 Plymouths are introduced

1961 The 1962 Chevrolets are introduced including the new Chevy II series

1961 The 1962 Ford Falcons, Galaxies, and station wagons are introduced

1962 American Motors announces a two-year, 24,000-mile warranty on its 1963 car lines

1963 The 1964 Chevrolet trucks are introduced

1965 The 1966 Plymouth Fury, Belvedere and Valiant are introduced

1966 The 1967 Chevrolets are introduced including the new Camaro "pony" car and the Caprice custom station wagon with simulated wood trip, the first for the marque since the 1954 model year

1966 The 1967 Chryslers and Imperials are introduced

1966 The 1967 Oldsmobiles are introduced

1966 The 1967 Plymouths and Plymouth Valiants are introduced

1970 The 1971 Cadillacs are introduced

1970 The 1971 Chevrolets cars and trucks are introduced, except for the new sub-compact Vega which had debuted nineteen days earlier

1980 Jean-Marc Lepeu is named Vice President of American Motors succeeding Wilson W. Sick

1983 Henry Ford II is inducted into the Automotive Hall of Fame in Midland, MI

1984 Kruse International begins the first liquidation auction of Harrah's Automobile Collection in Sparks, NV

1987 Henry Ford II dies of pneumonia in Detroit, MI at age 70

*This 1949 Mercury passing through the Chandelier Tree in northern California
was one of the first cars produced during the Henry Ford II era and
is one of the most nostalgia evoking symbols of the time.*

SEPTEMBER 30

1868 William E. Metzger is born in Peru, IL

1874 Herbert Randall Straight of the Cities Service Oil Company is born in Tidioute, PA

1889 Nicholas Dreystadt of General Motors is born in Germany

1897 The Central European Motor Vehicle Club is organized in Berlin, Germany

1901 Automobile license plates become mandatory in all of France

1907 The Ford Motor Company announces their first fiscal year with profits exceeding $1 million

1909 Robert Allen Boyer, Research Director of the Ford Motor Company 1930- 1943, is born in Toledo, OH

1912 The Ford Motor Company announces their first fiscal year with profits exceeding $10 million

1914 Ivo Colucci of Alfa Romeo is born in Livorno, Italy

1915 Charles Eckhart, first President of the Auburn Automobile Company, dies at age 74

1919 Racer Roberto Bonomi is born in Buenos Aires, Argentina

1922 Alonzo Hyatt Kelly Jr. of General Motors is born in Richlands, VA

1931 Automotive parts manufacturer James Richard Welton is born in Minneapolis, MN

1936 The General Motors Truck Company, manufacturing subsidiary of the Yellow Truck & Coach Manufacturing Company, is dissolved

1937 The last Duesenberg dealer closes its doors in New York City

The intersection of Hollywood and Vine in Hollywood, CA circa 1951 - the customized Duesenberg Model J convertible coupe was a 20 year old "used car" at the time. Its precise identity remains a mystery.

1937 The 1938 Packard Six, Eight, and Sixteenth Series Super Eight and Twelve are introduced

1941 Racer Reine Tore Lief Wisell is born in Motala, Sweden

1943 General Motors acquires the property and assets of the Yellow Truck & Coach Manufacturing Company

1943 Precision machinist Carl E. Johansson dies in Eskilstuna, Sweden at age 79

1944 Earl D. Sirrine, Sales Engineer for the Autocar Company since 1930, resigns due to failing health

1946 Racer Jochen Mass is born in Munich, Germany

1947 Charles P. Joy, a Packard dealer 1904-1947, dies in Saint Paul, MN at age 70

1951 Kathleen M. Hammer of the Ford Motor Company is born

1952 Frank Mundy wins his first AAA-sponsored race in Springfield, IL

1955 The last 1955 Hudson is produced

1955 Actor James Dean is killed at age 24 in a highway accident near Cholame, CA while driving his Porsche 550 Spyder

1957 The first race staged at the Bridgehampton Road Course on Long Island, NY, a 75-mile SCCA event, is won by Walt Hansgen in a Jaguar

1959 The Ford Motor Company announces plans to produce the compact "Comet"

1959 The London showrooms of Hooper & Company (Coachbuilders) Ltd. close after 63 years at the same location

1961 Racer Eric van de Poele is born in Verviers, Belgium

1964 The 1965 Chryslers and Imperials are introduced

1965 The 1966 Chryslers and Imperials are introduced

1966 The 1967 Fords are introduced

1966 The Mercury Cougar is introduced, based loosely on the Ford Mustang

1968 The 1969 Mercury Marquis is introduced as the new top-of-the-line series with a full range of body styles

1970 NASCAR stages its last race on a dirt track, the Homestate 200 at the Fairgrounds Speedway in Raleigh, NC, which is won by Richard Petty

1971 The cars of the late automotive historian Ken Purdy are sold at auction in Weston, CT

1973 The 1974 Mercedes-Benz models are introduced to the United States market

1974 Edward N. Cole retires as President of General Motors

1979 The Rebaque makes its only Formula 1 appearance in the Canadian Grand Prix, but the Type HR100 driven by Hector Rebaque retires with engine mounting problems

1986 The first British-built Nissan, a Bluebird (based on the Stanza), is completed and presented to HRH Charles, the Prince of Wales

1988 Al Holbert, 1986 and 1987 winner of the 24 Hours of Daytona, is killed at age 41 in an airplane accident in Columbus, OH

1990 Racer Rob Moroso is killed in a car accident in Mooresville, NC

1992 BMW begins construction on its new assembly plant in Spartanburg, SC

1996 The 90,000,000th Toyota, a silver Aristo 3.0V, is produced

OCTOBER 1

1826 Benjamin Berkely Hotchkiss, firearms manufacturer and namesake of the 1903-1955 French-built Hotchkiss, is born in Watertown, CT

1847 The world's first sale of pneumatic tires is made to Lord Lorane of Albany Park, Guildford, England - the rotting remains of the tires, built to the design of Robert William Thomson, are now owned by the Dunlop Rubber Company Ltd.

1860 Giovanni Ceirano, a cofounder of Fiat, is born in Cuneo, Italy

1876 Soviet automotive engineer Nikolai Romanovich Briling is born in Moscow, Russia

1883 Ormond Edson Hunt, a longtime Packard and General Motors official, is born in Saranac, MI

1883 Benz & Cie, Rheinische Gasmotorenfabrik in Mannheim is founded by Carl Benz, Friedrich Wilhelm Esslinger, and Heinrich Kleyer

1896 The Austrian Automobile, Motorcycle and Touring Club is organized

1901 J. Frank Duryea begins design work on the first Stevens-Duryea

1902 E. R. Thomas Motor Company is founded to replace the Buffalo Automobile and Auto-Bi Company, with the name of the marque changing from Buffalo to Thomas

1908 The Ford Model T is introduced

1908 Roy A. Fruehauf of the Fruehauf Trailer Company is born in Detroit, MI

1910 The 6th Vanderbilt Cup Race is held on Long Island, NY and won by Harry F. Grant in a 90-hp Alco for the second consecutive year - riding mechanics Charles Miller (with Louis Chevrolet) and Matthew Bacon (with Harold Stone) are killed during the race

1910 The 1911 Hudsons are introduced, including the new Model 33 designed by Howard E. Coffin that is often cited as the first true Hudson

1910 B. W. Burtsell is named Production Manager for the Packard Motor Car Company

1913 Eugene J. Farkas is put in charge of the experimental drafting room of the Ford Motor Company

1915 Henry Ford assigns Charles E. Sorensen to oversee the manufacture of an undesigned Ford farm tractor - Sorensen picks Eugene J. Farkas to be the Chief Engineer in charge of its design

1915 The Henry Ford Hospital opens in Detroit, MI

1925 George William Coombe Jr. of General Motors is born in Kearney, NJ

1928 Racer Willy Mairesse is born in Momignies, Belgium

1929 The 1930 Nashes are introduced, including the Series 490 which featured the marque's first 8-cylinder engine

1930 The 1931 Nashes are introduced, including the Series 870 which featured the new "Flathead Eight" engine

1931 A Model AA truck is the first vehicle produced at Ford's new Dagenham, England factory

1931 Packard's Canadian factory in Windsor, ON begins production

1932 Racer Frank Gardner is born in Sydney, NSW, Australia

1933 The 1934 Nashes are introduced featuring new styling by Count Alexis de Sakhnoffsky

1936 The 1937 Nashes are introduced

1936 The Yellow Truck & Coach Manufacturing Company becomes the actual truck manufacturing arm of General Motors, with the General Motors Truck Company responsible for sales

1938 The 1939 Hupmobile Senior Six and Eight are publicly introduced - a Junior Six based on the body dies of the Cord 810/812 did not proceed beyond a single prototype

1940 The 1941 Cadillacs are introduced, including the new Series 61, Series 63, and Series 67

1940 The 1941 Nashes are introduced, including the new Ambassador 600 with unitized body/frame construction

1941 The first 1942 Cadillac is produced

1941 The 1942 Nashes are introduced

1942 Racer Jean-Pierre Jabouille is born in Paris, France

1943 The GMC Truck & Coach Division of General Motors is created from the former Yellow Truck & Coach Manufacturing Company

1943 Eugene Gruenewald, President of the Ross Gear & Tool Company and former General Manager of R and V Engineering Company, manufacturers of sleeve valved engines, dies

1945 The 1946 Hudsons are introduced

1947 James E. Auten, an official with White, Cadillac 1914-1918, Lafayette, and Nash 1920-1938, dies at age 64

1949 With virtually no change to the 1949 specification, Packard begins marketing their Twenty-Third Series cars as 1950 models

1949 Ormond E. Hunts retires as Executive Vice President of General Motors

1953 S. H. "Wacky" Arnolt purchases the Bertone-styled Alfa Romeo B.A.T. 5

1953 Arthur R. Blood, a design engineer with Franklin before entering the farm tractor industry, dies at age 62

1954 The Packard Motor Car Company purchases the Studebaker Corporation - the Studebaker-Packard Corporation is organized with James J. Nance as President and Paul G. Hoffman as Chairman of the Board

1955 The Ohio Turnpike opens to the public

1956 Mack Trucks, Inc. acquires the Brockway Motor Truck Corporation of Cortland, NY

1957 Fina Petroleum Products Ltd. changes its name to Petrofina (Great Britain) Ltd.

1957 Racer Tony Longhurst is born in Sydney, NSW, Australia

1958 The 1959 Fiats are introduced to the United States market

1959 The 1960 Fiats are introduced to the United States market

1959 The 1960 British Fords are introduced to the United States market

1959 The 1960 German Ford Taunus is introduced to the United States market

1959 The 1960 German Goliaths are introduced to the United States market

1959 The 1960 Morris is introduced to the United States market

1959 The 1960 Oldsmobiles are introduced

1959 The 1960 Pontiacs are introduced

1959 General Motors stylists began developing the XP-727, a clay mock-up that would evolve into the front-wheel drive 1967 Cadillac Eldorado sport coupe

1959 Racer Brian Simo is born in Chicago, IL

1960 The 1961 Fiats are introduced to the United States market

1960 Jack W. Minor resigns from the Chrysler Corporation during the scandals that led to the ouster of President William C. Newberg

1961 The 1962 Fiats are introduced to the United States market

1961 Stuart Turner joins the British Motor Corporation as Competition Manager

1962 The 1963 Fiats are introduced to the United States market

1963 Racer Jean-Denis Deletraz is born in Geneva, Switzerland

1963 The Pontiac GTO is introduced as an option package for the deluxe Tempest

1964 The 1965 Ford Mustangs are officially introduced, including a new 2+2 fastback coupe

1964 Rolls-Royce begins a direct distributorship policy to the United States

1964 Racer Jerome Policand is born in Geneva, Switzerland

1965 The new four-wheel drive Ford Bronco is introduced

1965 The 1966 Ford Mustangs are introduced

1966 The 1967 Fords are introduced

1967 Stuart Turner joins the Ford Motor Company Ltd. as Competition Manager

1968 The 1969 AMC models are introduced, including the last cars to bear the historic Rambler name

1968 Kurt Lotz names Werner Holste as Technical Director of Volkswagenwerk AG

1970 The 1971 Jaguars are introduced to the United States market

1970 The 1971 Mercedes-Benz models are introduced to the United States market

1971 Alvin B. Anderson is named General Manager of the General Motors factory in Lordstown, OH

1971 Rudolf Leiding, President of Audi, is named as the new Chairman of Volkswagenwerk AG, replacing Kurt Lotz who had resigned September 24

1972 Pontiac General Manager F. James McDonald transfers to the same position at Chevrolet, with Martin J. Caserio replacing him at Pontiac

1972 American Motors organizes a subsidiary, the American Motors Leasing Corporation, to manage the leasing of cars to the public

1974 Elliott M. Estes is elected President of General Motors

1974 The 1975 Chevrolet trucks are introduced

1974 The 1975 Chryslers and Imperials are introduced

1974 The 1975 Dodges are introduced

1974 The 1975 Plymouths are introduced

1975 John J. Riccardo is elected Chairman of the Chrysler Corporation, replacing the retiring Lynn A. Townsend - Eugene A. "Gene" Cafiero is elected President and R. K. Brown becomes the new Executive Vice President in charge of North American operations

1976 The Bristol Britannia is introduced as the successor to the Bristol 603

1979 Henry Ford II retires as Chief Executive Office of the Ford Motor Company and is succeeded by Philip Caldwell

1980 The Rolls-Royce Silver Spirit is introduced to replace the Silver Shadow

1982 Henry Ford II retires as an employee of the Ford Motor Company

1985 The 1986 AMC Eagle is introduced

1985 Ninian Sanderson, winner of the 1956 24 Hours of Le Mans, dies from cancer in Glasgow, Scotland at age 60

1987 Diamandus Communications, Inc. purchases the CBS Magazine Division of CBS, Inc., including *Automobile Quarterly* magazine

1990 The Suzuki Motor Company, Ltd. of Shizuoka, Japan changes its name to the Suzuki Motor Corporation

OCTOBER 2

1869 Elisha Hilliard Cooper, longtime Chairman of the Fafnir Bearing Company, is born in Rockport, MA

1887 George Thurman Christopher of Packard is born in Cloverland, IN

1888 B. Edwin Hutchinson, Vice President and Treasurer of the Maxwell Motor Corporation 1921-1924 and the first Vice President of the Chrysler Corporation, is born in Chicago, IL

1907 The Moon Motor Car Company is incorporated with Joseph W. Moon as President, Stewart McDonald as Vice President and General Manager, Alfred F. Moberly as Treasurer, and George H. Schelp as Secretary

1912 Semon Emil "Bunkie" Knudsen of General Motors and the Ford Motor Company is born in Buffalo, NY

1912 The eighth Vanderbilt Cup is staged in Milwaukee, WI and won by Ralph DePalma in a Mercedes

1914 Henry Walter Welch of General Motors is born in Jefferson, OH

1919 Racer Jan Flinterman is born in the Netherlands

1921 Racer Mike Nazaruk is born in Newark, NJ

1921 Racer Giorgio Scarlatti is born in Rome, Italy

1923 The Nash 1922-1923 "Winged Wheel with Motometer" mascot is patented on behalf of manufacturer Stant Machine Company of Connersville, IN

1925 London, England allows double-deck, fully-enclosed buses after such vehicles had been banned for 16 years

1927 Racer Paul Goldsmith is born in Parkersburg, WV

1928 Eberhard von Kuenheim of BMW is born in Juditten, Germany

1930 Construction begins on the new Ford-Werke AG factory in Cologne, Germany

1930 Racer Jack Bowsher is born in Springfield, OH

1933 The Bentley 3 1/2 Litre is introduced, the first of the marque produced by the Rolls-Royce owned Bentley Motors (1931) Ltd.

1934 Gordon M. Buehrig is issued a United States patent for his automobile body that would be used by the 1936 Cord 810 and 1937 Cord 812

1934 The Plymouth 1933 "Goddess" mascot is patented by designer Herbert V. Henderson

1935 The Rolls-Royce Phantom III, featuring a V-12 engine, is announced

1936 The first Kenworth cab-over-engine truck is produced

1939 The Lincoln-Zephyr Continental is formally introduced at the Ford Rotunda in Dearborn, MI

1940 Freelan O. Stanley dies in Newton, MA at age 91

1940 Racer Giovanni Giuseppe Gilberto "Nanni" Galli is born in Bologna, Italy

1947 The Federation Internationale de l'Automobile (FIA) splits the Grand Prix competitions into Formula 1 and Formula 2

1948 The first automobile races are held at Watkins Glen, NY under the guidance of Cameron Reynolds Argetsinger and the Sports Car Club of America (SCCA) - Frank Griswold, driving a 2.9-liter pre-World War II Alfa Romeo, wins both events, a 26.4-mile Junior Prix, and the 52.8-mile Grand Prix

1948 The first modern British Grand Prix (and the first since 1927) is staged at Silverstone and won by Luigi Villoresi driving a Maserati 4CLT/48

1949 Racer Michael Bleekemolen is born in Amsterdam, the Netherlands

1953 The 1954 Hudsons are introduced

1953 William Fairhurst, Vice President of the Dana Corporation and a former employee of Packard and Denby trucks, dies in Wernersville, PA at age 61

1954 The last Detroit-built Hudson is produced

1954 The 100,000th Volkswagen Transporter is produced

1958 V. A. Crosby of the Climax Molybdenum Company dies at age 65

1959 Chevrolet introduces the Corvair, a rear-engined compact car line

1959 The Jaguar Mark 2 saloon is introduced

1962 The 1,000,000th Volkswagen Transporter is produced

1964 Tom Green, driving the Wingfoot Express, raises the land speed record to 413.20 mph at the Bonneville Salt Flats, UT

1965 Donaldson Brown, General Motors Vice President of Finance 1921-1937 and its Vice Chairman 1937-1946, dies at age 80

1967 The Japan Petroleum Development Corporation is established

1968 B. Brewster Jennings, Chairman of the Socony Mobil Oil Company 1955-1958, dies at age 70

1975 The 1976 Chevrolet trucks are introduced

1978 Groundbreaking ceremonies are held for the DeLorean Motor Car Company factory in Dunmurry, Northern Ireland

1983 A monument to Count Albert de Dion is dedicated in Puteaux, France

1988 Sir Alec Issigonis, designer of the Morris Minor and Mini, dies in Birmingham, England at age 81

England in the 1950's - the "woodie" parked on High Street in Aylesford, Kent is a Morris Minor Traveller.

OCTOBER 3

1869 Edgar Landon Apperson is born near Kokomo, IN

1873 Hugh Chalmers is born in Dayton, OH

Chalmers "30" Touring Car

1877 Oliver Edward Barthel, an associate of of Charles B. King and Henry Ford who was Chief Engineer of the Cadillac Motor Car Company in 1902 and formed the Barthel Motor Company in 1903, is born in Detroit, MI

1894 Edward J. Pennington of Cleveland, OH applies for a patent for his "motor vehicle", notable for its balloon tires

1896 The Paris-Marseille-Paris race ends during its tenth day with M. Mayade winning in his Panhard et Levassor

1912 Mortimer Roberts, driving a Mason, wins the 220.64 mile Pabst Blue Ribbon Trophy Race in Wauwatosa, WI, the first major victory for a car with a Duesenberg engine

1914 James William Grant of Paccar, Inc. is born in Ronan, MT

1916 James Scripps Booth resigns from the Scripps-Booth Company

1921 Erik Lennart Valdemar Johansson of Volvo is born in Goteborg, Sweden

1928 The Ford Motor Company announces its entry into the bus business

1931 George Theodorus Briggs, Sales Manager of the Wheeler-Schebler Carburetor Company, dies in Indianapolis, IN at age 55

1934 The National Automobile Chamber of Commerce reorganizes as the Automobile Manufacturers Association

1934 Dr. Calvin Winsor Rice, Executive Secretary of the American Society of Mechanical Engineers since 1906, dies

1936 Earl McCarty resigns as Vice President and General Manager of the Nash Motor Company

1937 Harry R. McMahon, founder in 1914 and President 1914-1936 of the Standard Steel Spring Company, dies in Coraopolis Heights, PA at age 64

1941 The first 1942 Mercury is produced

1941 The 1942 Buicks are introduced

A 1942 Buick Special 4-door sedan is parked between 1936 and 1941 Fords in Deerwood, MN.

1941 Racer Andrea de Adamich is born in Trieste, Italy

1943 D. A. Andrews of the Continental Motors Corporation dies at age 58

1945 The first post-World War II Chevrolet automobile is produced

1945 Truman H. Newberry, a Director of the Packard Motor Car Company since 1903, dies in Grosse Pointe Farms, MI at age 80

1946 The first post-World War II Salon de l'Automobile opens in Paris, France

1952 The Gordini 38 S sports car debuts at the Paris Motor Show

1955 The first 1956 Pontiac is produced

1955 William F. Pioch Sr., a manufacturing engineering consultant to the Ford Motor Company and an employee of the firm since 1912, dies

1956 The 1956 Ford Thunderbirds are introduced

1956 The last 1956 Pontiac is produced

1956 John G. Wood, Chief Engineer of Empire 1907-1913 and Chief Engineer of Chevrolet 1945-1949, dies at age 73

1956 Theron Bradshaw, former Chief Engineer of the Replacement Division, Perfect Circle Company, dies at age 65

1958 The first 1959 Ford Thunderbird is produced

1958 The 1959 Oldsmobiles are introduced

1960 The first 1961 Ford Thunderbird is produced

1962 The 1963 Plymouths are introduced

1963 The 1964 Pontiacs are introduced

1967 Robert C. Graham dies at age 82

1969 Racer Massimiliano "Max" Papis is born in Como, Italy

1969 Racer Alessandro Zampedri is born in Brescia, Italy

1970 Pierre Veyron, winner of the 1939 24 Hours of Le Mans, dies in Cap d'Eze, France at age 67

1990 Clarence W. Avery is inducted into the Automotive Hall of Fame to note his design of the first moving assembly line as implemented by the Ford Motor Company

1995 Comercial Sicocar SA, the Toyota distributor for Ecuador, opens their new administration, sales, and service facility building in Guayaquil

OCTOBER 4

1858 Leon Serpollet is born in Culoz, France

1866 Pioneer automobile designer Francis "Frank" Jaszkowiak is born

1876 Herbert Champion Harrison, founder of the Harrison Radiator Company, is born in Calcutta, India

1886 B. B. Bachman of Autocar is born

1902 Frederic Garrett Donner of General Motors is born in Three Oaks, MI

Among the first cars manufactured during the nine-year General Motors chairmanship of Frederic G. Donner were these two 1959 Chevrolets parked near the public school in Donnybrook, ND. Their "seagull wing" tailfins and "cat's eye" taillights may have been a bit bizarre, but unlike most cars the 1959 Chevy was unmistakable from behind.

1902 Ralph Campbell Mark of General Motors is born in Jackson, MI

1912 Racer David Bruce-Brown is killed at age 22 when his Fiat crashes during a practice run for the Milwaukee (WI) Grand Prize race

1919 The first post-World War I Rolls-Royce is imported into the United States

1919 Philip H. McMillan, Secretary of the Packard Motor Car Company and an original investor of the company, dies at age 46

1924 The Montlhery race track near Paris, France opens with a two-day series of races

1927 Racer Roberto Bussinello is born in Pistoia, Italy

1928 Racer Bob Scott is born in Watsonville, CA

1928 The Checker Model K is introduced

1933 Charles Thompson, a cofounder of the Cleveland Cap and Screw Company in 1901 and developer of an improved process for manufacturing automobile engine valves that led to his company being purchased by the Winton Motor Carriage Company in 1903, dies in Cleveland, OH at age 63 - Winton failed in 1924, but the subsidiary survived to evolve into TRW, Inc.

1937 Russell Joseph Saunders of the Freightliner Corporation is born in San Mateo, CA

1941 Charles L. Bowden, Sales Manager for the Elmore Manufacturing Company 1910-1912 and a leading proponent of two-cycle automobile engines, dies in Valparaiso, IN at age 75

1944 Pierre Lefaucheux is appointed President of Renault succeeding Louis Renault

1945 The first post-World War II Pontiac is officially produced, although production records indicate that actual production had begun on September 13

1946 Racer Barney Oldfield dies of a cerebral hemorrhage in Beverly Hills, CA at age 68

1948 Racer Bob Morris is born in Australia

1951 The first Willys Aero is produced

1954 The first 1955 Pontiac is produced featuring the division's new Strato Streak V-8 engine

1955 The Continental Mark II is introduced by William Clay Ford

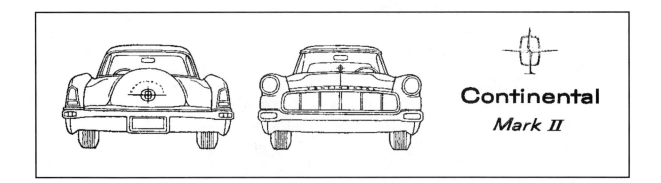

Continental
Mark II

1955 The completed Bugatti Type 251 race car makes its first test run at the aerodrome in Entzheim, France with Pierre Marco at the wheel

1956 Tooling is approved for the 1957 Packard Clipper using a slightly modified Studebaker body shell

1956 Leo L. Williams, a design engineer whose automotive career included stints with Lambert, Peerless, Chandler, Hupmobile, and GMC, dies

1958 Walter E. Lyon of the Firestone Tire & Rubber Company dies at age 55

1961 Deutz AG of Germany acquires a license to build diesel engines using the Wankel rotary engine theories

1962 The 1963 Oldsmobiles are introduced

1962 The 1963 Pontiacs are introduced

1962 Studebaker announces a two-year, 24,000-mile warranty on its 1963 car lines

1970 Emerson Fittipaldi driving a Lotus wins the United States Grand Prix in Watkins Glen, NY to clinch the World Champion Driver title for his deceased teammate, Jochen Rindt, the first time the award had been given posthumously

1970 Racer Curtis M. Turner is killed at age 46 in an airplane crash near Punxsutawney, PA

1973 The Ford Motor Company announces plans to build a factory in Valencia, Spain

1975 The cornerstone is laid for the Iola, WI headquarters of Krause Publications, publishers of *Old Cars* newspaper

1983 Richard Noble driving the Rolls-Royce powered Thrust 2 as designed by John Ackroyd raises the land speed record to 633.468 mph at Black Rock Desert, NV

1984 UAW President Owen Bieber is elected to the Chrysler Corporation Board of Directors

1992 Racer Denis Hulme dies at age 56 from a heart attack suffered while driving a BMW M3 in the Bathurst 1000 in New South Wales, Australia

1993 Harold A. Poling announces his retirement as Chairman of the Ford Motor Company

OCTOBER 5

1826 Henry Studebaker is born in East Berlin, PA

1841 John Simson Gray, first President of the Ford Motor Company, is born in Edinburgh, Scotland

1857 Richard Dudgeon's first steam vehicle is destroyed in the fire at the Crystal Palace in New York City

1892 Warren Packard II, the only son of William D. Packard, is born

1899 Marcus Wallenberg of Saab-Scania AB is born in Stockholm, Sweden

1900 The prototype Black steamer is taken for its first test drive in West Chester, PA by designer Stephen C. Black

1916 Automotive parts manufacturer Robert George Wingerter is born in Detroit, MI

1916 The Henry Ford Trade School officially opens in Highland Park, MI

1917 Automobile parts manufacturer Eugene I. Anderson is born in Crothersville, IN

1919 Enzo Ferrari makes his racing debut, finishing 11th in the Parma-Poggio di Berceto hillclimb in his C.M.N.

1921 The 1922 Nashes are introduced

1922 Racer Jose Froilan Gonzalez is born in Arrecifes, Argentina

1924 J. G. Parry Thomas sets the first Montlhery, France lap record of 131.89 mph in his Leyland

1926 The Dort Motor Car Company is officially dissolved

1931 Hans Graf von der Goltz of BMW is born in Bad Marienberg, Germany

1933 Jack Dow Rutherford of the International Harvester Company is born in Greenland, AR

1937 Howard G. Young, an official with Peerless and White before entering the electric utility industry, dies at age 50

1940 The DeSoto S-8 series is introduced, featuring "Rocket" bodies

1940 Bryon Forbes "Barney" Everitt dies in Detroit, MI at age 67

1944 Dr. Carl Claus, a German-born authority on powder metallurgy and Vice President of the Bound Brook Oil-Less Bearing Company, dies at age 60

1945 The first post-World War II Studebaker is produced, a 1946 Skyway Champion sedan

1949 George D. Keller, President of Keller Motors, Inc. of Huntsville, AL, dies of a heart attack at age 56

1949 Hugh J. Ferry becomes President of the Packard Motor Car Company, although the deposed George T. Christopher would officially hold the office until December 31, 1949

1949 Racer Klaus Ludwig is born in Roisdorf, West Germany

1950 Fred J. Schaefer of Franklin, Chevrolet, and Ford dies in Detroit, MI at age 53

1954 Henry J. and Edgar Kaiser sign a contract to produce Kaiser cars, Willys cars and trucks, and Jeeps in Argentina

1960 The 1961 Ramblers are introduced

1962 The 1963 Ramblers are introduced

1962 Racer Michael Mario Andretti is born in Bethlehem, PA, the son of racer Mario Andretti

1964 The 1965 Hillman Minx is introduced to the United States market

1964 Art Arfons, driving the Green Monster, raises the land speed record to 434.02 mph at the Bonneville Salt Flats, UT

1964 The special Lincoln Continental convertible involved in the assassination of John F. Kennedy in 1963 is returned to service after being remodeled by the Ford Motor Company and Hess & Eisenhardt of Cincinnati, OH

1969 Graham Hill makes his record 90th consecutive Grand Prix start

1981 The six year production run of the Triumph TR7 ends as the last of 111,648 cars is completed at the Rover factory in Solihull, Warwickshire, England

OCTOBER 6

1859 Tire manufacturer Franklin Augustus Seiberling is born in Western Star, OH

1866 Brothers Henry A. and James A. House drive their House steam car from Hartford to Stratford, CT

1893 Max Ronald Burnell of General Motors is born in Metamora, MI

1906 The third Vanderbilt Cup Race, held on Long Island, NY, is won by Louis Wagner in a 100-hp, 12.7-litre Darracq

1910 Orazio Satta Puliga of Alfa Romeo is born in Turin, Italy

1917 George W. Houk, an automobile wheel manufacturer who introduced Rudge-Whitworth detachable wire wheels in the United States, dies in Hollywood, CA at age 51

1918 Racer Andre Pilette is born in Paris, France of Belgian ancestry

1918 Racer Max de Terra is born in Switzerland

1919 The Mercer Automobile Company is reorganized as the Mercer Motors Company with E. S. Hare as President

1926 Duesenberg, Inc. is organized by E. L. Cord to design and manufacture a top-of-the-line car, introduced two years later as the Duesenberg Model J

1927 Roger P. Deschamps, a Belgian importer of United States automobile and agricultural equipment, dies in New York City at age 35

1931 The 1931 Oldsmobile "Eagle" mascot is patented by designer William Schnell

1933 The last 1933 Pontiac is produced

1938 Edsel B. Ford chooses "Mercury" as the name of the new marque under development by the Ford Motor Company

A park ranger poses proudly with his 1940 Ford Deluxe station wagon.

1939 The 1940 Fords are introduced featuring styling by Eugene Gregorie

1940 Thomas Neal of General Motors dies at age 82

1940 Frank Griswold, driving an Alfa Romeo, wins the World's Fair Grand Prix staged on the exposition grounds in Flushing, NY

1940 Edwin "Eddie" Pullen, pioneer driver for the Mercer racing team, dies in Los Angeles, CA at age 57

1941 Racer John Nicholson is born in Auckland, New Zealand

1941 Thomas J. Litle Jr., former Chief Engineer of Lincoln and Marmon who served as President of the Society of Automotive Engineers in 1926, dies in South Bend, IN at age 66

1942 Racer Edgar Doren is born in Wuppertal, Germany

1944 Racer Jose Carlos Pace is born in Sao Paulo, Brazil

1951 Sir Henry Lovell Goldsworthy Gurney, British High Commander for Malaya, is assassinated at age 53 by Communist rebels near Kuala Lumpur while he was riding in a Rolls-Royce Silver Wraith Park Ward limousine, the only time that the British marque has been involved in such an incident

1952 The 700,000th automobile is produced by the Kaiser-Frazer Corporation

1952 Racer Manfred Winkelhock is born in Waiblingen, West Germany

1954 The 1955 Studebakers are introduced

1955 The Lincoln Continental Mark II is introduced in Europe at the Paris Auto Show

1955 The first Citroen DS is produced

1956 Race Mike McLaughlin is born in Waterloo, NY

1959 Mickey Thompson, driving the Challenger I, sets a land speed record for automobile engine powered vehicles of 363.67 mph

1960 The 1961 Oldsmobiles are introduced, including the new compact F-85

1960 The 1961 Pontiacs are introduced, including the new compact Tempest series

1961 The 1962 Ramblers and Rambler Americans are introduced

DS-21 PALLAS

So there are really only two kinds of cars in the world today: Citroën and the rest."
ROAD & TRACK MAGAZINE

SALES AND SERVICE THROUGHOUT THE U.S.A. AND CANADA. CHECK THE YELLOW PAGES. FOR DEALER LIST, LITERATURE, AND/OR EUROPEAN DELIVERY BROCHURE, WRITE: CITROEN CARS CORPORATION, F437. 641 LEXINGTON AVE., NEW YORK, N.Y. 10022. WEST: 8423 WILSHIRE BOULEVARD, BEVERLY HILLS, CALIF. 90211.

1962 Jack Brabham, in the second Formula 1 appearance with his new Brabham, finishes 4th in the United States Grand Prix, becoming the first driver to earn championship points driving a car of his own design

1963 The 1964 Ramblers are introduced, featuring Adjust-O-Tilt steering as an option

1963 The Stebro makes its only Formula 1 appearance in the United States Grand Prix in Watkins Glen, NY with the Type 4 car driven by Peter Broeker finishing in seventh place

1966 The 1967 Cadillacs are introduced, including the new front-wheel-drive Fleetwood Eldorado sport coupe

1966 The 1967 Ramblers are introduced

1969 The 1970 British Fords are introduced to the United States market

1970 The 1971 AMC models are introduced

1970 The 1971 full-sized Plymouths are introduced

1971 Automotive journalist W. F. Bradley dies in Condom-en-Armagnac, France at age 95

1972 Warren Walter Fitzgerald, Supervisor of Automotive Information Services for the General Motors Design Staff, dies of cancer in Pontiac, MI

1973 Racer Francois Cevert is killed at age 29 when his Tyrrell-Cosworth crashes during a practice run for the United States Grand Prix in Watkins Glen, NY

1974 Racer Helmuth Koinigg is killed at age 25 when his Surtees-Cosworth crashes during the United States Grand Prix in Watkins Glen, NY

1977 The 1978 Pontiacs are introduced

1981 Esso UK PLC is registered in Great Britain

1988 Chrysler Corporation and Fiat SpA form a joint venture to market the Alfa Romeo in the United States

1989 B.R. "Woody" Woodill, a Downey, CA Dodge dealer who designed and built the 1952-1956 Willys-powered Woodill Wildfire sports car, dies in McAllen, TX at age 73

1995 Racer Russell Phillips is killed at age 26 when his Oldsmobile crashes during the Winston 100 NASCAR Sportsman Series race at the Charlotte Motor Speedway in Concord, NC

OCTOBER 7

1888 H. E. Hund, General Manager of the Briggs Manufacturing Company 1929-1934 and later President of Reo Motors, Inc., is born in East Detroit, MI

1907 A Walter driven by Joe Parkin Jr. wins a 10-hour race at the Trenton (NJ) Inter-State Fairgrounds - this event hastened the evolution of the marque into the Mercer

1912 Racer Peter Walker is born in Huby, Leeds, Yorkshire, England

1913 The world's first moving assembly line starts at the Highland Park, MI factory of the Ford Motor Company

1913 Camille Jentazy, winner of the 1903 Gordon Bennett Trophy and former land speed record holder, dies at age 44 from an accidental shooting while on a wild boar hunt

1919 James Noel Johnson of the A. O. Smith Corporation is born in Stevens Point, WI

1928 Thomas L. Raymond, an cofounder of the Kent Motors Corporation in Newark, NJ, at which time he was that city's mayor, dies at age 53

1930 The Cadillac 1930-1932 "Heron" mascot is patented by designer J. W. Hession Jr.

1930 Racer Bernard Collomb is born in Nice, France

1930 Race car mechanic Curtis Wade Crider is born in Charleston, SC

1935 John R. Cobb driving a Napier-Railton sets the alltime Brooklands (England) lap record for Class A (unlimited) of 143.44 mph

1935 The Wayland Grand Prix, the first race at the Wayland track near Boston, MA and the first race staged by the Automobile Racing Club of America (ARCA), is won by Langdon Quimby in a Willys 77

1935 Emery H. Fahrney, a pioneer designer of automobile engines and spark plugs, dies at age 59

1939 The 1940 Fords are introduced

1945 The 1946 Buicks are introduced

1955 The 1956 Dodges are introduced

1959 James D. Vaseau, Truck Product Engineer for the Ford Division of the Ford Motor Company, dies at age 46

1960 The first episode of the television program *Route 66* airs

1962 The Ford Mustang I show car is unveiled in Watkins Glen, NY

1962 Racer Henri Oreiller dies at age 36 from injuries suffered when he crashes during a race at the Montlhery circuit in France

1962 The Ford Mustang I show car is unveiled in Watkins Glen, NY

1963 The Ford Mustang II show car is unveiled in Watkins Glen, NY - unlike its predecessor, the Mustang II was more prototype than show car and closely resembled the production Mustang that would be introduced in 1964

1965 Racer Marco Apicella is born in Bologna, Italy

1965 Racer Richard Dean is born in Great Britain, the son of racer Tony Dean

1965 The 1966 Chevrolets are introduced

1965 The 1966 Pontiacs are introduced

1965 The 1966 Ramblers are introduced

1966 Racer Vincenzo Sospiri is born in Sorli, Italy

1973 The first national meet of the Pontiac-Oakland Club International is held in Camp Hill, PA

1981 The Triumph Acclaim, a badge-engineered Honda, is introduced and would be produced until 1984 when the Triumph marque was discontinued

1983 Allen W. Merrell, Ford Motor Company Vice President for Civic and Government Affairs 1963-1973, dies in Charlottesville, VA at age 67

1983 The Dodge Brothers' Club is formed in Hershey, PA to serve enthusiasts of Dodge and Graham vehicles manufactured through the 1938 model year

1984 The Grand Prix of Europe is the first race at the newly-rebuilt Nurburgring in Germany

1995 Racer Louis Meyer dies in Las Vegas, NV at age 91

OCTOBER 8

1869 James Franklin Duryea is born in Washburn, IL

1884 William Robert Wilson of the Reo Motor Car Company is born in Chicago, IL

1887 Marvin E. Coyle, President and General Manager of Chevrolet 1933-1946, is born in Centerville, PA

1890 Edward Vernon "Eddie" Rickenbacker (nee Rickenbacher), World War I flying ace, automobile racer, airlines executive, and namesake of the 1922-1927 Rickenbacker automobile, is born in Columbus, OH

1903 Racer Yves Giraud-Cabantous is born in Saint-Gaudens, Garonne, France

1904 The first Vanderbilt Cup race is held on Long Island, NY, with the Panhard et Levassor driven by George Heath edging out Albert Clement in his Clement-Bayard - this race marked the last official appearance of the Packard Gray Wolf, which finished fourth in the hands of Charles Schmidt

1909 Racer Everitt Saylor is born in Brookville, OH

1910 Len Zengle, driving a Chadwick, wins the 200-mile Founder's Day Cup Race at Fairmount Park in Philadelphia, PA, the first racing win by a car with a supercharged engine

1913 George Wahl of the Wahl Motor Company commits suicide

1916 Mercer records its last racing victory as a Model 22-70 Raceabout wins the Giant's Despair Hillclimb in Wilkes-Barre, PA

1917 The first Fordson tractor is produced

1919 Racer John James "Jack" McGrath is born in Los Angeles, CA

1920 The Marland Oil Company is incorporated in Delaware - the firm would evolve into Conoco Inc.

1922 T. L. Hausmann of Lakewood, OH is appointed receiver of the Templar Motors Corporation

1926 Racer Hollingsworth "Worth" McMillion is born in Virginia

1929 A United States design patent is issued to racer Wade Morton for his "A Combination Automobile Body, Hood and Radiator", the basic design of the Auburn Cabin Speedster prototype

1929 The Packard "Adonis" mascot, otherwise known as "Daphne at the well" or "sliding boy", is patented by designer Edward McCarten, who based his work on a 1927 design by French sculptor Emil Antoine Bourdelle

1929 Jack W. Corn of the Quaker State Corporation is born in Cobb County, GA

1931 The last Oakland, a Series 301 sedan, is produced

1931 Automobile headlight designer Karl Dumas Chambers dies in Oteen, NC at age 38

1936 The first 1937 Pontiac Deluxe Eight is produced

A 1937 Pontiac negotiates a passage through the Drive-Way Stump near Pepperwood, CA.

1938 Edsel B. Ford makes a public announcement that full production of the new Mercury marque has begun at five United States plants

1940 The 1941 DeSotos are introduced, featuring an optional "Simplimatic" semi-automatic transmission

1944 Peter E. Martin of the Ford Motor Company dies in Detroit, MI at age 62

1946 Racer Wayne Anderson is born in Yaphank, NY

1949 British occupation authorities transfer the ownership and management of Volkswagenwerk GmbH to the West German government

1953 The 1954 Dodges are introduced

1954 George W. Mason, Chairman, President, and General Manager of American Motors and a former employee of Studebaker and the Chrysler Corporation, dies in Detroit, MI at age 63

1954 Racer Fulvio Maria Ballabio is born in Milan, Italy

1954 Racer Huub Rothengatter is born in Bussum, the Netherlands

1955 Racer William C. "Wild Bill" Elliott is born in Cumming, GA

1955 Racer Alain Ferte is born in Falaise, France

1955 Automobile designer Joseph Vollmer dies in Brunswick, Germany at age 84

1955 Alfred Moorhouse, Vice President of Technical Assistants Inc. whose previous automotive career included stints with Hudson, Cadillac, and Chalmers, dies at age 71

1956 The 1957 Hillman Husky is introduced to the United States market

1958 The 1959 German Ford Taunus is introduced to the United States market

1958 The 1959 Rambler and Rambler American are introduced

1958 William V. C. Ruxton, namesake of the 1929 front-wheel-drive Ruxton, dies in New York City at age 67

1958 Ray Lemke opens the first independent Datsun dealership in the United States in San Diego, CA

1959 The 1960 Fords, including the new compact Falcon, are introduced

1960 The 1961 Chevrolets are introduced

1961 John D. Hertz, founder of the Hertz Rent-A-Car System, Inc. in 1924 and the Yellow Cab Company, dies in Los Angeles, CA at age 82

1965 The Budd Automotive Company of Canada is established in Kitchener, ON

1968 Henry Jervis Mulliner, founder and namesake of the British coachbuilding firm and the last surviving charter member of the Royal Automobile Club, dies in Bexhill-on-Sea, East Sussex, England at age 97

CHISWICK   H.J. Mulliner & Co., Ltd.   LONDON

1973 Robert Pass of Passport Transportation Ltd., a St. Louis, MO truking firm specializing in shipping collectible automobiles, purchases a 1940 Mercedes-Benz 770K reputedly once owned by Adolf Hitler for $176,000 at an auction in Lancaster, PA - the price set a new record for collector car auctions, and marked the second time in eight months that this car had established the record

1974 Paul G. Hoffman, Chairman of the Studebaker Corporation 1953-1954 and the Studebaker-Packard Corporation 1954-1956, dies in New York City at age 83

1996 The Ford Motor Company's 250,000,000th vehicle is produced

OCTOBER 9

1623 Automobile pioneer Ferdinand Verbiest is born in Pittem, Belgium

1833 Internal combustion engine pioneer Eugen Langen is born in Cologne, Germany

1896 Ralph Thomas, a Michigan tourism official whose early career included stints with Maxwell, Chalmers, Lincoln, and Winton, is born in Roanoke, VA

1897 Henry Sturmey, Editor of *The Autocar*, begins the first Great Britain end-to-end automobile trip - his Coventry Daimler would cover the 929 miles from John O'Groats to Land's End in ten days

1899 The world's first full-sized gasoline-powered buses, two 12-hp German- built Daimlers, go into service in London, England

1903 Mary Doud Packard, mother of William D. Packard and James W. Packard, dies

1909 The Alabama Legislature approves an act requiring automobile owners to register with their county probate judge

1911 The last of four Founders Day Races staged by the Quaker City Motor Club at Fairmount Park in Philadelphia, PA is won by Erwin Bergdoll in a Benz

1915 The Sheepshead Bay Speedway opens in Brooklyn, NY with the running of the 350-mile Vincent Astor Cup won by Gil Anderson in a Stutz at an average speed of 102.60 mph, a record for such a distance

1919 Hare's Motors, Inc. is formed to coordinate the management of Mercer, Locomobile and Simplex

1920 Jack Webb Minor of the Chrysler Corporation is born in Kansas City, MO

1922 Emile Coquille, the French director of Rudge-Whitworth Wheels, and Georges Durand, Secretary-General of L'Automobile-Club de l'Ouest, initiate plans to stage a 24-hour race at Le Mans, France

1928 Racer Pat O'Connor is born in North Vernon, IN

1930 The Reo Royale is introduced

1931 The last Pontiac Fine Six is produced

1937 The 1938 Oldsmobiles are introduced

1937 Racer David Prophet is born in Hong Kong of British ancestry

1938 The 1939 Buicks are introduced

1943 Leo Drobig, an automotive design engineer in his native England as well as in Germany and the United States, dies

1953 The Chrysler Corporation sells its New York City real estate including the art-deco Chrysler Building

1958 The 1959 Pontiacs are introduced featuring "Wide-Track" stance

1959 The 1960 Dodge four-wheel-drive trucks are introduced

1959 Earl S. Twining, retired head of the Racing Division of the Champion Spark Plug Company, dies at age 67

1961 Racer Julian Bailey is born in Cobham, Kent, England

1962 The 1,000,000th Volkswagen Transporter is produced

1962 Racer Paul Radisich is born in Auckland, New Zealand

1963 Alfred J. Fisher of the Fisher Body Company dies in Detroit, MI at age 70

1967 Great Britain's "breathalyser law" goes into effect

1968 The Ford Motor Company purchases Willys-Overland do Brasil

1971 The Milestone Car Society is formed in Hershey, PA by 16 charter members

1988 Felix Wankel, inventor of the rotary engine, dies in Lindau, Germany at age 86

1989 Frederic A. Bush of the Sinclair Petroleum Company dies at age 85

1992 A 1980 Chevrolet Malibu is struck by a football-sized meteorite, the only such incident ever recorded

OCTOBER 10

1804 Steam vehicle pioneer Nicolas Cugnot dies in Paris, France at age 79

1833 John Mohler Studebaker is born in Gettysburg, PA

1877 William Richard Morris (later Baron Nuffield of Nuffield), founder of W. R. M. Motors, Ltd., manufacturers of the Morris in Cowley, Oxfordshire, England, is born in Worcestershire, England

The "bullnose" Morris Cowley, introduced in 1915, was one of Great Britain's most popular cars. The driver of this 1923 tourer has paused curbside in Great Yarmouth on the east cost of England.

1884 Gustav Waldemar Carlson, developer of the two-speed axle, is born in Holland, Sweden

1900 The first Packard magazine advertisement appears

1901 Henry Ford wins his first race driving "999", defeating Alexander Winton in a 10-mile match race at the Grosse Pointe (MI) Race Track

1903 The Packard Motor Car Company officially closes its Warren, OH plant as the last shipment of supplies and equipment leaves for Detroit, MI

1904 The Ford Motor Company approves development of the Model E, a commercial "Delivery Car" version of the Model C passenger car

1904 The Ford Motor Company of Canada Ltd. begins production in the former factory of the Walkerville Wagon Company

1904 E. C. di Bricherasio of Fiat dies in Aglie, Italy at age 35

1907 The Pierce Great Arrow wins the Chicago Motor Club's 200-Mile Economy Run to win the Knight Trophy

1908 The first races are staged at the Long Island (NY) Motor Parkway - winner of the 10-lap Sweepstakes is Herbert Lytle in an Isotta-Fraschini

1908 The first Founders' Day Cup Race held in Fairmount Park, Philadelphia, PA is won by George Robertson in a Locomobile

1914 William Sherman Blakeslee Jr. of the Chrysler Corporation is born in Grand Rapids, MI

1922 The Ford Model T Fordor Sedan is announced to dealers

1930 Racer Eugenio Castelotti is born in Milan, Italy

1932 John Thomas Hackett of the Cummins Engine Company is born in Fort Wayne, IN

1932 The last M.G. 18/80 Mk II is completed

1934 The 1,000,000th 1934 General Motors vehicle is produced

1936 Frank R. Hickman of Locomobile dies in Fairfield, CT at age 75

1939 W. J. Sommers of Mack and White dies in Manhasset, NY at age 51

1944 The first post-liberation Renault is produced

1947 Racer Gerardo Martinez is born in Mexico

1948 Racer Bill Scott is born in the United States

1948 Racer Ted Horn is killed at age 38 during a race in DuQuoin, IL

1952 Racer Siegfried Stohr is born in Rimini, Italy of German-Italian ancestry

1954 H. E. Hund, General Manager of the Briggs Manufacturing Company 1929-1934 and President of Reo Motors, Inc. 1940-1949, dies at age 66

1958 The 1959 Dodges are introduced

A 1959 Dodge Custom Royal Lancer 2-door hardtop is nearest the camera in this view of Memorial Hospital in Karlstad, MN. Dodge was one of several marques that reached its zenith of garish styling in 1959.

1983 The Ford Motor Company acquires a 30% equity in Otosan Otomobil Sanayi As PK, the first automobile manufacturer in Turkey

1988 The first 1989 Ford Thunderbird and Mercury Cougar are produced at the Ford Motor Company's Lorain, OH factory

1995 Toyota Motor Manufacturing Canada Inc. opens their new engine plant in Cambridge, ON

OCTOBER 11

1875 Hobart Cutler Dickinson of the Society of Automotive Engineers is born in Bangor, ME

1885 Herman Liveright Moekle of the Ford Motor Company is born in Pittsburgh, PA

1887 Delmar Gerle "Barney" Roos, Locomobile design engineer 1912-1920, Chief Engineer of Pierce-Arrow 1920-1921, Vice President of Locomobile 1921-1925, Chief Engineer of Marmon in 1925, Chief Engineer & Vice President of Studebaker, plus advisory positions with other automobile companies in the United States and England, is born in New York City

1889 Alexander Fraser of the Shell Union Oil Corporation is born in Glasgow, Scotland

1891 Arthur G. Phelps of General Motors is born in Chicago, IL

1895 The Ames automobile, designed by D. J. Ames, President of the Owatonna Manufacturing Company, in collaboration with partner Frank LaBare, is test driven in Owatonna, MN

1901 A White steamer driven by Rollin H. White wins the 5-mile and 10-mile races in Detroit, MI, often cited as the first "serious" track races in the United States

1904 A. Atwater Kent is issued the first of several United States patents that he would receive for automotive ignition equipment

1909 Members of various European automobile clubs sign an agreement creating the International Travelling Pass system of identifying cars with oval tags, generally black on white, noting the country of registration

1911 Racer Nello Pagani is born in Milan, Italy

1917 The assets of the defunct Emerson Motors Company are transferred to the newly formed Campbell Motor Car Company

1920 Automobile historian Sidney Fine is born in Cleveland, OH

1924 Hall Marmon, son of Walter C. Marmon and heir apparent of the Nordyke & Marmon Company, is killed at age 25 in an automobile accident near Avon, IN - the younger Marmon had been in charge of experimental work for the company and was returning from an unsuccessful attempt to test a new braking system at the Pikes Peak (CO) Auto Highway

1926 Wunibald Kamm is issued a German patent for his automobile body design, the only patent ever held personally by the aerodynamics pioneer

1926 Richard Hale Leet of the Amoco Corporation is born in Maryville, MO

1928 Racer Alfonso de Portago is born in London, England as the Spanish nobleman Don Alfonso Cabeza de Vaca y Leighton, Carvajal y Are, 13th Conde de la Mejorada, 17th Marquis de Portago

1930 Sir Michael Owen Edwardes, Chairman of Jaguar and BL Cars Ltd., is born in South Africa

1932 The Mack trucks "Bulldog" mascot used continuously since 1932 is patented by designer A. F. Masury

1935 The 1936 Cadillac Series 90 (V-16) is introduced

1948 The Kaiser-Frazer Corporation produces its 300,000th car

1950 George S. Case Sr., Chairman of the Lamson & Sessions Company since 1938 and an official in the automotive parts industry since 1904, dies

1951 George M. Bicknell, Chief Engineer of the Carter Carburetor Corporation 1917-1951 who previously had worked for Chalmers, Selden, Winton, and American Underslung, dies in Daytona Beach, FL at age 64

1954 The first 1955 Ford is produced

1954 The Jeep CJ-3B and trucks are introduced

1954 The first Jeep CJ-5 is produced

1957 Donald E. Montgomery of the United Auto Workers dies in Washington, DC at age 60

1959 J. J. Powelson, Chief Automotive Engineer for the Esso Standard Oil Company, dies at age 63

1964 Racers Franco Patria and Peter Lindner plus three track officials are killed during a race in Montlhery, France

1965 Ira A. Weaver, a developer of automobile maintenance equipment, dies in Springfield, IL at age 94

1972 C. W. Van Ranst dies at age 79

1974 AB Volvo purchases a controlling interest of Van Doorne's Personenautofabriek Daf B.V., the Dutch manufacturers of the compact Daf featuring the unique "Variomatic" transmission

1979 The 1980 Pontiacs are introduced

1982 Coachbuilder and stylist Thomas L. Hibbard dies in Rockport, ME at age 84

1990 General Motors unveils their new marque, the Saturn

1995 Jaguar enthusiast Peter Francis dies

OCTOBER 12

1860 Elmer Ambrose Sperry, builder of the Sperry Electric 1899-1901 and a pioneer developer of disc brakes, is born in Cortland, NY

1868 August Horch, founder of the Horch and Audi marques, is born in Winningen on the Mosel, Germany

1880 Lammot DuPont of General Motors is born in Wilmington, DE

Illustrated below is a Fleetwood conception of the Town Brougham, mounted on the Cadillac V-16 chassis. V-16 prices range from $5,350 to $15,000

Of all the reasons why the Cadillac V-16 has met with such favor, none is more important than the fact that it permits complete expression of the purchaser's preference as to body style and appointments. Fleetwood has executed more than thirty V-16 body types, each one highly distinctive in its basic design, and available in a variety of finishes and interior fabrics. In addition, special custom creations may be had in any mode the purchaser specifies. Any Cadillac-La Salle dealer will gladly provide complete information.

CADILLAC V 8 12 16

Chairman of General Motors 1929-1937, Lammot DuPont succeeded his brother in this position. The Cadillac V-16, perhaps the most outstanding car ever produced by General Motors, was introduced during his term.

1894 Cecil Benton Thomas of the Chrysler Corporation is born in Fredericktown, OH

1903 The National Automobile & Motor Company of Oshkosh, WI is liquidated

1906 Racer Piero Taruffi is born in Albano Laziale, Rome, Italy

1911 Sir William J. Crossley, cofounder of Crossley Brothers, Ltd. (later Crossley Motors, Ltd.), dies at age 67

1912 Riding mechanic Tony Scudelari dies from injuries suffered twelve days earlier when the Fiat driven by David Bruce-Brown crashed during practice for the Grand Prize race in Milwaukee, WI

1922 John B. Foote, founder and President of the Foote Brothers Gear & Machine Company of Chicago, IL, dies at age 57

1928 Racer Fred Comer dies

1929 Dr. Hans Liebold of Daimler-Benz AG is born in Germany

1931 Stephen Salsbury, a biographer of Pierre S. DuPont, is born in Oakland, CA

1932 Racer Ned Miller Jarrett is born on a farm near Newton, NC

1935 The last regular production Rolls-Royce Phantom II is completed

1936 The first Vanderbilt Trophy race is staged at the Roosevelt Raceway in Westbury, NY and won by Tazio Nuvolari in an Alfa Romeo - George Vanderbilt, a cousin of William K. Vanderbilt Jr., is the patron of the reborn classic race, and a ceremonial first lap is driven by track manager Colonel George Robertson in the Locomobile "Old 16", they being the winning driver and car of the 1908 Vanderbilt Cup

1937 Racer Robert Paul Hawkins is born in Melbourne, Victoria, Australia

1937 Samuel F. Arbuckle, inventor of double-filament headlight and tail light bulbs, dies in New York City at age 52

1940 Cowboy actor Tom Mix, a fancier of exotic automobiles, is killed when his 1937 Cord 812 convertible crashes near Florence, AZ

1940 The Packard Nineteenth Series is introduced

1941 Racer Morgan Shepherd is born in Ferguson, NC

1943 Racer Bertil Roos is born in Goteborg, Sweden

1946 Ettore Bugatti marries Genevieve Delcuze as his second wife after fathering two children by her

1947 Production of the "step-down" 1948 Hudson begins

1950 The 500,000th car is produced by the Kaiser-Frazer Corporation, a 1951 Kaiser Deluxe sedan

1950 The Society of Motion Picture Art Directors names the 24th Series Packard (1951 model year) as "the most beautiful car of the year"

1952 William G. Ireland of the Bundy Tubing Company dies at age 55

1954 The 1955 Chevrolets are introduced

1954 George W. Romney is elected Chairman and President of American Motors

1956 The first MGA coupe prototype is completed

1956 Racer Mark Dismore is born in Greenfield, IN

1958 Paul S. Dean of The Texas Company dies at age 65

1960 Toyo Kogyo Company, Ltd. President Tsuneji Matsuda reaches an agreement with NSU of Germany to produce Wankel rotary-engined automobiles

1961 The 1962 Ford Thunderbirds are introduced

1968 Racer Bill Auberlen is born in Redondo Beach, CA

1981 Porsche president Peter Schutz and Ron Dennis of McLaren sign a contract to jointly develop a V-6 Grand Prix engine

1983 Paul H. Stern of Manheim, PA, a noted collector of Chrysler Corporation products, dies at age 81

1985 Racer Duke Dinsmore dies in Daytona Beach, FL at age 72

1986 Benetton records its first Formula 1 victory with Gerhard Berger winning the Mexican Grand Prix

1995 Toyota Zimbabwe (Pvt.) Ltd. opens their new service center in Msasa

1996 Race car builder Edward "Eddie" Kuzma dies in Tigard, OR at age 85

OCTOBER 13

1850 John Gaine Rumney, a designer and manufacturer of automobile springs, is born in Detroit, MI

1884 James E. Hale of the Firestone Tire & Rubber Company is born in Manchester, NH

1899 Piero Dusio of Cisitalia is born in Scurzolengo d'Asti, Italy

1902 The Ohio Automobile Company reorganizes as the Packard Motor Car Company, with James W. Packard remaining as President and Henry B. Joy joining the firm as a major investor

1915 James Couzens resigns as Vice President and Treasurer of the Ford Motor Company, but retains his 11% ownership and seat on the Board of Directors

1916 The General Motors Corporation is incorporated in Delaware - in 1917 it would acquire the stock of the original General Motors Company founded in 1908

1918 Barney Oldfield competes in his last official automobile race

1921 The Alfa Romeo Tipo RL is introduced at the Milan Auto Show

1923 Alvis makes its racing debut at Brooklands, with Major Maurice Harvey winning the 200-mile race at a record 93.29 mph

1928 Donald Owen Dulude, President of the Kuhlman Corporation, a Troy, MI automobile parts manufacturer, is born in Bay City, MI

1933 Ralph Dale Gray, the biographer of Elwood Haynes, is born in Otwell, IN

1934 Whitney Straight, driving a Duesenberg, sets the alltime Brooklands record for Class C (under 5000 cc) of 138.15 mph

1940 The 1941 Buicks are introduced, featuring a twin-carburetion "Fireball" engine and a two-way hood

1948 Charles F. Meyer, President of the Standard Oil Company of New York 1928- 1931, dies in Rancho Santa Fe, CA at age 84

1949 The first Borgward Hansa 1500 is produced

1949 Racer Patrick Neve is born in Brussels, Belgium

1953 The Virginia Museum of Fine Arts introduces the Artmobile, the world's first mobile art gallery

1954 The first Hudson Rambler is produced at the Kenosha, WI factory

1956 Jaguar Cars Ltd. announces its withdrawal from racing

1958 Chassis engineer Alfred L. Stem of the Ford Motor Company dies at age 63

1959 Woldemar G. Schultz, an automotive engineer with the Ford Motor Company, dies at age 64

1961 Edward R. Dye, the inventor of the "cloverleaf" highway interchange and an advocate of seat belts, dies in Orchard Park, NY at age 59

1962 The Korea Oil Corporation is incorporated in Seoul, South Korea

1964 Craig Breedlove, driving the Spirit of America at the Bonneville Salt Flats, UT, raises the land speed record to 468.72 mph

1964 Racer Nestor Gabriel Furlan is born in Argentina

1967 Fukio Nakagawa, President of the Toyota Motor Company, Ltd., dies

1968 The first race staged at the Michigan Speedway in Irish Hills is won by Ronnie Bucknum in the Weinberger Homes Special

1981 Racer Philippe Etancelin dies in Neuilly-sur-Seine, France at age 84

1982 The British Post Office issues four commemorative stamps featuring a vintage and current Austin, Ford, Jaguar, or Rolls-Royce

1989 Racer Fred Agabashian dies in Alamo, CA at age 76

OCTOBER 14

1857 Elwood Haynes is born in Portland, IN

1893 Race car designer Charles Cooper is born in Paris, France

1897 Emil Jellinek of Nice, France takes delivery of a belt-drive Daimler, leading to his association with the marque and its name change to Mercedes

1905 The second Vanderbilt Cup Race is held on Long Island, NY and won by Victor Hemery driving an 80-hp Darracq

1909 Racer and exotic car dealer George Curtis Rand is born in Short Hills, NJ

1909 Racer Bernd Rosemeyer is born in Lingen, Lower Saxony, Germany

1911 The first road race staged in Santa Monica, CA, the 202-mile Free for All, is won by Harvey Herrick in a National

1911 The eighth Glidden Tour begins in New York City, with a planned route through Atlanta, GA to Jacksonville, FL

1914 Lucius B. Packard of Salem, MA, builder of the 1895-1898 Packard, dies - of no known relationship to James W. and William D. Packard, the total output of this firm appears to have been an 1895 gasoline-powered car and two later electrics

1925 Harold Arthur "Red" Poling of the Ford Motor Company is born in Troy, MI

1925 Automotive parts designer William M. Meyers, Sales Engineer of the Johnson Company, dies in Detroit, MI at age 44

1927 John Richard Edman of General Motors is born in Brighton, MI

1927 Automotive steel manufacturer Frank L. Brown dies in Philadelphia, PA at age 50

1927 Prince William of Sweden is presented with a new Nash Advanced Six by Scandinavian-ancestry employees of the Nash Motors Company

1933 Johnny Gerber competes in and wins his last race in Bel Air, MD

1937 The 31st International Motor Exhibition opens in London, the first to be held at Earls Court

1938 The first contracts are awarded for construction of the Pennsylvania Turnpike

1939 Ralph Lauren, fashion designer and noted automobile collector, is born in the Bronx, NY

1940 Henry H. Timken, Chairman of the Board of the Timken Roller Bearing Company since 1928, dies at age 72

1947 Racer Rikki von Opel is born in New York City

1950 John J. Raskob of General Motors dies in Centreville, MD at age 71

1951 Everett Welles Frazar, an import-export executive who represented Henry Ford in Asia, dies at age 84

1953 Herbert Demel of Audi and Volkswagen is born in Vienna, Austria

1959 The 1960 Rambler and Rambler American are introduced

1962 Racer Pat Pigott dies from race-incurred injuries

1965 The second-generation 1966 Buick Riviera is introduced

1965 The 1966 Cadillacs are introduced

1965 The 1966 Oldsmobiles are introduced, including the new front-wheel-drive Toronado

1968 Harvey C. Fruehauf of the Fruehauf Trailer Company dies at age 74

1968 The United States Secret Service accepts delivery of a modified 1969 Lincoln Continental for presidential service - its hypothetical $500,000 retail price resulted in it often being cited as the world's most expensive car

1969 The government of Japan allows foreign investment of up to 50% in Japanese automobile companies

1973 Jackie Stewart announces his retirement from racing

1980 Henry Ford II marries Kathy DuRoss in Carson City, NV

1983 Automotive historian Michael Sedgwick dies in Midhurst, West Sussex, England at age 57

OCTOBER 15

1840 E. A. Colburn, namesake of the 1906-1911 Colburn automobile made in Denver, CO, is born in New York state

1884 Roy F. McConnell of the Standard Oil Company is born in Detroit, MI

1895 The first British automobile show is staged by Sir David Salomans on the grounds of his home near Tunbridge Wells and features five exhibitors

1899 Racer Adolf Brudes von Breslau is born in Germany

1901 Hermann J. Abs, Chairman of the Daimler-Benz AG Supervisory Board 1955-1970, is born in Germany

1904 The first Reo is completed and taken for its initial test drive by Ransom E. Olds

1904 The Smith Automobile Company in incorporated in Kansas by Clement Smith, L. Anton Smith, Terry Stafford, Leni Smith, Adele A. Smith and Laura A. Strait

1908 The Detroit (MI) Fire Department receives its first motorized fire truck

1919 Racer Chuck Stevenson is born in Sidney, MT

1920 Motor sports television announcer Chris Economaki is born in Brooklyn, NY

1921 Racer Al Pease is born in Canada

1924 Lido Anthony "Lee" Iacocca of the Ford Motor Company and the Chrysler Corporation is born in Allentown, PA

1926 The Willys-Overland Company acquires rights to the independent front suspension system developed by Sizaire Freres of France

1927 Thomas Harold Corson of Coachmen Industries, Inc., a manufacturer of recreational vehicles, is born in Elkhart, IN

1929 The Greenfield, MI post office opens at the Henry Ford Museum

1930 Alfred R. Glancy resigns as General Manager of Oakland-Pontiac, and is replaced by Irving J. Reuter who transfers from the same position with Chevrolet

1933 James Charles Cotting, President and Chief Executive Office of the Navistar International Corporation 1987-1995, is born in Winchester, MA

1935 The 1936 Nash Series 3640A and second-series LaFayettes are introduced

1936 The last Rolls-Royce Phantom II is completed per special order of Dowager Lady Fox, more than a year after production had officially ceased

1936 The 30th International Motor Exhibition opens in London, England, the last to be held at Olympia

1937 The 1938 Nashes are introduced

The 1938 Nash coupe in the foreground reflects the styling influences of the Lincoln-Zephyr, and appropriately is parked at the Zephyr Cove Resort on the shore of Lake Tahoe in Nevada.

1938 The 1939 Nashes are introduced, featuring new styling by George W. Walker

1938 The Pak-Age-Car delivery van originally conceived by Stutz is introduced by the Aviation & Transportation Corporation, a successor of the Cord Corporation, bearing the Diamond T logo

1944 Henry May, a cofounder of the Pierce-Arrow Motor Car Company, dies in Buffalo, NY at age 83

1945 The Automotive Council for War Production is deactivated

1945 Production of the post-World War II 1946 Oldsmobiles begins

1951 The 1952 Dodge Power Wagons are introduced

1953 The 1954 Plymouths are introduced

1955 The 1956 British Fords are introduced to the United States market

1957 The 1958 Studebakers are introduced along with the Studebaker-based 1958 Packard Hawk

1957 Stanley Whitworth, English-born Vice President of the Studebaker Corporation 1933-1947 who designed the Stutz Bearcat in 1910, dies at age 76

Among the various Studebakers manufactured during the Stanley Whitworth era was this circa 1947 truck operated by the Lake to Lake Dairy Cooperative in Kiel, WI.

1959 The 1960 Edsels are introduced

1960 The 1961 Hillmans are introduced to the United States market

1961 The Chaparral makes its racing debut with designer Jim Hall finishing third in the *Los Angeles Times* Grand Prix in Riverside, CA

1964 The 1965 Jaguars are introduced to the United States market

1964 Fiberglass-bodied automobile pioneer R. Games Slayter dies at age 67

1964 Craig Breedlove, driving the Spirit of America, raises his own 2-day-old land speed record to 526.28 mph at the Bonneville Salt Flats, UT, although a crash after clearing the timing area demolishes the car

1966 The United States Department of Transportation is established as a cabinet level agency with Alan S. Boyd appointed as its first Secretary of Transportation by President Lyndon B. Johnson

1976 The United States Congress passes legislature establishing the Corporate Average Fuel Economy (CAFE) requiring all new automobiles manufactured to have an average of 18 mpg

1978 Lee Iacocca is fired as President of Ford Motor Company

1979 William Clay Ford Jr. joins the Ford Motor Company as a product planning analyst

1981 Racer Philip Fotheringham-Parker dies at age 74

1982 Jaguar Car Holdings Ltd. is organized

OCTOBER 16

1885 Rembrandt Bugatti is born in Milan, Italy - the younger brother of Ettore Bugatti and an artist by trade, he is best remembered in automotive circles as the creator of the standing elephant mascot designed in 1916 and later used on the Bugatti Type 41 Royale

1896 Donald Ewan Montgomery of the United Auto Workers is born in Asbury Park, NJ

1899 A Marsh steam car built by brothers Alonzo R. and William Townsend Marsh and driven by the latter covers a flying mile in 1 minute, 34 4/5 seconds (37.97 mph) in Whitman, MA to set what they believed to be a land speed record

1918 Racer A. P. R. "Tony" Rolt is born in Bordon, Hampshire, England

1930 The Bentley 8 Litre is introduced at the Olympia Motor Show in London

1934 Racer Peter Ashdown is born in Danbury, Essex, England

1934 Henry Brewer Schacht of the Cummins Engine Company is born in Erie, PA

1937 Racer Sir John Whitmore is born in Great Britain

1944 The Hewson Pacific Corporation is organized in Los Angeles, CA by W. Sherman Hewson, Burton Chalmers, and John V. Shanley to manufacture the 3-wheeled Rocket - only a single protype would be produced

1949 Pioneer tire designer and manufacturer Charles B. Whittelsey dies in Hartford, CT at age 80

1950 The 1951 Hudsons are introduced including the new Hornet series that would dominate NASCAR events for several years

A 1951 Hudson transports North Dakota Governor and Mrs. Norman Brunsdale during a parade in Bismarck. Hudson convertibles of this era were, and still are, great parade vehicles.

1954 The Lincoln Continental Owners Club holds its first national meeting with special guest William Clay Ford announcing that the Continental Mark II would appear within one year

1955 Elbert L. Potter Jr., an experimental engineer with Hupmobile 1925-1929 and later an official with the Houdaille-Hershey Corporation, dies

1957 The 1958 Plymouths are introduced

1957 Peter J. Shuttleworth, a mechanical engineer at the General Motors Proving Grounds, dies at age 23

1958 The Chevrolet El Camino is introduced as the answer to the Ford Ranchero

1963 Howard A. Lewis, a Vice President of the Nash-Kelvinator Corporation and American Motors, dies at age 72

1978 Philip Caldwell is named President and Chief Executive Office of the Ford Motor Company

OCTOBER 17

1846 Joseph Lowthian Hudson is born in Newcastle-upon-Tyne, England

1863 Charles Herman Metz is born in Utica, NY

1885 Automotive parts manufacturer William Woodward Sloane is born in Canajoharie, NY

1890 The Union Oil Company of California is incorporated

1893 Evangeline Cote Dahlinger of the Ford Motor Company is born in Detroit, MI

1895 James Pullinger and John Henry Knight of Farnham, Surrey, England are arrested for operating a motor vehicle in that city - the two men were cited for disturbing the peace in the first motoring arrest made in Great Britain

1901 Roy Samuel Evans of the American Austin Car Company is born in Bartow, GA

1902 The first Cadillac is completed and taken for a test drive by Alanson P. Brush with Wilfred Leland as his passenger

1904 Malcolm Williams Welty of the Ford Motor Company is born in Wamego, KS

1910 Powel Crosley Jr. marries Gwendolyn Bakewell Aiken

1917 Clarence H. Booth, President of the Scripps-Booth Company, resigns

1918 E. S. Hare is named Vice President of the Packard Motor Car Company

1919 The prototype supercharged Mercedes is taken for its first test drive by Karl Schopper, W. Schwerdtfeger, and Jakob Kraus on the road between Degerloch and Echterdingen, south of Stuttgart, Germany

1919 The Fisher Body Company of Ohio is incorporated for the purpose of expanding corporate operations into Cleveland, OH

1922 The 1923 Nashes are introduced

1924 H. H. Kohlsaat, Publisher of the *Chicago Times-Herald* 1894-1901 and the sponsor in 1895 of the first automobile race staged in the United States, dies at age 71

1925 William Livingstone Jr., a Detroit, MI banker involved in the formation of the Ford Motor Company, dies at age 81

1926 Buick President Harry H. Bassett dies in Neuilly, France at age 51, having contracted pneumonia while attending the Paris Salon

1926 Racer Roberto Lippi is born in Rome, Italy

1926 George Henry Turnbull, a longtime British automobile executive with Standard, Triumph, British Leyland Ltd., and "father" of the Korean-built Hyundai, is born

1933 Barney Oldfield becomes the first to drive a farm tractor more than a mile-a-minute, reaching 64.2 mph in a special Allis-Chalmers in Dallas, TX - the event was staged to attract financing for a planned land speed record attempt

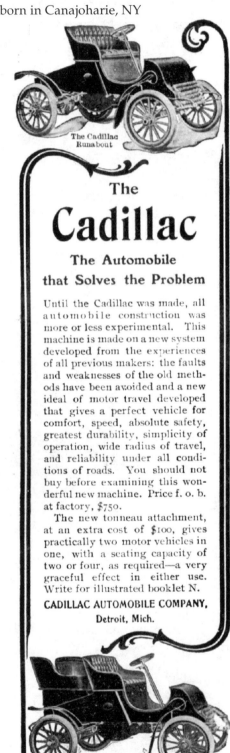

The Cadillac Runabout

The Cadillac

The Automobile that Solves the Problem

Until the Cadillac was made, all automobile construction was more or less experimental. This machine is made on a new system developed from the experiences of all previous makers: the faults and weaknesses of the old methods have been avoided and a new ideal of motor travel developed that gives a perfect vehicle for comfort, speed, absolute safety, greatest durability, simplicity of operation, wide radius of travel, and reliability under all conditions of roads. You should not buy before examining this wonderful new machine. Price f. o. b. at factory, $750.

The new tonneau attachment, at an extra cost of $100, gives practically two motor vehicles in one, with a seating capacity of two or four, as required—a very graceful effect in either use. Write for illustrated booklet N.

CADILLAC AUTOMOBILE COMPANY, Detroit, Mich.

With detachable tonneau

—434—

1935 The Rolls-Royce Phantom III, featuring the marque's first V-12 engine, is officially introduced at the Olympia Motor Show in London, England

1937 H. W. Kent, President of the Kenworth Motor Truck Corporation 1927-1937, dies in Seattle, WA at age 55

Roseburg, OR circa 1950. Why the Kenworth firetruck and White Freightliner COE tractor appear to be getting serviced on a busy downtown street is unknown.

1945 The first post-World War II Cadillac is completed 54 days after last M-24 tank is produced by the company

1946 Racer Enzo Coloni is born in Italy

1951 Frederick O. Bezner, an pioneer executive in both the automotive and aviation industries, dies in Norwalk, CT at age 73

1952 The 1953 Henry J is introduced

1955 The first 1956 Ford Thunderbird is produced

1955 Racer Joel Wolfe Thorne Jr. dies at age 40 in a plane crash near Los Angeles, CA

1956 The first 1957 Pontiac is produced

1956 The MGA coupe is introduced at the London (England) Motor Show at Earls Court

1958 The 1959 Fords are introduced as "The World's Most Beautifully Proportioned Cars"

1962 Leonard Lee, Chairman of Coventry Climax Engines Ltd., announces the company's withdrawal from Grand Prix racing - public support would reverse this decision two months later

1962 The Daimler 2.5-litre V-8 saloon is introduced at the Earls Court Motor Show in London, the first new model of the marque since its acquistion by Jaguar

1966 Racer Tom Kendall is born in La Canada, CA

1969 K. M. Knuppenburg, President of the Michigan Rivet Corporation, dies

1971 The Arthur Fred Austria Simple Garage Collection, a large holding of antique and classic cars assembled by the late Art Austria, is sold at auction by Sotheby, Parke-Bernet in Los Angeles, CA

1981 The first Las Vegas (NV) Grand Prix is staged on a makeshift course in the parking lot of Caesars Palace casino, and is won by Alan Jones in a Williams-Ford

1981 Directors of the Bridgehampton (NY) Road Races Corporation vote to sell their site for real estate development, ending a 32-year tradition of sports car racing at the venue

OCTOBER 18

1730 Antoine de la Mothe, Sieur de Cadillac dies in Castle Sarrazin, France at age 70 - an explorer of North America who established a settlement at the present site of Detroit, MI, he is remembered today as the namesake of the top-of-the-line General Motors marque originally introduced in 1903

1873 Automobile ball bearing designer Frederick E. Muller is born in Aix-la-Chapelle, France (now Aachen, Germany)

1885 J. E. Garlent, an official of Brush, Oakland, Hupmobile, King, and the Harroun, is born in Brantford, ON, Canada

1898 Racer Clemente Biondetti is born in Budduro, Sardinia, Italy

1912 Thomas W. Wilby, assisted by factory driver F. V. Haney, arrives in Victoria, BC in his Reo to complete the first trans-Canada automobile trip

1915 Robert B. Ward, founder in 1905 and President of the Ward Motor Vehicle Company, dies in New Rochelle, NY at age 62 - many of his electric trucks were used in his own huge bakery business

1919 Rolls-Royce of America, Inc. is established in Springfield, MA

1919 Racer Hans Klenk is born in Kunzelsau, Germany

1931 Thomas A. Edison dies in West Orange, NJ at age 84 - the great inventor, a friend of Henry Ford, devoted much effort to improving the electric car but met with limited success

1931 The first automobile race is held at the Oakland (CA) Speedway

1932 The Studebaker Corporation purchases the White Motor Company

1932 Automotive parts manufacturer Harvey Allen Ludwig is born in Chicago, IL

1933 Racer Ludovico Scarfiotti is born in Turin, Italy, the grandson of the first president of Fiat

1934 The 1935 Buicks are introduced

1936 The 1937 Buicks are introduced

1938 Construction begins on the Pennsylvania Turnpike

1943 Arthur C. Brauer, Assistant Chief Draftsman for the Hudson Motor Car Company, dies at age 55

1945 Automotive historian Douglas Charles Nye is born in Guildford, England

1951 The first DeSoto is produced with the Firedome V-8 engine

Third Street, Tracy, MN circa 1962. At far left is a 1952 DeSoto, an aging but still formidable automobile with its Firedome V-8.

1955 Melbourne L. Carpentier, Assistant Chief Chassis Engineer for the Chrysler Corporation, dies

1966 Jean-Pierre Peugeot, President of SA des Automobiles Peugeot 1945-1964, dies in Paris, France at age 79

1975 The first auction sale of cars from the collection of B. J. "Barney" Pollard is held in Detroit, MI

1977 Daimler-Benz AG executive Hans-Martin Schleyer is murdered by members of the so-called Baader-Meinhof gang six weeks after they had kidnapped him

1982 The British government closes the DeLorean factory in Northern Ireland

1984 General Motors acquires the EDS Corporation for $2.5 billion

OCTOBER 19

1860 An internal combustion engine designed by Eugenio Barsanti and Felice Matteucci is installed at the Maria Antonia railway station in Florence, Italy, the first instance where such an engine was put into practical usage

1888 Lawrence Peter Fisher is born in Norwalk, OH

1896 Sherrod E. Skinner, Oldsmobile General Manager 1940-1950, is born in New Britain, CT

1897 Henry Sturmey completes a 929-mile trip from John O'Groats to Land's End in his Coventry Daimler, becoming the first person to cross Great Britain end-to-end by automobile

1897 John Melancthon Hickerson, the biographer of Ernest R. Breech, is born in Hatfield, MO

1914 Otto Zipper, a Los Angeles, CA Ferrari and Porsche dealer and a longtime sponsor of racing cars, is born in Vienna, Austria

1917 Robert M. Rodger of the Chrysler Corporation is born in Hammond, NY

1923 Delage & Cie. is reorganized as a public corporation

1924 Count Louis Zborowski is killed at age 29 when his Mercedes crashes during the Italian Grand Prix in Monza

1927 Frank Raymond Faraone of General Motors is born in San Francisco, CA

1927 Francis Birtles leaves London, England in his 14-hp Bean beginning the first overland trip by car from England to Australia

1931 Joseph Bijur, founder of the Bijur Lubricating Corporation, dies in Long Island City, NY at age 57

1934 Archie M. Andrews is elected Chairman of the Hupp Motor Car Corporation

1935 The Squire makes its second and final racing appearance with Luis Fontes finishing third in the Second Mountain Handicap race at Brooklands, England

1945 Packard introduces its first post-World War II cars, the Clipper Eight Standard and Clipper Eight Deluxe

1948 The 1949 Kaisers are announced to the public

1953 Harold Clutterbuck, Technical Officer to the Society of Motor Manufacturers and Traders and an employee of that organization since 1922, dies in London, England at age 63

1954 The 1955 Pontiacs are introduced

1956 Racer Didier Theys is born in Nivelles, Belgium

1958 Mike Hawthorn driving a Ferrari Dino 246 in his final race finishes second in the Moroccan Grand Prix at the Ain-Diab circuit in Casablanca behind the Vanwall driven by Stirling Moss, but clinches the World Champion Driver title to become the first Briton to win this honor

1961 Gustav W. Carlson, developer of the two-speed axle, dies in Cleveland, OH at age 77

1962 The 6,000,000th Volkswagen is produced

1963 Automotive historian William A. Simonds dies in Sun City, AZ at age 76

1965 Racer John Jones is born in Thunder Bay, Ontario, Canada

1971 Tire manufacturer Alberto Pirelli dies in Casciano, Italy at age 89

1976 Eleanor Clay (Mrs. Edsel B.) Ford dies at age 80 at the Henry Ford Hospital in Detroit, MI

1976 Aston Martin Lagonda introduces their new 4-door saloon at the London (England) Motor Show at Earls Court

1981 SA des Automobiles Peugeot President Jean Boillot announces the appointment of Jean Todt as Competition Director

1982 One day after his Northern Ireland factory was closed, John Z. DeLorean is arrested in Los Angeles, CA and charged with racketeering and drug trafficking

1986 General Motors cancels its plastic car project

1987 Racer Hermann Lang dies in Bad Canstatt, West Germany at age 78

1990 Zenon C. R. Hansen of Mack dies at age 81

1990 Fred L. Hartley, longtime President and Chairman of the Union Oil Company of California, dies at age 73

1996 Richard Louis "Dick" Larson, an official of the Lincoln Continental Owners Club, dies at age 61

OCTOBER 20

1867 George William Davis, founder of the George W. Davis Motor Car Company in 1908, is born in Winchester, IN

1888 Edward T. Jones, an experimental engineer with the H. H. Franklin Manufacturing Company who later was a successful aeronautical engineer, is born in Saratoga Springs, NY

1896 Reginald Claud Rootes is born

1898 The world's first one-marque race is staged as Pierre Levegh wins the St. Germain-Vernon-St. Germain (France) road race in his Mors

1908 William M. Eaton succeeds George E. Daniels as President of General Motors

1912 Walter John Simons of the Chrysler Corporation is born in New York City

1917 Conover T. Silver completes plans for the Silver Apperson four-passenger speedster, a stillborn car that would later materialize as the Kissel Gold Bug Speedster

1918 Forrest Arthur Hainline Jr. of American Motors is born in Rock Island, IL

1921 Racer Manuel Ayulo is born in Los Angeles, CA

1926 Francis W. Davis publicly demonstrates power steering in Detroit, MI

1926 Edward John Barrington Douglas-Scott-Montagu, 3rd Baron Montagu of Beaulieu, a British automobile historian and museum curator, is born

1927 Henry Ford stamps "A 1" into the first Ford Model A engine

1929 Wolfgang Roller of Daimler-Benz AG is born in Uelsen, Lower Saxony, Germany

1932 Giovanni Pirelli, founder in 1872 of the first rubber factory in Italy, dies in Milan, Italy at age 83

1938 Chris Staniland driving a Multi-Union sets the alltime Brooklands (England) record for Class D (under 3000 cc) of 141.45 mph

1943 Enrique A. Touceda, a Cuban-born automotive malleable iron authority and professor of metallurgy, dies at age 81

1943 Racer Carlos Ruesch is born in Argentina

1951 The first Charles D. Miller Memorial Handicap Trophy Race is staged at the Convair Airport in Allentown, PA with the main event won by Gus Ehrman in a M.G. TD

1952 The 1953 Jeep pickup trucks are introduced

1952 The 1953 Willys four-wheel-drive wagons are introduced

1954 The first General Motors fully-automated assembly line begins producing Pontiac's new Strato Streak V-8 engine

1957 Frank A. Best, retired President of Standard Products of Canada, dies at age 71

1963 The first Chaparral appears in its last race, an event in Laguna Seca, CA in which driver Skip Hudson fails to finish

1965 The last Volvo PV544 is produced - longtime test driver Nils Wickstrom drives the car off the Lundby, Sweden assembly line in the presence of surviving AB Volvo cofounder Gustaf Larson

1978 Gerald C. Meyers is elected Chairman of American Motors

1978 Racer Gunnar Nilsson dies from cancer in London, England at age 29

1980 Advertising executive Joseph Fewsmith Jr. presents the promotional archives of the Jordan Motor Car Company to the Western Reserve Historical Society

1995 James K. Gaylord, who with his brother Edward conceived the 1955 Gaylord luxury sports car, dies in Phoenix, AZ at age 69

OCTOBER 21

1874 Richard Benz, younger son of Carl Benz, is born

1875 George N. Pierce marries Louisa Day

1877 William A. Chryst of Delco is born in Dayton, OH

1877 Russell Huff of Packard and Dodge is born in Leesburg, OH

1887 Elwood Haynes marries Bertha Beatrice Lanterman in Portland, IN

1888 Rodolfo Ogarrio of Texaco, Inc. is born in Ciudad Juarez, Chihuahua, Mexico

1897 The Pittsburgh Motor Vehicle Company is organized by Louis Semple Clarke along with his brothers John S. and James K., his father Charles, and mutual friend William Morgan to build the Pittsburgh - in 1900 the firm would relocate to Ardmore, PA as the Autocar Company

1925 Alfa Romeo ends their factory racing program after dominating the year's grand prix schedule, opting to devote the racing budget to improvement of the production program

1927 Production of the new Ford Model A begins

1927 General Motors stylist Charles Morrell "Chuck" Jordan is born in Whittier, CA

1929 The Edison Institute Museum (renamed the Henry Ford Museum in 1947) in Dearborn, MI is dedicated to coincide with the fiftieth anniversary of the invention of the light bulb by Thomas A. Edison

1932 Racer Cesare Perdisa is born in Bologna, Italy

1933 Automotive journalist Brock Wendel Yates is born in Buffalo, NY

1942 Racer Allan Grice is born in Australia

1948 Alain Madle of Graham and General Motors, a developer of the variable speed transmission, dies at age 57

1953 A Jaguar XK120 driven by Norman Dewis sets a stock car record of 172.412 mph at Jabbeke, Belgium

1954 The Ford Motor Company of Canada, Ltd. moves its headquarters from Windsor, ON to Toronto

1955 The 1956 Chryslers and Imperials are introduced

1955 The 1956 Plymouths are introduced

1955 The 1956 Pontiacs are introduced

1956 Jud Larson makes his USAC debut, winning a 100-mile race in Sacramento, CA driving the John Zink Special

A 1956 Chrysler New Yorker sedan at Dolaskie's Grocery Store in Shingleton, MI.

1956 Paul de Kuzmik, Hungarian-born design engineer with Stutz who later was an airlines executive in Brazil, dies at age 62

1960 Dealer Robert J. Castle of Syracuse, NY drops his plan to import Soviet automobiles

1960 Racer Gary Evans is born in Great Britain

1971 Hendry S. M. Burns of the Shell Oil Company dies at age 71

1973 Racer Nasif Estefano dies at age 40

1977 Roy D. Chapin Jr. resigns from active managment of American Motors while retaining his Chairman of the Board position - Gerald C. Meyers is elected to succeed Chapin as President and Chief Executive Officer

1978 The Duesenberg II, a fiberglass-bodies replica of the original 1930's Duesenberg Model J boattail speedster, is introduced in Elroy, WI by the Elite Heritage Motors Corporation

1980 The last International Scout is produced, bringing the total to 532,674 over the 20-year run

1987 The Ford Motor Company acquires a majority equity in AC Cars, Ltd.

OCTOBER 22

1868 Andrew Lawrence Riker is born in New York City

1879 John Lee Pratt of General Motors is born in Aspen Grove, VA

1890 Howard Augustus Lewis of American Motors is born in Faribault, MN

1899 The first automobile race is held in Austria - the 5,500 meter race at the Trabrennbahn in Vienna is won by Baron Theodor von Liebieg driving the Nesseldorf Wien

1903 The ALAM sues the Ford Motor Company for violating the Selden Patent

1906 Henry Ford is elected President of Ford Motor Company succeeding the late John S. Gray

1910 Prince Francis of Teck, Chairman of the Royal Automobile Club, dies at age 40

1920 Andre Dubonnet takes delivery of his first Hispano-Suiza, a marque he would frequently use as a basis for automotive experiments

1928 Alexis de Sakhnoffsky arrives in New York City to begin his United States career as an automobile stylist

1928 The Pep Auto Supply Company changes its corporate name to Pep Boys - Manny Moe & Jack

1931 Reno Haibe, whose automobile career included stints with Maxwell-Briscoe, Stoddard-Dayton, Empire, Federal, Cole, and Kissel, dies at age 48

1932 The Franklin Olympic is introduced as a 1933 model

1936 James Couzens of Ford dies in Detroit, MI at age 64

1941 Racer Gus Schrader is killed in Shreveport, LA at age 46

1944 Robert E. Manly, President of the Remco Products Corporation, dies at age 69

1945 The first post-World War II Plymouth, a P15S Deluxe sedan, is produced

1945 The Lincoln-Mercury Division of the Ford Motor Company is established

1946 Charles C. Hanch, an official with Marmon, Studebaker, and Maxwell, dies in Chicago, IL at age 78

1949 The last Lancia Aprilia is completed

1952 Dodge introduces its Red Ram V-8, claimed to have more horsepower per cubic inch than any other volume-produced engine

1952 The Healey 100 is introduced at Earls Court, London - Leonard Lord, Chairman of the newly formed British Motor Corporation, immediately began negotiations with Donald Healey that would lead to the Austin-Healey

1952 Two Packard Monte Carlo showcars are completed by the Henney Motor Company

1954 The 1955 Ford Thunderbird is introduced as a new sub-marque

1954 The Studebaker-Packard Corporation acquires the Murray Body Company, a longtime independent producer of automobile bodies

1955 Daimler-Benz AG officially withdraws from racing

1955 George R. Ericson, Patent Counsel since 1928 for the Carter Carburetor Corporation and himself a holder of many patents, dies in St. Louis, MO

1957 The 1958 Ramblers and Rambler Americans are introduced

1958 Capt. Maurice Hudlass, Chief Engineer of the Royal Automobile Club, dies at age 56

1965 Racer Earl Cooper dies in Atwater, CA at age 79

1969 The Datsun 240Z sports car is introduced

1978 Leo D. Welch, Chairman of the Standard Oil Company of New Jersey 1960- 1963, dies near Cuernevaca, Mexico at age 80

1993 Innes Ireland, winner of the 1961 United States Grand Prix and later an automotive journalist, dies in Reading, Berkshire, England from cancer at age 63

1996 The Museum of Automobile History, owned by automotive literature dealer Walter Miller, opens in Syracuse, NY

OCTOBER 23

1762 Steam engine pioneer Samuel Morey is born in Hebron, CT

1868 Frederick William Lanchester is born in Hove, Sussex, England

1883 John Will Anderson, an inventor of automotive parts who founded the Anderson Company in 1918, is born in Woodland, IL

1885 Edward Whitten Isom of the Sinclair Refining Company is born in Toledo, OH

1889 Stylist Amos E. Northup is born in Bellevue, OH

1896 William Jennings Bryan, riding in a Mueller-Benz provided by local dealer and manufacturer Henry Mueller, becomes the first presidential candidate to campaign in an automobile during a stop in Decatur, IL

1998 Ceirano & Cie, Societa per la Costruzione di Campioni per la Fabbricazione di Vetture Automobili is founded in Turin, Italy - located in a building owned by the parents of Vincenzo Lancia, this firm would evolve into Fiat SpA

1911 Production of the Ford Model T begins at the new Ford Motor Company Ltd. factory in Trafford Park, Manchester, England

1914 Stephen J. Tompkins of Dodge is born in Ravena, NY

1918 Automotive historian James Potvin Barry is born in Alton, IL

1927 Edward Joseph Dunn, President of the Eclipse Machine Company and an advocate of the Bendix drive for electric starting devices, dies in Elmira, NY at age 61

1933 Harlow H. Curtice is named General Manager of Buick

1937 The 1938 Chevrolets are introduced

1937 Racer Giacomo "Geki" Russo is born in Milan, Italy

1938 The Marmon-Herrington Company, Inc. purchases the Indianapolis, IN factory used since 1921 for the manufacture of the Duesenberg

1941 Race car designer Gerard Ducarouge is born in Paray-le-Monial, France

1941 Racer Rene Metge is born in Montrouge, France

1946 Rolls-Royce Ltd. completes their first post-World War II car, a Bentley Mark VI standard saloon

1951 Stunt driver Bengt Norberg, holder of the world's distance record for driving a car on two side wheels, is born in Appelbo, Sweden

1952 The 1953 Dodges are introduced, featuring the marque's first V-8 engines

1953 Chrysler Corporation acquires the Briggs Manufacturing Company of Detroit, MI, automobile body manufacturers

1955 Tony Brooks makes his Formula 1 debut driving a Connaught B-Type at the Syracuse Grand Prix in Sicily, and becomes the first British driver in a British car to win a Grand Prix since Sir Henry Segrave's victory in a Sunbeam at San Sebastian in 1924

1962 Racer John E. "Jack" Scales dies at age 76

1966 Racer Alessandro "Alex" Zanardi is born in Bologna, Italy

1970 Gary Gabelich, driving the Blue Flame, raises the land speed record to 622.407 mph at the Bonneville Salt Flats, UT

1973 Racer Ralph Mulford dies in Worcester, MA at age 88

OCTOBER 24

1864 Claude Goodman Johnson of Rolls-Royce is born in Datchet, England

1887 George William Borg, a cofounder of the Borg-Warner Corporation, is born in West Burlington, IA

1900 The Ohio Automobile Company, manufacturers of the Packard, holds its first board meeting and elects James W. Packard as President, George L. Weiss as Vice President, and William D. Packard as Treasurer

1900 The first Thomas automobile is tested by F. P. Nehrbas

1903 Robert M. Lockwood joins the Ford Motor Company as Export Manager

1903 The first 6-cylinder Napier is introduced

1908 The fourth Vanderbilt Cup Race is held on Long Island, NY and won by George Robertson in a Locomobile, a car later owned by artist Peter Helck and generally known as "Old 16"

1908 Frederick E. Moskovics is elected to SAE membership

1910 Automotive parts manufacturer Lester Clinton Tiscornia is born in Oakland, CA

1914 Race car mechanic Clay Smith is born in Phoenix, AZ

1915 William B. Pratt and George B. Pratt reorganize the Pratt Motor Car Company as the Elkhart (IN) Carriage & Motor Car Company, with the new firm's automobile to be called the Elcar

1921 Charles C. Rappleyea of Chalmers and Overland dies in Allentown, PA at age 43

1924 Racer George Amick is born in Vernonia, OR

1928 Racer Jerry Titus is born in Johnson City, NY

1928 Willard Lamb Velie Sr. dies in Moline, IL

1930 Joseph Boyer, a Director of the Packard Motor Car Company 1903-1904, dies

1936 The 1937 Buicks introduced featuring the "Aerobat" carburetor

Downtown Hood River, OR circa 1948 - the parked car nearest the camera at left is a 1937 Buick sedan.

1937 Juan Manuel Fangio makes his racing debut

1938 The Mercury is previewed for the press in Dearborn, MI where it is announced that the new marque will officially be the "Mercury", not the "Ford-Mercury" as originally suggested by Edsel B. Ford

1943 Caleb S. Bragg, pioneer racer and co-inventor with Victor W. Kliesrath of the Bragg-Kliesrath brake, dies in New York City at age 58

1944 Louis Renault dies at age 67 in a Paris, France military prison hospital as a result of torture administered due to alleged Nazi collaboration

1946 Automotive historian Jane Wexler Stern is born in New York City

1948 Dr. Giuseppe Farina wins the Circuito di Garda race at Lago di Garda, Italy in a Ferrari 125, the first victory for a monoposto example of the marque

1951 Michelin & Cie. is issued a French patent for its radial tires

1952 Joseph G. Swain, a consulting engineer to the Goodyear Tire & Rubber Company and a longtime manufacturer of automobile wheel rims, dies in Akron, OH at age 73

1955 The 1956 Cadillac Sedan DeVille and Eldorado Seville coupe are introduced

1957 Racer Tracy Leslie is born

1958 The 1959 Chryslers are introduced

1958 The 1959 Dodge four-wheel-drive trucks are introduced

1958 Samuel P. Hess, retired Sales Manager of the Detroit Steel Products Company, dies at age 73

1959 Automotive literature dealer Barry J. Schiff is born in Providence, RI

1960 Racer Joachim Winkelhock is born in Waiblingen, West Germany, the younger brother of racer Manfred Winkelhock

1965 Richie Ginther driving a Honda wins the Mexican Grand Prix in Mexico City, the only Formula 1 victory for the driver and first for the marque

1971 Racer Jo Siffert is killed at age 35 when his BRM P160 crashes during the Rothmans Victory Race at Brands Hatch, England

1971 Automotive historian Jay G. Hayden dies at age 86

1974 Jack Head, Chief Executive Officer of the Ford-owned Carrozzeria Ghia, announces that production of the DeTomaso Pantera at the Ford-run Carrozzeria Vignale factory in Grugliasco, Italy would be discontinued

1976 The first Japanese Grand Prix is staged in Fuji and won by Mario Andretti in a Lotus 77-Ford - the Kojima makes its Formula 1 debut with the Type KE007 car financed by Matsuhisa Kojima, designed by Masao Ono, and driven by Masahiro Hasemi finishing in 11th place

1980 Traditional M.G. production ends as a white MGB is completed at the Abingdon, England factory - total production for the 51-year history of the marque was 1,155,032, although the marque would soon be revived in various badge-engineered forms

1985 Racer Richie Evans is killed at age 44 when he crashes during a race at the Martinsville (VA) Speedway

OCTOBER 25

1864 John Francis Dodge is born in Niles, MI

Among the casualties of the tornado that devastated Fergus Falls, MN on June 22, 1919 was this 1918 Dodge Model 30 Roadster.

1873 John North Willys is born in Canandaigua, NY

1882 Carl Benz forms his first automotive venture, Gasmotorenfabrik Mannheim AG, but the firm would dissolve within three months

1898 Harry C. Stutz marries Clara Marie Dietz

1902 Barney Oldfield driving the Ford "999" in his automobile racing debut wins the Manufacturers' Challenge Cup match race in Grosse Pointe, MI

1910 Barney Oldfield driving a 60-hp Knox easily defeats heavyweight boxing champion Jack Johnson driving a 90-hp Thomas in a bizarre match race at the Sheepshead Bay track in Brooklyn, NY that was promoted as a contest between the white and black races

1917 Dodge Brothers begins full-scale truck production

1934 Baron Kent Bates of Chrysler and Volkswagen is born in Los Angeles, CA

1936 The 3,000,000th Buick is presented to Arthur Lee Newton, President of the Glidden Buick Corporation in New York City, the marque's largest dealer

1944 The Packard Motor Car Company board authorizes $2.8 million to begin the conversion to post-World War II automobile production

1949 George M. Fisher is named President of Keller Motors, Inc.

1954 Regular production of the 1955 Ford begins

1954 The Austin Model A50 is introduced in United States

1956 The 1957 Hudsons, destined to be the last of the marque, are introduced

1956 The 1957 Plymouths are introduced

1958 Racer Stuart Lewis-Evans dies in East Grinstead, Sussex, England at age 28 from injuries suffered six days earlier when his Vanwall crashed during the Moroccan Grand Prix at Ain-Diab near Casablanca

1958 Robert M. Tullos, General Service Manager of the Reo Division, White Motor Company, dies at age 47

1960 Harry G. Ferguson, the Irish-born designer of automobiles, airplanes, and farm tractors, dies in Abbotswood, Gloucestershire, England at age 75

1961 Gilbert J. Loomis, builder of the 1900-1904 Loomis who later was a design engineer for Payne-Modern, Pope-Tribune, and Speedwell, dies in Englewood Cliffs, NJ

1961 Racer Ward Burton is born in Danville, VA

1970 Automotive historians Michael Stern and Jane Wexler marry

1972 Racer Johnny Mantz dies at age 54

1974 Edouard Bertrand of Bugatti dies in Wolxheim, France at age 79

1978 Mitsubishi announces plans to purchase Chrysler Australia

OCTOBER 26

1878 William Kissam Vanderbilt Jr., patron of automobile racing and the Long Island Motor Parkway, is born in New York City

1881 Eugene Jeno Farkas of the Ford Motor Company is born in Kald, Hungary

1888 John Ferdinand Oberwinder, an advertising executive who was closely associated with the tire industry, is born in St. Louis, MO

1895 Automotive historian Joseph Floyd Clymer is born in Indianapolis, IN

1908 Albert Champion organizes the Champion Ignition Company in Flint, MI, which evolved into the AC Spark Plug Division of General Motors

1909 General Motors purchases the Cartercar Company of Pontiac, MI, and gives William C. Durant permission to attempt the purchase of the Ford Motor Company

1911 The eighth Glidden Tour ends in Jacksonville, FL, and is won by a Maxwell driven by a team of drivers from Tarrytown, NY - a Reo truck that followed the cars with baggage and spare tires was fitted with pneumatic tires, the first time they were ever installed on a motor truck

1917 The Briggs-Detroiter Company is liquidated after six years of production

1917 Automotive historian Michael Frostick is born in Hove, Sussex, England

1918 Charles S. Beach of the Willys-Overland Company dies in New York City

1920 A. H. M. J. Ward resigns as a Director of Bentley Motors, Ltd. - Charles Frederick Stead and Charles Frederick Boston join the board, with Boston acting as Chairman

1922 William H. Little, who worked for Locomobile, Orient, and Buick before founding the Little Motor Car Company and serving as the first President of the Chevrolet Motor Company, dies in Detroit, MI at age 48

1926 The Auburn Automobile Company acquires Duesenberg Automobile and Motors Corporation

1927 Stuart de la Rue, Chairman of Bentley Motors, Ltd. in 1923, dies at age 44

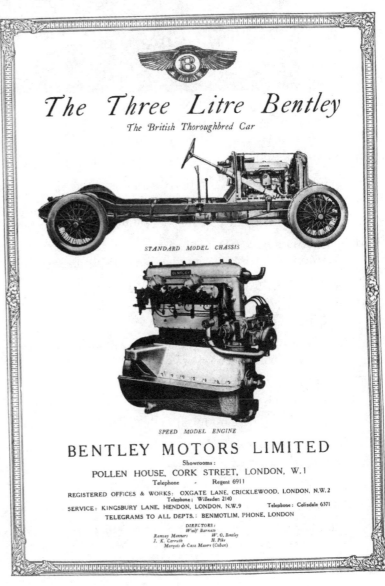

The Three Litre Bentley
The British Thoroughbred Car

STANDARD MODEL CHASSIS

SPEED MODEL ENGINE

BENTLEY MOTORS LIMITED
Showrooms :
POLLEN HOUSE, CORK STREET, LONDON, W.1
Telephone - Regent 6911
REGISTERED OFFICES & WORKS: OXGATE LANE, CRICKLEWOOD, LONDON, N.W.2
Telephone : Willesden 2140
SERVICE: KINGSBURY LANE, HENDON, LONDON, N.W.9   Telephone : Colindale 6371
TELEGRAMS TO ALL DEPTS.: BENMOTLIM, PHONE, LONDON
DIRECTORS:
Woolf Barnato
Ramsay Manners   W. O. Bentley
J. K. Carruth   H. Pike
Marquis de Casa Maury (Cuban)

1929 Thomas J. Litle Jr. resigns as Chief Engineer of Marmon

1938 S. P. Worthington, cofounder in 1923 and President since 1929 of the Tiona Petroleum Company, dies at age 46

1942 Racer Jonathan Williams is born in Cairo, Egypt, the son of a Royal Air Force bomber pilot

1945 The 1946 Fords are introduced to the public on what is billed as "V-8 Day"

A 1946 Ford Super Delux convertible, purchased new by Ernest Hanson of Robinson, ND.

1947 British racer Ian Ashley is born in Wuppertal, Germany

1951 Thomas H. White, Vice President of the White Motor Company 1921-1927, dies at age 57

1953 The Kaiser-Frazer Corporation discontinues the Allstate marque

1954 The Lancia D50 makes its racing debut at the Spanish Grand Prix in Barcelona - Alberto Ascari qualifies the car in the pole position, but retires early due to clutch and oil seal problems

1954 Sir Algernon Arthur St. Lawrence Lee "A. Lee" Guinness, pioneer racer, Steward of the Royal Automobile Club, and brother of land speed record setter K. Lee Guinness, dies at age 71

1955 Racer Sammy Swindell is born in Bartlett, TN

1961 Daimler-Benz AG acquires a license to manufacture gasoline-powered Wankel rotary engines of greater than 50-hp

1965 Craig Breedlove, driving the Spirit of America at the Bonneville Salt Flats, UT, raises the land speed record to 555.127 mph

1970 California becomes the first state to offer vanity license plates as Governor Ronald Reagan presents the special plates with "AMIGO" to Mr. and Mrs. Robert E. Klees of Fullerton

1970 The 1971 Opels are introduced to the United States market

1971 The Mercedes-Benz ESF 05, the second of five experimental safety vehicles, is introduced to the public

1976 The new Ford Motor Company plant in Valencia, Spain is dedicated by Henry Ford II and King Juan Carlos

1979 Ray P. Dinsmore of the Goodyear Tire & Rubber Company dies at age 86

1980 Victor Galindez, a former light-heavyweight boxing champion turned race car driver, is killed at age 31 when he crashes during a race in DeMayo, Argentina

1995 The 100,000th Toyota Avalon is produced at the Georgetown, KY plant

OCTOBER 27

1864 John M. Mack, founder of Mack trucks, is born in Mount Cobb, PA

1873 James R. Cardwell, a Director of the Diamond T Motor Car Company, is born in Concord, VA

1877 Everett Scott Cameron is born in Shubenacadie, Nova Scotia, Canada

1878 Martin Wilhelm Torkelson, a pioneer developer of highway bridge standards, is born in Jackson County, WI

1891 Walter C. Baker marries Fannie Elizabeth White, daughter of Rollin C. White

1911 Packard is issued a United States patent for its first special radiator cap

1913 Racer Luigi Piotti is born in Italy

1924 The Charlotte (NC) Board Speedway stages its first event, a 250-mile race won by Tommy Milton in a Miller

1926 AB Volvo occupies the former Nordiska Kullagerfabriken factory in Hisingen, Sweden (near Goteborg) for the purpose of beginning the production of automobiles

1927 O. L. Arnold of the Ford Motor Company joins General Motors as Vice President and Director of Truck Sales for the General Motors Truck Company

1927 Albert Champion, founder and President 1908-1927 of the AC Spark Plug Company, dies in Paris, France at age 49

1930 Automotive tool manufacturer Louis Schwab dies at age 53

1936 The Packard 110, a low-priced 6-cylinder car, is introduced

1936 South African racer Dave Charlton is born in Redcar, Yorkshire, England

1937 The 1938 Cadillac Series 90 is introduced featuring a totally redesigned 135-degree V-16

1937 Bernd Rosemeyer reaches 238.7 mph in his Auto Union on a German autobahn

1941 Racer Dick Trickle is born in Wisconsin Rapids, WI

1945 The first post-World War II Nash is produced

1945 Ferdinand Porsche is arrested by United States military officials for alleged pro-Nazi activities during World War II - he would later be turned over to French officials and held for nearly two years

1946 The first major post-World War II race, the revived Pena Rhin Grand Prix staged in Barcelona, Spain, is won by Giorgio Pelassa in a Maserati 4CL

1947 The 1948 Hudsons featuring "Step-Down" styling are introduced at the Detroit (MI) Masonic Temple

1947 Samuel Crowther, collaborator with Henry Ford on several books, dies in Boston, MA at age 67

1948 The Jaguar XK120, Austin Atlantic, and Morris Minor are introduced at the Earls Court show in London, England

1948 Rolls-Royce Ltd. reacquires the original 1907 Rolls-Royce Silver Ghost

1957 Archibald G. Danielson, Assistant Chief Engineer of the Diamond T Motor Car Company and an employee of the firm for 37 years, dies at age 62

1958 The 1959 Ford Thunderbirds are introduced

1964 Art Arfons driving the Green Monster raises the land speed record to 536.71 mph at the Bonneville Salt Flats, UT

1965 Cadillac announces a one-day production record of 1,017 cars

1971 William Murray Gray of Gray-Dort dies in Chatham, ON, Canada at age 80

1977 Anton "Tony" Hulman Jr., owner of the Indianapolis Motor Speedway since 1945, dies in Indianapolis, IN at age 76

1978 The United States Environmental Protection Agency bans methlycyclopentadienyl manganese tricarbonyl (MMT) as an octane booster in unleaded fuel

OCTOBER 28

1879 Charles Bedell Rose, an industrial consultant whose career included executive positions with Oldsmobile, Velie, Fageol, and American LaFrance, is born in Burton, MI

1893 O. B. Higgins of the Ford Motor Company is born in Bayonne, NJ

1908 The Rolls-Royce 40/50-hp Balloon Car, known within the company as "The Cookie", is delivered to the Hon. C. S. Rolls in Derby, England

1909 The Elmore Manufacturing Company is incorporated in Ohio, although it had been manufacturing Elmore automobiles since 1900

1909 The Springfield Motor Car Company incorporates in Springfield, IL with Harry C. Medcraft as President, Rudolph Haas as Vice President, Edward Everett Staley as Secretary, and racer Otis Funderburk as Sales Manager - the new firm was a reorganization of the Med-Bow Automobile Company of Springfield, MA, but actual production was only about ten cars

1913 Malcolm Lawrence Denise of the Ford Motor Company is born in Decatur, MI

1918 As a result of World War I, Nesselsdorf in the Austro-Hungarian empire becomes Koprivnice, Czechoslovakia, leading to the Nesselsdorf automobile being being renamed as the Tatra

1919 Racer Walter Edwin Hansgen is born in Westfield, NJ

1929 David Charles Collier of General Motors is born in Hardisty, AB, Canada

1931 Racer Bernie Ecclestone is born in St. Peters, Suffolk, England

1934 James Anthony Capolongo of the Ford Motor Company is born in Syracuse, NY

1937 Henry Gulick, an authority on automotive materials, dies at age 74

1938 Piston ring manufacturer John E. Ruth dies at age 50

1945 Edward James Gulda of the Ford Motor Company is born in Detroit, MI

1945 The first post-World War II English sprint races are held at Filton Aerodrome near Bristol - class winners included Bob Gerard in an E.R.A. and Sir Alec Issigonis in the "Lightweight Special"

1947 E. J. Sadler, Vice President of the Standard Oil Company of New Jersey 1930-1942, dies at age 68

1951 Juan Manuel Fangio, driving an Alfa Romeo Type 159, wins the Spanish Grand Prix at the Pedralbes circuit, the last Formula 1 victory for the marque - Talbot-Lago makes its last Formula 1 appearance with an entry of six cars, but only Louis Rosier in 7th place and Philippe Etancelin in 8th place complete the race

1952 The Packard Twenty-Sixth Series is introduced

1954 The 1955 Chevrolets are introduced, featuring completely new styling and the marque's first V-8 engine since 1918

1955 Col. Elbert J. Hall, whose Hall-Scott aviation engines powered the super luxury Fageol car of 1917 and in 1930 was a cofounder with Norman DeVaux of the DeVaux-Hall Motors Corporation, manufacturers of the economy DeVaux of 1931-1932, dies in Los Gatos, CA at age 73

1955 Sir Arthur P. DuCros, founder in 1901 of the Dunlop Rubber Company Ltd., dies in Oxhey, Hertfordshire, England at age 84

1955 Earle H. Gould of the Lincoln-Mercury Division of the Ford Motor Company, whose previous automotive career included stints with Studebaker, Chandler, Hupmobile, Chrylser, Packard, and Willys-Overland, dies

1965 Nicholas Kelley, the interim first President of the Chrysler Corporation who later served as its General Counsel and Vice President 1937-1957, dies at age 80

1975 Charles L. McCuen, a longtime research engineer with General Motors whose early career included time with Packard and Rickenbacker, dies at age 83

1981 The 1982 Pontiac Phoenix and T100 compacts are introduced

OCTOBER 29

1904 Barney Oldfield, driving the Peerless Green Dragon at Yonkers, NY, wins the so-called "World's Championship" by defeating three European cars in a match race

1912 Norsk-Engelsk Mineralolie AS is registered - the firm would evolve into AS Norske Shell in 1940

1914 William B. Chenoweth begins the world's first intercity truck service between Colorado Springs, CO and Snyder, TX

1917 A Mack 3 1/2-ton truck driven by J. A. Stoner successfully ascends Mount Wilson, CA carrying a 10-ton load, an accomplishment that strengthened the marque's reputation as well as that of the motor truck industry in general

1922 George Chaffee Dillon, Chairman of the Manville Corporation, a Denver, CO automobile parts manufacturer, is born in Kansas City, MO

1923 Walter M. Murphy announces the creation of the newsletter *Murphy Service* to promote both his custom coachbuilding efforts and the Ford products sold by his five California dealerships

1929 The stock market crash abruptly ends contract negotiations between New Era Motors, Inc. and the Marmon Motor Car Company to have the latter produce the Ruxton

To ensure that the potential customer would appreciate the low profile of the Ruxton, the graphic artist supplied a five-foot measurement guide... and cut off the heads of the couple admiring the revolutionary and controversial car.

1932 Racer Alex Soler-Roig is born in Barcelona, Spain

1934 William B. Young, Engineering Manager for the Perfect Circle Product Division of the Dana Corporation, is born in Harrison, MI

1942 G. B. Upton, a professor of automotive engineering at Cornell University, dies at age 60

1949 George Mertz Slocum, Publisher of *Automotive News*, dies in Detroit, MI at age 60

1951 Racer Tiff Needell is born in Havant, Hampshire, England

1952 Racer Guillermo Maldonaldo is born in Argentina

1953 Oil executive Frederick B. Koontz dies at age 64

1954 The last 1954 Hudson is produced - many consider this the end of the "real" Hudson, although the marque continued to be produced until 1957 as a badge-engineered Nash

1954 J. Lester Dryden, Vice President of the Borg-Warner Corporation who in 1921 designed the single-disc clutch universally adopted by the industry and was the principal advocate of automotive grilles to protect radiators and add beauty, dies at age 73

1956 The 1957 Chryslers are introduced, including the first 300C convertible

1956 Racer Louis Rosier, father of racer Jean-Louis Rosier, dies at age 50 from injuries suffered three weeks earlier when his Ferrari crashed during the Coupe du Salon race at the Montlhery circuit in France

1959 The Valiant compact car is introduced by the Chrysler Corporation, at first considered to be a new marque but beginning with the 1961 model year as a Plymouth series

1962 The Chrysler Corporation begins its Consumer Delivery Program as a public hands-on test of the semi-production Chrysler Turbine Car

1962 Eger V. Murphree, President of the Standard Oil Development Company 1947-1962, dies in Summit, NJ at age 63

1965 Racer Paul Stewart is born in Geneva, Switzerland, the son of racer Jackie Stewart

1968 Herman D. Palmer, Chief Engineer of Kissel 1906-1930, dies in Hartford, WI

While the Duesenberg brothers were beginning their automotive design careers in Rockford, IA, about 40 miles away in Grundy Center the Lower brothers - Monroe Laverne, Milo S., and Orville E. - were establishing themselves as dealers. Their new garage opened February 7, 1914 and featured a complete line of Maxwell and Kissel automobiles. Exiting the service bay in this photograph is a 1912 Kissel touring car designed by Herman D. Palmer.

1974 Don Heinisch, President of the FWD Corporation since 1968, dies at age 51

1975 Sir Alfred Owen of BRM dies at age 67

1976 The Automotive Hall of Fame is dedicated in Midland, MI

1984 Philip Caldwell retires as Chairman of the Ford Motor Company

1991 The 30,000,000th Pontiac is produced, a white Bonneville SSEi built at the Wentzville (MO) Assembly Center

OCTOBER 30

1875 Clarence Winfred Spicer, inventor of the first practical automobile driveshaft, is born in West Hallock (now Edelstein), IL

1882 Bayard Dickenson Kunkle of General Motors is born in Steelton, PA

1888 Frederick James Lamborn of Dodge is born in Springfield, OH

1893 The Waltham Manufacturing Company is established by Charles H. Metz, William Parrot, and Herbert L. Thompson to produce bicycles - the firm would later produce automobiles and motorcycles

1899 The first Packard engine is completed and found to produce 7.1 horsepower

1900 Walter F. Rockwell of the Timken-Detroit Axle Company is born in Boston, MA

1900 The Remington automobile is introduced

1904 Neil Holser McElroy of the Chrysler Corporation is born in Berea, OH

1906 Racer Giuseppe "Nino" Farina is born in Turin, Italy

1909 The fifth Vanderbilt Cup Race is held on Long Island, NY and won by Harry F. Grant in a 90-hp Alco

1909 Corbin records its first racing victory as Frank Free wins a race at Ascot Park, CA with a four-cylinder model

1911 The Little Motor Car Company is incorporated in Flint, MI by William H. Little, Charles M. Begole, and William S. Ballenger

1914 The Abner Doble Motor Vehicle Company is founded in Waltham, MA

1917 Racer Maurice Trintignant is born in Sainte-Cecile-les-Vignes, France

1918 Percy Wheeler Tracy of Premier dies in Washington, DC at age 39

1926 Racer Jacques Swaters is born in Brussels, Belgium

1927 M.G. makes its official racing debut with Alberto Sanchez Cires driving a 14/28 to victory in a race at San Martin, Argentina

1928 The 1928 Hudson/Essex "Winged God" mascot is patented by designer F. C. Ruppel

1951 Burns Dick, Chief Automotive Engineer for the Wagner Electric Corporation and an employee of the firm since 1913, dies at age 68 aboard the USS Mauretania while returning from a visit to his native England

1952 The 1953 Chryslers are introduced

1952 William H. Graves of the Packard Motor Car Company contracts with the Ionia Manufacturing Company of Ionia, MI to produce 500 Packard Caribbean convertible bodies for the 1953 model year

1954 Wilbur Shaw, winner of the 1937 Indianapolis 500 and President of the Indianapolis Motor Speedway Company since 1951, is killed at age 51 in an airplane crash near Decatur, IN

1956 The 1957 Chryslers and Imperials are introduced

1956 The 1957 DeSotos are introduced

1956 The 1957 Dodge cars and four-wheel-drive trucks are introduced, with the cars featuring torsion-bar front suspension

A 1957 Dodge has just cleared customs at the international city of Nogales straddling the border between Sonora, Mexico and Arizona, USA.

1956 The 1957 Plymouths are introduced

1957 Harry K. Reinoehl, Chief Product Engineer of the International Harvester Company, dies at age 67

1959 York Noble Industries Ltd. of London, England announces that the Noble 200 will soon be assembled at a new plant in Israel

1959 Frithiof V. Timm, Truck & Bus Manager for General Motors International A/S in Copenhagen, Denmark and a proponent of motor transport in Denmark and Norway, dies at age 60

1961 Maschinen Augsburg-Nurnburg of Germany, makers of MAN trucks, acquires a license to manufacture Wankel rotary engines

1963 The Lamborghini is introduced

1967 Edward N. Cole is elected President and Chief Operating Office of General Motors

1967 Eiji Toyoda is named President of the Toyota Motor Company, Ltd.

1968 Automotive historian Rose Wilder Lane dies in Danbury, CT at age 80

1970 The 1971 Ford trucks are introduced

1978 Charles A. Chayne, Chief Engineer of Buick 1936-1951, dies in Carmel, CA at age 80 - he is remembered for saving the Bugatti Type 41 Royale Weinberger cabriolet and later donating it to the Henry Ford Museum

OCTOBER 31

1866 Edwin Hoyt Lockwood, a leading authority on fuel utilization in internal combustion engines, is born in New Canaan, CT

1885 Automobile bearing manufacturer John D. Cutter is born in Orange, NJ

1888 Belfast, Ireland veterinarian John B. Dunlop is issued a British patent for his pneumatic tires

1893 Alfred Lindley Boegehold of General Motors is born in Mount Vernon, NY

1901 Packard uses its famous "Ask the man who owns one" slogan in their advertising for the first time

1902 Racer Warren Wilbur Shaw is born in Shelbyville, IN

1904 The first and only Wick automobile is sold at auction to Roy York

1905 Amedee Bollee Jr. is issued a French patent for his automatic splash lubrication system

1910 The Panama Canal Zone requires all automobiles to be registered

1913 A National Day of Celebration is staged to officially dedicate the Lincoln Highway

1920 W. O. Bentley resigns from Bentley and Bentley Ltd. to devote full time to his position as Chief Engineer for Bentley Motors, Ltd.

1922 Clarence A. Earl resigns as President of Earl Motors, Inc. of Jackson, MI

1924 The last Marmon Model 34 is produced

1925 The Ford Motor Company establishes a one-day production record as 9,109 Ford Model T's come off the assembly line

1925 The Rockingham Board Speedway in Salem, NH stages its first event, a 250-mile race won by Peter DePaolo in a Duesenberg

1935 The 1,000,000th Ford V-8 is produced during the calendar year, a 1935 Fordor Touring Sedan with body by Briggs

Unusual roadside architecture flourished in the 1930's - an 8-piece band and their Ford Deluxe Phaeton pose in front of a sombrero-shaped diner somewhere (presumably) in Mexico.

1939 The 1940 Chryslers, DeSotos, Dodges, and Plymouths are introduced at the Chrysler Building in New York City

1939 Racer Tom Bigelow is born

1939 Automobile photographer and historian Alan Sweigert is born in Cleveland, OH

1940 George W. Hanson dies at age 65

1941 Racer Derek Bell is born in Pinner, Middlesex, England

1941 The Divco-Twin Truck Company of Canada Ltd., a subsidiary of the Divco-Twin Truck Company, is liquidated

1943 Racer Elliott Forbes-Robinson is born in San Francisco, CA

1945 The last Inskip-bodied Rolls-Royce Phantom III is delivered to P. Fishbacher of Rye, NY

1952 The Kaiser Dragon, an upscale version of the standard Kaiser Deluxe, is introduced on Halloween Day as a mid-year model

1954 A prototype 1955 Packard Patrician sedan completes a 25,000-mile endurance run at the Packard Proving Grounds in Utica, MI at an average speed of 104.737 mph

1955 Walter R. Grant resigns as Treasurer of the Studebaker-Packard Corporation

1956 The last Detroit, MI board meeting of the Studebaker-Packard Corporation is held, with all corporate activities now shifting to South Bend, IN

1957 The Chevrolet Impala is introduced

1957 The 1958 Dodge four-wheel-drive trucks are introduced

1958 The 1959 Edsels are introduced

1965 The Rockingham (SC) Speedway stages its first event, a 500-mile NASCAR race won by Curtis Turner in a Ford

1965 Roy A. Fruehauf of the Fruehauf Trailer Company dies at age 57

IMPALA—excitement on wheels

THE IMPALA CONVERTIBLE

1967 Racer Buddy Lazier is born in Vail, CO, the son of racer Bob Lazier

1967 Frederic G. Donner retires as Chairman and Chief Executive Officer of General Motors, to be succeeded the following day by President James M. Roche

1967 The Borg-Warner Corporation is reorganized in Delaware, succeeding the company of the same name incorporated in Illinois in 1928

1971 Roy T. Hurley, Chairman of the Curtiss-Wright Corporation 1952-1961 who engineered the "Joint Progam" with the Studebaker-Packard Corporation in 1956, dies in Santa Barbara, CA

1989 The Ford Motor Company acquires Associates First Capital Corporation

1992 General Motors stylist Charles M. Jordan retires

1995 The Ford Motor Company announces that Norm Ehlers will retire as a Vice President at the end of the year

NOVEMBER 1

1866 Charles G. Young of Willys is born in Bath, NY

1868 Comfort Avery Adams, a consulting engineer with the coachbuilding firm Edward G. Budd Manufacturing Company, is born in Cleveland, OH

1889 Madame Louise Sarazin is named exclusive distributor for Daimler engines in France, succeeding her late husband Edouard Sarazin

1895 The first United States automobile club, the American Motor League, is formed in Chicago, IL with Dr. J. Allen Hornsby acclaimed as its Chairman

1895 Wilhelm Maybach joins Daimler Motoren-Gesellschaft as Chief Engineer

1898 Racer Arthur Legat is born in Haine St. Paul, Belgium

1899 The first automobile show in the United States opens in New York City as part of a general technology exposition

1901 The Apperson Brothers Automobile Company is founded

1901 Automotive historian Henry Bolles Lent is born in New Bedford, MA

1904 William C. Durant and the Durant-Dort Carriage Company purchase majority interest in the Buick Motor Company - Charles M. Begole is named President, succeeding James H. Whiting

1905 The 1906 Auburn Model C is introduced

1905 Groundbreaking ceremonies are held in Flint, MI for the new Buick Motor Company factory

1908 The first Hupmobile is completed, a Model 20 runabout

1913 The Scripps-Booth Cyclecar Company is organized in Detroit, MI by William E. Scripps, George G. Booth, and James Scripps Booth

1916 Edsel B. Ford marries Eleanor Lowthian Clay in Detroit, MI - she was a niece of Joseph L. Hudson, namesake of the Hudson motor car

1918 Racer Ken Miles is born in Sutton Coldfield, Warwickshire, England, the son of United States citizens

1925 E. L. Cord becomes President of the Auburn Automobile Company

1927 The 2,000,000th Buick is produced, a 1928 coupe

1928 The Ford Motor Company becomes the first mass producer of automobiles to use safety glass as standard equipment

1928 Racer Ted Whiteaway is born in Feltham, Middlesex, England

1930 Maurice Olley joins General Motors as a design engineer with Cadillac

1931 Auto Union AG is established as a legal entity, although the actual formation of the corporation did not occur until June 29, 1932

1931 The Soviet Ford factory near Nizhni Novgorod (now Gor'kiy), Russia, USSR is completed

1932 Work begins on the Pierce Silver Arrow show cars

1932 Hochleistungsfahrzeugbau GmbH is founded by Ferdinand Porsche and Adolf Rosenberger with the sole purpose to build a Grand Prix car in the new unlimited classification - the proposed design would be built by the newly-formed Auto Union AG

1934 Umberto Agnelli of Fiat is born in Lausanne, Switzerland

1936 Racer Jack Rex "Jackie" Lewis is born in Stroud, Glouscestershire, England

1939 Great Britain implements gasoline rationing due to World War II

1940 The Hupp Motor Car Corporation is reorganized under bankruptcy

1940 Automotive parts manufacturer Hugh Walter Sloan Jr. is born in Princeton, NJ

1941 The Texas Corporation changes its name to The Texas Company

1942 John L. Gonard, the inventor of a device for preventing retrograde movement of motor vehicles, dies at age 75

1945 The first post-World War II Lincoln is produced

1945 The first post-World War II Mercury is produced

1945 The Kaiser-Frazer Corporation moves into the Willow Run administration building

1946 James A. Bohannon, former President of the Peerless Motor Car Company, presents the unique Peerless V-16 to the Thompson Products Museum in Cleveland, OH

1947 Unsold 1947 Fords are officially redesignated as 1948 models

1947 The 1948 Lincolns and Lincoln Continentals are introduced

1948 General Motors resumes management control of Adam Opel AG

1948 The 1949 Packard Twenty-Second Series is introduced

1949 The West Rock Tunnel in New Haven, CT, the state's first automobile tunnel, opens to the public

1950 Automobile parts manufacturer Arthur G. Drefs dies at age 62

1951 The Henry J is introduced as a new marque by the Kaiser-Frazer Corporation

1951 The 1952 Packard Twenty-Fifth Series is introduced

1954 The first 1955 Packard is produced

1955 William E. Paris, Vice President of the Willys-Overland Company 1946-1955, dies at age 61

1956 The Divco Corporation acquires the Wayne Works, Inc. and changes its name to the Divco-Wayne Corporation

1957 The 1958 Chryslers are introduced

1957 The 1958 Dodges are introduced

1957 The 1958 Fiats are introduced to the United States market

1957 The 1958 Lincolns are introduced

1961 The 1962 International Scout is introduced

1961 Charles L. Tutt, President of the Pikes Peak Auto Highway Company, dies at age 72

1962 The 1963 International Scout is introduced

1962 Racer Ricardo Rodriguez is killed at age 20 when his Lotus-Climax crashes during a practice run for the first Mexican Grand Prix in Mexico City

1966 The 1967 International Scout is introduced

1967 General Motors elects James M. Roche as Chairman/Chief Executive Officer and Edward N. Cole as President/Chief Operating Officer

1968 Designer Rudolf Hruska takes the first test drive in an Alfasud

1971 The 1972 Fiats are introduced to the United States market

1972 The Mercedes-Benz 280C is introduced to the United States market

1972 The Standard Oil Company of New Jersey changes its name to the Exxon Corporation

1974 Robert D. Lund is named General Manager of Chevrolet

1977 Giuseppe Morandi, winner of the 1927 Mille Miglia, dies at age 83

1979 The Ford Motor Company purchases a 25% equity in the Toyo Kogyo Company, Ltd., Japanese manufacturers of the Mazda

1979 The Subaru 360 Drivers' Club is organized for owners of 2-cylinder Subarus

1982 Honda production begins in the United States as a 1982 Accord rolls off the assembly line at the Marysville, OH plant of the Honda of America Manufacturing Company

1982 Rolls-Royce historian Harold Nockolds dies at age 75

1993 Alexander J. Trotman is elected as Chairman, President, and Chief Executive Officer of the Ford Motor Company

1995 Michael A. Grimaldi is appointed Vehicle Line Executive (VLE) for full-sized trucks and is elected to the Board of Directors of General Motors

1995 Toyota Motor Finland Oy is established with M. Ennevaara as President

NOVEMBER 2

1865 Spencer Penrose, a mining engineer who built the Manitou & Pikes Peak (CO) Railr Peak Auto Highway, is born in Philadelphia, PA

1874 George S. Cawthorne of Rambler is born in Chicago, IL

1881 W. Ledyard Mitchell of the Chrysler Corporation is born in Cincinnati, OH

1889 Robert Fager Black, President of the White Motor Company who previously had held executive positions with Mack and Brockway, is born in Harrisburg, PA

1893 Coachbuilder Battista "Pinin" Farina is born in Turin, Italy

1894 Count Albert de Dion holds a meeting of pioneer automobilists at his home to lay plans for a Paris-Bordeaux (France) race

1895 George B. Selden is issued a United States patent giving him full rights as the inventor of the gasoline automobile

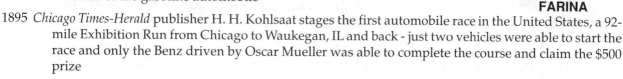

FARINA

1895 *Chicago Times-Herald* publisher H. H. Kohlsaat stages the first automobile race in the United States, a 92-mile Exhibition Run from Chicago to Waukegan, IL and back - just two vehicles were able to start the race and only the Benz driven by Oscar Mueller was able to complete the course and claim the $500 prize

1895 The first issue of *The Autocar* is published in Coventry by John James Henry Sturmey

1896 The first automobile insurance in Great Britain is written by the General Accident Company

1899 James W. Packard and George L. Weiss open a new machine shop separate from other Packard family businesses to produce automobiles

1902 The first gasoline-powered Locomobile is sold to M. M. Riglander of New York City and delivered personally by designer Andrew L. Riker

1908 The Fort Pitt Motor Manufacturing Company of New Kensington, PA registers its "castle" trademark for the Pittsburgh Six automobile produced 1908-1911 - the castle noted its principal promoter, B. G. von Rottweiler, who claimed to be a German baron

1908 Russel Abner Frisbie and G. Stanley Heft of the Frisbie-Heft Motor Company acquire a factory in Middletown, CT but only a single four cylinder prototype is produced as the company decides to build marine engines as a principle endeavour

1915 B. Robert "Woody" Woodill is born in California

1920 Robert Anderson of Plymouth is born in Columbus, NE

1922 Ferdinand P. J. Beickler of Opel is born in Mainz, Germany

1929 The Hungerford rocket-powered car built by brothers Floyd and Daniel Hungerford makes its maiden run in Elmira, NY

1932 The Plymouth Model PC is introduced to its dealers via a 90-minute CBS radio program narrated by commentator Lowell Thomas

1935 The Cord 810 is introduced at the National Automobile Show in New York City - President Franklin D. Roosevelt had urged car manufacturers to advance their introductions of new models by two months to help alleviate the traditional slump in employment during the fall months

1935 The 1936 Chevrolets are introduced

1935 The 1936 Chryslers are introduced

1935 The 1936 DeSotos are introduced

1935 The 1936 Dodges are introduced

1935 The 1936 Hudsons and Terraplanes are introduced

*A 1936 Hudson convertible coupe at the Brown Derby Restaurant
in Hollywood, CA - the good life of the mid-1930's.*

1935 The 1936 Pierce-Arrows are introduced

1935 The 1936 Studebakers are introduced

1942 Ormand E. Hunt is named Executive Vice President of General Motors and placed in charge of the company's mobilization efforts for World War II

1944 Thomas Midgley Jr., a longtime associate of Charles F. Kettering in the development of "Ethyl" gasoline, dies in Worthington, OH at age 55

1946 Racer Alan Jones is born in Melbourne, Victoria, Australia, the son of racer Stan Jones

1950 Ford Motor Company establishes the Office of Defense Products to oversee company participation in the Korean War effort

1951 The first 1952 Pontiac is produced

1954 The first 1955 Willys is produced

1956 Racer Tomas Kaiser is born in Sweden

1959 The first section of the M1 motorway in Great Britain opens to the public

1963 Racer Larry Pearson is born

1965 Craig Breedlove driving the rebuilt Spirit of America-Sonic I raises the land speed record to 555.127 mph at the Bonneville Salt Flats, UT

1968 George P. Dorris, manufacturer of the 1906-1926 Dorris and 1912-1926 Dorris truck, dies at age 95

1969 Automobile historian Frank Ernest Hill dies in New York City at age 81

1978 Lee Iacocca joins the Chrysler Corporation as President and Chief Executive Officer

1989 Carmen Fasanella ends his 68-year career as a taxicab owner and driver in Princeton, NJ

1992 John F. "Jack" Smith Jr. is elected President and Chief Executive Officer of General Motors

1994 Privatization of Renault begins

NOVEMBER 3

1850 Erwin Ross Thomas, founder of the E. R. Thomas Motor Company, is born in Webster, PA

1861 William Doud Packard is born in Warren, OH

1864 Alvaro S. Krotz, designer of the 1908-1912 Sears auto buggy, is born in a log cabin near Defiance, OH

1884 Linwood Andrews Miller, Vice President of the Willys-Overland Company 1920-1933, is born in Salem, NJ

1888 Sir William Fraser, longtime British oil executive, is born in Glasgow, Scotland

1889 Charles Bridgen Lansing, an employee of the Simplex Automobile Company who later served as Vice Chairman of the Colorado Highway Commission, is born in Colorado Springs, CO

1898 Eger Vaughan Murphree of the Standard Oil Development Company is born in Bayonne, NJ

1900 The first National Automobile Show opens at Madison Square Garden in New York City

1904 Charles J. Glidden donates a trophy to the American Automobile Association to be awarded to the winner of the upcoming Glidden Tour, a reliabilty run for automobiles

A 1910 advertising postcard promoting the E-M-F and the Glidden Tour was perhaps most effective in pointing out the urgent need for improved roads.

1908 Kenneth Sholl Ferrand Corley of Joseph Lucas Industries, Ltd. is born in Birmingham, England

1910 The first Colby is completed

1910 Philip Corbin, namesake of the 1905-1912 Corbin, dies - the Corbin Motor Vehicle Company was a subsidiary of the American Hardware Corporation which was controlled by the Corbin family

1911 The Chevrolet Motor Car Company is incorporated with William H. Little as President, William C. Durant as Vice President, and Curtis R. Hatheway as Treasurer

1919 The H.C.S. Motor Company of Indianapolis, IN is incorporated with James C. Murdock as Chairman of the Board, Harry C. Stutz as President, Samuel T. Murdock as Vice President, A. Gordon Murdock as Secretary, and Henry F. Campbell as Treasurer

1919 Peter Morgan, Managing Director of the Morgan Motor Company Ltd. and son of founder H. F. S. Morgan, is born

1928 Attorney Andre de Pfyffer, a Director of Automobile Volvo SA, is born in Lucerne, Switzerland

1930 Trevor Owen Jones, director of the General Motors Proving Grounds 1974-1978 and Chairman of the Libbey-Owens-Ford Company 1987-1994, is born in Maidstone, Kent, England

1943 Racer Gary Irvin is born

1945 T. H. Augustus Duncombe, a medical doctor and motoring enthusiast who invented free wheeling, dies in Pontiac, MI at age 78

1948 Racer Helmuth Koinigg is born in Vienna, Austria

1950 K. T. Keller is elected Chairman of the Chrysler Corporation

1952 Racer Greg Sacks is born in Mattituck, NY

1953 The Dodge Firearrow show car with body by Carrozzeria Ghia is introduced

1953 The first 1954 Henry J is produced

1953 John Davenport Siddeley, Lord Kenilworth,
        Chairman of the Armstrong- Siddeley Motors
        Ltd., dies in Jersey, Channel Islands at age 87

1955 The 1956 Packard Fifty-Sixth Series is introduced

1957 Racer Akihiko Nakaya is born in Japan

1962 Harlow H. Curtice, President of Buick 1933-1948 and President of General Motors 1953-1958, dies in
        Flint, MI at age 69

*Harlow H. Curtice is arguably the most important figure in Buick history, and
this 1951 Special sedan displays the look that this marque attained during his
career. The car is parked at Sylvan Lodge in Wasagaming, Manitoba, Canada, the
headquarters townsite in Riding Mountain National Park.*

1970 David M. Klausmeyer, Design Engineer for the Barley Motor Company 1922-1924, a Chevrolet
        executive 1924-1946, and President of the Marmon-Herrington Company, Inc. 1946-1963,
        dies at age 68

1975 Consolidated Industries, Inc. purchases the Diamond-Reo Truck Division of the White Motor Corporation

1977 Reid Railton, designer of land speed record cars and the Hudson-based 1933-1950 Railton sports car,
        dies in Berkeley, CA at age 82

1979 Evangeline Cote Dahlinger of the Ford Motor Company dies in Port Huron, MI at age 86

1986 General Motors Vice President W. Robert Price resigns

1995 The United States Postal Service issues five antique automobile stamps in New York City - the Ken
        Dallison-designed stamps portray an 1893 Duryea, 1894 Haynes, 1898 Columbia, 1899 Winton, and
        1901 White

NOVEMBER 4

1841 Benjamin Franklin Goodrich is born in Ripley, NY

1868 Camille Jenatzy, land speed record setter and manufacturer of the 1898- 1903 Jenatzy, is born in Brussels, Belgium

1881 G. W. Smith, designer of the Jeffrey Quad truck and later a design engineer with the Nash Motors Company, is born in Foxburg, PA

1884 Harry George Ferguson is born in Dromore, County Down, Northern Ireland

1886 Earle Frederick Johnson of General Motors is born in Moosic, PA

1891 Automobile parts manufacturer Melville C. Mason is born in Rupert, VT

1892 Edward Lane Shea, President and Chairman of the Ethyl Gasoline Corporation, is born in Nashua, NH

1899 Paul Cedric Ackerman of Doble and the Chrysler Corporation is born in Erie, PA

1899 William Collins Whitney and Col. Albert A. Pope reach an agreement with George B. Selden to manufacture automobiles using the Selden patent with royalties of $15 per vehicle (minimum $5,000 per year)

1902 James W. Packard and William A. Hatcher are issued a United States patent for their "H-slot" gearshift gate

1904 John Tilden Robinson, manufacturer of the Robinson in Hyde Park, MA 1900- 1902 before joining with Edward W. Pope to produce the Pope-Robinson, dies

1904 The Indianapolis Auto Racing Association stages its first races at the Indianapolis Fairgrounds - Carl G. Fisher wins the 5-mile handicap race in a Premier, and Jan Clemens wins the 100-mile feature race in a National, setting a dirt track record for that distance of 52.93 mph

1919 Racer Eric Thompson is born in Surbiton, Middlesex, England

1923 William Pettigrew Benton of the Ford Motor Company is born in Laurinburg, NC

1927 The first Marmon V-16 engine is tested

1927 Automotive historian James Michael Laux is born in LaCrosse, WI

1931 Production of the Peerless is suspended

1935 The Antique Automobile Club of America is founded in Philadelphia, PA

1936 James T. Kennedy of the B. F. Goodrich Tire & Rubber Company dies at age 62

1938 The 1939 Fords are introduced

1938 The 1939 Mercury, a new marque manufactured by the Ford Motor Company, is introduced to the public

1939 Packard introduces automobile air conditioning at the 40th National Automobile Show in Chicago, IL

1943 Samuel M. Havens, Vice President of the Wyman-Gordon Company, dies at age 66

1943 Racer Bob Wollek is born in Strasbourg, France

1944 The Scuderia Ferrari factory in Modena, Italy is bombed by the allies

1953 The first General Motors Hydra-Matic transmission is produced at the Willow Run factory, a portion of which was leased from the Kaiser-Frazer Corporation following the August 12th fire at General Motors' Livonia, MI transmission plant

1954 Detroit, MI area dealers are given a preview look at the 1955 Plymouths with "Forward Look" styling by Virgil M. Exner

A 1955 Plymouth Belvedere with "Forward Look" styling and a 1951 Plymouth reflecting K.T. Keller's influence occupying adjoining spaces in front of the First Baptist Church in Brooksville, FL. The difference in visual effect is striking.

1955 Racer Jacques Villeneuve (Sr.) is born in Chambly, Quebec, Canada, the younger brother of racer Gilles Villeneuve

1956 Racer Ross Bentley is born in Vancouver, BC, Canada

1956 Parry H. Paul, an executive of the Autocar Company and antique automobile historian, dies

1956 E. O. Dixon, former Chief Metallurgist of the International Harvester Company, dies

1957 The 1958 Mercurys are introduced

1961 The first races are held at the Kyalami track near Johannesburg, South Africa

1963 Transmission designer Howard W. Simpson dies in Dearborn, MI at age 71

1964 The 3,000,000th Cadillac is produced, a 1965 Fleetwood Brougham

1965 Lee Ann Roberts Breedlove, wife of land speed record holder Craig Breedlove, becomes the first woman to exceed 300 mph reaching 308.50 mph in the Spirit of America at the Bonneville Salt Flats, UT

1968 Racer Derrick Cope is born in San Diego, CA

1968 Racer Horace Gould dies in Southmead, England at age 47

1973 Paul W. Hayes, a Southampton, NY Packard enthusiast and owner of an auto upholstery business, dies in New York City

1976 Racer Toni Ulmen dies in Dusseldorf, West Germany at age 70

NOVEMBER 5

1863 James Ward Packard is born in Warren, OH

1864 Truman Handy Newberry, a director of the Packard Motor Car Company 1903- 1945, is born in Detroit, MI

1870 Albert E. Doman, a designer of automobile electrical equipment, is born in Maiden Bradley, England

1893 William Edward Paris of the Willys-Overland Company is born in Toledo, OH

1895 Raymond Fernand Loewy, an industrial designer long associated with the Studebaker marque, is born in Paris, France

1895 George B. Selden is issued United States Patent #549,160 for his "Road Engine" even though he had never actually built a vehicle or interested another party enough to try his theories which were almost universally thought to be impractical

1895 The Automobile Club de France is founded by Count Albert de Dion, Baron Zuylen de Nyevelt, and journalist Paul Meyan, with Baron de Nyevelt serving as its first President

1896 The Hill & Boll coachbuilding firm registers the Yeovil Motor Car & Cycle Company in Yeovil, Somset, England to manufacture complete cars to the designs of Percival W. Petter

1902 Henri Fournier, driving a Mors at Dourdan, France, raises the land speed record to 76.60 mph

1903 Arthur Duray, driving a 100-hp Gobron-Brillie at Dourdan, France, raises the land speed record to 84.73 mph

1905 Racer Louis Rosier is born in Puy de Dome, Auvergne, France

1914 Philip John Monaghan of General Motors is born in Detroit, MI

1918 In his most ambitious political effort Democrat Henry Ford loses a United States Senate race to Republican Truman H. Newberry by about 7,500 votes out of over 430,000 votes cast

1921 Racer Kurt Adolff is born in Stuttgart, Germany

1926 The Buick 1927 "Goddess" mascot is patented by designer by William Schnell

1938 Automotive parts manufacturer John Miles Burke is born in Glendale, CA

1943 David Beecroft, President of the Society of Automotive Engineers, dies in South Bend, IN at age 68

1950 The first Pebble Beach (CA) Road Races are staged, with the main event won by Phil Hill in a Jaguar XK120

1952 Racer Joe James is killed at age 25 when he crashes during a race in San Jose, CA

1955 John A. Carnie of the Dodge Truck Division, Chrysler Corporation dies

1956 Racer Freddie Dixon dies at age 64

1958 The first MAZ 525 truck is produced at the Byelorussian Automobile Factory in Zhodino, USSR (now Belarus)

1958 Racer Tomas Mezera is born in Australia of Czech ancestry

1959 Paul Galvin, the Motorola executive who popularized the car radio, dies at age 64

1959 Racer Elton Sawyer is born

1965 The prototype Shelby GT 350H is shipped to the Hertz Corporation for testing, the first of 936 Ford Mustang-based muscle cars that would be built to order for the rental car firm

1986 Racer Adolf Brudes dies at age 87

1987 Kutztown Publishing Company purchases *Automobile Quarterly* magazine from Diamandis Communciations, Inc., formerly CBS Magazines

NOVEMBER 6

1878 Frank Ballou Stearns is born in Berea, OH

1893 Edsel Bryant Ford is born in Detroit, MI

1894 Motor truck manufacturer Harold Orwig Hoffman, an executive with White, Autocar, and Indiana, is born in Cleveland, OH

1899 The first Packard is completed and test driven in Warren, OH

1907 Clyde M. Vandeburg, Assistant to the President of the Packard Motor Car Company 1939-1942, is born in Montrose, CO

1907 The first track records are set at Brooklands in England - Frank Newton in a 25.6-hp Napier covers the flying 1/2 mile at 77.92 mph and H. C. Tryon in a 38.4-hp Napier raises this record to 86.75 mph later in the day

1909 Construction begins on the new Springfield Motor Car Company factory in Springfield, IL

1911 Michael Ference Jr. of the Ford Motor Company is born in Whiting, IN

1915 The "Lescina" name is registered as a trademark by the Lescina Automobile Company of Newark, NJ - its name was coined from that of its principal designer, Siegfried Leschziner

1930 Production begins at the Moscow (USSR) Automotive Plant

1933 English Racing Automobiles Ltd. is founded by Raymond Mays to build E.R.A. cars using modified Riley engines

1934 David Noel McCammon of the Ford Motor Company is born in Topeka, KS

1936 The Henry B. Joy, President 1909-1916 of the Packard Motor Car Company, dies in Grosse Pointe Farms, MI at age 71

1936 The Ford Motor Company holds its dealer preview for the 1937 Fords at the Detroit (MI) Coliseum

1939 The Rolls-Royce Ltd. Repairs and Service Departments are relocated to new premises in Willesden, England as the Derby works are entirely devoted to World War II government contract work - the Willesden works would be utilized for special coachwork construction after 1984

1940 George Alan Peapples of General Motors of Canada Ltd., is born in Benton Harbor, MI

1947 The first shipment of post-World War II Rolls-Royce and Bentleys arrives in the United States

1949 Racer Rex Mays is killed at age 36 when his Novi crashes during a race in Del Mar, CA

1951 Production begins at the Zeran Automobile Factory in Warsaw, Poland - the state-owned Fabryka Samochodow Osobowych initially manufactures the Warszawa, based heavily on the Russian Pobieda

1951 The Kuwait Oil Company (London) Ltd. is registered

1953 The first Arnolt Aston Martin is completed by Carrozzeria Bertone

1954 Construction of the Cadillac Park Avenue show car begins - the car with modifications would later be produced as the ultra-luxuray Eldorado Brougham

1954 Automotive historian Garet Garrett dies in Atlantic City, NJ at age 76

1955 Racer Jack McGrath is killed at age 36 during a race in Phoenix, AZ

1970 Edwin Foster Blair, a Director of the Packard Motor Car Company 1950-1957 (the Studebaker-Packard Corporation after 1954), dies at age 68

1978 Buick General Manager David C. Collier is promoted to executive in charge of General Motor's new finance group, and is succeeded at Buick by General Motors of Canada Ltd. President Donald H. McPherson

1986 Alfa Romeo rejects Ford Motor Company's acquisition bid, and approves a takeover offer from Fiat

1987 The Henry Ford Museum's "The Automobile in American Life" opens

1995 Buick General Manager Edward H. Mertz announces "US Olympic Gold" versions of the 1996 Buick Regal and Skylark models to commemorate General Motors' sponsorship of the 1996 United States Olympic Team

NOVEMBER 7

1865   Automobile wheel manufacturer George W. Houk is born in Wellsboro, PA

1869   Wilfred Chester Leland is born in Worcester, MA

1877   Lamonte Judson Belnap, President of Rolls-Royce of America, Inc. 1919-1925, is born in Burr Oak, MI

1880   John Nicol of Federal, GMC, and Divco is born in Detroit, MI

1883   Owen Milton Nacker, designer of the Cadillac V-16 engine, is born in Highland, MI

1890   Wilfred Leland joins his father's precision machining partnership with Robert C. Faulconer and Charles H. Norton

1896   Barthold Theodoor Wilhelm Van Hasselt of the Royal Dutch/Shell Group is born in Leiden, the Netherlands

1897   Norman Clare Damon, a former Hudson official and organizer of the Automotive Safety Foundation, is born in Gerry, NY

1900   Packard's first full-page magazine advertisement appears in *The Horseless Age*

1911   Racer Frankie Del Roy (nee Frank DeRosa) is born in Philadelphia, PA

1918   E. Ralph Estep, first Editor of *The Packard*, dies in Sedan, France

This 1918 Packard Twin Six touring fits perfectly into the 1916-1920 era when this was the only model offered by Packard and arguably was one of the world's best cars.

1918 Alfred P. Sloan Jr. is elected to the board of General Motors

1924 The Ford Motor Company acquires C. E. Johansson, Inc., manufacturers of "Joe Blocks" precision gauging equipment

1924 The first AMO F-15 trucks are produced at the Moscow Automotive Plant

1925 Alan Herbert Foster of American Motors is born in Somerville, MA

1928 The Packard "Daphne at the Well" mascot is patented

1930 Automotive journalist David E. Davis Jr. is born

1932 Automobile historian John Jerome is born in Tulsa, OK

1933 Gordon M. Buehrig does two pencil sketches of a "baby Duesenberg", a proposition that would evolve into the 1936 Cord 810

1936 The 1937 Chevrolets are introduced featuring Unisteel Bodies by Fisher

1937 The Horseless Carriage Club of America is founded in Los Angeles, CA by W. Everett Miller, Arthur E. Twohy, and William E. Wakefield

1939 John Leopold Egan of Jaguar is born in Rawtenstall, Lancashire, England

1940 The Tacoma (WA) Narrows Bridge collapses

1941 J. B. Franks Jr., a longtime official with the White Motor Company, dies in Chestnut Hill, PA

1943 Harry J. Worthington, an antiques dealer who acquired many items on behalf of Henry Ford for the Henry Ford Museum and Greenfield Village, dies in Doylestown, PA at age 73

1943 Max L. Tost, German-born official of the American Bosch Corporation since 1910, dies at age 63

1945 Gus Edwards, composer of the 1905 song "In My Merry Oldsmobile", dies at about age 64

1948 Racer Alex Ribeiro is born in Belo Horizonte, Brazil

1949 The Kaiser-Frazer Corporation changes the serial number plates on all unsold 1949 Frazers and introduces them as 1950 models

1950 Wallace T. Holliday, Chairman of the Standard Oil Company of Ohio 1949-1950, dies in Cleveland, OH at age 66

1951 George W. Proctor, a Chevrolet employee and official since 1919, dies in Detroit, MI at age 58

1952 The last 1952 Pontiac is produced

1956 The 9,000,000th Buick is produced

1956 Racer Jonathan Palmer is born in London, England

1957 The first Trabant is produced in the former Horch works in Zwickau, DDR with the name of the new marque commemorating the recent Russian-launched earth satellite, the Sputnik

1957 The 1958 Fords are introduced

1958 Jack F. Chrysler, an official of the Chrysler Corporation 1934-1937 and Vice President of the W. P. Chrysler Building Corporation 1939-1953, dies at age 46

1960 Racer Red Byron dies in Chicago, IL from a heart attack at age 44

1965 Art Arfons, driving the Green Monster at the Bonneville Salt Flats, UT, raises the land speed record to 576.553 mph

1967 Racer Ian Raby dies in London, England at age 46 from injuries suffered on July 30th during a Formula 2 race in Zandvoort, the Netherlands

1969 Georges Roesch of Talbot dies at age 78

1974 Josef Rust of Volkswagen resigns as Chairman of the Supervisory Board and is replaced by Hans Birnbaum

1975 Piero Dusio of Cisitalia dies in Buenos Aires, Argentina at age 76

1988 William E. Prior is ousted as President of Global Motors, Inc., the United States importers of the Yugo

1995 Racer Bill Stroppe dies at age 76

NOVEMBER 8

1864 Abraham Lincoln is elected to his second term as President of the United States - one of Lincoln's supporters is 21-year-old Henry M. Leland, who would refer to his first presidential vote as the inspiration for naming the luxury marque that he began producing in 1920

1866 Herbert Austin, founder of the Austin Motor Company Ltd. in 1905, is born in Little Missenden, Buckinghamshire, England

1883 Carl M. Breer of the Chrysler Corporation is born in Los Angeles, CA

1908 The Hupp Motor Car Corporation is organized in Detroit, MI with J. Walter Drake as President along with Robert C. Hupp, Edward Denby, Charles D. Hastings, Otto von Bachelle, Joseph R. Drake, John E. Blake, and Emil A. Nelson in other executive positions

1908 Electric automobile pioneer William Edward Ayrton dies in London, England at age 61

1909 Victor Hemery, driving the Blitzen Benz at Brooklands, England, records an official timing of 125.95 mph, the land speed record for gasoline- powered cars but just short of the 1906 speed set by Fred Marriott in the Stanley steam-powered "Wogglebug"

1913 A. R. Welch, manufacturer of the 1903-1911 Welch, dies during a hunting vacation when his canoe capsizes during a sudden storm

1915 Robert M. Burns of the Holley Carburetor Company is born in Spurgeon, IN

1915 John N. Willys establishes the Guaranty Securities Company, a pioneer firm specializes in financing retail automobile sales

1916 The International Motor Company reorganizes as the International Motor Truck Corporation, with their principal business the manufacture of Mack trucks

1918 The McLaughlin Motor Car Company of Canada is absorbed by General Motors

1921 Oakland General Manager George Hannum announces that testing of the new copper-cooled engine has been unsuccessful

1930 Stanford A. Smith of Maxwell and Lexington dies at age 40

1930 Neumaticos Goodyear SA is established in Buenos Aires, Argentina

1931 Racer Peter Collins is born in Kidderminster, England

1933 Racer Peter John Arundell is born in Ilford, Essex, England

1938 Harry Laurance Fuller of the Amoco Corporation is born in Moline, IL

1946 Racer Richard Scott is born in Aberdeen, Scotland

1947 Racer Giorgio Francia is born in San Giorgio di Plano, Bologna, Italy

1954 Ralph L. Busse, retired Vice President of the Timken-Detroit Axle Company and an employee of the firm since 1915-1951, dies at age 64

1955 The West Virginia Turnpike opens to the public

1956 The Ford Motor Company selects "Edsel" as the name of its new marque to be introduced for the 1958 model year

1957 The 1958 Oldsmobiles are introduced - among the cars actually produced on this day is the marque's 6,000,000th, a Holiday Ninety-Eight four-door hardtop

1957 James R. McClelland of the Imperial Oil Company Ltd. dies at age 57

1971 William Klein Jr., a chocolate manufacturer and noted collector of classic Rolls-Royce and Bentleys, dies in Harrisburg, PA at age 54

1978 Buick Chief Engineer Lloyd E. Reuss is promoted to the same position with Chevrolet, and is succeeded at Buick by Robert J. Schultz

1984 Sir Michael Edwardes of British Leyland Ltd. is named Chairman of the Dunlop Rubber Company Ltd.

1985 Masten Gregory, winner of the 1965 Le Mans 24 hour race, dies in Rome, Italy at age 53

NOVEMBER 9

1861 Jules Semon Bache of the Chrysler Corporation is born in New York City

1865 Charles Leonard Bowden, Sales Manager for the Elmore Manufacturing Company 1910-1912, is born in Ogdensburg, NY

1872 W. A. Brush of Buick and Packard is born in Detroit, MI

1875 Artemus Ward Jr., President of the King Motor Car Company 1912-1920, is born in Philadelphia, PA

1893 Clyde Colvin DeWitt, a chemist with the Ford Motor Company 1916-1917, is born in Hyndman, PA

1908 The first Cactus Derby, a 511-mile desert road race from Los Angeles, CA to Phoenix, AZ, begins and is won by F. C Fenner and H. D. Ryus driving a White steamer

1917 Race promoter John Clarence Holman is born in Nashville, TN

1926 John W. Swan contracts with General Motors for the use of his Swan intake manifold

1928 Automotive parts manufacturer Bernard Harvey Marrington is born in Vancouver, BC, Canada

1929 Racer Joe Lee Johnson is born in Cowpens, SC

1932 The Pierce-Arrow V-12 is introduced

1932 The A & K Petroleum Company is incorporated in Delaware - the firm would evolve into the Kerr-McGee Corporation

1937 Waldo D. Waterman is issued a United States patent for his Arrowbile, a combination automobile/airplane

1938 Goldie Gardner driving the M.G. EX135 on the Dessau (Germany) Autobahn sets Class G records for the mile (187.62 mph) and the kilometer

1952 William N. Booth of the Kelsey-Hayes Wheel Corporation dies in Lake Worth, FL at age 86

1955 Racer Rick Carelli is born

1955 The 1956 Ford Thunderbirds are introduced

1956 The 1957 Oldsmobiles are introduced

1956 The 1957 Pontiacs are introduced

1960 Robert S. McNamara is named President of the Ford Motor Company by Chairman Henry Ford II

1960 The 4,000,000th Volkswagen is produced

A circa-1960 gathering at the summit of the Grimsel Pass in southern Switzerland includes an interesting group of European cars including a Land Rover, a Citroen, and of course a Volkswagen.

1960 Ford Motor Company establishes the Automotive Assembly Division to operate 17 car and truck assembly plants within the company

1962 The Ford Rotunda in Dearborn, MI is destroyed by fire - 13,189,694 people had visited the landmark since its 1953 reopening

NOVEMBER 10

1855 Pierre-Alexandre Darracq is born in Bordeaux, France

1885 Paul Daimler completes a two-mile round trip between Canstatt and Unterturkheim, Germany on the two-wheeled gasoline-powered vehicle recently built by his father, Gottlieb Daimler - although of little practical value, this event is often cited as the first motorcycle drive

1890 Carl F. W. Borgward is born in Altona (now a part of Hamburg), Germany

1894 John Raymond Davis of the Ford Motor Company, is born in Oil City, PA

1910 A Hupmobile begins a promotional round-the-world trip

1910 Oscar Alexis Lundin of General Motors is born in Detroit, MI

1924 Michael Humenik of the Ford Motor Company is born in Garfield, NJ

1925 James V. Rose of the Chrysler Corporation is born in Detroit, MI

1926 Racer Art Bisch is born in Mesa, AZ

1929 Automotive historian William Edward Butterworth III is born in Newark, NJ

1930 The Marmon Sixteen debuts at the Chicago (IL) Auto Show

1930 The Moon Motor Car Company closes its St. Louis, MO factory

1933 Giustino Cattaneo resigns from the Fabbrica Automobili Isotta-Fraschini Board of Directors

1934 Racer Lucien Bianchi is born in Milan, Italy

1935 Charles T. Jeffery of the Thomas B. Jeffery Company dies

1937 The Ford Motor Company holds its dealer preview for the 1938 Fords in Louisville, KY

1940 Edsel authority Leroy Murry Walker is born in Zap, ND

1942 The first GMC amphibious truck, dubbed the "Duck", is completed

1949 The 1950 Pontiacs are introduced

A Texaco service station, Steve's Cafe, and a 1950 Pontiac Catalina hardtop coupe in Chenoa, IL on Route 66 - mid 20th century Americana at its best.

1950 Col. Herbert W. Alden of the Timken-Detroit Axle Company, often cited as the designer of the first army tank, dies in Trenton, MI at age 79

1951 The 1952 Dodges are introduced

1953 The Kaiser-Frazer Corporation sells its Willow Run factory to General Motors

1954 Alvin G. Tanner of the Socony-Vacuum Oil Company dies at age 65

1956 Harry F. Sinclair, founder of the Sinclair Oil Company in 1916, dies in Pasadena, CA at age 80

1960 The 1961 Ford Thunderbirds are introduced

1965 Racer Eddie Irvine is born in Conlig, Northern Ireland

1977 California antique car collector M. L. "Bud" Cohn dies in London, England at age 81 during his third visit to the London-Brighton Run with his 1893 Benz Velo

1978 The 1,000,000th Mazda Wankel rotary engine is produced

1988 Gerald Greenwald is named Vice Chairman of the Chrysler Corporation

1989 Donald E. Petersen, President of the Ford Motor Company, resigns and is succeeded by Harold A. Poling

1992 The 250,000th Mazda Miata is produced

NOVEMBER 11

1852 Robert Boyd Ward, founder of the Ward Motor Vehicle Company, is born in New York City

1874 Clement Orville Miniger, a developer of automobile batteries, is born in North East, PA

1886 Alice Huyler Ramsey, the first woman to drive an automobile across the United States, is born in Hackensack, NJ

1906 Peugeot makes its official racing debut finishing 3rd, 4th, and 8th in a 126.1-mile race in Rambouillet, France

1907 Gunnar Ludwig Engellau of Volvo is born in Sweden

1908 Racer Don Parker is born in Ramsgate, Kent, England

1909 Racer Piero Scotti is born in Florence, Italy

1912 Thomas Clifton Mann of the Automobile Manufacturers Association is born in Laredo, TX

1916 The A. O. Smith Corporation is reorganized in New York, succeeding the 1904 company founded by Arthur Oliver Smith

1922 Walter P. Chrysler signs a contract with the ZSB Engineering Company to develop ZSB's car design as the 1924 Chrysler Six

1923 William D. Packard dies in Warren, OH at age 62

1925 Bamford & Martin Ltd., manufacturers of the Aston Martin, is forced into receivership

1925 John H. Dohner, inventor of the Dohner compression coupling, dies in Dayton, OH at age 63

1926 The Midwest Aircraft Corporation is established as a subsidiary of the Marmon Motor Car Company to design and develop a V-16 automobile engine in total secrecy

1926 Racer Maria-Teresa de Filippis is born in Italy

1926 Louis Meyer makes his racing debut in Charlotte, NC

1926 Robert Blake Jackson, biographer of F. E. and F. O. Stanley, is born in Hartford, CT

1928 Racer William Edgar Justice is born in Forsyth County, NC

1930 The Chrysler 1931-1932 "Winged Cap/Gazelle" mascot is patented by designer Herbert V. Henderson

The 1931 Chrysler Imperial Eight - marketed as "The Masterpiece" - carried Herbert V. Henderson's new mascot.

1933 Racer Martino Finotto is born in Italy

1934 The Briarcliff Trophy Race in Briarcliff, NY is staged for the first time since 1908 with the 99-mile race being won by Langdon Quimby in a Willys 77

1935 The Ford Motor Company exhibit at the California-Pacific Exposition in San Diego, CA closes after hosting 2,552,199 visitors

1937 Racer Vittorio Brambilla is born in Monza, Italy, the younger brother of racer Tino Brambilla

1937 Racer Samuel David "Sam" McQuagg is born in Columbus, GA

1940 John F. Klink, promoter of the 1907-1910 Klink manufactured in Dansville, NY, dies at age 71

1940 The first Willys-built Jeep prototype is presented to the United States Army for testing

1942 John J. Klein, assistant to President Arthur W. Herrington of the Marmon-Herrington Company, Inc., dies from pneumonia at age 32

1946 The 1947 Packards are introduced

The classic Packard grille is still prominent on this 1947 Clipper photographed in Monterey, Mexico.

1946 Racer Al Holbert is born in Pennsylvania

1952 Richard W. Jackson, a Vice President of the Hudson Motor Car Company, is shot to death in Detroit, MI at age 40

1957 Racer Dean Hall is born in Palo Alto, CA

1967 Racer Gil de Ferran is born in Paris, France

1967 Racer Roy Payne is born in Alvin, TX

1973 Racer Rob Morgan is born in Conway, AR

1976 Billy Arnold, winner of the 1930 Indianapolis 500 in which he became the first winner to average better than 100 mph while driving without relief, dies at age 70

1972 Ronnie Hoseholder, a racer and Chrysler Corporation executive, dies of cancer in Detroit, MI

1978 Mazda produces its 1,000,000th Wankel rotary engine

1989 The Ford Motor Company acquires Jaguar PLC for $2.5 billion

1989 Robert A. Boyer of the Ford Motor Company dies in Dunedin, FL at age 80

NOVEMBER 12

1879 Leonard Pinkney Steuart, a longtime Washington, DC automobile dealer, is born in Branchville, MD

1901 Automobile stylist Alexis de Sakhnoffsky is born in Kiev, Ukraine, the son of Count Wladimir de Sakhnoffsky, aide to Czar Nicholas II

1902 Sven E. Dithmer of General Motors is born in Bucharest, Romania

1904 Max Edwin Hoffman, a leading United States importer of foreign cars, is born in Vienna, Austria

1908 General Motors purchases all common stock of the Olds Motor Works, with Olds executives Frederick L. Smith and Henry Russel joining the General Motors Board of Directors

1909 The Daimler Motoren Gesellschaft registers the "Mercedes" name (without accents) as a trademark

1912 The United States Supreme Court rules that the Selden patent is "valid but not violated", effectively ending its impact on the domestic automobile industry

1914 Racer Peter Whitehead is born in Menston, Yorkshire, England

1916 Racer Paul Emery is born in Chiswick, Great Britain

1920 Frank H. Ball, builder of two Ball automobiles in 1903 and with his son Fred O. Ball the inventor of the Ball & Ball carburetor as manufactured by the Penberthy Injector Company, dies in Detroit, MI at age 73

1927 The 2,000,000th Dodge is produced

1928 Racers Earl de Vore and Norman Batten, winning codriver of the 1925 Indianapolis 500, are lost at sea enroute to South Africa aboard the SS Vestris

1932 W. Hubert Beal, President of the Lycoming Manufacturing Company, is named President of the Auburn Automobile Company to succeed E. L. Cord who would remain as Chairman of the Board

1934 Albert E. Doman, a designer of automobile electrical equipment, dies in Elbridge, NY at age 64

1943 Rally driver Bjorn Waldergard is born in Sweden

1945 Racer George Eaton is born in Toronto, ON, Canada

1949 The Volkswagen Type 2, later named the Transporter, is introduced

1953 Dodge introduces its Firearrow sports roadster, a one-off concept car that would appear at upcoming United States automobile shows

1954 The 1955 Jeep CJ-5 is introduced

1956 The Ford Ranchero is introduced in Quitman, GA

1956 Peerless Motor Car Company design engineer Elverton W. Weaver dies in Cleveland Heights, OH

1960 The 1961 Ford Thunderbird is introduced, the third generation of the sub-marque

1964 Paula Murphy, driving Art Arfons' J46 rocket-powered car at the Bonneville Salt Flats, UT, sets a women's land speed record of 226.37 mph

1965 Bob Summers of Ontario, CA raises the LSR for axle-drive, piston-engined automobiles to 409.277 mph in the Chrysler-powered "Goldenrod" at the Bonneville Salt Flats, UT, regaining the record for the United States after 37 years of British ownership

1966 Racer Don Branson is killed at age 46 when he crashes during a midget race at the Ascot Motor Speedway in Gardena, CA

1967 Ernest C. Kanzler of the Ford Motor Company dies in Grosse Pointe Farms, MI at age 75

1978 The Central Mississippi Valley Chapter of the Hudson-Essex-Terraplane Club, Inc. holds its first meeting in Burlington, IA

1986 The United States introduction of the Bentley Eight is held in New York City

1987 William Clay Ford is named Chairman of the Finance Committee for the Ford Motor Company

NOVEMBER 13

1824 Joseph Staggi, a Roman Catholic priest who built the first automobile in Florence, Italy in the 1850's, is born in Italy

1860 Charles Henry John Chetwynd-Talbot, 20th Earl of Shrewbury, is born in London, England - in 1903 the Earl began importing the Clement designed by the Frenchman Adolphe Clement, and by year's end the marque was being manufactured in London as the Talbot

1877 Automobile accessories manufacturer Samuel Alexander Fulton is born in Clay County, IL

1878 Carlton R. Mabley of S & M Simplex is born in Detroit, MI

1893 Charles Tell Lawson of American Motors is born in White Stone, VA

1896 The Arnold prototype, a German-made Benz with an engine designed by William Arnold, makes its initial test run from East Peckham, Kent, England to Bromley and return

1903 Sales Manager Charles A. Wardle is dismissed because it was found "his services can be dispensed with" - he was the first employee of the Ford Motor Company to be terminated

1904 P. Baras, driving a Darracq at Ostend, Belgium, raises the land speed record to 104.52 mph

1908 The Ford Model T is introduced into Europe with a showing in London, England

1909 Automotive historian Albert Robert Bochroch is born in Philadelphia, PA

1910 The first Colby automobile is tested in Mason City, IA

THE COLBY MODEL H. FORE DOOR
FIVE-PASSENGER TOURING CAR
$1,750.00. TOP, $85.00 EXTRA

During the pre-1930 era hundreds of small automobile companies were conceived.
The Colby of Mason City, IA seemed to be one of the more promising
of this lot but lasted only until 1914.

1916 E. L. Cord wins his first automobile race, a 273-mile run from Douglas to Phoenix, AZ driving a Paige

1917 William Mahony O'Brien of the Chrysler Corporation is born in Chicago, IL

1927 The Holland Tunnel between New York City and Jersey City, NJ officially opens to traffic

1928 Capt. George White of the Army Air Corps stages the first United States test of rocket-powered vehicles at the Velodrome in New York City, but his unmanned motorcycle reaches just 17 mph

1933 Auto Union's new Grand Prix car is taken for its first test drive by Willy Walb at the Nurburgring in Germany

Two Auto Union C-Types and a Mercedes-Benz W125 occupy the front row with more of the same in the rear. Grand Prix racing in the late 1930's was dominated to unprecedented levels by these two marques.

1934 The 10,000,000th Chevrolet is produced, a 1935 Standard 4-door Sedan built in Flint, MI that would later be presented to the Flint Police Department

1940 The Willys-Overland Company completes its first prototype Jeep based on the design created by American Bantam Car Company

1943 Henri Toutee, Chief Engineer of Chenard-Walcker, dies at age 59

1945 Racer Masahiro Hasemi is born in Tokyo, Japan

1947 The 20,000,000th Chevrolet is produced

1954 Raymond S. Saddoris, and official of the A. O. Smith Corporation since 1921, dies at age 56

1954 William N. Hinds, a sales official with Hudson, Ford, and Willys-Overland before starting his own business in 1953, dies at age 59

1955 Carleton H. Schlesman, an official with the Standard Oil Company of New York and the Socony-Vacuum Oil Company before joining the Naval Ordnance Laboratory in 1948, dies

1956 Robert W. Lea of the Stephens Motor Car Company dies at age 70

1958 Dr. Heinz Nordhoff, President of Volkswagenwerk AG, and the late Dr. Ferdinand Porsche are given the 1958 Elmer A. Sperry Award for the design of the Volkswagen

1965 A. G. Elliott of Rolls-Royce dies at age 84

1966 Racer Dick Atkins dies from injuries suffered the previous day during a race at the Ascot Motor Speedway in Gardena, CA

1969 Racer Jeret Schroeder is born in Queens, NY

1973 The Copper Development Association leases their experimental CDA Electric van to the Birmingham, MI Water Meter Department to test the vehicle's feasibility under real-world conditions

1978 LeRoy Spencer of Packard dies in San Francisco, CA at age 85

1984 Racer Cliff Woodbury dies

1986 Racer Franco Cortese, winner of the 1951 Targa Florio, dies at age 83

1988 The Saudi Arabian Oil Company is incorporated to succeed the Arabian American Oil Company (Aramco)

1995 The Ford Motor Company announces that Louis R. Ross will retire as Vice Chairman and Chief Technical Officer at the end of the year

NOVEMBER 14

1861 Crankshaft manufacturer Lyman Francis Gordon is born in Worcester, MA

1896 Thirty motorists drive from London to Brighton, England to celebrate the Emancipation Act that lifted most anti-automobile restrictions - two Duryea cars participate as part of the English introduction of the marque

1899 A. Horch & Cie. is organized in Cologne-Ehrenfeld, Germany

1905 The Packard Motor Car Company is granted a trademark for its "Packard" script logo

1910 Racer William H. Sharp dies two days after his Sharp-Arrow crashed during the American Grand Prize race in Savannah, GA - his car would become the basis for the Mercer Raceabout

1914 The first Dodge, a tourer later named "Old Betsy", is completed and shipped to a customer in Nashville, TN

1920 The prototype Duesenberg Model A, the first passenger car to bear the Duesenberg name, is introduced in unpainted form at the Automobile Salon held in the Hotel Commodore in New York City

1922 Earl A. Thompson is issued a patent for his "Automatic Gear Shifting Mechanism for Sliding Gear Transmission" later known as "Synchro-Mesh" for trademark purposes

1927 Automotive historian William M. "Bill" Libby is born in Atlantic City, NJ

1928 The Bayerische Motoren-Werke (BMW), an Eisenach, Germany motorcycle manufacturer, purchases the Dixi-Werke AG from Gothaer Waggonfabrik AG to enter the automobile industry

1929 Racer DeWayne Louis "Tiny" Lund is born in Harlan, IA

1930 The Veteran Car Club, the world's first organization dedicated to the preservation of antique automobiles, is founded by S. C. H. "Sammy" Davis, J. A. Master, and J. A. Wylie

1931 The 1932 Buicks are introduced

1936 The 1937 Fords are introduced in two series with different V-8 engines

1940 The Alvis plant in Coventry, England is one of 21 factories destroyed during a Nazi air raid, although the overall productive capacity of the city's automotive industry is not seriously affected

1943 Author Craig Thomas Norback, a frequent contributor to the Chilton Company's automobile guides, is born in Pittsburgh, PA

1944 Racer Joe Saldana is born

1945 Anton "Tony" Hulman purchases the Indianapolis Motor Speedway Company from Edward V. Rickenbacker for $750,000

1945 Racer Robert Brett Lunger is born in Wilmington, DE

1946 Racer Irv Hoerr is born in Peoria, IL

1951 The 1952 Packard 25th Series is introduced on a nationwide television comedy special hosted by Red Skelton

1954 Racer Eliseo Salazar is born in Santiago, Chile

1955 Thomas Carney, retired Chief Engineer for the International Harvester Company whose previous automotive career included stints with Anderson Electric, Packard, and Willys-Overland, dies

1955 Racer Ted Prappas is born in Santa Monica, CA

1962 The Jeep Wagoneer is introduced

1965 Hap Sharp, driving a Chaparral, wins the first race at the Stardust Road Course in Las Vegas, NV

1977 George Schoeneck, designer of the 1919-1924 Climber manufactured in Little Rock, AR, dies in Gastonia, NC

1990 Shigeo Shingo of Toyota dies in Tokyo, Japan at age 81

1995 Renato Ambrosini of Siata dies at age 70

1996 The first regular production General Motors EV-1 electric-powered coupe rolls off the assembly line in Lansing, MI

NOVEMBER 15

1839 Steam-powered vehicle pioneer William Murdock dies at Sycamore Hill near Soho, England at age 85

1853 Automotive journalist Horace M. Swetland, the first member of the Society of Automotive Engineers, is born in Erie County, PA

1874 David Roger Wilson of the Willys-Overland Company is born in Warren, OH

During his 5-year term as Willys-Overland President David R. Wilson concentrated on small cars with modest success. The 1937 Willys sedan parked at left in Redwood Falls, MN is typical of the Wilson era.

1875 Amedee Bollee Sr. successfully tests his Bollee-Dalifol vehicle in a run from La Villette to Belleville, France

1898 Fowler McCormick of the International Harvester Company is born in Chicago, IL

1903 George L. Weiss resigns as a Director and Vice President of the Packard Motor Car Company

1908 Carlo (nee Karl) Abarth is born in Vienna, Austria

1909 The first prototype Detroit-Dearborn designed by Paul Arthur is test driven - the Detroit-Dearborn Motor Car Company of Dearborn, MI was organized by Edward Bland, Arthur L. Kiefer, Elmer W. Foster, and Samuel D. Lapham, but would be bankrupt before the end of 1910 after producing 110 cars

1909 The 1,000th Hupmobile is produced

1911 The Mora Motor Car Company of Newark, NY is liquidated at auction with its factory, nine acres of land, 50 cars, and assorted parts realizing $120,000

1912 Automotive parts manufacturer Horace Armor Shepard is born in Purvis, MS

1916 Carl M. Breer begins his automotive career as head of the new Engineering Research Department of the Studebaker Corporation

1917 Frederick H. Clarke, Dr. Henry F. Clarke, F. J. Nagel, and J. H. Simpson are convicted of mail fraud in connection with the affairs of the Kent Motors Corporation of Newark, NJ

1924 The Murray Body Company is founded in Detroit, MI to manufacture automobile bodies

1927 Race car designer Harry A. Miller is issued a United States patent for his front wheel drive mechanism

1930 The 1931 Chevrolets are introduced

*A 1931 Chevrolet Independence Series AE Cabriolet (one of 23,077 built),
a mobile home, and a dog no doubt made this man a happy camper.*

1930 The Moon Motor Car Company is placed into receivership

1935 The 1936 Nash Ambassador Series 3610 and 3680 are introduced

1938 Herbert Howard Rice, President and General Manager of the Cadillac Motor Car Company 1921-1925, dies at age 68

1939 Jaakko Ihamuotila of Neste OY is born in Helsinki, Finland

1950 The 1951 Lincolns are introduced

1950 Ernest J. Sweetland, inventor of the Purolator oil filter manufactured by Motor Improvement, Inc. of Newark, NJ, dies in San Francisco, CA at age 70

1959 Hooper & Company (Coachbuilders) Ltd. closes after 154 years

1959 Fred I. Tone, designer of the American Underslung, dies at age 81

1960 Karl E. Scott is elected President of Ford Motor Company of Canada Ltd.

1961 George W. Romney resigns from American Motors to pursue a political career

1962 Roy Abernethy, President, General Manager, and Chief Operating Officer of American Motors, is given the additional title of Chief Executive Officer

1965 The 1966 Opels are introduced to the United States market

1965 Craig Breedlove driving the Spirit of America-Sonic I raises the land speed record to 600.601 mph at the Bonneville Salt Flats, UT

1965 Warren C. MacFarlane, former Auburn official and longtime President of the Minneapolis-Moline Company, dies in Minneapolis, MN at age 82

1966 The 1,000,000th automobile is registered in Rome, Italy

1968 Cyrus R. Osborn of General Motors dies at age 71

1970 Tsuneji Matsuda, President of the Toyo Kogyo Company, Ltd. and creator of the Mazda automobile, dies

1973 The 1974 Fiats are introduced to the United States market

1974 The 1975 AMC models are introduced

1977 The 100,000,000th United States-built Ford Motor Company vehicle, a 1978 Ford Fairmont Futura 4-door sedan, is produced at the Mahwah, NJ plant

NOVEMBER 16

1881 Herbert Alfred Gidney of the Gulf Oil Company is born in Boston, MA

1885 James Walter Tiscornia, the developer of disc brakes, is born in San Andreas, CA

1887 Investment banker Charles Fisher Glore, a Director of the Studebaker Corporation and the Stewart-Warner Corporation, is born in Eureka Springs, AR

1888 Charles W. McKinley of the Willys-Overland Company is born in Toledo, OH

1888 Taizo Ishida of Toyota is born in Kosugai, Chita, Aichi, Japan

1901 Andrew L. Riker, driving a Riker electric car at Coney Island in Brooklyn, NY, sets a United States record for the mile run of 57.14 mph, but is well behind the effort of Frenchman Henri Fournier, who reaches 69.498 mph in his Mors

1904 Los Angeles, CA records its first automobile theft, a White steam-powered touring car, which is later recovered

1906 Frank Clifford McCoard of the Ford Motor Company is born in Payette, ID

1909 Gasmotorenfabrik Deutz AG notifies Ettore Bugatti that the company will terminate his license agreement as of December 15, 1909

1911 Ettore Bugatti signs a contract with Peugeot to produce his 30th design as the Peugeot Bebe

1915 Pierre S. DuPont succeeds Thomas Neal as Chairman of General Motors, with Charles W. Nash continuing as President

1916 The eleventh and last Vanderbilt Cup race is held in Santa Monica, CA and won by Dario Resta in a Peugeot

1918 Automotive historian Joergen Ditlev Scheel is born in Denmark

1920 Hare's Motors, Inc. announces the acquisition of the Kelly-Springfield Motor Truck Company

1934 David Perry Williams of the Edward G. Budd Manufacturing Company is born in Detroit, MI

1936 Gianpaolo Dallara of Lamborghini and Iso is born in Verano, Italy

1936 Frank Henry Mason III of the Ford Motor Company born in Paris, TN

1936 Racer Skip Barber is born in Carlisle, PA

1936 Racer John Mahler is born

1937 Ferdinand Porsche is issued a United States patent for his torsion-bar suspension

1946 Robert E. Healy of Martin Wasp dies at age 63

1946 Earl W. Kimball, an employee of Franklin who in 1919 helped organize and was Vice President of the Ostendorf Motor Corporation and later was an executive in the oil industry, dies

1950 Cadillac achieves six-figure model year production for the first time - the 100,000th 1950 Cadillac is a Fleetwood Sixty Special Sedan

1954 John W. Whitehead, the Australian-born President of the Norwalk Tire & Rubber Company, dies in Norwalk, CT at age 64

1955 Leonard Dyer, inventor of the "H-pattern" gearshift gate and other automobile improvements, dies in Winter Park, FL at age 82

1956 Racer Terry Labonte is born in Corpus Christi, TX

1956 E. Waldo Stein of the Firestone Tire & Rubber Company dies at age 65

1958 Racer Roberto Guerrero is born in Medellin, Colombia

1959 R. K. Braunsdorff of the Tung-Sol Electric Company, a developer of automotive directional signal lights and sealed-beam headlights, dies at age 63

1961 The 1962 Ford Fairlane is introduced as a new mid-sized series

1962 Racer Mike Groff is born in Van Nuys, CA

1964 The 1965 Opels are introduced to the United States market

1967 Eiji Toyoda is appointed as a Vice President of the Japan Automobile Manufacturers Association (JAMA)

1984 John Cote Dahlinger, the alleged illegitimate son of Henry Ford, dies of cancer in Saginaw, MI at age 61

1996 A monument honoring brothers John F. & Horace E. Dodge is dedicated at the site of their birthplace in Niles, MI

NOVEMBER 17

1861 John Gary Anderson, manufacturer of the 1910 Rock Hill and 1916-1924 Anderson cars, is born in Lawsonville, NC

1865 William Meriam Burton of the Standard Oil Company of Indiana is born in Cleveland, OH

1902 Augieres, driving a Mors at Dourdan, France, raises the land speed record to 77.13 mph

1906 Soichiro Honda is born in Iwata-Gun (now Tenryu City), Shizuoka Prefecture, Japan

1916 The Edward G. Budd Manufacturing Company of Philadelphia, PA produces its 100,000th steel body for Dodge touring cars

1918 Automotive parts manufacturer Robert Joseph Mason is born in Muskegon, MI

1920 The Hebb Motor Company is forced into bankruptcy

1921 Frederick Wise Bowditch of General Motors is born in Jamaica, Long Island, NY

1924 Automobile historian George Smith May is born in Ironwood, MI

1925 Thomas J. Litle Jr. is named Chief Engineer of Lincoln

1939 Racer Chris Craft is born in Porthleven, Cornwall, England

1943 Frank A. Ross, Senior Vice President of the Stewart-Warner Corporation, dies at age 60

1945 Racer Damien Magee is born in Belfast, Antrim, Northern Ireland

1948 William H. Evans, an English-born design engineer with the Briggs Manufacturing Company and the Willys-Overland Company, dies

1949 Edward G. Seubert, President of the Standard Oil Company of Indiana 1927- 1944, dies in Chicago, IL at age 73

1950 The Kaiser Golden Dragon is introduced

1950 The last 1950 Pontiac is produced

1952 The first 1953 Pontiac is produced

1954 Chrysler Corporation introduces its 1955 Chrysler, DeSoto, Dodge, and Plymouth automobiles featuring "Forward Look" styling by Virgil M. Exner

---

CHRYSLER CORPORATION ➤ THE *FORWARD* LOOK
PLYMOUTH · DODGE · DE SOTO · CHRYSLER · IMPERIAL

1955 The 1956 Nashes are introduced, featuring "Speedline" styling

1961 Automobile body manufacturer William J. Meinel dies in Philadelphia, PA at age 68

1966 The 1967 Opels are introduced to the United States market

1966 Art Arfons, driving the Green Monster at the Bonneville Salt Flats, UT, crashes at better than 600 mph in what would be his last attempt at raising the land speed record

1967 Racer Domenico "Mimmo" Schiattarella is born in Milan, Italy

1970 The Soviet Union lands the first wheeled vehicle on the surface of the Moon, and later in the day the Lunokhod I is driven around Mare Imbrium by remote control from the Earth

1986 Georges Besse, President of Renault since 1982 and its Chairman since 1985, is assassinated in Paris at age 58

NOVEMBER 18

1880 John W. Thomas of the Firestone Tire & Rubber Company is born in Tallmadge, OH

1881 Bertram Ward Burtsell of Packard is born in Brooklyn, NY

1888 Stanwood W. Sparrow of Stevens-Duryea, Metz, and Studebaker is born in Middleborough, MA

1890 Joseph Morrell Dodge, a director of the Packard Motor Car Company 1942-1947, is born in Detroit, MI

1892 Racer Tazio Giorgio Nuvolari is born in Castel d'Ario, Mantua, Lombardy, Italy

1894 Tire manufacturer Frank George Schenuit is born in Baltimore, MD

1904 Automotive artist Melbourne Brindle is born in Australia

1906 Automobile designer Alexander Arnold Constantine "Alec" Issigonis is born in Smyrna (now Izmir), Turkey

1907 Pierre Dreyfus of Renault is born in Paris, France

1907 The Napier Motor Car Company of America, located in Jamaica Plain, MA, is dissolved - the firm would be reorganized in 1909 but production of the American Napier would end in 1912

1908 The Overland Automobile Company and other business interests controlled by John N. Willys are consolidated as the Willys-Overland Company

1912 Rodney Weir Markley Jr. of the Ford Motor Company is born in Denver, CO

1914 Joseph W. Frazer marries Lucile Frost

1916 The American Grand Prix staged in Santa Monica, CA is won by Howdy Wilcox in a Peugeot

1918 Harry W. Ford, President of the Saxon Motor Car Company 1914-1918, dies in New York City from pneumonia at age 38

1925 The Chevrolet 1929-1931 "Viking" mascot is patented by designer William Schnell

1927 Henry Edmunds, the man who arranged the first meeting between H. F. Royce and Hon. C. S. Rolls, dies in Hove, England at age 74

1930 The Pontiac 1932 "Eagle" mascot is patented by designer William Schnell

1932 Racer Nasif Estefano is born in Concepcion, Tucuman, Argentina

1934 Pliny E. Holt, builder in 1896 of the first automobile in California and later an executive with the Caterpillar Tractor Company, dies at age 62

1936 Supercharging is offered as a $415 extra-cost option on the Cord 812

1940 The 4,000,000th Buick is produced

1940 The Richardson Pan-American Highway Expedition begins in Detroit, MI as a modified 1941 Plymouth driven by Sullivan Richardson, Arnold Whitaker, and Kenneth C. Van Hee departs Detroit, MI on the first automobile trip from North America to Punta Arenas, Magallanes, Chile at the southern tip of South America

1941 Racer Gary Bettenhausen is born in Tinley Park, IL, the son of racer Tony Bettenhausen (Sr.)

1949 The 1950 Hudson Pacemakers are introduced as a lower priced, slightly shorter variant of the Super-Six series

1955 The balance of the 1956 Cadillacs are introduced, joining two models that had debuted on October 24

1959 Harry W. Anderson of General Motors dies at age 67

1960 Chrysler Corporation announces the termination of the DeSoto marque after 32 years of production

1968 Gary Bettenhausen wins the Phoenix 200 at the Phoenix International Raceway on his 27th birthday for his first major victory

1982 Frank Litherland, longtime promoter of the Hoosier Auto Show & Swap Meet, dies in Brownsburg, IN

1987 The Ford Motor Company purchases United States Leasing International

1987 A 1963 Ferrari 250 GTO hardtop coupe sets a public auction record of $1,600,000

1991 Chrysler Corporation and Fiat SpA announce the termination of their agreement to distribute the Alfa Romeo in the United States

1992 David C. Hill succeeds David McLellan as Chevrolet Corvette Chief Engineer

NOVEMBER 19

1867 Charles Connard Hanch of Marmon, Studebaker, and Maxwell is born in Maywood, IN

1869 Alexander Brownell Cullen Hardy of General Motors is born in Ypsilanti, MI

1884 Automobile designer Harry A. Marchant is born in Aylmer, Ontario, Canada

1885 Nelson S. Pringle of Autocar is born in Newark, NJ

1904 Automobile engineer and designer Wellington Everett Miller is born in Los Angeles, CA

1906 Tom Cooper, a longtime associate of Barney Oldfield and onetime owner of the Ford "999", is killed in an automobile accident in New York City

1912 Thomas Neal becomes the first Chairman of General Motors and is succeeded as President by Charles W. Nash

1921 Ormand E. Hunt is appointed Chief Engineer of Chevrolet

1922 Automotive historian Walter A. Musciano is born in New York City

1928 Carlos C. Booth, M.D., a surgeon who in 1895 designed the first car in Ohio (his Booth-Crouch was actually built by machinist W. Lee Crouch of New Brighton, PA), dies in Youngstown, OH at age 66

1935 Packard receives a United States patent for a special One Twenty mascot designed by Howard F. Yeager

1937 George Eyston driving the Thunderbolt at the Bonneville Salt Flats, UT raises the land speed record to 312.35 mph

1938 Racer Lothar Motschenbacher is born in Cologne, Germany

1947 Racer Frank Garbutt dies in Los Angeles, CA at age 78

1951 The last 1951 Pontiac is produced

1954 Racer Spike Gehlhausen is born

1954 The 1955 Buicks are introduced

1954 The 1955 Oldsmobiles are introduced

1956 Henry Ford II announces that the Ford Motor Company's new marque will be called the Edsel and the Special Products Division will become the Edsel Division

1956 The 1957 Pontiacs are introduced

1959 The last Edsel is produced - the Mercury-Edsel-Lincoln Division of the Ford Motor Company was officially recreated as the "new" Lincoln-Mercury Division with Ben D. Mills continuing as General Manager

1955 BUICK
41 Special Sedan

1961 Racer Al Keller is killed at age 41 when he crashes during the Bobby Ball Memorial Race in Phoenix, AZ

1967 Arensio "Dodgie" Laurel, winner of the 1962 and 1963 Macau Grand Prix, is killed in Macau when he crashes on the Guia Circuit during the 1967 Macau Grand Prix

1969 Racer Philippe Adams is born in Mouscron, Belgium

1986 Antique automobile collector George Hall Waterman Jr., best remembered as the co-owner of the 1866 Dudgeon steam vehicle, dies in Providence, RI

1989 Racer Grant Adcox is killed when he crashes during the Atlanta (GA) 500

NOVEMBER 20

1860 Warren Packard marries Mary E. Doud - their sons William D. Packard and James W. Packard would become the founders and namesakes of the United States luxury marque

1901 The Krastin Automobile Manufacturing Company is organized in Cleveland, OH with Charles S. Beardslee as President and designer August Krastin as General Manager - the firm would go bankrupt in 1904

1905 Automotive parts manufacturer Maynard Brewster Terry is born in Brooklyn, NY

1908 The first Velie is taken for its inaugural test drive in Moline, IL - the car, known as "Old Maud" still exists

1919 The 20,000th Essex, a 2-passenger roadster, is produced

1919 Racer Alan Brown is born in Malton, Yorkshire, England

1924 Peerless introduces the Equipoised Eight

PEERLESS
PEERLESS HAS ALWAYS BEEN A GOOD CAR

The Peerless Equipoised Eight
with Custom Bodies

4-Pass. Phaeton	$2845
7-Pass. Phaeton	2895
4-Pass. Victoria	3245
5-Pass. Coupe	3295
5-Pass. Sedan	3495
5-Pass. Brougham	3495
7-Pass. Sedan	3595
Limousine	3795

The Peerless Six

5-Pass. Phaeton	$1895
7-Pass. Phaeton	1995
Sport Roadster	2195
5-Pass. Coupe	2295
5-Pass. Sedan	2395
7-Pass. Sedan	2595
Limousine	2695

All Prices F. O. B. Factory

1924 Automotive historian Irwin Stambler is born in Brooklyn, NY

1934 Arthur W. Herrington is issued a United States patent for his "Driving Mechanism for Steering Wheels of Motor Vehicles" four years after the application had been made

1935 Harold E. Larsen of the Timken-Detroit Axle Company dies in San Mateo, CA

1940 The first 6-cylinder Ford car is produced since the unsuccessful Model K of 1906-1908

1943 Charles J. Marks, a tool engineer with the Simplex Automobile Company who later was an executive in the aeronautical industry, dies at age 67

1946 The American Central Manufacturing Company and the Aviation Corporation, two former divisions of the old Cord Corporation, merge

1948 Racer Gunnar Nilsson is born in Halsingborg, Sweden

1951 The Kaiser-Frazer Corporation and Sears, Roebuck & Company agree to produce and market a variant of the Henry J through Sears as a new marque, the Allstate

1951 Racers Jose Estradad Menocal and Miguel Gonzalez are killed near Oaxaca, Mexico during the Pan-American Road Race

1952 General Motors President Charles E. Wilson resigns to become Secretary of Defense in the administration of Dwight D. Eisenhower - Harlow H. Curtice is named Acting President

1952 The 1953 Plymouths are introduced

The business district of Princeton, IL in 1955 - the parked car at far left is a 1953 Plymouth Cranbrook Club Coupe.

1953 The last Henry J is produced

1953 The last 1953 Pontiac is produced - the division officially drops the Sedan Delivery body style

1953 The first Volvo Duett PV445DS van is produced

1955 Frank E. Payne, cofounder, President 1917-1951, and Chairman of the Board of the Crane Packing Company, and an authority on mechanical packings and seals, dies in Glencoe, IL at age 72

1957 Racer Stefan Bellof is born in Giessen, Germany

1957 Racer Carlos Guerrero is born in Mexico City, DF, Mexico

1959 The British Ford Anglia is introduced to the United States market

1960 The legendary Maserati 250F, winner of more than 30 Grand Prix races, makes its last official competitive appearance as Bob Drake finishes 13th at the Grand Prix of the United States in Riverside, CA

1961 Racer Tim Harvey is born in Farnborough, Hampshire, England

1965 Racer Jimmy Vasser is born in Canoga Park, CA

1988 Racer Cale Yarborough announces his retirement

NOVEMBER 21

1844 Smith S. Griffith of Marmon is born near Winchester, KY

1848 Politician William Cotter Maybury, a frequent financial backer of young Henry Ford, is born in Detroit, MI

1872 William Joseph McAneeny of Hudson is born in Newport, NY

1882 Edward Stanlaw "Ned" Jordan is born in Merrill, WI

1903 John Wallace Raisbeck of American Motors is born in Coronel, Chile

1903 L'Ebe Bugatti, eldest daughter of Ettore Bugatti, is born in Milan, Italy

1907 George H. Day, General Manager of the ALAM and President of the Electric Vehicle Company 1900-1907, dies in Daytona Beach, FL at age 56

1911 Norman Henry Bell of the White Motor Company of Canada is born in Brantford, ON

1912 The Warren Motor Car Company is reorganized with Homer Warren reelected as President and Vice President C. R. Wilson, Secretary F.T. Lewis, Treasurer L.M. Hamlin, and Gereral Manager R.W. Allen as new officers

1919 The Fox Motor Company is organized in Philadelphia, PA by Ansley H. Fox, inventor of the Fox shotgun

1925 Ralph Arthur Iorio of General Motors is born in Rochester, NY

1925 Roy Thomas Lawrie of American Motors is born in Windsor, ON, Canada

1927 The first Dodge Victory Six is produced

1929 The Mercer Motors Corporation is incorporated in Delaware to revive the Mercer marque but only one car, a 1931 convertible coupe with body by the Merrimac Body Company, was built

1937 Howard E. Coffin, Vice President and Chief Engineer of the Hudson Motor Car Company 1909-1930, is killed at age 64 by an accidental gunshot wound in Sea Island Beach, GA

1939 Clarence W. Spicer, builder of the prototype 1903 Spicer while a student at Cornell University in Ithaca, NY, and later the inventor of the first practical automotive driveshaft and a manufacturer of universal joints, dies in Miami, FL at age 64

1943 Racer Jacques Laffite is born in Magny-Cours, France

1945 John Edward Aldred, an investment banker associated with numerous firms including Rolls-Royce of America, Inc., dies

1947 F. M. Small, founder of the Martin-Parry Corporation, manufacturers of automobile and truck bodies, dies in York, PA at age 69

1951 Racer Carlos Panini is killed near Oaxaca, Mexico during the Pan-American Road Race

1952 The 1953 Packard 26th Series is introduced

1953 Racer Felice Bonetto is killed at age 50 when his Lancia crashes near the village of Silao, Mexico during the Carrera Panamericana

1955 The Bugatti Type 251 race car is introduced at the Entzheim Aerodrome near Molsheim, France with Roland Bugatti, Maurice Trintignant, and Pierre Marco taking the car for demonstration drives

1959 Automobile historian Ralph C. Epstein dies at age 60

1962 Irving R. Bacon, an artist who was the "court painter" for Henry Ford, dies in El Cajon, CA at age 86

1966 Guy W. Vaughan, a pioneer racer and automobile designer who later was an executive in the aeronautical industry, dies at age 82

1970 The Ford Mustang Boss 351 is introduced at the Detroit (MI) Auto Show

1993 Racer Stephane Proulx dies in Ste. Adele, PQ, Canada at age 27

1994 Automotive journalist Dean Batchelor dies at age 72

1996 Elmo Langley, a NASCAR racer 1955-1978 and official since 1980, dies at age 68 from a heart attack suffered while testing an Acura NSX-R at the Suzuka circuit in Japan

NOVEMBER 22

1643 Rene Robert Cavalier, Sieur de La Salle, explorer and namesake of the 1927-1940 Cadillac-produced companion marque, is born in Rouen, France

1826 The Blanchard steam carriage is successfully tested in Springfield, MA by designer Thomas Blanchard

1847 Georges Thadee Bouton is born in Paris, France

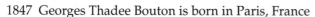

The original LaSalle trademark adopted in 1927

1866 James Brewster, founder of the coachbuilding firm that would be closely associated with Rolls-Royce of America, Inc., dies in New Haven, CT at age 78

1893 General Motors stylist Harley Jefferson Earl is born in Los Angeles, CA

1894 James Sims Reid, founder of the Standard Products Company and the inventor of numerous automotive products, is born in Yazoo City, MS

1898 Hon. Evelyn Ellis resigns as a Director of the Daimler Motor Company, Ltd.

1899 William Francis Marande of the Eaton Manufacturing Company is born in Bay City, MI

1900 The prototype Mercedes car built by the Daimler Motoren Gesellschaft to the specifications of Emil Jellinek is given its first test drive by Gustav Vischer

1905 Henry Ford and James Couzens establish the Ford Manufacturing Company as a means of ousting Alexander Y. Malcomson from the Ford Motor Company

1912 The Grabowsky Power Wagon Company is declared bankrupt

1915 The Hupp Motor Car Corporation acquires the American Gear Company of Jackson, MI, converting the firm to the production of axles

1918 Enzo Ferrari makes his racing debut driving a 3-litre C.M.N. to a third place finish in the first Parma-Berceto (Italy) race

1927 James Hector McNeal Jr. of the Edward G. Budd Manufacturing Company is born in Dover, DE

1934 Racer Jackie Pretorious is born in Potchefstroom, South Africa

1937 Stanley Krall of the Fisk Rubber Corporation dies in Longmeadow, MA at age 43

1942 Tubeless tires are successfully tested by their developer, John B. McGay of Tulsa, OK

1946 A. B. C. Hardy of General Motors dies in Flint, MI at age 77

1947 Racer Salt Walther is born

1951 Sharon D. Dudzinski of the Chrysler Corporation is born

1942 Rollin Abell, holder of 40 patents for automotive parts, dies at age 73

1957 Enzo Ferrari introduces the Ferrari 250 Testa Rossa

1957 Sir Kenneth Crossley, Chairman of Crossley Motors, Ltd., dies in Whitchurch, England at age 80

1963 William Clay Ford purchases the Detroit Lions professional football team

1967 Racer Peter Aslund is born in Karlstad, Sweden

1986 The Centro Tecnologico-Cultural y Museo del Automovilismo Juan Manuel Fangio opens in Balcarce, Argentina

1995 The last M.G. RV8 is produced in Cowley, England

NOVEMBER 23

1851 Charles Hotchkiss Norton, a business partner of Henry M. Leland, is born in Plainville, CT

1852 George Adelman Matthews of the Jackson Automobile Company is born in in Thompson, OH

1864 Henry Bourne Joy of Packard is born in Detroit, MI

1897 Ransom E. Olds is issued a United States patent for a "Motor Carriage", his first gasoline-powered vehicle that had been completed the prior year

1898 Claude Arlington Pauley of the Firestone Tire & Rubber Company is born in Toledo, OH

1901 The Twentieth Century Motor Company, Ltd. is registered in Penge, England by E. H. Owen to manufacture the Owen automobile

1910 James J. Storrow replaces William M. Eaton as President of General Motors

1911 Charles Franklin Jones of the Humble Oil & Refining Company is born in Bartlett, TX

1913 M. B. Gilman of Minneapolis, MN announces plans to manufacture the Arrow cyclecar

1919 Seymour A. Lippmann, a research associate with Uniroyal Inc., is born

1920 B. F. Tobin, founder and Chairman of the Continental Motors Corporation, dies in Grosse Pointe, MI at age 54

1927 Otis Chandler, *Los Angeles Times* publisher and collector of classic and high-performance cars, is born in Los Angeles, CA

1929 The first Oakland V-8 is produced

1932 The Dodge Series DP is introduced

1932 Giustino Cattaneo assumes principal management of Fabbrica Automobili Isotta-Fraschini

1940 The Ford Motor Company completes its first prototype Jeep based on the design of the American Bantam Car Company

1942 Col. Azel Ames, a manufacturer of electrical equipment for motor vehicles since 1909, dies in Yonkers, NY at age 69

1951 The first Warszawa, based on the Soviet Pobieda, is completed by the Fabryka Samochodow Osobowych of Warsaw - this is often cited as the first automobile to be manufactured in Poland

1954 The 50,000,000th General Motors automobile is produced, a 1955 Chevrolet Bel Air Sport Coupe

1954 The 1954 Hudson Ramblers are introduced as badge-engineered Nash Ramblers that would be the only cars available to Hudson dealers for three months

1954 The 1955 Lincolns are introduced

1957 Herman L. Moekle, an official of the Ford Motor Company 1913-1947, dies at age 72

1959 Aaron L. Sapiro, an attorney connected with the Ford Motor Company, dies at age 75

1969 Racer Olivier Beretta is born in Monte Carlo, Monaco

1979 Carlo Abarth dies in his native Austria at age 71

1983 Joseph A. Petnel, the inventor of the automobile turn signal in 1924, dies at age 94

NOVEMBER 24

1849 John Froelich, inventor of the gasoline-powered farm tractor, is born

1866 Banker William Glanton Irwin, a cofounder of the Cummins Engine Company, is born in Columbus, IN

1867 Alvin Carr McCord, an inventor of automobile and railway devices, is born in Paris, IL

1900 The first Pierce gasoline-powered automobile, actually a heavily modified DeDion-Bouton of French manufacture, is taken for its first test drive in Buffalo, NY

When this registered letter left the George N. Pierce Company in 1904, the humble Pierce Motorette was evolving into the Pierce-Arrow, one of the world's great luxury marques until its demise in 1938.

1903 Clyde Jay Coleman of New York City is issued a United States patent for an automobile self starter - although impractical, rights to the design were sold to Delco and formed the basis for the work of Charles F. Kettering

1909 Richard Charles Gerstenberg, Chairman of General Motors 1972-1974, is born in Little Falls, NY

1921 Petroleum research chemist Robert Louis Banks is born in Piedmont, MO

1922 J. A. Joyce, driving a modified A.C., covers 101 miles, 696 yards in one hour, becoming the first "light car" to reach 100 miles in sixty minutes

1938 Automotive parts manufacturer Edward L. Valance dies at age 56

1951 Ernest E. Wemp, holder of more than 100 patents relating to automobile clutches, dies

1952 Paul Gaeth, the German-born manufacturer of the Gaethmobile 1902-1904 and Gaeth 1905-1910, and one of the first people to restore antique cars, dies in Cleveland, OH at age 79

1975 Ernesto Maserati dies in Bologna, Italy at age 77

1979 Prominent antique automobile collector Owen Owens dies in Berkeley, CA at age 49

1993 Mercury Marine of Stillwater, OK produces its last LT-5 engine, the Chevrolet/Lotus-designed V-8 that was used in the Corvette ZR-1 produced 1990-1995

NOVEMBER 25

1844 Carl (nee Karl) Friedrich Benz is born in Pfaffenrot, Baden, Germany

1888 Clifford Boles Longley of the Ford Motor Company is born in Chicago, IL

1909 The Elmore Manufacturing Company of Clyde, OH, named for its original location in Elmore, OH, is acquired by General Motors

1912 Frank H. McKinney joins the Packard Motor Car Company

1915 Hyundai cofounder Chung Ju Yung is born in Asan, Tongcho, Kangwon Province, Korea

1920 Gaston Chevrolet is killed at age 37 when he crashes during a race at the Beverly Hills, CA board track - Chevrolet's riding mechanic, Lyall Jolls, is also killed in the accident

1925 The first Ford Motor Company airplane is completed

1926 The first Salmson GSC is sold

1936 Albert C. Schulz, Assistant Chief Engineer of the Locomobile Company of America 1905-1916 and later the Chief Engineer of the Mercer Motors Company, dies in Bridgeport, CT at age 61

1942 George H. Hunt, a principal developer of automotive safety glass, dies

1946 Racer Tommy "Slim" Borgudd is born in Borgholm, Sweden

1949 The 1,000,000th Cadillac is produced, a 1950 Coupe deVille

1949 William Brewster, builder of the Brewster car 1915-1925 and a custom coachbuilder primarily associated with Rolls-Royce of America, Inc., dies in Bridgeport, CT at age 83

1949 The last 1949 Plymouth is produced followed by the first 1950 Plymouth, a P20 Special Deluxe sedan

A 1949 Plymouth P17 3-Passenger Coupe awaits it owner at the Skyway Terminal in Government Camp, OR. This unusual bodystyle was Plymouth's lowest priced offering for the model year and enjoyed a run of 13,715 units.

1951 The 1,933-mile Pan-American Road Race from Tuxtla Gutierrez to Ciudad Juarez, Mexico is won by Piero Taruffi in a Ferrari

1953 Emerson J. Luxmoore, a body designer with Chevrolet for 27 years, is killed in a traffic accident at age 50

1958 Charles F. Kettering of General Motors dies in Dayton, OH at age 82

1963 Sherwood H. Egbert resigns as President of the Studebaker Corporation and is succeeded by Byers A. Burlingame

1965 The 1966 Plymouth Barracuda is introduced to complete the marque's lineup

1966 The 1967 Plymouth Barracuda is introduced to complete the marque's lineup

1982 Racer Walt Ader dies at age 68

1988 Vittorio Ghidella, Managing Director of Fiat SpA, resigns

NOVEMBER 26

1836 John Loudon Macadam, a developer of improved road paving materials, dies in Dumfriesshire, Scotland at age 80

1845 Edward Waldron Pope, a partner in the manufacture of the Pope-Robinson, is born in Boston, MA

1858 Jefferson Seligman, a New York City banker who in 1906 ordered the first Rolls-Royce Silver Ghost to be exported, is born in New York City

1877 Charles Cassius Gates, founder and President of the Gates Rubber Company in Denver, CO, is born in Waterford, MI

1878 Richard Ralph Hallam Grant of General Motors is born in Ipswich, MA

1882 Emlen Spencer Hare is born in Philadelphia, PA

1884 Charles E. Wetherald, a longtime General Motors executive who was active in the formation of the Chevrolet Motor Company, is born in Wilson, NY

1887 Racer Pietro Bordino is born in Turin, Italy

1895 Industrial engineer Clarke Demorest Pease, whose automotive career included time with Studebaker, Packard, and Hispano-Suiza, is born in Big Rapids, MI

1899 Herbert Willetts of the Mobil Oil Corporation is born in Troy, NY

1908 The first American Grand Prize race, staged in Savannah, GA by the Automobile Club of America (ACA), is won by Louis Wagner in a Fiat

1917 Racer Wilfried Edgar Barth is born in Herold-Erzgebirge, Germany

1920 Racer Eddie O'Donnell dies in Beverly Hills, CA from injuries suffered the previous day when his Duesenberg collided with the Frontenac driven by Gaston Chevrolet

1927 The Ford Model A is announced

1927 The Chrysler Imperial Series L80 is introduced

New Imperial 7-passenger Sedan, illustrated. Also available in 5-passenger Sedan, Sedan-Limousine, Town Sedan, Roadster and other custom-built body models.

1929 Leonard C. Baldwin, a Standard Oil Company of New Jersey sales engineer who had been involved in the production of Hispano-Suiza and Bugatti aero engines during World War I, is killed at age 31 in an automobile accident

1940 Allan A. Ryan, whose 1916 effort to corner the stock of the Stutz Motor Car Company of America ended in personal bankruptcy and disinheritance by his father, dies in San Francisco, CA at age 60

1941 A. E. Wetterborg of the Federal-Mogul Corporation dies

MAKE REPLACEMENTS WITH GENUINE
FEDERAL-MOGUL STANDARD PARTS

*"They're Standard Equipment
With Over 150 Manufacturers"*

The Complete
Line Includes
Bronze Back Babbitt
Lined Bearings
Die Cast Babbitt
Bearings and
Bushings
Bronze Bushings
Bronze Washers
Bronze Cored and
Solid Bars
Babbitt Metals
Bolts, Nuts, Shims
and Screws

FEDERAL·MOGUL CORPORATION
A consolidation of the Federal Bearing and Bushing
Corporation and the Muzzy-Lyon Company
Detroit   Michigan

Mogul
FEDERAL

1943 Automobile radiator authority Glen Grover Holt, Vice President of the Perfex Corporation, dies at age 47

1946 The Dearborn Motors Corporation is organized to market Ford tractors

1946 Hearse manufacturer John W. Henney, owner of the Henney Motor Company, dies in Freeport, IL

1948 The first Holden is produced

1951 The 1952 Crosleys are introduced

1951 John W. Thomas, President of the Firestone Tire & Rubber Company 1932-1941 and its Chairman 1941-1946, dies in Akron, OH at age 71

1953 Female racer Desire Wilson is born in Johannesburg, South Africa

1956 Racer Dale Jarrett is born in Conover, NC, the son of racer Ned Jarrett

1958 Harold Sydnor of the Esso Standard Oil Company dies at age 60

1958 Francis Edwin Cunningham, Vice President of James Cunningham Son & Company, Inc., dies in Rochester, NY at age 75

1962 The 3,000,000th post-World War II British Motor Corporation car is produced, a Vanden Plas Princess R saloon that was presented to the British Red Cross by BMC Chairman Sir George Harriman

1963 The Porsche Carrera GTS Type 904 is introduced

1967 Pettit's Museum of Motoring Memories in Natural Bridge, VA closes

1972 The Bertone X 1/9, a badge-engineered version of the discontinued Fiat X 1/9, is introduced at the Birmingham (UK) Motor Show

1980 Peter DePaolo, winner of the 1925 Indianapolis 500, dies at age 82

1984 The agricultural side of the International Harvester Company is sold to the Tenneco Corporation, with the truck side of the company continuing on a temporary basis as International Trucks

1995 Nick Curtin, Sales and Marketing Director of Burlen Fuel Systems Ltd., is killed in a motorcycle accident at age 41

1870 Joseph Sanford Mack of Mack trucks is born in Mount Cobb, PA

1885 Kaufman Thuma "K.T." Keller of the Chrysler Corporation is born in Mount Joy, PA

1889 Curtis P. Brady is issued a permit by the New York City Commissioner of Parks allowing him to drive his steam automobile through Central Park

1891 Paul Willard Garrett of General Motors is born in Lincoln, KS

1898 The first Chanteloup hillclimb held near Paris, France is won by Camille Jenatzy in an electric Jenatzy of his own design

1901 Clement Studebaker, President of the Studebaker Brothers Manufacturing Company since 1868, dies in South Bend, IN at age 70

1907 Carl E. Buchholzer of the Chrysler Corporation is born in Dayton, OH

1911 The seventh Vanderbilt Cup is held in Savannah, GA and won by Ralph Mulford in a Lozier

1913 Peter Paul Schilovsky, designer of the gyroscope-car, successfully tests the prototype at the Wolseley factory in Birmingham, England

1914 The Modoc Motor Company, a division of Montgomery Ward & Company, is dissolved after three years of operation

1924 Elaine Bond of *Road & Track* magazine is born

1928 Willard L. Velie Jr. announces that production of Velie automobiles will be discontinued with all efforts of the Velie Motor Corporation directed toward the manufacture of Monocoupe airplanes

1939 John W. Wilkinson of Franklin is presented with a lifetime membership in the Society of Automotive Engineers

1940 Automotive machine tool manufacturer Frank B. Hamerly dies in California at age 53

1941 J. Walter Drake, a cofounder and first President of the Hupp Motor Car Corporation, dies in Detroit, MI at age 66

1945 Racer Alain de Cadenet is born in Great Britain

1949 Hobart Cutler Dickinson, President of the Society of Automotive Engineers in 1933, dies in Washington, DC at age 74

1949 Racer Masanori Sekiya is born in Japan

1950 The first 1951 Pontiac is produced

1956 The Jeep FC-150 3/4-ton pickup is introduced as a 1957 model

1957 Racer Kenneth Acheson is born in Cookstown, Tyrone, Northern Ireland

1968 The 200,000th International Scout, a 1969 800A equipped with a 304-cid V-8, is produced at the Fort Wayne, IN plant

1972 The 16,000,000th Pontiac is produced, a blue 1973 Catalina sedan

1975 Charles A. Dana, founder of the Dana Corporation, an automobile parts manufacturer, dies at age 94

1980 James Jerome Bradley, curator of the National Automotive History Collection of the Detroit (MI) Public Library, dies in Royal Oak, MI at age 58

1985 Joseph E. Cappy, Executive Vice President of American Motors, announces that production of the Jeep CJ series will end in 1986

1989 Automotive historian Hugh G. Conway dies at age 75

1990 The Toyota Motor Company Ltd. announces that they will build a second factory at their Georgetown, KY location

1996 The last Cadillac Fleetwood is produced in Arlington, TX - this car would mark the discontuance of the rear wheel drive Cadillac and the name of the once independent custom coachbuilder

NOVEMBER 28

1837 John Wesley Hyatt, the inventor of the roller bearing, is born in Starkey, NY

1873 Frank Phillips, founder of the Phillips Petroleum Company, is born in Greeley County, NE

*Page, ND circa 1950 - with a population of just 482, the local Phillips 66 dealer
had to compete with both Texaco and Standard for business.*

1880 D'Orsay McCall White, Chief Engineer of Cadillac 1914-1919 and the designer of its first V-8 engine, is born in Glasgow, Scotland

1890 The Daimler Motoren-Geselschaft is founded

1895 The *Chicago Times-Herald* Contest is won by J. Frank Duryea in his motor carriage, although the Gold Medal is awarded to the Morris & Salom Electrobat II for alleged greater ease of operation

1910 The first test forgings are produced at the new Dodge Brothers, Inc. plant in Hamtramck, MI

1911 The Briggs-Detroiter Company is incorporated in Michigan

1927 The Ford Motor Company begins a massive advertising campaign in advance of the introduction of the Model A scheduled for December 2, 1927

1938 John Paul McTague of the Ford Motor Company is born in Jersey City, NJ

1939 H. W. Linneen of the Sinclair Refining Company dies at age 44

1950 James E. Hale of the Firestone Tire & Rubber Company and President-elect for 1951 of the Society of Automotive Engineers, dies in Akron, OH at age 66

1954 James T-B Bowles of the Crown Central Petroleum Corporation dies at age 72

1956 Arthur J. Scaife, English-born design engineer with White and Autocar who served as President of the Society of Automotive Engineers in 1932, dies in St. Petersburg, FL at age 81

1958 Racer Hideki Okada is born in Tokyo, Japan

1962 Racer Ken Johnson is born in the United States

1963 Lee Wallard, winner of the 1951 Indianapolis 500, die in St. Petersburg, FL at age 53

1990 Racer Chico Godia-Sales dies in Barcelona, Spain at age 69

NOVEMBER 29

1865 Benjamin Franklin Tobin, founder of the Continental Motors Corporation, is born in Chicago, IL

1866 Automotive engineer Arthur Benjamin Browne is born in Cambridge, MA

1875 Artist Irving Ruben Bacon, the "court painter" for Henry Ford, is born in Fitchburg, MA

1895 The American Motor League adopts its constitution and elects officers

1896 Carl J. Snyder of the Chrysler Corporation is born in York, PA

1906 Vincenzo Lancia and Claudio Fogolin form a partnership to produce motor cars in Turin, Italy

1908 Harold Gibson Warner of Cadillac is born in Yankton, SD

Harold G. Warner served as Cadillac's General Manager 1960-1966, an era when the trademark tailfins began to shrink and eventually disappear. This 1961 Sedan de Ville parked near Trinity Hospital in Minot, ND still sports rather adequate fins, but their days would be numbered.

1915 Racer Helmut Niedermayr is born in Germany

1916 Automobile ball bearing manufacturer Joseph Robert Tomlinson is born in Philadelphia, PA

1922 Former Ford Motor Company executive James Couzens is appointed to the United States Senate to replace Truman H. Newberry, who had defeated Henry Ford for the seat in 1918

1923 Racer Chuck Daigh is born in Long Beach, CA

1929 All real property of the defunct Velie Motor Corporation in Moline, IL including the family's Villa Velie mansion is sold at auction

1942 William Stamps Farish, President of the Standard Oil Company of New Jersey, dies in Millbrook, NY at age 61

1944 Racer Lee Kunzman is born

1948 The Holden FX is introduced, the first complete automobile manufactured by General Motors-Holden's Pty Ltd. in Melbourne, Victoria, Australia

ALLARD

1954 The last Allard is produced

1954 Phillip H. Patchin of the Standard Oil Company dies in San Mateo, CA at age 70

1965 The last Bentley S3 chassis is completed and delivered to the coachbuilder

1975 Racer Graham Hill is killed in an airplane crash near Arkley, Hertfordshire, England - also killed were racer Tony Brise, age 23, Hill-Cosworth team manager Ray Brimble, designer Andy Smallman, and race mechanics Terry Richards and Tony Alcock

1981 James S. Reid, a physician who later developed and manufactured automobile parts, dies at age 87

1988 James T. Crow, Editor of *Road & Track* magazine 1966-1974, dies at age 65

1996 Volkswagenwerk AG executive Jose Ignacio Lopez resigns as a result of an industrial espionage legal action brought by General Motors, his former employer

NOVEMBER 30

1872 Herbert Andrew Montagu-Douglas-Scott (Lord Herbert Scott), Chairman of Rolls-Royce Ltd., is born

1899 Leopoldo Alphonso "Leo" Villa, a master mechanic long associated with the land speed record efforts of Sir Malcolm and Donald Campbell, is born in London, England of a Swiss father and Scottish mother

1901 The Henry Ford Company is organized to continue the work of the defunct Detroit Automobile Company

1903 Pioneer British motoring enthusiast Sir Frederick Bramwell dies at age 85

1907 The first exclusive show for motor trucks opens in Chicago, IL with 29 exhibitors

1910 AB Scania-VABIS is organized in Sodertalje, Sweden

1917 The Detroiter Motor Car Company is sold to a financial trustee

Södertälje · Sweden
SCANIA-VABIS

1920 William C. Durant attends his final General Motors board meeting, losing his corporate presidency for the last time as well as $90,000,000 of his personal wealth

1921 The Willys-Overland Company enters receivership

1921 After disappointing tests General Motors officially cancels the development of the "copper-cooled" 6-cylinder Oakland

1928 The Hupp Motor Car Corporation purchases the Chandler-Cleveland Motors Corporation

1929 Frederick Tasker Burgess, Chief Designer of Bentley Motors, Inc., dies

1931 Racer Richard Leon "Dick" Hutcherson is born in Keokuk, IA

1933 The first National Automobile Dealers Association (NADA) used car value guide becomes effective to comply with new government regulations

1935 Racer Trevor Blondyk is born in Krugersdorp, South Africa

1936 The General Motors Truck & Coach Division of the Yellow Truck & Coach Manufacturing Company is formed to handle sales of GMC trucks

1940 The General Motors AC Delco factory in Southampton, England is destroyed during a Nazi air raid

1943 James R. Hughes, English-born automobile body engineer with Ford, Studebaker, and Pierce-Arrow, dies at age 55

1946 Coachbuilder Edward G. Budd dies in Germantown, PA at age 75

1949 Julius P. Heil, President 1906-1946 and Chairman 1946-1949 of the Heil Company, manufacturers of truck and trailer tanks, and Governor of Wisconsin 1939-1943, dies near Milwaukee, WI at age 73

1950 L. L. Colbert is elected President of the Chrysler Corporation

1954 Racer Prince Raimondo Lanza Di Trabia dies in Rome, Italy at age 39

1955 The 1956 Hudson Wasps, Hornet Sixes, and Hornet V-8's are introduced

1955 The Houdaille-Hershey Corporation changes its name to Houdaille Industries, Inc.

1960 The 1960 Lincoln Continentals are introduced, the first of a new design that would redefine automobile styling during the 1960's

1960 The last DeSoto is produced

1960 The first International Scout is produced

1963 Henry Cave, a pioneer designer for the Daimler Motor Syndicate Ltd. and the Imperial Autocar Manufacturing Company Ltd. in England who came to United States to work with Andrew L. Riker and later founded the SKF Ball Bearing Company, dies in Hartford, CT at age 89

1969 Racer Marc Goossens is born in Belgium

1970 Carl W. Cenzer, developer of unitized body construction while at Hudson and American Motors, dies

1972 Neil H. McElroy, a Director of the Chrysler Corporation, dies at age 68

1973 The Mercury Bobcat is introduced as a badge-engineered Ford Pinto by the Ford Motor Company of Canada, Ltd. one year before the car would be available in the United States

1974 Richard C. Gerstenberg retires as Chairman and Chief Executive Officer of General Motors

1979 The "last" Buick V-8 engine block is produced at the Buick foundry, an action thought to signal the end of Buick V-8 cars, but the availabilty of this type of engine continued without model year interruption

1984 The Toyo Kogyo Company, Ltd. announces plans to build a Mazda factory in Flat Rock, MI

DECEMBER 1

1861 Carlos Charles Booth, who in 1895 designed the first car in Ohio now identified as the Booth-Crouch, is born in Greene, OH

1865 Charles Louis Eugene Virion, a sculptor and designer of automobile mascots, is born in Ajaccio, Corsica, France

1879 W. DeGroff Wilcox of the Edward G. Budd Manufacturing Company is born in Valparaiso, IN

1883 Benz & Cie, Rheinische Gasmotorenfabrik, the automotive venture of Carl Benz, is registered as a company name in Mannheim, Germany

1888 Clarence Francis, Chairman of the Studebaker-Packard Corporation for three months in 1960, is born in Port Richmond, Staten Island, NY

1893 Henry Ford is promoted to Chief Engineer of the Edison Illuminating Company of Detroit, MI

1894 The premier issue of the world's first automobile magazine, *La Locomotion Automobile*, is published in Paris, France by Raoul Vuillemont

1897 John N. Willys marries Isabel Irene Van Wie

1898 Raymond Hendry Laird of the Ford Motor Company is born in Detroit, MI

1900 The National Association of Automobile Manufacturers is organized in New York City with Samuel T. Davis of Locomobile as its first President

1903 The Reid Manufacturing Company of Detroit, MI begins production of the Wolverine

1905 Hans Ledwinka, following a three-year employment in Paris, returns to the Nesseldorf Wagenbau-Fabriks-Gessellschaft as head of the automobile department

1906 The American Tourist and Roadster, produced by the American Motor Car Company of Indianapolis, IN, debut at the 7th ACA show in New York City

1907 Hugh Chalmers is named President of the E. R. Thomas-Detroit Company

1908 The Marinette Automobile Company of Marinette, WI, manufacturers of the Thayer as designed by Harry Thayer, is forced into bankruptcy

1908 Automotive supply company executive James MacClymont Hannan is born in Lincoln, NE

1913 The Gulf Refining Company opens the world's first drive-in service station in Pittsburgh, PA

1916 The 1917 Hudsons are introduced

1917 The 1918 Hudsons are introduced

1918 The 1919 Hudsons are introduced as the Series M, slightly modified versions of the 1918 offerings - the redesigned Series O cars were unveiled six months later and were also marketed as 1919 Hudsons

1919 The 1920 Hudsons and Essex Fours are introduced

1919 John L. Pratt joins General Motors as an assistant to President William C. Durant, beginning a 56-year career with the firm

1920 Pierre S. DuPont succeeds William C. Durant as President of General Motors and names Alfred P. Sloan Jr. as Executive Vice President

1920 The 1921 Hudsons are introduced, although the company was attempting to discourage year-dating its cars under the assumption that depreciation would be reduced, protecting the owners' investment

1921 The Trask steam car, promoted by former Stanley distributor O. C. Trask, is announced by the Detroit Steam Motors Corporation

1923 The 1924 Essex Sixes are introduced

1926 Thomas J. Litle Jr. is named Chief Engineer of the Marmon Motor Car Company

1927 Veteran racer Ralph Mulford, driving a Chandler touring car, makes the first automobile ascent of Mount Tom, MA

1928 The Duesenberg Model J is introduced at the New York Automobile Salon

1928 Robert McClements Jr. of the Sun Oil Company is born in Philadelphia, PA

1929 Harold Keith Sperlich of the Ford Motor Company and Chrysler Corporation is born in Detroit, MI

1929 Scuderia Ferrari is formed by Enzo Ferrari, Alfredo Caniato and Mario Tadini to manage the racing program for Alfa Romeo

1930 Ferdinand Porsche starts his own engineering firm in Stuttgart, Dr. Ing. h.c. Ferdinand Porsche GmbH, Konstruktionsburo fur Motoren-, Fahrzeug-, Luftfahrzeug- und Wasserfahrzeugbau, with initial work involving the Wanderer marque

1931 The 1931 Franklin "Stylized Bird" mascot is patented by designer Raymond H. Dietrich

1932 The 1933 Nashes are introduced

1933 Ugo Gobbato is named Managing Director of Alfa Romeo

1935 Don E. Ahrens is named General Sales Manager of Cadillac

1935 Carol Wettlaufer Gelderman, a biographer of Henry Ford, is born in Detroit, MI

1935 The Nissan Diesel Motor Company, Ltd. is established in Japan

1939 The "Sunshine Special", a highly modified Lincoln used by United States Presidents Franklin D. Roosevelt and Harry S. Truman 1939-1950, is leased to the government by the Ford Motor Company

1942 World War II gasoline rationing begins in the United States to conserve fuel and rubber

1942 Eugene Holman is named Vice President of the Standard Oil Company of New Jersey

1943 Charles F. Kettering of General Motors is awarded the John Fritz Medal for notable scientific and industrial achievement by the American Society of Mechanical Engineers

1943 Warren J. Belcher, holder of over 40 patents relating to automotive chains, dies at age 75

1946 General Motors executive Frank R. Pierce is named as the first President of Dearborn Motors Corporation, Ford Motor Company's new subsidiary formed to manage the manufacturing and sales of Ford tractors

1947 Officina Specializzata Costruzione Automobili, manufacturers of the OSCA 1947-1967, is founded in Bologna, Italy by brothers Ernesto, Ettore, and Bindo Maserati

1948 Racer Guy Tumner is born in Ficksburg, South Africa

1948 The 1948 Plymouth Model 15 officially becomes a 1949 model - these cars are now called "First Series" to differentiate them from the redesigned true 1949's that would appear in March

1953 The 1954 Henry J is introduced

1953 The 1954 Jeep CJ is introduced

1953 The first 1954 Pontiac is produced

1955 The Saab 93 is introduced

1955 The 1956 Hudson Wasp and Hornet are introduced, featuring the new American Motors V-8 engines instead of the Packard V-8's used in 1955, and special "Hudson" styling by Richard Arbib

1955 Volvo's 5-year "PV" warranty is extended to light trucks

1955 The first segment of the Ohio Turnpike is opened to the public

1955 The Vacuum Oil Company Ltd. changes its name to the Mobil Oil Company Ltd.

1955 Drury Adams of the Shell Oil Company dies in Honolulu, HI

1959 Harley J. Earl retires as head of General Motors' Styling Section and is succeeded by William L. Mitchell - Robert M. Critchfield, Vice President of General Motors and General Manager of Pontiac 1952-1956 also retires

For better than 30 years all General Motors cars reflected the styling genius of Harley J. Earl. This 1941 Oldsmobile 76 Dynamic Cruiser entering the famous Turnaround at the end of the Lewis & Clark Trail in Seaside, OR exhibits both Mr. Earl's "torpedo" look of the 1940's and his flair for catchy names.

1963 Wendell Scott wins the Grand National race in Jacksonville, FL for his only NASCAR victory but the first by a black driver

1963 Racer Marco Greco is born in Sao Paolo, Brazil

1969 The 1970 Jaguars are introduced to the United States market

1971 Racer Christian Pescatori is born in Brescia, Italy

1972 The Pollock Auto Showcase in Philadelphia, PA opens to the public

1974 Thomas A. Murphy is elected Chairman and Chief Executive Officer of General Motors

1980 Automobile writer and historian Robert W. Irvin dies at age 47

1981 The Imperial Palace Auto Collection in Las Vegas, NV, owned by Ralph Engelstad and the Imperial Palace Hotel & Casino, opens to the public

1986 H. Ross Perot is ousted from the General Motors Board of Directors

1986 Donald J. Atwood is named Chairman of the General Motors Technical Group

1996 Racing journalist Denis Jenkinson dies at age 75

DECEMBER 2

1804 Internal combustion engine pioneer Philippe Lebon dies in Paris, France at age 37

1870 Giuseppe Gaetano Stefanini, an Isotta-Fraschini engineering consultant, is born in Lodi, Italy

1898 Ronald J. Waterbury of Chevrolet is born in Ionia County, MI

1899 John Rhodes Cobb, racer and land speed record setter, is born in Hackbridge, Surrey, England

1902 Leon Levavasseur is issued a French patent for his V-8 engine, the world's first operational engine with this configuration

1916 The Uniontown (PA) Board Speedway stages its first event, a 112.5-mile race was won by Louis Chevrolet driving a Frontenac - Hughie Hughes is killed during the race

1916 Livio Nicolis of Alfa Romeo is born in Brescia, Italy

1924 E. Ellsworth Wood Jr. of the Miniature Incandescent Lamp Company dies at age 26

1927 The Ford Model A is introduced

1928 The 1929 Auburn Series 6-80 and 8-90 are introduced

1930 Racer David Piper is born in Edgware, Middlesex, England

1931 Horst W. Herke of Adam Opel AG is born in Mainz, Germany

1934 Donald Lee Gothard of General Motors is born in Madison, WI

1936 The first Inskip-bodied Rolls-Royce Phantom III is delivered to E. W. Bill of New York City

1937 Racer Chris Bristow is born in London, England

1938 The Veteran Motor Car Club of America is founded

1939 L. W. Moulton of Franklin dies at age 48

1940 Frederick C. Kroeger is named a Vice President of General Motors

1947 Racer Andy Rouse is born in Dymock, Gloucestershire, England

1949 Charles Henry Wondries of the Studebaker Corporation dies in Pasadena, CA at age 61

1950 The last 1950 Plymouth is produced

1952 Hans A. Boehringer, German-born General Motors design engineer, dies in Saginaw, MI at age 48

1954 The 1955 Mercurys are introduced

1956 Pontiac announces plans to produce a limited edition model with standard fuel injection

1969 American Motors and Kaiser Industries Corporation sign an agreement whereby KIC would sell their Kaiser-Jeep operation to AMC

1974 The government of Kuwait purchases a 14.6% interest in Daimler-Benz AG

1976 Robert B. Roberts of Hudson, NC becomes the 75,000th subscriber to *Old Cars* newspaper

1981 The 1982 Pontiac 6000 and Firebird are introduced

1982 The Ford Robotics and Automation Applications Consulting Center opens in Dearborn, MI

1982 John S. Bugas of the Ford Motor Company dies at age 74

1983 Prominent antique automobile collector Louis A. "Jack" Frost dies in Rochester, MI at age 81

1993 Pehr G. Gyllenhammar resigns as Chairman of AB Volvo, with Bo Rydin named as his interim successor - the company announces that their planned merger with Renault has been abandoned

DECEMBER 3

1873 Arthur Atwater Kent, a radio manufacturer who earlier had developed and manufactured improved automobile ignition equipment, is born in Burlington, VT

1890 Albert George Elliott of Rolls-Royce is born

1900 NASCAR official James Alexander "Pat" Purcell is born in Grand Forks, ND

1905 John Thomas "Tom" Mahoney, biographer of George W. Romney, is born in Dallas, TX

1909 The Stafford Motor Car Company is incorporated in Missouri by Terry Stafford

1910 The first (Panama) Canal Zone automobile license plate is issued to Natalio Ehrman

1913 Robert Fargo Draper of Hurst Performance, Inc. is born in Deerfield, WI

1915 Racer Robert "Red" Byron is born in Boulder, CO

1917 The Quebec Bridge near Quebec, PQ, Canada, the world's longest cantilever truss span, opens to the public

1918 Donald Duane Lennox of the International Harvester Corporation is born in Pittsburgh, PA

1920 The first Washington is completed by designer Otto M. Shipley

1924 Byron C. Foy marries Thelma Chrysler, daughter of Walter P. Chrysler

1924 Racer Roberto Mieres is born in Mar del Plata, Argentina

1925 The Murray Body Company is forced into receivership

1932 The 1933 Buicks are introduced

1932 Clement Studebaker Jr. dies at age 61

1932 Racer Gaetano Starrabba, an Italian prince, is born in Palermo, Sicily

1936 William E. Warwick of the Standard Oil Company of Indiana dies at age 74

1937 Racer Robert Arthur "Bobby" Allison is born in Miami, FL

1938 Racer Walker Evans is born

1939 Racer Tom Bagley is born

1948 The Kaiser-Frazer Corporation purchases the Willow Run, MI factory that it had leased since 1945 for $15.1 million

1949 Harold B. Harvey, a manufacturer of aluminum, brass, and copper automobile forgings, dies at age 65

1949 A. Atwater Kent, a manufacturer of automobile ignition systems who later was a leading manufacturer of radios, dies on his 76th birthday

1951 The 1952 Pontiacs are introduced

1951 Racer Rick Rayon Mears is born in Wichita, KS

1951 George W. Davies, English-born General Sales Manager of the Sealed Power Corporation, dies in Muskegon, MI at age 62

1964 Racer Bobby Marshman is killed at age 28 while testing a Lotus-Ford at the Phoenix International Speedway

1979 The last AMC Pacer is produced

1981 The Ford Ranger is announced by Harold A. Poling, Executive Vice President of the Ford Motor Company

1979 AMC Pacer

DECEMBER 4

1880 Garfield Arthur "Gar" Wood, designer of the Miss America racing boats but also influential in automotive affairs, is born in Mapleton, IA

1881 Barbara Maria Giuseppnia Mascherpa Bolzoni, later Mrs. Ettore Bugatti, is born in Milan, Italy

1883 Automotive metallurgist Mason P. Rumney is born in Detroit, MI

1904 Ludovico Prinetti withdraws from the Isotta Fraschini partnership

1905 The Gates-Osborne Carriage Company of Indianapolis, IN reorganizes as the Cole Carriage Company, evolving in 1909 into the Cole Motor Car Company

1911 Warren Johnson, inventor of the electric thermostat and manufacurer of Johnson trucks since 1901 and Johnson cars since 1905, dies in Milwaukee, WI

1914 Coachbuilder Wilhelm Karmann Jr., is born

1915 The Ford Peace Ship, Henry Ford's personal effort to end World War I, departs from Hoboken, NJ on its voyage to Europe

1939 Paul Robert Verkuil of the American Automobile Association is born in Staten Island, NY

1944 Racer Francois Migault is born in Le Mans, France

1947 Leo C. Conradi, Technical Director of Research and Development for the Standard Steel Spring Company, dies in Sewickley, PA at age 57

1951 The Willys Aero sedan is announced

1952 The 1953 Dodge Power Wagons are introduced

1952 The Packard Clipper Sportster is introduced

1955 Joseph A. Galamb of the Ford Motor Company dies in Detroit, MI at age 74

1957 Racer Raul Boesel is born in Curitiba, Brazil

1961 The 5,000,000th Volkswagen is produced

1963 Steam car pioneer George E. Whitney dies in Manchester, NH at age 101

1964 Racer Thomas Danielsson is born in Kungsbacka, Sweden

1974 Race car designer Leo Goossen dies in Los Angeles, CA at age 82

1984 General Motors announces that they are discontinuing the production of diesel-engined automobiles

1992 David C. Hill assumes his duties as Chief Corvette Engineer

1995 General Motors announces the election of corporate President and Chief Executive Office John F. Smith Jr. as Chairman to succeed John G. Smale on January 1, 1996 - Harry J. Pearce is elected Vice Chairman and John D. Finnegan is elected Vice President and Treasurer, succeeding Heidi Kunz in the latter position

DECEMBER 5

1866 William Sylvester Ballenger of Little, Mason, and Chevolet is born in Cambridge City, IN

1887 Rose Wilder Lane, a biographer of Henry Ford, is born in DeSmet, SD - she was the daughter of Laura Ingalls Wilder, author of the *Little House on the Prairie* series

1917 Racer Ken Downing is born in Chesterton, Staffordshire, England

1920 Automobile historian John Nixon Brooks is born in New York City

1925 The Olympia Speedway in Maroubra, NSW, Australia opens

1926 Racer James Roy "Jim" Paschal is born in High Point, NC

1928 Gerald Carl Meyers of American Motors is born in Buffalo, NY

1931 The 1932 Chevrolets, marketed as the Confederate Series BA, are introduced

1931 William L. McLellan, a distributor of Willys and Willys-Knight cars and President of the Edmonton Auto Service Club, dies in Edmonton, Alberta, Canada at age 32 following a major operation

1932 The first Ford Model C is produced, featuring Ford's first 4-cylinder engine with a counter-balanced crankshaft

1932 Racer Jim Hurtubise is born in North Tonawanda, NY

1932 Romano Artioli of Bugatti Automobili, manufacturers of the Bugatti 110, is born in Mantua, Italy

1932 The Lorain-Carnegie Bridge (now the Hope Memorial Bridge) in Cleveland, OH opens to the public

1933 Charles Nelson Pogue of Winnipeg, Manitoba, Canada is issued the first of three United States patents for his Pogue Carburetor, said to increase gas mileage to as high as 200 mpg

This restored 1932 Chevrolet Confederate Series BA Convertible Cabriolet (photographed at the 1988 Medora, ND Car Show) clearly shows its Eagle Mascot.

1936 Austin W. Deyo, designer of the Larabee truck and an official of the Larabee-Deyo Motor Truck Company 1915-1917, dies at age 46

1938 The Champion Spark Plug Company is reorganized in Delaware to succeed the original company founded in 1910

1946 Racer Sarel van der Merwe is born in Port Elizabeth, South Africa

1948 B. M. Leece, President of the Leece-Neville Company and a pioneer in the manufacturing of automotive lighting equipment, dies in Cleveland, OH at age 72

1949 The first 1950 Plymouth P19 Deluxe and P20 Deluxe are produced

1951 Chester S. Ricker, a pioneer employee of Henderson and Stutz who was the official scorer for the first Indianapolis 500 race in 1911 and had performed this function at the event ever since, dies at age 63

1955 George Ebling, personal photographer for Henry Ford, dies in Dearborn, MI at age 69

1958 The first British limited-access highway, the Birmingham-Carlisle Motorway, is officially opened by Prime Minister Harold Macmillan

1958 William J. Foster of Chevrolet dies at age 67

1960 Stylist Walter Dorwin Teague (Sr.) dies in Flemington, NJ at age 76

1970 Racer Jordi Gene is born in Barcelona, Spain

1977 The Plymouth Horizon is introduced as the first front-wheel-drive small car manufactured in the United States

DECEMBER 6

1822 Ignaz Schustala is born in Nesseldorf, Austria-Hungary (now the Czech Republic)

1876 Friedrich Samuel "Fred" Duesenberg is born in Lippe state, Germany

1889 Robert Winship Woodruff of the White Motor Company is born in Columbus, GA

1905 Giuseppe Luraghi of Alfa Romeo is born in Milan, Italy

1909 Hugh Chalmers purchases the Chalmers-Detroit Motor Company interests of Roy D. Chapin, Howard E. Coffin, and Frederick O. Bezner for $788,000 while the three latter men purchase Chalmers' interest in the Hudson Motor Car Company for $80,040, resulting in the separation of the two firms

1916 The first American LaFrance cetrifugal pumper is delivered to Troy (NY) Fire Department

1918 Capt. Harry Colburn Turner, a founder of the Southern California Automobile Club in 1900 and the first to drive an automobile from Los Angeles to San Francisco, dies in the military hospital in Abbeville, France at age 45

1919 Samuel C. Pandolfo of the Pan Motor Company is convicted of fraud

1922 Automobile journalist James T. Crow is born in Vincennes, IN

1929 Construction is completed on the Royal Gorge Bridge near Canon City, CO, the world's highest bridge at 1,053 feet above the Arkansas River

1931 Earl H. Hecht, a design engineer of automotive parts and tires, dies in Mansfield, OH at age 39

1933 The 1934 Fords are previewed by the press in Dearborn, MI

1939 The Rolls-Royce "Silver Ripplet", a small prototype with 3.5 litre six- cylinder engine, is completed

1941 Hart O. Berg, manufacturer of the 1903-1905 Berg designed by Robert Jardine and the 1903-1904 Euclid designed by James G. Heaslet, dies in New York City at age 76

1946 The California Texas Corporation is incorporated in Delaware

1948 Racer Keijo "Keke" Rosberg is born in Stockholm, Sweden of Finnish parents

1955 The United States government standardizes the size of automobile license plates

1957 Robert Wellesley Anthony Brewer, credited with design improvements for automobiles and airplanes, dies in Philadelphia, PA at age 80

1961 Racer Manuel Reuter is born in Mainz, West Germany

1962 Graeme K. Howard of General Motors dies in Norfolk, CT at age 66

1963 The first 426 Hemi engine is successfully tested by the Chrysler Corporation

1971 Richard C. Gerstenberg is elected Chairman and Chief Executive Officer of General Motors

1973 A blue 1974 Buick Electra Limited sedan is the first of the marque to be equipped with a factory-installed passive air bag restraint

1974 Citroen and Peugeot merge

1976 Kitty O'Neil (later Mrs. Hambleton) records a speed of 524.016 mph at the Alvard Desert, OR driving the rocket-powered Motivator SM1 - her two-way average of 512.710 mph establishes a new womens land speed record

1989 Centre International de l'Automobile Museum opens in Paris, France

DECEMBER 7

1874 Leon Turcat, builder with his brother-in-law Simon Mery of the 1898-1928 Turcat-Mery, is born in Marseille, France

1875 Automobile upholstery manufacturer Jared Warner Stark is born in Plymouth, PA

1884 Charles Helm Vincent, head of the Packard Proving Grounds in Utica, MI 1928-1947 and brother of Packard executive Jesse G. Vincent, is born in Mountain Grove, MO

1892 Alfred Joseph Fisher is born in Norwalk, OH

1892 Cornelius Willett Van Ranst is born in Syracuse, NY

1896 Automobile body manufacturer Magnus Mallory Burgess is born in Detroit, MI

1903 Svante Holm of Saab is born in Oslo, Norway

1917 Herbert L. Misch, an engineer with Packard and Cadillac prior to becoming Vice President of the Ford Motor Company in charge of the newly established Environmental and Safety Engineering section, is born

1917 Racer Ottorino Volonterio is born in Orselina, Switzerland

1920 Automobile bearing manufacturer Julius A. Perkins dies at age 72

1924 Racer John Love is born in Bulawayo, Southern Rhodesia (now Zimbabwe)

1925 Racer Hermanos "Nano" da Silva Ramos is born in Paris, France with dual French/Brazilian citizenship

1928 Racer Marian Lee "Mickey" Thompson is born in San Fernando, CA

1928 The Ford Motor Company Ltd. is organized to transfer more management of company activities to British citizens

1929 Bentley Motors, Ltd. appoints Lt. Col. Thomas Barwell Barrington as Chief Designer one week after the death of F. T. Burgess

1931 The last Ford Model A is produced on the same day that Henry and Edsel Ford would make a commitment to the V-8 as the marque's primary engine

1931 Robert C. Hupp, a cofounder of Hupmobile in 1908 who later was involved with the R,C.H., the Hupp-Yeats electric, and the Monarch, dies in Detroit, MI at age 55

1932 The first 1933 Pontiac Straight 8 is produced

1935 Rally driver Gunnar Haggbom is born in Sweden

1936 Racer Bob Tullius is born in Rochester, NY

1939 Spencer Penrose, builder of the Pikes Peak (CO) Auto Highway, dies at age 74

1944 Clyde E. Bonnett of the B. F. Goodrich Company, a participant in several of the original Glidden Tours, dies at age 62

1947 The 1948 Hudsons, featuring "step-down" styling, are introduced

1952 Automotive artist Anne Peyton is born in Fort Collins, CO

1953 The Mercury Sun Valley coupe is introduced featuring a transparent roof over the front seat

1953 Charles I. Hall, a General Electric Company researcher holding 739 patents including the automobile thermostat, dies in Boston, MA at age 65

1958 Racer Juan Carlos Giacchino is born in Argentina

1965 The 3,000,000th Chevrolet is produced during the calendar year, the first time that the marque had reached this milestone

1977 Racer Georges Grignard dies at age 72

1984 Racer Lee Roy Yarbrough dies in Jacksonville, FL at age 46

1995 General Motors and Elabuga Automotive Works announce a joint venture to produce up to 50,000 Chevrolet Blazers at the Elabuga, Tatarstan, Russia factory

1997 Robert R. "Bob" Knapp, founder of the Deer Park Winery Automobile Collection, dies at age 64

DECEMBER 8

1861 William Crapo Durant is born in Boston, MA

1863 Automobile engine designer Leon-Marie-Joseph-Clement Levavasseur is born in Mesnil Val, Seine Maritime, France

1884 Jay G. Hayden, biographer of James Couzens, is born in Cassopolis, MI

1892 Arthur Landis of the Auburn Automobile Company is born in Oxford, NC

1896 Marsden Ware of Packard is born in Millville, NJ

1909 Charles Rayfield applies for a United States patent for his carburetor, a design that would become the favorite of race car designers and drivers and standard equipment on several well known marques

1913 Arthur Duray driving the 300-hp Super Fiat at Ostend, Belgium records a one-way run at 132.37 mph, faster than the existing land speed record but not officially recognized

1915 The Diamond T Motor Car Company of Chicago, IL registers both the "diamond" logo and a large "T" as trademarks

1918 Racer John Aitken dies during the influenza epidemic

1921 Carroll A. Hochwalt creates tetrathyl lead (TEL) by combining zinc ethyl and lead chloride, leading to the development of "ethyl" gasoline

1926 Clinton Dillman Lauer, a Ford Motor Company executive 1971-1992, is born in Joliet, IL

1926 Pierre Fenaille is issued a French patent for a CV U-joint considered essential for a successful front-drive automobile

1928 Haakan H. J. Frisinger of Volvo is born in Skovde, Sweden

1930 A United States patent application is filed by E. L. Cord, Herbert C. Snow, and Don C. Hollister to protect the design of the 1931 Auburn radiator shell

1931 The 1932 Graham Blue Streak series is introduced featuring new styling by Amos E. Northup and William H. Neely

1931 The first Pontiac Series 402 Six is produced

1932 The first Pontiac is produced with the new straight-8 engine designed by Benjamin Anibal

1934 The White Motor Company again becomes an independent concern after two years as part of the Studebaker Corporation

1936 Automotive historian Andrew John Appleton Whyte is born

1940 Racer George Snider is born

1942 Industrial architect Albert Kahn dies in Detroit, MI at age 73

1945 The Toyota Motor Company, Ltd. receives permission from military occupation authorities to resume bus and truck production

1951 Porsche makes its first successful United States racing effort when the 1500-cc car sponsored by Max Hoffman and Walter Glockler, the marque's Frankfurt, Germany agent, dominates a race at Palm Beach Shores, FL until retiring with valve gear troubles

1952 The 1953 Hudsons are introduced

1953 The 1953 Dodge Sierra 4-door station wagon is introduced as a mid-year model

1957 The first Sunday newspaper section devoted entirely to automobile advertising appears featuring the 1958 Packard, Studebaker, and Mercedes-Benz lines

1957 George A. Kopatzke, an official of the Wagner Electric Corporation since 1921, dies at age 53

1958 Racer Michel Ferte, younger brother of racer Alain Ferte, is born in Falaise, France

1964 Great Britain's worst automobile accident occurs near Wigan with more than 100 vehicles involved, three deaths, and about 120 injuries

1968 Grease gun manufacturer Oscar U. Zerk dies in Kenosha, WI

1980 Anthony "Tony" Giamo, a specialist in the restoration of the Franklin marque, dies in Thousand Oaks, CA at age 77

1981 Mitsubishi debuts in the United States under its own name

RAYFIELD CARBURETOR
More power - Less fuel - Wider range
FINDEISEN & KROPF MFG. CO.
21ST & ROCKWELL STS., CHICAGO, ILL.

DECEMBER 9

1875 Race car designer Harry Arminius Miller is born in Menomonie, WI

1881 Harry Walter Kent of Kenworth trucks is born in Lockport, NY

1896 Russell Games Slayter, a pioneer developer of fiberglass-bodied automobiles, is born in Argos, IN

1896 The George N. Pierce Company is incorporated in New York state by George N. Pierce, Henry May, Samuel J. Thompson, E. Clifford Potter, and Lorenzo B. Somerby

1907 Ernest Marples, British Minister of Transport 1959-1964 and a proponent of legislating older vehicles off public roads, is born

1917 General Motors reports that they have formed a "close alliance" with the Scripps-Booth Company which had recently been taken over by William C. Durant and the Chevrolet Motor Company

1920 Racer Doug Serrurier is born in Germiston, South Africa

1921 Thomas A. Boyd working under the supervision of Dr. Thomas Midgley Jr. successfully tests tetraethyl gasoline

1925 Will M. Caldwell of the Ford Motor Company is born in Detroit, MI

1927 Victor and Mildred Bruce begin a record-setting 10-day endurance run at the Montlhery track in France in their 2.0-litre A.C. - the type would later be marketed as the A.C. Montlhery

1928 Racer Andre Milhoux is born in Bressoux, Belgium

1936 Racer Ben Pon is born in Leiden, the Netherlands

1937 Automobile spring and bumper manufacturer Floyd E. Badger dies at age 52

1938 George W. Smith of Jeffery, Nash, and Buick is killed at age 58 in an automobile accident near Toledo, OH

1941 Richard Goodyear of the Chrysler Corporation is born in New Haven, CT

1941 George C. Rand, President of the Automobile Racing Club of America, suspends all activities due to World War II - the club was never reactivated

1942 Racer Sheldon Kinser is born

1946 The first 1947 Hudson is produced

1950 The 1951 Chevrolets are introduced

1951 Hudson announces their intent to produce a "light car", the Jet

1954 David N. Miller of Mack, Autocar, and Reo dies at age 58

1954 Alvaro S. Krotz, designer of the 1903-1904 Krotz Electric, the 1908-1912 Sears, and the 1908-1911 Krotz Gas-Electric, dies in Beloit, WI at age 90

1957 Russell E. MacKenzie of the Studebaker-Packard Corporation dies at age 59

1959 Leland W. Fox of the Firestone Tire & Rubber Company dies at age 65

1963 The last United States-built Studebaker is produced as corporate officials announce the closing of the South Bend, IN factory

1969 The AC Spark Plug Division of General Motors in Flint, MI begins developing the catalytic converter under the direction of General Manager George W. Chestnut, Chief Engineer Thomas E. Hustead, and General Motors President Edward N. Cole

DECEMBER 10

1826 William Ford, father of Henry Ford, is born in Ballinascarthy, County Cork, Ireland

1845 R. W. Thomson of London, England is issued a British patent for his "improvement in carriage wheels", in effect the world's first pneumatic tires

1862 Theodore Arthur Willard, the inventor of the storage battery, is born in Castle Rock, MN

1895 The Self Propelled Traffic Association, the first automobile club in Great Britain, is organized in London with Sir David Salomans as President, and John Philipson, Sir Frederick Bramwell, Alexander Siemens, and the 12th Earl of Winchilsea as Vice Presidents

1907 John F. Dodge weds Matilda Rausch in his second marriage

1908 Clifford Maurice MacMillan of the Studebaker Corporation is born in Hebron, IN

1910 Automotive parts manufacturer Urban Theodore Kuechle is born in Milwaukee, WI

1912 Charles W. Nash is elected President of General Motors succeeding Thomas Neal

1915 The 1,000,000th Ford Model T is produced

1915 Thomas Aquinas Murphy, Chairman of General Motors 1974-1980, is born in Hornell, NY

1917 The Nakajima Aircraft Company is organized in Japan - the firm would evolve into Fuji Heavy Industries, Ltd., manufacturers of the Subaru

1920 Horace E. Dodge dies in Palm Beach, FL at age 52

1929 The Cadillac V-16 is announced to dealers in a letter from division President Lawrence P. Fisher

1940 Racer Bentley Warren is born in Gloucester, MA

1942 Automotive historian Huw Beynon is born in Ebbw Vale, Wales

1945 Racer Robert McDonough dies

1947 Racer Jurgen Barth is born in Thoum, Germany

1951 The 1952 Jeep pickup trucks are introduced

1951 The 1952 Willys four-wheel-drive wagons are introduced

A late 1914 Ford Model T touring car with 1915 California license plates on tour in the Sierra Nevada Mountains — Model T production was nearing the one million mark, an unthinkable goal only a few years before.

1954 Racer Price Cobb is born in Dallas, TX

1957 Thorsten Y. Olsen, Chairman of the Board of the Tinius Olsen Testing Machine Company and an employee of the firm since 1903, dies at age 78

1961 Louis G. Hupp of Hupmobile dies in Detroit, MI at age 89

1963 Purfina SA changes its name to Fina SA

1968 Peter Monteverdi completes the design of his first four-place car, the Monteverdi Type 375 L

1970 Lee Iacocca is elected President of the Ford Motor Company

1981 The Rouge Steel Company is formed as a subsidiary of the Ford Motor Company

DECEMBER 11

1818 Jerome Increase Case is born in Williamstown, NY

1874 George H. Lanchester is born

1877 William Packard, grandfather of William D. Packard and James W. Packard, dies in Kernville, CA at age 74

1894 The Exposition Internationale de Velocipedie et de Locomotion Automobile, the world's first automobile show, opens in Paris, France with four exhibitors

1904 James E. Goodman of General Motors is born in Union City, IN

1905 The Ford Motor Company, having lost a patent suit, contracts with inventor Frederick W. Ball for the use of his planetary transmission

1905 Joseph A. Galamb is hired C. Harold Wills of the Ford Motor Company

1906 Rolls-Royce records its first export sale of a Silver Ghost, taking an order for a Barker bodied phaeton from Jefferson Seligman of New York City

1906 The first completed KisselKar, a 1907 Model C, is shipped to Joseph McDuffee, a Chicago, IL automobile dealer

1915 The Hudson Super-Six is previewed to dealers

1919 The first Bentley prototype is registered

1920 Denis Jenkinson, the winning navigator with driver Stirling Moss in the 1955 Mille Miglia, is born in London, England

1921 The San Carlos Board Speedway in San Francisco, CA stages its first races - the 250-mile main event is won by Jimmy Murphy driving a Duesenberg

1922 Bentley and Bentley Ltd. is liquidated

1926 The Goodyear Tyre & Rubber Company (Australia) Ltd. is established in Sydney, NSW, Australia

1926 John William Oldham of the Chrysler Corporation and American Motors is born in Roseville, MI

1934 Buick engineer John Dolza is issued a United States patent for his Roller automatic transmission, but its usage in production vehicles is rejected by division President Harlow H. Curtice

1935 Edford M. Walter, Assistant Sales Manager of the Ethyl Gasoline Corporation, is killed at age 41 when his airplane crashes near Nunda, NY

1937 The Auburn Automobile Company and its subsidiary, Lycoming Manufacturing Company, file for reorganization under bankruptcy protection in United States District Court in Fort Wayne, IN

1940 William Francis Powers of the Ford Motor Company is born in Philadelphia, PA

1941 Buick reduces prices on all of its new cars to compensate for the lack of a spare tire and tube due to World War II restrictions

1941 Walter L. Marr, Chief Engineer of Buick from 1903 into the 1920's, dies in Signal Mountain, TN at age 76

1950 The first 1951 Plymouth, a Cranbrook sedan, is produced

1951 Kirke K. Hoagg of General Motors dies in Scarsdale, NY at age 62

1953 Willard A. Stearns, an oil seal and synthetic rubber specialist whose automotive career included stints with Packard and Buick, dies at age 54

1961 The Philco Corporation is acquired as a subsidiary of the Ford Motor Company

1961 Racer Philippe Favre is born in Geneva, Switzerland

1963 Ethyl Gasoline Corporation executive Edward L. Shea dies in New York City at age 71

1966 Rover and Alvis are acquired by the Leyland Group

1967 The Lincoln Continental Mark III is previewed by the press

1975 Continental Automotive Associates buy the assets of the bankrupt Bricklin Canada Ltd.

1981 Edgar F. Kaiser dies in San Francisco, CA at age 73

1986 AB Volvo and General Motors sign an agreement whereby Volvo will assume responsibility for the production of GMC heavy-duty trucks

1995 Cesare Romiti is named Chairman of Fiat SpA, succeeding Gianni Agnelli

DECEMBER 12

1873 Henry Jones Fuller of Rolls-Royce of America, Inc. is born in St. Johnsbury, VT

1879 August Samuel Duesenberg is born in Kirchheide, Lipfe Detmold, Germany

1885 Ward Murphey Canaday, Chairman of Willys-Overland, Inc. 1936-1946 and a principal developer of the Jeep, is born in New Castle, IN

1905 Terry Stafford is issued a United States patent for his solid-unit drive train

1906 The first Brooklands Automobile Racing Club meeting is held with Lord Lonsdale as President

1906 Antique automobile collector Clarion Elroy Larson is born in Randall, IA

1909 Classic car collector Andrew Davidson Darling is born

1911 Christian Werner joins the Daimler Motoren-Gesellschaft as an engineer and test driver

1912 Herbert M. Dawley applies for a United States patent on his fender- mounted headlights design that would become a hallmark of the Pierce-Arrow marque

1916 The Studebaker Corporation breaks ground for its new factory in South Bend, IN

1922 The Flower City Specialty Company of Rochester, NY is issued a United States patent for its Self-Closing Monkey Links tire chain repair kit

1922 Automotive parts manufacturer Wernert Edward Mischler is born in Pittsburgh, PA

1923 The 1,000,000th Dodge is produced

1936 Racer Wally Dallenbach (Sr.) is born

1946 Racer Emerson Fittipaldi is born in Sao Paulo, Brazil

1946 Racer Renzo Zorzi is born in Turin, Italy

1948 Racer Roelof Wunderink is born in Eindhoven, the Netherlands

Dodge Brothers logos changed frequently in the early years - this one appeared in late 1921

1950 High-performance engine designer Ernest Henry dies in Paris, France at age 65

1951 William D. Allison contracts with the Packard Motor Car Company to develop torsion bar suspension

1951 Russell A. Firestone, a Director of the Firestone Tire & Rubber Company and second son of Harvey S. Firestone, dies in New York City at age 50

1952 The 1953 Fords are introduced

1956 James Frank Chapman, a development engineer with the Flxible Company, dies

1957 A. J. Rowledge of Rolls-Royce dies at age 81

1959 Bruce McLaren driving a Cooper-Climax wins the United States Grand Prix in Sebring, FL, at age 22 years, 104 days the youngest driver to win a Formula 1 championship race - the Kurtis makes its only Formula 1 appearance, but the car driven by Rodger Ward retires with clutch problems - the Tec-Mec, designed by Valerio Colotti based on the Maserati 250F, makes its only Formula 1 appearance, but driver Fritz d'Orey retires with an oil leak

1959 F. P. Zimmerli of the Associated Spring Corporation dies at age 65

1964 Joseph M. Dodge, a Director of the Packard Motor Car Company 1942-1947, dies at age 74

1964 William E. Rootes, 1st Baron Rootes of Ramsbury, GBE, KBE, dies in London at age 70

1965 Racer Stephane Proulx is born in Quebec, PQ, Canada

1975 Two months after his Canadian-based factory went bankrupt, Malcolm Bricklin files for personal bankruptcy in Scottsdale, AZ

1985 Shoichiro Toyoda announces plans to build a Toyota factory in Canada

1994 Ronald L. Zarrella, President and Chief Operating Officer of Bausch & Lomb Inc., is elected as a Vice President of General Motors in charge of the North American Vehicle Sales, Service, and Marketing Group

1995 Classic car collector Andrew Darling dies on his 86th birthday

DECEMBER 13

1873 Automobile bearing manufacturer F. M. Germane is born in Chicago, IL

1885 J. F. Winchester of the Hewitt Motor Company and the Standard Oil Company of New Jersey is born in Walpole, MA

1892 Heber Wallace Peters of Packard and Cadillac is born in New Bedford, MA

1896 Philco Corporation executive William Balderston, a pioneer in the commercialization of automobile radios, is born in Boise, ID

1904 Frank V. Whyland and Clarence P. Hollister, manufacturers of the Berkshire, are issued a United States patent for their progressive three-speed transmission

Berkshire Automobiles
HIGH CLASS TOURING CARS
MADE AND TESTED IN THE BERKSHIRE HILLS

THREE MODELS
16 H. P. $2,000   25 H. P. $2,500   40 H. P. $4,500
The car that will do in the Berkshire Hills will do anywhere on this earth
Berkshire Cars are a modern, up-to-date American product.
No Agents. Entire output handled direct by
DOUGLAS ANDREWS COMPANY, Selling Agents
1623 Broadway, NEW YORK
Branch Stores : CHICAGO,   BOSTON,   BROOKLINE,   PITTSFIELD

1909 John Otto Zimmerman of the General Motors Acceptance Corporation is born in New York City

1909 The Gramm-Logan Motor Car Company of Bowling Green, OH registers its name as a trademark, said to be styled in handwriting of Benjamin A. Gramm - the firm built only trucks and was dissolved in 1910

1914 Automotive historian Carey Stillman Bliss is born in Albany, NY

1916 Packard's board of directors rejects the offer of Charles W. Nash and James J. Storrow to purchase the company

1918 Racer William "Bill" Vukovich (nee Vucerovich) is born in Alameda, CA

1920 Sizaire Freres et Naudin is reorganized as the Societe des Nouveaux Etablissements Sizaire et Naudin, with Francois-Zavier Belas as President

1920 Philip Sidney Egan, a member of the Tucker design team and an historian of the marque, is born in Oak Park, IL

1921 Most of the Templar Motors Corporation factory in Cleveland, OH is destroyed by fire

1922 William L. Kissel and J. Friedrich "Fritz" Werner are issued a United States patent for their "Convertible Automobile Body", a removable top that could convert an open touring car into a closed car and had been offered on the KisselKar and Kissel since 1914

1923 Purfina SA is incorporated in Antwerp, Belgium

1927 The Peerless 1927-1928 "Eagle's Head" mascot is patented by designer F. C. Ruppel

1928 The Goodyear Tire & Rubber Company of Alabama, a subsidiary of the Goodyear Tire & Rubber Company, is established in Gadsden, AL

1929 Theodor Kollinek, a director of the Automobil und Flugtechnische Gesellschaft and a prolific contributor to German and Austrian automotive trade journals, dies in Berlin, Germany at age 40

1934 Frank B. Averill of the Studebaker Corporation of Canada Ltd. dies

1935 Duesenberg, Inc. announces that assembly of the Duesenberg Model J has been completed and that most of their employees are being laid off indefinitely

1935 Racer Earl Franklin "Bomber" Balmer is born in Floyds Knobs, IN

1935 Maurice Wolfe, President of the Meteor Motor Car Company, manufacturers of funeral cars, dies in Piqua, OH at age 59 - he was a pioneer Cadillac salesman who claimed the first sale of an automobile to an American Indian, and later was designer/manufacturer of the 1907-1909 Wolfe, the 1910-1913 Wilcox, and the 1910-1912 Clark

Longtime owner Clarion E. Larson and his rare 1907 Wolfe at the North Dakota Centennial car show in Bismarck in 1989. This car was recently acquired by General Motors executive Harry J. Pearce, a friend of the Larsons.

1935 Charles R. Bissell, a pioneer exporter of United States automobiles, dies

1935 Lars G. Nilson, a Swedish-born consulting engineer and former President of the Nilson-Miller Company, dies in Hoboken, NJ at age 73

1939 The first production Lincoln Continental is completed

1944 Racer Mike Mosley is born in California

1945 Racer Brian McGuire is born in Melbourne, Victoria, Australia

1957 The last 2-seat Ford Thunderbird is produced

1960 The 1960 Opels are introduced to the United States market

1960 Ford Motor Company President Robert S. McNamara resigns to accept the nomination of President-elect John F. Kennedy to become Secretary of Defense

1971 The 1972 Jaguars are introduced to the United States market

1973 John D. Biggers, President of the Libbey-Owens-Ford Glass Company 1930- 1953 and its Chairman 1953-1960, dies at age 84

1973 Charles R. Feldmann, longtime owner of the Henney Motor Company, dies in Connecticut at age 75

1979 The Shell-D'Arcy Petroleum Company of Nigeria Ltd. changes its name to the Shell Petroleum Development Company of Nigeria

1985 Renault executive Pierre Semerena is named Chairman of American Motors

DECEMBER 14

1884 Hugh Joseph Ferry of Packard is born in Grand Rapids, MI

1903 Karl Alexander Roesch of the White Motor Company is born in Cleveland, OH

1909 The famous brick surface is completed at the Indianapolis Motor Speedway

1914 Henry J. Kaiser forms his first company, the Henry J. Kaiser Company, specializing in road construction

1914 The Societa Anonima Officine Alfieri Maserati is founded in Bologna, Italy

1922 The 1923 Auburns are introduced, featuring new engines manufactured by the Weidely Motors Company of Indianapolis, IN

1924 The J. I. Case Threshing Machine Company introduces the Jay-Eye-See as a scaled-down companion marque to its Case line of automobiles

1924 The Culver City (CA) Board Speedway stages its first event, a 250-mile race won by Bennett Hill driving a Miller

1924 Racer Bob Drake is born in the United States

1929 The first Pontiac Model 6-30-B and New Series Big Sixes are produced

1930 The Ford Model A Victoria is introduced

1931 Bentley Motors (1931) Ltd. is organized as a subsidiary of the British Equitable Central Trust, a paper organization acting on the behalf of Rolls-Royce Ltd.

1936 Racer Charlie Hayes is born in Chevy Chase, MD

1941 The Nazi-occupation government in France orders that all automobiles registered before December 1925 must be destroyed as a supply of materiel for the armaments industry

1943 William G. Irwin, the financial backer of diesel engine manufacturer Clessie L. Cummins, dies in Indianapolis, IN

1943 Pioneer automobile design engineer Joseph A. Anglada dies in Abington, PA at age 63

1944 The Pierce-Arrow Motor Car Company is legally dissolved

1947 Louis Delage dies in Paris, France at age 73

1947 Racer Howdy Holmes is born in Ann Arbor, MI

1947 The National Association for Stock Car Auto Racing (NASCAR) is founded at the Streamline Hotel in Daytona Beach, FL, with Bill France Sr. chosen as the organization's first President

1951 The 1952 Chryslers are introduced

1954 Racer Alan Kulwicki is born in Greenfield, WI

1962 Highway engineer Herbert S. Fairbank dies in Baltimore, MD at age 74

1966 Racer Fabrizio Giovanardi is born in Sassuolo, Italy

1978 The 150,000,000th Ford Motor Company vehicle, a 1979 Ford Mustang, is produced at the Dearborn, MI plant

1979 Edgar William Garbisch and his wife, the former Bernice Chrysler, die

1987 The last American Motors-designed Eagle station wagon is produced, in effect the final act of the last "independent" United States automobile producer

1991 Henry Austin Clark, antique automobile collector, owner of the Long Island Automotive Museum, and automobile historian, dies in Glen Cove, NY at age 74

1995 Gerhard Liener, former Finance Director for Daimler-Benz AG who had resigned under pressure in July, commits suicide at his home in Bavaria

1995 Fiat SpA names Paolo Cantarella to succeed Cesare Romiti as President

DECEMBER 15

1852 Ignaz Schustala obtains official permission to begin construction of a carriage factory in Olmutz, Moravia, Austria-Hungary (now Olomouc, Czech Republic) - this enterprise would evolve into the Tatra automobile works

1861 Charles Edgar Duryea is born in Canton, IL

1868 August Charles Fruehauf is born in Fraser, MI

1870 Charles Newton Teetor, founder of the Teetor-Hartley Motor Company and the Perfect Circle Company, is born in Hagerstown, IN

See that groove

See that slot

It Takes Both
to *Regulate* the Oil

Neither can do the job alone. 1000 miles to the gallon of oil. Standard equipment in more than 140 motor cars, trucks and buses.

Oil Regulating Type, 60c and Up
Compression Type, 30c and Up

THE PERFECT CIRCLE CO.
HAGERSTOWN   **INDIANA**

PERFECT CIRCLE
Oil-Regulating Piston Rings
Patented March 29, 1910; May 2, 1922

C.N. Teetor was the patriarch of a family that has distinguished itself as automotive manufacturers, inventors, and historians for three generations.

1893 Harvey Charles Fruehauf, a cofounder in 1915 with his father August C. Fruehauf of the Fruehauf Trailer Company, manufacturers of truck trailers, is born in Grosse Pointe Park, MI

1896 Stephen M. Balzer of the Bronx, NY is issued a United States patent for his tiny voiturette manufactured in 1894

1898 Thomas Oscar McLaughlin of General Motors is born in Sheridan, WY

1901 Edwin Foster Blair, a director of the Packard Motor Car Company 1950- 1957, is born in Weatherford, TX

1903 Edward Charles Quinn of the Chrysler Corporation is born in Detroit, MI

1908 Bernard Alfred Chapman of American Motors is born in Detroit, MI

1909 Ettore Bugatti resigns as chief designer of Gasmotorenfabrik Deutz AG of Cologne, Germany

1913 Racer Walt Ader is born in Califon, NJ

1914 Alanson P. Brush is issued a United States patent for his automobile frame concept developed specifically for the Marmon Model 34

1915 The Hercules Motor Manufacturing Company is organized

1915 Marius Albert van Merkensteijn of Kaiser-Frazer, Willys-Overland, Studebaker, and American Motors is born in Rotterdam, the Netherlands

1917 The first Moore is produced by the Moore Motor Vehicle Company of Minneapolis, MN - George L. Moore, the local Ford dealer, hoped that his car would compete favorably against Henry Ford's Model T

1917 The Scripps-Booth Model Six-39 is introduced

1918 John E. Genn of the Stewart-Warner Speedometer Corporation dies in New York City at age 35

1919 The Astra Motors Corporation is organized in Saint Louis, MO with B. R. Parrott as President and Treasurer, A. J. Kessinger as Secretary, and V. C. Kloepper as Chief Engineer to manufacture the Astra, a car designed by New York City engineer Andre Mertzanoff

1919 The Locomobile Company is organized by E. S. Hare to acquire the assets of the Locomobile Company of America

1927 The first Marmon V-16 is roadtested in a temporary chassis

1934 The 1935 Chevrolets are introduced, featuring "Turret Top" styling

1935 Stylist William L. Mitchell joins General Motors

1940 Automotive starting motor and generator manufacturer Arthur A. Skinner dies at age 55

1941 The last 1942 Pontiac Chieftain is produced

1942 Massachusetts issues the first plastic license plate tabs

1945 Paul Daimler, Chief Engineer of Mercedes-Benz, dies in Berlin, Germany at age 76

1949 The first Saab is produced

1949 Raymond Mays and Ken Richardson test drive the first BRM V-16 race car in its public debut at Folkingham Airfield, Bourne, England

1949 The assets of the Linn Manufacturing Company are sold at public auction

1949 Elbridge F. Bacon, Assistant Chief Engineer of the AC Spark Plug Division of General Motors, dies at age 51

1949 Roy Noll of the Ford Motor Company dies in Dearborn, MI at age 66

1950 Deutsch-Amerikanische Petroleum Ges changes its name to Esso AG

1951 The 1952 Henry J Vagabond is introduced

1951 The 1952 Kaisers are introduced - these cars were actually modified 1951 cars that were marketed as Virginians

1951 Packard terminates its longtime advertising contract with Young & Rubicon, embarking on a massive national advertising campaign under the direction of Maxon, Inc.

1952 The 1953 Willys Aero-Eagle and Aero-Lark are introduced

1955 The 1956 Hudson Ramblers are introduced

1957 Former United States Representative Leonidas C. Dyer (R-MO), the author of the Auto Theft Act of 1919, dies in St. Louis, MO at age 86

1966 Racer Massimiliano "Max" Angelelli is born in Italy

1980 Peter Gregg, winner of the 1976 Daytona 24-hour race, dies in Ponte Vedra, FL at age 40

DECEMBER 16

1872 Clarence Alfred Musselman, a cofounder of the automotive publisher Chilton Company in 1899, is born

1883 Gottlieb Daimler is issued German patent #28002 for his "Gasmotor" featuring hot-tube ignition and most basic concepts of the modern four- stroke gasoline engine

1890 Marvin L. Gosney of the Sinclair Oil Company is born in Paris, MO

1894 Elbert L. Smith of McIntyre and Barley is born in Otsego, MI

1904 The Timken Roller Bearing Axle Company is reorganized in Canton, OH to succeed the original company of the same name that had been incorporated in New Jersey in 1902

1906 Henry A. Barnes, a designer of traffic control equipment, is born in Newark, NJ

1906 James Michael Roche of General Motors is born in Elgin, IL

1914 The Chevrolet 490, designed by Alfred Sturt, is announced as William C. Durant's first serious competitor of the Ford Model T - its model number noted the current price of the Ford car

1918 Roy Post Trowbridge of General Motors is born in Sacramento, CA

1920 Racer Les Leston is born in Nottingham, Nottinghamshire, England

1921 Automotive parts manufacturer William Henry Patterson Jr. is born in Toledo, OH

1923 Chester Lee Krause, publisher of *Old Cars Weekly*, is born in Iola, WI

1925 Assar Gabrielsson and Gustaf Larson sign a written agreement defining their plan to mass produce an automobile, which would evolve into AB Volvo

1929 The K-D Motor Company, founded in 1912 by Miss Margaret E. Knight and Mrs. Beatrice Davidson, is legally "dissolved by Proclamation", having ceased production of the K-D in 1913

1931 The Buick 1931-1932 "Winged 8" mascot is patented by designer by K. Forbes

1932 Racer Henry Taylor is born in Shefford, Bedfordshire, England

1934 Scuderia Ferrari conceives the plans for the 16-cylinder Alfa Romeo Bimotore race car

1938 C. L. Jacobsen, Chrysler Division Sales Manager, announces that the sun roof option is being discontinued after just three months due to lack of demand

1941 Charles D. Cutting, designer of the 1910-1914 Cutting automobile and later a manufacturer of automotive parts, dies in Detroit, MI

1945 Giovanni Agnelli, the founder of Fiat, dies in Turin, Italy at age 79

1953 The 1954 Canadian Mercurys are introduced

1954 Maxwell E. McDowell of the Standard Oil Company dies in Scarsdale, NY at age 60

1960 J. W. Tiscornia, an automobile parts manufacturer who is credited with the development of disc brakes, dies in Saint Joseph, MI at age 75

1977 Peugeot executive Andre Gasparoux is murdered by leftist terrorists in Buenos Aires, Argentina

1981 Orville Wick, a design engineer with the AC Spark Plug Division of General Motors 1941-1963 credited with many product improvements, dies in Garrison, ND at age 79

1982 Colin Chapman, founder and Chairman of the Lotus Engineering Company, later Lotus Cars Ltd., dies in Norfolk county, England at age 54

1982 Osmond F. Rivers, an executive with Hooper & Company (Coachbuilders) Ltd. 1911-1959, dies in Copenhagen, Denmark at age 87

1985 The Ford Motor Company acquires First Nationwide Financial Corporation

1986 Raymond Levy is named Chairman of Regie Nationale des Usines Renault

1987 Peter Schutz resigns as Chairman of Dr. Ing. h.c. F. Porsche KG

1989 Racer Oscar Galvez dies in Buenos Aires, Argentina at age 76

DECEMBER 17

1872 Giuseppe Merosi of Alfa Romeo is born in Piacenza, Italy

1892 Internal combustion engine pioneer George Bailey Brayton dies at age 53 while on a business trip in England

1908 The Lansing (MI) Fire Department acquires their first motorized fire truck

1908 Automobile racing historian Charles Lancaster Betts Jr. is born in Philadelphia, PA

1909 The Indianapolis Motor Speedway holds its grand opening, complete with the ceremonial laying of the last "golden" brick by Indiana Governor Thomas R. Marshall

1910 William Charles Newberg of the Chrysler Corporation is born in Seattle, WA

1910 Charles F. Kettering, William A. Chryst, and William P. Anderson successfully test the first automobile self-starter

1919 The International Motor Truck Corporation, manufacturers of the Mack truck, acquires the assets of the Wright-Martin Aircraft Corporation including their main engine plant in New Brunswick, NJ

1924 James T. McCleary, an advocate of the Lincoln Highway and former United States Congressman from Minnesota, dies in LaCrosse, WI at age 71

1925 "The New Stutz Vertical Eight, with Safety Body", the first Stutz designed during the Frederic E. Moskovics era, is unveiled to dealers

1931 Bentley Motors (1931) Ltd. is incorporated as a subsidiary of Rolls-Royce Ltd.

1931 The 1932 Cadillacs and LaSalles are introduced at the Cadillac National Convention for dealers and sales personnel in Detroit, MI

1934 Ransom E. Olds resigns from the Executive Committee of the Reo Motor Car Company

1940 The American Bantam Car Company completes its initial contract to supply seventy prototype Jeeps to the federal government

1945 William F. Milward, designer of the Charron-Laycock automobile, dies at age 66

1948 Racer Leonel Friedrich is born in Brazil

1952 The Austin Motor Company Ltd. and Morris Motors Ltd. merge to form the British Motor Corporation with Leonard Lord as Chairman

1955 Dodge introduces the Coronet station wagon and the Royal Lancer 2-door hardtop coupe as mid-year models

1956 The first 1957 Packard, its appearance heavily influenced by Studebaker, is produced at the Studebaker plant in South Bend, IN

1956 Great Britain begins emergency gasoline rationing because of the Suez Canal crisis in Egypt

1963 Theodore V. Houser, a longtime Sears, Roebuck & Company executive who conceived the idea of the 1952-1953 Allstate, a badge-engineered Henry J, dies at age 71

1963 Harry B. Kenyon, inventor of the headlight dimmer switch, dies in Miami, FL

1963 The United States Congress enacts the first national legislation regarding air pollution controls on automobiles

1968 Racer Paul Tracy is born in Toronto, ON, Canada

1973 A Buick Apollo with a reworked 1960's V-6 engine is driven by Chief Engineer Phillip C. Bowser from Flint, MI to the General Motors' building in Detroit, MI where President Edward N. Cole drives it to the former Kaiser-Jeep Corporation plant in Toledo, OH - the end result was Buick's return to the V-6 engine and one of the more successful reactions to the OPEC crisis

1979 Stan Barrett, driving the Budweiser Rocket car at Rogers Dry Lake, CA, reaches 739.666 mph in an unofficial one-way run, the first time that the sound barrier had been broken on land

1983 The Lincoln Continental Mark VII is introduced

1986 John Z. DeLorean is acquitted of fraud

1986 Giulio Ramponi, winner of the Mille Miglia in 1928 and 1929, dies in South Africa at age 84

1991 The last Rolls-Royce Phantom VI is completed, a Mulliner Park Ward landaulette that was later sold to His Majesty Haji Hassanal Bolkiah Mu'izzaddin Waddaulah, the Sultan of Brunei

DECEMBER 18

1864 Frederick William Barker, the patent attorney who represented Henry Ford in the Selden suit, is born in London, England

1880 Earle C. Anthony, a Los Angeles, CA Packard dealer 1905-1956 and a Director of the company 1948-1956, is born in Washington, IL

1883 Automobile stylist Walter Dorwin Teague is born in Decatur, IN

1898 The first official land speed record is set at 39.245 mph by Count Gaston de Chasseloup-Laubat driving a Jeantaud at the world's first sprint races in Acheres Park near Paris, France - this car is usually credited with introducing the steering wheel, which would soon replace the then ubiquitous tiller

1898 Theodore Parsons Hall, developer of the Hall flying automobile, is born in Wallingford, CT

1899 Jack F. Wolfram, Oldsmobile General Manager 1951-1964, is born in Pittsburgh, PA

1907 Racer Bill Holland is born in Philadelphia, PA

1913 The Standard Motor Company of Minneapolis, MN purchases the Colby Motor Company of Mason City, IA

1916 Douglas Andrew Fraser, President of the United Auto Workers 1977-1983, is born in Glasgow, Scotland

1919 Racer Henri Fournier dies in Paris, France at age 48

1921 Clarence E. Rogers of Amplex, Sun, and Crow-Elkhart dies in Elkhart, IN at age 36

1924 The Bendix Corporation, a leading manufacturer of automobile brakes, is organized with Vincent H. Bendix as President

1930 Henry A. House, who helped build the House steam car in Bridgeport, CT in 1866 but achieved more success in England with the Lifu steam cars and trucks of 1899-1902, dies in Bridgeport at age 90

1938 Paul Kleiber, manufacturer of the Kleiber truck 1914-1937 and Kleiber automobile 1924-1929, dies in San Francisco, CA

1941 Racer Wayne Baker is born

1942 George Riley Thurston Jr. of the Cummins Engine Company is born in Rushville, IN

1945 Racer Mike Walker is born in Birmingham, England

1946 The Austin Princess limousine is announced

1953 The 1954 Pontiacs are introduced

1955 Racer Ted Musgrave is born in Franklin, WI

1956 The 1957 Plymouth Fury sport coupe is introduced to complete the marque's model lineup

1979 The Reo Clubhouse in Lansing, MI is demolished

1982 The first TAG turbo V-6 racing engine developed jointly by Porsche and McLaren is tested in preparation for use in the McLaren MP4/1D chassis

1984 The New United Motor Manufacturing, Inc. (NUMMI), a joint venture between General Motors and Toyota in Fremont, CA, introduces its first car to be sold in the United States as the Chevrolet Nova

1991 Racer George Abecassis dies in Ibstone, Buckinghamshire, England at age 78

1995 Henry Banks, racer and USAC official 1959-1984, dies at age 81

DECEMBER 19

1752 Francois Isaac de Rivaz, internal combustion engine pioneer, is born in Paris, France

1877 James Chase Rappleyea of Chalmers and Overland is born in Rochester, NY

1888 John David Biggers, a longtime executive with the Libbey-Owens-Ford Glass Company who previously had been associated with Dodge Brothers, Inc., the Graham Brothers Company, and the Graham-Paige Motors Corporation, is born in St. Louis, MO

1895 Automobile parts manufacturer William Frederic Wise is born in Lima, OH

1915 Automotive historian Herbert Lozier is born in New York City

1917 The Detroiter Motor Car Company is declared bankrupt

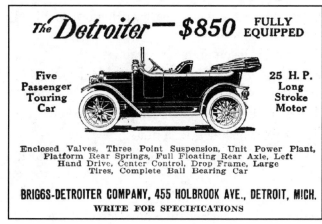

Things looked very good for the one-year-old Detroiter marque when this advertisement appeared in 1912, but the company went through several name changes on its way to oblivion in 1919.

1918 General Motors acquires the McLaughlin Motor Car Company of Oshawa, ON to establish itself in the Canadian market

1918 John F. Reno of the Moline Automobile Company, an advocate of Knight sleeve-valve engines, dies in East Moline, IL at age 35

1923 Luigi Innocenti of Innocenti is born

1923 Racer Onofre Augustin Marimon is born in Buenos Aires, Argentina

1924 The last British-made Rolls-Royce Silver Ghost, a touring car with custom body by Barker, is sold to John Henry Thomas of London

1925 Raymond H. Dietrich contracts to be a "Body Critic" for Packard

1937 Nathaniel Thomas Dawes Jr., a collector and historian of Studebaker and Packard, is born in Newburgh, NY

1938 Henry Ford II is elected to the Ford Motor Company Board of Directors

1939 Benjamin Copf of Ford-Japan, Yoshisuke Ayukawa of Nissan, and Risaburo Toyoda of Toyota sign a joint venture agreement to manufacture cars in Japan

1940 Fred R. Nohavec, an authority on automotive air cleaners, dies at age 49

1951 The Kuwait Oil Company (London) Ltd. changes its name to the Kuwait Oil Company Ltd.

1954 Racer Jeff Allam is born in Epsom, Great Britain

1956 The Kelsey-Hayes Wheel Corporation changes its name to the Kelsey-Hayes Company

1966 Two Sunbeam Tiger II production prototypes are completed

1979 Regie Nationale des Usines Renault acquires a 10% share of AB Volvo

1983 Tojiro Okamoto of Toyota dies at age 94

1994 Rolls-Royce announces that they have reached an deal with BMW to utilize the German company's new V-12 as its future engine supply

DECEMBER 20

1867 Myron Francis Hill, the inventor of antifriction bearings and founder of the American Roller Bearing Company, is born in Milford, MA

1868 Harvey Samuel Firestone is born in Columbiana County, OH

1870 Herbert Watson Alden, an automotive parts executive who is credited with designing the first army tank, is born in Lyndonville, VT

1892 Alexander T. Brown and George F. Stillman are issued a patent for their pneumatic automobile tires

1895 The world's first gasoline-powered bus service connecting Siegen, Netphen, and Deuz, Germany is discontinued after nine months, having transported approximately 10,600 paying customers

1911 The Piston Ring Company is founded in Muskegon, MI by Charles E. Johnson and Paul R. Beardsley - the firm would evolve into the Sealed Power Corporation

1912 The Stewart-Warner Speedometer Company is incorporated in Virginia

1914 Lyman F. Gordon, founder of the Wyman-Gordon Company, dies in Grafton, MA at age 53, at which time his firm made approximately 90% of the automobile crankshafts in the United States

1920 Jean Maddern Pitrone, biographer of John and Horace Dodge, is born in Ishpeming, MI

1922 New York City's last horsedrawn fire appartus makes its final run

1923 Ransom E. Olds retires as President of the Reo Motor Car Company and is succeeded by Richard H. Scott

1929 The last Stearns-Knight is produced

1931 Automotive ball bearing manufacturer J. William Schatz is murdered at age 57 at his home in Poughkeepsie, NY

1940 The 1,000th Volkswagen Kubelwagen is produced

1945 World War II tire rationing ends in the United States

1946 Richard Edson Marston, Chief Engineer of the Selden Truck Company whose earlier career included stints with Marmon and Packard, dies

1947 Horace T. Thomas, the Chief Engineer of the Olds Motor Works who helped design the Oldsmobile Curved Dash, and Vice President of the Reo Motor Car Company 1914-1947 who designed the first Reo automobile and Reo Speed Wagon truck, dies in Lansing, MI at age 73

1951 The 1952 Henry J is introduced

1951 The Allstate, a badge-engineered Henry J, is introduced as a new marque to be sold by Sears, Roebuck & Company

1957 The first 1958 Ford Thunderbird, the first car completely designed by the styling team headed by George W. Walker and the first of the submarque to have four seats, is produced

1959 Racer Scott Goodyear is born in Toronto, ON, Canada

1963 The last United States-built Studebaker is produced

1968 Racer Karl Wendlinger is born in Kufstein, Austria

1974 Rudolf Leiding resigns as Managing Director of Volkswagenwerk AG

1975 John Lee Pratt, a 56-year employee of General Motors and the first in the company to hold the title of Executive Vice President, dies in Fredericksburg, VA at age 96

1976 J. Frank Drake of the Gulf Oil Company dies at age 96

1977 British automobile executive Sir Reginald Rootes dies in London at age 81

1982 Automobile historian George W. Risley dies in Detroit, MI at age 70

1993 Bert-Olof Svanholm is named Chairman of AB Volvo, replacing interim Chairman Bo Rydin

DECEMBER 21

1886 Edmund Ewald Hans, credited with many improvements in automobile heating systems, is born in Altura, MN

1895 The 1,000th Daimler is produced

1909 Automobile battery manufacturer Harry Joseph Noznesky is born in Kennett Square, PA

1914 Dr. J. W. Carhart, builder of the 1871 Carhart steamer "The Spark" while a resident of Racine, WI, dies in San Antonio, TX

1918 Automobile historian Griffith Borgeson is born in Berkeley, CA

1921 Racer Gunther Bechem is born in Germany

1921 Racer Bernd Nacke is born in Germany

1926 The first United States-built Rolls-Royce Phantom I is completed and delivered to Harry C. Orndorff of Providence, RI

1931 The Kissel Motor Car Company of Hartford, WI is liquidated at auction

1932 The first 1933 Cadillac 452C (V-16) is completed

1933 The first 1934 Pontiac is produced

1935 Racer Lorenzo Bandini is born in Barce, Cyrenaica (now El Marj, Libya)

1937 The Lincoln Tunnel under the Hudson River between New York City and Weehawken, NJ is officially dedicated and opened to traffic

1939 Victor W. Kliesrath, inventor of transmission improvements and the vacuum booster brake, dies in Manhasset, NY at age 58

1950 Michael Bruce Urquehart Dewar, Chairman of British Timken Ltd., dies at age 64

1955 Frederick W. Heisley, Vice President of Allied Wheel Products Inc., dies

1956 Carl B. Parsons, Swedish-born Chief Body Engineer for Mitchell, Nash, Cadillac, and Studebaker who is credited with designing the first closed sedan passenger car body (for a 1910 Marion), dies at age 72

1959 A. T. Roblin of the Imperial Oil Company, Ltd. dies at age 63

1966 The 100,000th Porsche is produced

1969 William A. Fisher dies in Detroit, MI at age 83

1970 Carl M. Breer, Chrysler Corporation engineer 1925-1949, dies in Detroit, MI at age 87

Among the many cars designed by Chrysler Corporation's "Three Musketeers" - Zeder, Breer, and Skelton - was this rare 1942 Dodge 4-door sedan parked in front of Rutland (VT) High School.

1979 Congress approves $1.5 billion in federal guaranteed loans as a bailout for the ailing Chrysler Corporation

1994 Peter Ward resigns as Chief Executive of Rolls-Royce Motors

DECEMBER 22

1856 Charles Edward Test of National is born in Richmond, IN

1885 Wilhelm Kissel of Daimler-Benz AG is born in Hassloch, Germany

1887 Louis Paul Lochner, biographer of Henry Ford, is born in Springfield, IL

1891 J. I. Case dies in Racine, WI at age 73

1896 Fahrzeug-Fabrik Eisenach, an ancestor of BMW, is organized

1900 One month after its initial test drive as a prototype, finish work on the new 35-hp Daimler built to the designs of Emil Jellinek is completed by Wilhelm Maybach - the car is named for Jellinek's daughter, Mercedes

1905 Racer Pierre Levegh (nee Pierre Bouillon) is born in Paris, France - he later had his name legally changed to that of his uncle, a pioneer racer for Mors who had no male heir

1910 The Fisher Closed Body Company is established by brothers Frederick J. Fisher and Charles T. Fisher

1920 The Moore Motor Vehicle Company of Danville, IL is liquidated at auction after production of 612 cars since 1916 in Minneapolis, MN and Danville

1920 Genevieve Marguerite Delcuze, the second wife of Ettore Bugatti, is born in Courbevoie, France

1921 Reuben Rolland Jensen of General Motors is born in Ainsworth, NE

1922 An agreement is reached between H. W. Kent, Edgar K. Worthington, and Captain F. A. Keen to acquire the stock of the Gersix Manufacturing Company as a basis for organinzing the Kenworth Motor Truck Corporation

1928 The Marmon Motor Car Company announces its new marque, the Roosevelt, as the "World's First Eight Under $1000"

1931 The first Pontiac V-8 is produced

1931 Noel Goutard, Chairman of the French automobile parts manufacturer Valeo SA, is born in Casablanca, Morocco

1934 Racer David G. Pearson is born in Woodruff, SC

1937 Edsel B. Ford announces the appointment of John R. "Jack" Davis as General Sales Manager of the Ford Motor Company, replacing William C. Cowling

1938 Racer Bob Lazier is born in the United States

1948 The last 1948 Pontiac is produced

1952 Johan Jan Beeckmans of ITT Automotive Inc. is born in Antwerp, Belgium

1954 The 1955 Plymouth Suburban station wagons are introduced to complete the marque's model year lineup

1957 Frank G. Woollard, a consulting engineer who introduced the continuous production assembly line in Great Britain, dies at age 74

1960 The 1,000,000th Morris Minor is produced - introduced in 1948, this was the first British car to achieve such a milestone

1961 Scheib, Inc. is organized in Delaware to succeed the automobile painting business founded by Earl A. Scheib in 1937

1962 Francis B. Davis, Chairman of the United States Rubber Company 1929-1949, dies in Wilmington, DE at age 79

1962 Racer Bertrand Gachot is born in Luxembourg, Luxembourg

1963 Horace E. Dodge Jr. dies in Detroit, MI at age 63

1965 A 70 mph speed limit is imposed in Great Britain by Minister of Transport Tom Fraser

1973 Stylist Virgil M. Exner Sr. dies in Birmingham, MI at age 64

1974 The Parts and Service Division of the Ford Motor Company is formed

1977 Forest R. McFarland, a design engineer with Packard and Buick, dies in Grand Blanc, MI at age 78

1983 General Motors and Toyota announces plans to build a jointly-owned factory in Fremont, CA

1995 Jim Selwa is named President of Lotus Cars U.S.A.

DECEMBER 23

1862 Automobile parts manufacturer Herman J. Hass is born in Cincinnati, OH

1868 E. H. Belden, Chief Engineer of the Willys-Overland Company, is born in Jackson, MI

1872 Claud Hanscomb Foster, the inventor of the automobile horn and founder of the Gabriel Manufacturing Company, is born in Brooklyn, OH

1894 Carlyle Fraser, a longtime manufacturer of automotive parts who served as President of the National Automotive Parts Association 1941-1942, is born in Cornwall on the Hudson, NY

1904 Hon. C. S. Rolls contracts with Royce, Ltd. to take all automobiles of 2-cylinders/10 hp through 6-cylinders/30 hp manufactured by the latter company

1911 Frederick K. Thayer and A. E. Schnitker organize the Rayfield Motor Company as part of a plan to move the struggling Rayfield Motor Car Company from Springfield to Chrisman, IL

1915 The Marmon Model 34 is announced

1915 William C. Durant, acting through the Chevrolet Motor Company, announces his plans to to purchase a controlling interest in General Motors

1915 The White Motor Company is incorporated in Ohio

1922 Salmson #001, rebodied after a racing accident, is sold in England

1923 A Rolls-Royce Silver Ghost Pall Mall tourer, serial #80JH, is presented by friends to former United States President Woodrow Wilson on his birthday

1925 Charles L. Nedoma, Secretary to the Chief Engineer of the Cadillac Motor Car Company, dies in Detroit, MI at age 49

1933 Wilson William Sick Sr. of the Ford Motor Company and American Motors is born in Wayland, NY

1936 Racer Todd Gibson is born

1939 Edmund Coleman Craft of the Borg-Warner Corporation is born in Plainfield, NJ

1941 The last pre-World War II Buick is produced at the Linden, NJ factory

1944 Lloyd R. Smith, Chairman of the A. O. Smith Corporation, manufacturers of automobile frames, dies in Milwaukee, WI at age 61

1947 The Tri-Wheel Motor Company is organized in Oxford, NC with Clarence D. Gill as President and General Manager, B. C. Pragerson as Vice President, Joseph A. Watkins as Secretary, and J. J. Medford as Treasurer

1951 William H. Watkins, an employee of Dodge and Hudson who later was an axle manufacturer in Canada, dies at age 57

1956 Racer Michele Alboreto is born in Milan, Italy

1957 Russell Stuart Begg, retired Chief Engineer of General Motors-Holden's Ltd. in Melbourne, Victoria, Australia, and Chief Engineer of the Jordan Motor Car Company in Cleveland, OH 1916-1923, dies at age 70

1959 Racer Tobey Butler is born in Kannapolis, NC

1966 The first Sunbeam Tiger II is produced

1969 Racer Gianantonio Pacchioni is born in Italy

1971 Alessandro Cagno, winner of the first Targa Florio, dies at age 88

1974 Renault announces plans to build a factory in Iran

1985 Racer Prince Birabongse "B. Bira" dies in London, England at age 71

1990 Wendell Scott, the most successful black racer in the United States, dies in Danville, VA at age 69

DECEMBER 24

1801 Richard Trevithick, with seven passengers aboard, makes the first test drive in his three-wheeled steam-powered vehicle in Camborne, Cornwall, England

1873 Sir Harry Brittain of Napier is born

1876 Automobile parts manufacturer Lon R. Smith is born in Brownsburg, IN

1887 Edouard Sarazin, pioneer automobile designer and French agent for the Daimler, dies

1889 Henry Grady Weaver, a draftsman with the Haynes Automobile Company in Kokomo, IN 1913-1916, Assistant General Manager of the Sun Motor Car Company in Elkhart, IN 1916-1917, and longtime General Motors Director of Customer Research, is born in Eatonton, GA

1893 Henry Ford, with his wife Clara's assistance, test his first gasoline engine in their kitchen

1898 Maitre Viot, after being given a test drive by Louis Renault, becomes the first to purchase a Renault

1903 The first British license plate, number "A1", is issued to Earl Russell, brother of the philosopher Bertrand Russell, for his Napier

1903 Alvan T. Fuller acquires the Packard agency for Boston, MA, which would be one of the nation's most successful

1904 The (Societa Anonima) Fabbrica Automobili Isotta-Fraschini assumes the assets of the original 1900 Isotta-Fraschini organization

1904 Henry M. Leland agrees to assume a management leadership role with the Cadillac Motor Car Company

1908 Dean Burt Hammond of the Kaiser-Frazer Corporation is born in Saline, MI

1910 The Pierce-Arrow 5-ton truck is introduced, the world's first motor truck with worm-gear drive

1918 Ernest Ballot forms the Etablissements Ballot to produce racing cars

1920 Automobile parts manufacturer Chester E. Clemens dies near Madison, OH at age 57

1924 The Ford Model T 8-foot platform-stake truck is introduced

1924 Peter E. Martin is appointed First Vice President in Charge of Manufacturing for the Ford Motor Company

1924 Automotive historian Jack Scagnetti is born in Piney Fork, OH

1925 The citizens of Springwells, MI vote to change the city's name to Fordson

1930 The unique Rolls-Royce Phantom I with custom "windblown" coupe body by Brewster is completed and delivered to owner Tommy Manville

1931 Racer Michael Johnson "Mike" Parkes is born in Richmond, Surrey, England, the son of John Joseph Parkes, Chairman of the Alvis Car and Engineering Company Ltd.

1941 Racer James Howden Ganley is born in Hamilton, New Zealand

1943 Frank C. Campsall is named to the Board of Directors of the Ford Motor Company

1946 Racer Bobby Olivero is born

1949 Racer Warwick Brown is born in Sydney, NSW, Australia

1953 The first prototype Lincoln Continental Mark II is completed

1953 Herman Charles Schultz, General Manager of the Diamond T Truck Company, dies at age 50

1956 Frank Rycamber, General Foreman and Inspector for the Cadillac Motor Car Division, General Motors, dies at age 45

1960 Clyde Tingley, Plant Superintendent for the Gramm Motor Company in Bowling Green, OH who served as Governor of New Mexico 1934-1938, dies in Albuquerque, NM at age 77

1961 General Motors styling chief William L. Mitchell has his self-proclaimed "greatest moment" as Buick accepts his design for the 1963 Riviera and Chevrolet accepts his design for the 1963 split-window Corvette

1963 S. H. "Wacky" Arnolt, designer of modified M.G.'s and Bristols, dies in Chicago, IL at age 56

1983 Prominent antique automobile hobbyist John C. Slade dies at age 81

DECEMBER 25

1878 Louis Joseph Chevrolet is born in La Chaux-de-Fonds, Switzerland

Involvement in the company bearing his name was minimal, but countless millions of Chevrolets, including this 1938 Master Deluxe Business Coupe parked in Carson City, NV, will perpetuate the memory of Louis Chevrolet.

1891 Harry Warren Anderson of General Motors is born in Cadillac, MI

1903 The first Maxwell is successfully tested in Detroit, MI

1906 Terry Stafford is issued a United States patent for his rear brakes design

1909 Zora Arkus-Duntov (nee Zachary Arkus), the first Chevrolet Corvette Chief Engineer, is born near Brussels, Belgium of Russian parents

1923 Alan Francis Bethell of Standard, Triumph, and American Motors is born in Sudbury, England

1926 Richard Frank Tucker of the Mobil Corporation is born in New York City

1927 Georges Noel Besse of Renault is born in Clermond-Ferrand, France

1929 Clessie L. Cummins tests his first diesel-powered automobile, a converted 1925 Packard limousine

1934 The 1935 Chevrolet "Unicorn" mascot is patented by designer B. E. Lemm

1934 Racer Giancarlo Baghetti is born in Milan, Italy

1934 Thomas Midgley, London-born inventor of pneumatic tire improvements and father of Ethyl gasoline developer Thomas Midgley Jr., dies in Bradenton, FL at age 74

1943 Racer Wilson Fittipaldi is born in Sao Paolo, Brazil

1946 The first Ford Sportsman is delivered to actress Ella Raines

1954 Evan H. Wright, head of the Bus Engineering Department of the Ford Motor Company since 1948, dies in Birmingham, MI

1963 Automotive engineer Axel J. Jansson dies in Detroit, MI at age 78

1970 Louis R. Mack of Packard dies at age 83

1973 Gabriel Voisin dies in Moulin d'Ozenay, France at age 93

1978 Duesenberg stylist Jesse Herbert "Herb" Newport dies at age 72

1994 Pierre Dreyfus, Chairman of Renault 1955-1975, dies in Paris at age 87

1996 Audrey Moore (later Mrs. Maurice Hodges), designer of the post-World War II Studebaker hood ornament and the interior of the 1948 Tucker, dies in Bloomington, IN at age 78

DECEMBER 26

1903 Race official Mary Guidice Momo is born in Turin, Italy

1908 The Four Wheel Drive Auto Company, later the FWD Corporation, is founded in Clintonville, WI

1910 General Motors stylist James Ross Shipley is born in Marion, OH

1923 Automobile stylist Richard A. Teague is born in Fernwood, CA

1923 The 9,000,000th Ford Model T is produced

Closed Model T's - a Center Door Sedan and Coupe parked here in front of the court house in Perry, OK - were becoming very popular by the time production reached 9,000,000. In 1923 nearly half of the world's motor cars were Model T Fords.

1926 Major C. Court Treatt and his party arrive in Cairo, Egypt in two military-style Crossleys, having taken 27 months to complete the first overland car trip from Capetown, South Africa

1933 The Nissan Motor Company Ltd. is organized in Tokyo, Japan

1935 Racer Bill Brack is born in Toronto, Ontario, Canada

1936 Racer Trevor Patrick Taylor is born in Wickersley, Yorkshire, England

1944 Joseph A. Jeffery, an official of the Champion Spark Plug Company who is credited with many improvements in spark plug design, dies in Detroit, MI at age 71

1949 Racer Keiji Matsumoto is born in Kyoto, Japan

1955 Benjamin F. Hopkins, founder of the Cleveland Graphite Bronze Company, its President 1919-1948, and its Chairman of the Board 1948-1953, dies at age 79

1956 Preston Tucker dies of cancer in Ypsilanti, MI at age 53

1985 The Ford Taurus and Mercury Sable are introduced

1987 The first front-wheel drive Lincoln Continental is introduced

1988 The 1989 Ford Thunderbird and Mercury Cougar are introduced

1992 The Lincoln Mark VIII is introduced

DECEMBER 27

1848 Tire manufacturer Giovanni Battista Pirelli is born in Varenna, Como, Lombardy, Austria-Hungary (now Italy)

1876 Franklin Fay Chandler of the Ross Gear & Tool Company is born in Indianapolis, IN

1887 Ernest W. Seaholm, Chief Engineer of Cadillac 1923-1943, is born in Michigan

1888 Diesel-engine manufacturer Clessie Lyle Cummins is born in Honey Creek, IN

1900 Racer Hans Stuck von Villiez is born in Warsaw, Poland of German/French Hugenot ancestry

1904 Rene Bonnet of Automobiles Deutsch-Bonnet is born Vaumas, France

1904 Henry M. Leland is officially named General Manager of the Cadillac Motor Car Company

1905 Racer Antonio Brivio is born in Biella, Italy

1922 Dutch automobile designer Charles Marie Van Eugen joins Lea & Francis Ltd. of Coventry, England

1923 The Packard Second Series Six is introduced

1927 The Paige-Detroit Motor Car Company is reorganized as the Graham-Paige Motors Corporation

1929 The Cadillac V-16 is introduced

1932 Willis Paul Tippett Jr., Chairman of American Motors 1982-1985, is born in Cincinnati, OH

1932 Eddie Miller driving a modified Auburn 12-160 Speedster at Muroc Dry Lake, CA sets speed records ranging from 1 kilometer to 1,000 miles

1933 The 1934 Buicks are introduced, the first with independent front suspension

1934 Racer and rallyist Patricia Moss Carlsson, sister of racer Stirling Moss and wife of rallyist Erik Carlsson, is born in Thames Ditton, England

1935 H. F. S. Morgan enters a prototype Morgan 4/4 in the London to Exter (England) Trial, the public debut of the Morgan four-wheeler

1938 Calvin B. Bridges, a geneticist who designed streamlined cars as a hobby, dies in Los Angeles, CA at age 49

1943 Curtis H. Veeder, inventor of the odometer and tachometer, dies at age 81

1948 Edsel Bryant Ford II, the only son of Henry Ford II, is born in Detroit, MI

1950 Col. Jesse G. Vincent resigns as Executive Vice President of the Packard Motor Car Company

1951 A Crosley, the first right-hand drive car made in the United States specifically for city mail delivery, goes into service in Cincinnati, OH

1969 Edward D. Rollert of Buick is killed in a hunting accident in rural South Dakota at age 57

1971 Heber W. Peters of Packard and Cadillac dies at age 79

1976 Frank W. Jenks, an employee of the International Harvester Company since 1914 who served as its Chief Executive Officer 1958-1962, dies at age 79

1979 Honda Motor Company Ltd. and BL Cars Ltd. (formerly British Leyland Ltd.) announce plans to form a joint venture to produce automobiles

1983 Howard Hoelscher, an antique car collector and automobile literature dealer in Parsippany, PA, dies in Boonton, NJ at age 66

1985 Jean Rondeau, designer of the Rondeau race car who in 1980 became the first French racer to win the 24 Hours of Le Mans in a car of his own design, is killed at age 39 in a car-train accident in the Champagne region of France

1993 Racer Andre Pilette, the father of racer Teddy Pilette, dies at age 75

DECEMBER 28

1870 Steel automobile body pioneer Edward Gowan Budd is born in Smyrna, DE

1872 Philip Hamilton McMillan of Packard is born in Detroit, MI

1872 Harold Edward Snagge of Napier is born

1877 Thomas P. Henry of the American Automobile Association is born in Brookhaven, MA

1884 Racer Ralph K. Mulford is born in Brooklyn, NY

1896 Racer Philippe "Phi Phi" Etancelin is born in Rouen, France

1902 Albert C. Moore of Buick, Packard, Dodge, Plymouth, and Ford is born in Marion, MI

1908 The Buick Motor Company and the Olds Motors Works merge under the General Motors corporate heading

1909 Racer David Murray is born in Edinburgh, Midlothian, Scotland

1915 The Hudson Motor Car Company is issued a United States patent for "the Super-Six principle" relating to automobile engines

1915 The newly formed White Motor Company acquires the stock of The White Company to complete a reorganization for legal purposes

1920 Frederick S. and August S. Duesenberg are issued a United States patent for their internal combustion engine incorporating their "walking beam" principle

1925 The first Pontiac is produced, a Series 6-57 coupe

1926 The Pontiac 1926 "Indian Head" mascot is patented by designer William Schnell

1928 Donald L. Stephens, Chief Engineer for Peterbilt 1970-1977, is born in Seattle, WA

1929 United Auto Workers official Owen Frederick Bieber is born in North Dorr, MI

1934 The 1935 Studebakers are introduced, featuring the new Planar Front Wheel Suspension system

1936 Ransom E. Olds retires as Chairman of the Reo Motor Car Company following several years of policy disputes with company President Richard H. Scott

1939 Racer Conny Andersson is born in Stockholm, Sweden

1949 The 1950 Buicks are introduced

1952 Arthur W. Ambrose, President of the Cities Service Oil Company since 1946, dies at age 63

1953 The 30,000,000th Chevrolet is produced, a 1954 Bel Air convertible

1953 After an initial run of 300 cars in Flint, MI, production of the Chevrolet Corvette is shifted to the plant in St. Louis, MO

1953 J. H. Ballard, retired Chief Technical Engineer for the Sealed Power Corporation, dies in Long Beach, CA at age 67

1954 Production of the 1955 Nash-based Hudson Hornets and Wasps begins

1956 Pontiac announces three different optional triple two-barrel carburetor setups

1957 The 2,000,000th Volkswagen is produced

1957 Racer Hisashi Yokoshima is born in Ibaraki, Japan

1957 Lewis P. Kalb, Executive Vice President of the Continental Motors Corporation 1942-1950 and holder of many patents, dies at age 69

1960 Clarence Francis resigns as Chairman of the Studebaker-Packard Corporation, having held the position for just three months - Sherwood H. Egbert is elected President, succeeding Harold E. Churchill

1962 The 11,000,000th Buick is produced

1965 Racer Joe Thomas dies

1983 Racer Eugene Chaboud, winning codriver of the 1938 24 Hours of Le Mans, dies in Montfermeil, France at age 76

DECEMBER 29

1800 Charles Goodyear, the inventor of vulcanization, is born in New Haven, CT

1877 Maurice Hippolyte Sizaire is born in Paris, France

1878 William John Cameron of the Ford Motor Company of Canada, Ltd. is born in Windsor, ON

1883 A. K. Brumbaugh of Autocar and White is born in Hagerstown, MD

1890 Automobile parts manufacturer Nicholas Peter Thul is born in Berkeley Heights, NJ

1907 The 10,000th Ford is produced

1908 Otto Zachow and William A. Besserdich of Clintonville, WI are issued a United States patent for their "power applying mechanism" which established the basic design for four-wheel braking systems

1916 Robert Grenfall Courter of General Motors is born in Saranac, MI

1917 Racer David Hampshire is born in Mickleover, Derbyshire, England

1918 Richard L. Terrell of General Motors is born in Dayton, OH

1924 George Thomas Harris, designer of the 1891 Harris omnibus, dies in Charlottesville, VA at age 69

1929 Wilhelm Maybach dies in Stuttgart, Germany at age 83

1931 The Auburn 1931-1934 "Winged Man" mascot is patented by designer K. E. Stant

1932 Hiroshi Okuda of Toyota is born

1938 Racer Helmut Kelleners is born in Germany

1939 Marie Luhring, a mechanical engineer with Mack Trucks, Inc. and the first female member of the Society of Automotive Engineers, dies in Plainfield, NJ at age 47

1940 Thomas A. Russell, General Manager of the Russell Motor Car Company Ltd. and President of Willys-Overland Ltd. 1918-1933, dies in Toronto, Ontario, Canada at age 63

1942 John H. Tuttle is issued a US patent for an automobile body with an open rear-seat passenger section that could be covered with a removable padded roof panel - his design had been introduced on the new 1939 Checker taxicab line

1947 The first 1948 Pontiac is produced

1949 Hugh J. Ferry is elected to succeed George T. Christopher as President of the Packard Motor Car Company - the company announces the discontinuance of its six cylinder automobile production

1951 Walter A. Kull, a design engineer with General Motors who worked on the development of four-wheel brakes, dies near Bridgeport, MI at age 60

1953 Chrysler Corporation purchases the Briggs Manufacturing Company for $35,000,000

1954 William M. Burton, President of the Standard Oil Company of Indiana 1918-1927, dies in Miami, FL at age 89

1955 William E. Kemp of the Kingston Products Corporation, the inventor of the compensating spring speed governor for truck engines, dies

1958 Edward S. "Ned" Jordan dies in New York City at age 76

1958 Harold F. Blanchard, Technical Editor of *Motor* magazine, dies at age 68

1958 O. L. Anderson, retired engine designer for Oldsmobile, dies at age 65

1962 The LDS makes its Formula 1 debut in the South Africa Grand Prix in East London, but the car designed and driven by Doug Serrurier retires with a radiator leak

1967 The Hyundai Motor Company is registered as a separate entity from the parent Hyundai Construction by brothers Chung Ju Yung and Chung Se Yung

1969 Racer Allan McNish is born in Dumfries, Dumfries, Scotland

1974 Richard E. Krafve, a Ford Motor Company official who served as General Manager of the Edsel Division 1955-1958, dies at age 67

1983 Racer Max de Terra dies at age 64

1988 Racer Mike Beuttler dies in San Francisco, CA at age 45

1991 Automobile stylist Alex Sarantos Tremulis dies at age 77

DECEMBER 30

1897 Automobile headlight manufacturer Edward Y. Davidson Jr. is born in Washington, DC

1899 James W. Packard, William D. Packard, and George L. Weiss establish Packard & Weiss, a formal partnership agreement that would evolve into the Packard Motor Car Company

1904 The Upton Motor Company is incorporated in New Jersey - this was the second automotive venture of Colcord Upton, but production at the Lebanon, PA factory would end in 1907

1905 Victor Hemery, driving a Darracq between Arles and Salon, France, raises the land speed record to 109.65 mph

1907 Leon Charles Greenebaum of the Hertz Corporation is born in New York City

1911 Racer Walt Brown is born in Springfield, NY

1915 William Turnor Lewis, former President of the Mitchell Motor Company, dies

1915 Miss Eleanor Velasco Thornton, believed by many to have been Charles Sykes' model for his Rolls-Royce "Spirit of Ecstasy" mascot, drowns after the SS Persia was torpedoed by the German submarine U-38 off the coast of Crete in the Mediterranean Sea

1916 The All-Steel Motor Car Company is reorganized by Hunter Woodson and F. V. Smith as the Macon Motor Car Company of Macon, MO

1918 The Camden Motors Corporation of Camden, NJ registers its "Frontmobile" trademark - the marque's original producer, the Safety Motor Company of Grenloch, NJ had just abandoned production after two years, and the Camden venture was an attempt at continuation by the car's designer, C. H. Blomstrom, which ended in 1922 without a single car being produced

1918 Henry Ford resigns as President of the Ford Motor Company

1920 Charles F. Kettering is appointed to the Board of Directors of General Motors

1921 Edmund Rumpler is issued a German patent for his "Tropfen-Auto"

1925 The first circumnavigation of Australia by automobile is completed

1929 The F. B. Stearns Company is dissolved

1929 The last Gardner is produced

The distinctive Griffin logo of the Gardner

1932 Edward N. Cole joins General Motors at age 23

1934 Racer Fred Lorenzen is born in Elmhurst, IL

1936 Racer Michael Henderson "Mike" Spence is born in Croydon, Surrey, England

1939 The United States Rubber Company acquires the Fisk Rubber Corporation of Chicopee Falls, MA

1940 C. Harold Wills, Chief Engineer 1903-1919 of the Ford Motor Company and builder of the 1921-1927 Wills Sainte Claire, dies in Detroit, MI from a diabetic coma at age 62

1941 The last Packard Custom Super Eight 180 is produced

1942 Racer Guy Edwards is born in Liverpool, England

1946 The 1947 Pontiacs are introduced

1951 L. B. Billings, an employee and official of the Goodyear Tire & Rubber Company since 1916, dies in Birmingham, MI at age 59

1956 Racer Francois Hesnault is born in Neuilly-sur-Seine, France

1960 Fifty special 1961 Ford Thunderbird convertibles are produced for use in the upcoming inaugural parade of President John F. Kennedy

1960 Racer Alfonso Garcia de Vinuesa is born in Spain

1964 The 9,000,000th Volkswagen is produced

1969 Racer Emmanuel Clerico is born in Paris, France

1974 Aston Martin Lagonda Ltd. announces that it is going into voluntary bankruptcy

1976 Racer Rudi Fischer dies at age 64

1983 Willis Ward, a pioneer black executive with the Ford Motor Company, dies in Detroit, MI at age 71

DECEMBER 31

1870 William A. Hatcher, a pioneer designer for the Packard Motor Car Company, is born in South Bend, IN

1870 Dr. Benjamin F. Goodrich establishes Goodrich, Tew & Company, a firm that would evolve into the B. F. Goodrich Company in 1880

1876 Norman DeVaux is born in Michigan

1879 Carl Benz successfully tests his first gasoline engine

1890 Don E. Ahrens of General Motors is born in Lodgepole, NE

1903 William Munger Heynes of Jaguar is born in Leamington Spa, Warwickshire, England

1914 The Dodge Brothers, Inc. contract to provide powertrain components to the Ford Motor Company is terminated

1918 General Motors officially acquires the United Motors Corporation, which combined the scattered interests of William C. Durant into a single corporate entity

1922 John Frank Bookout Jr. of Royal Dutch/Shell Group is born in Shreveport, LA

1923 Philip Eglin Benton Jr. of the Ford Motor Company is born in Charlottesville, VA

1925 Nicola Romeo is ousted as Managing Director of Alfa Romeo, and is succeeded by Pasquale Gallo

1928 Ferdinand Porsche resigns from Daimler-Benz AG

1930 General Motors acquires the Electro-Motive Company of Cleveland, OH, partly to enter the railroad locomotive business but primarily to acquire the services of its chief engineers, Richard Dilworth and Harold L. Hamilton

1931 Production of the Cord L29 ends after a three-year run of 4,429 cars - the marque would be dormant until the introduction of the "coffin-nose" Cord 810 in 1935

1932 Jose Joseph Dedeurwaerder of American Motors and Renault is born in Halle, Belgium

1933 Dominion Motors Ltd. of Toronto, ON officially discontinues production of the Frontenac autombile after a three-year run

1941 The use of chrome plating for United States cars ends for the duration of World War II

1941 George L. Hawn Sr., an official with the Olds Motor Works, Continental Motors Corporation, Piston Ring Company, and the Sealed Power Corporation, dies at age 70

1945 Electric automobile pioneer Pedro G. Salom dies in Philadelphia, PA at age 89

1948 The first redesigned "second series" 1949 Plymouth is produced

1948 Malcolm Campbell dies at age 63

1949 Although on leave of absence since the October board meeting, George T. Christopher officially retires as President of the Packard Motor Car Company with Hugh J. Ferry assuming that office

1950 K. T. Keller retires as President of the Chrysler Corporation

1950 The Sam Collier Memorial Grand Prix of Endurance is staged by Alec Ulmann, the first race held at Hendrick Field in Sebring, FL - the winner is a Crosley Hot Shot driven by Fritz Koster and Ralph Deshon

1951 The Henry J Vagabond is introduced

1955 A. G. Elliott, Vice Chairman of Rolls-Royce Ltd., retires after 43 years with the company

1964 Coachmen Industries, Inc., a manufacturer of recreational vehicles, is founded in Middlebury, IN

1964 James D. Tew, President of the B. F. Goodrich Tire & Rubber Company 1928- 1937, dies at age 82

1971 James M. Roche retires as Chairman/Chief Executive Officer of General Motors

1980 Thomas A. Murphy retires as Chairman/Chief Executive Officer of General Motors

1985 General Motors acquires the Hughes Aircraft Company and combines it with the recently acquired EDS Corporation to form a subsidiary, the GM Hughes Electronics Corporation

1992 Lee Iacocca retires as Chairman of the Chrysler Corporation

INDEXES

Automobile History Day By Day can be referenced by any of the five following indexes: Marque, Company/Organization, Personal Name, Place Name, and Illustration.

The Indexes are tabulated by date, NOT by page number. The main reason I've done this is to allow for the compilation of the Indexes to be perpetual as new, enhanced, and corrected entries are added in anticipation of future editions. Needless to say any new editions will have an almost total change of page numbers for repeated entries. The Illustrations Index is presented in a consistent style even though this index will be unique to the First Edition - no illustrations will be repeated in any future editions.

The dates are listed by number in what I call "United States civilian" usage, e.g. June 1st shown is as "6/1", not "1/6" or "1.6" as is typical in Europe and the military services.

INDEX 1 - MARQUES

"Marque" is one of many French terms universally used by the automobile industry and simply means brand name. Sub-marques, series, model names, etc. are not itemized in this index.

Abarth 5/12
A.C. 1/5, 2/16, 6/20, 11/24, 12/9
Acme 6/9
Acura 11/21
Adams-Hewitt 2/19, 6/20
Adler 8/16
Aerocar 2/23
AFM 5/18
AGS 9/7
Ahrens-Fox 1/9, 9/28
Airmobile 4/19
Ajax (1) 2/28
Ajax (2) 5/1, 7/17, 9/12
Albatross 1/8
Alco 6/4, 6/27, 8/22, 10/1, 10/30
A.L.F.A. 1/1, 9/21
Alfa Romeo 1/2, 1/3, 1/9, 1/13, 1/16, 3/10,
    3/12, 3/25, 3/28, 3/30, 3/31, 4/9, 4/18,
    4/19, 4/22, 4/24, 4/28, 5/5, 5/6, 5/11, 5/12,
    5/13, 5/15, 5/20, 5/21, 5/25, 5/29, 6/2, 6/9,
    6/10, 6/11, 6/13, 6/14, 6/15, 6/17, 6/18,
    6/19, 6/21, 6/25, 6/28, 6/30, 7/1, 7/2, 7/9,
    7/10, 7/11, 7/12, 7/13, 7/16, 7/26, 7/31,
    8/1, 8/3, 8/7, 8/8, 8/9, 8/10, 8/16, 8/19,
    8/20, 9/1, 9/5, 9/8, 9/10, 9/11, 9/12, 9/14,
    9/21, 9/26, 9/30, 10/1, 10/2, 10/6, 10/12,
    10/13, 10/21, 10/28, 11/6, 11/18, 12/1,
    12/2, 12/6, 12/16, 12/17, 12/31
Alfasud 1/2, 5/20, 11/1
Allard 4/12, 9/7, 11/29
Alldays & Onions 6/28
Allen 7/3, 8/29
Allen-Kingston 4/24
Allis-Chalmers 10/17
Allstate 4/23, 9/3, 10/26, 11/20, 12/17, 12/20
Alpine 6/15
Alta 5/13, 5/27
Alvis 3/28, 4/21, 4/27, 6/24, 10/13, 11/14
AMC 1/15, 1/21, 2/24, 2/28, 3/1, 3/9, 3/11,
    3/23, 4/1, 4/7, 5/11, 5/20, 6/1, 6/6, 6/20,
    6/30, 7/1, 7/8, 7/18, 7/26, 8/5, 8/21, 9/21,
    9/22, 9/25, 9/27, 9/26, 10/1, 10/6, 11/15,
    12/3, 12/14, 12/31
American 12/1
American Austin 2/28, 5/21, 6/3
American Bantam 6/2, 6/19, 6/22, 12/17
American LaFrance 3/10, 6/10, 6/12, 8/4, 8/27,
    10/28, 12/6
American Napier 11/18
American Steam Car 5/31, 6/10
American Underslung 7/3, 10/11, 11/15
Ames 10/11
Amilcar 7/15
AMO 11/7
Amon 4/28
Amphicar 4/1
Amplex 8/24, 9/23, 12/18
Anderson 11/17
Anderson Electric 11/14
Andrea Moda 5/31
Ansaldo 5/22
Apperson 5/12, 5/24, 7/20, 10/20
Ardsley 5/16
Argo 7/6
Armstrong-Siddeley 11/3
Arnold 1/28, 11/13

Arrol-Johnston 9/14
Arrow 11/23
Arrowbile 2/20, 11/9
Arrows 1/29
A.S.A. 4/5, 8/10
Aston-Butterworth 6/22
Aston Martin 1/5, 5/2, 5/10, 5/13, 5/24, 5/31,
    6/21, 9/15, 11/6, 11/11
Aston Martin Lagonda 10/19
Astra 2/16, 12/15
Asuna 2/12
ATS (UK) 1/15
ATS (I) 2/11, 6/9
Atterbury 9/26
Auburn 1/2, 1/4, 1/5, 1/15, 1/18, 2/11, 2/12,
    2/16, 2/20, 2/24, 2/26, 3/5, 3/18, 3/23,
    5/22, 6/4, 6/15, 7/1, 7/6, 7/14, 7/27, 7/31,
    8/15, 8/23, 8/24, 8/29, 9/10, 10/8, 11/1,
    11/15, 12/2, 12/8, 12/14, 12/27, 12/29
Audi 1/1, 3/25, 5/31, 8/26, 9/11, 10/1, 10/14
Austin (UK) 1/1, 1/3, 2/19, 2/27, 3/1, 3/3,
    4/25, 5/4, 5/20, 5/23, 5/29, 8/26, 9/17,
    10/13, 10/25, 10/27, 12/18
Austin (US) 3/31, 5/9
Austin-Healey 6/11, 9/2, 10/22
Austro-Daimler 1/1, 4/30, 6/28
Auto-Bi 1/15
Autocar 1/6, 1/16, 1/30, 2/2, 4/14, 5/26, 6/18,
    6/20, 6/29, 7/3, 7/7, 9/19, 10/4, 10/21,
    11/6, 11/19, 11/28, 12/9, 12/29
Autolandplane 2/8
Automatic Air 6/12
Auto Union 1/1, 1/12, 1/28, 3/6, 4/11, 5/6,
    5/21, 5/27, 6/10, 6/25, 6/29, 7/5, 7/15,
    7/26, 8/26, 9/3, 9/11, 10/27, 11/13
Available 7/10
Ayres 5/3

Bailey 2/12
Bailey Electric 3/6, 4/18
Baker Electric 4/26
Baldwin Steam 4/19
Ball 11/12
Ballot 4/17, 7/4, 8/6, 9/4
Balzer 12/15
Barley 1/29, 2/2, 8/7, 12/16
Barthel 10/3
Bay State 4/16, 9/4
Bean 7/15, 10/19
Bellasi 8/16
Belmont 5/6
Bendix 1/31
Benetton 10/12
Bentley 1/10, 1/18, 2/19, 2/27, 3/4, 3/5, 3/23,
    4/12, 4/17, 5/14, 5/29, 5/30, 6/8, 6/14,
    6/17, 6/21, 6/22, 6/29, 6/30, 7/8, 7/11,
    7/18, 7/26, 8/13, 8/28, 9/17, 10/2, 10/16,
    10/23, 11/6, 11/8, 11/12, 11/29, 12/11
Benz 1/29, 3/14, 3/16, 3/18, 4/4, 4/8, 4/23,
    5/1, 5/6, 5/19, 6/24, 6/28, 7/3, 8/12, 9/7,
    10/9, 11/2, 11/8, 11/10, 11/13
Benz Sohne 3/9, 9/19
Berg 6/12, 12/6
Bergius 6/4
Berkshire 12/13
Bersey 8/19

Bertone 11/26
Bianchi 9/23
Biautogo 9/13
Biddle-Murray 2/20
Bignan-Sport 4/20
Bizzarrini 6/6
Black 10/5
Blanchard 11/22
B.L.M. 7/7
BMW 1/1, 2/15, 3/1, 3/7, 3/15, 4/15, 4/23,
    5/15, 5/16, 6/14, 6/22, 6/26, 7/20, 7/21,
    8/1, 8/2, 8/3, 9/25, 9/30, 10/2, 10/4, 10/5,
    11/14, 12/19, 12/22
Bollee 11/15
Bonner 7/15
Booth-Crouch 11/19, 12/1
Borgward 8/1, 10/13
Brabham 4/12, 5/15, 6/28, 7/16, 8/5, 8/14,
    9/8, 9/25, 10/6
Bradfield 8/20
Brasier 7/5
Breeze Midget 7/16
Breeze-Paris 7/16
Brewster 3/22, 4/20, 5/2, 6/2, 11/25
Bricklin 2/2, 5/9, 6/25
Briscoe 1/20, 6/16, 6/21, 6/26, 7/4, 10/22
Bristol 10/1, 12/24
BRM 1/8, 3/2, 4/8, 4/22, 5/13, 5/25, 5/31,
    7/28, 9/12, 10/24, 10/29, 12/15
Brockway 8/7
Brooks 3/14
Brotz 4/13
Brough Superior 1/12
BRP 6/9
Brush 2/11, 3/6, 4/1, 4/2, 7/1, 10/18
Buchet 1/15
Buffalo 10/1
Bugatti (1) 1/11, 1/18, 2/10, 3/3, 3/20, 3/30,
    4/4, 4/9, 4/11, 4/14, 4/15, 4/24, 5/1, 5/9,
    5/25, 5/26, 6/10, 6/12, 6/20, 6/26, 6/27,
    6/29, 6/30, 7/1, 7/11, 7/15, 7/27, 8/3, 8/7,
    8/11, 8/15, 8/25, 8/27, 8/30, 9/7, 9/9,
    9/10, 9/14, 9/21, 9/26, 10/4, 10/10, 10/16,
    10/25, 10/30, 11/21, 11/26
Bugatti (2) 9/14, 12/5
Buick 1/1, 1/5, 1/13, 1/14, 1/15, 1/16, 1/19,
    1/20, 1/25, 1/26, 1/29, 2/1, 2/3, 2/4, 2/7,
    2/18, 2/21, 2/28, 3/5, 3/6, 3/16, 3/17,
    3/18, 3/21, 3/29, 4/5, 4/8, 4/9, 4/19, 4/22,
    5/1, 5/3, 5/9, 5/12, 5/13, 5/15, 5/19, 5/20,
    5/27, 5/28, 6/1, 6/2, 6/10, 6/13, 6/14, 6/17,
    6/22, 6/24, 6/25, 6/27, 7/1, 7/2, 7/9, 7/17,
    7/18, 7/22, 7/26, 7/27, 7/28, 7/29, 8/1, 8/8,
    8/9, 8/11, 8/13, 8/14, 8/15, 8/19, 9/4, 9/5,
    9/9, 9/11, 9/12, 9/16, 9/17, 9/19, 9/20,
    9/21, 9/22, 9/24, 9/26, 9/27, 9/28, 10/3,
    10/7, 10/9, 10/13, 10/14, 10/17, 10/18,
    10/23, 10/24, 10/25, 10/26, 11/1, 11/3,
    11/5, 11/6, 11/7, 11/8, 11/9, 11/14, 11/18,
    11/19, 11/30, 12/3, 12/9, 12/11, 12/16,
    12/17, 12/22, 12/23, 12/24, 12/27, 12/28
Burlingame 2/9

Cadillac 1/1, 1/2, 1/4, 1/6, 1/7, 1/8, 1/13,
    1/15, 1/19, 1/25, 1/29, 2/1, 2/3, 2/4, 2/7,
    2/12, 2/17, 2/25, 2/28, 2/29, 3/1, 3/5, 3/6,
    3/11, 3/12, 3/13, 3/17, 3/25, 4/1, 4/2, 4/8,

4/13, 4/15, 4/16, 4/21, 4/28, 5/1, 5/4, 5/5, 5/10, 5/11, 5/12, 5/15, 5/19, 5/21, 5/29, 5/31, 6/1, 6/3, 6/5, 6/10, 6/11, 6/13, 6/19, 6/24, 6/26, 6/27, 7/1, 7/7, 7/8, 7/10, 7/15, 7/22, 7/29, 7/30, 8/1, 8/5, 8/6, 8/7, 8/8, 8/22, 8/24, 8/26, 8/27, 8/28, 9/1, 9/15, 9/16, 9/18, 9/19, 9/21, 9/22, 9/24, 9/26, 9/29, 10/1, 10/6, 10/7, 10/8, 10/11, 10/14, 10/17, 10/18, 10/24, 10/27, 11/1, 11/4, 11/6, 11/7, 11/18, 11/22, 11/25, 11/27, 11/28, 11/29, 12/1, 12/7, 12/10, 12/13, 12/17, 12/21, 12/24, 12/27

Cameron 1/2, 4/16
Car DeLuxe 3/1, 4/1
Cardinal 3/2
Carhart 1/15, 12/21
Carroll 2/23
Carter 5/19
Cartercar 2/3, 4/6, 5/22, 5/31, 8/17, 9/26
Case 4/6, 6/13, 12/14
CDA Electric 11/13
Century 2/18
Chadwick 2/26, 3/7, 4/27, 5/30, 8/20, 10/8
Chalmers (-Detroit) 1/25, 1/28, 4/2, 4/15, 6/2, 6/6, 6/12, 6/28, 8/2, 10/8, 10/9, 10/11, 10/24, 12/19
Chandler 2/18, 2/26, 3/14, 4/1, 4/13, 4/15, 5/28, 6/11, 7/30, 10/3, 10/28, 12/1
Chaparral 6/5, 7/12, 10/15, 10/20, 11/14
Charron-Laycock 12/17
Checker 1/12, 2/16, 5/2, 6/18, 7/9, 7/12, 7/15, 9/1, 9/3, 10/4, 12/29
Chenard-Walcker 5/27, 6/13, 8/18, 11/13
Chevrolet 1/2, 1/4, 1/7, 1/11, 1/15, 1/16, 1/19, 1/20, 1/26, 1/27, 1/28, 1/30, 2/1, 2/2, 2/3, 2/8, 2/15, 2/20, 2/21, 2/22, 2/25, 2/26, 2/27, 2/28, 3/1, 3/7, 3/14, 3/15, 3/24, 3/25, 3/26, 4/1, 4/5, 4/9, 4/15, 4/16, 4/19, 4/21, 4/24, 4/28, 4/29, 4/30, 5/1, 5/2, 5/10, 5/11, 5/12, 5/14, 5/15, 5/22, 5/28, 5/30, 5/31, 6/1, 6/2, 6/3, 6/4, 6/5, 6/6, 6/12, 6/25, 6/26, 6/27, 6/29, 6/30, 7/1, 7/2, 7/9, 7/10, 7/14, 7/16, 7/17, 7/24, 7/26, 7/31, 8/1, 8/6, 8/7, 8/11, 8/20, 8/24, 8/25, 8/28, 8/29, 9/1, 9/2, 9/4, 9/7, 9/8, 9/10, 9/11, 9/13, 9/14, 9/18, 9/20, 9/21, 9/22, 9/23, 9/24, 9/26, 9/27, 9/28, 9/29, 10/1, 10/2, 10/3, 10/5, 10/7, 10/8, 10/9, 10/12, 10/15, 10/16, 10/23, 10/28, 10/31, 11/1, 11/2, 11/3, 11/7, 11/8, 11/13, 11/15, 11/18, 11/19, 11/23, 11/24, 11/25, 12/2, 12/4, 12/5, 12/7, 12/9, 12/15, 12/16, 12/24, 12/25, 12/28
Christie 5/6, 5/7, 5/28, 9/5
Chrysler 1/1, 1/2, 1/5, 1/16, 1/21, 1/28, 1/29, 1/30, 1/31, 2/1, 2/2, 2/4, 2/5, 2/6, 2/9, 2/10, 2/12, 2/13, 2/18, 2/20, 2/24, 3/1, 3/2, 3/9, 3/10, 3/11, 3/13, 3/16, 3/18, 3/19, 3/24, 3/25, 3/30, 4/1, 4/2, 4/3, 4/4, 4/10, 4/11, 4/17, 4/19, 4/23, 4/28, 4/30, 5/1, 5/12, 5/13, 5/15, 5/16, 5/20, 5/23, 5/26, 5/27, 5/30, 6/2, 6/3, 6/4, 6/6, 6/9, 6/11, 6/12, 6/13, 6/16, 6/17, 6/18, 6/22, 6/26, 6/30, 7/1, 7/2, 7/3, 7/7, 7/8, 7/12, 7/13, 7/15, 7/16, 7/18, 7/21, 7/22, 7/25, 7/26, 7/27, 7/28, 7/30, 7/31, 8/1, 8/3, 8/4, 8/5, 8/6, 8/7, 8/9, 8/13, 8/20, 8/28, 9/14, 9/17, 9/19, 9/20, 9/23, 9/24, 9/26, 9/29, 9/30, 10/1, 10/21, 10/24, 10/25, 10/28, 10/29, 10/30, 10/31, 11/1, 11/2, 11/8, 11/11, 11/12, 11/17, 11/26, 11/27, 12/1, 12/14, 12/16, 12/21
Cisitalia 3/9, 4/10, 4/30, 5/15, 8/7, 9/3, 9/16
Citroen 4/13, 4/24, 5/28, 6/1, 6/4, 7/3, 7/12, 7/14, 7/22, 7/23, 7/27, 8/4, 8/8, 9/23, 10/6, 12/6
Clark 12/13
Clement 11/13

Clement-Bayard 10/8
Clement-Talbot 7/3
Cleveland 2/26, 4/1, 6/11
Clough 8/2
C.M.N. 10/5, 11/22
Coates-Goshen 9/19
Colburn 10/15
Colby 3/14, 3/24, 11/3, 11/13
Cole 4/3, 6/22, 10/22
Coloni 9/27
Columbia 4/3, 5/1, 6/28, 7/2, 8/22, 9/2, 11/3
Comet 9/7
Commer 4/9
Connaught 5/19, 7/9, 7/19, 9/21, 10/23
Continental 6/24
Cooper 1/19, 2/29, 4/3, 4/24, 5/2, 5/9, 5/13, 5/17, 6/5, 6/15, 6/19, 6/22, 7/14, 7/16, 7/18, 7/27, 8/1, 8/23, 9/7, 9/10, 12/12
Corbin 3/8, 4/15, 9/25, 10/30, 11/3
Cord 1/6, 1/27, 2/3, 2/8, 2/12, 2/16, 3/6, 3/23, 5/1, 5/10, 5/17, 5/30, 6/15, 6/17, 7/6, 7/10, 7/19, 7/27, 8/7, 8/21, 8/25, 9/3, 9/14, 10/1, 10/2, 10/12, 11/2, 11/7, 11/18, 12/31
Cosworth 5/24, 6/21
Coyote 5/29, 9/6
Crane (-Simplex) 2/27, 4/27, 6/16, 7/7
Crosley 3/28, 4/29, 6/19, 7/3, 7/7, 11/26, 12/27, 12/31
Crossley 1/29, 2/17, 2/26, 4/22, 9/23, 11/22, 12/26
Crow-Elkhart 9/23, 12/18
Croxton-Keeton 4/1
CTA-Arsenal 9/21
Cunningham 5/17, 7/31

Daf 1/31, 3/23, 5/3, 5/23, 10/11
Daimler (D) 2/14, 3/4, 3/17, 3/29, 3/30, 4/1, 4/2, 4/3, 4/14, 5/1, 5/29, 6/2, 6/9, 6/11, 7/9, 7/21, 8/16, 9/29, 10/9, 10/14, 11/1, 12/21, 12/22, 12/24
Daimler (UK) 1/14, 1/29, 2/2, 2/23, 3/18, 3/22, 3/28, 4/15, 4/22, 5/16, 5/22, 5/26, 6/6, 6/7, 6/17, 6/26, 7/3, 8/9, 8/12, 8/28, 10/9, 10/17, 10/19
Dale 4/12, 5/28, 8/14
Dallara 5/1
Daniels 3/24, 6/25
Darracq 1/4, 1/29, 2/10, 2/17, 5/7, 5/28, 10/6, 10/14, 11/13, 12/30
Datsun 1/9, 4/29, 10/8, 10/22
daVinci 9/13
Davis 7/22, 7/23, 8/15
D.B. 7/14, 9/6
De Dietrich 6/12, 6/26
DeDion-Bouton 1/31, 2/26, 3/9, 5/1, 6/12, 6/15, 7/11, 7/22, 8/20, 11/24
DeDion, Bouton & Trepardoux 4/28
Deidt 5/30
Delage 1/10, 3/12, 3/22, 3/25, 4/20, 4/25, 5/30, 7/4, 7/6, 8/7, 9/18
Delahaye 4/10, 6/14, 8/15, 8/22, 9/18
Delaunay-Belleville 5/12
DeLorean 2/19, 10/18
Denby 1/20, 10/2
Derby 8/6
Desberon 8/15
DeSoto 1/1, 1/2, 1/5, 1/11, 1/25, 1/26, 1/27, 1/30, 1/31, 2/9, 2/10, 2/18, 3/4, 3/9, 3/12, 3/25, 4/23, 5/6, 5/21, 6/20, 6/28, 7/1, 7/7, 7/13, 7/21, 8/2, 8/4, 8/8, 8/15, 9/1, 9/23, 10/5, 10/8, 10/18, 10/30, 10/31, 11/2, 11/17, 11/18, 11/30
DeTomaso 6/21, 7/2, 10/24
Detroit-Dearborn 1/20, 11/15

Detroit Electric 6/25
Detroiter 3/1, 7/15
Deutsch-Bonnet 12/27
Deutz 1/1, 1/5
DeVaux 4/1, 4/8, 8/25, 10/28
DeWitt 4/15, 5/5
D.F.P. 1/15, 6/8
Diamond-Reo 11/3
Diamond T 2/15, 2/22, 5/12, 5/18, 6/28, 9/19, 10/15, 12/8
Diana 6/25
Disbrow 6/23
Divco 6/28, 11/7
Dixi 1/1
Dixie Flyer 2/21
DKW 1/1, 5/7
Doble 1/1, 1/5, 2/4, 11/4
Dodge (Brothers) 1/1, 1/2, 1/4, 1/7, 1/11, 1/14, 1/15, 1/20, 1/26, 1/29, 2/7, 2/11, 2/18, 2/20, 2/26, 2/29, 3/1, 3/18, 3/20, 3/22, 3/24, 3/25, 4/1, 4/4, 4/5, 4/6, 4/8, 4/15, 4/19, 4/25, 4/28, 4/30, 5/6, 5/10, 5/19, 5/28, 6/1, 6/2, 6/6, 6/7, 6/11, 6/16, 6/25, 6/28, 7/1, 7/10, 7/11, 7/13, 7/15, 7/17, 7/27, 7/30, 8/7, 8/12, 8/31, 9/6, 9/21, 9/22, 9/23, 9/24, 9/25, 9/28, 10/1, 10/6, 10/7, 10/8, 10/9, 10/10, 10/15, 10/21, 10/22, 10/23, 10/25, 10/30, 10/31, 11/1, 11/2, 11/3, 11/5, 11/10, 11/12, 11/14, 11/17, 11/21, 11/23, 12/4, 12/8, 12/12, 12/17, 12/19, 12/22, 12/23, 12/28, 12/31
Dorris 11/2
Dort 1/2, 1/5, 1/26, 3/13, 5/8, 5/17, 6/25, 7/17, 9/10
Dover 7/1
Dual-Ghia 6/13, 6/28
Dudgeon 1/25, 11/19
Duesenberg 1/1, 1/2, 2/7, 2/9, 2/12, 2/16, 2/22, 2/28, 2/29, 3/8, 3/28, 4/3, 4/11, 4/13, 4/20, 4/25, 4/27, 5/9, 5/20, 5/21, 5/30, 6/1, 6/9, 6/17, 6/18, 6/26, 7/2, 7/4, 7/6, 7/22, 7/26, 7/28, 8/1, 8/6, 8/7, 8/20, 8/25, 8/31, 9/4, 9/12, 9/30, 10/3, 10/6, 10/13, 10/21, 10/23, 10/26, 10/31, 11/7, 11/26, 12/1, 12/11, 12/13, 12/25
Duesenberg II 10/21
duPont 4/16
Durant 1/12, 3/14, 3/19, 4/1, 7/10, 8/1, 9/4
Duryea (UK) 1/16
Duryea (US) 3/11, 4/6, 4/19, 5/30, 6/11, 8/14, 9/21, 11/3, 11/14, 11/28

Eagle (1) 3/12, 6/18
Eagle (truck) 9/26
Earl 1/25
Eckhardt & Souter 3/9
Edsel 1/15, 2/3, 4/9, 4/18, 6/7, 9/4, 9/22, 10/15, 10/31, 11/8, 11/10, 11/19, 12/29
Edwards 4/16, 4/20
Eifelland 3/4
Elcar 1/3, 2/9, 7/2, 10/24
Elliott 9/13
Ellis & Turner 8/14
Elmore 7/10, 10/28
Emeryson 7/14
E-M-F 1/1, 6/2, 8/16, 8/26, 9/5
Empire 4/3, 4/4, 7/12, 10/3, 10/22
Enger 1/4, 5/24
Ensign 7/1
Epperly 5/30
E.R.A. 1/1, 4/30, 5/7, 6/3, 8/7, 8/8, 8/10, 8/17, 9/2, 9/7, 10/28, 11/6
Erie & Sturgis 5/30

Erskine 7/1
Essex 1/11, 1/16, 1/27, 6/21, 6/22, 6/23, 6/25, 7/21, 7/24, 10/30, 11/12, 11/20, 12/1
Euclid 12/6
EuroBrun 4/3
Evans Steam 7/13
Everitt 9/20
Excalibur 1/5, 5/10

Fageol 4/8, 10/28
Falcon-Knight 3/16, 5/31, 6/19
Federal 2/6, 4/11, 7/4, 10/22, 11/7
Ferguson 7/8, 7/15, 9/23
Ferrari 1/7, 1/10, 1/12, 1/13, 1/18, 1/22, 1/29, 2/1, 2/6, 2/13, 2/22, 2/28, 3/1, 3/6, 3/14, 3/21, 3/28, 4/4, 4/5, 4/7, 4/24, 4/25, 4/26, 4/28, 4/30, 5/1, 5/8, 5/10, 5/11, 5/12, 5/18, 5/20, 5/25, 5/26, 5/29, 5/30, 6/3, 6/14, 6/17, 6/20, 6/21, 6/22, 6/30, 7/3, 7/5, 7/6, 7/7, 7/11, 7/14, 7/21, 7/23, 7/31, 8/1, 8/3, 8/9, 8/15, 8/17, 8/18, 9/3, 9/4, 9/5, 9/7, 9/10, 9/18, 9/23, 9/25, 10/7, 10/19, 10/24, 10/29, 11/18, 11/22, 11/25
Fiat (F.I.A.T.) 1/7, 1/16, 1/22, 2/23, 2/26, 3/8, 3/10, 3/12, 3/19, 3/20, 3/21, 3/23, 3/24, 3/30, 3/31, 4/7, 4/9, 4/10, 4/14, 5/4, 5/19, 5/20, 5/27, 5/31, 6/1, 6/8, 6/14, 6/21, 6/22, 6/24, 6/27, 7/1, 7/4, 7/5, 7/11, 7/12, 7/14, 7/28, 8/8, 8/9, 8/13, 8/15, 8/25, 8/30, 9/1, 9/3, 9/4, 9/7, 9/9, 9/16, 10/4, 10/10, 10/12, 10/18, 11/1, 11/6, 11/15, 11/26, 12/8, 12/16
Firestone-Columbus 2/22
Fittipaldi 1/12
Flanders 4/15, 6/16
Flint 6/9
Fondmetal 6/16
Ford (Australia) 3/31
Ford (Canada) 5/11, 5/12, 5/13, 6/3, 8/10
Ford (Germany) 3/20, 4/14, 5/4, 5/17, 8/27, 10/1, 10/8
Ford (Japan) 12/19
Ford (Spain) 2/1
Ford (USSR) 11/1
Ford (UK) 3/18, 3/27, 4/17, 4/18, 5/16, 8/10, 8/25, 9/1, 9/15, 10/1, 10/6, 10/13, 10/15, 10/23, 11/20
Ford (US) 1/1, 1/3, 1/4, 1/5, 1/6, 1/9, 1/10, 1/11, 1/12, 1/13, 1/14, 1/15, 1/16, 1/18, 1/19, 1/20, 1/21, 1/22, 1/23, 1/25, 1/27, 1/28, 1/30, 1/31, 2/1, 2/3, 2/4, 2/6, 2/7, 2/9, 2/10, 2/11, 2/12, 2/13, 2/15, 2/16, 2/17, 2/19, 2/20, 2/22, 2/23, 2/24, 2/25, 2/26, 2/27, 2/28, 2/29, 3/2, 3/4, 3/5, 3/7, 3/8, 3/9, 3/10, 3/12, 3/13, 3/15, 3/16, 3/17, 3/18, 3/19, 3/22, 3/23, 3/25, 3/26, 3/29, 3/31, 4/1, 4/2, 4/5, 4/6, 4/7, 4/8, 4/9, 4/10, 4/11, 4/12, 4/13, 4/14, 4/15, 4/16, 4/17, 4/18, 4/21, 4/22, 4/24, 4/25, 4/26, 4/27, 4/28, 4/29, 4/30, 5/1, 5/3, 5/4, 5/5, 5/6, 5/7, 5/8, 5/9, 5/10, 5/11, 5/12, 5/13, 5/14, 5/17, 5/18, 5/20, 5/21, 5/22, 5/23, 5/24, 5/25, 5/26, 5/27, 5/28, 5/29, 5/30, 5/31, 6/1, 6/2, 6/3, 6/4, 6/6, 6/7, 6/8, 6/9, 6/10, 6/12, 6/13, 6/14, 6/16, 6/17, 6/18, 6/19, 6/20, 6/21, 6/22, 6/23, 6/24, 6/27, 6/28, 6/29, 6/30, 7/1, 7/2, 7/3, 7/5, 7/6, 7/7, 7/8, 7/9, 7/11, 7/13, 7/15, 7/17, 7/20, 7/23, 7/24, 7/26, 7/27, 7/28, 7/31, 8/1, 8/2, 8/3, 8/4, 8/8, 8/10, 8/11, 8/23, 8/13, 8/14, 8/17, 8/18, 8/20, 8/21, 8/22, 8/24, 8/26, 8/27, 8/28, 8/30, 9/2, 9/3, 9/4, 9/6, 9/8, 9/9, 9/10, 9/12, 9/13, 9/14, 9/15, 9/16, 9/17, 9/18, 9/19, 9/21, 9/22, 9/24, 9/25, 9/26, 9/27, 9/28, 9/29, 9/30, 10/1, 10/3, 10/5, 10/6, 10/7, 10/8, 10/10, 10/11, 10/12, 10/16, 10/17, 10/20, 10/22, 10/24, 10/25, 10/26, 10/27, 10/29, 10/30, 10/31, 11/1, 11/4, 11/5, 11/6, 11/7, 11/9, 11/10, 11/12, 11/13, 11/14, 11/15, 11/16, 11/19, 11/20, 11/21, 11/26, 11/28, 11/30, 12/1, 12/2, 12/3, 12/5, 12/6, 12/7, 12/10, 12/12, 12/13, 12/14, 12/15, 12/16, 12/20, 12/22, 12/24, 12/25, 12/26, 12/28, 12/29, 12/30
Ford-Gregorie 9/21
Fordson 2/3, 10/8
Franklin 1/27, 2/10, 2/11, 3/11, 3/16, 3/24, 4/1, 4/4, 4/16, 5/1, 5/11, 5/22, 5/28, 5/29, 6/9, 6/19, 6/23, 6/25, 6/30, 7/1, 7/5, 10/1, 10/5, 10/22, 11/16, 11/27, 12/1, 12/2, 12/8
Frazer 1/20, 2/1, 2/6, 3/1, 3/3, 3/23, 3/28, 4/9, 4/19, 4/28, 5/26, 5/29, 6/22, 6/28, 6/29, 7/17, 7/25, 7/26, 8/8, 8/9, 8/14, 9/26, 11/7, 12/15
Frazer-Nash 8/17
Frontenac (Canada) 12/31
Frontenac (US) 3/14, 4/5, 5/30, 11/26, 12/2
Frontmobile 12/30
F.R.P. 2/8
Fry 7/18
Fryckman 1/12, 5/15
Fuller 2/16
FWD 1/18, 3/18, 9/14

Gaeth 11/24
Gaethmobile 11/24
Gardner 12/30
Garford 1/23, 8/4
Gaylord 10/20
GAZ 1/1
General Motors 1/4, 11/14
Gilby 7/15
GMC 1/5, 1/30, 2/6, 2/11, 2/21, 2/26, 3/10, 3/20, 4/2, 4/6, 5/9, 5/27, 6/1, 7/3, 7/5, 7/12, 8/1, 8/2, 8/15, 8/16, 9/1, 9/14, 9/16, 9/19, 9/26, 10/4, 11/7, 11/10, 11/30, 12/11
GN 5/21
Gobron-Brillie 3/28, 3/31, 7/17, 7/21, 11/5
Goliath 10/1
Gordini 1/28, 3/21, 6/23, 7/13, 7/18, 8/5, 10/3
Gordon/Gordon-Keeble 3/10
Graham (Brothers) 1/6, 1/16, 2/11, 5/5, 5/12, 6/25, 7/10, 7/15, 7/27, 9/3, 9/14, 10/7, 10/21, 12/8, 12/19
Graham-Paige 1/5, 1/6, 2/1, 2/6, 2/11, 5/12, 6/10, 6/12, 6/19, 7/7, 7/15, 8/7, 8/11, 8/14, 12/19
Gramm-Logan 12/13
Grant 5/11, 8/24
Gray 9/15
Gray-Dort 3/13, 4/10, 8/8, 10/27
Great Smith 1/1
Green Bay 7/16
Greifzu 8/3
Grout 9/9
G.W.K. 5/28

Hall 3/17
Halliday 5/28
Handley-Knight 7/1
Hanson 2/27, 6/15
Harris 6/12, 12/29
Harrison 1/17
Harroun 10/18
Hatfield 5/20
Haynes 4/13, 5/24, 6/18, 7/4, 11/3, 12/24
HCM 2/26
H.C.S. 11/3
Healey 10/22
Heck 8/3
Heine-Velox 1/7, 4/28

Henderson 12/5
Henry J 2/26, 6/26, 9/3, 9/28, 10/17, 11/1, 11/3, 11/20, 12/1, 12/15, 12/17, 12/20, 12/31
Hercules 1/24
Herreshoff 5/28
Herschmann 5/20
Hesketh 3/30
Hewitt 2/19, 6/20
Hill 4/27
Hillman 6/17, 8/15, 8/21, 9/15, 10/5, 10/8, 10/15
Hilton 8/13
Hindustan 5/11
Hispano-Suiza 1/18, 2/28, 3/8, 3/15, 4/18, 4/19, 5/12, 6/14, 8/8, 10/22, 11/26
Hofmann 1/20, 2/16, 5/17
Holden 3/20, 6/18, 7/14, 11/26, 11/29
Holland 4/26
Hollier 2/24
Holsman 4/15, 5/15
Hol-Tan 5/12
Honda 1/1, 3/1, 3/24, 4/26, 5/10, 5/26, 6/4, 6/23, 7/7, 7/13, 8/2, 8/5, 8/10, 9/10, 10/7, 10/24, 11/1
Horch 4/29, 11/7
Horlacher 3/4
Hotchkiss 2/13, 10/1
Houpt 1/19
Houpt-Rockwell 1/19, 8/27
House 10/6, 12/18
Howard 4/5
Hudson 1/1, 1/2, 1/11, 1/14, 1/15, 1/16, 1/18, 1/27, 2/5, 2/6, 2/10, 2/11, 2/16, 2/17, 2/23, 2/24, 2/25, 3/1, 3/5, 3/6, 3/13, 3/20, 3/24, 4/1, 4/9, 4/10, 4/12, 4/18, 4/25, 5/1, 5/2, 5/21, 5/23, 5/27, 5/31, 6/16, 6/19, 6/20, 6/21, 6/25, 7/1, 7/3, 7/6, 7/13, 7/15, 7/18, 7/29, 8/3, 8/5, 8/7, 8/8, 8/9, 8/12, 8/23, 8/25, 8/28, 8/30, 9/1, 9/6, 9/13, 9/23, 9/24, 9/28, 9/30, 10/1, 10/2, 10/8, 10/12, 10/13, 10/16, 10/25, 10/27, 10/29, 10/30, 11/7, 11/11, 11/12, 11/13, 11/18, 11/21, 11/30, 12/1, 12/7, 12/8, 12/9, 12/11, 12/15, 12/23, 12/28
Hungerford 11/2
Hupmobile 1/3, 1/5, 1/24, 1/28, 2/5, 2/8, 2/20, 2/29, 3/8, 4/2, 4/22, 5/22, 6/21, 6/27, 7/1, 7/7, 7/11, 7/13, 7/27, 8/3, 8/25, 9/1, 9/2, 9/3, 9/14, 9/15, 10/1, 10/4, 10/18, 10/16, 10/28, 11/1, 11/8, 11/10, 11/15, 12/7, 12/10
Hupp-Yeats 12/7
HWM 5/27
Hyundai 1/15, 2/1, 8/6, 10/17, 11/25

Impact 2/3, 4/18
Imperial (1) 8/6
Imperial (2) 2/2, 4/29, 5/1, 6/12, 7/1, 7/18, 8/11, 9/23, 9/24, 9/25, 9/29, 9/30, 10/1, 10/21, 10/30, 11/26
Indiana 5/31, 11/6
Innes 8/16
Innocenti 6/21, 12/19
International 1/16, 1/18, 1/30, 2/20, 2/28, 3/1, 4/9, 4/16, 4/25, 4/28, 5/1, 5/3, 5/28, 6/3, 6/14, 6/24, 7/14, 7/15, 7/31, 8/1, 8/6, 8/20, 9/15, 9/26, 10/21, 11/1, 11/27, 11/30
Inter-State 2/5
Iso 2/13, 2/21, 3/21, 6/27, 7/24, 8/21, 8/25, 8/28, 11/16
Isotta-Fraschini 1/9, 1/13, 1/24, 2/21, 2/22, 3/19, 3/26, 6/2, 6/5, 6/12, 6/26, 6/27, 7/3, 8/2, 9/2, 9/7, 10/10, 11/10, 11/23, 12/2, 12/4, 12/24
Itala 5/9, 8/10, 9/10
Isuzu 4/29, 8/12

Iveco 2/13
Jackson 7/19
Jaguar 1/14, 1/19, 1/20, 1/30, 2/8, 2/12, 2/14, 3/3, 3/16, 3/27, 3/28, 3/29, 4/1, 4/3, 4/4, 4/9, 4/12, 4/15, 5/20, 5/26, 5/30, , 6/10, 6/14, 6/15, 6/21, 7/10, 7/15, 7/21, 8/1, 8/24, 9/1, 9/4, 9/9, 9/19, 9/21, 9/30, 10/1, 10/2, 10/11, 10/13, 10/15, 10/17, 10/21, 10/27, 11/7, 12/1, 12/13, 12/31
Jaskowiak 4/8
Jaxon 7/19
Jay-Eye-See 12/14
JBW 7/18
Jeantaud 1/17, 3/4, 12/18
Jeep (Jeepster) 1/1, 1/10, 1/20, 1/28, 2/5, 2/23, 2/27, 2/28, 3/7, 3/10, 3/19, 3/25, 4/3, 4/7, 5/13, 5/20, 6/16, 6/19, 7/13, 7/17, 7/19, 7/25, 8/15, 8/17, 9/19, 9/23, 10/5, 10/11, 10/20, 11/11, 11/12, 11/13, 11/14, 11/23, 11/27, 12/1, 12/10, 12/12, 12/17
Jeffery 6/12, 7/13, 11/4, 12/9
Jenatzy 1/17, 1/27, 3/28, 4/29, 11/27, 11/28
Jensen 5/8, 5/21, 8/18
Jewett 1/12
Johnson 12/4
Jones 2/20
Jordan (1) 3/12, 6/23, 7/3, 9/18
Jordan (2) 3/10
JPW 3/30, 6/16, 7/27

Kaiser 1/3, 1/6, 1/9, 1/17, 1/20, 1/29, 1/30, 2/1, 2/3, 2/5, 2/6, 2/16, 2/22, 2/26, 3/1, 3/3, 3/7, 3/14, 3/20, 3/23, 3/28, 4/7, 4/8, 4/9, 4/10, 4/19, 4/27, 4/28, 4/19, 5/2, 5/9, 5/14, 5/15, 5/26, 5/28, 5/29, 6/22, 6/28, 6/29, 6/30, 7/17, 7/19, 7/25, 7/26, 7/29, 8/6, 8/8, 8/9, 8/14, 8/29, 9/19, 9/25, 9/26, 10/5, 10/12, 10/19, 10/31, 11/17, 12/15
K-D 12/16
Keeton 4/1
Keller 10/5
Kelly-Springfield 4/16, 6/24
Kelsey 5/17
Kenworth 1/22, 2/1, 10/2, 12/9
Keystone 1/9
Kimball 7/27
King 3/6, 6/23, 8/28, 10/18
Kingston 1/15
Kissel/KisselKar 2/26, 2/29, 6/10, 8/20, 10/20, 10/22, 10/29, 12/11, 12/13
Kleiber 12/18
Klenk 8/1
Kline Kar 5/20
Klink 7/8, 11/11
Knickerbocker 2/18
Knox 2/15, 3/8, 5/1, 5/20, 6/2, 6/12, 10/25
Kojima 10/24
Krotz Electric 12/9
Krotz Gas-Electric 12/9
Kurtis 1/25, 5/3, 5/30, 12/12
Kuzma 5/30

Lafayette 1/29, 7/8, 10/1
LaFayette (Nash) 1/10, 6/15, 10/15
Lagonda 2/10, 4/9, 6/17
La Licorne 1/15
Lambert 10/4
Lamborghini 3/10, 4/23, 4/28, 10/30, 11/16
Lanchester 3/8, 6/6, 7/22, 8/28
Lancia 1/16, 1/20, 1/22, 5/2, 5/5, 5/10, 5/12, 5/22, 6/3, 6/20, 6/27, 6/29, 7/1, 9/1, 10/22, 10/26, 11/21
Landrey-et-Beyroux 5/1
Lane Steam 1/3

Land Rover 4/30
Larrousse 3/1
LaSalle 1/1, 1/3, 3/5, 3/20, 5/1, 5/5, 5/9, 8/6, 8/26, 12/17, 11/22
LDS 12/29
Lec 6/5
Leach 9/17
Lescina 11/6
Lexington 5/10, 11/8
Lexus 5/1
Leyland 4/6, 10/5
Liberty 1/28, 7/27
Lifu 12/18
Ligier 1/25, 6/19
Lincoln (Continental, Zephyr) 1/1, 1/4, 1/10, 1/15, 1/26, 1/30, 2/3, 2/4, 2/6, 2/8, 2/12, 2/13, 3/24, 3/25, 3/26, 3/27, 3/29, 4/1, 4/2, 4/5, 4/15, 4/16, 4/18, 4/21, 4/22, 5/8, 5/20, 6/9, 6/12, 6/13, 6/19, 6/23, 6/25, 7/1, 7/7, 7/17, 7/21, 8/31, 9/9, 9/13, 9/14, 9/16, 9/17, 9/20, 10/2, 10/4, 10/5, 10/6, 10/9, 10/14, 10/16, 10/20, 11/1, 11/8, 11/15, 11/17, 11/19, 11/23, 11/30, 12/1, 12/11, 12/13, 12/17, 12/24, 12/26
Lincoln Highway 1/5
Linn 5/7
Lister 5/19
Little 1/21, 4/2, 12/5
Lloyd 2/2, 9/1, 9/15
Locomobile 1/3, 1/14, 1/23, 2/1, 2/26, 2/27, 3/10, 4/15, 4/16, 4/22, 5/1, 5/18, 6/17, 6/24, 7/7, 7/29, 7/31, 8/12, 8/25, 9/10, 10/9, 10/10, 10/11, 10/12, 10/24, 10/26, 11/2, 12/1
Lola 4/27, 5/9, 5/17, 5/19, 5/20, 5/26, 6/9, 6/11, 9/28
Long Steam 7/10
Loomis 10/25
Lorraine-Dietrich 4/11
Lotus 1/1, 1/22, 2/15, 3/13, 3/23, 4/3, 4/7, 4/21, 4/23, 5/7, 5/18, 5/19, 5/29, 5/30, 5/31, 6/5, 6/17, 6/18, 6/19, 6/30, 7/2, 7/14, 7/15, 7/20, 7/30, 8/18, 8/27, 9/5, 9/10, 9/11, 9/22, 10/4, 10/24, 11/1, 11/24, 12/3, 12/16
Lozier 1/23, 2/3, 2/14, 2/17, 3/19, 4/3, 4/24, 5/6, 5/25, 5/28, 6/11, 7/29, 8/27, 11/27
Lunar Roving Vehicle (LRV) 3/17, 7/31, 8/8
Lutzmann 1/21
Luverne 3/20
Luxford 3/13
Lyncar 7/19

Maccar 2/15
Mack 1/1, 1/16, 1/23, 2/13, 3/1, 3/14, 4/14, 5/17, 5/30, 6/3, 6/20, 7/21, 7/24, 8/4, 8/7, 8/28, 9/16, 9/20, 10/10, 10/11, 10/19, 10/27, 10/29, 11/8, 11/27, 12/9, 12/17
Macon 5/17
Maja 8/2
MAN 10/30
Marathon 1/1
March 3/7, 4/19, 4/27, 5/24, 6/20, 7/29, 8/19
Marcos 6/8
Marcus 4/16
Marion 12/21
Marmon 1/3, 1/8, 1/21, 2/2, 2/18, 2/20, 2/26, 2/28, 3/13, 3/15, 3/30, 4/4, 4/6, 4/7, 5/1, 5/9, 5/17, 5/24, 5/30, 6/13, 7/24, 7/29, 8/5, 8/31, 9/6, 9/21, 9/25, 10/6, 10/11, 10/26, 10/29, 10/31, 11/4, 11/10, 11/19, 11/21, 12/15, 12/20, 12/23
Marquette (1) 4/9
Marquette (2) 6/1, 6/27, 6/30, 10/22, 11/19
Marsh 10/16

Martini 5/21
Martin Wasp 1/3, 1/31, 3/25, 4/1, 6/2, 7/2, 7/6, 11/16
Maserati 1/17, 1/19, 3/29, 4/10, 4/24, 4/25, 5/6, 5/10, 5/19, 5/22, 5/30, 6/4, 6/15, 6/27, 7/4, 7/6, 7/14, 7/28, 7/31, 8/4, 8/9, 8/18, 9/5, 9/7, 9/28, 10/2, 10/27, 11/20
Mason 1/12, 2/19, 3/26, 6/25, 6/26, 7/14, 7/31, 8/16, 10/3, 12/5
Matheson 2/11, 8/12
Mathis 4/1, 4/15, 6/13
Matra 1/10, 1/11, 2/10, 2/29, 5/6, 5/21, 5/29, 6/18, 6/23, 7/1, 7/4
Maxwell 1/11, 1/20, 2/25, 5/30, 6/6, 6/9, 6/15, 6/16, 6/21, 6/26, 7/4, 7/5, 7/9, 8/7, 9/18, 10/9, 10/22, 10/26, 11/8, 11/19, 12/25
Maybach 2/7, 3/23, 4/1
Maytag 3/26
MAZ 8/9, 11/5
Mazda 1/30, 4/8, 4/25, 5/30, 6/23, 7/4, 7/13, 7/26, 8/6, 8/21, 9/16, 9/28, 11/1, 11/10, 11/11, 11/15, 11/30
McFarlan 4/17
McGuire 8/29
McIntyre 1/29, 12/16
McLaren 5/12, 6/2, 6/6, 6/9, 7/3, 7/27, 9/14, 10/12, 12/18
McLaughlin 1/6
Mecca 4/14
Mercedes 1/21, 1/25, 1/27, 2/23, 2/26, 3/25, 3/29, 4/1, 4/2, 4/7, 4/20, 4/21, 4/27, 5/25, 6/10, 6/23, 6/28, 7/2, 7/4, 7/7, 7/11, 7/12, 7/20, 9/2, 9/10, 9/13, 10/2, 10/14, 10/17, 10/19, 11/12, 11/22, 12/22
Mercedes-Benz 1/6, 1/16, 1/23, 1/28, 2/6, 2/7, 2/15, 2/23, 2/25, 3/4, 3/12, 3/13, 3/26, 3/29, 4/1, 4/4, 4/7, 4/10, 4/11, 4/16, 4/30, 5/1, 5/2, 5/7, 5/15, 5/20, 5/26, 5/31, 6/3, 6/8, 6/10, 6/11, 6/12, 6/13, 6/15, 6/19, 6/25, 6/28, 7/4, 7/15, 7/16, 7/19, 7/24, 7/29, 8/1, 8/2, 8/3, 9/2, 9/3, 9/11, 9/12, 9/28, 9/30, 10/1, 10/8, 10/12, 10/26, 11/1, 12/8, 12/15
Mercer 1/1, 1/3, 2/8, 2/9, 2/27, 2/28, 3/10, 4/16, 8/20, 8/22, 8/26, 8/27, 10/6, 10/7, 10/8, 10/9, 11/14, 11/21
Mercury (Canada) 11/30, 12/16
Mercury (US) 1/6, 1/7, 1/15, 1/21, 1/30, 2/2, 2/3, 2/8, 2/10, 2/12, 2/17, 2/18, 2/19, 2/22, 3/17, 3/20, 3/27, 3/29, 4/1, 4/18, 4/22, 5/3, 5/12, 5/26, 7/1, 7/3, 7/5, 8/8, 8/26, 8/31, 9/4, 9/9, 9/21, 9/22, 9/30, 10/3, 10/6, 10/8, 10/10, 10/24, 10/28, 11/1, 11/4, 11/19, 11/30, 12/2, 12/7, 12/26
Merkel 7/7
Merzario 1/15
Messerschmitt 6/26, 9/15
Meteor 7/10
Metropolitan 2/14, 4/9, 4/24
Metz 6/21, 6/29, 7/19, 8/3, 11/18
Metzger 4/15
M.G. 1/20, 2/4, 2/9, 2/18, 3/25, 3/27, 3/28, 4/12, 4/25, 5/5, 5/7, 5/31, 6/2, 6/21, 7/1, 7/15, 7/21, 7/24, 8/27, 9/15, 9/23, 10/10, 10/12, 10/17, 10/20, 10/24, 10/30, 11/9, 11/22, 12/24
Michigan 8/6
Mighty Mite 1/1
Miller 4/16, 4/23, 4/25, 4/30, 5/1, 5/3, 5/4, 5/30, 6/14, 6/15, 6/16, 7/8, 7/11, 8/6, 8/9, 9/15, 10/27, 12/14
Minardi 4/7
Minerva 6/27
Mirage 4/25, 5/1
Mitchell 1/23, 2/19, 2/27, 4/2, 4/19, 6/12, 12/21

Mitsubishi 1/9, 1/11, 2/7, 3/13, 4/30, 5/24, 6/2, 9/6, 10/25, 12/8

Monarch (US) 12/7

Monarch (Canada) 3/23, 5/12

Monroe 4/24, 8/1

Monteverdi 6/7, 9/11, 12/10

Moon 1/3, 2/3, 2/12, 4/7, 6/27, 7/15

Moore 12/15

Morgan 3/27, 5/13, 7/1, 12/27

Morris 2/14, 3/27, 3/28, 5/11, 6/19, 7/1, 8/26, 8/29, 10/1, 10/2, 10/10, 10/27, 12/22

Morris & Salom 11/28

Mors 3/7, 4/9, 4/12, 5/24, 5/29, 6/29, 7/4, 7/28, 8/5, 10/20, 11/5, 11/16, 11/17, 12/22

Moskvitch 5/31

Motorette 1/9, 5/17

Mueller (-Benz) 4/24, 10/23

Multimobile 5/28

Multi-Union 10/20

Muntz 6/20, 6/29

Murray 9/5

Napier 1/24, 1/25, 1/29, 2/5, 2/10, 2/19, 2/24, 3/11, 5/11, 5/12, 6/8, 6/26, 7/6, 7/28, 8/7, 8/10, 9/18, 10/7, 10/24, 11/6, 12/24, 12/28

Nash 1/1, 1/3, 1/14, 1/21, 1/29, 1/30, 2/1, 2/3, 2/11, 2/14, 2/22, 2/27, 3/1, 3/11, 3/13, 3/14, 3/17, 3/24, 4/1, 4/2, 4/9, 4/12, 4/14, 4/18, 4/19, 4/23, 4/27, 5/1, 5/16, 5/20, 5/22, 5/27, 5/30, 6/1, 6/6, 6/16, 6/18, 6/23, 6/28, 7/1, 7/6, 7/8, 7/17, 7/20, 7/29, 8/1, 8/15, 8/20, 8/23, 9/1, 9/15, 9/22, 9/28, 10/1, 10/2, 10/5, 10/14, 10/15, 10/17, 10/27, 10/29, 11/15, 11/17, 12/1, 12/9, 12/21, 12/28

National 2/22, 7/8, 8/7, 10/14, 11/4, 12/22

Nelson 2/20, 5/1

Nesseldorf 5/21, 5/22, 6/9, 8/1, 10/22, 10/28

Nissan 1/29, 2/2, 2/12, 3/1, 3/3, 3/26, 3/29, 5/9, 5/20, 8/3, 9/11, 9/15, 9/30, 12/19

Noble 10/30

North American 7/10

Northern 2/22, 4/28, 6/1

Novi 5/15, 5/16, 11/6

NSU 10/12

Oakland 1/3, 1/9, 1/20, 1/24, 1/28, 2/1, 2/11, 2/21, 2/25, 3/2, 3/6, 3/8, 3/15, 3/22, 3/24, 4/2, 4/8, 4/9, 4/16, 5/1, 6/7, 6/13, 6/17, 6/22, 7/4, 7/9, 7/12, 8/1, 8/4, 8/12, 8/15, 8/28, 9/29, 10/8, 10/15, 10/18, 11/8, 11/23, 11/30

Oldfield 5/30

Oldsmobile 1/1, 1/5, 1/8, 1/14, 1/20, 1/25, 2/5, 2/15, 2/18, 2/19, 2/20, 2/22, 2/25, 3/1, 3/9, 3/16, 3/28, 4/1, 4/2, 4/5, 4/8, 4/29, 5/1, 5/4, 5/8, 5/11, 5/13, 5/14, 5/16, 5/22, 5/28, 5/30, 6/3, 6/4, 6/5, 6/10, 6/16, 6/27, 6/28, 7/5, 7/11, 7/19, 7/23, 7/27, 8/9, 8/21, 8/24, 8/25, 8/28, 8/31, 9/5, 9/10, 9/11, 9/12, 9/13, 9/14, 9/20, 9/22, 9/24, 9/26, 9/27, 9/29, 10/1, 10/3, 10/4, 10/6, 10/9, 10/14, 10/15, 10/19, 10/28, 11/7, 11/8, 11/9, 11/12, 11/19, 12/18, 12/20, 12/29

O.M. 3/26, 4/18, 9/23

Onyx 5/28

Opel 1/1, 1/5, 1/17, 1/18, 1/21, 1/28, 2/20, 3/12, 3/18, 4/3, 4/8, 4/11, 4/17, 4/29, 5/18, 5/20, 5/23, 6/24, 7/26, 8/2, 8/3, 8/27, 9/1, 9/6, 9/15, 9/21, 9/24, 10/26, 11/2, 11/15, 11/16, 11/17, 12/13

Orient 10/26

Orient Electric 6/17

Orlo 7/19

OSCA 4/7, 9/13, 12/1

Osella-Cosworth 3/1, 6/13

Oshkosh (1) 7/16, 7/24

Oshkosh (2) 4/1, 5/1

Otto 9/5

Overland 2/12, 3/31, 4/8, 6/15, 10/24, 12/19

Owen (1) 11/23

Owen (2) 4/29

Owen Magnetic 4/29, 5/22

Oxford 1/30

Pacific 3/27

Packard (1) 6/25, 10/14

Packard (2) 1/1, 1/2, 1/3, 1/4, 1/5, 1/6, 1/9, 1/10, 1/11, 1/15, 1/16, 1/17, 1/18, 1/19, 1/20, 1/22, 1/24, 1/25, 1/27, 1/29, 1/31, 2/2, 2/3, 2/4, 2/5, 2/6, 2/9, 2/10, 2/11, 2/12, 2/14, 2/15, 2/18, 2/19, 2/20, 2/22, 2/23, 2/24, 2/25, 2/26, 2/27, 2/28, 3/1, 3/2, 3/3, 3/4, 3/5, 3/8, 3/10, 3/11, 3/14, 3/15, 3/16, 3/17, 3/18, 3/20, 3/21, 3/22, 3/23, 3/24, 3/25, 3/26, 3/27, 3/29, 3/31, 4/1, 4/6, 4/9, 4/10, 4/11, 4/12, 4/13, 4/14, 4/15, 4/16, 4/17, 4/18, 4/19, 4/20, 4/22, 4/23, 4/26, 4/30, 5/1, 5/2, 5/4, 5/5, 5/7, 5/8, 5/9, 5/11, 5/12, 5/16, 5/19, 5/22, 5/25, 5/30, 5/31, 6/1, 6/3, 6/5, 6/7, 6/9, 6/10, 6/14, 6/16, 6/17, 6/19, 6/20, 6/21, 6/22, 6/23, 6/25, 6/26, 6/27, 6/28, 7/1, 7/2, 7/3, 7/6, 7/7, 7/8, 7/9, 7/12, 7/13, 7/16, 7/19, 7/22, 7/23, 7/24, 7/25, 7/26, 7/27, 7/29, 7/30, 7/31, 8/1, 8/2, 8/4, 8/5, 8/6, 8/8, 8/10, 8/13, 8/14, 8/15, 8/17, 8/19, 8/20, 8/21, 8/22, 8/23, 8/24, 8/25, 8/26, 8/27, 8/28, 8/30, 8/31, 9/1, 9/2, 9/3, 9/4, 9/6, 9/8, 9/10, 9/11, 9/13, 9/15, 9/16, 9/17, 9/19, 9/20, 9/22, 9/23, 9/25, 9/26, 9/27, 9/29, 9/30, 10/1, 10/2, 10/4, 10/5, 10/8, 10/10, 10/12, 10/13, 10/15, 10/19, 10/21, 10/22, 10/24, 10/25, 10/27, 10/28, 10/30, 10/31, 11/1, 11/3, 11/4, 11/6, 11/7, 11/9, 11/11, 11/13, 11/14, 11/15, 11/18, 11/19, 11/21, 11/23, 11/25, 11/26, 12/1, 12/4, 12/7, 12/8, 12/11, 12/12, 12/13, 12/14, 12/15, 12/17, 12/18, 12/19, 12/20, 12/22, 12/24, 12/25, 12/27, 12/28, 12/30, 12/31

Paige (1) 8/9

Paige (-Detroit) 1/21, 2/11, 5/5, 6/10, 7/15, 8/16, 11/13

Pak-Age-Car 10/15

Pan 1/27, 9/29

Panhard 7/20, 7/28, 10/8

Panhard et Levassor 2/10, 2/17, 2/25, 4/8, 4/14, 4/23, 5/11, 5/17, 5/24, 5/27, 5/29, 6/1, 6/12, 6/14, 7/12, 7/13, 7/14, 7/16, 7/24, 7/31, 10/3, 10/8

Paragon 8/28

Parnelli 9/22

Parry 3/17, 7/28

PAT-PAF 3/27

Patriot 1/10, 7/26

Patterson-Greenfield 9/23

Payne-Modern 10/25

Peck 9/6

Peerless 5/30, 6/12, 6/30, 8/6, 8/8, 8/28, 10/4, 10/5, 10/29, 11/1, 11/20, 12/13

Pegaso 5/15, 8/19

Penske 8/15, 9/22

Peterbilt 12/28

Petter 5/26, 7/18

Peugeot 1/4, 3/6, 3/8, 3/18, 3/20, 3/23, 3/24, 4/2, 4/8, 4/21, 4/24, 5/21, 5/26, 5/30, 6/3, 6/10, 6/11, 6/19, 6/25, 6/26, 7/2, 7/22, 7/26, 8/6, 8/7, 9/4, 9/6, 9/16, 9/19, 9/23, 11/11, 11/16, 11/18, 12/6, 12/16

Phantom Corsair 4/23, 5/29

Phelps 8/24

Pierce-Arrow 1/1, 1/2, 1/9, 1/21, 2/1, 2/4, 2/9, 2/11, 2/24, 2/28, 3/2, 3/16, 3/19, 3/28, 4/16, 4/26, 4/27, 4/30, 5/1, 5/12, 5/13, 5/15, 5/22, 5/23, 5/29, 6/2, 6/24, 7/22, 7/28, 7/30, 8/7, 8/15, 8/19, 8/21, 8/25, 8/26, 9/18, 9/19, 9/20, 9/21, 10/10, 10/11, 10/15, 11/1, 11/2, 11/9, 11/24, 11/30, 12/12, 12/24

Pierce-Racine 1/30, 4/6

Pittsburgh Six 11/2

Plass 1/7

Playboy 3/13, 4/3, 4/14, 5/20, 6/3

Plymouth 1/1, 1/4, 1/7, 1/12, 1/14, 1/24, 1/28, 1/31, 2/4, 2/23, 3/3, 3/7, 3/14, 3/15, 3/25, 3/30, 3/31, 4/1, 4/2, 4/4, 4/5, 4/6, 4/7, 4/13, 4/17, 4/19, 5/6, 5/10, 6/4, 6/8, 6/11, 6/14, 6/15, 7/1, 7/7, 7/10, 7/11, 7/13, 7/17, 7/18, 7/28, 8/6, 8/8, 8/20, 8/24, 9/14, 9/15, 9/18, 9/19, 9/20, 9/21, 9/23, 9/25, 9/26, 9/27, 9/28, 9/29, 10/1, 10/2, 10/3, 10/6, 10/15, 10/16, 10/21, 10/22, 10/25, 10/27, 10/29, 10/30, 10/31, 11/2, 11/4, 11/10, 11/17, 11/18, 11/20, 11/25, 12/1, 12/2, 12/5, 12/11, 12/18, 12/22, 12/28, 12/31

Pobieda 11/6, 11/23

Pontiac (1) 7/13

Pontiac (2) 1/1, 1/3, 1/5, 1/7, 1/9, 1/10, 1/11, 1/12, 1/14, 1/16, 1/19, 1/20, 1/22, 1/27, 1/28, 1/31, 2/2, 2/6, 2/10, 2/11, 2/12, 2/13, 2/23, 2/26, 3/1, 3/2, 3/6, 3/8, 3/11, 3/14, 3/15, 3/20, 3/22, 3/28, 4/1, 4/9, 4/13, 4/18, 4/19, 4/20, 4/24, 5/1, 5/7, 5/21, 6/3, 6/10, 6/12, 6/18, 6/20, 6/22, 6/23, 6/27, 6/30, 7/1, 7/4, 7/5, 7/6, 7/13, 7/15, 7/16, 7/18, 7/20, 7/30, 7/31, 8/4, 8/5, 8/8, 8/10, 8/11, 8/12, 8/15, 8/17, 8/18, 8/20, 8/21, 8/22, 8/23, 8/24, 8/26, 8/28, 8/31, 9/1, 9/3, 9/4, 9/6, 9/8, 9/11, 9/13, 9/15, 9/16, 9/18, 9/20, 9/21, 9/23, 9/24, 9/25, 9/26, 9/27, 9/28, 10/1, 10/3, 10/4, 10/6, 10/7, 10/8, 10/9, 10/11, 10/15, 10/17, 10/19, 10/20, 10/21, 10/28, 10/29, 11/2, 11/7, 11/9, 11/17, 11/18, 11/19, 11/20, 11/27, 12/1, 12/2, 12/3, 12/7, 12/8, 12/14, 12/15, 12/16, 12/18, 12/21, 12/22, 12/28, 12/29, 12/30

Pope 4/19, 4/20, 4/28, 5/13, 5/20, 5/27

Pope-Hartford 3/8, 4/19, 5/20, 8/25

Pope-Robinson 11/4, 11/26

Pope-Toledo 1/30, 4/1, 7/2

Pope-Tribune 10/25

Porsche 1/10, 1/17, 1/31, 2/4, 2/16, 3/6, 3/15, 3/17, 3/20, 3/21, 4/9, 4/16, 4/20, 4/27, 4/30, 5/14, 5/16, 5/24, 6/8, 6/13, 6/14, 6/22, 7/8, 7/20, 8/1, 8/3, 8/7, 8/12, 8/17, 8/18, 8/23, 8/28, 9/1, 9/3, 9/17, 9/19, 9/30, 10/12, 10/19, 11/26, 12/8, 12/18, 12/21

Powell 4/17

Praga 1/1, 5/4

Pratt (-Elkhart) 7/2

Premier 4/3, 6/30, 10/30, 11/4

Prinetti & Stucchi 3/14

Protos 7/1, 7/26, 7/30

Pullman 5/20, 7/24

Pungs-Finch 5/9

Railton 6/24, 8/7, 8/23, 9/15, 9/16, 10/7, 11/3

Rainier 1/25, 3/29

Ralt-Cosworth 3/24

RAM 3/13

Rambler 2/1, 2/5, 2/19, 3/1, 4/1, 4/2, 4/14, 5/22, 6/10, 6/23, 6/28, 6/30, 9/22, 10/1, 10/5, 10/6, 10/7, 10/8, 10/13, 10/14, 10/22, 11/2

Ranger 9/26

Rapid 8/1, 8/2
Rayfield 1/5, 2/1, 2/8, 2/14, 5/26, 8/31
R.C.H. 7/25, 12/7
Rebaque 9/30
Reed Steam 7/22
Reeves 8/25
Regal 7/4
Relay 2/3
Reliance 8/1
Remington 10/30
Renault 1/1, 1/7, 1/17, 1/21, 2/11, 3/6, 3/8,
    3/9, 3/21, 3/30, 3/31, 4/9, 4/13, 4/21,
    4/27, 5/24, 5/31, 6/26, 6/28, 6/29, 7/1, 7/2,
    7/5, 7/8, 7/9, 7/16, 7/18, 8/5, 8/12, 9/5,
    9/9, 9/22, 9/27, 10/4, 10/10, 11/2, 11/17,
    11/18, 12/13, 12/16, 12/22, 12/23, 12/24,
    12/25, 12/31
Reo 1/3, 1/13, 1/21, 3/11, 3/18, 4/16, 4/17,
    4/29, 5/11, 5/18, 5/30, 6/2, 7/15, 7/23,
    8/9, 8/16, 8/28, 9/3, 10/9, 10/15, 10/18,
    10/25, 10/26, 12/19, 12/20
ReVere 2/7, 3/2, 5/1, 7/15, 8/25, 9/12
Rial 4/3
Richard-Brasier 6/17
Rickenbacker 5/10, 7/6, 7/25, 10/8, 10/28
Riker 3/4, 6/1, 9/7, 11/16
Riley 6/9, 9/2, 11/6
Roamer 4/22, 8/7
Robinson 11/4
Rochet-Schneider 2/4
Rocket 10/16
Rockford 4/11
Rock Hill 11/17
Rockne 3/4, 3/22, 3/31, 9/16
Roger (-Benz) 8/17
Rolls-Royce 1/1, 1/3, 1/7, 1/10, 1/14, 1/17,
    1/22, 1/23, 1/25, 1/26, 1/28, 1/31, 2/1, 2/4,
    2/5, 2/6, 2/12, 2/19, 2/26, 2/28, 3/7, 3/9,
    3/13, 3/15, 3/16, 3/20, 3/22, 3/27, 4/2, 4/9,
    4/10, 4/11, 4/13, 4/15, 4/17, 4/20, 4/21,
    4/22, 4/23, 4/24, 5/1, 5/2, 5/4, 5/9, 5/11,
    5/12, 5/18, 5/20, 5/23, 5/26, 5/28, 6/2, 6/3,
    6/6, 6/7, 6/12, 6/14, 6/17, 6/18, 6/21, 6/24,
    6/25, 6/27, 6/28, 6/29, 7/1, 7/9, 7/13, 7/14,
    7/15, 7/19, 7/25, 7/30, 8/1, 8/2, 8/8, 8/13,
    8/14, 8/25, 8/26, 8/27, 8/29, 8/30, 9/2, 9/5,
    9/20, 9/22, 9/27, 10/1, 10/2, 10/4, 10/6,
    10/12, 10/13, 10/15, 10/17, 10/24, 10/27,
    10/28, 10/31, 11/1, 11/6, 11/7, 11/8, 11/21,
    11/22, 11/25, 11/26, 11/30, 12/2, 12/3, 12/6,
    12/11, 12/12, 12/17, 12/19, 12/21, 12/23,
    12/24, 12/30
Romano Eagle 8/12
Rondeau 6/13, 12/27
Roosevelt 2/20, 5/15, 12/22
Roots & Venables 7/7
Rover 3/5, 3/23, 5/3, 5/13, 8/9, 10/5
Royal Tourist 6/12
Royce 2/3, 2/26, 3/27, 4/1, 4/22
Rumpler 6/18
Russell 1/27, 4/17, 5/1
Russo-Baltique 5/30
Rutenber 2/26
Ruxton 2/8, 5/6, 6/27, 7/26, 8/1, 9/14, 10/8,
    10/29

Saab 3/6, 3/15, 3/17, 4/2, 5/6, 6/10, 8/28,
    9/22, 12/1, 12/7, 12/15
Salmson 4/13, 4/15, 4/29, 5/4, 5/21, 6/7, 9/10,
    11/25, 12/23
Samson 6/3
Saturn 1/4, 1/7, 1/26, 4/19, 7/30, 7/31, 8/22,
    10/11
Sauber 3/14
Saurer 3/1, 8/2

Saxon 2/23, 5/4, 7/4
Scarab 2/25, 5/29, 6/19, 7/24
S.C.A.T. 5/26
Scirocco 6/9
Scripps-Booth 1/12, 4/22, 5/27, 6/13, 9/13,
    12/15
Seagrave 6/27
Searchmont 1/9
Sears 11/3, 12/9
Sefac 8/15
Selden 5/8, 10/11
Serpollet 3/6, 4/13, 4/21, 5/19
Shadow-Cosworth 3/3, 3/5, 3/22, 8/14
Shannon 7/16
Sharp-Arrow 11/14
Sheffield 9/8
Shelby 1/27, 2/16, 3/1, 11/5
Sheridan 8/1
Siata 11/14
Simca 1/18, 1/28, 5/6, 7/18, 8/5
Simplex 3/10, 4/21, 5/19, 7/7, 9/15, 10/9
Simtek 3/27
Singer 5/24
Sintz 5/9
Sir Vival 3/20
Sizaire-Berwick 6/20, 8/20
Sizaire et Naudin 6/1
Sklarek 5/19
Skoda 1/1, 3/28, 9/4
S & M Simplex 9/17, 11/13
Speedwell 10/25
Sperry 6/16, 10/12
Spicer 11/21
Spirit 7/16
Springfield 5/26
Spyker 2/21, 4/1, 8/16
Squire 1/17, 7/6, 9/17, 9/20, 10/19
S.S. 9/21
Standard 2/10, 10/17, 12/25
Stanley 1/26, 3/25, 4/2, 5/12, 5/30, 5/31, 6/1,
    6/10, 6/17, 7/17, 7/20, 8/18, 8/19, 8/22,
    8/31, 9/20, 11/8, 12/1
Star 1/10, 3/10, 7/24, 8/1
Stearns (-Knight) 3/8, 4/6, 7/9, 8/15, 9/2, 9/6,
    12/20
Stebro 10/6
Stephens 5/8
Sterling (1) 7/3
Sterling (2) 8/9
Sterling-Knight 4/6, 5/30, 7/5, 9/2
Sterling-New York 5/1
Stevens-Duryea 4/2, 4/4, 8/13, 8/29, 10/1, 11/18
Stoddard-Dayton 8/14, 10/22
Stout Scarab 1/16, 2/24, 3/16, 3/20, 6/19
Strang 8/31
Studebaker 1/1, 1/2, 1/3, 1/6, 1/10, 1/11, 1/14,
    1/22, 1/23, 1/24, 1/30, 1/31, 2/1, 2/4, 2/5,
    2/11, 2/12, 2/14, 2/15, 2/16, 2/18, 2/19,
    2/24, 2/25, 2/27, 2/29, 3/4, 3/5, 3/8, 3/9,
    3/12, 3/16, 3/18, 3/23, 3/26, 3/30, 3/31,
    4/1, 4/6, 4/8, 4/9, 4/12, 4/13, 4/16, 4/19,
    4/21, 4/26, 4/27, 4/30, 5/1, 5/4, 5/8, 5/15,
    5/16, 5/17, 5/26, 6/6, 6/7, 6/22, 6/26, 7/1,
    7/2, 7/9, 7/12, 7/14, 7/16, 7/19, 7/22, 7/23,
    7/24, 7/26, 7/27, 7/28, 7/31, 8/4, 8/7, 8/11,
    8/13, 8/14, 8/15, 8/17, 8/19, 8/20, 8/22,
    8/24, 8/26, 8/30, 8/31, 9/1, 9/2, 9/3, 9/4,
    9/8, 9/14, 9/19, 9/20, 9/24, 10/1, 10/4,
    10/5, 10/6, 10/8, 10/11, 10/15, 10/22, 10/28,
    10/31, 11/2, 11/5, 11/6, 11/16, 11/18, 11/19,
    11/26, 11/30, 12/1, 12/8, 12/9, 12/15, 12/17,
    12/19, 12/20, 12/21, 12/25, 12/28
Studebaker-Garford 7/22
Stutz 1/9, 2/2, 2/9, 2/18, 4/3, 4/4, 4/15, 4/18,

    5/5, 5/18, 6/11, 6/26, 6/26, 7/8, 9/3, 9/4,
    9/9, 9/18, 10/9, 10/15, 10/21, 11/26, 12/5,
    12/17
Subaru 1/10, 2/15, 6/30, 7/15, 11/1, 12/10
Sun 9/23, 12/18, 12/24
Sunbeam 1/16, 3/16, 3/29, 4/29, 5/17, 5/23,
    6/27, 7/3, 7/17, 7/21, 7/26, 9/2, 9/11,
    9/17, 9/25, 10/23, 12/19, 12/23
Sunset 4/18
Supreme 5/31
Surtees 7/18, 10/6
Suzuki 1/30, 8/12
Swallow Doretti 1/6

Talbot (-Lago) 1/1, 4/15, 5/17, 7/23, 7/26, 9/3,
    9/9, 9/21, 10/28, 11/7, 11/13
Tarkington 6/1
Tatra 1/1, 1/29, 2/13, 3/2, 3/5, 3/29, 5/13,
    10/28, 12/15
Tec-Mec 12/12
Templar 1/3, 5/30, 6/16
Terraplane 8/1, 11/12
Texmobile 3/27, 8/5
Thayer 12/1
Theodore 3/4
Thomas 1/20, 1/27, 2/22, 2/28, 4/28, 5/1,
    5/28, 7/4, 7/16, 7/18, 7/22, 7/30, 9/5,
    9/17, 9/20, 10/1, 10/24, 10/25
Thomas-Detroit 2/28
Thornycroft 1/2, 2/21
Thrif-T 1/18
Token 5/12
Toledo 5/27
Toleman 9/13
Tosi 8/30
Toyota 1/9, 2/27, 3/1, 4/18, 5/28, 6/1, 6/13,
    8/1, 8/2, 8/4, 8/6, 8/24, 9/1, 9/12, 9/30,
    10/26, 11/14, 11/16, 12/12, 12/16, 12/19,
    12/22, 12/29
Trabant 7/10, 11/7
Trask 12/1
Treser 8/26
Triumph 2/10, 5/2, 10/5, 10/7, 10/17, 12/25
Trojan 4/28
Trumbull 5/7
Tucker 1/29, 3/3, 3/21, 3/30, 4/7, 5/6, 5/29,
    6/10, 6/19, 6/29, 7/5, 7/7, 7/19, 12/13,
    12/25
TVR 1/4
Twyman 7/12
Tyrrell-Cosworth 4/18, 8/5, 9/20, 10/6

Valiant 1/31, 7/13, 8/8, 9/21, 10/29
Vanden Plas 4/21, 5/6, 6/19, 7/2, 9/17, 11/26
Vanguard 2/21
Vanwall 5/6, 5/19, 7/3, 7/17, 7/20, 8/18,
    10/19, 10/25
Vaughan 8/15
Vauxhall 4/4, 6/20, 8/27
VAZ 3/24
Velie 1/10, 2/23, 3/20, 5/19, 6/1, 7/2, 7/24,
    10/24, 10/28, 11/20, 11/27, 11/29
Veritas 3/3, 5/27, 7/4, 8/1, 8/2
Victor 5/18
Voisin 2/5, 4/4, 6/1
Volga 6/14
Volkswagen 1/1, 1/3, 1/5, 1/10, 1/15, 1/17,
    1/18, 1/24, 2/12, 2/15, 2/17, 3/4, 3/10,
    3/23, 3/26, 3/28, 4/7, 4/12, 4/14, 4/15,
    4/23, 4/27, 5/9, 5/11, 5/14, 5/15, 5/20,
    5/25, 5/26, 5/28, 6/16, 7/1, 7/3, 7/10, 7/14,
    7/17, 7/21, 7/31, 8/1, 8/5, 8/25, 9/1, 9/15,
    9/16, 9/17, 9/18, 9/24, 10/1, 10/2, 10/9,

10/14, 10/19, 10/25, 11/7, 11/9, 11/12,
11/13, 12/4, 12/20, 12/28, 12/30
Volpini 9/28
Volvo 1/1, 1/5, 1/24, 2/3, 4/14, 4/23, 4/24,
4/28, 5/6, 5/9, 5/17, 5/21, 5/22, 6/2, 6/9,
6/22, 6/27, 7/3, 7/4, 7/19, 7/22, 7/31,
8/23, 8/25, 8/28, 9/1, 9/9, 9/13, 9/27,
10/3, 10/11, 10/20, 11/11, 11/20, 12/1,
12/8, 12/11, 12/16

Walter 1/1, 10/7
Waltham Steam 6/17
Walton 8/22
Wanderer 1/1
Ward Leonard 2/18
Ware 7/5
Warren 2/28, 6/11
Warszawa 11/6, 11/23
Wartburg 4/14
Washington 2/22, 12/3
Watson 5/30
Waverley Electric 3/31
Welch 1/5, 1/26, 4/1, 4/24, 11/8
Welleyes 7/11
Wells 4/22
Westcott 1/11, 4/3
Wetteroth 5/30
White 1/10, 1/16, 2/10, 2/15, 3/1, 4/1, 4/8,
4/9, 4/10, 5/3, 5/20, 5/27, 6/21, 6/29, 7/3,
7/4, 7/5, 7/7, 7/8, 7/10, 8/16, 8/25, 8/28,
9/18, 9/19, 10/1, 10/5, 10/10, 10/11, 11/3,
11/6, 11/9, 11/16, 11/28, 12/6, 12/29
Wick 10/31
Wilcox 12/13
Williams 4/27, 5/1, 7/14, 7/15, 8/10, 9/22,
10/17
Wills Sainte Claire 6/1, 7/12, 12/30
Willys 1/6, 1/10, 1/15, 1/18, 1/24, 1/31, 2/15,
2/16, 3/5, 3/7, 3/8, 3/17, 3/21, 4/14, 4/28,
5/4, 5/14, 5/25, 6/16, 6/17, 7/15, 7/19,
7/29, 8/6, 8/14, 8/15, 9/26, 10/4, 10/5,
10/6, 10/7, 10/20, 11/1, 11/2, 11/11, 12/4,
12/5, 12/10, 12/15
Willys-Knight 5/31, 12/5
Willys-Overland 1/6, 1/10, 1/19, 2/15, 2/18,
2/27, 3/10, 3/11, 3/23, 4/15, 4/20, 4/22,
4/28, 4/29, 5/12, 5/19, 5/30, 7/13, 7/24,
8/16, 9/20, 9/21, 10/15, 10/28, 11/13,
11/14, 11/15, 12/12, 12/15
Winther 3/15
Winton 2/11, 2/19, 2/26, 3/1, 3/21, 3/28, 4/1,
4/6, 4/11, 5/23, 5/30, 6/10, 6/17, 6/20,
6/22, 7/3, 7/26, 8/1, 8/4, 8/13, 10/7, 10/9,
10/11, 11/3
Wisner 9/3
Wolf 1/9
Wolfe 12/13
Wolseley 7/1, 11/27
Wolverine 12/1
Woodill 10/6
Worthington 7/2

Yellow Cab 3/24, 6/17, 6/29, 7/14
Yugo 1/29, 8/26, 11/7

Zakspeed 4/21
Zhiguli 9/9
ZIL 3/26, 6/26
ZIM 6/14
Zimmer 5/10
ZIS 6/26, 7/8
Zust 9/17

INDEX 2 - COMPANIES AND ORGANIZATIONS

A & K Petroleum Company 11/9
AC Cars, Ltd. 10/21
Accurate Machine Company 4/6
Acme Motor Car Company 6/9
AC Spark Plug Company 9/20, 10/27
Aermore Manufacturing Company 1/23
Aerocar Motor Company 2/23
Aerojet Engineering Company 3/28
Aerolite Piston Company, Ltd. 1/19, 4/23, 6/29
Aeronutronic Systems, Inc. 6/24
Ahrens-Fox Company 1/26
Air Cooled Motors Company 3/21, 7/11
Albany Hardware Specialty Manufacturing Company 1/10
Albatross Motor Car Company 1/8
Allen Motor Car Company 7/3, 9/20
Allied Corporation 9/24
Allied Wheel Products Inc. 12/21
All-Steel Motor Car Company 12/30
Alvis Car and Engineering Company Ltd. 4/27, 6/24, 12/24
Amcar 5/22
Amerada Corporation 2/7
Amerada Hess Corporation 3/13, 6/20
Amerada Petroleum Corporation 6/20
American Austin Car Company 2/28, 10/17
American Automobile Association (AAA) 3/3, 3/4, 4/1, 5/9, 6/12,
   8/1, 8/3, 8/8, 8/27, 9/4, 9/7, 9/18, 9/30, 11/3, 12/4, 12/28
American Automobile Company 9/10
American Bantam Car Company 6/2, 6/19, 6/22, 9/23, 11/13, 11/23,
   12/17
American Bearing Company 8/6
American Bosch Corporation 4/25, 7/16, 11/7
American Bosch Magneto Corporation 6/4, 8/4
American Bugatti Club 2/10
American Car Association (ACA) 9/9, 12/1
American Central Manufacturing Company 3/3, 11/20
American Cyclecar Manufacturers' Association 1/27
American Darracq Automobile Company 5/28
American Gear Company 11/22
American Hardware Corporation 11/3
American Honda Motor Company 6/4
American LaFrance Fire Engine Company 3/10, 8/4
American Locomotive Automobile Company 6/27, 8/22
American Locomotive Company 6/4, 6/22, 6/27
American Metal Products Company 3/25
American Motor Body Company 9/3
American Motor Car Company 12/1
American Motor Car Manufacturers Association (AMCMA) 1/13, 2/8,
   2/24
American Motor League 11/1, 11/29
American Motors Corporation 1/4, 1/9, 1/14, 1/15, 1/21, 2/4, 2/5,
   2/6, 2/7, 2/12, 2/14, 2/16, 2/24, 2/28, 3/1, 3/9, 3/10, 3/12, 3/20,
   3/21, 3/23, 3/27, 4/7, 4/9, 4/24, 5/1, 5/6, 5/20, 5/27, 5/31, 6/1,
   6/6, 6/13, 6/20, 6/22, 7/1, 7/8, 7/26, 8/5, 8/12, 8/22, 8/28, 8/31,
   9/2, 9/6, 9/19, 9/20, 9/21, 9/28, 9/29, 10/1, 10/8, 10/12, 10/16,
   10/20, 10/21, 10/22, 11/7, 11/13, 11/15, 11/21, 11/27, 11/30, 12/1,
   12/2, 12/5, 12/11, 12/13, 12/14, 12/15, 12/23, 12/25, 12/27, 12/31
American Motors Leasing Corporation 10/1
American National Red Cross 4/29
American Roller Bearing Company 12/20
American Society of Mechanical Engineers (ASME) 10/3, 12/1
American Steel Foundries 5/31
American Swiss Company 6/27
American Trucking Association 2/3

American Truck Museum and Library 9/27
AM General 3/21, 4/12
Amoco Corporation 1/1, 4/21, 4/23, 10/11, 11/8
Amplex Motor Car Company 1/20, 5/12
Anderson Company 10/23
Anderson Motor Company 2/27, 5/22
Anglo American Oil Ltd. 4/27
Anglo-Persian Oil Company, Ltd. 4/14
Angus Automobile Company 2/16
Anonima Lombarda Fabbrica Automobili 1/1, 9/21
Ansted Motor Company 8/26
Antique Automobile Club of America 4/17, 5/31, 11/4
Antique Truck Club of America 1/21
Apperson Brothers Automobile Company 3/28, 7/20, 11/1
Arabian American Oil Company (Aramco) 11/13
Arabian Oil Compay Ltd. 2/10
Ardsley Motor Car Company 5/16
Argo Electric Vehicle Company 4/6, 6/24, 7/6
Argonne National Laboratory 5/1
Armstrong-Siddeley Motors Ltd. 6/15, 11/3
Arnsted Engineering Company 5/10
AS Norske Shell 10/29
Associated Spring Corporation 6/18, 12/12
Associates First Capital Corporation 10/31
Association of Licensed Automobile Manufacturers (ALAM) 2/24, 3/5,
   4/28, 7/2, 8/6, 9/9, 10/22, 11/21
Association of Spark Plug Manufacturers 1/29
Aston Martin Lagonda Ltd. 1/5, 12/30
Aston Martin Ltd. 8/31
Aston Martin Owners Club 5/25
Astra Motors Corporation 12/15
Atlantic Refining Company 4/29, 5/3, 6/15, 9/15
Atlantic Richfield Company 5/3, 6/17
Auburn Automobile Company 1/18, 2/2, 2/19, 3/3, 3/10, 3/23, 4/20,
   5/13, 6/16, 6/25, 7/1, 7/6, 7/27, 7/31, 8/7, 8/24, 9/1, 9/15, 9/28,
   9/30, 10/26, 11/1, 11/12, 12/8, 12/11
Auburn Central Manufacturing Company 3/3, 3/10, 5/13
Auburn-Cord-Duesenberg Museum 7/6, 9/15
Audi NSU Auto Union AG 1/1
Austin Automobile Company 1/8, 3/31
Austin Motor Company Ltd. 3/3, 6/22, 11/8, 12/17
Arthur Fred Austria Simple Garage Collection 10/17
Austrian Automobile Association (ARBO) 5/18
Austrian Automobile, Motorcycle, and Touring Club 10/1
Autobianchi SA 9/23
Autocar Company 1/1, 1/6, 1/16, 2/1, 2/2, 2/29, 6/18, 7/25, 8/23,
   8/25, 8/28, 9/30, 10/21, 11/4
Autocostruzioni Societa per Anzioni 4/5
Autodromo Nazionale di Monza 6/29
Automatic Air Carriage Company 6/12
Automobile Association (AA) 2/25, 6/26
Automobile Club de France (ACF) 6/26, 11/5
Automobile Club of America (ACA) 3/4, 5/20, 11/26, 12/1
Automobile Club of Great Britain and Ireland (ACGBI) 8/10
Automobile Club of Michigan 1/28, 8/16
Automobile Club of Western New York 6/25
Automobile Company of America 6/17, 7/29, 9/10
Automobile Manufacturers Association 2/15, 2/27, 4/27, 10/3, 11/11
Automobile Manufacturers' Association (RDA) of Germany 6/22
Automobile Movie Theatre 6/6
Automobile Old Timers 8/8
Automobile Quarterly 10/1, 11/5

Automobile Racing Club of America (ARCA) 10/7, 12/9
Automobiles Delage 1/10
Automobiles Deutsch-Bonnet 7/14, 12/26
Automobiles Talbot SA 1/1
Automobile Topics 7/17
Automobile Volvo SA 11/3
Automobili Ferruccio Lamborghini 8/1
Automobili Serenissima SpA 2/11
Automobili Turismo e Sport 2/11
Automobil und Flugtechnische Gesellschaft 12/13
Automotive Affair 4/1
Automotive & Aviation Parts Mfrs., Inc. 2/20
Automotive Development Company 9/22
Automotive Equipment Company 5/11
Automotive Gear Works 8/15
Automotive Hall of Fame 6/25, 9/29, 10/3, 10/29
Automotive News 1/26, 10/29
Automotive Safety Foundation 2/20, 11/7
Auto-Owners Insurance Company 2/14
Auto Union AG 1/1, 4/11, 6/29, 11/1
Autoworld 7/4
Available Truck Company 7/10
AVCO Corporation 2/8, 4/9
AVCO Manufacturing Corporation 3/25, 4/9, 5/26
Aviation and Transportation Corporation (ATCO) 2/11, 2/12, 10/15
Aviation Corporation 2/19, 11/20
Ayres Gasoline Engine & Automobile Works 5/3

Back Bay Cycle & Motor Company 5/24
Badger Four Wheel Drive Auto Company 1/9
Bahrain National Oil Company 2/23
Bailey Automobile Company 2/12
Baker Motor Vehicle Company 2/17, 5/13, 6/3, 6/27, 7/5
Baker Rauch & Lang Company 2/17, 5/13
Baker-Raulang Company 2/17, 5/13
Baldwin Automobile Company 4/19
Bamford & Martin Ltd. 11/11
Barber-Colman Company 6/12
Barber-Greene Company 4/3
Barley Motor Company 11/3
Barrett-Jackson Collector Car Auction 9/28
Barthel Motor Company 10/3
Bausch & Lomb Inc. 12/12
Bayerische Flugzeugwerke AG (BFW) 3/7, 7/21
Bayerische Motoren-Werke (BMW) 3/7, 3/15, 3/31, 7/21, 8/13, 11/14
Belmont Automobile Manufacturing Company 5/6
Bendix Aviation Corporation 2/24, 4/13
Bendix Corporation 1/31, 4/13, 9/24, 12/18
Bentley and Bentley Ltd. 5/1, 6/29, 10/31, 12/11
Bentley Motors, Ltd. 1/18, 1/26, 1/31, 2/6, 3/2, 3/23, 4/14, 6/9, 6/17,
    7/3, 7/8, 7/10, 7/11, 7/27, 10/26, 10/31, 11/30, 12/7
Bentley Motors (1931) Ltd. 3/5, 7/27, 10/2, 12/14, 12/17
Benz & Cie 3/18, 4/21, 5/1, 6/28, 10/1, 12/1
Carl Benz & August Ritter Mechanische Werkstatte 8/9
C. Benz Sohne 3/9, 9/19
Benzoline Motor Fuel Company 3/31
Berghoff Brewing Corporation 3/1
Biddle-Murray Manufacturing Company 2/20
Biddle & Smart Company 1/21, 3/6
Bijur Lubricating Company 10/19
Black & Decker Corporation 5/15
BL Cars, Ltd. 5/5, 10/11, 12/27
BL Public Limited Company 2/8, 3/30
BMW (US) Holding Corporation 6/4
Boeing Aircraft Company 6/5
Bohman & Schwartz 3/22
Bombardier, Inc. 6/19, 6/23
Borg & Beck Company 5/9
Borg-Warner Corporation 1/12, 2/21, 2/27, 3/6, 3/25, 4/1, 5/9, 7/2,
    7/15, 8/25, 9/24, 10/24, 10/29, 10/31, 12/23
Robert Bosch GmbH 7/1
Robert Bosch North America 7/1

Boston Woven Hose & Rubber Company 3/9
Bound Brook Oil-Less Bearing Company 9/14, 10/5
BP America Inc. 5/13, 9/13
BP France 2/7
BP North America Inc. 5/13
Bradfield Motors, Inc. 8/20
Brewster & Company 4/20, 5/2, 6/2, 6/24, 8/18
J. B. Brewster and Company 6/8
Bricklin Canada Ltd. 9/25, 12/11
Bridgeport Body Company 1/7
Bridgestone/Firestone Inc. 5/16
Bridgestone Tire Company Ltd. 3/1
Briggs Cunningham Automotive Museum 2/8
Briggs-Detroiter Company 1/20, 3/1, 7/15, 8/13, 10/26, 11/28
Briggs Manufacturing Company 1/17, 7/3, 7/20, 10/7, 10/10, 10/23,
    11/17, 12/29
British-American Oil Company Ltd. 4/1
British Automobile Association 2/12, 8/5
British Equitable Central Trust 12/14
British Goodrich Rubber Company Ltd. 1/31
British Institution of Mechanical Engineers 6/25
British Leyland Ltd. 8/11, 10/17, 11/8, 12/27
British Leyland Motor Corporation Ltd. 1/9, 1/17, 2/8, 3/5, 3/22, 5/3,
    8/9, 9/11
British Leyland Motors, Inc. 3/30, 4/22, 8/11
British Motor Corporation (BMC) 7/2, 7/12, 7/27, 9/13, 10/1, 10/22,
    11/26, 12/17
British Motor Holdings Ltd. 1/17, 2/8, 7/12
British Petroleum Company PLC 4/14, 6/23, 7/24, 8/18
British Racing Motors, Ltd. 3/2
British Red Cross 11/26
British Timken Ltd. 12/21
British Tire & Rubber Company Ltd. 8/30
Brockway Motor Truck Corporation 3/26, 3/29, 8/7, 9/1, 10/1
Brooklands Automobile Racing Club 12/12
Brooks (Steam) Motors Ltd. 3/14
Brown-Lipe Gear Company 9/4
W. W. Brown Machine Works 6/14
Brown & Sharpe Manufacturing Company 6/4
Brummer Seal Company 6/29
Brunswick Ordnance Corporation 6/1
Brush Runabout Company 4/1
Buda Company 2/3, 6/14, 7/15, 7/25, 8/17, 8/23, 8/31
Edward G. Budd Manufacturing Company 1/20, 2/18, 2/21, 3/28,
    4/1, 5/20, 5/24, 6/21, 7/12, 7/15, 7/20, 8/23, 9/18, 11/1, 11/16,
    11/17, 11/22, 12/1
Budd Automotive Company of Canada 4/2, 10/8
Budd Canada Inc. 4/2
Buffalo Automobile and Auto-Bi Company 10/1
Buffalo Automobile Club 7/24
Ettore Bugatti Automobilfabrik 1/1
Bugatti Automobili 1/18, 9/6, 12/5
Bugatti International S.A.H. 8/27
Bugatti Owners' Club 5/9
Bugatti SpA 9/14
Buick Auto-Vim and Power Company 8/1
Buick Manufacturing Company 2/18
Buick Motor Company 1/13, 1/19, 5/12, 5/19, 6/1, 6/7, 7/9, 7/29,
    8/1, 9/3, 9/4, 9/9, 9/11, 9/29, 11/1, 12/28
Bundy Tubing Company 5/27, 9/10, 10/12
Burlen Fuel Systems Ltd. 11/26
Burmah Oil Company 5/15, 7/10
Business Hall of Fame 4/25
Byelorussian Automobile Factory 11/5

Cadillac-LaSalle Club 8/6
Cadillac Motor Car Company 1/6, 1/8, 2/23, 4/13, 5/31, 6/1, 6/7,
    7/1, 7/12, 7/29, 8/15, 8/22, 8/27, 9/15, 10/3, 11/15, 12/23, 12/24,
    12/27
California Department of Public Works 3/6
California Texas Corporation 1/1, 12/6
California Texas Oil Corporation 1/1

Caltex Petroleum Corporation 1/1
Camden Motors Corporation 12/30
Campbell-Ewald Company 1/9
Campbell Motor Car Company 10/11
Canadian Automotive Trade 3/27
Car Classics 1/1
Car Illustrated 5/28
Carroll Motor Car Company 2/23
Carrosserie Schutter & van Bakel 7/1
Carrozzeria Bertone 1/13, 2/25, 11/6
Carrozzeria Ghia 5/15, 10/24, 11/3
Carrozzeria Pininfarina 4/3, 9/16
Carrozzeria Touring 3/3, 9/6
Carrozzeria Vignale 10/24
Carter Carburetor Corporation 9/23, 10/11, 10/22
Cartercar Company 2/3, 10/26
Carter Motor Car Corporation 5/19
J. I. Case Threshing Machine Company 4/6, 12/14
Casco Motors Inc. 1/24
Caterpillar Tractor Company 11/18
CBS, Inc. 10/1
CBS Magazines 11/5
Ceirano & Cie, Societa per la Costruzione di Campioni per la
    Fabbricazione di Vetture Automobili 10/23
Central European Motor Vehicle Club 9/30
Central Manufacturing Company 1/15, 5/10
Centre International de l'Automobile, Museum 12/6
Centro Tecnologico-Cultural y Museo del Automovilismo Juan Manuel
    Fangio 11/22
Chadwick Engineering Works 3/7
Chalmers-Detroit Motor Company 3/4, 12/6
Chalmers Motor Company/Corporation 6/2, 8/15
Champion Home Builders Company 8/14
Champion Ignition Company 10/26
Champion Spark Plug Company 1/18, 2/9, 3/27, 4/18, 6/2, 6/24, 7/6,
    8/24, 9/12, 10/9, 12/5, 12/26
Chandler-Cleveland Motors Corporation 11/30
Chandler Motor Car Company 2/18, 3/3, 4/1, 4/13
Chattanooga Times 1/29
Checker Cab Manufacturing Corporation 1/12, 2/19, 3/14
Checker Motors Corporation 2/16, 3/14, 5/2, 7/7, 7/9
SA des Ans. Etx. Chenard et Walcker 6/13
Chevrolet Brothers Manufacturing Co. 4/5
Chevrolet Motor Company 2/4, 2/28, 4/15, 5/2, 7/14, 8/9, 9/1, 10/26,
    11/3, 11/26, 12/9, 12/23
Chevrolet Motor Company of Delaware 9/23
Chevron Corporation 7/1, 9/23
Chevron Oil Italiana SpA 3/8
Chevyland USA 3/28
Chicago Historical Antique Automobile Museum 8/11
Chicago Motor Club 10/10
Chicago Motor Coach Company 7/23
Chicago Times-Herald 4/24, 10/17, 11/2, 11/28
Chilton Company 1/3, 6/18, 11/14, 12/16
CH Industrials 1/5
Chloride Batteries Ltd. 2/20
Christie Direct Action Motor Car Company 2/21
Christie's 2/25, 5/11
Chrysler Australia 10/25
W. P. Chrysler Building Corporation 1/7, 11/7
Chrysler Corporation 1/1, 1/2, 1/5, 1/7, 1/8, 1/9, 1/10, 1/13, 1/18,
    1/21, 1/22, 1/26, 1/28, 2/1, 2/2, 2/4, 2/6, 2/9, 2/12, 2/13, 2/20,
    2/23, 2/24, 3/1, 3/2, 3/3, 3/4, 3/5, 3/9, 3/10, 3/13, 3/16, 3/19, 3/24,
    3/30, 4/1, 4/2, 4/3, 4/4, 4/5, 4/6, 4/10, 4/11, 4/17, 4/18, 4/19, 4/23,
    4/28, 4/30, 5/1, 5/3, 5/6, 5/9, 5/12, 5/13, 5/15, 5/20, 5/21, 5/25,
    5/27, 5/28, 5/30, 6/2, 6/6, 6/7, 6/9, 6/11, 6/12, 6/13, 6/16, 6/18,
    6/20, 6/21, 6/22, 6/26, 6/30, 7/1, 7/2, 7/3, 7/7, 7/8, 7/11, 7/12,
    7/13, 7/15, 7/17, 7/18, 7/21, 7/22, 7/25, 7/27, 7/30, 8/2, 8/3, 8/4,
    8/5, 8/6, 8/7, 8/8, 8/9, 8/10, 8/11, 8/13, 8/15, 8/18, 8/21, 8/25,
    8/30, 8/31, 9/3, 9/5, 9/7, 9/10, 9/11, 9/14, 9/15, 9/18, 9/20, 9/21,
    9/22, 9/25, 10/1, 10/2, 10/4, 10/6, 10/8, 10/9, 10/10, 10/12, 10/15,
    10/18, 10/19, 10/20, 10/23, 10/28, 10/29, 10/30, 11/2, 11/3, 11/4,
    11/5, 11/7, 11/8, 11/9, 11/10, 11/11, 11/13, 11/17, 11/18, 11/22,
11/27, 11/29, 11/30, 12/1, 12/6, 12/9, 12/11, 12/15, 12/17, 12/21,
    12/29, 12/31
Chrysler Corporation Ltd. of Canada 2/10, 2/13, 3/25, 6/17, 6/30,
    7/16, 7/17, 7/28
Chrysler Export Corporation 6/11
Chrysler Institute of Engineering 5/16
Chrysler United Kingdom 1/16
Chrysler-Zeder, Inc. 3/14
Cie Financiere Belge des Pertoles Petrofina SA 2/25
Cincinnati Reds 3/28
Cities Service Oil Company 3/8, 4/20, 5/4, 5/19, 9/30, 12/28
Cities Service Oil Company Ltd. 1/20, 7/8
Classic Car Club of America 1/11, 3/14, 8/5
Clement-Talbot, Ltd. 2/6, 5/17
Cleveland Automobile Company 4/1, 6/24
Cleveland Cap and Screw Company 1/2, 10/4
Cleveland Graphite Bronze Company 2/3, 6/5, 6/13
Cleveland Plain Dealer 9/3
Climax Molybdenum Company 4/7, 10/2
Clymer Manufacturing Company 5/15
Coachcraft, Ltd. 4/17
Coachmen Industries, Inc. 10/15, 12/31
Coates-Goshen Automobile Company 9/17
Coca-Cola Company 3/7
Colby Motor Company 3/14, 3/24, 12/18
Cole Carriage Company 12/4
Cole Motor Car Company 6/22, 12/4
Colgate University 6/10
Collectible Automobile 6/12
Collins & Aikman Corporation 1/14
Columbia Broadcasting System (CBS) 7/15
Columbia University 3/25
Comercial Sicocar SA 10/3
Commercial Car Journal 2/15
Commission Sportive Internationale 2/28
Compagnie Generale des Etablissements Michelin 4/4, 8/25
Compagnie Nationale d'Automobiles 7/11
Conoco Inc. 8/2, 10/8
Consolidated Industries, Inc. 11/3
Consolidated Motors Corporation 4/7
Continental Automotive Associates 12/11
Continental-Divco Company 4/10, 5/2
Continental Motors Corporation 9/7
Continental Motors Corporation (2) 1/9, 1/25, 2/10, 2/28, 3/1, 3/3,
    3/29, 4/9, 6/24, 7/1, 7/5, 8/1, 8/7, 8/25, 9/23, 10/3, 11/23, 11/29,
    12/28, 12/31
Continental Oil Company 2/13, 4/3, 5/31
Cooke Auto School 5/4
Cooper Tire & Rubber Company 7/1, 7/19, 8/9
Copper Development Association 11/13
Corbin Screw Corporation 9/25
Corbin Motor Vehicle Company 11/3
Cord Automobile Company 3/6
Cord Corporation 2/3, 2/8, 2/19, 3/25, 4/9, 6/17, 7/14, 8/4, 8/26,
    8/28, 10/15, 11/20
Cornell University 10/29
Corvair Society (CORSA) 3/7
Cosmopolitan 5/30, 6/17, 9/10
Coventry Climax Engines Ltd. 10/17
Crane & Breed 6/15
Crane Motor Car Company 7/7
Crane Packing Company 11/20
Craven Foundation 2/29, 6/21
Frederick C. Crawford Auto-Aviation Museum 3/19
Crosley Automobile Club 7/7
Crosley Motors Inc. 3/28, 6/22
Crossley Brothers, Ltd. 4/22, 10/12
Crossley Motors, Ltd. 10/12, 11/22
Crown Central Petroleum Corporation 3/20, 11/28
Cummins Engine Company 2/3, 2/18, 3/2, 5/15, 5/26, 7/10, 7/14,
    8/18, 10/10, 10/16, 11/24, 12/18
James Cunningham Son & Company, Inc. 7/31, 11/26

Cupples Company 8/13
Curtiss-Wright Corporation 3/23, 5/8, 6/3, 7/26, 7/27, 8/6, 9/1, 10/31
Cyclecar Club of New Jersey 6/13

Daf B.V. 4/3
Daihatsu Motor Company Ltd. 3/1
Daimler and Lanchester Owners' Club 6/6
Daimler-Benz AG 1/1, 1/14, 1/16, 1/24, 1/30, 2/16, 3/14, 3/18, 3/26,
    3/29, 4/1, 4/5, 4/11, 4/16, 5/18, 5/20, 6/15, 6/28, 7/6, 7/8, 7/13,
    7/18, 7/22, 7/27, 9/5, 9/12, 9/15, 9/23, 10/12, 10/15, 10/18, 10/20,
    10/22, 10/26, 12/2, 12/14, 12/22, 12/31
Daimler-Benz of North America 1/1
Daimler Motor Company, Ltd. 3/22, 4/15, 4/17, 5/15, 5/26, 6/7, 11/22
Daimler Motor Company of New York 9/29
Daimler Motoren-Gesellschaft 3/4, 4/1, 4/2, 6/23, 6/28, 8/14, 9/24,
    11/1, 11/12, 11/22, 11/27, 12/12
Daimler Motor Syndicate, Ltd. 1/14, 2/23, 4/22, 11/30
Dana Corporation 2/25, 10/2, 10/29, 11/27
Daniels Motor Car Company 3/24, 6/25, 9/8
Davis Motor Car Company 7/22, 7/23
George W. Davis Motor Car Company 5/3, 10/20
Dayton Metal Products Company 9/25
Dearborn Motors Corporation 3/29, 5/30, 11/26, 12/1
Deep Rock Oil Company 8/17
Deer Park Winery Automobile Collection 12/7
De Industrieele Maatschappij Trompenburg 4/1
Delage & Cie. 4/20, 8/22, 10/19
Delco (Dayton Engineering Laboratories Company) 3/12, 3/24, 4/10,
    4/29, 5/11, 6/4, 7/1, 7/22, 10/21, 11/24, 11/30
DeLorean Manufacturing Company Ltd. 2/19
DeLorean Motor Car Company 10/2
DeLuxe Motor Car Company 3/1
Denby Truck Company 1/20
Desberon Motor Company 8/15
Detroit Athletic Club 6/19
Detroit Automobile Company 1/12, 1/25, 2/7, 6/1, 8/5, 11/30
Detroit Automotive Products Corporation 5/17
Detroit-Dearborn Motor Car Company 11/15
Detroiter Motor Car Company 7/15, 11/30, 12/19
Detroit Free Press 4/6
Detroit Lions 1/23, 11/22
Detroit-Oxford Motor Company 1/30
Detroit Public Library 3/1, 9/9, 11/27
Detroit Steam Motors Corporation 12/1
Detroit Steel Products Company 10/24
Detroit Tigers 1/17, 7/3
Deutsch-Amerikanische Petroleum Ges 12/15
Deutsche Bank 1/14
Deutz AG 8/1, 10/4
DeVaux-Hall Motors Corporation 10/28
DeWitt Motor Car Company 5/5
Diamandus Communications, Inc. 10/1, 11/5
Diameda Argentina SA de Petroleo 6/30, 8/22
Diamond Chain & Manufacturing Company 2/24, 8/30
Diamond Reo Trucks, Inc. 5/30
Diamond-Star Motors 3/13
Diamond T Motor Car Company 2/3, 4/1, 4/10, 6/28, 9/19, 10/27, 12/8
Diamond T Truck Company 12/24
Diana Motors Company 6/25
Dietrich, Inc. 2/12, 8/4
Dill Manufacturing Company 5/26
Dillon, Read & Company 4/30, 7/30
Divco Corporation 1/16, 11/1
Divco-Twin Truck Company 1/16, 4/10, 10/31
Divco-Twin Truck Company of Canada Ltd. 10/31
Divco-Wayne Corporation 11/1
Dixi-Werke AG 11/14
Doble Steam Motors 1/1, 2/4
Abner Doble Motor Vehicle Company 10/30
Dodge Brothers Corporation 3/10, 7/2
Dodge Brothers, Inc. 1/11, 3/20, 3/26, 4/30, 7/1, 7/2, 7/6, 7/17, 7/30,
    11/28, 12/19

Dodge Brothers' Club 10/7
Dominion Motors Ltd. 3/14, 12/31
Dort Motor Car Company 1/1, 1/5, 3/13, 10/5
Dow Jones Services 4/23
Duesenberg Automobile & Motors Company 1/1, 1/2, 3/8, 10/26
Duesenberg Brothers 8/1
Duesenberg Corporation 1/27
Duesenberg, Inc. 6/1, 10/6, 12/13
Duesenberg Motor Company 5/9
Dukes of Hazzard 8/16
Dunlop Rubber Company Ltd. 1/26, 3/2, 5/7, 10/1, 10/28, 11/8
Dunlop Rubber Company (Scotland) Ltd. 1/17, 2/6
Dunlop Tire & Rubber Goods Company Ltd. 8/28
Duplex Engine Governor Company 1/21
DuPont Company 8/27
DuPont Motor Manufacturing Company 9/26
Durant-Dort Carriage Company 11/1
Durant Motors, Inc. 1/12, 2/18, 3/10, 3/19, 4/1, 8/1
Durant Motors of Canada 3/14
Duryea Motor Wagon Company 1/18, 9/2, 9/21
Duryea Power Company 4/6

Eagle Motor Truck Corporation 9/26
Earl Motors, Inc. 1/25, 10/31
Early Ford V8 Club of America 2/10
Easton Manufacturing Company 9/13
Eaton Axle & Spring Company 4/17, 7/28
Eaton Corporation 4/21
Eaton Manufacturing Company 5/12, 8/4, 11/22
Eaton Yale & Towne Inc. 4/21
Eberhard Manufacturing Company 4/16
Echlin Inc. 5/8, 7/21
Eclipse Machine Company 10/23
Edison Illuminating Company 8/15, 12/1
Edison Institute Museum 10/21
Edison Storage Battery Company 2/1
Edmonton Auto Service Club 12/5
EDS Corporation 10/18, 12/31
Edsel Owners Club, Inc. 2/3
Elabuga Automotive Works 12/7
Elcar Motor Company 1/3
Elco Lubricant Corporation 2/8
Electric Autolite Company 1/28, 5/1, 8/21
Electric Cab Company 9/23
Electric Storage Battery Corporation 3/15, 5/19
Electric Vehicle Company 2/17, 11/21
Electro-Motive Company 12/31
Elite Heritage Motors Corporation 10/21
Elkhart Carriage & Motor Car Company 10/24
Ellingson Car Museum 4/24
Ellis & Turner Company 8/14
Elmore Manufacturing Company 10/4, 10/28, 11/9, 11/25
Emerson Motors Company 4/29, 6/4, 10/11
Empire Motor Car Company 7/12
Enger Motor Car Company 1/4, 5/24
English Racing Automobiles Ltd. 11/6
Enterprise Automobile Company 8/8
Ernst & Ernst 4/9
Esso AG 12/15
Esso Export Corporation 9/25
Esso Petroleum Company 9/1
Esso Standard Oil Company 10/11, 11/26
Esso UK PLC 4/27, 10/6
Etablissements Ballot 7/4, 12/24
Ethyl Gasoline Corporation 2/9, 3/26, 7/7, 8/11, 9/6, 9/9, 9/19, 11/4,
    12/11
Everitt-Metzger-Flanders Company 1/1, 2/14, 3/9, 4/15, 6/2
Excel Corporation 6/5
Exxon Corporation 2/10, 2/12, 2/19, 3/1, 5/3, 8/2, 8/13, 11/1

Fabbrica Automobili Isotta-Fraschini 1/9, 2/25, 9/24, 11/10, 11/23,
    12/24

Fabbrica Italiana Automobili Torino 3/8, 7/1, 7/11
Fabryka Samochodow Osobowych 11/6, 11/23
Fafnir Bearing Company 1/4, 3/11, 10/2
Fageol Motors Company 4/5, 9/14
Fahrzeug-Fabrik Eisenach 12/22
Falcon Motor Corporation 5/31
Federal Bearing & Bushing Corporation 5/1
Federal-Mogul Corporation 1/4, 2/11, 4/6, 5/1, 11/26
Federal Motor Company 7/12
Federal Motor Truck Company 3/1, 3/21
Federation Internationale de l'Automobile (FIA) 10/2
Ferrari SpA 9/7
Fiat Motors of North America, Inc. 5/1
Fiat SpA 3/8, 3/12, 6/21, 6/24, 9/7, 9/23, 10/6, 10/23, 11/18, 11/25,
    12/11, 12/14
Fina Petroleum Products Ltd. 1/20, 10/1
Fina PLC 6/4
Fina SA 12/10
Firestone Tire & Rubber Company 1/1, 2/1, 2/13, 2/26, 2/28, 3/4, 3/14,
    4/5, 4/14, 6/11, 8/3, 9/4, 9/6, 9/16, 10/4, 10/13, 11/16, 11/18,
    11/23, 11/26, 11/28, 12/9
First Czecho-Moravian Machinery Factory 5/4
First Nationwide Financial Corporation 12/16
Fish Carburetor Corporation 5/8
Fisher Body Company 2/23, 3/15, 3/28, 3/31, 6/30, 7/14, 7/22, 8/12,
    8/21, 9/3, 10/9
Fisher Body Company of Canada Ltd. 8/21
Fisher Body Company of Ohio 10/17
Fisher Closed Body Company 8/21, 12/22
Fisk Rubber Corporation 11/22, 12/30
Fitz Gibbon & Crisp, Inc. 1/16
Fleetwood Metal Body Company 1/1, 4/1, 5/9, 6/5
Fleming Manufacturing Company 5/22
Flint Road Cart Company 9/28
Flint Wagon Works 5/12
Flower City Specialty Company 12/12
Flugwerke Deutschland 3/31
Flxible Company 12/12
Foote Brothers Gear & Machine Company 10/12
Ford & Malcomson Company 6/16
Ford Archives 5/7
Ford Foundation 1/11, 1/15, 5/8
Ford International Capital Corporation 3/7
Ford International Finance Corporation 2/26
Ford-Japan 12/19
Ford Manufacturing Company 11/22
Ford Manufacturing Company of Australia 3/31
Fordmobile Company, Ltd. 6/16
Ford Motor Company 1/1, 1/2, 1/3, 1/4, 1/5, 1/6, 1/7, 1/9, 1/10, 1/12,
    1/13, 1/14, 1/15, 1/16, 1/17, 1/18, 1/20, 1/21, 1/22, 1/24, 1/25,
    1/26, 1/27, 1/28, 1/29, 1/30, 1/31, 2/1, 2/2, 2/3, 2/4, 2/5, 2/6, 2/7,
    2/10, 2/11, 2/12, 2/13, 2/15, 2/16, 2/18, 2/19, 2/20, 2/22, 2/24,
    2/25, 2/26, 2/27, 3/1, 3/2, 3/3, 3/4, 3/6, 3/7, 3/8, 3/9, 3/13, 3/15,
    3/16, 3/18, 3/19, 3/21, 3/22, 3/23, 3/24, 3/25, 3/28, 3/31, 4/1, 4/6,
    4/7, 4/8, 4/9, 4/10, 4/11, 4/12, 4/14, 4/15, 4/16, 4/17, 4/18, 4/20,
    4/21, 4/22, 4/23, 4/24, 4/25, 4/26, 4/27, 4/28, 4/29, 4/30, 5/1, 5/2,
    5/3, 5/4, 5/5, 5/9, 5/10, 5/11, 5/12, 5/13, 5/14, 5/18, 5/20, 5/21,
    5/22, 5/24, 5/25, 5/26, 5/29, 5/30, 5/31, 6/1, 6/3, 6/4, 6/7, 6/8, 6/9,
    6/12, 6/13, 6/14, 6/16, 6/17, 6/19, 6/20, 6/23, 6/24, 6/28, 7/1, 7/2,
    7/3, 7/5, 7/6, 7/7, 7/8, 7/9, 7/10, 7/11, 7/12, 7/13, 7/14, 7/15, 7/17,
    7/18, 7/20, 7/21, 7/22, 7/24, 7/26, 7/27, 7/28, 7/29, 7/31, 8/1, 8/2,
    8/5, 8/7, 8/8, 8/9, 8/10, 8/11, 8/12, 8/13, 8/14, 8/15, 8/18, 8/21,
    8/23, 8/25, 8/26, 8/29, 8/30, 8/31, 9/1, 9/2, 9/3, 9/4, 9/7, 9/8, 9/9,
    9/10, 9/11, 9/12, 9/13, 9/14, 9/15, 9/17, 9/18, 9/19, 9/20, 9/21,
    9/23, 9/26, 9/30, 10/1, 10/2, 10/3, 10/4, 10/5, 10/6, 10/7, 10/8,
    10/9, 10/10, 10/11, 10/13, 10/14, 10/15, 10/16, 10/17, 10/21, 10/22,
    10/24, 10/26, 10/27, 10/28, 10/29, 10/31, 11/1, 11/2, 11/3, 11/4,
    11/6, 11/7, 11/8, 11/9, 11/10, 11/11, 11/12, 11/13, 11/15, 11/16,
    11/18, 11/19, 11/22, 11/23, 11/25, 11/28, 12/1, 12/2, 12/3, 12/4,
    12/7, 12/8, 12/9, 12/10, 12/11, 12/13, 12/14, 12/16, 12/19, 12/22,
    12/23, 12/24, 12/25, 12/29, 12/30, 12/31
Ford Motor Company A-S (Denmark) 3/28
Ford Motor Company Ltd. 3/8, 3/18, 4/16, 4/18, 5/16, 6/7, 6/17,
    8/10, 10/1, 10/23, 12/7

Ford Motor Company Navy Service School 9/16
Ford Motor Company of Australia, PL 3/31, 4/5, 7/1
Ford Motor Company of Canada, Ltd. 2/3, 3/5, 3/18, 3/23, 5/11, 5/12,
    5/13, 6/3, 6/30, 7/10, 8/4, 8/10, 8/17, 8/25, 9/8, 9/9, 9/18, 10/10,
    10/21, 11/15, 11/30, 12/29
Ford Motor Credit Company 1/10, 2/20, 4/9, 5/1, 8/9, 8/21, 8/24
Ford News 9/19
Ford of Europe, Inc. 4/12
Ford of Spain 2/1
Ford Research and Engineering Center 6/16
Ford Robotics and Automoation, Applications Consulting Center 12/2
Ford SA Francaise 2/28
Ford Times 4/2, 4/15
Ford-Werke AG 1/31, 5/4, 5/17, 7/31, 8/27, 10/2
Henry Ford Company 3/12, 8/22, 8/27, 11/30
Henry Ford Hospital 1/17, 10/1, 10/19
Henry Ford Museum & Greenfield Village 1/14, 2/18, 6/1, 6/3, 6/12,
    7/11, 7/20, 8/31, 9/27, 10/15, 10/21, 10/30, 11/6, 11/7
Henry Ford & Son Inc. 7/27
Henry Ford Trade School 7/1, 8/1, 8/19, 10/5
Fort Pitt Motor Manufacturing Company 11/2
Four Wheel Drive Auto Company 1/31, 8/10, 12/26
Fox Motor Company 11/21
Fram Corporation 2/29, 5/22, 6/16, 8/20
Fram Oil Filter Company 5/22
H. H. Franklin Manufacturing Company 6/30, 7/1, 7/11, 10/20
Franklin Automobile Company 3/21, 5/15
Freightliner Corporation 10/4
Frisbie-Heft Motor Company 11/2
Frost & French Inc. 4/27
Fruehauf Corporation 3/27, 5/2
Fruehauf Trailer Company 2/27, 4/29, 5/2, 5/11, 5/16, 5/22, 6/8, 10/1,
    10/14, 10/31, 12/15
Fruehauf Trailer Company of Canada Ltd. 1/14
Fuji Heavy Industries, Ltd. 7/15, 12/10
FWD Corporation 6/28, 8/10, 8/23, 10/29, 12/26

Gabriel Manufacturing Company 6/21, 12/23
Gardner Motor Company 3/16, 9/17
Gasmotorenfabrik Deutz AG 1/1, 1/5, 9/1, 11/16, 12/15
Gasmotorenfabrik Mannheim AG 10/25
Gates-Osborne Carriage Company 12/4
Gates Rubber Company 3/31, 11/26
General Accident Company 11/2
General Electric Company 3/14, 6/27, 12/7
General Motors Acceptance Corporation 1/6, 1/29, 5/21, 8/9, 8/11, 9/2,
    9/11, 9/28, 12/13
General Motors Acceptance Corporation de Mexico 5/9
General Motors Company/Corporation 1/1, 1/2, 1/3, 1/4, 1/5, 1/6,
    1/7, 1/8, 1/10, 1/11, 1/13, 1/14, 1/15, 1/16, 1/17, 1/19, 1/20, 1/21,
    1/22, 1/25, 1/26, 1/28, 1/31, 2/1, 2/2, 2/3, 2/6, 2/8, 2/9, 2/10, 2/11,
    2/13, 2/14, 2/15, 2/16, 2/17, 2/19, 2/20, 2/21, 2/22, 2/23, 2/24, 2/26,
    2/28, 3/1, 3/2, 3/4, 3/5, 3/6, 3/8, 3/10, 3/12, 3/13, 3/14, 3/15, 3/16,
    3/18, 3/19, 3/21, 3/24, 3/25, 3/26, 3/28, 3/29, 4/1, 4/2, 4/3, 4/5, 4/6,
    4/7, 4/9, 4/10, 4/12, 4/13, 4/14, 4/15, 4/16, 4/18, 4/19, 4/20, 4/21,
    4/22, 4/23, 4/24, 4/25, 4/26, 4/27, 4/29, 5/2, 5/3, 5/4, 5/5, 5/8, 5/10,
    5/11, 5/12, 5/13, 5/17, 5/18, 5/19, 5/21, 5/22, 5/23, 5/25, 5/29, 5/31,
    6/1, 6/2, 6/3, 6/6, 6/7, 6/9, 6/10, 6/12, 6/14, 6/16, 6/18, 6/21, 6/22,
    6/23, 6/24, 6/25, 6/26, 6/27, 6/28, 6/30, 7/1, 7/2, 7/5, 7/6, 7/7, 7/9,
    7/10, 7/11, 7/12, 7/14, 7/15, 7/16, 7/17, 7/18, 7/22, 7/24, 7/29, 7/30,
    7/31, 8/1, 8/2, 8/3, 8/4, 8/5, 8/6, 8/7, 8/8, 8/10, 8/12, 8/13, 8/15,
    8/17, 8/18, 8/20, 8/23, 8/26, 8/27, 8/28, 8/29, 8/30, 8/31, 9/1, 9/3,
    9/4, 9/6, 9/8, 9/10, 9/11, 9/12, 9/14, 9/16, 9/17, 9/19, 9/21, 9/22,
    9/23, 9/24, 9/25, 9/26, 9/27, 9/28, 9/29, 9/30, 10/1, 10/2, 10/3, 10/4,
    10/6, 10/10, 10/11, 10/12, 10/13, 10/14, 10/16, 10/18, 10/19, 10/20,
    10/21, 10/26, 10/27, 10/28, 10/30, 10/31, 11/1, 11/2, 11/3, 11/4, 11/5,
    11/6, 11/7, 11/8, 11/9, 11/10, 11/12, 11/15, 11/16, 11/17, 11/18,
    11/19, 11/20, 11/21, 11/22, 11/23, 11/25, 11/26, 11/27, 11/29, 11/30,
    12/1, 12/2, 12/6, 12/7, 12/9, 12/10, 12/11, 12/12, 12/15, 12/16,
    12/17, 12/18, 12/19, 12/20, 12/22, 12/23, 12/24, 12/25, 12/26, 12/28,
    12/29, 12/30, 12/31
General Motors de Mexico, SA 9/23
General Motors Europe 1/22, 4/29
General Motors Export Corporation 1/15, 6/18, 9/24

General Motors-Holden's Ltd. 12/23
General Motors-Holden's Pty Ltd. 11/29
General Motors Institute 6/22, 8/5
General Motors International A/S 10/30
General Motors of Canada Ltd. 1/6, 1/10, 2/12, 2/26, 3/1, 6/5, 8/9, 9/8, 11/6
General Motors Overseas Corporation 9/21
General Motors Proving Grounds 11/3
General Motors Research Corporation 5/8, 6/12, 8/1
General Motors Technical Center 5/16, 9/30
General Motors Truck Company 8/1, 9/1, 9/30, 10/1, 10/27
General Petroleum Corporation 4/19, 5/23
General Tire & Rubber Company 1/29, 2/28, 3/28, 4/18, 8/21, 9/4
General Vehicle Company 4/15
Genuine Part Company 9/12
Georgia Institute of Technology 5/15
German-American Automobile Company 1/21, 1/22
Gersix Manufacturing Company 12/22
Gideon Society 1/2
Glasspar of USA 6/2
Glidden Buick Corporation 10/25
Global Motors, Inc. 1/29, 4/15, 11/7
GMC Truck Talk 5/27
GM Hughes Electronics Corporation 12/31
Goliath-Werke GmbH 8/10
Goodman Manufacturing Company 9/8
B. F. Goodrich Company 2/12, 5/1, 5/17, 6/6, 7/29, 8/19, 9/6, 9/10, 9/18, 9/29, 12/7, 12/31
B. F. Goodrich Tire & Rubber Company 5/2, 5/11, 6/5, 6/17, 6/22, 11/4, 12/31
B. F. Goodrich Tire & Rubber Company of Canada Ltd. 5/21, 6/16
Goodrich, Tew & Company 12/31
Goodyear Tire & Rubber Company 1/6, 2/1, 2/28, 3/12, 3/18, 4/9, 4/24, 4/27, 4/29, 5/20, 5/30, 7/8, 7/26, 8/11, 8/13, 8/24, 8/25, 8/29, 9/1, 9/12, 9/20, 10/24, 10/26, 12/13, 12/30
Goodyear Tire & Rubber Company, Ltd. (Java) 1/26
Goodyear Tire & Rubber Company of Alabama 12/13
Goodyear Tire & Rubber Company of Canada Ltd. 7/27
Goodyear Tyre & Rubber Company (Australia) Ltd. 12/11
Goodyear Tyre & Rubber Company (Great Britain) Ltd. 9/24
Gor'kiy Automobile Plant 1/1, 5/2, 6/14
Gotfredson Truck Corporation Ltd. 6/29
Gothaer Waggonfabrik AG 11/14
Gould & Eberhardt, Inc. 7/18
Grabowsky Power Wagon Company 11/22
Graham Brothers Company 5/5, 6/21, 9/12, 12/19
Graham-Paige Motors Corporation 1/5, 1/6, 2/5, 2/10, 4/20, 5/5, 6/10, 6/21, 7/7, 7/10, 7/15, 9/3, 9/12, 9/14, 12/19, 12/27
Gramm-Logan Motor Car Company 12/13
Gramm Motor Company 1/5, 2/3, 12/24
Grant Motor Car Corporation 5/11
Gray-Campbell Company 8/8
Gray-Dort Motors Ltd. 3/13, 4/10, 8/8
Gray Line Tours 6/15
Gray Motor Company 4/6, 7/5
Greenfield Tap & Die Corporation 4/15
Greyhound Corporation 2/5, 5/22
Grosse Pointe Yacht Club 9/15
Group Lotus PLC 1/22
Grout Brothers Automobile Company 4/20
Guaranty Securities Company 11/8
Gulf Oil Canada Ltd. 4/1
Gulf Oil Company 4/10, 5/3, 7/21, 8/30, 9/1, 9/12, 11/16, 12/20
Gulf Refining Company 12/1
Gurney Ball Bearing Company 4/21
Gustav Otto Flugmaschinenfabrik Munchen 3/15

Hackney Brothers Body Company 5/7
C. M. Hall Lamp Company 8/18
Handley Motors, Inc. 7/1
Hanson Motor Company 6/15
Hare's Motors, Inc. 1/25, 2/27, 3/10, 10/9, 11/16

Harrah's Automobile Collection 2/24, 6/27, 7/8, 9/29
Harrison Radiator Company 3/6, 10/4
Harrison Wagon Works 1/17
Hartford Rubber Works Company 3/16
Harvey Metal Corporation 6/20
Hatfield Motor Vehicle Company 5/20
Hayes Manufacturing Company 2/22
Haynes-Apperson Company 5/25
Haynes Automobile Company 2/28, 6/24, 9/2, 9/6, 12/24
H.C.S. Motor Company 11/3
Hebb Motor Company 1/10, 3/13, 6/23, 7/23, 11/17
A. G. Hebb Auto Company 2/2, 4/1, 9/17
Heil Company 3/5, 7/24, 11/30
Hemmings Motor News 1/2
Henney Motor Company 1/18, 2/8, 2/15, 9/10, 10/22, 11/26, 12/13
Hercules Motor Manufacturing Company 6/8, 12/15
Hercules Motors Corporation 1/24, 2/19, 6/8, 7/31, 9/26
Hershey Corporation 1/30
Hertz Corporation 2/6, 3/25, 6/15, 11/5, 12/30
Hertz Rent-A-Car System, Inc. 4/10, 10/8
Hess & Eisenhardt 10/5
Hewitt Motor Company 6/20, 12/13
Hewson Pacific Corporation 10/16
Hill & Boll 11/5
Hillman-Coatalen Motor Car Company Ltd. 6/17
Hindustan Motors Ltd. 5/11, 8/1
Hinkley Motors Corporation 7/15
Hispano-Suiza Society 5/12
Hochleistungsfahrzeugbau GmbH 11/1
Holley Carburetor Company 6/27, 7/16, 11/8
Holsman Automobile Company 4/15
Honda Motor Company Ltd. 4/26, 5/10, 6/4, 7/13, 8/5, 9/24, 12/27
Honda of America Manufacturing Company 9/19, 11/1
Hood Rubber Company 4/13, 8/17
Hoof Products Company 8/8
Hooper & Company (Coachbuilders) Ltd. 9/30, 11/15, 12/16
Hoosier Auto Show & Swap Meet 11/18
Hoover Universal, Inc. 5/12
A. Horch & Cie. 11/14
A. Horch & Co., Motorwagenwerke AG 4/29
Horlacher AG 3/4
Horseless Age 2/9, 3/11
Horseless Carriage Club of America 4/4, 6/26, 11/7
Hotpoint 5/7, 6/19
Houdaille Corporation 1/30
Houdaille-Hershey Corporation 1/16, 1/30, 6/10, 10/16, 11/30
Houdaille Industries, Inc. 11/30
Houde Engineering Corporation 2/4
H. S. Houpt Manufacturing Company 1/19
Houston Astros 6/8
Howard Motor International Corporation 4/5
Huck Axle Corporation 7/9
Hudson-Essex-Terraplane Club, Inc. 11/12
Hudson Motor Car Company 1/1, 1/11, 1/14, 2/23, 2/24, 2/25, 3/1, 3/4, 3/6, 3/24, 4/18, 5/1, 5/21, 6/21, 7/1, 7/13, 7/14, 7/15, 7/18, 8/8, 8/9, 9/6, 9/8, 9/23, 10/18, 11/11, 11/21, 12/6, 12/28
Hughes Aircraft Company 12/31
Humble Oil and Refining Company 2/11, 3/25, 4/30, 6/16, 8/9, 9/22, 11/23
Humble Oil Company 2/8, 7/30, 8/26
Hupp Corporation (1) 7/25
Hupp Corporation (2) 6/21, 7/1
Hupp Motor Car Corporation 2/8, 3/8, 4/15, 7/1, 7/7, 7/11, 8/7, 9/8, 9/27, 10/19, 11/1, 11/8, 11/22, 11/27, 11/30
Hurst Performance, Inc. 12/3
Husey Drop Forging & Manufacturing Company 2/23
Hvid Company 2/3
Hyatt Roller Bearing Company 5/10
Hydraulic Brake Company 7/17
Hyundai Construction 5/25, 12/29
Hyundai Engineering & Construction Co. 1/10
Hyundai Motor Company 1/4, 2/1, 8/6, 12/29

Imperial Autocar Manufacturing Company Ltd. 11/30
Imperial Motor Car Company 8/6, 9/4
Imperial Oil Company, Ltd. 7/26, 8/7, 9/6, 9/8, 11/8, 12/21
Imperial Palace Auto Collection 12/1
Imperial Palace Hotel & Casino 12/1
Inalfa Hollandia Inc. 7/22
Indianapolis Auto Racing Association 11/4
Indianapolis Motor Speedway Company 2/9, 5/7, 7/15, 8/15, 10/30, 11/14
Indiana Truck Corporation 5/31
Indian Motorcycle Company 9/26
Industrias Kaiser Argentina SA (IKA) 1/20
Institut Francasis du Petrole 2/23
Institution of Automobile Engineers 3/6
International Automotive Hall of Fame 5/25
International Brewing Corporation 6/2
International Business Machines 5/3
International Harvester Company 1/1, 1/6, 1/7, 2/19, 3/14, 3/17, 4/9, 4/16, 5/2, 5/10, 8/7, 8/12, 8/17, 9/14, 9/19, 10/5, 10/30, 11/4, 11/14, 11/15, 11/26, 12/3, 12/27
International Motor Car Company 5/26
International Motor Company 4/4, 6/20, 11/8
International Motor Contest Association 8/1
International Motor Sports Association 7/4
International Motor Truck Corporation 4/12, 11/8, 12/17
International Plainfield Motor Company 6/1
International Travelling Pass 10/11
International Truck Restorers Club 6/21
International Trucks 11/26
Interstate Battery System of America 5/21
Inter-State Motor Company 2/5
Ionia Manufacturing Company 10/30
Iraq National Oil Company 2/8
Irish Automobile Club 1/22, 8/9
Isuzu Motors Ltd. 4/9, 4/29
ITT Automotive Inc. 9/18, 12/22

Jackson Automobile Company 2/24, 4/5, 4/10, 5/14, 7/23, 11/23
Jaguar Car Holdings Ltd. 7/3, 10/15
Jaguar Cars Ltd. 3/3, 4/1, 5/26, 7/12, 8/9, 9/4, 10/13
Jaguar/Group 44, 6/15
Jaguar PLC 7/3, 9/1, 11/11
Jaguar Rover Triumph Inc. 3/30
Japan Automatic Transmission Company 1/28
Japan Automobile Manufacturers Association (JAMA) 11/16
Japan National Oil Corporation 6/27
Japan Petroleum Development Corporation 6/27, 10/2
Thomas B. Jeffery Company 3/1, 6/10, 7/13, 7/29, 11/10
Jensen Cars Ltd. 1/1
Jewett Motors Inc. 1/12
C. E. Johansson, Inc. 11/7
T. G. John Ltd. 4/27
Johnson Bronze Company 2/12
Johnson Company 10/14
Johnson Controls, Inc. 5/12
Johnson Service Company 12/4
Jones Motor Car Company 2/20
Jordan Motor Car Company 4/5, 10/20, 12/23

Henry J. Kaiser Company 12/14
Kaiser-Frazer Corporation 1/11, 1/20, 2/5, 2/7, 2/10, 3/1, 3/3, 3/23, 3/28, 4/14, 4/28, 5/26, 6/28, 7/17, 7/26, 8/9, 8/11, 9/21, 9/26, 9/28, 10/6, 10/11, 10/12, 10/26, 11/1, 11/4, 11/7, 11/10, 11/20, 12/3, 12/24
Kaiser-Frazer Owners Club International 4/19
Kaiser Industries Corporation 3/7, 3/14, 3/15, 3/21, 5/2, 12/2
Kaiser-Jeep Corporation 2/4, 2/5, 3/7, 4/7, 12/17
Kaiser Manufacturing Corporation 4/28
Kaiser Motors Corporation 3/14, 5/26, 6/30, 7/29
Wilhelm Karmann GmbH 7/21
Karosserie Glaser 7/21

K-D Motor Company 12/16
Keller Motors, Inc. 10/5, 10/25
Kelly-Springfield Truck & Bus Corporation 6/24
Kelly-Springfield Tire & Rubber Company 2/23
Kelly-Springfield Motor Truck Company 11/16
Kelsey-Hayes Company 2/20, 8/11, 12/19
Kelsey-Hayes Wheel Corporation 1/17, 4/25, 11/9, 12/19
Kelsey Wheel Company 1/19, 6/12, 8/23
Kelvinator Corporation 1/4
Kent Motors Corporation 1/28, 4/26, 5/29, 9/16, 10/7, 11/15
Kenworth Motor Truck Corporation 1/22, 3/1, 10/17, 12/22
Kerr-McGee Corporation 3/20, 4/29, 9/15, 11/9
Keyes Supply Company Ltd. 2/4
Kinetic Chemical Company 8/27
King Motor Car Company 11/9
Kingsbury Aviation Company 8/23
Kingston Products Corporation 12/29
Kissel Motor Car Company 2/29, 4/28, 6/25, 9/6, 9/19, 12/21
Klink Motor Car Manufacturing Company 7/8
Knight Rider 9/26
Knox Automobile Compay 2/15, 3/6, 5/1, 5/12, 6/12, 6/21
Knox Motors Company 5/1
Kohler Company 4/13
Korea Oil Corporation 10/13
Krastin Automobile Manufacturing Company 11/20
Krause Publications 10/4
S. S. Kresge Company 1/28
Krit Motor Car Company 9/3
Kruse International 9/29
Kuhlman Corporation 4/25, 10/13
Kuhlman Electric Company 4/25, 6/1
Kutztown Publishing Company 11/5
Kuwait Oil Company Ltd. 12/19
Kuwait Oil Company (London) Ltd. 11/6, 12/19

Laboratory Equipment Company 8/27
Lagonda Ltd. 6/17
La Locomotion Automobile 12/1
Lamson & Sessions Company 10/11
Langen, Otto, & Rosen 6/30
Larabee-Deyo Motor Truck Company 12/5
Lea & Francis Ltd. 12/27
L'Automobile-Club de l'Ouest 10/9
LeBaron Carrossiers 1/7
LeBaron Inc. 1/7, 3/7, 5/9
Lecoq and Fernie 1/15, 2/14
Leece-Neville Company 1/12, 12/5
Lehigh University 8/4
Lehman Brothers 5/4
Leland, Faulconer, and Norton 9/19
Lendrum & Hartman 9/5
Lescina Automobile Company 11/6
Letourneur & Marchand 5/4
Lewis Spring and Axle Company 2/24
Lexington Motor Company 5/10
Leyland Group 1/17, 12/11
Leyland Historic Vehicles Ltd. 9/2
Leyland Motor Corporation Ltd. 2/8, 6/17
Leyland Motors Ltd. 6/18
Libbey-Owens-Ford Company 8/27, 11/3
Libbey-Owens-Ford Glass Company 1/9, 1/15, 2/1, 5/28, 8/27, 9/14, 12/13, 12/19
Libbey-Owens Glass Company 5/18, 5/28
Limousine Body Company 9/15
Lincoln Continental Owners Club 10/16, 10/19
Lincoln Highway Association 7/1, 8/10
Lincoln Memorial Road Association 4/22
Lincoln Motor Company 1/26, 2/4, 3/29, 4/1, 6/7, 6/13, 8/29
Linn Manufacturing Company 5/7, 12/15
Little House on the Prairie 12/5
Little Motor Car Company 1/21, 2/4, 10/26, 10/30
Little Motor Kar Company 8/5

Llandudno Motor Touring Company 8/2
Lloyd Motoren-Werke GmbH 2/2
Locke & Company 4/16, 6/18
Locomobile Company of America 2/1, 5/18, 7/28, 8/26, 8/31, 11/25, 12/15
Locomotive & Machine Company of Montreal Ltd. 6/19
London Electric Cab Company 8/19
Harley C. Loney Company 9/20
Long Island Automotive Museum 8/1, 8/27, 9/1, 12/14
Long Island Motor Parkway Company 6/16
Los Angeles Times 10/15, 11/23
Lotus Cars Ltd. 12/16
Lotus Cars U.S.A. 12/22
Lotus Engineering Company 1/1, 12/16
Lozier Motor Company 2/3, 2/14, 5/6, 5/25, 7/29
Lubrizol Corporation 3/14, 4/5
Lucas Industries PLC 4/1
Joseph Lucas Industries, Ltd. 11/3
Ludlow Valve Manufacturing Company 3/23
Luftfahrzeug-Motoren GmbH 3/23
Luverne Automobile Company 1/9
Luverne Motor Truck Company 7/23
Lycoming Manufacturing Company 11/12, 12/11
Lycoming Motors Corporation 2/19, 9/15

Macbeth-Evans Glass Company 8/16
Mack Brothers Company 7/26
Mack Brothers Motor Car Company 1/8, 1/9, 2/1, 4/29
Mack-International Motor Truck Corporation 2/15
Mack Manufacturing Corporation 6/1
Mack Motor Truck Corporation 6/1
Mack Trucks, Inc. 1/1, 1/21, 1/22, 1/26, 2/13, 3/14, 3/29, 4/12, 5/17,
    5/29, 6/1, 6/2, 6/10, 6/18, 7/13, 7/21, 7/23, 8/7, 9/6, 9/20, 9/27,
    10/1, 12/29
Macon Motor Car Company 5/17, 12/30
R. H. Macy Company 6/19
Magee-Hale Parking Meter Company 1/1
Magee Museum 6/16
Magyar Autoklub 3/27
Manitou & Pikes Peak Railroad 11/2
Mann Egerton, Ltd. 4/12
Mansfield Tire & Rubber Company 8/12
Manufacturers Contest Association 3/3
Manville Corporation 10/29
Marathon Motor Works 1/1
Marinette Automobile Company 12/1
Marland Oil Company 10/8
Marmon Club 5/5
Marmon-Herrington Company, Inc. 2/18, 3/13, 8/5, 9/1, 10/23, 11/3,
    11/11
Marmon Motor Car Company 2/2, 4/6, 5/1, 10/29, 11/11, 12/1, 12/22
Marmon Motor Company 3/15
Marquette Motor Car Company 4/9
Martin-Parry Corporation 7/13, 8/2, 9/20, 11/21
Martin-Wasp Corporation 4/1, 6/2
Marvel Carburetor Company 5/9
Maschinen Augsburg-Nurnburg (MAN) 10/30
Mason Automobile Company 1/12
Mason Motor Car Company 3/26, 8/16
Mason Motor Company 7/14, 7/31, 9/9
Massachusetts Institute of Technology 2/5, 9/24
Master Tire & Rubber Corporation 3/26, 7/1
Matra SA 2/10, 7/15
Maxim Motor Company 8/8
Maxon, Inc. 12/15
Maxwell-Briscoe Motor Company 5/17, 6/16, 6/21, 7/4
Maxwell Motor Corporation 1/11, 4/6, 6/6, 6/15, 6/26, 10/2
Maybach Motoren-Werke GmbH 3/23
Mazda Motor Corporation 5/1, 8/20
McLaughlin Motor Car Company 1/6, 9/8, 11/8, 12/19
McQuay-Norris Manufacturing Company 2/3, 4/5
Meccas Manufacturing & Specialty Co. 4/14
Med-Bow Automobile Company 10/28

Meldrum & Fewsmith, Inc. 3/12, 4/1
Mercer Automobile Company 1/1, 4/15, 5/31, 9/7, 10/6
Mercer Motors Company 9/24, 10/6, 11/25
Mercer Motors Corporation 11/21
Mercury Marine 11/24
Merrimac Body Company 11/21
Meteor Motor Car Company 12/13
Metz Company 5/21, 8/3
Metzger Motor Car Company 6/20, 9/20
M.G. Car Company Ltd. 1/20, 7/1, 7/21
Michelin & Cie. 6/4, 10/24
Michelin Tire Corporation 3/24
Michigan Buggy Company 8/6
Michigan Rivet Corporation 8/15, 9/2, 10/17
Mid-America Research Corporation 1/1
Midas International Corporation 4/8
Midlands Automobile Club 8/12
Midstates Jeepster Association 9/19
Midwest Aircraft Corporation 11/11
Milestone Car Society 4/30, 5/18, 10/9
A. J. Miller Company 3/19
Harry A. Miller Manufacturing Company 7/8
Miniature Incandescent Lamp Company 12/2
Minneapolis-Moline Company 11/15
Minsk Automobile Plant 8/9
Mitchell-Lewis Motor Company 2/19, 2/24, 4/8
Mitchell Motor Company 2/27, 4/2, 9/12, 12/30
Mitsubishi Heavy Industries Ltd. 4/22
Mitsubishi Motors Corporation 4/22, 5/1, 9/22
Mitsubishi Motors New Zealand Ltd. 5/1
Miyata Works, Ltd. 1/21
Mobil Corporation 3/5, 6/18, 7/14, 12/25
Mobil Oil Australia Ltd. 2/1, 4/2
Mobil Oil Company Ltd. 12/1
Mobil Oil Corporation 5/18, 6/18, 7/5, 11/26
Modernistic Industries, Inc. 2/12, 2/28
Modine Manufacturing Company 3/15, 6/23
Modoc Motor Company 11/27
Moline Automobile Company 12/19
Moline Plow Company 5/8
Molotov Automobile Plant 6/14
Monroe Auto Equipment Company 3/1, 3/30, 8/16, 8/26
Monroe Body Company 8/1
Monroe Motor Company 4/24, 8/1
Montgomery Ward & Company 11/27
Moon Motor Car Company 1/3, 2/3, 2/11, 4/7, 6/25, 6/27, 7/1, 8/13,
    10/2, 11/10, 11/15
Moon-Ruxton Company 2/3
Moore Motor Vehicle Company 12/15, 12/22
Mora Motor Car Company 11/15
Moreland Motor Truck Company 4/8
Morgan Motor Company Ltd. 9/5, 11/3
Morris Garages 7/21
Morris Motors Ltd. 7/1, 12/17
Morse Chain Company 3/25
Moscow Automotive Plant 11/6, 11/7
Moskovskii Zavod Malolitrajnikh Avtomobilei 5/31
Motometer Company 5/17
Motor 2/22, 12/29
MoToR 4/2
Motor & Accessory Manufacturers Association 2/24
Motor Age 1/20, 2/19, 3/23
Motorcar Company 9/26
Motor Improvement, Inc. 11/15
Motor Institute of America 5/4
Motorola 6/29, 11/5
Motor Products Corporation 1/3, 2/15
Motor Sales & Service Corporation 8/13
Motor Trend 1/23, 9/10
Motor Vehicle Review 9/27
Motor Wheel Corporation 1/17, 2/17, 6/9, 9/8
Mueller Manufacturing Company 4/24

H. J. Mulliner, Park Ward Ltd. 5/15
Murphy Service 10/29
Walter M. Murphy Company, Coachbuilders 2/24, 3/22, 7/4
Murray Body Company 5/13, 6/17, 10/22, 11/15, 12/2
Murray Corporation 8/14
Musee de l'Anthologie Automobile 5/1, 6/11
Musee National de l'Automobile 7/7, 7/27
Museum of Automobile History 10/22
Museum of Automobiles 5/1
Muskegon Motor Specialities Company 7/17
Muzzy-Lyon Company 5/1

Nakajima Aircraft Company 12/10
Napco Detroit, Inc. 3/1
Napco Industries, Inc. 3/1
D. Napier & Son, Ltd. 2/18, 3/19, 5/10, 7/9
Napier Motor Car Company of America 11/18
Nash-Kelvinator Corporation 1/4, 1/14, 2/27, 3/23, 3/24, 3/29, 4/1,
    5/1, 5/22, 5/30, 6/18, 10/16
Nash Motors Company 1/4, 1/20, 2/3, 2/24, 2/27, 3/13, 4/2, 4/12,
    5/1, 5/16, 5/27, 7/8, 7/29, 8/1, 9/12, 10/3, 10/14, 11/4
National Acme Company 5/8
National Association of Automobile Dealers 2/2
National Association of Automobile Manufacturers (NAAM) 12/1
National Association for Stock Car Auto Racing (NASCAR) 2/6, 2/11,
    2/15, 2/19, 2/21, 3/8, 3/26, 4/1, 4/2, 4/5, 4/24, 5/2, 5/3, 5/6, 5/24,
    5/28, 6/1, 6/17, 6/19, 7/1, 7/4, 7/13, 7/31, 8/6, 8/11, 9/1, 9/4, 9/5,
    9/7, 9/13, 9/15, 9/22, 9/26, 9/30, 10/6, 10/16, 10/31, 11/21, 12/1,
    12/3, 12/14
National Automobile & Casualty Company 2/22
National Automobile Chamber of Commerce 1/1, 3/2, 10/3
National Automobile Dealers Association (NADA) 4/16, 6/27, 11/30
National Automobile & Motor Company 10/12
National Automotive Parts Association 1/25, 12/23
National Aviation Hall of Fame 7/21
National Corvette Museum 9/2
National Corvette Restorers Society 3/24
National Cycle & Automobile Company, Ltd. 2/26
National Hot Rod Association (NHRA) 5/7
National Malleable & Steel Castings Company 8/24
National Motor Carriage Company 8/1, 9/2
National Motor Vehicle Company 1/16, 6/21
National Motor Museum 4/9, 5/22, 7/4
National Sales Engineering Corporation 7/19
National Truck Driving Rodeo 2/3
Naval Ordnance Laboratory 11/13
Navistar International Corporation 1/7, 3/20, 10/15
Nederlandsche Automobiel Club 7/3
Nelson Muffler Corporation 5/15, 5/23, 7/10
Nesselsdorfer Wagenbau-Fabriks-Gesellschaft 6/3, 9/1, 12/1
Neste OY 1/9, 11/15
Neumaticos Goodyear SA 11/8
New Departure Manufacturing Company 2/28, 3/26, 6/28
New Era Motors, Inc. 2/3, 4/7, 4/16, 10/29
Newcomb, Endicott and Company 1/12
New United Motor Manufacturing, Inc. 2/17, 12/18
New Venture Gear Inc. 8/30
New York Herald 5/10, 5/14
New York Herald-Tribune 4/2
New York Times 4/2
New York Trade School 4/6
Nigerian National Oil Corporation 4/1
Nigerian National Petroleum Corporation 4/1
Nilson-Miller Company 12/13
Nippon Oil Company Ltd. 5/10
Nissan Diesel Motor Company, Ltd. 12/1
Nissan Motor Company, Ltd. 1/28, 3/29, 4/27, 6/27, 8/3, 9/8, 9/12, 12/26
Nissan Motor Corporation in USA 9/28
Nissan Motor Manufacturing Company 3/26, 5/9
Nordiska Kullagerfabriken 10/27
Nordyke & Marmon Company 2/2, 5/17, 6/27, 10/11
Norge Corporation 2/26

Norma-Hoffmann Bearings Corporation 2/25, 3/10, 4/28, 9/21
Norsk-Engelsk Mineralolie AS 10/29
North American Motors Inc. 7/10
Northwestern Auto Parts Company 3/1
Northwood Institute 7/3
Norwalk Tire & Rubber Company 11/16
Notre Dame University 3/4, 3/31
Nuova Automobili Ferruccio Lamborghini SpA 9/1
NV Koninklijke Nederlandsche Mij tot Expolitatie van
    Petroleumbronnen in Nederlandsch-Indie 2/14, 6/16

Oakes Products Corporation 1/30
Oakland Motor Car Company 2/14, 4/9, 8/1, 8/28, 9/23
Officina Specializzata Costruzione Automobili (OSCA) 12/1
Officine Meccaniche SA 9/23
Ohio Automobile Company 1/23, 3/8, 4/12, 9/10, 9/29, 10/13, 10/24
Ohio State University 9/23
Oilgear Company 4/16
Old Cars (Weekly) 6/16, 9/22, 9/25, 10/4, 12/2, 12/16
R. E. Olds Company 8/16, 9/27
Olds Gasoline Engine Works 5/8
P. F. Olds & Son, Inc. 7/31
Olds Motor Vehicle Company 5/8, 8/21
Olds Motor Works 1/1, 1/5, 2/19, 3/1, 3/9, 5/7, 5/8, 5/13, 5/18, 8/1,
    8/7, 9/27, 11/12, 12/20, 12/28, 12/31
Olender Sales & Engineering Company 9/8
Tinius Olsen Testing Machine Company 12/10
Omnibus Corporation 8/31
Adam Opel AG 3/13, 3/18, 4/8, 11/1, 12/2
Organization of the Petroleum Exporting Countries (OPEC) 9/14, 12/17
Oshkosh Truck Corporation 4/1, 4/22, 5/1
Ostendorf Motor Corporation 11/16
Osterreichische Automobil-Gesellschaft 8/2
Osterreichisches Daimler Motoren AG 1/1, 4/30
Otis Auto Dynatester, Inc. 7/9
Otosan Otomobil Sanayi As PK 10/10
N. A. Otto & Cie 2/13
Overland Automobile Company 1/9, 3/31, 11/18
Overman Wheel Company 5/18
Owatonna Manufacturing Company 10/11
Owens-Corning Fiberglass 2/25, 4/25

P & G Manufacturing Company 7/17
Paccar, Inc. 2/1, 3/3, 4/21, 8/9, 8/11
Pace Petroleum 1/5
Pacific Car & Foundry Company 2/1
Pacific Coast Oil Company 1/27
Packard Automobile Classics 4/11
Packard Club 8/23
Packard Electric Company 6/5
Packard Federal Corporation 5/5
Packard Motor Car Company 1/1, 1/9, 1/16, 1/17, 1/20, 1/24, 1/27,
    1/29, 1/31, 2/1, 2/3, 2/4, 2/6, 2/9, 2/11, 2/15, 2/17, 2/27, 2/28,
    3/1, 3/3, 3/10, 3/14, 3/15, 3/17, 3/21, 3/24, 3/26, 3/31, 4/6, 4/10,
    4/16, 4/17, 4/19, 4/20, 4/22, 4/27, 5/1, 5/7, 5/8, 5/12, 5/16, 5/19,
    5/22, 5/25, 5/26, 6/1, 6/7, 6/10, 6/12, 6/20, 6/22, 6/25, 7/1, 7/5,
    7/20, 7/22, 7/27, 7/29, 7/30, 8/6, 8/8, 8/13, 8/18, 8/22, 8/25, 9/1,
    9/2, 9/4, 9/5, 9/8, 9/11, 9/14, 9/21, 9/24, 9/25, 10/1, 10/3, 10/5,
    10/10, 10/13, 10/17, 10/24, 10/25, 10/30, 11/5, 11/6, 11/14, 11/15,
    11/18, 11/25, 12/12, 12/15, 12/27, 12/29, 12/30, 12/31
Packard News 6/1
Packard & Weiss 9/10, 12/30
Paige-Detroit Motor Car Company 1/12, 1/20, 5/5, 6/7, 6/10, 12/27
Pakistan Petroleum Ltd. 6/5
Pan Motor Company 1/27, 9/29, 12/6
Paragon Motor Company 8/28
Parker Motor Company 2/28
Park Ward & Company Ltd. 6/30
Parry Automobile Company 3/26, 5/12, 7/28
Passport Transportation Ltd. 10/8
Patriot Manufacturing Company 7/23
C. R. Patterson & Sons 9/23
Paxton Products Company 3/18

Peerless Corporation 6/30
Peerless Motor Car Company 3/28, 5/18, 6/12, 6/25, 6/30, 8/6, 11/1, 11/12
Penberthy Injector Company 11/12
Peninsular Metal Products Corporation 9/22
Pennsylvania Rubber Company 7/4
Pennzoil Company 2/10, 6/1, 7/21, 9/6
Pennzoil United Inc. 4/1, 6/1
Pep Auto Supply Company 1/19, 10/22
Pep Boys - Manny Moe & Jack 10/22
Perfect Circle Company 3/10, 3/29, 5/2, 8/17, 8/23, 10/3, 12/15
Perfection Metal Silo Company 5/29
Perfex Corporation 11/26
Peru Auto Parts Manufacturing Company 2/12
Petersen Automotive Museum 6/11
Petrofina (Great Britain) Ltd. 4/1, 10/1
Petrofina SA 2/25
Pettit's Museum of Motoring Memories 11/26
Petrofina (UK) Ltd. 4/1, 6/4
Peugeot SA 8/6, 9/4
Phantom III Technical Society 5/1
Philco Corporation 7/25, 9/13, 12/11, 12/13
Phillips Petroleum Company 1/3, 2/19, 3/30, 4/7, 4/15, 6/13, 6/17, 8/1, 8/6, 8/15, 8/23, 8/31, 9/1, 11/28
Pichon-Parat 4/12
Pierce-Arrow Motor Car Company 3/28, 5/1, 5/13, 6/6, 6/21, 6/24, 8/7, 8/15, 8/26, 8/30, 10/15, 12/14
George N. Pierce Company 1/31, 2/4, 4/26, 8/12, 9/1, 12/9
Pierce Motor Company 4/6
Pikes Peak Auto Highway Company 1/9, 11/1
Pirelli SpA 3/2, 3/21
Peter Pirsch & Company 7/14
Piston Ring Company 12/20, 12/31
Pittsburgh Motor Vehicle Company 8/28, 10/21
Plass Motor-Wagon Company 1/7
Playboy Motor Car Corporation 4/3, 4/14, 5/20, 6/3
Plymouth Factory Service School 5/22
Pollock Auto Showcase 12/1
Pontiac-Oakland Club International 1/1, 10/7
Pontiac Spring & Wagon Works 7/13
Pope Manufacturing Company 3/6, 4/14, 5/13, 8/10
Pope Motor Car Company 5/27
Dr. Ing. h.c. Ferdinand Porsche GmbH Konstruktionsburo fur Motoren-, Fahrzeug-, Luftfahrzeug- und Wasserfahrzeugbau 12/1
Dr. Ing. h.c. F. Porsche KG 12/16
Porsche Leasing GmbH 4/1
Porsche Salzburg 5/14
Powell Manufacturing Company 4/17
Powell Muffler Company 6/9
Prague Automobile Factory, Ltd. 3/27
Pratt Motor Car Company 10/24
E. L. Pratt Automobile Company 4/1
Pratt & Whitney 9/17
Pressed Steel Company 5/27, 7/25
Prest-O-Lite Company 3/15, 7/15
Prest-O-Lite Storage Battery Company of Canada Ltd. 4/25
Princess Homes, Inc. 5/10
Proctor & Gamble Company 8/7
Prvni Ceskomoravska Tovarna na Stroje v Praze 5/4
PSA Peugeot-Citroen 8/10
Pullman Motor Company 7/24
Pure Oil Company 5/23
Purfina SA 12/10, 12/13
Puritan Machine Company 2/27

Quaker City Motor Club 10/9
Quaker State Corporation 3/5, 7/1, 10/8
Quaker State Oil Refining Corporation 7/1
Quinlan Motors 7/15

Ragtime Car and Boat Museum 5/15
Rainier Motor Company 1/25

Rand McNally & Company 2/13, 7/31, 8/17
R and V Engineering Company 10/1
Rapid Motor Vehicle Company 9/26
Ray Day Piston Company 4/12
Rayfield Motor Car Company 2/8, 2/14, 5/26, 12/23
Rayfield Motor Company 12/23
Reading Automobile Company 2/3
Regie Nationale des Usines Renault 1/1, 1/17, 1/21, 3/31, 12/16, 12/19
Reid Manufacturing Company 12/1
Relay Motor Car Company 2/3
Remco Products Corporation 10/22
Renault SA 9/6
Renwick & Bertelli, Ltd. 5/13
Reo Clubhouse 12/18
Reo Motor Car Company 1/11, 3/5, 3/11, 3/17, 3/18, 4/17, 5/18, 6/1, 7/15, 9/4, 9/27, 10/8, 12/17, 12/20, 12/28
Reo Motors, Inc. 1/3, 10/7, 10/10
Republic Rubber Company 9/15
Reutter 3/21
Revere Copper & Brass, Inc. 6/1
ReVere Motor Car Company 2/7, 7/15
Rheinische Gasmotorenfabrik Benz & Cie 3/16
Richfield Oil Corporation 5/3
Rickenbacker Motor Company 7/25
Ring & Hoffman 4/29
W. A. Roach Company 3/31
Road & Track 1/27, 3/15, 4/5, 6/15, 7/20, 7/25, 8/4, 9/28, 11/27, 11/29
Roamer Motor Car Company 4/22, 8/7
Rockford Automobile & Engine Company 4/11
Rolls-Royce Distributing Ltd. 3/16
Rolls-Royce Enthusiasts Club 5/18
Rolls-Royce Ltd. 1/7, 1/14, 1/25, 1/31, 2/1, 2/3, 2/4, 2/6, 2/12, 2/23, 3/13, 3/15, 4/11, 4/19, 4/21, 4/23, 4/24, 5/4, 5/17, 6/7, 6/16, 6/17, 6/27, 7/9, 7/16, 7/19, 8/28, 9/9, 9/23, 10/23, 10/27, 11/6, 11/30, 12/14, 12/17, 12/31
Rolls-Royce Motors, Inc. 3/9, 9/14
Rolls-Royce Motors Ltd. 6/25, 7/25, 12/21
Rolls-Royce of America, Inc. 1/1, 1/7, 2/1, 3/9, 3/22, 4/21, 6/18, 6/24, 8/10, 8/13, 8/18, 8/29, 9/24, 10/18, 11/7, 11/21, 11/22, 11/25, 12/12
Rolls-Royce Owners' Club 5/1, 5/12
Rollway Bearing Company 3/5
Roots Oil Motor & Motor Car Company, Ltd. 7/7
Ross Gear & Tool Company 4/6, 7/9, 10/1, 12/27
Rouge Steel Company 12/10
Rover Group PLC 3/5, 5/3, 8/9
Royal Automobile Club (RAC) 2/29, 3/22, 4/22, 5/18, 8/10, 9/14, 9/15, 10/8, 10/22, 10/26
Royal Dutch Oil Company 9/6
Royal Dutch/Shell Group 2/14, 6/16, 6/29, 8/19, 9/1, 11/7, 12/31
Royal Irish Automobile Club 1/22
Royce, Ltd. 12/23
Sir Henry Royce Foundation 5/18
Ruckstell Sales & Manufacturing Company 5/29
Rudge-Whitworth Wheels 10/6, 10/9
Russell Motor Car Company Ltd. 12/29
Rutenber Motor Company 5/31
R. W. M. Investment Company 3/1

Saab AB 5/16
Saab Automobile AB 1/1
Saab-Scania AB 1/1, 5/16, 9/13, 10/5
Saab-Scania of America 3/17
SA Andre Citroen 8/8
Sacred Heart Auto League 9/14
SA des Automobiles Peugeot 1/1, 10/18, 10/19
SAEIC 7/27
Safety Motor Company 12/30
St. Louis Cardinals 5/10, 7/26
SA Minerva Motors 6/27
Sandberg Ranch 9/10
Saturday Evening Post 2/15, 3/31
Saturn Corporation 1/7, 1/26, 7/30

Saudi Arabian Oil Company 11/13
Saxon Motor Car Company 5/4, 11/18
AB Scania-VABIS 11/30
Scania AV 5/16
Schaefer, Inc. 3/5
Scheib, Inc. 12/22
A. Schrader's Son 2/22, 8/28
Scintilla Magneto Company 3/3
Scripps-Booth Company 2/26, 5/6, 7/28, 9/24, 10/3, 10/17, 12/9
Scripps-Booth Cyclecar Company 11/1
Scripps Motor Company 6/12
Scuderia Ferrari 9/1, 11/4, 12/1, 12/16
Seagrave Corporation 1/5, 6/28
Sealed Power Corporation 6/9, 12/3, 12/20, 12/28, 12/31
Seaman Body Corporation 1/30, 9/8
Seaman Motors 9/19
Sears, Roebuck & Company 9/3, 11/20, 12/17, 12/20
Seattle Chamber of Commerce 7/12
Seattle Times 3/17, 5/29
Seiberling Tire & Rubber Company 2/1, 7/3, 8/11
Selden Truck Company 12/20
Self Propelled Traffic Association 12/10
Walden W. Shaw Corporation 1/31, 6/29
Walden W. Shaw Livery Company 8/25
Sheepshead Bay Speedway Corporation 1/23, 8/27
Shelby Automobiles, Inc. 3/1
Shell Canada Ltd. 7/1
Shell Company of Canada Ltd. 8/7, 8/26
Shell Company of the United Kingdom Ltd. 4/1, 4/4
Shell-D'Arcy Petroleum Company of Nigeria Ltd. 9/11, 12/13
Sheller-Globe Corporation 9/28
Shell Marketing Company Ltd. 1/17, 4/30
Shell Oil Company 1/31, 2/16, 4/28, 5/18, 6/16, 7/20, 9/22, 10/21, 12/1
Shell Oil Company of Canada Ltd. 1/25, 7/1, 8/26
Shell Petroleum Development Company of Nigeria 12/13
Shell Refining & Marketing Company Ltd. 1/17, 5/8
Shell Refining Company Ltd. 4/1, 5/8
Shell Research Ltd. England 7/29
Shell UK Ltd. 4/4
Shell Union Oil Company 2/8, 5/6, 9/22, 10/11
Siam Motors Company, Ltd. 8/3
Simplex Automobile Company 5/12, 7/7, 7/25, 11/3, 11/20
Sinclair Consolidated Oil Company 9/22
Sinclair Gulf Corporation 9/22
Sinclair Oil Company 9/21, 11/10, 12/16
Sinclair Oil & Refining Company 9/22
Sinclair Petroleum Company 3/10, 10/9
Sinclair Refining Company 1/4, 1/10, 1/22, 4/5, 5/5, 6/27, 8/20, 8/24, 9/4, 9/21, 10/23, 11/28
Singapore Airlines 8/14, 9/28
Sizaire-Berwick (France) Ltd. 6/20
Sizaire Freres 10/15
Sizaire Freres et Naudin 6/1, 12/13
Skelly Oil Company 4/11
SKF Ball Bearing Company 7/10, 11/30
SKF Industries, Inc. 7/6
Alfred P. Sloan Museum 9/4
Sloan-Kettering Institute 8/7
Smalley Auto Company 8/11
SMH 3/4
Smith Automobile Company 1/1, 5/29, 8/26, 10/15
A. O. Smith Corporation 2/22, 5/31, 9/9, 9/16, 10/7, 11/11, 11/13, 12/23
Smithsonian Institution 4/23, 7/4, 7/26, 7/27, 8/19
Snap-On Wrench Company 4/10
So-Cal Speed Shop 3/22
Sociedad Hispano-Suiza Fabrica de Automoviles SA 6/14
Societa Anonima Carburatore Zenith 7/6
Societa Anonima Italiana Nicola Romeo e C. 9/21
Societa Anonima Officine Alfieri Maserati 12/14
Societa Generale per l'Industria Metallurgica e Meccanica 6/21
Societa Milanese d'Automobili Isotta-Fraschini & C. 1/24
Societa Petrolifera Italinana SpA 7/16

Societe A. Darracq 1/4
Societe Alacienne de Construction Mechanique (SACM) 4/1
Societe des Anciens Etablissements Panhard et Levassor 7/16
Societe des Automobiles Pilain 9/7
Societe des Ingenieurs de l'Automobile 1/17
Societe des Nouveaux Etablissements Sizaire et Naudin 12/13
Societe Generale des Huiles de Petrole 2/7
Societe Industrielle de Mecanique et Carrosserie Automobile (Simca) 1/18
Societe Nouvelle des Automobiles Delage 9/18
Societe Renault Freres 3/30
Society of Automobile Engineers 1/18, 9/21
Society of Automotive Engineers (SAE) 1/10, 1/15, 1/16, 2/9, 3/11, 3/23, 3/26, 3/27, 4/9, 6/4, 6/15, 7/1, 7/12, 7/21, 7/26, 9/4, 9/15, 10/11, 10/24, 11/5, 11/15, 11/27, 12/29
Society of Motion Picture Art Directors 10/12
Society of Motor Manufacturers 1/2
Society of Motor Manufacturers and Traders 10/19
Socony Mobil Oil Company 4/29, 5/18, 10/2
Socony-Vacuum Oil Company 2/23, 2/28, 4/28, 4/29, 5/2, 5/3, 5/9, 5/29, 5/31, 6/9, 11/10, 11/13
Sotheby, Parke-Bernet 10/17
South African Motor Car Company 3/13
South African Motor Corporation 5/22
Southern California Automobile Club 12/6
Southern California Freight Lines Ltd. 9/16
South Wales Motor Car & Cycle Company 1/1
Spaulding Manufacturing Company 1/20
Sperry Rand Corporation 6/16
Sports Car Club of America (SCCA) 2/26, 3/25, 6/11, 9/2, 9/30, 10/2
Sport Velocipedique Metropolitaine 4/28
Springfield Manufacturing Company 6/24, 8/29
Springfield Motor Car Company 5/26, 10/28, 11/6
Spring Industries 7/1
Squire Car Manufacturing Company Ltd. 7/6
Stafford Motor Car Company 12/3
Standard Automobile Supply Company 8/8
Standard Machinery Company 7/9
Standard Motor Company 12/18
Standard Motor Company Ltd. 2/10
Standard Oil Company 2/13, 2/26, 3/10, 3/19, 3/29, 4/4, 4/13, 5/3, 5/10, 5/23, 5/27, 5/31, 6/24, 6/25, 7/8, 9/9, 9/11, 9/28, 10/15, 11/29, 12/16
Standard Oil Company of Brazil 3/22
Standard Oil Company of California 1/27, 1/30, 2/1, 3/5, 7/1, 9/1
Standard Oil Company of Indiana 1/13, 1/18, 2/24, 3/2, 3/11, 4/23, 5/3, 6/18, 6/20, 8/28, 9/25, 11/17, 12/3, 12/29
Standard Oil Company of New Jersey 1/6, 1/9, 2/7, 2/23, 3/19, 4/4, 4/22, 5/1, 5/2, 6/18, 6/24, 7/17, 7/31, 8/5, 8/10, 8/12, 8/17, 8/27, 9/13, 9/25, 10/22, 10/28, 11/1, 11/26, 11/29, 12/1, 12/13
Standard Oil Company of New York 6/9, 8/10, 9/24, 10/13, 11/13
Standard Oil Company of Ohio 1/10, 4/18, 4/22, 5/13, 6/1, 7/11, 8/1, 11/7
Standard Oil Development Company 10/29, 11/3
Standard Products Company 6/27, 11/22
Standard Products of Canada 10/20
Standard Screw Company 6/14
Standard Steel Spring Company 6/13, 10/3, 12/4
Standard Wheel Company 6/13
Stanley Motor Carriage Company 2/16, 8/18
Stant Machine Company 10/2
State College (PA) High School 2/17
F. B. Stearns Company 5/17, 8/15, 12/30
Stephens Motor Car Company 1/18, 5/8, 11/13
Sterling Motor Car Company 7/28
Sterling Motor Company 8/9
Sterling Motor Truck Company 3/16, 6/1
Sterling-Knight Motors Company 4/6, 5/31
J. Stevens Arms and Tool Company 8/29
Stewart Motor Company 7/19
Stewart-Warner Corporation 4/2, 5/19, 11/16, 11/17
Stewart-Warner Speedometer Corporation 1/6, 3/13, 3/22, 4/1, 4/2, 12/15, 12/20
Stout Engineering Laboratories 1/10

Stout Metal Airplane Company 8/1
Streator Motor Car Company 5/28
Studebaker Brothers Manufacturing Company 1/1, 2/14, 5/26, 11/27
H. & C. Studebaker 2/16
Studebaker Corporation 1/1, 1/3, 2/4, 2/14, 2/15, 2/18, 3/4, 3/8, 3/9,
    3/18, 4/13, 4/17, 4/26, 6/7, 6/22, 7/1, 7/2, 7/5, 7/12, 7/14, 7/25,
    8/4, 8/7, 8/14, 8/15, 8/17, 8/23, 8/26, 9/1, 9/24, 10/1, 10/8, 10/15,
    10/18, 11/15, 11/16, 11/25, 12/8, 12/10, 12/12
Studebaker Drivers Club 6/7
Studebaker Corporation of Canada Ltd. 2/26, 12/13
Studebaker-Packard Corporation 1/10, 2/1, 2/11, 2/15, 2/19, 2/24, 3/1,
    3/5, 3/16, 3/18, 3/23, 3/26, 4/9, 4/16, 4/26, 5/8, 5/10, 5/20, 6/3,
    7/2, 7/10, 7/12, 7/22, 7/24, 7/26, 7/27, 7/31, 8/6, 8/19, 8/31, 9/1,
    9/2, 9/3, 10/1, 10/8, 10/22, 10/31, 11/6, 12/1, 12/9, 12/28
Stutz Motor Car Company of America 2/3, 2/18, 4/3, 11/26
Subaru 360 Drivers' Club 1/10, 6/30, 11/1
Subaru of America, Inc. 2/15, 3/21
Sunbeam Motor Car Company Ltd. 1/16
Sun Motor Car Company 12/24
Sun Oil Company 2/23, 7/2, 12/1
Sunset Automobile Company 4/18
Superior Coach Corporation 8/29
Supreme Motor Company 5/31
Sutton & Company 6/6
Suzuki Motor Company, Ltd. 1/30, 10/1
Suzuki Motor Corporation 10/1
Svenska Kullagerfabriken 6/22
Swallow Sidecar Company 9/4
Swan Carburetor Company 9/17

T & N Industries Inc. 4/9
Tarkington Motor Company 6/1
Technical Assistants Inc. 10/8
Teetor-Hartley Motor Company 5/2, 12/15
Templar Motors Corporation 1/4, 2/14, 6/16, 10/8, 12/13
Tenneco Corporation 11/26
Texaco Canada Inc. 7/14, 8/20
Texaco, Inc. 2/15, 2/27, 3/21, 4/30, 6/11, 9/4, 10/21
Textron Corporation 3/23
The Autocar 10/9, 11/2
The Horseless Age 11/7
Theo Masui Ltd. 3/13, 5/6, 6/17
The Packard 6/16, 11/7
The Texas Company 1/11, 2/11, 2/19, 3/13, 4/30, 8/10, 8/26, 10/12,
    11/1
Thomas Cook & Son 7/11
E. R. Thomas-Detroit Company 12/1
E. R. Thomas Motor Company 2/28, 7/15, 8/19, 10/1, 11/3
Thompson Products Inc. 3/11, 3/20, 5/10, 8/14, 8/31, 9/26
Thompson Products Museum 11/1
J. I. Thornycroft & Company, Ltd. 9/6
Tillotson Manufacturing Company 9/1
Timken Company 4/21
Timken-Detroit Axle Company 3/18, 3/31, 4/19, 6/5, 10/30, 11/8, 11/10,
    11/20
Timken Roller Bearing Axle Company 6/5, 12/16
Timken Roller Bearing Company 1/1, 2/26, 4/3, 4/21, 4/25, 6/5, 6/11,
    8/10, 8/22, 8/28, 9/20, 10/14
Tiona Petroleum Company 10/26
Todd Motors Corporation Ltd. 5/1
Tokyo Ishikawajima Shipbuilding & Engineering Company, Ltd. 4/9
Torbensen Gear & Axle Company 7/28
Toyoda Automatic Loom Works 8/18
Toyo Kogyo Company, Ltd. 1/28, 1/30, 2/27, 3/17, 4/8, 4/25, 5/1,
    7/4, 8/6, 10/12, 11/1, 11/15, 11/30
Toyota Motor Company, Ltd. 2/17, 3/27, 4/18, 6/3, 6/10, 7/1, 8/18,
    8/28, 10/13, 10/30, 11/27, 12/8
Toyota Motor Corporation 7/1, 7/10, 8/6
Toyota Motor Corporation Australia Ltd. 9/12
Toyota Motor Finland Oy 11/1
Toyota Motor Manufacturing Canada Inc. 10/10
Toyota Motor Manufacturing USA 8/4
Toyota Motor Philippines Corporation 8/2

Toyota Motor Sales Company 7/1
Toyota USA 8/24
Toyota Zimbabwe (Pvt.) Ltd. 10/12
Travelers Insurance Company 2/1
Treser Automobiltechnik und Design 1/1
Trinidad Oil Company 7/17
Tri-Wheel Motor Company 1/18, 3/15, 6/22, 12/23
Trumbull Motor Car Company 5/7
TRW Inc. 1/2, 10/4
Tucker Automobile Club 7/19
Tucker Corporation 3/3, 3/21
Tung-Sol Electric Company 11/16
T.V.R. Engineering Ltd. 1/4
Twentieth Century Motor Car Company 4/12, 8/14
Twentieth Century Motor Company, Ltd. 11/23
20/Ghost Club 5/26
Twin Coach Company 4/5, 9/14

UAW-Ford National Development and Training Center 9/28
Union Oil Company 6/21, 8/1
Union Oil Company of California 1/16, 3/18, 6/13, 6/22, 6/27, 7/6,
    10/17, 10/19
Uniroyal, Inc. 2/27, 3/30, 11/23
United Automobile, Aerospace, and Agricultural Implement Workers
    of America (UAW) 1/1, 1/10, 1/14, 1/22, 2/11, 2/14, 2/15, 3/14,
    3/20, 4/18, 5/9, 5/13, 5/18, 5/26, 6/9, 6/14, 6/20, 8/6, 8/15, 8/23,
    9/1, 10/4, 10/11, 10/16, 12/18, 12/28
United Engine & Machine Company 8/30
United Motors Corporation 5/11, 12/31
United States Axle Company 4/11
United States Auto Club (USAC) 2/18, 4/23, 6/1, 6/14, 7/1, 7/3, 7/22,
    8/18, 9/16, 9/28, 10/21, 12/18
United States Gauge Company 7/7, 7/15
United States Leasing International 11/18
United States Motor Company 1/11, 9/12
United States Rubber Company 1/25, 2/19, 2/27, 3/30, 8/16, 12/22,
    12/30
Universal Motor Oils Company 8/19
Universal Oil Products Company 5/8, 5/29
University of Illinois 1/10
University of Michigan 9/1, 9/7
Unocal Corporation 3/18, 4/1
Upton Motor Company 12/30
Urals Automotive Plant 7/8
U. S. Ball Bearing Manufacturing Company 1/23

Vacuum Oil Company Ltd. 3/31, 4/2, 5/13, 12/1
Valeo SA 12/22
Vanadium Corporation of America 6/18
Vanden Plas (England) Ltd. 2/26, 3/13, 4/21, 5/6, 6/17
Vanden Plas (England) 1923 Ltd. 7/2, 9/8
Van Doorne's Automobielfabrik NV 1/31, 5/3
Van Doorne's Bedrifswagenfabrick Daf B.V. 4/3
Van Doorne's Personenautofabriek Daf B.V. 10/11
Van Horn's Truck Museum 5/6
Vauxhall Motors Ltd. 3/27, 7/1
Vauxhall Motors (1914) Ltd. 5/12
Veeder Manufacturing Company 1/31, 9/4
Velie Carriage Company 2/6, 6/1
Velie Motor Corporation 2/23, 11/27, 11/29
Velie Motor Vehicle Company 7/2
Verein Deutscher Ingenieure 1/1
Veteran Car Club 6/7, 9/18, 11/14
Veteran Motor Car Club of America 3/13, 8/19, 8/24, 12/2
Vickers Son & Company Ltd. 4/17, 6/25
Villanova University 6/7
Virginia Museum of Fine Arts 10/13
Volga Automobile Works 1/9, 3/24
Volkswagen de Mexico 1/15
Volkswagen Manufacturing Corporation of America 7/31
Volkswagen of America 4/19, 4/29, 7/31
Volkswagen USA 9/27
Volkswagenwerk AG 1/3, 1/10, 3/26, 3/28, 4/23, 5/9, 5/28, 7/1, 9/6,

9/13, 9/15, 9/24, 10/1, 10/8, 11/13, 11/29, 12/20
AB Volvo 1/1, 1/5, 1/31, 4/28, 7/31, 9/13, 10/11, 10/20, 10/27, 12/2, 12/11, 12/16, 12/19, 12/20

Wagenhals Motor Car Company 9/27
Wagner Electric Corporation 1/15, 3/20, 7/18, 10/30, 12/8
Wahl Motor Company 10/8
C. C. Wakefield & Company Ltd. 1/15
Walker Body Company 3/10, 8/24
Walkerville Wagon Company 10/10
Walter Automobile Company 1/1, 5/31
Walter Car Company 1/1
Walter Treser Automobilbau GmbH 8/26
Waltham Manufacturing Company 8/3, 10/30
Wanderer-Werke AG 1/1
Wankel GmbH 7/4
Ward, Hayden & Satterlee 9/10
Ward LaFrance Truck Corporation 2/15
Ward Motor Vehicle Company 6/35, 10/18, 11/11
Warner Gear Company 3/30, 4/1, 5/9, 8/16
Warner Instrument Company 3/13, 3/22
Warren Motor Car Company 6/11, 11/21
Waukesha Motor Company 1/4, 1/7, 3/28, 4/8, 5/31, 8/20, 8/31
Wausau Motor Parts Company 6/4
Wayne Corporation 3/19
Wayne Works, Inc. 11/1
Weidely Motors Company 12/14
Welch Motor Car Company 1/5, 4/1
West Bend Aluminum Company 2/29
Westcott Motor Car Company 1/11, 7/18
Western Auto Supply Company 4/7, 5/14
Western Motor Car Company 2/22
Western Reserve Historical Society 10/20
Wheeler-Schebler Carburetor Company 10/3
White Company 12/28
White Consolidated Industries, Inc. 1/31, 6/21
White Motor Company 1/3, 1/8, 1/11, 2/26, 2/29, 3/7, 3/11, 4/1, 4/9, 4/10, 4/20, 4/26, 4/27, 5/3, 5/8, 5/24, 6/1, 6/2, 6/30, 7/1, 7/8, 7/16, 8/4, 8/8, 8/17, 8/21, 8/25, 9/1, 9/4, 9/8, 9/17, 9/29, 10/18, 10/25, 10/26, 11/2, 11/3, 11/7, 12/6, 12/8, 12/14, 12/23, 12/28
White Motor Company of Canada 11/21
White Sewing Machine Company 7/5, 7/6
J. C. Whitney & Company 6/25
Wickes Companies 1/14
Willard Storage Battery Company 1/26, 1/27, 2/3, 3/18, 5/30, 9/6
William Foster & Company Ltd. 9/6
Wills Sainte Claire, Inc. 9/24
Willys Motors Inc. 2/20, 2/26, 3/7, 3/15, 5/4
Willys-Overland Company 1/6, 1/10, 1/16, 1/18, 1/19, 2/12, 2/15, 2/27, 3/10, 3/11, 3/21, 3/23, 4/14, 4/20, 4/22, 4/23, 4/28, 5/11, 5/17, 5/19, 5/30, 7/13, 7/14, 7/23, 7/24, 9/1, 9/21, 10/15, 11/1, 11/3, 11/5, 11/13, 11/15, 11/16, 11/17, 11/18, 11/30, 12/12, 12/23
Willys-Overland do Brasil 10/9
Willys-Overland Ltd. 12/29
C. R. Wilson Body Company 8/14
Wilson Foundry & Machine Company 6/1
Winnebago Industries, Inc. 2/28
Winton Engine Company 6/30
Winton Motor Car(riage) Company 2/11, 3/1, 3/5, 4/1, 10/4
Wire Wheel Corporation 4/9
Wisconsin Duplex Auto Company 5/1
Wolseley Motors Ltd. 7/1
Wright-Martin Aircraft Corporation 12/17
W. R. M. Motors, Ltd. 3/28, 10/10
Wyman-Gordon Company 5/21, 11/4, 12/20

Yale University 4/16
Yanama Diesel Company 2/25
Yellow Cab Company 4/10, 5/29, 8/25, 10/8
Yellow Cab Manufacturing Company 1/2, 1/31, 3/31, 6/29, 8/17, 8/26
Yellow Truck & Coach Manufacturing Company 7/14, 7/23, 8/26, 9/1, 9/30, 10/1, 11/30

Yeovil Motor Car & Cycle Company 11/5
York Noble Industries Ltd. 10/30
Yorkshire Motor Car Company, Ltd. 9/25
Young & Rubicon 12/15

Zavod Imieni Likhacheva 3/26, 6/26
Zavod Imieni Molotova 6/14
Zavod Imieni Stalina 6/15, 6/26
Zenith Carburetor Company 4/7, 9/15
Zenith Radio Corporation 3/11, 5/15
Zeran Automobile Factory 11/6
Zimmer Corporation 5/10
ZSB Engineering Company 11/11

INDEX 3 - PERSONAL NAMES

Names are listed per most common usage. As a general rule full names, when known, are recorded only with the birth entry in the main text of the book. Entries marked with an asterisk (*) are birth dates, while those marked with a plus sign (+) are death dates.

Aaltonen, Rauno 1/17*
Abarth, Carlo 11/15* 11/23+
Abate, Carlo 7/10*
Abecassis, George 3/21* 12/18+
Abell, Rollin 11/22+
Abernethy, Roy 1/9, 2/12, 2/28+ 9/29* 11/15
Abodaher, David J. 2/1*
Abrams, Frank W. 6/24* 7/17+ 7/18
Abresch, Charles 4/28+
Abs, Hermann J. 10/15*
Acheson, Kenneth 11/27*
Ackerman, Paul C. 11/4*
Ackroyd, John 10/4
Adair, Neal G. 2/22+
Adamich, Andrea de 10/3*
Adamowicz, Tony 5/2*
Adams, Comfort A. 2/21+ 11/1*
Adams, Drury 12/1+
Adams, Joseph E. 2/26*
Adams, Kenneth S. 3/30+ 8/31*
Adams, Philippe 11/19*
Adams, Ralph L. 1/20+
Adams, Ruth 4/22
Adamson, John F. 2/16*
Adcox, Grant 11/19+
Addy, Frederick S. 1/1*
Adelman, Sam 1/23+
Ader, Clement 4/2* 5/8, 9/3
Ader, Walt 11/25+ 12/15*
Adolff, Kurt 11/5*
Agabashian, Fred 8/21* 10/13+
Agajanian, J. C. 5/5+ 6/16*
Agg, Thomas R. 5/7+ 5/17*
Agnelli, Edoardo 7/14+
Agnelli, Gianni 3/12* 12/11
Agnelli, Giovanni 4/9, 7/1, 7/11, 7/14, 8/13*
    12/16+
Agnelli, Umberto 11/1*
Ahrens, Don E. 7/10, 12/1, 12/31*
Ahrens, Hermann 3/14* 9/12
Ahrens, Kurt Jr. 4/19*
Aiello, Lauent 5/23*
Aitken, John 9/4, 12/8+
Akin, Bob 3/6*
Albert, Paul 5/15+
Alboreto, Michele 12/23*
Alborn, Frank 1/3+
Alcock, Tony 11/29+
Alden, Herbert W. 11/10+ 12/20*
Alderman, Frank R. 8/5
Aldington, H. J. 8/17
Aldred, J. E. 11/21+
Aldrich, Fred A. 1/1, 8/9
Alesi, Jean 6/11*
Alexander, Donald 6/21* 7/20+
Alexander, Henry C. 8/1*
Alfonso XIII 2/28+ 5/17*
Alger, Russell 1/24+ 2/27* 9/8
Algie, John 4/11+
Allam, Jeff 12/19*
Allard, Sydney 4/12+
Allday, G. James 6/7+

Allen, Carl E. 3/13*
Allen, Carlos H. 2/8+
Allen, George B. 7/1
Allen, Loy 4/7*
Allen, Michael 1/1
Allen, R. W. 11/21
Allen, W. D. 5/22+
Alley, Tom 5/30
Alliot, Philippe 5/24, 7/27*
Allison, Bobby 2/25, 6/1, 6/19, 12/3*
Allison, Cliff 2/8* 5/18, 6/18
Allison, Davey 2/25* 5/3, 7/13+
Allison, Donnie 9/7*
Allison, James A. 2/9, 8/15, 9/12
Allison, Mike 7/4*
Allison, Robert 3/21, 4/1
Allison, William D. 12/12
Allman, Scott 3/2
Altenau, Alan G. 5/16*
Althouse, C. W. 7/4
Alzen, Uwe 8/18*
Amati, Giovanna 7/20*
Ambrose, Arthur W. 4/20* 12/28+
Ambrosini, Renato 11/14+
Ames, Azel 11/23+
Ames, D. J. 10/11
Ames, Harold T. 2/16* 6/2+ 6/15, 7/19
Amick, George 4/9+ 10/24*
Ammann, Othmar H. 3/26* 9/22+
Amon, Chris 4/26, 4/28, 6/9, 6/18, 7/20*
Anderson, Alvin B. 10/1
Anderson, Bob 5/19* 8/14+
Anderson, Eugene I. 10/5*
Anderson, Gary 3/10
Anderson, Geordie 6/6+
Anderson, Gil 4/18, 10/9
Anderson, Harry W. 11/18+ 12/25*
Anderson, Iain M. 5/11*
Anderson, J. G. 11/17*
Anderson, John W. 9/28+ 10/23*
Anderson, Joseph A. 2/26*
Anderson, O. L. 12/29+
Anderson, Robert 11/2*
Anderson, Wayne 10/8*
Anderson, William P. 12/17
Anderson, Wingate M. 3/22+
Andersson, Conny 12/28*
Andersson, Peggan 8/15*
Andreini, Joseph I. 3/1*
Andres, Emil 7/22*
Andretti, Aldo 2/28*
Andretti, John 3/12*
Andretti, Mario 2/28* 4/1, 4/25, 9/22, 10/5,
    10/24
Andretti, Michael 10/5*
Andrew, J. Ernest 9/19+
Andrews, Allen 4/25*
Andrews, Archie M. 4/7, 4/16, 6/27+ 10/19
Andrews, D. A. 10/3+
Andrews, Keith 5/15+ 6/15*
Andrey, Gaston 8/8*
Andruet, Jean-Claude 8/13*

Angelelli, Max 12/15*
Angelis, Elio de 3/26* 5/15+
Angell, Chester M. 9/29+
Angell, William R. 1/25+ 2/10*
Anglada, Joseph A. 1/29* 5/1, 12/14+
Angle, Glenn D. 1/5* 1/26+
Anibal, Benjamin 1/1, 1/24, 3/2, 3/15, 6/22+
    12/8
Anthony, Earle C. 2/22, 3/10, 8/6+ 9/19, 12/18*
Apicella, Marco 10/7*
Apperson, Edgar 5/12+ 10/3*
Apperson, Elmer 3/28+ 5/25, 6/12, 7/4, 8/13*
Apperson, Mrs. Elmer 6/12
Arbib, Richard 2/22+ 3/29, 12/1
Arbuckle, Samuel F. 10/12+
Archer, Thomas P. 3/1* 8/10+
Arfons, Art 2/3* 10/2, 10/5, 10/27, 11/7, 11/12,
    11/17
Arfons, Craig 7/9+
Arfons, Walt 7/9
Argetsinger, Cameron 10/2
Arkus-Duntov, Zora 4/21+ 5/1, 7/2, 12/25*
Armstrong, Douglas 3/22*
Armstrong, Frank G. 9/19*
Armstrong, Frank T. 1/15+
Armstrong, J. C. R. 4/15+
Arnheim, Alvin J. 4/17+
Arno, Peter 1/8* 2/23+
Arnold, Billy 11/11+
Arnold, Charles F. 9/1
Arnold, Fred 5/4
Arnold, O. L. 10/27
Arnold, Walter 1/28
Arnold, William 11/13
Arnolt, Wacky 4/28* 10/1, 12/24+
Arnoux, Rene 5/21, 7/4*
Artese, Alessandro 8/1
Arthur, Paul 11/15
Artioli, Romano 9/14, 12/5*
Artzet, Didier 2/10*
Arundell, Peter 4/3, 11/8*
Ascari, Alberto 1/18, 3/27, 4/28, 5/26+ 6/27,
    6/28, 7/13* 9/3, 9/28, 10/26
Ascari, Antonio 5/6, 6/9, 6/28, 7/13, 7/26+
    8/16, 9/15*
Ash, L. David 2/6, 9/10
Ashdown, Peter 10/16*
Ashley, David 4/5*
Ashley, Ian 10/26*
Ashmore, Gerry 7/25*
Askins, Wallace B. 6/2*
Aslund, Peter 11/22*
Assheton, Edward (Lord Howe) 3/25
Aston, Bill 3/4+ 3/29*
Atkins, Dick 11/13+
Atterbury, George W. 9/26*
Attwood, Richard 4/4*
Atwood, Donald J. 1/25, 5/25* 12/1
Auberlen, Bill 10/12*
Augieres 11/17
Ault, Thomas J. 6/23*
Aument, Carroll 2/23
Auspitzer, Julius 3/31

Austin, Herbert 1/3, 5/23+ 6/22, 11/8*
Austin, Walter S. 1/8, 3/31, 5/9+
Austria, Art 10/17
Auten, James E. 7/8* 10/1+
Averell, S. G. 6/23
Averill, David M. 1/1, 7/17+
Averill, Frank B. 12/13+
Avery, Clarence W. 2/15* 4/17, 5/13+ 10/3
Avrin, Gary 7/14+
Aycock, Nathaniel M. 1/11+
Ayrton, William E. 11/8+
Ayukawa, Yoshisuke 12/19
Ayulo, Manuel 5/17+ 10/20*

Babbitt, Isaac 5/26+ 7/26*
Babcock, Irving B. 6/25* 9/1
Babitch, Abraham M. 5/25+
Bacciagaluppi, Giuseppe 6/29
Bache, J. S. 11/9*
Bachelart, Eric 2/28*
Bachelle, Otto von 11/8
Bachman, B. B. 10/4*
Bacon, Elbridge F. 12/15+
Bacon, John H. 4/2* 8/14+
Bacon, Irving R. 11/21+ 11/29*
Bacon, Matthew 10/1+
Badder, Luca 1/25*
Badger, Floyd E. 12/9+
Baghetti, Giancarlo 4/5, 6/9, 6/20, 12/25*
Bagley, Tom 12/3*
Bailey, Bertram 2/12
Bailey, Edwin W. M. 3/6+ 4/18*
Bailey, Julian 10/9*
Bailey, Robert M. 4/8*
Baillairge, Charles 5/10+ 9/29*
Bain, Lowell S. 5/10*
Baird, Craig 7/22*
Baits, Stuart G. 8/28*
Baker, Arthur 4/22*
Baker, Buck 3/4*
Baker, Buddy 1/25* 3/24, 5/2
Baker, Cannon Ball 3/12* 5/5, 5/10+ 5/18,
    7/29, 9/12
Baker, G. L. 8/7
Baker, Hines H. 9/22*
Baker, Kim 3/2
Baker, S. Frank 5/17+
Baker, Walter C. 4/26+ 6/27* 10/27
Baker, Mrs. Walter C. 10/27
Baker, Warren L. 5/9*
Baker, Wayne 12/18*
Bakken, James K. 4/17*
Balderston, William 7/25+ 12/13*
Baldi, Mauro 1/31*
Baldwin, Jack 5/31*
Baldwin, Leonard C. 11/26+
Balestrero, Renato 4/18
Ball, Bobby 2/27+ 8/26*
Ball, F. C. 2/5
Ball, Frank H. 5/21* 11/12+
Ball, Fred O. 11/12
Ball, Frederick W. 4/9, 12/11
Ballabio, Fulvio 10/8*
Ballard, J. H. 12/28+
Ballenger, William S. 2/28+ 10/30, 12/5*
Ballot, Ernest 7/4, 12/24
Ballot-Lena, Claude 8/4*
Balmer, Bomber 6/7, 12/13*
Balough, Charles 1/24+ 2/13*
Balough, Gary 9/16*
Ballot, Ernest 1/5
Balsa, Marcel 1/1* 8/3, 8/11+

Balzer, Stephen M. 12/15
Bandini, Lorenzo 4/5, 5/10+ 9/28, 12/21*
Banker, Oscar H. 5/31*
Banks, Henry 6/14* 12/18+
Banks, John V. 1/17*
Banks, Robert L. 1/3+ 11/24*
Banks, Warwick 7/12*
Banting, Rod 5/31*
Baracca, Count 6/17
Baracca, Countess 6/17
Baras, P. 11/13
Barbazza, Fabrizio 4/2*
Barber, Amzi Lorenzo 6/17, 6/22*
Barber, Bob 8/19
Barber, John 4/22*
Barber, Skip 11/16*
Barberis, F. F. 7/16*
Barbieri, Cesare 5/25+
Barcella, Ernest L. 6/7*
Barenyi, Bela 1/23
Barford, V. G. 9/6+
Barilla, Paolo 4/20*
Barit, A. E. 2/25, 3/13, 5/1, 5/21, 6/16, 7/14+
    8/30*
Barke, Allen 4/16*
Barker, Carl 5/18*
Barker, Frederick W. 7/8+ 12/18*
Barley, Albert C. 8/7
Barnard, Harry 8/26+ 9/5*
Barnato, Woolf 3/2, 3/5, 6/22, 7/27+
Barnes, Claire L. 1/16+
Barnes, Fuller F. 6/18+
Barnes, Henry A. 9/16+ 12/16*
Barrett, N. S. 8/27*
Barrett, Stan 12/17
Barrett, Tom H. 8/13*
Barrett, William F. 3/15*
Barrichello, Rubens 5/23* 8/28
Barringer, George 9/1+
Barrington, T. B. 12/7
Barron, D. D. 6/7*
Barrow, Clyde 5/23+
Barrow, L. T. 6/16*
Barry, James P. 10/23*
Barsanti, Eugenio 10/19
Barson, John 8/11
Bartels, Michael 3/8*
Barth, Edgar 5/20+ 8/2, 11/26*
Barth, Jurgen 12/10*
Barthel, Oliver E. 8/28+ 10/3*
Bartlett, Kevin 5/25*
Barvajel 9/29
Bassett, Harry H. 1/13, 5/1, 9/11* 10/17+
Bassett, William H. 7/21+
Bassi, Giorgio 1/20*
Batchelder, C. K. 7/9+
Batchelor, Dean 11/21+
Bates, Baron K. 10/25*
Bates, Donald E. 4/17
Bates, George H. 2/3*
Batten, Norman 5/30, 11/12+
Battenberg, J. T. III 4/24
Bauer, Erwin 6/2+ 7/17*
Bauer, John 9/14*
Bauer, Rudolf 4/25
Bauer, Wilhelm 3/30+
Bauman, John N. 3/11*
Baumann, Gustave 6/27*
Baxter, C. Kenneth 8/17*
Bayliff, Bud 5/4
Bayol, Elie 2/28*
Bazin, F. 8/8

Beach, Charles S. 10/26+
Beach, William N. 1/22
Beacham, Charles R. 6/17*
Beachey, Lincoln 1/10
Beal, W. Hubert 3/3+ 11/12
Beall, F. F. 4/6+ 9/15*
Beam, Herman 4/29
Beamer, George R. 7/7* 7/15+
Beardslee, Charles S. 11/20
Beardsley, Paul R. 12/20
Beat, Fehr 6/18+
Beauchamp, Albert 9/14+
Beaufort, Carel de 4/10* 8/3+
Beaujon, Michel 1/25
Beauman, Don 7/9+ 7/26*
Beaver, Harry C. 4/2+ 8/13*
Bechem, Gunther 12/21*
Becker, Burton A. 7/10+
Becker, Helmut 7/24*
Bedard, Patrick 8/20*
Bedford, Thomas A. 2/7*
Beeckmans, Johan Jan 12/22*
Beecroft, David 11/5+
Beekhuis, Jon 3/31*
Begg, Russell S. 12/23+
Begole, Charles M. 10/30, 11/1
Behra, Jean 2/16* 7/28, 8/1+
Beickler, Ferdinand P. J. 1/22, 11/2*
Beissbarth 4/14
Belas, Francois-Zavier 12/13
Belcher, Warren J. 12/1+
Belcourt, George A. 4/22* 5/31+ 7/5
Belden, E. H. 12/23*
Belfry, William G. 7/14*
Bell, Derek 3/13, 10/31*
Bell, Norman 4/28+
Bell, Norman H. 11/21*
Bellasi, Vittorio 8/16
Belloc, Jean-Philippe 4/24*
Bellof, Stefan 9/1+ 11/20*
Belmondo, Paul 4/23*
Belnap, Lamonte J. 8/10+ 11/7*
Belsey, Adrian 5/26
Belso, Tom 8/27*
Beltoise, Jean-Pierre 1/10, 2/29, 4/26* 7/1, 7/4
Beltz, John B. 1/25* 5/1, 5/14+
Benard, A. P. 8/19*
Bendix, Vincent H. 3/27+ 8/12* 12/18
Benjafield, John 8/6*
Bennett, Frederick Stanley 9/18
Bennett, Harry H. 1/4+ 1/17* 9/27
Bennett, James Gordon 5/10* 5/14+
Bennett, Roy F. 3/18*
Benneteau-Desgrois, Felix 5/9*
Benoist, Robert 3/21* 6/7, 6/20, 8/8, 9/14+
Benson, John R. 8/31*
Benson, Johnny 6/27*
Bentley, Alfred 6/29
Bentley, Alvin M. 4/10+ 8/30*
Bentley, H. M. 1/18, 2/14, 4/10+ 4/23, 5/1, 7/8
Bentley, Ross 11/4*
Bentley, W. O. 1/1, 1/15, 1/18, 2/14, 3/2, 4/10,
    4/19, 4/23, 5/1, 5/10, 6/8, 6/17, 7/8, 8/13+
    9/16* 10/31
Bentley, Mrs. W. O. (1) 1/1
Benton, Philip E. Jr. 3/1, 12/31*
Benton, William P. 11/4*
Benz, Carl 1/1, 1/29, 3/9, 4/4+ 4/21, 5/1, 5/5,
    7/3, 7/20, 8/9, 9/19, 10/1, 10/21, 10/25,
    11/25* 12/1, 12/31
Benz, Mrs. Carl 5/5+ 7/20
Benz, Eugen 3/9+ 5/1*

Benz, Richard 9/19+ 10/21*
Beretta, Olivier 11/23*
Berg, Allen 8/1*
Berg, Edward E. 4/6+
Berg, Egon G. 4/3+
Berg, Hart O. 12/6+
Bergdoll, Erwin 10/9
Berger, Fred H. 3/24+ 6/17*
Berger, Georges 8/23+ 9/14*
Berger, Gerhard 8/27* 10/12
Bergius, Walter 6/4+
Bernard, Eric 8/24*
Bernitt, Elmer W. 5/6*
Bernstein, David 6/10*
Berry, John H. 9/24*
Bertaggia, Enrico 6/19*
Bertone, Nuccio 2/25+
Bertram, Oliver 8/5
Bertrand, Edouard 10/25+
Berwick, F. W. 6/20
Besse, Georges 1/21, 11/17+ 12/25*
Besserdich, William A. 5/1, 9/7, 9/29, 12/29
Best, Frank A. 10/20+
Bethell, Alan F. 12/25*
Bettenhausen, Gary 11/18*
Bettenhausen, Tony (Sr.) 5/12+ 9/12*
Betti, John A. 1/6*
Betts, Charles L. 12/17*
Beuck, August 9/19
Beuttler, Mike 4/13* 12/29+
Beynon, Huw 12/10*
Beyreis, Don 2/6
Bezner, Frederick O. 2/28, 10/17+ 12/6
Bezy, Gregory A. 9/14+
Bianchi, Lucien 3/30+ 8/5, 11/10*
Bible, Lee 3/13+
Bicknell, George M. 10/11+
Biddle, William E. 1/21+
Bide, Austin 3/5, 9/11*
Bidwell, Bennett E. 2/4, 6/22*
Bieber, Owen 5/18, 10/4, 12/28*
Biela, Frank 2/8* 9/11
Bienfait, Johan 4/1
Bigalke, Werner 5/21
Bigelow, Charles 2/9
Bigelow, Tom 10/31*
Biggers, John D. 12/13+ 12/19*
Biggers, Robert L. 1/8*
Bijur, Joseph 10/19+
Bill, E. W. 12/2
Bill, Harry L. 4/15+
Billi, Giorgio 2/11
Billings, J. F. 1/1
Billings, L. B. 12/30+
Billman, Mark 5/30+
Binder, Hans 6/12*
Biondetti, Clemente 2/24+ 4/4, 10/18*
Bira, B. 7/15* 8/10, 12/23+
Bird, Anthony 4/26*
Bird, C. A. 7/3
Birge, Raymond B. 9/1
Birger, Pablo 1/6* 3/9+
Birkigt, Marc 3/8* 3/15+
Birkin, Tim 3/4, 6/22+ 6/29, 7/26*
Birla, G. P. 8/2*
Birnbaum, Hans 11/7
Birrell, Gerry 6/23+ 7/30*
Birtles, Francis 7/15, 10/19
Bisch, Art 7/6+ 11/10*
Bishop, Arthur G. 1/22+
Bishop, John 7/4
Bissell, Charles R. 12/13+

Bissell, Louis G. 5/17*
Bizzarini, Giotto 4/5, 6/6*
Black, Charles G. 9/28+
Black, Clarence A. 8/5
Black, Fred L. 1/26* 3/23+
Black, John P. 2/10*
Black, Keith 5/13+
Black, Robert F. 11/2*
Black, Stephen C. 10/5
Black, W. M. 5/9
Blackburn, Bunkie 4/22*
Blackburn, S. L. 2/27+ 5/22*
Blackmore, George 9/22
Blaine, James G. 1/10*
Blair, Benjamin H. 9/13+
Blair, Edwin Foster 2/9, 11/6+ 12/15*
Blair, James C. 1/9* 2/1+
Blake, John E. 11/8
Blakeslee, William S. Jr. 10/10*
Blanc, Jean 7/24+
Blanch, Edward J. 3/16*
Blanchard, Harold F. 12/29+
Blanchard, Harry 1/31+
Blanchard, Thomas 11/22
Bland, Edward 11/15
Bleekemolen, Michael 10/2*
Blees, R. W. 2/12
Bleicher, Clarence E. 3/25* 9/23+
Bliss, Carey S. 3/18+ 12/13*
Bliss, Henry B. 9/13+
Bliss, Mike 4/5*
Bliven, Frederick 9/12+
Bloch, Robert 4/18
Blomqvist, Stig 7/29*
Blomstrom, C. H. 3/1, 12/30
Blondyk, Trevor 11/30*
Blood, Arthur R. 10/1+
Blood, Howard E. 2/26*
Blood, Robert R. 6/12
Blood, Roderic M. 3/13+
Blundell, Mark 4/8*
Blythin, Robert 1/10* 3/21+
Bochroch, Albert R. 11/13*
Bock, Carl J. 4/2+
Boddie, William 7/31
Bodine, Brett 1/11*
Bodine, Geoff 4/18*
Bodine, Todd 2/27*
Bodley, Fred 1/23+
Bodman, Henry E. 3/3+ 3/10, 3/17, 8/8*
Boegehold, Alfred L. 10/31*
Boehringer, Hans A. 12/2+
Boerlage, G. D. 6/29+
Boesel, Raul 12/4*
Boesen, Victor 9/7*
Bogle, Henry C. 3/10, 5/1
Bohannon, James A. 11/1
Bohmrich, John J. 2/4*
Boillot, Andre 6/10+
Boillot, Georges 5/21+
Boillot, Jean 10/19
Boisset, Yves 1/4, 3/18
Bojalad, Joe 1/5
Bollee, Amedee Jr. 10/31
Bollee, Amedee Sr. 11/15
Bollman, Jim 7/7
Bolster, John 1/13+
Bolton, Peter 6/20
Bombardier, J. A. 6/23
Bonaparte, Napoleon 4/20
Bond, Colin 8/15*
Bond, Elaine 4/5+ 11/27*

Bond, Frank A. 7/3+
Bond, John R. 7/20+ 7/25*
Bondurant, Bob 4/27*
Bonetto, Felice 6/9* 11/21+
Bonner, Clarence E. 7/15
Bonnet, Rene 12/27*
Bonnett, Clyde E. 12/7+
Bonnett, Neil 2/11+ 7/30*
Bonnier, Jo 1/31* 4/9, 5/31, 6/11+
Bonomi, Roberto 9/30*
Booher, Joe 2/12+
Bookout, John F. Jr. 12/31*
Boole, David 1/30+
Booth, Carlos C. 11/19+ 12/1*
Booth, Clarence H. 10/17
Booth, George G. 9/24+ 11/1
Booth, James Scripps 5/31* 9/13+ 10/3
Booth, William N. 11/9+
Boothby, Clinton R. 1/28+
Bordinat, Gene 2/10* 8/11+
Bordino, Pietro 4/15+ 9/3, 9/4, 11/26+
Borel, Jean-Marc 9/6*
Borg, George W. 2/21+ 10/24*
Borgeson, Griffith 12/21*
Borghese, Scipione 8/10
Borgudd, Tommy 11/25*
Borgward, Carl F. W. 2/2, 7/28+ 8/10, 11/10*
Borzacchini, Baconin 9/10+ 9/28*
Bosch, Robert 3/9+ 9/23* 9/24
Boston, C. F. 10/26
Botha, Luki 1/16*
Bott, Frederick V. 1/19+
Bott, George R. 8/14+
Bott, Helmut 5/14+ 8/23*
Bouchut, Christophe 9/24*
Boudarel, Albert 9/19*
Bouillon, Pierre ("Levegh") 12/22*
Boullion, Jules 2/6*
Bourdelle, Emil A. 10/8
Bourque, William A. 8/19+
Bourquin, James F. 4/9* 7/1+
Bouton, Georges 1/1, 4/28, 11/22*
Boutsen, Thierry 7/13*
Bouwer, Gerry 2/6, 6/4
Bowden, Charles L. 10/4+ 11/9*
Bowden, Gregory Houston 7/1*
Bowden, Herbert L. 1/25
Bowditch, Frederick W. 11/17*
Bowe, John 4/16*
Bowen, Lem W. 7/12* 8/22
Bower, Ferdinand A. 6/7
Bowles, James T-B 3/20* 11/28+
Bown, Jim 6/24*
Bowser, Phillip C. 12/17
Bowsher, Jack 10/2*
Boyd, Alan S. 10/15
Boyd, Johnny 8/19*
Boyd, Thomas A. 12/9
Boyd, Virgil E. 1/1, 2/20
Boyer, Harold R. 2/25*
Boyer, Joe 5/30, 9/1+
Boyer, Joseph 10/24+
Boyer, Robert A. 9/30* 11/11+
Bozic, Milivoj 8/7
Brabazon, Lord 2/8* 5/17+
Brabham, David 3/27, 9/5*
Brabham, Gary 3/29*
Brabham, Geoff 3/20*
Brabham, Jack 3/20, 3/29, 4/2* 5/2, 5/12, 7/16, 8/5, 8/27, 9/5, 10/6
Bracco, Giovanni 6/6* 8/6+
Brack, Bill 12/26*

Brack, Kenny 3/21*
Bradfield, H. C. 8/20
Bradley, Albert 4/2, 5/29* 8/31, 9/11+
Bradley, James J. 11/27+
Bradley, Thomas M. 3/8, 7/11
Bradley, W. F. 3/8* 10/6+
Bradshaw, Theron 10/3+
Brady, Curtis P. 11/27
Brady, James J. 2/28, 3/9
Bragg, Caleb 10/24+
Brakov, Yevgeny A. 3/26
Braley, Witt H. 6/16+
Bramberry, Harry M. Sr. 1/11+
Brambilla, Tino 1/31* 11/11
Brambilla, Vittorio 11/11*
Bramley, Matthew F. 1/4* 5/30+
Bramwell, Frederick 3/7* 11/30+ 12/10
Branca, Toni 5/10+ 9/15*
Brancatelli, Gianfranco 1/18*
Brandon, Eric 7/18* 8/8+
Branitzki, Heinz 4/23*
Bransome, Edwin D. 6/18*
Branson, Don 6/2* 11/12+
Brassfield, Darin 9/16*
Brauchitsch, Manfred von 5/15, 6/3, 8/15* 9/3
Brauer, Arthur C. 10/18+
Braunsdorff, R. K. 11/16+
Brayton, George 4/2, 6/2, 12/17+
Brayton, Scott 2/20* 4/30, 5/17+
Breadon, Sam 5/10+ 7/26*
Breech, Ernest R. 1/2, 1/25, 2/24* 7/1, 7/3+
 7/13, 10/19
Breedlove, Craig 3/23* 8/5, 10/13, 10/15, 10/26,
 11/2, 11/4, 11/15
Breedlove, Lee Ann Roberts 11/4
Breer, Carl M. 4/30, 7/14, 11/8* 11/15, 12/21+
Breese, Sidney S. 7/7
Breeze, Robert P. 5/6* 7/16+
Breitschwerdt, Werner 7/13, 9/23*
Brennan, Martin J. 5/30+
Brett, Riley 2/4+
Brewer, Edward E. 7/19* 8/9+
Brewer, Robert W. A. 12/6+
Brewster, Henry 5/19* 9/19+
Brewster, James 8/6* 11/22+
Brewster, James B. 3/9+ 6/8*
Brewster, William (1) 6/2* 9/1, 11/25+
Brewster, Mrs. William 9/1
Brewster, William (2) 5/12* 8/1+
Bricherasio, E. C. di 7/1, 8/25* 10/10+
Bricker, Mead L. 1/28+ 4/24*
Bricklin, Malcolm 4/15, 12/12
Bridger, Tommy 6/24* 7/30+
Bridges, Calvin B. 1/11* 12/27+
Briggs, A. H. 3/15
Briggs, Clare E. 8/25*
Briggs, Claude S. 3/1+ 8/13* 9/3
Briggs, George T. 10/3+
Briggs, Leon E. 1/31*
Briggs, Walter O. 1/17+ 2/27*
Briggs, Walter O. Jr. 1/20* 7/3+
Bright, Rinehart S. 5/21*
Brilli-Peri, Gastone 3/22+ 3/24*
Briling, N. R. 3/15+ 10/1*
Brimble, Ray 11/29+
Brindle, Melbourne 11/18*
Brinker, John H. 5/31* 9/16+
Brion, Adolph E. 1/25+ 3/19*
Briscoe, Benjamin 5/24* 6/21, 6/27+ 7/4
Brise, Tony 3/28* 11/29+
Bristow, Chris 6/19+ 12/2+
Brittain, Harry 2/18, 7/9+ 12/24*

Britten, Clyde H. 4/5+
Brivio, Antonio 12/27*
Broad, Michael 9/28
Broad, Tom 9/25
Broadley, Eric 5/20
Brock, Peter 8/17*
Brockbank, Russell 4/13*
Brockway, George A. 3/26* 9/1
Brodie, George H. 9/1*
Broeker, Peter 5/15* 10/6
Broers, Samuel 1/1*
Bronson, A. E. 5/26+
Brooks, George A. 5/11*
Brooks, Gerard W. 7/13*
Brooks, John 12/5*
Brooks, Tony 2/25* 7/20, 10/23
Brotje, Robert J. Jr. 4/18*
Brotz, Anton F. Sr. 4/13+
Brough, George 1/12+
Brough, James 8/14*
Brougham, Henry Peter 5/7+ 9/19*
Browaldh, Tore 8/23*
Brown, Alan 11/20*
Brown, Alexander T. 12/20
Brown, Barton 9/21*
Brown, Bruce K. 3/2+ 5/4*
Brown, D. Carlton 2/2
Brown, David 5/10*
Brown, Dick 6/13+
Brown, Donaldson 2/1* 10/2+
Brown, E. A. 1/9
Brown, Edwin F. 1/26*
Brown, Frank L. 10/14+
Brown, George H. 3/1
Brown, George L. 3/17*
Brown, H. A. 3/1, 6/5*
Brown, J. L. 5/26
Brown, John 3/6
Brown, John L. Jr. 3/10*
Brown, R. K. 10/1
Brown, Samuel 5/27
Brown, W. W. 6/14+ 7/17
Brown, Walt 7/29+ 12/30*
Brown, Warwick 12/24*
Brown, Will H. 4/2+
Browne, Arthur B. 9/16+ 11/29*
Brownell, Dave 2/17*
Browning, Albert J. 7/2+ 9/27*
Brownlie, William 9/7+
Bruce, James G. 3/27+
Bruce, Mildred 12/9
Bruce, Victor 12/9
Bruce-Brown, David 3/23, 10/4+ 10/12
Brudes, Adolf 10/15* 11/5+
Bruhn, Richard 6/29
Brumbaugh, A. K. 6/29+ 12/29*
Brundage, Jim 3/8*
Brundle, Martin 6/1* 6/21
Brunei, Sultan of 12/17
Bruner, Johnny 2/19*
Brunn, Hermann A. 9/21+
Brunn, Hermann C. 1/1* 9/27+
Brush, Alanson P. 2/2, 2/10* 3/6+ 3/29, 8/28,
 10/17, 12/15
Brush, Mrs. Alanson P. 3/29
Brush, W. A. 11/9*
Brussel, John W. 2/11
Bryan, Jimmy 1/28* 5/30, 6/19+ 6/29
Bryant, E. E. 5/15
Bryant, Peter 4/3*
Bryant, Thos L. 6/15*
Bryce, James W. 3/27+ 9/5*

Bucci, Clemar 9/4*
Buchholzer, Carl E. 11/27*
Buck, David 8/25+
Buck, Fred 7/6
Buckendale, L. Ray 4/19*
Buckert, William P. 7/17+
Buckingham, Earle 9/4*
Buckminster, Philip 2/20
Bucknum, Ronnie 4/5* 4/22+ 8/2, 10/13
Budd, Edward G. 6/17, 11/30+ 12/28*
Budd, Edward G. Jr. 3/23* 5/20+
Buddrus, Edward 8/1*
Budlong, Milton J. 7/6+
Bueb, Ivor 6/6* 8/1+
Buehrig, Gordon M. 1/22+ 1/28, 2/28, 5/17,
 6/5, 6/18*, 8/15, 8/28, 10/2, 11/7
Bugas, John S. 4/26* 12/2+
Bugatti, Carlo 2/16*
Bugatti, Ettore 2/16, 2/25, 3/14, 4/1, 4/11,
 4/15, 5/1, 5/25, 6/12, 6/26, 6/29, 7/1,
 7/31, 8/21+ 8/28, 9/1, 9/14, 9/15*, 10/12,
 10/16, 11/16, 11/21, 12/15, 12/22
Bugatti, Mrs. Ettore (1) 2/25, 7/21+ 12/4*
Bugatti, Mrs. Ettore (2) 10/12, 12/22*
Bugatti, Giuseppe 3/1*
Bugatti, Jean 1/15* 4/4, 8/11+
Bugatti, L'Ebe 7/31+ 11/21*
Bugatti, Rembrandt 1/8+ 10/16*
Bugatti, Roland 3/29+ 8/28* 11/21
Buhl, Charles 8/23+
Buhl, Robbie 9/2*
Buick, David D. 3/6+ 7/9, 8/1, 8/16, 9/17*
Buick, James G. 9/9*
Buick, Thomas 7/9
Buist, H. Massac 4/5+ 4/16*
Bullard, James H. 3/26+ 5/14*
Bullard, Stanley H. 3/23+ 7/4*
Bundy, Harry W. 6/2+
Buquor, A. P. 7/13+ 9/20*
Burch, Lyndon W. 2/9*
Burgaller, Ernst Gunther 7/15
Burger, Bob 5/1
Burgess, F. T. 1/18, 4/14, 11/30+ 12/7
Burgess, John W. 5/12+
Burgess, Ian 7/6*
Burgess, Magnus M. 8/14+ 12/7*
Burgin, R. S. 3/6+ 5/2*
Burke, C. E. 6/15
Burke, John J. 1/29+
Burke, John M. 6/21+ 11/5*
Burkhardt, Otto M. 1/21*
Burlingame, Abraham 2/9+
Burlingame, Byers A. 8/30+ 11/25
Burman, Bob 2/21, 4/8+ 4/23* 7/26, 9/7
Burnell, Max R. 9/19+ 10/6*
Burness, Tad 7/11*
Burnett, E. L. 7/8, 8/24
Burns, Hendry S. M. 4/28* 10/21+
Burns, Robert M. 11/8*
Burns, William T. 4/3+ 7/9*
Burr, E. E. 1/3
Burr, Reginald G. 6/2+
Burrows, William F. 4/27*
Burst, Carl W. 2/3, 4/7
Burt, Kelvin 9/7*
Burt, Patsy 9/14
Burton, Jeff 6/29*
Burton, Ward 10/25*
Burton, William M. 11/17* 12/29+
Burtsell, B. W. 1/1, 7/20+ 10/1, 11/18*
Busby, Jim 6/14*
Buschmann, Siegfried 7/12*

Bush, Earl J. 5/12*
Bush, Frederic A. 3/10* 10/9+
Bush, George 1/25
Busse, Ralph L. 11/8+
Bussinello, Roberto 10/4*
Busso, Guiseppe 1/3
Butler, Don 2/19+ 3/11*
Butler, Tobey 12/23*
Butterfield, H. K. 6/25
Butterworth, W. E. 11/10*
Buzard, Ralph M. 8/17*
Byrne, Charles 7/31
Byrne, Tommy 5/6*
Byroade, Henry A. 7/24*
Byron, Red 2/15, 4/14, 11/7+ 12/3*

Cabenelas, Sidonio 1/28+
Cabianca, Giulio 2/19* 6/15+
Cabral, Mario 1/15*
Cade, Phil 7/12*
Cadenet, Alain de 11/27*
Cadillac, Antoine de la Mothe 3/5* 10/18+
Caesar, Orville S. 5/22*
Caffi, Alex 3/18* 5/1
Cafiero, Eugene A. 3/1, 6/13* 7/8, 10/1
Cagno, Alessandro 5/2* 5/9, 6/29, 12/23+
Calderari, Enzo 4/18*
Caldwell, Philip 1/27* 2/1, 3/13, 4/14, 6/8,
    9/14, 10/1, 10/16, 10/29
Caldwell, Will M. 12/9*
Calhoun, Chad F. 8/6*
Caliri, Giacomo 4/7
Calkins, Buzz 5/2*
Calle, Chris 9/28
Calvet, Jacques 9/4, 9/19*
Calvo, Umberto 7/21*
Cameron, Everett S. 1/15, 10/27*
Cameron, Forrest F. 1/15
Cameron, Frederick 4/26+
Cameron, William J. 8/4+ 12/29*
Cameron, William T. 1/4+ 4/9*
Campari, Giuseppe 6/8* 6/13, 8/3, 9/10+
Campbell, Dewey H. 7/17+
Campbell, Donald 1/4+ 3/23* 7/17, 11/30
Campbell, Edwin R. 8/9
Campbell, Fred J. 2/10* 5/23+
Campbell, George N. 4/29, 8/6
Campbell, Henry F. 11/3
Campbell, Malcolm 2/4, 2/5, 2/19, 2/22, 2/24,
    3/7, 3/11* 3/23, 4/11, 6/17, 7/21, 9/3,
    9/17, 9/25, 11/30, 12/31+
Campbell, Theodore A. 4/29, 8/6
Campbell, Wallace R. 2/3* 8/10+
Campbell-Jones, John 1/21*
Campos, Adrian 6/17*
Campsall, Frank C. 1/2* 3/2, 3/16+ 6/1,
    12/24
Canaday, Ward M. 1/19, 2/27+ 5/19, 9/1,
    12/12*
Caniato, Alfredo 12/1
Cannon, John 6/21*
Cannon, Larry 4/13*
Cannon, Terry 4/1
Cantarella, Paolo 12/14
Cantlon, Shorty 5/30+
Capelli, Ivan 5/24* 9/7
Capelli, Pier Giorgio 6/22
Caplan, John D. 3/5*
Capolongo, James A. 10/28*
Cappy, Joseph E. 5/15, 11/27
Caracciola, Rudolf 1/28, 1/30* 4/7, 5/7, 5/15,
    6/19, 7/11, 7/18, 7/19, 7/24, 7/29, 8/29+

Caraffa, Gino 8/4+
Carbiener, Harvey D. 6/5+
Carcasci, Paulo 1/7*
Cardwell, James R. 10/27*
Carelli, Rick 11/9*
Carey, Bob 4/16+ 9/24*
Carhart, George C. 1/1+
Carhart, J. W. 12/21+
Carillo, Paul 1/25
Carini, Piero 3/6* 5/30+
Carkhuff, Stacy G. 4/14
Carlisle, Clifton H. 7/27+
Carlson, Billy 5/30, 7/5+
Carlson, Donald H. E. 8/25*
Carlson, Eric S. 1/2
Carlson, Gustav W. 10/10* 10/19+
Carlson, Lewis H. 8/1*
Carlson, Willie 7/4+
Carlsson, Erik 3/5* 3/15, 7/9, 12/27
Carlton, Clarence C. 5/17* 6/9+
Carmichael, G. Elizabeth 4/12, 5/28, 8/14
Carmichael, Harry J. 1/10, 3/1
Carney, Thomas 11/14+
Carnie, John A. 11/5+
Carnot, Nicolas 6/1* 8/24+
Carolin, E. R. 8/11+
Carpenter, Arthur W. 3/30*
Carpenter, Walter S. Jr. 1/8*
Carpenter, Walter W. 4/13+ 6/26*
Carpentier, Melbourne L. 10/18+
Carpentier, Patrick 8/13*
Carr, Ray 6/1
Carroll, Charles F. 5/16+
Carroll, Rick 6/22+
Carron, Harold G. 3/15+
Carruth, J. K. 3/2
Carter, Byron J. 1/18, 3/10, 4/6+ 5/31, 7/19,
    8/17*, 9/21, 9/26
Carter, Duane 5/5* 6/11+ 9/16
Carter, Howard O. 5/19
Carter, Jimmy 1/7
Carter, Ken 4/16
Carter, Pancho 6/11*
Cartwright, John P. 6/7*
Casaroll, Eugene A. 6/13* 6/28
Case, George S. Sr. 10/11+
Case, J. I. 12/11* 12/22+
Caserio, Martin J. 7/18* 10/1
Casner, Lucky 4/10+
Caspers, Albert 7/31
Casstevens, Bill 1/14
Casteele, Dennis 8/8+
Castellotti, Eugenio 1/16, 3/14+ 10/10*
Castiglioni, Camillo 8/13
Castle, Robert J. 10/21
Castles, Soapy 1/10* 4/1
Castoldi, Mario 2/26* 5/31+
Caton, John J. 5/16+
Cattaneo, Giustino 6/12, 6/26, 8/2* 11/10,
    11/23
Caughey, Frank T. 9/26
Cave, Henry 7/10* 11/30+
Cawthorne, George S. 2/19+ 11/2*
Caze, Robert la 2/26*
Cecotto, Johnny 1/25*
Cederleaf, Fred W. 9/24+
Ceirano, Ernesto 2/23+ 9/9*
Ceirano, Giovanni 10/1*
Ceirano, Giovanni Battista 3/30+ 6/14* 7/11
Ceirano, Matteo 1/22* 3/19+
Cenzer, Carl W. 11/30+

Cermak, Joseph 2/3+
Cevert, Francois 2/25* 6/20, 10/6+
Chaboud, Eugene 4/12* 12/28+
Chadwick, Frank B. 7/11+
Chadwick, John L. 8/14*
Chadwick, Lee S. 2/26*
Chalmers, Burton 10/16
Chalmers, Hugh 6/2+ 8/22, 10/3* 12/1, 12/6
Chalmers, Mrs. Hugh 8/22
Chamasrour, Joseph A. 7/18*
Chamberlain, G. P. 5/15
Chambers, Karl D. 10/8+
Chaminade, Leon A. 6/26+
Champeau, Dave 7/4+
Champion, Albert 4/2* 10/26, 10/27+
Chandler, Alfred D. Jr. 9/15*
Chandler, Franklin F. 4/6+ 12/27*
Chandler, Frederick C. 2/18+ 7/30
Chandler, Otis 11/23*
Chapin, Roy D. 2/16+ 2/19, 2/23* 2/25, 2/28,
    3/1, 3/4, 8/8, 8/22, 12/6
Chapin, Roy D. Jr. 1/9, 6/1, 9/21* 10/21
Chapman, Bernard A. 12/15*
Chapman, Colin 1/1, 5/19* 12/16+
Chapman, Hazel Williams 1/1
Chapman, James F. 12/12+
Charbonneaux, Philippe 2/18*
Charles, Prince of Wales 9/30
Charles, G. W. 5/25
Charlton, Dave 10/27*
Charron, Fernand 5/24, 6/14, 7/13, 8/13+
Chase, Julian 2/14+
Chase, Mike 4/17*
Chasseloup-Laubat, Gaston de 1/17, 3/4,
    12/18
Chauvet, Pierre 7/21*
Chaves, Pedro 2/27*
Chayne, Charles A. 1/1, 2/6* 7/11, 10/30+
Cheek, J. D. Picksley Sr. 7/6
Cheesbourg, Bill 6/12*
Cheever, Eddie 1/10* 3/1, 4/12, 6/26
Cheever, Ross 4/12*
Chenea, Paul F. 5/17*
Chenoweth, William B. 10/29
Chesebrough, Harry E. 7/13*
Chester, William M. Jr. 3/5*
Chestnut, George W. 12/9
Chevrolet, Arthur 4/5, 4/16+
Chevrolet, Gaston 11/25+ 11/26
Chevrolet, Louis 4/5, 5/20, 5/30, 6/6+ 10/1,
    12/2, 12/25*
Chicoine, Lionel M. 4/21*
Chiesa, Andrea 5/6*
Chimeri, Ettore 2/27+
Chinetti, Luigi 7/17* 8/17+
Chirico, Domenico 6/11*
Chiron, Louis 5/12, 5/22, 6/22+ 8/3* 8/7,
    9/13, 9/21
Choate, Allen E. 9/7
Choheco, Jose 6/3, 6/11
Christ, George W. 8/26+
Christie, Bob 4/4*
Christie, J. Walter 1/11+ 2/21, 3/27, 5/6* 9/5
Christopher, George T. 4/22, 6/7+ 9/4, 10/2*
    10/5, 12/29, 12/31
Christy, James Jr. 8/3
Chrysler, Jack F. 1/7* 11/7+
Chrysler, Walter P. 1/5, 1/6, 1/7, 3/25, 4/2*
    6/6, 6/9, 6/17, 7/14, 7/22, 8/18+ 11/11,
    12/3
Chrysler, Mrs. Walter P. 6/6, 8/8+
Chrysler, Walter P. Jr. 9/19+

Chryst, William A. 6/4+ 7/22, 10/21* 12/17
Chudakov, E. A. 8/20* 9/19+
Chung Ju Yung 5/25, 11/25* 12/29
Chung Mong Kyu 1/4*
Chung Se Yung 1/4, 8/6* 12/29
Church, H. D. 4/16* 9/1
Churchill, Charles W. 2/10+
Churchill, Harold E. 2/1, 2/24, 7/26, 9/2, 12/28
Ciobanu, Mihai P. 3/1*
Cires, Alberto Sanchez 10/30
Citroen, Andre 2/5* 5/28, 6/1, 7/3+ 7/14
Claes, Johnny 2/3+ 8/11*
Claremont, Ernest A. 3/15
Clark, Dugald 8/1
Clark, Earl 1/6
Clark, Edgar M. 7/31+
Clark, Frank G. 8/11
Clark, Harrison 4/8*
Clark, Henry Austin 8/1, 8/27* 9/1, 12/14+
Clark, Jim 1/1, 3/4* 4/7+ 5/30, 6/3, 6/5, 6/17, 8/18
Clark, Oliver H. 4/2, 6/3, 6/4, 7/31
Clark, T. J. 2/25*
Clark, William H. 4/25+
Clarke, Edgar 6/10+
Clarke, Frederick H. 5/29, 9/16, 11/15
Clarke, Henry F. 5/29, 9/16, 11/15
Clarke, Louis Semple 1/6+ 8/23*
Clarkson, Coker F. 6/4+
Claus, Carl 10/5+
Clayden, A. Ludlow 2/23+
Cleland, John 7/15*
Clemens, Chester E. 7/12* 12/24+
Clemens, Jan 11/4
Clement, Adolphe 11/13
Clement, Albert 10/8
Clement, Frank C. 5/16
Clement, Walter 9/5
Clements, Frank O. 5/8+
Clerico, Emmanuel 12/30*
Clifton, Charles 3/2, 6/21+ 9/20*
Clingan, R. E. 3/11+
Clo, J. Harry 2/22+
Clough, Albert L. 9/21+
Clough, Enos 2/28* 8/2+
Clusserath, Bud 6/10+
Clutterbuck, Harold 10/19+
Clymer, Floyd 1/22+ 10/26*
Clymer, John 1/29*
Coatalen, Louis 3/29, 5/23+ 6/17, 9/11*
Coates, Joseph S. 9/17* 9/19+
Cobb, John R. 8/7, 8/23, 9/15, 9/16, 9/29+ 10/7, 12/2+
Cobb, Price 12/10*
Cobb, William G. 8/31
Cochrane, John M. 5/11*
Cochrane, Walter S. 5/9+
Coffey, Irven E. 9/23+
Coffin, Howard A. 2/28+ 6/11*
Coffin, Howard E. 2/28, 9/6* 10/1, 11/21+ 12/6
Cogan, Kevin 3/31*
Cohn, M. L. 2/25, 11/10+
Cohn, Nudie 5/8+
Colbert, L. L. 6/13* 7/27, 9/22+ 11/30
Colburn, E. A. 10/15*
Colby, William M. 3/14* 3/24+
Cole, Edward N. 5/1, 5/2+ 6/5, 9/17* 9/30, 10/30, 11/1, 12/9, 12/17, 12/30
Cole, Joseph J. 6/22
Cole, Roy E. 1/14* 4/19+
Cole, Tom 6/14+
Coleman, Clyde J. 2/17, 11/24

Coletta, Robert 2/1
Collard, Emmanuel 4/3*
Colley, Robert H. 6/15*
Collier, Barron Jr. 7/11
Collier, David C. 10/28* 11/6
Collier, Henry D. 1/30+ 3/29*
Collier, Peter 6/2*
Collier, Sam 9/23+ 12/31
Collins, Gary 1/24*
Collins, George C. 8/14+
Collins, Peter 6/3, 7/17, 8/3+ 11/8*
Collins, Richard H. 6/26
Collomb, Bernard 10/7*
Collyer, John L. 9/18*
Colombo, Alberto 2/23*
Colombo, Gioachino 1/9* 4/24+
Coloni, Enzo 10/17*
Colotti, Valerio 12/12
Colucci, Ivo 9/30*
Colville, David 2/19
Comar, Jerome M. 5/20*
Comas, Erik 9/28*
Combs, Robert H. 4/25+
Combs, Rodney 3/27*
Comer, Fred 10/12+
Comotti, Gianfranco 5/10+ 7/24*
Compton, W. Dale 1/7*
Comstock, George C. 1/25
Conde, John A. 8/31
Conder, Robert W. 8/25*
Conlon, James L. 1/14+
Connelly, John S. 8/11
Conner, E. B. 7/26
Conner, George 8/16*
Connor, Allen C. 6/22
Conquest, A. U. 9/16
Conradi, Leo C. 12/4+
Conrath, Adolphe 3/9+
Constantine, George 2/22*
Contreras, Enrique 5/21*
Converse, Frederick 4/15
Conway, Hugh G. 1/25* 11/27+
Cook, Kenneth N. 3/5+
Cook, L. M. 6/17*
Cook, Raymond F. 4/17+
Cook, Sidney A. 5/18*
Cooke, B. W. 5/4+
Cooksey, Will 4/28
Cooley, Eugene F. 8/21
Coolidge, Calvin 2/28
Coombe, George W. Jr. 10/1*
Cooper, Charles 10/14*
Cooper, Earl 1/9, 9/4, 9/9, 10/22+
Cooper, Elisha H. 1/4+ 10/2*
Cooper, Howard 6/27+
Cooper, John 9/7
Cooper, Oz 4/13*
Cooper, Peter 6/20
Cooper, Tom 11/19+
Cooper, William O. 2/14*
Cope, Derrick 11/4*
Cope, Mike 5/6*
Copeland, Lammot 5/19*
Copeland, Lucius D. 4/5
Copf, Benjamin 12/19
Coppola, Francis Ford 4/7*
Coppuck, Gordon 6/9
Coquille, Emile 10/9
Corace, Joseph R. 7/22*
Corbin, Philip 11/3+
Cord, E. L. 1/2+ 1/3, 1/6, 2/2, 2/3, 2/8, 4/9, 5/10, 5/30, 6/2, 6/17, 7/15, 7/20* 8/4,

8/18, 9/15, 9/19, 10/6, 11/1, 11/12, 11/13, 12/8
Cord, Mrs. E. L. (1) 9/19
Cord, Mrs. E. L. (2) 1/3
Cordts, John 7/23*
Cork, Kenneth 2/19
Corker, Joseph E. 7/12
Corley, Kenneth 11/3*
Corliss, George H. 2/21+ 6/2*
Corn, Jack W. 10/8*
Cornwall, Evelyn 3/13*
Corr, Albert C. 3/31+
Corson, Thomas H. 10/15*
Cortese, Franco 2/10* 3/9, 5/11, 5/25, 11/13+
Cortesi, Gaetano 5/29
Corum, L. L. 5/30
Cosgrove, R. J. 9/16
Costanzo, Alfredo 1/3*
Costin, Frank 6/8*
Cotes, M. F. 9/8*
Cottaz, Didier 5/23*
Cottenham, 6th Earl of 5/29* 7/19+
Cotting, James C. 3/20, 10/15*
Cotton, Billy 8/7
Cottrell, James W. 2/15+
Coulombe, Joseph C. 4/16+
Coulon, Jacques 1/15*
Coulson, George H. 8/20+
Coulthard, David 3/27*
Courage, Piers 5/27* 6/21+
Courter, Robert G. 12/29*
Couture, Alan B. 7/21+
Couzens, James 1/5, 2/24, 8/26* 9/5, 10/13, 10/22+, 11/22, 11/29, 12/8
Cowan, Andrew 9/28
Cowen, William M. 4/23
Cowie, Ernest S. 7/20* 8/7+
Cowles, Edward P. 1/6, 7/16
Cowling, William C. 12/22
Cox, Claude E. 3/31, 6/13
Cox, Glenn A. Jr. 8/6*
Cox, Len W. 4/23
Coyle, Marvin E. 9/27+ 10/8*
Coyne, David 3/31*
Cozette, Rene 8/20+
Crabb, Richard 1/20*
Craft, Chris 11/17*
Craft, Edmund C. 12/23*
Craig, Burt J. 5/12, 6/1, 8/7* 9/2+
Cram, C. J. 8/28
Cram, Leroy V. 4/26+
Crane, Henry M. 6/16* 6/21+ 7/25, 7/30
Crane, J. E. 5/1, 8/10, 9/13*
Crank, James D. 8/19
Craun, William H. 6/7
Craven, Ricky 5/24*
Crawford, Charles S. 1/28+ 4/3*
Crawford, Clarence H. 1/30
Crawford, Frederick C. 3/19*
Crawford, James M. 6/1, 8/29* 9/23+
Crawford, Jim 2/13*
Crawford, William W. 2/19+
Creighton, Charles 9/5
Cresto, Sergio 5/2+
Crichton-Stuart, Charles 3/10*
Crider, Curtis 10/7*
Crimmins, Philip P. 8/1*
Crinelli, Patrick 8/5*
Crist, Harold 1/1
Crist, Russell A. 3/10*
Critchfield, Robert M. 12/1
Critchley, J. S. 4/17, 6/26

Crittenden, Kenneth 9/3
Croceri, Fernando 1/6*
Crocker, Sewall E. 5/23, 7/26
Cronkhite, L. J. 5/22+
Crook, Tony 2/16*
Crosby, F. Gordon 8/21+
Crosby, V. A. 10/2+
Crosley, Powel Jr. 3/28+ 4/29, 6/22, 9/18* 10/17
Crosley, Mrs. Powel Jr. 10/17
Cross, Richard E. 2/12, 6/6, 9/20*
Crossley, Geoffrey 5/11* 5/13
Crossley, Kenneth 2/17* 11/22+
Crossley, William J. 4/22* 10/12+
Crouch, W. Lee 11/19
Crow, James T. 11/29+ 12/6*
Crow, Stuart 8/21*
Crowther, Samuel 10/27+
Crum, Roy W. 4/9*
Crusoe, Lewis D. 2/25*
Cruz, Adolfo 6/28*
Cudini, Alain 4/19*
Cugnot, Nicolas 9/25* 10/10+
Cummings, Bill 2/8+ 3/2
Cummins, Clessie L. 2/7, 3/20, 4/20, 8/18+
    12/14, 12/25, 12/27*
Cummins, Don 2/18+
Cuneo, Terence 1/3+
Cunningham, A. J. 5/17* 7/31+
Cunningham, Edna 3/18
Cunningham, Francis E. 11/26+
Curcio, John B. 5/29*
Cureton, Thomas 1/16
Curran, John C. Jr. 8/21*
Curtice, Harlow H. 2/2, 7/22, 8/15* 8/31,
    10/23, 11/3+, 11/20, 12/11
Curtin, Nick 11/26+
Curtiss, Glenn H. 1/23, 2/8, 5/21* 7/23+
Curzon, Francis 7/26+
Cutler, E. H. 3/6* 6/21+
Cutler, Edward J. 1/14, 3/8+ 8/12*
Cutter, John D. 3/11+ 10/31*
Cutting, Charles D. 12/16+
Czaykowski, Stanislaus 9/10+

Dabrera, Robin 3/1+
Dacco, Guido 9/10*
Dahlinger, Evangeline Cote 10/17* 11/3+
Dahlinger, John Cote 4/9* 11/16+
Dahlinger, Raymond C. 4/7, 7/3*
Daigh, Chuck 6/19, 11/29*
Daimler, Adolf 3/24+ 9/8*
Daimler, Anna 4/14
Daimler, Emilie 4/14*
Daimler, Gottlieb 3/4, 3/6+ 3/17* 3/24, 4/1,
    4/3, 4/14, 4/18, 6/9, 6/30, 7/8, 7/9, 8/1,
    8/15, 8/29, 9/8, 9/13, 9/29, 11/10, 12/16
Daimler, Mrs. Gottlieb 7/8
Daimler, Paul 1/1, 4/1, 9/13* 11/10, 12/15+
D'Alene, Wilbur 9/4
Dallara, Gianpaolo 5/1, 11/16*
Dall'Ave, Orlando 1/23+
Dallenbach, Wally 5/23, 12/12*
Dallenbach, Wally Jr. 5/23*
Dallest, Richard 2/15*
Dallison, Ken 3/23* 4/2, 6/11, 8/25, 11/3
Dalmas, Yannick 7/28*
Dalton, Hubert K. 7/26+
Daly, Derek 3/11*
Damon, Norman C. 8/6+ 11/7*
Dana, Charles A. 4/25* 11/27+
Dance, Charles 2/21
Dangerfield, Edmund 5/31

Daniell, J. F. 3/12* 3/13+
Daniels, George E. 3/24+ 6/25, 9/22, 10/20
Danielson, Archibald G. 10/27+
Danielsson, Thomas 12/4*
Danner, Christian 4/4*
Daponte, Jorge 6/5*
Darin, Frank 2/16*
Darling, Andrew 12/12*+
Darracq, Alexandre 1/4, 11/10*
Darrin, Howard A. "Dutch" 1/3+ 2/16, 3/14,
    4/17, 4/30, 5/16*, 6/15, 9/26
Dauch, Robert E. 4/11
Dauer, Jochen 1/10*
Davenport, Thomas 2/25, 7/6+ 7/9*
David, Donald K. 2/15*
Davidson, Beatrice 12/16
Davidson, Edward Y. Jr. 8/16+ 12/30*
Davidson, W. J. 9/4+
Davies, E. G. 1/19
Davies, G. L. 8/4
Davies, George W. 12/3+
Davies, Jimmy 6/11+ 8/18*
Davies, Ralph K. 9/9*
Davis, Albert F. 7/7*
Davis, Charles S. 7/2+
Davis, Colin 7/29*
Davis, Darrell L. 8/8*
Davis, David E. Jr. 11/7*
Davis, Ernest F. 8/25+
Davis, Floyd 5/31*
Davis, Francis B. 9/16* 12/22+
Davis, Francis W. 4/16+ 8/19* 10/20
Davis, Gary 7/22, 8/15+
Davis, George W. 5/3+ 10/20*
Davis, John D. 7/13
Davis, John R. "Jack" 11/10* 12/22
Davis, Louise Hitchcock 7/13
Davis, S. C. H. "Sammy" 1/9*+ 4/15, 5/25,
    6/9, 7/29, 11/14
Davis, Samuel L. 8/3*
Davis, Samuel T. 1/14, 8/31+ 12/1
Davis, William H. 7/27*
Davison, Lex 2/14+
Dawes, Nathaniel T. 12/19*
Dawley, Herbert M. 2/24, 8/15+ 12/12
Dawson, J. Gordon 2/3*
Dawson, Joe 6/18+ 8/2
Day, George H. 4/3* 11/21+
Day, Graham 3/5, 5/3*
Day, J. Wentworth 4/21*
Day, Joseph 4/14
Day, William L. 9/1
Dean, Hugh 5/1, 9/19*
Dean, James 9/30+
Dean, Paul S. 10/12+
Dean, Richard 10/7*
Dean, Tony 10/7
DeBerry, E. P. 5/10+
de Bruyne, Dirk 9/1*
de Campi, John W. 2/4*
de Caters, Pierre 5/25, 7/29
de Causse, J. Frank 5/10+
de Cesaris, Andrea 4/3, 5/31*
DeCrane, Alfred C. Jr. 6/11*
de Dietrich, Eugene 6/26
de Dion, Albert 1/1, 3/9* 5/1, 7/22, 8/19+
    10/2, 11/2, 11/5
Dedeurwaerder, Jose J. 1/15, 9/28, 12/31*
Deeds, Edward A. 3/12* 5/11, 7/1+ 7/22
Deere, John 5/19, 7/2
de Ferran, Gil 11/11*
de Florez, Luis 3/4*

deForest, Baron 7/4
de Graffenried, Emmanuel 5/18*
de Kuzmik, Paul 10/21+
Delage, Louis 1/10, 3/22* 12/14+
DeLand, Charles S. 1/7
Delaney, George A. 1/1, 2/11* 7/15+
DeLaRossa, Don 2/6
de la Rue, Stuart 5/29* 7/3, 10/26+
DeLaval-Crow, T. C. 6/28+
Deletraz, Jean-Denis 10/1*
Delius, Ernst von 7/26+
Delong, James E. 1/7, 5/31*
de Looze, John 3/16
DeLorean, John Z. 1/6* 2/1, 3/1, 4/2, 6/16,
    6/26, 7/1, 8/16, 10/19, 12/17
DeLorenzo, A. G. 8/26*
Del Roy, Frankie 11/7*
Demel, Herbert 10/14*
Demogeot, Victor 1/29
Dempsey, James 8/28
Dempsey, John S. 6/14* 8/17+
Denby, Edward 11/8
Denise, Malcolm L. 10/28*
Dennis, Ron 10/12
de Nyevelt, Zuylen 11/5
Depailler, Patrick 8/1+ 8/9*
DePalma, Ralph 1/5, 1/23* 2/12, 2/18, 2/26,
    2/27, 3/19, 3/31+ 4/24, 5/30, 7/16, 9/17,
    10/2
DePaolo, Peter 2/22, 4/15* 4/20, 4/30, 5/30,
    7/11, 10/31, 11/26+
Derham, Enos J. 1/3* 3/11+
Dernier, Leon 7/26+
DeRosa, Frank 11/7*
Derr, Thomas S. 5/31+ 6/10*
Deschamps, Roger P. 10/6+
Deshon, Ralph 12/31
Deslex, Gustav 7/1
de Soto, Hernando 5/21+
De Tomaso, Alejandro 1/13, 7/10*
Deukmejian, George 9/7
Deutsch, Charles 9/6*
DeVaux, Norman 10/28, 12/31*
Devenow, Chester 3/3*
Devine, John M. 5/13*
de Vizcaya, Augustin 1/1
de Vizcaya, Pierre 7/15
de Vore, Earl 11/12+
DeWaard, John 3/30*
Dewar, Michael 12/21+
DeWaters, E. A. 7/22*
Dewey, James F. 2/12* 8/1+
DeWindt, Edward M. 3/31*
Dewis, Norman 1/20, 10/21
DeWitt, Clyde C. 11/9*
DeWitt, Virgil L. 4/15
Deyo, Austin W. 12/5+
Dezendorf, Nelson C. 4/23*
d'Humbersin, Philippe 9/28
Dibley, Hugh 4/29*
Dibos, Eduardo 4/12*
DiCerto, Joseph J. 2/27*
Dick, Burns 10/30+
Dickens, Stanley 5/7*
Dickinson, Hobart Cutler 10/11* 11/27+
Dickson, Larry 9/6*
Dieringer, Yancy 6/1*
Diesel, Rudolf 2/23, 2/28, 3/18* 7/26, 9/29+
Dietrich, Raymond H. 1/7, 1/11, 2/12, 2/15*
    3/19+ 12/1, 12/19
Dieudonne, Pierre 3/24*
Digneit, William 1/15+

Dillon, George C. 10/29*
Dilworth, Richard 12/31
Di Misurata, Giovanni Volpi 2/11
Dingley, Bert 4/7+ 6/12, 6/30, 8/5
Diniz, Pedro 5/22*
Dinkel, John 8/1*
Dinsmore, Duke 4/10* 10/12+
Dinsmore, Ray P. 4/24* 10/26+
di Palma, Jose Luis 3/31*
Disbrow, Louis 6/13
Dismore, Mark 10/12*
Dithmer, Sven E. 11/12*
Di Trabia, Raimondo 11/30+
Dixon, E. O. 11/4+
Dixon, Freddie 11/5+
Doble, Abner 4/19, 4/28, 7/16+
Docker, Bernard 5/22+ 8/9*
Dodge, Daniel R. 7/19+
Dodge, Horace E. 2/28, 5/17* 6/2, 7/17, 7/19,
    7/29, 8/27, 11/16, 12/10+
Dodge, Mrs. Horace E. 6/2+ 7/29
Dodge, Horace E. Jr. 8/2* 12/22+
Dodge, John F. 1/14+ 4/20, 7/17, 7/19,
    8/27, 9/18, 9/22, 10/25* 11/16, 12/10, 12/20
Dodge, Mrs. John F. (1) 9/22
Dodge, Mrs. John F. (2) 4/20, 9/18+ 12/10
Dodge, Joseph M. 11/18* 12/12+
Doehler, Robert 5/17+
Doenin, V. N. 9/11*
Doerfner, Willian H. 4/12*
Dohanos, Steven 5/18*
Dohner, John H. 5/31* 11/11+
Dolhem, Jose 4/16+ 4/26*
Dolnar, Hugh 4/27, 7/27
Dolza, John 12/11
Doman, Albert E. 11/5* 11/12+
Doman, Carl 3/24, 4/19
Domonoske, Arthur B. 1/1* 1/5+
Donaldson, Benjamin R. 7/18*
Donaldson, George R. 6/16+
Donaldson, J. A. 6/10*
Donnelly, Joseph A. 3/9+
Donnelly, Martin 3/26*
Donner, Frederic G. 1/1, 1/5, 2/28+ 9/1, 10/4*
    10/31
Donohue, Mark 3/18* 7/3, 8/19+ 9/22
Donovan, Frank 6/6* 9/26+
Donovan, Leo 4/6+
Dooley, Channing R. 4/4* 6/25+
Doren, Edgar 10/6*
Doret, Marcel 2/5+
d'Orey, Fritz 3/25* 12/12
Dorman, A. D. 6/3* 6/27+
Dorn, Robert L. 5/1
Dorpmuller, Julius 7/5+ 7/24*
Dorris, George P. 4/2* 11/2+
Dort, J. Dallas 1/1, 2/2* 5/8, 5/17+ 8/9, 9/10,
    9/28
Dort, Mrs. J. Dallas 5/8
Dory, Pedro van 4/3+
Dotter, Bobby 7/11*
Doty, Leonidas Jr. 6/4+
Dougall, Rad 9/7*
Douglas, Albert L. 2/15+
Douglas, Theodore 1/21+ 3/2*
Downing, Jim 1/4*
Downing, Ken 7/19, 12/5*
Doyle, William 2/15*
Drake, Albert D. 3/26*
Drake, Bob 4/18+ 11/20, 12/14*
Drake, Dale 7/10+
Drake, Edwin 8/27

Drake, J. Frank 9/1* 12/20+
Drake, J. Walter 9/27* 11/8, 11/27+
Drake, Joseph R. 11/8
Drakeford, William 4/15
Draper, Robert F. 12/3*
Drefs, Arthur G. 4/5* 11/1+
Dresser, Ivan C. 9/23
Dreyfus, Pierre 11/18* 12/25+
Dreyfus, Rene 1/11, 4/10, 5/6* 6/13, 8/15,
    8/16+
Dreystadt, Nicholas 6/1, 6/4, 9/3+ 9/30*
Driscoll, Bridget 8/17
Driver, Paddy 5/19*
Drobig, Leo 10/9+
Drogo, Piero 4/28+ 8/8*
Drury, Charles E. 2/24*
Dryden, J. Lester 1/2* 10/29+
Dryver, Bernard de 9/19*
Dube, William 5/23+
Dubonnet, Andre 4/19, 10/22
Ducarouge, Gerard 1/25, 10/23*
Du Cros, Arthur P. 1/26* 10/28+
Dudgeon, Richard 10/5
Dudzinski, Sharon D. 11/22*
Duerksen, Menno 6/23*
Duerr, Carl 5/8
Duesenberg, August S. 1/18+ 3/8, 3/28, 8/1,
    9/4, 12/12*, 12/28
Duesenberg, Frederick S. 2/7, 2/19, 3/8, 4/27,
    6/26, 7/2, 7/26+ 8/1, 8/16, 12/6* 12/28
Duesenberg, Mrs. Frederick S. 4/27
Duesenberg, Fritz 3/28
Duff, Robert H. 3/5+
Dufresne, Artaud 6/1
Dufresne, Louis 6/1
du Gast, Camille 6/27
Duggan, Tom O. 3/20+
Dulude, Donald O. 10/13*
Duman, Ronnie 6/9+
Dumfries, Johnny 4/26*
Duncan, Isadora 9/14+
Duncombe, T. H. Augustus 6/4* 11/3+
Dundee, Chris 7/10
Dunham, George W. 2/17+ 3/1
Dunk, A. O. 3/5+ 7/1* 7/15
Dunlap, James L. 8/20*
Dunlop, John B. 2/5* 10/31
Dunlop, Robert G. 7/2*
Dunn, Edward J. 10/23+
Dunn, Joseph M. 8/9*
DuPont, E. Paul 9/26+
DuPont, Lammot 3/27, 5/3, 7/24+ 10/12*
DuPont, Pierre S. 1/15* 3/27, 4/5+ 5/10,
    10/12, 11/16, 12/1
DuPuy, Harry W. 7/4+ 9/27*
Dur, Philip A. 6/22*
Durand, Georges 10/9
Durant, William C. 1/11, 1/12, 2/8, 2/18, 3/18+
    4/7, 4/25, 5/2, 5/11, 5/30, 6/1, 6/9, 6/17,
    7/1, 7/24, 7/28, 8/1, 8/9, 8/15, 9/4, 9/10,
    9/16, 9/23, 9/26, 9/28, 9/29, 10/26, 11/1,
    11/3, 11/30, 12/1, 12/8* 12/9, 12/16, 12/23,
    12/31
Durant, Mrs. William C. 6/17
Duray, Arthur 7/4, 7/17, 11/5, 12/8
Duray, Leon 4/16, 4/30* 5/12+ 6/14
Duryea, Charles E. 3/28, 4/6, 4/19, 6/11, 8/13,
    9/21, 9/28+ 12/15*
Duryea, Mrs. Charles E. 8/13
Duryea, J. Frank 2/15+ 4/19, 5/30, 8/29, 9/10,
    9/21, 10/1, 10/8* 11/28
Dusinberre, Samuel B. 3/26+
Dusio, Piero 5/15, 9/3, 10/13* 11/7+

Duttenhofer, Max von 8/14+
Dye, Edward R. 3/10* 10/13+
Dyer, Leonard 5/13* 8/8, 11/16+
Dyer, Leonidas C. 6/11* 12/15+
Dyke, A. L. 5/26+
Dykstra, John 3/2+ 4/10, 4/12, 4/16* 4/30
Dykstra, Nicholas 1/1* 7/21

Earhart, Amelia 7/7, 7/21
Earl, Bob 1/13*
Earl, Clarence A. 10/31
Earl, Harley J. 3/10+ 6/23, 9/3, 11/22* 12/1
Earnhardt, Dale 4/29*
Earp, Clifford 7/28
Eastman, John R. 9/28*
Eaton, George 11/12*
Eaton, George H. 9/15+
Eaton, Joseph O. 7/28*
Eaton, Robert J. 2/13* 3/16
Eaton, William M. 10/20, 11/23
Eberhardt, Fred L. 7/18+
Ebling, George 3/18* 12/5+
Ebstein, Joseph 5/12*
Ecclestone, Bernie 10/28*
Eckel, Earle S. 4/17+
Eckhardt, John 3/9
Eckhart, Charles 9/30+
Eckhart, Morris 6/25, 7/1
Economaki, Chris 10/15*
Eddins, Daniel S. 4/13* 8/24+
Eddy, Arthur L. 9/1
Edgar, Graham 9/9+ 9/19*
Edge, S. F. 2/10+ 3/29* 5/11, 5/12, 6/26, 6/29
Edison, Thomas A. 2/11* 2/18, 10/18+ 10/21
Edman, John R. 10/14*
Edmunds, Henry 3/20+ 5/4, 11/18+
Edsell, Arthur J. 8/17
Edward VII 2/14, 6/26
Edward VIII 6/22
Edwardes, Michael 10/11* 11/8
Edwards, Charles E. 7/19*
Edwards, Frank W. 4/10* 4/29+
Edwards, Gus 11/7+
Edwards, Guy 12/30*
Edwards, Sterling 4/16
Edwards, Wallace W. 5/9*
Effmann, Karl H. 3/10* 8/23+
Egan, John 3/27, 4/1, 8/9, 11/7*
Egan, Philip S. 12/13*
Egbert, Sherwood H. 2/1, 7/24* 7/31+ 11/25,
    12/28
Egerton, Hubert W. 4/12*
Egginton, Enoch J. 5/23+
Egloff, Gustav 5/8+
Ehlers, Norm 10/31
Ehrich, Terry 1/2
Ehringer, Frank J. 3/3*
Ehrman, Edwin H. 6/14+
Ehrman, Gus 10/20
Ehrman, Natalio 12/3
Eisengrein, Henry D. 2/15+
Eisenhower, Dwight D. 1/26, 4/14, 8/7, 11/20
Ekstrom, Erik 1/12+
Elbert, J. L. 4/11+ 5/21*
Elder, Ray 8/19*
Eldridge, Ernest A. D. 7/12
Elfes, Harold L. 2/15+
Elford, Vic 6/10*
Elges, George R. 1/1, 6/22, 7/1, 8/1
Elgh, Eje 6/15*
Elisian, Ed 8/30+
Ellingson, Charles 3/17

Ellingsworth, Jesse 5/30
Elliott, A. G. 11/13+ 12/3* 12/31
Elliott, Bill 10/8*
Elliott, Robert 8/9*
Elliott, Robert B. 7/8*
Elliott, W. L. 9/13
Ellis, Carleton 1/13+ 9/20*
Ellis, Charles C. 2/2* 9/26+
Ellis, Evelyn 7/12, 11/22
Ellis, George H. 2/28
Ellor, James E. 7/16+
Elwart, Joan Potter 8/27*
Emerson, Victor L. 5/6+
Emerson, Willis G. 4/29
Emery, Don 9/1*
Emery, Grace 9/20
Emery, Paul 2/3+ 7/14, 8/5, 11/12*
Emmert, Rodger J. 1/15*
Emmert, Theodore J. 9/9*
Emrick, Terry L. 8/24*
Enever, Sydney 2/9+ 3/25*
Engel, Elwood P. 2/10* 5/15
Engel, Lyle K. 5/12* 8/10+
Engellau, Gunnar 1/5+ 11/11*
Engelstad, Ralph 12/1
Enger, Frank J. 1/4+
England, Lofty 5/30+ 8/24*
England, Paul 3/28*
English, Herdis G. 2/20+
Ennevaara, M. 11/1
Enos, Robert C. 4/17*
Epstein, Ralph C. 9/25* 11/21+
Erickson, Harry J. 6/15+
Ericson, George R. 10/22+
Erie, James Philip 5/30
Erskine, Albert R. 1/24* 7/1+ 8/7
Ertl, Harald 4/7+ 8/31*
Escobedo, Manuel G. 5/9*
Esders, Armand 4/4, 7/27
Eskridge, Joseph W. 5/31* 8/9
Esslinger, Friedrich 5/1, 10/1
Estabrook, Edward L. 5/10*
Estefano, Nasif 10/21+ 11/18*
Estep, E. Ralph 6/16, 11/7+
Estes, Elliott M. 1/7* 1/31, 3/24+ 6/22, 7/1,
    10/1
Etancelin, Philippe 9/3, 9/26, 10/13+ 10/28,
    12/28*
Etzler, Eugene E. 9/17+
Eubanks, Joe 5/2
Euser, Cor 4/25*
Evans, Bob 6/11*
Evans, Dave 2/7, 5/30
Evans, Garrett 1/19*
Evans, Gary 10/21*
Evans, Leigh R. 1/27* 5/1+
Evans, Oliver 4/15+ 5/19, 7/13, 9/13*
Evans, Richie 7/23* 10/24+
Evans, Robert B. 1/9, 6/6
Evans, Ronald K. 6/12+ 8/17*
Evans, Roy S. 6/2, 10/17*
Evans, Walker 12/3*
Evans, William D. 4/20+
Evans, William H. 11/17+
Everitt, Barney 6/2, 7/25, 9/20, 10/5+
Evernden, Ivan 8/11*
Ewald, Henry T. 1/9+ 4/20*
Ewell, E. G. 1/26*
Exner, Virgil M. Jr. 4/17*
Exner, Virgil M. Sr. 3/28, 9/24* 11/4, 11/17,
    12/22+
Eyston, George 4/29, 6/20* 7/18, 8/27, 9/16, 11/19

Fabi, Corrado 4/12*
Fabi, Teo 3/9* 4/12, 9/3
Fabre, Pascal 1/9*
Faccioli, Aristide 7/11
Facetti, Carlo 6/26*
Fageol, Frank R. 9/14*
Fagioli, Luigi 6/9* 6/20+ 7/1
Fahrney, Emery H. 10/7+
Fairbank, Herbert S. 9/16* 12/14+
Fairbanks, Avard 3/2*
Fairfield, Pat 1/1
Fairhurst, William 10/2+
Fairman, Jack 3/15* 7/8, 7/15
Falbe-Hansen, Viggo 3/28*
Falchetto, Benoit 9/14
Fales, Frederick S. 2/26* 9/24+
Falkenhausen, Alex von 5/18
Fallesen, Christian 7/1
Fallon, Ivan 6/26*
Faloon, Bryon 1/8+
Fanelli 6/19+
Fangio, Juan Manuel 1/16, 1/17, 1/19, 2/23,
    4/10, 5/21, 6/24* 7/1, 7/4, 7/6, 7/17+
    7/18, 8/4, 8/18, 9/19, 10/24, 10/28, 11/22
Fangio, Juan Manuel II 9/9*
Faraone, Frank R. 10/19*
Farina, Battista "Pinin" 3/10, 4/3+ 11/2*
Farina, Giuseppe "Nino" 5/5, 5/13, 6/25,
    6/30+ 9/1, 10/24, 10/30*
Farish, William S. 2/23* 11/29+
Farkas, Eugene J. 2/24+ 10/1, 10/26*
Farley, James I. 2/24* 6/16+ 6/25, 7/1
Farlow, A. G. 7/8
Farman, Henri 2/10, 2/17, 7/18+
Farman, Maurice 2/17, 2/25+ 3/21*
Farmer, L. G. T. 5/13*
Farmer, Moses G. 2/9* 5/25+ 7/26
Farrand, A. M. 7/16, 7/24
Fasanella, Carmen 2/1, 2/19* 11/2
Faulconer, Robert C. 9/19, 11/7
Faulkner, George 3/21+
Faulkner, Roy H. 2/3, 2/11* 8/15+ 8/24
Faulkner, Walt 2/16* 4/22+
Faurote, F. L. 9/5+
Faussier, Paul 4/28
Favre, Philippe 12/11*
Fay, S. M. 7/14*
Federmann, Simone 5/29
Fedewa, Tim 5/9*
Feldmann, Charles R. 1/18, 2/8* 12/13+
Felker, W. B. 8/12
Fellows, Ron 9/28*
Fenaille, Pierre 12/8
Fendell, Bob 8/24*
Fengler, Harlan 4/1+
Fenner, F. C. 11/9
Ference, Michael Jr. 11/6*
Fergus, John C. 9/18*
Ferguson, Harry 7/15
Ferguson, Harry G. 5/24, 10/25+ 11/4*
Ferguson, William H. 7/23
Fergusson, David 1/31, 2/4, 4/27+
Fergusson-Wood, Harry 1/22*
Fermor-Hesketh, Alexander 6/22
Fernandez, Adrian 4/20*
Ferrari, Claudio 5/1
Ferrari, Dino 1/19* 6/30+
Ferrari, Enzo 2/14, 2/18* 5/20, 6/14, 6/17,
    7/13, 8/9, 8/14+ 10/5, 11/22, 12/1
Ferris, Walter 4/16+
Ferry, Hugh J. 1/1, 2/4+ 2/11, 5/1, 6/1, 6/19,

10/5, 12/14* 12/29, 12/31
Ferte, Alain 6/10, 10/8* 12/8
Ferte, Michel 12/8*
Fetch, Tom 6/20, 8/21
Fewsmith, Joseph 3/12+ 4/1, 5/18*
Fewsmith, Joseph Jr. 10/20
Fields, Joseph E. 3/12+ 4/19*
Figgie, Harry E. 6/13+
Filippis, Maria-Teresa de 6/15, 11/11*
Fine, Sidney 10/11*
Fink, Emil C. 1/1+
Finnegan, John D. 12/4
Finotto, Martino 11/11*
Firestone, Clinton 2/22+
Firestone, Harvey S. 2/7+ 6/21, 8/3, 12/12,
    12/20*
Firestone, Harvey S. Jr. 4/20* 6/1+
Firestone, Harvey S. III 5/5+
Firestone, Raymond C. 9/6*
Firestone, Russell A. 12/12+
Fischer, Friedrich von 5/1
Fischer, Rudi 4/19* 12/30+
Fish, Calvin 7/22*
Fish, Frederick S. 2/5* 8/13+
Fish, John R. 5/8+
Fishbacher, P. 10/31
Fisher, Albert 1/2* 3/15* 7/22
Fisher, Alfred J. 8/2, 8/22, 10/9+ 12/7*
Fisher, Carl G. 1/12* 2/9, 2/22, 4/22, 7/15+
    8/15, 8/27, 9/12, 11/4
Fisher, Charles T. 2/16* 7/22, 8/8+ 8/22,
    12/22
Fisher, Edward F. 1/17+ 2/23* 8/2, 8/22
Fisher, Frederic J. 1/2* 7/14+ 7/22, 8/22,
    12/22
Fisher, George M. 10/25
Fisher, Howard A. 3/31+ 8/22
Fisher, James B. 4/8+
Fisher, John K. 8/6
Fisher, Lawrence P. 5/1, 5/31, 7/30, 8/2, 8/22,
    9/3+, 10/19* 12/10
Fisher, William A. 6/30, 8/2, 8/22, 9/21*
    12/21+
Fishleigh, Walter T. 1/19* 2/23+ 7/8, 8/24
Fisichella, Giancarlo 2/15*
Fiske, Charles P. 5/21* 8/9+
Fitch, John 8/4*
Fittipaldi, Christian 1/18*
Fittipaldi, Emerson 1/18, 9/10, 10/4, 12/12*
Fittipaldi, Wilson 1/12, 1/18, 12/25*
Fitzau, Theo 3/18+
Fitzgerald, Warren W. 10/6+
Fitzpatrick, John 6/9*
Flaherty, Pat 1/6* 5/30
Flaherty, Patrick J. 2/12+
Flanders, Walter E. 4/15, 6/2, 6/16+ 7/25
Flannery, J. P. 3/30*
Fleener, Lon A. 6/30*
Fleming, John M. 4/4*
Fleuelling, Lewis E. 8/24*
Flick, Friedrich 4/11
Flink, James J. 5/1*
Flinterman, Jan 10/2*
Flintermann, Carl H. L. 1/18+
Flock, Fonty 3/21* 3/26, 7/15+
Flock, Tim 5/11*
Flockhart, Ron 4/12+ 6/16*
Florio, Vincenzo 9/10
Flynn, James W. 3/28+
Fogg, Charles E. 6/20+
Fogolin, Claudio 11/29
Foitek, Gregor 3/27*

Folberth, Fred G. 9/22+
Follis, Ralph G. 2/1*
Follmer, George 1/27* 3/3
Fontes, Luis 10/19
Foote 7/9
Foote, John B. 4/6* 10/12+
Forbes, K. 12/16
Forbes, Myron E. 5/15+ 8/7
Forbes-Robinson, Elliott 10/31*
Ford, Anne McDonnell 2/12
Ford, Benson 1/30, 4/18, 7/20* 7/27+
Ford, Bruce 6/3* 8/10+
Ford, Edsel B. 1/1, 2/18, 2/28, 4/29, 5/16, 5/26+
    6/13, 6/19, 7/9, 8/10, 9/4, 9/17, 9/21, 10/6,
    10/8, 10/24, 11/1, 11/6*, 12/7, 12/22
Ford, Mrs. Edsel B. 10/19+ 11/1
Ford, Edsel B. II 1/1, 1/7, 1/15, 4/9, 12/27*
Ford, Edsel Henry 2/3
Ford, Harry W. 5/4* 11/18+
Ford, Henry 1/1, 1/12, 1/13, 1/15, 1/20, 2/2,
    2/7, 2/19, 2/28, 3/7, 3/12, 4/7+, 4/9, 4/10,
    4/11, 4/15, 5/7, 5/8, 5/11, 5/25, 6/1, 6/4,
    6/8, 6/10, 6/21, 6/25, 7/8, 7/9, 7/12, 7/21,
    7/26, 7/30* 8/5, 8/15, 8/17, 8/20, 9/4,
    9/17, 9/19, 9/25, 9/27, 10/1, 10/3, 10/10,
    10/18, 10/20, 10/22, 11/5, 11/21, 11/22,
    11/29, 12/1, 12/2, 12/4, 12/5, 12/7, 12/10,
    12/18, 12/22, 12/24, 12/30
Ford, Mrs. Henry 4/11* 9/17, 9/25, 9/29+
    12/24
Ford, Henry II 1/7, 1/11, 2/12, 2/19, 2/22,
    3/13, 4/10, 4/14, 4/29, 5/8, 5/10, 5/11,
    5/20, 5/22, 6/13, 6/16, 6/19, 6/27, 6/30,
    7/13, 8/3, 9/4* 9/9, 9/11, 9/13, 9/21, 9/27,
    9/29+ 10/1, 10/14, 10/14, 10/26, 11/9,
    12/19, 11/19, 12/27
Ford, Mrs. Henry II (1) 2/12, 7/13, 8/3
Ford, Mrs. Henry II (2) 2/19
Ford, Mrs. Henry II (3) 10/14
Ford, James W. 2/1*
Ford, John A. 6/21*
Ford, Mary Litogot 3/29+ 4/25
Ford, Perley H. 1/24+
Ford, William 4/25, 12/10*
Ford, Mrs. William 4/25
Ford, William Clay 1/23, 2/27, 3/14* 4/1, 4/10,
    5/12, 6/4, 6/21, 7/1, 7/17, 7/24, 9/8, 10/4,
    10/16, 11/12, 11/22
Ford, Mrs. William Clay 6/21
Ford, William Clay Jr. 1/15, 5/1, 3/7, 9/8, 10/15
Forini, Franco 9/22*
Forsyth, Frederick J. 4/19
Foster, Alan H. 11/7*
Foster, Billy 1/20+
Foster, Claud H. 6/21+ 12/23*
Foster, Cuthbert 6/30
Foster, Elmer W. 11/15
Foster, Lloyd H. 9/16
Foster, William J. 12/5+
Fotheringham-Parker, Philip 9/22* 10/15+
Fournier, Henri 5/29, 6/29, 11/5, 11/16, 12/18+
Fox, Ansley H. 11/21
Fox, Charles H. 1/26+
Fox, Dowager Lady 10/15
Fox, Edwin 2/26+ 9/8*
Fox, Jack C. 6/3+ 7/25*
Fox, Leland W. 12/9+
Fox, Ray 5/28*
Fox, Roland 4/21+
Foxworth, John E. Jr. 4/6*
Foy, Byron C. 6/20* 6/28+ 12/3
Foy, Mrs. Byron C. (Chrysler) 8/20+ 12/3
Foyt, A. J. 1/16* 5/12, 5/29, 5/30
Frame, Fred 4/25+

France, Bill Sr. 2/21, 6/17+ 9/26* 12/14
Franchi, Carlo "Gimax" 4/14*
Francia, Giorgio 11/8*
Francis, Clarence 9/3, 12/1* 12/28
Francis, Peter 10/11+
Frank, Larry 1/31, 4/29*
Frank, Len 6/28+
Franklin, Herbert H. 4/16+
Franklin, Stanley H. 6/16+
Franks, J. B. Jr. 11/7+
Franquist, Gustav E. 5/19* 9/15+
Franzen, Paul 7/5+
Franz Ferdinand 6/28+
Fraschini, Oreste 7/3+ 7/15*
Fraser, Alexander 10/11*
Fraser, Carlyle 9/12+ 12/23*
Fraser, Douglas A. 5/13, 12/18*
Fraser, Tom 12/22
Fraser, William 11/3*
Frazar, Everett Welles 8/17* 10/14+
Frazer, Joseph W. 2/26, 3/4* 6/19, 7/17, 7/25,
    7/26, 7/28, 8/7+ 8/9, 11/18
Frazer, Mrs. Joseph W. 11/18
Frazer-Nash, Archie 3/10+
Frazier, John P. 3/2*
Fredericks, George 7/4+
Free, Frank 10/30
Freedlander, A. L. 6/6*
Freeman, Andrew L. 1/18+ 3/10*
Freers, George H. 1/21* 2/26, 6/30
Freers, Howard P. 8/13*
Freeston, Herbert G. 7/29+
French, Hubert C. 4/5+
French, John S. 1/5*
Frentzen, Heinz-Harald 4/27, 5/3*
Freon, Franck 3/16*
Frere, Patrick 7/11
Frere, Paul 1/30*
Frew, Lawson H. 1/31+
Frey, Donald N. 3/13* 4/17
Frey, Stuart M. 2/13*
Friderich, Ernest 8/30
Friede, Julian S. 6/27
Friedrich, Leonel 12/17*
Fries, Robert E. 5/25+
Frisbie Russel A. 11/2
Frisinger, Haakan 1/1, 12/8*
Frismuth, Harriet 9/17*
Fritsch, Karl Friedrich 9/10
Friz, Max 3/1
Froelich, John 5/23+ 11/24*
Frost, Jack 12/2*
Frostick, Michael 10/26*
Frua, Pietro 6/2* 6/28+
Fruehauf, August C. 5/16+ 12/15*
Fruehauf, Harry R. 4/29+ 6/8*
Fruehauf, Harvey C. 10/14+ 12/15*
Fruehauf, Roy A. 10/1* 10/31+
Fry, David 7/18
Fry, Joe 7/29+
Frykman, August 1/12+ 8/8*
Fuchs, A. J. 5/26
Fukuyama, Hideo 8/13*
Fuller, Alvan T. 2/27* 3/1, 4/30+ 12/24
Fuller, Harry L. 11/8*
Fuller, Henry J. 4/21+ 12/12*
Fuller, Peter 3/1
Fuller, R. Buckminster 7/1+ 7/12*
Fulton, Samuel A. 1/2+ 11/13*
Fults, Leon A. 5/14
Funderburk, Otis 10/28
Furlan, Nestor 10/13*

Furlow, James W. 3/4+ 8/4*

Gabbiani, Beppe 1/2*
Gabelich, Gary 8/29* 10/23
Gabriel, Fernand 5/24
Gabrielsson, Assar 1/1, 12/16
Gache, Philippe 5/31*
Gachot, Bertrand 3/10, 3/27, 6/23, 12/22*
Gadd, Charles W. 4/6*
Gaebelein, Paul W. 8/6+ 8/21*
Gaeth, Paul 11/24+
Gaffke, William J. 5/22+
Gaillard, Patrick 2/12*
Galamb, Joseph A. 2/3* 4/10, 12/4+ 12/11
Gale, Dan 9/2
Gale, Thomas C. 6/18*
Galica, Divina 8/13*
Galindez, Victor 10/26+
Gallagher, Ralph W. 5/27* 7/31+
Gallaher, Edward B. 1/9+
Gallatin, John T. 4/1+
Galles, Jamie 2/3*
Galli, Nanni 10/2*
Gallinger, A. 7/16
Gallo, Pasquale 12/31
Galvez, Oscar 8/17* 12/16+
Galvin, Paul 6/29* 11/5+
Gamble, Fred 3/17*
Ganley, Howden 12/24*
Gansey, Gilbert 6/24
Ganss, Julius 5/1
Gant, Harry 1/10* 5/6, 6/17, 9/1, 9/7, 9/15,
    9/22
Garbisch, Edgar W. 12/14+
Garbisch, Bernice Chrysler 2/14+
Garbo, Greta 9/4
Garbutt, Frank 4/5* 11/19+
Garcea, Giampaolo 6/10*
Gardham, Joe 8/2
Gardner, Frank 10/1*
Gardner, Goldie 5/31, 6/2, 7/24, 8/25+ 8/27,
    11/9
Gardner, Russell E. 3/16* 9/17+
Gardner, Vincent E. 5/14+
Garford, Arthur L. 1/23+ 8/4*
Garfunkel, Ira 6/26+
Garlent, J. E. 10/18*
Garrett, Garet 2/19* 11/6+
Garrett, Paul 11/27*
Gartner, Jo 1/24* 6/1+
Gasparoux, Andre 12/16+
Gates, Charles C. 11/26*
Gatti, Cesare 7/1
Gault, S. C. 1/6*
Gauntlett, Victor 1/5
Gaydon, Peter 5/6*
Gaylord, Edward 10/20
Gaylord, James K. 10/20+
Gaze, Tony 2/3*
Gebby, Jerry 4/3+ 7/28*
Geddes, Norman Bel 4/27* 5/8+
Geddes, Reay 3/2, 5/7*
Geer, William C. 6/17*
Gegen, Bob 9/15
Gehlhausen, Spike 11/19*
Geki (Giacomo Russo) 6/18+ 10/23*
Gelderman, Carol 12/1*
Gendebien, Olivier 1/12*
Gene, Jordi 12/5*
Genn, John E. 12/15+
Genoa, Duke of 3/19
Gentilozzi, Paul 2/6*

Gentzel, Perry H. 2/16+
George V 3/18, 6/26
George VI 6/16
George, Elmer 5/30+ 7/15*
Gerard, Bob 1/19* 1/26+ 10/28
Gerber, J. W. 1/9
Gerber, Johnny 4/11+ 5/30, 10/14
Gerini, Gerino 4/5, 8/10*
German, Jacob 5/20
Germane, F. M. 12/13*
Germann, Steven J. 9/4*
Gerstenberg, Richard C. 1/1, 11/24* 11/30, 12/6
Gerstenmaier, John H. 7/8+ 8/24*
Gery, Paul E. 1/16+
Gethin, Peter 2/21*
Gettrust, Joseph F. 7/10+
Ghia, Giacinto 2/21+ 9/18*
Ghidella, Vittorio 11/25
Ghinzani, Piercarlo 1/16*
Giacchino, Juan Carlos 12/7*
Giacomelli, Bruno 9/10*
Giacosa, Dante 3/31+ 1/3*
Giamo, Tony 12/8+
Gibson, Charles C. 9/12*
Gibson, Dick 4/16*
Gibson, Todd 12/23*
Gidney, Herbert A. 11/16*
Giffard, Pierre 7/22
Gilbaud, Theodule 7/6+
Gilbert, Henry H. 2/12*
Gilbert, Joseph 7/1
Gilbert-Scott, Andrew 6/11*
Gilfillan, Sennet W. 3/5+
Gill, A. K. 4/1*
Gill, Clarence D. 12/23
Gillan, Paul W. 1/2, 9/27
Gillen, Stanley J. 8/10*
Gillespie, Dean M. 5/3*
Gillespie, King W. 2/2
Gillies, George 2/4
Gillies, Hugh A. 4/23+
Gilliland, Stan 7/19
Gilman, M. B. 11/23
Gilman, Max M. 1/22, 2/28+ 4/17, 4/22, 7/19*
Gilmour, Allan D. 3/1, 6/17*
Gimax (Carlo Franchi) 4/14*
Ginther, Richie 5/29, 8/5* 9/28+ 10/24
Giovanardi, Fabrizio 12/14*
Girardot, Leonce 5/29
Giraud-Cabantous, Yves 3/31+ 10/8*
Girl, Christian 6/10+
Giroix, Fabien 9/17*
Giron, Louis 4/9
Giugiaro, Giorgetto 8/7*
Giulioli, Gene P. 9/2
Giunti, Ignazio 1/10+ 8/30*
Giuntini, Frederick 7/14
Giuppone, Cesare 9/16+
Glancy, Alfred R. 2/1, 7/17* 8/4+ 10/15
Glatz, Fritz 7/21*
Gleason, Jimmy 9/12+
Glidden, Charles J. 8/10, 8/29* 9/11+ 9/18, 11/3
Glockler, Walter 12/8
Glore, Charles F. 11/16*
Glotzbach, Charlie 6/19*
Glover, Frederic S. 1/13+ 3/18*
Glowacke, Ed 3/17, 4/1* 5/4, 5/25+
Gloy, Tom 6/11*
Goad, Louis C. 2/9*
Gobbato, Ugo 4/28+ 7/16* 12/1
Godfrey, Edward R. 5/25*
Godia-Sales, Chico 3/21* 11/28+

Goethals, Christian 8/4*
Goeudevert, Daniel 1/31*
Goldsmith, Paul 10/2*
Golze, Hermann 3/18
Gomez, Guillaume 7/25*
Gomm, Mo 1/14+
Gonard, John L. 11/1+
Gonzalez, Froilan 7/14, 10/5*
Gonzalez, Miguel 11/20+
Good, Alan P. 2/10+ 4/9* 6/17
Good, Charles w. 9/7+
Goodman, James E. 12/11*
Goodman, Walter L. 4/19* 5/23+
Goodrich, B. F. 8/3+ 11/4* 12/31
Goodrich, David M. 5/17+ 6/22*
Goodson, R. E. 4/22*
Goodspeed, Leland F. 4/22
Goodwillie, David H. 1/15*
Goodyear, Charles 3/26, 5/8, 7/1+ 7/18, 12/29*
Goodyear, Richard 12/9*
Goodyear, Scott 12/20*
Goossen, Leo 12/4+
Goossens, Marc 11/30*
Gordini, Aldo 5/20*
Gordini, Amedee 1/1, 3/21, 6/23* 8/5
Gordon, Jeff 8/4* 8/6
Gordon, John F. 1/6+ 5/15* 5/31, 6/1, 6/5, 9/1
Gordon, Lyman F. 11/14* 12/20+
Gordon, Monk 5/30+
Gordon, Robby 1/2*
Gordon, Steven S. 8/29*
Gornick, Alan L. 9/23*
Gorrell, Edgar S. 2/3*
Gosney, Marvin L. 12/16*
Gossett, William T. 9/9*
Gothard, Donald L. 12/2*
Gottingus, Joseph 5/12+
Goudard, Maurice 1/17+
Gould, Earle H. 10/28+
Gould, Horace 9/20* 11/4+
Gounon, Jean-Marc 1/1*
Goutard, Noel 12/22*
Goux, Jules 5/30, 9/4
Grabner, John 2/28+
Grabowsky, Max 9/26+
Graef, Charles D. 5/20*
Graf, Hans 10/5*
Graham, Erwin H. 1/28*
Graham, Joseph B. 1/5, 1/16, 6/10, 7/5+ 9/12*
Graham, Ray A. 1/5, 4/18, 5/28* 6/10, 8/11+
Graham, Mrs. Ray A. 4/18
Graham, Robert C. (1) 1/5, 5/15, 6/10, 7/15, 8/21* 10/3+
Graham, Mrs. Robert C. 5/15
Graham, Robert C. (2) 6/7*
Graham, Walker Ryan A. 7/13*
Gramm, Benjamin A. 12/13
Granatelli, Andy 3/18* 8/14
Grant, Harry F. 10/1, 10/30
Grant, James W. 10/3*
Grant, Jerry 1/23*
Grant, Richard H. 9/24+ 11/26*
Grant, Walter R. 6/1, 10/31
Grass, J. A. 1/29+ 7/1*
Grater, Alfred E. 1/11+ 1/21*
Graves, William H. 4/30* 9/1, 10/30
Gravett, Robb 5/2*
Gray, Christian H. 1/7
Gray, Jack 2/21+
Gray, John S. 7/6+ 10/5* 10/22
Gray, Ralph D. 10/13*
Gray, Robert (1) 3/13, 4/10

Gray, Robert (2) 2/12*
Gray, William M. 3/13, 10/27+
Greco, Marco 12/1*
Green, David 1/28*
Green, E. R. 5/30
Green, George A. 2/21+
Green, Heatley 9/20+
Green, Tom 10/2
Greene, Keith 1/5* 7/15
Greenebaum, Leon C. 3/25+ 12/30*
Greenleaf, William 7/1*
Greenwald, Gerald 5/30, 9/11* 11/10
Gregg, Peter 5/4* 12/15+
Gregoire, Rene 6/4*
Gregoire, Stephan 5/14*
Gregorie, Eugene 10/6
Gregory, Benjamin F. 6/7
Gregory, Masten 2/29* 5/19, 11/8+
Greifzu, Paul 8/3
Grettenberger, John 2/1
Grey, Andrew D. 6/18+
Grice, Allan 10/21*
Grier, Samuel 6/18
Griffin, Robert T. 3/13, 7/3*
Griffith, Daniel B. 8/30*
Griffith, Pat 1/28+
Griffith, S. S. 11/21*
Grignard, Georges 7/25* 12/7+
Grim, Bobby 9/4*
Grimaldi, Michael A. 11/1
Grimm, Goetz 3/16*
Grisham, Rita 4/9*
Grissom, Steve 6/26*
Griswold, Frank 10/2, 10/6
Groff, J. L. E. 2/23+
Groff, Mike 11/16*
Grohs, Harald 1/28*
Grouillard, Olivier 6/16, 9/2*
Grout, C. B. 4/20
Grout, Carl 4/20
Grout, Fred 4/20
Grout, William L. 4/20+
Grover-Williams, William 8/2
Gruenewald, Eugene 10/1+
Gruger, Frederick R. 8/2*
Grundy, Gordon E. 2/26*
Grylls, S. H. 7/19
Gubby, Brian 4/17*
Gubitz, Werner H. A. 6/1, 7/29*
Gueiros, Marcos 5/11*
Guelfi, Andre 5/6*
Guernsey, Charles O. 9/1
Guerra, Miguel 8/31*
Guerrero, Carlos 11/20*
Guerrero, Roberto 5/9, 11/16*
Gugelmin, Mauricio 4/20*
Guilbaud, Theodule 7/6+
Guinness, A. Lee 5/11* 10/26+
Guinness, K. Lee 5/11, 5/17, 10/26
Guippone, Giouse 3/8, 9/16+
Guitteny, Lucien 6/17*
Gulbenkian, Calouste 7/20+
Gulbenkian, Nubar 1/10+ 6/2*
Gulda, Edward J. 10/28*
Gulick, Henry 10/28+
Gulotta, Tony 8/31
Gunn, George Jr. 4/10*
Gurnett, C. H. 5/11+ 7/24*
Gurney, Chuck 4/20*
Gurney, Dan 3/12, 4/9, 4/13* 6/18, 6/28, 7/3, 7/5, 7/8

Gurney, F. W. 4/21*
Gurney, Goldsworthy 2/14* 2/21, 2/28+
Gurney, Henry 10/6+
Gurschner, Gustave 9/28*
Gusloff, O. F. 5/15
Gustaf Adolf VI 4/24
Gustafson, Stanley W. 2/18*
Gustin, Lawrence R. 5/26*
Guth, Wilfried 7/8*
Guthrie, Janet 3/7* 5/22
Guthrie, Jim 9/13*
Guthrie, Randolph H. 6/7
Guyot, Albert 4/20
Gyllenhammar, Pehr G. 4/28* 12/2

Haas, Rudolph 10/28
Haba, Leonard Allen 8/11*
Habbel, Wolfgang R. 3/25*
Hackett, John T. 10/10*
Hackworth, Donald E. 2/19*
Haddon, J. William 3/4+ 3/20, 5/24* 8/11
Haener, Arnold 7/8, 8/24
Hafstad, Lawrence R. 6/18*
Haggbom, Gunnar 12/7*
Hague, Robert W. 4/6*
Hahn, Carl 3/28, 7/1*
Hahn, Heinz W. 2/13*
Hahne, Armin 9/10*
Hahne, Hubert 3/28*
Haibe, Reno 10/22+
Hailwood, Mike 3/23+ 4/2*
Hainline, Forrest A. Jr. 10/20*
Hakkinen, Mika 9/28*
Halbleib, Edward A. 8/16
Halbleib, Joseph C. 8/16+
Halderman, Gail 9/10
Hale, James E. 10/13* 11/28+
Haley, William J. 8/27* 9/25+
Halford, Bruce 5/18*
Hall, Charles I. 12/7+
Hall, Dean 11/11*
Hall, Elbert J. 4/8* 10/28+
Hall, Jim 6/5, 7/23* 10/15
Hall, John R. 6/11+
Hall, Theodore P. 3/17+ 12/18*
Halle 7/15+
Halle, Hiram J. 5/29+
Hallett, John 3/28
Hallinan, M. J. 8/28
Hallock, Edward F. 2/23+
Hambleton, Kitty 12/6
Hamerly, Frank B. 11/27+
Hamilton, Bobby 5/29*
Hamilton, Davey 6/13*
Hamilton, Duncan 4/30* 5/13+ 6/14
Hamilton, Harold L. 5/3+ 6/14* 12/31
Hamilton, Harry G. 7/13
Hamilton, Hugh 8/26+
Hamilton, Pete 7/20*
Hamlin, L. M. 11/21
Hamlin, Ralph 7/5+
Hammel, Albert 4/26, 7/14* 9/3+
Hammer, Kathleen M. 9/30*
Hammers, Morgan J. 4/19* 4/28*
Hammes, Michael N. 5/15
Hammond, Dean B. 3/28, 7/17+ 12/24*
Hammond, Elmer C. 1/10, 2/2
Hammond, Eugene I. 7/6, 9/17
Hampshire, David 8/25+ 12/29*
Hampson, Robert J. 9/11
Hanai, Masaya 6/10+ 8/1*

Hanawa, Yoshikazu 6/27
Hanch, Charles C. 6/15, 6/20, 10/22+ 11/19*
Hanchett, Benton 4/6* 6/24+ 7/6
Hancock, Thomas 3/26+ 5/8*
Handley, J. I. 7/1
Haney, F. V. 10/18
Hankinson, Ralph A. 8/1*
Hanks, Sam 5/7, 6/27+ 7/13*
Hannagan, Steven 2/5+
Hannan, James M. 5/22+ 12/1*
Hannaway, Brett 5/7
Hannum, George 11/8
Hanon, Bernard 1/7* 1/21
Hans, Edmund 7/8+ 12/21*
Hansen, Ivan W. 5/29+
Hansen, Mel 6/5+
Hansen, Richard A. 7/10*
Hansen, Zenon C. R. 1/21, 7/23* 10/19+
Hansford, Gregg 3/5+
Hansgen, Walt 4/7+ 9/19, 9/30, 10/28*
Hanson, George W. 9/11* 10/31+
Hansten, Huschke von 1/3* 3/6+
Hardee, Sam W. 8/19+
Harden, Orville 4/4* 8/17+
Harder, Delmar S. 3/19*
Harding, Warren G. 2/28, 3/4
Hardy, A. B. C. 1/21, 4/19, 4/25, 5/28, 8/13, 11/19*, 11/22+
Hardy, Bill 8/26*
Hardy, William E. 7/23
Hare, E. S. 1/1, 2/27, 3/10+ 6/1, 7/29, 10/6, 10/17, 11/26* 12/15
Hargis, James 9/5
Harkey, Bob 6/23*
Harkness, Harry 1/23+ 5/17, 7/12, 7/20, 8/27
Harmsworth, A. C. W. 7/15* 8/14+
Harrah, William F. 6/30+ 9/2*
Harriman, George 3/3* 5/29+ 11/26
Harrington, George J. 2/13*
Harris, Charles N. 6/3+ 8/6
Harris, David B. 8/9*
Harris, George T. 6/12, 12/29+
Harris, Harry E. 4/4*
Harris, Leon 6/20*
Harris, Mike 5/25*
Harrison, Cuth 1/22+ 7/6*
Harrison, Herbert C. 3/6+ 10/4*
Harroun, Ray 1/12* 1/19+ 5/30, 9/25
Hart, Brian 9/7*
Hartford, Edward V. 5/28* 6/30+
Hartley, Fred L. 1/16* 10/19+
Hartman, F. W. 9/5+
Hartmann, William V. 9/12*
Hartz, Harry 5/1, 9/26+
Hartz, Paul F. 8/20*
Harvey, Harold B. 6/20* 12/3+
Harvey, Maurice 10/13
Harvey, Tim 11/20*
Hasemi, Masahiro 2/2, 10/24, 11/13*
Haskell, Raymond 4/6+
Haspel, Wilhelm 1/1
Hass, Herman J. 2/12+ 12/23*
Hassan, Wally 4/12*
Hassard-Short, Frederick W. 2/12+ 8/5*
Hasse, Rudi 5/30*
Hassler, Friday 2/17+
Hastings, Charles D. 8/7+ 8/25* 11/8
Hatch, Darwin S. 1/20+ 2/19*
Hatcher, William A. 1/27, 7/3, 7/7, 11/4, 12/31*
Hatfield, Charles B. Jr. 5/20
Hatfield, Charles B. Sr. 5/20
Hathaway, Stewart S. 7/25*

Hatheway, Curtis R. 8/9, 9/10, 11/3
Hattori, Naoki 6/13*
Haugdahl, Sig 2/4+ 3/8, 4/7
Haugwitz-Reventlow, Kurt von 2/24
Haupt, Willie 5/30
Hausmann, T. L. 6/16, 10/8
Havemeyer, John Francis 6/15+
Havens, Samuel M. 11/4+
Hawkes, W. D. 5/30
Hawkins, Norval 5/2, 7/10* 8/18+
Hawkins, Paul 5/26+ 10/12*
Hawn, George L. Sr. 12/31+
Haworth, H. F. 6/18+
Hawthorn, Mike 1/22+ 4/10* 6/22, 7/5, 9/2, 10/19
Hayden, Billy 1/19* 3/27
Hayden, Jay G. 10/24+ 12/8*
Hayek, Nicolas 3/4
Hayes, Charlie 12/14*
Hayes, H. Jay 4/23* 8/14+
Hayes, Paul W. 11/4+
Hayes, Walter 4/12*
Hayje, Boy 5/3*
Haylett, Robert E. 6/13+
Hayner, Stuart 3/2
Haynes, A. R. 8/7*
Haynes, Elwood 4/13+ 5/25, 7/4, 10/13, 10/14* 10/21
Haynes, Mrs. Elwood 10/21
Haynes, Frederick 1/11
Haynes, Robert B. 2/25+
Haynes, Ronald 9/9*
Hayward, Nathaniel 1/19* 7/18+
Haywood, Hurley 5/4*
Hazell, Robert T. 1/14+
Head, Jack 10/24
Healey, Donald 1/13+ 4/29, 10/22
Healey, Geoffrey 4/29+
Healy, Robert E. 3/25* 6/2, 11/16+
Hearley, Tim 1/5
Hearne, Eddie 2/9+ 8/14, 9/4
Hearne, Richie 1/4*
Heaslet, James G. 8/30, 12/6
Heath, George 10/8
Hebb, A. G. 1/10, 2/2, 4/1, 7/26*
Hecht, Earl H. 12/6+
Hedlund, Roger 8/23
Heeks, Willi 2/13*
Heft, G. Stanley 11/2
Heftler, Victor R. 9/15+
Hegbourne, Tony 7/1+ 7/24*
Heger, Altfrid 1/24*
Heil, Julius P. 7/24* 11/30+
Heimbach, Elmer F. 6/29+
Heine, Gustav 1/7* 4/28+
Heinen, Paul A. 1/9*
Heinisch, Don 8/23* 10/29+
Heinmuller, Dwight 5/16*
Heins, Bino 6/15+
Heintz, Leo I. 7/8+
Heinzelman, Reginald 6/28
Heise, Richard A. 8/13*
Heisley, Frederick W. 12/21+
Helary, Eric 8/10*
Helck, Peter 4/22+ 6/17* 10/24
Held, John Jr. 1/10* 3/2+
Helder, Roger J. 7/7*
Heldt, Peter M. 2/9, 3/11+
Helfrich, Theo 4/29+ 5/13* 8/1
Heller, J. R. 2/8+
Hemery, Victor 5/19, 9/9+ 10/14, 11/8, 12/30
Hemmings, E. R. 1/2

Henderson, Herbert V. 3/1, 3/15, 7/17, 7/21, 8/2, 10/2, 11/11
Henderson, Peter 5/30
Henderson, Thomas W. 3/1
Henn, Edwin C. 8/20+
Henne, Ernst 6/14
Hennecke, Earle V. 5/11+
Hennessey, Patrick 4/18*
Henney, John W. 11/26+
Henning, Harold P. 9/12+
Henricy, John 3/2
Henry, Ernest 1/2* 9/28, 12/12+
Henry, Leslie R. 8/31
Henry, Thomas P. 9/7+ 12/28*
Hensley, Charles J. 6/12
Henton, Brian 9/13, 9/19*
Hepburn, Ralph 5/16+
Herbert, Jean 9/5
Herbert, Johnny 6/23, 6/25*
Herd, Robin 3/7, 6/9
Hering, Charles E. 5/8+
Herke, Horst W. 12/2*
Herreshoff, Charles F. 1/30+ 5/28*
Herreshoff, Francis L. 8/23+
Herrhausen, Alfred 1/30*
Herrick, Harvey 10/14
Herrington, Arthur W. 1/5, 3/30* 8/5, 9/6+ 11/11, 11/20
Herrmann, Hans 2/23* 8/2
Hershey, Franklin Q. 1/7, 7/23*
Herta, Bryan 5/23*
Hertz, John D. 2/6, 4/10* 8/25, 8/26, 10/8+
Hery, Louis 7/28+
Hesnault, Francois 12/30*
Hess, Donald P. 4/25*
Hess, Henry 3/23+
Hess, Leon 3/13*
Hess, Samuel P. 10/24+
Hession, J. W. Jr. 10/7
Heuer, Georg 7/21+
Heumann, Jules 5/12
Heussner, Carl E. 1/2+
Heveron, Doug 3/29*
Hewitt, Edward R. 2/19+ 6/20*
Hewson, W. Sherman 10/16
Heyer, Hans 3/16*
Heynes, William 7/10+ 12/31*
Hezemans, Toine 4/14*
Hibbard, Thomas L. 5/9, 10/11+
Hickerson, J. Mel 10/19*
Hickman, Frank R. 10/10+
Hicks, Harold A. 4/12+
Hicks, Roger W. 6/15*
Hieronimus, Otto 4/1
Higgins, O. B. 10/28*
Hight, Franklin R. 3/28+
Hildenbrand, Kenneth W. 3/1+
Hill, Bennett 12/14
Hill, Claude 7/15
Hill, Damon 9/17*
Hill, David C. 1/15* 11/18, 12/4
Hill, Frank Ernest 8/29* 11/2+
Hill, Graham 2/15* 4/12, 4/15, 6/18, 9/17, 10/5, 11/29+
Hill, Herbert E. 7/3+
Hill, L. T. 1/25+
Hill, Myron F. 12/20*
Hill, Phil 4/20* 6/9, 7/6, 9/4, 9/7, 11/5
Hillin, Bobby 6/5*
Hillman, William 6/17
Hills, Herbert H. 3/15, 7/23* 7/27, 8/13, 8/25
Hinds, William N. 11/13+

Hines, Anthony L. 9/19*
Hinkley, Carl C. 7/15* 8/23+
Hinman, James H. 1/7
Hinnershitz, Tommy 4/6*
Hirahara, Yoshito 8/2+
Hirashima, Chick 5/4*
Hirschler, Horace L. 5/24+
Hirt, Peter 3/30* 5/27
Hiss, Mike 7/7*
Hitler, Adolf 4/10, 5/26, 10/8
Hives, Ernest W. 4/21* 4/24+ 5/23, 6/16
Hoagg, Kirke K. 12/11+
Hoban, Carl L. 9/19+
Hobbs, David 6/9*
Hobgood, Will 2/7*
Hobrock, Raymond H. 9/10+
Hochwalt, Carroll A. 12/8
Hodges, Hayden 6/17
Hodgetts, Chris 6/12*
Hodgman, Clare E. 9/7+
Hodkin, David 8/17
Hoeler, William 4/4+
Hoelscher, Howard 12/27+
Hoelzle, Eugene C. 3/22*
Hoerr, Irv 11/14*
Hoffa, James R. 2/14*
Hoffman, Arthur H. 8/13+
Hoffman, H. O. 11/6*
Hoffman, Max 5/20, 6/21, 7/10, 7/17, 11/12* 12/8
Hoffman, Paul G. 2/4, 3/9, 4/13, 4/26* 7/26, 10/1, 10/8+
Hoffmann, Ingo 2/18*
Hofheinz, Roy M. 6/8
Hofmann, Fred 3/23+
Hofmann, Josef 1/20* 2/16+ 5/17
Hogan, Henry M. 3/18* 6/2+
Hogg, Tony 1/27* 8/4+
Hoglund, Ellis S. 7/29*
Hoglund, William E. 1/26, 6/28, 8/22*
Hohensee, Frederick W. 7/24+
Holbert, Al 9/30+ 11/11*
Holcomb, Harry 8/19+
Holden, E. H. 6/2
Holden, Edward W. 3/20, 6/18+ 8/14*
Holden, Mrs. Edward W. 3/20
Holden, James 1/22
Holder, William G. 3/15*
Holland, Bill 5/20+ 12/18*
Holland, Samuel 4/26*
Hollander, E. R. 5/12
Hollertz, Rose Ann 3/28+
Holley, George M. 4/14* 6/27+
Holliday, Wallace T. 3/10* 11/7+
Hollingshead, Richard M. Jr. 6/6
Hollister, Clarence P. 12/13
Hollister, Don C. 12/8
Holm, Svante 12/7*
Holman, Eugene 1/6, 5/2* 8/12+ 12/1
Holman, John 5/25, 11/9*
Holmes, Howdy 12/14*
Holmgrain, E. O. 2/6+
Holsman, Henry K. 5/15+
Holste, Werner 10/1
Holt, Glen Grover 11/26+
Holt, Pliny E. 8/27* 11/18+
Holtback, Roger 1/1
Honda, Soichiro 7/10, 8/5+ 11/17*
Honold, Gottlob 9/24
Hood, Wallace A. 9/16
Hoof, A. C. 8/8+
Hooker, Harry H. 8/4+

Hooven, Frederick J. 9/4
Hoover, Herbert 2/28, 3/4, 5/30, 8/8
Hoover, Vernon C. 6/1+ 7/19*
Hope, Bob 9/1
Hope, Harry 9/1
Hopkins, Benjamin F. 6/13* 12/26+
Hopkins, Cecil 5/22*
Hopkins, F. T. 1/1
Hopkins, Spencer D. 5/5*
Hopkirk, Paddy 4/14*
Horch, August 2/3+ 4/29, 10/12*
Horikoshi, Jiro 1/11+
Horine, Merrill C. 1/23+
Horn, Ted 2/27* 10/10+
Hornaday, Ron Jr. 6/20*
Horne, John R. 3/20
Horning, Harry L. 1/4+ 3/28*
Hornsby, J. Allen 11/1
Hornsted, L. G. 6/24
Horowitz, Louis 4/3
Horrocks, Raymond 1/9*
Horstemeyer, Bill 8/22+
Horter, Earl 3/29+
Horton, E. P. 6/16* 8/15+
Horton, Robert B. 8/18*
Hosac, W. E. 2/1
Hoshino, Kazuyoshi 2/2, 7/1*
Hotchkiss, Benjamin B. 2/14+ 10/1*
Hough, C. M. 4/23+ 5/18* 9/15
Hough, Richard 5/15*
Houk, George W. 10/6+ 11/7*
Hoult, Charles 2/14
Houpt, Harry S. 1/19
House, Henry A. 4/23* 10/6, 12/18+
House, James A. 10/6
Householder, Ronnie 11/11+
Houser, Theodore V. 9/3* 12/17+
Houston, Tommy 1/29*
Howard, Charles S. 2/28* 6/6+
Howard, Earl 1/6
Howard, Graeme K. 3/4* 12/6+
Howard, Harold F. 1/7+
Howard, J. W. 8/1
Howard, Max L. 3/16+
Howard, Norman 5/14*
Howard, O. O. 8/1
Howard, Ray L. 1/29+
Howard, Walter S. 7/27+
Howe, Lord 3/25
Howell, K. J. 9/24+
Howland, Alfred 2/10
Hoy, Will 4/2*
Hruska, Rudolf 1/2+ 1/16, 7/2* 11/1
Huartson, Craig 8/26*
Hubman, Tim 6/28*
Huck, Louis C. 7/9+
Hucul, Cliff 8/21*
Hudlass, Maurice 10/22+
Hudson, Joseph L. 2/24, 7/15+ 10/17* 11/1
Hudson, Skip 10/20
Huebner, George J. Jr. 3/25, 4/19
Huff, Russell 3/26+ 10/21*
Hufstader, W. F. 6/25*
Hughes, Arthur M. 4/7*
Hughes, Hughie 8/27, 12/2+
Hughes, James R. 2/28, 11/30+
Hughes, Jim 3/26+
Hughes, Louis R. 4/6
Hughson, William L. 4/16+
Hull, J. Byron 8/24+
Hulman, Tony 10/27+ 11/14
Hulme, Denis 6/18* 10/4+

Humbert, Jack N. 3/2+
Hume, James W. 4/9+
Humenik, Michael 7/15+ 11/10*
Humlhanz, Albert F. 5/21*
Hund, H. E. 10/7* 10/10+
Hungerford, Daniel 11/2
Hungerford, Floyd 11/2
Hunt, George H. 11/25+
Hunt, J. H. 3/24*
Hunt, J. W. 1/7+
Hunt, James 3/30, 6/15+ 6/22, 8/29*
Hunt, Lester C. 6/19+ 7/8*
Hunt, Ormond E. 1/4+ 10/1* 11/2, 11/19
Hunter, Lee 4/27*
Hunter, Robert E. 6/12*
Hunter, Rudolph M. 3/20+ 6/20*
Huntoon, George 6/11
Hupp, Louis G. 12/10+
Hupp, Robert C. 4/29, 6/2* 11/8, 12/7+
Huppert, Willard L. 3/12+
Hurd, Reverdy L. 9/7
Hurlburt, Mike 4/3*
Hurley, Roy T. 6/3* 10/31+
Hurn, James E. 8/12+
Hurtubise, Jim 1/6+ 12/5*
Huss, Theodore 7/6
Hussey, Patrick L. 2/23+
Hussong, F. R. 2/2
Hustead, Thomas E. 12/9
Husted, Seymour L. Jr. 6/12
Hutcherson, Dick 11/30*
Hutchings, Lester 2/12+ 4/7*
Hutchinson, B. Edwin 10/2*
Hutchinson, Charles M. 7/24
Hutchinson, Richard A. 9/19*
Hutchison, Gus 4/26*
Hutton, Barbara 2/24
Huxley, T. C. Jr. 2/3+
Huygens, Christian 4/14* 7/8+
Hyatt, John W. 5/10+ 11/28*
Hyde, Charles K. 3/23*
Hyde, Harlow 4/4+
Hylton, James 8/26*
Hytten, Mario 4/20*

Iacocca, Lee 2/1, 3/9, 4/14, 4/29, 7/13, 7/18,
    8/8, 9/5, 9/11, 9/20, 10/15* 11/2, 12/10,
    12/31
Iacoponi, Stefano 8/20*
Ibanez, Jose Maria 2/1*
Ickes, Elwood T. 4/17+
Ickx, Jacky 1/1* 5/1, 7/7
Ickx, Jacques 1/1
Iglesias, Jesus 2/22*
Ihamuotila, Jaakko 11/15*
Iliff, Warren J. 8/21+
Ingold, Ernest 3/26*
Innes, Henry 8/16+
Innocenti, Ferdinando 6/21+
Innocenti, Luigi 12/19*
Inoue, Taki 9/5*
Inskip, John S. 2/1, 3/22, 9/7+
Instone, E. M. C. 8/12
Iorio, Ralph A. 11/21*
Ireland, Innes 5/31, 6/9, 6/12* 10/22+
Ireland, William E. 5/21+
Ireland, William G. 10/12+
Irimajiri, Shoichiro 5/10
Irvan, Ernie 1/13*
Irvin, Gary 11/3*
Irvin, Robert W. 12/1+
Irvine, Eddie 11/10*

Irving, J. S. 3/11
Irwin, Chris 6/27* 7/16
Irwin, James B. 3/17* 7/31, 8/8+
Irwin, W. G. 11/24* 12/14+
Isaac, Bobby 8/1* 8/14+
Isbrandt, Ralph H. 4/9*
Ishibashi, Kanichiro 3/1*
Ishida, Taizo 11/16*
Ishihara, Takashi 3/3* 9/28
Isler, Jacques 8/14*
Isom, Edward W. 1/22+ 10/23*
Isotta, Cesare 7/2, 9/9
Issigonis, Alec 2/19, 8/26, 10/2+ 10/28, 11/18*
Iwasaki, Yataro 1/9* 2/7+
Iwasawa, Masaji 4/25*

Jabouille, Jean-Pierre 6/25, 7/1, 7/16, 10/1*
Jackson, Brian 9/28+
Jackson, Edwin B. 4/15+
Jackson, H. Nelson 1/14+ 5/23, 7/26
Jackson, Jimmy 9/10
Jackson, Reggie 5/18*
Jackson, Richard W. 5/23* 11/11+
Jackson, Robert B. 11/11*
Jackson, Roy 9/3*
Jacobs, Steve 8/25+
Jacobs, Walter L. 2/6+ 6/15*
Jacobsen, C. L. 9/14, 12/16
Jacobsen, William Jr. 1/9
Jacoby, George A. 5/13*
Jacquemart, Patrick 7/9+
Jacques, Leo G. 1/3*
Jaeger, Herman J. 3/7+ 4/29*
Jahnke, Charles B. 5/6+
Jakob, Victor 6/9
Jakobsen, Jakob K. 8/7*
James, Joe 11/5+
James, John 5/10*
James, William S. 2/29+ 9/3*
Jamieson, Tom 5/7+
Jamison, Andrew 8/22+
Janicke, Edward S. 4/7+
Jano, Vittorio 3/12+ 4/22* 6/9
Jansson, Axel J. 2/2* 12/25+
Jaquays, Chuck 6/25
Jaray, Paul 3/10* 7/31
Jardine, Robert 6/12+ 12/6
Jarier, Jean-Pierre 1/15, 7/10*
Jarrett, Dale 11/26*
Jarrett, Ned 10/12* 11/26
Jarrott, Charles 4/8, 5/25, 7/31
Jaskowiak, Frank 4/8, 7/30+ 10/4*
Jaussaud, Jean-Pierre 6/3*
Jay, Frank 8/18+
Jay, Webb 5/20, 5/27, 7/4
Jeffery, Charles T. 6/10, 11/10+
Jeffery, Joseph A. 6/27* 12/26+
Jeffery, Thomas B. 2/5* 4/2+
Jelinski, Frank 5/23*
Jellinek-Mercedes, Andree 8/2*
Jellinek (-Mercedes), Emil 1/21+ 3/30, 4/2,
    4/6* 4/10, 8/2, 9/2, 10/14, 11/22, 12/22
Jellinek, Mercedes 2/23+ 8/2, 12/22
Jellinek (-Mercedes), Guy 4/10*
Jenatzy, Camille 1/17, 1/27, 3/28, 4/9, 4/29,
    7/2, 10/7+ 11/4* 11/27
Jenkins, Ab 1/25* 3/2, 7/2, 7/22, 8/6, 8/9+,
    8/31, 9/4, 9/18, 9/19
Jenkinson, Denis 5/1, 12/1+ 12/11*
Jenks, Frank W. 8/7* 12/27+
Jennings, B. Brewster 6/9* 10/2+
Jennings, William F. 9/14+

Jensen, Reuben R. 12/22*
Jenter, John C. 8/26+
Jerome, John 11/7*
Jerome, Walter C. 3/20*
Jewett, Harry M. 1/12, 5/5, 6/10, 7/29
Jimenez, Cesar 7/4*
Johansson, Carl E. 3/15* 9/30+
Johansson, Lennart 10/3*
Johansson, Micke 5/13*
Johansson, Stefan 5/28, 7/16, 9/8*
Johncock, Gordon 8/25*
Johns, Bobby 5/22*
Johnson, Amos 4/9*
Johnson, Basil 1/14, 1/31, 4/23
Johnson, Carl W. 6/5+
Johnson, Charles E. 12/20
Johnson, Claude 3/15, 4/11+ 4/23, 9/22, 10/24*
Johnson, Dick 4/26*
Johnson, E. A. 7/1
Johnson, E. D. 6/7+
Johnson, Earle F. 7/24+ 11/4*
Johnson, Eddie 2/10*
Johnson, Elmer W. 5/2* 6/27+
Johnson, G. R. 3/22, 4/12
Johnson, H. D. 7/22
Johnson, Jack 10/25
Johnson, James N. 10/7*
Johnson, Joe Lee 11/9*
Johnson, John E. 3/30+ 8/16*
Johnson, Joseph 4/10
Johnson, Junior 6/28*
Johnson, Ken 11/28*
Johnson, Leslie 6/8+
Johnson, Lyndon B. 1/16
Johnson, Philip G. 9/12+
Johnson, Richard L. 5/5*
Johnson, Van 7/19+
Johnson, Walter P. 2/20+
Johnson, Warren S. 12/4+
Johnston, Edward A. 3/1*
Johnstone, Bruce 1/30*
Johnstone, Parker 3/27*
Jolls, Lyall 11/25+
Jones, Alan 8/14, 10/17, 11/2*
Jones, B. Frank 1/8+ 9/19*
Jones, Bubby 6/5*
Jones, Charles F. 4/30+ 11/23*
Jones, Davy 6/1*
Jones, Edward M. 2/3*
Jones, Edward T. 10/20*
Jones, Gerald F. 9/20*
Jones, Halsey R. 8/28+
Jones, John 10/19*
Jones, P. J. 4/23*
Jones, Parnelli 4/23, 8/12*
Jones, Stan 11/2
Jones, Trevor O. 11/3*
Jones, Walter M. 8/31+
Jonsson, Niclas 8/4*
Jordan, Charles M. 10/21* 10/31
Jordan, Eddie 3/10
Jordan, Edward S. "Ned" 2/2, 11/21* 12/29+
Jordan, Mrs. Ned 2/2
Jost, Reinhold 4/24*
Jourdain, Michel Jr. 9/2*
Joy, Basil H. 3/6
Joy, Charles P. 9/30+
Joy, Henry B. 1/9, 1/23, 1/24, 3/14, 7/4, 8/26,
    9/11, 10/13, 11/6+ 11/23*
Joyce, J. A. 11/24
Joyce, William J. Jr. 8/10*

Juan Carlos 10/26
Judd, Morton F. 6/28+
Judge, John E. 5/5*
Junek, Elisabeth 9/7
Junek, Vinzenz 7/15+
Justice, Bill 11/11*

Kachlein, George F. Jr. 4/1+ 5/9*
Kageyama, Masahiko 8/8*
Kahn, Albert 1/1, 1/4, 1/9, 3/21* 5/26, 12/8+
Kaiser, Edgar F. 1/11, 3/28, 5/4, 7/29* 10/5, 12/11+
Kaiser, Henry J. 4/8, 4/10, 5/9* 7/17, 7/25, 7/26, 8/9, 8/24+ 10/5, 12/14
Kaiser, Mrs. Henry J. (1) 3/14+ 4/8
Kaiser, Mrs. Henry J. (2) 4/10
Kaiser, Henry J. Jr. 5/2+
Kaiser, Herman 1/12
Kaiser, Tomas 11/2*
Kalb, Lewis P. 6/24* 12/28+
Kamm, Wunibald 4/26* 5/7, 10/11
Kane, Forrest H. 1/28+
Kankkunen, Juha 4/2*
Kannady, Arthur H. 9/1+
Kanzler, Ernest C. 1/20, 5/29* 6/13, 6/19, 7/26, 11/12+
Kanzler, Mrs. Ernest C. 6/19
Karch, Oswald 3/6*
Karczewski, Zbigniew J. 4/13+
Karl, Jerry 4/29*
Karmann, Wilhelm Jr. 12/4*
Karmann, Wilhelm Sr. 9/28+
Karnstadt, C. 2/26
Karolevitz, Robert F. 4/26*
Katayama, Ukyo 3/1, 5/29*
Katayama, Yutaka 9/15* 9/28
Kaufman, Daniel W. 3/1
Kaufman, Nathan M. 3/1
Kautz, Christian 7/4+
Kawamata, Katsuji 3/1* 3/29+
Kawamoto, Nobuhiko 3/24* 5/10
Kawazoe, Soichi 9/28
Kazato, Hiroshi 3/13*
Kearfott, Arman J. 5/5+
Kearns, Henry 4/30* 6/5+
Keating, Thomas H. 2/25+
Keech, Ray 4/22, 5/30, 6/15+
Keegan, Rupert 2/26*
Keen, F. A. 12/22
Keeton, Forrest M. 4/1+
Kehrl, Howard H. 2/2* 5/1
Keigwin, W. S. 6/17
Keiller, Alexander 6/20
Keizan, Eddie 9/12*
Kelleners, Helmut 12/29*
Keller, Al 5/2, 11/19+
Keller, George D. 10/5+
Keller, Harry L. 4/8+
Keller, Jason 4/23*
Keller, K. T. 1/21+ 4/1, 4/17, 7/22, 11/3, 11/27* 12/31
Kelley, George L. 7/25+
Kelley, Nicholas 6/26, 7/12* 10/28+
Kelly, Alonzo H. Jr. 9/30*
Kelly, Joe 3/13*
Kelly, Sherman L. 8/21+
Kelly, Sidney 1/26*
Kelly, William E. 6/2
Kelsey, Carl 2/13, 5/17+ 7/20*
Kelsey, John 1/19+ 6/20*
Kemp, A. P. 6/25, 7/1
Kemp, William E. 12/29+

Kemper, H. G. 2/10*
Kempton, Stephen 9/23+
Kempton, Steve 2/8*
Kendall, Tom 10/17*
Kenilworth, Lord 11/3+
Kennedy, David 1/15*
Kennedy, James T. 11/4+
Kennedy, John F. 5/20, 10/5, 12/13, 12/30
Kennicott, Jay A. 1/9
Kenny, William F. 8/13+
Kent, Duke of 9/14
Kent, A. Atwater 3/4, 10/11, 12/3*+
Kent, H. W. 1/22, 10/17+ 12/9* 12/22
Kenyon, Harry B. 12/17+
Kenyon, Mel 4/15*
Kerr, Maurice L. 7/8+
Kesling, Peter C. 1/1*
Kessel, Loris 4/1*
Kessenger, A. J. 12/15
Kessler, Jean B. A. 6/16*
Kessler, Robert L. 4/7
Kettering, Charles F. 1/6, 1/10, 1/13, 2/1, 2/8, 2/17, 4/17, 5/11, 6/2, 6/4, 6/12, 6/13, 6/15, 7/22, 8/7, 8/17, 8/29* 9/15, 9/25, 11/2, 11/24, 11/25+ 12/1, 12/17, 12/30
Keyes, Corlis G. 2/4+
Keys, Walter C. 1/25+
Kidder, Donald E. 1/30*
Kidston, Glen 6/22
Kiefer, Arthur E. 11/15
Kieft, Milton 6/3+
Killebrew, George W. 1/1
Killefer, Tom 1/7*
Kimball, Earl W. 11/16+
Kimball, Fred M. 7/27
Kimber, Cecil 2/4+ 3/27, 4/12* 7/21
Kimberly, Jim 7/23
Kimes, Beverly Rae 8/17*
Kincaid, W. G. 4/15+
King, Anita 6/10+
King, Charles B. 1/18, 2/2* 3/6, 6/23+ 10/3
King, Joe H. 9/25*
King, Robert S. 7/21*
Kingsford, Edward G. 1/24
Kingston, R. I. 5/31
Kinnear, James W. III 3/21*
Kinnunen, Leo 8/5*
Kinser, Sheldon 12/9*
Kirby, Frank E. 8/28
Kirkham, George 1/3
Kishline, F. F. 1/6
Kissel, George A. 6/25, 9/19
Kissel, Louis 4/28+
Kissel, Otto P. 6/25
Kissel, Wilhelm 6/28, 7/18+ 12/22*
Kissel, William L. 2/29, 9/6+ 12/13
Kissinger, Walter B. 6/21*
Kittredge, Lewis H. 3/28+
Klauser, Hans 3/21
Klausmeyer, David M. 2/2* 6/30, 11/3+
Klees, Robert E. 10/26
Kleiber, Paul 12/18+
Klein, Aaron E. 7/8*
Klein, Chris J. 2/26, 5/29
Klein, John J. 11/11+
Klein, William Jr. 1/10* 11/8+
Kleinert, George H. 6/12+
Klemperer, Wolfgang 7/31
Klenk, Hans 8/1, 10/18*
Klerk, Peter de 3/16*
Kleyer, Heinrich 10/1
Kliesrath, Victor W. 5/30, 10/24, 12/21+

Kline, James A. 5/20*
Klinedinst, Louis M. 8/10+
Kling, Karl 7/4, 9/16*
Klingler, Harry J. 1/5, 7/5*
Klingmann, Horst 3/24
Klink, John F. 7/8, 11/11+
Klodwig, Ernst 4/15+ 5/23* 8/3
Kloepper, V. C. 12/15
Klotzburger, Edwin C. 3/14+ 4/1*
Klug, C. T. 1/27+
Knap, Herschel B. 2/1+ 7/1*
Knape, Hans 7/26
Knapp, Bob 12/7+
Knight, Charles Y. 3/22, 5/4+ 6/6, 8/15
Knight, John 3/28
Knight, John Henry 10/17
Knight, Margaret E. 12/16
Knoblock, Alvin F. 9/1+
Knowles, Don 3/2
Knox, Harry A. 1/19* 5/20, 6/2+ 7/13
Knudsen, Semon E. 1/31, 2/6, 7/1, 9/2, 9/11, 10/2*
Knudsen, William S. 1/6, 1/11, 1/15, 2/22, 3/25* 4/27+, 5/3, 6/21, 7/1, 9/3
Knudson, Richard L. 6/4*
Knuppenburg, K. M. 9/2, 10/17+
Knyff, Rene de 7/24
Koci, Ludwig F. 5/3*
Kocich, Weldon C. 2/28
Koenig, Len 6/12+
Koeppen, Hans 7/26
Kohlsaat, H. H. 3/22* 10/17+ 11/2
Koinigg, Helmuth 10/6+ 11/3*
Kojima, Matsuhisa 10/24
Kollinek, Theodor 12/13+
Kolzow, Hans 1/1
Komenda, Erwin 4/27
Konecke, Fritz 1/16* 3/26+
Konrad, Franz 6/8*
Koontz, Frederick B. 7/14* 10/29+
Koopman, Henry E. 6/17*
Kopatzke, George A. 12/8+
Kopka, Donald F. 8/21*
Kopper, Hilmar 3/13*
Korenz, Wilhelm 8/14
Kosiski, Steve 3/28*
Koster, Fritz 12/31
Kountz, Clark H. 8/24*
Koussevitsky, Serge 4/15
Kox, Peter 2/23*
Kozarowitsky, Mikko 5/17*
Krafve, Richard E. 4/18, 9/22* 12/29+
Krages, Louis 8/2*
Krall, Stanley 11/22+
Krarup, Marius C. 6/20, 8/21
Krastin, August 11/20
Kraus, G. A. 6/24+
Kraus, Jakob 10/17
Krause, Chester L. 1/1, 12/16*
Krause, Rudolf 3/30* 4/11+ 8/3
Krause, Walter F. 2/25, 4/25
Kreis, Oscar C. 7/5+
Kremer, Erwin 6/26*
Krenzke, William F. 1/23+
Kress, Ralph H. 7/10*
Kresteller, Mort 5/22+
Kretz, Anna S. 9/24*
Krisiloff, Steve 7/7*
Kristensen, Tom 7/7*
Kroeger, Frederick C. 8/10+ 12/2
Krosnoff, Jeff 7/14+ 9/24*
Krotz, Alvaro S. 11/3* 12/9+

Krumm, Michael 3/19*
Kryder, George M. 6/11+
Kuechle, Urban T. 12/10*
Kuehn, Werner 8/9+
Kuenheim, Eberhard von 10/2*
Kuepfer, Matthew C. 9/26+
Kuhler, Otto A. 7/31*
Kulick, Frank 2/17
Kull, Walter A. 12/29+
Kulwicki, Alan 4/1+ 12/14*
Kume, Tadashi 1/1*
Kume, Yutaka 5/20*
Kunkle, Bayard D. 9/14+ 10/30*
Kunz, Heidi 12/4
Kunzman, Lee 11/29*
Kurtis, Frank 1/25*
Kurtz, J. C. 4/19
Kurtz, Wilhelm 8/15
Kuser, Frederick 1/1
Kuser, John L. 1/1, 5/31
Kutz, Nicholas J. 5/9
Kuwashima, Masami 9/14*
Kuzma, Eddie 10/12+
Kyes, Roger M. 2/13+ 3/6*
Kynoch, Charles W. 7/11+
Kyrides, Lucas P. 4/13*

LaBare, Frank 10/11
Labonte, Bobby 5/8*
Labonte, Terry 11/16*
Labrousse 7/1
Lace, A. C. 5/7
Lacey, Robert 1/3*
LaDue, A. D. 1/9
Laffite, Jacques 1/25, 6/19, 11/21*
Lafosse, Jean-Louis 6/13+
Lagache, Andre 5/27
Lagardere, Jean-Luc 2/10*
Lagasse, Scott 3/2
Lagorce, Franck 9/1*
Lagrace, Jean 6/16+
Laing, Allen B. 4/2+ 4/25*
Laird, Raymond H. 6/1, 8/29+ 12/1*
Lalique, Rene 4/6* 5/5+
Lamb, Jim 4/2*
Lamberjack, Dominique 4/5
Lambert, Chris 7/28+
Lambertus, Peter 8/6+
Lamborghini, Ferruccio 2/20+ 4/28*
Lamborn, Frederick J. 10/30*
Lambury of Northfield, Lord 9/13+
Lammers, Jan 6/2*
Lamplough, Robs 6/4*
Lamy, Pedro 3/20*
Lanchester, Frank 7/22* 3/28+
Lanchester, Frederick W. 3/8+ 10/23*
Lanchester, George H. 12/11*
Lancia, Vincenzo 2/15+ 2/26, 6/22, 6/27, 7/1, 8/24*, 10/23, 11/29
Landi, Chico 6/7+ 7/14*
Landis, Arthur 12/8*
Landis, Omar 6/16
Lane, Frederick Van Z. 5/8+
Lane, Mills B. Jr. 1/29* 5/7+
Lane, Rose Wilder 10/30+ 12/5*
Lane, William J. 1/3+
Lanfranchi, Tony 7/25*
Lang, Hermann 4/6* 4/7, 4/10, 5/7, 5/15, 7/21, 7/24, 8/1, 10/19+
Langen, Eugen 8/1, 10/9*
Langes, Claudio 7/20*
Langhammer, Anthony J. 6/21*

Langley, Elmo 11/21+
Langworth, Richard M. 7/7*
Lanier, Randy 9/22*
Lannert, Robert C. 3/14*
Lansdale, Henry R. 1/25+
Lansing, Charles B. 11/3*
Lapeyre, Xavier 4/13*
Lapham, Samuel D. 11/15
Larini, Nicola 3/10, 3/19* 9/27
LaRoche, Frederick A. 5/28
Larrauri, Poppy 8/19*
Larrousse, Gerard 5/23*
Larsen, Harold E. 11/20+
Larson, Carl F. W. 7/2*
Larson, Clarion E. 12/12*
Larson, Dick 10/19+
Larson, Gustaf 7/31, 10/20, 12/16
Larson, Jud 1/21* 6/11+ 10/21
Larzelere, Harold B. 4/27
La Salle, Robert Cavalier de 3/20+ 11/22*
Lasky, Victor 1/7* 2/22+
Lassig, Jurgen 2/25*
Lauda, Niki 2/22* 8/17
Lauer, Bob 1/12
Lauer, Clinton D. 12/8*
Laurel, Dodgie 11/19+
Lauren, Ralph 10/14*
Laurent, Roger 2/21*
Lautenschlager, Christian 1/3+ 4/13* 7/7
Laux, James M. 11/4*
Lavery, George L. 1/11+ 2/18*
Lawrence, Charles L. 7/7
Lawrence, Chris 7/27*
Lawrie, Roy T. 11/21*
Lawson, Charles T. 11/13*
Lawson, Eddie 3/11*
Lawson, Harry J. 1/14, 2/23*
Lazarnick, Nathan 1/20+
Lazier, Bob 10/31, 12/22*
Lazier, Buddy 10/31* 12/22
Lazurenko, Lydia B. 6/6*
Lea, Robert W. 1/18* 11/13+
Leach, Clayton B. 9/6*
Leak, David K. 3/18*
Leamy, Alan H. 6/4* 8/20
Lear, William P. 5/14+ 6/26* 8/9
Leasher, Glenn 9/10+
Leboissetier, Nicolas 6/5*
Lebon, Philippe 5/29* 12/2+
Leclere, Michel 3/18*
LeCocq, Louis 5/30+
Lecot, Francois 7/22, 7/23
Lederle, Neville 9/25*
Ledwinka, Hans 2/14* 3/2+ 9/1, 12/1
Ledwinka, Joseph 6/17
Lee, Leonard 10/17
Leece, B. M. 3/17* 12/5+
Lees, Geoff 5/1*
Lees, George C. 3/24* 4/11+
Leet, Richard H. 10/11*
Lefaucheux, Pierre 2/11+ 3/31, 10/4
Lefebvre, Gordon 1/27* 6/27+
Legat, Arthur 2/23+ 11/1*
Legros, Augustin 3/12+
Lehmann, Otto R. 4/10+
Lehto, J. J. 1/31* 3/14
Leicher, Al 1/9, 3/20* 7/23
Leicher, Edward L. 1/9, 7/23
Leicher, Larry 7/23
Leicher, Robert 7/23
Leiding, Rudolf 10/1, 12/20
Leiningen, Hermann zu 9/21

Leisen, Frederick A. 5/9
Leitzinger, Butch 2/28*
Leiviska, George 9/26+
Leland, Henry M. 2/16+ 3/26+ 6/1, 6/13, 7/1, 8/22, 8/29, 9/19, 9/25, 11/8, 12/24, 12/27
Leland, Mrs. Henry M. 9/25
Leland, Wilfred 1/17+ 6/13, 10/17, 11/7*
Lemaitre, Georges 3/23, 7/22
Lemaux, Daryl F. 8/6+
Lemke, Ray 10/8
Lemke, Robert F. 9/25
Lemm, B. E. 2/13, 9/26, 12/25
Lennon, John 6/29
Lennox, Donald D. 12/3*
Leno, Jay 4/28*
Lenoir, Jean 1/12* 1/24, 3/19, 8/4+
Lent, Henry B. 11/1*
Lentz, Rea 8/12
Lenz, Arnold W. 1/1, 7/13+
Leonard, H. J. 3/8* 5/17+
Leonard, Joe 8/4* 9/6
Leonard, Jonathan Norton 5/15+ 5/25*
Leonard, Michael A. 8/3*
Leonard, Rene 5/27
Leonard, Ward 2/8* 2/18+
Leonardis, Giulio de 1/11, 5/18+
Leoni, Lamberto 5/24*
Lepage, Kevin 6/26*
Lepeu, Jean-Marc 9/29
Leschziner, Siegfried 11/6
Leslie, Tracy 10/24*
Lessells, John M. 2/5* 5/17+
Leston, Les 7/27, 12/16*
Le Sueur, Richard V. 9/6+
Letourneur, Jean-Marie 4/1
Letts, William M. 2/25+ 2/26*
Levassor, Emile 1/21* 4/14+ 5/17, 8/24
Levassor, Mrs. Emile 5/17, 11/1
Levavasseur, Leon 12/2, 12/8*
Levegh, Pierre (1) 7/28, 10/20, 12/22
Levegh, Pierre (2) 6/11+ 12/22*
Leven, Bruce 9/27*
Levy, George M. 6/26* 7/19+
Levy, Raymond 6/28* 12/16
Lewis, Charles 2/24* 4/10+ 7/19
Lewis, Charles H. 3/5+
Lewis, Dave 5/13+
Lewis, David L. 4/5*
Lewis, F. T. 11/21
Lewis, Howard A. 10/16+ 10/22*
Lewis, Jackie 5/17, 11/1*
Lewis, Paul E. 4/21+
Lewis, Paul M. 4/19
Lewis, Ralph G. 1/15+
Lewis, William Mitchell 2/19
Lewis, William Turnor 12/30+
Lewis-Evans, Stuart 4/20* 5/19, 10/25+
Lhamon, George M. 3/3*
Libby, Bill 6/16+ 11/14*
Libertiny, George Z. 6/14*
Liddell, George J. 4/2+
Liebieg, Theodor von 10/22
Liebold, Ernest G. 3/4+ 3/16*
Liebold, Hans 4/4, 10/12*
Liedtke, John H. 2/10*
Liener, Gerhard 7/27, 12/14+
Liesen, Klaus 4/15*
Ligier, Guy 1/25, 7/12*
Likhachev, Ivan A. 6/15* 6/24+ 6/26
Lilley, Tom 8/13*
Lillieqvist, Gustav A. 5/31+
Lincoln, Abraham 2/12* 4/15+ 11/8

Lindenthal, Albert G. 1/29+
Linder, Dick 4/19+ 7/19
Lindfield, Henry 2/13+
Lindner, Peter 10/11+
Link, Robert A. 7/1*
Linn, H. H. 5/7*
Linneen, H. W. 11/28+
Lipe, Willard C. 9/4+
Lipford, Roque E. 8/16*
Lippi, Roberto 10/17*
Lippincott, Oliver 6/24
Lippmann, Seymour A. 11/23*
List, Hans 4/30*
Litchfield, Paul W. 3/18+ 7/26* 9/1
Litherland, Frank 11/18+
Litle, Thomas J. Jr. 10/6+ 10/26, 11/17, 12/1
Little, Chad 4/29*
Little, William H. 1/21, 2/4* 10/26+ 10/30, 11/3
Livezey, William S. 3/27
Livingston, William B. 7/3+
Livingstone, William Jr. 1/21* 10/17+
Lloyd, Bill 7/12*
Lochner, Louis P. 1/8+ 12/22*
Lochridge, Lloyd P. 1/10+
Locke, Justus V. 3/2* 4/16+
Lockhart, Frank 4/25+
Lockton, Cedric P. 2/20+
Lockwood, E. H. 4/16+ 10/31*
Lockwood, Robert M. 10/24
Loewy, Raymond 1/5, 4/30, 7/14+ 11/5*
Lof, Dries van der 5/24+ 8/23*
Lombard, Andre 5/21
Lombard, Jacques 7/12*
Lombardi, Claudio 5/12*
Lombardi, Lella 3/3+ 3/26* 4/27
Lombardini, Luciano 1/20+
Loney, Harley C. 9/20+
Long, Archie M. 6/24*
Long, George A. 7/10
Long, J. C. 8/22*
Long, John B. 2/18
Long, Ray A. 6/28*
Long, Richard H. 4/16+ 9/4*
Longaker, Edgar L. 8/29+
Longhurst, Tony 10/1*
Longley, Clifford B. 7/15+ 11/25*
Lonsdale, Lord 12/12
Loof, Ernst 3/3+ 7/4* 8/1
Loofbourrow, Alan G. 6/9*
Loomis, Gilbert J. 10/25+
Lopez, Jose Ignacio 1/18* 4/24, 11/29
Loquasto, Al 6/21*
Loraine-Barrow, Claude 4/10, 6/12+
Lorane, Lord 10/1
L'Orange, Prosper 3/14, 3/18
Lord, Leonard P. (Lord Lambury) 9/13+ 10/22, 12/17
Lorenz, Paul F. 6/1*
Lorenzen, Fred 4/5, 4/24, 12/30*
Lorrilard, Ernest E. 8/1
Lory, Albert 9/21
Losh, J. Michael 3/2, 4/24
Lott, Antone L. 2/15*
Lotz, Kurt 4/12, 9/13, 9/18* 9/24, 10/1
Louckes, Theodore N. 5/4*
Loudon, Jonkheer Hugo 9/6+
Louveau, Henri 1/7+ 1/25*
Love, George H. 7/25+ 9/21
Love, John 12/7*
Lovejoy, William J. 9/2*
Lovell, Brian 5/8+
Lovely, Pete 4/11*
Lovett, Benjamin B. 2/2* 9/2+

Lovstad, Anton J. 3/15
Loyer, Roger 3/24+ 8/5*
Lozier, Harry (Jr.) 7/29
Lozier, Henry A. (Sr.) 2/27, 5/28+
Lozier, Herbert 12/19*
Luby, Chester G. 4/29
Lucas, Jean 4/25*
Lucke, Charles E. 3/25+
Ludlow, H. D. 1/15
Ludvigsen, Karl E. 4/24* 5/1
Ludwig, Harvey A. 10/18*
Ludwig, Klaus 10/5*
Luhring, Marie 4/9, 12/29+
Lund, Robert D. 1/1, 3/15, 5/11, 11/1
Lund, Tiny 2/24, 8/17+ 11/14*
Lundin, Oscar A. 11/10*
Lundvall, Bjoern 9/22+
Lundy, J. Edward 1/6+
Luneburg, William V. 1/9, 1/21+
Lunger, Brett 11/14*
Luptow, Frank 9/21+
Luraghi, Giuseppe 12/6*
Lutz, Robert A. 2/12*
Lux, John A. 7/19+
Luxmoore, Emerson J. 11/25+
Luyendyk, Arie 9/21*
Lynch, James E. 8/31+
Lyon, Walter E. 10/4+
Lyons, William 2/8+ 3/3, 9/4* 9/9
Lytle, Herbert 10/10

Maag, Oscar L. 8/22+
Maas, Ernest 7/26
Maassen, Sasha 9/28*
Mabley, Carlton R. 9/17+ 11/13*
Macadam, John L. 9/21* 11/26+
MacArthur, A. P. 9/23
MacArthur, Fred A. 8/1+
MacArthur, Samuel E. 4/8*
Macauley, Alvan 1/16+ 1/17* 2/27, 3/17,
    3/31, 4/10, 4/17, 4/19, 4/22, 5/16, 6/25
Macauley, Alvan Jr. 9/6*
Macauley, Edward 5/16
MacCachren, Rob 3/24*
MacDonald, Arthur E. 1/25
MacDonald, Dave 5/30+
MacDonald, Harold C. 6/20*
MacDowel, Mike 9/13*
Macerone, Francis 7/18
MacFarlane, Warren C. 1/18* 11/15+
MacGregor, P. H. 4/1, 10/27
Mack, Augustus F. 7/1, 7/14*
Mack, John M. 3/14+ 7/1, 10/27*
Mack, Joseph S. 7/24+ 11/27*
Mack, Louis R. 1/24* 12/25+
Mack, William C. 2/13+
Mackaye, H. D. W. 1/5
Mackay-Fraser, Herbert 6/23* 7/14+
MacKenzie, Doc 8/8
MacKenzie, Gordon B. 7/12*
MacKenzie, Russell E. 12/9+
MacKichan, Clare M. 2/20+
Mackie, Duane 6/12+
Macklin, Lance 6/11, 9/2* 9/15
MacMillan, Clifford M. 12/10*
Macmillan, Harold 12/5
MacNaughton, James 1/22
MacPherson, Earle S. 1/6, 1/28+ 3/21, 5/1, 7/6*
MacPherson, Jeff 6/9*
MacTavish, Don 2/22+
Madle, Alain 10/21+
Magee, Carlton C. 1/1, 1/5* 1/31+ 7/19

Magee, Damien 11/17*
Maggi, Aymo 3/26, 6/5
Maggs, Tony 2/9* 4/3, 7/15
Maglioli, Umberto 6/5* 6/20
Magnusson, Jan 7/4*
Mahler, John 11/16*
Mahone, Barbara Jean 4/19*
Mahoney, J. Allan 2/19+
Mahoney, Tom 7/17+ 12/3*
Maier, Andrew C. 8/27+ 9/15*
Mairesse, Guy 4/24+ 8/10*
Mairesse, Willy 9/2+ 10/1*
Makinen, Timo 3/18*
Makino, Isao 8/24
Malachinski, Joe 2/7
Malcher, Jean-Pierre 2/19*
Malcomsom, Alexander Y. 2/28, 6/7* 7/12,
    8/1+ 8/20, 11/22
Maldonaldo, Guillermo 10/29*
Malkin, Colin 9/28
Mallock, Ray 4/12*
Malloy, Jim 5/18+
Malon, Leon 7/28+
Malone, Stephen P. 5/1
Maltby, John N. 7/10*
Malumphy, Frank T. 1/19+ 4/14*
Manautou, Oscar 9/9*
Mancheski, Frederick J. 7/21*
Mandel, Leon 7/31*
Manderville, Roger 9/22*
Manly, Robert E. 10/22+
Mann, Thomas C. 11/11*
Manners, Ramsey 1/26+ 3/2
Mannes, Lee 6/19
Manney, Henry N. III 3/15+ 3/27*
Manning, Donald W. 2/9*
Manning, Lucius B. 4/9+ 6/17, 8/18*
Mansell, Nigel 8/8*
Mansfield, John D. 1/1, 6/17
Mantovani, Sergio 5/22*
Mantz, Johnny 9/4, 9/18* 10/25+
Manville, Tommy 12/24
Manzon, Robert 4/12*
Marande, William F. 5/12+ 11/22*
Marang, Ido 5/25+
Marcelo, Jovy 5/15+ 7/21*
Marcenac, James 2/14+
Marchand, Jean-Arthur 4/1
Marchant, Harry A. 6/7+ 11/19*
Marchesi, Enrico 7/1
Marcis, Dave 3/1*
Marco, Pierre 7/15, 10/4, 11/21
Marcus, Siegfreid 4/16, 9/18*
Marestaing, Albert 6/16
Marimon, Onofre 7/31+ 12/19*
Marinoni, Attilio 6/18+
Mark, Ralph C. 10/4*
Markewich, Robert 2/6
Markham, Erwin F. 3/28
Markin, David R. 2/16*
Markin, Morris 7/7+ 7/15*
Markley, Rodney W. Jr. 11/18*
Markmann, Charles L. 4/16*
Marko, Helmut 4/27* 6/13
Marko, Paul M. 1/13+
Marks, Charles J. 11/20+
Marks, Ed 4/19
Marks, James H. 1/6* 2/6+
Marlin, Sterling 6/30*
Marmon, Daniel 5/9+
Marmon, Hall 6/4* 10/11+
Marmon, Howard C. 1/30, 2/26, 2/28, 4/4+

5/24* 6/27, 7/14
Marmon, Walter C. 5/17, 6/4, 8/26* 8/29+ 10/11
Marples, Ernest 12/9*
Marquat, William F. 3/17* 5/29+
Marquis, Samuel S. 1/25, 6/8* 6/21+
Marr, Leslie 8/14*
Marr, Walter L. 7/9, 8/14* 12/11+
Marrington, Bernard H. 11/9*
Marriott, Fred H. 1/26, 8/19, 11/8
Marsh, Alonzo R. 10/16
Marsh, Tony 7/20*
Marsh, William T. 10/16
Marshall, Albert M. 7/6
Marshall, Thomas R. 12/17
Marshall, W. H. 6/7* 8/22+
Marshman, Bobby 12/3+
Marston, John 1/16
Marston, Richard E. 12/20+
Marten, Emil R. 7/16+
Martin, Carlos J. 1/31+
Martin, Earl 2/10+
Martin, Eugene 3/24*
Martin, George E. 4/10+
Martin, Homer 1/22+ 8/15*
Martin, Jean-Michel 6/19*
Martin, John 3/20*
Martin, Karl H. 1/31* 6/2, 7/2, 7/6+
Martin, Lionel 5/24
Martin, Mark 1/9*
Martin, Peter E. 1/3, 4/17* 7/10, 10/8+ 12/24
Martin, Royce G. 5/1+ 6/7*
Martin, Truman J. 2/1, 7/2
Martinez, Gerardo 10/10*
Martini, Giancarlo 4/23, 8/16*
Martini, Mauro 5/17*
Martini, Pierluigi 4/7, 4/23*
Marvin, Bob 4/7+
Marvin, Dan 8/13*
Marx, Oscar B. III 1/3*
Marzotto, Giannino 4/13* 4/26
Maserati, Alfieri 3/3+ 4/25
Maserati, Bindo 3/26, 12/1
Maserati, Ernesto 11/24+ 12/1
Maserati, Ettore 12/1
Masetti, Giulio 4/25+
Mason, Arthur C. 7/31
Mason, Edward R. (1) 1/12, 8/16
Mason, Edward R. (2) 7/12+
Mason, Frank H. III 11/16*
Mason, George R. 9/9+
Mason, George W. 1/4, 2/27, 3/12* 5/1, 5/30, 6/16, 10/8+
Mason, Melville C. 11/4*
Mason, Robert J. 11/17*
Mass, Jochen 1/15, 9/30*
Mast, Rick 3/4*
Masters, J. A. 11/14
Masui, Theo 6/17
Masury, A. F. 10/11
Materassi, Emilio 9/9+
Materazzi, Nicola 1/18*
Matheson, Charles W. 3/21* 8/12+
Matheson, Frank F. 2/11+ 6/27*
Mathis, Emil 4/1
Mathis, Herman 7/21+
Mathues, Thomas O. 1/26*
Matschoss, Conrad 1/1
Matsuda, Jujiro 8/6*
Matsuda, Tsuneji 10/12, 11/15+
Matsumoto, Keiji 12/26*
Matsushita, Hiro 3/14*

Matteucci, Felice 10/19
Matthaei, Frederick Sr. 3/25+ 9/17*
Matthews, Albert S. 5/5+
Matthews, Banjo 2/14*
Matthews, George A. 5/14+ 7/19, 11/23*
Matthews, Gordon L. 9/7
Max, Jean 7/27*
Maxim, Ernest L. 8/8+
Maxim, Hiram P. 2/17+ 9/2*
Maxwell, Archibald M. 4/18+ 4/22*
Maxwell, John F. 5/22+
Maxwell, Jonathan D. 3/8+ 6/21, 7/4, 9/3* 9/18
Maxwell, Mrs. Jonathan D. 9/18
May, George S. 11/17*
May, Henry 3/19* 10/15+ 12/9
May, Michael 8/18*
Mayade, M. 2/10, 10/3
Maybach, Karl 2/7+ 3/23, 7/6*
Maybach, Wilhelm 1/1, 2/7, 2/9* 3/23, 4/1, 4/18, 9/13, 11/1, 12/22, 12/29+
Maybury, William C. 11/21*
Mayer, Tim 2/22* 2/29+
Mayfield, Jeremy 5/27*
Maynes, Robert 5/26
Mayo, Alfred N. 6/12+
Mayo, William B. 1/7* 2/1+
Mays, L. N. 9/1
Mays, Raymond 1/8+ 3/2, 5/13, 6/3, 8/7, 8/8, 9/2, 9/7, 11/6, 12/15
Mays, Rex 11/6+
Maytag, Elmer H. 3/26
Maytag, Frederick L. 3/26+ 7/14*
Mazaud, Robert 7/28+
Mazet, Francois 2/26*
McAfee, Ernie 4/22+
McAlpine, Ken 7/19, 9/21*
McAneeny, William J. 3/24+ 11/21*
McCahill, Tom 5/10+
McCalmont, A. W. 4/5+
McCammon, David N. 11/6*
McCarroll, Hudson 2/20* 3/31+ 7/17
McCarten, Edward 10/8
McCarthy, Perry 3/3*
McCarty, Earl 10/3
McCaslin, Henry C. 8/11
McCleary, James T. 2/5* 4/22, 12/17+
McClelland, James R. 11/8+
McClements, Robert Jr. 12/1*
McCloud, J. Lansford 7/26+ 7/29*
McCluggage, Denise 1/20*
McClure, Donald L. 9/14+
McClure, John Q. 2/22*
McClure, Roy D. 1/17* 3/31+
McCluskey, Roger 8/24* 8/29+
McCoard, Frank C. 11/16*
McComb, F. Wilson 2/9* 2/24, 4/19+
McCombs, Doug 8/20
McConkey, M. W. 7/17+
McConnell, Roy F. 2/13+ 10/15*
McConnell, William A. 1/3*
McConville, C. C. 8/10+
McCord, Alvin C. 8/6+ 11/24*
McCormick, Fowler 1/6+ 11/15*
McCoy, Larry 8/18*
McCrea, Charles H. 8/24+
McCuen, Charles L. 5/22* 6/2, 10/28+
McCulla, William R. 6/20
McCullough, Donald F. 5/6*
McCurry, Robert B. Jr. 7/10*
McDaniel, James S. 8/1
McDewell, H. S. 4/6+ 7/9*
McDonald, Eugene F. Jr. 3/11* 5/15+

McDonald, F. James 2/1, 3/1, 8/3* 8/31, 10/1
McDonald, Stewart 1/3+ 10/2
McDonough, Robert 12/10+
McDougal, Taine G. 9/20*
McDougall, John 7/3*
McDowell, Maxwell E. 12/16+
McDuffe, Paul 9/5+
McDuffee, J. H. 5/12+
McDuffee, Joseph 12/11
McDuffie, J. D. 8/11+
McEachern, Steve 9/16*
McElreath, Jimmy 2/18* 9/6
McElroy, Neil H. 8/7, 10/30* 11/30+
McFarland, Forest R. 12/22+
McGay, John B. 11/22
McGee, Dean A. 3/20* 9/15+
McGrath, Jack 6/16, 10/8* 11/6+
McGrath, John 4/16+ 6/9*
McGraw, Fred V. 4/12+ 8/30*
McGuire, Brian 8/29+ 12/13*
McInerney, James M. 1/8*
McInerney, William K. 9/26*
McIntosh, Charles L. 4/6+
McIntyre, Charles S. 8/26+
McKee, Garnet 1/3+ 9/7*
McKenna, R. M. 6/18
McKinley, Charles W. 11/16*
McKinley, William 8/22
McKinney, Frank H. 6/7+ 11/25
McLane, John 4/4
McLaren, Bruce 4/1, 5/22, 6/2+ 6/6, 6/9, 6/18, 7/18, 8/30* 12/12
McLaughlin, M. S. 4/17
McLaughlin, Mike 10/6*
McLaughlin, Robert S. 1/6+ 9/8*
McLaughlin, Thomas O. 12/15*
McLean, Bob 3/26+
McLellan, David 11/18
McLellan, William L. 12/5+
McLernon, James W. 9/27
McMahon, Harry R. 10/3+
McMechan, Jervis B. 3/27*
McMillan, B. H. 5/31+
McMillan, James T. 4/20* 9/4+
McMillan, Philip H. 9/8, 10/4+ 12/28*
McMillen, Dave 5/5*
McMillion, Worth 6/23, 10/8*
McMullen, Eugene J. 8/24+
McMurtry, Alden L. 1/15* 7/26+
McNally, Andrew (Jr.) 5/20+ 7/31*
McNally, Andrew 3rd 2/13, 8/17*
McNamara, Francis 8/17*
McNamara, Ray 6/30
McNamara, Robert S. 6/9* 11/9, 12/13
McNeal, James H. Jr. 11/22*
McNish, Allan 5/19, 12/29*
McPherson, Donald H. 11/6
McPherson, Frank A. 4/29*
McQuagg, Sam 11/11*
McRae, Graham 3/5*
McTague, John P. 11/28*
Mears, Otto E. 1/9, 4/29
Mears, Rick 12/3*
Mecke, Theodore H. Jr. 3/6*
Medcraft, Harry C. 10/28
Medford, J. J. 12/23
Medhurst, George 8/2
Mehta, Shekhar 6/20*
Meier, George 6/25
Meinel, William J. 7/3* 11/17+
Meister, H. O. K. 6/10+
Melanowski, Leo 3/1

Meldrum, Barclay 4/1
Melton, James 1/2* 4/21+
Melton, Major 1/25*
Mendelssohn, Louis 3/28+ 8/12*
Menditeguy, Carlos 4/27+ 8/10*
Menocal, Jose Estradad 11/20+
Menu, Alain 8/9*
Meraw, Francis P. 2/15
Merkel, Joseph F. 7/7+
Merkes, Marshall 5/20*
Merosi, Giuseppe 1/1, 12/17*
Merrell, Allen W. 10/7+
Merrill, Kenneth C. 2/20* 4/9, 5/1
Merrill, S. Clifford 9/20+
Merrill, Thomas S. 2/16*
Merry, Donald H. 5/26+
Merryweather, George E. 6/8+
Mertz, Edward H. 2/1, 11/6
Mertzanoff, Andre 12/15
Mery, Simon 5/24*
Merz, Charles 7/6* 7/8+
Merz, Otto 5/19+ 6/28, 7/18, 9/12
Merzario, Arturo 1/15, 3/11*
Messerschmitt, Willy 6/26* 9/15+
Metge, Rene 10/23*
Metz, Charles H. 6/29+ 7/19, 8/3, 10/17*
    10/30
Metz, Edwin H. 5/21+
Metz, Walter 7/19
Metzger, William E. 4/11+ 6/2, 7/25, 8/22,
    9/20, 9/30*
Meyan, Paul 11/5
Meyer, Charles F. 10/13+
Meyer, Louis 5/30, 10/7+ 11/11
Meyers, Gerald C. 1/15, 10/20, 10/21, 12/5*
Meyers, William M. 10/14+
Mezera, Tomas 11/5*
Miaskiewicz, Rick 3/22*
Michael, Jerry Dean 8/14
Michelin, Andre 1/16* 4/4+
Michelin, Edouard 6/23* 8/25+
Michelin, Francois 7/3*
Michelin, Edouard 6/11
Middlekamp, John H. 8/28*
Midgley, Thomas 12/25+
Midgley, Thomas Jr. 5/18* 11/2+ 12/9, 12/25
Mieres, Roberto 12/3*
Migault, Francois 4/27, 12/4*
Mikkola, Hannu 5/24*
Miles, John 6/14*
Miles, Ken 2/6, 8/17+ 11/1*
Miles, Samuel 3/23
Milhoux, Andre 12/9*
Millen, Steve 2/17*
Miller, Adolph G. 6/18+
Miller, Arjay R. 2/6, 3/4* 4/10, 5/1
Miller, Charles 10/1+
Miller, Charles D. 10/20
Miller, Chet 5/15+
Miller, David N. 12/9+
Miller, Eddie 7/1, 12/27
Miller, Ethel 8/8
Miller, Harry A. 1/30, 5/3+ 5/4, 6/16, 11/15,
    12/9*
Miller, J. F. 5/26
Miller, Jack 6/14
Miller, Joseph I. 5/26*
Miller, Linwood A. 11/3*
Miller, Noel H. 3/15+
Miller, Paul A. 8/10*
Miller, Robert S. 2/24, 8/15*
Miller, Sam 4/15*

Miller, W. Everett 4/6+ 11/7, 11/19*
Miller, Walter 10/22
Mills, Ben D. 4/24* 11/19
Milner, Roy 3/15
Milton, Taliaferro 3/26*
Milton, Tommy 4/27, 5/30, 7/10+ 9/17, 10/27
Milward, William F. 12/17+
Mimran, Patrick 9/1
Mims, Donna Mae 9/2
Minard, Ernest E. 7/19+
Miniger, Clement O. 4/23+ 11/11*
Minneker, Jim 3/2
Minshall, Charles 6/13
Minoia, Ferdinando 3/26, 6/2* 6/27+
Minor, Jack W. 10/1, 10/9*
Misch, Herbert L. 12/7*
Mischler, Wernert E. 12/12
Miskowski, Lee R. 3/27*
Mitchell, Bert J. 5/31* 6/15+
Mitchell, Grover Ira 5/28+
Mitchell, W. Ledyard 11/2*
Mitchell, William L. 7/2* 7/31, 9/12+ 12/1,
    12/15, 12/24
Mitchell, William R. 5/8+
Mitter, Gerhard 8/1+ 8/30*
Mix, M. W. 1/20
Mix, Tom 10/12+
Moberly, Alfred F. 10/2
Mobila, Jean Pierre 6/13+
Mobius, Karl 5/20*
Modena, Stefano 4/3, 5/12*
Moekle, Herman L. 10/11* 11/23+
Mogi, Kazuo 2/2*
Moll, Guy 8/15+
Momberger, August 5/27
Momo, Alfred 3/17, 9/12*
Momo, Mary 3/17+ 12/26*
Monaghan, Philip J. 11/5*
Monaghan, Thomas S. 3/25*
Monahan, Gordon J. 2/29+
Monier, Emile 7/10*
Monroe, R. F. 4/24, 8/1, 8/28
Montagu, Douglas Scott 3/30+ 6/10* 7/9
Montagu of Beaulieu, Edward 10/20*
Montaignac, Marquis de 5/1+
Montariol, M. de 5/1
Montermini, Andrea 5/30*
Monteverdi, Peter 6/7* 9/11, 12/10
Montezemolo, Luca di 2/6
Montgomerie-Charrington, Robin 6/22*
Montgomery, Major General 8/28
Montgomery, Donald E. 10/11+ 10/16*
Montgomery, Patricia 8/1
Moodie, John 4/6
Moon, Dean 2/16
Moon, Joseph W. 2/11+ 10/2
Moon, Stanley 4/7
Mooney, James D. 1/19, 2/18* 4/20, 6/18, 9/21+
Moore, Albert C. 12/28*
Moore, Audrey 12/25+
Moore, Bud 5/26*
Moore, C. Harrington 8/10
Moore, C. J. 3/8
Moore, George L. 12/15
Moore, Greg 4/22*
Moore, Jerry J. 6/27
Moore, Lou 3/25+ 9/12*
Moore, Meade F. 4/12+ 8/22
Moorhouse, Alfred 10/8+
Mora, Luigi 6/21+
Moran, Daniel J. 4/3+ 5/31*
Moran, Rocky 2/3*

Morandi, Guiseppe 3/26, 11/1+
Morbidelli, Gianni 1/13*
More, William M. 4/6+
Moreland, H. 5/18
Moreland, Watt L. 4/8+
Moreno, Roberto 2/11* 5/31
Morey, Samuel 4/1, 4/17+ 10/23*
Morgan, Brian 7/8*
Morgan, Charles G. Jr. 2/3+
Morgan, Dave 8/7*
Morgan, H. F. S. 5/13, 6/15+ 11/3, 12/27
Morgan, J. R. 3/14, 5/29
Morgan, John Pierpont 6/21
Morgan, Peter 11/3*
Morgan, Rob 11/11*
Morgen, Heinrich-Joachim von 5/28+ 9/21
Morimoto, Akio 9/24*
Moroso, Rob 9/30+
Morris, Bob 10/4*
Morris, G. Ronald 8/30*
Morris, Henry G. 1/19
Morris, William R. (Lord Nuffield) 4/9, 7/1,
    7/21, 8/22+ 8/29, 10/10*
Morris, Mrs. W. R. (Lady Nuffield) 4/9
Morris-Goddall, Mort 5/25
Morrison, Roger L. 3/23+ 8/28*
Morrison, Tommy 3/2
Morrow, Mrs. M. S. 8/14
Morse, Frank L. 3/25+
Morse, O. F. 7/16
Mortimer, Wyndham 8/23+
Morton, Allen W. 8/1*
Morton, John 2/17*
Morton, Wade 3/18, 7/1, 10/8
Mose, Carl C. 3/8
Moser, H. C. 7/23+ 9/1*
Moser, Silvio 4/24* 5/26+ 8/16
Moskovics, Frederic E. 1/5, 2/18+ 5/23* 10/24,
    12/17
Mosley, Mike 3/3+ 12/13*
Mosling, Bernard A. 5/1, 9/29
Moss, Cruse W. 4/7*
Moss, Pat (Carlsson) 7/9, 12/27*
Moss, Stirling 1/19, 4/23, 5/1, 5/9, 5/27, 5/29,
    6/5, 7/9, 7/15, 7/16, 7/20, 8/17, 8/18,
    8/23, 9/17* 9/23, 10/19, 12/11, 12/27
Motschenbacher, Lothar 11/19*
Mott, Charles S. 2/20+ 2/22, 6/2*
Moulton, Arthur J. 7/7+
Moulton, L. W. 12/2+
Moulton, Vern 1/28+ 2/14*
Mowrey, Paul W. 7/27
Mueller, Henry 10/23
Mueller, Hieronymus 4/24
Mueller, Oscar 3/25* 4/24+ 11/2
Muir, Brian 9/11+
Mulcahy, B. Mark 4/2
Mulford, Ralph 1/21, 4/10, 8/7, 8/27, 10/23+
    11/27, 12/1, 12/28*
Muller, Frederick E. 2/25+ 10/18*
Muller, Herbert 5/11* 5/24+
Muller, Jorg 9/3*
Muller, William J. 2/8+ 4/7, 7/26*
Muller, Yvan 8/16*
Mullin, Roger W. Jr. 6/2*
Mulliner, H. J. 10/8+
Mullins, William H. 1/30* 3/6+
Munari, Sandro 3/27*
Munaron, Gino 4/2*
Mundy, Frank 6/8* 9/30
Munekuni, Yoshihide 5/10
Muntz, Earl 6/20+ 6/29

Murdock, A. Gordon 11/3
Murdock, James C. 11/3
Murdock, Samuel T. 11/3
Murdock, William 8/21* 11/15+
Murphree, Eger V. 10/29+ 11/3*
Murphy, Edward M. 8/28
Murphy, Jimmy 2/28, 5/30, 6/18, 7/26, 9/15+ 12/11
Murphy, Paula 11/12
Murphy, Thomas A. 12/1, 12/10* 12/31
Murphy, Walter M. 10/29
Murphy, William H. 8/5
Murphy, William T. 6/1* 7/9+
Murray, Allen E. 3/5*
Murray, Arthur T. 1/23* 4/24+
Murray, David 4/5+ 12/28*
Murray, Fred H. 1/1
Murray, Ian G. 6/18*
Murray, Willis G. 9/5
Musciano, Walter A. 11/19*
Musgrave, Charles R. 8/15*
Musgrave, Ted 12/18*
Musselman, C. A. 1/3+ 12/16*
Musso, Luigi 1/22, 4/28, 7/6+ 7/29*
Mutchler, E. Michael 4/24
Muzzy, H. Gray 2/21*
Myers, Pop 3/13+

Nab, Herb 4/1*
Nacke, Bernd 8/3, 12/21*
Nacker, Owen M. 2/2, 11/7*
Nader, Ralph 2/27*
Nadig, Henry A. 1/10+
Nagasaka, Naoki 4/24*
Nagel, Adolph 9/18+
Nagel, F. J. 9/16, 11/15
Nakagawa, Fukio 10/13+
Nakagawa, Ryoichi 4/27*
Nakajima, Satoru 2/23*
Nakako, Osami 8/20*
Nakaya, Akihiko 11/3*
Nallinger, Fritz 6/13
Nance, James J. 1/15, 2/15, 2/19* 3/26, 5/1,
    5/7, 5/12, 6/19, 6/26, 7/22+ 7/26, 9/4,
    10/1
Nannini, Alessandro 7/7*
Napier, John S. 9/14
Napier, Montague 1/22+
Narvaez, Maurizio de 5/18*
Nash, Charles W. 1/4, 1/28* 4/23, 6/1, 6/6+
    7/13, 7/29, 8/1, 9/9, 11/16, 11/19, 12/10,
    12/13
Nash, Mrs. Charles W. 4/23
Nash, E. O. 4/27
Naspetti, Emanuele 2/24*
Natili, Massimo 7/28*
Naudin, Louis 6/1, 6/20
Nave, Henry J. 1/21, 8/8*
Naylor, Brian 3/24* 7/18, 8/8+
Nazaruk, Mike 5/1+ 10/2*
Nazzaro, Felice 2/26, 3/21+ 6/8
Ndahura, D. 3/28+
Neal, Thomas 1/26, 2/16, 9/27* 10/6+ 11/16,
    11/19, 12/10
Nedoma, Charles L. 8/15, 12/23+
Needell, Tiff 10/29*
Neely, William H. 12/8
Neerpasch, Jochen 2/4
Negishi, Masakazu 1/21+
Negri, Osvaldo Jr. 5/29*
Nehrbas, F. P. 7/16, 10/24
Neil, Edmund B. 8/30+
Nelson, A. C. 7/19

Nelson, Bill 3/17
Nelson, Boyce 9/4+
Nelson, Charles E. (1) 8/20*
Nelson, Charles E. (2) 5/15* 5/23+
Nelson, Craig T. 4/4*
Nelson, Emil A. 2/20* 9/1, 11/8
Nelson, Gunner 5/12+
Nelson, John E. 8/30*
Nelson, Norm 1/30*
Nelson, S. B. 1/9
Nelson, Walter H. 3/23*
Nemechek, Joe 9/26*
Neubauer, Alfred 3/29* 9/12
Neve, Patrick 10/13*
Nevin, J. J. 2/13*
Nevins, Allan 3/5+ 5/20*
New, Leo 9/2+
Newberg, William C. 4/28, 6/30, 10/1, 12/17*
Newberry, Truman H. 10/3+ 11/5* 11/29
Newby, Arthur C. 2/9
Newcomb, Edward C. 7/25+
Newhall, Arthur B. 3/12+ 8/17*
Newman, Paul 1/26*
Newport, Herb 12/25+
Newton, Arthur L. 10/25
Newton, Frank 6/8, 11/6
Ney, Alfred M. 1/31*
Neyhart, Amos E. 2/17, 8/11
Nicandros, C. S. 8/2*
Nicholas II 11/12
Nichols, Byron J. 2/20, 7/15*
Nicholson, E. Rupert 2/4
Nicholson, John 7/19, 10/6*
Nicol, John 11/7*
Nicolis, Livio 12/2*
Niedermayr, Helmut 4/3+ 11/29*
Nielsen, John 2/7*
Nielsen, Lauritz F. 9/5+
Niemann, Brausch 11/3*
Nieppe, Edmond de la 6/17
Nierop, Kees 3/16*
Nilson, Lars G. 12/13+
Nilsson, Gunnar 10/20+ 11/20*
Nissen, Kris 7/20*
Nitske, W. Robert 3/29*
Nixon, St. John C. 6/7+ 8/17*
Nixon, Stuart 6/9+
Noble, Richard 10/4
Nockolds, Harold 6/28* 11/1+
Noda, Hideki 3/7*
Nogues, Antony 4/14
Nohavec, Fred R. 12/19+
Nolan, William F. 3/6*
Noll, Roy G. 12/15+
Nolte, Henry R. Jr. 3/3*
Nones, Walter M. 3/10+
Norback, Craig T. 11/14*
Norberg, Bengt 5/24, 10/23*
Norberg, Carl F. 5/19+
Norberg, Rudolph C. 3/18* 9/6+
Nordhoff, Heinz 1/1, 1/6* 1/24, 4/12+ 9/17,
    11/13
Norris, George L. 4/13+
North, Albert G. 7/13
Northcliffe, Lord 7/15* 8/14+
Northey, Percy 4/10
Northup, Amos E. 2/15+ 10/23* 12/8
Norton, Charles H. 9/19, 11/7, 11/23*
Norton, H. E. 6/23*
Nostrand, Caroline 2/24
Nottingham, William B. 8/5

Nourry 6/15
Novais, Jorge 1/25*
Novak, James M. 9/1*
Noyes, W. C. 1/9
Noznesky, Harry J. 12/21*
Nuckey, Rodney 6/26*
Nuffield, Lord (William R. Morris) 4/19, 7/1,
    8/22+ 8/29, 10/10*
Nutt, Arthur 2/6*
Nutt, Frank N. 6/24+
Nuvolari, Tazio 4/10, 5/12, 5/22, 6/21, 7/2,
    7/14, 8/9, 8/10+ 9/3, 9/11, 10/12, 11/18*
Nye, Doug 10/18*
Nyland, John R. 7/16*

Oakes, Harlan J. 2/6+
Oakland, Ralph E. 1/12*
Oberle, Frank G. 7/16+
Oberwinder, J. Ferdinand 10/26*
O'Brien, William M. 11/13*
Ochs, Milton B. 1/29*
O'Connell, Johnny 7/24*
O'Connell, Robert T. 6/28, 7/7*
O'Connor, Pat 5/30+ 10/9*
O'Donnell, Eddie 7/1, 11/26+
Odor, Keith 9/11+
Offenhauser, Fred 2/11* 8/18+
Ogarrio, Rodolfo 10/21*
Ogawa, Hitoshi 2/15* 5/24+
Ohinouye, Tsuneo 3/13*
Ohno, Taiichi 5/28+
Okada, Hideki 11/28*
Okamoto, Tojiro 12/19+
Okuda, Hiroshi 12/29*
Oldfield, Barney 1/10, 2/27, 3/6, 3/16, 4/8,
    4/23, 5/21, 5/28, 5/30, 6/3* 6/19, 7/25,
    8/6, 8/9, 8/28, 9/5, 10/4+ 10/13, 10/17,
    10/25, 10/29, 11/19
Oldham, John W. 12/11*
Oldham, W. J. 8/25+
Olds, Pliny F. 7/1+ 7/31
Olds, Ransom E. 1/5, 2/4, 4/17, 5/8, 5/11,
    6/3*, 6/5, 7/1, 7/10, 7/23, 7/28, 7/31, 8/11,
    8/16, 8/21, 8/26+ 9/1, 10/15, 11/23,
    12/17, 12/20, 12/28
Olds, Mrs. Ransom E. 6/5, 6/6* 9/1+
Olen, Walter A. 1/18+ 1/31*
Olender, Frank J. 8/9* 9/8+
Oliver, Jack 8/14*
Oliver, Smith Hempstone 8/19*
Olivero, Bobby 12/24*
Olley, Maurice 6/12* 7/1, 11/1
Olmsted, Clarence E. 9/4*
Olofsson, Anders 3/31*
Olsen, Rolf L. 5/24+
Olsen, Thorsten Y. 12/10+
Olson, Robert S. 1/10* 8/9+ 8/24
Olson, Sidney 4/30*
O'Malley, John M. 3/6+
O'Neil, Kitty (Hambleton) 12/6
O'Neil, Thomas F. 4/18*
O'Neil, William F. 8/21* 9/4+
Ong, John D. 9/29*
Ongais, Danny 5/21*
Ono, Masao 10/24
Opel, Adam 5/4, 9/8+
Opel, Fritz von 4/8+ 4/27, 5/4* 5/23, 9/24
Opel, G. von 5/18
Opel, Rikki von 7/1, 10/14*
Opel, Wilhelm von 5/2+
Opperman, Jan 2/9*
Oreiller, Henri 10/7+

Orford, Ian 1/1
Orndorff, Harry C. 12/21
Oros, Joe 3/19, 9/10
Orr, Rodney 2/14+
Osborn, Cyrus R. 8/27* 11/15+
Osella, Enzo 3/1
Osiecki, Bob 8/28
Oster, Thomas H. 2/6*
Ostrander, Stanley W. 9/21*
Ostreich, Markus 7/3*
Oswald, Robert 7/1
O'Toole, R. J. 2/22*
Otto, Gustav 3/7, 3/15
Otto, Nikolaus A. 1/2, 3/15, 5/9, 6/14* 8/1, 8/4, 8/14
Otto, Wilhelm 1/2
Owen, Alfred 4/8* 4/22, 10/29+
Owen, Arthur 3/23*
Owen, E. H. 11/23
Owen, Raymond M. 4/29+ 5/22*
Owens, Cotton 5/21*
Owens, James S. 3/27*
Owens, Owen 5/15, 11/24+

Pacchioni, Gianantonio 12/23*
Pace, Carlos 3/18+ 10/6*
Packard, Elizabeth A. 1/19+
Packard, James W. 1/6, 1/16, 2/12, 3/20+ 4/11, 6/1, 6/5, 6/10, 7/22, 7/28, 8/4, 8/13, 8/31, 9/8, 9/11, 10/9, 10/13, 10/14, 10/24, 11/2, 11/4, 11/5* 11/20, 12/11, 12/30
Packard, Mrs. James W. 1/19+ 8/31
Packard, Lucius B. 6/25, 10/14+
Packard, Mary E. (Doud) 10/9+ 11/20
Packard, Warren 6/1* 7/28+ 11/20
Packard, Mrs. Warren 11/20
Packard, Warren II 8/26+ 10/5*
Packard, William 12/11+
Packard, William D. 6/1, 6/5, 6/11, 7/28, 8/4, 9/27, 10/5, 10/9, 10/14, 10/24, 11/3* 11/11+, 11/20, 12/11, 12/30
Packard, Mrs. William D. (1) 6/11
Packard, Mrs. William D. (2) 9/27
Packer, C. Edward 1/20+
Packer, William M. 1/31
Pagani, Nello 3/29, 6/4, 10/11*
Page, DeWitt 2/28+
Page, Robert P. Jr. 1/30* 6/18+
Page, Victor W. 4/1+
Paige, Edison W. 8/9
Paige, Fred O. 1/20+
Paillet, Charles 3/20*
Paletti, Riccardo 6/13+ 6/15*
Palm, Torsten 7/23*
Palmer, Herman D. 2/26, 10/29+
Palmer, Jonathan 4/21, 11/7*
Palmer, Louis H. 5/31+
Palmer, Randall A. 9/26
Palmer, Thomas W. 1/25* 6/1+
Pampyn, Jose-Luis 1/16+
Panch, Marvin 1/31, 5/28*
Pandolfo, Samuel C. 1/27+ 12/6
Panhard, Hippolyte 7/16
Panhard, Rene 5/27* 7/16+
Panini, Carlos 11/21+
Panis, Olivier 9/2*
Panke, Helmut 6/4
Panny, William P. 4/18*
Paoli, Jean-Pierre 5/3*
Papin, Denis 8/22*
Papis, Max 10/3*
Parayre, Jean-Paul 7/5* 9/4

Pardington, A. R. 6/6
Pareja, Jesus 3/6*
Paris, Auguste J. Jr. 1/31*
Paris, William E. 11/1+ 11/5*
Parish, Neff E. 6/25
Parish, William F. 3/7+
Parke, Frederick K. 1/10*
Parker, Bonnie 5/23+
Parker, Charles L. 2/28
Parker, Don 4/16, 11/11*
Parker, Earle D. 6/12+
Parker, Frank L. 2/28
Parker, George 2/28
Parker, John R. 9/9*
Parker, Philo W. 4/13*
Parker, Robert 3/17
Parkes, J. J. 12/24
Parkes, Mike 5/1, 7/18, 8/28+ 12/24*
Parkhurst, Red 9/15
Parkin, Joe Jr. 10/7
Parnell, Reg 1/7+ 6/25, 7/2*
Parnell, Tim 6/25*
Parrish, Clarence H. Jr. 6/17+
Parrot, William 10/30
Parrott, B. R. 12/15
Parry, David M. 3/26* 3/31, 5/12+ 7/28
Parsons, Benny 7/12*
Parsons, Carl B. 12/21+
Parsons, Harry 3/24
Parsons, Johnnie 7/4* 8/26, 9/8+
Parsons, Johnny 8/26*
Parsons, Phil 6/21*
Partridge, Albert G. 3/12+ 8/25*
Pary, M. 1/31
Paschal, Jim 12/5*
Pass, Robert 10/8
Patchin, Phillip H. 9/11* 11/29+
Pate, James L. 9/6*
Paton, Clyde R. 1/7* 1/18, 7/24, 8/26+
Patrese, Riccardo 1/29, 4/17* 9/22
Patria, Franco 10/11+
Patterson, Fred 9/23
Patterson, Jas 1/8*
Patterson, W. D. 4/20*
Patterson, William H. 12/16*
Pattison, Jim 6/29
Patty, Frank A. 1/11*
Paul, John Jr. 2/19*
Paul, John Sr. 2/19
Paul, Parry H. 11/4+
Paul, Robert G. 3/5*
Pauley, Claude A. 11/23*
Paulus, Max G. 9/25*
Pawley, Dennis K. 4/11
Paxton, Thomas B. 5/11
Payne, Frank E. 11/20+
Payne, Matt 2/6+
Payne, Roy 11/11*
Peake, Alonzo W. 5/3* 8/28+
Peapples, George A. 11/6*
Pearce, Austin W. 9/1*
Pearce, Harry J. 8/20* 12/4
Pearson, David 7/13, 12/22*
Pearson, Larry 11/2*
Pearson, Lester 1/16
Pease, Al 10/15*
Pease, Clarke D. 11/26*
Peck, Barton L. 9/6+
Peck, D. Cameron 3/31* 4/19+
Pedersoli, Oscar 4/3*
Peer, Edward F. 8/16
Pelassa, Giorgio 10/27

Pelletier, Alfred W. 1/22*
Pelletier, LeRoy E. 9/5+
Pemberton, Max 2/22+ 6/19*
Pence, Harry E. 3/29+
Penfield, Edward 2/8+ 6/2*
Pennington, Edward J. 3/5+ 10/3
Penrose, Spencer 8/12, 11/2* 12/7+
Penske, Roger 2/20*
Pepper, Donald 9/23
Pepys, Mark 5/29* 7/19+
Percival, L. A. D. 9/16
Percy, Win 9/28*
Perdisa, Cesare 10/21*
Perez, Luis 5/15*
Perkins, Bill 4/29+
Perkins, James A. 2/12
Perkins, Jim 5/1
Perkins, Julian L. 2/12
Perkins, Julius A. 12/7+
Perkins, Larry 3/18*
Perlman, Louis H. 2/4
Perot, H. Ross 12/1
Perouse, Augustin 2/28
Perrin, John G. 2/17+ 4/24
Perrot, Xavier 2/1*
Perry, Percival 3/18* 6/17+
Pescarolo, Henri 5/6, 7/15, 9/25*
Pescatori, Christian 12/1*
Pesenti-Rossi, Alessandro 8/31*
Pestillo, P. J. 3/22*
Petard, Rene M. 4/8+
Peters, Heber W. 8/25, 12/13* 12/27+
Peters, Josef 9/16*
Peters, Robert J. 2/27+
Petersen, Donald E. 2/1, 3/1, 9/4* 11/10
Petersen, Robert E. 9/10*
Peterson, Peter 9/16*
Peterson, Ronnie 2/14* 9/11+
Petillo, Kelly 5/30, 6/30+
Petit, Pierre 9/27*
Petnel, Joseph A. 11/23+
Petter, Ernest W. 5/26* 7/18+
Petter, Percival W. 7/18, 11/5
Pettit, Paul 5/2
Petty, Kyle 3/14, 6/2* 7/2
Petty, Lee 2/22, 3/14* 5/22, 6/14
Petty, Richard 2/18, 2/23, 3/14, 6/2, 6/15, 7/2* 7/4, 7/6, 7/12, 8/1, 9/30
Peugeot, Jean-Pierre 10/18+
Peugeot, Pierre 6/11*
Peugeot, Rodolphe 4/2*
Peugeot, Roland 3/20*
Peyton, Anne 12/7*
Pfau, Hugo 3/7*
Pfennig, Ernst 7/15, 7/23
Pflum, William 9/27
Pfyffer, Andre de 11/3*
Phelps, Alva W. 1/17*
Phelps, Arthur G. 5/1+ 10/11*
Phelps, L. J. 8/25
Philion, Achille 9/13
Philipson, John 12/10
Phillips, Frank 8/23+ 11/28*
Phillips, Noel 9/27
Phillips, Russell 10/6+
Phillipson, Brainerd F. 3/24* 4/7+
Piane, Paolo delle 5/1*
Picard, Fernand 3/6
Picard, Francois 4/26*
Pickett, Greg 1/8*
Piech, Ferdinand 1/1, 3/28
Pierce, Bert 4/2*

Pierce, Frank R. 3/29* 12/1
Pierce, George N. 1/9* 5/23+ 10/21, 12/9
Pierce, Mrs. George N. 10/21
Pierce, Percy 7/22, 7/28, 8/26+
Pieterse, Ernest 7/4*
Pietsch, Paul 6/20*
Piggins, W. S. 9/3
Pigott, C. M. 4/21*
Pigott, Pat 10/14+
Pike, Hubert 3/2
Pilain, Francois 9/7*
Pile, J. Howard 8/31+
Pilette, Andre 7/26, 10/6* 12/27+
Pilette, Teddy 7/26* 12/27
Pimm, Ed 5/3*
Pioch, William F. Sr. 10/3+
Piotti, Luigi 4/19+ 10/27*
Piper, David 12/2*
Piper, Perry 2/3
Piquero, Jose M. 2/25
Piquet, Nelson 8/10, 8/17* 9/25
Pirelli, Alberto 4/28* 10/19+
Pirelli, Giovanni 10/20+ 12/27*
Pirelli, Leopoldo 3/2, 8/27*
Pirelli, Piero 1/27* 8/7+
Pirocchi, Renato 3/26*
Pironi, Didier 3/26* 5/4, 8/23+
Pirro, Emanuele 1/12*
Pirsch, Peter 3/2* 7/14+
Pischetsrieder, Bernd 2/15*
Pitkin, Albert J. 6/4
Pitrone, Jean Maddern 12/20*
Pizer, Vernon 2/20*
Place, Bion C. 3/29+
Planche, Etienne 1/1, 3/15, 5/31
Plass, Reuben H. 1/7
Plastow, David 5/9*
Plimpton, Raymond E. 6/9+
Plonski, Henry 9/22+
Plowright, Denny 4/1
Poberejsky, Michel 6/16*
Poege, Willy 5/12+
Poele, Eric van de 9/30*
Pogue, Charles N. 12/5
Polak, Vasek 4/16+
Policand, Jerome 10/1*
Poling, Forrest K. 2/26*
Poling, Harold A. 2/1, 3/1, 10/4, 10/14* 11/10, 12/3
Polis, Nancy E. 2/26
Pollard, Art 5/5* 5/12+
Pollard, Barney 1/9+ 10/18
Pollet, Jacques 7/2*
Polley, J. W. 5/25
Pomeroy, Andrew L. 3/11* 5/10+
Pon, Ben 12/9*
Pontiac 4/20+
Poore, Dennis 2/12+ 7/19, 8/19*
Pope, Albert A. 5/20* 8/10+ 11/4
Pope, Edward W. 11/4, 11/26*
Pope, George 1/9* 4/19*
Pope, Harold L. 4/14+
Pope, John C. 8/11+
Pope, N. B. 7/17*
Pope, Winslow B. 9/18+
Pordes, Dore 6/15
Porsche, Ferdinand 1/1, 1/12, 1/30+ 4/27, 4/30, 6/22, 8/2, 8/5, 8/7, 8/11, 9/3* 9/6, 9/19, 10/27, 11/1, 11/13, 11/16, 12/1, 12/31
Porsche, Ferry 1/10, 9/17, 9/19*
Porsche, Mrs. Ferry 1/10
Portago, Alfonso de 5/12+ 10/11*

Portenga, Steve 5/22*
Porter, Finlay Robertson 2/8+
Portman, John 5/22
Posey, Sam 5/26*
Postal, Fred 9/26
Postlethwaite, Harvey 3/30
Potter, David S. 1/16*
Potter, E. Clifford 12/9
Potter, Elbert L. Jr. 10/16+
Potter, Horace W. 5/25
Potter, Wallace 2/28
Potterat, Julien 5/30
Pound, Arthur 1/14+ 6/1*
Powell, William S. 8/27+
Powelson, J. J, 10/11+
Power, A. F. 7/11*
Powers, Ray 7/1
Powers, William F. 12/11*
Pozzi, Charles 8/27*
Pragerson, B. C. 12/23
Prappas, Ted 11/14*
Pratt, George B. 7/2, 10/24
Pratt, John L. 10/22* 12/1, 12/20+
Pratt, Philip W. 7/27
Pratt, William B. 7/2, 10/24
Pray, Glenn 3/6
Presbrey, Otis 7/9+
Pressley, Robert 4/8+
Pretorius, Jackie 11/22*
Price, Hickman Jr. 8/14*
Price, W. Robert 11/3
Price, Willis J. 9/23*
Prince, Charles 8/8+
Prince, Talmadge 2/19+
Prinetti, Ludovico 12/4
Pringle, Nelson S. 2/2+ 11/19*
Prinz, Gerhard 4/5*
Prior, Frank O. 1/18+ 8/28*
Prior, William E. 11/7
Probst, Karl K. 7/25+
Proctor, George W. 11/7+
Prophet, David 3/29+ 10/9*
Prost, Alain 2/24* 7/5
Proulx, Stephane 11/21+ 12/12*
Prudhomme, Don 5/7
Pruett, Scott 5/24*
Pruitt, Raymond S. 3/23, 6/17, 7/31* 9/1+
Pryce, Tom 3/5+ 5/12, 6/11*
Pugh, John Vernon 1/18*
Pughe, Earle W. 3/23+
Pulcher, Martin L. 3/21*
Pullen, Eddie 2/28, 10/6+
Pullinger, James 10/17
Purcell, Pat 4/4+ 6/1, 12/3*
Purdy, Ken 4/28* 6/7+ 7/2, 9/30
Purley, David 1/26* 6/5, 7/2+
Puterbaugh, Bill 6/6*
Putnam, Al 9/15+

Quail, Frank Jr. 3/12+
Quandt, Herbert 6/22*
Queiroz, Aldebert De 1/28*
Quester, Dieter 5/30*
Quiggle, Charles C. 7/23
Quimby, Langdon 10/7, 11/11
Quinlan, John 7/15
Quinn, Edward C. 12/15*
Qvale, Kjell 5/8

Raby, Ian 7/30, 9/22* 11/7+
Rackham, Horace H. 6/13+
Radclyffe, C. R. 1/1

Radford, Harry R. 9/26
Radford, William H. 1/30
Radisich, Paul 10/9*
Rae, Allen 8/28+
Rae, John B. 3/21*
Raggio, Carlo 9/10
Ragnotti, Jean 8/29*
Ragsdale, Edward T. 5/15* 6/17+
Rahal, Bobby 1/10*
Railton, Reid 6/24* 11/3+
Raines, Ella 12/25
Rainier, John T. 1/25, 3/29+
Raisbeck, John W. 11/21*
Ramos, Nano 12/7*
Ramponi, Giulio 8/7, 12/17+
Ramsey, Alice Huyler 6/9, 8/7, 9/10+ 11/11*
Rand, George C. 10/14* 12/9
Randak, Arthur S. 5/5+
Randall, Hugh 7/1+
Rankin, Luther M. 3/8
Raphanel, Pierre-Henri 5/27*
Rapilly, Yves 4/24*
Rapp, Karl 3/7, 7/21
Rappleyea, James C. 10/24+ 12/19*
Raskob, John J. 3/19* 10/14+
Rasmussen, Carl A. 3/1
Rasmussen, Eldon 7/7*
Rasmussen, Jorgen S. 6/29
Rathbone, Monroe J. 3/1* 8/2+
Rathman, Dick 5/2
Rathmann, Jim 7/16*
Ratzenberger, Roland 4/30+ 7/4*
Rausch, Ray R. 3/4*
Ravaglia, Roberto 5/26*
Raviolo, Victor G. 6/20*
Rayfield, Charles 12/8
Rayfield, Frederick 2/14
Rayfield, George 2/14
Rayfield, John 2/14
Rayfield, William 2/14, 5/26
Raymond, Charles B. 2/12* 7/29+
Raymond, Lee R. 8/13*
Raymond, Thomas L. 4/26* 9/16, 10/7+
Rea, S. C. 1/9
Read, Nathan 1/20+ 7/5* 8/26
Reagan, Ronald 7/4, 10/26
Reardon, M. D. 2/7+
Rebaque, Hector 2/5* 9/30
Reber, James C. 6/9
Redman, Brian 3/9* 9/28
Reece, Jimmy 9/28+
Reed, David Allen 8/1
Reed, John A. 7/22
Reed, W. H. 5/25
Rees, Alan 1/12*
Rees, Gareth 3/12*
Reese, Clarence 8/1, 8/25*
Reese, Sephaniah 5/31
Reeves, Milton O. 8/25*
Reeves, Stevie 5/16*
Regazzoni, Clay 3/21, 3/28, 7/14, 9/5*
Reichenstein, Murray L. 9/18
Reickert, Erick A. 8/30*
Reid, Anthony 6/21*
Reid, F. Malcolm 5/11+
Reid, Gordon 4/20+
Reid, James S. 11/22* 11/29+
Reid, James S. Jr. 1/15*
Reid, Thomas R. 4/20*
Reid, Walter C. 5/30+
Reifel, George C. 8/6*
Reindel, John D. 9/24*

Reiners, Neville 7/10*
Reinhardt, Robert D. 8/5*
Reinhart, John 2/5+ 8/24
Reinoehl, Harry K. 10/30+
Reins, Ralph 9/18*
Reis, J. F. 3/23*
Reith, Francis C. "Jack" 7/3+ 9/4*
Renault, Fernand 3/30
Renault, Louis 1/12* 1/17, 3/30, 10/4, 10/24+ 12/24
Renault, Marcel 3/30, 5/14* 5/24+ 6/29
Reno, John F. 12/19+
Renting, E. A. 7/28
Renwick, Robert W. 2/25+
Renzetti, Aurelius M. 2/2
Reso, Sidney J. 2/12* 5/3+
Ress, Albert 6/13
Resta, Dario 3/6, 6/26, 8/7, 9/2+ 11/16
Reuckstell, Grover E. 5/29+
Reuss, Lloyd E. 4/3, 9/22* 11/8
Reutemann, Carlos 1/29, 4/12*
Reuter, Edzard 2/16* 7/22
Reuter, Irving J. 2/26* 4/21+ 10/15
Reuter, Manuel 12/6*
Reuther, Roy L. 1/10+
Reuther, Victor G. 1/1*
Reuther, Walter 5/9+ 9/1*
Reventlow, Lance 2/24* 5/29, 6/19, 7/24+
Reville 7/2
Revson, Peter 2/27* 3/22+
Rexford, Bill 3/14*
Reynolds, E. T. 2/11*
Reynolds, J. S. 1/7
Rhoads, Paul J. 6/26+
Rhodes, John 8/18*
Ribbs, Willie T. 5/19
Ribeiro, Alex 11/7*
Ribeiro, Andre 1/18*
Ricardo, Harry 1/26* 5/18+ 6/4
Ricart, Wifredo P. 3/31, 5/15* 8/19+
Riccardo, John J. 1/8, 7/2* 7/8, 10/1
Rice, Calvin W. 10/3+
Rice, Francis E. 2/19*
Rice, Herbert H. 5/12, 11/15+
Rice, Horace E. 6/4* 8/4+
Richard, Eugene C. 2/18, 4/8*
Richards, Elmer E. 2/27*
Richards, Jim 9/2*
Richards, Terry 11/29+
Richards, Thomas O. 5/17+
Richards, Walter 9/18*
Richardson, Ken 12/15
Richardson, Sullivan 7/28, 11/18
Richenbaugh, Raymond L. 1/21
Richmond, Everett E. 7/31+
Richmond, Tim 8/13+
Rickenbacker, Edward V. 1/1, 5/30, 7/4, 7/5, 7/23+ 7/25, 8/15, 9/18, 10/8* 11/14
Ricker, Chester S. 12/5+
Rieber, Torkild 3/13* 8/10+
Riegel, F. Alexander 4/22+
Rieser, O. O. 5/10+
Riess, Fritz 7/11*
Rightmyer, Holden W. 6/27+
Riglander, M. M. 11/2
Rigolly, Louis 3/28, 3/31, 7/21
Rigsby, Jim 8/31+
Riker, Andrew L. 1/14, 3/4, 4/9, 6/1+ 8/28, 9/5, 9/7, 9/18, 10/22* 11/2, 11/16, 11/30
Riker, Mrs. Andrew L. 4/9
Riley, Brett 7/30*
Riley, Edward 1/7+ 6/30*

Rindt, Jochen 3/25, 4/12, 4/18* 9/5+ 10/4
Rines, John R. 8/3*
Rinland, Sergio 5/1
Rippingille, Edward V. Sr. 3/24+
Risley, George W. 2/21* 3/1, 9/9, 12/20+
Ritchie, John A. 3/16+ 8/26
Rivaz, Isaac de 1/30, 4/8, 4/10, 7/30+ 12/19*
Rivers, Osmond F. 12/16+
Rivolta, Renzo 6/27, 8/21+
Robarts, Richard 9/22*
Robbins, Brian G. 3/6
Robbins, John 8/3
Roberts, E. F. 9/4, 9/24+
Roberts, Fireball 1/20* 5/24, 7/2+
Roberts, Floyd 5/30+
Roberts, M. V. 6/9*
Roberts, Mason M. 1/4*
Roberts, Montague 9/20+
Roberts, Mortimer 10/3
Roberts, Ralph S. 1/7
Roberts, Robert B. 12/2
Roberts, Ross H. 2/3*
Roberts, Roy S. 3/12, 4/6
Robertson, George 7/3+ 8/27, 10/10, 10/12, 10/24
Robertson, Steve 7/4*
Robinson, Chip 3/29*
Robinson, John T. 11/4+
Robinson, W. Dean 7/20+
Roblin, A. T. 12/21+
Robson, George 9/1, 9/2+
Roche, James M. 1/1, 2/7, 6/1, 7/10, 10/31, 11/1 , 12/16* 12/31
Rock, John D. 1/1
Rockefeller, John D. 5/23+ 5/31, 7/8*
Rockefeller, William 5/31* 6/24+
Rockefeller, Winthrop 2/22+ 5/1*
Rockelman, Fred 5/6*
Rockne, Knute 3/4* 3/31+
Rockwell, Albert F. 1/19
Rockwell, C. L. 3/28
Rockwell, Stanley P. 8/11+
Rockwell, Walter F. 5/29+ 10/30*
Rockwell, Willard F. 3/31*
Rockwell, Willard F. Jr. 3/3*
Rocky, Glen 9/12+
Rodee, Chuck 5/14+
Rodes, Harold P. 6/22
Rodez, Pierre 5/24+ 6/12
Rodger, David W. 1/4+
Rodger, Robert M. 2/12+ 10/19*
Rodgers, William S. S. 2/19*
Rodriguez, Alberto 1/14* 3/11+
Rodriguez, Pedro 1/18* 7/11+
Rodriguez, Ricardo 2/14* 4/7, 6/17, 11/1+
Roe, Michael 8/8*
Roebling, Charles 5/31
Roebling, Ferdinand W. 5/31
Roebling, Washington A. II 1/1, 4/15+
Roeder, Dale 7/27*
Roesch, Georges 4/15* 11/7+
Roesch, J. Albert Jr. 4/27+
Roesch, Karl A. 7/7+ 12/14*
Roesing, Walter H. 9/12+
Roger, Emile 3/16
Rogers, Clarence E. 9/23* 12/18+
Rogers, Walter S. 1/16+
Rohde, Otto C. 6/2+
Rohrl, Walter 3/7*
Rol, Franco 6/5* 6/18+
Roller, Wolfgang 10/20*

Rollert, Edward D. 3/16* 6/24, 12/27+
Rollinson, Alan 5/15*
Rolls, C. S. 3/7, 3/15, 3/20, 4/9, 4/23, 5/4, 5/11, 7/11+ 8/27* 8/30, 9/27, 10/28, 11/18, 12/23
Rolls, John Allan 8/30
Rolph, Samuel W. 3/8* 4/7+
Rolt, L. T. C. 2/11* 5/9+
Rolt, Tony 6/14, 10/16*
Romberg, Henry E. 2/22+
Romeo, Nicola 4/28* 6/15, 8/15+ 12/31
Romiti, Cesare 6/24* 12/11, 12/14
Rommel, Erwin 8/12
Romney, George W. 2/12, 4/1, 7/8* 7/26+ 8/22, 10/12, 11/15, 12/3
Rondeau, Jean 12/27+
Rooney, Tom 4/18
Roos, Barney 2/13+ 10/11*
Roos, Bertil 10/12*
Roosevelt, Franklin D. 9/10, 12/1
Roosevelt, Theodore 8/22
Rootes, Nicholas G. 7/12*
Rootes, Reginald 10/20* 12/20+
Rootes, William E. 8/17* 12/12+
Rootes, William G. 1/16+ 6/14*
Roots, Francis M. 9/25
Roots, J. D. 7/7
Roots, Philander H. 9/25
Roper, Jim 6/19
Roper, Sylvester H. 6/1+
Rosberg, Keke 3/4, 9/23, 12/6*
Rose, Charles B. 5/27+ 10/28*
Rose, James V. 5/30+ 11/10*
Rose, Mauri 1/1+ 5/26* 5/30
Rose, Max Kaspar 5/1
Rosemeyer, Bernd 1/28+ 5/14, 7/5, 10/14* 10/27
Rosenbaum, Lewis N. 1/9+ 3/29*
Rosenberger, Adolf 6/19, 11/1
Rosier, Jean-Louis 10/29
Rosier, Louis 7/23, 10/28, 10/29+ 11/5*
Roslerstamm, Hugo von 6/3+ 8/1
Ross, Arthur 4/29+
Ross, Edward A. 7/9+
Ross, Frank Jr. 2/8*
Ross, Frank A. 11/17+
Ross, James H. 9/13*
Ross, Louis R. 3/23* 11/13
Ross, T. J. 5/27+ 7/27*
Rothengatter, Huub 10/8*
Rouse, Andy 12/2*
Row, E. C. 1/10* 2/13
Rowan, Robert D. 3/27*
Rowland, George R. 2/11+
Rowledge, A. J. 7/30* 12/12+
Roy, Ross 7/22* 8/16+
Royce, F. H. 2/3, 3/15, 3/16, 3/20, 3/27* 4/1, 4/22+ 5/4, 6/19, 6/26, 6/27, 9/16, 9/23, 11/18
Royce, Mrs. F. H. 3/16
Ruby, Lloyd 1/12* 2/6
Rudd, Ricky 9/12*
Rude, T. Morey 5/27+
Ruesch, Carlos 10/20*
Ruffia, Biscaretti di 7/1
Rugg, Harry M. 7/17+
Rumford, George W. 8/2+
Rumney, John G. 4/29+ 10/13*
Rumney, Mason P. 12/4+
Rumpler, Edmund 1/4* 6/18, 9/7+ 12/30
Runge, Robert F. 7/6+
Runk, Lee H. 3/10*

Ruppel, F. C. 1/27, 5/22, 5/31, 6/19, 10/30, 12/13
Rush, Ken 9/13
Rush, Thomas E. 1/8, 1/16* 6/3+
Rushmore, Samuel W. 8/16+
Rusinol, Pedro 2/25
Russel, Henry 2/25+ 5/16* 11/12
Russell, Bertrand 12/24
Russell, Earl 12/24
Russell, George 3/15*
Russell, Jim 5/28*
Russell, Thomas A. 4/17* 12/29+
Russell, Thomas F. 4/7*
Russo, Geki 6/18+ 10/23*
Russo, Paul 2/15+ 4/10*
Rust, Josef 11/7
Ruth, Babe 4/7
Ruth, John E. 10/28+
Ruthenburg, Louis 3/20*
Rutherford, Jack D. 10/5*
Rutherford, Johnny 3/12*
Ruttman, Troy 3/11* 5/17* 5/30, 7/4
Ruxton, William V. C. 5/6* 10/8+
Ryan, Allan A. 11/26+
Ryan, Peter 6/10* 7/2+
Ryan, Walter D'Arcy 3/14+
Rycamber, Frank 12/24+
Rydell, Rickard 9/22*
Rydin, Bo 5/7* 12/2, 12/20
Ryus, H. D. 11/9

Sabin, Arthur J. 9/21*
Sabine, Thierry 1/14+
Sachs, Eddie 5/28* 5/30+
Sackett, Ray C. 3/9
Sacks, Greg 11/3*
Saddoris, Raymond S. 11/13+
Sadler, Bill 9/3*
Sadler, E. J. 5/1* 10/28+
Sadler, Hermie 4/24*
Sagan, John 3/9*
Sage, Fred L. 6/11+
Said, Bob 5/5*
Said, Boris 9/18*
St. Germain, J. Ross 9/6+
St. James, Lyn 3/13*
St. John, Anthony P. 1/13*
Sakhnoffsky, Alexis de 1/25, 4/27+ 10/1, 10/22, 11/12*
Sakhnoffsky, Wladimir de 11/12
Salamano, Carlo 1/19+ 9/9
Salazar, Eliseo 3/13, 11/14*
Saldana, Joe 11/14*
Sale, Rhys M. 3/5*
Salles, Gaulter 9/28*
Sallustro, Oberdan 3/21, 4/10+
Salo, Mika 9/25*
Salom, Pedro G. 1/19, 4/12* 12/31+
Salomans, David 4/19+ 6/28* 10/15, 12/10
Salsbury, Stephen 10/12*
Salvadori, Roy 5/2, 5/12* 5/20, 5/25, 5/31
Samuels, Benjamin 3/31* 5/29+
Samuels, William 8/28+
Sanchez, Joseph J. 1/7, 1/26+
Sanders, Sol 7/10*
Sanderson, Ninian 5/14* 10/1+
Sandoz, Ed. M. 8/21*
Sanesi, Consalvo 3/28* 9/12
Santoni, Antonio 3/14
Sapiro, Aaron L. 2/5* 11/23+
Sarazin, Edouard 5/17, 11/1, 12/24+
Sarles, Roscoe 9/17+

Sarto, Jorma O. 1/26*
Satta, Orazio 1/3, 10/6*
Sauerbrey, Paul C. 3/3+
Sauereisen, Christian F. 5/5* 5/14+
Saunders, Russell J. 10/4*
Saurer, Adolphe 3/1
Savage, Swede 7/2+ 8/26*
Saveniers, Jean 7/24+
Sawyer, Elton 11/5*
Sayer, Malcolm 9/9
Saylor, Everitt 10/8*
Scaglione, Franco 6/19+ 9/26*
Scagnetti, Jack 12/24*
Scaife, Arthur J. 11/28+
Scales, Jack 10/23+
Scanlon, Charles J. 7/14*
Scarborough, Carl 5/30+
Scarfiotti, Ludovico (1) 4/9, 7/1
Scarfiotti, Ludovico (2) 5/1, 6/8+ 9/4, 10/18*
Scarlatti, Giorgio 7/2, 10/2*
Scarratt, Albert W. 4/16*
Schacht, Henry B. 7/14, 10/16*
Schadt, Ewald K. 8/8+
Schaefer, Fred J. 10/5+
Schaefer, John M. 3/8+
Schafer, Edward T. 8/8*
Schakel, Raymond A. 8/30+
Schamberger, Duffy 4/14
Schatz, Herrman A. 3/16+
Schatz, J. William 12/20+
Scheckter, Ian 8/22*
Scheckter, Jody 1/9, 1/29* 5/12, 5/22, 8/22
Schecter, Roy 1/31
Scheel, J. Ditlev 2/14+ 11/16*
Scheib, Earl A. 12/22
Schell, Harry 5/13+ 6/29*
Schelp, George H. 10/2
Schemansky, Joe 1/12
Schenck, Robert B. 7/1
Schenken, Tim 4/28, 9/26*
Schenuit, Frank G. 3/30+ 11/18*
Scherrer, Albert 2/28* 7/5+
Schiattarella, Mimmo 11/17*
Schick, Edward M. 6/16+
Schiff, Barry J. 10/24*
Schiller, Heinz 1/25*
Schilovsky, Peter 11/27
Schindler, Bill 3/6* 9/20+ 9/25
Schiske, Rudolf 6/15
Schlecht, Richard 1/25
Schlegel, Alfred 5/9
Schlesman, Carleton H. 11/13+
Schlesser, Jean-Louis 9/12*
Schlesser, Jo 5/18* 7/7+ 9/12
Schleyer, Hans-Martin 9/5, 10/18+
Schlumpf, Fritz 3/30, 7/7
Schmiding, Walter F. 9/7
Schmidt, Charles 1/2, 4/12, 5/5, 9/3, 10/8
Schmidt, Herman H. A. Jr. 6/24+
Schmidt, William F. 2/6
Schmuecker, Toni 1/10, 4/23*
Schneider, Bernd 7/20*
Schneider, Louis 9/27+
Schneider, Marvin N. 1/26+
Schneider, Theodore 2/4+
Schnell, William 1/2, 1/3, 2/12, 3/14, 6/3, 7/14, 9/21, 10/6, 11/5, 11/18, 12/28
Schnitker, A. E. 2/14, 12/23
Schoeller, Rudolf 3/7+ 4/27*
Schoeneck, George 11/14+
Schon, Pierre 8/2+
Schopper, Karl 9/2, 10/17

Schornstein, Dieter 6/28*
Schoup, Bert 5/30+
Schrader, Gus 5/22* 10/22+
Schrader, Ken 5/29*
Schreiber, G. A. 8/16+
Schreiber, John M. 7/18+
Schrempp, Jurgen E. 9/15*
Schroeder, Dorsey 2/5*
Schroeder, Eric 4/8+
Schroeder, Jeret 11/13*
Schroeder, Rob 5/11*
Schubert, Frank R. 2/4+
Schulenberg, Count von der 5/26
Schultz, Arthur B. 5/1+
Schultz, Herman C. 12/24+
Schultz, John L. 1/22
Schultz, Robert J. 11/8
Schultz, Woldemar G. 10/13+
Schultze, Herbert 7/12+
Schulz, Albert C. 11/25+
Schumacher, Michael 1/3* 2/14
Schumann, John J. 8/11+ 9/11*
Schupp, Otto 7/6
Schuppan, Vern 3/19*
Schustala, Ignaz 1/29+ 12/6* 12/15
Schuster, George 2/4* 7/4+ 7/30, 8/16
Schutz, Peter 10/12, 12/16
Schwab, Louis 10/27+
Schwartz, Maurice 3/22+
Schwartz, Robert 3/9*
Schwarz, Elmer H. 2/21+
Schweikert, John F. 7/8*
Schweitzer, Louis 7/8*
Schweizer, Paul 3/4
Schwenke, Robert 7/24
Schwerdtfeger, W. 10/17
Schwitzer, Lew 8/14
Scott, Benny 2/4*
Scott, Bert 6/23
Scott, Bill 10/10*
Scott, Bob 7/5+ 10/4*
Scott, C. F. 5/30*
Scott, Dave 5/14*
Scott, David R. 7/31
Scott, Herbert 1/25, 6/17+ 8/28, 11/30*
Scott, Joseph V. 1/23*
Scott, Karl E. 11/15
Scott, Kenneth N. 4/1, 9/1
Scott, Richard 11/8*
Scott, Richard H. 3/11+ 4/17, 7/23* 12/20, 12/28
Scott, Wendell 8/29* 12/1, 12/23+
Scott-Brown, Archie 5/13* 5/19+
Scotti, Piero 2/14+ 11/11*
Scott-Moncreiff, David 6/28+ 7/1*
Scott-Montagu, John 7/3
Scripps, William E. 5/6* 6/12+ 11/1
Scudelari, Tony 10/12+
Seaholm, Ernest 4/16, 12/27*
Seaman, Dick 2/4* 6/25+ 7/11, 7/24
Seaman, Harold H. 1/30+ 9/8*
Seaman, Harry J. 5/8+
Seaman, Richard J. 9/19*
Searle, Frederick E. 7/1, 8/1* 8/19+
Sears, David 2/16
Sears, Jack 2/16*
Sears, Stanley E. 2/16, 5/26, 9/17+
Sears, Stephen W. 7/27*
Seaton, Laurence F. 1/10
Seaton, Walter W. 3/22*
Sebert, John 5/12
Secrest, Fred G. 8/25*

Sedgwick, Michael 3/20* 10/14+
Seeley, Dana Elisha 8/28+ 9/25*
Seeley, Halstead H. 4/19*+
Segrave, Henry 3/11, 3/16, 3/29, 5/20, 5/23,
    5/27, 6/13+ 9/22* 10/23
Seiberling, Charles W. 1/26* 9/20+
Seiberling, Francis 2/1+ 9/20*
Seiberling, Frank A. 8/11+ 10/6*
Seiberling, James P. 7/3*
Seidel, Wolfgang 3/1+ 7/4*
Seidemann, William A. 4/10
Seiler, Paul W. 8/15* 9/1
Sekiya, Masanori 11/27*
Selden, George B. 1/17+ 3/5, 5/8, 9/14* 9/15,
    11/2, 11/4, 11/5
Seligman, Jefferson 6/18+ 11/26* 12/11
Selwa, Jim 12/22
Semerena, Pierre 6/20* 12/13
Semon, Waldo L. 9/10*
Senechal, Robert 8/7
Senna, Ayrton 3/21* 4/21, 5/1+
Serafini, Dorino 7/22*
Sergay, Boris Peter 6/1+
Serpollet, Leon 2/1+ 4/13, 4/21, 5/19, 10/4*
Serra, Chico 2/3*
Serrurier, Doug 12/9* 12/29
Servoz-Gavin, Johnny 1/18*
Seton, Barry 5/5
Seton, Glenn 5/5*
Settember, Tony 6/9
Setzer, Dennis 2/27*
Seubert, Edward G. 6/20* 11/17+
Seward, Clarence W. 1/7
Shacket, Sheldon R. 4/3*
Shafer, Harvey G. 7/24*
Shakespeare, John W. 3/30
Shank, Louis W. 3/26+
Shanley, James J. 6/26+
Shanley, John V. 10/16
Sharp, Hap 1/1* 11/14
Sharp, Scott 2/14*
Sharp, William H. 11/14+
Shattuck, Albert R. 3/27
Shaver, G. F. 7/25
Shaw, Dale 4/9*
Shaw, David A. 5/12+ 8/24*
Shaw, Walden W. 8/25
Shaw, Wilbur 5/30, 10/30+ 10/31*
Shawe-Taylor, Brian 1/29*
Shea, Edward L. 11/4* 12/11+
Sheets, Harold F. 5/2* 5/29+
Shelby, Carroll 1/11* 1/27, 2/16, 3/1, 5/31
Shellenbarger, Dale 5/4
Shelly, Tony 2/2*
Shelton, Steve 5/16*
Shepard, Everett H. 7/16+
Shepard, Horace A. 11/15*
Shepherd, Lee 3/11+
Shepherd, Morgan 10/12*
Sheppy, Charles L. 5/1+ 9/21*
Sherman, Don 9/28
Sherman, Joe 4/19*
Sherman, Vernon W. 4/7*
Sherry, Peter J. 4/20*
Shettler, Reuben 8/16
Shields, John H. 8/29*
Shingo, Shigeo 11/14+
Shinoda, Larry 3/25*
Shipley, James R. 1/10+ 12/26*
Shipley, Otto M. 12/3
Shobe, Vernon I. 4/7+
Shomer, Frank A. 7/16, 7/24

Short, Charles R. 5/8+
Shrewsbury, Earl of 5/17+ 11/13*
Shriner, Eileen 4/23+
Shriner, Herb 4/23+ 5/29*
Shulman, Harry 3/14* 3/20+
Shurcliff, Sidney 1/19+ 3/24* 5/12
Shuttleworth, Dick 9/14
Shuttleworth, Peter J. 10/16+
Sibley, B. E. 2/13+ 9/1
Sick, Wilson W. 9/29, 12/23*
Siddeley, John Davenport 11/3+
Sidgreaves, Arthur F. 1/14, 4/23, 6/7+ 6/12*
Siegling, Elmer 9/26+
Siemens, Alexander 1/22* 2/16+ 12/10
Siena, Eugenio 5/15+
Siffert, Jo 3/7, 4/23, 7/7* 7/20, 8/17, 10/24+
Silas, Cecil J. 4/15*
Siler, William A. 1/8+
Silver, Conover T. 10/20
Silvestre, Paul 2/17*
Simms, Frederick R. 2/14, 4/22+ 5/16, 6/7,
    7/12, 8/10
Simo, Brian 10/1*
Simon, Andre 1/5*
Simon, D. A. G. 7/24*
Simon, Dick 9/21*
Simon, Peter 7/28
Simonds, William A. 1/13, 1/31, 3/1, 9/19* 10/19+
Simone, Fabrizio de 3/30*
Simoni, Giampiero 9/12*
Simons, Walter J. 10/20*
Simonsen, Richard 9/8+
Simpson, Howard W. 1/29, 5/8* 7/1, 11/4+
Simpson, J. H. 9/16, 11/15
Sinatra, Frank 8/11
Sinclair, Earle W. 5/5* 9/21+
Sinclair, Harry F. 7/6* 9/21, 11/10+
Sinclair, Robert J. 3/17*
Sinclair, Walrond 1/31, 8/30+
Sinclair, William 1/17* 2/6+
Singleton, William D. 2/7* 7/29+
Sinsabaugh, Christopher 1/26+
Sintz, Clark 5/9* 7/14
Sintz, Claude 7/14+
Sirois, Frenchy 4/16
Sirois, Jigger 4/16*
Sirrine, Earl D. 2/1, 7/25+ 9/30
Sisler, Louis E. 8/3
Sislo, C. L. 9/26
Sivocci, Ugo 9/8+
Sizaire, Georges 5/8* 5/12+ 6/1, 6/20
Sizaire, Maurice 1/28+ 6/1, 6/20, 12/29*
Skaife, Mark 4/4*
Skelly, William G. 4/11+ 6/10*
Skelton, Betty 6/16, 6/28*
Skelton, Owen R. 2/9* 7/14, 7/22+
Skelton, Red 11/14
Skinner, A. E. 2/3*
Skinner, Arthur A. 12/15+
Skinner, Clarence O. 2/20*
Skinner, Mike 6/28*
Skinner, Sherrod E. 1/5, 8/5, 10/19*
Sklarek, Clifford 2/28+ 5/19*
Skoda, Karl Ritter von 6/9
Skramstad, Harold K. 6/3*
Slade, John C. 12/24+
Slater, Bob 6/5+
Slater, Martin 7/19
Slauson, Harold W. 7/22+
Slayter, R. Games 2/25, 4/25, 10/15+ 12/9*
Sligh, Tom S. Jr. 3/30+ 5/17*
Sloan, Alfred P. Jr. 1/11, 2/17+ 2/21, 4/2, 5/3,

    5/10, 5/23* 6/3, 8/2, 8/7, 9/29, 11/7, 12/1
Sloan, George A. 5/20+ 5/30*
Sloan, Hugh W. Jr. 11/1*
Sloane, William W. 9/8+ 10/17*
Slocum, George M. 10/29+
Sloper, Thomas 1/7
Smale, John G. 1/1, 8/1* 12/4
Small, F. M. 8/24* 11/21+
Smalley, J. Sheppard 8/11+
Smallman, Andy 4/27, 11/29+
Smiley, Gordon 5/15+
Smith, A. O. 11/11
Smith, Adele A. 10/15
Smith, Arthur 9/13
Smith, Ben D. 9/14+
Smith, Chris 9/4*
Smith, Clay 9/6+ 10/24*
Smith, Clement 1/31, 5/17, 6/7, 10/15
Smith, Clyde J. 1/30
Smith, D. Myrle 2/6+
Smith, Earl H. 3/1
Smith, Edgar W. 4/1* 9/17+
Smith, Elbert L. 1/29+ 12/16*
Smith, F. Llewellyn 7/25*
Smith, F. V. 12/30
Smith, Frederick L. 1/5, 5/8, 11/12
Smith, Frederick Robertson 6/15+
Smith, G. W. 11/4*
Smith, George 9/10
Smith, George H. 4/17
Smith, George W. 12/9+
Smith, Herbert E. 8/16*
Smith, James H. 3/26*
Smith, Jimmy 6/23
Smith, John F. 2/1
Smith, John F. Jr. 1/1, 1/4, 2/1, 4/6* 6/28, 11/2,
    12/4
Smith, John T. 1/17* 9/28+
Smith, Joseph N. 2/5+ 3/9*
Smith, L. Anton 10/15
Smith, Leni 10/15
Smith, LeRoi Tex 1/1*
Smith, Lloyd L. 8/19*
Smith, Lloyd R. 8/21* 12/23+
Smith, Lon R. 12/24*
Smith, Louise 7/31*
Smith, Mark 4/10*
Smith, Oscar A. 8/20+ 9/7*
Smith, Roger B. 1/1, 4/3, 4/18, 7/12* 7/31, 8/1
Smith, Roscoe M. 1/22* 4/16+ 9/11
Smith, Samuel L. 1/5, 5/7+ 5/8, 5/11, 6/28*
Smith, Stanford A. 11/8+
Smithey, Wayne H. 7/8*
Smyth, Bill 6/1
Snagge, Harold 3/19+ 5/10, 12/28*
Sneva, Jerry 5/23*
Sneva, Tom 6/1*
Snider, George 12/8*
Snipe, Cyril 5/25
Snobeck, Dany 5/2*
Snow, Herbert C. 12/8
Snyder, Carl J. 6/30+ 11/29*
Snyder, Clifford L. 5/2+
Snyder, J. Rush 8/31+
Snyder, Jimmy 6/29+
Sobey, Albert 8/5*
Soderman, Sven-Erik 8/2, 9/26*
Sofield, Hilton W. 8/13
Solana, Moises 7/27*
Soler-Roig, Alex 10/29*
Solheim, Carl 7/7
Somerby, Lorenzo B. 12/9

Sommer, Raymond 7/13, 8/31* 9/10+
Sommers, W. J. 10/10+
Sonnecken, Edwin H. 7/22*
Soper, Steve 9/27*
Sorensen, Charles E. 3/2, 3/13, 5/11, 6/1,
    8/11+ 9/7*, 10/1
Sospiri, Vincenzo 10/7*
Souders, George 7/26+
Soules 7/2
Sourd, Marc 4/27*
South, Stephen 2/19*
Southgate, Tony 5/25*
Soutter, Arthur W. 1/7+ 3/9*
Spangler, Lester 5/30+
Sparken, Mike 6/16*
Sparrow, Edward W. 8/21
Sparrow, Stanwood W. 8/14+ 11/18*
Spaulding, Henry W. 1/20+
Speed, Lake 1/17*
Speers, William H. 4/8+
Spence, Bill 5/30+
Spence, Mike 4/24, 5/7+ 12/30*
Spence, Russell 1/3*
Spencer, Carleton B. 3/23
Spencer, Jimmy 2/15*
Spencer, LeRoy 1/10, 7/29, 11/13+
Sperlich, Harold K. 2/2, 2/4, 12/1*
Sperry, Elmer A. 6/16+ 10/12*
Spice, Gordon 4/18*
Spicer, Clarence W. 10/30* 11/21+
Spiegelberg, Charles J. 8/3
Spijker, Hendrik 2/21+
Spiller, David H. 5/8*
Spoon, George A. 7/17+
Spray, Judd W. 4/25+
Spring, Frank S. 3/13
Springer, Neil A. 5/2*
Spurrier, Henry 6/16* 6/17+
Spychiger, Tommy 4/25+
Squire, Adrian 9/20+
Squire, John 7/18
Stacey, Alan 6/19+ 8/29*
Stafford, Terry 1/1, 5/17, 9/4, 10/15, 12/3,
    12/12 , 12/25
Staggi, Joseph 3/27+ 11/13*
Stahl, Ben 9/7*
Staiger, John G. 3/20*
Staley, E. E. 2/14, 5/26, 10/28
Stambaugh, A. A. 6/1* 7/11+
Stambaugh, H. J. Jr. 4/24+
Stambler, Irwin 11/20*
Staniland, Chris 10/20
Stanley, Carlton F. 3/25+
Stanley, Clarance 1/14*
Stanley, Francis E. 1/1, 3/25, 5/30, 6/1* 6/17,
    7/20, 7/31+ 9/20, 11/11
Stanley, Mrs. Francis E. 1/1
Stanley, Freelan O. 3/25, 6/1* 6/17, 8/31,
    10/2+ 11/11
Stanley, Raymond W. 4/1* 9/20+
Stant, K. E. 12/29
Stapp, Babe 9/17+
Stark, Jared W. 3/24+ 12/7*
Starkman, Ernest S. 2/1
Starrabba, Gaetano 12/3*
Stauffer, Richard G. 7/3+
Stead, C. F. 10/26
Stead, E. T. 4/7, 5/24+
Stearns, Frank B. 7/5+ 8/15, 11/6*
Stearns, Willard A. 12/11+
Stebbins, Arthur C. 8/21
Steele, Lynn H. 2/16+

Stefanini, Giuseppe 12/2*
Stegemeier, Richard J. 4/1*
Steichen, Edward 3/25+ 3/27*
Stein, E. Waldo 11/16+
Steinkuhler, Franz 5/20*
Steinman, David B. 6/11* 8/22+
Steinway, William 9/29
Stella, Ugo 1/1
Stem, Alfred L. 10/13+
Stempel, Robert C. 2/1, 4/3, 5/25, 7/5* 8/1,
    9/1
Stephens, Donald L. 12/28*
Stephens, H. Morton 9/23+
Stephens, George W. 8/12+
Sterling, James G. "Pete" 4/6, 5/31, 9/2+
Sterling, Ross 2/11* 3/25+
Stern, Jane Wexler 10/24* 10/25
Stern, Michael 10/25
Stern, Paul H. 10/12+
Stern, Philip Van Doren 7/31+ 9/10*
Stern, Richard Ritter von 6/2
Sternberg, Ernest R. 7/3*
Sternberg, William G. Jr. 3/16+
Sternbergh, Herbert M. 4/6
Steuart, Leonard P. 1/17+ 11/12*
Stevens, Brooks 1/4+ 7/22
Stevens, Claud L. 1/18+
Stevens, Samuel B. 7/24, 7/29
Stevenson, Chuck 10/15*
Stewart, Frank G. 8/8+
Stewart, Gwenda 8/6
Stewart, Ian 7/15*
Stewart, Jackie 3/6, 3/7, 4/18, 4/19, 6/11*
    6/23, 7/12, 8/5, 9/12, 9/20, 10/14, 10/29
Stewart, Jimmy 3/6*
Stewart, Norman J. 8/9*
Stewart, Paul 10/29*
Stewart, Robert G. 1/27*
Stewart, Robert W. 2/24+ 3/11*
Stewart, Tony 5/20*
Stewart, William L. 6/21+
Stewart, William L. Jr. 6/27* 8/1+
Stieglitz, William I. 2/2
Stillman, George F. 12/20
Stillman, Walter 12/20+
Stirano, Giorgio 3/1
Stivender, Donald L. 5/8*
Stoddard, Harry G. 5/21+ 9/13*
Stoessel, Rudy 4/17*
Stohr, Siegfried 10/10*
Stokes, Donald G. 3/22*
Stoll, Herman 2/19+
Stommelen, Rolf 2/4, 3/4, 4/27, 5/24+ 7/11*
Stone, Harold 10/1
Stoner, J. A. 10/29
Stoner, Richard B. 5/15*
Storrow, James J. 1/21* 1/26, 3/13+ 7/29,
    11/23, 12/13
Stout, Richard H. 7/10+
Stout, William B. 2/25, 3/16* 3/20+ 4/25,
    6/19
Strachan, Douglas A. 8/6*
Stradella, Charles G. 1/6, 1/29*
Straight, Herbert R. 5/4+ 9/30*
Straight, Laura A. 10/15
Straight, Whitney 7/11, 10/13
Stranahan, Robert A. 2/9+ 7/7*
Strang, Colin 8/31
Strang, Lewis 3/19, 7/20+ 9/7
Stratingh, Sibrandus 9/3
Strauss, A. M. 9/28
Strauss, L. Z. Morris 8/4*

Streiff, Phillippe 6/26*
Strelinger, Charles A. 9/19
Stricker, Adam K. Jr. 6/28*
Stricklin, Hut 6/24*
Stringer, Clyde W. 3/25+
Strom, Walter H. 1/23+
Strombotne, Richard L. 5/6*
Strong, Edward T. 6/1
Stroppe, Bill 1/15* 5/3, 11/7+
Struhatschek, Rudolf 6/9
Stryker, James W. 4/20*
Stuart, Donald R. 1/10, 3/1
Stubblefield, Stubby 5/21+
Stuck, Hans 1/1, 2/9+ 3/6, 5/18, 6/10, 8/26,
    12/27*
Stuck, Hans-Joachim 1/1* 6/14
Studebaker, Clement 2/16, 3/12* 11/27+
Studebaker, Clement Jr. 8/11* 12/3+
Studebaker, Henry 2/16, 10/5*
Studebaker, Jacob F. 5/26*
Studebaker, John C. 6/7
Studebaker, John M. 1/2, 3/16+ 7/22, 10/10*
Studebaker, Mrs. John M. 1/2
Studebaker, Peter E. 4/1*
Stureson, Per 3/22*
Sturgis, Samuel D. 5/30
Sturmey, Henry 5/15, 10/9, 10/19, 11/2
Sturt, Alfred 12/16
Stutz, Harry C. 6/26+ 9/12* 10/25, 11/3
Stutz, Mrs. Harry C. 10/25
Sudo, T. 1/15
Sullivan, Danny 3/9*
Sulprizio, D. 8/30+
Sulzback, Jacob 1/8, 1/9
Summers, Bob 11/12
Sundberg, Severt 2/22+
Sundblom, H. H. 6/22*
Sundling, C. Stanley 8/27+
Surace, Filippo 3/28*
Surer, Marc 9/18*
Surtees, John 2/11* 5/6, 5/20, 7/18, 9/10
Sussman, Victor H. 7/26*
Sutcliffe, Andy 5/9*
Sutherland, James D. 1/26+
Sutton, Edward O. 5/1
Sutton, Len 3/30, 8/9*
Sutton, R. M. V. 5/30
Suzuki, Aguri 9/8*
Suzuki, Keiichi 3/21*
Suzuki, Osamu 1/30*
Suzuki, Toshio 2/2, 3/10*
Svanholm, Bert-Olof 12/20
Svenson, Charles W. 9/25+
Swain, Joseph G. 10/24+
Swan, Harry L. 8/23*
Swan, John W. 9/17, 11/9
Swanson, Bob 6/13+ 8/20*
Swaters, Jacques 10/30*
Swayne, Alfred H. 4/5* 4/16+
Sweatlund, Charles 9/5+
Sweet, Ernest E. 9/15+
Sweetland, Ernest J. 5/26* 11/15+
Sweigert, Al 10/31*
Sweikert, Bob 5/20* 6/17+
Swensrud, Sidney A. 8/1*
Swetland, Horace M. 6/15+ 11/15*
Swiener, Wallace 7/7+
Swift, Clarence B. 7/8+
Swindell, Sammy 10/26*
Swinehart, James A. 8/3
Swinscoe, John 6/10+
Sydnor, Harold 11/26+

Sykes, Charles 1/26, 2/6, 3/16, 4/15, 12/30
Symington, William 3/22+
Sytner, Frank 6/29*
Szanto, Frank W. 9/23+
Szews, Charles 4/1
Szisz, Ferenc 6/26

Tabacu, Ion P. 7/22*
Taber, George H. Jr. 1/4* 8/20+
Taber, Melbert W. 2/17+
Tadini, Mario 12/1
Takahara, Noritake 6/6*
Takahashi, Kenji 5/18*
Takahashi, Kunimitsu 1/29*
Talbott, Willard 2/1
Tambay, Patrick 6/25*
Tamburini, Antonio 9/15*
Tangeman, C. H. 5/12
Tangeman, G. P. 5/12
Tanner, Alvin G. 5/3* 11/10+
Tarasov, Aleksandr M. 5/4
Taravilla, Rafael 1/16+
Tarkington, Joseph A. 2/26
Tarquini, Gabriele 3/2*
Tarrant, Harley 3/12
Taruffi, Piero 1/12+ 5/12, 5/18, 10/12* 11/25
Tassin, Thierry 1/11*
Taylor, Arnold N. 8/18+
Taylor, Charles F. 9/24*
Taylor, Dennis 6/2+ 6/12*
Taylor, Frank 1/1
Taylor, Frederick W. 3/20* 3/21+
Taylor, Geoffrey 5/13, 7/2
Taylor, Henry 12/16*
Taylor, Henry Seth 1/7+ 4/9*
Taylor, Ian 1/28* 6/7+
Taylor, Joe 9/5+
Taylor, John 3/23* 9/8+
Taylor, Mike 4/24*
Taylor, Reese H. 6/22+ 7/6*
Taylor, Trevor 1/1, 7/16, 12/26*
Taylor, Wayne 7/15*
Teagle, Walter C. 1/9+ 5/1*
Teague, Al 8/21
Teague, Kerry 1/12*
Teague, Marshall 2/11+ 5/22*
Teague, Richard A. 1/4, 2/6, 3/1, 4/18, 5/5+
    9/2, 12/26*
Teague, Walter Dorwin 5/29, 12/5+ 12/18*
Teck, Francis of 1/9* 10/22+
Teetor, C. N. 3/29, 5/2+ 12/15*
Teetor, Lothair 3/30*
Teetor, Ralph R. 2/15+ 8/17*
Tell, William K. Jr. 2/27*
Temperino, Maurizio 1/26* 1/31+
Tempero, Bill 1/16*
Temple, Herbert A. 9/8+
Tenney, Perry L. 8/22+
Tenni, Omobono 7/4+
terHorst, Jerald F. 7/11*
Terra, Max de 10/6* 12/29+
Terrell, Richard L. 12/29*
Terry, Maynard B. 11/20*
Terry, Sydney L. 4/5*
Test, Charles E. 6/22+ 12/22*
Testemolle, M. 6/4
Tetzlaff, Teddy 3/19, 7/5, 8/12
Tew, James D. 5/2* 12/31+
Thackwell, Mike 3/24, 3/30* 9/28
Thayer, Frederick K. 2/1* 2/14, 12/23
Thayer, Harry 12/1
Thery, Leon 6/17, 7/5

Theys, Didier 10/19*
Thiim, Kurt 8/3*
Thomas, Cecil B. 6/11+ 10/12*
Thomas, Charles A. 2/15*
Thomas, Charles D. 4/3
Thomas, Charles R. 3/8+ 3/29*
Thomas, E. R. 2/27, 7/16, 9/13+ 11/3*
Thomas, Mrs. E. R. 2/27
Thomas, Edwin J. 4/27*
Thomas, Evelyn 5/30
Thomas, H. Kerr 4/30
Thomas, Herb 2/6, 4/6* 5/2
Thomas, Horace T. 3/28, 8/9* 12/20+
Thomas, J. G. Parry 3/3+ 4/6* 4/27, 4/28, 10/5
Thomas, J. Henry 6/3, 12/19
Thomas, Joe 12/28+
Thomas, John W. 11/18* 11/26+
Thomas, L. D. 4/21*
Thomas, Larry 1/25+
Thomas, Lowell 11/2
Thomas, Ralph 10/9*
Thomas, Rene 3/7* 5/30, 7/6, 9/23+
Thomas, Rolland Jay 4/18+ 6/9*
Thompson, Charles 7/16* 10/4+
Thompson, Craig S. 5/24*
Thompson, Dick 5/1
Thompson, Earl A. 3/9, 4/29+ 11/14
Thompson, Eric 7/19, 11/4*
Thompson, Fred C. 3/6+
Thompson, Frederick R. 9/1
Thompson, Herbert L. 10/30
Thompson, Joe 4/21+ 9/27*
Thompson, Mickey 3/16+ 5/14, 9/9, 10/6, 12/7*
Thompson, Samuel J. 12/9
Thompson, Speedy 4/2+ 4/3*
Thompson, William D. 2/9+
Thoms, Louis 6/21+
Thomson, Johnny 4/9* 9/24+
Thomson, R. W. 10/1, 12/10
Thorne, Joel 7/8, 10/17+
Thorne, Leslie 6/23* 7/13+
Thornley, John 7/15+
Thornton, Eleanor 4/15* 12/30+
Thul, Nicholas P. 2/8+ 12/29*
Thurman, Arthur 5/30+
Thursby, Ray 4/4*
Thurston, George R. Jr. 12/18*
Tibbett, Lawrence 1/6
Tibbetts, Milton E. 6/1, 7/27* 8/27+
Tice, Percival S. 5/19+
Till, Brian 3/26*
Tillotson, Harry C. 9/1+
Tilt, Charles A. 6/28* 9/19+
Timken, Henry 3/16+ 6/28, 8/16*
Timken, Henry H. 10/14+
Timken, William R. 6/11+
Timm, Frithiof V. 10/30+
Timmerman, Arthur H. 3/20, 7/18+
Timpy, Jack J. 1/4*
Tingelstad, Bud 4/4* 7/30+
Tingle, Sam 8/24*
Tingley, Clyde 1/5* 12/24+
Tinker, George M. 6/17*
Tippett, W. Paul Jr. 1/15, 7/1, 9/28, 12/27*
Tiscornia, J. W. 11/16* 12/16+
Tiscornia, Lester C. 10/24*
Tisdale, Wright 3/24*
Titchener, Walter E. 5/7+
Tito, Josip Broz 8/7
Titterington, Desmond 5/1*
Titus, Jerry 8/5+ 10/24*
Tjaarda, John 6/25, 7/10

Tobin, B. F. 11/23+ 11/29*
Todghma, Ron W. 7/16
Todt, Fritz 2/8+ 7/5, 9/4*
Todt, Jean 10/19
Togo, Yukiyasu 8/24
Toivonen, Henri 5/2+
Tojo, Teruo 9/6
Tolentino, Mario 4/3
Tolley, James 6/29
Tomlinson, Joseph R. 11/29*
Tompkins, Stephen B. 4/14+
Tompkins, Stephen J. 10/23*
Toms, Harvey 7/8
Toncray, Millard H. 9/8+
Tone, Fred I. 7/3, 11/15+
Tongue, Reggie 5/6
Tooker, John C. 1/3
Torkelson, Martin W. 4/2+ 10/27*
Tornaco, Charles de 6/7* 9/18+
Tost, Max L. 11/7+
Touceda, Enrique A. 10/20+
Toutee, Henri 8/18* 11/13+
Towell, Thomas W. 1/6, 9/28*
Townsend, Lynn A. 4/19, 5/12* 7/3, 7/27, 10/1
Toyoda, Eiji 9/12* 10/30, 11/16
Toyoda, Kiichiro 3/27+
Toyoda, Risaburo 6/3+ 12/19
Toyoda, Shoichiro 2/27* 12/12
Toyoda, Tatsuro 6/1*
Tracy, Joe 3/10, 3/20+ 3/22*
Tracy, Paul 12/17*
Tracy, Percy W. 10/30+
Trainer, James E. 9/16*
Trask, O. C. 12/1
Treatt, C. Court 9/23, 12/26
Tremear, Charles H. 7/20+
Tremulis, Alex 5/16, 8/28, 12/29*
Trepardoux, Charles 1/1, 2/26+
Treser, Walter 1/1, 8/26
Trevithick, Richard 4/13* 4/22+ 12/24
Trichel, G. W. 9/10*
Trickle, Dick 10/27*
Trimmer, Tony 1/24*
Trintignant, Maurice 7/1, 8/5, 10/30* 11/21
Triplett, Ernie 3/5+
Trips, Wolfgang von 5/4* 9/10+
Troberg, Picko 1/1*
Trolle, Michel 6/23*
Trosize, Rocky 3/1+
Trossi, Carlo Felice 5/9+
Trotman, Alexander J. 7/22* 11/1
Trowbridge, Roy P. 12/16*
Truman, Harry S. 7/3, 12/1
Trumbull, Isaac B. 5/7+
Tryon, H. C. 7/6, 11/6
Tucker, Preston 1/22, 3/21, 5/29, 6/10, 7/5,
    9/21*, 12/26+
Tucker, Richard F. 12/25*
Tucker, Stanley 3/2, 4/14
Tudor, Frederic 9/1
Tuke, J. E. 9/25
Tullius, Bob 12/7*
Tullos, Robert M. 10/25+
Tumner, Guy 12/1*
Turcat, Leon 12/7*
Turley, Everett W. 9/6+
Turnbull, George H. 10/17*
Turner, Arthur 7/3
Turner, Curtis 4/12* 10/4+ 10/31
Turner, Harry C. 12/6+
Turner, Hughes C. 9/27
Turner, Stuart 1/14* 10/1

Turner, Walter J. 5/1*
Tutt, Charles L. 1/9* 11/1+
Tuttle, Holmes P. 6/16+ 6/17*
Tuttle, John H. 12/29
Twining, Earl S. 10/9+
Twohey, Arthur E. 4/4+ 11/7
Twohey, John 7/9+
Tyrrell, Ken 3/5*

Ugnon, Pierre Gilbert 4/26+
Ugolini, Nello 8/9*
Uhlenhaut, Rudolf 5/18, 6/13
Ulmann, Alec 4/23+ 5/12, 6/16* 12/31
Ulmen, Toni 1/25* 11/4+
Ulrich, Franz Heinrich 7/6*
Unser, Al Jr. 4/19* 8/9
Unser, Al Sr. 5/17, 5/24, 5/29*
Unser, Bobby 2/20*
Unser, Jerry 5/17+
Unser, Louis 9/3
Upton, Colcord 12/30
Upton, G. B. 10/29+
Urich, Harold C. 5/9
Utley, John E. 2/20*
Utz, J. G. 3/4*

Vaccarella, Nino 3/4* 5/5, 9/10
Vadier, Fernand 8/6+ 9/28*
Vail, Ira 4/21+ 9/5
Valade, Gary C. 5/6
Valance, Edward L. 11/24+
Valier, Max 5/17+ 7/26
Valk, Robert E. 8/21*
Valletta, Vittorio 5/4, 7/28* 8/9+
Valton, Charles 1/26* 5/21+
Van Alstyne, Milton H. 4/13+
van Bakel, Willem 7/1
Vance, Harold S. 2/15, 3/9, 8/22* 8/31+
Vancil, Bruce 5/26
Van Damm, Sheila 8/23+
Vandeburg, Clyde M. 11/6*
Vanderbilt, George 10/12
Vanderbilt, William K. Jr. 1/8+ 1/27, 4/21, 8/5,
    10/12, 10/26*
van der Merwe, Sarel 12/5*
Vanderpleyn, Christian 9/7
Vanderveen, Bart H. 5/5*
Vandervell, Tony 7/3
van der Woude, Reinier G. A. 5/6*
vanderZee, Abram 7/10+ 7/15, 8/18*
VanDerzee, Norman K. 4/1, 9/23
van Doorne, Hub 5/23+
Van Dusen, Charles B. 1/28* 8/16+
Vane, H. T. 2/18
Van Eck, S. C. van Pantheleon 2/16+
Van Etten, Bob 6/29+
Van Eugen, Charles M. 12/27
Van Fleet, Frederick A. 6/12* 6/25+
Van Hasselt, Barthold T. W. 11/7*
Van Hee, Kenneth C. 7/28, 11/18
Van Horn, Lloyd 5/6
Van Lennep, Gijs 3/16* 6/13
van Merkensteijn, M. A. 12/15*
Van Ranst, C. W. 6/25, 10/11+ 12/7*
van Rooyen, Basil 4/19*
Van Sicklin, Willis L. 2/12
van Twist, G. 9/12+
Van Valkenburgh, Paul 4/8*
Van Zandt, Newton E. 3/8, 5/1+
Varley, Harold 1/18
Varzi, Achille 5/6, 6/30+ 8/8* 9/7
Vaseau, James D. 10/7+

Vasser, Jimmy 5/26, 11/20*
Vatter, George 7/19
Vaughan, Clifford J. 4/24
Vaughan, Guy W. 8/15* 11/21+
Vauthier 5/24+
Vazquez, Siro 2/10* 2/19+
Veeder, Curtis H. 1/31* 12/27+
Velez, Fermin 4/3*
Velie, Willard L. 5/19, 7/2, 10/24+
Velie, Willard L. Jr. 2/23, 3/20+ 11/27
Velie, Mrs. Williard L. Jr. 2/23
Venediger, Herbert 1/1
Vennerholm, Gosta 9/8+
Verbiest, Ferdinand 1/28+ 10/9*
Verkuil, Paul R. 9/18, 12/4*
Vermirovsky, Josef 5/13
Verreault, George T. 7/18
Verstappen, Jos 3/4+
Veyron, Pierre 10/3+
Viano, David C. 5/7*
Vickery, Sharlene A. 2/26
Vico, Carole 1/23
Victor Emmanuel III 9/12
Vignale, Alfredo 6/15*
Vilas, Homer A. 4/16
Villa, Leo 11/30*
Villeneuve, Gilles 1/18* 4/9, 5/8+ 11/4
Villeneuve, Jacques (Jr.) 1/18, 4/9*
Villeneuve, Jacques (Sr.) 1/18, 4/9, 11/4*
Villoresi, Luigi 5/16* 6/27, 10/2
Villota, Emilio de 7/26*
Vincent, Charles H. 12/7*
Vincent, Jesse G. 1/1, 2/10* 4/20+ 5/30, 7/29,
    7/30, 12/7, 12/27
Vinuesa, Alfonso Garcia de 12/30*
Viot, Maitre 12/24
Virion, Charles 12/1*
Vischer, Gustav 11/22
Vodovnik, Raymond F. 1/31*
Vogelsong, George E. 7/12+
Voiculescu, Ion A. 6/17*
Voisin, Gabriel 2/5* 6/1, 12/25+
Volkhart, Kurt 3/12, 4/11, 4/17
Vollmer, Joseph 2/13* 10/8+
Volonterio, Ottorino 12/7*
von Bachelle, Otto 4/2
Vonlanthen, Jo 5/31*
von Neumann, Johnny 4/20
von Rottweiler, B. G. 11/2
Vos, Simon J. 7/17+
Vuillemont, Raoul 12/1
Vukovich, Bill (Sr.) 3/29, 5/30+ 12/13*
Vukovich, Bill III 3/29
Vukovich, Billy (Jr.) 3/29*

Wachtler, William B. 7/7+
Wacker, Fred (Jr.) 7/10*
Wada, Takao 6/24*
Wade, Billy 1/5+
Wagenhals, W. G. 9/27
Wagner, Honore 5/23+
Wagner, James K. 7/27*
Wagner, Louis 8/7, 10/6, 11/26
Wagner, Thomas J. 7/28*
Wahl, George 10/8+
Wahlberg, Nils 1/20+ 8/20*
Wainwright, Hugh 1/1
Wainwright, Lucius M. 2/24+
Wakefield, C. C. 1/15+
Wakefield, William E. 11/7
Walb, Willy 7/18, 11/13
Waldergard, Bjorn 11/12*

Waldon, Sidney 1/20+ 1/29*
Walker, Dave 6/10*
Walker, George W. 5/2, 10/15, 12/20
Walker, Helm 4/7
Walker, James H. 3/10+ 8/24*
Walker, John Brisben 5/30, 6/17, 7/7+ 9/10*
Walker, Leroy 11/10*
Walker, Mike 12/18*
Walker, Peter 3/1+ 4/30, 10/7*
Walkerley, Rodney 4/2*
Walkinshaw, Tom 8/14*
Wall, W. G. 1/16+ 8/7*
Wallace, Andy 2/19*
Wallace, Kenny 8/23*
Wallace, Mike 3/10*
Wallace, Rusty 8/14*
Wallace, William H. 8/23+
Wallard, Lee 9/7* 11/28+
Wallbillich, John J. 3/13+
Wallenberg, Marcus 9/13+ 10/5*
Walling, Z. B. 7/1
Walmsley, William 9/4
Walsh, William J. 2/3* 8/31+
Walter, Edford M. 12/11+
Walter, Heini 7/28*
Walter, William 1/1
Walters, Dean A. 2/20+
Walther, Salt 11/22*
Walton, William L. 8/22*
Waltrip, Darrell 2/5* 5/25
Waltrip, Michael 4/30*
Wanger, Norman F. 4/10+
Wankel, Felix 8/13* 10/9+
Ward, A. H. M. J. 1/18, 4/23, 5/1, 6/17, 6/29,
    10/26
Ward, Artemus Jr. 11/9*
Ward, James A. 6/9*
Ward, Peter 12/21
Ward, Robert B. 10/18+ 11/11*
Ward, Rodger 1/10* 5/30, 12/12
Ward, Willis 12/30+
Wardle, Charles A. 11/13
Ware, Marsden 9/10+ 12/8*
Warner, A. P. 3/22+ 4/18*
Warner, C. H. 1/6+ 3/13*
Warner, Frederic W. 2/14+
Warner, Harold G. 6/1, 9/15, 11/29*
Warner, John A. C. 7/1, 7/12*
Warren, Alex M. 8/4*
Warren, Bentley 12/10*
Warren, Charles C. 5/1
Warren, Homer 11/21
Warren, Louis B. 8/30*
Warrington, Jesse 2/28
Warwick, Derek 1/29, 8/27*
Warwick, Paul 1/29* 7/21+
Warwick, William 1/30, 7/12, 9/19
Warwick, William E. 1/13* 12/3+
Washington, George 2/22
Washington, Martha 2/22
Waterbury, Ronald J. 7/9+ 12/2*
Waterfall, Thornton E. 3/2*
Waterman, George H. Jr. 11/19+
Waterman, Waldo D. 2/20, 11/9
Watkins, Joseph A. 12/23
Watkins, Sidney 9/6*
Watkins, William H. 1/9* 12/23+
Watney, Walter 8/22
Watson, A. J. 5/8*
Watson, Granville S. 7/17+
Watson, James W. 6/22*
Watson, John 5/4* 6/6, 8/15

Watson, John H. Jr. 8/17+ 9/1*
Watson, P. A. 2/26+
Watson, R. A. 4/6+
Watt, James 1/19* 6/25, 8/25+
Wattles, Stan 7/24*
Watts, Frank E. 4/22, 5/22*
Watts, George 6/22
Weatherly, Clay 5/30+
Weatherly, Joe 1/21+ 5/29*
Weaver, Elverton W. 11/12+
Weaver, Henry G. 1/3+ 12/24*
Weaver, Ira A. 1/29* 10/11+
Weaver, James 4/4*
Webb, Earle W. 2/9* 7/7+
Weckler, Herman L. 1/26+ 8/31*
Weed, Harry D. 8/23
Weeks, Robert G. 7/14*
Wegner, Victor A. 5/3+
Weidler, Volker 3/18* 6/23
Weiger, Ralph J. 1/21*
Weinhardt, Robert A. 9/26+
Weir, Thomas A. 4/28+
Weisberger, Bernard A. 8/15*
Weiss, Carl W. 9/14+
Weiss, Erwin A. 6/14* 7/8+
Weiss, George L. 2/19* 4/11, 4/13, 6/17, 8/4,
    9/25+, 10/24, 11/2, 11/15, 12/30
Weiss, Sammy 6/4+
Weith, Warren 1/26*
Weitz, John 5/25*
Welch, A. R. 11/8+
Welch, Henry W. 10/2*
Welch, Leo D. 4/22* 10/22+
Weller, Harry D. Jr. 2/26*
Wells, Fred 4/22+ 8/10*
Wells, Henry 5/30
Welsh, Frederic E. 4/7
Welsh, William L. 1/2+
Welton, James R. 9/30*
Welty, Malcolm W. 10/17*
Wemblyn 7/14
Wemp, Ernest E. 11/24+
Wendler, Paul H. 3/8*
Wendlinger, Karl 12/20*
Wenk, William C. 3/16+ 5/29*
Werner, Calvin J. 7/1, 8/27* 9/1
Werner, Christian 4/27, 5/19* 6/17+ 6/19, 12/12
Werner, Helmut 9/2*
Werner, J. F. 12/13
Werner, Marco 4/27*
Werner, Wilhelm 3/25, 3/29
Westbury, Peter 5/26*
Westcott, Burton J. 1/11+ 7/18*
Westwood, Noel 8/4
Wetherald, Charles E. 7/31, 11/26*
Wetterborg, A. E. 11/26+
Weyl, Pierce A. 5/18+
Weymann, Charles 4/18
Wexler, Jane 10/25
Whalley, J. Irving 3/8+ 9/14*
Wharton, Clifton R. Jr. 1/12
Wharton, Ken 1/12+ 3/21* 8/17
Wheatley, Richard C. 8/21*
Wheaton, Paul R. 6/13*
Wheeler, Frank H. 2/9
Whitaker, Arnold 7/28, 11/18
Whitbeck, J. V. 5/28*
White, Albert E. F. 8/5
White, D. McCall 1/29+ 5/19, 11/28*
White, Edward P. 2/28+
White, Fred R. 2/17* 5/13+
White, George 11/13

White, Lawrence J. 6/1*
White, Mike 7/2*
White, Rollin C. 6/3* 7/5+ 10/27
White, Rollin H. 7/1, 7/11* 9/2, 9/10+ 10/11
White, Mrs. Rollin H. 9/2
White, Samuel O. 4/1+
White, Thomas H. 8/4* 10/26+
White, Walter C. 4/8, 9/8* 9/29+
White, William K. 7/1*
White, Windsor T. 4/9+ 8/28*
Whiteaway, Ted 11/1*
Whitehead, Graham 1/15+ 4/15* 9/21
Whitehead, John W. 11/16+
Whitehead, Peter 9/21+ 9/22, 11/12*
Whitehouse, Bill 4/1* 4/16, 7/14+
Whiting, C. H. 9/7
Whiting, James H. 5/12* 7/9, 11/1
Whitlock, George E. 3/20*
Whitman, Henry G. 2/12
Whitman, Lester L. 7/6, 9/17
Whitmore, John 10/16*
Whitney, George E. 6/10* 12/4+
Whitney, William C. 11/4
Whittelsey, Charles B. 3/16* 10/16+
Whittington, Bill 1/23, 9/11*
Whittington, Dale 1/23
Whittington, Don 1/23*
Whitworth, Stanley 10/15+
Whyland, Frank V. 9/7, 12/13
Whyte, Andrew 5/3+ 12/8*
Wibel, Albert M. 4/11+ 5/3, 7/17
Wick, Henry B. 9/29
Wick, Orville 9/14* 12/16+
Wickins, David A. 2/15*
Wickman, Carl E. 2/5+
Wickstrom, Nils 10/20
Widdows, Robin 5/27*
Widman, Charles H. 6/17*
Widman, Michael F. Jr. 8/14+
Wieland, Arthur J. 3/21+ 5/11*
Wiese, Warren M. 4/14*
Wiess, Harry C. 2/8, 7/30* 8/26+
Wietzes, Eppie 5/28*
Wik, Reynold M. 3/19*
Wilber, D. J. 3/3+
Wilby, Thomas W. 8/27, 10/18
Wilcock, F. W. 9/5
Wilcox, Howdy 5/30, 9/23+ 11/18
Wilcox, W. DeGroff 5/24+ 12/1*
Wilder, Laura Ingalls 12/5
Wilds, Mike 1/7*
Wiles, Ivan L. 3/6, 6/13*
Wilford, J. W. 4/7+
Wilkins, Mira 6/1*
Wilkinson, Fred 7/18
Wilkinson, John 2/11* 6/25+ 7/1, 11/27
Wilks, Peter 6/25
Willard, Edward A. 6/12
Willard, Theodore A. 2/3+ 12/10*
Willem, Andre 6/20+
Willetts, Herbert 7/5+ 11/26*
William of Sweden 10/14
"Williams" 4/14, 8/2
Williams, Calvin C. 6/25
Williams, David P. 11/16*
Williams, Edson P. 7/31*
Williams, G. Mennen 4/18
Williams, George M. 4/6* 5/17
Williams, Jonathan 10/26*
Williams, Jules 3/23
Williams, Leo L. 10/4+
Williams, Wendell M. Jr. 5/15*

Williamson, James W. 9/2*
Williamson, Roger 2/2* 7/29+
Wills, C. Harold 3/15, 6/1* 9/24, 12/11, 12/30+
Willys, John N. 1/9, 3/17, 5/30, 7/30, 8/26+
    10/25*, 11/8, 11/18, 12/1
Willys, Mrs. John N. (1) 12/1
Willys, Mrs. John N. (2) 7/30
Wilmer, E. J. 4/30
Wilson, C. R. 11/21
Wilson, Charles E. 1/6, 1/26, 2/2, 6/3, 6/6,
    7/18*, 9/26+ 11/20
Wilson, David R. 3/11+ 11/15*
Wilson, Desire 11/26*
Wilson, Ernest E. 1/22+
Wilson, John D. 4/18
Wilson, Keith 1/18*
Wilson, Odbert P. 9/21+
Wilson, Paul C. 4/21*
Wilson, Porterfield 7/12*
Wilson, Vic 4/14*
Wilson, William R. 3/5, 10/8*
Wilson, Woodrow 2/28, 7/11, 8/10, 12/23
Wimille, Jean-Pierre 1/28+ 2/26* 2/28, 3/30,
    6/16, 6/20, 8/11, 9/9, 9/21
Winans, Earl W. 7/4+
Winch, J. Russell 3/14+
Winchell, Frank 1/15*
Winchester, J. F. 12/13*
Winchester, W. S. 7/30
Winchilsea, 12th Earl of 3/28* 9/7+ 12/10
Windham, Walter G. 7/5+
Wing, Dennis 2/27+
Wingerter, Robert G. 10/5*
Wingrove, Gerald 8/16*
Winkelhock, Joachim 10/24*
Winkelhock, Manfred 8/12+ 10/6* 10/24
Winn, Bill 8/20+
Winnai, Fred 6/17
Winship, Loyd A. 1/10
Winslow, Arthur S. 8/1
Winslow, Dallas E. 8/18
Winter, John 8/2*
Winterbotham, Joseph 2/24* 4/19+
Winther, Martin P. 3/15+
Winton, Alexander 1/2, 2/26, 3/1, 3/28, 5/4,
    6/10, 6/20* 6/22+ 6/30, 7/22, 10/10
Wirth, Nick 5/31
Wise, Karl M. 6/6+
Wise, William F. 4/18+ 12/19*
Wisell, Reine 9/30*
Wishart, Spencer 8/22+ 8/26
Wisner, Charles H. 9/3
Witchell, R. S. 1/31
Wolf, Walter 1/9
Wolfe, Maurice 5/16* 12/13+
Wolfe, Stewart J. 9/6*
Wolfram, Jack F. 1/1, 1/8, 12/18*
Wollek, Bob 11/4*
Wondries, Charles H. 12/2+
Wood, C. B. D. 5/27+
Wood, Charles 9/4
Wood, E. Ellsworth Jr. 6/26* 12/2+
Wood, F. Derwent 6/27
Wood, Gar 6/20+ 12/4*
Wood, J. T. 5/28
Wood, Jeff 1/20*
Wood, John G. 10/3+
Wood, John M. 1/10+
Wood, Jonathan 1/18*
Wood, Quentin E. 3/5*
Woodbury, Cliff 11/13+
Woodcock, Leonard 2/15*

Woodhead, James H. 4/14*
Woodill, B. R. 10/6+ 11/2*
Woodruff, Robert W. 3/7+ 12/6*
Woodson, Hunter 12/30
Woodward, L. L. 1/16+ 4/21*
Wooler, Ernest 1/1, 2/26* 6/24+
Woolfe, John 6/14+
Woollard, Frank G. 12/22+
Woolson, Harry T. 9/20*
Woolson, L. Irving 3/4+ 6/27*
Woolson, Lionel M. 2/15, 4/23+
Woolworth, F. W. 2/24
Worthington, Edgar K. 1/22, 12/22
Worthington, Harry J. 11/7+
Worthington, S. P. 10/26+
Woudenberg, Paul R. 9/1*
Wridgway, Charles 5/30
Wright, Benjamin F. 3/10+
Wright, C. O. 1/9
Wright, Evan H. 12/25+
Wright, J. Patrick 6/16*
Wright, James O. 9/4*
Wright, Newell S. 8/18
Wright, Orville 7/21
Wright, Phil 1/18
Wright, Warwick 6/17
Wrightsman, Warren 7/4
Wunderink, Roelof 12/12*
Wurges, Daniel 5/30
Wyckoff, Paul W. 6/12*
Wydler, John J. 5/19+
Wyer, John 4/25, 5/1
Wylie, Frank W. 7/3*
Wylie, J. A. 11/14
Wynn, A. E. 8/27
Wyss, Wallace A. 9/19*

Xydias, Alex 3/22* 8/24

Yamamoto, Kenichi 9/16*
Yamasaki, Yoshiki 4/8*
Yarborough, Cale 3/27* 11/20
Yarbrough, Lee Roy 2/26, 9/17* 12/7+
Yates, Ballard A. 7/9*
Yates, Brock 10/21*
Yeager, Howard F. 5/11, 11/19
Yealin, Richard A. 9/3*
Yeltsin, Boris 3/26
Yntema, Theodore O. 4/8* 8/24, 9/18+
Yokich, Stephen P. 6/14
Yokoshima, Hisashi 12/28*
Yont, Charles A. 8/12
York, Jerome B. 5/3, 5/6
York, Roy 10/31
Young, Charles G. 6/17+ 11/1*
Young, DuBois 4/15
Young, Fred M. 4/29*
Young, George A. 9/26
Young, Howard G. 10/5+
Young, Robert R. 1/25+ 2/14*
Young, William B. 10/29*
Youngren, Harold T. 5/1* 8/1

Zachow, Otto 3/24, 12/29
Zahn, Joachim 1/24*
Zakowski, Peter 5/13*
Zampedri, Alessandro 10/3*
Zanardi, Alex 6/23, 10/23*
Zarrella, Ronald L. 12/12
Zava, Bruno 4/3
Zborowski, Elliott 4/1+
Zborowski, Louis 2/20* 6/16, 8/23, 10/19+

Zeder, Fred M. 2/24+ 3/2, 3/19* 4/17, 7/14
Zeder, Fred M. II 3/14*
Zeder, James C. 4/17* 4/30, 5/25+
Zehender, Goffredo 1/7+
Zeller, Frank Jr. 9/4
Zengle, Len 10/8
Zerbi, Tranquillo 3/10+
Zerk, Oscar U. 12/8+
Zerneri, Guido 6/21+
Zethrin, Val E. 1/17
Zewalk, Bob 4/30+
Zientowski, Walter C. 2/15
Zimmer, P. H. 5/10
Zimmer, Richard R. 4/27+
Zimmerli, F. P. 12/12+
Zimmerman, John 7/1
Zimmerman, John O. 12/13*
Zimmerman, O. B. 5/10+
Zimmerman, Paul G. 5/12*
Zimmermans, Adolphe 5/19
Zipper, Otto 1/17, 2/2+ 10/19*
Zoboli, Vittorio 6/24*
Zorzi, Renzo 5/10, 12/12+
Zuccarelli, Paul 6/19+
Zunino, Reggio 3/8*
Zunino, Ricardo 4/13*
ZurSchmiede, W. Tom 3/10, 6/12*

INDEX 4 - PLACE NAMES

Places are listed by country with only precise locations included. The names of states, provinces, counties, etc. are included in this index when known even though such designations often are not included in the main text. Countries listed reflect 1997 status - country names and boundaries, especially in Europe, have gone through many changes during the age of the automobile.

ALGERIA
Algiers, Alger 5/27
Batna, Constantine 5/12

ARGENTINA
Arrecifes, Buenos Aires 10/5
Balcarce, Buenos Aires 6/24, 9/19, 11/22
Buenos Aires, Buenos Aires 1/6, 1/10,
  1/12, 1/13, 1/14, 1/15, 1/16, 1/17, 1/18,
  1/19, 1/20, 1/22 1/28, 1/31, 3/9, 4/13,
  4/27, 6/5, 6/28, 7/10, 8/10, 8/13, 8/31,
  9/30, 11/7, 11/8, 12/16, 12/19
Concepcion, Tucuman 11/18
DeMayo 10/26
Mar del Plata, Buenos Aires 1/31, 12/3
Pergamino, Buenos Aires 2/22
Rosario, Santa Fe 8/19
San Martin, Mendoza 10/30
Santa Fe, Santa Fe 4/12, 9/4

AUSTRALIA
Adelaide, South Australia 8/14
Altona, Victoria 9/12
Bathurst, NSW 10/4
Booleroo, South Australia 3/19
Cowangie, Victoria 3/18
Geelong, Victoria 7/1
Hobart, Tasmania 2/27, 3/1
Hurstville, NSW 4/2
Longford, Tasmania 2/29
Marouba, NSW 12/5
Melbourne, Victoria 2/3, 4/12 10/12 11/2
  11/29, 12/13, 12/23
Perth, Western Australia 9/8
Phillip Island, Victoria 3/5
Sandown Park, Victoria 2/14
Sydney, NSW 3/19, 3/20, 3/29, 6/10, 7/15,
  7/21, 8/14, 9/26, 9/28, 10/1, 12/11, 12/24

AUSTRIA
Baden, Lower Austria 6/9
Gmund, Carinthia 3/20, 6/8
Gmunden, Upper Austria 5/30
Graz, Styria 4/27, 6/8, 6/9, 8/19
Innsbruck, Tirol 6/26
Klosterneuburg, Vienna 2/4, 2/14
Kufstein, Tirol 12/20
Linz, Upper Austria 6/2
Salzburg, Salzburg 5/14, 6/2, 7/4
Vienna, Vienna 1/4, 1/24, 1/29, 2/22,
  2/23, 3/11, 4/16, 5/21, 5/30, 6/2, 6/3,
  6/17, 6/24, 6/26, 6/29, 7/2, 7/7, 8/2,
  10/14, 10/19, 10/22 11/3, 11/12 11/15
Wiener-Neustadt, Lower Austria 4/30, 9/19
Worgl, Tirol 8/27
Zell-am-Ziller, Tirol 6/12
Zeltweg, Styria 8/19

BAHAMAS
Nassau, New Providence 6/17

BAHRAIN
Awali 2/23

BARBADOS 3/6

BELGIUM
Antwerp, Antwerp 6/27, 12/13, 12/22
Bastogne, Luxembourg 7/31
Bressoux, Liege 12/9

Brussels, Brabant 1/1, 1/12, 2/3, 2/25,
  2/28, 3/24, 4/9, 6/7, 7/13, 7/26, 8/5, 9/14,
  9/18, 9/19, 10/13, 10/30, 11/4, 12/25
Chimay, Hainaut 5/25
Haine St. Paul 11/1
Haine St. Pierre, Hainaut 2/23
Halle, Brabant 12/31
Jabbeke, West Flanders 5/30, 7/24, 10/21
Leuven, Brabant 5/8
Liege, Liege 2/21
Momignies, Hainaut 10/1
Mouscron, West Flanders 11/19
Mussy-la-Ville 1/12
Nieuwpoort, West Flanders 7/21
Nivelles, Brabant 10/19
Ostend, West Flanders 5/25, 7/17, 7/21,
  9/2 11/13, 12/8
Pittem, West Flanders 10/9
Spa (-Francorchamps), Liege 1/7, 5/1, 5/6,
  5/15, 5/19, 5/24, 6/7, 6/9, 6/15, 6/16,
  6/17, 6/18, 6/19, 6/22, 6/25, 6/28, 7/1,
  7/26, 9/1
Verviers, Liege 9/30
Zolder, Limburg 5/4, 5/8, 5/9, 5/21, 6/5

BELARUS
Krugloye, Mogilev 3/14
Minsk, Minsk 8/9
Zhodino 11/5

BOSNIA & HERZEGOVINA
Sarajevo, Sarajevo 6/28

BRAZIL
Belo Horizonte, Minas Gerais 11/7
Curitiba, Parana 12/4
Indaiatuba, Sao Paulo 8/6
Joinville, Santa Catarina 4/20
Mairipora, Sao Paulo 3/18
Rio de Janeiro, Guanabara 1/29, 2/11, 4/3,
  8/17, 9/28
Sao Paulo, Sao Paulo 1/18, 2/3, 2/18, 3/21,
  5/22, 5/23, 6/7, 7/14, 10/6, 12/1, 12/12,
  12/25

CANADA

Alberta
  Calgary 8/1
  Edmonton 8/25, 12/5
  Hardisty 10/28

British Columbia
  Maple Ridge 4/22
  Nanaimo, Vancouver Island 4/6
  Vancouver 1/16, 7/26, 9/18, 11/4, 11/9
  Victoria, Vancouver Island 10/18

Manitoba
  Winnipeg 3/18, 12/5

New Brunswick
  Shediac 5/31

Newfoundland
  Saint John's 3/2, 4/14

Nova Scotia
  Schubenacadie 10/27

Wolfville 5/9

Ontario
  Ailsa Craig 5/11
  Alliston 6/4
  Aylmer 2/3
  Brantford 10/18, 11/21
  Cambridge 10/10
  Chatham 8/8, 8/11, 8/26, 10/27
  Corunna 9/27
  Dundas 1/21
  Enniskillen 9/8
  Essex 1/2, 4/17
  Goderich 9/4
  Hamilton 1/2, 1/20, 4/6
  Ingersoll 2/5, 7/24
  Kingston 7/22, 9/3
  Kitchener 10/8
  Listowel 8/1
  London 4/1, 8/12
  Mosport Park 6/6, 6/13, 8/12, 8/27, 9/22
  Niagara Falls 4/13, 6/21, 9/17
  Oakville 5/11
  Oshawa 1/6, 12/19
  Ottawa 3/8
  Peterborough 2/29, 8/22
  Saint Catherines 9/3
  Saint Thomas 8/24
  Sandwich 9/7
  Silverstone 8/14
  Stratford 3/14
  Thunder Bay 10/19
  Tillsonburg 3/17
  Toronto 1/5, 1/22, 2/4, 2/25, 2/26, 2/29,
    3/24, 4/17, 4/25, 5/12, 7/14, 7/27, 8/6,
    8/9, 8/12, 9/6, 9/24, 10/21, 12/17, 12/20,
    12/26, 12/29, 12/31
  Walkerville 10/10, 11/12
  Wallaceburg 4/17
  Waterford 6/4
  Wheatley 7/4
  Windsor 2/3, 2/13, 3/5, 4/29, 6/29, 6/30,
    7/29, 8/10, 8/11, 8/14, 8/17, 9/17, 9/28,
    10/1, 10/21, 11/21, 12/29

Prince Edward Island
  Rusticoville 7/5

Quebec
  Bay du Febvre 4/22
  Berthierville 1/18
  Chambly 11/4
  Montreal 4/21, 6/13, 6/19, 7/9, 9/23, 9/26
  Mont-Tremblant 6/16
  Quebec 5/10, 9/29, 12/3, 12/12
  Ste. Adele 11/21
  Stanstead Plain 4/9
  Ville Lasalle 8/13

CHILE
Coronel, Concepcion 11/21
Punta Arenas, Magallanes 7/28, 11/18
Santiago, Santiago 11/14

CHINA
Peking, Hopeh 6/10, 8/10
Shanghai, Kiangsu 8/17

COLOMBIA
  Medellin, Antioquia 11/16

CROATIA
  Motovun, Istria 2/28

CUBA
  Havana, Havana 2/23, 5/5

CZECH REPUBLIC (CZECHOSLOVAKIA, BOHEMIA)
  Brno, Jihomoravsky 5/13, 9/21, 9/22
  Koprivnice, Silesia 10/28
  Liberec, Severocesky 9/3
  Nesseldorf, Silesia 5/21, 10/28, 12/6
  Olomouc, Severomoravsky 12/15
  Plzen-Tremosna, Zapadocesky 9/7
  Prague, Prague 3/5
  Ruttka 4/10
  Schonlinde, Sudetenland 8/30

DENMARK
  Arnum 7/20
  Bording Sogn 8/7
  Copenhagen, Copenhagen 3/25, 3/28, 4/23, 7/14, 8/23, 9/7, 10/30, 12/16
  Fano Island, Jutland 6/24
  Varde, Ribe 2/7
  Vojens, Haderslev 8/3

ECUADOR
  Guayaquil, Guayas 10/3

EGYPT
  Cairo, Cairo 4/13, 8/13, 9/23, 10/26, 12/26
  Gezira Island, Cairo 3/9
  Port Said, Canal 8/2

FINLAND
  Helsinki, Uusimaa 3/18, 5/17, 9/25, 9/28, 11/15
  Tampere, Hame 8/5
  Turku, Turku-Pori 1/17

FRANCE
  Abbeville, Somme 2/5, 12/6
  Ablis, Yvelines 4/21, 8/5
  Acheres Park, Yvelines 1/17, 1/27, 3/4, 4/9, 4/29, 12/18
  Aix-en-Provence, Bouches-du-Rhone 3/29
  Ajaccio, Corsica 12/1
  Albi, Tarn 7/13, 7/14, 8/5
  Ales, Gard 1/16
  Amiens, Somme 6/19
  Arles, Bouches-du-Rhone 12/30
  Arpajon, Essonne 7/6, 7/12
  Aubenas, Ardeche 1/1
  Aublet, Gers 2/10
  Auffargis 3/21
  Auxerre, Yonne 7/12
  Avignon, Vaucluse 5/31, 6/11
  Ay, Marne 4/6
  Belleville, Rhone 11/15
  Belleville-sur-Saone 2/5
  Billancourt, Hauts-de-Seine 1/17, 3/30
  Bleneau, Yonne 8/18
  Blois, Loir-et-Cher 8/22
  Bois-Colombes, Hauts-de-Seine 1/7
  Bordeaux, Gironde 5/23, 5/24, 5/29, 6/11, 6/19, 11/2 11/10
  Boulogne-sur-Mer, Pas-de-Calais 7/2
  Boulogne-sur-Seine, Hauts-de-Seine 9/19
  Bourgoin, Isere 5/23
  Brachay 5/29
  Cadours, Haute-Garonne 9/10
  Caen, Calvados 7/28
  Cannes, Alpes-Maritimes 1/10, 5/7
  Cap d'Eze, Alpes-Maritimes 10/3
  Carpentras, Vaucluse 6/20, 8/29
  Carquefou, Loire-Atlantique 3/9

Castle Sarrazin 10/18
Chambery, Savoie 6/30
Champigny-sur-Marne, Val-de-Marne 7/14, 9/6
Charenton-le-Pont, Val-de-Marne 7/10
Chateauroux, Indre 6/10
Chinon, Indre-Loire 5/21
Clermont-Ferrand, Puy-de-Dome 7/3, 7/5, 8/1, 8/9, 12/25
Cognac, Charente 3/22
Concarneau, Finistere 9/11
Condom-en-Armagnac 10/6
Corte, Corsica 5/2
Couhe-Verac, Vienne 5/24
Courbevoie, Hauts-de-Seine 1/10, 5/12, 6/20, 12/22
Culoz, Ain 10/4
Desvres, Pas-de-Calais 9/16
Dieppe, Seine-Maritime 7/7
Dijon-Prenois, Cote-d'Or 7/5
Dorlisheim, Bas-Rhin 8/28
Dourdan, Essonne 11/5, 11/17
Draveil, Essonne 8/19
Entzheim, Bas-Rhin 10/4
Falaise, Calvados 10/8, 12/8
Gap, Haute Alpes 9/6
Gueux, Marne 7/4, 7/5, 7/6
Grenoble, Isere 1/18, 6/26
Illkirch-Grafenstaden, Bas-Rhin 4/1
Istres, Bouches-du-Rhone 8/24
La Capelle, Aisne 8/10
La Chatre, Indre 6/10
Lapalud, Vaucluse 4/14
La Turbie, Alpes-Maritimes 3/29, 3/30, 4/1, 4/7
La Villette, Seine 11/15
Le Beausset, Toulon 7/28
Le Castellet, Var 5/15
Le Havre, Seine-Maritime 1/30, 7/28
Le Mans, Sarthe 3/30, 4/7, 4/10, 4/25, 5/26, 5/27, 6/1, 6/10, 6/11, 6/13, 6/14, 6/15, 6/16, 6/18, 6/19, 6/20, 6/21, 6/22, 6/23, 6/25, 6/26, 7/26, 7/27, 7/28, 8/11, 8/30, 10/1, 10/9, 11/8, 12/4, 12/27
L'Hay-les-Roses, Val-de-Marne 9/1
Libourne, Gironde 6/12
Liouville, Meuse 5/18
Lorient, Morbihan 7/5
Lyon, Rhone 1/9, 4/12, 5/23, 6/14, 7/4, 8/3, 9/2, 9/21
Magny-Cours, Nievre 11/21
Malmerspach 3/30
Marolles-en-Hurepoix, Essonne 1/21
Marseille, Bouches-du-Rhone 1/31, 2/28, 4/12, 4/14, 5/15, 5/24, 7/27, 9/24, 10/3, 12/7
Mensil Val, Seine Maritime 12/8
Millau, Aveyron 1/23
Molsheim, Bas-Rhin 1/1, 11/21
Montfermeil, Seine-Saint-Denis 12/28
Montfort, Ille-et-Vilaine 3/4
Montlhery, Essonne 4/24, 5/10, 6/25, 7/26, 8/15, 8/20, 10/4, 10/5, 10/7, 10/11, 10/29, 12/9
Montrouge, Hauts-de-Seine 5/23, 10/23
Moulin d'Ozenay 12/25
Moulins, Allier 3/20
Mulhouse, Haut-Rhin 7/7, 7/27
Muret, Haute-Garonne 4/2
Nancy, Meurthe-et-Moselle 9/12
Nantes, Loire-Atlantique 7/28
Neufchateau, Vosges 5/14
Neuilly, Yonne 8/21, 10/17
Neuilly-sur-Seine, Hauts-de-Seine 6/16, 10/13, 12/30
Neville en Caux 4/8
Nice, Alpes-Maritimes 1/21, 1/31, 2/10, 2/16, 3/23, 3/25, 3/28, 3/31, 4/5, 4/10, 4/13, 5/6, 5/28, 9/2, 9/14, 10/7, 10/14
Niedebronn, Bas-Rhin 6/26
Nimes, Gard 3/30
Orleans, Loiret 4/7, 7/25
Paray-le-Monial, Saone-et-Loire 10/23

Paris, Seine 1/5, 1/8, 1/12, 1/14, 2/1, 2/4, 2/7, 2/10, 2/12, 2/14, 2/17, 2/25, 2/26, 3/6, 3/16, 3/18, 3/21, 4/1, 4/2, 4/3, 4/4, 4/5, 4/14, 4/23, 4/26, 4/28, 5/4, 5/5, 5/6, 5/8, 5/9, 5/15, 5/15, 5/18, 5/24, 5/27, 5/29, 6/1, 6/7, 6/10, 6/11, 6/12, 6/14, 6/16, 6/24, 6/25, 6/26, 6/27, 6/28, 6/29, 7/1, 7/2, 7/3, 7/4, 7/8, 7/10, 7/13, 7/14, 7/18, 7/21, 7/22, 7/25, 7/26, 7/28, 7/30, 8/2, 8/4, 8/14, 8/16, 8/19, 8/24, 8/31, 9/3, 9/9, 9/14, 9/17, 9/19, 9/20, 9/23, 9/24, 9/25, 10/1, 10/3, 10/4, 10/6, 10/10, 10/14, 10/17, 10/18, 10/24, 10/27, 11/2 11/5, 11/11, 11/12, 11/17, 11/18, 11/22 11/27, 12/1, 12/2, 12/6, 12/7, 12/11, 12/12 12/14, 12/18, 12/19, 12/25, 12/29, 12/30
Pau, Basses-Pyrenees 1/26, 2/10, 2/17, 3/29, 4/10, 4/23, 9/21, 9/26
Perigueux, Dordogne 3/7, 5/1
Peyrehorade, Landes 2/10
Poitiers, Vienne 9/28
Pontcharra, Isere 7/4
Puteaux, Hauts-de-Seine 6/1, 10/2
Puy de Dome, Auvergne 11/5
Rambouillet, Yvelines 11/11
Reims, Marne 1/31, 5/1, 7/1, 7/2, 7/4, 7/5, 7/6, 7/14, 7/18
Romans-sur-Isere, Drome 9/28
Rouen, Seine-Maritime 6/26, 7/7, 7/22, 11/22, 12/28
Saint-Berain, Saone-et-Loire 9/7
Saint-Brieuc, Cotes-du-Nord 4/24
Saint-Chamond, Loire 2/24
Saint-Dizier, Haute-Marne 2/11
Saint-Etienne, Loire 4/16, 5/30
Saint-Frion 1/1
Saint-Gaudens, Garonne 10/8
Saint-Germain, Hauge-Saone 10/20
Saint-Maur-des-Fosses, Val-de-Marne 9/17
Sainte-Cecile-les-Vignes, Vaucluse 10/30
Salon, Bouches-du-Rhone 12/30
Samer, Pas-de-Calais 6/4
Sedan, Ardennes 11/7
Strasbourg, Bas-Rhin 4/29, 7/15, 11/4
Suresnes, Hauts-de-Seine 1/4, 3/24
Thomery, Seine-et-Marne 6/19
Tivoli 6/19
Toulouse, Haute-Garonne 7/28, 9/2
Touzac 9/28
Uzes, Gard 1/16
Valentigney, Doubs 3/20, 6/11
Varenne-St. Hilaire 8/4
Vaumas 12/27
Verdun, Meuse 5/21
Vernon, Eure 10/20
Vichy, Allier 7/12
Velizy-Villacoublay, Yvelines 2/29
Villecresnes, Val-de-Marne 3/26
Villefranche-sur-Saone, Rhone 4/26
Villiers-en-Lieu 6/11
Void, Meuse 9/25
Voiron, Isere 9/24
Voves, Eure-et-Loir 7/27
Wolxheim, Bas-Rhin 10/25

GERMANY
  Aachen, North Rhine-Westphalia 6/28, 7/28, 10/18
  Abtsteinach, Hesse 4/24
  Albeck, Wurttemberg 9/23
  Altona, Hamburg 11/10
  Avus, Brandenburg 1/12, 3/6, 5/19, 5/23, 5/27, 7/11, 8/1, 9/10, 9/11, 9/24
  Bad Canstatt, Wurttemberg 4/6, 6/17, 10/19
  Baden-Baden, Baden 2/13, 6/28, 7/7
  Bad Marienberg, Westerwald 10/5
  Bad Nauheim, Hesse 5/12
  Bad Reichenhall, Bavaria 9/17
  Berlin, Berlin 2/15, 2/16, 3/6, 5/4, 5/17,

5/23, 5/25, 5/27, 5/29, 6/27, 7/18, 7/24,
8/1, 8/26, 9/7, 9/10, 9/30, 12/13, 12/15
Bingen, Rhineland-Palatinate 6/17
Bissingen, Bavaria 3/23
Bonn, North Rhine-Westphalia 3/3
Borna, Saxony 5/20
Brandenburg, Brandenburg 1/1
Bremen, Bremen 2/2, 7/28, 8/2, 8/10, 8/16
Brunswick, Lower Saxony 4/19, 10/8
Buchenwald, Thuringia 9/14
Canstatt, Wurttemberg 3/4, 3/6, 5/14, 6/10,
11/10
Chemnitz, Saxony 7/1
Cologne, North Rhine-Westphalia 1/1, 1/5,
5/4, 5/17, 6/14, 7/6, 9/1, 9/2 10/2 10/9,
11/14, 11/19, 12/15
Darmstadt, Hesse 1/28, 5/19
Degerloch, Wurttemberg 10/17
Dessau, Halle 5/31, 6/2 11/9
Deuz 3/18, 12/20
Dillenburg, Hesse 3/25
Diplom-Kaufmann 1/30
Dresden, Saxony 3/26, 7/21
Dusemond-on-the-Mosel 7/24
Dusseldorf, North Rhine-Westphalia 1/25,
9/16, 11/4
Echterdingen, Wurttemberg 10/17
Ehrenfeld, North Rhine-Westphalia 11/14
Eisenach, Thuringia 8/2, 9/25
Emden, Lower Saxony 1/18
Essen, North Rhine-Westphalia 1/24, 1/28, 7/12
Esslingen, Wurttemberg 3/4
Felsberg, Hesse 6/10
Frankfurt am Main, Hesse 1/28, 5/13, 5/19,
6/26, 9/7, 9/11, 12/8
Frechen, North Rhine-Westphalia 4/23
Freiburg, Wurttemberg 8/7, 9/15
Friedrichshafen, Wurttemberg 2/7, 3/23
Fuerth, Bavaria 6/21
Fulda, Hesse 7/3
Gabelbach 7/29
Giessen, Hesse 4/7, 9/16, 11/20
Gotha, Thuringia 3/16
Gronau, North Rhine-Westphalia 1/1, 2/9
Halle, Halle 1/3
Hamburg, Hamburg 7/29, 8/15, 11/10
Hannover, Lower Saxony 1/16, 1/22, 5/23,
6/24, 8/3
Hassloch, Rhineland-Palatinate 12/22
Heidelberg, Baden 3/18
Heilbronn am Neckar, Wurttemberg 2/9
Herold-Erzgebirge 11/26
Herzogenaurach, Bavaria 4/17
Hildesheim, Lower Saxony 1/6
Hockenheim, Baden 4/7, 5/18, 8/1, 8/23
Homburg, Saarland 6/17
Horrem, North Rhine-Westphalia 5/4
Hurth-Hermuhlheim, North Rhine-
Westphalia 1/1
Ingelheim, Hesse 5/15
Ingolstadt, Bavaria 1/1
Juditten 10/2
Karlsruhe, Baden 9/13
Kirchheide, Lipfe Detmold 12/12
Kirchheim, Wurttemberg 8/23
Koblenz, Rhineland-Palatinate 5/12, 9/8
Kunzelsau, Wurttemberg 10/18
Ladenburg, Baden 4/4
Lahr, Baden 8/13
Leipzig, Leipzig 4/6
Lenderscheid 9/18
Lindau, Allgau, Bavaria 10/9
Lingen, Lower Saxony 10/14
Loerrach 3/24
Ludwigsburg, Wurttemberg 5/20
Ludwigshafen, Rhineland-Palatinate 3/6
Magdeburg, Altmark 6/27
Magstadt, Wurttemberg 4/13
Mainz, Rhineland-Palatinate 4/18, 11/2,
12/2, 12/6

Malchin, Mecklenburg-Schwerin 9/18
Malente, Schleswig-Holstein 7/5
Mannheim, Baden 3/16, 7/3, 8/9, 8/31, 10/1,
10/25, 12/1
Meissen, Saxony 1/21
Moers, North Rhine-Westphalia 3/28, 9/10
Moorlage 2/13
Morfelden, Hesse 1/28
Muhldorf, Bavaria 9/28
Mulheim-am-Rhein, North Rhine-
Westphalia 1/15
Munchberg, Bavaria 2/3
Munchen Gladbach, North Rhine-
Westphalia 3/16
Munich, Bavaria 2/15, 3/2, 3/23, 4/4, 4/14,
5/3, 5/7, 5/26, 7/21, 9/15, 9/30
Munsingen-Buttenhausen, Wurttemberg 5/14
Neindorf, Lower Saxony 7/4
Netphen, North Rhine-Westphalia 3/18, 12/20
Neuss, North Rhine-Westphalia 2/8
Neustadt, Rhineland-Palatinate 6/20
Nieder-Ingelheim, Hesse 5/15
Niehl, Rhineland-Palatinate 5/17
Norisring, Bavaria 7/11
Nurburgring, Rhineland-Palatinate 5/12,
5/21, 5/23, 5/24, 5/28, 6/2, 6/14, 6/19,
7/12, 7/15, 7/17, 7/19, 7/24, 7/26, 7/31,
8/1, 8/2, 8/3, 8/4, 8/5, 8/8, 8/18, 8/21,
8/23, 9/8, 9/27, 10/7, 11/13
Nuremberg, Bavaria 1/10, 7/11
Osnabruck, Lower Saxony 7/21
Pfaffenrot, Baden 11/25
Pforzheim, Baden 7/20, 9/4
Plettenberg, North Rhine-Westphalia 3/8
Pritzwalk, Brandenburg 6/22
Regensburg, Bavaria 3/7
Remagen, Rhineland-Palatinate 1/30
Remscheid, North Rhine-Westphalia 7/31
Rhaunen, Westphalia 3/21
Roisdorf 10/5
Rossfeld 6/8
Rostock, Mecklenburg 8/9
Russelsheim, Hesse 1/21, 2/13, 3/12, 3/13,
4/11, 4/27, 5/4
Ruthestein 7/21
Saarbrucken, Saarland 7/20
Schorndorf, Wurttemberg 3/17
Siegen, North Rhine-Westphalia 3/18, 7/11,
12/20
Siegmar-Schonau, Saxony 1/1
Solingen, North Rhine-Westphalia 4/5
Steige 7/26
Stuttgart, Wurttemberg 1/30, 2/23, 3/4,
3/6, 3/9, 3/20, 3/26, 4/14, 5/19, 8/15,
8/18, 9/12, 9/23, 10/17, 11/5, 12/1, 12/29
Thoum 12/10
Tuttlingen, Wurttemberg 2/25
Uberlingen, Wurttemberg 7/18
Uelsen, Lower Saxony 10/20
Unterturkheim, Wurttemberg 1/3, 4/1, 11/10
Uslar, Lower Saxony 3/14
Vierkrug 1/7
Waiblingen, Wurttemberg 10/6, 10/24
Wiesbaden, Hesse 1/8, 5/2, 5/15
Winningen, Rhineland-Palatinate 10/12
Wolfsburg, Lower Saxony 2/17, 4/12, 5/25,
5/26
Wuppertal-Elberfeld, North Rhine-
Westphalia 1/24, 7/16, 10/6, 10/26
Wurzburg, Bavaria 5/20
Zuffenhausen, Wurttemberg 3/21
Zulz, Upper Silesia 4/23
Zwickau, Saxony 11/7

GREECE
Athens, Central Greece and Euboea 2/13

HONG KONG 4/29, 10/9

HUNGARY
Budapest, Pest-Pilis 5/23, 6/21
Homak 3/29
Kald 10/26
Mako, Csongrad 2/3
Nagylak 2/13
Szolnok, Szolnok 6/14

INDIA
Calcutta, West Bengal 5/11, 8/2 10/4

INDONESIA
Bogor, West Java 1/26

IRAQ
Baghdad, Baghdad 2/8, 9/14

IRELAND
Athy, Kildare 7/2
Ballinascarthy, Cork 12/10
Ballinascorney 5/28, 9/23
Chapelizod, Dublin 7/15
Cork, Cork 4/30
Drogheda, Louth 5/6
Dublin, Dublin 1/22, 1/26, 1/29, 3/11, 5/28,
7/4, 8/9, 9/17, 9/23
Dunrod 9/15
Longhurst 3/6
Portmarnock, Dublin 9/17
Sligo, Sligo 1/15
Waterford, Waterford 8/9
Wexford, Wexford 6/26
Wicklow, Wicklow 7/9

ITALY
Aglie, Turin, Piedmont 10/10
Albano Laziale, Rome 10/12
Allesandria, Piedmont 4/15, 5/12, 7/17
Ancona, Marche 2/24
Arezzo, Tuscany 9/15
Argenta, Emilia-Romagna 5/24
Arona, Novara, Piemont 9/12
Asti, Piedmont 5/29, 7/17
Avandaro 4/7
Bazzano, Emilia-Romagna 6/23
Berceto, Emilia-Romagna 11/22
Bergamo, Lombardy 5/10, 8/31
Biella, Piedmont 6/5, 6/6, 12/27
Bobbio, Emilia-Romagna 6/14
Bologna, Emilia-Romagna 2/11, 4/28, 5/1,
5/20, 6/24, 10/2, 10/7, 10/21, 10/23, 11/24,
12/1
Borgo Pancarale, Lombardy 9/10
Brescia, Lombardy 3/1, 3/14, 3/26, 6/29,
7/20, 7/24, 9/4, 9/9, 9/23, 10/23, 12/1,
12/2
Bresso, Lombardy 6/27
Budduro, Sardinia 8/18
Caldogno 8/2
Campogalliano, Emilia-Romagna 9/14
Casciano 10/19
Cascina, Pisa, Tuscany 8/20
Caserta, Campania 6/18
Castel d'Ario, Lombardy 11/18
Cavarzere, Venetia 3/27
Civenna 3/11
Colle della Maddelena 8/7
Como, Lombardy 10/3
Cormano, Lombardy 6/26
Cremona, Lombardy 6/9, 9/28
Cuneo, Piedmont 1/22, 6/14, 8/7, 9/9, 10/1
Fanfullo, Lombardy 6/8
Fiorano, Emilia-Romagna 2/14
Florence, Tuscany 2/24. 5/12, 6/15, 9/26,
10/19, 11/11, 11/13
Fobello di Valsesia 8/24
Frugarolo, Piedmont 3/26
Galliate, Novara, Piedmont 8/8
Garda, Verona, Venetia 5/22
Genoa, Liguria 7/14

Grugliasco, Piedmont 10/24
Guidizzolo, Lombardy 5/12
Guilianova Lido 3/2
Imola, Emilia-Romagna 4/27, 4/30, 5/1
LaCassa, Piedmont 3/30
Lago di Garda, Lombardy 10/24
Lavezzola 8/16
Legnano, Milan, Lombardy 1/9
Lido di Camaiore, Tuscany 3/19
Limiate 9/10
Limone, Piedmont 1/26
Livorno, Tuscany 7/31, 8/7
Lodi, Lombardy 12/2
Lugo, Emilia-Romagna 4/23
Madonie, Sicily 4/25
Magreglio 8/15
Manerbio, Lombardy 6/9
Mantua, Lombardy 5/6, 8/10, 12/5
Maranello, Emilia-Romagna 7/21
Mestre, Venetia 5/26
Milan, Lombardy 1/1, 1/20, 1/27, 1/31,
 2/16, 2/25, 3/3, 3/9, 3/26, 4/5, 4/12, 4/20,
 4/28, 5/6, 5/9, 5/16, 5/22, 5/24, 6/2, 6/15,
 6/18, 6/21, 7/13, 7/14, 7/15, 7/17, 7/31,
 8/7, 9/4, 9/6, 9/11, 9/12, 9/15, 9/16, 9/23,
 10/8, 10/10, 10/11, 10/13, 10/16, 10/20,
 11/10, 11/17, 11/21, 12/4, 12/6, 12/23,
 12/25
Modena, Emila-Romagna 2/18, 3/14, 6/5,
 6/15, 6/30, 8/14, 9/18, 9/28, 11/4
Mont Cenis, Savoie 6/27
Montebelluna, Venetia 1/25
Monte Pellegrino, Emilia-Romagna 4/10
Montevarchi, Tuscany 3/24
Montona (Motovun, Croatia) 2/28
Monza, Lombardy 1/31, 2/26, 4/2, 4/25,
 5/26, 6/14, 6/27, 6/29, 8/28, 9/3, 9/4, 9/5,
 9/7, 9/8, 9/9, 9/10, 9/11, 9/12, 9/13,
 10/10, 10/19, 11/11
Moratica di Benferraro 9/15
Mugello, Tuscany 6/13
Naples, Campania 4/28
Nardo, Apulia 4/4, 6/12, 6/21
Noale, Venetia 6/19
Notaresco, Abruzzi 3/26
Oggebbio, Piedmont 2/10
Osimo, Marche 6/9
Ospedaletti, Liguria 6/27
Padua, Venetia 4/17, 6/10, 7/1, 7/2
Palermo, Sicily 3/4, 12/3
Parma, Emilia-Romagna 10/5, 11/22
Passo del Penice 6/14
Pavia, Lombardy 8/21
Perugia, Umbria 2/20
Pesaro, Marche 1/13, 7/22
Pescara, Abruzzi 7/13, 8/15, 8/18
Piacenza, Emilia-Romagna 1/2, 5/11, 7/16,
 12/17
Pistoia, Tuscany 10/4
Poggio di Berceto, Lombardy 10/5
Pompeii, Campania 4/2
Quercianella 6/6
Ravenna, Emilia-Romagna 6/17
Reggio, Calabria 3/28, 6/11
Renazzo di Cento, Emilia-Romagna 4/28
Rimini, Emilia-Romagna 10/10
Riviera d'Adda, Lombardy 1/16
Rome, Latium 1/3, 1/11, 1/12, 2/15, 2/18,
 3/15, 3/23, 4/12, 5/18, 5/25, 5/31, 6/12,
 6/24, 7/20, 7/29, 8/10, 8/30, 10/2, 10/17,
 11/8, 11/15, 11/30
Ronciglione, Latium 7/28
Rovato, Brescia, Lombardy 3/18
Salerno, Campania 1/18, 7/24
Sampierdarena, Liguria 7/28
San Giorgio Canavese, Piedmont 4/22
San Giorgio di Plano, Emilia-Romagna 11/8
San Prospero 5/12
San Remo, Liguria 6/27
Sant'Antimo, Campania 4/28

Sassi 5/15, 6/22
Sassuolo, Emilia-Romagna 5/30, 12/14
Scurzolengo d'Asti 10/13
Siena, Tuscany 7/7
Sondrio, Lombardy 3/6
Sorli 10/7
Stresa, Novara, Piedmont 9/12
Superga 5/15, 6/22
Susa, Turin, Piedmont 6/27
Suvereto, Tuscany 6/19
Syracuse, Sicily 10/23
Terni, Umbria 9/28
Terranova Bracciolini 3/28
Trieste, Venezia Giulia 9/3, 10/3
Troia, Apulia 1/23
Turin, Piedmont 1/18, 2/15, 2/21, 2/23,
 2/25, 3/8, 3/10, 3/12, 3/19, 3/21, 3/31,
 4/2, 5/2, 5/11, 5/15, 5/29, 6/15, 6/22,
 6/28, 7/1, 7/3, 7/6, 7/10, 7/17, 8/25, 8/28,
 9/5, 9/12, 9/18, 10/6, 10/18, 10/23, 10/30,
 11/2 11/26, 11/29, 12/12 12/16, 12/26
Valentino 3/27
Varedo, Liano 2/23
Varenna, Lombardy 12/27
Varese, Lombardy 3/26, 6/18, 9/12
Venice, Venetia 3/8
Verano, Emilia-Romagna 11/16
Verona, Venetia 2/19, 3/14
Vicenza, Venetia 7/1
Vignola, Emilia-Romagna 8/9
Villar Perosa, Piedmont 8/13
Volpago del Montello, Venetia 7/16
Zibido San Giacomo, Lombardy 2/26

JAPAN
 Cero, Gifu 1/30
 Fuji, Shizuoka 10/24
 Hachiioji City, Tokyo 7/10
 Hiroshima, Hiroshima 1/30, 2/27, 4/8, 8/6
 Hyogo, Hyogo 3/24, 9/24
 Ibaraki, Osaka 12/28
 Kinjo, Nishi Kasugai, Aichi 9/12
 Kobe, Hyogo 3/14, 9/5
 Kosugai, Chita, Aichi 11/16
 Kumamoto, Kumamoto 9/16
 Kurume, Fukuoka 3/1
 Kyoto, Kyoto 12/26
 Nagoya, Aichi 2/27, 6/1
 Odate, Akita 4/25
 Okazaki, Aichi 2/23
 Osaka, Gifu 3/1, 3/7
 Owase, Mie 8/13
 Shizuoka, Shizuoka 10/1, 11/17
 Suzuka, Mie 5/24, 11/21
 Tenryu City, Shizuoka 11/17
 Tokyo 1/21, 1/29, 2/7, 2/10, 2/15, 3/3, 3/13,
  3/29, 4/9, 4/29, 5/20, 5/29, 6/6, 6/7, 7/1,
  8/2, 8/5, 8/12, 9/8, 9/15, 11/13, 11/14,
  11/28, 12/26
 Tosa, Kochi 1/9
 Toyota City 5/28, 6/10
 Yokkaichi, Mie 6/13
 Yokohama 1/15

KENYA
 Nairobi 2/5

KOREA (SOUTH)
 Asan, Tongcho, Kangwon 8/6, 11/25
 Seoul, Kyonggi 1/10, 6/13, 10/13

LATVIA
 Liepaja, Kurzeme 1/10
 Riga, Vidzeme 5/30

LEBANON
 Beirut 7/18

LIBYA
 El Marj (Barce), Cyrenaica 12/21

Tripoli 3/24, 4/18, 5/5, 5/7, 5/10, 5/12,
 5/15, 6/22

LUXEMBOURG
 Luxembourg 8/27, 12/22

MACAU
 Macau 11/19

MACEDONIA
 Skopje 1/20

MALAYSIA (MALAYA, STRAITS SETTLEMENTS)
 Kuala Lumpur, Selangor 10/6

MALI
 Timbuktu 1/14

MEXICO
 Ciudad Juarez, Chihuahua 10/21, 11/25
 Colona Dublan, Chihuahua 7/8
 Cuernavaca, Morelos 10/22
 La Paz, Baja California Sur 6/26
 Mexico City, Distrito Federal 1/18, 2/5, 2/14,
  4/20, 5/28, 6/16, 6/18, 9/2 10/24, 11/1,
  11/20
 Oaxaca, Oaxaca 11/20, 11/21
 Puebla, Puebla 5/15
 Silao, Guanajuato 11/21
 Tuxtla Gutierrez, Chiapas 11/25
 Valle de Bravo, Mexico 7/27
 Zacatecas, Zacatecas 5/9

MONACO
 Monte Carlo 1/23, 3/7, 3/27, 4/14, 5/10,
  5/11, 5/12, 5/18, 5/19, 5/21, 5/22, 5/29,
  5/31, 6/2, 6/18, 6/20, 6/22, 7/14, 8/3, 8/15,
  11/23

MOON
 Hadley Rille 7/31
 Mare Imbrium 11/17

MOROCCO
 Casablanca 10/19, 10/25, 12/22

NETHERLANDS (HOLLAND)
 Amersfoort, Utrecht 4/15
 Amsterdam, North Holland 1/1, 4/1, 4/30,
  5/3, 5/6, 7/1, 7/13, 10/2
 Assen, Drenthe 5/5
 Bloemendaal, North Holland 3/16
 Born, Limburg 5/3
 Bussum, North Holland 10/8
 Dordrecht, South Holland 9/12
 Eindhoven, North Brabant 1/31, 4/14, 12/12
 Emmen, Drenthe 8/23
 Enschede, Overijssel 5/24
 Groningen, Groningen 9/3
 Haarlem, North Holland 4/25
 the Hague, South Holland 4/14, 6/16, 6/21, 7/8
 Hook of Holland, South Holland 2/21
 Leiden, South Holland 11/7, 12/9
 Maarsbergen Castle 4/10
 Rotterdam, South Holland 9/1, 12/15
 Sommelsdyk, South Holland 9/21
 Stiens, Friesland 4/16
 Utrecht, Utrecht 7/3
 Zandvoort, North Holland 5/20, 5/31,
  6/2, 6/21, 6/22, 6/23, 7/23, 7/29, 7/30,
  8/5, 8/17, 11/7

NEW ZEALAND
 Ardmore 1/12
 Auckland, North Island 1/8, 3/30, 8/30,
  10/6, 10/9
 Bulls, North Island 7/20
 Hamilton, Waikato, NI 12/24
 Nelson, South Island 6/18
 Wellington, North Island 2/2, 3/5

NORWAY
Kristiansund, More og Romsdal 9/16
Oslo, Oslo 12/7
Voss, Hordaland 3/4, 3/13

PAKISTAN
Karachi 6/5

PANAMA
Colon, Colon 6/18
Panama City, Panama 5/25, 6/18

PERU
Lima 4/12

POLAND
Biala, Opole 4/23
Krakow, Krakow 1/20
Warsaw 11/6, 11/23, 12/27

PORTUGAL
Aldeia Galega 3/20
Algarve 9/17
Estoril, Estremadura 4/21, 6/18
Lisbon, Estremadura 7/20, 8/23
Mangualde, Viseu 7/27
Oporto, Douro Litoral 1/25, 2/27

PUERTO RICO
San Juan 6/17

ROMANIA
Bucharest, Bucharest 11/12
Nadlac, Arad 2/13
Pitesti, Arges 6/16

RUSSIA (USSR)
Elabuga, Tatarstan 12/7
Gor'kiy, Gor'kiy 1/1, 5/2, 6/14, 11/1
Miass, Chelyabinsk 7/8
Moscow, Moscow 2/1, 2/4, 3/15, 5/19,
    5/31, 6/15, 6/24, 6/26, 6/28, 8/26, 9/19,
    10/1, 11/6, 11/7
Nizhni Novgorod, Gor'kiy 5/2 11/1
St. Petersburg (Leningrad), St. Petersburg
    1/31, 5/19, 5/30, 6/16
Sergievskoe, Tula 8/20
Tol'iatti, Kuibyshev 1/9, 3/24, 9/9
Venev Raion (Ozertzy), Tula 6/15

SENEGAL
Dakar 1/14

SERBIA (YUGOSLAVIA)
Belgrade 9/3

SOUTH AFRICA
Capetown, Cape of Good Hope 2/6, 3/13,
    6/4, 9/23, 12/26
Durban, Natal 1/7, 1/30, 6/18
East London, Cape of Good Hope 1/1, 1/29,
    8/22 12/29
Ficksburg, Orange Free State 12/1
Germiston, Transvaal 12/9
Johannesburg, Transvaal 4/19, 5/19, 9/12,
    11/4, 11/26
Krugersdorp, Transvaal 11/30
Kyalami, Transvaal 3/1, 3/3, 3/4, 3/5, 3/7,
    3/14, 3/22, 3/30, 11/4
Parow-Bellville, Cape of Good Hope 7/4
Pilgrims Rest, Transvaal 3/16
Port Elizabeth, Cape of Good Hope 7/15,
    12/5
Potchefstroom, Transvaal 11/22
Pretoria, Transvaal 2/9
Somerset West-Strand, Cape of Good Hope
    3/13
Theunissen, Orange Free State 9/25

SPAIN
Amorebieta, Vizcaya 1/18
Barcelona, Barcelona 3/21, 4/3, 5/15, 10/26,
    10/27, 10/29, 11/28, 12/5
Cadiz, Cadiz 9/17
Jarama, Madrid 4/28
Las Palmas, Canary Islands 4/5
Madrid, Madrid 3/6, 4/28, 5/15, 5/17, 5/24,
    6/12, 7/26
Marbella, Malaga 8/8
Montjuich Park, Barcelona 4/27
Pedrables, Barcelona 10/28
San Sebastian, Giupuzcoa 7/18, 10/23
Valencia, Valencia 6/17, 10/4, 10/26

SWEDEN
Anderstorp, Jonkoping 6/19
Appelbo 10/23
Borgholm, Oland, Kalmar 11/25
Burtrask, Vasterbotten 2/22
Eskilstuna, Sodermanland 9/30
Falkenberg, Halland 8/15
Farila, Gavleborg 5/7
Frotuna, Vastmanland 3/15
Goteborg, Goteborg och Bohus 1/5, 4/14,
    4/28, 6/2 10/3, 10/12, 10/27
Halsingborg, Kristianstad 11/20
Hisingen, Goteborg och Bohus 10/27
Holland 10/10
Karlskoga, Orebro 6/15
Karlstad, Varmland 11/22
Kristinehamn, Varmland 7/23
Kungsbacka, Halland 12/4
Lindesberg, Orebro 7/29
Lundby 10/20
Mora, Kopparberg 8/2
Motala, Ostergotland 9/30
Orebro, Orebro 2/14
Rattvik, Kopparberg 5/24
Skovde, Skaraborg 12/8
Sodertalje, Stockholm 11/30
Sorredsdalen 4/24
Stockholm, Stockholm 1/31, 3/18, 8/22, 10/5,
    12/6, 12/28
Sundsvall, Vasternorrland 1/1
Torsby, Varmland 8/8
Trollhattan, Skaraborg 3/5
Vasteras, Vastmanland 8/23
Vaxjo, Kronoberg 9/8

SWITZERLAND
Airolo, Ticino 9/5
Arbon, Thurgau 3/1
Aresdorf 9/18
Basel, Baselstadt 3/20, 4/26, 8/21
Bellinzona, Ticino 4/24
Berne, Berne 3/4, 5/18, 6/4, 1/30, 7/4
Bienne, Berne 4/18
Binningen, Baselland 6/7
Bremgarten, Berne 5/27, 8/26
Clarens, Vaud 7/20
Frauenfeld, Thurgau 1/25
Fribourg, Fribourg 7/7
Geneva, Geneva 1/2, 1/21, 2/28, 3/4, 3/6,
    3/8, 3/10, 3/16, 3/17, 3/20, 4/15, 7/8,
    8/9, 10/1, 10/29, 12/11
Goschenen, Uri 9/5
Klausen 8/7
Kreuzlingen, Thurgau 3/7
La Chaux-de-Fonds, Neuchatel 12/25
Lausanne, Vaud 3/4, 4/3, 11/1
Lucerne, Luzern 11/3
Lugano, Ticino 4/1, 9/5, 9/28
Mohlin, Aargau 3/4
Orselina 12/7
Reinach, Aargau 5/11
Ruti, Zurich 7/28
Saint Moritz, Graubunden 4/8
Saint-Ursanne, Berne 5/31
Schaffhausen, Schaffhausen 3/26

Sierre, Valais 5/10
Versoix, Geneva 3/15
Zurich, Zurich 1/22, 2/1, 2/12, 3/4, 3/27,
    3/31, 4/19, 7/12, 7/23, 8/14

THAILAND (SIAM)
Bangkok, Phra Nakhon 7/15

TUNISIA
Carthage 5/6

TURKEY
Bursa, Bursa 4/13
Izmir (Smyrna), Izmir 11/18
Moonjoosoon 5/31

UKRAINE
Kiev, Kiev 11/12
Yalta, Crimea 9/11

UNITED KINGDOM

Channel Islands
Jersey 11/3

England
Abbotswood, Gloucestershire 10/25
Abingdon-on-Thames, Berkshire 1/20, 10/24
Aintree, Lancashire 7/15, 7/16, 7/18, 7/20
Alderley Edge, Cheshire 6/24
Alresford, Essex 8/27
Alwalton, Lincolnshire 3/27
Arkley, Hertfordshire 11/29
Aston Clinton, Buckingham 5/24, 6/8
Atherstone, Warwickshire 5/1
Barnet, Hertfordshire 4/8
Basildon, Berkshire 1/15
Baslow, Derbyshire 5/11
Beaulieu, Hampshire 4/9, 5/22, 7/4
Beckenham, Kent 8/17
Bexhill-on-Sea, Sussex 5/19, 10/8
Birkenhead, Cheshire 3/18
Birmingham, Warwickshire 1/18, 2/2, 4/22,
    5/13, 6/9, 6/19, 7/8, 7/27, 8/25, 9/7, 10/2,
    11/3, 11/26, 11/27, 12/5, 12/18
Blackburn, Lancashire 5/29
Blackpool, Lancashire 1/4, 7/28, 9/4
Bognor Regis, Sussex 1/26, 7/2
Bordon, Hampshire 10/16
Bourne, Kesteven, Lincoln 1/8, 4/16, 4/22
    12/15
Bournemouth, Hampshire 7/11
Bradford, Yorkshire 9/25
Brands Hatch, Kent 3/12, 3/21, 4/16, 5/17,
    7/2, 7/20, 8/29, 9/25, 10/24
Brentwood, Essex 6/25
Bretford, Warwickshire 3/18
Brighton, Sussex 2/13, 5/15, 6/5, 6/28, 7/2,
    7/19, 9/2, 9/5, 9/7, 9/14, 9/17, 11/10,
    11/14
Bristol, Bristol 3/18, 4/23, 9/20, 10/28
Bromley, Middlesex 11/13
Bromsgrove, Worcestershire 5/23
Brooklands, Surrey 2/29, 3/4, 3/11, 3/25,
    4/11, 4/15, 4/30, 5/6, 5/7, 5/16, 5/17,
    5/20, 6/8, 6/9, 6/17, 6/24, 6/29, 7/6, 7/18,
    8/3, 8/5, 8/6, 8/7, 8/8, 8/27, 9/2, 9/7,
    10/7, 10/13, 10/19, 10/20, 11/6, 11/8,
    12/12
Broomfield, Essex 8/29
Burnaston, Derbyshire 4/18
Burnley, Lancashire 11/9
Bushey, Middlesex 8/18
Camborne, Cornwall 12/24
Carlisle, Cumberland 12/5
Cheltenham, Gloucester 2/21
Chertsey, Middlesex 3/21, 5/17
Chester, Cheshire 1/22, 2/11
Chesterton, Staffordshire 12/5
Chichester, Sussex 2/4, 2/24

Chislehurst, Kent 1/17, 3/11
Chiswick, Essex 11/12
Chobham, Surrey 9/21
Clipston, Nottingham 3/7
Cobham, Kent 10/9
Coddenham, Suffolk 3/30
Colchester, Essex 4/1, 5/27, 6/14
Colden Common, Hampshie 3/25
Compton Verney, Warwickshire 6/26
Coniston Water, Lancashire 1/4
Cookham Dean, Berkshire 6/11
Coventry, Warwickshire 1/14, 1/16, 1/17,
   2/2, 2/23, 4/15, 4/27, 5/25, 5/26, 7/3,
   8/28, 10/2, 11/2 11/14, 12/27
Cowley, Oxford 3/28, 7/25, 10/10, 11/22
Crewe, Cheshire 6/6
Croydon, Surrey 12/30
Dagenham, Middlesex 2/19, 5/16, 10/1
Danbury, Essex 10/16
Dartford, Kent 3/28, 4/22
Datchet, Buckingham 7/12 10/24
Derby, Derby 1/7, 6/25, 6/27, 7/2, 7/9, 9/19,
   10/28, 11/6
Dovercourt, Essex 5/12
Downham Market, Norfolk 5/28
Dukinfield, Cheshire 2/25
Dulwich, Middlesex 4/12
Durham, Durhamshire 8/14
Dymock, Gloucestershire 12/2
Eastbourne, Sussex 8/25
East Grinstead, Sussex 10/25
East Marden, Sussex 4/19
East Peckham, Kent 1/28, 11/13
Edgware, Middlesex 9/8, 12/2
Enfield, Middlesex 9/7
Epsom, Surrey 1/21, 2/3, 4/17, 12/19
Esher, Surrey 7/10
Ewell, Surrey 2/21
Exeter, Devonshire 12/27
Exning, Suffolk 4/21
Farnborough, Hampshire 11/20
Farnham, Surrey 10/17
Farningham, Kent 4/16
Farnsworth, Lancashire 2/26
Feltham, Middlesex 11/1
Fowey, Cornwall 6/7
Fulham, Middlesex 8/11
Gallops 2/10
Gloucester, Gloucestershire 2/21, 5/18, 6/4
Goodwood, Sussex 3/13, 4/3, 4/7, 4/23, 6/2
Great Milton, Oxfordshire 4/2
Great Yarmouth, Norfolkshire 9/13
Grimsby, Lincolnshire 5/9
Guildford, Surrey 1/3, 1/22 10/1, 10/18
Hackbridge, Surrey 12/2
Hackney, Middlesex 9/23
Halifax, Yorkshire 3/20
Hampstead, Middlesex 2/15, 4/16, 9/17
Hampton-in-Arden, Warwickshire 5/18
Handsworth, Birmingham, Warwickshire 8/21
Harrogate, Yorkshire 4/15
Harrow, Middlesex 2/19, 9/27
Havant, Hampshire 10/29
Hendon, Durham 5/19
Henley-on-Thames, Oxfordshire 8/22
Hereford, Hereford 1/17, 4/4
Hounslow, Middlesex 3/23
Hove, Sussex 7/22 10/23, 10/26, 11/18
Huby, Leeds, Yorkshire 10/7
Huddersfield, Yorkshire 5/10
Hungerford, Berkshire 1/16
Hyde, Cheshire 3/24
Ibstone, Buckingham 12/18
Ilford, Essex 11/8
Illogan, Cornwall 4/13
Ipswich, Suffolk 5/18
Islington, Middlesex 6/14
Kibworth Beauchamp, Leicester 2/12
Kidderminster, Worcestershire 11/8
King's Lynn, Norfolk 6/1

Kingston Hill, Surrey 3/23
Kingston-upon-Hull, Yorkshire 4/14
Kingston-upon-Thames, Middlesex 3/10
Knaresborough, Yorkshire 8/27
Knutsford, Cheshire 4/1
Kop Hill, Buckinghamshire 3/28
Lake Windermere, Lancashire 6/13
Land's End, Cornwall 10/9, 10/19
Leamington Spa, Warwickshire 6/9, 12/31
Leeds, Yorkshire 8/27
Leicester, Leicestershire 1/19, 2/2, 3/23
Lincoln, Lincolnshire 9/6
Lindley, Yorkshire 1/20
Lingfield, Sussex 3/4
Little Missenden, Buckingham 11/8
Liverpool, Lancashire 3/18, 6/29, 9/6, 12/30
London, Middlesex 1/2, 1/5, 1/9, 1/15,
   1/18, 1/19, 1/21, 1/26, 1/27, 1/29, 2/6,
   2/12, 2/14, 2/15, 2/23, 2/24, 2/25, 2/26,
   3/3, 3/6, 3/10, 3/12, 3/22, 3/23, 3/30,
   4/1, 4/3, 4/4, 4/8, 4/10, 4/11, 4/18, 4/22,
   4/24, 4/25, 4/26, 5/2, 5/9, 5/13, 5/17,
   5/25, 5/26, 5/26, 5/27, 5/31, 6/4, 6/6,
   6/7, 6/9, 6/10, 6/14, 6/15, 6/17, 6/20,
   6/21, 6/22, 6/23, 6/26, 6/27, 6/30, 7/1,
   7/3, 7/4, 7/6, 7/7, 7/9, 7/10, 7/14, 7/16,
   7/17, 7/18, 7/19, 7/24, 7/29, 8/6, 8/10,
   8/14, 8/17, 8/19, 8/23, 8/27, 8/30, 9/2,
   9/10, 9/11, 9/13, 9/16, 9/17, 9/22, 9/23,
   9/27, 9/28, 9/30, 10/2 10/9, 10/11, 10/14,
   10/15, 10/16, 10/17, 10/19, 10/20, 10/22,
   10/27, 10/30, 11/7, 11/8, 11/10, 11/13,
   11/14, 11/30, 12/2 12/10, 12/11, 12/12,
   12/18, 12/19, 12/20, 12/23, 12/27
Longbridge, Warwickshire 2/19
Loose, Kent 6/14
Loudwater, Buckingham 8/16
Maiden Bradley, Wiltshire 11/5
Maidstone, Kent 11/3
Malmesbury, Wiltshire 8/13
Malton, Yorkshire 11/20
Manchester, Lancashire 2/14, 2/16, 3/8,
   3/9, 4/1, 5/4, 6/6, 6/18, 7/9, 8/24, 10/23
Marlborough, Wiltshire 5/8
Mauldslie 8/14
Melton Mowbray, Leicester 2/20
Menston, Yorkshire 11/12
Mexborough, Yorkshire 4/10
Micheldever, Hampshire 7/12
Mickleover, Derbyshire 12/29
Midhurst, Sussex 10/14
Mildenhall, Suffolk 5/9
Millbrook, Bedfordshire 9/17
Newcastle-upon-Tyne, Northumberland 10/17
Newent, Gloucestershire 6/11
New Milton, Hampshire 7/18
Newton Solney, Derbyshire 8/25
Northampton, Northampton 2/16
Norwich, Norfolk 7/22
Nottingham, Nottinghamshire 2/8, 7/10, 12/16
Oulton Park, Cheshire 4/15, 5/26, 7/21, 9/23
Oundle, Northampton 4/2
Oxford, Oxfordshire 2/19
Oxhey, Hertfordshire 10/28
Packwood, Warwickshire 5/10
Paddington Wharf, Lancashire 7/18
Paulerspury 5/18
Peckham, Middlesex 6/10
Penge, Kent 11/23
Peterborough, Huntingdon & Peterborough
   7/30
Petersfield, Hampshire 5/14
Pinner, Middlesex 10/31
Plymouth, Devonshire 9/1
Porthleven, Cornwall 11/17
Portishead, Somerset 8/18
Prescot, Mersey, Lancashire 5/9, 7/27, 8/31
Preston, Lancashire 6/17
Ramsgate, Kent 11/11
Ranelagh, Middlesex 7/14

Rawtenstall, Lancashire 11/7
Reading, Berkshire 1/18, 4/21, 10/22
Redcar, Yorkshire 6/17, 10/27
Reeds, Cornwall 2/28
Rhodes Green 4/16
Richmond, Surrey 5/19, 12/24
Romford, Essex 8/14
Royston, Yorkshire 4/2
St. Peters, Suffolk 10/28
Salford, Oxfordshire 3/24
Scarborough, Yorkshire 3/8, 6/12
Sheffield, Yorkshire 1/22, 7/6
Shefford, Bedfordshire 12/16
Shelsley Walsh, Worcester 5/23, 6/3, 7/3,
   7/11, 8/12
Shepton Mallet, Somerset 8/7
Sherborne, Dorset 5/13
Silverstone, Northampton 3/24, 3/29, 4/26,
   5/2, 5/6, 5/13, 5/19, 7/8, 7/14, 7/19, 8/14,
   10/2
Smallfield, Surrey 3/15
Smethwick, Staffordshire 3/21
Snetterton, Norfolk 4/24
Soho, Middlesex 11/15
Solihull, Warwick 10/5
Southampton, Hampshire 11/30
South Croxton, Leicestershire 1/26
South Harting, Hampshire 7/26
Southmead 9/20, 11/4
Southport, Lancashire 3/16
Southsea, Hampshire 8/23
Spread Eagle 6/28
Stafford, Staffordshire 3/29
Steeple, Essex 9/22
Stockwell 4/15
Stoke Damerel, Devonshire 2/5
Stoke Newington, Middlesex 3/26
Stourbridge, Gloucestershire 7/20
Stroud, Gloucestershire 11/1
Style Kop, Staffordshire 8/29
Sudbury, Middlesex 12/25
Sunderland, Durham 9/8
Surbiton, Middlesex 11/4
Sutton, Surrey 8/29
Sutton Coldfield, Warwick 11/1
Swindon, Wiltshire 7/13
Tamworth-in-Arden 3/23, 6/12
Tatsfield, Surrey 2/11
Tavistock, Devonshire 4/4
Thames Ditton, Surrey 12/27
Thruxton, Hampshire 4/12
Tolpuddle, Dorset 9/28
Treator, Cornwall 2/28
Tunbridge Wells, Kent 10/15
Upton-on-Severn, Worcester 8/8
Wallasey, Cheshire 9/24
Walsall, Staffordshire 5/15
Warwick, Warwickshire 2/8, 6/26
Welbeck Park, Nottingham 5/11
Welwyn, Hertford 6/24
Westcliff, Essex 7/23
West Kingsdown, Kent 1/24
West Wittering, Sussex 4/22, 9/23
Weybridge, Surrey 6/17
Whitchurch, Shropshire 11/22
Wickersley, Yorkshire 12/26
Wigan, Lancashire 12/8
Willesden, Middlesex 11/6
Wimbledon, Middlesex 3/29, 9/5
Winchester, Hampshire 6/17, 8/28
Windsor, Berkshire 3/22
Winscombe, Somerset 4/10
Withington, Gloucestershire 6/8
Witney, Oxfordshire 5/27
Woking, Surrey 8/13
Wolverhampton, Staffordshire 1/16, 4/4,
   8/18, 9/24
Worcester, Worcestershire 3/1
Yeovil, Somerset 7/18, 11/5

Isle of Man
  Douglas 5/12
  Port Vuillen 5/11

Northern Ireland
  Ballyclare, Antrim 8/10
  Belfast, Antrim 3/26, 4/14, 5/4, 5/24, 7/3,
    10/31, 11/17
  Conlig, Down 11/10
  Cookstown, Tyrone 11/27
  Craigantlet 5/24
  Cultra, Down 5/1
  Dromore, Down 11/4
  Dunmurry, Antrim 10/2

Scotland
  Aberdeen, Aberdeenshire 4/28, 11/8
  Aboyne, Aberdeenshire 7/30
  Arbroath, Angus 9/17
  Ardrishaig, Argyll 6/17
  Ayr, Ayrshire 9/21
  Bowling, Dunbarton 3/6
  Dalry, Ayrshire 6/7
  Dreghorn, Ayrshire 2/5
  Dundee, Angus 8/28
  Dunfermline, Fife 2/5, 2/13
  Dumfries, Dumfries 12/29
  Edinburgh, Midlothian 5/15, 6/16, 7/15,
    9/19, 10/5, 12/28
  Glasgow, Lanark 3/15, 3/21, 6/4, 10/1,
    10/11, 11/3, 1/28, 12/18
  Grangemouth, Stirling 6/20
  Greenock, Renfrewshire 1/19, 6/23
  Helensburgh, Dunbarton 8/30
  Inveraray, Argyll 6/17
  John O'Groats, Caithness 10/9, 10/19
  Kilmany, Fifeshire 3/4
  Kirkcudbright, Kirkcudbright 6/12
  Loch Ness, Iverness 9/29
  Milton, Dunbarton 6/11
  Old Cumnock, Ayrshire 8/21
  Paisley, Renfrew 5/13
  Rothesay, Bute 4/26
  Troon, Ayrshire 7/13
  Twynholm, Kirkcudbright 3/27
  Wick, Caithness 1/17
  Wishaw, Lanark 7/15

Wales
  Bethesda, Caernarvon 8/2
  Builth Wells, Radnor 7/5
  Cardiff, Glamorgan 1/2
  Ebbw Vale, Monmouth 12/10
  Llandudno, Caernarvon 2/25, 8/2
  Llanrwst, Denbigh 8/2
  Newport, Monmouthshire 1/12
  Pendine Sands, Carmarthen 2/4, 3/3, 4/27,
    4/28, 7/21, 9/25
  Penmaenmawr, Caernarvon 8/2
  Penryhn, Caernarvon 8/2
  Ruthin, Denbighshire 6/11
  Wrexham, Denbigh 4/6

UNITED STATES OF AMERICA

Alabama
  Birmingham 2/19
  Calera 6/24
  Demopolis 9/10
  Fort Payne 3/21, 5/11
  Gadsden 6/26, 9/13, 12/13
  Huntsville 1/24, 10/5
  Montgomery 6/1
  Notasulga 4/19
  Selma 5/18
  Talladega 3/24, 5/2, 5/3, 5/6, 7/13, 8/17,
    9/13

Alaska
  Fairbanks 1/27

Arizona
  Chandler 1/30
  Douglas 11/13
  Florence 10/12
  Mesa 11/10
  Phoenix 1/10, 1/27, 1/28, 2/27, 3/10, 3/18,
    3/20, 4/5, 4/12, 5/3, 5/12, 7/31, 8/26,
    10/20, 10/24, 11/6, 11/9, 11/13, 11/18,
    11/19, 12/3
  Scottsdale 12/12
  Sedona 3/23
  Sun City 10/19
  Tucson 1/25, 2/8, 4/3, 4/10, 4/19, 5/20,
    6/12, 6/30, 9/21

Arkansas
  Arkansas City 5/21
  Batesville 1/9
  Charleston 2/10
  Conway 11/11
  Eureka Springs 11/16
  Fayetteville 9/19
  Greenland 10/5
  Monticello 3/29, 4/20
  Morrilton 5/1
  Mountain Home 9/19
  Texarkana 8/12, 8/31

California
  Alameda 2/1, 12/13
  Alamo 1/8, 10/13
  Alhambra 4/5
  Altadena 4/4
  Anaheim 5/21
  Angel Island 2/2
  Artois 1/1
  Ascot Park 10/30
  Atwater 10/22
  Azusa 3/28
  Bakersfield 8/20
  Banning 7/16
  Berkeley 7/11, 11/3, 11/24, 12/21
  Beverly Hills 2/3, 2/28, 6/6, 10/4, 11/25, 11/26
  Bradbury 3/16
  Canoga Park 11/20
  Carlsbad 5/7
  Carmel 10/30
  Caruthers 8/19
  Cerritos 1/2
  Cholame 9/30
  Chula Vista 4/14
  Compton 1/1
  Corona 4/8, 9/9
  Costa Mesa 2/8, 3/23
  Covina 9/10
  Culver City 1/5, 3/31, 4/20, 5/21, 12/14
  Del Mar 4/16, 11/6
  Downey 10/6
  El Cajon 11/21
  El Centro 3/5
  El Dorado 6/28
  El Mirage Lake 5/16
  Emeryville 1/10, 2/4, 5/15
  Escondido 7/20, 8/28
  Fallbrook 5/5
  Fernwood 12/26
  Fremont 12/18, 12/22
  Fresno 3/29, 4/30, 5/5, 9/17
  Fullerton 10/26
  Gardena 11/12 11/13
  Garden Grove 9/25
  Germantown 1/1
  Glendale 1/4, 1/6, 4/21, 5/4, 6/29, 8/18,
    11/5
  Hawthorne 8/23
  Hillsborough 6/6
  Hollywood 1/20, 6/2, 6/10, 8/5, 10/6
  Kernville 12/11
  La Canada 10/17
  Laguna Seca 10/20

Lennox 8/31
Little Shasta 6/14
Lockeford 4/20
Long Beach 1/15, 3/28, 6/38, 9/28, 11/29,
  12/28
Los Angeles 1/6, 1/7, 1/9, 1/11, 1/17, 1/22,
  2/4, 2/9, 2/22, 2/25, 3/3, 3/4, 3/5, 3/19,
  3/22, 3/25, 3/28, 3/30, 4/4, 4/6, 4/8, 4/16,
  4/27, 5/5, 5/10, 5/13, 5/20, 5/28, 5/30,
  6/4, 6/11, 6/13, 6/15, 6/29, 7/1, 7/5, 7/6,
  7/8, 7/16, 7/25, 7/31, 9/5, 9/10, 9/16,
  9/17, 9/19, 10/6, 10/8, 10/15, 10/16,
  10/17, 10/19, 10/20, 10/25, 11/8, 11/9,
  11/16, 11/19, 11/22 11/23, 12/4, 12/6,
  12/18, 12/27
Los Gatos 1/4, 3/27, 10/28
March Air Force Base 5/14
Mendocino 5/4
Menlo Park 3/5
Modesto 8/21
Mount Hamilton 9/13
Mount Wilson 7/16, 10/29
Muroc Dry Lake 12/27
Newhall 8/26
North Hollywood 5/8
Oakland 5/1, 5/2, 7/9, 8/4, 9/13, 9/14,
  10/12 10/18, 10/24
Ontario 6/28, 9/6, 11/12
Orange 3/20
Pacific Grove 8/4
Palm Springs 2/22, 3/12, 4/16, 5/29, 8/15
Palo Alto 6/3, 6/29, 11/11
Pasadena 1/1, 2/3, 2/24, 4/30, 6/5, 8/6,
  11/10, 12/2
Pebble Beach 4/20, 4/22, 8/25, 11/5
Pico Rivera 6/22
Porterville 10/26
Rancho Mirage 6/2, 6/20
Rancho Santa Fe 10/13
Redondo Beach 10/12
Redwood City 8/19
Richmond 9/21
Riverside 1/21, 1/27, 4/3, 5/24, 6/5, 8/17
  10/15, 11/20
Rogers Dry Lake 12/17
Rosamond 3/23
Sacramento 5/24, 10/21, 12/16
Salinas 1/13, 6/4
San Andreas 11/16
San Bernardino 8/16
San Diego 1/9, 1/30, 2/7, 2/9, 3/16, 3/17,
  4/16, 4/20, 5/5, 5/18, 5/29, 6/1, 7/24,
  8/4, 10/8, 11/4, 11/11
San Fernando 12/7
San Francisco 1/30, 2/1, 2/5, 2/9, 3/1, 3/6,
  3/22, 3/26, 3/29, 4/6, 4/16, 4/18, 5/12,
  5/22, 5/23, 5/24, 5/28, 6/9, 6/16, 6/20,
  6/27, 7/4, 7/6, 7/9, 7/17, 7/26, 7/29, 8/4,
  8/6, 8/7, 8/24, 8/30, 9/9, 9/12, 9/13, 9/24,
  10/19, 10/31, 11/13, 11/15, 11/26, 12/6,
  12/11, 12/18, 12/29
San Jose 4/8, 8/16, 8/29, 11/5
San Leandro 8/30
San Marino 1/6
San Mateo 5/7, 9/27, 10/4, 11/20, 11/29
San Pedro 8/29
Santa Ana 6/9, 6/25, 9/19
Santa Barbara 2/16, 10/31
Santa Fe Springs 2/16
Santa Monica 1/3, 1/23, 2/20, 2/27, 2/28,
  8/22, 10/14, 11/14, 11/16, 11/18
Santa Paula 6/27, 9/4
Santa Rosa 7/16
Sausalito 8/18
Sonoma 4/16
Southgate 2/7
South Laguna 2/28
South Laguna Beach 2/24
South Pasadena 3/31, 9/2
Stockton 5/22

Sunnyvale 1/19
Sunol 4/28
Thousand Oaks 12/8
Torrance 4/23, 5/2
Torrey Pines 7/20
Turlock 8/8
Upland 3/11
Vallejo 4/22, 8/4
Van Nuys 2/14, 5/11, 7/22, 7/23, 11/16
Victorville 9/14
Watsonville 10/4
Westminster 6/16
Whittier 3/1, 8/27, 10/21
Yosemite National Park 6/24, 8/23

Colorado
Boulder 12/3
Buena Vista 2/13
Buick 9/19
Canon City 12/6
Colorado Springs 1/9, 8/23, 8/26, 9/3, 10/29, 11/3
Crested Butte 1/25
Denver 3/1, 5/2, 6/15, 7/22 10/15, 11/18, 11/26
Fort Collins 12/7
Fruita 4/1
Lafayette 4/14
LaJunta 2/17
Leadville 9/23
Manitou Springs 8/3
Montrose 11/6
Pikes Peak 6/14, 7/17, 8/2, 8/12, 9/3, 9/6, 10/11, 11/2 12/7
Pueblo 3/1, 4/27, 6/12, 9/5
Vail 10/31

Connecticut
Bethel 4/1
Bridgeport 6/15, 6/17, 9/4, 11/25, 12/18
Bristol 3/22
Brooklyn 4/3
Colchester 7/18
Danbury 3/24, 10/30
Fairfield 3/23, 6/1, 10/10
Farmington 1/2
Greenwich 2/18, 2/28, 7/26, 8/15, 9/11
Hamden 3/20, 5/12, 6/7
Hartford 1/29, 4/10, 5/22, 5/29, 8/22, 9/4, 10/6, 10/16, 11/11, 11/30
Hebron 10/23
Kent 1/19
Manchester 6/10
Meriden 9/7
Middletown 11/2
New Britain 10/19
New Canaan 8/14, 10/31
New Haven 1/17, 1/26, 3/16, 5/19, 5/23, 6/8, 6/21, 7/7, 7/22 11/1, 11/22 12/9, 12/29
New London 7/24
New Milford 4/14
Norfolk 12/6
Norwalk 1/9, 1/23, 2/14, 2/17, 7/7, 10/17, 11/16
Old Saybrook 2/15
Plainville 11/23
Preston 8/6
Putnam 7/12
Sharon 3/22
Stamford 4/28, 9/18
Stonington 8/1
Stratford 10/6
Thompson 9/2
Torrington 3/18, 5/12
Wallingford 12/18
Watertown 10/1
Weston 9/30
Westport 4/29, 9/7
Winsted 2/27

Delaware
Dover 7/6, 9/15, 11/22
Guyencourt 9/15
Newport 9/13
Smyrna 12/28
Wilmington 1/15, 4/5, 5/19, 10/12 11/14, 12/22

District of Columbia
Washington 1/13, 1/17, 1/20, 1/24, 2/8, 2/10, 2/16, 2/22, 2/28, 3/2, 3/4, 3/10, 3/28, 4/5, 4/6, 4/15, 4/21, 5/9, 5/13, 5/19, 6/3, 7/4, 7/7, 7/13, 7/26, 7/27, 8/25, 8/31, 10/11, 10/30, 11/12 11/27, 12/30

Florida
Apopka 1/20
Bal Harbour 2/25
Bradenton 4/24, 12/25
Clearwater 1/16, 2/14
Clermont 3/15
Daytona Beach 1/2, 1/5, 1/21, 1/25, 1/27, 1/31, 2/2, 2/4, 2/5, 2/6, 2/7, 2/11, 2/12, 2/14, 2/15, 2/16, 2/17, 2/18, 2/19, 2/21, 2/22, 2/23, 2/24, 2/26, 3/2, 3/7, 3/8, 3/11, 3/13, 3/16, 3/20, 3/23, 3/28, 3/29, 4/7, 4/9, 4/10, 4/14, 4/20, 4/22, 4/23, 4/25, 4/27, 5/22, 6/15, 7/4, 8/28, 9/6, 9/7, 9/30, 10/11, 10/12 11/21, 12/14, 12/15
Delray Beach 4/23
Dunedin 11/11
Dunnellon 6/27
Fort Lauderdale 3/3, 4/4, 6/24
Hialeah Park 2/28
Hobe Sound 9/10
Hollywood 2/25
Jacksonville 2/4, 4/18, 4/20, 8/16, 9/17, 10/14, 10/26, 12/1, 12/7
Lakeland 2/11
Lake Worth 11/9
Marianna 7/25
Miami 2/6, 2/12, 3/11, 3/28, 4/12, 4/15, 4/20, 6/2, 6/10, 6/20, 7/15, 8/10, 8/13, 9/7, 11/21, 12/3, 12/17, 12/29
Miami Beach 1/13, 1/17, 2/7, 2/19, 2/21, 2/22, 2/24, 7/15, 9/17
Naples 9/22, 9/26
Nokomis 2/20
Oldsmar 7/10
Opa Locka 9/15
Orlando 3/25
Ormond Beach 1/7, 1/23, 1/26, 1/29, 5/23
Palm Beach 1/6, 2/28, 7/22, 12/10
Palm Beach Shores 12/8
Pensacola 6/28
Pompano Beach 3/8, 5/10
Ponte Vedra 12/15
Punta Gorda 8/29
Saint Petersburg 3/11, 3/26, 11/28
Sarasota 6/17, 7/31
Sebring 3/21, 3/25, 3/26, 4/1, 4/23, 7/9, 12/12, 12/31
Tequesta 2/28
West Palm Beach 2/6, 3/12
Winter Haven 9/4
Winter Park 11/16
Zephyrhills 5/23

Georgia
Americus 8/4
Atlanta 1/4, 2/15, 2/27, 3/27, 3/28, 4/5, 4/13, 4/26, 4/27, 6/8, 6/15, 7/6, 7/8, 7/10, 7/15, 7/21, 9/1, 9/2, 9/12, 9/21, 10/14, 11/19
Augusta 8/4
Bartow 10/17
Buena Vista 10/17
Columbus 11/11, 12/6
Cumming 10/8
Decatur 2/3

Eatonton 12/24
Jekyll Island 6/1
Marietta 2/28
McRae 6/17
Moultrie 1/2
Quitman 11/12
St. Simons Island 4/15
Savannah 1/29, 3/16, 3/19, 5/7, 11/14, 11/26, 11/27
Sea Island Beach 11/21
Thomasville 5/5
Tifton 1/25

Hawaii
Honolulu, Oahu 5/21, 7/26, 8/24
Wailuku, Maui 3/23

Idaho
Boise 1/17, 12/13
Moscow 2/15
Nampa 6/13
Payette 11/16
Weiser 3/5

Illinois
Albany 2/24
Alton 4/1, 10/23
Antioch 2/16
Aurora 8/17
Beecher City 9/9
Belleville 9/22
Berwyn 7/10
Bethalto 4/5
Bloomington 7/1
Buda 6/14
Cahokia 4/20, 6/29
Camp Point 5/20
Canton 5/19, 12/15
Carbondale 3/13
Chicago 1/8, 1/12, 1/15, 1/19, 1/20, 1/23, 1/27, 1/29, 2/3, 2/4, 2/8, 2/11, 2/13, 2/14, 2/15, 2/16, 2/19, 2/21, 2/22, 2/23, 2/28, 3/1, 3/9, 3/14, 3/23, 3/24, 3/25, 3/26, 3/31, 4/4, 4/3, 4/4, 4/6, 4/8, 4/15, 4/19, 4/20, 4/24, 4/26, 4/28, 5/1, 5/3, 5/4, 5/8, 5/10, 5/11, 5/20, 5/25, 5/26, 5/27, 5/30, 6/1, 6/2, 6/11, 6/12, 6/14, 6/15, 6/17, 6/19, 6/25, 6/26, 6/28, 6/30, 7/3, 7/10, 7/13, 7/14, 7/15, 7/16, 7/22, 7/23, 7/29, 7/31, 8/7, 8/8, 8/11, 8/13, 8/16, 8/17, 8/20, 8/21, 8/23, 8/25, 8/31, 9/1, 9/5, 9/7, 9/19, 9/21, 9/25, 9/26, 10/1, 10/2 10/8, 10/10, 10/11, 10/12, 10/17, 10/18, 10/22 11/1, 11/2, 11/4, 11/7, 11/10, 11/13, 11/15, 11/17, 11/25, 11/28, 11/29, 11/30, 12/8, 12/11, 12/13, 12/24
Chrisman 1/7, 2/1, 7/15, 8/31, 12/23
Crete 3/16
Crystal Lake 8/27
Danville 12/22
Decatur 3/25, 10/23
DeKalb 1/28, 4/15
DuQuoin 9/6, 10/10
East Moline 12/19
East Saint Louis 8/30
Edelstein 10/30
Elgin 7/14, 8/22, 8/25, 8/26, 8/27, 12/16
Elmhurst 12/30
Evanston 2/20, 2/27, 4/27, 7/13
Freeport 2/10, 5/8, 9/10, 11/26
Galesburg 4/9, 8/17
Georgetown 3/20
Glencoe 11/20
Goreville 8/15
Harvard 6/29
Harvey 6/14
Highland Park 9/1
Hinsdale 8/8
Hoffman 3/30

Isabel 7/8
Joliet 2/24, 5/1, 12/8
Litchfield 9/26
Mason City 4/5, 6/18
Melrose Park 3/17, 9/17
Moline 5/19, 6/1, 8/12 10/24, 11/8, 11/20, 11/29
Mount Sterling 9/6
Mount Vernon 7/8
Normal 3/13
Oak Park 1/15, 2/20, 12/13
Ottawa 1/6
Pana 2/19
Paris 3/20, 7/15, 11/24
Peoria 2/13, 7/28, 8/14, 9/8, 11/14
Peru 9/30
Quincy 1/2, 3/16
Rantoul 6/2
Ravenswood 2/28
Rochelle 5/2
Rockford 1/9, 1/12, 3/5, 4/11, 5/15, 6/1
Rock Island 3/8, 10/20
Secor 4/19
Skokie 2/20
Smithboro 9/9
Springfield 5/26, 8/20, 8/22, 9/30, 10/11, 10/28, 11/6, 12/22 12/23
Streator 2/1
Tinley Park 9/12 11/18
Walshville 5/5
Washburn 10/8
Washington 12/18
Waukegan 11/2
West Hallock 10/30
Wilmette 8/26
Winnetka 8/28
Woodland 10/23

Indiana
Anderson 1/4, 1/19, 9/24
Angola 3/24
Argos 12/9
Attica 8/8
Auburn 4/30, 5/14, 7/6, 8/24, 9/15, 9/28
Avon 10/11
Bloomington 12/25
Bridgeport 2/12
Brownsburg 11/18, 12/24
Cambridge City 12/5
Camby 1/18
Cloverland 10/2
Coal City 9/4
Columbus 2/3, 5/26, 11/24
Connersville 1/15, 2/8, 5/10, 8/26, 9/25, 10/2
Crothersville 10/5
Decatur 10/30, 12/18
Elkhart 10/15, 10/24, 12/18, 12/24
Evansville 1/15, 7/7
Floyds Knobs 12/13
Fort Wayne 2/19, 3/1, 5/2, 5/28, 6/1, 6/21, 7/15, 8/11, 9/28, 10/10, 11/27, 12/11
Goodland 6/13
Greenfield 10/12
Greensburg 7/12
Hagerstown 2/15, 3/30, 5/2, 8/17, 12/15
Hamilton 2/24
Hammond 1/21, 4/16
Hebron 9/18, 12/10
Honey Creek 12/27
Hudson 8/15
Indianapolis 1/1, 1/11, 1/12, 1/16, 1/18, 1/19, 1/27, 1/28, 2/5, 2/9, 2/26, 3/2, 3/13, 3/20, 3/28, 4/2, 4/3, 4/4, 4/18, 4/25, 4/29, 5/3, 5/7, 5/9, 5/10, 5/12, 5/14, 5/15, 5/16, 5/17, 5/18, 5/19, 5/20, 5/21, 5/22, 5/24, 5/28, 5/29, 5/30, 5/31, 6/1, 6/2, 6/3, 6/4, 6/14, 6/15, 6/17, 6/19, 6/20, 6/22, 6/26, 6/27, 6/30, 7/2, 7/6, 7/12, 7/15, 7/24, 7/26, 7/28, 7/30, 8/4, 8/6, 8/14, 8/15, 8/19, 8/25, 8/29, 9/2, 9/12, 9/15,

9/23, 9/25, 9/27, 10/3, 10/23, 10/27, 10/30, 11/3, 11/4, 11/11, 11/12 11/14, 11/26, 11/28, 12/1, 12/4, 12/5, 12/14, 12/17, 12/27
Kentland 2/19
Kokomo 2/28, 4/13, 5/25, 7/4, 7/20, 8/13, 10/3, 12/24
Ladoga 5/15
Lafayette 4/6, 8/17
LaPorte 1/1, 5/15
Lawrenceburg 3/12
Linton 3/10
Logansport 7/15, 8/25
Marion 7/3
Maywood 11/19
Middlebury 12/31
Mishawaka 1/20
Morgantown 6/30
Muncie 2/5, 2/19, 3/30, 7/13, 7/25, 8/1, 8/25
New Augusta 7/8
New Castle 12/12
North Manchester 5/5
North Vernon 10/9
Otwell 10/13
Peru 2/12, 5/3
Petersburg 2/9
Pierceton 6/5
Plainfield 9/7
Plymouth 6/22
Portland 6/23, 10/14, 10/21
Richmond 3/15, 5/3, 5/24, 6/22, 6/27, 7/8, 8/15, 8/26, 12/22
Rockville 4/4
Rosewood 5/16
Rushville 4/23, 5/20, 12/18
Russiaville 9/3
Shelbyville 10/31
South Bend 2/14, 2/16, 2/20, 3/30, 4/9, 4/17, 4/19, 5/3, 5/16, 6/6, 7/1, 7/13, 7/16, 8/11, 8/13, 8/15, 8/30, 10/31, 11/5, 11/27, 12/9, 12/12 12/17, 12/31
Spurgeon 11/8
Terre Haute 1/21, 2/12, 3/31, 5/30, 6/13
Union City 12/11
Valparaiso 7/16, 10/4, 12/1
Vincennes 12/6
Wabash 1/20
Washington 5/28, 8/21, 9/12
Whiting 11/6
Winchester 10/20
Winimac 3/13
Zionsville 5/31

Iowa
Burlington 11/12
Cedar Rapids 3/11, 4/14
Charles City 7/12
Clarion 1/6
Council Bluffs 2/19
Davenport 4/11
Des Moines 1/26, 2/19, 6/5, 6/26, 8/7, 8/16, 9/4, 9/11, 9/20
Fairfield 5/17
Fort Dodge 7/10
Grinnell 1/20
Harlan 11/14
Iowa City 3/7
Jesup 2/10
Keokuk 11/30
Mapleton 12/4
Marion 1/27
Marshalltown 3/4
Mason City 3/14, 3/24, 5/6, 11/13, 12/18
Mount Pleasant 3/24
Muscatine 8/11
Northwood 8/1
Randall 12/12
Sioux City 7/4
Washington 8/13
Waterloo 8/20

West Burlington 10/24

Kansas
Bazaar 3/31
Beloit 1/10
Coffeyville 3/12
El Dorado 1/20
Ellis 6/6
Fairfax 7/18
Great Bend 1/13
Horton 8/31
Humboldt 3/20
Lawrence 1/11
Lincoln 11/27
Marysville 4/8
Meriden 5/30
Parsons 4/19
Pittsburg 6/17
Russell 8/1
Salina 5/3
Sedan 8/15
Topeka 5/12, 5/29, 8/13, 11/6
Wamego 4/2 10/17
Wellington 7/19
Wichita 1/20, 2/20, 3/6, 9/12 12/3

Kentucky
Bowling Green 4/28, 7/2, 7/31, 9/2
Covington 6/21
Georgetown 9/12 10/26, 11/27
Hickman 3/16
Hodgenville 2/12
Hopkinsville 5/15
Lexington 5/1
Louisville 2/21, 3/2, 3/9, 3/20, 9/23, 11/10
McKinney 3/27
Owensboro 1/28, 2/5, 4/30, 5/27
Pleasureville 5/13
Scott County 2/15
Winchester 11/21

Louisiana
Baton Rouge 6/11, 8/2
Castor 6/17
Metairie 2/8
New Orleans 2/12, 2/21, 4/25
Norwood 9/26
Plaindealing 5/21
Ruston 5/17
Shreveport 10/22 12/31
Slidell 4/16
Trichel 9/10
Velie 7/24

Maine
Auburn 1/26
Bangor 10/11
Belfast 1/20
East Pittston 4/18
Kingfield 4/2, 6/1
Newburgh 5/24
Parkman 6/20
Portland 8/30
Rockland 2/26
Rockport 10/11
Sanford 1/24
Thomaston 7/17
Washburn 5/7
West Falmouth 5/22
York Harbor 9/20

Maryland
Abingdon 8/4
Arlington 6/4
Baltimore 2/1, 2/2, 2/3, 3/30, 5/16, 6/12, 7/23, 8/3, 8/7, 9/16, 9/22, 9/25, 11/18, 12/14
Bel Air 10/14
Bethesda 6/22, 8/11
Branchville 11/12
Camp Holabird 9/23

Centreville 10/14
Chevy Chase 12/14
Cumberland 8/28
Derwood 9/15
Hagerstown 12/29
Iron Hill 6/21
Laurel 7/11
Silver Spring 8/14
Worton 3/8

Massachusetts
Amesbury 3/6, 8/24
Ashland 3/6
Athol 9/13
Boston 1/1, 1/9, 1/21, 1/25, 2/13, 2/15,
    2/18, 2/20, 2/26, 2/27, 3/1, 3/3, 3/14,
    3/24, 3/31, 4/4, 4/9, 4/15, 4/30, 5/20,
    5/24, 5/30, 6/1, 6/10, 7/2, 7/25, 7/26,
    7/27, 8/5, 9/11, 9/18, 10/7, 10/27, 10/30,
    11/16, 12/7, 12/8, 12/24
Brookhaven 12/28
Brookline 6/10, 9/1
Cambridge 4/16, 9/16, 11/5, 11/29
Chatham 1/7
Chicopee Falls 5/18, 12/30
Cohasset 8/10
Concord 1/21
Easton 1/19
Fall River 2/17
Fitchburg 11/29
Gloucester 12/10
Grafton 12/20
Great Barrington 3/31
Haverhill 5/25
Hingham 8/24
Hyde Park 11/4
Ipswich 11/26
Jamaica Plain 11/18
Lawrence 6/30
Lenox 8/27
Lincoln 3/13
Longmeadow 11/22
Lowell 3/30, 9/7
Lynn 3/9, 5/21, 8/17
Malden 2/27
Marston's Mills 5/12, 6/29
Maynard 5/25
Merrimac 3/10
Middleborough 6/11, 11/18
Milford 12/20
Milton 5/6, 7/12
Mount Tom 12/1
Nantucket 5/16
New Bedford 4/1, 11/1, 12/13
New Braintree 4/21
Newburyport 7/31
Newton 4/1, 6/4, 8/18, 10/2
Northfield 7/10
Orange 8/28
Pittsfield 1/14, 3/23, 5/3, 9/1
Rockport 10/2
Salem 6/25, 10/14
Somerville 5/25, 7/3, 11/7
South Weymouth 9/4
Springfield 1/18, 2/12, 2/17, 3/5, 4/19,
    5/14, 5/28, 5/30, 6/18, 8/19, 9/21, 10/18,
    10/28, 11/22
Taunton 3/24, 7/26
Tewksbury 4/24
Waban 5/31
Walpole 12/13
Waltham 4/16, 7/14, 10/30
Warren 7/2, 8/26
Watertown 3/2, 3/19, 4/13
Wayland 10/7
Wellesley Hills 4/2
Wenham 7/31
Westboro 2/4
Westfield 1/19, 3/8, 8/1
West Newton 3/13

Weymouth 9/4
Whitman 10/16
Winchester 3/10, 10/15
Winthrop 7/9
Worcester 2/9, 4/6, 5/21, 7/11, 10/23, 11/7, 11/14

Michigan
Adrian 4/27
Algonac 6/28
Almont 1/7
Ann Arbor 1/17, 3/25, 4/7, 4/19, 5/29, 8/1,
    9/24, 12/14
Battle Creek 1/4, 1/26, 8/13
Bay City 3/19, 3/31, 4/17, 10/13, 11/22
Beaver Island 6/2
Bellaire 7/22
Benton Harbor 11/6
Berlin 9/17
Big Rapids 8/17, 11/26
Birch Run 9/6
Birmingham 6/7, 8/26, 11/13, 12/22 12/25,
    12/30
Bloomfield Hills 4/29, 5/25, 7/26, 9/10
Bridgeport 12/29
Brighton 10/14
Britton 1/9
Brooklyn 5/26, 6/15
Burr Oak 11/7
Burton 10/28
Cadillac 6/12, 8/3, 12/25
Cambria Mills 6/12
Capac 9/21
Cassopolis 12/8
Cheboygan 7/27
Chelsea 6/16
Coldwater 2/20
Cranbrook 6/21
Dansville 2/15
Davidson 7/23
Dearborn 1/6, 1/15, 1/16, 1/28, 2/7, 2/26,
    3/2, 3/29, 4/7, 4/9, 4/29, 5/7, 5/16, 6/16,
    9/3, 9/26, 9/28, 10/2, 10/21, 10/24, 11/4,
    11/9, 11/15, 12/2, 12/5, 12/6, 12/14, 12/15
Decatur 10/29
Detroit 1/1, 1/2, 1/3, 1/4, 1/5, 1/6, 1/9,
    1/10, 1/11, 1/12, 1/13, 1/17, 1/18, 1/19,
    1/20, 1/21, 1/24, 1/25, 1/26, 1/28, 1/30,
    2/1, 2/2, 2/3, 2/4, 2/5, 2/6, 2/9, 2/10,
    2/11, 2/12, 2/15, 2/16, 2/17, 2/20, 2/21,
    2/23, 2/24, 2/27, 2/28, 3/1, 3/2, 3/3, 3/5,
    3/6, 3/9, 3/10, 3/14, 3/15, 3/16, 3/18,
    3/23, 3/24, 3/26, 3/27, 3/31, 4/1, 4/3, 4/4,
    4/6, 4/7, 4/9, 4/10, 4/11, 4/13, 4/15, 4/19,
    4/20, 4/21, 4/25, 4/27, 4/29, 5/3, 5/6, 5/8,
    5/9, 5/13, 5/16, 5/19, 5/22, 5/23, 5/24,
    5/27, 5/30, 5/31, 6/1, 6/4, 6/5, 6/6, 6/7,
    6/12, 6/16, 6/20, 6/22, 6/25, 6/26, 6/28,
    7/1, 7/2, 7/3, 7/6, 7/9, 7/12, 7/14, 7/15,
    7/20, 7/22, 7/23, 7/28, 7/29, 8/1, 8/2, 8/5,
    8/6, 8/7, 8/8, 8/10, 8/15, 8/18, 8/20, 8/22,
    8/23, 8/25, 8/26, 8/27, 8/28, 8/29, 9/1,
    9/2, 9/3, 9/4, 9/5, 9/7, 9/8, 9/9, 9/11,
    9/14, 9/15, 9/16, 9/17, 9/18, 9/19, 9/20,
    9/21, 9/22, 9/23, 9/24, 9/25, 9/26,
    9/29, 10/1, 10/3, 10/5, 10/9, 10/10, 10/10,
    10/11, 10/13, 10/14, 10/15, 10/17, 10/18,
    10/19, 10/20, 10/22 10/23, 10/26, 10/27,
    10/28, 10/29, 10/31, 11/1, 11/5, 11/6, 11/7,
    11/8, 11/9, 11/10, 11/11, 11/12, 11/13,
    11/15, 11/16, 11/18, 11/21, 11/22, 11/23,
    11/27, 12/1, 12/2 12/4, 12/7, 12/8, 12/9,
    12/10, 12/15, 12/16, 12/17, 12/20, 12/21,
    12/22 12/23, 12/25, 12/26, 12/27, 12/30
Dowagiac 8/28
East Detroit 10/7
East Lansing 8/22
Farmington 8/19
Flat Rock 11/30
Flint 1/19, 1/22, 2/4, 2/20, 2/28, 3/18,
    4/15, 4/24, 5/12, 5/17, 5/25, 5/26, 6/17,

6/18, 6/22, 6/30, 7/1, 7/4, 7/9, 7/27, 7/31,
    8/1, 8/13, 8/14, 9/3, 9/11, 9/19, 9/28,
    10/26, 10/30, 11/1, 11/3, 11/13, 11/22,
    12/9, 12/17, 12/28
Fordson 2/15, 12/24
Frankenmuth 3/18
Fraser 12/15
Grand Blanc 12/22
Grand Rapids 1/6, 1/8, 1/17, 2/9, 2/11,
    3/8, 3/21, 3/31, 4/1, 4/20, 5/9, 6/2, 6/27,
    7/7, 7/11, 7/18, 10/10, 12/14
Greenfield 4/11, 10/15
Greenfield Village 6/25
Grosse Pointe 4/21, 4/29, 6/2, 6/11, 6/28,
    8/8, 9/15, 10/10, 10/25, 11/23
Grosse Pointe Farms 10/3, 11/6, 11/12
Grosse Pointe Park 7/14, 9/15, 12/15
Grosse Pointe Shores 5/26, 8/16
Grosse Pointe Woods 3/4
Hamtramck 1/4, 9/21, 11/28
Hancock 8/5
Harrison 10/29
Hastings 8/5, 8/25
Highland 11/7
Highland Park 1/1, 1/21, 6/11, 7/10, 10/5, 10/7
Hillsdale 8/25
Holland 3/27, 4/8
Imlay City 1/5, 4/23
Inkster 2/2
Ionia 10/30
Irish Hills 10/13
Ironwood 11/17
Ishpeming 2/26, 5/19, 12/20
Jackson 1/18, 2/24, 3/26, 5/14, 5/22, 7/19,
    8/6, 8/17, 10/4, 10/31, 11/22 12/23
Kalamazoo 4/24, 5/8, 6/27, 7/9, 7/1, 7/12,
    7/22, 8/6, 8/7, 9/15
Kingsford 1/24
Lake St. Clair 1/12, 2/17
Lansing 1/25, 1/26, 2/18, 2/20, 2/23, 3/9,
    3/11, 3/22, 5/4, 5/13, 5/14, 5/18, 6/5,
    7/15, 7/25, 7/31, 8/11, 8/16, 8/21, 8/26,
    9/4, 11/14, 12/17, 12/18, 12/20
Lapeer 7/13
Laurium 7/18
LeRoy 2/14
Leslie 4/30
Lexington 8/14
Livingston County 9/25
Livonia 6/25, 8/12 11/4
Ludington 1/4, 7/13
Mackinac Island 8/28
Marion 12/28
Marne 9/12, 9/17
Mendon 1/7, 5/2
Metamora 10/6
Midland 7/3, 9/29, 10/29
Milford 7/17
Monroe 8/16
Mount Clemens 3/21, 6/12, 7/10, 8/1
Muir 4/23
Muskegon 4/18, 4/29, 6/22, 8/1, 8/21,
    11/17, 12/3
Niles 5/17, 10/25, 11/16
North Dorr 12/28
Onaway 9/8
Oscoda 4/7
Otsego 12/16
Oxford 1/30
Pellston 5/9
Petoskey 2/26
Petrieville 8/15
Pinckney 6/6
Plainwell 5/13
Plymouth 3/8
Pontiac 1/3, 1/5, 2/10, 3/11, 3/28, 4/1, 4/6,
    4/18, 4/24, 5/9, 6/1, 6/18, 7/5, 7/13, 8/1,
    8/27, 8/28, 10/6, 10/26, 11/3
Portage 6/3
Port Huron 8/22, 8/25, 11/3

Rochester 5/3, 12/2
Roseville 12/11
Royal Oak 1/6, 1/22, 6/14, 7/3, 11/27
Saginaw 1/25, 4/12, 4/21, 5/12, 5/29, 7/1,
   7/6, 7/16, 8/3, 9/15, 11/16, 12/2
Saint Clair 7/5
Saint Clair Shores 6/19
Saline 12/24
Saint Joseph 12/16
Saranac 3/24, 10/1, 12/29
Sault Sainte Marie 3/30
Southfield 3/2, 7/21
Springwells 12/24
Sturgis 9/27
Three Oaks 10/4
Three Rivers 9/9
Trenton 11/10
Troy 10/13, 10/14
Utica 6/14, 6/22, 8/5, 9/2 10/31, 12/7
Vanderbilt 5/1
Warren 5/16, 5/23, 6/27, 8/15
Waterford 11/26
Wayne 5/23
Whittemore 9/21
Willow Run 1/31, 3/28, 5/29, 6/22, 6/23,
   6/28, 9/21, 11/1, 11/4, 11/10, 12/3
Wixom 6/9, 7/11
Ypsilanti 2/27, 4/9, 7/10, 11/19, 12/26

Minnesota
   Altura 12/21
   Castle Rock 12/10
   Chisholm 1/31
   Edina 7/27
   Faribault 10/22
   Fort Snelling 9/4
   Frazee 4/4
   Hibbing 7/23
   Minneapolis 3/1, 1/12, 3/14, 3/29, 6/7,
      6/18, 7/11, 7/31, 8/20, 9/5, 9/14, 9/22,
      9/30, 11/15, 11/23, 12/18, 12/22
   Mora 2/25
   Owatonna 10/11
   Parkers Prairie 7/2
   Pipestone 9/4
   Rochester 4/14, 6/24, 6/30
   Rogers 4/24
   Saint Cloud 9/29
   Saint Paul 4/16, 8/24, 9/30
   Virginia 6/20

Mississippi
   Edwards 9/12
   Jackson 1/17
   Mayersville 2/23
   Purvis 11/15
   Winona 5/31
   Yazoo City 11/22

Missouri
   Cape Girardeau 6/3, 8/6
   Centerview 2/11
   Clinton 4/11
   Excelsior Springs 4/7
   Fenton 5/29, 8/14
   Hannibal 6/26
   Hatfield 10/19
   Kansas City 2/29, 3/6, 4/18, 5/3, 5/12, 5/14,
      5/29, 6/14, 7/12, 7/20, 7/30, 8/1, 8/7, 9/3,
      9/17, 10/9, 10/29
   Kirkwood 2/5
   Knob Noster 5/4
   Lebanon 2/24
   Macon 2/12, 5/17, 12/30
   Maplewood 9/5
   Maryville 10/11
   Mountain Grove 12/7
   Paris 12/16
   Piedmont 11/24
   Saint Joseph 5/30, 6/1

Saint Louis 1/10, 2/3, 2/16, 3/4, 3/10, 3/13,
   3/15, 4/1, 4/5, 4/15, 4/27, 5/10, 5/26, 6/25,
   7/17, 7/25, 7/26, 7/31, 8/9, 8/10, 8/13,
   8/28, 9/11, 9/26, 10/8, 10/26, 11/10, 12/15,
   12/19, 12/28
Sedalia 8/6
Thayer 5/31
Warrensburg 7/20
Webster Groves 1/8
Wentzville 10/29

Montana
   Glacier National Park 7/11, 7/19
   Great Falls 4/16
   Miles City 1/18
   Ronan 10/3
   Sidney 10/15

Nebraska
   Ainsworth 12/22
   Angus 2/16
   Central City 9/19
   Columbus 11/2
   Elm Creek 3/28
   Havelock 1/10
   Lincoln 1/10, 4/1, 7/4, 12/1
   Lodgepole 12/31
   Nebraska City 7/22
   Ogallala 7/8
   Omaha 3/28, 6/10, 7/5, 9/2
   Shelby 3/4
   Springfield 8/6

Nevada
   Black Rock Desert 10/4
   Carson City 5/26, 10/14
   Jean 7/28
   Las Vegas 2/2 10/7, 10/17, 11/14, 12/1
   Reno 1/2, 5/14
   Sparks 2/24, 6/27, 7/8, 9/29

New Hampshire
   Boscawen 2/9
   Bretton Woods 7/12, 7/28
   Center Conway 4/9
   Dover 7/26
   Hanover 6/27
   Hinsdale 6/27
   Laconia 8/2
   Lebanon 4/19
   London 8/27
   Manchester 8/29, 10/13, 12/4
   Mount Washington 7/5, 7/11, 7/12, 7/20,
      8/25, 8/31
   Nashua 6/17, 11/4
   Oxford 4/1
   Pelham 5/28
   Pittsfield 9/1
   Salem 10/31
   Springfield 2/28
   West Swanzey 2/2
   Winchester 6/21

New Jersey
   Amatol 5/1
   Asbury Park 3/13, 9/3, 10/16
   Atlantic City 3/9, 3/18, 3/23, 5/1, 7/1, 8/23,
      11/6, 11/14
   Bayonne 7/5, 7/7, 8/24, 10/28, 11/3
   Berkeley Heights 12/29
   Boonton 12/27
   Califon 12/15
   Camden 6/6, 7/14, 12/30
   Cranford 5/16
   East Orange 4/26, 7/25
   Edgewater 4/8
   Elizabeth 1/10, 2/11, 6/9, 6/26
   Englewood Cliffs 10/25
   Flemington 12/5
   Garfield 11/10

Grenloch 12/30
Guttenberg 9/18
Hackensack 11/11
Hoboken 7/4, 8/8, 8/21, 12/4, 12/13
Jersey City 2/13, 6/25, 8/18, 11/13, 11/28
Kearney 10/1
Linden 12/23
Lyndhurst 9/14
Mahwah 6/20, 11/15
Middletown 4/29
Millville 12/8
Monmouth Beach 8/30
Montclair 3/27, 5/6
Morristown 9/17
Newark 2/5, 2/10, 3/3, 5/10, 5/29, 6/2,
   6/26, 8/10, 9/13, 9/16, 9/20, 10/7, 11/6,
   11/10, 11/15, 11/19, 12/16
New Brunswick 1/24, 5/23, 7/7, 12/17
Old Bridge 5/6
Orange 3/14, 5/24, 5/28, 7/18, 10/31
Palmyra 6/12
Passaic 9/20
Phillipsburg 5/16
Plainfield 2/8, 4/2, 4/25, 8/16, 12/23, 12/29
Princeton 2/1, 2/19, 11/1, 11/2
Ringwood Manor 6/20
River Edge 5/6
Riverton 8/13
Roseland 4/15
Salem 11/3
Short Hills 10/14
Somerville 2/13
Summit 3/18, 10/29
Teaneck 1/9, 6/13
Trenton 1/1, 3/30, 4/19, 7/5, 7/13, 9/28, 10/7
Trenton Junction 1/16
Wanamassa 7/31
Wayne 4/15
Weehawken 3/7, 12/21
Westfield 10/28
West Orange 10/18

New Mexico
   Albuquerque 1/5, 2/3, 2/20, 3/19, 4/19,
      5/29, 8/30, 12/24
   Silver City 3/10, 9/20

New York
   Albany 6/12 12/13
   Alexandria Bay 8/10, 8/15
   Attica 4/23
   Auburn 2/11
   Babylon 3/4, 8/22
   Batavia 8/9
   Bath 11/1
   Bayshore 8/15
   Beacon 2/8, 6/2
   Boston Corners 4/22
   Brentwood 4/22
   Briarcliff 6/23, 11/11
   Bridgehampton 6/11, 9/30, 10/17
   Brighton Beach 8/27, 9/5, 9/7
   Brockport 3/1, 5/1
   Bronx 5/20, 7/4, 9/20, 10/13, 12/15
   Bronxville 1/11, 2/18
   Brooklyn 1/7, 2/15, 3/19, 5/17, 5/24, 6/2,
      6/3, 6/16, 7/1, 7/27, 8/1, 8/28, 9/2 10/9,
      10/15, 10/25, 11/16, 11/18, 11/20, 12/18,
      12/28
   Buffalo 1/23, 1/31, 2/1, 2/28, 3/9, 3/10,
      4/3, 4/5, 4/6, 4/14, 4/16, 5/1, 5/22, 5/23,
      6/3, 6/9, 6/21, 6/25, 7/2, 7/7, 7/9, 7/12,
      7/16, 7/23, 7/24, 8/10, 8/11, 8/12, 8/26,
      9/1, 9/7, 9/8, 9/13, 9/20, 10/2 10/15,
      10/21, 11/24, 12/5
   Canajoharie 10/17
   Canandaigua 10/25
   Canastota 8/23
   Caneadea 9/28
   Central Islip 4/22

Chelsea-on-Hudson 9/18
Chemung 2/27
Clarkson 9/14
College Point 1/21
Conewango Valley 3/14
Cortland 3/29, 8/7, 9/1, 10/1, 10/12
Croton on the Hudson 6/11, 12/23
Dansville 7/8, 11/11
Delhi 3/19
East Aurora 7/19
Easton 6/2
Elbridge 11/12
Elmira 1/11, 3/10, 4/18, 8/4, 10/23, 11/2
Flushing 10/6
Forest Hills 4/29, 8/14
Fort Edward 9/16
Georgetown 4/13
Gerry 11/7
Glen Cove 5/12, 7/24, 9/21, 12/15
Glenham 4/4
Goshen 9/17, 9/19
Gratwick 9/21
Great Neck 8/18
Greenport 7/17
Hamden 8/24
Hamilton 6/10
Hammond 10/19
Hammondsport 5/21
Harrison 5/15
Hewlett Harbor 3/29
Homer 3/26
Hornell 12/10
Hudson 8/15
Irvington-on-Hudson 5/30
Ithaca 11/21
Jamaica 11/17
Jamestown 5/2, 8/25
Johnson City 10/24
Keene 9/20
Kings 9/6
Kingston 8/15
Lake George 9/4
Larchmont 6/23
Liberty 1/7
Lido Beach 7/16
Little Falls 7/2 11/24
Liverpool 3/29
Lockport 3/19, 12/9
Long Island City 1/1, 1/10, 3/20, 4/1, 9/29, 10/19
Manhasset 10/10, 12/21
Manhattan 2/8
Mattituck 11/3
Middletown 9/12
Millbrook 11/29
Mineola 9/25
Montauk 7/9
Mount Kisco 5/17
Mount Vernon 1/23, 2/25, 10/31
Newark 11/15
Newburgh 12/19
New Castle 6/16
Newport 11/21
New Rochelle 4/9, 4/28, 5/6, 5/24, 8/15, 9/24, 10/18
New York City 1/1, 1/2, 1/3, 1/4, 1/5, 1/6, 1/7, 1/8, 1/9, 1/10, 1/11, 1/13, 1/14, 1/15, 1/16, 1/17, 1/18, 1/19, 1/20, 1/21, 1/22, 1/23, 1/25, 1/26, 1/29, 1/30, 1/31, 2/4, 2/6, 2/8, 2/12, 2/13, 2/14, 2/16, 2/17, 2/19, 2/22, 2/27, 3/1, 3/3, 3/4, 3/5, 3/7, 3/9, 3/10, 3/13, 3/17, 3/18, 3/25, 3/26, 3/27, 3/29, 3/30, 4/2, 4/3, 4/4, 4/5, 4/6, 4/7, 4/8, 4/13, 4/14, 4/15, 4/16, 4/17, 4/18, 4/21, 4/22, 4/23, 4/25, 4/29, 4/30, 5/1, 5/4, 5/5, 5/6, 5/8, 5/10, 5/11, 5/12, 5/14, 5/15, 5/17, 5/18, 5/20, 5/25, 5/26, 5/28, 5/30, 5/31, 6/1, 6/2, 6/3, 6/6, 6/7, 6/8, 6/9, 6/11, 6/12, 6/13, 6/15, 6/16, 6/17, 6/18, 6/19, 6/20, 6/21, 6/23, 6/27, 6/28, 6/29, 6/30, 7/1, 7/2, 7/3, 7/4, 7/5, 7/6, 7/7, 7/8, 7/10, 7/11, 7/12, 7/13, 7/17,
7/22, 7/24, 7/25, 7/26, 7/28, 7/30, 7/31, 8/2, 8/7, 8/12, 8/16, 8/20, 8/21, 8/24, 8/25, 9/1, 9/5, 9/11, 9/13, 9/15, 9/16, 9/17, 9/19, 9/20, 9/21, 9/24, 9/28, 9/30, 10/5, 10/6, 10/8, 10/11, 10/12 10/14, 10/20, 10/22 10/24, 10/24, 10/25, 10/26, 10/31, 11/1, 11/2 11/3, 11/4, 11/9, 11/11, 11/12, 11/13, 11/18, 11/19, 11/24, 11/26, 11/27, 12/1, 12/2 12/5, 12/6, 12/11, 12/12, 12/15, 12/19, 12/20, 12/25, 12/29, 12/30
North Tonawanda 1/29, 7/20, 12/5
Nunda 6/12 12/11
Ogdensburg 6/17, 11/9
Orchard Park 10/13
Peekskill 9/9
Plattsburgh 2/3, 5/25
Port Jefferson 4/13
Port Jervis 4/14
Port Morris 7/26
Port Richmond 12/1
Poughkeepsie 1/3, 7/17, 7/24, 8/1, 12/20
Queens 11/13
Ravena 10/23
Rensselaer 4/8
Richford 5/31, 7/8
Ripley 11/4
Riverdale 8/26
Rochester 1/15, 1/17, 4/22, 4/27, 5/17, 6/17, 7/7, 7/31, 8/9, 11/21, 11/26, 12/7, 12/12 12/19
Rockville Center 6/24
Rye 5/27, 7/7, 9/25, 10/31
Salamanca 5/27
Saratoga Springs 7/9, 7/28, 10/20
Sayville 6/14
Scarborough 1/21, 6/4
Scarsdale 12/11, 12/16
Schenectady 3/14, 9/7
Schuyler Falls 1/11
Seaford 6/26
Shelter Island 6/10
Sodus 5/28
Southampton 2/8, 4/23, 8/1, 8/27, 9/1, 11/4
Springfield 3/4, 12/30
Springville 7/4
Sprout Brook 5/9
Starkey 11/28
Staten Island 8/4, 12/4
Summitville 3/6
Syracuse 1/31, 2/11, 3/11, 3/21, 3/24, 4/16, 4/19, 6/20, 6/25, 6/30, 7/11, 9/4, 9/12, 9/15, 10/21, 10/22 10/28, 12/7
Tarrytown 6/24, 7/4, 10/26
Troy 7/12 10/14, 11/26, 12/6
Utica 3/16, 6/9, 9/11, 10/17
Waterloo 7/17, 10/6
Watkins Glen 7/12, 8/11, 9/19, 9/22, 9/23, 10/2, 10/4, 10/6, 10/7
Wayland 12/23
Wellsville 3/30
Westbury 7/5, 7/19, 10/12
Westchester 4/24
Westernville 7/23
Westfield 2/3
Whitestone 8/14
Williams Grove 7/29
Williamstown 12/11
Wilson 11/26
Yaphank 10/8
Yonkers 5/16, 5/30, 7/24, 7/25, 7/28, 10/29, 11/23

North Carolina
Asheville 4/8, 4/21
Beaufort 3/29
Canton 4/22
Catawba 8/1
Charlotte 4/2, 5/22, 5/24, 5/25, 6/14, 6/19, 7/2, 10/27, 11/11
Concord 1/12 10/6
Conover 11/26

Ferguson 10/12
Gastonia 11/14
Hickory 8/14
High Point 12/5,
Hudson 12/2
Kannapolis 4/29, 12/23
Laurinburg 1/25, 11/4
Lawsonville 11/17
Level Cross 7/2
Monroe 4/3
Mooresville 9/30
Morehead City 2/9
Newton 2/27, 10/12
Old Fort 5/2
Oteen 10/8
Oxford 12/8, 12/23
Pinehurst 3/10
Raleigh 4/7, 7/4, 9/19, 9/30
Randleman 3/14, 6/2
Ronda 6/28
Taylorsville 1/10
Timmonsville 3/27
Vaughndale 5/22
Washington 1/26
Waynesville 2/22

North Dakota
Bismarck 4/8, 7/30, 8/8, 8/20
Carrington 8/11
Fargo 4/19
Garrison 12/16
Grafton 5/5
Grand Forks 1/18, 6/28, 12/3
Malcolm 9/14
Neche 8/22
Park River 4/26
Sharon 3/17
Souris 1/12, 5/15
Upham 3/10
Valley City 3/12
Zap 11/10

Ohio
Akron 2/1, 2/3, 2/12, 2/14, 4/5, 4/9, 4/27, 4/29, 5/11, 5/15, 5/17, 6/1, 6/5, 6/22, 7/3, 8/3, 8/11, 8/19, 8/21, 8/23, 9/4, 9/6, 10/24, 11/26, 11/28
Ansonia 9/12
Ashland 4/1, 5/26
Ashtabula 4/17, 8/16
Avon Lake 9/12
Bedford 5/22
Bellebrook 1/17
Bellefontaine 3/19, 6/24
Bellevue 6/21, 10/23
Berea 7/19, 10/30, 11/6
Bourneville 1/27
Bowling Green 8/24, 12/13, 12/24
Brooklyn 12/23
Brookville 10/8
Canton 6/21, 8/22 12/16
Carrolton 1/2
Centerburg 3/1
Champaign 5/31
Chillicothe 6/27
Cincinnati 1/4, 1/26, 1/29, 2/8, 2/27, 3/28, 5/11, 5/16, 5/24, 6/14, 6/15, 7/3, 9/4, 9/12, 9/18, 11/2 12/23, 12/27
Circleville 2/19
Cleveland 1/10, 1/15, 1/26, 2/13, 2/17, 2/18, 2/19, 2/20, 2/23, 2/26, 3/1, 3/3, 3/4, 3/10, 3/14, 3/17, 3/19, 3/20, 3/28, 4/5, 4/6, 4/13, 4/26, 4/30, 5/1, 5/10, 5/11, 5/12, 5/13, 5/16, 5/18, 5/25, 5/30, 6/8, 6/11, 6/13, 6/15, 6/30, 7/1, 7/2, 7/5, 7/10, 7/11, 8/4, 8/5, 8/24, 9/1, 9/3, 9/4, 9/8, 9/17, 9/29, 10/3, 10/4, 10/11, 10/17, 10/19, 10/31, 11/1, 11/6, 11/7, 11/17, 11/20, 11/24, 12/5, 12/14, 12/23, 12/31
Cleveland Heights 5/8, 9/2 11/12
Clyde 11/25

Columbia Station 1/14
Columbus 1/14, 2/13, 2/19, 4/12, 5/4, 5/8,
    5/26, 6/9, 6/19, 6/27, 6/28, 7/2, 7/12,
    7/13, 8/10, 8/14, 9/18, 9/30, 10/8
Copley 8/19
Cygnet 5/31
Dayton 1/26, 2/1, 3/15, 3/25, 3/29, 4/20,
    4/29, 5/12, 7/1, 7/21, 7/25, 8/1, 8/27,
    8/31, 9/4, 9/6, 10/3, 10/21, 11/11, 11/25,
    11/27, 12/29
Defiance 11/3
Delaware 3/18
Dixon 2/26
Dover 7/27
East Palestine 1/10, 3/6, 6/9
Edgerton 2/9
Elmore 11/25
Elyria 1/23, 5/31
Findlay 4/6, 7/19
Fredericktown 10/12
Gates Mills 4/27
Geneva 6/3
Georgetown 4/10
Granville 3/12
Greene 12/1
Greenfield 9/23
Greenwich 8/17
Independence 1/4
Ironton 2/19
Jefferson 10/2
Kent 4/5, 4/7, 9/14
Lakewood 5/30, 7/27, 8/25, 10/8
Leesburg 10/21
Lexington 8/17
Lima 7/15, 7/27, 12/19
London 1/5
Lorain 5/18, 10/10
Lordstown 6/1, 10/1
Loudonville 8/29
Madison 12/24
Mansfield 5/8, 12/6
Marietta 6/22, 9/6
Marion 12/26
Marysville 9/19, 11/1
Medina 1/10
Miamisburg 5/20
Miamiville 7/17
Milan 2/11
Minerva 7/18
Mount Gilead 4/13
Mount Vernon 5/6
New Lexington 9/20
Norwalk 2/23, 9/21, 10/19, 12/7
Norwood 2/2, 8/11
Ottawa 9/28
Painesville 8/20, 9/22
Penfield 9/18
Perrysburg 5/4
Peru 1/2
Piney Fork 12/24
Piqua 1/15, 3/19, 12/13
Reynoldsburg 7/10
St. Marys 1/10
Salem 3/6
Sandusky 1/2, 2/16, 5/11, 7/10
Shaker Heights 2/20
Sharon 6/8
Springfield 1/11, 2/25, 5/28, 7/15, 10/2, 10/30
Tallmadge 11/18
Thompson 11/23
Tipp City 6/7
Toledo 1/9, 1/10, 2/6, 2/9, 2/10, 2/27, 4/14,
    4/18, 4/23, 4/25, 4/28, 5/17, 5/27, 5/29,
    5/30, 6/13, 7/8, 7/13, 7/19, 8/8, 8/9, 8/10,
    8/21, 9/30, 10/23, 11/5, 11/16, 11/23, 12/9,
    12/16, 12/17
Uhrichsville 9/29
Van Wert 2/10
Warren 1/3, 5/31, 6/5, 7/30, 9/5, 9/10, 9/14,
    10/10, 11/3, 11/5, 11/6, 11/11, 11/15
Wauseon 6/3

Wellsville 2/14
Western Star 10/6
West Milton 9/6
West Unity 8/6
Williamsport 7/9
Willoughby 3/13
Wooster 1/6, 6/6
Worthington 11/2
Xenia 8/8
Youngstown 1/24, 3/9, 4/24, 9/14, 9/29, 11/19

Oklahoma
    Altus 9/19
    Ardmore 3/11
    Bartlesville 1/3
    Cleveland 1/1
    Hinton 9/12
    Hockerville 7/15
    Mooreland 3/11
    Oklahoma City 1/1, 7/19
    Stillwater 11/24
    Stilwell 4/29
    Tulsa 1/1, 2/10, 3/6, 4/11, 8/17, 9/24, 11/7,
        11/22
    Tuttle 6/17
    Vian 4/24
    Weatherford 6/23

Oregon
    Aims 8/9
    Alvard Desert 12/6
    Grants Pass 4/4
    Milton 5/17
    Portland 3/26, 4/23, 5/30, 6/12, 6/23, 7/10,
        8/15
    Tigard 10/12
    Vernonia 10/24

Pennsylvania
    Abington 12/14
    Allegheny (Pittsburgh) 1/31, 2/11, 9/27
    Allentown 1/10, 2/19, 9/20, 9/24, 9/27, 10/15,
        10/20, 10/24
    Altoona 6/15, 6/24, 9/1, 9/4, 9/23
    Ardmore 1/1, 2/2
    Aspinwall 5/14
    Barnesboro 9/14
    Bellevue 1/7
    Berwick 2/15
    Bethlehem 3/12, 5/28, 8/4, 10/5
    Bloomsburg 6/16
    Braddock 2/6
    Bradford 8/24, 9/20
    Bryn Mawr 3/11, 6/16, 6/18
    Butler 5/20, 6/19, 6/22
    Camp Hill 10/7
    Carlisle 11/16
    Centerville 10/8
    Chalfont 5/21
    Charleroi 8/16
    Chestnut Hill 11/7
    Connellsville 4/19
    Coraopolis Heights 10/3
    Dallas 2/27
    Dalton 2/22
    Delmont 9/1
    Doylestown 11/7
    East Berlin 10/5
    Easton 1/27, 4/17
    Elizabethtown 1/10
    Elkins Park 1/11
    Ellwood City 6/7
    Erie 6/10, 7/3, 10/16, 11/4
    Exton 2/29
    Fleetwood 1/1, 4/1, 6/5
    Foxburg 11/4
    Frackville 8/1
    Franklin 1/4
    Friendsville 1/9
    Germantown 8/19, 11/30
    Gettysburg 3/12 10/10

Harrisburg 2/6, 7/19, 11/2 11/8
Havertown 6/20
Hazleton 5/29
Hershey 10/7, 10/9
Hummelstown 5/20
Hyndman 11/9
Jeanette (spelling ?) 3/11, 7/4
Johnstown 7/26
Kennett Square 12/21
Kutztown 11/5
Lancaster 1/6, 2/26, 4/21, 10/8
Langhorne 4/7, 5/1, 5/2, 6/12, 6/17, 6/19,
    7/1, 8/8
Lebanon 12/30
Ligonier Mountain 7/2
Lima 4/2
Locustdale 2/12
Long Pond 6/17, 7/3
Mahanoy City 4/20
Manheim 10/12
McAllisterville 8/13
Mechanicsburg 3/5
Moosic 11/4
Mount Cobb 7/14, 10/27, 11/27
Mount Joy 11/27
Nazareth 4/25
New Brighton 11/19
New Chester 6/7
New Germantown 6/1
New Kensington 11/2
New Stanton 5/28
Norristown 8/29
North East 11/11
Oil City 11/10
Oxford 8/4
Parsippany 12/27
Penfield 7/17
Philadelphia 2/8, 2/9, 2/13, 1/28, 3/6,
    3/11, 3/17, 3/20, 3/23, 3/31, 4/8, 4/12,
    4/16, 4/17, 5/6, 5/18, 5/26, 6/4, 6/9, 7/3,
    7/6, 7/8, 7/9, 7/13, 7/15, 8/2, 8/10, 8/27,
    9/15, 9/17, 9/19, 9/28, 10/8, 10/9, 10/10,
    10/14, 11/4, 11/7, 11/9, 11/13, 11/17,
    11/21, 11/26, 11/29, 12/1, 12/6, 12/11,
    12/17, 12/18, 12/31
Pittsburgh 1/5, 1/15, 2/11, 3/4, 3/17, 3/21,
    4/27, 5/5, 5/13, 7/25, 8/23, 8/28, 8/31,
    9/3, 9/27, 10/11, 10/21, 11/14, 12/1, 12/3,
    12/12, 12/18
Plymouth 5/31, 12/7
Pocono 6/19
Port Carbon 3/21, 4/1
Pottstown 3/7, 4/11
Punxsutawney 10/4
Reading 2/3, 4/6, 6/9, 6/11, 6/25
Scranton 1/23
Sharon 8/8
Sewickley 12/4
Spartansburg 1/12
State College 2/17, 2/28
Steelton 10/30
Strasburg 2/23
State College 2/16
Stroudsburg 8/13
Sunbury 7/19
Tidioute 9/30
Tipton 9/1
Titusville 8/27
Uniontown 12/2
Weatherly 3/14
Webster 11/3
Wellsboro 11/7
Wernersville 10/2
West Chester 10/5
West Monterey 9/29
Westmoreland 9/15
Wheatland 1/1, 6/3
Whitpain 9/10
Wilkes-Barre 1/8, 5/12, 5/30, 10/8
Williamsport 9/4, 9/15
Wyalusing 9/10
Wyncote 5/18

York 1/29, 7/1, 8/24, 11/21, 11/29

Rhode Island
  Auburn 7/9
  Narragansett Park 9/7, 9/18
  Newport 7/7, 8/7, 8/8, 8/19, 8/27, 9/6, 9/7
  Pawtucket 2/28
  Providence 2/15, 2/21, 6/1, 6/4, 6/27, 9/18,
    10/24, 11/19, 12/21

South Carolina
  Aiken 5/17
  Bishopville 4/6
  Cedar Creek 2/7
  Charleston 7/19, 10/7
  Columbia 3/26
  Cowpens 11/9
  Darlington 7/5, 9/1, 9/4, 9/5
  Florence 1/25
  Greenville 4/1
  Hartville 3/4
  Rock Hill 2/27
  Rockingham 10/31
  Spartanburg 5/26, 9/30
  Summerville 5/1
  Woodruff 12/22

South Dakota
  Brandon 5/10
  DeSmet 12/5
  Gettysburg 7/31
  Iroquois 5/12
  Norbeck 3/19
  Pierre 1/7
  Watertown 5/6, 8/13
  Yankton 4/26, 11/29

Tennessee
  Bartlett 10/26
  Bristol 4/1
  Chattanooga 1/29
  Columbia 6/30
  Knoxville 4/22
  Memphis 9/17
  Mountain City 4/29
  Murfreesboro 8/1
  Nashville 1/1, 3/4, 4/2, 5/29, 5/30, 7/6,
    8/14, 11/9, 11/14
  Newport 8/30
  Paris 11/16
  Signal Mountain 12/11
  Spring Hill 7/30, 7/31
  Smyrna 3/26, 5/9
  Woodbury 4/9

Texas
  Abilene 7/23
  Alvin 11/11
  Anahuac 2/11
  Arlington 2/18, 6/3, 11/27
  Bartlett 11/23
  Beaumont 1/10, 7/30
  Canadian 2/14
  Center 5/14
  Clint 6/7
  Corpus Christi 5/8, 11/16
  Dallas 2/7, 2/15, 3/18, 5/20, 5/21, 6/15,
    6/20, 7/8, 7/18, 8/9, 10/17, 12/3, 12/10
  Denton 3/15
  Fort Stockton 3/2
  Fort Worth 6/14, 8/5
  Gainesville 2/3, 9/9
  Goldthwaite 9/22
  Grand Prairie 1/21, 7/10
  Holland 4/7, 6/8
  Houston 1/16, 3/26, 6/27, 9/14, 9/26
  Laredo 11/11
  Leesburg 1/11
  Manor 6/16
  McAllen 10/6
  Midland 6/5

Oakwood 6/13
Port Arthur 1/6
San Angelo 5/2, 9/28
San Antonio 4/6, 6/10, 12/21
Snyder 10/29
Troy 8/9
Waco 4/13
Weatherford 12/15
Wichita Falls 1/12

Utah
  Bonneville Salt Flats 3/2, 4/29, 7/2, 7/17,
    7/22, 8/5, 8/6, 8/12, 8/14, 8/19, 8/20,
    8/21, 8/23, 8/24, 8/27, 8/31, 9/3, 9/4,
    9/5, 9/9, 9/10, 9/15, 9/16, 9/18, 9/19,
    9/28, 10/3, 10/5, 10/13, 10/15, 10/23,
    10/26, 10/27, 11/2 11/4, 11/7, 11/12,
    11/15, 11/17, 11/19
  Kelton 7/26
  Ogden 9/27
  Provo 3/2
  Salt Lake City 1/10, 4/30, 8/9, 9/4
  Spanish Fork 1/25

Vermont
  Bennington 3/25, 6/2, 7/6
  Bradford 9/1
  Brandon 2/25
  Burke 6/17
  Burlington 1/14, 12/3
  Danville 2/16
  East Braintree 2/26
  Fairlee 4/17
  Lyndonville 12/20
  McIndoe Falls 7/16
  Newbury 8/9
  Poultney 5/14
  Putney 6/3
  Rupert 11/4
  St. Johnsbury 12/12
  Salisbury 7/6
  Waterbury 5/1
  Williamstown 7/9

Virginia
  Aspen Grove 10/22
  Berryville 3/26
  Boyce 1/30
  Charlottesville 10/7, 12/29, 12/31
  Cherrydale 9/9
  Chesapeake 9/12, 9/13
  Chesapeake Beach 4/15
  Concord 10/27
  Danville 10/25, 12/23
  Elkton 4/2
  Falls Church 1/11
  Floyd 4/12
  Fredericksburg 12/20
  Harrisonburg 2/10
  Horsepen 9/26
  Kiptopeke 4/15
  Lexington 3/4
  Martinsville 9/22, 10/24
  Natural Bridge 11/26
  Norfolk 9/4
  Oak Grove 5/29
  Onancock 5/5
  Richlands 9/30
  Richmond 1/27, 2/7, 2/10, 8/1, 8/7, 9/7
  Roanoke 10/9
  South Boston 6/23, 6/29
  White Stone 11/13

Washington
  Ellensburg 1/29
  Seattle 1/16, 1/22, 1/30, 2/15, 2/28, 3/1,
    3/17, 4/21, 5/29, 6/1, 6/15, 6/23, 7/12,
    7/24, 7/26, 9/19, 9/21, 10/17 12/17, 12/28
  Spokane 4/4, 4/29, 5/4, 6/1, 7/29, 8/20, 9/19
  Tacoma 4/10, 4/16, 5/9, 7/5, 8/18, 11/7

West Virginia
  Bluefield 8/13
  Charleston 8/4
  Lost Creek 3/27
  New Martinsville 7/14
  Parkersburg 3/1, 10/2
  Wheeling 1/1, 1/17, 5/5, 7/6, 9/1
  White Sulphur Springs 6/13
  Williamstown 4/10

Wisconsin
  Beloit 3/22, 7/15
  Berlin 9/19
  Brodhead 8/12
  Chase 3/20
  Clinton 1/6, 3/13
  Clintonville 1/9, 1/18, 5/1, 6/28, 8/10, 12/26,
    12/29
  Deerfield 12/3
  Edgerton 8/26
  Elkhart Lake 7/23, 8/5
  Elroy 10/21
  Franklin 12/18
  Genoa City 5/15
  Green Bay 7/12, 7/16, 7/24
  Greenfield 12/14
  Hartford 6/25, 9/6, 10/29, 12/21
  Iola 10/4, 12/16
  Janesville 2/21, 4/21, 5/10, 6/3, 9/15
  Kenosha 3/2, 4/10, 5/27, 6/13, 6/25, 6/30,
    7/14, 10/13, 12/8
  LaCrosse 11/4, 12/17
  Loganville 3/20
  Madison 1/3, 5/23, 7/16, 7/24, 8/11, 9/20,
    12/2
  Marinette 12/1
  Menominee 5/28
  Menomonie 12/9
  Merrill 11/21
  Milwaukee 1/2, 1/4, 1/16, 2/4, 3/5, 4/9,
    4/10, 4/28, 5/8, 5/17, 6/13, 6/17, 6/25,
    7/8, 7/17, 8/9, 8/18, 9/8, 9/11, 10/2, 10/4,
    10/12, 11/30, 12/4, 12/10, 12/23
  Mount Horeb 4/17
  Oshkosh 7/16, 10/12
  Plymouth 7/19
  Racine 2/27, 4/2, 4/6, 6/11, 6/23, 12/21, 12/22
  Rice Lake 5/22
  Stevens Point 3/27, 7/21, 10/7
  Trout Lake 9/19
  Waukesha 5/31, 6/22, 8/20, 9/19
  Wausau 3/1
  Wauwatosa 3/28, 10/3
  Wequiock 7/16
  West Allis 6/9, 6/13, 8/18, 8/30
  Winneconne 1/31
  Wisconsin Dells 5/25
  Wisconsin Rapids 10/27
  Woodville 1/18

Wyoming
  Cheyenne 9/20
  Creston 7/4
  Rock Springs 4/26
  Sheridan 12/15

VENEZUELA
  Caracas, Distrito Federal 1/25, 2/10
  Vignale Monferrato 8/8

VIETNAM
  Hanoi, Hadong 7/13

ZAMBIA (NORTHERN RHODESIA)
  Mufulira, Western 5/25

ZIMBABWE
  Bulawayo 12/7
  Msasa 10/12

INDEX 5 - ILLUSTRATIONS

This index includes people, places, marques, and organizations depicted in the illustrations or mentioned in the captions.

Abarth 11/23
A.C. 11/24
Acme 6/9
Aermore 1/23
Alfa Romeo 5/11
Allan, Fred 5/30
Allard 11/29
Alldays & Onions 6/28
Alvis 4/21
AMC 4/1, 9/25, 12/3
American Austin 5/21
American Underslung 7/3
Antique Automobile Club of America 11/4
Apperson 3/28
Argo Electric 7/6
Arizona
   Nogales 10/30
Armstrong-Siddeley 11/3
Aston Martin 6/21
Auburn 7/14, 8/7
Auburn Automobile Company 9/15
Austin (UK) 12/18
Austin (US) 3/31
Autocar 2/1, 8/23
Auto Union 11/13

Badger Bumpers 12/9
Baker Electric 4/26
Bay State 9/4
Bean 7/15
Bendix Brakes 8/12
Bentley 3/7, 5/15, 10/26
Benz 4/4
Berkshire 12/13
BMW 8/13
Borgward 7/28
Bosch 9/23
Boyce Moto-Meter 3/17
Brewer, Edward E. 8/9
Brewster 6/2
Brunn 1/7
Brunsdale, Norman 10/16
Buda Motor 6/14
Buffalo/Auto-Bi 1/15
Bugatti 7/31
Buick 3/6, 3/21, 5/12, 5/20, 8/1, 10/3, 10/24,
   11/3, 11/19
Buick Motor Company 9/16
Buick, David D. 3/6

Cadillac 1/13, 2/17, 2/29, 3/26, 5/10, 5/17,
   6/15, 7/7, 8/7, 10/12, 10/17, 11/29
Caesar, Orville S. 5/22
California
   Big Basin 10/6
   Carpinteria 4/26
   Chandelier Tree 6/25, 9/29
   Corona 9/9
   Garberville 3/5
   Hollywood 9/30, 11/2
   Los Angeles 6/26
   San Francisco 4/9, 8/8
   Yosemite National Park 4/2

Canada
   Abbotsford, BC 7/10
   Vancouver, BC 1/6
   Boissevain, MB 1/15
   Wasagaming, MB 11/3
   Huntsville, ON 6/10
   Wiarton, ON 4/13
Cartercar 2/3
Case 8/7
Champion Spark Plug 1/14, 7/7
Chandler 4/15
Checker 3/14
Chevrolet 1/7, 1/15, 1/30, 2/20, 2/26, 3/28,
   4/19, 6/12, 8/6, 9/10, 10/4, 10/12, 10/31,
   11/15, 12/5, 12/25
Chevrolet, Louis 12/25
Chilton 1/3
Chrysler 3/19, 9/7, 9/14, 10/21, 11/11, 11/17,
   11/26
Chrysler Corporation 8/6, 11/17, 12/21
Citroen 2/5, 10/6, 11/9
Clement 5/17
Cleveland 4/15
Clymer, Floyd 10/26
Colby 11/13
Cole 6/22, 12/4
Colorado
   Estes Park 1/10
   Fort Collins 1/10
   Fort Lupton 5/2
   Ovid 8/1
   Virginia Dale 3/13
Columbia 9/2
Connecticut
   Danbury 8/14
Continental Motors 8/7
Cooper Tires 8/9
Cord 1/2, 1/6, 8/21
Crosley 9/18
Curtice, Harlow H. 11/3

Daf 3/23
Daimler (D) 9/29
Daimler (UK) 6/6
Darracq 10/6
Datsun 1/9
DeDion-Bouton 8/19
Delage 10/19
DeLorean, John Z. 7/1
Denby 1/20
DeSoto 1/2, 1/27, 3/12, 4/23, 8/4, 10/18, 11/17
De Tomaso 7/10
Detroit Diamond 2/15
Detroiter 12/19
DeVaux 8/7
D.F.P. 6/8
Diamond T 6/28
Dietrich, Inc. 8/4
Doble-Detroit 7/16
Dodge 9/7, 9/22, 10/10, 10/23, 10/25, 10/30,
   11/17, 12/21
Dodge Brothers 12/12
Dolson 2/29
Donner, Frederic G. 10/4
Dorris 11/2

Duesenberg 7/26, 9/30
Duesenberg, Fred 6/26
Dunlop 1/26
DuPont, Lammot 10/12
Duryea 9/28

Earl, Harley J. 12/1
Edsel 7/3
Elkhart 7/1
Elmore 10/28
E-M-F 11/3
Empire 7/12
Enger 1/4

Fafnir 1/4
Farina 11/2
Federal-Mogul 11/26
Ferrari 8/14
Fiat 3/31
Firestone 2/7
Fisher 7/14
Fithen, Frank E. 4/16
Florida
   Brooksville 11/4
   Fort Myers 3/11
   St. Augustine 2/15
   West Palm Beach 9/22
Ford 1/17, 2/3, 2/15, 2/28, 3/18, 3/28, 4/2,
   4/6, 4/7, 4/15, 4/29, 5/20, 5/21, 5/26, 6/9,
   6/10, 6/16, 7/10, 7/15, 7/30, 7/31, 8/1, 8/8,
   8/18, 9/2, 9/22, 9/27, 10/3, 10/6, 10/26,
   10/31, 12/10, 12/26
Ford, Edsel B. 5/26
Ford, Henry 2/7, 7/31
Ford, Henry II 9/29
Franklin 2/10, 4/16, 6/19, 6/25
Frazer 1/20
FWD 3/23

Gardner 12/30
Garford 8/4
General Motors 4/29, 8/20, 9/16, 10/4, 10/12,
   12/1, 12/13
Georgia
   Manchester 9/9
Germany
   Heidelberg/Mannheim 7/5
Giacosa, Dante 3/31
GN 5/21
Goodyear 3/18
Graham 1/16
Graham-Paige 1/5, 6/10
Gray-Dort 10/27
Greyhound 5/22
Grout 9/9
Gurney Nutting 8/1

Haiti
   Port-au-Prince 2/13
Hanson 9/11
Hanson, Ernest 10/26
Harrah's Automobile Collection 6/30
Hawkins, Norval 8/18
Haynes 4/13
Haynes, Elwood 4/13

Helck, Peter 1/14
Henderson, Herbert V. 11/11
Henry J 9/28
Herreshoff 5/28
Hertz 2/6
Highway Post Office 2/10
Hispano-Suiza 3/15
Holley 4/14
Honda 3/1
Houk, George W. 11/7
Hudson 3/5, 8/30, 10/16, 11/2
Hupmobile 7/7

Idaho
    Porthill 7/30
    Wallace 2/19
Illinois
    Chenoa 11/10
    Coleta 6/10
    Elburn 4/7
    Princeton 11/20
Imperial (1) 8/6
Imperial (2) 11/11, 11/17, 11/26
Indiana
    South Bend 3/4
International 9/19
Iowa
    Clear Lake 8/9
    Des Moines 6/26
    Essex 9/4
    Grundy Center 10/29
    Hampton 3/26
    Lineville 7/31
    Mason City 11/13
    Rockford 10/29
    West Union 3/19
Iso 8/28
Isotta-Fraschini 9/24

Jackson 5/14
Jaguar 9/1
Jeep 11/27
Jensen 5/21
Johnson Bronze 2/12
Jordan 7/3, 8/7

Kaiser 5/9
Keeton 4/1
Keller, K. T. 11/4
Kentucky
    Somerset 5/22
Kenworth 10/17
Kettering, Charles F. 6/15
Kissel 10/29
Kline Kar 5/20
Knox 1/19, 6/2
Konecke, Fritz 3/26
Krit 9/3

Lagonda 2/10
Lanchester 3/28, 6/6
Lancia 8/24
Land Rover 11/9
Larson, Clarion E. 12/13
LaSalle 5/5, 11/22
Leland, Henry M. 3/26
Lincoln 1/7, 3/26, 6/18, 9/14

Lincoln Continental 5/26, 10/4
Lincoln Highway 5/2
Lincoln-Zephyr 6/25, 8/8, 10/15
Lloyd 9/15
Locomobile 1/14, 6/1, 9/10
Lotus 7/20
Lower brothers 10/29
Lozier 2/17

Macauley, Alvan 4/10
Mack 5/30, 7/1
Magee, Carlton C. 1/31
Marathon 1/1
Marmon 1/3
Marmon-Herrington 3/13
Martin-Parry 7/13
Maryland
    Baltimore 5/19
Maserati 5/22
Mason 6/26
Matheson 6/27
Matheson brothers 6/27
Maxwell 6/21, 9/1, 10/29
Maybach 2/8
Mercedes-Benz 3/26, 7/19, 11/13
Mercer 4/15
Mercury 2/19, 8/8, 9/9, 9/29, 10/24
Meteor 7/10
Mexico
    Mexico City, DF 1/18
    Monterey, Nuevo Leon 11/11
    Nogales, Sonora 10/30
M.G. 7/21
Michigan
    Detroit 8/7
    Flint 9/16
    Iron Mountain 5/12
    Petoskey 1/16
    Shingleton 10/21
Minnesota
    Barnesville 5/20
    Canby 3/6
    Deerwood 10/3
    Elizabeth 1/18
    Fergus Falls 10/25
    Glenwood 1/8
    Karlstad 10/10
    Long Prairie 6/8
    Madelia 5/26
    Ortonville 1/16
    Redwood Falls 11/15
    St. Louis Park 6/16
    Spicer 3/28
    Tracy 10/18
Missouri
    Kansas City 6/30
Mitchell 2/19
Montana
    Big Timber 9/21
Moon 7/5, 8/7
Morgan 6/15
Morris 10/1, 10/2, 10/10
Motor Products 2/15
H. J. Mulliner 10/8
Myers, Ethel M. 6/10

Napier 1/22
NASCAR 2/21
Nash 5/16, 7/8, 9/1, 10/15
Nash-Kelvinator 2/1
Nebraska

Aurora 4/19
Nevada
    Carson City 12/25
    Zephyr Cove 10/15
New Mexico
    Hot Springs 1/30
    Tularosa 6/9
    White Sands 8/8
    White's City 9/22
New York
    Governor's Island 7/17
    Long Island City 9/29
    New York City 1/17
    Pennelville 6/25
    Skaneateles 4/1
    Syracuse 4/16
North Dakota
    Beulah 7/3
    Bismarck 1/17, 5/5, 5/31, 10/16, 12/13
    Crosby 1/20
    Donnybrook 10/4
    Jamestown 1/31
    Mandan 2/29, 9/19
    Medora 12/5
    Minot 9/3, 11/29
    Page 11/28
    Robinson 10/26
    Tuttle 5/30
    Valley City 8/30

Oakland 1/24, 3/28, 4/16, 6/27
Ohio
    Steubenville 4/16
Oklahoma
    Perry 12/26
    Turner Falls 4/11
Olds, Ransom E. 9/4
Oldsmobile 1/1, 1/8, 4/1, 5/7, 5/18, 12/1
Opel 1/5
Oregon
    Government Camp 11/25
    Hillsboro 9/28
    Hood River 10/24,
    Roseburg 10/17
    Seaside 12/1
Orient 10/30
Overland 2/12, 5/27

Packard 1/6, 1/16, 1/18, 4/9, 4/10, 4/23, 5/5,
    5/11, 5/17, 6/17, 8/8, 11/7, 11/11
Paige 6/10
Paige-Detroit 6/10
Palmer, Herman D. 10/29
Pearce, Harry J. 12/13
Peerless 6/12, 11/20
Perfect Circle 12/15
Peugeot 7/26
Peyton, Ernie 1/10
Phillips 66, 11/28
Pierce-Arrow 1/9, 5/17, 9/20, 11/24
Plastow, David 5/9
Playboy 4/3
Plymouth 1/27, 1/30, 6/8, 6/11, 7/17, 8/8, 8/30,
    9/7, 11/4, 11/17, 11/20, 11/25
Pontiac 2/13, 3/28, 6/20, 6/27, 7/1, 7/30, 8/17,
    9/3, 9/16, 10/8, 11/10
Pope-Hartford 4/19
Pope-Toledo 5/27
Porsche 3/21
Pratt 7/2

Railton 6/24
Rambler 2/29, 7/8
Rand McNally 5/20
Rayfield 12/8
R.C.H. 7/25
Renault 6/25
Reo 3/5, 9/4
Rickenbacker 5/10, 7/23
Riker 9/7
Riker, Andrew L. 6/1
Riley 6/9
Rockne 3/4
Rolls-Royce 1/17, 2/6, 5/9, 6/2, 8/14, 9/23
Romney, George W. 7/8
Roosevelt 5/15
Rover 5/13
Ruckstell Axle 5/29
Rudge-Whitworth 11/7
Ruxton 10/29

Salmson 11/25
Samson 3/18
Saxon 7/4
Scania-Vabis 11/30
Schafer, Edward T. 2/17
Schwiddle, Charley 9/4
Selden 9/14
Shell 9/22
Skelly 4/11
SKF 7/10
Sloan, Alfred P. Jr. 2/17
Socony 5/31
South Dakota
    Hecla 2/3
    Rapid City 3/18
    Wall 1/27, 7/8
    Yankton 2/28
Speedwell 10/25
Standard Oil 11/28
Star 7/24
Stearns-Knight 5/17, 8/15
Steele Rubber 2/16
Steinway 9/29
Sterling (2) 8/9
Stevens-Duryea 8/29
Studebaker 2/12, 4/13, 4/26, 5/22, 10/15
Studebaker-Packard 3/26
Stutz 6/26, 9/12
Sunbeam-Talbot 5/17
Surinam
    Paramaribo 4/14
Switzerland
    Grimsel Pass 11/9

Talbot 5/17
Teetor, C. N. 12/15
Tennessee
    Manchester 1/7
Texaco 3/13, 11/10, 11/28
Texas
    McAllen 1/13
    Weslaco 1/31
Thornycroft 1/2
Timken 8/16
Touring 3/3, 9/6
Toyota 2/27, 8/28
Triumph 5/2
Tucker 12/26
T.V.R. 1/4

United Kingdom
    Aylesford, England 10/2
    Great Yarmouth, England 10/10
United States Tires 2/27
Utah
    Kanab 4/6
Vanden Plas 4/21
Vauxhall 3/27, 6/20
Veeder 12/27
Velie 7/2, 8/7
Vermont
    Rutland 12/21
Veteran Motor Car Club of America 12/2
Victor 5/18
Volkswagen 4/7, 4/14, 4/19, 11/9
Volvo 11/11

Walker, Leroy 7/3
Warner 3/22
Warner, Harold G. 11/29
Washington
    Everett 3/12
Wheeler-Schebler Carburetor 10/3
Whippet 5/30
White 1/10, 9/29, 10/11
White Freightliner 10/17
Whitworth, Stanley 10/15
Wick, Carl J. 7/15
Wick, Marvin 6/16
Willard 2/3
Willys 3/11, 5/27, 9/21, 11/15
Willys, John N. 5/30
Willys-Overland 5/17, 5/31
Wilson, David R. 11/15
Winnebago 2/28
Winton 4/6, 6/20
Wisconsin
    Barron 5/9
    Black River Falls 3/6
    Kiel 10/15
    Oakfield 4/15
    Racine 2/19
    Tomah 1/1
Wolfe 12/13
Wolfram, Jack F. 1/8
Wyoming
    Lusk 8/18
    Rock Springs 5/2
    Worland 7/8

Yellow 1/31

EPILOGUE

So there it is. *Automobile History Day By Day* may not be a "history" in the strictest sense of the word, but it surely is a collection of trivial factoids quite unlike anything previously available.

The first century of the automotive industry has been nothing short of a miracle. Millions of mostly honorable men and women working for thousands of mostly reputable organizations have produced countless millions of mostly excellent automobiles. A natural result of all this has been the development of an equally important network of parts manufacturers, aftermarket suppliers, maintenance and repair experts, etc. The invention of such things as drive-in restaurants, motels, and roadmaps would not have been necessary without the meteoric worldwide acceptance of the motor car. The automotive industry is not the most important - I'd rank agriculture, medicine, and perhaps some others above it - but its influence in shaping today's culture is second to none.

The automobile world of my youth (Bismarck, ND in the 1950's) was quite a different scene from that of today. Personal vehicles were almost 100% cars (pickups and larger trucks were for work only), and these cars were almost 100% home grown. Dr. Carl J. Baumgartner, a local obstetrician who delivered yours truly, owned a Jaguar saloon during these years. As I remember it his Jaguar was the only foreign car in Bismarck at the time. Automotive styling of this era has been both praised and criticized for its excesses, but this was probably the only time in history that cars could be easily identified by a six-year-old. I know... I was one!

I've long been involved in the old car hobby, but I've always tried to stay up to speed with current models as well. Are today's cars better than those of years ago? Of course they are. I think overall quality bottomed out in the 1970's but has rapidly recovered to what might be an all time high. Much of this can be traced to necessity as the established American and European industries had to meet the challenges of the new world automotive power, the Japanese. As late as the 1970's reaching 100,000 miles with an automobile was a rare accomplishment. Today this is expected of even the lowest form of car. The cloth driver's seat in my 1972 Cadillac was disintegrating when the rest of the car was still very presentable. By contrast, the synthetic velour upholstery in my 1979 Cadillac was still nearly as new when the car was nearing 200,000 miles and the end of its useful life. Yes, the cars of yesterday, whether you're talking about 1900 or 1950 or whatever, were wonderful and will always remain among the most nostalgic symbols of their eras, but current cars are much more user friendly and are just plain better than their ancestors.

The automobile industry, of course, has not gone unnoticed. Governments in general just simply can't leave it alone. Incrementally imposed legislation, regulations, and mandates on the car companies would have smothered a weaker industry. Individuals such as Ralph Nader, Al Gore, and Ted Kaczynski have labeled the automobile as everything from unsafe to the greatest menace facing mankind. As this is being written those of this mindset are attacking the success story of the 1990's - sport utility vehicles - knowing full well that SUV's represent the industry's and the consumer's reaction to attempts to make all of us drive identical "econoboxes". It seems that diversity is a virtue except when it comes to our motor vehicles.

Will the automobile survive into the next century and beyond? The answer to this question had better be obvious. Will the car of 2007, 2047, or 2097 look like the car of 1997? While the basic arrangement of the automobile really has not changed that much since the earliest days of the industry, the answer to this question is equally obvious. What will be the biggest change in motor cars in the next century? My guess would be in the area of fuel.

I was educated to be an accountant and definately cannot speak as a scientist, but I've always believed that in the big picture fossil fuels are only a temporary solution. I applaud the recent electric car efforts of General Motors and others and hope that a real breakthrough might be made - imagine the public response to an electric car with a range of 500 miles that could be recharged in the time and at the cost now required to fill a car's gas tank. Cars powered by alcohol have proven themselves in certain parts of the world and universally in bigtime racing. Steam cars continue to have a small but enthusiastic group of believers, yet all of the above probably represent 20th century thinking.

It is almost obligatory that I comment here about living to see a man on the moon, but in a more down to earth development I've witnessed the dawning of the computer age and the changes that it has brought to the business world. I've also witnessed the invention of the compact disc and its virtually overnight conquest of the world of recorded sound, not to mention its adaptation by the above mentioned computer. Is an automotive fuel breakthrough comparable to the computer or compact disc on the horizon? I think so, and feel confident that it will happen in the 21st century. I hope that it happens in my lifetime.

In the meantime, happy motoring.